READINGS IN
ABNORMAL PSYCHOLOGY

7 DAY LOAN

READINGS IN ABNORMAL PSYCHOLOGY

Jill M. Hooley
Harvard University

John M. Neale
State University of New York at Stony Brook

Gerald C. Davison
University of Southern California

WILEY
John Wiley & Sons
New York   Chichester   Brisbane   Toronto   Singapore

To Ernest and Marguerite,
Gail,
Aaron and Ida

Acquisitions Editor, Deborah Moore
Managing Editor, Joan Kalkut
Production Manager, Deborah Herbert
Production Supervisor, Gilda Stahl
Editorial Supervisor, Gilda Stahl
Manufacturing Manager, Robin Garmise
Designer, Michael Jung

Library of Congress Cataloging in Publication Data:

Readings in abnormal psychology / [edited by] Jill M. Hooley, John M. Neale, Gerald C. Davison.
    p.   cm.
    References
    ISBN 0-471-63107-8
  1. Psychology, Pathological. I. Hooley, Jill M. II. Neale, John M., 1943–   . III. Davison,
Gerald C.
RC454.R373 1989
616.89—dc19   88-26796
                                                 CIP

Printed in the United States of America

10 9

Preface

The ability to distill a large body of research and theory into a single volume of well-organized, readable text is the hallmark of any good textbook writer. Unfortunately, what gets lost in this distillation process—even with the best of authors—is a full appreciation of the subtlety and complexity of the research endeavor and the excitement and controversy that surrounds the pursuit of knowledge. For this reason, course instructors often seek to expose students to a sampling of original, undistilled sources. At the same time, students are also often interested in reading more widely but lack the knowledge and expertise to select wisely from the thousands of original articles available.

In this volume we have attempted to provide a collection of readings in abnormal psychology that is sensitive to the needs of instructors and students alike. For the instructor we aimed to provide a diverse selection that focuses on current issues in contemporary psychopathology. For students we tried to select high-interest articles that are both accessible and challenging.

Thirty-six articles are reprinted in this volume. The number of articles is large because, as the field of psychopathology develops, the number of articles required to provide an understanding of the major issues and trends grows proportionally. This is not to say, however, that we consider the articles in this book to cover everything that is important in abnormal psychology today. Rather, we aimed to provide readers with a sense of the issues and questions that are currently attracting theoretical and empirical attention.

It is our hope that, regardless of their level of ability or special area of interest, the majority of readers will find something of significance in the articles we have chosen. We hope also that instructors of psychopathology, regardless of their orientations or preferred textbooks, will be able to find articles suitable to their course objectives. The articles represent a wide range of academic and popular sources and include research reports, review articles, theoretical discussions, as well as first-person accounts of psychopathology written by patients themselves.

The articles in this volume were selected by the three editors after a thorough combing of representative publications in the field. In all cases an article had to have at least two supporters in order to remain a candidate for selection. In evaluating each article's suitability for reprinting, we tried to balance the needs of students and their instructors. Many articles that are included (as well as a number that were rejected) were field-tested on our own students. Some that we wanted to reprint had to be omitted because of space considerations. Others, although important, were simply too detailed or dry to be both accessible and interesting to all but the most tenacious.

The book is divided into seven sections,

although the boundaries between these are far from rigid. In many cases articles appearing in one section could easily be placed elsewhere. Wherever possible, however, we have tried to keep conceptually related articles together. Thus, Section 1 focuses on the investigation and diagnosis of psychopathology, whereas Sections 2 and 3 cover schizophrenia and mood disorders, respectively. Anxiety disorders and reactions to stress are covered in Section 4. This is then followed by a consideration of substance abuse and interpersonal disorders (Section 5). In Section 6 we have included articles that discuss developmental disorders such as hyperactivity, and bulimia. Finally, in Section 7, a number of articles designed to convey the nature of current clinical practice are highlighted. Introductory comments preceding each section are designed to provide students with enough general background and/ or overview information to ease them into the topic areas.

A number of people assisted in the preparation of this book. In particular, the invaluable help of John Richters is acknowledged. He provided comments on the introductory sections, made suggestions about specific articles, and provided support throughout the whole project. Thanks are also extended to Mary Tays and Laura Hillman. Their secretarial talents and organizational skills helped keep things running smoothly. Last, but by no means least, we acknowledge our debt to the writers of the articles themselves. Without their creative talents this book would not be possible.

Jill M. Hooley
John M. Neale
Gerald C. Davison

July 1988

CONTENTS

Section 4

Section 5

Section 6

Contents

SECTION 1

Investigation and Diagnosis of Psychopathology

The classification systems we employ both reflect and influence how we think about important phenomena. This is no less true in the study of mental disorders than in the study of medicine, chemistry, physics, or biology. Classification systems are critical to all domains of scientific inquiry.

An easily forgotten fact about classification systems is that they are not discovered; rather, they are created to suit particular purposes. Books in a library, for example, can be classified by author, publication date, subject, or even size. It is meaningless to ask which is the correct or "true" way to classify them. The answer to that question rests heavily on the needs of the library user. Utility is thus the yardstick by which any classification system is measured. In science, classification systems are evaluated according to how well they guide scientists in their pursuit, interpretation, and application of knowledge.

Before the scientific study of psychopathology, numerous classification systems for mental disorders had been introduced by philosophers and physicians over the centuries. Beginning with Hippocrates' tripartite classification system of mania, melancholia, and phrenitis (brain fever), each new system reflected a distillation of the needs and knowledge of its historical period. Each in a limited sense was useful, if only because it provided some starting point for thinking about and dealing with the recognized disorders of the time. But many of these systems were also based on and wedded to specific theories of mental disorder that were then current. For this reason, and because they were constructed in the absence of any systematically developed body of information about symptom patterns, intra inter-individual histories, prevalence rates, and such, there was little basis for evaluating their relative usefulness in comparison to alternative systems. Many classification systems were therefore destined to fall by the wayside as new theories and systems were introduced.

The late nineteenth century marked the recognition of a need for more systematic and cumulative inquiry into the nature, origins, and treatment of mental disorders. Whereas the usefulness of a classification system before the late nineteenth century was often measured by its promise, the scientific criterion for usefulness would become progress. By today's standards, the utility of a diagnostic classification system is judged by its ability to assist researchers and clinicians in their diagnosis, understanding, treatment of, and communication about mental disorders. Coming to grips with these different needs in a single diagnostic classification system has not been an easy task. During the past few decades, however, considerable progress has been made toward realization of this goal.

1

We focus first on the two most widely accepted classification systems for mental disorders in use today. One of these, the Diagnostic and Statistical Manual (DSM), is used throughout the United States. The other, the International Classification of Diseases (ICD), is the product of the World Health Organization. It has been adopted throughout Europe and is also used in various other parts of the world. By considering briefly the development and current status of these systems, we hope to sensitize readers to some of the problems and assumptions inherent in the diagnostic endeavor. In so doing, this overview will provide a conceptual framework within which the four articles selected for this section can be understood and integrated.

ICD and DSM

In 1939, the World Health Organization (WHO) began to include mental disorders in what was then known as the International List of Causes of Death (ICD). The number of mental disorders recognized by the WHO became even more comprehensive in 1948 when this classification system underwent a further expansion and became known as the International and Statistical Classification of Diseases, Injuries, and Causes of Death. Despite this change in name, however, the ICD still remained a nomenclature. It was at that time (and is today) simply an approved list of diagnostic categories and titles.

At around the same time, steps to address the problem of classification diversity were also being taken in the United States. The American Psychiatric Association attempted to resolve the problem through the publication of an official manual that described and classified various kinds of psychopathological conditions. The first of these—the *Diagnostic and Statistical Manual of Mental Disorders* (DSM—appeared in 1952. Importantly, unlike the ICD, the DSM also attempted to provide working definitions or brief descriptions of the syndromes it listed.

Problems still remained, however. Many influential clinicians criticized the diagnostic system and, despite a call to the contrary, DSM did not succeed in becoming widely adopted.

The revision of DSM (DSM-II) in 1968 was designed to bring the American diagnostic system into closer alignment with that used by clinicians in other parts of the world. The diagnostic categories in DSM-II were based on the nomenclature of the seventh revision of the ICD (ICD-8), which came into official use in 1969. For their part, the British, through the addition of a glossary that attempted to describe the typical clinical features of the disorders listed in the ICD, also incorporated an important aspect of the American classification system. By the early 1970s, therefore, efforts had been made on both sides of the Atlantic to develop, refine, and adopt standard systems of diagnostic classification for mental disorders. Although the DSM and ICD systems appeared to be quite similar at the time, a major study of diagnostic differences between the researchers in the United States and the United Kingdom revealed otherwise.

The US–UK Cross National Study

This study (Professional Staff, 1974) focused on the diagnosis of schizophrenia in New York and London. Of particular interest were large differences in the number of schizophrenics being admitted to public mental hospitals in the United States relative to the United Kingdom. Whether this reflected a real difference in the number of schizophrenics in New York compared to London, or merely represented differences in the criteria used by American versus British psychiatrists for diagnosing schizophrenia, became a principal focus of interest.

The results of this collaborative endeavor were impressive. Compared with their British colleagues, American psychiatrists applied the diagnosis of schizophrenia to a much wider variety of symptom patterns, including those that the British were likely to diagnose as manic depressive illness. This became most evident when American and British psychiatrists assigned different diagnoses to the same patients after viewing the same videotaped diagnostic interviews.

The US–UK Cross National project made it clear that British and American conceptualizations of the same disorder did not reliably lead to the same patients being identified as schizophrenic. The American concept of schizophrenia reflected in DSM-II was relatively broad and was based on psychoanalytic notions of its etiology and dynamics. The ICD system endorsed by the British, on the other hand, employed a much more narrow and descriptive definition of schizophrenia that was relatively free from etiologic assumptions. As a result of these differences, researchers in the United States were applying the schizophrenic label to different symptom patterns than were their British counterparts. Obviously, this made the comparison and interpretation of data generated by schizophrenia researchers in the two countries extremely difficult. Moreover, there were even differences in the diagnosis of schizophrenia among psychiatrists from different regions of the United States who employed the same (DSM) classification system. If researchers were really to speak a common language, it was clear that a number of major changes needed to be made.

DSM-III and Beyond

In the United States, the most significant of these changes came with the publication of DSM-III in 1980. Unlike DSM-II, which reflected the psychodynamic underpinnings of American psychiatry, the authors of DSM-III made efforts to adopt a more atheoretical stance. In this sense, there was a move toward the more descriptive approach that had been Kraepelin's legacy to European clinicians. Important steps were also taken to

deal head-on with one of the most important sources of diagnostic error—the problem of criterion variance. Instead of the rather vague statements that had characterized the earlier editions, DSM-III listed specific inclusion and exclusion criteria for each diagnosis in an explicit and precise fashion. No longer was it the responsibility of each clinician to translate the manual's description of illnesses into diagnostic criteria; DSM-III clearly described, defined, and detailed the type and number of symptoms that were required to be present in order to make a specific diagnosis. It became, in other words, a true diagnostic manual. This did much to improve agreements in diagnosis among psychiatrists and heralded a new era of optimism about diagnostic reliability.

Studies during the past decade have demonstrated that many of the diagnostic categories within the DSM can be identified reliably. Nonetheless, the value of DSM and ICD (now ICD-9, 1977) as taxonomies of mental illness is still subject to question. In the final analysis, the utility of these classification systems will rest on the extent to which they are capable of integrating new research findings and guiding future empirical and theoretical efforts. At the present time, both diagnostic systems are best viewed as research and clinical tools. As we pointed out earlier, they are creations that are useful only to the extent that they serve the purposes of researchers and clinicians. It should therefore come as no surprise that work still continues on refining the DSM and the ICD classification systems. A revision of DSM-III (DSM-III-R) appeared in 1987, and work is already well underway on DSM-IV. Researchers are simultaneously working toward the ninth revision of the ICD (ICD-10). Whether future generations of researchers and clinicians will ultimately witness the merging of these two taxonomies into one standard and universal diagnostic system is not yet clear. What is clear, however, is that as our knowledge of psychopathology changes, so also must our taxonomies of mental disorders.

Basic Assumptions in the Classification of Psychopathology

The goal of a universal diagnostic classification system that can serve the needs of researchers and clinicians is predicated on two basic assumptions. The first, of course, is that mental disorders do indeed exist and are therefore classifiable. The second is that mental illnesses manifest themselves in similar ways across time and in diverse cultures. Thus, even though the concept of mental illness is largely defined within a social context, some general agreement regarding what is and what is not pathological must not only be demonstrated but must also be shown to transcend cultural boundaries.

The first two articles in this section concern these assumptions. In selection 1, Gorenstein examines the proposition made by Szasz (1960) almost 30 years ago that mental illness is a myth. In the intervening decades, according to Gorenstein, little progress had been made toward addressing the charges in Szasz's position. Accordingly, Gorenstein's article attempts to reduce the age-old debate over the existence of mental illness to "manageable proportions." In so doing, it clarifies some interesting and important issues.

Gorenstein's article is followed by the oldest paper in the book. This is a 1976 article by Murphy (selection 2) that critically examines psychiatric labeling theory from a cross-cultural perspective. Murphy focuses in particular on the nature of abnormal behavior among Bering Sea Eskimos and the Yoruba of Nigeria. The examples cited by Murphy underscore the fact that certain types of behavior are considered abnormal across wide variations in social and cultural contexts.

The third selection is an article by Matarazzo concerning the important issue of diagnostic reliability. Matarazzo's article (which has been abridged for inclusion in this collection) documents some of the important efforts that have been made in the search for diagnostic reliability. This is followed by a discussion of one of the most widely used psychiatric interviews of the 1970s, the Schedule for Affective Disorders and Schizophrenia (SADS). Since the publication of Matarazzo's article, the Structured Clinical Interview for DSM-III-R (SCID-R, 1987) has also been developed and has become the instrument of choice for many clinical researchers. Nonetheless, the development of both the SADS and the Present State Examination (PSE) are of historical importance because they represent early efforts to decrease another important source of diagnostic error: error due to differences in the information obtained from patients during diagnostic interviews.

Finally, we end the section with an article by Myers and colleagues (selection 4). This describes the results of the Epidemiological Catchment Area (ECA) project—a major study into the prevalence of psychiatric and psychological difficulties in the general population. This large-scale research effort, which was funded by the National Institute of Mental Health, included research teams in three different geographic locations and interviews with more than 9500 community residents. The article yields valuable insights into the strategies and techniques used by epidemiological researchers. It also documents the prevalence of various disorders, many of which are discussed in later sections of the volume. We hope the material presented in this article will also sensitize readers to the number of lives that are affected by psychopathology in its many manifestations.

References and Suggested Additional Readings

American Psychiatric Association (1987). *Diagnostic and statistical manual of mental disorders* (3rd ed., revised). Washington, DC: Author.

Endicott, J., and Spitzer, R. L. (1978). A diagnostic interview: The schedule for affective disorders and schizophrenia. *Archives of General Psychiatry, 35,* 837–844.

EYSENCK, H. J. (1986). A critique of contemporary classification and diagnosis. In T. Millon & G. L. Klerman, *Contemporary directions in psychopathology: Toward the DSM-IV.* New York: Guilford Press.

FINN, S. E. (1982). Base rates, utilities, and DSM-III: Shortcomings of fixed-rule systems of psychodiagnosis. *Journal of Abnormal Psychology, 91,* 294–302.

HOROWITZ, L. M., POST, D. L., FRENCH, R. D., WALLIS, K. D., AND SIEGELMAN, E. Y. (1981). The prototype as a construct in abnormal psychology: 2. Clarifying disagreement in psychiatric judgments. *Journal of Abnormal Psychology, 90,* 575–585.

KENDELL, R. E. (1975). *The role of diagnosis in psychiatry.* Oxford, England: Blackwell.

PROFESSIONAL STAFF OF THE US–UK CROSS-NATIONAL PROJECT (1974). The diagnosis and psychopathology of schizophrenia in New York and London. *Schizophrenia Bulletin, 1,* 80–102.

SPITZER, R. L., WILLIAMS, J. B. W., AND GIBBON, M. *Structured clinical interview for DSM-III-R—patient version (SCID-P, 4/1/87).* Biometrics Research Department, New York State Psychiatric Institute, New York.

SZASZ, T. S. (1960). The myth of mental illness. *American Psychologist, 15,* 113–118.

WING, J. K., COOPER, J. E., AND SARTORIOUS, N. (1974). *Measurement and classification of psychiatric symptoms:* London: Cambridge University Press.

WORLD HEALTH ORGANIZATION (1977). *Manual of the international statistical classification of diseases, injuries and causes of death* (9th rev.). Geneva: Author.

1

Debating Mental Illness: Implications for Science, Medicine, and Social Policy

Ethan E. Gorenstein

Abstract: The debate over the existence of mental illness is into its third decade without any real progress toward resolution. Resolution is possible, however, if two wholly unrelated issues are separated from one another. These are (a) the conceptual status of the psychological variables determining deviant behavior and (b) the appropriate response of society to individuals exhibiting certain behavioral characteristics. Regarding the first issue, sound philosophy of science dictates that the psychological variables determining deviant behavior are not physical structures but hypothetical constructs. Neither side of the mental illness debate seems to have any quarrel with this conclusion. Regarding the second issue, the two sides of the debate do not seem to have any fundamental disagreement over behavioral ideals. Moreover, they appear to agree that methods of achieving such ideals be selected for specific efficacy. The real disagreement seems to be over professional prerogatives and the legal/ethical status of the behaviorally aberrant. I suggest that these issues be addressed directly and the empty debate over the existence of mental illness be abandoned.

Ethan E. Gorenstein. Debating mental illness: Implications for science, medicine, and social policy. *American Psychologist*, 1984, Vol. 39, No. 1, pp. 50–56.

It will soon be a quarter of a century since Thomas Szasz (1960) advanced his controversial thesis that mental illness is a myth. During that time, Szasz's position has alternately been denounced (e.g., Ausubel, 1961; Chodoff, 1976; Kety, 1974) and applauded (e.g., Laing, 1964; Rosenhan, 1973; Sarbin, 1968; Scheff, 1966), but always, the issues have been intractable to resolution. As the debate continues to unfold (e.g., Szasz, 1982a), the mental health field is still unable to establish, except as a matter of faith, whether or not there is such a thing as mental illness.

Gradually, though, the views of Szasz and like-minded commentators have had a subtle but detectable impact on a field that remains staunchly medical in orientation. The standard terminology of the past—"mental disease," "insanity"—is now considered archaic by most mental health professionals. Even "mental illness," once considered the locution of enlightenment, is increasingly avoided in the scientific literature. In the psychiatric sphere, practitioners have begrudgingly resigned themselves to elections as the only feasible means of establishing the medical status of controversial behavior patterns. In education, textbooks on psychiatry and abnormal psychology now suggest that mental illness or abnormality, although it surely is real, is exceedingly difficult to define absolutely.

Thus, the mental health field has made uneasy adjustments to accommodate its most important contemporary challenge. But the basic issues do not go away (e.g., Szasz, 1982b), and one wonders why there has been no real progress in resolving so fundamental a debate as whether or not mental illness exists.

I think most who have studied this problem would agree that one of the principal difficulties has been the failure to isolate the separate questions that need to be addressed (cf. Sarason & Ganzer, 1968). However, I think this problem has been compounded by the failure of the various interested parties—science, medicine, and social welfare—to understand the limitations of their respective domains. The result has been such misrepresentation of the issues that opponents cannot even recognize those points on which they actually agree.

It is hard to tell if the debate over the existence of mental illness is ripe for a solution. It does seem clear, however, that this debate is ready to be reduced to manageable proportions. In so doing, we may examine some important issues that seem already to have been solved and identify the remaining issues and appropriate avenues to their resolution.

Mental Illness: The Definitional Challenge

A protracted debate was set in motion by Thomas Szasz (1960) when he suggested that "mental illness," originally a summary term for certain behavioral phenomena treated by health professionals, had become reified as a *cause* of the very phenomena that the term had been coined to represent. In other words, the concept of a diseased mind was based on a logical fallacy.

Not only could the concept of mental illness be criticized on logical grounds, but also, according to Szasz, there were some

factual reasons why the notion of "illness" had doubtful application to mental phenomena. First of all, it was unlikely that organic brain damage could account for the content of an individual's thoughts (and, in any event, organic etiology would imply a *brain* disease, but not mental illness). Second, Szasz suggested that there was a fundamental distinction between the procedures used to diagnose physical diseases and the procedures used to identify mental disorders. In the former case, a diagnosis was based on objective criteria, but in the latter, completely subjective judgments were demanded. Finally, Szasz proposed that mental illness functioned as a pretext for exonerating irresponsible behavior and was objectionable from the point of view of social justice.

Szasz concluded that the term "mental illness" had outlived its usefulness and suggested that deviant behavior patterns be recognized simply as "problems in living."

The responses to Szasz's statement were of many types. An initial rebuttal, offered by David Ausubel (1961), captured what was probably the predominant sentiment among mental health professionals at the time. To begin with, Ausubel offered plausible counterarguments to many of Szasz's factual claims. In addition, he denounced the moral implications of Szasz's proposal that the concept of mental illness be abolished. However, refutation of Szasz's central thesis, that mental illness did not exist, proved elusive. Ausubel was able to do no better than proclaim the existence of mental illness as a manifest truth. Mental illness could be defined, he declared, as "behavior that is either seriously distorted or sufficiently unadaptive to prevent normal interpersonal relations and vocational functioning," in other words, "a gross deviation from a designated range of desirable behavioral variability" (p. 72). This definition, of course, simply begged the question: What is normal? What is desirable?

To refute Szasz's position effectively, it seemed that an unequivocal definition of mental illness had to be formulated. However, Ausubel's failure to define the phenomenon in question foreshadowed certain difficulties that would be encountered in any attempt to specify the parameters of psychological abnormality. Subsequently, it has become standard practice for abnormal psychology texts to introduce the field by enumerating various means of defining mental illness or abnormality and various deficiencies associated with each of them (e.g., Bootzin & Acocella, 1980; Gottesfeld, 1979; Kazdin, Bellack, & Hersen, 1980; Sue, Sue, & Sue, 1981).

The Definitions

The so-called "statistical" method of defining mental illness is typically presented first as one plausible approach that inevitably raises more questions than it answers. According to this definition, mental illness is determined by the relative frequency of certain characteristics or behaviors in the general population. Phenomena that are relatively rate—in the case of a normal distribution this amounts to phenomena that are dimensionally extreme—are considered indexes of mental illness. For example, individuals whose level of trait anxiety is two standard deviations above the population mean might be considered abnormal or mentally ill according to this definition.

Needless to say, this method of defining mental illness is fraught with deficiencies, the most obvious, though probably the least problematic (see Rimland, 1969), being the dependence on arbitrary cutoff points. The greatest inadequacy is the definition's complete lack of content. On what basis are the psychological dimensions to be chosen? Is anxiety a relevant dimension? Is intelligence? The notion that some psychological characteristics are statistically rare obviously does very little to clarify the boundaries of mental illness.

An alternative method of defining mental illness, the textbooks have noted, is the use of social norms. The social definition is similar to the statistical definition in that statistical rarity usually characterizes those psychological features judged abnormal, but now the relevant dimensions of behavior are specified, in particular, in terms of the values of society at large. Behavior that is beyond the bounds of social acceptability would be considered a manifestation of mental illness by this definition. The textbooks have generally been quick to emphasize the totalitarian implications of this approach and suggest that it must ultimately be rejected on these grounds. Yet, the social definition seems to capture some essential ingredients in the way the concept of mental illness is applied.

A third means of defining mental illness is to draw on psychological theory. As the textbooks usually note, numerous theoretical persuasions have sprouted up in the mental health field, each with its particular notion of what constitutes psychological abnormality or mental illness. Although some schools of thought do not use the term *illness* explicitly, each identifies certain undesirable psychological states or behaviors that merit professional intervention. Unconscious conflicts dominating an individual's behavior are "pathological" according to psychoanalytic theory; ineffective responding for reinforcers defines the patient for some learning theorists; among the humanists, it is marked incongruence of the introjected self-concept and the actual self; for the gestalt therapist, it is an excessive dissociation of components of experience. The list is virtually endless, and there is a tremendous variety of viewpoints expressed. Unfortunately, the theoretical assortment is so great that it would be impossible to formulate any broadly acceptable definition of mental illness.

This is not to imply that all theories are equally meritorious. Clearly, some theories may be considered superior to others on either formal or empirical grounds. But even the most advanced psychological theory currently available falls far short of the kind of comprehensiveness and validation that could justify authoritative pronouncements regarding the parameters of abnormality. Were an adequate theory to be developed, it is still not clear that a definition of mental illness would result. After all, a valid psychological theory would merely afford the explanation of psychological or behavioral outcomes in accordance with postulated causal mechanisms. Such outcomes would still have to be evaluated as positive or negative according to some criteria. Deciding on the relevant criteria entails nothing less than posing the original question: What is abnormal?

Most textbooks recognize, therefore, that theory-based definitions of mental illness amount to an alternate form of the social definition. The only difference is that the norms are derived from the implicit values of a particular school of thought as opposed to society at large, and of course, often there is more than casual correspondence between the two.

A fourth principal method of defining illness or abnormality is to use the criterion of subjective discomfort. According to this approach, individuals are identified as mentally ill by their own admission of psychological distress. Of all the means of defining abnormality, this is perhaps the most analogous to the approach taken in the practice of physical medicine. Medical conditions are identified primarily because an individual seeks treatment for physical discomfort. Alternatively, a nonpainful condition is targeted for treatment because it is known ultimately to lead to physical discomfort (or death), and of course, some conditions are treated merely because the patient desires a change, as in the case of cosmetic surgery.

Psychiatry, however, has been notoriously resistant to accepting a role for its patients in determining illness. Indeed, the traditional clinical lore held that a disorder's severity was measured in direct proportion to the patient's lack of awareness of the underlying psychological processes. It is this theoretical climate that enabled many in the field to accept uncritically a study in the early 1960s purporting to show that over 80% of an unsuspecting metropolitan population exhibited psychiatric symptoms and almost one quarter were "impaired" (Srole, Langner, Michael, Opler, & Rennie, 1962).

The textbooks have generally recognized some merit in the subjective discomfort definition but have concluded that it falls far short of a satisfactory definition of mental illness. As a sole criterion, it would exclude many of the so-called personality disorders as well as such psychotic states as mania and schizophrenia. A principal feature of these diagnostic categories is a lack of insight into the problematic nature of one's mental condition. More generally, the textbooks observe, almost anyone's understanding of mental illness includes the notion that the affected individual might have some impairment in rational judgment, especially as applied to himself or herself. Thus, a subjective discomfort definition of mental illness appears to violate certain intuitive understandings of the concept.

What Are We Attempting to Define?

If the statistical definition, the social definition, the theory-based definition, and the subjective discomfort definition all fall short of an adequate representation of mental illness, it seems reasonable to wonder if we really know just what we are trying to define.

An opinion on this subject is offered by several theorists of a sociological bent who contend that the social definition of mental illness, for all its unsavory connotations of conformism, actually comes closer to the mark than we are willing to admit. To make their point, theorists such as Braginsky, Braginsky, and Ring (1969), Sarbin (1967, 1968), and Scheff (1966, 1970) have brought the full weight of Goffman's (1959, 1961, 1963) social identity theory into the mental health arena.

Scheff (1970), for example, published a statement in the then newly formed journal *Schizophrenia Bulletin*, denouncing its very rationale. Schizophrenia, he contended, is not an illness but an ideology, a label conferred on individuals who commit offenses against the public order. The nature of the transgression is the failure to maintain society's implicit standards of self-presentation in public encounters, a violation of "residual rules."

The social deviance perspective of Scheff suggests, perhaps, why the mental health field gropes so ineffectually for a definition of mental illness yet senses intuitively that the concept has some validity. A definition is elusive because deviance itself has no inherent properties; it is strictly a normative phenomenon. Yet, deviation from social norms is so deeply understood by every member of society that any conceptual abstraction to pin it down strikes a responsive chord. The illness or medical model enjoys currency because the contemporary approach to regulating deviance is through treatment by medical personnel.

It is important to note—and this is often not understood by the many detractors of Scheff and like-minded theorists—that Scheff's position acknowledges the potential role of psychological, environmental, and even genetic or biochemical factors in producing deviant behavior. Scheff's quarrel is not with the putative causes of behavior but with the identification and characterization of the outcome. Specifically, what is condemned is the application of medical terminology to a phenomenon identified by social criteria.

Despite these qualifications, many behavioral scientists, particularly those with medical training (e.g., Kety, 1974; Spitzer, 1975, 1976), bristled at the continuing insinuations by Scheff, Szasz, and others (e.g., Laing, 1967; Rosenhan, 1973) that they had been devoting their careers to the research and treatment of a myth. Seymour Kety's (1974) paper, entitled "From Rationalization to Reason," took up the defense of the medical model as an empirical challenge. Specifically, he outlined the results of his investigation of psychopathology in the biological and adoptive relatives of schizophrenic and control adoptees. The results indicated that schizophrenia (as defined by DSM-II) was three and a half times more prevalent among the biological relatives of schizophrenic adoptees than among all other groups of relatives, including those with whom the index case had actually been

raised. If there were any doubts as to the implications of these findings, they could be dispelled by subsequent analyses restricted to paternal half-siblings (who do not share even their prenatal environment). Among these relatives, it was found that those related to a schizophrenic index case were seven times more likely then controls to be diagnosed as schizophrenic. The only factor that could conceivably account for this result is genetic overlap among biological relatives. As Kety was compelled to conclude, "If schizophrenia is a myth, it is a myth with a strong genetic component!" (p. 961).

Two Questions

Kety's study was a classic contribution to the body of evidence now generally accepted as incontrovertibly demonstrating a genetic component of schizophrenia.

But did the study establish the existence of mental illness?

I suggest that Kety's study did not even address this issue, at least not in the way it had been formulated by Szasz, Scheff, and others. As we shall see, the principal reason that the myth versus illness dispute continues unresolved is that advocates of the two perspectives are actually in substantial agreement with each other on most basic points without realizing it. To understand this, we must first consider what is really meant by the proposition that mental illness is a myth.

This proposition actually raises two very different questions, and unless they are separated, any systematic or rational analysis of the issues is completely obstructed.

The questions are, in effect: (a) What is the conceptual status of the psychological variables determining deviant behavior? and (b) How should society respond to individuals exhibiting certain psychological or behavioral characteristics?

Mental Illness, Medicine, and Science

The first question is not one that the so-called medical model can speak to, though science can. Unfortunately, many theorists and researchers erroneously equate medicine with science, thus presuming that if the scientific validity of a term such as schizophrenia is established, then schizophrenia is automatically installed within the purview of medicine.

In fact, medicine has only a derivative relationship to science. It is a technology developed to deal with pragmatic problems as defined by individuals and social policy. Thus, when the genetic basis of schizophrenia gradually came to light, this no more established it as a medical condition than the genetic basis of eye color established brown eyes as a medical condition. That a particular phenomenon has a cause in no way implies it is a disease.

Disease and illness are not scientific concepts. They are merely categories that comprise the ever-expanding range of conditions treated by health professionals. As Meehl (1977) observed:

> **One can discern nothing obviously in common—in the postulated causal structure, in the statistical relations between signs or symptoms and the defining etiology, and in the approach to prophylaxis and treatment—among the following conditions, all of which are recognized as "disease entities": Huntington's disease, pellagra, measles, rheumatoid arthritis, subacute bacterial endocarditis, congenital aneurysm, idiopathic epilepsy, general paresis, dementia senilis, obesity, diabetic gangrene, appendicitis, gout, cerebral fat embolism following bone-crushing trauma. So far as I have been able to ascertain, no general systematic clarification has been done within organic medicine on the metaquestion "When does a disease entity exist?" (pp. 194–195)**

The conceptual status of psychological variables can hardly be elucidated by a so-called model devoid of any unifying conceptual framework.

Some medically trained researchers might dispute such a characterization, suggesting that a basic medical model with substantial

heuristic value does in fact exist. As Kety (1974) stated in defending the proposition that schizophrenia is a disease:

> **The medical model is an evolving intellectual process, consonant with the scientific method, which involves long periods of observation and description, increasingly sharper differentiation, and research rather than wishful thinking.**
>
> **The medical model of an illness is a process that moves from the recognition and palliation of symptoms to the characterization of a specific disease in which the etiology and the pathogenesis are known and the treatment is rational and specific. That process depends on the acquisition of knowledge and may often take many years or centuries. (p. 959)**

But what process is it that Kety is actually describing here? Students of nonmedical fields will recognize it, not as a "process consonant with the scientific method," but as the scientific method itself, as it is applied in physics, chemistry, biology, psychology, economics or any other empirical field. Atom, molecule, genotype, cognition, market value: Are these diseases? Indeed they are not. They are theoretical entities or constructs that have been inferred following systematic observation of their presumed effects. The scientific method may be useful in discovering causes and developing cures for medical conditions, but this in no way implies the converse: that a particular state constitutes a medical condition because it is amenable to scientific analysis.

The point, then, is that the "medical model," as Kety uses the concept, is synonymous with the scientific method, which objectively does not provide recommendations regarding the necessity of treatment by medical personnel.

If medicine has nothing to say about the conceptual status of psychological variables, then where does science stand vis-à-vis the proposition that mental illness is a myth?

Far from disputing such a claim, science presents itself as a chief proponent. Science, after all, is built on myths. Its very progress depends on the development and refinement of the many outlandish creations—otherwise known as theories—that afford prediction and control of natural phenomena. Accordingly, the psychological variables determining deviant behavior are regarded by scientists (cf. Neale & Oltmanns, 1980), not as diseases but as theoretical or hypothetical constructs (Cronbach & Meehl, 1955). Hypothetical constructs are not presumed to exist as physical structures (though the basis of their effects may be presumed to reside ultimately in physical mechanisms). Rather, they are conceptual abstractions that are developed to account for observable phenomena. Terms such as schizophrenia, depression, anxiety, psychopathy—in short, all the so-called mental disorders—are products of just such an inferential process.

Those who defend the illness model of mental disorders do so principally in the interest of preserving an enlightened scientific approach to the research and treatment of deviant behavior. Though their idiom is medical, we may presume that they do not intend to quarrel with sound philosophy of science regarding the conceptual status of inferred entities. Kety's own words, quoted earlier, clearly reveal his commitment to the tentative "evolving intellectual process" that scientific inference entails.

Therefore, regarding the conceptual status of psychological variables determining deviant behavior, there is no real impediment to a negotiated settlement between the medical and the myth ideologues. Both camps implicitly accept the proposition that psychological variables—mental conditions or diagnostic entities—are theoretical constructs subject to modification and refinement in accordance with acceptable standards of inductive inference (see Szasz, 1960, p. 113).

Where the two factions often differ, though the level of polemic rarely advances this high, is in their reading of the empirical status of specific diagnostic categories. Critics of the medical perspective have typically underscored limitations in the reliability and predictive validity of psychiatric diagnoses (e.g., Braginsky et al., 1969; Rosenhan, 1973; Scheff, 1970), whereas its advocates (e.g., Kety, 1974; Spitzer, 1975) have understandably sought to emphasize the successes.

But even this difference of opinion is not as great as it often seems. Sophisticated advocates of the medical perspective are acutely aware of the tenuous empirical status of most diagnostic categories. For example, in their analysis of the diagnostic reliability of DSM-II, Spitzer and Fleiss (1974) concluded that, even under the best of circumstances, levels of interrater agreement were quite unsatisfactory. Although reliability in the most recent DSM appears to be substantially improved, the authors of the manual recognize that the predictive validity of even reliable categories is hardly assured (see American Psychiatric Association, 1980, pp. 1–12).

The empirical status of current diagnostic entities is really beside the point. Even entities with proven construct validity (Cronbach & Meehl, 1955) are myths in the sense of their being abstract creations. Unlike other myths, however, valid constructs can lay claim to some measure of "verisimilitude" (Popper, 1972).

Mental Illness and Social Policy

What of the second aspect of the myth versus illness debate: How should society respond to individuals exhibiting certain (deviant) psychological or behavioral characteristics?

Now we are in a realm to which science brings no special expertise, for this is a matter of social policy. Science can, of course, provide information that will aid the public in making an educated decision, but such information conveys only the empirical relations between independent and dependent variables, that is, between therapeutic actions and behavioral outcomes. As to which actions or outcomes are desirable, cost-efficient, egregious, misguided, or anything else, these questions must be referred to organs of the public will that are customarily charged with formulating social policy in accordance with society's basic values. To some extent, we already have something of a codified policy in effect, as reflected in competency hearings and insurance practices, though we need not dwell on the very controversial and very incomplete nature of such policy as it now stands.

By and large, the formulation and execution of policy for psychological intervention has fallen, by default, on the various professional groups claiming expertise in the modification of psychological or behavioral abnormalities: medicine, clinical psychology, social work, and pastoral counseling. Needless to say, such policy has never been explicitly delineated, and most mental health practitioners are hardly ever reminded that implicit values are espoused whenever a decision is made to initiate or terminate treatment of a given individual. The question of values is rarely raised because, by and large, members of society seem to agree fairly well what constitutes desirable versus undesirable behavioral outcomes. Occasionally (and not inconsequentially), conflicts do arise, as when a hospitalized patient (described as having "loss of insight") refuses to accept treatment or when a segment of society (e.g., homosexuals) is no longer willing to have its behavioral practices considered grounds for medical intervention.

But for better or worse, there seems to be minimal conflict over many fundamental ideals of human existence—for example, that one should be physically comfortable, emotionally happy, kind to others, and in touch with events—and these shared ideals are reflected every day in the treatment goals endorsed by patients and therapists alike.

By the same token, there is no real disagreement between the myth and the medical ideologues over behavioral ideals themselves. Neither group views the aimless wandering of hallucinating vagrants through New York City as a desirable behavioral outcome (however, see Laing, 1967, for a possible exception). Rather, the dispute has arisen over medicine's labeling as "diseases" those behavioral practices that

fall short of consensually accepted standards. As we have already seen, this is an empty dispute in terms of its conceptual or scientific significance—there is no scientific basis for labeling a hypothetical construct "diseased." In terms of practical significance, proponents of the medical versus the myth position are in conflict essentially over the following question: What are the particular methods, both in terms of effectiveness and moral acceptability, that should be adopted to help individuals achieve levels of behavioral adjustment consistent with common values?

Supporters of the disease perspective have maintained that medical treatment is the appropriate strategy of intervention, whereas their opponents have insisted that deviant behavior be addressed as "problems in living" (Szasz, 1960). But here again the difference between the medical versus the myth ideologues may be more apparent than real.

Indeed, how does verbal psychotherapy—a practice that has traditionally posed a medical treatment—really differ from alternative modes of intervention aimed at problems in living? We need not review the classic comparative studies of psychotherapeutic practice (e.g., Frank, 1973; Levy, 1963; Schofield, 1964) to surmise that the two approaches would not differ at all in any qualitative sense. Whatever its pretensions to the medical imprimatur, psychotherapy remains a verbal exchange between two individuals, intended ultimately to help one of the individuals overcome the very problems in living that Szasz has underscored.

Even the various somatic treatments advocated by medical psychiatry are not inherently anathema to the problems-in-living perspective. The antimedical movement is not bent on denying the palliative benefits of chemical compounds to those who suffer. The principal objection has to do with ultimate effectiveness: that such treatments are used as nonspecific custodial measures that fail to achieve any permanent remedy. The use of psychotropic medications is considered doubly injurious because these medications not only entail serious (sometimes permanent) side effects, but also are far too readily (and fallaciously) interpreted as affirming a simple organic model, thereby dampening efforts to explore alternatives or adjuncts to medication that are more specifically effective (Szasz, 1976).

Despite these objections, Szasz and others do not articulate any absolute principle that would bar somatic treatment as a component of the therapeutic armamentarium if an undeniably positive contribution to alleviating problems in living could be demonstrated. By the same token, serious thinkers in psychopharmacology acknowledge that treatments are ideally devised to address proximate causes specifically, whether through somatic, psychological, or social means (Barchas, Berger, Ciaranello, & Elliott, 1977).

If the myth and the medical ideologues are largely able to agree on behavioral ideals, and if they agree in principle that methods of achieving these ideals be selected for specific efficacy, then where does the dispute really lie?

By now it should be clear that the dispute lies in the only real meaning that the term "illness" has acquired when applied to an individual's emotions or behavior, namely, (a) the authorization of care by a physician and, in some cases, (b) the assignment of a legal/ethical status that denies certain freedoms while conferring special protections. Professional and regulatory practices like these (and ultimately, their social consequences, e.g., Sarbin, 1967) are at the heart of the debate over the existence of mental illness.

The issues raised are enormously controversial, and the depth of disagreement between adversaries cannot be minimized. Szasz's position, for example, is fundamentally irreconcilable with that of the medical establishment. Whereas Szasz denounces involuntary commitment categorically, the medical establishment generally supports it as legitimate and even desirable (cf. Chodoff, 1976).

Society must come to grips with the many questions that are raised by its avowed intention not to ignore deviant behavior. For example: Who is entitled to conduct treatment? When can treatment be applied forcibly? When can an individual's rights be abridged? When is an individual absolved from responsibilities?

These are serious questions, difficult questions, but what ultimately must be faced is that they are not theoretical or empirical questions. They are questions of social regulation that must be addressed directly, not concealed within a specious debate over the existence of an undefined abstraction.

References

AMERICAN PSYCHIATRIC ASSOCIATION. (1980). *Diagnostic and statistical manual of mental disorders* (3rd ed.). Washington, DC: Author.

AUSUBEL, D. P. (1961). Personality disorder *is* disease. *American Psychologist, 16,* 69–74.

BARCHAS, J. D. BERGER, P. A., CIARANELLO, R. D., AND ELLIOTT, G. R. (1977). *Psychopharmacology: From theory to practice.* New York: Oxford University Press.

BOOTZIN, R. R., AND ACOCELLA, J. R. (1980). *Abnormal psychology: Current perspectives* (3rd ed.). New York: Random House.

BRAGINSKY, B. M., BRAGINSKY, D. D., AND RING, K. (1969). *Methods of madness: The mental hospital as a last resort.* New York: Holt, Rinehart & Winston.

CHODOFF, P. (1976). The case for involuntary hospitalization of the mentally ill. *American Journal of Psychiatry, 133,* 496–501.

CRONBACH, L. J., AND MEEHL, P. E. (1955). Construct validity in psychological tests. *Psychological Bulletin, 52,* 281–302.

FRANK, J. D. (1973). *Persuasion and healing* (2nd ed.). Baltimore, MD: Johns Hopkins University Press.

GOFFMAN, E. (1959). *The presentation of self in everyday life.* New York: Doubleday.

GOFFMAN, E. (1961). *Asylums: Essays on the social situation of mental patients and other inmates.* Chicago: Aldine.

GOFFMAN, E. (1963). *Stigma: Notes on the management of spoiled identity.* Englewood Cliffs, NJ: Prentice-Hall:

GOTTESFELD, H. (1979). *Abnormal psychology: A community mental health perspective.* Chicago: Science Research Associates.

KAZDIN, A. E., BELLACK, A. S., AND HERSEN, M. (Eds.). (1980). *New perspectives in abnormal psychology.* New York: Oxford University Press.

KETY, S. S. (1974). From rationalization to reason. *American Journal of Psychiatry, 131,* 957–963.

LAING R. D. (1964). Is schizophrenia a disease? *International Journal of Social Psychiatry, 10,* 184–193.

LAING, R. D. (1967). *The politics of experience.* New York: Pantheon.

LEVY, L. H. (1963). *Psychological interpretation.* New York: Holt, Rinehart & Winston.

MEEHL, P. E. (1977). Specific genetic etiology, psychodynamics, and therapeutic nihilism. In P. E. Meehl (Ed.), *Psychodiagnosis: Selected papers.* New York: Norton.

NEALE, J. M., AND OLTMANNS, T. F. (1980). *Schizophrenia.* New York: Wiley.

POPPER, K. R. (1972). *Objective knowledge: An evolutionary approach.* London: Oxford University Press.

RIMLAND, B. (1969). Psychogenesis versus biogenesis: The isssues and the evidence. In S. C. Plog & R. B. Edgerton (Eds.), *Changing perspectives in mental illness.* New York: Holt, Rinehart & Winston.

ROSENHAN, D. L. (1973). On being sane in insane places. *Science, 179,* 250–258.

SARASON, I. G., AND GANZER, V. J. (1968). Concerning the medical model. *American Psychologist, 23,* 507–510.

SARBIN, T. R. (1967). On the futility of the proposition that some people be labeled "mentally ill." *Journal of Consulting Psychology, 31,* 447–453.

SARBIN, T. R. (1968). Notes on the transformation of social identity. In L. M. Roberts, N. S. Greenfield, & M. H. Miller (Eds.), *Comprehensive mental health: The challenge of evaluation.* Madison: University of Wisconsin Press.

SCHEFF, T. J. (1966). *Being mentally ill: A sociological theory.* Chicago: Aldine.

SCHEFF, T. J. (1970). Schizophrenia as ideology. *Schizophrenia Bulletin, 2,* 15–19.

SCHOFIELD, W. (1964). *Psychotherapy: The purchase of friendship.* Englewood Cliffs, NJ: Prentice-Hall.

SPITZER, R. L. (1975). On pseudoscience in science, logic in remission, and psychiatric diagnosis: A critique of Rosenhan's "On being sane in insane place." *Journal of Abnormal Psychology, 84,* 442–452.

SPITZER, R. L. (1976). More on pseudoscience in science and the case for psychiatric diagnosis. *Archives of General Psychiatry, 33,* 459–470.

SPITZER, R. L., AND FLEISS, J. L. (1974). A re-analysis of the reliability of psychiatric diagnosis. *American Journal of Psychiatry, 125,* 341–347.

SROLE, L., LANGNER, T. S., MICHAEL, S. T., OPLER, M. K., AND RENNIE, T. A. C. (1962). *Mental health in the metropolis* (Vol. 1). New York: McGraw-Hill.

SUE, D., SUE, D. W., AND SUE, S. (1981). *Understanding abnormal behavior.* Boston: Houghton Mifflin.

SZASZ, T. (1960). The myth of mental illness. *American Psychologist, 15,* 113–118.

SZASZ, T. (1976). *Schizophrenia: The sacred symbol of psychiatry.* New York: Basic Books.

SZASZ, T. (1982a). The psychiatric will: A new mechanism for protecting persons against "psychosis" and psychiatry. *American Psychologist, 37,* 762–770.

SZASZ, T. (1982b, February 16). Vagrancy and vagrants. *The New York Times,* p. 19.

2

Psychiatric Labeling in Cross-Cultural Perspective

Jane M. Murphy

In recent years labeling (or societal reaction) theory has aroused strong interest among people concerned with mental illness. From the perspective of labeling theory, the salient features of the behavior patterns called mental illness in countries where Western psychiatry is practiced appear to be as follows: (i) these behaviors represent deviations from what is believed to be normal in particular sociocultural groups, (ii) the norms against which the deviations are identified are different in different groups, (iii) like other forms of deviation they elicit societal reactions which convey disapproval and stigmatization, (iv) a label of mental illness applied to a person whose behavior is deviant tends to become fixed, (v) the person labeled as mentally ill is thereby encouraged to learn and accept a role identity which perpetuates the stigmatizing behavior pattern, (vi) individuals who are powerless in a social group are more vulnerable to this process than others are, and (vii) because social agencies in modern industrial society contribute to the labeling process they have the effect of creating problems for those they treat rather than easing problems.

Jane M. Murphy. Psychiatric labeling in cross-cultural perspective. SCIENCE, Vol. 191, March 12, 1976, pp. 1019–1028. Copyright © 1976 by the American Association for the Advancement of Science. Reprinted by permission.

This school of thought emerged mainly within sociology, as an extension of studies of social deviance in which crime and delinquency were originally the major focus (1). It is also associated with psychiatry through, for example, Thomas Szasz and R. D. Laing (2). These ideas have come to be called a "sociological model" of mental illness, for they center on learning and the social construction of norms. They began to be formulated about 25 years ago (3), commanded growing attention in the late 1960's, and have been influential in recent major changes in public programs for psychiatric care, especially the deinstitutionalization which is occurring in a number of states (4, 5).

Several aspects of the theory receive support from a study reported in *Science* by David Rosenhan (6), based on the experiences of eight sane subjects who gained admission to psychiatric hospitals, were diagnosed as schizophrenic, and remained as patients an average of 19 days until discharged as "in remission." Rosenhan argues that "we cannot distinguish insanity from sanity" (6, p. 257). He associates his work with "anthropological considerations" and cites Ruth Benedict (7) as an early contributor to a theme he pursues, which is that "what is viewed as normal in one culture may be seen as quite aberrant in another" (6, p. 250). He indicates that the perception of behavior as being schizophrenic is relative to context, for "psychiatric diagnosis betrays little about the patient but much about the environment in which an observer finds him." He argues that, despite the effort to humanize treatment of disturbed people by calling them patients and labeling them mentally ill, the attitudes of professionals and the public at large are characterized by "fear, hostility, aloofness, suspicion, and dread." Once the label of schizophrenia has been applied, the "diagnosis acts on all of them"—patient, family, and relatives—"as a self-fulfilling prophecy. Eventually, the patient himself accepts the diagnosis, with all of its surplus meanings and expectations, and behaves accordingly" (6, p. 254).

The research to be described here presents an alternative perspective derived from cross-cultural comparisons, mainly of two widely separated and distinctly contrasting non-Western groups, Eskimos of northwest Alaska and Yorubas of rural, tropical Nigeria. It is concerned with the meanings attached to behaviors which would be labeled mental illness in our society. I interpret these data as raising important questions about certain assumptions in the labeling thesis and therefore as casting doubt on its validity as a major explanation of mental illness, especially with respect to schizophrenia. These cross-cultural investigations suggest that relativism has been exaggerated by labeling theorists and that in widely different cultural and environmental situations sanity appears to be distinguishable from insanity by cues that are very similar to those used in the Western world.

The Labeling Orientation

As Edwin Schur (8) points out, if labeling theory is conceived broadly it is the application of George Herbert Mead's theories about self–other interactions to a definition of social deviance extended to include human problems ranging from crime to blindness. Labeling theory emphasizes the social meanings imputed to deviant behavior and focuses on the unfolding processes of inter-

action whereby self-definition is influenced by others. Further, "it is a central tenet of the labeling perspective that neither acts nor individuals are 'deviant' in the sense of immutable, 'objective' reality without reference to processes of social definition." Schur states that "this relativism may be viewed as a major strength" of labeling theory (8, p. 14).

Edwin Lemert's concept of secondary deviance (9) is of critical importance in linking self–other considerations to deviations. Secondary deviation occurs when a person learns the role and accepts the identity of a deviant as the basis of his life-style. It is a response to a response; negative feedback from significant others reinforces and stabilizes the behavior that initially produced it. Applied to criminality, this idea has created general awareness of a process whereby a young person on being labeled a juvenile delinquent may enter a network of contingencies that lead ultimately to his learning criminal activities and "hardening" as a criminal rather than to the correction of behavior.

In *The Making of Blind Men*, Robert Scott points to a similar process regarding a very different type of deviance (10). If a person is labeled blind by certain administrative criteria he is likely to become enmeshed in care-giving agencies that encourage him to accept a definition of himself as helpless and to learn to play the role of the blind man. These experiences may even inhibit the use of residual vision. Scott shows that institutions for the blind vary in the degree to which they encourage acceptance or rejection of the deviant role and that these differences are related to differences in the life-style of blind men. Insofar as the labeling concept has been employed in this way I believe it is sound and has disclosed new and valuable information.

The application of labeling ideas to mental illness has tended to take a different course (11) and has aroused considerable controversy, as indicated, for example, in the continuing exchange between Thomas Scheff and Walter Gove *et al.* (12–15). One question in this controversy is whether mental illness should be considered a "pure case" of secondary deviation or a more complex case. Lemert's formulation of the concept of secondary deviation was influenced by his investigation of stuttering, and he suggests that stuttering represents the pure case: "Stuttering thus far has defied efforts at causative explanation. . . . It appears to be exclusively a process-product in which, to pursue the metaphor, normal speech variations, or at most, minor abnormalities of speech (primary stuttering) can be fed into an interactional or evaluational process and come out as secondary stuttering" (9, p. 56).

The important point here is that primary deviance is considered to be normal variation or only "minor abnormalities," and the influence of societal reactions is considered genuinely causative. Societal reactions "work on" and "mold" normal variations of speech to "create" stuttering. For mental illness the labeling theorists have tended to use the "pure case" model rather than the more complex model represented by blindness, where lack or loss of sight is primary deviance and the role of blind man is secondary deviance.

Scheff has provided the most systematic theoretical statement regarding labeling and mental illness, and in his formulation the primary deviations that are fed into interactional processing to come out as mental illness are described as "amorphous," "unstructured," and "residual" violations of a society's norm (11, pp. 33, 82). Rosenhan suggests that the behaviors labeled schizophrenic might be " 'sane' outside the psychiatric hospital but seem insane in it . . . [because patients] are responding to a bizarre setting" (6, p. 257). Lemert says that social exclusion can "create a paranoid disposition in the absence of any special character structure" (9, p. 198). Further, many have posited that behavior we call mental illness might be considered normal in a different culture or in a minority social class. Thus, the primary deviations of mental illness are held to be for the most part insignificant, and societal reactions become the main etiological factor.

This view is reminiscent of ideas about human plasticity, cultural determinism, and cultural relativism which were prominent in what used to be called the culture-personality studies of anthropology. In fact the influence of culture-personality on labeling theory is explicitly stated by Lemert, who was trained jointly in sociology and anthropology and who has drawn on non-Western studies throughout his career. The influence is equally acknowledged by Rosenhan (6). It seems to me that numbers of proponents of labeling theory assume that the expanding body of data from non-Western areas has supported the relativist propositions put forth by Benedict and others in the 1930's and '40's (16). Indeed, it was my own assumption when I began anthropological work with Eskimos. I thought I would find their conception of normality and abnormality to be very different, if not opposite, from that held in Western Culture. This did not prove to be the case, and my experience is not unique. Anthropologists who have been conducting field research in recent years using more systematic methods but continuing to work on the relations between individual behavior and cultural context tend to hold a greatly modified view of the extent of individual plasticity and the molding force of culture (17, 18).

It would be misleading on my part to imply that all theory building and investigation regarding the relation of labeling and mental illness have followed the pure-case model. In their studies on mental retardation Robert Edgerton and Jane Mercer use moderate labeling ideas and show that social reactions are related to differences in the ways subnormal individuals are able to function both in and outside of institutions (19). A growing number of studies of alcoholism, many of them influenced by labeling views, have demonstrated that social attitudes and the variable meanings attached to drinking are correlated with marked differences in alcoholism rates in various cultural groups (20). There are, in addition, numbers of studies of the social pathways leading to hospitalization, the impact of hospitalization, attitudes toward discharged mental patients, and so on which reveal important outcomes from the mentally ill without imputing to societal reactions the degree of significance given them in the more deterministic formulations.

Most labeling studies of mental illness have been carried out in the United States and the United Kingdom. Variations in the definition and tolerance of mental illness have mainly been studied in groups at different social class levels in industrialized society (21). Since cultural relativism is one of the main elements of the orientation, it seems useful to put some of the basic labeling questions to non-Western data. As background for this, I quote from four contributors to labeling theory: Scheff, Erving Goffman, Theodore Sarbin, and David Mechanic. These references do not encompass the breadth and elaboration of each contributor's own approach to the problem of mental illness, but they do reflect the view of cultural relativity which runs throughout the labeling orientation.

Scheff says that "the culture of the group provides a vocabulary of terms for categorizing many norm violations" (11, pp. 33, 81). These designate deviations such as crime and drunkenness. There is a residual category of diverse kinds of deviations which constitute an affront to the unconscious definition of decency and reality uniquely characteristic of each culture. Scheff posits that the "culture provides no explicit label" for these deviations but they nevertheless take form in the minds of societal agents as "stereotypes of insanity." When people around a deviant respond to him in terms of these stereotypes, "his amorphous and unstructured rule-breaking tends to crystallize in conformity to these expectations." Scheff further suggests that these cultural stereotypes tend to produce uniformity of symptoms within a cultural group and "enormous differences in the manifest symptoms of stable mental disorder between societies."

It has been pointed out that there appears to be a contradiction in one aspect of Scheff's theory (12, p. 876; 22). It is difficult to accept that a socially shared image of behavior that can influence action and has the concrete-

ness of a stereotype should lack a name. It is possible Scheff meant that in the evolution of language a label for insanity was the last to emerge because it refers to a residue of norm violations. The dating of words is beyond the scope of the data to be presented here, but it will be possible to see whether an explicit label currently exists in the two cultures studied, a hunting-gathering culture (Eskimo) and an agricultural society (Yoruba), neither of which developed a written language. If a word for insanity occurs we can then investigate the kinds of behaviors therein denoted.

Regarding our own society, Goffman stresses that the "perception of losing one's mind is based on culturally derived and socially engrained stereotypes as to the significance of symptoms such as hearing voices, losing temporal and spatial orientation, and sensing that one is being followed" (23). He further indicates that there is cultural variation in this kind of imagery and differential encouragement for such a view of oneself. This makes it appropriate to ask whether hallucinations, delusions, and disorientations are present or absent from the conception of losing one's mind in Yoruba and Eskimo cultures, assuming they have a stereotype of insanity at all.

Labeling theorists express considerable dissatisfaction with the concept of mental illness, pointing out that it is a vague and euphemistic metaphor and ties together phenomena that are neither "mental" nor "illness." They argue that mental illness is a myth developed in Western societies, that the term represents an abortive effort to improve the treatment of people previously called lunatics, that in the name of this myth we continue to incarcerate, punish, and degrade people for deviating from norms. Sarbin suggests that defining behavioral aberrations as illness occurred in medieval Europe as a way to relabel people who might otherwise have been burned at the stake as witches (24). He further suggests that it was during this phase of Western history that the concept of mind came into being. It was used as a way to explain perplexing behavior that could not be related to occurrences external to the person. It is *"as if* there are states of mind" that cause these patterns of conduct. The "as if" was transmuted into the myth that the mind exists as a real entity and can therefore be sick or healthy.

In the data to be given, it will be possible to ask whether the idea of an inner state that influences conduct is found in these non-Western groups and, since both groups believe in witchcraft, whether a stereotype of insanity is associated with the conduct of witches. Everywhere that witchcraft has been systematically studied the role of the witch involves deviances that are heavily censured. The witch carries out practices that are believed to harm people through supernatural means. If the insane person and the witch are equated in the beliefs of non-Western groups, it would appear to follow that in those groups mental illness is thought of as social deviance; and this would be a telling point for labeling theory.

Mechanic makes the point that "although seemingly obvious, it is important to state that what may be viewed as deviant in one social group may be tolerated in another, and rewarded in still other groups" (25). He emphasizes that the social response may influence the frequency with which the deviant behavior occurs. It has been hypothesized by a number of researchers that holy men, shamans, or witch doctors are psychotics who have been rewarded for their psychotic behavior by being made incumbents of highly regarded and useful roles (26). This is the obverse of the possibility that the insane are thought of as witches. The role of the healer carries great power and approval. The idea of social rewards for mental illness underscores the lengths to which relativity can be carried, for it suggests that the social definition of one kind of behavior can turn it into such opposing roles as the defamed witch or the renowned shaman. Mechanic's points make it appropriate, therefore, to ask whether the shamans in Eskimo culture and the healers in Yoruba culture are thought by the people to be mentally ill and whether the rates of such mental illness in these groups are similar to or different from those in the West.

Scheff, Goffman, Sarbin, and Mechanic share the view that in our society the appellation "mentally ill" is a "stigmatizing" and "brutalizing" assessment. It robs the individual of identity through profound "mortification" and suggests that he is a "nonperson." It forces him into an ascribed role, exit from which is extremely difficult. Thus another question is posed. If Eskimos and Yorubas have a stereotype of insanity, are they less harsh than we with those defined as insane?

To illustrate the model I have in mind for exploring these questions I will first describe a non-Western event which suggests that certain aspects of labeling theory are valid. It does not concern mental illness but it demonstrates the use of labels as arbitrary social definitions in the labeling theory sense. The case is reported by W. H. R. Rivers in connection with his analysis of the concept of death among the Melanesians (27):

Some persons who are seriously ill and likely to die or who are so old that from the Melanesian point of view they are ready to die are labeled by the word *mate*, which means "dead person." They become thereby subjects of a ceremonial live burial. It can be argued that the Melanesians have a concept of death which is a social fiction. It embodies what they arbitrarily agree to define as death and is a distortion of reality as seen by most cultural groups. The label *mate* involves a degradation ceremony in which an elderly person is deprived of his rights and is literally "mortified." He is perceived *"as if* dead" and then buried. The linguistic relativist might even say that this use of the word *mate* shows that the Melanesians do not perceive death by means of the indicators of vital functioning applied in Western society (28).

Rivers's own conclusion is that the Melanesians view death the way we do and are cognizant of the difference between biological and social *mate*. Biological *mate* is by far the commoner phenomenon. In their practice of live burials the Melanesians in fact take close note of two typical precursors of death—old age and illness.

It seems clear, however, that socially sanctioned acts based on symbolic meanings, such as those involved in social *mate,* are powerful in influencing the course of human affairs. They can be treacherously abused and lead to what we think of as cruel outcomes. Rivers says that the practice is not conceived to be cruel or degrading by the Melanesians because in their meaning the burial relieves the person of a worn-out earth-life so that he can enter the higher status of the spiritual afterlife. By our standards the Melanesian interpretation would nevertheless be considered a collective rationalization of "geronticide." Whatever the intent, the socially defined death of elderly Melanesians is a myth and serves as a model of what I understand the labeling theorists to mean by the "myth of mental illness." Thus a final question: Do the Eskimos and Yorubas subscribe to such fictions about mental illness through which they perpetrate inhumanity and degradation?

Method of Study

The data to be presented derive mainly from a year of field work, in 1954–55, in a village of Yupik-speaking Eskimos on an island in the Bering Sea, and an investigation of similar length, in 1961 and 1963, among Egba and Yorubas. I also draw on shorter periods of field work in Gambia, Sudan, and South Vietnam.

Some of the Eskimo data came from a key informant, who systematically described the life experiences of the 499 Eskimos who constituted a total village census over the 15 years previous to and including the year of investigation. In addition, a dictionary of Eskimo words for illness and deviance was developed. Extended life histories of a small number of Eskimos were gathered. Also daily observations and comments from Eskimos about Eskimos (both in their own village and in other areas known to them) were recorded for the purpose of understanding their conceptions of behavior (29).

The approach among the Yorubas was different in that I worked with a group of three native healers and a member of an indige-

nous cult. Interviews were directed toward understanding Yoruba concepts of behavior in the abstract and centered on actual people only to the extent that acquaintances and patients were brought into the discussion as illustration (30).

The Eskimo data served as the base for an epidemiological study of the village in 1955, and the Yoruba data constituted one of the first phases of a larger epidemiological study carried out with a group of Nigerian and U.S. colleagues in which we studied 416 adults, of whom 245 constituted a representative sample from 14 villages (31).

In *The Social Meanings of Suicide,* a study affiliated with the labeling tradition, Jack Douglas has shown the weakness of official statistics as a basis for judging the social significance of behavioral phenomena in groups (32). The Eskimo and Yoruba studies reflect a similar orientation about the inadequacies of mental hospital statistics for the purposes at hand. As has been done in many labeling studies, I relied on participant observation and interviewing about microcultural events. The focus was on indigenous meanings. These meanings were then used as a basis for counting similar behavior patterns, so that they were defined from within a cultural group rather than by imposed criteria.

In these studies I have considered language to be the main repository of labels. Insofar as there is a counterpart to the official recognition of mental illness involved in hospital commitment in a Western society, it resides in what Eskimos and Yorubas say are the kinds of people treated by shamans and native healers.

Labeled Behavior Patterns

The first specific question is: Do Eskimos and Yorubas have labels for psychological and behavioral differences that bear any resemblance to what we mean by mental illness? These groups clearly recognize differences among themselves and describe these in terms of what people do and what they say they feel and believe. Some of the differences lead people to seek the aid of healers and some do not, some differences arouse sympathy and protection while others arouse disapproval, some are called sickness and others health, some are considered misconduct and others good conduct. Some are described by a single word or nominative phrase. Some that seem to have common features are described in varying circumlocutions and sentences. If a word exists for a complex pattern of behavior it seems acceptable to assume that the concept of that pattern has been crystallized out of a welter of specific attributes and that the word qualifies as an explicit label.

Of major importance is whether or not the Yorubas and Eskimos conceptualize a distinction between body and mind and attribute differences in functioning to one or the other. The first indication of such a distinction arose early in the Eskimo census review when a women was described in these terms: "Her sickness is getting wild and out of mind. . . but she might have had sickness in her body too." The Eskimo word for her was *nuthkavihak*. It became clear from other descriptions that the word refers to a complex pattern of behavioral processes of which the hallmark is conceived to be that something inside the person—the soul, the spirit, the mind—is out of order. Descriptions of how *nuthkavihak* is manifested include such phenomena as talking to oneself, screaming at someone who does not exist, believing that a child or husband was murdered by witchcraft when nobody else believes it, believing oneself to be an animal, refusing to eat for fear eating will kill one, refusing to talk, running away, getting lost, hiding in strange places, making strange grimaces, drinking urine, becoming strong and violent, killing dogs, and threatening people. Eskimos translate nuthkavihak as "being crazy."

There is a Yoruba word, *were*, which is also translated as insanity. The phenomena include hearing voices and trying to get other people to see their source though none can be seen, laughing when there is nothing to laugh at, talking all the time or not talking at all, asking oneself questions and answering them, picking up sticks and leaves for no purpose except to put them in a pile, throwing away food because it is thought to contain *juju*, tearing off one's clothes, setting fires, defecating in public and then mushing around in the feces, taking up a weapon and suddenly hitting someone with it, breaking things in a state of being stronger than normal, believing that an odor is continuously being emitted from one's body.

For both *nuthkavihak* and *were* indigenous healing practices are used. In fact, among the Yorubas some native healers specialize in the treatment of *were* (33, 34).

The profile of *were* behaviors is based not only on what the healers described in the abstract but also on data concerning two members of the sample identified as *were* by the village headman and a group of 28 *were* patients in the custody of native healers and in a Nigerian mental hospital. The profile of *nuthkavihak* is built from information about four individuals within the 15-year population of 499 persons and six Eskimos from earlier times and from a related Eskimo settlement in Siberia.

Of paramount significance is the fact that *were* and *nuthkavihak* were never used for a single phenomenon such as hearing voices, but rather were applied to a pattern in which three or four of the phenomena described above existed together. It is therefore possible to examine the situations in which a person exhibited one or another of the listed behaviors but was not labeled insane.

The ability to see things other people do not see and to look into the future and prophesy is a clearly recognized and highly valued trait. It is called "thinness" by Eskimos. This ability is used by numerous minor Eskimo diviners and is the outstanding characteristic of the shaman. The people called "thin" outnumber those called insane by at least eight to one. Moreover, there were no instances when a "thin" person was called *nuthkavihak*.

When a shaman undertakes a curing rite he becomes possessed by the spirit of an animal; he "deludes" himself, so to speak, into believing that he is an animal. Consider this description (35):

The seance is opened by singing and drumming. After a time the shamaness falls down very hard on the floor. In a while, the tapping of her fingers and toes is heard on the walrus skin floor. Slowly she gets up, and already she is thought to "look awful, like a dog, very scary." She crawls back and forth across the floor making growling sounds. In this state she begins to carry out the various rites which Eskimos believe will cure sickness, such as sucking the illness out of the body and blowing it into the air. Following this the shamaness falls to the floor again and the seance is over.

Compare this to the case, reported by Morton Teicher, of a Baffin Island Eskimo who believed that a fox had entered her body (36). This was not associated with shamanizing but was a continuous belief. She barked herself hoarse, tried to claw her husband, thought her feet were turning into fox paws, believed that the fox was moving up in her body so that she could feel its hair in her mouth, lost control of her bowels at times, and finally became so excited that she was tied up and put into a coffin-like box with an opening at the head through which she could be fed. This woman was thought to be crazy but the shamaness not. One Eskimo summarized the distinction this way: "When the shaman is healing he is out of his mind, but *he is not crazy.*" Figure 1 is a picture selected by an Eskimo to illustrate the shaman's appearance during a seance (37).

This suggests that seeing, hearing, and believing things that are not seen, heard, and believed by all members of the group are sometimes linked to insanity and sometimes not. The distinction appears to be the degree to which they are controlled and utilized for a specific social function. The inability to control these processes is what is meant by a mind out of order; when a mind is out of

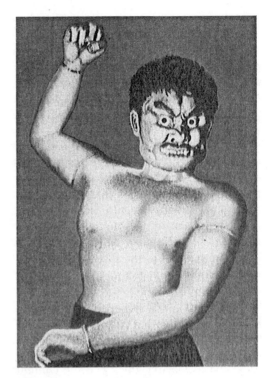

FIGURE 1
The shaman during seance: "he is out of mind but not crazy."

order it will not only fail to control sensory perception but will also fail to control behavior. Another Eskimo who was asked to define *nuthkavihak* said that it means "the mind does not control the person, *he is crazy.*" I take this to mean that volition is implicated, that hearing voices, for example, can be voluntary or involuntary, and that it is mainly the involuntary forms that are associated with *were* and *nuthkavihak.*

In cultures such as Eskimo and Yoruba, where clairvoyant kinds of mental phenomena are encouraged and preternatural experiences are valued, something similar to what we might call hallucinations and delusions can probably be learned or simulated. A favorable audience reaction is likely to stabilize the performance of the people who fill the roles of fortune-teller and faith healer. For example, the shamaness described above was unable to keep her patient alive but her performance was considered to have been well executed; she was said to have done "all her *part, acting* like a dog." The Eskimos believe that a person can learn to be a shaman. Their view of *nuthkavihak* is something that befalls the person, a pattern of behavioral processes that can appear and disappear, lasting a long time with some people and a short time with others.

A number of researchers in the field of cross-cultural psychiatry take the position that the underlying processes of insanity are the same everywhere but that their specific content varies between cultural groups (38). A psychotic person, it is thought, could not make use of the imagery of Christ if he had not been exposed to the Christian tradition and he could not elaborate ideas about the *wittiko* cannibalistic monster if not exposed to Cree and Ojibwa Indian traditions (39). It would seem that if a culture-specific stereotype of the content of psychosis exists in a group it might have the kind of influence suggested in labeling theory. If the content stereotype were applied to the unstructured delusions of a psychotic his thought productions might be shaped and stabilized around the theme of that stereotype.

There have been several attempts to study phenomena such as *wittiko* and *pibloktoq*, the former being thought of as the culturally defined content of a psychotic process in which the person believes himself to be a cannibalistic monster and the latter as a culture-specific form of hysteria found in the arctic (40, p. 218;41). The evidence of their existence comes from early ethnographies. It has been difficult in the contemporary period to locate people who have these illnesses (42). If the availability of a content stereotype has the effect one would expect from labeling theory, the stereotype should have sustained the pattern, but in fact these content patterns seem to have disappeared.

Prominent in the descriptions of the images and behavior of people labeled *were* and *nuthkavihak* were cultural beliefs and practices as well as features of the natural environment. Eskimo ideation concerned arctic animals and Eskimo people, objects, and spirits. The Yoruba ideation was based on tropical animals and Yoruba figures. The cul-

tural variation was, in other words, general. There was no evidence that if a person were to become *were* or *nuthkavihak* he would reveal one specific delusion based on cultural mythology. In this regard I reach the same conclusion as Roger Brown did when he set out to see how far labeling ideas would aid his understanding of hospitalized schizophrenics: "Delusions are as idiosyncratic as individual schizophrenics or normals. . . . There seems to be nothing like a standard set of heresies, but only endless variety" (15, p. 397).

The answer to the first specific question, whether Eskimos and Yorubas have labels for psychological and behavioral differences resembling what we call mental illness, is to my mind a definite yes. The expanding ethnographic literature on this topic indicates that most other non-Western groups also have such labels [in addition to the papers already cited see (43)]. From this broad perspective it appears that (i) phenomenal processes of disturbed thought and behavior similar to schizophrenia are found in most cultures; (ii) they are sufficiently distinctive and noticeable that almost everywhere a name has been created for them; (iii) over and above similarity in processes, there is variability in content which in a general way is colored by culture; and (iv) the role of social fictions in perceiving and defining the phenomena seems to have been very slight.

Unlabeled Behavior Patterns

The questions of this section are: Do phenomena labeled mental illness by us go unlabeled elsewhere, and if so what are the consequences? Are there natural experiments of culture which allow us to gain some understanding of the effects of not labeling? From the linguistic relativist's viewpoint, if phenomena are not named they are screened out of the perception of the people who speak that language; thus not only would mental illness go unrecognized if unlabeled but also the negative effects of labeling could not pertain.

Although one cannot speak of mental illness without reference to insanity and psychoses, most people in our culture mean more by the term and include some or all of the phenomena described in a textbook of psychiatry. Elsewhere I have presented data about Eskimo and Yoruba terms, lack of terms, and levels of generalization for mental retardation, convulsions, and senility (30, 44). According to the healers with whom I worked, the Yorubas have no word for senility but they recognize that some old people become incapable of taking care of themselves, talk to themselves, are agitated, wander away and get lost. In such cases they are watched, fed, and protected in much the same way as might be done in a nursing home. The lack of an explicit label seems to make little difference in how they are treated.

In contemporary Western society psychoneurotic patterns are thought of as one of the main types of mental illness, yet neurosis has a minor role in the labeling theory literature (45). Since labeling theory is addressed to the concept of mental illness per se, one feels it ought to apply to the neurotic as well as the psychotic.

In working with the Eskimos and Yorubas I was unable to find a word that could be translated as a general reference to neurosis or words that directly parallel our meaning of anxiety and depression. On the other hand, their words for emotional responses that we might classify as manifestations of anxiety or depression constitute a very large vocabulary. The Yoruba lexicon includes, for example, words for unrest of mind which prevents sleep, being terrified at night, extreme bashfulness which is like a sense of shame, fear of being among people, tenseness, and overeagerness. The Eskimo terms are translated as worrying too much until it makes the person sick, too easy to get afraid, crying with sadness, head down and rocking back and forth, shaking and trembling all over, afraid to stay indoors, and so on. The point is that neither group had a single word or explicit label that lumped these phenomena together as constituting a general class of illness by virtue of their underlying sim-

ilarities or as a pattern in which several components are usually found in association (46). In the terms of this article, these symptoms are unlabeled but they do exist. People recognize them and try to do something about them. Some of them are conceived as severely disabling and cause people to give up aspects of their work (such as being captain of a hunting boat); others appear to be less serious. Some of them are transient; others are life-long characteristics.

Of special significance to the problem at hand is the fact that most of these emotional phenomena are definitely thought of as illnesses for which the shaman and witch doctor have effective cures. The number of people who exhibit these phenomena is considerably in excess of those labeled *were* and *nuthkavihak*. Among the Yorubas the ratio is approximately 12 to 1 and among the Eskimos 14 to 1. In the clientele of a typical shaman or healer a large proportion would be people who came with symptoms such as "unrest of mind that prevents sleep" or "shaking and trembling all the time."

The answer to the question whether phenomena we label mental illness go unlabeled elsewhere is thus also yes. These Eskimos and Yorubas point out a large number of psychological and behavioral phenomena which we would call neuroses but which they do not put together under such a rubric. The consequence is not, however, a reduction in the number of persons who display the phenomena or great difference in how they are treated. The fact that these peoples cannot categorically define someone as "a neurotic" or that the Yorubas do not talk about "a senile" appears mainly to be a classification difference, and I am led to conclude that the phenomena exist independently of labels.

Evaluation of Behavior Patterns

Do non-Western groups evaluate the labeled behaviors of mental illness negatively or positively? Are they more tolerant of deviance than we are? I shall consider first the related institutional values of the culture, its roles and ceremonies, and then the noninstitutionalized actions and attitudes toward the mentally ill.

As pointed out earlier, it has been proposed that the shaman role is a social niche in which psychopathology is socially useful and that therefore mental disorder is positively valued. Since the Eskimos do not believe the shaman is *nuthkavihak*, it cannot be insanity that invests the role with prestige in their eyes. It could be, however, that some other form of mental illness, possibly a neurotic disorder like hysteria, is considered essential to what a shaman does and therefore is accorded the same respect that the role as a whole commands.

Among the 499 Eskimos 18 had shamanized at some time in their lives. None was thought to be *nuthkavihak*. No other personality characteristic or emotional response was given as typical of all of them, and in these regards the shamans seemed to be a random sample of the whole. The only feature I was able to determine as common to the group was that they shamanized, and they did that with variable success.

The Yoruba healer has not been described in the literature as a mentally ill person, though some of the Yoruba healing cults consist of individuals who have been cured and thereafter participate in curing others. The healers known to me and my conversations with Yorubas about their healers gave no evidence that mental illness was a requisite. Thus as far as the groups reported here are concerned, mental illness does not appear to be venerated in these roles. If the shaman is to be considered either psychotic or hysterical it seems to require that a Western definition be given to the portion of behavior specific to shamanizing.

If not institutionalized in an esteemed role, is mental illness institutionalized in a contemptible role? Both the Yorubas and the Eskimos have a clearly defined role of witch as the human purveyor of magically evil influences. Though feared, the man or woman who is believed to use magic in this way is held in low esteem.

Is insanity or other mental illness prima facie evidence that a person is a witch? If one tries to answer this by identifying the people labeled *were* or *nuthkavihak* and then the people labeled witches and comparing the two groups to see how much they overlap in membership, as I did regarding the shamans, a serious problem arises. The difficulty is in identifying the witches. Unlike shamanizing, which is a public act, the use of evil magic is exceedingly secretive. I did note, however, that there was no correspondence between the group of Eskimos said to have been insane at some point in their lives and the six people named as *auvinak* (witch) by a least one Eskimo.

In the more generalized information from the Yoruba healers it was evident that insanity was often believed to result from the use of evil magic but an insane person was rarely believed to use it against others. Thus my interpretation of whether mental illness is built into the role of witch is similar to the view presented about the role of healer. Some insane people have probably been accused of being witches, but it has been by happenstance, not because witching and insanity are considered to be the same thing and equally stigmatized.

In these regards the Eskimos and Yorubas seem to have much in common with the Zapotecs studies by Henry Selby (47, pp. 41–42). His work focuses on witchcraft as a major form of social deviance, and he interprets his information as supporting labeling ideas (48), especially the vulnerability of outsiders to labeling. He found that accusations of witchcraft are more likely to be leveled at someone outside the immediate group of kin and neighbors than at a group member. However, after "talking about deviance for months" with his Zapotec informants, Selby realized that he had no information on mental illness. He explored this topic separately and "found out that there were people who were 'crazy'" and that the condition was defined as having "something to do with the soul and was symptomized by agitated motor behavior, ataraxia, violent purposeless movement, and the inability to talk in ways that people could readily understand." Clearly, the Zapotecs have a conception of insanity, and, like Eskimos and Yorubas, they do not classify it in the same frame of reference with such norm transgressions as witching, envy, stinginess, and adultery.

Another way in which a culture might institutionalize a negative view of mental illness is through a degradation ceremony or ritual slaying, as in the case of the Melanesian social *mate*. Ceremony is a preservative of custom, and there is voluminous information on ceremonies for healing, ceremonies for effecting fertility of land, animals, and humans, and rites of passage, as well as ceremonies in which various forms of human sacrifice are carried out.

In view of the wide elaboration of customs whereby groups of people enact their negative and positive values, it is perhaps surprising that no groups seem to have developed the idea of ceremonially killing an insane person in the prime of life just because he is insane. Infanticide has sometimes been conducted when a child was born grossly abnormal in a way which might later have emerged as brain damage, and senility may have been a contributing factor in live burials. Also there is no doubt that insane people have sometimes been done away with, but that is different from ritual sacrifice. There is no evidence as far as I can determine that killing the insane has ever been standardized as a custom. There are, on the other hand, numerous indications from non-Western data that the ceremony appropriate for people labeled mentally deranged is the ceremony of healing (34, 36, 38, 43). Even the word "lunatic" associates the phenomena with healing, since it was usually the healer who was believed to have power over such cosmic forces as the lunar changes which were thought to cause insanity.

Regarding informal behavior and attitudes toward the mentally ill it is difficult to draw conclusions, because there is evidence of a wide range of behaviors that can be conceptualized as audience reactions. Insane people have been objects of certain restrictive measures among both the Eskimos and the Yorubas. The Eskimos physically restrain insane people in violent phases, follow them around, and force them to return home if they run away; and there is one report of an insane man's being killed in self-defense when, after killing several dogs, he turned on his family. In describing the Chukchee, a Siberian group known to these Bering Strait Eskimos, Waldemar Bogoras reports the case of an insane woman who was tied to a pole during periods of wildness (49). Teicher describes, in addition to the coffin-like box mentioned earlier, the use of an igloo with bars across the opening through which food could be passed (36). This is again similar to Selby's observations of Zapotecs who barred the door of a bamboo hut as a way of restraining a psychotic man (47).

The Yoruba healer of *were* often has 12 to 15 patients in custody at one time. Not infrequently he shackles those who are inclined to run off, and he may use various herbal concoctions for sedation. In Nigeria, where population is much denser than in the arctic, it was not uncommon to see *were* people wandering about the city streets, sometimes naked, more often dressed in odd assortments of tattered clothing, almost always with long, dirt-laden hair, talking to themselves, picking up objects to save. In studying a group of such vagrant psychotics Tolani Asuni noted that they usually stayed in one locale, that people fed them generously, allowed them to sleep in the market stalls, teased them mildly or laughed at them for minor deviations, and took action to control them only if the psychotics became violent (50).

A case I encounterd in Gambia illustrates the complexities of the situation and indicates that compassion and rejection are sometimes both engaged. The case is of a man, identified as insane, who lived some 500 yards outside a village. The villagers lived in thatched mud houses. The madman lived on an abandoned anthill. It was about 2.5 meters long and 1.5 meters high and the top had been worn away to match the contours of his body (Fig. 2). Except for occasional visits to the village, he remained on

FIGURE 2
A man living on an abandoned anthill: "He is out of mind and crazy."

difference between Western and non-Western groups in intolerance of the mentally ill. Furthermore, there seems to be little that is distinctively cultural in the attitudes and actions directed toward the mentally ill, except in such matters as that an abandoned anthill could not be used as an asylum in the arctic or a barred igloo in the tropics. There is apparently a common range of possible responses to the mentally ill person, and the portion of the range brought to bear regarding a particular person is determined more by the nature of his behavior than by a preexisting cultural set to respond in a uniform way to whatever is labeled mental illness. If the behavior indicates helplessness, help tends to be given, especially in food and clothes. If the behavior appears foolish or incongruous (in the light of the distinctive Eskimo and Yoruba views of what is humorous), laughter is the response. If the behavior is noisy and agitated, the response may be to try to quiet, sometimes by herbs and sometimes by other means. If the behavior is violent or threatening, the response is to restrain or subdue.

The answer to the question posed at the beginning of this section seems to be that the patterns these groups label mental illness (*were* or *nuthkavihak*) are not evaluated in either a starkly positive or starkly negative way. The flavor and variability of the audience reactions to mental illness suggest the word "ambivalence." Two recent studies in the United States also indicate that stigma is not automatically and universally applied to mental illness and that complex responses are typical in our society as well (51).

this platform through day and night and changing weather. His behavior was said to have become odd when he was a young man, and when I saw him he had not spoken for years, although he sometimes made grunting sounds. In one sense he was as secluded and alienated from his society as patients in back wards are in ours. On the other hand, the villagers always put food out for him and gave him cigarettes. The latter act was accompanied by laughter, because the insane man had a characteristic way of bouncing several leaps into the air to get away from anyone who came close to him, and that was considered amusing. Once a year someone would forceably bathe him and put new clothes on him.

If one defines intolerance of mental illness as the use of confinement, restraint or exclusion from the community (or allowing people to confine or exclude themselves), there does not appear to be a great deal of

Norm Violations

If these Eskimos and Yorubas are ambivalent about mental illness, do they strongly condemn any behaviors at all? Both groups have words for theft, cheating, lying, stinginess, drunkenness, and a large number of other behaviors which they consider to be specific acts of bad conduct. These, like the practice of witchcraft, are thought of as transgressions against social standards and are negatively sanctioned.

In addition, the Eskimos have a word, *kunlangeta,* which means "his mind knows what to do but he does not do it." This is an abstract term for the breaking of many rules when awareness of the rules is not in question. It might be applied to a man who, for example, repeatedly lies and cheats and steals things and does not go hunting and, when the other men are out of the village, takes sexual advantage of many women— someone who does not pay attention to reprimands and who is always being brought to the elders for punishment. One Eskimo among the 499 was called *kunlangeta.* When asked what would have happened to such a person traditionally, an Eskimo said that probably "somebody would have pushed him off the ice when nobody else was looking." This suggests that permissiveness has a limit even in a cultural group which in some respects, such as attitude toward heterosexual activity, is very lenient. The Yorubas have a similarly abstract word, *arankan,* which means a person who always goes his own way regardless of others, who is uncooperative, full of malice, and bullheaded.

There are parallels between *kunlangeta* and *arankan* and our concept "psychopath"—someone who consistently violates the norms of society in multiple ways. Also, some of the specific acts of wrongdoing which Eskimos and Yorubas recognize might in our society be called evidence of "personality disorders." In Western psychiatry, this term refers to sexual deviations, excessive use of drugs or alcohol, and a variety of behaviors that primarily cause trouble for other people rather than for the doer.

It is of considerable interest that *kunlangeta* and *arankan* are not behaviors that the shamans and healers are believed to be able to cure or change. As a matter of fact, when I pressed this point with the Yoruba healers they specifically denied that these patterns are illness. Both groups, however, believe that specific acts of wrongdoing may make an individual vulnerable to illness or other

misfortune. For example, Eskimos hold to a hunting ethic which prescribes ownership and sharing of animals; cheating in reference to the hunting code is thought of as a potential cause of physical or mental illness. The social codes among the Yorubas are somewhat different, but they also believe that breaking taboos can cause illness. It has been recognized by anthropologists for nearly half a century that among peoples who believe in magic there is remarkable similarity in the explanations of illness, and that transgression as well as witchcraft ranks high in the accepted etiology of many non-Western groups (52). Believing that transgression causes illness is nevertheless quite different from believing that transgression *is* illness.

Thus the answer to the question of this section appears to be that these groups do have strong negative sanction for a number of behaviors. A difference between their opinions and those embodied in Western psychiatry is that the Eskimos and Yorubas do not consider these transgressions symptomatic of illness or responsive to the techniques used for healing.

Prevalence

Is the net effect of a non-Western way of life such that fewer people suffer from something they label mental illness than is the case in the West? In view of the focus on *were* and *nuthkavihak,* attention will mainly be directed to this pattern of behavior and it will be compared with schizophrenia.

There are available now a number of epidemiological studies of mental illness in different countries and cultures. Warren Dunham has compared prevalence rates for schizophrenia from 19 surveys in Europe, Asia, and North America; Table 1 is adapted from tables he presents (53). Like several others who have studied these figures, Dunham concludes that the prevalence rates "are quite comparable" despite the fact that some are based on hospital data and some on population surveys, despite differences in defi-

TABLE 1 Compilation of Prevalence Rates for Schizophrenia, from Dunham (53)

Investigator	Date	Place	Population	Cases No.	Rate per 1000
Brugger	1929	Thuringia, Germany	37,546	71	1.9
Brugger	1930–31	Bavaria, Germany	8,628	22	2.5
Stromgren	1935	Bornholm, Denmark	45,930	150	3.3
Kaila	1936	Finland	418,472	1,798	4.2
Bremer	1939–44	Northern Norway	1,325	6	4.5
Sjogren	1944	Western Sweden	8,736	40	4.6
Böök	1946–49	Northern Sweden	8,931	85	9.6
Fremming	1947	Denmark	5,500	50	9.0
Essen-Möller	1947	Rural Sweden	2,550	17	6.6
Mayer-Gross	1948	Rural Scotland	56,000	235	4.2
Uchimura	1940	Hachizo, Japan	8,330	32	3.8
Tsugawa	1941	Tokyo, Japan	2,712	6	2.2
Akimoto	1941	Komoro, Japan	5,207	11	2.1
Lin	1946–48	Formosa, China	19,931	43*	2.1
Cohen and Fairbank	1933	Baltimore, U.S.	56,044	127	2.3
Lemkau	1936	Baltimore, U.S.	57,002	158	2.9
Roth and Luton	1938–40	Rural Tennessee, U.S.	24,804	47	1.9
Hollingshead and Redlich	1950	New Haven, U.S.	236,940	845†	3.6
Eaton and Weil	1951	Hutterites, U.S.	8,542	9*	1.0

*Inactive as well as active cases.   †Cases treated six months or more.

nitions and methods, and despite the cultural variation involved.

The rates of *were* and *nuthkavihak* can be compared to rates of schizophrenia in two Western surveys, one in Sweden and one in Canada. The Swedish study was carried out by Erik Essen-Möller and colleagues in two rural parishes for which a population register existed. Each member of the population was interviewed by a psychiatrist. A prevalence rate of schizophrenia is reported, with figures for cases in the community and cases in a hospital during a specific year (54). This design is similar to the one I used among the Eskimos, where a census register provided the base for determining the population, and each person was systematically described by at least one other Eskimo. Focusing on the people living in the specified year reduces the Eskimo population studied from 499 to 348.

The Canadian study, in which I was one of the investigators, was based on a probability sample of adults in a rural county (55). We designed the Yoruba study to explore the possibilities of comparing mental illness rates, and so used similar sampling procedures. The rates in these two surveys are based on compilations of interview data with selected respondents as well as systematic interviews about those respondents with local physicians in Canada and local village headmen in Nigeria.

The results of comparing these studies is that the proportion of people who exhibited or had at some time exhibited the pattern of behavior called schizophrenia, *were*, or *nuthkavihak* appears to be much the same from group to group (Table 2). At the time these studies were carried out, mental hospitals existed all over the world. The Canadian and Swedish populations are similar to the

TABLE 2 Rates of nonhospitalized schizophrenia in two Western samples and of indigenously defined insanity in two non-Western samples. Rates are per 1000 population after adjustment by the Weinberg method (58).

Group	Date	Size	Cases No.	Rate per 1000
Swedish	1948	2550	12	5.7
Eskimo	1954	348	1	4.4
Canadian	1952	1071	7	5.6
Yoruba	1961	245	2	6.8

United States in having a sizable number of large mental hospitals. The Eskimo population was considered to be in the catchment area served by a mental hospital in the United States, and the Yoruba villages were in the vicinity of two mental hospitals (56). For the Canadian and Yoruba studies we do not know the number of people who might otherwise have been in the communities but were hospitalized during the period when prevalence was surveyed. The Swedish and Eskimo studies, by virtue of starting with census registers, provide information on this point. The age-adjusted prevalence rate in the Swedish survey is 8.1 per 1000 when hospitalized schizophrenics are included and the Eskimo rate of *nuthkavihak* is increased to 8.8 when the one hospitalized case is added.

The number of schizophrenics, *were* and *nuthkavihak* in a population is small, but this comparison suggests that the rates are similar. With a broader definition of mental illness which I have explained elsewhere (it includes the neurotic-appearing symptoms, the senile patterns, and so on) the total prevalence rates for the three groups I have studied are: Canadian, 18 percent; Eskimo, 19 percent; and Yoruba, 15 percent (57).

The answer to the last question above seems thus to be that the non-Western way of life does not offer protection against mental illness to the point of making a marked difference in frequency. The rates of mental illness patterns I have discussed are much more striking for similarity from culture to culture than for difference. This suggests that the causes of mental illness, whether genetic or experiential, are ubiquitous in human groups.

Summary and Conclusions

Labeling theory proposes that the concept of mental illness is a cultural stereotype referring to a residue of deviance which each society arbitrarily defines in a distinct way. It has been assumed that information from cultures that are markedly different from Western society supports the theory. This paper presents systematic data from Eskimo and Yoruba groups, and information from several other cultural areas, which instead call the theory into question.

Explicit labels for insanity exist in these cultures. The labels refer to beliefs, feelings, and actions that are thought to emanate from the mind or inner state of an individual and to be essentially beyond his control; the afflicted persons seek the aid of healers; the afflictions bear strong resemblance to what we call schizophrenia. Of signal importance is the fact that the labels of insanity refer not to single specific attributes but to a pattern of several interlinked phenomena. Almost everywhere a pattern composed of hallucinations, delusions, disorientations, and behavioral aberrations appears to identify the idea of "losing one's mind," even though the content of these manifestations is colored by cultural beliefs.

The absence of a single label among Eskimos and Yorubas for some of the phenomena we call mental illness, such as neuroses, does not mean that manifestations of such phenomena are absent. In fact they form a major part of what the shamans and healers are called upon to treat. Eskimos and Yorubas react to people they define as mentally ill with a complex of responses involving first of all the use of healing procedures but including an ambivalent-appearing mixture of care giving and social control. These reactions are not greatly dissimilar from those that occur in Western society. Nor does the amount of mental illness seem to vary greatly within or across the division of Western and non-Western areas. Patterns such as schizophrenia, *were* and *nuthkavihak* appear to be relatively rare in any one human group but are broadly distributed among human groups. Rather than being simply violations of the social norms of particular groups, as labeling theory suggests, symptoms of mental illness are manifestations of a type of affliction shared by virtually all mankind.

References and Notes

1. H. S. BECKER, *Outsiders* (Free Press, New York, 1963), reprinted in 1973 with a new chapter, "Labelling theory reconsidered."

2. T. S. SZASZ, *The Myth of Mental Illness: Foundations of a Theory of Personal Conduct* (Hoeber-Harper, New York, 1961); R. LAING AND A. ESTERSON, *Sanity, Madness, and the Family* (Basic Books, New York, 1964).

3. Notably in E. LEMERT's distinction between primary and secondary deviance, which appeared initially in his book *Social Pathology* (McGraw-Hill, New York, 1951).

4. "In California, labeling theory itself contributed to the formulation of the Lanterman-Petris-Short act, a law which makes it difficult to commit patients to mental hospitals, and still more difficult to keep them there for long periods of time" (5, p. 256).

5. T. SCHEFF, *Am. Sociol. Rev.* **40**, 252 (1975).

6. D. ROSENHAN, *Science* **179**, 250(1973).

7. R. BENEDICT, *J. Gen. Psychol.* **10**, 59(1934).

8. E. SCHUR, *Labelling Deviant Behavior. Its Sociological Implications* (Harper & Row, New York, 1971).

9. E. LEMERT, *Human Deviance Social Problems and Social Control* (Prentice-Hall, Englewood Cliffs, N.J., 1967).

10. R. SCOTT, *The Making of Blind Men* (Russell Sage Foundation, New York, 1969).

11. T. SCHEFF, *Being Mentally Ill: A Sociological Theory* (Aldine, Chicago, 1966).

12. W. GOVE, *Am. Sociol. Rev.* **35**, 873 (1970).

13. ———— AND P. HOWELL, *ibid.* **39**, 86 (1974); W. GOVE, *ibid.* **40**, 242 (1975); R. CHAUNCEY, *ibid.*

248; T. SCHEFF (5, 14). In addition to the Rosenhan study (6), Scheff (14) evaluates the following six investigations as strongly supporting labeling: J. GREENLEY, *J. Health Soc. Behav.* **13**, 25 (1972); A. LINSKY, *Soc. Psychiatr.* **5**, 166 (1970); W. RUSHING, *Am. J. Sociol.* **77**, 511 (1971); M. TEMERLIN, *J. Nerv. Ment. Dis.* **147**, 349 (1968); W. WILDE, *J. Health Soc. Behav.* **9**, 215 (1968); D. WENGER AND C. FLETCHER, *ibid.* **10**, 66 (1969). For several articles unfavorable to labeling theory see W. GOVE, Ed., *The Labelling of Deviance, Evaluating a Perspective* (Wiley, New York, 1975). Also not favorable are R. BROWN (15); N. DAVIS, *Sociol. Q.* **13**, 447 (1972); J. GIBBS, in *Theoretical Perspectives on Deviance*, R. SCOTT AND J. DOUGLAS, Eds. (Basic Books, New York, 1972), p. 39; S. KETY, *Am. J. Psychiatr.* **131**, 957 (1974); R. SPITZER, *J. Abnorm. Psychol.* **84**, 442 (1975); D. AUSUBEL, *Am. Psychol.* **16**, 69 (1961).

14. T. SCHEFF, *Am. Sociol. Rev.* **39**, 444 (1974).

15. R. BROWN, *Am. Psychol.* **28**, 395 (1973).

16. R. BENEDICT, *Patterns of Culture* (Houghton Mifflin, Boston, 1934); M. MEAD, *Sex and Temperament in Three Primitive Societies* (Morrow, New York, 1935); *Male and Female* (Morrow, New York, 1949).

17. W. CAUDILL, in *Transcultural Research in Mental Health*, W. LEBRA. Ed. (Univ. Press of Hawaii, Honolulu, 1972), p. 25; R. EDGERTON, in *Changing Perspectives in Mental Illness*, S. PLOG AND R. EDGERTON, Eds. (Holt, Rinehart & Winston, New York, 1969), p. 49; R. LEVINE, *Culture, Personality and Behavior* (Aldine, Chicago, 1973); M. FIELD, *Search for Security, An Ethnopsychiatric Study of Rural Ghana* (Northwestern Univ. Press, Chicago, 1960); A. WALLACE, *Culture and Personality* (Random House, New York, 1970); B. WHITING AND J. WHITING, *Children of Six Cultures* (Harvard Univ. Press, Cambridge, Mass., 1975).

18. J. HONIGMANN, *Personality in Culture* (Harper & Row, New York, 1967).

19. R. EDGERTON, *The Cloak of Competence* (Univ. of Califoirnia Press, Berkeley, 1967); J. MERCER, *Labeling the Mentally Retarded* (Univ. of California Press, Berkeley, 1973).

20. R. JESSOR, T. GRAVES, R. HANSON, S. JESSOR, *Society, Personality and Deviant Behavior* (Holt, Rinehart & Winston, New York, 1968); J. LEVY AND S. KUNITZ, *Indian Drinking* (Wiley, New York, 1974); H. MULFORD, in *The Mental Patient: Studies in the Sociology of Deviance*, S. SPITZER AND N. DENZIN, Eds. (McGraw-Hill, New York, 1968), p. 155; D. PITTMAN AND C. SNYDER, *Society, Culture and Drinking Patterns* (Wiley, New York, 1962).

21. S. SPITZER AND N. DENZIN, Eds., *The Mental Patient: Studies in the Sociology of Deviance* (McGraw-Hill, New York, 1968).

22. C. FLETCHER AND L. REYNOLDS, *Sociol. Focus* **1**, 9 (1968).

23. E. GOFFMAN, *Asylums: Essays on the Social Situation of Mental Patients and Other Inmates* (Aldine, Chicago, 1962), p. 132.

24. T. SARBIN, in *Changing Perspectives in Mental Illness*, S. PLOG AND R. EDGERTON, Eds. (Holt, Rinehart & Winston, New York, 1969), pp. 11, 15, 19.

25. D. MECHANIC, *Ment. Hyg.* **46**, 68 (1962).

26. G. DEVEREUX, in *Some Uses of Anthropology: Theoretical and Applied*, J. CASAGRANDE AND T. GLADWIN, Eds. (Anthropological Society of Washington, Washington, D.C., 1956), p. 23; A. KROEBER, *The Nature of Culture* (Univ. of Chicago Press, Chicago, 1952), pp. 310–319; R. LINTON, *Culture and Mental Disorders* (Thomas, Springfield, Ill., 1956), pp. 98, 118–124; J. SILVERMAN, *Am. Anthropol.* **69**, (No. 1), 21 (1967).

27. W. RIVERS, *Psychology and Ethnology* (Harcourt Brace, New York, 1926), pp. 38–50.

28. B. WHORF, *Language, Thought and Reality* (Technological Press of MIT, Cambridge, Mass., 1956).

29. J. HUGHES [Murphy], thesis, Cornell University (1960). The recording of Eskimo words was conducted by Charles C. Hughes. The spelling given here follows the principles used in C. HUGHES (with the collaboration of J. MURPHY), *An Eskimo Village in the Modern World* (Cornell Univ. Press, Ithaca, N.Y., 1960). The census of 1940 which served as a baseline was prepared by Alexander Leighton and Dorothea Leighton. The extended statements by Eskimos and Yorubas which appear in quotation marks in the text are taken from my unpublished field notes, 1954–55, 1961, 1963. Most of the Eskimo and Yoruba phrases are also taken directly from these sources. In a few instances I have needed to paraphrase for intelligibility and therefore I have not used quotation marks for phrases.

30. A. LEIGHTON AND J. MURPHY, in *Comparability in International Epidemiology*, R. ACHESON, Ed. (Milbank Memorial Fund, New York, 1965), p. 189.

31. A. LEIGHTON, T. LAMBO, C. HUGHES D. LEIGHTON, J. MURPHY, D. MACKLIN, *Psychiatric Disorder among the Yoruba* (Cornell Univ. Press, Ithaca, N.Y., 1963).

32. J. DOUGLAS, *The Social Meanings of Suicide* (Princeton Univ. Press, Princeton, N.J., 1967).

33. Prince found that *were* was defined for him in terms almost identical to those I present here; he studied 46 *were* specialists (34, p. 84).

34. R. PRINCE, in *Magic, Faith, and Healing*, A. KIEV, Ed. (Free Press of Glencoe, New York, 1964).

35. J. MURPHY, in *Magic, Faith, and Healing*. A. KIEV, Ed. (Free Press of Glencoe, New York, 1964), p. 53.

36. M. TEICHER, *J. Ment. Sci.* **100**, 527 (1954).

37. In looking through a magazine with me, an Eskimo pointed to a picture and said that it resembled the shaman in seance; Fig. 1 is a photograph of that picture retouched to eliminate garments which the Eskimo said were irrelevant to the similarity.

38. A. DE REUCK AND R. PORTER, Eds., *Ciba Foundation Symposium: Transcultural Psychiatry* (Churchill, London, 1965); A. KIEV, *Transcultural Psychiatry* (Free Press, New York, 1972).

39. S. PARKER, *Am. Anthropol.* **62**, 603 (1960).

40. Z. GUSSOW, in *Psychoanalytic Study of Society*, W. MUENSTERBERGER, Ed. (International Univ. Press, New York, 1960), p. 218.

41. M. TEICHER, *Windigo Psychosis* (American Ethnological Society, Seattle, 1960).

42. Gussow (40) provides a description of *pibloktoq* based on 14 recorded cases, mainly from explorers and ethnographers in the area from Greenland to the west coast of Alaska during the first part of this century. Recently a serious attempt was made to study *pibloktoq* properly and measure its prevalence. Ten cases were located from a population of 11,000 Innuit Eskimos. These cases were found on further study to be exceedingly heterogeneous; "Several subjects had epilepsy; several were diagnosed as schizophrenic, most had low normal serum calcium levels; one had hypomagnesemia and possible alcoholism." [E. FOULKS, *The Arctic Hysterias of the North Alaskan Eskimo* (American Anthropological Association, Washington, D.C., 1972), p. 117]. This information suggests that *pibloktoq* is and may always have been a rare and ill-defined phenomenon. Regarding *wittiko* my assessment of the evidence is similar to Honigmann's when he says, "I can't find one [case] that satisfactorily attests to someone being seriously obsessed by the idea of committing cannibalism" (18, p. 401).

43. M. BEISER, J. RAVEL, H. COLLOMB, C. EGELHOFF, *J. Nerv. Ment. Dis.* **155**, 77 (1972); M. MICKLIN, M. DURBIN, C. LEON, *Am. Ethnol.* **1**, 143 (1974); H. KITANO, in *Changing Perspectives in Mental Illness*, S. PLOG AND R. EDGERTON, Eds.

(Holt, Rinehart & Wintson, New York, 1969), p. 256; R. EDGERTON, *Am. Anthropol.* **68**, 408 (1966); the following in *Magic, Faith, and Healing*, A. KIEV, Ed. (Free Press of Glencoe, New York, 1964): S. FUCHS, p. 121; K. SCHMIDT, p. 139; M. GELFAND, p. 156; B. KAPLAN AND D. JOHNSON, p. 203; M. WHISSON, p. 283.

44. J. MURPHY AND A. LEIGHTON, in *Approaches to Cross-Cultural Psychiatry*, J. MURPHY AND A. LEIGHTON, Eds. (Cornell Univ. Press, Ithaca, N.Y., 1965), p. 64.

45. A. ROSE, in *Human Behavior and Social Processes*, A. ROSE, Ed. (Houghton Mifflin, Boston, 1962), p. 537.

46. Western society also lacked a comprehensive concept of neurosis prior to Freud's influence, but at the present time neurotic patterns hold a firm position in the official classifications of Western psychiatry; see *Diagnostic and Statistical Manual of Mental Disorders* (American Psychiatric Association, Washington, D.C., 1968).

47. H. SELBY, *Zapotec Deviance, The Convergence of Folk and Modern Sociology* (Univ. of Texas Press, Austin, 1974).

48. Much of the support for labeling theory which Selby finds in his evidence stems from the following statement: "To the villagers, witches have an objective reality 'out there.' To me, they do not. I, the sociologist-anthropologist, do not believe that there are people in the world who have the capacity to float foreign objects through the air, insert them into my body, and make me sick or kill me" (47, p. 13). He concludes, "We create the deviants; they are products of our minds and our social processes." It seems to me this is a mistaken conclusion. I agree that the people who use witchcraft do not actually kill their victims by their incantations, burning effigies, boiling nail parings, and so on. The question, however, is whether some people actually carry out these maliciously intended acts. My work with Eskimos and Yorubas suggests that the idea of witchcraft is widely available to these groups just as the idea of lethal weapons is to us and that a few people in such groups really do conduct the rites that they believe will harm others (the artifacts of witchcraft attest to this), that they are genuinely deviant in these practices, and that they are the brunt of strong disapproval because of them. In this regard witchcraft involves real acts. It just happens that because these acts are by definition secret they give rise to distortions, false accusations, and misidentifications.

49. W. BOGORAS, in *The Jesup North Pacific Expedition*, F. BOAS, Ed. (Memoir of the Amerian Museum of Natural History, New York, 1904–1909), p. 43.

50. T. ASUNI, in *Deuxième Colloque Africain de Psychiatrie* (Association Universitaire pour le Développement de l'Enseignement et de la Culture en Afrique et à Madagascar, Paris, 1968), p. 115.

51. W. BENTZ AND J. EDGERTON, *Soc. Psychiatr,* **6**, 29 (1971); H. SPIRO, I. SIASSI, G. CROCETTI, *ibid* **8**, 32 (1973).

52. F. CLEMENTS, *Primitive Concepts of Disease* (Univ. of California Publications in American Archeology and Ethnology, Berkeley, 1932).

53. W. DUNHAM, *Community and Schizophrenia, An Epidemiological Analysis* (Wayne State Univ. Press, Detroit, 1965), pp. 18, 19. Dunham indicates that 21 cases of schizophrenia were discoverd in the Essen-Möller study. I use 17 of these (those for whom the author had high confidence that the pattern was schizophrenia). For comparability between Tables 1 and 2, I recalculated the rate for this one study. See also T. LIN, *Psychiatry* **16**, 313 (1953), for a similar use and interpretation of several of the studies cited here.

54. E. ESSEN-MÖLLER, *Individual Traits and Morbidity in a Swedish Rural Population* (Ejnar Munksgaard, Copenhagen, 1956). The rates for schizophrenia in the community and in the hospital were calculated from information on pp. 85–86.

55. A. LEIGHTON, *My Name is Legion* (Basic Books, New York. 1959); D. LEIGHTON, J. HARDING, D. MACKLIN, A. MACMILLAN, A. LEIGHTON, *The Character of Danger* (Basic Books, New York, 1963).

56. T. LAMBO, in *Magic, Faith, and Healing*, A KIEV, Ed. (Free Press of Glencoe, New York, 1964), p. 443; T. ASUNI, *Am. J. Psychiatry* **124**, 763 (1967).

57. J. MURPHY, in *Transcultural Research in Mental Health*, W. LEBRA, Ed. (Univ. Press of Hawaii, Honolulu, 1972), p. 213.

58. W. WEINBERG, *Arch. Rassen. Gesellschaftsbiol,* **11**, 434 (1915). The Weinberg method of adjusting the rate of mental illness for the probable age period of susceptibility is useful when the age distributions of the populations compared are different. Comparison of Western and non-Western populations particularly need such adjustment. The age of susceptibility for schizophrenia is assumed by Weinberg to be 16 to 40 years; I used 20 to 40 years because that age breakdown is available in the four studies compared.

59. The Eskimo and Yoruba studies which form

the core of this paper, and the Canadian study used for comparison, have been carried on as part of the Harvard Program in Social Psychiatry directed by Alexander H. Leighton and supported by funds from the Social Science Research Center of Cornell (for the Eskimo studies), the National Institute of Mental Health, the Ministry of Health of Nigeria, and the Social Science Research Council (for the Yoruba studies), the Carnegie Corporation of New York, the Department of National Health and Welfare of Canada, the Department of Public Health of the Province of Nova Scotia, the Ford Foundation, and the Milbank Memorial Fund.

3

The Reliability of Psychiatric and Psychological Diagnosis*

Joseph D. Matarazzo

Abstract: Experience suggests that many psychologists and psychiatrists, as well as most attorneys, judges, and other individuals whose work requires a knowledge of the extent of the reliability of psychologic and psychiatric diagnosis are not aware that recent research has dramatically influenced the conclusions one may draw in regard to the fallability of such human judgments. The purpose here is to provide a brief introduction of the history of such diagnostic judgments from the time of the early Greek philosophers through the decade of the 1960s. This will be followed by a review of a series of important studies from several research centers which were published during the past decade and which presented the first robust evidence that such clinician-to-clinician diagnoses have now attained remarkably high levels of reliability. . . .

*For ease of exposition only, the adjectives psychiatric and psychological diagnosis are included in this title. Nevertheless, all licensed mental health professionals and their full time research colleagues use diagnostic terms which they select from one or several common pools of such terms (e.g., DSM III). As is apparent in the text, these classificatory schemes were produced and refined by investigators and clinicians from each of the behavioral sciences.
Joseph D. Matarazzo. The Reliability of Psychiatric and Psychological Diagnosis. Reprinted (abridged) by permission from *Clinical Psychology Review*, Vol. 3, 1983. Copyright © 1983, Pergamon Journals, Ltd.

The history of the use of verbal and observational cues in early forms of the "mental status" examination as a basis for classification, nosology, and diagnosis is intimately intertwined with the history of medicine, psychiatry, and psychology, dating back to the earliest records of the human race. An excellent historical review of the actual nosological system in use for psychiatric *classification* and *diagnosis* in each era from the period 2,600 B.C., through Hippocrates and Plato of the classic Greek period (5th and 4th century B.C.), through early Christianity, the Dark Ages, the Renaissance, through the great writers of the 16th, 17th and 18th century medicine, and finally, the 19th and 20th centuries is provided in rich and detailed text in Zilboorg (1941). In addition, one appears in neat but comprehensive outline in the appendix of the book by Menninger, Mayman, and Pruyser (1963). The latter includes the *specific* diagnostic classifications used by each of the well-known and lesser giants, including Hippocrates, Plato, Galen, Avicena, Saint Thomas Aquinas, Paracelsus, Sydenham, Linneaus, Kant, Pinel, Rush, Esquirol, Maynert, Wernicke, Kraepelin, Bleuler, Freud, and Meyer. The outline ends with the system of William Menninger, whose work in World War II was incorporated in the American Psychiatric Association's 1952 *Diagnostic and Statistical Manual of Mental Disorders* (DSM I) and also served as the prototype for DSM II (which was published in 1968). No one of these earlier systems directly contributed to DSM III, which was published in 1980 by the American Psychiatric Association with input from hundreds of psychiatrists, clinical psychologists, and other mental health specialists.

We turn first to an examination of some of the issues involved in determining the reliability and, thus ultimately, the validity of the diagnosis reached by mental health professionals, who use the interview for classifying their patients by use of any of the nosological systems now extant for such diagnosis.

Early History of Psychiatric Diagnosis

The word diagnosis is derived from the Greek preposition *dia* (apart) and *gnosis* (to perceive or to know). Thus, to know the nature of something requires at the same time distinguishing it from others. Ancient Egyptian and Sumerian records of 4500 years ago include scattered references which reveal that, as far back as 2600 B.C., writers of that era could describe with modern sounding precision the two clinical syndromes which we today call melancholia and hysteria. One thousand years later, in the famous Ebers papyrus (1500 B.C.), one finds excellent descriptions of two other still currently recognized clinical conditions: alcoholism and senile deterioration. One of the earliest systematized psychiatric classification schemes was contributed a thousand years later by Hippocrates who, working in the fourth century B.C., divided all mental illnesses into the following diagnostic categories: (1) phrenitis, (2) mania, (3) melancholia, (4) epilepsy, (5) hysteria, and (6) scythian disease, or, what we today call "transvestitism." As cited above, Menninger et al. (1963, pp. 449–489), in a clearly presented and extensive outline, trace the changes next introduced in such "psychi-atric" diagnoses from the time of Plato, through the Dark Ages and Renaissance, through Kraepelin, and then up to the present. A reader following this history cannot help but be impressed with the observation that, despite the mixture from ancient times through the eighteenth century of demonology and science in attempts by a succession of writers to describe the *etiology* of such psychiatric conditions, most of the diagnostic names themselves (namely psychosis, epilepsy, alcoholism, senility, hysteria and other neuroses, and mental retardation) and the description of their clinical features have changed little during the last 2500 years. The promulgation of *specific* subcategories (e.g., schizophrenic versus manic depressive types of psychoses) within these global general categories has, however, varied considerably from one era to another, despite the lack of much change in these larger, more global diagnostic classifications (e.g., psychosis).

Notwithstanding the fact that global classifications of insanity were consistently recognized throughout all epochs, psychiatry and clinical psychology were very undeveloped disciplines until this century. A beginning empiricism did not come to the mental health sciences until five decades ago, not until the first few hundred pre and post World War II clinical psychologists and psychiatrists entered the field and began to give definition to their respective, newly developing professions. As their increasing numbers made it possible, a few stalwarts began to seek empirical evidence that the human judgment called diagnosis was a reliable (stable and reproducible) datum. The requirement that one should check the accuracy across another examiner (or oneself at a later time) of one's *specific* diagnostic classification of a mentally ill person most likely *was* perceived throughout each successive era in the long history which predated the modern era of empiricism in psychiatric diagnosis. However, such empirical research on one clinician's test-retest congruence in classification was not carried out until the recent era. Nevertheless, from humankind's earliest recorded times, there no doubt were recognized pathognomonic features of mental illness that one could almost take for granted as signs of severe mental derangement, and, thus, all observers would agree on this global diagnosis. The convulsive symptom of epilepsy probably was one such universally recognized datum, as no doubt also was hallucination a classic datum indicating the presence of psychosis or similarly grave mental derangement. It probably would be a fair guess that, in the early history of modern clinical psychiatry and psychology, few clinicians would not agree that a person who heard a voice which no one else heard was hallucinating and, in the absence of data that the individual was a mystic, an alcoholic, a drug addict, or had a brain tumor, conclude that such a person was psychotic. Furthermore, such experienced clinicians quite likely would have believed as a matter of faith that if any two of them independently interviewed this patient, they no doubt would get the same history of hallucination and, with such history, each reach the same diagnosis. That is, their interrater agreement on the diagnosis of psychosis would be perfect, or near perfect, in this and similar patients. However, in the absence of empirical evidence it was equally likely that, despite demonstrable similarity in their professional training and their avowed allegiance to the same diagnostic classification system such as the American Psychiatric Association's then current one, two experienced clinicians interviewing the same patient might disagree and, empirically, reveal *little* interrater agreement or reliability.

The earliest empirical studies on this issue were conducted between 1930–1965 and indicated that this latter was true. In fact, until 1967, the number of research workers who found diagnostic judgments based on psychiatric interviews unreliable outnumbered those who reported studies showing that they were reliable. Early investigators who believed interviewer-based psychiatric and psychological diagnosis to be unreliable were Ash (1949), Boisen (1938), Eysenck (1961), Masserman and Carmichael (1938),

Mehlman (1952), Pasamanick, Diniz, and Lefton (1959), Scott (1958), and Zubin (1967). Arrayed against them were these early defenders of the reliability of interview-based psychiatric and psychological diagnosis: Hunt, Wittson, and Hunt (1953), Foulds (1955), Schmidt and Fonda (1956), Seeman (1953), Kreitman et al. (1961), Beck (1962), Beck, Ward, Mendelson, Mock, and Erbaugh (1962), Wilson and Meyer (1962), Sandifer, Pettus, and Quade (1964), and Matarazzo (1965). In addition, several early authors also contributed excellent theoretical and review articles in this general area: Beck (1962), Caveny, Wittson, Hunt, and Herrmann (1955), Eysenck (1961), and Zigler and Phillips (1961). These last papers did much to clarify the pertinent issues in the reliable-unreliable debate. Rotter (1954, pp. 250–257) actually outlined steps for improving the reliability of interview-derived judgments.

In the past decade, considerable sophistication has been introduced into reliability research of this type, and the bases that served to pit one group of these experts against the other have given way to highly sophisticated empirical research. However, because of its pertinence to these newest studies, we will first examine some of this earlier research before reviewing the most recent empirical work.

Early Studies Showing the Unreliability of Psychiatric Diagnosis

A study which involved several diagnoses arrived at simultaneously, although reasonably independently, was reported by Ash (1949). In his study, 52 white males were evaluated in a government-related clinic in a joint interview by two or three psychiatrists who worked full time in this clinic. Typically, one of the psychiatrists conducted a physical examination of each man and then called his colleague(s) in for the psychiatric interview. The psychiatric interview was jointly conducted, each psychiatrist asking whatever questions he wished. However, each psychiatrist recorded his diagnosis independently. Specific diagnoses were not discussed.

Ash presented his results for *pair* combinations of the three psychiatrists for varying combinations (Ns of 38 to 46) of the 52 cases, and jointly for all *three* raters for only the 35 out of 52 cases, which were seen simultaneously by all three psychiatrists. An earlier, pre-1952 version of the official nomenclature of the American Psychiatric Association (1952) was used for their diagnostic judgments. This involved five *major categories* (mental deficiency, psychosis, psychopathic personality, neurosis, and "normal range but with predominant personality characteristic") and some sixty *specific* diagnostic subcategories. Agreement levels among the three psychiatrists in the 35 cases (examined by all *three* in simultaneous conference) for the *major* category diagnosis was 45.7%; for *specific subcategory* diagnosis it was only 20%. As might be expected, two out of the three of these psychiatrists, in different combinations of two, showed agreement levels higher than these: 51.4% and 48.6%, respectively.

Matarazzo (1965) pointed out in an earlier review of this reliability versus unreliability literature that, in essence, these results show that three psychiatrists could agree completely in 45.7% of the cases for five broad categories (where chance expectation would be 1 in 5, or 20%, if the base rates of the five conditions were known and equal—

which they certainly were not) and in 20% of the cases in specific categories (where chance expectation would be 1 in 60, or 1.7% if the base rates again were known and equal). However, Matarazzo pointed out that, with an N as small as 35, considerations of base rates appeared overly refined even if such base rates could have been determined by Ash. As will be discussed below, lack of consideration of the base rates of each psychiatric or psychological diagnosis in a sample will lead to higher apparent levels of reliability and agreement. Thus, even these relatively poor levels of agreement obtained by combinations of either two or three psychiatrists in Ash's study for the major diagnoses (namely 51.4% and 45.7% agreement, respectively) are values that are inflated and higher than they would be if agreements simply by "chance" had been partialed out.

During the next two decades four additional reliability studies were published. Each reported percentage agreements which, while higher than those obtained by Ash, still were considered as evidence of unacceptably low reliability by mental health professionals. These studies were reported by Schmidt and Fonda (1956), Kreitman et al. (1961), Beck, Ward, Mendelson, Mock, and Erbaugh (1962), and Sandifer et al. (1964). The results of these four studies are summarized in Table 1, along with those of Ash.

Although the levels of agreement in the *major* diagnostic categories shown in Table 1 may be considered by some readers as evi-

TABLE 1 Percent Agreement on Psychiatric Diagnoses Obtained by Two Independent Psychiatrists

	Ash (1949)	Schmidt and Fonda (1956)	Kreitman et al. (1961)	Beck et al. (1962)	Sandifer et al. (1964)
Number of patients	35	426	90	153	91
Agreement in major category	51	84	78	70	–
Agreement in specific diagnosis	49	55	63	54	57

dence of the reliability of such diagnoses, specialists working in this field concluded otherwise. In fact, although these higher reliabilities for the *major* as against the *specific* diagnoses were acknowledged, most experts were pessimistic in their interpretation even of the results obtained with such major categories. Thus, after reviewing the interrater reliability studies conducted through 1964 and summarized here in our Table 1, Zubin (1967) offered the following conclusions:

> **The findings indicate that the degree of overall agreement between different observers with regard to specific diagnoses is too low for individual diagnosis. The overall agreement on general categories of diagnosis, although somewhat higher, still leaves much to be desired. The evidence for low agreement across specific diagnostic categories is all the more surprising since, for the most part, the observers in any one study were usually quite similar in orientation, training and background. [p. 383].**

The reader interested in a lucid and most convincing set of hypotheses about the types of personal and highly idiosyncratic factors which led to the relatively low reliabilities of psychiatric diagnosis in the era before 1965 will find these in the in-depth studies of the proclivities of individual mental health diagnosticians carried out by Raines and Rohrer (1955, 1960) and the discussion of these two provocative papers by Matarazzo (1965). Furthermore, factors other than the idiosyncracies of the individual clinician also were operating, and a review of these was provided by Blum (1978). However, as alluded to above, from a research point of view it was not only the problems associated with the reported levels of reliability of the diagnosticians' judgments that were troublesome in the pessimistic reaction to these relatively low inter-judge reliability values for the now clearly less than trustworthy specific diagnoses being used daily by this nation's mental health clinicians. There also

was a methodological problem dealing with "base rates" which had not been addressed.

The Problem of Base Rates

In an earlier review of the literature on the reliability of such psychiatric diagnoses, Matarazzo (1965, p. 421) was struck by the fact that the studies summarized in Table 1 had not concerned themselves with a serious potential methodological flaw: namely the issue of base rates. That is, the assessments of the degree of interrater agreement shown in Table 1 had neglected to take into account the frequency with which any particular specific diagnosis did or did not occur in a population or sample of patients. H. F. Hunt (1950), in an early annual review chapter, was one of the first to highlight the importance of the problem of base rates. Subsequently, the New York State Psychiatric Institute (Columbia University) team of Cohen (1960), Spitzer, Cohen, Fleiss, and Endicott (1967), and Fleiss (1971) elaborated further on the issue of base rates and developed statistical procedures (the Kappa statistic) for handling a number of other problems involved in such interrater research, including how to control for the percentage of agreement two independent diagnosticians should reach on the basis of *chance* alone. During the past decade, Spitzer, Fleiss, Cohen, Endicott, and their colleagues in New York, and Robins, Guze and their colleagues at the Washington University School of Medicine in St. Louis each have used the Kappa statistic and related sophisticated methodology. Therefore, as will be shown in later sections, they have improved considerably the quality of research on the reliability and validity of psychiatric diagnosis. Formulas for kappa (K) and weighted kappa (Kw) have been published, and hypothetical examples have been furnished by both groups. The formula for K is as follows:

$$K = \frac{p_o - p_c}{1 - p_c}$$

where p_o is the observed proportion of agreement, and p_c is the agreement expected by chance alone. The hypothetical data in our Table 2, cited by Helzer, Robins, Taibleson, Woodruff, Reich, and Wish (1977) of the St. Louis group, illustrate the use of kappa. In this hypothetical study of the reliability of the psychiatric diagnosis of schizophrenia, two clinicians independently examine the same 100 patients and give each patient one of two diagnoses: "Schizophrenia" or "not schizophrenia." From these judgments there are three possibilities regarding diagnostic agreement: (1) both clinicians agree on schizophrenia, (2) both agree on nonschizophrenia, and (3) they disagree. The latter category can be broken down further into those patients for whom the first examiner diagnosed schizophrenia whereas the second did not; and where the second examiner diagnosed schizophrenia and the first did not, thus making the four possible combinations shown in Table 2.

All the data needed to compute kappa are given in Table 2. The proportion of observed agreement (p_o) is based on the total number of interviews (all 200) rather than on the total number of patients (100). Table 2 shows that the frequency with which both clinicians were in full agreement was 20 + 72, or 92 patients. Thus p_o is (20 + 72) dividend by 100, or .92. The proportion of agreement (frequency) based on chance alone (p_o) in this sample of 200 interviews

is 48 patients. It is based on the number of times or frequency that a diagnosis (in this case, schizophrenia) was made by either examiner in the 200 interviews. Thus, there were 40 (20 + 20) such instances in the first row, six instances in the third row, and two instances in the fourth row. That is, a positive diagnosis (the diagnosis of schizophrenia) was given 48 times out of 200 interviews, yielding a proportion of 48 divided by 200 or .24. The proportion of times the diagnosis of nonschizophrenia was given in this sample of patients likewise was 152 out of 200 interviews, yielding a proportion of .76. That is, if the two examiners had not even seen the patients at all but, instead, had merely assigned each one the diagnosis of schizophrenia, they would have been correct with 24 of the 100 patients.

Likewise, if they each diagnosed each of the 100 patients as nonschizophrenic without seeing any of them, they would have correctly identified 76 of them correctly because there were that many in the sample to begin with. The proportion p in the formula is designed to offer a correction for such chance "hits" and is computed in our example as $p_c = (48 \div 200)^2 + (152 \div 200)^2$ equals $(.24)^2 + (.76)^2$, or .64. The values of .92 and .64, when entered in the formula for kappa given above, yield $K = (.92 - .64) \div (1 - .64)$, or $K = .28 \div .36$, for a

TABLE 2 Hypothetical Values for Agreement by Two Randomly Selected Clinicians for the Diagnosis of Schizophrenia

	First Examiner	Second Examiner	No. Patients Involved	No. of Interviews Involved
Both clinicians diagnose schizophrenia in the same patient	20	20	20	40
Both clinicians diagnose not schizophrenia in the same patient	72	72	72	144
First clinician diagnoses schizophrenia; second clinician says not	6	0	6	12
Second clinician diagnoses schizophrenia; first clinician says not	0	2	2	4
Total			100	200

final value of $K = .78$. Thus, the reliability of psychiatric diagnosis of our two clinicians in Table 2, with appropriate statistical correction and control, is .78. Until kappa was introduced by Cohen (1960) and became widely accepted only a decade ago, investigators such as those discussed in Table 1 would have inflated the degrees of agreement shown in our Table 2, concluding, most likely, that the level of agreement between the two clinicians shown in our Table 2 was .92 and not .78 as revealed by kappa after chance hits are excluded.

Kappa was applied in several actual clinical studies in the early 1970s, and we shall examine these studies and results shortly. Additionally, in an important methodological contribution, Spitzer and Fleiss (1974) reanalyzed the data in each of the studies summarized here in our Table 1, substituting kappa as the statistic in each instance. Not surprisingly, inasmuch as they now controlled after the fact for chance agreement in each of these earlier published studies, they found the levels of agreement to be considerably *lower* than those shown in our Table 1. However, before we review the use of kappa in new samples of patients studied on the reliability issue after the early 1970s, we must first examine another methodological issue. This methodological refinement had at its core the necessary stipulation that, before two clinicians go about testing the reliability of their diagnostic classification, they must first agree on what it actually is that they will be examining for in their patients. In other words, how objectively specificable were each of the supposedly distinct psychiatric and psycholological diagnoses found in the 1952 DSM I or the 1968 DSM II, or in any of the other then currently extant classificatory systems?

The Era of Operational Definitions in Psychiatric Diagnoses

During the early 1950s, Robins and Guze and their colleagues at the Washington University School of Medicine had concluded that the problem of low interrater reliability in psychiatric and psychological diagnosis arose out of the inability of two examiners to write down (and therefore agree in advance) what symptoms or other behaviors had to be present before a specific diagnosis of, for example, schizophrenia, hysteria, anxiety neurosis, manic-depressive psychosis, or alcoholism could be made. Clearly, a diagnosis or other classification can be no better than the classifier's knowledge and understanding of the specifics of the phenomena he or she is classifying. Most persons would agree that an individual who experiences hallucination is mentally ill. Beyond this quite likely universally agreed-on observation, the data summarized here in Table 1, inflated as we now know they are, make quite clear that broadly educated and highly trained mental health professionals agreed less and less as the categories and classifications of the behavior disorders they must discriminate become progressively more specific. Professionals of comparable experience disagreed on the particulars required for any given diagnosis not only from one hospital to another but also with each other in the same institution where, it might have been assumed, there would be a fairly high level of agreement as to definition of various disorders.

It was disagreements of this type, evident even in the staff of a single psychiatric hospital or facility, that demanded that some common yardstick or measuring instrument be devised if future research were to be improved. The St. Louis group thus set about patiently and painstakingly during the 1950s, 1960s, and 1970s to develop a *structured interview* by use of which they standardized the method for *eliciting* data from each patient and, next, classified the products of this interview into *explicitly enumerated* clinical criteria for each of 16 psychiatric disorders in DSM II. Their explicit criteria for individual diagnostic classifications (such as hysteria, alcoholism, depression, schizophrenia) were published in a series of individual papers, and the whole was then integrated and reproduced in a single article by Feighner, Robins, Guze, Woodruff, Winokur, and Munoz (1972). To provide the reader with an example of their approach, the 1972 Feighner et al. operational definition of the symptoms which an interviewer had to elicit or observe before making the diagnosis of *depression* is reproduced here in our Figure 1. Each of the many psychiatric conditions contained in the 1968 DSM II was not as clearly defined by Feighner et al. as was depression. Yet, a large enough number of the important psychiatric conditions (16 plus an all-important residual category called "undiagnosed psychiatric illness") was such that, with the additional clinical and research data contained in the separate chapters of a book published by Woodruff, Goodwin, and Guze (1974), by 1972–1974 it began to be possible for other investigators to begin to use the definitions of the St. Louis group (and, as will be described below, those provided by the New York State Psychiatric Institute and St. Louis collaborative team of Spitzer, Endicott, and Robins and colleagues). The publication of these definitions markedly enhanced research by removing the critical barrier of disagreement in the definition of what was being classified which had impeded prior research on the reliability of psychiatric and psychological diagnosis. The potential gain from the use of their operationally explicit criteria was so strikingly obvious that this approach, despite considerable initial resistance (see Spitzer & Williams, 1980, p. 1054), would become the basis around which DSM III, introduced officially in 1980, would be built. This latter history will be presented shortly.

In a collaborative study involving the St. Louis and New York State Psychiatric Institute groups, with funding from the National Institute of Mental Health, Spitzer, Endicott, and Robins (1978) shortly thereafter expanded, modified, and added to the 1972 Feighner et al. criteria for a selected group of 23 functional psychiatric disorders, and demonstrated that the use of 23 (plus those of a number of subtypes of these 23) operational definitions increased rater-to-rater reliability considerably. These definitions are a further refinement of those in the Feighner et al. (1972) version, and they served as the

tools of one of the first reliability studies employing operational definitions of the disorders. We now turn to that study.

A 1977 Reliability Study Using Operational Definitions and Kappa: St. Louis Group

We should first indicate, however, that when we commented earlier on the methodological flaw involving base rates and agreement by chance alone inherent in the studies summarized here in our Table 1, we indicated that Spitzer and Fleiss (1974) *reanalyzed* the data from those studies by applying the kappa statistic correction to them. They also tabulated many more specific diagnoses than we show in our Table 1. Spitzer and Fleiss then computed an average kappa across the studies and the results are summarized here in the *last* column of our Table 3. Spitzer and Fleiss (1974) offered the following conclusion regarding the results reproduced here in the last column of Table 3:

> **There are no diagnostic categories for which reliability is uniformly high. Reliability appears to be only satisfactory for three categories: Mental deficiency, organic brain syndrome (but not its subtypes), and alcoholism. The level of reliability is no better than fair for psychosis and schizophrenia and is poor for the remaining categories (p. 344).**

It must be remembered that this 1974 conclusion by Spitzer and Fleiss related to reliability studies (those in our Table 1) which had been conducted *before* the Feighner et al. (1972) classificatory criteria had been published. A study of the utility of the explicit and operational criteria, which in the interim had been offered by the St. Louis group to improve diagnostic reliability, was subsequently published by that group (Helzer, Clayton, Pambakian, Reich, Woodruff, & Reveley, 1977), and the results were compared by them to the results of the earlier studies in the format shown in our Table 3.

In their 1977 reliability study, one destined to become a classic, Helzer et al. utilized three psychiatrists: a first year resident,

1972 Feighner Criteria for Depressive Disorder

Depression. The following three requirements *must* be met:

1. *Dysphoric mood* characterized by symptoms such as the following: depressed, sad, despondent, hopeless, feeling "down in the dumps," irritable, fearful, worried, or discouraged.

2. *At least 5 of the following 8 criteria:* (a) Poor appetite or weight loss of 2 pounds a week or 10 pounds or more a year when not dieting. (b) Difficulty in sleeping, including insomnia or hypersomnia. (c) Loss of energy, namely fatigability, tiredness. (d) Agitation or retardation. (e) Loss of interest in usual activities, or decrease in sexual drive. (f) Feelings of self-reproach or guilt (either may be delusional). (g) Complaints of or actually diminished ability to think or concentrate, such as slow thinking or mixed-up thoughts. (h) Recurrent thoughts of death or suicide, including thoughts of wishing to be dead. (*Note:* If only 4 of these 8 criteria are found, diagnose as "probable depression" rather than "depression.")

3. *A psychiatric illness lasting at least one month with no preexisting conditions* such as schizophrenia, anxiety neurosis, phobic neurosis, obsessive, compulsive neurosis, hysteria, alcoholism, drug dependency, antisocial personality, homosexuality and other sexual deviations, mental retardation, or organic brain syndrome.

(*General Note:* Patients with life-threatening or incapacitating medical illness preceding and paralleling the depression do not receive the diagnosis of primary depression.)

1978 RDC Criteria for Depressive Disorder

A. One or more distinct periods with dysphoric mood or pervasive loss of interest or pleasure. The disturbance is characterized by symptoms such as the following: depressed, sad, blue, hopeless, low, down in the dumps, "don't care any more," or irritable. The disturbance must be prominent and relatively persistent but not necessarily the most dominant symptom. It does not include momentary shifts from one dysphoric mood to another dysphoric mood, eg, anxiety to depression to anger, such as are seen in states of acute psychotic turmoil.

B. At least five of the following symptoms are required to have appeared as part of the episode for definite and four for probable (for past episodes, because of memory difficulty, one less symptom is required): 1. Poor appetite or weight loss or increased appetite or weight gain (change of 0.5 kg a week over several weeks or 4.5 kg a year when dieting); 2. Sleep difficulty or sleeping too much; 3. Loss of energy, fatigability, or tiredness; 4. Psychomotor agitation or retardation (but not mere subjective feeling of restlessness or being slowed down); 5. Loss of interest or pleasure in usual activities, including social contact or sex (do not include if limited to a period when delusional or hallucinating) (The loss may or may not be pervasive); 6. Feeling of self-reproach or excessive or inappropriate guilt (either may be delusional); 7. Complaints or evidence of diminished ability to think or concentrate, such as slowed thinking, or indecisiveness (do not include if associated with marked formal thought disorder); 8. Recurrent thoughts of death or suicide, or any suicidal behavior.

C. Duration of dysphoric features at least one week, beginning with the first noticeable change in the subject's usual condition (definite if lasted more than two weeks, probable if one to two weeks).

D. Sought or was referred for help from someone during the dysphoric period, took medication, or had impairment in functioning with family, at home, at school, at work, or socially.

E. None of the following that suggest schizophrenia is present: 1. Delusions of being controlled (or influenced), or of thought broadcasting, insertion, or withdrawal (as defined in this manual); 2. Nonaffective hallucinations of any type (as defined in this manual) throughout the day for several days or intermittently throughout a one-week period; 3. Auditory hallucinations in which either a voice keeps up a running commentary on the subject's behaviors or thoughts as they occur, or two or more voices converse with each other; 4. At some time during the period of illness had more than one month when he exhibited no prominent depressive symptoms but had delusions or hallucinations (although typical depressive delusions such as delusions of guilt, sin, poverty, nihilism, or self-deprecation, or hallucinations with similar content are not included); 5. Preoccupation with a delusion or hallucination to the relative exclusion of other symptoms or concerns (other than typical depressive delusions of guilt, sin, poverty, nihilism, self-deprecation or hallucinations with similar content); 6. Definite instances of marked formal thought disorder (as defined in this manual), accompanied by either blunted or inappropriate affect, delusions or hallucinations of any type, or grossly disorganized behavior.

F. Does not meet the criteria for schizophrenia, residual subtype.

FIGURE 1

Definition of depression: 1972 Feighner criteria versus 1978 Spitzer research diagnostic criteria. Adapted from "Diagnostic Criteria for Use in Psychiatric Research" by J.P. Feighner, et al., *Archives of General Psychiatry*, 1972, 26, 57–63, and from "Research Diagnostic Criteria" by R.L. Spitzer, et al., *Archives of General Psychiatry*, 1978, 35, 773–782. Copyright 1972 and 1978 by the American Medical Association. Reprinted by permission.

TABLE 3 Diagnostic Frequency and Interrater Concordance

Diagnosis	Frequency of Diagnosis, in %	Overall Agreement, in %	Specific Agreement, in %	Kappa (N = 101)	Kappa (N = 71)	From Spitzer & Fleiss (1974)
Depression	81	86	84	.55	.70	.41
Mania	13	96	73	.82	.93	.33
Anxiety neurosis	35	89	73	.76	.84	.45
Schizophrenia	5	96	43	.58	.66	.57
Antisocial personality	15	95	72	.81	.85	.53
Alcoholism	35	88	71	.74	.73	.71
Drug dependence	15	96	76	.84	.85	—
Hysteria (female subjects only)	18	88	68	.72	.72	—
Obsessional illness	7	97	67	.78	.79	—
Homosexuality	3	99	75	.85	.79	—
Organic brain syndrome	6	92	20	.29	.36	.77
Undiagnosed psychiatric illness	18	76	20	.19	—	—
Average concordance	—	92	62	.66	.75	—

Note. Adapted from "Reliability of Psychiatric Diagnosis: II" by J. E. Helzer, P. J. Clayton, R. Pambakian, T. Reich, R. A. Woodruff, and M. A. Reveley, *Archives of General Psychiatry*, 1977, *34*, 136–141. Copyright 1988 by the American Medical Association. Reprinted by permission.

a junior medical school staff psychiatrist, and a senior faculty psychiatrist. Each of 101 new patients admitted to the psychiatric service of the medical school in St. Louis was interviewed twice: once within 24 hours of admission by one of the three psychiatrists and again, independently, by a second psychiatrist about 24 hours later. Each psychiatrist saw about an equal number of patients, and each interviewer came first or second about equally. The results shown in our Table 3 are the kappa levels of agreement achieved by different combinations of *pairs* of the three psychiatrists being studied.

The frequency of diagnosis shown in the first column is based on the 202 interviews (101 patients seen twice), Thus, acknowledging multiple diagnoses (the average per patient was 2.5) in the 202 interviews conducted by a series of two interviewers, a diagnosis of current or past depression was made 164 times or 81% of the total. Because an average of 2.5 diagnoses were made per patient, this latter figure does *not* mean that 81% of the 101 patients were diagnosed primary affective disorder, depressed type. That is, inasmuch as diagnoses were non-preemptive in this study, any given patient might (and some in fact did) have another psychiatric illness clearly antecedent to depression. This first column in Table 3 merely catalogs the percent of the 202 interviews which included depression as one of the diagnoses among the 2.5 generated per each of the 202 such interviews. After depression, anxiety and alcoholism (each with 35%) were the next most frequently assigned diagnoses as shown in the first column of Table 3.

The second and third columns of Table 3 show percentage of overall agreement (the raw percentage of agreement in individual cases by the two interviewers) and specific agreement (the percentage of agreement after excluding the 18% undiagnosable cases shown in the second from the bottom row). *The fourth column presents the test-retest reliability (kappa) for the 101 patients across the two interviewers for each diagnostic category.* Inasmuch as the St. Louis group believed the classification *"undiagnosed psychiatric illness"* was an operationally defined category which should be used at this early state of research, they encouraged its use whenever a clinician was unsure of the diagnosis. As shown in the second from the bottom row of our Table 3, the two interviewers used this category in 18% of the 202 interviews. The authors recomputed kappa for their data excluding these patients, and the values of kappa for the 71 patients for whom both interviewers gave a positive diagnosis are shown in the second from the last column of Table 3.

Whether one examines the values of kappa for specific diagnosis on all 101 patients or the values of kappa only on the smaller sample of 71 patients, they show strikingly higher interrater reliability for specific psychiatric diagnosis than published heretofore (see the results of earlier research in our Table 1). In fact, even when these earlier results in our Table 1 are corrected and kappa is applied, as was done by Spitzer and Fleiss for six of the earlier reliability studies (and reproduced here in the last column of our Table 3), the 1977 kappa values obtained by the St. Louis group (see the fifth and sixth columns in Table 3) were found in direct comparison by them to be markedly higher in all categories except organic brain syndrome. Helzer et al. (1977) indicated that this surprisingly low value for organic brain syndrome resulted in their study because there were too few such organic patients: namely, only 6% of the interviews, and also because, in the mid 1970s, their operational criteria for this category were not yet well defined.

NIMH Collaborative Research Program and Increased Reliability

Investigators working in the same general area but located in different settings frequently pool their talents and produce a product neither could have produced alone. With federally funded support from an NIMH grant to study the psychobiology of depression, psychiatrist Spitzer and psychologist Endicott and their colleagues at the New York State Psychiatric Institute were able to join forces in furthering research on the reliability and validity of psychiatric diagnosis with Robins in St. Louis, as well as

with colleagues at the Harvard and Iowa medical schools. Together, these collaborators produced by 1977 two important research and clinical tools: (1) a manual of *Research Diagnostic Criteria* consisting of explicit relatively easy to utilize operational definitions of 25 psychiatric disorders, many of which they hoped would become part of DSM III (Spitzer, Endicott, & Robins, 1978) and, as described above, (2) a *standardized interview schedule for eliciting* the history and related present status and clinical information needed to determine in which of these categories a given patient with an affective disorder or schizophrenia should be classified (Endicott & Spitzer, 1978). In the present section we will present only the empirical findings on reliability and defer until a later section a more complete description of the content of the Research Diagnostic Criteria (the expanded list of operational definitions which constitutes the RDC) and the standardized interview called the standardized Schedule of Affective Disorders and Schizophrenia (SADS) necessary to elicit the information upon which an RDC diagnosis is made.

In their next reliability study, this collaborative team of investigators utilized new patients from their four settings and applied their recently developed research tools in what, after the Helzer et al. (1977) study, appeared to be one of the best-designed investigations up to that time on the reliability of psychiatric and psychological diagnosis. Two of the three studies in this 1978 report involved joint interviews whereby one rater conducted the interview and the other merely observed, with each giving an independent diagnosis. The third study utilized two different and independent interviewers and a test-retest interval which ranged from 1 day to 1 week for different patients. The results of these three reliability studies were reported by Spitzer, Endicott, and Robins (1978) and are shown in Table 4. Inasmuch as this collaborative team could begin with and then improve on the operational definitions and the structured interview earlier utilized in St. Louis by Helzer, Clayton, Pam-

TABLE 4 Kappa Coefficients of Agreement for Major Diagnostic Categories Using the Research Diagnostic Criteria (RDC)

	Joint Interviews		Test-Retest
	Study A (N = 68)	Study B (N = 150)	(n = 60)
Present Episode			
Schizophrenia	.80	—	.65
Schizo-affective Disorder, Manic Type	—	—	.79
Schizo-affective Disorder, Depressed Type	.86	.85	.73
Manic Disorder	.82	.98	.82
Major Depressive Disorder	.88	.90	.90
Minor Depressive Disorder	—	.81	—
Alcoholism	.86	.97	1.00
Drug Abuse	.76	.95	.92
Life-time			
Schizophrenia	.75	.91	.73
Schizo-affective Disorder, Manic Type	—	—	—
Schizo-affective Disorder, Depressed Type	.94	.87	.70
Manic Disorder	.89	.93	.77
Hypomanic Disorder	.85	—	.56
Major Depressive Disorder	.97	.91	.71
Minor Depressive Disorder	—	.68	—
Alcoholism	.88	.98	.95
Drug Abuse	.89	1.00	.73
Obsessive Compulsive Disorder	—	1.00	—
Briquet's Disorder	.79	.95	—
Labile Personality	—	—	.70
Bipolar I	.93	.95	.40
Bipolar II	.79	.85	—
Recurrent Unipolar	.81	.83	.80
Intermittent Depressive Disorder	—	.85	.57

Note. Adapted from "Research Diagnostic Criteria" by R. L. Spitzer, J. Endicott, and E. Robins, *Archives of General Psychiatry*, 1978, **35**, 79. Copyright 1978 by the American Medical Association. Reprinted by permission.

bakian, Reich, Woodruff, and Reveley (1977), the resulting even higher reliability values from their three studies shown in our Table 4 relative to Table 3 may not be too surprising.

The test-retest correlations for *specific* psychiatric diagnoses shown in the whole of Table 4 and in the second from the last column of Table 3 are at levels which traditionally have characterized the best *psychological tests from the psychometric standpoint;* namely, the Wechsler Intelligence Scales, the Minnesota Multiphasic Person-

ality Index, and similar instruments. These same 1978 correlations for *specific* diagnoses reported in Table 4 (and Table 3) are also at or above the relatively high levels of reliability reached for the *major* diagnostic categories in the earlier (1940–1967) period of reliability research reviewed in Table 1. If investigators in other settings next could demonstrate the same degree of reliability across independent clinicians for the diagnostic categories which had been painstakingly operationally defined by the collaborative project group and the St. Louis group, a major barrier would have been overcome in the history of psychiatric and psychological diagnoses. However, in their 1977 study, Helzer et al. acknowledged that two elements of their research design may have artificially increased their values of kappa shown in Table 3: (1) They permitted an average of 2.5 diagnoses per interview, and (2) the results they obtained by use of the structured interview were reviewed by a research faculty member to see if the interviewer had failed to record a datum that, in fact, had come out in the interview. Those cautions being acknowledged, if future research could show that these two factors did increase the values of kappa, then Helzer et al. would have helped identify two operationally specifiable factors that had impeded prior research, and these should be studied in greater detail in future studies. The results published in 1977 and shown here in Table 3 seemed, however, to one reviewer (Matarazzo, 1978, p. 68) to have resulted as much from the use of very explicit operational definitions as from these two potentially contaminating factors highlighted by Helzer et al. in the St Louis study.

The results of the 1978 collaborative study between New York State Psychiatric Institute and the St. Louis group (Spitzer, Endicott, and Robins, 1978), described above and summarized here in our Table 4, however, were among the first to suggest that the high levels of reliability being attained by 1978 were true values and were not inflated as a result of the methodological shortcomings considered by Helzer et al. in 1977. Subsequent research published between 1978–1981 would dispell any lingering doubt that this was so. However, before reviewing these most recent reliability studies per se, it is necessary to present in more detail the pivotal role played by the development of a longer list of operational definitions of the various disorders. Also to be noted is introduction of standardized interviews in these 1977 and 1978 reliability studies shown in our Tables 3 and 4, as well as the even more striking reliability values which would be found in the subsequent reliability studies published between 1978 and 1981.

Structured Interviews and the Reliability of Psychiatric and Psychological Diagnosis: 1978–1981

The Present State Examination (PSE)

The St. Louis Group of the 1950s and early 1960s, consisting of Eli Robins, Guze, Winokur, Murphy and their younger colleagues, clearly was well aware that its attempts to develop operationally explicit, objectively denotable and, thus, reliable criteria for the psychiatric disorders was a risky undertaking. One of the biggest hurdles they knew they faced was the strongly held intuitive belief of the individual psychiatrist or psychologist that *his* or *her* criteria for making the diagnosis of schizophrenia or anxiety neurosis, for example, perforce was more or less universally accepted (despite published evidence to the contrary in such judgments as reviewed above). The resistance posed by these beliefs was a risk the St. Louis group accepted as they worked, year after year, to develop the specifiable criteria for each of a number of recognized psychiatric conditions. However, one risk they recognized they might never surmount, despite their painstaking effort, was whether or not they could ever develop operationally explicit, reliable criteria which would have clinical face validity and, in time, demonstrable clinical predictive validity and, thus, utility. As we briefly noted above, subsequent history, including importantly the contributed effort of colleagues working in other clinical and research centers, would indicate that, during the 1970s, these hopes and effort of the St. Louis group would be rewarded. We shall now examine more closely how this came about.

In the early 1960s, Wing, Birley, and Cooper (1967), working in Great Britain, published evidence that it was possible to develop a structured interview, which they called the *Present State Examination* (PSE), which allowed a clinician to conduct a mental status examination and provide a more reliable psychiatric diagnosis for *schizophrenia* and the *affective disorders* than had heretofore been possible. In fact, the PSE was developed in joint effort by clinicians in the United Kingdom and the United States under the auspices of the World Health Organization. This was explicitly done to reduce the empirically documented unreliability in the diagnosis of schizophrenia then characterizing psychiatric diagnosis throughout the world. Although subsequent research during the next decade (Luna & Berry, 1979; Spitzer & Williams, 1980, pp. 1047–1048) would establish the reliability and effectiveness of this crossnational instrument (PSE), today its use has not even become extensive, particularly in the United States. However, in America, the research effort which began in St. Louis and later paralleled that on the PSE was aimed at developing operational definitions for a much larger number of psychiatric conditions than merely schizophrenia or affective disorder.

As discussed above in relation to Table 3, the first solid evidence that the efforts of the St. Louis group working in the United States would be rewarded came in the early 1970s with publication by Feighner et al. (1972) of an explicit, operationally denotable definition of 16 psychiatric conditions. An example of the criteria needed to make the diagnosis of depression is given at the top of Figure 1. The importance of this publication for improvement in the reliability of psychiatric diagnosis was immediately recognized in scientific circles and the term "Feighner criteria" (pronounced "finer criteria"!) soon became part of the lexicon of research workers whose hope it was to make psychiatric diagnosis a science rather than a highly idiosyncratic judgmental activity. Furthermore, to teach medical students and residents these Feighner criteria, a small book was published by Woodruff, Goodwin, and Guze (1974) which both described each

of these 16 clinical conditions in more detail and provided the explicit Feighner operational diagnostic criteria for each. The book was updated and revised by Goodwin and Guze (1979). However, it had become clear by 1972 to a small cadre of U.S. research psychiatrists that operationally definable criteria for psychiatric disorders were possible. In fact, the Feighner criteria led to an immediate, dramatic improvement in clinician–clinician diagnostic reliability as demonstrated soon thereafter in the study shown here in Table 3 and conducted by Helzer et al. (1977).

However, although Feighner et al. wrote explicit, denotable criteria for some of the most common psychiatric conditions, this impressive feat did not assure that clinicians in other settings would know how *to elicit the necessary information* from a clinical interview to permit them *to apply* it to these reliable criteria. As suggested above, expanding the list of explicitly defined conditions and also providing a clinically useful aid for eliciting this required information were the next steps in this clinical-scientific odyssey.

More Refined Operational Criteria: Research Diagnostic Critera (RDC)

Intramural and extramural experts associated with the National Institute of Mental Health had recognized by 1970 that the psychiatric condition known as *depression* appeared to have a strong psychobiologic component. As a result, the large scale NIMH collaborative study of the biology and psychology of depression described earlier was launched. This federally funded collaborative study on depression provided a vehicle for Robins and his St. Louis group and their colleagues from the Columbia, Harvard, and Iowa medical centers to modify (and thereby improve upon) the Feighner criteria, if possible; not only for depression but for other disorders as well. Indeed, the record indicates they accomplished that task. Specifically, by 1977, the collaborators from these four medical centers had produced a manual of Research Diagnostic Criteria (RDC) which contained explicit, relatively easy to apply operational descriptions of 25 diagnostic categories plus a 26th category (never mentally ill). As earlier had been the case with the Feighner criteria, the description of each of these 26 diagnostic categories subsequently was published in the scientific literature (Spitzer, Endicott, & Robins, 1978); and the impressive kappa reliability values for 24 of the 26 diagnostic categories also were included (see our Table 4) in that publication.

The extent of progress to develop denotably explicit criteria between the 1972 Feighner criteria and the 1978 Spitzer, Endicott and Robins RDC may be appreciated by comparing the 1972 and 1978 descriptions of the same disorder: *depression*. To this end, the reader should contrast the 1972 Feighner description of depression reproduced in the top half of Figure 1 with the 1978 Spitzer, Endicott, and Robins description of the same syndrome shown in the bottom half of the same figure. A comparison of these two indicates that RDC employs not only *inclusive* criteria which must be present (e.g., the presence of sadness, poor appetite, sleep disturbance) but also, and equally important, *exclusive* criteria (e.g., the presence of specific kinds of delusions or hallucinations) whose presence rules out the diagnosis of depression and helps rule in another equally explicitly defined syndrome such as schizoaffective disorder, depressed subtype.

The development of both inclusive and exclusive criteria for the descriptions of specific syndromes contained in the Research Diagnostic Criteria clearly was an epochal event in the history of psychiatric and psychological classification. However, as Spitzer and Williams (1980) point out, the RDC descriptions, including the one for depression reproduced here in Figure 1, are technically *not* strictly operational definitions or criteria for diagnosing each disorder. The reason they are not, strictly speaking, operational definitions is that "they do not specify the operations that a clinician must perform—

for example, specific questions to be asked—to make clinical judgments. Hence, it is more accurate to refer to them as diagnostic criteria. In research settings, clinicians were expected to use the criteria regardless of their own *personal concepts* of the disorders" (Spitzer & Williams, 1980, p. 1049) and *the type of interview* they are using in eliciting the diagnostic information. However, this requirement presented a major methodological problem because the theoretical and clinical framework within which mental health clinicians elicited clinical information from the same patient varied so much from one clinician to another. That is, if clinicians of widely differing theoretical orientations (e.g., psychoanalytic versus nondirective versus pharmacobiologic) each conducted a diagnostic interview *in his or her own idiosyncratic manner*, there would be less likelihood that the resulting clinical information needed to apply a binary (yes–no) decision to one or another of the RDC criteria of the type shown in Figure 1 would have been elicited by each such clinician from the same patient.

Therefore, as suggested earlier, to better insure that clinicians in the same or different settings conduct a clinical interview and examination which maximizes the chance that the clinical material needed to apply the RDC criteria is elicited, it was necessary to develop a generally acceptable interview format which would structure or *standardize* the questions asked by each interviewer. Thus, concurrent with development of the RDC, and building upon the experience gained in the transnational collaboration which produced the Present State Examination (PSE), colleagues working with these same St. Louis and New York research groups set about to develop *structured interview schedules* which would remove as much as possible the unreliablity in the resulting psychiatric diagnosis introduced by differences in the way clinicians elicit clinical information. [The following section focuses on one of these diagnostic interviews, the] *Schedule for Affective Disorders and Schizophrenia* (*SADS*), developed at Columbia by the psychologist—

psychiatrist team of Endicott and Spitzer et al. . . .

Schedule for Affective Disorders and Schizophrenia (SADS)

This interviewing tool also was developed through the cooperation of researchers and clinicians at the four medical centers collaborating in the NIMH study of depression. It was employed as a standardized interviewing tool that produced the remarkable increases in the reliability of diagnosis shown above in our Table 4. There are three versions of the SADS (Endicott & Spitzer, 1978). One measures *current* status (SADS), the second, *lifetime* psychiatric status (SADS-L), and the third, *change* from a former state (SADS-C).

In the interests of space, only the first (current status) will be described here. The SADS is organized into two parts. Part 1 is designed to yield a very detailed description of the subject's *current* psychiatric and psychological episode and status as well as his or her functioning *during the week prior* to the interview. In addition, interview questions comprising Part 1 are explicitly designed to elicit descriptions of the current episode of illness when the former were *their most severe*. Part 2 of this same version of the SADS uses questions which will elicit descriptions of *past* psychiatric and psychologic disturbance.

The organization of the SADS is similar to that of a clinical interview focused on differential diagnosis. The schedule provides for a progression of questions, items, and operationally explicit criteria that systematically rule in and rule out each of the growing list of RDC diagnoses (Endicott & Spitzer, 1978). For example, Figure 2 includes the five items in the SADS which are used by the interviewer to screen in (or out) the RDC diagnosis called "manic syndrome." As may be seen from the items on the left side of Figure 2, the SADS provides the next set of *standardized* questions which are to be asked *after* the clinician makes the binary judgment that a dysphoric mood is present. Based on

the answers elicited to these items, as shown in the top right quadrant of Figure 2, the clinician *next* makes a clinical judgment about the severity of the phenomenon (i.e., from not or slightly depressed through extremely elated). In reaching these complex decisions, the clinician using the 1978 SADS is instructed to use all available sources of information and, most important, as many *additional* general or specific questions as are necessary to render a judgment about each item in this structured interview schedule. Not surprisingly, then, when first introduced, the SADS was described as a tool which is best used by *experienced* clinical or research psychiatrists, psychologists, psychiatric social workers and nurses, and their colleagues from other behavioral science disciplines.

Improvement in the reliability of psychiatric and psychological diagnosis made possible by using the SADS structured interview to elicit the clinical material, and then applying the judgments made from the latter to the explicitly described diagnostic categories contained in the Research Diagnostic Criteria, was readily obvious. Within a decade, what had been only moderate reliability in the pre-1970 categories of *major* psychiatric and psychologic conditions, plus disappointedly poorer reliability in the *specific* diagnostic categories subsumed under these major ones (see our Table 1), was replaced by published evidence (see Table 4) that the reliability across clinicians using the Schedule for Affective Disorders and Schizophrenia plus the Research Diagnostic Criteria for a number of major *and* specific diagnostic categories had reached scientifically accepted levels of magnitude and significance. This high level of reliability held across two clinicians conducting independent interviews on the same day as well as between a single clinician (or two clinicians) on two test-retest occasions separated by months. The pertinent reliability data were reported in two publications (Endicott & Spitzer, 1978; Spitzer, Endicott, & Robins, 1978). The three patient samples consisted of 68 jointly interviewed inpatients newly admit-

The next 5 items are screening items to determine the presence of manic-like behavior. If any of the items are judged present, inquire in a general way to determine how he was behaving at that time with such questions as, *When you were this way, what kinds of things were you doing? How did you spend your time?* Do not include behavior which is clearly explainable by alcohol or drug intoxication.

If the subject has only described dysphoric mood, the following questions regarding the manic syndrome should be introduced with a statement such as: *I know you have been feeling (depressed). However, many people have other feelings mixed in or at different times so it is important that I ask you about those feelings also.*

Elevated mood and/or optimistic attitude toward the future which lasted at least several hours and was out of proportion to the circumstances.

Have (there been times when) you felt very good or too cheerful or high—not just your normal self?

If unclear: *When you felt on top of the world or as if there was nothing you couldn't do?*

(Have you felt that everything would work out just the way you wanted?)

If people saw you would they think you were just in a good mood or something more than that?

0 No information

1 Not at all, normal, or depressed

2 Slight, e.g., good spirits, more cheerful than most people in his circumstances, but of only possible clinical significance

3 Mild, e.g., definitely elevated mood and optimistic outlook that is somewhat out of proportion to his circumstances

4 Moderate, e.g., mood and outlook are clearly out of proportion to circumstances

5 Severe, e.g., quality of euphoric mood

6 Extreme, e.g., clearly elated, exalted expression and says "Everything is beautiful, I feel so good"

PAST WEEK 1 2 3 4 5 6

(What about during the past week?)

Less need for sleep than usual to feel rested (average for several days when needed less sleep).

Have you needed less sleep than usual to feel rested?
(How much sleep do you ordinarily need?)
(How much when you were [are] High?)

0 No information

1 No change or more sleep needed

2 Up to 1 hour less than usual

3 Up to 2 hours less than usual

4 Up to 3 hours less than usual

5 Up to 4 hours less than usual

6 4 or more hours less than usual

PAST WEEK 1 2 3 4 5 6

(What about during the past week?)

Unusually energetic, more active than his usual level without expected fatigue.

Have you had more energy than usual to do things?

(More than just a return to normal or usual level?)

(Did it seem like too much energy?)

0 No information

1 No different than usual or less energetic

2 Slightly more energetic but of questionable significance

3 Little change in activity level but less fatigued than usual

4 Somewhat more active than usual with little or no fatigue

5 Much more active than usual with little or no fatigue

6 Unusually active all day long with little or no fatigue

(What about during the past week?)

PAST WEEK 1 2 3 4 5 6

FIGURE 2

SADS probes for screening manic syndrome. Adapted from "A Diagnostic Interview" by J. Endicott and R. L. Spitzer, *Archives of General Psychiatry*, 1978, 35, 839. Copyright 1978 by the American Medical Association. Reprinted by permission.

ted to the New York State Psychiatric Institute, plus 150 patients who were jointly assessed in the four medical centers collaborating in the NIMH depression project, in addition to 60 additional patients who were interviewed in a test-retest design by interviewers in the same four participating medical centers.

Table 5 presents the very impressive intraclass correlation co-efficients of reliability reported by Endicott and Spitzer (1978) for the summary scale scores for dimensions of psychopathology achieved by use of the SADS in conjunction with the RDC for eight operationally defined categories. In their introduction to the results presented for the dimensions of psychopathology shown here in Table 5, and the *major* diagnostic categories shown in Table 4 (as well as Table 6), Spitzer, et al. (1978) made the following comment:

The choice of which diagnostic categories to include in the RDC, and how they should be operationally defined, was based on our judgment of the major problems of current diagnostic research. First of all, we selected categories that primarily are of interest to investigators in the broadly defined areas of affective disorders and schizo-

phrenia. Second, we included other categories of major importance for differential diagnosis of these conditions. Finally, we attempted to define the categories so as to maximize the possibility of testing various diagnostic hypotheses. Thus, the affective disorders were subdivided into nonmutually exclusive subtypes that allow each subject to be evaluated for each subtype . . . Furthermore, when a diagnostic concept, such as psychotic depression, seemed to involve several different domains (reality testing, endogenous features, incapacitation), each of these different features was used to define separate subtypes (pp. 775–776).

That the SADS-RDC combination could produce extraordinarily high reliability values for the *major* diagnostic classifications has been shown in the results presented in our Tables 4 and 5. However, even more extraordinary, given the poor pre-1970 results reviewed in our Table 1, these same two standardized tools produced almost as high joint-interview and test-retest reliability values for the *specific subtypes* of major depressive disorder. Those results are shown in Table 6. In commenting on the reliability values shown in Table 6, Spitzer et al. (1978

TABLE 5 Cronbach Alpha Coefficients of Reliability for Summary Scales of the Schedule for Affective Disorders and Schizophrenia

	Intraclass R		
Summary Scales	Joint Interview (N = 150)	Test-Retest (N = 60)	Internal Consistency (N = 150)
Depressive mood and ideation	.95	.78	.87
Endogenous features	.96	.83	.80
Depressive-associated features	.96	.88	.79
Suicidal ideation and behavior	.97	.83	.80
Anxiety	.94	.67	.58
Manic syndrome	.99	.93	.97
Delusions-hallucinations	.97	.91	.87
Formal thought disorder	.82	.49	.47

Note. Adapted from "Research Diagnostic Criteria" by R. L. Spitzer, J. Endicott, and E. Robins, *Archives of General Psychiatry,* 1978, *35,* 842. Copyright 1978 by the American Medical Association. Reprinted by permission.

TABLE 6 Kappa Coefficients of Agreement on Subtypes of Major
Depressive Disorder

	Joint Interviews		
	Study A (N = 68)	Study B (N = 150)	Test-Retest (N = 60)
Present illness only			
Primary	0.78	0.80	0.86
Secondary	0.65	0.79	0.95
Psychotic	0.59	0.87	0.70
Incapacitating	0.55	0.62	0.66
Endogenous	0.48	0.80	0.58
Agitated	0.74	0.69	0.59
Retarded	0.54	0.74	—
Situational	0.63	0.72	0.78
Simple	—†	0.75	0.77
Lifetime diagnosis			
Bipolar with mania	0.93	0.95	—*
Bipolar with hypomania	0.79	0.85	—*
Recurrent unipolar	0.81	0.83	0.80

†Not in the RDC at the time.   *Less than 5%
Note. Adapted from "Research Diagnostic Criteria" by R. L. Spitzer, J. Endicott, and E. Robins,
Archives of General Psychiatry, 1978, *35*, 780. Copyright 1978 by the American Medical Association.
Reprinted by permission.

indicated "they are somewhat lower than the major categories given in Table 3 [our Table 4] but, for the most part, are quite satisfactory for research use, and much higher than generally reported. On the basis of these studies, some minor revisions have been made in the [RDC] criteria for schizo-affective disorders, schizophrenia, and the agitated, incapacitating, endogenous, and retarded subtypes of major depressive disorder" (p. 780). In addition these SADS-RDC results led Spitzer Endicott and Robins (1978, p. 780) to report in 1978 that the results of a soon-to-be-published study by Helzer et al. (1981) would show that these RDC-SADS "test-retest kappa coefficients are higher than those recently reported from a study using the St. Louis Feighner criteria for the five major diagnostic categories included in both studies."

In a subsequent study of the RDC and SADS from the same NIMH collaborative study on depression, Andreasen and col-leagues (1981) from that collaborative group completed an intensive study of the reliability of the *lifetime* version of the SADS using experienced research clinicians and interviewers from all facilities and patients from the Iowa City and Boston collaborating institutions; currently symptomatic patients; as well as those whose symptoms were in remission and who were thus functioning as normals (nonpatients) and relatives of the patients who may or may not have been ill in the past or currently. A clinician from one center interviewed each of 50 patient and nonpatient subjects in the morning, another clinician from the second center (Iowa City) independently saw that same individual that afternoon, and in the evening, the two interviewers compared their diagnostic judgments and reached a third (consensus) diagnosis. The 50 subjects also had been diagnosed at the local center (25 in Iowa City and 25 in Boston) by the RDC-SADS method during the previous 6 months, mak-

TABLE 7 Test-Retest Study of Lifetime SADS-L* and RDC Diagnosis

SADS-L-RDC Lifetime Diagnosis	Base Rate%	Intraclass R	
		Morning vs Afternoon	Initial vs Consensus
Bipolar 1	10	1.00	.88
Bipolar 2	6	.62	.06
Major depressive disorder	44	.87	.75
Primary	33	.70	.59
Secondary	6	.60	.51
Recurrent	15	.78	.21
Psychotic	9	.79	.24
Incapacitating	9	.19	.40
Alcoholism	25	.94	.72
Never mentally ill	33	.70	.63

*SADS-L indicates the Schedule for Affective Disorders and Schizophrenia-Lifetime Version.
Note. Adapted from "Reliability of Lifetime Diagnosis" by N. C. Andreasen, W. M. Grove, R. W. Shapiro, M. B. Keller, R. M. Hirschfield, and P. McDonald-Scott. *Archives of General Psychiatry,* 1981, *38,* 402. Copyright 1981 by the American Medical Association. Reprinted by permission.

ing it possible to compare the reliability of that initial diagnosis on that person with the evening consensus-diagnosis arrived at 6 months later by the two clinicians working in concert. Table 7 presents the test-retest reliability results for the major diagnostic categories studied, including one for individuals (33%) who had never been mentally ill. Table 8 summarizes test-retest reliability values for those SADS-L *specific* items and interview probes which diagnose a *depressive* episode as well as those items needed for the diagnosis of a *manic* syndrome. As may be seen, the reliability results for the several *major* categories and for the depressive and manic syndrome items of this Collaborative Project Reliability Study conducted in Iowa City and Boston were generally of the same high order of magnitude found in the initial 1978 reliability studies reported by Spitzer et al. (1978) (those shown in our Tables 5 and 6). Andreasen et al. (1981) conclude that the reliability of *lifetime* psychiatric diagnoses made on never mentally ill individuals or on former depressed or manic patients who currently are in remission is remarkably good, almost as high as for *cur-*

rent patients assessed by the SADS. It also is important to note that, although not shown in tabular form here, Andreasen et al. found considerably lower clinician-to-clinician reliability values for the 10 *specific* individual items which operationally define the global diagnosis of *anxiety disorder* in that same 1981 study, although they concurrently found quite good inter-judge reliability for *individual* items which make up the diagnoses of *substance* abuse, *suicidal behavior,* and *personality makeup* (e.g., suspicious, inhibited and cheerful).

. . . During the period of development of the SADS by Endicott and Spitzer (1978) and the RDC by Spitzer, Endicott and Eli Robins (1978), Lee Robins and her associates (1981) at Washington University also were developing the Diagnostic Interview Schedule (DIS). Further, Helzer and his associates (1981) at Washington University were concurrently developing the Renard Diagnostic Interview (RDI). Inasmuch as the DIS and RDI do not *require* the use of experienced clinicians for reaching a diagnosis. . . . these two additional contributions by the St. Louis Group are of con-

TABLE 8 Test-Reliability of SADS-L Items that Characterize Depressive Episodes and the Manic Syndrome

		Intraclass R	
SADS-L Depressive Syndrome Items*	Base Rate,† %	Morning vs Afternoon	Initial vs Consensus
Depressed mood	54	.71	.59
Impaired functioning	50	.80	.67
Appetite or weight change	44	.77	.79
Sleep disturbance	38	.70	.53
Tiredness	25	.72	.44
Loss of interest	33	.92	.60
Guilt	29	.71	.60
Trouble concentrating	31	.85	.50
Thoughts of death or suicide, suicide attempt	17	.80	.65
Agitation-retardation	19	.42	.38
No. of symptoms	—	.92	.74
No. of episodes of depressive syndrome	—	1.00	− .01
No. of episodes of major depressive disorder	—	.18	− .01
Age at onset	—	1.00	.64
Age at last episode	—	.30	.96
Hospitalized	10	.88	.78
Received medication	25	.95	.56
Preceded or followed by mania, hypomania	8	.88	.64
Incapacitated	8	.19	.19
Suicidal gesture	6	.91	.56
Associated with pregnancy	10	.73	.49
SADS-L Manic Syndrome Items*			
Elevated mood	38	.84	.60
More active	17	.67	.67
More talkative	15	.77	.84
Thoughts race	13	.91	.91
Grandiosity	13	.88	.78
Less need for sleep	15	.85	.77
Distractibility	8	.64	.56
Poor judgment	10	.78	.78
No. of symptoms	—	.92	.94
Impairment	10	1.00	.90
Age at onset	—	1.00	.94
Age at last episode	—	1.00	.99
Hospitalized	6	1.00	.85
Received medication	10	1.00	.90
Preceded or followed by depression	8	.88	.78
Incapacitated	6	.49	.55

*SADS-L indicates the Schedule for Affective Disorders and Schizophrenia—Lifetime Version.   †Base rate is given if the rating is dichotomous.

Note. Adapted from "Reliability of Lifetime Diagnosis" by N. C. Andreasen, W. M. Grove, R. W. Shapiro, M. B. Keller, R. M. Hirschfield, and P. McDonald-Scott, *Archives of General Psychiatry,* 1981, **38**, 402. Copyright 1981 by the American Medical Association. Reprinted by permission.

siderable importance. Due to space limitations, however, they are not discussed further here. Instead, we will examine the manner in which the contributions of each of the workers from the four participating medical centers, plus the effort of scores of other contributors, eventuated in the development and publication in 1980 of DSM III by the American Psychiatric Association.

DSM III

Background and Development

Although not originally a partner in the early research on the 1972 Feighner criteria, or the 1978 Research Diagnostic Criteria and the Schedule for Affective Disorders and Schizophrenia, the leadership of the American Psychiatric Association was not unaware of the potential of the effort of these several research groups for improving the reliability of the diagnostic judgments of American psychiatrists, clinical psychologists, and colleagues from related mental health fields. In the context of a description of the events leading to DSM III, Spitzer and Williams (1980) provide a brief and lucid history of psychiatric classification and diagnosis. They chronicle the development by the World Health Organization (WHO) of the 1948 predecessor of the current (ninth edition) Manual for the International Classification of Disease (ICD), and the development by the American Psychiatric Association of DSM I (1952) and DSM II (1968). Using these historical landmarks in classification as background, Spitzer and Williams (1980) and Spitzer, in his introductory chapter to the DSM III Manual (American Psychiatric Association, 1980, pp. 1–12), go on to describe the specific steps and processes involved in the development of DSM III. These steps included the appointment in 1974 of an American Psychiatric Association Task Force on Nomenclature and Statistics, with Robert L. Spitzer as its chairperson, whose charge it was to serve as a steering committee for the development of DSM III. The Task Force included psychiatrists as members, and epidemiologists, psychologists, and others as consultants. Subsequently, in an attempt to include as wide participation as possible, the American Psychological Association was invited to appoint a liaison committee of three psychologists in 1976 to provide input into DSM III (Schacht & Nathan, 1977). To help with this massive interdisciplinary undertaking, the American Psychiatric Association ultimately enlisted the help of 14 Advisory Committees on specific disorders, plus other consultants and helpers: The names of these committees and individuals are given in the opening pages of DSM III (APA, 1980).

Before DSM III would become a reality 6 years later, the various phases of its development required the effort not only of these committee members and consultants but of that of hundreds of additional specialists. Additional input came from the annually changing Board of Trustees of the parent APA, the full APA Assembly, and many of its other committees and regional branches. Furthermore, liaison with still other groups with a potential vested interest in DSM III (e.g., the American Psychoanalytic Association) also was required. Finally, as DSM III began to take shape, its various draft forms were tried out in field trials that, between 1976 and 1980, involved a total of 800 clinicians. In fact, the final field trial, financially supported by an agency of the federal government (NIMH), required 2 years and involved almost 400 such clinicians in more than 120 facilities as well as 80 clinicians in private practice (representing all parts of the United States). Spitzer has described, in what clearly must be an understatement, the series of political as well as professional and scientific dilemmas which his Task Force had to overcome before DSM III became available to mental health workers in 1980 (APA, 1980, pp. 1–12: Spitzer & Williams, 1980). Schacht and Nathan (1977) also describe a bit of the political drama as it was perceived by the discipline of psychology in the earliest days of the interdisciplinary effort which went into the development of DSM III.

No one reading these accounts can be other than impressed with the enormity of this collective accomplishment by American psychiatrists and their colleagues from several allied professions. Nor can anyone reading this 1974–1980 history of the development of DSM III be other than impressed by the manner in which the hundreds of persons involved in the development of DSM III discarded the earlier largely unreliable, purely clinical descriptions of psychiatric disorders which constituted DSM II and, instead, made explicit, operationally denotable definitions of *each* disorder the hallmark of DSM III. One example of a difference between the 1968 DSM II and the 1980 DSM III should suffice here to indicate the progress that was made in the 12 years separating forms II and III. Figure 3, which juxtaposes the two, provides a comparison of the DSM II and DSM III definitions of schizophrenia, and clearly exemplifies the progression from a *vague clinical statement* in DSM II to the list in DSM III of *well defined inclusive and exclusive criteria* which must be met before the diagnosis of schizophrenia may be made. The final version of DSM III (APA, 1980) contains equally explicit definitions of 16 such *major* diagnostic disorders and 187 *specific* disorders. The reader interested in the differences and similarities between DSM II and DSM III for many other specific disorders will find this annotated list in Spitzer and Williams (1980, pp. 1061–1069), and in more detail in the DSM III Manual (APA, 1980, pp. 371–395).

Given that many of the persons involved in the development of DSM III also had been, or concurrently were, involved in the development of the 1972 Feighner criteria, the 1978 Research Diagnostic Criteria, the 1978 Schedule for Affective Disorders and Schizophrenia, the 1981 Diagnostic Interview Schedule, and the 1981 Renard Diagnostic Interview, as well as other explicit criteria for psychiatric classification and diagnosis, it was only to be expected that the fruits of some of these approaches designed to improve the reliability of a clinician's diagnosis would be incorporated into DSM III.

In fact, Spitzer and Williams (1980) acknowledge that:

The criteria in the RDC provided a preliminary basis for those RDC categories that were included in DSM III. For some disorders—such as panic disorder, manic episode of bipolar disorder and obsessive-compulsive disorder—the criteria are virtually the same in both RDC and DSM III. For other categories—such as schizophrenia, schizoaffective disorder, and major depression—there are significant differences resulting from experience with the RDC and the interpretation of recent research findings (p. 1049).

However, despite the fact that DSM III has a degree of filial relationship to RDC and these other mentioned classificatory schemas, it is clear that in its final form, DSM III, as a classificatory schema designed to improve diagnostic agreement, is the offspring of no single former tool. DSM III might best be considered on an equal footing with these earlier operationally defined diagnostic classification systems. For that reason we will next consider the makeup of DSM III and then proceed to examine its clinician-to-clinician reliability.

The Composition of DSM III

DSM I and DSM II consisted of a single classificatory scheme encompassing the whole range of psychiatric diagnostic categories. DSM III departs from that format and instead utilizes *five separate axes* to constitute a considerably more comprehensive scheme for classifying the individual patient with a psychiatric or psychological disturbance. The earlier single axis scheme for differential psychiatric and psychological diagnosis (which constituted DSM I and DSM II) is now broken up into two axes. Together they encompass all the earlier mental disorders of DSM I and II, plus other categories introduced in the recent past. Axis I includes *all the psychiatric disorders with the exceptions of two major subsets*. These latter conditions, which

DSM-II Description of Schizophrenia*

This large category includes a group of disorders manifested by characteristic disturbances of thinking, mood and behavior. Disturbances in thinking are marked by alterations of concept formation which may lead to misinterpretation of reality and sometimes to delusions and hallucinations, which frequently appear psychologically self-protective. Corollary mood changes include ambivalent, constricted and inappropriate emotional responsiveness and loss of empathy with others. Behavior may be withdrawn, regressive and bizarre. The schizophrenias, in which the mental status is attributable primarily to a *thought* disorder, are to be distinguished from the *Major affective illnesses* (q.v.) which are dominated by a *mood* disorder. The *Paranoid states* (q.v.) are distinguished from schizophrenia by the narrowness of their distortions of reality and by the absence of other psychotic symptoms.

DSM-III Diagnostic Criteria for Schizophrenia†

A. At least one of the following during a phase of the illness:
   (1) Bizarre delusions (content is patently absurd and has *no* possible basis in fact), such as delusions of being controlled, thought broadcasting, thought insertion, or thought withdrawal.
   (2) Somatic, grandiose, religious, nihilistic or other delusions without persecutory or jealous content.
   (3) Delusions with persecutory or jealous content, if accompanied by hallucinations of any type.
   (4) Auditory hallucinations in which either a voice keeps up a running commentary on the individual's behavior or thoughts, or two or more voices converse with each other.
   (5) Auditory hallucinations on several occasions with content of more than one or two words having no apparent relation to depression or elation.
   (6) Incoherence, marked loosening of associations, markedly illogical thinking or marked poverty of content of speech, if associated with at least one of the following:
      (a) blunted, flat or inappropriate affect
      (b) delusions or hallucinations
      (c) catatonic or other grossly disorganized behavior.
B. Deterioration from a previous level of functioning in such areas as work, social relations, and self-care.

C. *Duration:* Continuous signs of the illness for at least six months at some time during the person's life with some signs of the illness at present. The six-month period must include an active phase during which there were symptoms from A, with or without a prodromal or residual phase, as defined below:

Prodromal phase: A clear deterioration in functioning before the active phase of the illness not due to a disturbance in mood or to a Substance Use Disorder, and involving at least *two* of the symptoms noted below.

Residual phase: Persistence following the active phase of the illness, of at least *two* of the symptoms noted below, not due to a disturbance in mood or to a Substance Use Disorder.

Prodromal or Residual symptoms:
   (a) social isolation or withdrawal
   (b) marked impairment in role functioning as wage-earner, student, or homemaker
   (c) markedly peculiar behavior (e.g., collecting garbage, talking to self in public, hoarding food)
   (d) marked impairment in personal hygiene and grooming
   (e) blunted, flat, or inappropriate affect
   (f) digressive, vague, overelaborate, circumstantial, or metaphorical speech
   (g) odd or bizarre ideation, or magical thinking, e.g., superstitiousness, clairvoyance, telepathy, "sixth sense," "others can feel my feelings," overvalued ideas, ideas of reference
   (h) unusual perceptual experiences, e.g., recurrent illusions, sensing the presence of a force or person not actually present

Examples: Six months of prodromal symptoms with 1 week of symptoms from A: no prodromal symptoms with six months of symptoms from A: no prodromal symptoms with two weeks of symptoms from A and six months of residual symptoms: six months of symptoms from A, apparently followed by several years of complete remission, with 1 week of symptoms in A in current episode.
D. The full depressive or manic syndrome (criteria A and B of major depressive or manic episode), if present, developed after any psychotic symptoms, or was brief in duration relative to the duration of the psychotic symptoms in A.
E. Onset of prodomal or active phase of the illness before age 45.
F. Not due to any Organic Mental Disorder or Mental Retardation.

FIGURE 3

Comparison of DSM II and DSM III definitions of schizophrenia.
*Adapted from *Diagnostic and Statistical Manual of Mental Disorders*, ed. 2. American Psychiatric Association, Washington, D.C., 1968. †Adapted from *Diagnostic and Statistical Manual of Mental Disorders*, ed. 3. American Psychiatric Association, Washington, D.C., 1980.

now constitute Axis II, are the *personality disorders* and the *specific developmental disorders of childhood*. Axis III in DSM III is to be used to classify *physical disorders and conditions*, which co-exist with Axis I and II conditions (e.g., dementia secondary to brain tumor, or childhood conduct disorder secondary to juvenile diabetes).

In recording a diagnosis, the clinician will use Axes I (mental), II (personality), or III (physical) for classifying the patient being evaluated. A patient may be given a single diagnosis on one of these three Axes or, as relevant, may be assigned a diagnosis on two or on all three of the axes concurrently. For example, on Axis I, major depression and alcohol dependence; Axis II, dependent personality disorder; and Axis III, alcoholic cirrhosis of liver, all may be given as a description of *one* patient.

Axes IV and V are unique to DSM III as an official classificatory system and were included primarily "for use in special clinical or research settings [to] provide information additional to the official DSM III diagnoses (Axes I, II and III) that is of value for treatment planning and predicting outcome" (APA, 1980, p. 8). Axis IV is used to specify the judged *Severity of Psychosocial Stressors*. It consists of an 8-point rating scale (from no apparent psychosocial stressor at one end to evidence for the role of a catastrophic stressor such as a concentration camp experience in leading to the present diagnostic disorder(s) classified on Axes I, II or III). The examples of stressors provided for the intermediate steps on this 8-point scale include change of job, divorce, and death of a parent. Therefore, they are not unlike those stressors assigned a numerical value from 1 to 100 in the Schedule of Recent Events developed by Holmes and Rahe (1967).

Axis V, *Highest Level of Adaptive Functioning Past Year*, assesses in a single composite rating on a 5-point scale (from superior to poor) the degree of adaptive success in three major areas of life: social relations, occupational functioning, and use of leisure time. It is believed by the developers of DSM III (APA, 1980, p. 28) that "this information

frequently has prognostic significance, because usually an individual returns to his or her previous level of adaptive functioning after an episode of illness."

For each psychiatric or psychological disorder to be rated on Axes I and II, the text in the DSM III Manual begins with a clinical description of the disorder, including its essential features, associated features, age at onset, course, typical level of impairment, complications, predisposing factors, prevalence, sex ratio and family pattern. The discussion of each disorder ends with a box in which are summarized the operationally denotable diagnostic criteria for that disorder which the clinician using DSM III should apply. These operationally specified criteria resemble those for manic depressive disorder shown at the bottom of our earlier Figure 2 and for schizophrenia reproduced in Figure 3. To emphasize the still evolving nature of this 1980 classificatory system, the following caveat precedes the list of diagnostic classifications which are included in DSM III (APA, 1980):

> **These criteria are offered as useful guides for making the diagnosis, since it has been demonstrated that the use of such criteria enhances diagnostic agreement among clinicians. It should be understood, however, that for most of the categories the criteria are based on clinical judgment, and have not yet been fully validated; with further experience and study, the criteria will, in many cases undoubtedly be revised (p. 31).**

The Reliability of Diagnosis with DSM III

DSM III Reliability Using Professional Clinicians

Spitzer and his colleagues have to date published the clinician-to-clinician kappa reliability coefficients for DSM III in two separate publications on what appears to be an overlapping data set: namely, from the first field trial (Phase One) using the January 15, 1978 draft of DSM III, and from a second field trial (Phase Two) most likely conducted in 1978–1979. The latter trial used what one may presume was the final draft of DSM III. The reliability results of the 1978 field trial are summarized in a paper by Spitzer, Forman, and Nee (1979). That publication reports the reliability findings on Axes I and II. A companion paper by Spitzer and Forman (1979) reports the reliability of Axes IV and V. Some of the same data for Axes I, II, IV and V, presented in a slightly different format, also are reported in the DSM III *Manual* itself (APA, 1980, pp. 467–472). This *Manual* (pp. 470–472) includes the reliability results obtained in Phase Two with the 1980 version of DSM III.

Inasmuch as the reliability results presented in the *Manual* are not too dissimilar from those published in the two 1979 publications, and because those in the *Manual* are too numerous for inclusion here, only the 1978 Phase One results reported in the two publications by Spitzer and his colleagues will be reviewed here.

In that Phase-One reliability study, Spitzer and his colleagues (1979a; 1979b) provided volunteer clinicians from all parts of the country with working copies of DSM III and asked each of them first to practice using it on 15 patients from his or her own patient population. Following this, the clinician, paired with another local clinician, was to carry out at least four reliability evaluations, with each clinician using each of the five axes in the evaluation. With few exceptions, the reliability interviews were conducted as part of the initial evaluation of a patient neither clinician had seen previously. As to format, the two clinicians could either be present at the same evaluation, following which they independently recorded their judgments (joint interview method), or if that was inconvenient, separate evaluations could be done, preferably within a day of the first interviewer's evaluation (test–retest interview method). Spitzer et al. (1979, p. 817) report that 40% of these test-retest interviews were done within one day of each

other, whereas almost half had a test-retest interval of more than 3 days. In either format, both clinicians were instructed *to make use of all the material available on the patient*, such as case records, letters of referral, nursing notes, and family information.

In all, 274 clinicians out of 365 recruited participated in the Phase One field trial using the January 15, 1978 draft and, together, they evaluated 281 adult patients. A total of 71 children and adolescents also were evaluated in Phase One; 55 more were seen in Phase Two. The reliability results from these children are published only in the 1980 *Manual* (APA, pp. 471–472). An additional 331 adult patients were evaluated in Phase Two using the last draft of DSM III and those results also are published only in the 1980 *Manual* (APA, pp. 470–472).

Table 9 from Spitzer, Forman and Nee (1979) presents the results of the two types of reliability studies on Axes I and II carried out by the 274 clinicians on the 281 adult patients evaluated on the basis of the January 15, 1978 draft of DSM III. As may be seen, 150 patients were assessed in the two clinicians present (joint) reliability study format. An additional 131 patients were evaluated in the test-retest study format. In Table 9, the 15 major diagnostic categories comprising Axis I are *indented* one space to the left of the individual specific categories subsumed under each of them, thus permitting the reader more readily to discern the reliability of the major diagnostic classification and each of its components.

One clear conclusion may be drawn from the results presented in Table 9. That is, unlike DSM I and II, DSM III is a much more reliable system for classifying the psychiatric and psychological disorders included in Axes I and II. The overall reliability of the 15 *major* categories making up Axis I is shown (second from the bottom row) to be .78 for the joint interview method and .66 for the test-retest method. As shown in the bottom rows, comparable kappa reliability values for the single major category of personality disorders making up Axis II are .61 and .54 respectively.

TABLE 9   The Reliability of DSM III Diagnosis Using Experienced Clinicians and Adult Patients: Kappa Coefficients of Agreement

Diagnostic Class	Percent of Total*	Interview Model	
		Joint (N = 150)	Test-Retest (N = 131)
Disorders of infancy, childhood, or adolescence	5.6	.66	.81
Mental retardation	2.1	.66	.85
Disorders characteristic of late adolescence	1.4	1.00	.66
Eating disorders	2.1	−0.01	.85
Organic mental disorders	12.9	.74	.83
Senile and presenile dementias	3.1	1.00	.74
Substance-induced organic brain syndromes	7.7	.48	.74
Organic brain syndrome with unknown etiology	4.5	.56	.72
Substance use disorders	22.0	.90	.74
Schizophrenic disorders	12.9	.82	.82
Paranoid disorders	0.7	1.00	1.00
Schizoaffective disorders	4.5	.56	.53
Affective disorders	44.6	.77	.59
Major affective disorders	29.6	.70	.65
Chronic minor affective disorders	19.9	.64	.29
Psychoses not elsewhere classified	7.0	.85	.43
Anxiety disorders	10.5	.74	.43
Factitious disorders	1.4	.49	1.00
Somatoform disorders	4.2	.53	.66
Dissociative disorders	0.7	1.00	−.004
Psychosexual disorders	2.1	1.00	1.00
Paraphilias	0.7	1.00	1.00
Psychosexual dysfunctions	1.7	1.00	1.00
Adjustment disorders	11.2	.74	.60
Disorders of impulsive control not elsewhere classified	1.7	−0.01	−0.01
Overall kappa for major classes, axis I		.78	.66
Overall kappa for personality disorders, axis II	60.6	.61	.54

*Percent of all subjects given diagnosis by at least one clinician. Because some subjects received diagnoses from two minor classes within a major class (e.g., a major affective disorder and a chronic minor affective disorder), the total percent of subjects in minor classes may exceed the percent of total subjects in the major class. Only in the case of substance use disorders was there an appreciable difference in percentages between the groups (joint = 28.7%, test-retest = 14.5%).

Note. Adapted from "DSM-III Field Trials: I. Initial Interrater Diagnostic Reliability" by R. L. Spitzer, J. B. W. Forman, and J. Nee, *American Journal of Psychiatry,* 1979, *136,* 815–817. Copyright 1979 by the American Psychiatric Association. Reprinted by permission.

Spitzer et al. (1979) indicate that inasmuch as the kappa reliability coefficients shown in Table 9 are corrected for chance agreements, a reader may conclude that:

high kappa (generally .70 and above) indicate good agreement as to whether or not the patient has a disorder within that diagnostic class, even if there may be a disagreement about the specific disorder within the class. For example, diagnoses of paranoid schizophrenia by two clinicians would be considered agreement on schizophrenia. The overall kappa for the major classes of Axis I indicates the extent to which there is agreement across all diagnostic classes for all patients given an Axis I diagnosis by at least one of the clinicians and is thus an overall index of diagnostic agreement (pp. 816–817).

A reader remembering the relatively low reliability values published only a decade ago on levels of agreement across two clinicians, despite the fact that the latter are inflated by uncorrected base rate (chance) agreements, cannot help but be impressed with the results shown in Table 9. If nothing else, the 11 coefficients in Table 9 which reach the heretofore unattainable value of 1.00 are a remarkable accomplishment.

In a classic understatement, at least for those of us in clinical settings who rarely see clinician-to-clinician reliability values above .30 or .40 for our judgments, Spitzer et al. (1979) evaluate the findings in Table 9 as follows:

For most of the classes, the reliability for both interview situations is quite good and, in general, is higher than that previously achieved using DSM I and DSM II. . . . It is particularly encouraging that the reliability for such categories as schizophrenia and major affective disorders is so high. . . . Although personality disorder is more reliably judged than previously, how to improve its reliability is not at all clear. As expected, the reliabilities are higher when the interviews are done

jointly. . . . Nevertheless, the drop in reliability for most of the classes is relatively small. Differences between reliabilities obtained under the two conditions may be due to different questions being asked by each interviewer as well as the patient's giving different responses to the same question asked at both interviews (p. 817).

Inasmuch as no structured interview schedule (such as the SADS, RDC, DIS, or RDI) seemed to have been included as the standardized method for eliciting the patient information in these DSM III studies, the reliabilities for Axis I and Axis II of DSM III shown in Table 9 are even more impressive. In the companion article on the remaining data of this same Phase One study, Spitzer and Forman (1979) report data comparable to those in Table 9 for Axis IV (stressors) and Axis V (adaptive functioning). Thus, for the same 281 patients interviewed by the same 274 clinicians represented in Table 9, the kappa coefficient of agreement for Axis IV was .62 for joint interviews and .58 for separate test-retest interviews. Reliability for Axis V was even better: namely, .80 for joint interviews and .69 for separate interviews. Also important, of relevance to the acceptability of DSM III among clinicians, Spitzer and Forman report that 81% of the 274 clinicians participating "judged the multiaxial system to be a useful addition to traditional diagnostic evaluation, although many indicated that they had difficulty quantifying severity of psychosocial stressor" (Spitzer & Forman, 1979, p. 818).

This Phase One study was followed by a Phase Two study which utilized the slightly changed, final version of DSM III. The interested reader will find the kappa coefficients for the major and specific diagnostic categories which comprise Axes I and II, and the ratings which comprise Axes IV and V, in a sample utilizing adults and a second sample utilizing children and adolescents in three tables in an Appendix to the 1980 Manual (APA, 1980, pp. 467–472). These Phase-Two results are too numerous to discuss here, therefore the following global statement (by Williams and Spitzer) must suffice to indicate their magnitudes: "It is noteworthy that the reliability in general improved in Phase Two, perhaps due to refinements in the criteria used in Phase Two" (APA, 1980, p. 468).

Detailed comparison of Phase One and Phase Two results reveals that the kappa values went down for some categories in Phase Two, although the overall trend was for a slight improvement. However, whether the reference be the Phase One or the Phase Two results, it is clear from the kappa values from these first studies that DSM III is a remarkably reliable classification scheme for the psychological and psychiatric disorders currently being evaluated by this country's mental health professionals.

*   *   *

References

American Psychiatric Association, *Diagnostic and statistical manual, mental disorders, first edition.* Washington, D.C.: Author, 1952.

American Psychiatric Association, *Diagnostic and statistical manual of mental disorders, third edition (DSM III).* Washington, D.C.: Author, 1980.

Andreasen, N. C., Grove, W. M., Shapiro, R. W., Keller, M. B., Hirschfeld, R. M., and McDonald-Scott, P. Reliability of lifetime diagnosis. *Archives of General Psychiatry,* 1981, *38,* 400–405.

Ash, P. The reliability of psychiatric diagnosis. *Journal of Abnormal and Social Psychology,* 1949, *44,* 272–277.

Beck, A. T. Reliability of psychiatric diagnoses: A critique of systematic studies. *American Journal of Psychiatry,* 1962, *119,* 210–216.

Beck, A. T., Ward, C. H., Mendelson, M., Mock, J. E., and Erbaugh, J. K. Reliability of psychiatric diagnoses, II. A study of consistency of clinical judgments and ratings. *American Journal of Psychiatry,* 1962, *119,* 351–357.

Blum, J. D. On changes in psychiatric diagnosis over time. *American Psychologist,* 1978, *33,* 1017–1031.

Boisen, A. Types of dementia praecox: A study in psychiatric classification. *Psychiatry,* 1938, *I,* 233–236.

Caveny, E. L., Wittson, C. L., Hunt, W. A., and Herrmann, R. S. Psychiatric diagnosis: Its nature and function. *Journal of Nervous and Mental Disease,* 1955, *121,* 367–373.

Cohen, J. A. Coefficient of agreement for nominal scales. *Educational and Psychological Measurement,* 1960, *20,* 37–46.

Endicott, J., and Spitzer, R. L. A. A diagnostic interview. *Archives of General Psychiatry,* 1978, *35,* 837–844.

Eysenck, H. J. Classification and the problem of diagnosis. In H. J. Eysenck (Ed.), *Handbook of abnormal psychology: An experimental approach,* New York: Basic Books, 1961.

Feighner, J. P., Robins, E., Guze, S. B., Woodruff, R. A., Winokur, G., and Munoz, R. Diagnostic criteria for use in psychiatric research. *Archives of General Psychiatry,* 1972, *26,* 57–63.

Fleiss, J. L. Measuring nominal scale agreement among many raters. *Psychological Bulletin,* 1971, *76,* 378–382.

Foulds, G. The reliability of psychiatric and validity of psychological diagnosis. *Journal of Mental Science,* 1955, *101,* 851–862.

Goodwin, D. W., and Guze, S. B. *Psychiatric diagnosis: Second edition.* New York: Oxford University Press, 1979.

Helzer, J. E., Clayton, P. J., Pambakian, R., Reich, T., Woodruff, R. A., and Reveley, M. A. Reliability of psychiatric diagnosis: II. *Archives of General Psychiatry,* 1977, *34,* 136–141.

Helzer, J. E., Robins, L. N., Croughan, J. L., and Welner, A. Renard diagnostic interview. *Archives of General Psychiatry,* 1981, *38,* 393–398.

Helzer, J. E., Robins, L. N., Taibleson, M., Woodruff, R. A., Reich, T., and Wish, E. D. Reliability of psychiatric diagnosis, I. A methodological review. *Archives of General Psychiatry,* 1977, *34,* 129–133.

Holmes, T. H., and Rahe, R. H. The social readjustment scale. *Journal of Psychosomatic Research,* 1967, *11,* 213–218.

Hunt, H. F. Clinical methods: Psychodiagnostics. In C. P. Stone and D. W. Taylor (Eds.). *Annual Review of Psychology,* 1950, *1,* 207–220.

Hunt, W. A., Wittson, C. L., and Hunt, E. B. A theoretical and practical analysis of the diagnostic process. In P. H. Hoch and J. Zubin (Eds.). *Current problems in psychiatric diagnosis.* New York: Grune & Stratton. 1953.

Kreitman, N., Sainsbury, P., Morrissey, J., Towers, J., and Scrivener. J. The reliability of psychiatric diagnosis. *Journal of Mental Science,* 1961, *107,* 887–908.

Luria, R. E., and Berry, R. Reliability and descriptive validity of PSE syndromes. *Archives of General Psychiatry,* 1979, **36**, 1187–1195.

MASSERMAN, J. H., AND CARMICHAEL, H. T. Diagnosis and prognosis in psychiatry: With a follow-up study of the results of short-term general hospital therapy in psychiatric cases. *Journal of Mental Science,* 1938, **84**, 893–946.

MATARAZZO, J. D. The interview. In B. B. WOLMAN (Ed.). *Handbook of clinical psychology.* New York: McGraw-Hill, 1965.

MATARAZZO, J. D. The interview: Its reliability and validity in psychiatric diagnosis. In B. B. WOLMAN (Ed.). *Clinical Diagnosis of Mental Disorders: A handbook,* New York: Plenum Press, 1978.

MEHLMAN, B. The reliability of psychiatric diagnosis. *Journal of Abnormal and Social Psychology,* 1952, **47**, 577–578.

MENNINGER, K., MAXMAN, M., AND PRUYSER, P. *The vital balance: The life process in mental health and illness.* New York: Viking, 1963.

PASAMANICK, B., DINIZ, S., AND LEFTON, M. Psychiatric orientation and its relation to diagnosis and treatment in a mental hospital. *American Journal of Psychiatry,* 1959, **116**, 127–132.

RAINES, G. N., AND ROHRER, J. H. The operational matrix of psychiatric practice. I. Consistency and variability in interview impressions of different psychiatrists. *American Journal of Psychiatry,* 1955, **111**, 721–723.

RAINES, G. N., AND ROHRER, J. H. The operational matrix of psychiatric practice. II. Variability in psychiatric impressions and the projection hypothesis. *American Journal of Psychiatry,* 1960, **117**, 133–139.

ROBINS, L. N., HELZER, J. E., CROUGHAN, J., AND RATCLIFF, K. S. National institute of mental health diagnostic interview schedule. *Archives of General Psychiatry,* 1981, **38**, 381–389.

ROTTER, J. *Social learning and clinical psychology.* Englewood Cliffs, N.J.: Prentice-Hall, 1954.

SANDIFER, M. G., PETTUS, C., AND QUADE, D. A study of psychiatric diagnosis. *Journal of Nervous and Mental Disease.* 1964, **139**, 350–356.

SCHACHT T., AND NATHAN, P. E. But is it good for the psychologists? Appraisal and status of DSM III. *American Psychologist,* 1977, **32**, 1017–1025.

SCHMIDT, H., AND FONDA, C. The reliability of psychiatric diagnosis: A new look. *Journal of Ab-normal and Social Psychology,* 1956, **52**, 262–267.

SCOTT, J. Research definitions of mental health and mental illness. *Psychological Bulletin,* 1958, **55**, 29–45.

SEEMAN, W. P. Psychiatric diagnosis: An investigation of interperson-reliability after didactic instruction. *Journal of Nervous and Mental Disease,* 1953, **118**, 541–544.

SPITZER, R. L., COHEN, J., FLEISS, J. L., AND ENDICOTT, J. Quantification of agreement in psychiatric diagnosis. *Archives of General Psychiatry,* 1967, **17**, 83–87.

SPITZER, R. L., ENDICOTT, J., AND ROBINS, E. Research diagnostic criteria. *Archives of General Psychiatry,* 1978, **35**, 773–782.

SPITZER, R. L., AND FLEISS, J. L. A re-analysis of the reliability of psychiatric diagnosis. *British Journal of Psychiatry,* 1974, **125**, 341–347.

SPITZER, R. L., AND FORMAN, J. B. W. DSM-III field trials: II. Initial experience with the multiaxial system. *American Journal of Psychiatry,* 1979a, **136**, 818–820.

SPITZER, R. L., FORMAN, J. B. W., AND NEE, J. DSM-III field trials: I. Initial interrater diagnostic reliability. *American Journal of Psychiatry,* 1979b, **136**, 815–817.

SPITZER, R. L., AND WILLIAMS, J. B. W. Classification in psychiatry. In A. KAPLAN, A. FREEDMAN, AND B. SADOCK (Eds.), *Comprehensive textbook of psychiatry; III.* Baltimore: Williams and Wilkins, 1980.

WILSON, M. S., AND MEYER, E. Diagnostic consistency in a psychiatric liaison service. *American Journal of Psychiatry,* 1962, **119**, 207–209.

WING, J. K., BIRLEY, J. L. T., AND COOPER, J. E. Reliability of a procedure for measuring and classifying "present psychiatric state." *British Journal of Psychiatry,* 1967, **113**, 449–515.

WOODRUFF, R. A., JR., GOODWIN, D. W., AND GUZE, S. B. *Psychiatric diagnosis.* New York: Oxford University Press, 1974.

ZIGLER, E., AND PHILLIPS, L. Psychiatric diagnosis: A critique. *Journal of Abnormal and Social Psychology,* 1961, **63**, 607–618.

ZILBOORG, G. *A history of medical psychology,* New York, Norton, 1941.

ZUBIN, J. Classification of the behavior disorders. In P. R. FARNSWORTH, O. McNEMAR, AND Q. McNEMAR (Eds.) *Annual review of psychology* (*Vol. 18*). Palo Alto, Calif.: Annual Reviews, Inc., 1967.

4

Six-Month Prevalence of Psychiatric Disorders in Three Communities:

1980 to 1982

Jerome K. Myers, Myrna M. Weissman, Gary L. Tischler, Charles E. Holzer III, Philip J. Leaf, Helen Orvaschel, James C. Anthony, Jeffrey H. Boyd, Jack D. Burke, Jr, Morton Kramer, and Roger Stoltzman

Six-month prevalence rates for selected *DSM-III* psychiatric disorders are reported based on community surveys in New Haven, Conn, Baltimore, and St. Louis. As part of the Epidemiologic Catchment Area program, data were gathered on more than 9,000 adults, employing the Diagnostic Interview Schedule to collect information to make a diagnosis. The most common disorders found were phobias, alcohol abuse and/or dependence, dysthymia, and major depression. The most common diagnoses for women were phobias and major depression, whereas for men, the most predominant disorder was alcohol abuse and/or dependence. Rates of psychiatric disorders dropped sharply after age 45 years.

Jerome K. Meyers, Myrna M. Weissman, Gary L. Tischler, Charles E. Holzer III, Philip J. Leaf, Helen Orvaschel, James C. Anthony, Jeffrey H. Boyd, Jack D. Burke, Jr., Morton Kramer, and Roger Stoltzman. Six-Month Prevalence of Psychiatric Disorders in Three Communities. *Archives of General Psychiatry*, 1984, Vol. 41, pp. 959–967. Copyright © 1984, American Medical Association. Reprinted by permission

Prevalence and incidence rates of specific psychiatric disorders derived from community-based surveys have important scientific and health policy implications. Variations in such rates can provide clues to etiology and can be used as base rates for family genetic studies. In health care policy, such rates are useful in planning health programs and in evaluating the impact of community treatment programs.

Population rates of psychiatric disorders have generally not been available in the United States because the post-World War II surveys of mental illness in the community assessed overall mental impairment or symptoms, without regard to specific diagnoses.[1] Accordingly, estimates for rates of discrete psychiatric disorders in the United States have been made on the basis of treated cases, have been inferred from studies that assessed rates of mental morbidity in general, or have been based on population surveys conducted in Europe.[2,3]

During the last decade, new techniques for improving the reliability and validity of diagnoses have been developed for use in community studies. Three diagnostic instruments have received particular attention in the United States: the Schedule for Affective Disorders and Schizophrenia (SADS) and the Research Diagnostic Criteria (RDC), developed by Spitzer and his colleagues[4,5] at the New York Psychiatric Institute; the Renard Diagnostic Interview, developed by Helzer et al.[6]; and the Present State Examination (PSE), developed by Wing et al.[7]

One of these instruments, the SADS, was employed in a pilot community study of about 500 persons by Weissman and Myers[3,8–10] in 1975 and 1976. This study demonstrated that it was feasible to employ diagnostically specific clinical instruments in the community to estimate rates of psychiatric disorder. However, highly trained interviewers with Master's level clinical education had to be employed as interviewers, since judgments were required in the administration of the SADS. Also, a lengthy training period covering several months was necessary. Thus, the instrument was not practical for use in large-scale surveys for ordinary survey interviewers. Furthermore, the size of the pilot study sample was small so that estimates for rates of disorders with small numbers were imprecise or unstable. Finally, persons interviewed were from the third wave of a study begun in 1967 and may not have continued to be representative of the population due to migration, deaths, and refusals.

Shortly after the conclusion of this pilot study, the Division of Biometry and Epidemiology, National Institute of Mental Health (NIMH), initiated the development of an adaptation of the SADS and Renard instruments to facilitate their use in general population studies. This new instrument, the Diagnostic Interview Schedule (DIS), has made possible large-scale epidemiologic community studies such as those being conducted as part of the Epidemiologic Catchment Area (ECA) research program described by Regier et al.[11]

The present article . . . [focuses] on the prevalence rates for the six-month period immediately preceding the interview. Data are presented by sex and age from the first of three waves of household sample surveys in New Haven, Conn., Baltimore, and St Louis. The overall design of the project has been described elsewhere,[11] as has the DIS used in the assessment of diagnostic status.[12] Certain aspects of the study, however, warrant elaboration, since they are crucial for the interpretation of the data presented in this report.

Methods

Overview

The original specifications for the ECA project called for each site to contact a random sample of approximately 4,000 household residents 18 years and older to obtain at least 3,000 interviews. The specific procedures for developing a sample frame varied from site to site along two important dimensions. First, the differences in the geographic areas to be surveyed and differences in available information about housing units influenced the sampling procedures at each site. Second, each site contained an oversampling of individuals to produce better estimates for specific subsets of the population.

The New Haven survey developed a list of all housing units and produced a systematic sample of household clusters using a random starting point. One adult from each household was selected at random. Elderly residents were oversampled. In Baltimore, blocks were selected with probability proportionate to size, and households were sampled systematically from blocks. One person between the ages of 18 and 64 years was selected from each household, with all persons 65 years and older also being selected to provide an oversample. In St Louis, census enumeration districts were selected from each of three catchment areas, with enumeration districts with a preponderance of blacks being oversampled. Two blocks were selected from each enumeration district (or clusters of enumeration districts) with probability proportionate to size followed by a systematic sampling of households. As in

New Haven, only one adult (18 years or older) was selected at random from each household.

Lay interviewers were recruited, trained, and supervised at each site. These interviewers gathered and recorded data on sociodemographic characteristics and mental status by following the highly standardized NIMH DIS. More than 3,000 interviews were conducted at each site with completion rates of between 76% and 80%. Common computer programs were used to analyze the data, ascertain cases of particular categories of mental disorder, and estimate prevalence rates and their variances.

DIS Issues

Briefly, the DIS is a highly structured interview designed for use by lay interviewers in epidemiologic studies and capable of generating computer diagnoses in terms of certain DSM-III, Feighner, or RDC criteria. According to Robins et al.[12], it is possible to make diagnoses by all three systems with a single interview because the three systems share a common heritage to the degree that they address diagnoses from a descriptive rather than etiologic perspective.

The DIS is designed to elicit the elements of a diagnosis, including symptoms, their severity, frequency, distribution over time, and whether or not they are explainable by physical illness, use of drugs or alcohol, or the presence of another psychiatric disorder. Both the questions and the probes are structured and precoded so that answers can be directly entered into the computer after editing. Diagnoses can be generated for current (last two weeks, one month, six months, one year) and lifetime prevalence. The DIS is relatively economical because it does not require a clinician, external data, coders, or a lengthy training program.

The rates presented in this report are based on the DSM-III diagnoses generated from the DIS. However, it is important to note that the DIS does not cover all DSM-III mental disorder categories. Its selective coverage was determined through careful

deliberations of a scientific advisory group, with decisions based primarily on expected prevalence, severity and clinical importance of the disturbances, research interest, and validity of the disorder category as suggested by treatment response, family studies, and follow-up studies. We have limited our presentation of DIS-based rates in this report to the following DSM-III categories that are covered by the DIS: agoraphobia, alcohol abuse/dependence, anti-social personality, drug abuse/dependence, dysthymia, major depression, manic disorder, obsessive-compulsive disorder, panic disorder, schizophrenia or schizophreniform disorder, simple phobia, social phobia, and somatization disorder. The Baltimore and St Louis research teams are able to report additional categories, but these are not included herein. The DSM-III exclusion criteria have not been used in arriving at diagnoses because of the difficulty in making the DSM-III exclusion concepts operational in a structured interview, particularly the concept that a group of symptoms for one disorder may be "due to" another disorder.

In addition to DSM-III diagnoses generated by the DIS, we shall present data on cognitive impairment based on Mini-Mental State Examination (MMSE) scores. The MMSE was developed by Folstein et al.[13] as a brief screening instrument for use as part of a clinical examination. It was designed to assess level of performance on cognitive tasks and it can be used as a screen for organic brain syndromes. As a screening instrument, it does not ascertain the criteria for making specific diagnoses of dementia, delirium, or any other specific organic brain syndrome. Therefore, we will use the term *cognitive impairment* to refer to poor performance on the test; we do not intend it as a label more suggestive of a particular clinical disorder.

When this collaborative research study was initiated, only a preliminary version of the DSM-III had been developed. Since Yale University (New Haven), the initial site for the ECA project, entered the field ahead of the other groups, it employed the version of the DIS that then existed, namely, DIS 2. Later, when field trials for the DSM-III were completed, the DIS was revised to incorporate the modifications to the DSM-III criteria. In the case of two diagnostic categories (phobia and schizophrenia), the version of the DIS (DIS 3) used in the first waves in St Louis and in Baltimore did not correspond exactly to the DIS 2 version employed in the first wave of interviews in New Haven. When we present data on those two diagnoses, we shall discuss the implications of these discrepancies. The third version of the DIS was employed in subsequent waves of interviewing in New Haven.

Prevalence Rate Estimation

The DIS determines DSM-III disorders with reference to several discrete time periods, including the two weeks prior to interview, one month, six months, and one year prior to interview, and the entire lifetime prior to interview. In this report, current mental status has generally been defined in terms of

disturbance that the DIS indicates as active in the six months prior to interview. One important reason for this definition is correspondence with the six-month period employed in the companion report by Shapiro et al.[14] on the topic of health and mental health care by persons with and without a DIS-classified mental disorder. A comparison of the overall rates by different time periods will be presented later in this article.

Two further comments about the data are in order before presenting the results. First, this is a survey of households only and does not include institutional cases. Second, the prevalence data presented should be seen as defined operationally by DIS approximations to DSM-III diagnostic categories.

The rates presented in this study are expressed as percentages. All differences in rates presented in the text are significant at the .05 level. Significance tests are based on the unequal variance t-test formula applied to cell-specific variance estimates obtained from the SESUDAAN program.[15] Table 1

TABLE 1 Number of Respondents and Confidence Bounds by Age and Sex*

	Men, Age Group, yr				Total Men	Women, Age Group, yr				Total Women	Total
	18–24	25–44	45–64	65+		18–24	25–44	45–64	65+		
					Sample Sizes						
New Haven, Conn.	176	542	337	236	1,291	247	692	453	375	1,767	3,058
Baltimore	201	467	303	351	1,322	303	745	539	572	2,159	3,481
St Louis	191	505	288	218	1,202	280	728	436	358	1,802	3,004
					Values for Constructing Confidence Limits, %						
0–0.49	0.1–0.7	0.3–0.5	0.2–0.9	0.2–0.9	0.2–0.4	0.1–0.8	0.1–0.8	0.1–0.5	0.2–0.7	0.2–0.4	0.1–0.3
0.5–0.99	0.9–1.8	0.7–1.1	1.0–1.1	0.8–1.1	0.4–0.7	0.8–1.4	0.6–0.7	0.5–1.3	1.0–1.3	0.3–0.5	0.3–0.4
1.0–2.49	1.2–2.8	0.7–1.7	1.2–2.0	1.3–1.7	0.5–1.1	1.1–2.3	0.8–1.5	0.8–1.5	1.0–1.7	0.5–0.8	0.3–0.7
2.5–4.99	2.5–3.4	1.5–2.3	2.0–2.4	2.3–3.4	0.8–1.2	1.5–2.8	1.2–1.6	1.8–2.7	1.1–3.1	0.8–1.4	0.7–1.0
5.0–9.99	3.3–4.8	2.2–2.4	2.4–4.5	2.2–3.9	1.5–1.9	3.1–4.1	2.0–2.2	1.9–3.5	2.2–3.9	0.9–1.8	0.7–1.1
10.0–19.99	4.5–7.6	2.9–4.4	3.3–5.2	3.7–7.2	2.0–2.6	3.9–5.5	2.5–3.4	3.1–4.5	2.8–5.8	1.7–2.2	1.3–1.8
20.0+	5.0–7.2	4.5–4.7	—	—	2.5–2.5	5.6–6.7	3.5–3.7	4.8–4.9	—	2.6–2.7	2.0–2.0

*This table consists of two parts. The upper portion presents actual sample sizes for each of the age and sex categories used in the analysis. As noted previously, the percentages presented in the main tables are based on weighted data. The lower portion of the table presents values to be used in constructing confidence bounds on the percentages reported in the main tables. For each age by sex category, there is a column of values to be used in constructing 95% confidence bounds. Along the left margin are ranges of percentage values that correspond to rates of reported disorder. To construct a 95% confidence bound for prevalence value, find the range of percentages along the left that corresponds to the prevalence percentage, and the column defined by the age by sex group. At their intersection are two numbers, a minimum and a maximum value to be used in the confidence bound. The 95% confidence bound will be the percentage value plus and minus the value given in the table. The confidence bound will be at least as big as the lower value and less than the larger value. For example, the New Haven prevalence for any disorder is 16.9% regardless of age and sex. Therefore, one looks in the right-hand column in the row with the range 10 to 19.99. The table values are 1.3 to 1.8. The lower 95% bound is as low as 16.9−1.8 = 15.1. The upper confidence bound for that figure is 16.9 + 1.8 = 18.7. Therefore, the true population percentage is expected to be between 15.1% and 18.7% for 95 of 100 samples from this population.

presents approximate confidence bounds and cell sizes that permit the reader to make further tests of significance among any of the rates presented.

Rates have been estimated by means of weighting and poststratification adjustment procedures so that the survey-based estimates for age, sex, and race distributions of the ECAs are comparable with the distributions indicated by the 1980 US census of these areas. These procedures are described more fully by Eaton et al. in this series of articles.[16] Nevertheless, there has been no standardization to remove differences in these distributions from one area to another. This must be considered when examining and interpreting variation in the rates from one site to another.

To summarize, the rates presented in this article are preliminary estimates of six-month prevalence rates derived from the first wave of adult household interviews at the three sites and are rates expressed as percentages. We shall present data for total weighted rates and by age and sex but not by any other sociodemographic variables.

Results

Total Rates and Prevalence by Sex

Affective Disorders. Table 2 presents the rates for the affective disorders by sex and age. Total rates vary from 4.6% in Baltimore to 6.2% in St Louis and 6.5% in New Haven. As measured by the DIS, major depression without bereavement is the most frequent current affective disorder, ranging from 2.2% in Baltimore to 3.5% in New Haven. Rates for the lifetime diagnosis of dysthymia are of approximately the same magnitude. A two-year period of depressed affect is required for dysthymia, but the DIS does not determine if one is currently in such a prolonged period of depression. Although this report deals with six-month prevalence we are presenting data on dysthymia, since it is a major affective disorder. The rates are significantly higher for women than for men at all sites for both major depression and dysthymia. Manic disorder is much less frequent, and there is little difference in its rates by sex. Major depressive episode in the pres-

TABLE 2 Six-Month Prevalence of DIS/DSM-III Affective Disorders by Sex and Age*

Site	Men, Age Group, yr				Total Men	Women, Age Group, yr				Total Women	Total
	18–24	25–44	45–64	65+		18–24	25–44	45–64	65+		
Major depressive episode without bereavement, %											
New Haven, Conn.	3.9	2.7	1.4	0.5	2.2	6.1	7.4	2.2	1.6	4.6	3.5
Baltimore	1.1	1.6	1.5	0.3	1.3	3.0	4.5	2.4	1.3	3.0	2.2
St Louis	1.1	2.8	1.3	0.1	1.7	5.2	5.2	4.9	1.0	4.5	3.2
Bereavement, %†											
New Haven	0.0	0.0	0.1	0.0	0.0	0.3	0.3	0.4	1.7	0.6	0.3
Baltimore	0.0	0.0	0.3	0.6	0.2	0.3	0.1	0.2	0.6	0.3	0.2
St Louis	0.0	0.2	0.0	0.0	0.1	0.0	0.1	0.0	0.6	0.2	0.1
Manic episode, %											
New Haven	1.3	1.0	0.0	0.0	0.6	2.0	1.2	0.6	0.0	0.9	0.8
Baltimore	0.0	1.1	0.0	0.0	0.4	0.3	0.7	0.3	0.0	0.4	0.4
St Louis	1.4	0.7	0.8	0.0	0.8	1.4	1.0	0.1	0.0	0.6	0.7
Dysthymia, %‡											
New Haven	3.0	3.0	2.1	1.8	2.6	2.3	5.1	3.0	3.1	3.7	3.2
Baltimore	0.4	1.3	1.8	0.6	1.2	1.0	4.3	3.5	1.3	2.9	2.1
St Louis	2.2	2.7	1.8	0.5	2.1	3.6	6.0	8.0	1.6	5.4	3.8
Any affective disorder, %§											
New Haven	7.5	5.4	3.0	2.2	4.6	9.1	11.4	5.6	5.0	8.2	6.5
Baltimore	1.5	3.7	3.1	1.2	2.7	4.5	8.9	6.3	3.1	6.0	4.6
St Louis	3.9	5.1	3.2	0.5	3.8	7.7	9.9	9.6	3.1	8.3	6.2

*DIS indicates Diagnostic Interview Schedule. †Respondents meeting criteria for major depressive episode, but explaining it as bereavement. ‡DIS 2 and 3 do not have recency probes for dysthymia, so these are lifetime figures. §Includes dysthymia.

TABLE 3 Six-Month Prevalence of DIS/DSM-III Panic and Obsessive-Compulsive Disorders by Sex and Age*

Site	Men, Age Group, yr				Total Men	Women, Age Group, yr				Total Women	Total
	18–24	25–44	45–84	65+		18–24	25–44	45–84	65+		
Panic, %											
New Haven, Conn.	0.0	0.5	0.3	0.0	0.3	0.7	1.6	0.6	0.4	0.9	0.6
Baltimore	1.0	0.5	1.4	0.0	0.8	1.0	1.9	1.0	0.2	1.2	1.0
St Louis	0.9	1.1	0.5	0.0	0.7	0.8	1.6	0.9	0.1	1.0	0.9
Obsessive-compulsive, %											
New Haven	0.9	1.3	0.4	1.2	0.9	2.7	2.8	0.8	0.4	1.7	1.4
Baltimore	2.1	1.7	2.4	0.9	1.9	2.6	3.1	1.3	1.2	2.2	2.0
St Louis	1.5	1.3	0.2	0.2	0.9	2.8	1.5	1.3	1.3	1.7	1.3

*DIS indicates Diagnostic Interview Schedule.

ence of bereavement is infrequent in absolute terms, although we do not have information on the relative rate of affective disorders among those who have been bereaved.

Panic and Obsessive-Compulsive Disorders. As can be seen in Table 3, the rates for panic and obsessive-compulsive disorders are similar at all three sites. Although rates for women are consistently higher, they are significant only for panic disorder in New Haven.

Substance Abuse and/or Dependence. The rates are rather similar for alcohol abuse and/or dependence at all sites, ranging from 4.5% in St Louis to 5.7% in Baltimore, as shown in Table 4. The rates for drug abuse and/or dependence are even more similar,

ranging from 1.8% in New Haven to 2.2% in Baltimore. At all sites, the rates for substance abuse and/or dependence are significantly higher for men than for women, especially for alcohol abuse and/or dependence.

Somatization and Antisocial Personality Disorder. As shown in Table 5, the prevalence of somatization disorder is low and was found only among women. In contrast, antisocial personality disorder was found to be significantly more frequent among men in Baltimore and St Louis.

Cognitive Impairment. Scores on the MMSE range from 0 correct to 30, a perfect score. For the purposes of this report, we define severe cognitive impairment as a score of 17 or less. In addition, we are pre-

TABLE 4 Six-Month Prevalence of DIS/DSM-III Substance Abuse/Dependence by Sex and Age*

Site	Men, Age Group, yr				Total Men	Women, Age Group, yr				Total Women	Total
	18–24	25–44	45–64	65+		18–24	25–44	45–64	65+		
Alcohol abuse/ dependence, %											
New Haven, Conn.	11.6	11.4	4.4	3.0	8.2	6.4	1.8	0.9	0.0	1.9	4.8
Baltimore	9.9	13.7	10.1	3.7	10.4	1.9	2.8	1.3	0.0	1.7	5.7
St Louis	8.6	11.7	5.9	3.0	8.5	2.3	0.8	0.5	0.7	1.0	4.5
Drug abuse/ dependence, %											
New Haven	11.0	1.6	0.0	0.0	2.5	6.1	0.8	0.0	0.0	1.3	1.8
Baltimore	6.3	4.8	0.2	0.0	3.0	5.0	1.9	0.0	0.0	1.6	2.2
St Louis	6.2	4.3	0.0	0.0	3.0	3.4	1.3	0.1	0.2	1.2	2.0

*DIS indicates Diagnostic Interview Schedule.

TABLE 5 Six-Month Prevalence of DIS/DSM-III Somatization and Antisocial Personality Disorder by Sex and Age*

Site	Men, Age Group, yr				Total Men	Women, Age Group, yr				Total Women	Total
	18–24	25–44	45–64	65+		18–24	25–44	45–64	65+		
Somatization disorder, %											
New Haven, Conn.	0.0	0.0	0.0	0.0	0.0	0.2	0.3	0.2	0.0	0.2	0.1
Baltimore	0.0	0.0	0.0	0.0	0.0	0.0	0.5	0.0	0.0	0.2	0.1
St Louis	0.0	0.0	0.0	0.0	0.0	0.6	0.3	0.2	0.0	0.3	0.1
Antisocial personality, %											
New Haven	1.2	1.0	0.3	1.1	0.8	0.6	0.6	0.0	0.0	0.3	0.6
Baltimore	0.9	3.4	0.2	0.0	1.5	0.1	0.3	0.0	0.0	0.1	0.7
St Louis	4.6	2.9	0.3	0.0	2.1	1.6	0.6	0.0	0.0	0.5	1.3

*DIS indicates Diagnostic Interview Schedule.

senting data on mild impairment as indicated by a score of 18 through 23. Scores of 24 and above represent little or no impairment.

As shown in Table 6, rates for both severe and mild cognitive impairment are rather similar at all sites, with rates for mild impairment being substantially higher. There is little difference in these rates by sex.

Schizophrenia/Schizophreniform Disorder. Intersite variation in the rates of schizophrenic disorders presented in Table 7 cannot be interpreted without considering that version 2 of the DIS (employed in New Haven) and DIS 3 (employed elsewhere) differ in their implementation of DSM-III criterion B for schizophrenia, deterioration from a previous level of functioning in such areas as work, social relations, and self-care. In addition, DIS 2 requirements for establishing auditory hallucinations were less

strict than the criterion used in version 3 of the DIS. Nevertheless, the total rates are not significantly different at the three sites. In fact, analysis of the data from St Louis, using the same criteria as in New Haven, produced a total rate of 1.3% compared with 1.1% in New Haven and an original rate of 0.6% in St Louis. Thus, rates may well be even more similar in the second wave of ECA surveys, since all sites have employed version 3 of the DIS in these follow-up interviews. There is little difference in rates by sex in St Louis, while rates are higher for women in New Haven and Baltimore.

Phobic Disorders. The data presented in Table 8 indicate significantly higher rates for phobic disorders in Baltimore (13.4%) than in New Haven (5.9%) and St Louis (5.4%) where rates are similar. Regardless of the specific rates or sites, rates for women are always significantly higher than for men.

TABLE 6 Six-Month Prevalence of Cognitive Impairment by Sex and Age

Site	Men, Age Group, yr				Total Men	Women, Age Group, yr				Total Women	Total
	18–24	25–44	45–64	65+		18–24	25–44	45–64	65+		
Severe, %											
New Haven, Conn.	0.7	0.6	0.8	6.3	1.4	0.3	0.1	1.4	4.2	1.2	1.3
Baltimore	0.0	0.0	1.1	5.7	1.1	0.4	0.5	1.1	4.8	1.4	1.3
St Louis	0.4	0.2	0.8	4.6	1.0	0.9	0.3	0.7	3.6	1.1	1.0
Mild, %											
New Haven	1.7	0.7	6.3	11.5	4.0	2.1	1.4	3.8	11.6	4.1	4.0
Baltimore	2.7	2.1	9.7	14.2	6.2	0.9	1.7	4.5	16.6	5.2	5.7
St Louis	4.0	2.5	5.2	18.4	5.5	1.6	2.5	9.2	15.0	6.2	5.9

TABLE 7 Six-Month Prevalence of DIS/DSM-III Schizophrenia or Schizophreniform Disorder by Sex and Age*

Site	Men, Age Group, yr				Total Men	Women, Age Group, yr				Total Women	Total
	18–24	25–44	45–64	65+		18–24	25–44	45–64	65+		
New Haven, Conn., %	2.1	0.6	0.3	0.0	0.7	1.6	2.6	0.7	0.9	1.6	1.1
Baltimore, %	1.3	0.7	0.8	0.0	0.7	1.0	3.2	0.9	0.2	1.6	1.2
St Louis, %	0.6	1.5	0.8	0.0	0.9	0.5	0.5	0.2	0.0	0.4	0.6

*DIS indicates Diagnostic Interview Schedule.

The degree of variability by site may arise partly from the fact that there is a much greater difference in the questions, their wording, probes, interviewer instructions, and the list of specific phobias presented to the respondents at the three sites than for any other diagnosis. For example, in New Haven, a shorter list of specific phobias was presented to respondents, and data were not collected to make a DSM-III diagnosis of social phobia. In Baltimore, the specific wording of questions made it easier to meet the DSM-III criteria than in New Haven or in St Louis, which appears to have had the strictest rules of any site. To illustrate, when the data were analyzed for Baltimore to approximate the questions from the version of the DIS employed in New Haven (exact comparison was not possible), the total rate in Baltimore dropped from 13.4% to 9.1% (compared with 5.9% in New Haven). In the follow-up interviews, the same version of the DIS was employed at all sites so that the cross-site variation in instrumentation and questionnaire administration noted previously will no longer apply.

Total Rates (Excluding Persons Who Had Only Phobias or Dysthymia)

Table 9 shows little intersite variability in the overall rates for any current disorder excluding persons having only phobia or dys-

TABLE 8 Six-Month Prevalence of DIS/DSM-III Phobias by Sex and Age*

Site	Men, Age Group, yr				Total Men	Women, Age Group, yr				Total Women	Total
	18–24	25–44	45–64	65+		18–24	25–44	45–64	65+		
Social phobia, %†											
Baltimore	2.3	2.1	0.8	1.5	1.7	4.3	2.7	1.8	1.9	2.6	2.2
St Louis	0.3	1.1	1.3	0.1	0.9	2.2	2.3	0.6	0.3	1.5	1.2
Simple phobia, %											
New Haven, Conn.	3.1	3.1	4.5	0.7	3.2	6.3	8.5	4.2	3.6	6.0	4.7
Baltimore	9.3	5.8	8.4	6.1	7.3	18.1	16.0	15.6	12.5	15.7	11.8
St Louis	2.1	2.2	2.8	1.5	2.3	5.6	10.2	4.5	1.9	6.5	4.5
Agoraphobia, %											
New Haven	0.7	1.4	1.2	0.5	1.1	5.3	6.0	3.3	1.2	4.2	2.8
Baltimore	3.9	2.6	4.1	3.3	3.4	7.3	8.8	8.3	5.5	7.8	5.8
St Louis	1.0	0.8	1.3	0.0	0.9	4.9	5.5	4.1	1.0	4.3	2.7
Total phobia, %‡											
New Haven	3.1	3.3	4.8	1.2	3.4	9.1	11.3	5.3	4.6	8.0	5.9
Baltimore	10.7	6.9	10.0	7.6	8.6	18.9	18.6	17.3	14.2	17.5	13.4
St Louis	2.5	3.0	3.3	1.5	2.8	8.4	11.2	5.3	2.6	7.7	5.4

*DIS indicates Diagnostic Interview Schedule.   †Data on social phobia were not collected in DIS 2 employed in wave 1 in New Haven.   ‡Some persons had more than one phobic diagnosis, so individual diagnostic categories do not add up to the rates presented in "total phobia."

TABLE 9 Six-Month Prevalence of Any of the Previous DIS/DSM-III Disorders and Severe Cognitive Impairment by Sex and Age Excluding Phobia*

Site	Men, Age Group, yr				Total Men	Women, Age Group, yr				Total Women	Total†
	18–24	25–44	45–64	65+		18–24	25–44	45–64	65+		
New Haven, Conn., %	23.4	17.0	7.6	11.6	14.5	20.7	14.4	6.6	8.9	12.1	13.2
Baltimore, %	18.3	19.5	12.2	9.6	15.7	12.2	13.2	6.7	7.4	10.0	12.6
St Louis, %	18.5	18.1	7.2	7.5	13.8	13.1	10.4	7.7	6.6	9.6	11.6

*Does not include dysthymia. DIS indicates Diagnostic Interview Schedule.   †Individual diagnoses total to more than the total rates since some persons have multiple diagnoses.

thymia, with a range from 11.6% in St Louis to 13.2% in New Haven. Rates for individual diagnoses in previous tables add up to more than these total rates, since some persons have multiple diagnoses. For example, in New Haven, 11.1% of respondents reported one diagnosis, 1.6% reported two diagnoses, and 0.5% reported three or more diagnoses.

Total Rates (Including Phobias)

Total rates for any current disorder (including phobias but excluding dysthymia) are shown in Table 10. New Haven and St Louis have similar rates, with Baltimore being higher because of the high rates for phobia.

In summary, as shown in Table 9, six-month prevalence rates for any DIS/DSM-III disorder we surveyed, but excluding phobias and dysthymia, varied from 11.6% in St Louis to 13.2% in New Haven. If phobias are included, as reported in Table 10, the rates are 14.8% in St Louis, 16.9% in New Haven, and 22.5% in Baltimore. The most common diagnoses are phobias, alcohol abuse and/or dependence, dysthymia, and major depression. There are important vari-ations by sex, however. For women, the four most common disorders are phobia, major depression, dysthymia, and obsessive-compulsive disorder. For men, on the other hand, alcohol abuse and/or dependence is by far the most common diagnosis, followed by phobia, drug abuse and/or dependence, and dysthymia.

Age Differences by Sex

As can be seen in Table 9, the rates for men and women for any diagnosis (excluding phobia and dysthymia) are substantially lower for persons 45 years and older than for the younger age groups. Note that the rates are about twice as high for persons younger than 45 years than those 45 years and older.

When the phobias are included, as presented in Table 10, the higher rates in Baltimore increase the total rates substantially for persons 45 years and older in that community, but these rates are still lower than for younger persons. There is still a ratio of about 2:1 in the rates for those under 45 years to those over 45 years in the other two

TABLE 10 Six-Month Prevalence of Any of the Previous DIS/DSM-III Disorders or Severe Cognitive Impairment by Sex and Age*

Site	Men, Age Group, yr				Total Men	Women, Age Group, yr				Total Women	Total†
	18–24	25–44	45–64	65+		18–24	25–44	45–64	65+		
New Haven, Conn. %	23.8	18.9	11.9	12.3	16.7	24.6	21.2	10.3	13.2	17.1	16.9
Baltimore, %	25.1	23.5	18.7	15.3	21.1	26.6	27.1	21.5	17.8	23.6	22.5
St Louis, %	18.9	19.8	9.4	8.8	15.4	17.8	17.2	10.9	8.8	14.3	14.8

*Does not include dysthmia. DIS indicates Diagnostic Interview Schedule.   †Individual diagnoses total to more than the total rates since some persons have multiple diagnoses.

sites. We shall now examine age differences by sex for the individual diagnostic categories and cognitive impairment as presented in Tables 2 through 8.

Affective Disorders. Affective disorders are generally less frequent in the age group 65 years and older. They are generally highest in the age groups 18 to 24 years and 25 to 44 years.

Panic and Obsessive-Compulsive Disorders. These disorders are more evenly distributed by age than the affective disorders. This is true for both sexes.

Substance Abuse and/or Dependence. This is a younger age disorder at all sites for both men and women. The rates decline substantially after age 44 years. Drug abuse and/or dependence is especially high in the youngest age group (18 to 24 years).

Somatization Disorder. This disorder is infrequent and was not found in persons aged 65 years and older. It is generally higher among persons younger than 44 years.

Antisocial Personality Disorder. Antisocial personality is clearly a young person's disorder, regardless of sex. The rates are generally low for persons younger than the age of 44 years.

Cognitive Impairment. Impaired cognitive mental status is an older person's disorder, regardless of sex, with highest rates being for persons aged 65 years and older and the next highest for persons aged 45 to 64 years, as would be expected. However, it is important to note that cognitive impairment was found in all age groups.

Schizophrenia. This is more common among persons younger than 44 years in both sexes. The rates are particularly low for persons 65 years and older.

Phobia. The phobias are more evenly distributed across the age span than most dis-

orders. However, the lowest rates are generally for persons aged 65 years and older.

In summary, while age distribution of disorders by sex is generally similar, there are some important differences, as shown in Table 11. The basis for ranking within age groups was the mean six-month prevalence rates for New Haven, Baltimore, and St Louis combined. Alcohol abuse and/or dependence predominates among men 18 to 24 years, followed close by drug abuse and/or dependence, whereas for women in this age group, phobias are the most common, followed by drug abuse and/or dependence and major depression. In the age group 25 to 44 years, alcohol abuse and/or dependence continues to be the most common disorder for men. However, phobias now are the second highest disorder covered, followed closely by drug abuse and/or dependence. For women, the most common disorders are phobias and major depression. In the age group 45 to 64 years, phobias remain the most frequent diagnosis for women, and nearly equals the rate of alcohol abuse and/or dependence for men. Dysthymia is the second most common diagnosis found among women. In the age group 65 years and older, severe cognitive impairment is the most common disorder for men, followed by phobia and alcohol abuse and/or dependence. For women in this age group, the most common disorder is phobia, followed by severe cognitive impairment.

When comparing the results of this study with the data presented in the Robins et al.[17] report in this series, we find generally comparable variation in lifetime and six-month prevalence rates by age and sex. Future reports will examine in detail the similarities and differences between such rates.

It is important to recognize that prevalence rates differ by the time period employed to measure them: the more current the time period, the lower the rates. As indicated earlier in this article, we chose a six-month period to have rates comparable with those used by Shapiro et al.[14] in their article on utilization. The variation in lifetime and

TABLE 11 Four Most Frequent DIS/DSM-III Psychiatric Disorders by Sex and Age Based on Six-Month Prevalence Rates*

Rank	18–24 yr	25–44 yr	45–64 yr	65+ yr	Total
			Men		
1	Alcohol abuse/ dependence	Alcohol abuse/ dependence	Alcohol abuse/ dependence	Severe cognitive impairment	Alcohol abuse/ dependence
2	Drug abuse/ dependence	Phobia	Phobia	Phobia	Phobia
3	Phobia	Drug abuse/ dependence	Dysthymia	Alcohol abuse/ dependence	Drug abuse/ dependence
4	Antisocial personality	Antisocial personality	Major depressive episode without grief	Dysthmyia	Dysthymia
			Women		
1	Phobia	Phobia	Phobia	Phobia	Phobia
2	Drug abuse/ dependence	Major depressive episode without grief	Dysthymia	Severe cognitive impairment	Major depressive episode without grief
3	Major depressive episode without grief	Dysthymia	Major depressive episode without grief	Dysthymia	Dysthymia
4	Alcohol abuse/ dependence	Obsessive-compulsive disorder	Obsessive-compulsive disorder	Major depressive episode without grief	Obsessive-compulsive disorder

*Dysthmia included. The basis for ranking was the mean six-month prevalence rates for New Haven, Baltimore, and St Louis combined. DIS indicates Diagnostic Interview Schedule.

more recent total prevalence rates can be seen in Table 12. For example, the total lifetime rate in New Haven for any disorder or severe cognitive impairment (but excluding dysthymia and phobia) drops from 24.2% to 15.2% for one year to 13.2% for six months, 9.5% for one month, and 8.6% for two weeks. Similar reductions in rates occur in St Louis and Baltimore, as is evident in Table

12. In future reports, we plan to discuss the details of the relationships between prevalence rates employing different time periods.

Table 13 presents summary rates for major classes and specific disorders in DSM-III. This table shows that the anxiety disorders accounted for some of the highest rates, even without the inclusion of generalized anxiety disorder and posttraumatic stress symptom,

TABLE 12 Comparison of Total Prevalence Rates of DIS/DSM-III Psychiatric Disorder by Time Period*

Site	Time Period				
	2 wk	1 mo	6 mo	1 yr	Lifetime
New Haven, Conn., %	8.6	9.5	13.2	15.2	24.2
Baltimore, %	8.8	10.6	12.6	14.3	23.0
St Louis, %	7.2	8.2	11.6	13.7	25.2

*Severe cognitive impairment included; dysthymia and phobia excluded. DIS indicates Diagnostic Interview Schedule.

TABLE 13 Six-Month Prevalence Rates of DIS/DSM III Disorders, Three ECA Sites*

Disorders	New Haven, Conn., % 1980–1981 (N = 3,058)	Baltimore, % 1981–1982 (N = 3,481)	St. Louis, % 1981–1982 (N = 3,004)
Any DIS disorder covered	18.4 (0.8)	23.4 (1.0)	16.8 (1.0)
Any DIS disorder except phobia	15.2 (0.8)	14.0 (0.7)	13.8 (0.9)
Any DIS disorder except substance use disorders	13.6 (0.7)	19.0 (0.9)	12.6 (0.9)
Substance use disorders	6.1 (0.4)	7.2 (0.6)	5.8 (0.5)
Alcohol abuse/dependence	4.8 (0.4)	5.7 (0.6)	4.5 (0.5)
Drug abuse/dependence	1.8 (0.3)	2.2 (0.3)	2.0 (0.3)
Schizophrenic/schizophreniform disorders	1.1 (0.2)	1.2 (0.2)	0.6 (0.2)
Schizophrenia	1.1 (0.2)	1.0 (0.2)	0.6 (0.2)
Schizophreniform disorder	0.1 (0.1)	0.2 (0.1)	0.1 (0.0)
Affective disorders	6.5 (0.6)	4.6 (0.4)	6.2 (0.6)
Manic episode	0.8 (0.2)	0.4 (0.1)	0.7 (0.2)
Major depression	3.5 (0.4)	2.2 (0.3)	3.2 (0.5)
Dysthymia	3.2 (0.4)	2.1 (0.2)	3.8 (0.4)
Anxiety/somatoform disorders	7.2 (0.4)	14.9 (0.8)	6.6 (0.6)
Phobia	5.9 (0.4)	13.4 (0.8)	5.4 (0.5)
Panic	0.6 (0.1)	1.0 (0.2)	0.9 (0.2)
Obsessive-compulsive	1.4 (0.2)	2.0 (0.3)	1.3 (0.3)
Somatization	0.1 (0.1)	0.1 (0.1)	0.1 (0.1)
Personality disorder Antisocial personality	0.6 (0.1)	0.7 (0.2)	1.3 (0.3)
Cognitive impairment (severe)	1.3 (0.2)	1.3 (0.2)	1.0 (0.2)

*DIS indicates Diagnostic Interview Schedule; ECA, Epidemiologic Catchment Area; numbers in parentheses indicate SEs.

two disorders that were not included in the original 15 DIS disorders but that have received increased attention in recent years. The substance abuse disorders are dominated by alcohol abuse/dependence and represent the first community rates as defined by DSM-III. Interestingly enough, these disorders have the best results on available criterion validity studies with the SADS-Lifetime version (SADS-L).[18] The affective disorders total does not reflect inclusion of cyclothymic, atypical, or adjustment reaction affective disorders. However, it does appear that the affective disorders, as a group, are relatively more prevalent in clinical populations (compared with anxiety and substance abuse disorders) than in community populations.

Table 13 should also facilitate comparison of six-month rates of DIS disorders with the lifetime rates of the Robins et al.[17] article and the services-utilization rates, as discussed in the article by Shapiro et al.[14] Since Table 13 includes dysthymia in the total rates, it is possible to determine the contribution of dysthymia to overall prevalence by comparing rates in Table 13 with those in Tables 9 and 10. Thus, the inclusion of dysthymia increases total rates by 0.9% to 2.0% in the three sites.

Comparisons With 1975 to 1976 New Haven Survey

Table 14 compares the current ECA findings with 1975 to 1976 data collected in New Haven in a study of 511 respondents in the third wave of interviews begun in 1967.[3,8–10] In the 1975 to 1976 study, the SADS and the RDC were used (not the DIS),

TABLE 14 Six-Month Prevalence of Psychiatric Disorder for New Haven, Conn, Baltimore, and St Louis

Disorder	New Haven, % 1975–1976 (N = 511)	New Haven, % 1980–1981 (N = 3,058)	Baltimore, % 1981–1982 (N = 3,481)	St Louis, % 1981–1982 (N = 3,004)
Major depression	4.3	3.5	2.2	3.2
Manic episode	0.6	0.8	0.4	0.7
Alcohol dependence	2.5	2.8	4.2	2.6
Drug dependence	1.0	1.1	0.8	1.1
Schizophrenia	0.4	1.1	1.0	0.6
Phobia	1.4	5.9	13.4	5.4
Panic	0.4	0.6	1.0	0.9
Obsessive-compulsive	0.0	1.4	2.0	1.3
Somatization	0.4	0.1	0.1	0.1
Antisocial	0.2	0.6	0.7	1.3

*1975 to 1976 diagnoses are based on Research Criteria; all other diagnoses are based on DIS/DSM-III. (DIS indicates Diagnostic Interview Schedule.)

so that comparisons of findings are rough. However, the similarity of findings is remarkable. The major difference is found in the phobias in which the rates of the current study are much higher, since the RDC criteria to make the diagnosis were much more stringent than are DSM-III criteria as made operational by the DIS.

We should point out some differences in the two studies. The earlier study was a cohort of respondents remaining in a third wave of a large community survey. As a result, there are no respondents in the earlier study who were aged 25 years or younger. Table 14 has not been standardized to take into account the differences in the age and sex of respondents. Rates in 1975 to 1976 were reported as current point prevalence, whereas the current study reports six-month prevalence. Finally, 1980 rates are weighted for age, sex, and race according to the US census statistics for the catchment area, whereas rates in the 1975 to 1976 study are unweighted. However, weighting makes little difference, as Eaton et al.[16] have pointed out. . . .

Conclusions

The comparison of DIS/DSM-III rates across the three ECA sites indicates considerable similarity of results at all sites. The only major discrepancy is the much higher rate of the phobic disorders found in Baltimore, which may be explained by methodological factors in the collection of data.

Summarizing our substantive findings, the most common disorders in the three communities studied are phobias, alcohol abuse and/or dependence, dysthymia, and major depression. In all three communities, there were similar sex and age differences in rates of disorder. The most common diagnoses for women were phobias and major depression, whereas for men, the predominant disorder was alcohol abuse and/or dependence. The total rates of disorder drop sharply after age 45 years. Most individual disorders follow the same pattern except cognitive impairment. The most striking but expected differences by age are that substance abuse and/or dependence and antisocial personality disorder are predominantly a younger person's disorder, whereas cognitive impairment is most prevalent in persons aged 65 years and older.

It is interesting to note the similarity of our findings with those of the 1975 to 1976 New Haven study. Although comparisons are rough because somewhat different instruments, time periods, and diagnostic criteria were used, the similarity of findings, with the exception of the phobias, is striking.

Future studies will examine in more detail the overall findings presented in this report. Of special interest will be variations in prevalence rates by time periods and the specific instances of age and sex differences. We shall also compare our findings with those in Los Angeles and North Carolina, the other two ECA sites that are still collecting data.

References

1. WEISSMAN MM, KLERMAN GL: The epidemiology of mental disorders: Emerging trends. *Arch Gen Psychiatry* 1978;35:705–712.
2. SILVERMAN C: *The Epidemiology of Depression.* Baltimore, Johns Hopkins University Press, 1968.
3. WEISSMAN MM, MYERS JK: Psychiatric disorders in a U.S. community: The application of Research Diagnostic Criteria to a resurveyed community sample. *Acta Psychiatr Scand* 1980;62:99–111.
4. SPITZER RL, ENDICOTT J, ROBINS E: Research Diagnostic Criteria: Rationale and reliability. *Arch Gen Psychiatry* 1978;35:773–782.
5. ENDICOTT J, SPITZER RL: A diagnostic interview: The Schedule for Affective Disorders and Schizophrenia. *Arch Gen Psychiatry* 1978;35:837–844.
6. HELZER JE, ROBINS LN, CROUGHAN JL, WELNER A: Renard diagnostic interview: Its reliability and procedural validity with physicians and lay interviewers. *Arch Gen Psychiatry* 1981;38:393–398.
7. WING JK, COOPER JE, SARTORIUS N: *Measurement and Classification of Psychiatric Symptoms.* New York, Cambridge University Press, 1974.
8. WEISSMAN MM, MYERS JK, HARDING PS: Psychiatric disorders in a U.S. urban community: 1975–1976. *Am J Psychiatry* 1978;135:459–462.
9. WEISSMAN MM, MYERS JK: Affective disorders in a U.S. urban community: The use of Research Diagnostic Criteria in an epidemiological survey. *Arch Gen Psychiatry* 1978;35:1304–1311.
10. MYERS JK, WEISSMAN MM: Psychiatric disorders and their treatment: A community survey. *Med Care* 1980;18:117–123.
11. REGIER DA, MYERS JK, KRAMER M, ROBINS LN, BLAZER DG, HOUGH RL, EATON WW, LOCKE BZ: The NIMH Epidemiologic Catchment Area program: Historical context, major objectives, and study population characteristics. *Arch Gen Psychiatry* 1984;41:934–941.
12. ROBINS LN, HELZER JE, CROUGHAN J, RATCLIFF KS: National Institute of Mental Health Diagnostic Interview Schedule: Its history, characteristics, and validity. *Arch Gen Psychiatry* 1981;38:381–389.
13. FOLSTEIN MF, FOLSTEIN SE, McHUGH PR: Mini Mental State: A practical method for grading the cognitive state of patients for the clinician. *J Psychiatr Res* 1975;12:189–198.
14. SHAPIRO S, SKINNER EA, KESSLER LG, VON KORFF M, GERMAN PS, TISCHLER GL, LEAF PJ, BENHAM L, COTTLER L, REGIER DA: Utilization of health and mental health services: Three Epidemiologic Catchment Area sites. *Arch Gen Psychiatry* 1984;41:971–978.
15. SHAH BV: *SESUDAAN: Standard Error Program for Computing of Standardized Rates for Sample Survey Data.* Research Triangle Park, NC, Research Triangle Institute, 1981.
16. EATON WW, HOLZER CE III, VON KORFF M, ANTHONY JC, HELZER JE, GEORGE L, BURNAM MA, BOYD JH, KESSLER LG, LOCKE BZ: The design of the Epidemiologic Catchment Area surveys: The control and measurement of error. *Arch Gen Psychiatry* 1984;41:942–948.
17. ROBINS LN, HELZER JE, WEISSMAN MM, ORVASCHEL H, GRUENBERG E, BURKE JD JR, REGIER DA: Lifetime prevalence of specific psychiatric disorders in three sites. *Arch Gen Psychiatry* 1984;41:949–958.
18. HESSELBROCK V, STABENAU J, HESSELBROCK M, MIRKIN P, MEYER R: A comparison of two interview schedules: The Schedule for Affective Disorders and Schizophrenia-Lifetime and the National Institute of Mental Health Diagnostic Interview Schedule. *Arch Gen Psychiatry* 1982;39:674–677.

Schizophrenia

Schizophrenia is a severe and often recurrent psychotic disorder characterized by hallucinations and delusions as well as by cognitive and affective disturbances. It directly affects the lives of slightly under 1% of the population, and, as is well illustrated by Murphy's (1976) article in the preceding section, it is found in all cultures.

Although we owe the term schizophrenia (literally, the shattering or splitting of the mind's functions) to Eugen Bleuler (1911), the syndrome was first recognized by Emil Kraepelin in 1898. Kraepelin called it dementia praecox—a term that described what he considered to be two important features of the disorder: an early age of onset and progressive intellectual deterioration.

For Kraepelin the course of the disorder was of paramount importance. Bleuler, in contrast, was concerned principally with schizophrenia's core or fundamental symptoms. These he referred to as the "4 A's": (1) loose Association of thoughts, (2) inappropriate Affect, (3) Autism, or the withdrawal of interest from the external to the internal world, and (4) Ambivalence, which was characterized by simultaneously holding contradictory feelings about people or situations.

These differences between Bleuler's and Kraepelin's views of schizophrenia are important because they are ultimately at the root of the diagnostic differences that were revealed by the US–UK Cross National Project

(discussed in the introduction to Section 1). Bleuler has been an extremely influential figure in American psychiatry; European psychiatry has been influenced considerably by the more descriptive approach of Kraepelin. Over the decades these differences in influence led to major differences in diagnostic practices and to a broadening of the diagnostic criteria for schizophrenia in the United States relative to Europe. With the advent of DSM-III (APA, 1980), however, American diagnostic criteria for schizophrenia were brought into much closer alignment with the narrower criteria used by clinicians in the rest of the world.

DSM-III-R Criteria for Schizophrenia

Although a number of different criteria (e.g., the Research Diagnostic Criteria; Spitzer, Endicott, & Robins, 1978) are still sometimes used to diagnose schizophrenia even within the United States, a general move toward the use of the DSM is now being reflected in the research literature. In their most recent form (DSM-III-R; APA, 1987) these criteria require the presence of at least two of the following symptoms during the active phase of the disorder: (1) delusions, (2) prominent hallucinations, (3) incoherence or marked loosening of the associations, (4) catatonic behavior, and (5) flat or grossly inappropriate affect. Some evidence of impaired functioning in work, social relations, or self-care is also needed in order to make the diagnosis. Finally, signs of disturbance are required to be continuously present for a period of at least 6 months.

The Experience of Schizophrenia

It is easy to describe the characteristic symptoms of schizophrenia in the abstract. However, it is considerably less easy to convey a flavor of what it is really like to experience the disorder firsthand. Most people have at times felt anxious or depressed; but most have not experienced hallucinations. We therefore begin this section with two "first-person accounts." Selection 5 (McGrath, 1984) was written by a 37-year old woman who was diagnosed as manifesting paranoid schizophrenia. Selection 6 (Lanquetot, 1984) was written by the daughter of a woman with the same diagnosis. Both accounts vividly illustrate the clinical features of the disorder and highlight the differences in functioning that can characterize two patients with the same diagnosis. They also describe the considerable efforts that patients and their families make to cope with recurrent psychosis and demonstrate the ambivalence that many patients feel toward antipsychotic medications.

Genetics and Neurobiology

Although our understanding of schizophrenia has developed considerably in recent decades, the cause of the disorder is still unknown. Few now doubt, however, that genetic factors are in some way implicated.

The studies that have led to this conclusion are well summarized by Nicol and Gottesman in selection 7. Following their introduction to the genetics of schizophrenia, Nicol and Gottesman provide a discussion of what is currently known about the

neurobiology of this disorder. Neurobiology has been at the center of some of the most important advances of recent years. Evidence continues to grow that the neurotransmitter dopamine is involved in at least some forms of schizophrenia.

Much attention is also now being directed to the study of the interaction of dopamine with two types of receptors. These, referred to as D1 and D2 receptors, are located on the membrane of the postsynaptic neuron. Most of the research now being done in this area is highly technical and demands a greater familiarity with biochemistry than the average informed reader is likely to command. Nicol and Gottesman have therefore rendered a valuable service by discussing recent advances in our understanding of the neurobiology of schizophrenia in a straightforward and reasonably accessible way.

The Search for Subtypes

One factor that complicates efforts to understand why some people develop schizophrenia is the likely etiologic heterogeneity of the disorder. Schizophrenia is often referred to as if it were a single, discrete disorder. Yet clinicians and researchers have long recognized that we may actually be dealing with a group of disorders that share a number of common features.

DSM-III-R (APA, 1987) currently recognizes four different subtypes of schizophrenia (paranoid, catatonic, disorganized, and undifferentiated). There is, however, no compelling evidence that supports the validity or usefulness of these diagnostic distinctions. This has prompted researchers to focus on alternative subtyping strategies. Currently attracting a great deal of attention is a dichotomy based on the distinction between positive and negative symptoms (Andreasen, selection 8).

Positive-symptom schizophrenia is characterized by prominent florid symptoms such as delusions and hallucinations, a generally favorable response to neuroleptic medication, and a course of illness that reflects periods of psychosis followed by periods of remission during which there is a return to relatively normal levels of functioning. Negative-symptom schizophrenia, on the other hand, is characterized by symptoms that reflect behavioral deficits rather than behavioral excesses (e.g., apathy, poverty of speech, and self-neglect). Negative symptoms tend to be more insidious in their onset and are less responsive to neuroleptic medication than the symptoms characteristic of positive-symptom schizophrenia.

Evidence for the existence of pure positive and negative subtypes of schizophrenia is still controversial; many patients diagnosed with schizophrenia manifest both types of symptoms. Nonetheless, the positive–negative distinction has a great deal of heuristic and theoretical appeal. Many of the distinctions between these two hypothesized subtypes cut across dimensions that researchers and clinicians have recognized in the past (e.g., process-reactive, good versus poor premorbid). In the final analysis, the success or failure of the positive versus negative symptom distinction will rest on the extent to which the classification of patients into these groupings provides new insights into the etiology of schizophrenia and contributes to the development of more effective forms of treatment.

The emphasis on neurobiologic factors that has characterized this section thus far accurately reflects the importance of this area in current schizophrenia research. It is not easy, however, to study the brains of schizophrenics. Ethical constraints clearly limit the kinds of investigations that can be conducted. In selection 9, Weinberger, Berman, and Zec (1986) provide an excellent example of how creative research designs and complex technology can combine to generate a method by which the function of the prefrontal cortex can be studied directly. Although the description of the methodology is technical, the results themselves are straightforward and highly provocative. As Weinberger et al. themselves point out, it is certainly tempting to view the data they present as evidence of a regionally specific dysfunction of brain physiology related to schizophrenia. How such a dysfunction may develop, however, is still an open question.

Treatment

Most advances in our understanding of the etiology of schizophenia in recent years have been the result of research in domains such as genetics and neurobiology. This emphasis is well represented in our choice of articles. Our discussion of schizophrenia would not be complete, however without reference to another very different area that is also attracting considerable attention. This concerns the role of the family in the aftercare treatment of schizophrenia.

At the center of this interest and activity is a characteristic of certain family members of schizophrenic patients called expressed emotion or EE (selection 10; Hooley, 1985). In brief, family members who are evaluated as being high in EE are those who express critical, hostile, or emotionally overinvolved attitudes about their schizophrenic family member during an interview about the patient. Precisely what is being captured in this EE measure is not yet clear. What is clear, however, is that patients living with family members rated high in EE are significantly more likely to suffer relapse during a 9-month period subsequent to discharge from the hospital. Recent evidence further suggests that living with a high-EE family member is also predictive of relapse in affectively disordered patients. The EE-relapse link thus does not seem to be specific to schizophrenia.

At present, it is not known whether a high expressed emotion rating in a relative tells us more about the relative or about the patient with whom he or she must cope. Much more basic research still needs to be done. However, it is certainly the case that the importance of the family in the management of psychiatric patients is now being recognized, and a number of psychosocial interventions based on the EE construct are being developed. A good example of the type of treatments that are being generated is provided by Hogarty and colleagues in selection 11. This article also provides a good illustration of the ways in which psychiatrists and psychologists can work together to combine pharmacologic and nonpharmacologic interventions to the greater benefit of psychotic patients.

References and Suggested Additional Reading

RICHTERS, J. E., AND WEINTRAUB, S. (1989). Beyond diathesis: Toward an understanding of high-risk environments. In J. ROLF, A. MAS-TEN, D. CICCHETTI, K. NUECHTERLEIN, AND S. WEINTRAUB (Eds.). *Risk and protective factors in the development of psychopathology.* New York: Cambridge University Press.

Schizophrenia Bulletin, 1987, *13,* 3. Special issue on high-risk research.

SPITZER, R. L., ENDICOTT, J., AND ROBINS, E. (1978). Research diagnostic criteria: Rationale and reliability. *Archives of General Psychiatry, 35,* 773–782.

WEINBERGER, D. R., WAGNER, R. L., AND WYATT, R. J., (1983). Neuropathological studies of schizophrenia: A selective review. *Schizophrenia Bulletin, 9,* 2, 193–212.

WONG, D. F., et al., (1986). Positron emission tomography reveals elevated D2 dopamine receptors in drug-naive schizophrenics. *Science, 234* (December), 1558–1563.

5

First Person Account: Where Did I Go?

Mary E. McGrath

The reflection in the store window—it's me, isn't it? I know it is, but it's hard to tell. Glassy shadows, polished pastels, a jigsaw puzzle of my body, face, and clothes, with pieces disappearing whenever I move. And, if I want to reach out to touch me, I feel nothing but a slippery coldness. Yet I sense that it's me. I just know.

I know I'm a 37-year-old woman, a sculptor, a writer, a worker. I live alone. I know all of this, but, like the reflection in the glass, my existence seems undefined— more a mirage that I keep reaching for, but never can touch.

I've been feeling this way for almost a year now, ever since I was diagnosed a paranoid schizophrenic. Sometimes, though, I wonder if I ever knew myself, or merely played the parts that were acceptable, just so that I could fit in somewhere. But the illness has certainly stripped me of any pretense now, leaving me, instead, feeling hollow, yet hurting. I twist and turn, hoping to find a comfortable position in which to be just me.

There are still occasional episodes of hallucinations, delusions, and terrible fears, and I have medication for these times. It relieves my mental stress, but I hate my bodily re-

sponses to it and the dulling of my healthy emotions. Therefore, I stop using the drug as soon as the storms in my mind subside. And I keep wondering why there isn't more emphasis on alternative therapies, such as the holistic programs used now by people with physical illnesses.

So I've searched, in library books and in articles about schizophrenia, hoping to find other solutions and answers to my why, how longs, what's the cure. Some of the information is frightening—the case histories of patients, the descriptions of symptoms. Some of it is confusing, reaming with speculations, yet with every author being certain that his written word is better than the last answer in print. Schizophrenia is genetic— no, no, it's surely biochemical—definitely nutritional—sorry, but it's caused by family interactions, maybe stress, etc. Now, with the worship of the technological gods, the explanation is that schizophrenia is a brain disease colorfully mapped out by the PET scanner. I suddenly feel that my humanity has been sacrificed to a computer printout, that the researchers have dissected me without realizing that I'm still alive. I'm not comfortable or safe in all their certain uncertainties—I feel they're losing me, the person, more and more.

In the most recently published book I've read, a doctor writes that psychotherapy is useless with schizophrenics. How could he even suggest that without knowing me, the

Mary E. McGrath. First person account: Where did I go? *Schizophrenia Bulletin*, 1984, Vol. 10, No. 4, pp. 638–640. Reprinted by Permission of the author.

85

one over here in this corner, who finds a lot of support, understanding, and acceptance with my therapist? Marianne is not afraid to travel with me in my fearful times. She listens when I need to release some of the "poisons" in my mind. She offers advice when I'm having difficulty with just daily living. She sees me as a human being and not only a body to shovel pills into or a cerebral mass in some laboratory. Psychotherapy is important to me, and it does help.

I sound angry—I guess I am—at the illness for invading my life and making me feel so unsure of myself . . . at the medical researchers who now only want to pick and probe into brains or wherever so they can program measurements into their computers while ignoring me, the person . . . at all the literature which shrouds schizophrenia in negativity, making any experience connected with it crazy and unacceptable . . . at the pharmaceutical industry for being satisfied that their pills keep me "functional" when all the while I feel drugged and unreal to myself. And I'm angry at me for believing and trusting too much in all this information and becoming nothing more than a patient, a victim of some intangible illness. It's no wonder to me anymore why I feel I've lost my self, why my existence seems a waning reflection.

But I'm still searching, questioning—looking inside now rather than on the library shelves—just wanting to feel a little comfortable. I know all the negatives: Schizophrenia is painful, and it is craziness when I hear voices, when I believe that people are following me, wanting to snatch my very soul. I am frightened too when every whisper, every laugh is about me; when newspapers suddenly contain curses, four-letter words shouting at me; when sparkles of light are demon eyes. Schizophrenia is frustrating when I can't hold onto thoughts; when conversation is projected on my mind but won't come out of my mouth; when I can't write sentences but only senseless rhymes; when my eyes and ears drown in a flood of sights and sounds . . . and on and on, always more. . . .

But I know I'm still me in the experience. And I'm creative, sensitive. I believe in mysteries, magic, rainbows, and full moons. I wonder why it's expected that I be quieted, medicated whenever it seems I'm stepping out of the boundaries of "reality." Should I let anyone know that there are moments, just moments, in the schizophrenia that are "special"? When I feel that I'm traveling to someplace I can't go to "normally"? Where there's an awareness, a different sort of vision allowed me? Moments which I can't make myself believe are just symptoms of craziness and nothing more.

What's so "special"? Well, the times when colors appear brighter, alluring almost, and my attention is drawn into the shadows, the lights, the intricate patterns of textures, the bold outlines of objects around me. It's as if all things have more of an existence than I do, that I've gone around the corner of humanity to witness another world where my seeing, hearing, and touching are intensified, and everything is a wonder.

Music, especially if I listen through headphones, envelops me and becomes alive, breathing high and low notes, and I'm floating on the movement.

Sometimes, in my schizophrenia, I go to the library, feeling like an explorer in a jungle of words and pictures. It can be frustrating because I capture nothing—not even one book chosen and checked out—but I scan the photos, the copied art works, even focus on a paragraph or two, as I venture along the shelves, my eyes jumping from book to book. I soon leave, emptyhanded, yet satisfied by having seen so much.

My illness is a journey of fear, often paralylzing, mostly painful. If only someone could put a bandaid on the wound . . . but where? Sometimes I feel I can't stand it any longer. It hurts too much, and I'm desperate to feel safe, comforted. It seems, at these times, when I reach bottom, that I'm given a message and I feel mystical, spiritual, and like a prophet who must tell anyone that there's really nothing to fear. A white light often appears, branding this message on my very soul, and those who are most afraid will see it in me and be at peace. And I somehow feel better for being the courier.

These "special" moments of mine—there are so few, but I look for them and use them to help me pass through the schizophrenic episodes. And I can't even predict when or if these moments will come. But I won't deny their existence; I won't tell myself it's all craziness.

I'm hopeful about the ongoing research to find an answer to schizophrenia, and I'm grateful for all the caring and the help of those in the mental health profession. But I know that I'm the schizophrenic living the experience, and I must look inside myself also for some ways to handle it. I have to be able to see me again as a real person and not a fading reflection.

The Author

Mary E. McGrath is a sculptor who has been working with wood for the past 7 years. She has just begun to exhibit her pieces in area galleries and shows. In addition she also works as a full-time employee of the Federal Government.

6

First Person Account: Confessions of the Daughter of a Schizophrenic

Roxanne Lanquetot

My mother is a paranoid schizophrenic. In the past I was afraid to admit it, but now that I've put it down on paper, I'll be able to say it again and again: Mother schizophrenic, Mother, paranoid, shame, guilt, Mother, crazy, different, Mother, schizophrenia.

I have been teaching inpatient children on the children's ward of Bellevue Psychiatric Hospital in New York City for 13 years, and yet I'm still wary of revealing the nature of my mother's illness. When I tell my friends about my mother, even psychiatrist friends, I regret my openness and worry that they will find me peculiar.

My profession is appropriate for the daughter of a schizophrenic; at least psychiatrists will think so. Since I often marveled that I escaped being a disturbed child, I decided to devote my life to helping difficult children. I have been successful in my work, which includes forming relationships with the mothers of my students, especially the schizophrenic ones, whom I visit on the wards during their periods of hospitalization.

I was born in Kansas City, Missouri, in 1933. When I was 5 years old, we moved to the Country Club section of the city, an area as spotlessly bourgeois as any residential area in the United States. The inhabitants of this region composed a homogeneous population of upper middle class citizens, all very similar in their life styles. Not even one unusual person could be found loitering on the streets of this hamlet, let alone a paranoid schizophrenic. If, according to the laws of probability, there were schizophrenics and other "crazies" scattered about in the population, they were well hidden.

On the outside our house resembled those of our neighbors, but on the inside it was so different that there was no basis of comparison. Our house was a disaster. Everything was a mess. Nothing matched, furniture was broken, dishes were cracked, and there were coffee rings and cigarette burns clear across our grand piano. I was ashamed of our house. It was impossible to bring friends home. I never knew what my mother might be doing or how she would look. She was totally unpredictable. At best she was working on a sculpture or practicing the piano, chain smoking and sipping stale coffee, with a dress too ragged to give to charity hanging from her emaciated body. At worst she was screaming at my father, still wearing her nightgown at 6 o'clock in the evening, a wild look on her face. I was never popular as a youngster, and I blamed my lack of popularity on my mother.

My friends had elegant, decorator homes

Roxanne Lanquetot. First person account: Confessions of the daughter of a schizophrenic. *Schizophrenia Bulletin*, 1984, Vol. 10, No. 3, pp. 467–471. Reprinted by permission of the author.

like the ones in *House Beautiful.* Their parents were caring, organized, but traditional. They provided for their children. Nothing was lacking. They were well-dressed, and their daughters had the kind of clothes I longed for, the kind that are sold at Saks Fifth Avenue. I attached a great importance to clothes, because I had to manipulate Mother to get them. It was not that we were poor. It was just that my mother didn't care about clothing. She was entirely oblivious to the fact that people wore clothes.

My mother didn't know how to cook. She was never at home to order groceries or plan meals, but she showed concern about proper nutrition for her children and hounded us to eat, or overeat. We dined out at least four times a week at the Fred Harvey restaurant in the Union Station where my grandfather had conveniently opened a charge account, and the rest of the week we ate broiled sirloin. The people who worked in the restaurant were used to us and paid no attention to Mother's idiosyncrasies. We children were allowed to purchase books at the station gift shop, and we read them at the table since no conversation with Mother was possible. Nancy Drew made an excellent dinner companion.

Mother was quite interested in music and ballet, and she took me to every ballet and concert in Kansas City. She always looked terrible when she went out, and more than once she arrived at the theatre in her bedroom slippers. I was embarrassed to be seen with her, and before we left home, I would try to convince her to dress properly. She never listened and sometimes became angry, but chic or not, I accompanied her. I loved music and dance as much as she did. I even gave up Saturday afternoons to stay home with her and listen to the Metropolitan Opera broadcasts, and I loved her most and felt closest to her sitting in front of a gas fire, feeling her bony arm around my shoulders as we listened to the music together. Throughout my childhood I was torn between my bizarre, but loving artist-mother and the conventional mothers of my friends.

Although Mother was rarely at home dur-

ing the day, she could be found at the ballet studio. I think that I was probably born at the studio, because I can't imagine that Mother could have gotten to the hospital in time to deliver. Although she continued to take classes until her psychotic break, as soon as I was born she unconsciously decided that I should become the *danseuse étoile* that had been her goal in life. I didn't have the talent to be promoted to such heights, but failing to understand this, she continued to nag me to take more classes and work harder.

Feelings of shame and fear overwhelmed me in those early years, shame that my friends would find out that my mother was "different" and fear that I would be "different" too. The fear of being like Mother must have prevented me from studying ballet and piano seriously. My mother played the piano and danced, and she was schizophrenic. If I played the piano and danced, I would be schizophrenic also. I was terrified that if I showed any signs of letting myself go and really working, my mother would close the doors of the studio and fasten them with a heavy, iron bar.

Mother and daughter were competitors in ballet and music. Mother, who had given birth to me when she was just 19 years old, looked young, mother and daughter looked alike, and we were taken for sisters. I didn't think that I could win a music or dance competition with Mother, and I wasn't interested anyway. I wanted to go to college, where I was assured success. Mother had always had trouble in school.

There were other problems in living with a schizophrenic mother. One was the lack of tranquility at home, the commotion, and chaos. My parents were constantly arguing, mainly about money. My mother had no idea of budgeting. She didn't need to learn, because her father was available to supply her with money as needed. My father didn't approve of limitless concert-going, dance classes, or book buying. He abhorred eating in restaurants everyday and expected Mother to stay home to take care of the house and prepare supper. I would be awakened at night by screaming and lie in bed pretending to be asleep, morbidly fascinated by my parents' quarrels.

Trying to make up for my mother's shortcomings was one of the major preoccupations of my early years. I was always cleaning and straightening up the house, vainly hoping to restore order, even as early as age 4, according to one of my aunts. I took care of my brothers, but I bitterly resented the fact that no one took care of me. I felt cheated by having to arrange my own birthday parties, ordering the cake, inviting friends, and choosing the present although I willingly organized parties for my younger brothers. After school I became the little mother who was furious about being deprived of her childhood.

One day, when I was 10, my mother vanished, and as if by magic, my father moved back to the house to take care of us. I resented his return. He had abandoned us, and I must have felt that he was responsible for Mother's problems. We were told that Mother was ill in a hospital in Burbank, California, where my grandfather's sister was a staff physician. I felt very lonely without her and began hanging around the ballet studio. Once the teacher put her arm around me and said, "Poor child, you miss your mother, don't you?"

Years later I learned that Mother had run away to New York without telling anyone she was leaving. She was making frenzied visits to the ballet schools there when a friend of the family phoned my grandparents to inform them of their daughter's strange behavior. My grandparents immediately set out for New York to rescue Mother. They brought her to Menninger's Clinic, which had not been in existence very long. At the time the hospital was located in old-fashioned red brick buildings that were already on the premises when the Menningers moved in. Equating building height and glass walls with hospital excellence, my grandparents took one look at the hospital and headed for California, where Mother was hospitalized for a year. She regained her physical health, but her mental health was

totally ignored. When she was discharged, we joined her in California, where we lived for the next 2 years. Mother was subdued and withdrawn from any human contacts outside of the family. Her withdrawal was less of a bane to our social life than her neurotic existence in Kansas City, but she lost something of the artist, her most interesting self.

When the family returned to the Midwest, we moved into a house in the country next to my grandparents, which made it easier for my grandfather to look after his beloved daughter. Mother was withdrawing more, spending the entire day lying on the bed, sleeping or doing exercises. She rarely left the house except to go next door to rant and rave at my grandmother while my grandfather stood nearby, patting her on the back and saying, "Bonnie, my dear little Bonnie, everything will be all right." Since neither of my grandparents would admit that their dear little Bonnie desperately needed help, we children could say nothing.

At the end of my junior year in high school I was in a serious automobile accident. I tend to think that my mother's consequent decompensation might have been precipitated by my being in a coma for 6 days, but I'm not certain. After I came home from the hospital, she became very strict with me, although she had never interfered in my social life previously. When I protested against her arbitrary, nonsensical restrictions on my dating, we began to have terrible fights. I could not make her accept the fact that a monastic existence was not for me.

Mother and I shared a room with twin beds. When Mother was lying down, she would start to moan as if she were talking in her sleep. "I can't stand that girl. She's evil; she's a bitch. She's just like her father." I was terrorized, but I dared not move. I felt I had to pretend to be asleep, because I didn't want her to know I was listening. I tried to deny the reality of Mother's illness by not acknowledging the outbursts. I used to lie in bed, wishing I were dead, believing that I was the worthless girl she was describing.

My oldest brother was the target of the

same kinds of insults, and we comforted each other. We were afraid to talk about Mother's behavior to our grandparents. They wouldn't admit that Mother was mentally ill. She was the "chosen one," and my brother and I took second place in the family—the opposite of a child's position in a normal grouping. We were frequently reminded that we would have to replace our grandparents as caretakers when we grew up.

I still remember with horror the night that I came in late from a date and decided to sleep on the couch in the living room in order not to wake Mother. I made an effort to avoid disturbing her, not because I was being considerate, but because I didn't want her to start moaning. As soon as I lay down, she came into the room and stood next to me, calling me a prostitute. When she spat on me, I grabbed her upper arm and bit it as hard as I could. The outline of my teeth etched in black and blue remained visible for over a week, but Mother never mentioned it. Even now when I think of the incident, I feel shame because of my loss of self-control and display of aggression toward my poor defenseless, crazy mother.

Next Mother began to insult strangers on the street. She would stop in front of a well-dressed bourgeois of Kansas City, fix her eyes on him for a few seconds, and snap angrily. "What's wrong with you? Why are you looking at me like that? I'm going to tell my lawyer." If my brother or I were with her, we'd be so embarrassed that we'd want to disappear into a crack in the sidewalk. No matter what we did, she wouldn't stop. Once she hit someone over the head with her pocketbook and another time notified the police that the neighbors were spying on her although they'd been gone for 3 months. In the sterile atmosphere of Kansas City, her outbursts upset everyone. In New York she wouldn't have been noticed.

My choice of colleges was based on their distance from Kansas City and Mother. I had to get away before I became crazy. I applied to the University of Chicago, Barnard, and Stanford and was accepted at all three. My grandfather refused to let me attend Chicago U. He said that Chicago was no place for a young girl, but I knew he refused because of Mother, who had attended the Chicago conservatory for 3 months before she returned home to Daddy. I decided against Barnard, because Mother liked New York. I was afraid that she might follow me there. That left Stanford.

Much to my dismay, Mother arrived in San Francisco during my sophomore year at Stanford. She came for a visit and decided to stay. The fantasy about being haunted by the specter of my schizophrenic mother had come true. She moved into a dumpy apartment two blocks from a dance studio and began taking Flamenco dancing from a Spaniard who taught there. She fell in love with her teacher, but he didn't care about her. Although he paid her less attention than he did the other students, she was always hanging around, gazing at him in abject adoration. She never realized how pathetic and absurd she appeared.

After I left Stanford, I went to Europe, distancing myself physically and emotionally from Mother. That same year it had been my oldest brother's turn to escape to college, and Mother was left with only my youngest brother to link her to the real world. This brother had always been her favorite anyway, due to his place in the birth order and the fact that he was born with his hip out of joint and therefore required extra care. He wasn't allowed the freedom of college, because Mother immediately followed him to Saint Louis and remained with him until he failed his courses and was asked to leave. Even a letter from my godmother in Saint Louis pleading with my grandparents to bring Bonnie back to Kansas City was not effective. They could not bring themselves to remove all of Mother's children. My youngest brother had to be the sacrificial lamb. When he became tired of his entrapment, he got married. The marriage was a failure, but it was obviously the only way he could free himself from Mother's stranglehold.

Mother's descent into chronic schizophrenia would take too long to describe. She was finally admitted to Menninger's where she improved during the first year and a half of treatment. Then her father died. She had always been her father's little girl, and her universe was shattered without him. The only person in the world she trusted had departed. After the funeral she refused to return to Menninger's. She had learned that no one had the right to send her to an out of state hospital against her will.

Two years later she had to return to the hospital. She was driving a car without brakes and insulting black people by loudly declaiming her theories about the inferiority of the black race. By her second admission it was too late. Mother had become a chronic schizophrenic. After the first year of hospitalization we were asked to remove her. The Menningers were only interested in patients whom they could cure. The family, for we remained a close family, rallied its forces to find another hospital, and we transferred her to a Mennonite Hospital in a small town in Western Kansas. We were grieved by the loss of Mother as a functional human being, a bereavement that was finalized by attaching "chronic" to her diagnostic category. I was especially horrified by the necessity of burying my mother in the country. My trepidation was intensified when Mother was moved to a halfway house near the hospital, where the only activity available to patients was filling mattresses.

When Mother began to threaten the doctor at the new hospital to find a lawyer to sue him, the family was forced to make the difficult decision to go to court to have her declared "incompetent," to openly admit that she was psychotic. We had to safeguard her trust fund from a shyster lawyer. My grandmother was devastated. Having avoided the truth for the greater part of her daughter's life, she couldn't face the fact that Bonnie was crazy. Since I was in Europe, my brother, my uncle, and the doctor testified that Mother was a danger to herself, Mother was declared "incompetent," and the judge appointed a guardian for her. According to Missouri law, a judge controlled every move made by an "incompetent."

Mother lost all liberty, all sense of self. Any step she took had to be authorized by the magistrate.

Once drug therapy came into being, Mother was force-fed Haldol against her wishes, and this resulted in a remission of symptoms. Feeling well enough to leave the hospital, she made the decision to go to Menninger's by herself to take an examination that she supposed would disprove her insanity. Of course, her guardian was forced by law to make her return to the hospital. She had not requested the judge's permission to make the journey. Later my brother accompanied her to Menninger's for an evaluation, the results of which showed that she was well enough to leave the halfway house in Kansas and come to New York to be near her children. They specified, however, that she would need to live in a structured environment.

Eventually the family received the authorization to have Mother's guardianship transferred to New York, and a "Committee" was appointed by the New York court. When Mother first joined us in the East, she behaved the way she did when she was discharged from the hospital in California— withdrawn, isolated from everyone but the family, yet able to profit from all the big city had to offer. Listening to music or watching ballet, she came back to life. Vital energy that had been absent for so long returned to her body. The results of changing her habitat were much better than we had ever expected.

Not only did Mother rediscover art and music in New York, but she soon became familiar with the liberal New York laws regarding "patients' rights." She refused to continue to take Haldol and slowly began the reverse trip to "No Man's Land," where she now dwells. The first sign of her decompensation was a refusal to come to my apartment, and then she rejected me completely. Next the manager of her middle class apartment hotel asked us to remove her. She was annoying the guests with her outbursts. She had become known to all the shopkeepers on the block as "The Crazy Lady of West

72nd Street." Looking like a zombie, she paraded down West 72nd Street, accusing aunts, uncles, and brother of stealing her father's fortune, screaming at people who frightened her, discernible from her New York counterparts only by a Midwestern accent and an absence of curse words.

Having been told over and over again in our youth that it was our duty to take care of Mother, my brother and I initially resented our burden. We felt that since Mother had not accepted the responsibility of her children, we should not have to be responsible for her. At that time it was difficult to admit that we actually loved our frail, unbalanced mother and wanted to help her. When we grew up, we began to understand why Mother was different, and our resentment lessened. On Haldol Mother's behavior improved tremendously, and we even harbored false hopes of her return to normal living. We never suspected that she might cease taking medication and regress. Whether or not it's preferable for her to be forcefed Haldol and incarcerated in Kansas or allowed to do as she pleases in liberal New York, as destructive as her life is now, is paradoxical. She was not able to enjoy life and pursue her artistic interests in the former situation, but she is even less able to do so in the latter. Without medication, she can only exist. I believe that basically she is less free in her present life, a prisoner of her delusions and paranoia. My brother, however, disagrees. He thinks that Mother is better off having the choice to live as she wishes, wandering aimlessly in the streets, constructing the world to fit her delusions.

The Author

Roxanne Lanquetot, M.A., M.S., has been teaching at P.S. 106M, Bellevue Psychiatric Hospital for the past 13 years. Her students are composed of the youngest group of children on the inpatient children's ward. She has begun a Ph.D. program in Educational Psychology at CUNY, and is also interested in writing, especially about children.

7

Clues to the Genetics and Neurobiology of Schizophrenia

Susan E. Nicol and Irving I. Gottesman

Cases of schizophrenia, one of the common forms of major psychiatric illness, have been reported almost since the beginning of recorded history, yet the cause of the disorder is still unknown. Our interpretation of the accumulated evidence from studies of families—both biological and adopted—of schizophrenics is that patients have a genetic predisposition to the disorder but that this predisposition by itself is not sufficient for the development of schizophrenia. This article can mention only some of the major findings from clinical genetics and promising leads in neurobiological research on schizophrenia; more detailed information can be found in the references, particularly in Gottesman and Shields (1982).

In discussing the neurobiology of schizophrenia, we should keep in mind the following findings from genetic and epidemiologic work on the disorder. First, no environmental causes have been discovered that will invariably, or even with moderate probability, produce schizophrenia in persons who are not related to a schizophrenic. The disorder occurs in both industrialized and undeveloped societies, and although within large urban communities the prevalence of schizophrenia rises dramatically in

the lower classes of society, this is true in general because individuals predisposed to the disorder tend to move downward through the social classes even before the onset of the illness (Goldberg and Morrison 1963).

Second, the risk of schizophrenia to the relatives of schizophrenics increases markedly with the degree of genetic relatedness (Bleuler 1978) even if the relatives have not shared a specific environment with the patient (Fig. 1). An identical twin of a schizophrenic is at least 3 times as likely as a fraternal twin to develop schizophrenia, and some 35–60 times as likely as an unrelated person from the same general population. However, fewer than half of the identical twins of schizophrenics in recent studies have schizophrenia themselves, although they share all their genes with schizophrenics, which demonstrates unequivocally the importance of environmental factors. The incomplete expression of genotypes, on the other hand, also plays a role, since the normal identical twins from discordant pairs transmit schizophrenia to their offspring at the same high rate as their schizophrenic twins do (Gottesman and Shields 1982).

Identical twins of schizophrenics are about as likely to develop schizophrenia whether they were reared apart from or together with their schizophrenic twins since childhood. Raising identical twins in different homes is a very rare event—only 12 pairs involving schizophrenia have been au-

Susan E. Nicol and Irving I. Gottesman. Clues to the genetics and neurobiology of schizophrenia. *American Scientist*, Vol. 71, pp. 398–404. Copyright © 1983, American Scientist.

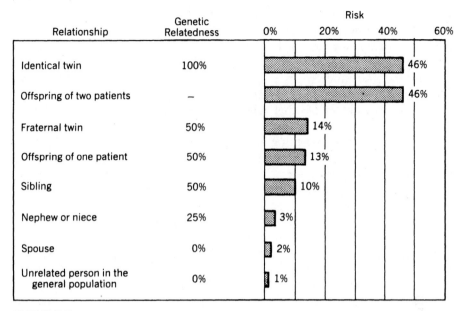

Relationship	Genetic Relatedness	Risk
Identical twin	100%	46%
Offspring of two patients	—	46%
Fraternal twin	50%	14%
Offspring of one patient	50%	13%
Sibling	50%	10%
Nephew or niece	25%	3%
Spouse	0%	2%
Unrelated person in the general population	0%	1%

FIGURE 1

Lifetime risks of developing schizophrenia are largely a function of how closely an individual is genetically related to a schizophrenic and not a function of how much their environment is shared. The observed risks, however, are much more compatible with a multifactorial polygenic theory of transmission than with a Mendelian model or one involving a single major locus, especially after allowance is made for some unsystematic environmental transmission. In the case of an individual with two schizophrenic parents, genetic relatedness cannot be expressed in terms of percentage, but the regression of the individual's "genetic value" on that of the parents is 1, the same as it is for identical twins. (Data from Gottesman and Shields 1982.)

thenticated; it may not be possible, therefore, to generalize the information yielded by these cases.

Data from other research strategies confirm the importance of genetics. For example, children of schizophrenics adopted by nonrelatives early in life still develop schizophrenia as adults at rates that are considerably higher than those of the population at large, and that sometimes are as high as the rates for children reared by their own schizophrenic parents (Heston 1966; Rosenthal et al. 1968). The adoptive parents and siblings of adoptees who became schizophrenics do not have significantly elevated rates of schizophrenia, but the schizophrenics' biological relatives do have high rates (Kety et al. 1976). Furthermore, children of normal parents adopted by a nonrelative who became schizophrenic after the adop-

tion do not show a significantly increased rate of schizophrenia (Wender et al. 1974).

Being a twin does not increase the risk for schizophrenia. Gender is not generally relevant in schizophrenia: the risk of developing the disorder among half-siblings of schizophrenic adoptees does not depend on whether the siblings share a father or mother with the schizophrenic (Kety et al. 1976), the offspring of male schizophrenics are as often schizophrenic as those of female schizophrenics, female identical twins of schizophrenics are not significantly more likely to develop the disorder than male identical twins, and opposite-sex fraternal twins of schizophrenics have the same risk as same-sex fraternal twins in recent studies. The one exception is that male schizophrenics, on average, develop the disorder earlier in life than female schizophrenics, but there are as many female as male schizophrenics by the end of the risk period, at age 65.

The observed risks for schizophrenia, however, are not compatible with any simple Mendelian genetic models, since they also vary with the severity of the schizophrenic's illness, the number of other relatives already affected by the disorder, and, in the case of the patient's offspring, the other parent's mental health (O'Rourke et al. 1982). The risks are compatible with a polygenic model of transmission similar to that used to study other common genetic diseases and congenital malformations, which involves the idea of a threshhold and a range of contributory factors, but theories that a single major genetic locus is responsible for some schizophrenia cannot be discarded completely (McGue et al., 1983).

Because no laboratory test can be equated with a schizophrenia genotype, it is not now possible to predict which individuals of those known to be at risk will develop the disorder. Hence, ambiguity and uncertainty haunt attempts to test specific models of genetic transmission. To complicate matters further, some psychoses that resemble schizophrenia are actually different conditions. These occur after head injuries or epileptic seizures, and the patients' relatives have the same low risk of schizophrenia as the population at large. Childhood psychoses that appear before puberty do not seem to be genetically related to schizophrenia.

Environmental factors continue to be important after the onset of schizophrenia. Excessively critical or overly intrusive behavior on the part of relatives of schizophrenics in remission increases their rate of relapse. Social intervention, therefore, should complement drug treatments of schizophrenics.

Biochemical Genetics

In theorizing about the biochemical genetics of schizophrenia, it is important to begin by considering what we know about other genetic diseases. Even with Huntington chorea, a relatively simple autosomal Mendelian

disease that is dominant and has complete penetrance, we cannot specify the exact nature of the genetic disorder at the molecular level. We infer the existence of an abnormal gene, but we are not yet able to isolate it by restriction enzymes. We cannot account for the variable age at onset of the disease, which covers the entire life span, and we cannot detect which of the offspring of affected individuals are destined to develop the disease, although 50% of them do so. For some 70% of other genetic disorders whose mode of transmission has been clearly identified as that of recessive inheritance, which we know to be associated with an enzyme deficiency, we cannot identify the enzyme (McKusick 1983). Although the pattern of inheritance of color blindness, one of the oldest known genetic disorders, was understood in the early 1700s, it was not assigned to the X chromosome until 1911 (Morgan 1911). In the 1980s we are still dependent on a behavioral test to identify the individuals who are color-blind, and we know little about the disorder's biological basis.

We know even less about the biochemical genetics of multifactorial disorders (Fraser 1981). However, the genes associated with these conditions are not qualitatively different from those underlying Mendelian traits at the molecular level: both groups of genes are subject to the same rules of inheritance because they are chromosomal and thus segregate, show dominance, can be suppressed or enhanced by other genes, and interact with their environment. Although from the beginning of this century geneticists have identified specific loci involved in polygenic conditions and have located them on specific chromosomes by linkage with major genes, these feats were accomplished with genetically tractable organisms such as wheat and fruit flies, not with humans.

Impressive recent advances in the biochemical genetics of common human illnesses including heart disease, diabetes, and hypertension have been made through the study of low-density lipoprotein receptors (e.g., Goldstein and Brown 1982), insulin receptors (e.g., Jarett 1979), and cation permeability, but genetic differences in receptor structure or function are only beginning to be explored as biochemical techniques such as high specific activity radioligands become available. Major genes partially responsible for diabetes and lupus erythematosus, however, have been identified (e.g., Fraser 1981).

Where does one begin the search for the biochemical differences that are implied by a genetic predisposition for schizophrenia? There are many studies of the biochemical parameters in schizophrenic patients, but as Kety (1980) has pointed out, differences between schizophrenics and controls often reflect not genetic differences but rather the patients' poor nutrition, chronic hospitalization, and history of medication.

Recent biochemical theorizing about schizophrenia has focused on dopamine, a catecholamine neurotransmitter. Evidence linking dopamine to schizophrenia may not be as strong as that for insulin and diabetes or cholesterol and cardiovascular disease, but it is compelling (Seeman 1980, 1985). Antipsychotic drugs called neuroleptics block dopamine receptors, and the effectiveness of the drugs in treating schizophrenics is highly correlated with how well they block the receptors. Further, neuroleptics produce symptoms similar to those seen in Parkinson's disease, a disorder known to be due to insufficient dopamine in specific neurons. L-dopa, which increases stores of dopamine and which is used to treat Parkinson's disease, produces a psychosis with features resembling schizophrenia in some persons (e.g., Meltzer and Stahl 1976). Another clue from biochemical pharmacology is that amphetamine, which releases stored dopamine and thus stimulates the receptors, worsens psychotic symptoms in some schizophrenics and elicits the same symptoms in certain of their nonschizophrenic relatives. Amphetamine can also produce a schizophrenia-like syndrome in some apparently normal users.

These observations have led to the hypothesis that there is an excess of dopaminergic activity in schizophrenic patients. How does one go about testing such a theory? If genetic contributors to schizophrenia involve altered activity in dopamine pathways, one would expect to find a large variation in enzyme activities, concentrations of precursors, neurotransmitters, or metabolites, or functions of the receptors in the human dopamine system. We will give a brief overview of what is currently known about dopamine neurons before discussing studies of the biochemical genetics of this pathway.

Dopamine Pathways

More is known about the enzymes involved in the synthesis and metabolism of dopamine than about the receptor proteins, in part because the enzymes either are soluble to begin with or can easily be made soluble in vitro, and thus they are more amenable to classical biochemical analysis. Dopamine is synthesized from tyrosine hydroxylase and dopa decarboxylase (Fig. 2). In noradrenaline neurons, the enzyme dopamine-B-hydroxylase (DBH) converts dopamine to norepinephrine. However, DBH is absent from dopamine neurons, where dopamine is metabolized by the mitochondrial enzyme monoamine oxidase (MAO) and aldehyde oxidase to dihydroxyphenylacetic acid, or by the enzyme catechol-o-methyl transferase (COMT) to 3-methoxytyramine (Cooper et al. 1974).

Dopamine is stored in vesicles in the transmitting neuron and is released into the synaptic cleft when these vesicles merge with the presynaptic membrane. As is the case with certain other neurotransmitters, the rate of dopamine release is thought to be determined not only by the electrical activity in presynaptic neurons, but also by feedback from autoreceptors on such neurons (Meltzer 1980). After it is released into the synaptic cleft, dopamine can bind to receptors on postsynaptic membranes or to the autoreceptors on the presynaptic membrane, it can be metabolized by COMT, or it can be taken back up into the presynaptic neuron, where it is either metabolized by MAO or stored again in vesicles for later release.

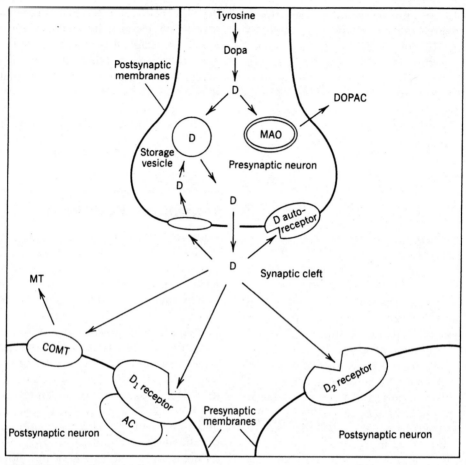

FIGURE 2

An excess of dopamine (D), which is synthesized from the amino acids tyrosine and dopa, may produce schizophrenic behavior. Dopamine can be metabolized to dihydroxyphenylacetic acid (DOPAC) by monoamine oxidase (MAO), or to 3-methoxy-tyramine (MT) by catechol-o-methyl transferase (COMT). After storage in the transmitting neuron, dopamine is released into the synaptic cleft, where it may bind to an autoreceptor and thus inhibit release of more dopamine. However, it may instead bind to a D_1 receptor associated with stimulating adenylate cyclase (AC), or to a D_2 receptor that inhibits AC; drugs that inhibit these receptors have proved effective in treating schizophrenia.

Dopamine has only recently been shown to interact with at least two types of postsynaptic receptors: D_1 receptors that are linked to the enzyme dopamine-stimulated adenylate cyclase (AC) (Kebabian and Calne 1979; Seeman 1980), and D_2 receptors that according to indirect evidence may be linked to dopamine-inhibited AC (Stoof and Kebabian 1981). In addition to differential as-sociation with AC, D_1 and D_2 sites have been distinguished by their relative affinity for dopamine agonists—agents that can imitate the actions of dopamine—and dopamine antagonists—agents that can block the effects of dopamine at receptor sites (Table 1). Seeman (1980) described two other dopamine sites identified by differing relative affinity for agonists and antagonists: the D_3 site

TABLE 1 Relative Affinity of Dopamine-sensitive Sites and Receptors for Dopamine (Agonist) and Spiperone (Antagonist)

Sites and receptors	Affinity (nM)	
	Dopamine	Spiperone
D_1 site (dopamine-sensitive adenylate cyclase)	~3,000	~2,000
D_2 receptor	~5,000	~0.3
D_3 site	~3	~1,500
D_4 site	~3	~1

Source: Seeman 1980.

and the D_4 site. It is known that at least a substantial proportion of D_1 and D_2 receptors are located on the postsynaptic neuron, but the location of D_3 and D_4 dopamine sites is less well established; there is some evidence that a proportion of D_3 receptors are found on the presynaptic neuron, perhaps as autoreceptors. Seeman distinguished dopamine sites from dopamine receptors based on the evidence that dopamine-related behaviors correlate best with activity of D_2 receptors. Other researchers do not make this distinction, referring to all sites where dopamine has the greatest affinity of any physiological compound as dopamine receptors.

Dopamine receptors were first identified biochemically in a peripheral tissue, the superior cervical ganglion (Greengard 1976). These receptors were shown to be associated with AC, as were the first dopamine receptors discovered in the brain. And it was the dopamine-sensitive AC in the brain that was first thought to be the site of action of the antipsychotic drugs (Clement-Cormier et al. 1974). Subsequent work demonstrated a good correlation between the clinical potency of the various phenothiazine antipsychotic drugs, such as chlorpromazine, and their inhibition of AC stimulated by dopamine, but the correlation between butyrophenone neuroleptics, such as haloperidol, and inhibition of this AC was not good (Fig. 3). The fact that the correlation between efficacy of both the phenothiazine and butyrophenone neuroleptics and their affinities for the D_2 receptor is excellent, as contrasted with the situation for the D_1 sites, definitively links the D_2 receptors to schizophrenia.

Dopamine and Genetic Liability

What changes in the dopamine pathway lead to schizophrenia? There are two ways this question can be asked with regard to neurons containing either dopamine or dopamine receptors: Of the many dopamine-containing neurons in the human body, which are relevant to schizophrenia? Of the many enzymes and receptors in these dopamine neurons, which may have pathological variations?

Although dopamine receptors exist both in the central nervous system and on its periphery, research on schizophrenia has focused primarily on the receptors in the brain. Investigations into the biochemical genetics of the disorder would be aided immeasurably if there were an easily sampled peripheral source of dopamine receptors, for instance on lymphocytes, platelets, or red blood cells. Impressive advances in the understanding of genetic and environmental influence on insulin receptor binding have been made with insulin receptors on blood cells (Jarrett 1979). However, peripheral dopamine receptors are in areas that are not easily sampled, and they may be biochemically different from central dopamine receptors (Creese et al. 1981).

Beyond the issue of which dopamine neurons may play a role in the genetic predisposition to schizophrenia is the question of which of the components of Figure 2 may be involved. The predisposition may represent a number of protein variations resulting in different relations between the proteins' structure and function. Each of these protein variants may, under proper environmental conditions, produce a schizophrenic syn-

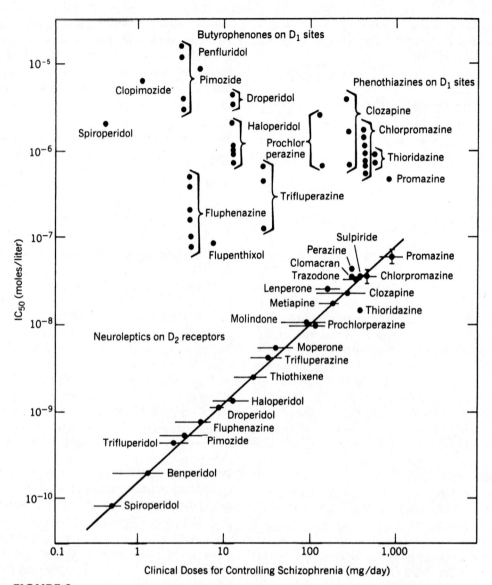

FIGURE 3

The average clinical doses of neuroleptics used in controlling the symptoms of schizophrenia correlate with the biochemical index (IC_{50}) of potency at D_2 dopamine receptors but not at D_1 sites. IC_{50} is a measure of the relative potency of the various antipsychotic drugs in blocking the dopamine sites. A range (*lines*) of clinical doses is depicted because of the variation reported for controlling the symptoms of schizophrenia in different individuals; the average doses are represented by dots. (After Seeman 1980.)

drome; alternatively, it may be the sum of variants at different loci that may place a person above the threshold of liability and lead to schizophrenia. We shall start the genetic overview with the synthetic and metabolic enzymes.

Genetic regulation of the catecholamine-synthesizing enzymes has been demonstrated by Ciaranello and Boehme (1982), working with inbred mouse strains. Studies of human biochemical genetics have focused on the metabolic enzymes in catecholamine neurons, COMT and MAO. Weinshilboum and Raymond (1977) demonstrated that low erythrocyte COMT activity is inherited as an autosomal recessive mechanism. The relation between differences in COMT activity and vulnerability to disease has yet to be established. Work on MAO has generally proceeded in the opposite direction: instead of first establishing base rates for differences in enzyme activity in the general population and then trying to associate MAO activity with the presence of disease, the literature on MAO has focused on comparisons of schizophrenics and normal subjects, with conflicting results (*Schizophrenia Bull.* 1980). There is evidence from a number of studies that chronic schizophrenics may have less platelet MAO than control groups do, but the relation between platelet and brain MAO and the functional significance of a decrease in enzyme activity of the magnitude detected remain in question (Rice et al. 1982).

In a study of dopamine-stimulated AC in the human brain, Carenzi and his colleagues (1975) reported no significant differences in enzyme activity between the postmortem tissue of schizophrenics and that of controls, but the activity was shown, in rats, to be a function of how long after death the tissue was frozen: the interval for the human schizophrenics' tissue was significantly longer than for the normal human tissue. However, Nicol and her co-workers (1981; McSwigan et al. 1980) found that dopamine-stimulated AC in rat brain tissue was stable for at least ten hours after death when enzyme activity was measured in washed membrane preparations. This suggested the loss of a soluble activator rather than the degradation of the membrane enzyme itself during this period. Therefore, it is feasible to examine these enzyme activities in schizophrenia and other disorders, using human brain tissue obtained after death.

Several research groups have reported that postmortem brain tissue from schizophrenics contains more D_2 receptors and that the receptors have less affinity for butyrophenone neuroleptics than tissue from control subjects (e.g., Reisine et al. 1980; Mackay et al. 1982). However, Mackay and

his colleagues (1982) have shown that the decrease in affinity of D_2 receptors for neuroleptics is reversed after the membranes are washed, which suggests that the decrease is due to the neuroleptic drugs the patients took before death. Whether the increase in the number of D_2 receptors is also an effect of the administration of neuroleptics before death remains controversial. Burt and his co-workers (1977) have established that long-term neuroleptic treatment does produce an increase in D_2 receptors in animals.

Lee and Seeman (1980) and Owen and his colleagues (1978) reported increases in D_2 receptors in tissue from a small number of schizophrenic patients who had been free of medication for at least a month before death. However, Mackay and his co-workers (1982) did not find any such increases in tissue from patients who had never taken neuroleptics, and concluded that the increases observed in medicated patients may be iatrogenic. There have been no reports of increases in the binding found at D_1 or D_3 receptors in postmortem brain tissue from schizophrenics, although these receptors have been less extensively studied (Seeman 1980).

A number of investigators have measured the levels of dopamine and its metabolite, homovanillic acid (HVA), in schizophrenic patients and have reported conflicting results (see Meltzer and Stahl 1976 for dopamine metabolites in cerebrospinal fluid, and Haracz 1982 for these substances in postmortem tissue). The work by Spokes (1979), Bird and his colleagues (1979), and Mackay and his co-workers (1982) on increased dopamine in the nucleus accumbens and caudate nucleus in the brain deserves special mention. Beginning with the paper examining factors influencing the measurement of dopamine and other neurotransmitters and enzymes in postmortem tissue (Spokes 1979), these investigators reported increased dopamine in specific subcortical structures. In contrast to the changes in the concentration of D_2 receptors, increased levels of dopamine do not appear to be related to any history of neuroleptic treatment.

Although there was no correlation between dopamine concentrations and the age at which the controls died, Mackay and his colleagues reported that schizophrenics who developed the disease early in life had the highest concentrations of dopamine after death. In their sample, an earlier age at death was also correlated with higher levels of dopamine in schizophrenics, and thus the relative importance of the age at onset of illness and the age at death is difficult to determine. However, the subjects who developed schizophrenia at an early age also had other biochemical abnormalities, such as decreased activity of the angiotensin-converting enzyme and low concentrations of gamma-amino-butyric acid (e.g., Arregui et al. 1980; Spokes et al. 1980).

These studies demonstrate both the existence of promising clues about the role of dopamine and the care with which such clues must be investigated. Many factors have to be controlled and analyzed. It may be that biochemical differences present in one group of schizophrenics, such as those who developed the disease at a young age, are not present in other groups. Alternatively, biochemical differences present at certain stages of the illness may not be present at other stages.

Crow (1980a, b) proposed two syndromes in schizophrenia. Type I, or acute schizophrenia characterized by "positive symptoms" (hallucinations, delusions, and disordered thought), is hypothesized to involve abnormalities in the dopamine pathway and to be responsive to neuroleptics. Type II, or chronic schizophrenia characterized by "negative symptoms" (reduced emotional response, poverty of speech, and loss of drive), is thought to involve structural changes in the brain and to be relatively resistant to neuroleptic medication. Crow emphasized, however, that both types often occur together, and that they are not separate disorders. Reports of structural abnormalities, such as enlarged cerebral ventricles, and neuropathological abnormalities in a proportion of schizophrenic patients give support to Crow's hypothesis of two syndromes (e.g., Johnstone et al. 1976; Weinberger and

Wyatt 1980; Stevens 1982). Knowledge of structural abnormalities may be important both for treatment of schizophrenic patients and for research design.

Although a number of biochemical and neuroendocrinolgial parameters have shown promise in predicting the response to treatment of depressed and manic patients, few such predictors are now known for schizophrenia (see Uytdenhoef et al. 1982 for review). Assessment of cerebral ventrical abnormalities by CT scan and of cerebral metabolic functioning (e.g., Jaffe 1982) should result in more homogeneous groups for study.

This review has focused primarily on the pathophysiology of dopamine, but other mechanisms, including cellular loss and structural abnormalities, have also been proposed as the underlying causes of some schizophrenic symptoms or of these symptoms in some schizophrenic patients. Researchers continue to explore other mechanisms. Rapid advances in our knowledge of endorphins has spurred research on these compounds in schizophrenics. Most promising are the reports of the neuroleptic-like activity of a peptide related to endorphin (de Wied et al. 1980), and the discovery that a subgroup of schizophrenic patients responded to treatment by these gamma-type endorphins (Van Praag et al. 1982).

Since there are hundreds of neurotransmitters and modulators, researchers could spend years examining the biochemical genetics of each of these systems in relation to schizophrenia and other disorders of the central nervous system with known genetic components. One way to short-cut the process of locating suspected gene products is with linkage analysis—i.e., the method of proving that a gene connected with a Mendelian trait is located on a chromosome near a genetic marker. With the advent of techniques using restriction endonucleases (e.g., Botstein et al. 1980), the number of known polymorphic loci available for linkage analyses should increase dramatically in the next few years. (For a discussion of the problems and the promise of such an approach to genetic analysis, see, for example, Gershon et al. 1981.)

Although we cannot yet describe the biochemical genetics of schizophrenia, many leads are being explored. It is important to keep in mind the information accumulated from work on clinical psychiatric genetics as the search continues for complementary, rational neurobiological data that will allow us to solve the puzzle of schizophrenia.

References

ARREGUI, A., A. V. P. MACKAY, E. G. SPOKES, AND L. L. IVERSEN. 1980. Reduced activity of angiotensin converting enzyme in basal ganglia in early onset schizophrenia. *Psychol. Med.* 10:307–13.

BIRD, E. D., E. G. S. SPOKES, AND L. L. IVERSEN 1979. Increased dopamine concentration in limbic areas of brain from patients dying with schizophrenia. *Brain* 102:347–60.

BLEULER, E. 1978. *The Schizophrenic Disorders: Long-Term Patient and Family Studies.* Trans. S. M. Clemens. Yale Univ. Press.

BOTSTEIN, D., R. L. WHITE, M. SKOLNICK, AND R. W. DAVIS. 1980. Construction of a genetic linkage map in man using restriction fragment length polymorphisms. *Am. J. Hum. Genet.* 32:314–31.

BURT, D. R., I. CREESE, AND S. H. SNYDER. 1977. Antischizophrenic drugs: Chronic treatment elevates dopamine receptor binding in brain. *Science* 196:326–28.

CARENZI, A., et al. 1975. Dopamine-sensitive adenylyl cyclase in human caudate nucleus. *Arch. Gen. Psychiat.* 32:1056–59.

CIARANELLO, R. D., AND R. E. BOEHME. 1982. Genetic regulation of neurotransmitter enzymes and receptors: Relationship to the inheritance of psychiatric disorders. *Beh. Genet.* 12:11–35.

CLEMENT-CORMIER, Y. C., J. W. KEBABIAN, G. L. PETZOLD, AND P. GREENGARD. 1974. Dopamine-sensitive adenylate cyclase in mamalian brain: A possible site of action of antipsychotic drugs. *PNAS* 71:113–17.

COOPER, J. R., F. E. BLOOM, AND R. H. ROTH, 1974. *The Biochemical Basis of Neuropharmacology.* Oxford Univ. Press.

CREESE, I., D. R. SIBLEY, S. LEFF, AND M. HAMBLIN. 1981. Dopamine receptors: Subtypes, localization and regulation. *Fed. Proc.* 40:147–52.

CROW, T. J. 1980a. Positive and negative schizophrenic symptoms and the role of dopamine. *Brit. J. Psychiat.* 137:383–86.

———. 1980b. Molecular pathology of schizophrenia: More than one disease process? *Brit. Med. J.,* 12 January, 66–68.

DE WIED, D., J. M. VAN REE, AND H. M. GREVEN. 1980. Neuroleptic-like activity of peptides related to [DES-TYR¹] γ-endorphin: Structure activity studies. *Life Sci.* 26:1575–79.

FRASER, F. C. 1981. The genetics of common birth defects and diseases. In *Genetic Issues in Pediatric and Obstetric Practice,* ed. M. KABACK, pp. 45–54. Chicago: Year Book Medical Publishers.

GERSHON, E. S., S. MATTHYSSE, X. O. BREAKEFIELD, AND R. D. CIARANELLO. 1981. *Genetic Research Strategies for Psychobiology and Psychiatry.* Pacific Grove, CA: Boxwood Press.

GOLDBERG, E. M., AND S. L. MORRISON. 1963. Schizophrenia and social class. *Brit. J. Psychiat.* 109:785–802.

GOLDSTEIN, J. L., AND M. S. BROWN. 1982. The LDL receptor defect in familial hypercholesterolemia: Implications for pathogenesis and therapy. *Med. Clinics of North Am.* 66:335–62.

GOTTESMAN, I. I., AND J. SHIELDS. 1982. *Schizophrenia: The Epigenetic Puzzle.* Cambridge Univ. Press.

GREENGARD, P. 1976. Possible role for cyclic nucleotides and phosphorylated membrane proteins in postsynaptic actions of neurotransmitters. *Nature* 260:101–08.

HARACZ, J. L. 1982. The dopamine hypothesis: An overview of studies with schizophrenic patients. *Schiz. Bull.* 8:438–69.

HESTON, L. L. 1966. Psychiatric disorders in foster home reared children of schizophrenic mothers. *Brit. J. Psychiat.* 112:819–25.

JAFFE, C. C. 1982. Medical imaging. *Am. Sci.* 70:576–85.

JARRETT, L. 1979. Pathophysiology of the insulin receptor. *Human Pathol.* 10:302–11.

JOHNSTONE, E. C., T. J. CROW, C. D. FRITH, J. HUSBAND, AND L. KREEL. 1976. Cerebral ventricular size and cognitive impairment in chronic schizophrenia. *Lancet,* 30 October, 924–26.

KEBABIAN, J. W., AND D. B. CALNE, 1979. Multiple receptors for dopamine. *Nature* 277:93–96.

KETY, S. S. 1980. The syndrome of schizophrenia: Unresolved questions and opportunities for research. *Brit. J. Psychiat.* 136:421–36.

KETY, S. S., D. ROSENTHAL, P. H. WENDER, AND F. SCHULSINGER. 1976. Studies based on a total sample of adopted individuals and their relatives: Why they were necessary, what they demonstrated and failed to demonstrate. *Schiz. Bull.* 2:413–28.

LEE, T., AND P. SEEMAN. 1980. Elevation of brain neuroleptics/dopamine receptors in schizophrenia. *Am. J. Psychiat.* 137:191–97.

McGUE, M., I. I. GOTTESMAN, AND D. C. RAO. 1983. The transmission of schizophrenia under a multifactorial threshold model. *Am. J. Hum. Genet.* 35:1161–1178.

MACKAY, A. V. P., et al. 1982. Increased brain dopamine and dopamine receptors in schizophrenia. *Arch. Gen. Psychiat.* 39:991–97.

McKUSICK, V. 1983. *Mendelian Inheritance in Man.* 6th ed. Johns Hopkins Univ. Press.

McSWIGAN, J. D., S. E. NICOL, I. I. GOTTESMAN, V. B. TUASON, AND W. H. FREY II. 1980. Effect of dopamine on activation of rat striatal adenylate cyclase by free Mg^{2+} and guanyl nucleotides. *J. Neurochem.* 34:594–601.

MELTZER, H. Y. 1980. Relevance of dopamine autoreceptors for psychiatry: Preclinical and clinical studies. *Schiz. Bull.* 6:456–75.

MELTZER, H. Y., AND S. M. STAHL. 1976. The dopamine hypothesis of schizophrenia: A review. *Schiz. Bull.* 2:19–76.

MORGAN, T. H. 1911. The origin of five mutations in eye color in drosophila and their modes of inheritance. *Science* 33:534–37.

NICOL, S. E., et al. 1981. Postmortem stability of dopamine-sensitive adenylate cyclase, guanylate cyclase, ATPase, and GTPase in rat striatum. *J. Neurochem.* 37:1535–39.

O'ROURKE, D., I. I. GOTTESMAN, B. K. SUAREZ, J. RICE, AND T. REICH. 1982. Refutation of the general single locus model for the etiology of schizophrenia. *Am. J. Hum. Genet.* 34:630–49.

OWEN, F., et al. 1978. Increased dopamine-receptor sensitivity in schizophrenia. *Lancet,* 29 July, 223–25.

REISINE, T. D., M. ROSSOR, E. SPOKES, L. L. IVERSEN, AND H. I. YAMAMURA. 1980. Opiate and neuroleptic receptor alterations in human schizophrenic brain tissue. In *Receptors for Neurotransmitters and Peptide Hormones,* ed. G. PEPEU, M. J. KUHAR, AND S. J. ENNA, pp. 443–50. New York: Raven.

RICE, J., P. McGUFFIN, AND E. G. SHASKAN. 1982. A commingling analysis of platelet monoamine oxidase activity. *Psychiat. Res.* 7:325–35.

ROSENTHAL, D., et al. 1968. Schizophrenics' offspring reared in adoptive homes. In *The Transmission of Schizophrenia,* ed. D. ROSENTHAL AND S. S. KETY, pp. 377–91. Pergamon Press.

Schizophrenia Bulletin. 1980. Schizophrenia and platelet monoamine oxidase (conf. proc.). 6:199–384.

SEEMAN, P. 1980. Brain dopamine receptors. *Phar. Rev.* 32:229–313.

———. 1985. Schizophrenia and dopamine receptors. In *A Method of Psychiatry,* 2nd ed., ed. S. E. GREBEN et al. Philadelphia: Lea and Febiger.

SPOKES, E. G. S. 1979. An analysis of factors influencing measurements of dopamine noradrenaline, glutamate decarboxylase and choline acetylase in human post-mortem brain tissue. *Brain* 102:333–46.

SPOKES, E. G. S., N. J. GARRETT, M. N. ROSSOR, AND L. L. IVERSEN. 1980. Distribution of GABA in post-mortem brain tissue from control, psychotic and Huntington's chorea subjects. *J. Neurol. Sci.* 48:303–13.

STEVENS, J. R. 1982. Neuropathology of schizophrenia. *Arch. Gen. Psychiat.* 39:1131–39.

STOOF, J. C., AND J. W. KEBABIAN. 1981. Opposing roles for D-1 and D-2 dopamine receptors in efflux of cyclic AMP from rat neostriatum. *Nature* 294:366–68.

UYTDENHOEF, P., P. LINKOWSKI, AND J. MENDLEWICZ. 1982. Biological quantitative methods in the evaluation of psychiatric treatment: Some biochemical criteria. *Neuropsychobiology* 8:60–72.

VAN PRAAG, H. M., W. M. A. VERHOEVEN, J. M. VAN REE, AND D. DE WIED. 1982. The treatment of schizophrenic psychoses with γ-type endorphins. *Biol. Psychiat.* 17:83–98.

WEINBERGER, D. R., AND R. J. WYATT. 1980. Schizophrenia and cerebral atrophy. *Lancet,* 24 May, 1130.

WEINSHILBOUM, R. M., AND F. A. RAYMOND. 1977. Inheritance of low erythrocyte catechol-o-methyltransferase activity in man. *Am. J. Hum. Genet.* 29:125–35.

WENDER, P. H., D. ROSENTHAL, S. S. KETY, F. SCHULSINGER, AND J. WEINER. 1974. Cross-fostering: A research strategy for clarifying the role of genetic and experiential factors in the etiology of schizophrenia. *Arch. Gen. Psychiat.* 30:121–28.

8

Positive vs. Negative Schizophrenia: A Critical Evaluation

Nancy C. Andreasen

Abstract: Discussion of the positive vs. negative distinction often fails to address whether this distinction refers to symptoms, syndromes, or diseases. Symptoms and syndromes are etiologically nonspecific, while diseases have a specific identifiable pathophysiology or etiology. The positive vs. negative distinction is sometimes discussed as a hypothesis for identifying discrete subtypes of disease within the schizophrenic syndrome. In this overview, the evidence supporting this approach to subtyping is critically reviewed, and modifications of the original form of the hypothesis are proposed.

Most investigators concur that the illness we usually call by a single name—"schizophrenia"—is probably a heterogeneous group of disorders that share the common features of psychotic symptoms, partial response to neuroleptics, and a relatively poor outcome. Patients who share these common features are, however, clinically quite diverse. Further, research investigations have repeatedly demonstrated that the most consistent finding one can obtain is a very large variance in any variable that may be measured in

Nancy C. Andreasen. Positive vs. negative schizophrenia: A critical evaluation. *Schizophrenia Bulletin,* Vol. 11, No. 3, pp. 380–389. Reprinted by permission of the author.

schizophrenia, ranging from cognitive to neurochemical (Andreasen 1979; Weinberger et al. 1980; Crow et al. 1982a, 1982b). The diversity in schizophrenia suggests that the disorders grouped under this general term may in fact represent several different specific diseases that may differ in important ways, such as the involvement of different neurotransmitter systems, different brain regions, or different etiological agents.

The search for discrete subtypes of schizophrenia did not make much progress until relatively recently, when the distinction between positive and negative symptoms, originally proposed by Hughlings Jackson (1931), was revived (Fish 1962; Strauss, Carpenter, and Bartko 1974; Andreasen 1979b, 1982; Angrist, Rotrosen, and Gershon 1980; Crow 1980; Lewine, Fogg, and Meltzer 1983). Because the distinction has clear heuristic and theoretical appeal, many researchers throughout the world are actively studying this approach to subtyping schizophrenia. Much of the appeal of this distinction is based on the fact that it unites phenomenology, cognitive features, pharmacology, and pathophysiology into a single comprehensive hypothesis. It also clarifies issues by simplifying and polarizing them, thereby permitting scientific testing and study. An obvious weakness of the distinction, which is only a handicap if it is accepted uncritically or naively, is that it oversimplifies what is clearly a complex problem. This overview reviews some of the evidence supporting the positive vs. negative distinction, as well as some of the potential criticisms of it.

Positive (Type I, Florid) Schizophrenia

As proposed by Crow (1980), type I or positive schizophrenia is characterized phenomenologically by prominent positive symptoms such as delusions and hallucinations. Patients with this disorder may have a relatively acute onset, and the course of the illness is characterized by exacerbations and remissions. Many patients with prominent positive features have relatively normal premorbid functioning before the onset of their symptoms, and when the symptoms are in remission their social functioning may be relatively good.

Cognitive Features

The two-syndrome theory hypothesizes that the positive symptoms of schizophrenia are not due to any underlying structural brain abnormality and that patients with positive symptoms should, therefore, have normal cognitive function. Various studies of structural brain abnormalities that can be visualized using computed tomography (CT) have supported this theory (Johnstone et al. 1976; Crow 1980; Andreasen et al. 1982b). That is, in general, the various CT studies have not been able to document any relationship between positive symptoms and various indices of brain abnormality such as ventricular enlargement, sulcal enlargement, or cerebellar atrophy. A single exception is one study that reports ventricular enlargement in patients classified as paranoid subtype (Nasrallah et al. 1982). One study has shown that, if anything, patients with positive symptoms may tend to have relatively small ventricles (Andreasen et al. 1982b). A single informative case of a patient with persistent treatment-refractory delusions of a persecutory and sexual nature suggests that patients with positive symptoms may have structural abnormalities, but not of the type associated with atrophy. This particular patient had marked enlargement of the corpus callosum and the septal nuclei; one might hypothesize that she had a "hyperconnection" syndrome or excessive activation of the limbic system (Andreasen, unpublished data).

In addition to CT scanning, neuropsychological testing has also been used to explore the cognitive features of the positive vs. negative subtypes. As in the case of CT scanning, rather consistently patients with positive symptoms have been found to perform normally on various neuropsychological tests (Crow 1980; Andreasen et al. 1982b).

Pharmacologic Features

The florid symptoms of schizophrenia, such as delusions, hallucinations, or bizarre agitated behavior, tend to respond relatively well to neuroleptics. The mechanism of action of these neuroleptics is blockade of dopamine transmission. Other drugs that facilitate dopamine transmission, such as the amphetamines, are likely to exacerbate positive symptoms (Angrist, Rotrosen, and Gershon 1980). These pharmacological features implicate dopamine as an important mechanism in producing positive symptoms. Further, it has been frequently noted clinically that patients with prominent positive symptoms require relatively high doses of neuroleptics to diminish their positive symptoms, and that they have remarkably few side effects in spite of these high doses. The tolerance for high-dose neuroleptics further supports some neurochemical abnormality in positive schizophrenia. On the other hand, while positive symptoms may remit partially or fully with neuroleptic treatment, sometimes defect or negative symptoms persist after treatment.

Pathophysiology

The pathophysiology of positive symptoms is unknown, but the above pharmacological evidence suggests that the abnormality may reside at least in part in the dopamine system. The "dopamine hypothesis" proposes that the symptoms of schizophrenia are due to excessive dopamine transmission (Randrup and Munkvad 1965, 1966, 1972; Snyder, Greenberg, and Yamamura 1974; Seeman et al. 1976, 1984; Snyder 1976). The mechanism for this hyperdopaminergic transmission is unknown. Some evidence suggests that the abnormality may be in the receptor portion of the synapse (Snyder 1976). Crow et al. (1982a), using ^{3}H-spiroperidol in post-mortem brains, have noted increased numbers of D_2 receptors in the area of the nucleus accumbens. In a postmortem brain study of neuropeptides, his team has also found increased vasoactive intestinal polypeptide (VIP) in the amygdala. Meltzer and colleagues have noted a relationship between low platelet monoamine oxidase (MAO) and high platelet 5-hydroxytryptamine (5HT) activity and positive symptoms (Meltzer et al. 1980; Jackman, Luchins, and Meltzer 1983). These latter findings suggest that other transmitters besides dopamine may be involved in producing positive symptoms. The platelet MAO and 5HT findings implicate serotonin, while the VIP findings suggest that acetyl choline could also be involved, since VIP and acetyl choline have been found to coexist and perhaps function as cotransmitters in autonomic ganglia (Krieger 1983). In any case, the underlying assumption concerning the pathophysiology of positive symptoms is that they are based primarily on a neurochemical rather than a structural abnormality. This hypothesis is supported in part by the mechanism of drug action and in part by the clinical observation that positive symptoms tend to be relatively reversible. The presumed area of abnormality is primarily subcortical, particularly temporolimbic.

Negative (Type II, Defect) Schizophrenia

The clinical features of negative schizophrenia tend to represent a mirror image to those of positive schizophrenia. The characteristic symptoms are negative or defect symptoms that represent a diminution of function rather than an excess. Typical negative symptoms include affective blunting, alogia (poverty of speech, poverty of content of speech), avolition and apathy, anhedonia and asociality, and attentional impairment. These symptoms usually begin insidiously without a clear onset, and patients therefore may have a long history of poor premorbid functioning. The course of the illness tends to be more chronic or deteriorating, and social functioning tends to be chronically impaired. Patients with prominent negative symptoms are often unable to hold a job and tend to remain socially isolated (Andreasen 1982b; Opler et al. 1984; Pearlson et al. 1984).

Cognitive Features

Brain-imaging techniques such as CT scanning have shown that schizophrenic patients in general have a higher rate of structural brain abnormalities than do control subjects (Johnstone et al. 1976; Weinberger et al. 1979a, 1980, 1981; Golden et al. 1980, 1981; Andreasen et al. 1982c; Nasrallah et al. 1982; Okasha and Madkour 1982; Reveley et al. 1982; Schulz et al. 1983). Studies that have focused on subtypes within the schizophrenia spectrum have noted that these structural brain abnormalities may occur more frequently in patients with prominent negative symptoms (Johnstone et al. 1976; Andreasen 1982b). The most common finding that has been noted is ventricular enlargement.

One study has also reported a relative increase in left-handedness among patients with prominent negative symptoms (Andreasen 1982b). This finding is important because it suggests something about the underlying mechanism that may lead to cerebral atrophy and cognitive impairment. Left-handedness may be either "genetic" or "pathological" (Satz 1972). Patients with genetic left-handedness tend to have a higher rate of left-handedness in other family members, while patients with pathological left-handedness develop it as a consequence of injury to their left hemisphere early in the developmental course (prenatally, perinatally, or within the first several years after birth). This injury to the left hemisphere produces a shift in the normal pattern of cerebral dominance. Normally the left hemisphere is used for the processing of fine motor activity and language. Because some injury has occurred to the left hemisphere early in life, however, patients with pathological left-handedness shift dominant processing to their uninjured right hemisphere, causing them to use the left hand for fine motor activity.

Patients with prominent negative symptoms also tend to have impaired performance on neuropsychological testing, using tests such as the Wechsler Adult Intelligence Scale (WAIS) (Rieder et al. 1979; Donnelly et al. 1980; Andreasen 1982b; Opler et al. 1984). While this impaired performance could be due to the inattention or lack of interest that characterize negative schizophrenia, it may also reflect actual cerebral injury. Patients with prominent negative symptoms tend to have a significantly lower educational achievement than do patients with prominent positive symptoms (Andreasen 1982b; Opler et al. 1984). Thus, there appears to be an association between the insidious onset of the illness, poor premorbid functioning, and cognitive impairment beginning early in life.

Pharmacological Features

Negative symptoms tend to respond less well to neuroleptic therapy than do positive symptoms. With aggressive treatment, hallucinations, positive thought disorder, and bizarre behavior can usually be markedly decreased in most patients. Delusions are frequently more treatment-refractory, but often respond as well. When these symptoms respond, the patient is sometimes left in a "defect state," characterized by alogia, avolition, and affective flattening. The picture is somewhat confused, however, by the fact that the extra-pyramidal side effects of neuroleptics frequently produce a picture similar to affective flattening.

The observation that many patients with positive symptoms continue to have negative symptoms after treatment has led some clinicians to conclude that negative symptoms are more likely to be treatment-refractory (Johnstone et al. 1978). Further, some patients present with a clinical picture characterized primarily or predominantly by negative symptoms, with a relative paucity of positive symptoms. These patients, likewise, tend to show a relatively poor response to neuroleptic treatment. One study has shown an association between poor treatment response and ventricular enlargement, further supporting the argument for a "structural" and therefore "irreversible" abnormality underlying negative symptoms (Weinberger et al. 1980).

An alternate hypothesis for the pharmacology of negative symptoms has been proposed, however. This point of view argues that the mechanisms underlying negative symptoms may also be neurochemical and therefore potentially reversible. For example, several investigators have proposed that negative symptoms may be due to a functional deficit in dopamine rather than an excess (Chouinard and Jones 1978; Lecrubier et al. 1980; Mackay 1980; Alpert and Friedhoff 1982). Such symptoms would, therefore, be more likely to respond to medications that facilitate or increase dopaminergic transmission, as neuroleptics have been reported to do in low doses (Puech, Simon, and Bossier 1978). Some investigators have experimented with the use of L-dopa (Buchanan et al. 1975; Gerlach and Lühdorf 1975; Inanaga et al. 1975). Others have proposed the use of "energizing" neuroleptics such as sulpiride (Lecrubier et al. 1980). Still other investigators have suggested that nonneuroleptic agents such as alprazolam may be useful in treating negative symptoms (Hollister, personal communication).

Pathophysiology

We know little that is definitive about the pathophysiology of negative symptoms, and as yet there is no widely accepted hypothesis similar to the dopamine hypothesis that can explain negative symptoms. The original explanation, proposed by Crow (1980), that negative symptoms are due to diffuse structural brain changes similar to those occurring in dementia appears to be an oversimplification. Not all patients with negative symptoms have ventricular enlargement or cortical atrophy, nor are negative symptoms consistently irreversible.

Reasoning a priori, one might argue that negative symptoms are most consistent with some type of frontal system disease. Patients who have experienced lesions in the prefrontal regions display symptoms remarkably similar to those that we have come to call negative symptoms: diminution in spontaneous movement and speech, loss of creativity, impaired attention and concentration, excessive concreteness, blunting of affect and emotional response, and profound apathy (Fuster 1980). One might argue simplistically that while positive symptoms might be due to a temporolimbic system abnormality, negative symptoms might be due to a frontal system abnormality. In fact, however, these two systems are interconnected through various major subcortical way-stations, such as the thalamus, and therefore subcortical dysfunction could explain both groups of symptoms.

The neurochemical mechanisms that might underlie negative schizophrenia are unclear. As described previously, some investigators have hypothesized that negative symptoms may reflect decreased dopaminergic transmission. This position has been argued from various vantage points by Lecrubier et al. (1980), Chouinard and Jones (1978), and Mackay (1980). Crow et al. (1982a) have shown that while the number of D_2 receptors is decreased in patients with positive symptoms, patients with negative symptoms have normal numbers of D_2 receptors, as measured in post-mortem brains. One problem with the hypodopaminergic theory of negative symptoms is that these symptoms sometimes coexist with positive symptoms in particular patients. While this theory can explain relatively "clean" instances of negative schizophrenia, it has more difficulty in accounting for the mixed patient.

Work in other centers has implicated the possible involvement of other transmitter systems. Lewine and Meltzer (1984) have observed an association between high platelet MAO and negative symptoms in male patients, thereby possibly implicating the serotonin system. Studying peptides, Ferrier et al. (in press) have observed decreased cholecystokinin (CCK) in the hippocampus and amygdala and somatostatin in the hippocampus of patients with prominent negative symptoms. If replicated, this finding would support a temporolimbic localization for negative symptoms as well. Further, since CCK and dopamine coexist in the midbrain as cotransmitters (Krieger 1983), this finding could provide further support for dopaminergic involvement.

The time may come soon when we can localize particular symptoms or syndromes of mental illness to transmitter or brain systems, but that time has not yet arrived. Attempting to localize these symptoms at present is like trying to solve a difficult and complex puzzle for which two or three pieces appear to be missing, lost, or unavailable.

Problems With the Positive vs. Negative Distinction

While theoretically appealing, and while supported by considerable evidence, the distinction between positive and negative schizophrenia just described nevertheless has a number of problems. It is best viewed as a heuristic approach to subtyping schizophrenia that lends itself to hypothesis testing and may be hypothesis generating. Investigators exploring this distinction must be aware of some of its conceptual and practical difficulties.

Failure to Distinguish Between Symptoms, Syndromes, and Diseases

The literature on the positive vs. negative distinction is often marred by a failure to recognize this basic distinction, which is fundamental to understanding phenomenology, diagnosis, and classification.

> *Symptoms* (as well as signs) are the clinical features of illness; they may occur in many different disorders (e.g., delusions). Symptoms can be added up as a continous measure and used to identify or define a syndrome and evaluate its severity.

> *Syndromes* are a set of clinical features that tend to occur together (e.g., dementia). Syndromes are phenomenologically similar, but may differ in etiology (e.g., multiinfarct dementia vs. Alzheimer's dementia).

> *Diseases* are discrete illnesses that differ in their pathophysiology or etiology (e.g., multiple sclerosis, neurosyphilis).

Since symptoms are relatively nonspecific, their presence does not necessarily have any predictive power. For example, the presence of a single negative symptom, or even several, does not necessarily indicate that a person has schizophrenia, nor does the presence of one or several positive symptoms. Depressed patients may have apathy or impaired attention, and they may also have delusions or hallucinations. To say that a symptom is nonspecific, however, is not to say that it is unimportant. Symptoms are the fundamental material with which diagnosticians and psychometricians must work.

Yet another problem that has not been adequately addressed is *how* to decide that a symptom is positive or negative. In most early work, the decision was simply made a priori. For some symptoms, this decision, based on "face validity," makes good sense. Items on the Brief Psychiatric Rating Scale (BPRS) (Overall and Gorham 1962) such as emotional withdrawal and blunted affect are rather clear negative symptoms, as are items on the Krawiecka scale (Krawiecka, Goldberg, and Vaughan 1977) such as affective flattening or poverty of speech. On the other hand, incongruity of affect moves back and forth from one study to another as a positive or negative symptom, and the place of psychomotor retardation or catatonic motor symptoms is also unclear. More work needs to be done on these symptoms, both through

various measures of internal consistency and through determining their predictive power in relation to various external validators.

Symptoms can be rated either categorically or continously; that is, they can either be scored as present vs. absent, or they can be rated by overall severity. The scales developed by Lewine, Fogg, and Meltzer (1983) based on the Rasch model use the former approach, while the Krawiecka scale and the Scale for the Assessment of Negative Symptoms (SANS) and the Scale for the Assessment of Positive Symptoms (SAPS) of Andreasen (1982a, 1984) use the latter approach. Scales that ask for a rating of present vs. absent may be simpler to use, although it is frequently difficult to identify the threshold for deciding that a symptom is present, particularly in the case of negative symptoms. On the other hand, scales that use continous measures, such as the SANS and the SAPS, lend themselves well to dimensional analyses that explore correlations.

As anyone with the most rudimentary knowledge of statistics is aware, however, the study of correlations permits only limited inferences. Correlations indicate the relationship between variables, but they do not permit one to draw any conclusions about causality. Ultimately, our goal is to determine the causes of psychiatric disorders, and the examination of correlations is only a first approximation to that goal. Although that fact is really quite rudimentary, all of us occasionally show some "cognitive slippage" in our eagerness to make inferences about relationships and assume that finding a correlation may help explain etiology.

If one wishes to attempt to identify either diseases or discrete subtypes of diseases, then one must posit a categorical approach. Instead of examining the relationship between symptoms and other variables, one must divide patients into groups and study some relevant correlate. Patients can be divided into groups on the basis of phenomenology (e.g., those with prominent negative symptoms and those who lack prominent negative symptoms), or they can be divided on the basis of some biological variable (e.g., those with high or normal numbers of D_2 receptors, or those with high vs. low platelet MAO). To speak of a disease or a subtype of disease implies that one is studying a phenomenon that is discontinuous from normality or that two subtypes of a disorder are discontinuous from one another.

Inadequately Developed Definitions of Symptoms

When interest in the positive vs. negative distinction was reawakened, investigators had few instruments at hand with which to measure negative symptoms. These symptoms had been in disfavor because of a frequently expressed concern that they could not be rated reliably. Initially, scales such as the Krawiecka or BPRS were used because they were the only ones available. The negative symptoms measured by these scales are relatively limited, and their psychometric properties with respect to the positive vs. negative distinction have not been adequately investigated. Unfortunately, however, much of the research described above is based on the use of these scales.

More recently, several new scales have been developed, such as the SANS, the SAPS, and the Lewine Scale. The SANS describes five major groups of negative symptoms (alogia, affective flattening, avolition-apathy, anhedonia-asociality, and attentional impairment). It has well-documented reliability and some external validity, such as correlation with premorbid functioning, ventricle-brain ratio, and cognitive impairment. The scale has good internal consistency. The SAPS, which is designed to provide similar measurements of relevant positive symptoms, is also available. These scales lend themselves well to repeated measures designs. The Lewine scale is derived from the Schedule for Affective Disorders and Schizophrenia (SADS) (Endicott and Spitzer 1978) and the Nurses' Observation Scale for Inpatient Evaluation (NOSIE) (Honigfeld et al. 1966). It also has good reliability. These two scales provide a much fuller description of the range of positive and negative symptoms than do those used previously.

Inadequately Developed Definitions of Syndromes and Diseases

While the two scales described above provide some relatively standard and comprehensive ways of measuring positive and negative symptoms, at present there are few well-conceptualized ways of defining positive and negative schizophrenia as a syndrome or disease. One set of criteria for defining positive, negative, and mixed schizophrenia has been proposed, and these criteria appear to have some predictive validity (Andreasen 1982b). Independent studies in other centers have also applied these criteria and found them to be valid and useful (Dion and Dellario 1985). One alternate approach is to classify patients as negative if they show *any* negative symptoms; this approach is based on the underlying assumption that negative symptoms must represent some type of "defect" that is of more theoretical significance than positive symptoms. Alternatively, one can add up scale scores on the various positive and negative symptom scales currently available and identify patients at extreme ends of the positive vs. negative continuum; this approach is clearly more syndromal in its orientation. Given our current state of knowledge, no method of defining patients as negative or positive can be considered preeminent. This is clearly an area where further investigation is needed.

Failure to Deal With the "Mixed" Patient

Early formulations of the positive vs. negative distinction failed to discuss the issue of the "mixed" patient. Positive and negative symptoms were treated as if they were distinct entities, and the fact that positive and negative symptoms frequently co-occur in a single patient was ignored. While it is possible that positive and negative schizophrenia are indeed two distinct disease entities with differing underlying pathophysiology or etiology or alternatively that they are syndromes at opposite ends of a continuum, in real life they are also groups of symptoms that may overlap in a single patient. If one speaks about positive vs. negative schizophrenia categorically, then how is one to explain the coexistence of positive and negative symptoms with a single patient?

Several explanations are possible. One is that while "pure negative" schizophrenia and "pure positive" schizophrenia may be distinct subtypes, patients with mixed symptoms represent yet another subtype, or even several different subtypes. A second possible explanation is that patients with mixed positive and negative symptoms are at an intermediate stage in the course of the illness; this hypothesis assumes that some patients may eventually evolve from a positive state to a negative state, and that the negative state represents the true or underlying disorder. Thus patients who are mixed are in fact negative, but the predominantly negative syndrome has not yet developed. A third explanation might be that the symptoms of schizophrenia could be due to multiple causes, and that some of these causes coexist in some patients; for example, patients with a mixture of positive and negative symptoms might represent those patients who have both suffered perinatal cerebral injury (producing atrophic damage and negative symptoms) and also suffer from a genetic tendency toward hyperdopaminergic transmission (leading to positive symptoms).

Yet another possible explanation is that there may be a single causative agent that affects different brain regions; for example, a slow virus might lead to patchy damage in different regions, and those patients who have a predominantly prefrontal lesion would have negative symptoms, while those with a predominantly temporolimbic localization would have positive symptoms, while some patients might have involvement in both areas. Yet another explanation might be that multiple neurochemical systems are involved in the production of the symptoms of schizophrenia, leading to various kinds of imbalance; for example, an excess of dopamine might lead to positive symptoms, an excess of γ-aminobutyric acid or serotonin might lead to negative symptoms, and a mixture of symptoms could be due to an imbalance of multiple systems. Some of these explanations are obviously theoretical or even a bit fanciful, but they serve to suggest that a single simple theoretical model will probably not be able to explain the symptoms, course, and classification of schizophrenia. A complex interactive model involving both environment and genetics, the involvement of multiple neurotransmitter systems, and the involvement of multiple brain regions is required.

Failure to Take Longitudinal Course Into Account

While the positive vs. negative distinction introduces some course variables into the model, such as poor premorbid functioning or poor outcome, it does not recognize the fact that the phenomenology of schizophrenia may vary dramatically over time. As described above, some patients with positive symptoms develop a defect state after the positive symptoms remit. Others clearly have a lifetime longitudinal course beginning with florid symptoms and later leading to deterioration. Some patients may begin with predominantly negative symptoms and remain in that state throughout their lives. To date, we have had relatively few studies on the longitudinal course of positive and negative symptoms over time. Work by Pfohl and Winokur (1982, 1983) indicates that the symptoms of schizophrenia do indeed vary. They studied a cohort of 52 chronic schizophrenic patients who were institutionalized before the era of antipsychotic medications and noted that during a 25-year period hallucinations and delusions became less frequent, while negative symptoms such as avolition, impaired social interaction, and affective flattening became more frequent. Thus, it appears that some schizophrenic patients do evolve from a positive to a negative state. Since the patients in this study were all institutionalized, it is not clear whether these findings are generalizable to patients with a less severe syndrome. Clearly, more longitudinal studies of the course of positive vs. negative symptoms are needed.

Conclusion

Schizophrenia may represent a single illness, or it may be a heterogeneous group of disorders referred to by a single name. If the latter is the case, and if research investigations fail to recognize the heterogeneity of the disorder and pool together unlike patients, then positive results will be lost because they are averaged out in a diverse sample. The large variance noted in most studies of schizophrenia supports this latter possibility. Consequently, efforts to identify discrete subtypes are of great importance.

The positive vs. negative approach to subtyping schizophrenia has recently aroused considerable interest, primarily because it synthesizes in a single theory many disparate observations and also makes "good clinical sense." In addition, it generates a number of scientifically interesting and testable hypotheses. One must add that like many useful theories (ranging from the catecholamine hypothesis through the Oedipus complex to negative cognitive sets), it represents an oversimplification. The tendency to oversimplify is both its strength and its weakness. We can use this approach best by recognizing that it is perhaps overly simplistic, but that it therefore permits the study of rather complex issues if applied intelligently and with caution.

The positive vs. negative distinction warrants much additional future study. Possible future directions include genetic and family studies to explore the prevalence and pattern of symptoms within families, detailed examination of the course of symptoms over time, application of new brain imaging technology to assist in the localization of positive vs. negative symptoms, attempts to define in more detail the brain regions and neurochemical systems involved, and detailed examination of pharmacological response with variable dose strategies and various types of medication.

References

ALPERT, M., AND FRIEDHOFF, A.J. An un-dopamine hypothesis of schizophrenia. *Schizophrenia Bulletin*, 6:380–387, 1982.

ANDREASEN, N.C. The clinical assessment of thought, language, and communication disorders: I. The definition of terms and evaluation of their reliability. *Archives of General Psychiatry*, 36:1315–1325, 1979a.

ANDREASEN, N.C. The clinical assessment of thought, language, and communication disorders: II. Diagnostic significance. *Archives of General Psychiatry*, 36:1325–1330, 1979b.

ANDREASEN, N.C. Negative symptoms in schizophrenia: Definition and reliability. *Archives of General Psychiatry*, 39:784–788, 1982a.

ANDREASEN, N.C. Negative *vs.* positive schizophrenia: Definition and validation. *Archives of General Psychiatry*, 39:789–794, 1982b.

ANDREASEN, N.C. *The Scale for the Assessment of Negative Symptoms (SANS)*. Iowa City, Iowa: The University of Iowa, 1983.

ANDREASEN, N.C. *The Scale for the Assessment of Positive Symptoms (SAPS)*. Iowa City, Iowa: The University of Iowa, 1984.

ANDREASEN, N.C.; DENNERT, J.W.; OLSEN, S.A.; AND DAMASIO, A.R. Hemisphere asymmetries and schizophrenia. *American Journal of Psychiatry*, 139:427–430, 1982a.

ANDREASEN, N.C.; OLSEN, S.A.; DENNERT, J.W.; AND SMITH, M.R. Ventricular enlargement in schizophrenia: Relationship to positive and negative symptoms. *American Journal of Psychiatry*, 139:297–302, 1982b.

ANDREASEN, N.C.; SMITH, M.R.; DENNERT, J.W.; JACOBY, C.G.; AND OLSEN, S.A. Ventricular enlargement in schizophrenia: Definition and prevalence. *American Journal of Psychiatry*, 139:292–296, 1982c.

ANGRIST, B.; ROTROSEN, J.; AND GERSHON, S. Differential effects of amphetamine and neuroleptics on negative *vs.* positive symptoms in schizophrenia. *Psychopharmacology*. 11:1–3, 1980.

BUCHANAN, F.H.; PARTON, R.V.; WARREN, J.W.; AND BAKER, E.P. Double blind trial of L-dopa in chronic schizophrenia. *Australian and New Zealand Journal of Psychiatry*, 9:269–271, 1975.

CHOUINARD, G., AND JONES, B.D. Schizophrenia as dopamine-deficiency disease. *Lancet*. I:99–100, 1978.

CROW, T.J. Molecular pathology of schizophrenia: More than one disease process? *British Medical Journal*, 280:66–68, 1980.

CROW, T.J.; CROSS, A.J.; JOHNSTONE, E.C.; OWEN, F.; OWENS, D.G.C.; BLOXHAM, C.; FERRIER, I.N.; MACREADIE, R.M.; AND POULTER, M. Changes in D_2 dopamine receptor numbers in post-mortem brain in schizophrenia in relation to the presence of the type I syndrome and movement disorder. In: COLLU, R., ed. *Brain Peptides and Hormones*. New York: Raven Press, 1982a. pp. 43–53.

CROW, T.J.; CROSS, A.J.: JOHNSTONE, E.C.; OWEN, F.; OWENS D.G.C.; AND WADDINGTON, J.C. Abnormal involuntary movements in schizophrenia: Are they related to the disease process or its treatment? *Journal of Clinical Psychopharmacology*, 2:336–340, 1982b.

DION, G., AND DELLARIO, D. "Symptom Subtypes in Institutionalized Schizophrenics: Comparison of Demographics, Outcome, and Functional Skills." Unpublished manuscript, 1985.

DONNELLY, E.F.; WEINBERGER, D.R.; WALDMAN, I.N.; AND WYATT, R.J. Cognitive impairment associated with morphological brain abnormalities on computed tomography in chronic schizophrenic patients. *Journal of Nervous and Mental Disease*, 168:305–308, 1980.

ENDICOTT, J., AND SPITZER, R.L. A diagnostic interview: The Schedule for Affective Disorders and Schizophrenia (SADS). *Archives of General Psychiatry*, 35:837–844, 1978.

FERRIER, I.N.; CROW, T.J.; AND ROBERTS, G.W. Alterations in neuropeptides in limbic lobe in schizophrenia. *Life Sciences*, in press.

FISH, F.J. *Schizophrenia*. Bristol: John Wright & Sons, Ltd., 1962.

FUSTER, J.M. *The Prefrontal Cortex*. New York: Raven Press, 1980.

GERLACH, J., AND LÜHDORF, K. The effect of L-dopa on young patients with simple schizophrenia treated with neuroleptic drugs: A double-blind cross-over trial with madopar and placebo. *Psychopharmacology*, 44:105–110, 1975.

GOLDEN, C.J.; GRABER, B.; COFFMAN, J.; BERG, R.; NEWLIN, D.; AND BLOCK, S. Structural brain deficits in schizophrenia: Identification by computed tomographic scan density measurements. *Archives of General Psychiatry*, 38:1014–1017, 1981.

GOLDEN, C.J.; MOSES, J.A.; ZELAZOWSKI, R.; GRABER, B.; ZATZ, L.M.; HORVATH, T.B.; AND BERGER, P.A. Cerebral ventricular size and neuropsychological impairment in young chronic schizophrenics. *Archives of General Psychiatry*. 37:619–623, 1980.

HONIGFELD, G.; GILLIS, R.D.: AND KLETT, C.J. NOSIE 30: A treatment-sensitive ward behavior scale. *Psychological Reports*, 19:180–182, 1966.

INANAGA, K.; NAKAZAWA, Y.; INOUE, K.; TACHIBANA, H.; OSHIMA, M.; KOTORII, T.; TANAKA, M.; AND OGAWA, N. Double-blind controlled study of L-dopa therapy in schizophrenia. *Folia Psychiatrica et Neurologica Japonica*, 29:123–143, 1975.

JACKMAN, H.; LUCHINS, D.; AND MELTZER, H.Y. Platelet serotonin levels in schizophrenia: Relationship to race and psychopathology. *Biological Psychiatry*. 18:887–902. 1983.

JACKSON, J.H. *Selected Writings*, Taylor, J., ed. London: Hodder & Stoughton, Ltd., 1931.

JOHNSTONE, E.C.; CROW, T.J.; FRITH, C.D.: HUSBAND, J.; AND KREEL, I. Cerebral ventricular size and cognitive impairment in chronic schizophrenia. *Lancet*, II:924–926, 1976.

JOHNSTONE, E.C.; CROW, T.J.; FRITH, C.D.; CARNEY, M.W.; AND PRICE, J.S. Mechanism of the antipsychotic effect in the treatment of acute schizophrenia. *Lancet*, I:848–851, 1978.

KRAWIECKA, M.; GOLDBERG, D.; AND VAUGHAN, M.A. Standardized psychiatric assessment for rating chronic patients. *Acta Psychiatrica Scandinavica*, 55:299–308, 1977.

KRIEGER, D.T. Brain peptides: What, where, and why? *Science*, 222:975–985, 1983.

LECRUBIER, Y.; PUECH, A.J.; SIMON, P.; AND WIDLÖCHER, D. Schizophrenie: Hyper ou hypofonctionnement du système dopa-minergique? Une hypothèse bipolaire. *Psychologie Medicale*, 12:2431–2441, 1980.

LEWINE, R.J.; FOGG, L.; AND MELTZER, H.Y. Assessment of negative and positive symptoms in schizophrenia. *Schizophrenia Bulletin*, 9:968–976, 1983.

LEWINE, R.J., AND MELTZER, H.Y. Negative symptoms and platelet monoamine oxidase activity in male schizophrenics. *Psychiatry Research*, 12:99–109, 1984.

MACKAY, A.V.P. Positive and negative schizophrenic symptoms and the role of dopamine: Discussion, 1. *British Journal of Psychiatry*, 137:379–383, 1980.

MELTZER, H.Y.; ARORA, R.C.; JACKMAN, H.; PSCHEIDT, G.; AND SMITH, M.D. Platelet monoamine oxidase and plasma amine oxidase in psychiatric patients. *Schizophrenia Bulletin*, 6:213–219, 1980.

NASRALLAH, H.A.; JACOBY, C.G.; McCALLEY-WHITTERS, M.; AND KUPERMAN, S. Cerebral ventricular enlargement in subtypes of chronic schizophrenia subtypes. *Archives of General Psychiatry,* 39:774–777, 1982.

OKASHA, A., AND MADKOUR, O. Cortical and central atrophy in chronic schizophrenia. *Acta Psychiatrica Scandinavica,* 65:29–34, 1982.

OPLER, L.A.; KAY, S.R.; ROSADO, V.; AND LINDENMAYER, J.P. Positive and negative syndromes in chronic schizophrenic patients. *Journal of Nervous and Mental Disease,* 172:317–325, 1984.

OVERALL, J., AND GORHAM, D. Brief Psychiatric Rating Scale. *Psychological Reports,* 10:799–812, 1962.

PEARLSON, G.D.; GARBACZ, D.J.; BREAKEY, W.R.; AHN, H.S.; AND DePAULO, J.R. Lateral ventricular enlargement associated with persistent unemployment and negative symptoms in both schizophrenia and bipolar disorder. *Psychiatry Research,* 12:1–9, 1984.

PFOHL, B., AND WINOKUR, G. The evolution of symptoms in institutionalized hebephrenic/catatonic schizophrenics. *British Journal of Psychiatry,* 141:567–572, 1982.

PFOHL, B., AND WINOKUR, G. The micropsychopathology of hebephrenic/catatonic schizophrenia. *Journal of Nervous and Mental Disease,* 171:296–300, 1983.

PUECH, A.J.; SIMON, D.; AND BOSSIER, J.R. Benzamides and classical neuroleptics: Comparison of their actions using apomorphine induced effects. *European Journal of Pharmacology,* 50:291–300, 1978.

RANDRUP, A.; AND MUNKVAD, I. Special antagonism of amphetamine induced abnormal behavior: Inhibition of stereotyped activity with increase of some normal activities. *Psychopharmacologia,* 7:416–422, 1965.

RANDRUP, A., AND MUNKVAD, I. Role of catecholamines in the amphetamine excitatory response. *Nature,* 211:540, 1966.

RANDRUP, A., AND MUNKVAD, I. Evidence indicating an association between schizophrenia and dopaminergic hyperactivity in the brain. *Orthomolecular Psychiatry,* 1:2–7, 1972.

REVELEY, A.M.; REVELEY, M.A.; CLIFFORD, C.A.; AND MURRAY, R.M. Cerebral ventricular size in twins discordant for schizophrenia. *Lancet,* 1:540–541, 1982.

RIEDER, R.O.; DONNELLY, E.F.; HERDT, J.R.; AND WALDMAN, I.N. Sulcal prominence in young chronic schizophrenic patients: CT scan findings associated with impairment on neuropsychological tests. *Psychiatry Research,* 1:1–8, 1979.

SATZ, P. Pathological left-handedness: An explanation. *Cortex,* 8:121–125, 1972.

SCHULZ, S.C.; KOLLER, M.M.; KISHORE, P.R.; HAMMER, R.M.; GEHL, J.J.; AND FRIEDEL, R.O. Ventricular enlargement in teenage patients with schizophrenia spectrum disorder. *American Journal of Psychiatry.* 140:1592–1595, 1983.

SEEMAN, P.; LEE, T.; CHANG-WONG, M.; AND WONG, K. Antipsychotic drug doses and neuroleptic/dopamine receptors. *Nature,* 261:717–719, 1976.

SEEMAN, P.; ULPIAN, C.; BERGERON, C.; RIEDERER, P.; JELLINGER, K.; GABRIEL, E.; REYNOLDS, G. P; AND TOURTELLOTTE, W.W. Bimodal distribution of dopamine receptor density in brains of schizophrenics. *Science,* 225:728–731, 1984.

SNYDER, S.H. The dopamine hypothesis in schizophrenia: Focus on the dopamine receptor. *American Journal of Psychiatry,* 133:197–202, 1976.

SNYDER, S.H.; GREENBERG, D.; AND YAMAMURA, H.U. Antipsychotic drugs and brain cholinergic receptors. *Archives of General Psychiatry,* 31:58–61, 1974.

STRAUSS, J.S.; CARPENTER, W.T., JR.; AND BARTKO, J.J. The diagnosis and understanding of schizophrenia: Part III. Speculations on the processes that underlie schizophrenic symptoms and signs. *Schizophrenia Bulletin,* 11:61–76, 1974.

TYRRELL, D.A.J.; PARRY, R.P.; CROW, T.J.; JOHNSTONE, E.; AND FERRIER, I.M. Possible virus in schizophrenia and some neurological disorders. *Lancet,* I:839–841, 1979.

WEINBERGER, D.R.; BIGELOW, L.B.; KLEINMAN, J.E.; KLEIN, S.T.; ROSENBLATT, J.E.; AND WYATT, R.J. Cerebral ventricular enlargement in chronic schizophrenia: An association with poor response to treatment. *Archives of General Psychiatry,* 37:11–13, 1980.

WEINBERGER, D.R.; DeLISI, L.E.; NEOPHYTIDES, A.M.; AND WYATT, R.J. Familial aspects of CT scan abnormalities in chronic schizophrenia. *Psychiatry Research,* 4:65–71, 1981.

WEINBERGER, D.R.; TORREY, E.F.; NEOPHYTIDES, A.M.; AND WYATT, R.J. Lateral cerebral ventricular enlargement in chronic schizophrenia. *Archives of General Psychiatry,* 36:735–739, 1979a.

WEINBERGER, D.R.; TORREY, E.F.; NEOPHYTIDES, A.M.; AND WYATT, R.J. Structural abnormalities in the cerebral cortex of chronic schizophrenic patients. *Archives of General Psychiatry,* 36:935–939, 1979b.

9

Physiologic Dysfunction of Dorsolateral Prefrontal Cortex in Schizophrenia

Daniel R. Weinberger, Karen Faith Berman, and Ronald F. Zec

To evaluate dorsolateral prefrontal cortex (DLPFC) physiology and function simultaneously, 20 medication-free patients with chronic schizophrenia and 25 normal controls underwent three separate xenon Xe 133 inhalation procedures for determination of regional cerebral blood flow (rCBF): first at rest, then while performing an automated version of the Wisconsin Card Sort (WCS), a DLPFC-specific cognitive test, and while performing a simple number-matching (NM) test. During rest, patients had significantly reduced relative, but not absolute, rCBF to DLPFC. During NM, no specific region differentiated patients from controls. During WCS, however, both absolute and relative rCBF to DLPFC significantly distinguished patients from controls. While controls showed a clear increase in DLPFC rCBF, patients did not. The changes were regionally specific, involving only DLPFC. Furthermore, in patients, DLPFC rCBF correlated positively with WCS cognitive performance, suggesting that the better DLPFC was able to function, the better patients could perform. Autonomic arousal measures, the pattern of WCS errors, and results of complementary studies suggest that the DLPFC finding is linked to regionally specific cognitive function and is not a nonspecific epiphenomenon.

The history of the frontal lobes and behavior includes a long chapter on the relevance of frontal lobe dysfunction in the pathogenesis of schizophrenia. Alzheimer[1] claimed that neuropathologic changes in layers II and III of frontal cortex were responsible for the illness. Both Kraepelin[2] and Bleuler[3] believed the frontal lobes to be a possible site for the pathologic changes of schizophrenia. One rationale for frontal leukotomy was to isolate a disturbed frontal lobe.[4] Even formulations of schizophrenia based on psychoanalytic principles have stressed frontal lobe function.[5]

In more recent theoretic discussions, it has been proposed that frontal lobe dysfunction, if not of primary pathogenic importance, may at least explain some of the clinical phenomena associated with schizophrenia.[6-9] For example, defect or so-called negative symptoms are similar to the impaired motivation, shallow affect, paucity of thought, and other features of frontal lobe disease.[10-14] The pattern of cognitive impairment in schizophrenia most consistently implicates the frontal lobes.[6,15-18] The same conclusion holds for the minor or "soft" neurologic signs often encountered in pa-

Daniel R. Weinberger, Karen Faith Berman, and Ronald F. Zec. Physiologic dysfunction of dorsolateral prefrontal cortex in schizophrenia. *Archives of General Psychiatry,* Vol. 43 (February 1986), pp. 114–124. Copyright © 1986, American Medical Association. Reprinted by Permission. (Because it is only meaningful if reproduced in color, Figure 3 of the original article is not reprinted here.)

tients with schizophrenia.[19-20] In addition, dysfunction in the frontal cortex has been proposed as an explanation for disordered smooth-pursuit eye tracking often seen in this illness.[21]

While these clinical observations and inferences are at most circumstantial evidence of frontal lobe dysfunction, findings from new techniques for directly studying regional brain physiology in living subjects are more provocative. Using radioactive xenon gas as a tracer of cerebral blood flow, a measure closely correlated with neuronal metabolism, Ingvar and Franzen[22-25] reported that medicated patients with schizophrenia failed to manifest the typical "hyperfrontal" pattern of regional cerebral blood flow (rCBF) seen in normal individuals. In spite of methodologic problems with these pioneering studies,[26] the investigators found an important correlation between blood flow pattern and clinical symptoms, in that patients who had the lowest frontal rCBF tended to be the most withdrawn, mute, and indifferent. Efforts to replicate these early rCBF studies using a noninvasive modification of the technique of Ingvar and Franzen have been inconsistent. While some reports have confirmed Ingvar and Franzen's observations,[27,28] others have not.[29,30] The results of positron emission tomography studies, which measure neuronal metabolism per se, have been as inconsistent as those of the rCBF studies.[31-35]

One explanation for the inconsistency of these results may involve the fact that patients were usually studied in what is called the "resting state." A problem with the resting state and with other conditions involving subjective, nonspecific stimulation is that the subject's mental experience and corresponding cerebral physiologic characteristics are poorly controlled and highly variable.[36-38] Thus, differences in rCBF during the resting state may be related to the subjective experience of having the test and not to abnormal cerebral physiologic features. Although two studies measured rCBF during prescribed cognitive activity,[24,30] neither attempted to control for those physiologic concomitants of the experience that were not specifically linked to the cognitive task.

Another possible reason for inconsistent results may involve a tendency to view the frontal lobe as a functionally homogeneous region. Thus, blood flow or glucose metabolism to the entire frontal lobe has been compared with posterior values[27-35] and not further differentiated into functional subdivisions. In some cases, this approach may have been dictated by limitations in the number of cortical areas surveyed.[27,29,30] Since the frontal lobe is a heterogeneous structure with respect to anatomy, physiology, and function,[10-13] it is reasonable to study discrete areas within the frontal lobe. The nonassociation cortex regions (eg, motor cortex, supplementary motor areas, and Broca's area) are of doubtful physiologic importance in schizophrenia, yet rCBF or metabolism in these areas may dilute differences in more relevant association cortex if the regions are lumped together. The problem is further complicated by the fact that even frontal association cortex is heterogeneous. Traditionally, it is differentiated into orbitomedial and dorsolateral aspects, based on anatomic and functional differences.[10-13] Recent neuroanatomic,[39,40] neurochemical,[40,41] and neuropharmacologic studies[42,43] suggest that this subdivision, though oversimplified, is valid and meaningful. It is also of potential importance in schizophrenia. The defect symptoms, pattern of cognitive impairment, and minor clinical signs are most suggestive of dysfunction of the dorsolateral aspect of prefrontal association cortex (DLPFC).[11,44-49] We attempted to evaluate rCBF and, by inference, neuronal metabolism in DLPFC during specific cognitive activation of this region, while controlling for the nonspecific physiological concomitants of the test procedure.

Subjects and Methods

Subjects

Twenty inpatients (15 men and five women) from the National Institute of Mental Health

(NIMH) research wards at St. Elizabeths Hospital, Washington, DC, volunteered and gave informed consent to participate in this study, which had the approval of both the institutional review board and the radiation safety committee. The patients fulfilled DSM-III criteria for chronic schizophrenia; for routine research purposes all medications were withdrawn and the patients remained medication free for a minimum of four weeks (range, four to six weeks) prior to the study. Research patients of the NIMH tend to be moderately to severely ill and to have shown an incomplete response to conventional treatment and require frequent institutional care. No patient with a history of alcohol or other drug abuse, brain injury, or diagnosable systemic or neurologic condition was included in the study.

The control sample consisted of 25 normal volunteers (16 men and nine women), 11 of whom were NIMH employees, while the remainder were paid respondents to an advertisement in the National Institutes of Health normal volunteer office. Control subjects who acknowledged a history of psychiatric, neurologic, or systemic illness with potential implications for cerebral blood flow (eg, hypertension, diabetes, and hyperlipidemia) were excluded.

There was no significant difference in age between patients (mean ± SEM, 28.9 ± 1.2 years) and controls (30.7 ± 1.7 years), or in handedness as assessed by preference for handwriting, various purposeful motor movements, and eye dominance. Moreover, the groups did not differ in height, weight, or mean resting blood pressure. The controls had completed significantly more years of school (16.8 ± 0.6 years; range, 12 to 20 years) than the patients had (12.5 ± 0.5 years; range, nine to 18 years) ($P < .0001$, t test, two-tailed).

rCBF Technique

The rCBF was determined by the noninvasive xenon Xe 133 inhalation technique developed by Obrist et al.[50] and modified by Deshmukh and Meyer[51] and Risberg.[52] Theoretic aspects and mathematics of this method have been described in detail.[53-55]

In the absence of a major disruption in cerebral autoregulation, blood flow to the cortex is determined primarily by neuronal metabolism.[56-59] Therefore, rCBF is a direct measure of cortical physiologic activity. In the present study, a measure of gray-matter rCBF, the initial slope (IS) of Obrist and Wilkinson[60] was used because this measure is relatively stable in pathologic conditions and at low count rates and because it may be particularly sensitive to changes related to cognitive activity.[61] The IS is an index (unitless) measure.

Our application of the ^{133}Xe inhalation rCBF technique involved several modifications of earlier studies. We used 32 head probes, radially arranged in 16 homologous pairs per hemisphere. Each subject's head was measured and marked to locate the F_{p1} and F_{p2} leads of the international 10–20 system of electroencephalographic electrode placement. These marks served as reproducible landmarks for applying the frontopolar head probes. To insure reproducible placement of the other probes, the inferior margin of the probe helmet was aligned parallel to the orbitomedial line. In our experience, most subjects found a snorkellike mouthpiece and a soft, foam nose clamp more comfortable and less threatening than the commonly used mask. More importantly, we found that this modification results in less gas leakage according to room radioactivity monitors and higher end-expiratory carbon dioxide partial pressure (P_{CO_2}). It is also better suited to the administration of activation procedures because there is minimal obstruction of the visual field, and since the nose is clamped, subjects do not smell the potentially disturbing odor of the plastic tubing in the gas delivery system. Patients were seated in a dentist's chair in a semireclining position (Fig. 1). This position may be more appropriate than a recumbent position for performing cognitive tasks.

FIGURE 1

Artist's schematized representation of subject undergoing xenon Xe 133 inhalation procedure for regional cerebral blood flow while taking automated version of Wisconsin Card Sort.

rCBF Test Conditions

Each subject underwent three separate rCBF determinations, each separated by approximately 40 minutes. Before beginning a determination, subjects were given approximately five minutes to become acclimated to the dimly lit room, the continuous low hum of computer fans and pump motors, and the feel of the chair, helmet, and mouthpiece.

Resting Condition. The first condition for each subject was always the resting state. Subjects were instructed to remain motionless, awake with eyes closed. Xenon inhalation began without the subjects' knowledge after several minutes of acclimation. This condition was not placed in counterbalanced sequence with the activation conditions because it was intended primarily as an opportunity for subjects to become at ease with the procedure before the more critical activation determinations.

Activation Conditions An important theoretic variable in this study was the selection of an activation procedure that would impose a specific physiologic load on the DLPFC. Although it is an oversimplification to assume that any cognitive task involves only a finely demarcated cortical region, in studies of patients with focal brain lesions, performance on the Wisconsin Card Sort (WCS) has shown a good correlation with DLPFC function.[45,48,49,62] Even within the frontal lobe itself, poor performance on the WCS correlates better with lesions of DLPFC than with lesions elsewhere. The WCS is an abstract reasoning, problem-solving test that involves achieving abstract sets, maintaining these sets, and then changing them. The test procedure and method for scoring are described in detail elsewhere.[62,63] It is unusual for normal individuals to have difficulty with this test, but patients with schizophrenia often have poor performance.[15-17] An automated version of the WCS was developed to suit the rCBF procedure. Instead of sorting cards, the subject responded to stimulus slides having the characteristic designs, which differed in color, shape, and number of elements. They were asked to match each stimulus to one of four switches labeled with the same designs and to determine how they were meant to make the match (ie, by color, number, or shape) on the basis of feedback (a green or red light) indicating whether each response was correct or incorrect (Fig 1). Once the correct rule for the match was discovered and a series of ten correct responses was made, the rule was changed without warning, and the subject was again required to determine the correct solution for the match. Responses were made with the right hand and a minimum of finger movement by pressing the appropriate switch. Before acclimation, the subject was read standard instructions for completing the test and given an opportunity to ask questions. Following the acclimation period, the subject began the test. Inhalation of ^{133}Xe began 90 s after the first response. The subject continued the WCS throughout the 12-minute data collection period. Gray-matter blood flow values in this study reflect primarily cortical activity approximately four to five minutes after beginning the WCS.

While some of the rCBF data acquired

during the WCS condition might reflect DLPFC function, other brain regions are undoubtedly affected by this test. For example, visual stimulation, eye scanning, and button pushing are likely to be associated with their own set of rCBF changes. Furthermore, the experience of taking a test in the blood flow laboratory environment might affect cortical metabolism. These aspects of the WCS condition were considered potentially serious impediments to data interpretation. We viewed them as "noise" that would be liable to obscure the "signal" relating to DLPFC physiologic characteristics.

For these theoretic reasons, we designed a control task, number matching (NM), as the third rCBF determination. This test was conceived as analogous to the blank in a biochemical assay. It was an effort to control for those physiologic aspects of the WCS condition that did not localize strongly to DLPFC, ie, the "noise" factors. The control task involved matching numbers from one to four that appeared on the identical view screen, having the same feedback lights at approximately the same frequency as the WCS stimuli, with similar numbers labeling the same response switches. For both tasks, stimulus presentation to the subject, the subject's indication or response, and the feedback were identical. To control for an order effect,[64–66] the WCS and NM conditions were administered in counterbalanced sequence from one subject to another.

Autonomic Arousal Measures

To assess a possible effect of nonspecific autonomic arousal on cortical blood flow, several arousal measures were monitored continuously during each procedure. A pulsimeter attached to the left ear and electrodes on the left hand permitted continuous polygraphic recording of pulse rate and skin conductance, respectively. Respiratory rate was taken from continuous capnographic recordings used to monitor end-expiratory P_{CO_2} concentration. For pulse and respiratory rate, the section of the recordings corresponding to the second to fourth min-

utes of the rCBF data collection period was isolated and a mean value taken as representative of that measure. We scored skin conductance from the same time period on a 0 to 4 scale. This scale was keyed to reference recordings showing deflections of increasing frequency and magnitude and was an attempt to simplify the traditional method of counting deflections while taking into account their magnitude. Autonomic arousal values were determined by an investigator who was unaware of the results of the rCBF data analysis. Due to occasional technical difficulty, each autonomic variable was not available for every study (see "Results" section).

rCBF Topographic Mapping

Each blood flow procedure resulted in rCBF values for 32 cortical regions. To present better a qualitative overview of the rCBF patterns and a visual orientation, we adapted a topographic mapping approach developed at the NIMH by Richard Coppola, PhD, and described in detail elsewhere.[67] This approach can be briefly summarized as follows. To determine x and y coordinates that defined the location of each head probe on a rectilinear grid of picture elements (pixels), we marked the probe locations on the heads of five individuals whose heads varied in size and shape. Using as references standard international 10–20 system electroencephalographic lead placements with predetermined x and y coordinates, mean head probe coordinates were established. Despite considerable differences in head size and shape, the SD of each coordinate was never greater than 10% of its mean. Figure 2 shows the approximate location of probes for the left hemisphere. Pixels between probes were then assigned blood flow values by computer based on a weighted interpolation of values from the four nearest probes. The results were keyed to a color scale for visual display. It should be emphasized that interpolated values (ie, those between probes) are used only for qualitative, pictorial representation. Statistical analyses are per-

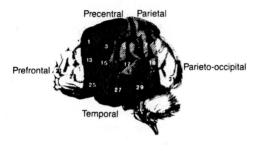

FIGURE 2

Location of left-hemisphere head probes and brain areas used for regional analyses. Homologous probe locations and regions for right hemisphere are not shown.

formed only on the actual values derived from the 32 clearance curves.

Statistical Analysis

The statistical analysis of rCBF data is complex and somewhat controversial.[55,68] Our approach was to analyze each condition separately, using multivariate analysis of variance (MANOVA) for across-group comparisons of multiple regions and univariate analysis of variance (ANOVA) for individual regions. Since the resting condition always came first and order may affect rCBF patterns,[64-66] the results of the resting condition were not compared with the results of the other conditions. Differences in visual stimulation, eye and hand movements, etc, would further compromise such a comparison. This approach best suits our main objective, to challenge DLPFC function specifically (ie, by WCS), with nonspecific activation (ie, by NM) as a baseline. All analyses were performed by computer using Statistical Analyses System Packages (SAS 82). General linear model routines were used for MANOVA and ANOVA.

Regional analysis. A straightforward approach to the data analysis is a group comparison of IS values in various brain regions per condition. To reduce the probability of MANOVA type II error and ANOVA type I error, the 32 probes were collapsed into five

functionally meaningful brain regions, shown in Fig 2. The mean of the probe values for each region determined the regional IS. Prefrontal region corresponded primarily to DLPFC, the region of primary theoretic interest in this study. The other frontal area, the precentral, is an interesting comparison region. It consists primarily of motor cortex, supplementary motor cortex, frontal eye fields, and Broca's area, regions less clearly implicated in schizophrenia. They may serve as a contrasting functional territory within the frontal lobe. The nonfrontal regions are additional reference areas to test a regional specificity hypothesis. Across-group analysis was done by MANOVA with regions as the multiple variables and by ANOVA for each region independently. Hemispheric analysis will be presented in a future report when a larger sample is available.

The regional across-group comparison of absolute rCBF values is complicated by the effect of blood P_{CO_2} concentrations on rCBF. Since rCBF varies directly with P_{CO_2},[69-71] differences in group rCBF comparisons may be an artifact of differences in ventilatory function. One approach to this problem has been to apply a correction factor routinely that will control for P_{CO_2} differences.[30,54,61] The magnitude of this factor, however, is controversial[69-71] and may depend on which measure of gray-matter flow is used.[54] Furthermore, while it is clear that acute changes in P_{CO_2} will significantly alter rCBF,[69-71] the importance of minor differences within the normal range that reflect chronic respiratory patterns is unclear. Group P_{CO_2} differences may represent not acute but chronic ventilatory patterns to which rCBF has adapted.[72] To further complicate this issue, P_{CO_2} levels measured in expired air may not always accurately reflect arterial P_{CO_2} because any leakage involved in gas delivery will result in lower P_{CO_2} values. In view of these considerations, the role of P_{CO_2} values in this study is uncertain and the interpretation of absolute rCBF data is difficult. Therefore, we have chosen to deemphasize absolute rCBF comparisons in favor of the ratio and change score approaches detailed below. For completeness, we present the results of regional comparisons of absolute rCBF data, correcting for P_{CO_2} only when P_{CO_2} was outside the range of standard laboratory values (>45 mm Hg), ie, a result not attributable to leakage or normal ventilatory function. When P_{CO_2} correction was performed, a 3% correction factor was used (ie, a change of 1 mm Hg in P_{CO_2} was equal to a 3% change in IS).[30]

Relative Distribution Analysis. Another approach to the analysis of rCBF data is to normalize regional values to a reference value for each brain.[52] Since P_{CO_2} affects whole-brain blood flow but does not appear to alter regional patterns,[70] P_{CO_2} is not a factor in this approach. In our analysis we derived two indexes consistent with our effort to test regional specificity within the frontal cortex. The prefrontal index (PFI) is a ratio of prefrontal regional flow (ie, in the DLPFC) to nonfrontal flow. The precentral index (PCI) corresponds to precentral regional flow divided by the same denominator, nonfrontal flow. These are measures of *relative* distribution of flow. Across-group comparisons per condition were done by ANOVA for each index.

Change Score Analysis. Because the NM condition was created as a control for the non-DLPFC aspects of the WCS condition, the analysis with the greatest potential for regional specialization is one that determines where these two tasks differ ("change score analysis"). Provided there are no within-group significant differences in P_{CO_2} between WCS and NM (which there were not, vide infra), the NM values can be subtracted from the WCS values for each region, for each subject. In other words, the WCS values can be "zeroed" with the NM results, highlighting the rCBF changes related to the WCS. Across-group regional comparisons of absolute IS change values by MANOVA and individual regions by ANOVA were performed. This approach is the crux of this study. It allows direct, nonratio comparisons and is not vulnerable to P_{CO_2} effects. In theory, it should have an advantageous signal-to-noise ratio for demonstrating a relationship between rCBF changes and cognitive function. In addition, the regional change scores were converted into prefrontal and precentral index percentage change scores, and an analysis of the *relative* distributional changes was performed by ANOVA.

Results
Resting State

Visual orientation maps of IS values [showed] that the overall rCBF patterns were not strikingly different in the resting state. One normal resting study had to be excluded due to technically poor data. Mean (±SEM) whole-brain gray-matter blood flow did not differ significantly between patients (71.5 ± 3.1) and controls (77.4 ± 2.5). There was a significant difference in respiratory rate and end-expiratory P_{CO_2} values (patients, 43.4 ± 1.2 mm Hg; controls, 47.3 ± 0.8 mm Hg; $P < .01$). Whether this group difference represents acute or chronic differences in respiratory patterns is unknown, but the P_{CO_2} levels suggest that breathing was atypical, and that hypoventilation occurred, especially in controls. Correcting IS values for P_{CO_2} difference did not affect the whole-brain blood flow comparison. It did, however, affect the regional analysis. For P_{CO_2} uncorrected data, the overall regional analysis (by MANOVA) was significant (Wilks' $\lambda = .72$, $F[5,38] = 2.95$, $P = .02$), and univariate ANOVA disclosed significantly lower rCBF in the patients only in the prefrontal region ($F = 4.5$, $P < .04$). Neither of these differences held following P_{CO_2} correction.

The results of the P_{CO_2} independent relative distribution analyses are shown in Fig. 3. While the PFI was significantly lower in patients, the PCI did not differ. These data suggest a subtle "resting" difference that appears to be limited to prefrontal cortex.

Activation States

Regional Analysis. While the overall rCBF pattern appeared similar for the NM condition, a dramatic qualitative difference was

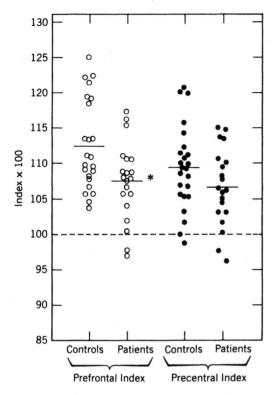

FIGURE 3
Regional indexes in resting state. Horizontal bars represent means. Asterisk indicates $F =$ 7.51, $P < .01$ by analysis of variance.

seen with the WCS. . . . Mean whole-brain IS values did not differ between groups on either condition. For patients IS was 76.1 ± 3.4 on the NM and 74.4 ± 3.2 on the WCS; for controls it was 77.3 ± 2.5 on the NM and 79.5 ± 2.2 on the WCS. In the NM condition, despite an overall difference in the regional analysis, no individual region stood out as different (Fig. 4, top). In contrast, during the WCS an overall difference and lower flow localized to both frontal regions characterized the patient group (Fig. 4, bottom). There were no group mean differences in baseline NM regional data; however, multivariate analysis of covariance (MANCOVA), covarying for initial NM IS values, strengthened the prefrontal group difference during WCS ($F[6,44] = 6.81$, $P = .01$). Mean P_{CO_2} values for both groups were within the normal range during both con-

ditions and did not differ across conditions within either group (Table 1).

Relative Distribution Analysis. The PFI values were similar during NM but differed significantly during WCS (Fig. 5). This difference appears to represent a failure of the PFI to increase in patients in WCS as compared with NM, an increase that was significant within the control group itself ($P = .02$). There were no significant group differences in PCI in either NM or WCS. Unlike PFI, PCI did not change in WCS as com-

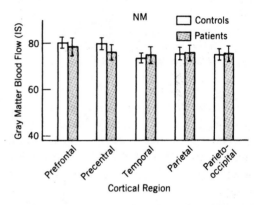

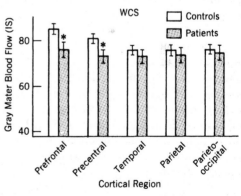

FIGURE 4
Regional analysis (mean ± SEM). IS represents initial slope. Top, Number matching (NM) condition. Wilks' $\lambda = 0.73$, $F(5, 39) = 2.69$, $P < .03$ by multivariate analysis of variance; individual regions not significant by univariate analysis of variance. Bottom, Wisconsin Card Sort (WCS) condition. Wilks' $\lambda = 0.44$, $F(5, 39) = 9.99$, $P < .0001$ by multivariate analysis of variance. Asterisk indicates prefrontal $F = 4.77$, $P = .03$, and precentral $F = 4.5$, $P < .04$ by univariate analysis of variance.

TABLE 1 Autonomic Variables in Medication-Free Wisconsin Card Sort (WCS) Study*

	Pco$_2$, mm Hg	Respirations/ min	Pulse, Beats/min	GSR (Scale Units)
Patients				
NM	39.9 ± 1.4	16.3 ± 0.9	85.6 ± 4.3 (N = 18)	2.9 ± 0.3 (N = 15)
WCS	41.2 ± 1.4	15.9 ± 1.0	84.5 ± 3.1 (N = 19)	2.8 ± 0.3 (N = 14)
Controls				
NM	45.0 ± 0.7	13.7 ± 0.7	67.4 ± 2.6 (N = 18)	2.1 ± 0.3 (N = 18)
WCS	44.1 ± 0.7	13.9 ± 0.07 (N = 24)	70.0 ± 2.2 (N = 18)	2.7 ± 0.3 (N = 18)

*Values are given as mean ± SEM. NM represents number matching; Pco$_2$, carbon dioxide partial pressure; and GSR, galvanic skin response. All across-group comparisons were significant ($P <$ .05, t test) except GSR during WCS. All within-group comparisons were not significant.

pared with NM within controls. These results suggest that in normal subjects, WCS produced an increase in relative flow that was localized within the frontal cortex to the DLPFC.

Change Score Analysis. Overall regional analysis for the IS change scores missed significance, but prefrontal change scores were significantly different (Table 2). Index percentage change score analysis disclosed clear differences in PFI with no differences in PCI (Fig. 6). The change score data emphasize that, compared with NM, WCS involved an increase in DLPFC blood flow in controls but not in patients. Indeed, patients appear to show the opposite trend in that mean rCBF actually decreased.

Autonomic Variables. Table 1 gives the results of the autonomic arousal variables. It is apparent that in every condition patients were at least as aroused as controls and usually more so. Furthermore, arousal measures did not differ significantly across activation conditions within each group.

WCS Performance and rCBF Correlations. On the WCS, patients made many more perseverative errors and achieved a

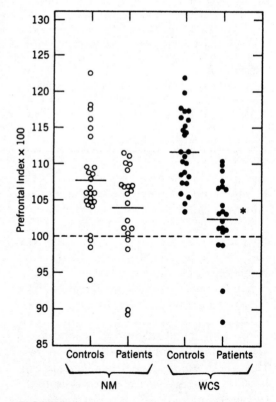

FIGURE 5

Prefrontal index during activation conditions. NM represents number matching; WCS, Wisconsin Card Sort. Asterisk indicates $F = 36.6$, $P < .0001$ by analysis of variance.

TABLE 2 Gray-Matter Blood Flow Change Values (WCS–NM)*

Region	Blood flow Change		ANOVA	
	Controls	Patients	F	P
Prefrontal	4.99 ± 1.7	− 2.31 ± 2.8	5.37	.025
Precentral	1.34 ± 1.4	− 2.50 ± 2.1	2.51	.12
Temporal	2.79 ± 1.7	− 1.44 ± 2.6	2.01	.16
Parietal	1.03 ± 1.3	− 1.53 ± 2.2	1.08	.31
Parieto-occipital	1.98 ± 1.5	0.21 ± 2.2	0.47	.5

*WCS represents Wisconsin Card Sort; NM, number matching; and ANOVA, analysis of variance. Wilks' λ = .81, $F(5,39)$ = 1.84, P = .13 by multivariate analysis of variance.

lower conceptual level than did controls (Table 3). In controls, while prefrontal index percentage change appeared to correlate positively (Pearson's r = .44, $P <$ .03) (Fig. 7) with percentage of perseverative error (ie, negatively with performance), this effect was determined by one outlier. When this outlier was excluded, the correlation disappeared (r = .04, $P <$ .8). In the patients a positive relationship between performance and DLPFC rCBF was found for both perseverative error (Fig. 7) and conceptual level (r = .47, $P <$ .04), a WCS score that varies inversely with perseverative error. This suggests that patients' performance was determined by how effectively they could activate DLPFC. Neither PFI percentage change nor any WCS performance measure correlated with years of education for either group. Also, PFI percentage change did not correlate with the number of responses made.

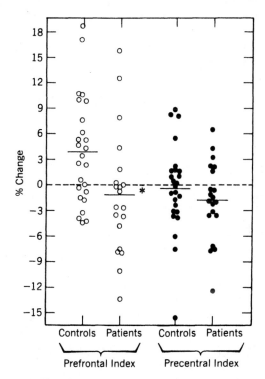

FIGURE 6

Percentage change in regional indexes: [(WCS-NM)/NM] × 100; WCS represents Wisconsin Card Sort, and NM, number matching. Asterisk indicates F = 6.35, $P <$ .02 by analysis of variance.

Comment

The results of this study suggest that patients with schizophrenia have a physiologic dysfunction of a specific region of the frontal lobe, the DLPFC, and that this pathophysiologic feature is linked to a particular manner of cognitive impairment often seen in this illness. In contrast to normal controls, patients did not have increased rCBF to this region while performing the WCS, a cognitive task that appears to be selective for DLPFC function. While a behavioral (ie, test performance) deficit together with a metabolic deficiency specific to the region critical for the behavior suggests such a clinical-pathophysiologic relationship, a number of issues must be considered in interpreting these results.

Before considering alternative interpre-

TABLE 3 Wisconsin Card Sort Performance Results

	Patients*	Controls
No. of categories correctly completed	1.5 ± 0.4	7.6 ± 0.5
% conceptual level	31.4 ± 5.5	79.2 ± 2.9
% perseverative error	27.4 ± 3.8	8.6 ± 1.0

*All comparisons, $P < .001$, t test.

tations of the data, several points will be reviewed. Differences in rCBF between patients and controls were consistently and almost exclusively confined to DLPFC. Whole-brain blood flow, as reported by Kety et al[73] more than 35 years ago and by Ingvar and Franzen[22-25] and others,[28-30] did not differ significantly between groups in either the resting state or the activation conditions. This finding conflicts with two recent rCBF studies[27,29] that found significantly lower whole-brain blood flow in the resting state in patients with schizophrenia. One possible explanation for the inconsistency is that neither of these two studies corrected for P_{CO_2}, a factor that can affect blood flow. As discussed above, however, the approach to

P_{CO_2} in inhalation rCBF studies is complex. To avoid the P_{CO_2} issue, the data analysis in our study emphasized relative rCBF distribution ratios and regional change values, using rCBF during the NM control task as a baseline against which the WCS rCBF was compared. The use of a baseline nonspecific activation task was an attempt to control for individual and/or group idiosyncracies and for those aspects of the rCBF experience not primarily related to the cognitive processing involved in the WCS, ie, non-specific activation factors such as anxiety, motor responses, visual stimulation, and eye scanning, and the subjective experience of undergoing the procedure. The results of both the rCBF relative distribution and the

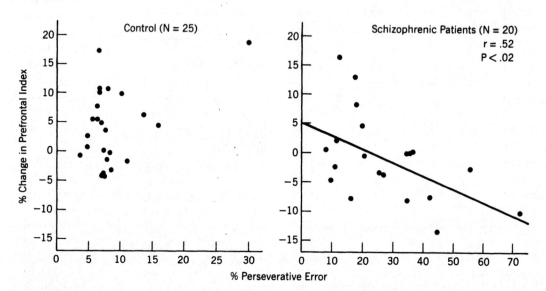

FIGURE 7
Correlation between regional cerebral blood flow and Wisconsin Card Sort performance for percentage change in prefrontal index. Pearson's product-moment correlation is shown.

change score analyses consistently singled out DLPFC as the only region differentiating patients from controls. This finding is strengthened by the observation that the precentral region, a functionally separate frontal area adjacent to DLPFC, did not differentiate patients from controls in these analyses.

Compared with the WCS activation condition, the resting state and the NM control task provided less clear evidence of between-group regional physiologic differences. Still, during resting, DLPFC flow as a ratio of nonfrontal flow (PFI) was lower in patients, but relative precentral flow (PCI) was not. In previous studies that did not find decreased relative frontal flow or metabolism in patients at rest, a separate analysis of DLPFC might have been productive. Nevertheless, interpretation of rCBF data during resting is problematic because of the poorly defined nature of the state.

Neither absolute nor relative DLPFC flow (PFI) differed between patients and controls during the NM task. Consistent with earlier studies,[29,30] patients with schizophrenia did not have reduced relative DLPFC blood flow under all conditions. Metabolism in the DLPFC during the NM task and other states not keyed to DLPFC function may be related to general frontal activity that is not task specific,[54,74,75] in contrast to the WCS state. Perhaps, since little DLPFC function is needed during NM, patients can meet the minimal demand. If the DLPFC deficit is subtle, as it appears to be, it should become more apparent when there is a specific physiologic load placed on DLPFC. This scenario appears to unfold during the WCS. When patients attempt the WCS, DLPFC metabolism fails to increase, a clear departure from the normal response. It is tempting to conclude that the demand for DLPFC function involved in the WCS exceeds the patients' capacity to activate the region. This would explain their poor performance on the test. The positive correlation between PFI and WCS performance in the patients is theoretically consistent with this assumption.

The Role of State Factors and Epiphenomena

While it is tempting to view these data as evidence of a regionally specific dysfunction of brain physiology related to schizophrenia, a number of other possible explanations for the findings must be considered. Alternative interpretations center around issues of patient interest, motivation, medication state, arousal, attention, and effort. Despite the use of a baseline control task, the results may still reflect differences in the subjective experience of undergoing the WCS procedure rather than pathophysiologic features. For example, it is possible that the patients were less interested in the test. Perhaps they were not trying as hard as they could or were unmotivated.[76] We have attempted to consider these possibilities and others through a variety of approaches. During each procedure an investigator observed the behavior of each patient. This investigator believed that patients were indeed involved and applying themselves to the task. The pattern of WCS errors (Table 3) is typical of those seen in patients having DLPFC lesions[48,62] and is not suggestive of random, disinterested responses. Furthermore, the correlations between PFI and WCS performance indicate that the changes in DLPFC relative flow were linked to performing the experimental task. After completing the procedure, patients were asked to explain what was required of them. In almost all cases they understood the instructions and seemed to appreciate the need for making abstract choices. In a manner similar to that described in patients with DLPFC pathologic changes,[48,62] the patients with schizophrenia had difficultly following through with this information.

Several investigators have considered arousal to be a critical variable in frontal blood flow.[54,74,75] However, differences in simple autonomic arousal do not seem to explain the WCS rCBF data. As Table 1 shows, measures of autonomic arousal were at least as great in patients as in controls during the WCS. Furthermore, no significant differences in arousal measures existed within either group in performing the WCS as compared with NM. State variables linked to medication status also did not appear to be major determinants of the findings, since in a companion study of medicated patients undergoing a similar WCS paradigm, the basic DLPFC differences between patients and controls persisted.[77]

One of the most difficult variables to assess in interpreting the data is attention. Disturbances of attention have been associated with both schizophrenia and pathologic changes in the DLPFC. If reduced flow to DLPFC is an epiphenomenon of inattention, similar findings in schizophrenia might be expected with any task in which attention is a critical variable. The negative results of our companion study of rCBF during two levels of a visual continuous performance task do not support this possibility.[77] Simply failing to perform well or to maintain attention up to normal standards does not appear to explain the WCS blood flow data.

Another possible explanation is that DLPFC rCBF is reduced in schizophrenia as a direct result not of impaired physiologic state but of impaired performance. This is, in essence, a variation on the chicken-vs-egg argument. According to this explanation, if the patients had performed better they would have shown more DLPFC flow. The obverse of this is that similar findings would be expected in any population who failed at the WCS. In a methodologically similar study of patients with Huntington's disease, an illness characterized by frontal lobe-type cognitive deficits probably based on pathologic changes in the caudate, DLPFC rCBF was normal despite very poor WCS performance.[78] It seems that poor performance alone is not sufficient reason for failure to activate DLPFC.

One of the more interesting findings in this study is the rCBF-performance correlations. In the controls, blood flow and performance did not correlate in a convincing manner. Since most controls had little difficulty with this task, they probably were not stressing their DLPFC functional "reserve."

In contrast, in the patients with schizophrenia, DLPFC rCBF and WCS performance showed a significant positive correlation. The more DLPFC was activated, the better patients performed. This correlation could be used to support either side of the chicken-vs-egg argument. While it suggests that patients performed only as well as their physiologic impairment allowed, it might mean that rCBF and performance were secondarily linked to another factor, such as effort, which varied for nonphysiologic reasons. Mental effort, whether purposeful or unconscious, is a particularly difficult variable to evaluate. Although it is possible that DLPFC activation is simply a function of nonspecific mental effort, which patients failed to apply during the WCS, the negative results of the continuous performance task experiment[77] suggest that nonspecific effort is not the determining factor. We are currently attempting to resolve further the role of effort with an analogous rCBF study using Raven's Progressive Matrices, a cognitive task that is more demanding but less specific for DLPFC function than is the WCS. In our experience with this task, a DLPFC deficit was not found.

Finally, it should be noted that because the rCBF method used is two dimensional and oriented around the cortical convexities, rCBF to other cortical surfaces (eg, orbital and medial) and subcortical structures (eg, thalamus and basal ganglia) could not be determined. These regions may play a modulatory role in DLPFC function or may be affected by DLPFC dysfunction. It would be of considerable interest to study DLPFC and subcortical structures simultaneously in a similar experiment using three-dimensional techniques such as single-photon-emission computed tomography and positron emission tomography.

DLPFC and Schizophrenia

The DLPFC is a highly evolved, unique region of human neocortex, about which detailed information has been accumulating steadily in the last decade. Virtually nonexistent in subprimate species, DLPFC serves perhaps more clearly than anything else as a hallmark of the human brain. Nevertheless, it is an uncommon site for focal pathologic changes. Classic notions about frontal lobe disease and personality changes such as "pseudopsychopathic" behavior, affective lability, and social disinhibition[4,11,14,79] are based on experience with lesions of orbitomedial cortex, a region much more frequently damaged by tumor, aneurysm, infarction, and psychosurgery.

The DLPFC is the last brain region to complete myelination, doing so primarily in the second and third decades of life. According to Yakovlev and LeCours,[80] it may continue to myelinate throughout life, suggesting a unique capacity for functional plasticity. The DLPFC has complex anatomic connections with virtually every lobe of the brain and every type of association cortex.[12,81] The DLPFC receives and sends projections to limbic, diencephalic, and mesencephalic nucleii important in the regulation of behavior. Recent experiments in monkeys indicated that there are unique and intriguing aspects to the subcortical connections of DLPFC.[39-41,82] For example, it is the only cortical region with direct projections to locus ceruleus and raphe nucleii,[40] suggesting that it can directly control its own noradrenergic and serotonergic input. Unlike orbitomedial frontal cortex, DLPFC receives dopaminergic and noradrenergic projections that do not ascend via the medial forebrain bundle pathways.[39-41] In fact, in addition to classic mesocortical dopamine projections from ventral tegmental area, DLPFC receives dopamine projections from substantia nigra,[39] a structure usually thought of in terms of subcortical dopamine systems.

The most frequent cause of pathologic changes confined to DLPFC is traumatic brain injury. Such patients show subtle changes in cognition and behavior.[11,44,83] These changes include flat affect, social withdrawal and ineffectiveness, impairment in goal-directed behaviors, poor motivation, diminished work capacity, inattentiveness, poor concentration, behavior dominated by here-and-now needs, a sense of psychic anergia, poor insight, diminished concern for personal hygiene, and an overall restriction in behavioral spontaneity. These changes are similar to what have been called the defect symptoms of schizophrenia. Patients with DLPFC pathologic changes also show slight reductions in IQ and difficulty with problem-solving cognitive tests such as the WCS.[13,45] This pattern of cognitive deficit is also similar to that seen in patients with schizophrenia.[16-18]

The results of the present study suggest that some patients with schizophrenia show this pattern of behavioral and cognitive impairment because they have a diminished capacity to increase DLPFC metabolism when there is specific need for it. It is apparent from the data that every patient does not demonstrate this physiologic finding, or at least that some show it more than others. This may correspond to the variability of defect and cognitive symptoms in schizophrenia. Future studies will examine the clinical implications of absent DLPFC activation.

Finally, assuming that the physiologic finding reflects brain disease, where is the lesion and how does it relate to other aspects of schizophrenia? Evidence from recent animal research suggests that a subtle structural lesion of the frontal lobes affecting its dopaminergic innervation could explain the findings of this study as well as many of the clinical and research aspects of schizophrenia. In monkeys, ablation of DLPFC produces selective and persistent cognitive deficits best demonstrated during delayed response tasks.[84] These tasks are animal models for human tests such as the WCS. The ability to perform delayed-response tasks involves fundamental processes in learning and cognition that include appreciation of time, sequence, and past experience. In the adult monkey, this ability depends on an intact DLPFC. More specifically, it appears to depend on intact dopaminergic innervation of DLPFC. Selective destruction of dopamine terminals in DLPFC by 6-hydroxydopamine results in delayed-response test deficits almost as severe as those caused by surgical ablation.[42] While destruction of dopamine cell bodies in ventral tegmental area also removes dopamine afferents to DLPFC and results in frontal cognitive deficits,[85] the behavioral effects of ventral tegmental area lesions tend to be more extreme than those of lesions confined to the DLPFC. It is tempting to propose that those symptoms of schizophrenia reminiscent of DLPFC dysfunction result from a subtle lesion in or near DLPFC that affects or is confined to its dopamine innervation.

Recent evidence of structural central nervous system pathologic changes in schizophrenia is consistent with the concept of a DLPFC lesion. Subtle frontal cortical atrophy has been reported in computed tomographic studies.[8,86] Pathologic changes in prefrontal cortex, particularly occurring during early development, may result in secondary structural changes in limbic and diencephalic nucleii,[84] because prefrontal cortex is anatomically linked with these regions. Postmortem findings of nonspecific degeneration[87] and/or atrophy[88] in periventricular limbic-diencephalic nucleii of schizophrenic brains are consistent with this possibility. Computed tomographic findings of ventricular enlargement are also explainable on this basis.[8] However, an equally intriguing possibility is that subcortical neuropathologic changes represent the primary abnormality and cortical atrophy and DLPFC dysfunction are secondary.[8] In other words, the lesion may be "upstream" from the DLPFC, involving dopamine as well as other projections from subcortical periventricular nucleii. The observation that DLPFC metabolism is not abnormal under all conditions but fails to "switch on" during specific cognitive demand may support this possibility.

While a link between the defect or "negative" features of schizophrenia and DLPFC pathologic changes might have been expected on intuitive grounds, it is a distinct departure to consider that the "positive" symptoms (ie, perceptual distortions, hallucinations, etc) also might be due to DLPFC pathologic features. Positive symptoms have traditionally been related to subcortical do-

pamine hyperactivity. This is consistent with the notion that the antipsychotic effects of neuroleptic drugs are based on their ability to block nigrostriatal and mesolimbic dopamine receptors.[89] In a recent experiment, Pycock et al[90] showed that 6-hydroxydopamine lesions of prefrontal cortex in the rat produced disinhibition of subcortical dopaminergic systems. They found an unusual pattern of both presynaptic and postsynaptic dopamine hyperactivity in nucleus accumbens and striatum, findings analogous to those described in some postmortem studies of patients with schizophrenia.[91] The findings of Pycock et al are consistent with those of Gunne et al,[92] who reported mesolimbic dopamine behavioral supersensitivity following prefrontal lesions.

This hypothetical condition of prefrontal cortical hypoactivity and limbic dopamine hyperactivity caused by a prefrontal cortical deafferentation lesion might also explain some aspects of the course and treatment of schizophrenia. For example, it might explain why neuroleptic medication typically produces greater improvement in positive than in defect symptoms.[93] It also might explain why defect symptoms tend to become more prominent with advancing age while the opposite tends to happen with positive symptoms. Since dopamine content in prefrontal cortex diminishes with age,[94] this could exaggerate the effects of an existing DLPFC lesion and increase defect symptoms. In similar fashion, subcortical dopamine receptor activity appears to regress with age,[95] and this may counteract the effect of the putative cortical lesion, leading to a reduction in positive symptoms.

The DLPFC lesion hypothesis may even shed light on one of the most physiologically mysterious aspects of schizophrenia—its tendency to appear in late adolescence. In monkeys, a perinatal DLPFC lesion does not impair performance on delayed response tasks until after sexual maturity.[96] This is analogous to what occurs with many congenital neurologic lesions (eg, seizure disorders and cerebral palsy), the clinical manifestations of which appear or change with maturation as the affected neural system comes "on line."

One uncertainty about this hypothesis is that it is not known whether a DLPFC lesion in primates causes subcortical dopamine disinhibition. If it does, will this subcortical change also become clinically apparent at sexual maturity, as is the case with the cortical deficit? These are important questions for further investigation. In humans, careful examination of DLPFC structure and neurochemistry in postmortem brain specimens is needed. The hypothesis of DLPFC hypoactivity as related to subcortical dopamine hyperactivity might be testable during life using positron emission tomography and several different ligands either simultaneously or in sequence. These research observations concerning DLPFC, in addition to addressing many clinical and biologic features of schizophrenia, may even explain in physiologic terms the psychodynamic formulation that schizophrenia involves inadequate ego defenses (ie, DLPFC deficit) in the face of overwhelming instinctual forces (ie, subcortical dopamine disinhibition).

References

1. ALZHEIMER A: Beitrage zur pathologischen Anatomie der Dementia Praecox. *Allgemeine Z Psychiatrie* 1913;70:810–812.

2. KRAEPELIN E: *Dementia Praecox and Paraphenia.* New York, RE Krieger Co, 1971, pp. 218–220.

3. BLEULER E: *Dementia Praecox or the Group of Schizophrenias.* New York, New York International Press, 1950, p. 467.

4. GREENBLATT M., SOLOMON HC: Concerning a theory of frontal lobe functioning, in GREENBLATT M, SOLOMON HC (eds): *Frontal Lobes and Schizophrenia.* New York, Springer Verlag, 1953, pp. 391–413.

5. PARFITT DN: The neurology of schizophrenia. *J Ment Sci* 1956, 102:671–718.

6. SEIDMAN LJ: Schizophrenia and brain dysfunction: An integration of recent neurodiagnostic findings. *Psychol Bull* 1983;94:195–238.

7. LEVIN S: Frontal lobe dysfunctions in schizophrenia: II. Impairments of psychological and brain functions. *J Psychiatr Res* 1984;18:57–72.

8. WEINBERGER DR: CAT scan findings in schizophrenia: Speculation on the meaning of it all. *J Psychiatr Res* 1984;18:477–490.

9. WEINBERGER DR: Clinical neuropathological correlations in schizophrenia: Theoretical implications, in ALPERT M (ed): *Controversies in Schizophrenia.* New York, Guilford Press, 1985; 92–106.

10. WARREN JM, AKERT K (eds): *The Frontal Granular Cortex and Behavior.* New York, McGraw-Hill Book Co, 1963.

11. LURIA AR: *Higher Cortical Functions in Man.* New York, Basic Books Inc, 1980.

12. FUSTER J: *The Prefrontal Cortex.* New York, Raven Press, 1980.

13. STUSS DT, BENSON, DF: Neuropsychological studies of the frontal lobes. *Psychol Bull* 1984;95:3–28.

14. HECAEN H, ALBERT ML: Disorders of mental functioning unrelated to frontal lobe pathology, in BENSON DF, BLUMER D (eds): *Psychiatric Aspects of Neurologic Disease.* New York, Grune & Stratton, 1975, pp. 137–149.

15. MALMO HP: On frontal lobe functions: Psychiatric patient controls. *Cortex* 1974;10:231–237.

16. KOLB B, WHISMAN IQ: Performance of schizophrenic patients on tests sensitive to left or right frontal temporal parietal function in neurological patients. *J Nerv Ment Dis* 1983;171:435–443.

17. TAYLOR MA, ABRAMS R: Cognitive impairment in schizophrenia. *Am J Psychiatry* 1984; 141:196–201.

18. LAWSON WB, WALDMAN IN, WEINBERGER DR: Schizophrenic dementia: Results of neuropsychological testing and clinical correlates. *J Clin Psychiatry,* in press.

19. QUITKIN F, RIFKIN A, KLEIN D: Neurologic soft signs in schizophrenia and character disorders. *Arch Gen Psychiatry* 1976;33:845–853.

20. WEINBERGER DR, WYATT RJ: Cerebral ventricular size: A biological marker for subtyping chronic schizophrenia, in USDIN E, HANIN I (eds): *Biological Markers in Psychiatry and Neurology.* New York, Pergamon Press, 1982, pp. 505–512.

21. MIALET JP, PICHOT P: Eye tracking patterns in schizophrenia. *Arch Gen Psychiatry* 1981; 38:183–186.

22. INGVAR DH, FRANZEN G: Distribution of cerebral activity in chronic schizophrenia. *Lancet* 1974;2:1484–1486.

23. INGVAR DH, FRANZEN G: Abnormalities of cerebral blood flow distribution in patients with chronic schizophrenia. *Acta Psychiatr Scand* 1974; 50:425–462,

24. FRANZEN G, INGVAR DH: Absence of activation in frontal structures during psychological testing of chronic schizophrenics. *J Neurol Neurosurg Psychiatry* 1975;38:1027–1032.

25. FRANZEN G, INGVAR DH: Abnormal distribution of cerebral activity in chronic schizophrenia. *J Psychiatr Res* 1975;12:199–214.

26. BERMAN KF, WEINBERGER DR, MORIHISA JM, ZEC RF: Xenon[133] inhalation regional cerebral blood flow: Application to psychiatric research, in MORIHISA JM (ed): *Brain Imaging in Psychiatry*. Washington, DC, American Psychiatric Association, 1984, pp. 41–64.

27. ARIEL RN, GOLDEN CJ, BERG RA, QUAIFE MA, DIRKSEN JW, FORSELL T, WILSON J, GRABER B: Regional cerebral blood flow in schizophrenia with the 133-xenon inhalation method. *Arch Gen Psychiatry* 1983;40:258–263.

28. MUBRIN A, KREZEVIC S, KORETIC D, LAZIC L, JAVARNIK N: Regional cerebral blood flow patterns in schizophrenic patients. *rCBF Bull* 1982; 3:43–46.

29. MATHEW RJ, DUNCAN GC, WEINMAN ML, BARR DL: Regional cerebral blood flow in schizophrenia. *Arch Gen Psychiatry* 1982;39:1121–1124.

30. GUR RE, SKOLNICK BE, GUR RC, CAROFF S, RIEGER W, OBRIST WD, YOUNKIN D, REIVICH M: Brain functions in psychiatric disorder: I. Regional cerebral blood flow in medicated schizophrenics. *Arch Gen Psychiatry* 1983;40:1250–1254.

31. BUCHSBAUM MS, INGVAR DH, KESSLER R, WATERS RN, CAPPELLETTI J, VAN KAMMEN DP, KING AC, JOHNSON JL, MANNING RG, FLYNN RN, MANN LS, BUNNEY WE, SOKOLOFF L: Cerebral glucography with positron tomography. *Arch Gen Psychiatry* 1982;39:251–259.

32. SHEPPHARD G, GRUZELIER J, MANCHANDA R, HIRSCH SR, WISE R, FRACKOWIAK R, JONES T: [15]O positron emission tomography scanning in predominantly never treated acute schizophrenic patients. *Lancet* 1983;2:1448–1452.

33. WIDEN L, BLOMGRIST G, DE PAULIS T, EHRIN E, ERIKSSON L, FARDE L, GREITZ T, HEDSTROM CG, INGVAR DH, LITTON JE, NILSSON JLG, OGREN SO, SEDVALL G, STONE-ELANDER S, WIESEL F-A, WIK G: Studies of schizophrenia with positron CT. *J Clin Neuropharmacol* 1984;7 (suppl 1):538–539.

34. FARCHAS T, WOLF AP, JEAGER J, BRODIE JD, CHRISTMAN DR, FOWLER JS: Regional brain glucose metabolism in chronic schizophrenia. *Arch Gen Psychiatry* 1984;41:293–300.

35. BUCHSBAUM MS, DELISI LE, HOLCOMB HH, CAPPELLETTI J, KING AC, JOHNSON J, HAZLETT E, DOWLING-ZIMMERMAN S, POST RM, MORIHISA J, CARPENTER W, COHEN R, PICKAR D, WEINBERGER DR, MARGOLIN R, KESSLER RM: Anteroposterior gradients in cerebral glucose use in schizophrenia and affective disorders. *Arch Gen Psychiatry* 1984;41:1159–1166.

36. DUARA R, BARKER W, APICELLA A, CHANG J, SIEGAL C, FINN R, GILSON A: Resting cerebral glucose metabolism: Intraindividual versus interindividual variability in young and elderly subjects, abstracted. *Neurology* 1985;35 (suppl 1):138.

37. DUARA R, SEVUSH S, GROSS-GLENN K, CHANG J, BARKER W, APICELLA A, GILSON A, FINN R: Intraindividual reliability of cerebral glucose metabolism in the resting state and during psychological activation, abstracted. *Neurology* 1985;35 (suppl 1):138.

38. LASSEN NA, ROLAND PE: Localization of cognitive function with cerebral blood flow, in KERTESZ A (ed): *Localization in Neuropsychology*. New York, Academic Press Inc, 1983, pp 141–152.

39. PORRINO LJ, GOLDMAN-RAKIC PS: Brainstem innervation of prefrontal and anterior cingulate cortex in the rhesus monkey revealed by retrograde transport of HRP. *J Comp Neurol* 1982; 205:63–76.

40. ARNSTEIN AFT, GOLDMAN-RAKIC PS: Selective prefrontal cortical projections to the region of the locus coeruleus and raphe nucleii in the rhesus monkey. *Brain Res* 1984;306:9–18.

41. MORRISON JH, MOLLIVER ME, GRZANNA R: Noradrenergic innervation of cerebral cortex: Widespread effects of cortical lesions. *Science* 1979;205:313–316.

42. BROZOSKI TJ, BROWN RM, ROSVOLD HE, GOLDMAN PS: Cognitive deficit caused by regional depletion of dopamine in prefrontal cortex of rhesus monkey. *Science* 1979;205:929–932.

43. BANYON MJ, WOLF ME, ROTH RH: Pharmacology of dopamine neurons innervating the prefrontal cingulate piriform cortices. *Eur J Pharmacol*, 1983;91:119–125.

44. KRETSCHMER E: Lokalisation und Beurteilung psychophysischer Syndrome bei Hirnverletzten, in REHWALD E (ed): *Das Hirntrauma*. Stuttgart, West Germany, Georg Thieme Verlag, 1956, pp 155–158.

45. STUSS DT, BENSON DF: Frontal lobe lesions and behavior, in KERTESZ A (ed): *Localization in Neuropsychology*. New York, Academic Press Inc, 1983, pp 429–454.

46. STUSS DT, BENSON DF, KAPLAN EF, WEIR WS, MALVA CD: Leucotomized and nonleucotomized schizophrenics: Comparison of tests of attention. *Biol Psychiatry* 1981;16:1085–1100.

47. STUSS DT, BENSON DF, KAPLAN EF, WEIR WS, NAESER MA, LIEBERMAN I, FERRILL D: The involvement of orbitofrontal cerebrum in cognitive tasks. *Neuropsychologia* 1983;21:235–248.

48. MILNER B: Effects of different brain lesions on card sorting. *Arch Neurol* 1963;9:100–110.

49. MILNER B: Interhemispheric differences in the localization of psychological processes in man. *Br Med Bull* 1971;27:272–277.

50. OBRIST WD, THOMPSON HK, WANG HS, WILKINSON WE: Regional cerebral blood flow estimated by 133 xenon inhalation. *Stroke* 1975; 6:245–256.

51. DESHMUKH VD, MEYER JS: *Noninvasive Measurement of Cerebral Blood Flow.* Englewood Cliffs, NJ, Prentice-Hall Inc, 1978.

52. RISBERG J: Regional cerebral blood flow measurements by 133 Xe-inhalation: Methodology and applications in neuropsychology and psychiatry. *Brain Lang* 1980;9:9–34.

53. EICHLING J: Noninvasive methods of measuring regional cerebral blood flow, in PRICE TR, NELSON B (eds): *Cerebrovascular Diseases.* New York, Raven Press, 1979, pp. 51–56.

54. PROHOVNIK I: *Mapping Brainwork.* Lund, Sweden, Liber, 1980.

55. PROHOVNIK I: Regional cerebral blood flow (rCBF), in MORIHISA JM (ed): *Brain Imaging in Psychiatry.* Washington, DC, American Psychiatric Association, 1984, pp 28–40.

56. ROY CS, SHERRINGTON CS: The regulation of the blood supply to the brain. *J Physiol* 1890;11:85–121.

57. ROSENBLUM WI: Cerebral microcirculation: A review emphasizing the interrelationship of local blood flow and neuronal function. *Angiology* 1965;16:485–507.

58. RAICHLE ME, GRUBB RL JR, GADO MH, EICHLING JO: Correlation between regional cerebral blood flow and oxidative metabolism. *Arch Neurol* 1976;33:523–526.

59. SOKOLOFF L: Relationships among local functional activity, energy metabolism and blood flow in the central nervous system. *Fed Proc* 1981; 40:2311–2316.

60. OBRIST WD, WILKINSON WE: The non-invasive Xe-133 method: Evaluation of CBF indices, in BES A, GERAUD G (eds): *Cerebral Circulation.* Amsterdam, Elsevier North Holland Inc, 1980, pp 119–124.

61. GUR RC, GUR RE, OBRIST WD, HUNGERBUHLER JP, YOUNKIN D, ROSEN AD, SKOLNICK BE, REIVICH M: Sex and handedness differences in cerebral blood flow during rest and cognitive activity. *Science* 1982;217:659–661.

62. MILNER B: Some effects of frontal lobectomy in man, in WARREN JM, AKERT K (eds): *The Frontal Granular Cortex and Behavior.* New York: McGraw-Hill Book Co, 1963, pp 313–334.

63. GRANT AD, BERG EA: A behavioral analysis of degree of reinforcement and ease of shifting to new responses in a Weigl-type card sorting problem. *J Exp Psychol* 1948;38:404–411.

64. RISBERG J, MAXIMILIAN V, PROHOVNIK I: Changes of cortical activity patterns during habituation to a reasoning test: A study of the 133 Xe inhalation technique for measurement of regional cerebral blood flow. *Neuropsychologia* 1977;15:793–798.

65. MCHENRY LC, MERORY J, BASS E, STUMP DA, WILLIAMS R, WITCOFSKI R, HOWARD G, TOOLE JF: Xenon 133 inhalation method for regional cerebral blood flow measurements: Normal values and test-retest results. *Stroke* 1978;9:396–399.

66. PROHOVNIK I, HAKANSSON K, RISBERG J: Observations on the functional significance of regional cerebral blood flow in 'resting' normal subjects. *Neuropsychologia* 1980;18:203–217.

67. COPPOLA R, BUCHSBAUM MS, RIGAL F: Computer generation of surface distribution maps of measures of brain activity. *Comput Biol Med* 1982;12:191–199.

68. WOOD F: Theoretical, methodological, and statistical implications of the inhalation rCBF technique for the study of brain-behavior relationships. *Brain Lang* 1908;9:1–8.

69. YAMAMATO M, MEYER JS, SAKAI F, YAMAGUCHI F: Aging and cerebral vasodilator responses to hypercarbia: Responses in normal aging and in persons with risk factors for stroke. *Arch Neurol* 1980;37:489–496.

70. MAXIMILIAN VA, PROHOVNIK I, RISBERG J: Cerebral hemodynamic responses to mental activation in normo and hypercapnia. *Stroke* 1980; 11:342–347.

71. DAVIS SM, ACKERMAN RH, CORREIA JA, ALPERT NM, CHANG J, BUONANNA F, KELLEY RE, ROSNER B, TAVERAS J: Cerebral blood flow and cerebrovascular CO_2 reactivity in stroke-age normal controls. *Neurology* 1983;33:391–399.

72. EVANS MC, CAMERON IR: Adaption of rCBF during chronic exposure to hypercapnia and to hypercapnia with hypoxia. *J Cereb Blood Flow Metab* 1981;1 (suppl 1):435–436.

73. KETY SS, WOODFORD RB, HARMEL MH, FREYHAN FA, APPEL KE, SCHMIDT CF: Cerebral blood flow and metabolism in schizophrenia: The effects of barbiturate semi-narcosis, insulin coma, and electroshock. *Am J Psychiatry* 1948;104:765–770.

74. INGVAR, DH: Functional landscapes of the

dominant hemisphere. *Brain Res* 1976;107: 181–197.

75. INGVAR DH: 'Hyperfrontal' distribution of the cerebral grey matter in resting wakefulness: On the functional anatomy of the conscious state. *Acta Neurol Scand* 1979;60:12–25.

76. RISBERG J, HALSEY JH, WILLS EL, WILSON EM: Hemispheric specialization in normal man studied by bilateral measurements of the regional cerebral blood flow. *Brain* 1975;98:511—524.

77. BERMAN KF, ZEC RF, WEINBERGER DR: Physiologic dysfunction of dorsolateral prefrontal cortex in schizophrenia: II. Role of neuroleptic treatment, attention, and mental effort. *Arch Gen Psychiatry* 1986;43:126–135.

78. WEINBERGER DR, BERMAN KF: Huntington's disease and subcortical dementia: rCBF evidence. *Neurology* 1985;35 (suppl 1):109.

79. DIMASCIO A: The frontal lobes, in HEILMAN KM, VALENSTEIN E (eds): *Clinical Neuropyschology*. New York, Oxford University Press, 1979, pp 360–412.

80. YAKOVLEV PI, LECOURS A-R: The myelogenetic cycles of regional maturation of the brain, in MINKOWSKI A (ed): *Regional Development of the Brain in Early Life*. Oxford, England, Blackwell Scientific Publications, 1964, pp. 3–70.

81. NAUTA WJH: The problem of the frontal lobe: a reinterpretation. *J Psychiatr Res* 1971;8:167–187.

82. GOLDMAN-RAKIC PS, SELEMON LD, SCHWARTZ MD: Dual pathways connecting the dorsolateral prefrontal cortex with the hippocampal formation and parahippocampal cortex in the rhesus monkey. *Neuroscience* 1984;12:719–743.

83. GRAFMAN J, VANCE SC, WEINGARTNER H, SALAZAR AM: Specific effects of orbito-frontal brain wounds upon regulation of mood. *Neurology*, in press.

84. GOLDMAN-RAKIC PS, ISSEROFF A, SCHWARTZ ML, BUGBEE NM: The neurobiology of cognitive development, in MUSSEN P (ed): *Handbook of Child Psychology: Biology and Infancy Development*. New York, John Wiley & Sons Inc, 1983, pp 281–344.

85. SIMON H, SCATTON B, LEMOAL M: Dopaminergic A10 neurones are involved in cognitive functions. *Nature* 1980;286:150–151.

86. SHELTON RC, INGRAHAM L, WEINBERGER DR: Cerebral structural pathology in schizophrenia: A new cohort. Presented as a scientific exhibit at the 40th annual convention and scientific program of the Society of Biological Psychiatry, Dallas, May 17, 1985.

87. WEINBERGER DR, WAGNER RL, WYATT RJ: Neuropathological studies of schizophrenia: A selective review. *Schizophr Bull* 1983;9:193–212.

88. BOGERTS B, MEERTZ E, SCHONFELDT-BAUSCH R: Basal ganglia and limbic system pathology in schizophrenia: A morphometric study. *Arch Gen Psychiatry* 1985;42:784–791.

89. KARSON CN, KLEINMAN JE, WYATT RJ: Biochemical conceptions of schizophrenia, in MILLON T, KLERMAN G (eds): *Contemporary Issues in Psychopathology*. New York, Guilford Press, in press.

90. PYCOCK CJ, KERWIN RW, CARTER CJ: Effect of lesion of cortical dopamine terminals on subcortical dopamine in rats. *Nature* 1980;286: 74–77.

91. BRACHA HS, KLEINMAN JE: Post mortem studies in psychiatry. *Psychiatr Clin North Am* 1984;7:473–485.

92. GUNNE LM, GROWDON J, GLAESER B: Oral dyskinesia in rats following brain lesions and neuroleptic drug administration. *Psychopharmacology* 1982;77:134–139.

93. BANNON MJ, ROTH RH: Pharmacology of mesocortical dopamine neurons. *Pharmacol Rev* 1983;35:53–68.

94. McGEER PL, McGEER EG: Neurotransmitters in the aging brain, in DARRISON AM, THOMPSON RHS (eds): *The Molecular Basis of Neuropathology*. London, Edward Arnold Ltd, 1981, pp 631–648.

95. WONG DF, WAGNER HN JR., DANNALS RF, LINKS JM, FROST JJ, RAVERT HT, WILSON AA, ROSENBAUM AE, GJEDDE A, DOUGLASS KH, PETRONIS JD, FOLSTEIN MF, TOUNG JKT, BURNS HD, KUHAR MJ: Effects of age on dopamine and serotonin receptors measured by positron emission tomography in the living human brain. *Science* 1984; 226:1393–1396.

96. ALEXANDER GE, GOLDMAN PS: Functional development of the dorsolateral prefrontal cortex: An analysis utilizing reversible cryogenic depression. *Brain Res* 1978;143:233–249.

10

Expressed Emotion: A Review of the Critical Literature

Jill M. Hooley

Abstract: Expressed Emotion (EE) reflects the attitude of a close relative toward a schizophrenic family member. Work carried out over the last decade has provided good evidence that the concept of EE is both valid and reliable. It is, moreover, an accurate predictor of relapse in schizophrenic patients. Since Kuipers's review of the area 6 years ago (Kuipers, 1979), research into EE has progressed rapidly. Not only have there been additional studies replicating the previously well documented relationship between EE of family members and relapse in schizophrenic patients, but issues relating to the interaction of EE with life events, its psychophysiological correlates, and to intervention procedures have also been explored. In view of these recent developments a reevaluation of the area is necessary. This article will review the progress made in the field to date and, in addition, suggest new directions for subsequent research.

The Origins of EE

The stimulus for the development of the EE concept came initially from work begun in

Jill M. Hooley. Expressed emotion: A review of the critical literature. Reprinted by permission from *Clinical Psychology Review*, Vol. 5, pp. 119–139, 1985. Copyright © 1985, Pergamon Press, Inc.

England by Brown and his colleagues (Brown, Carstairs, & Topping, 1958). Working with 229 discharged male patients, two thirds of whom had received a diagnosis of schizophrenia, Brown discovered that the patients' success or failure in the community seemed to be in some way associated with the kind of living group to which they returned (Brown, 1959; Brown et al., 1958). In particular, those patients discharged to live either in lodgings or at home with siblings survived better psychiatrically over the course of the subsequent year than those who went to live in large hostels or who returned to the parental or matrimonial home. This observation was itself suggestive, but was made all the more interesting when it was also noted that the amount of contact the patients usually had with their relatives was another important variable and one which was again related to outcome. Specifically, patients who experienced limited contact with their relatives, perhaps due to the employment of one or both outside the home, fared better over the next year than patients who, in contrast, spent longer periods of time with their families.

On the basis of these retrospective observations with an essentially heterogeneous group of subjects, Brown subsequently initiated a prospective study (Brown, Monck, Carstairs, & Wing, 1962) in an attempt to document with greater specificity those aspects of the living situation that make the most contribution to patient outcomes. To this end 128 male schizophrenic patients were recruited and interviewed at or around the time of their discharge from psychiatric hospital, 2 weeks after returning home, and again a full year later. In addition, the key female relative of each patient was also interviewed on three occasions. On the basis of these interviews, levels of emotion expressed, hostility and dominance were assessed both for relatives and patients. The ratings of the relatives alone were found to have most practical (predictive) utility. On the basis of whether the key relative was given a high rating on expressed emotion or was assessed as being high in hostility, patients were divided into dichotomous groups labelled high or low emotional involvement. Patients returning to homes high in emotional involvement were more likely to relapse over the 1-year follow-up period than those returning to live with relatives who had been rated as having low levels of emotional involvement.

Given this confirmation of part of the original findings (the previously found association between type of lodgings and relapse *not* being replicated), Brown et al. turned their attention toward improving the ratings of emotion, establishing reliable techniques of measurement, and investigating issues of validity (Brown & Rutter, 1966; Rutter & Brown, 1966). The result was the development of the Camberwell Family Interview (CFI), the nonschedule standardized interview in use today.

The Assessment of EE

The CFI, as Vaughn and Leff (1976b) point out, is concerned with obtaining information about events and activities in the home, and attitudes and feelings. Over the course of the interview, which in its shortened form (see Vaughn & Leff, 1976b) takes 1.5 to 2 hours to administer and is always audiotaped for later coding, the patient's key relative (usually a spouse or a parent, but occasionally a sibling or a son or daughter) is

asked questions pertaining to the emotional climate in the home 3 months prior to the patient's hospital admission. From the interviewee's perspective the aim of these questions is to gain information concerning: (a) the onset and development of the patient's present illness episode, and (b) the degree to which it has affected such aspects of family life as domestic tasks, atmosphere in the home, and so on. While this information is, in itself, a useful source of data relating to the episode, the most crucial aspect of the interview, from the researcher's perspective, concerns the assessment of the relatives' behavior, and in particular the feelings he or she expresses about the patient in the course of the interview. It is on the basis of the emotions expressed while the relative is talking about the patient that ratings of EE are made.

CFI ratings of relatives are based on five scales. These are criticism, hostility, emotional overinvolvement, warmth and positive remarks. Brief details of each of these scales will be given below.

Criticism

Criticism is the sum total of critical comments made about the patient, such remarks being judged as critical on the basis of content and/or voice tone. In order for a remark to be evaluated as critical on content alone there has to be a clear and unambiguous statement of resentment, disapproval or dislike (e.g, "I resent cooking a meal for her only to have her leave it untouched on the table"). A respondent can 'opt out' of a critical remark based solely on content by implying that his or her reactions are due, at least in part, to imperfections in himself/herself. A remark such as "It really annoys me when she does that but that's probably because I'm a rather intolerant person" would thus not be rated as critical since the respondent draws attention to the fact that the annoyance is his or her own fault, and thus does not blame the patient directly.

With critical remarks based on voice tone, however, no such opting out procedure can be exercised. Here criticism is evident in the pitch, speed and inflection imparted to the statement by the person making it, and the comment thus stands as critical even if it is subsequently qualified by self-deprecating sequelae.

Hostility

While criticism is situation specific, hostility involves a much more generalized negative feeling and is usually a remark critical of the patient *himself* rather than his specific actions or behaviors. Examples of hostility thus include aspects of generalization or rejection, as illustrated in the following comments.

1. "He is stupid. Everything he does is stupid."

2. "The farther I am away from him the better."

Whereas criticism is assessed simply by counting the number of critical remarks the relative makes about the patient, hostility is rated using a 4-point scale. Emotional overinvolvement is also assessed in this way, although typically a 6-point scale is utilized.

Emotional Overinvolvement

Emotional overinvolvement reflects an exaggerated emotional response to the patient's illness (e.g., "I said *what* hospital? Just imagine how I felt! I thought *I'd* have to go there myself from the shock."), or markedly overprotective behavior [("I haven't been out with my husband. I could go out if I wanted to but I don't go because I'm looking after Johnnie (aged 29 and working) you see, and I'm devoting my life to Johnnie because I think he needs me more.")].

Warmth and Positive Remarks

Although the two final assessments, warmth, and number of positive remarks, have been little discussed in the literature and empirically have been found to add little to the predictive power of EE ratings based on criticism, hostility and emotional overinvolvement (see Brown, Birley & Wing,

1972), they will be mentioned here both for the sake of completeness and also because they may be important in the future, in helping us understand why some patients fail to relapse despite living with high EE relatives. This is an idea which will be developed in more detail in later discussion. At this point, however, all that remains to be said is that, like criticism, warmth is rated by using voice tone although in this case the voice tone has to be clearly positive rather than clearly negative. Positive remarks are defined primarily by content and reflect, without ambiguity, praise, approval or appreciation (e.g., "He's a wonderful husband"). While the rating for positive remarks is based on the overall number of such remarks made during the course of the interview, the rating for warmth is assessed using a 6-point scale.

Reliability

Despite the fact that EE is rated on the basis of vocal and semantic qualities, it does appear to be a measure which can be assessed reliably by raters who receive adequate training. Provided that they have normal hearing ability, it appears to be possible for English speakers with a research or a clinical background to become reliable raters. Several native German speakers and two Hindi speakers with English as a second language have also been reliably trained using the English tapes.

In order to be able to work independently a minimum reliability co-efficient of .80 (Pearson product-moment correlation) is required for ratings of critical comments and emotional overinvolvement. None of the studies which appear in the literature have reliabilities lower than this. Brown et al. (1972) obtained inter-rater reliabilities ranging from .80 to .90 for the various scales of the CFI, while Vaughn and Leff (1976a) report an overall reliability for criticism of .86. EE can thus be considered to be a measure which, in the hands of individuals who have received approximately one month of training, can be rated reliably. Given that EE is primarily concerned with voice qualities such as tone, pitch and inflection, it is also likely that ratings might be made using techniques of structural voice analysis (e.g., Alpert, Kurtzberg, & Friedhoff, 1963), although at the present time this idea is not being explored.

Expressed Emotion and Relapse

A robust association has now been demonstrated between the level of EE expressed by the key relative at or during the patient's admission to hospital and psychiatric morbidity in the 9-month period subsequent to discharge. Using a cut-off of seven critical comments and/or marked emotional overinvolvement and/or hostility to divide relatives in the high or low EE groups, Brown et al. (1972) found a highly significant association between high EE and relapse rates. Of the 45 schizophrenic patients who lived with high EE relatives, 58% (26/45) showed either a change in state from nonschizophrenic to schizophrenic, as defined by the CATEGO clinical classification system, (Wing, Cooper, & Sartorius, 1974), or a marked exacerbation of symptoms, and were thus considered to have relapsed. In the patients living with low EE relatives, however, the relapse rate was only 16% (9/56). Since relapse was assessed using the Present State Examination (PSE) (Wing et al., 1974), instead of being determined by hospital readmission, it is unlikely that these findings simply reflect a tendency of high EE relatives to seek hospitalization for a patient more readily than low EE relatives. When relapse rates were reexamined using criticism, hostility and emotional overinvolvement separately rather than in a joint index of EE, the same significant association was found. (The rating of warmth was not used in the overall index and did not show a clear relation to relapse. The number of positive remarks was also not used in the analyses

since it was not rated in the earlier EE studies.) Moreover, the association between relapse and EE still held when factors such as the patients' degree of behavioral disturbance or level of work impairment in the 2 years before the key admission was controlled statistically. Evidence therefore suggests that the relation between EE and relapse is not spurious and cannot be accounted for by simply considering the patient's own behavior as a mediating variable.

The nature of these results, together with their practical and theoretical implications, made a replication of the work of Brown et al. (1972) highly desirable. In their study of 1976a, Vaughn and Leff therefore selected 37 schizophrenic inpatients together with a control group of 30 depressed patients and assessed relatives' EE levels using a much abbreviated form of the CFI (see Vaughn & Leff, 1976b). Despite the reduced length of the interview and the fact that it was only given to the key relative and not to both relative and patient, at first independently, and then jointly, as in Brown's (1972) study, (where only the relatives' responses from the interviews conducted individually were used in Brown's analysis), Vaughn and Leff successfully replicated Brown's results. Using a criticism threshold of seven or more critical comments and/or marked emotional overinvolvement (the rating of hostility being dropped, since in no case was it found in the absence of high criticism) to assign relatives into the high EE subgroup, Vaughn and Leff found a 9-month relapse rate of 50% in the high EE group compared with a 12% rate in the low EE group. In keeping with the earlier work of Brown et al. (1972), the PSE was again used to assess relapse, the interviewing psychiatrist being blind to the original level of EE in the relatives at the time of reassessment. When a lower criticism threshold of six critical comments was used, the relation between EE and relapse improved still further (48% relapse rate in the high EE group versus 6% in the low EE group). As before however, the degree of behavioral disturbance or level of previous work impairment did *not* predict relapse in these patients independently of EE. Thus, while no work-impaired patients living with low EE relatives relapsed, 55% of those living in high EE households did so.

One interesting finding to emerge from Vaughn and Leff's data is that the relation between relapse and EE does not seem to be unique to schizophrenia. This is suggested by results from a depressed control group. The criticism thresholds of seven and six which had been used for the schizophrenic patients did not reveal a significant association between EE and relapse when used on data from a depressed sample. When the cut-off was reduced however, and two or more critical comments were used to assign relatives into the high EE subgroup, a significant relationship did emerge. Specifically, 67% (14 of 21) of the depressed patients who had high EE relatives (when the reduced cut-off was employed) relapsed over the follow-up period. However, only 22% (2/9) of those living with low EE relatives did so. This suggested that EE might be a construct with some predictive validity for psychiatric groups other than schizophrenics. Since Vaughn and Leff's association between EE levels and relapse was determined by using a cut-off score which was decided upon post hoc, a replication of their study was needed before closer examination of the influence of EE in depressed populations became justifiable.

Such a replication has recently been completed (Hooley, Orley, & Teasdale, 1986) with encouraging results. Using a sample of 39 depressed and married psychiatric hospital inpatients, these investigators found spouses' EE levels to be significantly associated with relapse rates over a 9-month follow-up. Using the cut-off of two critical comments previously employed by Vaughn and Leff (1976a) to allocate relatives into the high or low EE groups, Hooley et al. found a relapse rate of 59% (20 of 34) in patients living with high EE spouses. None of the patients living with low EE spouses relapsed, however. This replication of Vaughn and

Leff's original work with depressed patients extends the utility of the EE construct and suggests that EE may well be a concept with predictive validity not only for schizophrenic patients but also for depressed individuals.

The reason why depressed patients, in comparison with schizophrenics, should relapse at such low rates of criticism is not yet clear. Vaughn and Leff suggest that depressed individuals may be more sensitive to criticism than schizophrenics. Certainly the literature is replete with evidence documenting the fact that depressives are more self-critical than nondepressed individuals (Beck, Rush, Shaw, & Emory, 1979; Kuiper, 1978; Lishman, 1972; Lunghi, 1972), and thus may show cognitive distortions which could lead them to exaggerate the negative aspects of their environments. Hooley et al. (1986) suggest another possible explanation however; specifically, the source of the criticism. All the depressed patients in this study and the majority of those in Vaughn and Leff's were being criticized by spouses. Most schizophrenics, on the other hand, are being criticized by parents. Since spouses are much more likely than parents to terminate relationships which are dissatisfying to them, criticism from a marital partner may be more threatening than criticism from a parent. Given this, small numbers of critical remarks from a spouse may be functionally equivalent to higher frequencies of criticism from a parent. While this issue has not yet been specifically addressed within EE research, it is clearly a topic which warrants further empirical study.

Within schizophrenic populations however, one pattern which is evident is that the relation between EE and relapse is not only a replicable phenomenon but also one which persists over a considerable follow-up period. Evidence for the former assertion comes from both Vaughn and Leff's (1976a) work, and also from research recently carried out by Vaughn, Snyder, Jones, Freeman, and Falloon, (1984) in the United States. Using a sample of 54 recently hospitalized schizophrenics from the Los Angeles area, these investigators found 9-month relapse rates of 56% in those patients living in high EE homes versus rates of 17% in patients from low EE families. When only the data from the 36 patients who lived with their key relatives continuously during the follow-up period were considered, the difference in relapse rates became even more impressive (high EE = 60%, low EE = 9%). These results thus provide striking confirmation of the British findings. Moreover, they suggest that the association between high EE and schizophrenic relapse retains its predictive validity cross-culturally. In a research field swamped by nonreplicable results, this is indeed an encouraging finding.

Data showing that EE is related to relapse over an extended period of time come from a 2-year follow-up study published in 1981 by Leff and Vaughn. Of the 26 nonrelapsed schizophrenic patients who formed their 1976 sample, Leff and Vaughn (1981) successfully managed to trace and obtain follow-up data on 25 former patients. Eleven of these were living with relatives assessed as high in EE, while 14 lived with low EE relatives. Although the relapse rate of patients from high EE families slows down considerably after the first 9 months at home, the rate is nevertheless still almost double (27% vs. 15%) the rate in the low EE homes where patients appear to relapse at low but constant rates over the whole of the 2-year period. The difference in the 2-year relapse rates of those patients who were well at 9 months does not reach statistical significance. However, since two of the patients in the high EE group who did not relapse had left home before the end of the follow-up period and were no longer living with their relatives, this lack of significance is perhaps not too surprising. The difference in the relapse rates is in the expected direction however and, as result, 2-year cumulative relapse rates still show a highly significant difference between the two groups of patients, with 62% of high EE group relapsing compared with only 20% of the low EE group.

Factors Interacting with EE

Although the association between EE and relapse remains strong even when such factors as type of clinical condition, degree of behavioral disturbance, and extent of work impairment are statistically controlled, there are currently data which suggest that three factors do interact with and modify the influence of relatives' emotional involvement. These factors are: (a) drugs, (b) the amount of face-to-face contact existing between the patient and the relative, and (c) independent life events.

The possibility that medication might serve to protect patients living with high EE relatives while having little or no effect on patients living in low EE homes was first suggested by Brown et al. (1972). Within Brown's study, 66% of the former group of patients who did not regularly take one of the major tranquilizing drugs for a large part of the follow-up period did, in fact, relapse. Patients living in high EE families and taking regular medication, however, showed a relapse rate of only 46%. Although this result only approached statistical significance, a significant result for maintenance medication was obtained in Vaughn and Leff's (1976a) replication. Here, 78% of patients not taking phenothiazines and living with high EE relatives relapsed, compared with only 25% of those also living with high EE relatives but regularly taking drugs.

Doses of maintenance medication therefore appear to exert a protective influence on patients exposed to highly critical or excessively emotionally overinvolved relatives. A similar protective effect also appears to operate in cases where patients spend reduced amounts of time (less than 35 hours per week) with such relatives. Brown's early work (Brown et al., 1962) had suggested this and the finding was replicated in his 1972 study (Brown et al., 1972) as well as being confirmed again 4 years later by Vaughn and Leff (1976a). In all cases, however, the protective effects of both drugs and reduced contact appear to operate only in situations where patients are living in high EE families; low EE relapse rates are seemingly unaffected by such influences.

Interestingly, the two protective effects appear to be additive. Using their own data together with that of Brown et al. (1972), Vaughn and Leff (1976a) were able to obtain relapse rates for high risk patients (the group comprised only of patients satisfying criteria for regular maintenance therapy) with and without the benefits of reduced contact with high EE relatives and regular medication. As can be seen from Figure 1, the highest relapse rates (92%) are found in patients who spend more than 35 hours per week with high EE relatives and who are, in addition, not taking neuroleptic drugs. When such patients are maintained on phenothiazines and have only limited contact with their high EE relatives, their relapse rates are comparable to those found in the low EE group (15%).

The finding that independent life events also interact with relatives' emotional attitudes in the period prior to a psychiatric episode is a more recent finding. Data pub-lished in 1980 by Leff and Vaughn suggest that while episodes of schizophrenia in patients living with high EE relatives are not preceeded by an excess of life events, those in patients from low EE homes are. This suggests that an episode of schizophrenia is associated with either high EE relatives or an elevated number of independent life events, and suggests that both may constitute unacceptable forms of stress for psychiatrically vulnerable individuals.

Validation of the Concept

In order to test the construct validity of the EE ratings, it will be necessary at some point to employ external validation criteria. Investigations of the actual behavior of relatives who are high or low in EE are an obvious first step. In recent years several studies have attempted to establish which aspects of intra-familial behavior are associated with high or low EE attitudes. Given the assumption that the critical attitude expressed by the high EE relative is reflected in com-

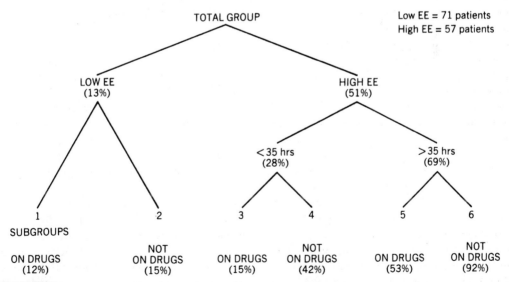

FIGURE 1

Nine month relapse rates of a total group of 128 schizophrenic patients. From "The influence of family and social factors on the course of psychiatric illness" by C.E. Vaughn and J.P. Leff, 1976, *British Journal of Psychiatry, 129*, p. 132. Copyright 1976 by the British Journal of Psychiatry. Reprinted by permission.

parable interpersonal behaviors between that relative and the patient during a direct interaction, it is comforting to note that some support for this idea was obtained in a recent study carried out by Valone, Norton, Goldstein, and Doane (1983). In a sample of 52 disturbed but nonpsychotic adolescents and their families, individual parents who expressed high EE attitudes made significantly more criticisms when involved in face-to-face interactions with their offspring than parents manifesting low EE attitudes. Neutral statements of an intrusive nature (e.g., "You say you're angry at us but I think you're really mad at yourself") or statements of support ("I want you to know that I care about you") did not differentiate between high and low EE parents. The study of Valone et al. (1983) thus provides some behavioral validation of the EE concept. However, while the results for criticism are encouraging, two minor methodological issues should be noted. First, the subjects used were not adult psychiatric patients but disturbed adolescents. Second, the parental assessments were carried out using the UCLA Parental Interview and not the CFI, customarily used for EE studies. The UCLA parental interview, a 144 item semi-structured interview described in full in Goldstein, Judd, Rodnick, Alkire, and Gould (1968) typically takes 1.5 to 2 hours to administer, and covers seven different areas of functioning: achievement, sociability, responsibility, communication, response to frustration, autonomy, and sex and dating. Generally, interviewers aim to pinpoint a specific issue existing between the parent and adolescent in each of these areas. As with the CFI however, the interviewee is allowed to elaborate and expand related ideas if he/she so chooses.

Like the Camberwell Family Interview, the UCLA interview is concerned with family behavior and recent events which have occurred in the home. One important difference however is that in the latter there is no specific avoidance of leading questions as in the CFI. Procedures for coding expressed

emotion from the interview have been developed by Norton (see Norton, 1982). While the data presented by Valone et al. must therefore be evaluated with these differences in mind, it is encouraging that EE ratings made from the UCLA interview do seem to have some validity. Thus, while the CFI provides a great deal of useful information to the clinician and researcher over and above that derived from the EE ratings, it may well be that other interviews, also designed to elicit information related to family functioning, might provide alternative ways of measuring the same phenomenon.

In addition to providing preliminary information about the behavior of high and low EE parents, the study of Valone et al. (1983) is of interest in that it examines triadic interactions (two parents and an adolescent offspring) where both parents are high in EE, and compares such interactions with those involving one high and one low EE parent (i.e., "mixed" parental dyads). Behavior was coded using the Affective Style (AS) coding system developed by Doane, West, Goldstein, Rodnick and Jones (1981). Within this system two kinds of critical remarks are possible. Benign criticisms are essentially remarks which would be coded as critical when making conventional EE ratings. They include such comments as "You have a bad attitude about school, John." Harsh criticisms however, are much stronger and are very similar to rejecting remarks which were discussed earlier (e.g., "You have an arrogant, stupid attitude").

Parental dyads where both mother and father are rated as high EE typically make more benign criticisms and more harsh criticisms than low EE parental dyads. Mixed parental pairs, however, express only high levels of benign criticism and their frequencies of harsh criticisms are much reduced. The presence of a low EE parent thus seems to moderate the expression of criticism in the high EE parent. This interesting finding has obvious implications for intervention, an issue which will be considered again in a later section.

A recent study by Miklowitz, Goldstein, Falloon, and Doane (1984), conducted with 42 families containing an offspring with an *established* diagnosis of schizophrenia, has confirmed that high EE parents ($n = 34$), produce a significantly greater number of negative affective statements than low EE parents ($n = 28$) when involved in face-to-face contact with their schizophrenic offspring. Moreover, the subdivision of the high EE group into high EE-critical ($n = 18$) and high EE-emotionally overinvolved ($n = 16$) also revealed differences in affective style patterns. While high EE-critical parents made more critical statements during interactions than low EE parents and (to a somewhat lesser extent) high EE-overinvolved parents, these latter parents were easily distinguishable from both high EE-critical and low EE parents by the high frequency of neutral-intrusive statements that they made. There thus seems to be a tendency, not only for high EE parents to behave in different ways than low EE parents, but also for parents within the high EE group to behave somewhat differently according to whether they are critical or emotionally overinvolved.

A study carried out by Kuipers, Sturgeon, Berkowitz, and Leff (1983) investigated not only the behavioral characteristics of high and low EE relatives but, in addition, examined the behavior of those schizophrenic patients who interacted with them. Analysis of the interactions which took place when the relatives and patients were interviewed by a third individual revealed that high EE relatives spent more time talking and less time looking at the patients than low EE relatives. Low EE relatives, on the other hand, were more prepared to be silent—a finding consistent with evidence that they are generally better listeners (Berkowitz, Kuipers, Eberlein-Vries, & Leff, 1981). Perhaps surprisingly, however, no patient differences were found in this study for any of the measures used.

The rather disappointing results of the work of Kuipers et al. (1983) may, to a large degree, be due to the inappropriateness of the measures selected. No attempt was made to code the content of the discussion, the only variables considered being duration of speech and looking time. Since the interaction took place under conditions where the patient and the relative were interviewed together by a third individual, the lack of natural behavior is also a problem. In a situation where depressed patients and their spouses were allowed to discuss topics about which they disagreed in the absence of others, marked differences in the behavior shown by high and low EE relatives (assigned to these groups on the basis of a median split) and patients emerged (Hooley, 1983). These differences were manifested in verbal as well as nonverbal behavior. Thus, when compared with low EE relatives, high EE relatives directed more critical remarks toward the patients, disagreed with them more frequently and were less accepting of what the patients had to say. The nonverbal behavior they exhibited was also more negative and less positive than that of low EE relatives. Patients interacting with high EE individuals, on the other hand, showed elevated levels of neutral nonverbal behavior and were less likely to make self-disclosing statements than patients who interacted with low EE family members. These data thus support the idea that interacting with a high EE relative may constitute a form of social stress for patients and suggest, moreover, that patients may respond to such stress by doing all they can, both verbally and nonverbally, to disengage themselves from the ongoing communication process.

In addition to work carried out within the behavioral domain, attempts to validate EE ratings have also been made, with some success, in the areas of psychophysiology. Work carried out in 1979 by Tarrier, Vaughn, Lader, and Leff demonstrated that the measure discriminating most successfully between patients from high and low EE homes was the rate of spontaneous fluctuations (SF) in skin conductance measured over a half-hour recording session. Using a design in which patients were tested on a variety of psychophysiological measures in the presence and absence of their key relative, Tarrier et al. were able to show that in the absence of the high and low EE relatives both patient groups showed highly aroused and indistinguishable physiological response patterns. Subsequent to the relatives entering the room, however, the responses of the low EE patients quickly habituated and their rates of spontaneous fluctuations in skin conductance soon approached normal levels. High EE patients, in contrast, showed no habituation when their relatives entered the room; their arousal levels remained high throughout the full 30 minutes of the recording session.

This intriguing result was later partially replicated by Sturgeon, Kuipers, Berkowitz, Turpin, and Leff (1981) using 20 patients suffering from acute schizophrenic episodes at the time of recording. While the spontaneous fluctuation rates of the acutely ill patients used by Sturgeon et al. were significantly greater than those found in the remitted patients studied by Tarrier et al., the calculation of individual regression lines allowed comparison of the high and low EE groups in both studies. A group of patients whose regression lines have a significantly negative mean slope are assumed to be showing habituation. This approach demonstrated a significant reduction in patients' SF activity *only* after the low EE relative entered the room in both the Tarrier et al. study and the Sturgeon et al. replication.

A more recent report by Sturgeon, Turpin, Kuipers, Berkowitz, and Leff (1984) now appears to contradict these findings. Adding a further 10 patients to the original 1981 sample and re-analysing the data using multivariate analysis of variance with skin conductance response (SCR) as the dependent variable, Sturgeon et al. now report a failure to replicate the finding of Tarrier et al. (1979) that low EE relatives have an apparently calming effect on schizophrenic patients. Since the two studies differ in a number of ways, the patient group of Sturgeon et al. (1984) being acutely ill, recorded during

hospitalization and including only patients in high face-to-face contact with their relatives, any one of these factors might be responsible for the discrepant findings. While Tarrier et al. (1979) reported no difference in remitted patients, Sturgeon et al. (1984) found the mean rate of SCRs in the high EE patient group to be almost twice that found in the low EE group. Since a 6-week delay typically occurred between hospital admission and testing, these researchers hypothesize that, while at admission both groups of patients have similarly high rates of SCR, the rise in SCR frequency in low EE patients is a relatively transient phenomenon. Sturgeon et al. (1984) suggest that the rapid decrease in the SCR frequency of low EE patients may be due to the fact that, in the majority of instances, onset of relapse in this group is preceded by the acute stress of a life event (see Leff & Vaughn, 1980). Patients from high EE families, on the other hand, have been exposed to a more chronic form of interpersonal stress. Because of this, it is suggested that their SCR frequencies may take longer to return to remission levels. During the recovery period, therefore, they are consequently at a higher risk of another schizophrenic episode due to this electrodermal vulnerability.

Clearly this is only speculation at the present time. However, more work is now in progress which is attempting to clarify some of the important issues. Before leaving research on psychophysiological correlates of EE however, one additional study deserves mention. While all the work that has been discussed thus far has been conducted in relatively artificial conditions (relative entering the room while the patient is being interviewed), a recent study by Valone, Goldstein, and Norton (1984), has examined the psychophysiological reactivity of both parents and their disturbed adolescent offspring during direct family confrontations. The study was conducted using 52 families who had sought help from the UCLA outpatient clinic some years before for problems relating to the adolescent family member. Psychophysiological data were collected on each adolescent before and during four emotionally charged discussions with the parents. Two of these took place with the mother and two with the father, each discussion averaging 5 minutes.

The use of disturbed but nonpsychotic adolescents considered to be at risk for schizophrenia spectrum disorders avoids one of the limitations of psychophysiological research employing diagnosed schizophrenics as subjects, since it permits the investigation of the emotional impact of high EE families on a presumably vulnerable but nonetheless psychiatrically intact individual. By this means the existence (or otherwise) of psychophysiological effects of high EE interactions prior to a schizophrenic episode can be investigated.

The results of Valone et al. provide empirical evidence that direct encounters between high EE individuals and their offspring are more emotionally arousing than the face-to-face interactions which take place within low EE families. Adolescents in the study who anticipated an initial interaction with a high EE parent showed higher levels of arousal (as measured by skin conductance) than adolescents expecting to interact with a low EE parent. Arousal levels of high EE parents were also significantly higher during the problem discussions than those measured in low EE parents. No differences in anticipatory arousal levels were in evidence within the parental group, however.

Generally, the results described by Valone et al. (1984) support findings from earlier studies and are of value in that they extend those findings to a nonschizophrenic population. Consequently, they provide evidence that the previously well-documented physiological reactivity to high EE relatives is not merely a phenomenon of the postpsychotic state. The data on parents also suggest that the elevated arousal levels typical of high EE interactions are not limited solely to the target of the criticism. While not showing any anticipatory arousal, high EE parents become highly aroused as they begin to become involved in the discussion and start to direct critical remarks toward their offspring.

Given the results of Valone et al. (1983), Hooley's (1983) behavioral observations and the psychophysiological data of Tarrier et al. (1979), Sturgeon et al. (1981, 1984) and Valone and his associates (1984), it seems clear that recent EE research has produced good evidence for its concurrent validity. This, in addition to the well documented predictive validity of the concept (Brown et al., 1972; Vaughn & Leff, 1976a; Vaughn et al., 1982, 1984) serves to make EE a conceptually sound and extremely exciting area for research. A crucial issue still remains however: specifically, the issue of the direction of cause and effect in the relationship between EE and relapse. It is to this key question that we shall now turn.

Establishing Causality: Experimental Manipulations of EE

Researchers in the area have always been fully cognizant of the need to establish the direction of the causal arrow linking relatives' EE and patients' relapse. To this end both Brown et al. (1972) and Vaughn and Leff (1976a) employed a variety of statistical approaches in their attempts to eliminate the possibility that certain mediating factors, such as the level of behavior disturbance manifested by the patients, might lead to both high EE in relatives and also to increased relapse in patients. This issue has also been addressed recently by Miklowitz, Goldstein, and Falloon (1983). In a study designed to examine the relation between relatives' EE and key patient attributes, symptom data were collected on 42 schizophrenics during hospitalization and also 2 to 4 weeks after discharge. In keeping with previous findings (Brown et al., 1972; Vaughn & Leff, 1976a) patients living in high EE families did not differ significantly from those living in low EE households with regard to their pre-morbid adjustment or the symptoms and syndromes they exhibited during hospitalization. Moreover, post-discharge measures also failed to discriminate between patients with low or high EE relatives. Thus, the general pattern of results suggests that patients with high or low EE families are essentially indistinguishable on measures of the severity of clinical condition.

In order to demonstrate convincingly the direction of the causal relationship, the hypothesized independent variable, (in this case EE) must be externally manipulated, and its resulting effect on the dependent variable (PSE-assessed relapse rates) closely monitored. Only when it is shown that relapse rates can be modified by changing relatives' EE can the direction of causality be considered to be established beyond reasonable doubt.

Clearly, ethical considerations do not permit studies designed to increase EE levels. However, in an ambitious trial of social intervention in the families of schizophrenic patients, Leff, Kuipers, Berkowitz, Eberlein-Vries and Sturgeon (1982) attempted to resolve the questions surrounding the issue of causality by reducing EE levels within high EE families. Patients who were living with and spending large periods of time in contact with high EE relatives and were therefore considered to be at high risk for relapse were randomly assigned to either an experimental group which received a package of social interventions, or a control group which received standard outpatient care ($n = 12$ in both cases). The aims of the social intervention were either to reduce the amount of face-to-face contact between relative and patient to below the crucial level of 35 hours per week, to change relatives' EE levels from high to low, or to do both, if possible. The social intervention package, details of which are given in Berkowitz et al. (1981), consisted of: (a) an educational program of four lectures on the etiology, course, treatment and management of schizophrenia, (see also Berkowitz, Eberlein-Vries, Kuipers, & Leff, 1984); (b) a relatives' group where both high and low EE relatives were encouraged

to talk about their problems; and (c) family sessions where a psychologist and a psychiatrist saw the patient and relatives together, at home, for 1 hour. The number of such sessions varied from family to family (range 1–25 sessions), and their content, while flexible, was essentially guided by the previously stated aims of the intervention procedure, namely, reducing EE and/or social contact. While members of the high EE experimental group received all three forms of social interventions, low EE experimental families did not receive any family sessions. All experimental families were encouraged to attend the two-weekly relatives' group sessions for the full 9 months of the study period.

How successful were these attempts to modify EE? Of the 11 high EE relatives followed up and reinterviewed 9 months subsequent to their induction to the study, five changed from high to low levels of criticism and three others showed some decrease. In contrast there was only a minimal, and nonsignificant, reduction in criticism levels in the controls.

The package of social interventions utilized by Leff et al. (1982) can therefore be considered to have successfully reduced levels of EE in the experimental families. Face-to-face contact between patient and relative also fell in five families, making the total success rate for the intervention 73% (8 out of 11 families). How, then, did this affect relapse rates in the experimental group patients? During the 9-month follow-up period a total of seven patients relapsed. Of these seven, six patients came from the control group. Thus the relapse rate in the controls was 50% while that in the experimental patients was 9%. The package of social interventions therefore produced a significant reduction in EE levels and also in subsequent relapse rates, providing strong evidence for the causal influence of high EE on relapse and also for the protective effect of lowered social contact between patient and relative.

The findings of Leff et al., based as they are on data from such a small number of families, are clearly in need of replication in a large scale clinical trial. Such a trial is currently being conducted in the United States by the National Institute of Mental Health. However, the results do point to the effectiveness of social interventions in the families of schizophrenics and, as a consequence, are of great practical importance. Since the effectiveness of the individual elements of the social intervention package was not evaluated, it still remains to be seen which aspects of this are most important for successful therapeutic intervention. Such practically related issues will no doubt form an active area of research in the years to come.

Summary and Suggestions for Future Research

Work carried out over the last decade has provided good evidence that the concept of EE is both valid and reliable. It is, moreover, an accurate predictor of relapse in schizophrenic patients and one which also seems to have good predictive validity for other groups of psychiatric patients, notably the depressed. In so far as it is not specific to schizophrenia, EE therefore seems to be a concept worthy of further and extensive investigation since it seems to be tapping aspects of the emotional climate within the home which have high salience for psychiatric patients.

Despite the strength of the association between EE and relapse and the information we have about its behavioral and interpersonal correlates, we still know little about the mechanism by which it might operate to produce an exacerbation of symptoms in patients. In other words, we are still some distance away from being able to answer two key questions: What *is* EE and how exactly does it work to bring about psychiatric relapse?

To date, the most realistic representation of the situation, and the one most congruent with the available data, is a model which either views high EE relatives as in some way constituting a form of increased social stress for vulnerable individuals, or one which

considers low EE relatives to be capable of lowering stress levels in vulnerable patients, or both. The schizophrenic patient is seen as an individual who, for whatever reason, is excessively sensitive to the effects of stress, be this caused by social interactions with close family members or by external life events.

Preliminary data from the University of Pittsburgh (Anderson, 1983) also support this view. Although no main effect of severity of illness on relapse was found for the 85 young schizophrenic patients studied, an interaction with EE was observed, relapse rates being highest in patients who had the most severe symptoms at the time they were discharged into high EE households. Thus, the more disturbed patients are when they return home, the less able they are to cope with the stresses imposed by such relatives.

The relations between vulnerability to schizophrenia, EE, and electrodermal arousal are still unclear. If the effects of EE are mediated by psychophysiological variables, it should be predicted that, in instances where relatives' EE levels are manipulated from high to low (as in the 1982 intervention trial of Leff et al.), electrodermal activity patterns of patients living with such relatives would also change, gradually becoming more like those of patients living in low EE families. Data reported by Sturgeon et al. (1984), however, do not support this prediction. While the intervention program described earlier did produce a significant effect on relapse rates in the schizophrenics studied, follow-up measures on 19 of the patients involved in the trial did not suggest that the therapeutic effects of the intervention package were mediated via SCR frequency.

Whether high EE relatives play a causal role in the development of schizophrenia is also not clear, although this is an issue currently under investigation (see Norton, 1982). What we do know, however, is that given a previous episode of schizophrenia, a subsequent episode is made more probable by prolonged contact with critical relatives. But what sort of factors make a particular relative high or low EE? Are there certain characteristics of such individuals which, if we could isolate them, would allow us to predict their response to the patient or is the reaction of the relative much more interactionally based?

In an attempt to discover why some families respond to patients with high levels of criticism and emotional overinvolvement while others appear to tolerate and support a mentally ill family member and refrain from behaving in ways which exacerbate the problem, Anderson, Hogarty, Bayer, and Needleman (1984), investigated the social networks of such families to see whether the high or low EE attitude could be related to external levels of social support. Brown's earlier work (Brown et al., 1972) had suggested that greater isolation from a support system might be a characteristic of high EE families. In view of this, Anderson et al. examined the social networks of both high and low EE families, hypothesizing that the networks of the former would be smaller, more dense, more disrupted and less satisfying than those of the latter. In the sample of 69 parents from 35 households containing a schizophrenic member, however, no significant difference emerged for either high and low EE individuals or high and low EE parental household groupings for any of the variables considered. The high or low EE attitude does not, thus, seem to be related, at least in any simple way, to the social support levels available outside the immediate family.

Perhaps, then, the EE attitude is more trait-like and is thus amenable to psychometric assessment. While the specific personality characteristics that may facilitate successful adaptation to the stress of coping with a chronically ill family member have not yet been investigated with respect to EE, recent work with the spouses of renal patients undergoing regular dialysis has indicated that certain personality variables might influence coping skills (Schoeneman, Reznikoff, & Bacon, 1983). What these researchers found in their investigation of the wives of haemodialysis patients was that,

contrary to expectation, good adjustment to living with chronic illness was not positively associated with an internal health locus of control (see Wallston, Wallston, & DeVellis, 1978 for details of the MHLC scale). This is in keeping with both Rotter's (1975) view and that of Wortman and Brehm (1975) that a strong perception that one is in control may not be functional in situations which are essentially uncontrollable.

Clearly this idea is of great interest with respect to EE and lends credibility to the hypothesis that high EE relatives, may, in fact, be individuals who attempt to cope by trying to exert control over what may actually be uncontrollable behavior in the patient. Certainly, high EE relatives, both by their own admission and as evidenced by the high levels of relapse in patients living with them, can be considered to be coping less well with the patient than low EE relatives. Moreover, sequential analyses of interactions involving depressed patients and their spouses (Hooley & Hahlweg, 1983), suggest that high EE spouses may be attempting to exert more control over their interactions with patients than low EE spouses.

The view of the high EE relatives as the controlling member of the relationship also fits in well with the general concept of EE. A relative is rated as being critical because they make it clear that there are aspects of the patient's personality or behavior that they would like to be different. High EE relatives, as judged by both their reported behavior toward the patient and their behavior during interview, are thus considered to be less tolerant and accepting of the patient (see also Vaughn & Leff, 1981). That they may actively work toward effecting the sorts of changes they desire is sometimes evidenced by the critical remarks they make. The following comments are all taken from Camberwell Family Interviews with high and low EE relatives, collected by the author (see Hooley, 1984).

I always say, 'why don't you pick up a book, do a crossword or something like that to keep your mind off it.' *That's even too much trouble.*

I've tried to jolly him out of it and pestered him into doing things. Maybe I've overdone it, I don't know.

He went round the garden 90 times, in the door, back out the door. I said "Have a chair, sit out in the sun." Well, he nearly bit my head off.

By contrast, the comments made by low EE relatives reveal a less intrusive attitude.

I know it's better for her to be on her own, to get away from me and try to do things on her own.

Whatever she does suits me.

I just tend to let it go because I know that when she wants to speak she will speak.

The idea of a high EE rating reflecting a controlling attitude toward the patient, while novel, appears to have good face validity. It also lends itself well to empirical investigation, both correlational and interventive. If a high EE relative is one who is more controlling, certain scales designed to measure locus of control (e.g., Rotter Internal–External Locus of Control scale, Rotter, 1966) should reveal differences between high and low EE individuals. It might also be predicted that certain patient-related behaviors, specifically those perceived as being amenable to external sources of influence, would be more likely to be the targets of the relatives' attempts to exert control and thus be more associated with criticism. If one symptom, for example, anergia (physical underactivity), is perceived by the relative as being more directly under the control of the patient (and consequently controllable by the relative as a result of their cajoling), than another symptom, for example, hallucinations, it would be predicted that high EE relatives would be more critical about the anergia than the hallucinatory behavior.

Symptoms likely to be considered by relatives as out of the realm of the patients' control are symptoms labelled as positive by Andreasen (1982). These positive symptoms include hallucinations, delusions, formal thought disorder or bizarre behavior. On the other hand, negative symptoms, such as alogia (infrequent or impoverished communication), apathy, attentional impairment or asociality, are all more likely to be seen by relatives as behaviors that the patient could do something about if he or she really wanted to. These symptoms might thus be expected to form more obvious targets for criticism.

Clearly, what is most needed at the present time is a study relating critical remarks to symptoms. We know from earlier studies (Brown et al., 1972; Miklowitz et al. 1983; Vaughn & Leff, 1976a) that criticism is not related to degree of behavioral disturbance per se. However, there is no a priori reason why it might not be related to specific symptoms or symptom combinations, and this issue deserves some attention from researchers in the future.

The idea of high EE relatives as highly controlling individuals also lends itself well to research concerned with the development of intervention techniques. It is quite possible that the most therapeutic feature of the social intervention trial of Leff et al. (1982) was to encourage discussion between high and low EE relatives and to allow the former to learn about and subsequently practice different, and possibly less overtly controlling, coping strategies. Moreover, the protective effect of reduced face-to-face contact between patient and relative may operate simply by reducing the opportunities the relative has to exert control over the patient or result in the relative seeing less of the objectional behavior typical of the patient.

The model of EE proposed above has its roots firmly in the interactions which take place between patient and relative and characterizes the high EE relative as an individual who is highly responsive to certain behaviors (or the lack of certain behaviors in the patient). It recognizes that not all high EE relatives may be as bad as a glance through the EE literature might suggest. Indeed some may be excessively controlling because they are *concerned* for the patient and his or her welfare. However, as the example given below indicates, their efforts to show this may not always be well received by the patient.

> **He got up one Sunday morning and he sat in the chair and I said, "What's the matter? Don't you feel well?" "No," he said. So I said, "Can I get you a drink?" "No." "Well it's not very warm. Don't you think I ought to get something to put on you?" "No." So I left him. I went back again to see that he was alright. He was still in the same position. This was nearly an hour later. So I thought, its not very warm, he *must* be getting cold. So I went out and got a blanket without asking him and put it on him. "I don't want it," he said. And then I did break down because I thought, well, what the devil can I do for him? And that's when it upsets me—when I can't do anything to help him like that.**

Of course, it is not realistic to view all high EE relatives as individuals who try to cope by making controlling attempts designed to restore the behavior of someone they care about to its previous level of functioning. In many instances, the relatives have long since given up, any remaining feelings being predominantly hostile.

> **It's just unbearable, sometimes to be with her.**

> **It's very difficult sometimes even to like her.**

It is likely, however, that relatives who are rated as critical but who do, in fact care about the patient, can be differentiated from those who are critical and uncaring by utilizing the CFI ratings made for warmth, positive remarks and hostility. The categorization of high EE relatives into caring and uncaring using such criteria may also have some predictive validity and might help explain why some patients fail to relapse despite living with highly critical relatives. An interactional analysis comparing the behavior of high EE/high warmth relatives with

high EE/low warmth relatives would be of value in helping us understand the possible differences between different high EE types, as also may independent consideration of high EE resulting from criticism and high EE due to emotional overinvolvement (Miklowitz et al., 1983). In addition, it might throw light on the factors underlying their high rate of criticism. The relation of such interactional data to patterns of relapse is also essential if we are to understand fully which aspects of the expressed emotion ratings are most psychologically toxic and/or supportive.

If EE is, as suggested by the present discussion, a measure of the responsiveness of certain individuals to particular symptoms or behavioral deficits in patients, it should also be an index which is sensitive to changes in the behavior of those patients. Of interest here is the finding of Miklowitz et al. (1983) that patients from critical families manifest moderately good levels of premorbid adjustment. Criticism may thus be a reaction to the reduced level of functioning shown by the patient during the illness phase. If this is the case, one might expect that the EE measure would be relatively unstable over time given symptomatic improvement in the patients. Preliminary data from West Germany (Köttgen, Mollenhauer, Sonnichsen, Jurth, & Hand, 1983) support the notion of lability of EE. Of 30 families rated as high EE, only 15 (50%) were rated as still being high in EE 6 months later. Of the 30 families initially rated as low EE, only 5 (17%) subsequently received a high rating. Unfortunately, it is not clear how these EE changes relate to behavioral change in the patients, although, in all cases, changes in EE (from high to low and from low to high) occurred with only very few treatment sessions.

The issue is obviously very interesting and merits more extensive investigation, especially since in their intervention study Leff et al. (1982) noticed a spontaneous change in attitude in two relatives from the control group despite the fact that neither had received any professional therapeutic help. A more detailed investigation of the factors involved in EE change (which seems more frequently to involve movement from high to low levels of criticism) would give obvious benefit to any intervention programs expressly designed to modify and lower high EE attitudes. The following comment was made spontaneously to the author by the high EE wife of a depressed patient. This woman had just viewed a videotaped recording of an interaction which had taken place between herself and her husband during his hospitalization some 3 months previously. The comment is of interest because it suggests that such a form of feedback may be of value in the modification of high EE attitudes and behavior. In addition, it provides a good illustration of the sensitivity to the changed behavior of the patient which, it is argued is an important characteristic of the high EE relative.

It was very salutary seeing that again. I didn't like how I was at all. I don't think I'd be like that again. I didn't like how I reacted to him. But of course if they're different, you're different aren't you?

The central issue behind the current discussion is, then, that EE should not be viewed as just another way of blaming families of schizophrenics. Potentially positive aspects of high EE and negative aspects of low EE deserve consideration. Because of the attitude they adopt, low EE relatives may actually tolerate levels of functioning well below the patient's capabilities. Those patients living with high EE relatives on the other hand, although perhaps exposed to greater stress from their families, may attain higher levels of functioning in between their more frequent episodes of illness. The time has now come for a thorough investigation of both the positive and negative components of relatives' critical attitudes. EE is a complex measure reflecting the interaction between a patient and a relative at a particular point in time. How stable this measure is, how it is influenced by changes in patient behavior and how it can be modified more

efficiently to prevent relapse in vulnerable patients are all key issues which must be addressed by researchers in the near future if we are to benefit fully from such a clearly valuable concept.

References

ALPERT, M., KURTZBERG, R., AND FRIEDHOFF, A. (1963). Transient voice changes associated with emotional stimuli. *Archives of General Psychiatry*, 8, 362–365.

ANDERSON, C. M. (1983, June). *EE as a predictor of the course of illness in young chronic patients*. Paper presented at the Schloss Ringberg EE conference in Munich.

ANDERSON, C. M., HOGARTY, G., BAYER, AND NEEDLEMAN, R. (1984). Expressed emotion and the social networks of parents of schizophrenic patients. *British Journal of Psychiatry*, 144, 247–255.

ANDREASEN, N. C. (1982). Negative and positive schizophrenia: Definition and validation. *Archives of General Psychiatry*, 39, 789–794.

BECK, A. T., RUSH, A. J., SHAW, B. F., AND EMERY, G. (1979). *Cognitive therapy of depression*. New York: Guilford Press.

BERKOWITZ, R., EBERLEIN-VRIES, R., KUIPERS, L., AND LEFF, J. (1984). Educating relatives about schizophrenia. *Schizophrenia Bulletin*, 10, 418–429.

BERKOWITZ, R., KUIPERS, L., EBERLEIN-VRIES, R., AND LEFF, J. (1981). Lowering expressed emotion in relatives of schizophrenics. In M. J. GOLDSTEIN (Ed.), *New developments in interventions with families of schizophrenics*. London: Jossey-Bass.

BROWN, G. W. (1959). Experiences of discharged chronic schizophrenic mental hospital patients in various types of living group. *Millbank Memorial Fund Quarterly*, 37, 105–131.

BROWN, G. W., BIRLEY, J. L. T., AND WING, J. K. (1972). Influence of family life on the course of schizophrenic disorders: A replication. *British Journal of Psychiatry*, 121, 241–258.

BROWN, G. W., CARSTAIRS, G. M., AND TOPPING, G. C. (1958). The post hospital adjustment of chronic mental patients. *The Lancet*, ii, 685–689.

BROWN, G. W., MONCK, E. M., CARSTAIRS, G. M., AND WING, J. K. (1962). The influence of family life on the course of schizophrenic illness. *British Journal of Preventative Social Medicine,* 16, 55–68.

BROWN, G. W., AND RUTTER, M. L. (1966). The measurement of family activities and relationships. *Human Relations,* 19, 241–263.

DOANE, J. A., WEST, K. L., GOLDSTEIN, M. J., RODNICK, E. H., AND JONES, J. E. (1981). Parental communication deviance and affective style: Predictors of subsequent schizophrenia spectrum disorders in vulnerable adolescents. *Archives of General Psychiatry,* 38, 679–685.

GOLDSTEIN, M. J., JUDD, L. L., RODNICK, E. H., ALKIRE, A., AND GOULD, E. (1968). A method for studying social influence and coping patterns within families of disturbed adolescents. *Journal of Nervous and Mental Disease,* 147, 223–251.

HOOLEY, J. M. (1983, June). *Interactions involving high and low EE relatives: A behavioural analysis.* Paper presented at the Schloss Ringberg EE conference in Munich.

HOOLEY, J. M. (1984). *Criticism and depression.* Unpublished doctoral dissertation, University of Oxford.

HOOLEY, J. M., AND HAHLWEG, K. (1983, June). *Patterns of interaction in high and low expressed emotion dyads.* Paper presented at the Schloss Ringberg EE conference in Munich.

HOOLEY, J. M., ORLEY, J., AND TEASDALE, J. D. (1986). Levels of expressed emotion and relapse in depressed patients. *British Journal of Psychiatry,* 148, 642–647.

KÖTTGEN, C., MOLLENHAUER, K., SONNISCHEN, I., JURTH, R., AND HAND, I. (1983). *The Camberwell Family Interview as a diagnostic and therapeutic tool.* Paper presented to the 7th International World Congress of Psychiatry, Vienna.

KUIPER, N. A. (1978). Depression and causal attributions for success and failure. *Journal of Personality and Social Psychology,* 36, 236–246.

KUIPERS, L. (1979). Expressed emotion: A review. *British Journal of Social and Clinical Psychology,* 18, 237–243.

KUIPERS, L., STURGEON, D., BERKOWITZ, R., AND LEFF, J. (1983). Characteristics of expressed emotion: Its relationship to speech and looking in schizophrenic patients and their relatives. *British Journal of Clinical Psychology,* 22, 257–264.

LEFF, J., KUIPERS, L., BERKOWITZ, R., EBERLEIN-VRIES, R., AND STURGEON, D. (1982). A controlled trial of social intervention in the families of schizophrenic patients. *British Journal of Psychiatry,* 141, 121–134.

LEFF, J., AND VAUGHN, C. (1980). The interaction of life events and relatives' expressed emotion in schizophrenia and depressive neurosis. *British Journal of Psychiatry,* 136, 146–153.

LEFF, J., AND VAUGHN, C. (1981). The role of maintenance therapy and relatives' expressed emotion in relapse schizophrenia: A two year follow-up. *British Journal of Psychiatry,* 139, 102–104.

LISHMAN, W.A. (1972). Selective factors in memory, part 2: Affective disorder. *Psychological Medicine,* 2, 248–253.

LUNGHI, M. E. (1977). The stability of mood and social perception measures in a sample of depressive in-patients. *British Journal of Psychiatry,* 130, 598–604.

MIKLOWITZ, D. J., GOLDSTEIN, M. J., AND FALLOON, I. R. H. (1983). Premorbid and symptomatic characteristics of schizophrenics from families with high and low levels of expressed emotion. *Journal of Abnormal Psychology,* 92, 359–367.

MIKLOWITZ, D. J., GOLDSTEIN, M. J., FALLOON, I. R. H., AND DOANE, J. A. (1984). Interactional correlates of expressed emotion in the families of schizophrenics. *British Journal of Psychiatry,* 144, 482–487.

NORTON, J. P. (1982). *Expressed emotion, affective style, voice tone and communication deviance as predictors of offspring schizophrenia spectrum disorders.* Unpublished doctoral dissertation, University of California, Los Angeles.

ROTTER, J. B. (1975). Some problems and misconceptions related to the construct of internal versus external control of reinforcement. *Journal of Consulting and Clinical Psychology,* 175, 43, 56–57.

ROTTER, J. B. (1966). Generalized expectancies for internal versus external control of reinforcement. *Psychological Monographs,* 80, (1, whole no. 609).

RUTTER, M., AND BROWN, G. W. (1966). The reliability and validity of measures of family life and relationships in families containing a psychiatric patient. *Social Psychiatry,* 1, 38–53.

SCHOENEMAN, S. Z., REZNIKOFF, M., AND BACON, S. J. (1983). Personality variables in coping with the stress of a spouse's chronic illness. *Journal of Clinical Psychology,* 39, 430–436.

STURGEON, D., KUIPERS, L., BERKOWITZ, R., TURPIN, G., AND LEFF, J. (1981). Psychophysiological responses of schizophrenic patients to high and low expressed emotion relatives. *British Journal of Psychiatry,* 138, 40–45.

STURGEON, D., TURPIN, G., KUIPERS, L., BERKOWITZ, R., AND LEFF, J. (1984). Psychophysiological responses of schizophrenic patients to high and low expressed emotion relatives: A follow-up study. *British Journal of Psychiatry*, 145, 62–69.

TARRIER, N., VAUGHN, C., LADER, M. H., AND LEFF, J. P. (1979). Bodily reactions to people and events in schizophrenia. *Archives of General Psychiatry*, 36, 311–315.

VALONE, K., GOLDSTEIN, M. J., AND NORTON, J. P. (1984). Parental expressed emotion and psychophysiological reactivity in an adolescent sample at risk for schizophrenia spectrum disorders. *Journal of Abnormal Psychology*, 93, 448–457.

VALONE, K., NORTON, J. P., GOLDSTEIN, M. J., AND DOANE, J. A. (1983). Parental expressed emotion and affective style in an adolescent sample at risk for schizophrenia spectrum disorders. *Journal of Abnormal Psychology*, 92, 399–407.

VAUGHN, C. E., AND LEFF, J. P. (1981). Patterns of emotional response in relatives of schizophrenic patients. *Schizophrenia Bulletin*, 7, 1, 43–44.

VAUGHN, C. E., AND LEFF, J. P. (1976a). The influence of family and social factors on the course of psychiatric illness. *British Journal of Psychiatry*, 129, 125–137.

VAUGHN, C. E., AND LEFF, J. P. (1976b). The measurement of expressed emotion in the families of psychiatric patients. *British Journal of Social and Clinical Psychology*, 15, 157–165.

VAUGHN, C. E., SNYDER, K., FREEMAN, W., JONES, S., FALLOON, I., AND LIBERMAN, R. (1982). Family factors in schizophrenic relapse: A replication. *Schizophrenia Bulletin*, 8, 425–426.

VAUGHN, C. E., SNYDER, K. S., JONES, S., FREEMAN, W. B., AND FALLOON, I. R. H. (1984). Family factors in schizophrenic relapse. *Archives of General Psychiatry*, 41, 1169–1177.

WALLSTON, K. A., WALLSTON, B. S., AND DEVELLIS, R. (1978). Development of the multidimensional health locus of control (MHLC) scales. *Health Education Monographs*, 6, 160–170.

WING, J. K., COOPER, J. E., AND SARTORIUS, N. (1974). *The description of psychiatric symptoms: An introduction manual for the PSE and catego system.* London: Cambridge University Press.

WORTMAN, C. B., AND BREHM, J. W. (1975). Responses to uncontrollable outcomes: An integration of reactance theory and learned helplessness model. In L. BERKOWITZ (Ed.), *Advances in experimental social psychology, Vol. 8.* New York: Academic Press.

11

Family Psychoeducation, Social Skills Training, and Maintenance Chemotherapy in the Aftercare Treatment of Schizophrenia

I. One-Year Effects of a Controlled Study on Relapse and Expressed Emotion

Gerard E. Hogarty, Carol M. Anderson, Douglas J. Reiss, Sander J. Kornblith, Deborah P. Greenwald, Carol D. Javna, and Michael J. Madonia

Relapse rates averaging 41% in the first year after discharge among schizophrenic patients receiving maintenance neuroleptic treatment led to the development of two disorder-relevant treatments: a patient-centered behavioral treatment and a psychoeducational family treatment. Following hospital admission, 103 patients residing in high expressed emotion (EE) households who met Research Diagnostic Criteria for schizophrenia or schizo-affective disorder were randomly assigned to a two-year aftercare study of (1) family treatment and medication, (2) social skills training and medication, (3) their combination, or (4) a drug-treated condition. First-year relapse rates among those exposed to treatment demonstrate a main effect for family treatment (19%), a main effect for social skills training (20%), and an additive effect for the combined conditions (0%) relative to controls (41%). Effects are explained, in part, by the absence of relapse in any household that changed from high to low EE. Only the combination of treatment sustains a remission in households that remain high in EE. Continuing study, however, suggests a delay of relapse rather than prevention.

Gerard E. Hogarty, Carol M. Anderson, Douglas J. Reiss, Sander J. Kornblith, Deborah P. Greenwald, Carol D. Javna, and Michael J. Madonia. Family Psychoeducation, Social Skills Training, and Maintenance Chemotherapy in the Aftercare Treatment of Schizophrenia. *Archives of General Psychiatry*, 1986, Vol. 43, pp. 633–642. Copyright © 1986, American Medical Association. Reprinted by permission.

In the late 1970s, a critical juncture had been reached in the aftercare treatment of schizophrenic disorders. A series of controlled studies that compared the injectible fluphenazine decanoate to an oral neuroleptic had convincingly demonstrated that the 35% to 40% relapse rate[1] observed among "drug assigned" schizophrenic patients in the first year after hospital discharge was *not* explained by drug noncompliance. Patients receiving either an oral neuroleptic or the injectible fluphenazine had *similar* relapse rates.[2-4]

Internationally, new investigational efforts sought to determine why such a large proportion of schizophrenic patients continued to relapse even though receipt of medication was assured by parenteral administration and whether successful attempts at relapse reduction could be made by means of more relevant therapeutic interventions addressed to environmental and personal factors associated with relapse.[5-7] A "psychosocial-biological" hypothesis of schizophrenic pathophysiology was reasoned, on which principles of clinical practice were formulated. As such, it was proposed that treatment strategies that reflected the current understanding of schizophrenic pathophysiology would be more appropriate and effective for patients and their families. This report represents the results of one of these investigations.

A comprehensive review of the theoretical bases underlying these new psychosocial interventions has been provided by us elsewhere.[8] Briefly, the literature appeared to indicate that the high expectations of certain psychosocial interventions (including an earlier trial by one of us[9]), embodied in the *therapeutic* environment, either precipitated relapse among selected outpatients or evoked long-dormant, psychotic symptoms in chronically hospitalized patients. Similarly, the expectations contained in more developed Western cultures, the demands of developmental epochs and life events, and the apparent stress generated by the selected "affects" of certain families[8,10,11] also suggested that stimulation from the *natural* environment of patients could exacerbate psychosis in vulnerable patients as well.

In our opinion, neither families, therapists, nor cultures could be "blamed" for the relapse of schizophrenic patients. Rather, these observations drew attention to the often severe psychobiological deficits of many schizophrenic patients when dealing with what might otherwise be ordinary life experiences for those not affected by the disorder. Further, it seemed to us that there was a *commonality* among the offending stimuli that were contained in the natural and the therapeutic environments of patients—a commonality that required the vulnerable patient to make an adaptive response to complex, vague, multiple, or emotionally charged expectations. The difficult task faced by the patient in correctly perceiving, processing, and responding selectively to stimuli seemed capable of precipitating a cognitive dysfunction (psychosis), perhaps secondary to affective or autonomic dysregulation.[12] The nature of schizophrenic vulnerability manifest during information-processing tasks[13] and in the regulation of arousal[14] had been amply documented over the past 50 years even though the functional significance of these deficits has remained incompletely understood. We reasoned that if either the demands of the environment *or* the underlying deficits were sufficiently severe, then these factors operating alone, or more likely together, might represent a sufficient cause for schizophrenic relapse—even when the receipt of antipsychotic medication was assured! Conversely, antipsychotic drug regulation of attention and arousal and/or the provision of a more benign, stimuli-modified environment, operating alone or together, might possibly result in the reduction of schizophrenic relapse.

With this "theory" as a basis, a program of family and individual behavioral intervention relevant to the needs of schizophrenic patients was formulated in 1977. Grant support was received in 1978, and the following study initiated in 1979. All patients and families had the opportunity to remain under treatment for at least one year by December 1984. This report describes the first-year outcome of a two-year trial.

Patients and Methods

Definitions of Treatment

Family Psychoeducation and Management. Our family approach was designed as an education and management strategy intended to lower the emotional climate of the home while maintaining reasonable expectations for patient performance. As frequently indicated to us by many relatives, this strategy should not be formally designated as "family therapy." Rather, through the provision of formal education about the disorder and strategies for managing more effectively, family members become allies in the treatment process as their anxiety and distress are decreased. More traditional attempts to promote disclosure, "insight," or direct modification of family systems, including the resolution of intergenerational and marital issues, were, for the most part, avoided. For ease of communication, we refer to the process as family treatment. The goal was to reduce both the positive and negative symptoms of schizophrenia that might be associated with the extremes of stimulation contained in either the therapeutic process or family life. Treatment sought to increase the stability and predictability of family life by decreasing the family's guilt and anxiety, increasing their self-confidence, and providing a sense of cognitive mastery through the provision of information concerning the nature and course of schizophrenia as well as specific management strategies thought to be helpful in coping with schizophrenic symptoms on a day-to-day basis. In that all families entered into this protocol of study were judged "high" in expressed emotion (EE) (a set of attitudes believed to be associated with schizophrenic relapse),[11] it was hypothesized that more direct efforts at a formal education concerning the illness and its management might alter unilateral views of the patient as being either "hopeless" or "obstructional," thereby reducing the understandable criticism, hostility, or emotional involvement that might follow on misinformation, frustration, and less effective coping skills.

Table 1 outlines the goals and treatment strategies of the family approach. The first three phases were most often employed during the first year after hospital admission. A detailed volume that describes both the rationale, content, structure, and process of this family approach is available elsewhere.[8]

Social Skills Training. The principles of social skills training employed were closely tied to the behavioral techniques elaborated by Liberman et al,[15] Wallace et al,[16] and Hersen and Bellack,[17] but differed from more traditional social skills training approaches in some important ways. The format, while highly structured relative to family therapy, was intentionally more flexible than traditional behavioral programs. For example, social skills therapists took into account the patients' progress in recovering from the psychotic episode when choosing the targets and pace for training. Further, emphasis was placed not only on the appropriate performance of social behaviors, but on the development of accurate social perception skills as well. The treatment process unfolded over a two-year period, rather than weeks or months. While the basic tactics of instruction, modeling, role play, feedback, and assigned homework characterized all phases of social skills training, psychotherapeutic strategies such as therapist support and empathy helped to underscore the therapist's alignment with the patient's concerns.

The goal of social skills training was to develop the social competence of patients by enhancing both verbal and nonverbal social behaviors as well as developing more accurate social perception and judgment. Training initially focused on improving the patient's social skills in dealing with family members. As treatment progressed, efforts were addressed to applying these skills to interpersonal relationships beyond the household, such as the social and vocational rehabilitation setting.

Initially, patients were instructed to avoid

TABLE 1 Overview of the Process of Family Treatment

Phases	Goals	Techniques
I. Connection	Connect with the family and enlist cooperation with program Decrease guilt, emotionality, negative reactions to the illness Reduction of family stresses	Joining Establishing treatment contract Discussion of crisis, history, and feelings about patient and illness Empathy Specific practical suggestions that mobilize concerns into effective coping mechanisms
II. Survival skills workshop	Increased understanding of illness and patient's needs by family Continued reduction of family stress Deisolation; enhancement of social networks	Multiple family (education and discussion) group Concrete data on schizophrenia Concrete management suggestions Basic communication skills
III. Reentry and application	Patient maintenance in community Strengthening of marital/parental coalition Increased family tolerance for low-level dysfunctional behaviors Decreased and gradual resumption of responsibility by the patient	Reinforcement of boundaries (generational and interpersonal) Task assignments Low-key problem solving
IV. Work/social adjustment	Reintegration into normal roles in community systems (work, school) Continued stabilization of basic functioning Increased focus on needs of other family members	Apply low-key environment techniques to work/social contacts outside home Task assignments Agency collaboration
V. Maintenance	Increased effectiveness of general family processes Decreased use of therapeutic resources for basic problems and tasks	Infrequent maintenance sessions Traditional or exploratory family therapy techniques

conflict and to decrease behaviors believed to elicit high EE in family members, particularly criticism. Early treatment efforts also focused on teaching patients to express positive feelings, which might decrease family dissatisfaction with the patient and to provide patients with a basic skill that could potentially elicit a favorable response from the family. As patients' performance and perception skills improved, they were trained to handle problems of increasing difficulty (eg, verbally responding to criticism, promoting resolution of conflicts). Social skills training thus represented an indirect attempt to "cool" the emotional climate of the household, in contrast to the more direct approach embodied in family treatment.

Table 2 describes the goals and techniques of this approach. A more detailed description of the rationale, content, structure and process of the social skills approach is available elsewhere.[18] In the first year of treatment, emphasis was essentially on phases I through III.

Control Group. Patients assigned to this condition received maintenance chemotherapy in the context of an individual, supportive, didactic relationship offered by a master's-level psychiatric nurse clinical

TABLE 2 Overview of the Process of Social Skills Training

Phases	Goals	Techniques
I. Stabilization and assessment	Establish therapeutic alliance Assess social performance and perception skills Assess behaviors that provoke expressed emotion	Empathy and rapport Behavioral role play assessment Self- and family reports of social performance
II. Social performance within family	Express positive feelings within family, ie, compliments, appreciation, interest in others Teaching strategies for coping with conflict: avoidance, verbal responses to criticism	Instruction, modeling, role play, feedback, homework (IMRFH) IMRFH: preferences; refusals; response to and expression of criticism via speech latency, voice tone, gaze, gestures, facial expression
III. Social perception within family	Correct identification of content, context, and meaning of messages	IMRFH: read message, label idea; summarize intent and response; consider timing and setting of response
IV. Extrafamilial relationships	Enhance socialization skills Enhance provocational and vocational skills	Assessment of assets needs, and network IMRFH: socialization: conversation and listening skills, dating; recreational activities; vocational: job interviewing; work habits; supervisor-employee relationship training
V. Maintenance	Skill generalization to new situations	IMRFH: social perception review

specialist. (Principles of supportive therapy similar to those employed have been elaborated elsewhere by Krauss and Slavinsky,[19] although our study is not a test of those authors' model.) It was designed as an individual treatment experience that patients might receive from better-trained professionals working in well-staffed outpatient clinics. As an active treatment, it thus had the potential to blur the differences in prophylactic effects between it and the more structured and disorder-specific individual and family treatment conditions. The same nurse clinicians provided similar supportive treatment and supervision of maintenance chemotherapy for all social skills and family treatment patients as well.

By design, patients in all cells were to be seen at least biweekly. Regular clinic attenders in experimental groups were, for the most part, seen weekly. Families were seen weekly during the acute phase of illness, then biweekly for several months, and monthly thereafter. Social skills patients were seen weekly in the first year and biweekly or monthly thereafter. Patients in the combined treatment cell, by definition, accumulated proportional increases in direct service. Details of the treatment contacts and the relationship to outcome will be presented elsewhere. Senior staff regularly monitored the experimental therapies for compliance to treatment protocol. It should be noted that selection of only high EE households allegedly placed patients at a risk of relapse greater than what one might expect in unselected samples.[20] Finally, while relationships with resocialization and vocational rehabilitation agencies were developed and sustained for experimental subjects, use of these resources was, in nearly all cases, reserved to the second year of treatment. Patient goals for the first treatment year were primarily the achievement and maintenance of remission from psychosis.

Study Design

Consecutive admissions to the inpatient service of Western Psychiatric Institute and Clinic, Pittsburgh, were recruited for study between February 1979 and December 1983. Patients met Research Diagnostic Criteria (RDC)[21] for either schizophrenia or schizoaffective disorder. We included schizoaffective disorder since the RDC requires that patients meet clear diagnostic criteria for schizophrenia as well as affective disorder. In addition, we required the presence of two schizophrenic symptoms (rather than one) to qualify for a diagnosis of definite schizoaffective disorder. We believe that the acute episode of schizoaffective disorder is a serious and increasingly common form[22] of psychotic illness (phenomenologically characteristic of patients who relapse while receiving maintenance chemotherapy),[23] and prefer to beg the question as to whether the "diagnosis" represents a variant of schizophrenia or affective disorder.

For at least one of the three months before admission, the patient had to reside in (and was likely to return to) a household defined as "high" in EE. A significant other residing in the patient's household was rated "high"[11] if he or she expressed six or more critical comments toward the patient, or had a rating of 4 or 5 on a global judgment of emotional overinvolvement, or had a positive rating of hostility. Ratings followed an audiotaped interview in which the abbreviated form of the Camberwell Family Interview (CFI) Schedule[24] was administered. All EE raters were trained to reliabilities of .8 or greater on the essential components of EE, using British criterion tapes. Training and experience in the use of the CFI schedule typically took six months before a rater began evaluating study relatives.

Patients were excluded from study if they were beyond the age range of 17 to 55 years, presented evidence of organic brain syndrome, or had a recent history of alcohol or substance abuse that, in the opinion of the diagnostician, could explain the presenting index psychotic episode. Further, patients who suffered renal, hepatic, or cardiovascular disease that precluded the use of antipsychotic medication were also excluded. Whenever possible, patients received maintenance therapy with injectible fluphenazine decanoate to avoid the confound between drug noncompliance and other variables that might be presumed to account for relapse. Patients not discharged from hospital within six months of admission were also excluded. All patients and their families signed informed consent statements and the study was approved by our institutional review board.

The family treatment/social skills study was one of two investigations being conducted concurrently. Assignment to either protocol was made on a calendar basis designed to accommodate available therapist time. Admission to either protocol was made on alternate weeks or months that were predetermined before eligible patients were actually admitted to the hospital. The study attempted to provide a "nested" drug-treated control group, ie, one in which the therapists themselves would be "blind" to the control condition. This design was sought based on the past experience of the investigator, which indicated that controls might be inconsistently treated. Sometimes, for example, it was not that experimental subjects had fared particularly well, but rather that controls did significantly less well than expected in the studies of drug and psychotherapy (as discussed in the "Comment" section). Thus, all diagnostically eligible and consecutively admitted patients living in high EE households were, at the point of hospital admission, first randomized to either the family treatment/social skills study or the control condition: a concurrent dosage study that investigated the potential interaction between EE, drug dose, and relapse. Within the psychosocial protocol, pa-

tients were further randomized to family treatment and medication, social skills training and medication, or a combination of family treatment, social skills training, and medication. Within the dosage study, high EE patients were randomized at the point of hospital admission to an aftercare trial that eventually hoped to contrast a physician-recommended standard dose of fluphenazine decanoate to an experimental low dose. Standard-dose, high EE patients thus served as controls for both the family treatment/social skills study and the dosage study. Patients were designated as controls for the two years of study regardless of whether they ultimately entered into the postdischarge, dosage-study protocol.

During the period of study intake, 134 patients were assigned to the experimental or control cells as soon after hospital admission as diagnosis and EE assessments could be completed (between two days and two weeks). Table 3 describes the disposition of all 134 patients. We provide these details because there is often concern expressed[25] as to how representative "study" patients are of the total population of eligible patients available for investigation at the research facility. Of the 134 patients, 103 actually consented to and entered protocol. Thirty-one patients were administratively terminated. Of these, ten patients were terminated before hospital discharge when late emerging evidence revealed a history of substance abuse, organicity, or bipolar disease. (There was pressure on diagnosticians to move quickly so as to permit family therapists to engage with families as soon as possible after hos-

TABLE 3 Disposition of All Potentially Eligible, Consecutively Admitted Patients

	No. Assigned (N = 134)	No. Entered (N = 103)	No. Administratively Terminated (N = 31)	Reason for Termination		
				No. With Wrong Diagnosis	No. Never Discharged	No. Refused
Family treatment	30	22	8	3	1	4
Social skills training	30	23	7	2	1	4
Family treatment and social skills	29	23	6	1	2	3
Controls	45	35	10	4	2	4

pital admission, should the patient be assigned to one of the family treatment cells.) Six patients were transferred to public mental hospitals and were not discharged within six months. Fifteen patients withdrew consent before discharge or refused protocol on discharge. The number of administrative terminations did not differ significantly across treatment cells. However, seven of 11 administratively terminated *female* patients "refused" protocol compared with eight of 21 administratively terminated *male* patients.

Among the 103 eligible patients and their families thus available for study, we differentiated subjects who met criteria for treatment exposure (treatment takers, N = 90) and those who either relapsed during the process of engagement (N = 11) or otherwise survived but failed to meet full criteria for treatment exposure (N = 2) (partial takers, N = 13). Minimal treatment exposure was defined as follows. Family treatment required attendance by the family at a psychoeducation workshop (usually within a month of admission), plus one example of attempting to implement a management procedure at home or, in a rare case, simply attending six or more family sessions. Minimal treatment exposure to social skills training required completing baseline assessments of social skill deficits (phase I) plus at least one session in skills rehearsal. Minimal treatment in the control condition represented at least two individual sessions of supportive therapy provided by the nurse clinician plus one continuous month of maintenance oral neuroleptic medication, or three consecutive injections of fluphenazine. We distinguish between "treatment takers" and "partial takers" because the latter patients are rarely mentioned (or, in fact, are dropped from analyses) in published studies, but their inclusion in the analyses does influence the interpretation of results, as will be shown.

Whenever possible, the same family member was reevaluated one year after the patient's discharge on the CFI schedule to approach the question of differential treatment effects on the initial level of high EE.

For purposes of this report, two types of schizophrenic relapse are evaluated. Type I relapse represents a change from being "nonpsychotic" at hospital discharge to "psychotic" according to the RDC criteria for schizophrenia or schizoaffective disorder. A type II relapse represented a team consensus that a severe clinical exacerbation of persistent psychotic symptoms had occurred. Otherwise, there were 13 patients, equally distributed across cells who manifested persistent psychosis over the year of observation. However, 12 of these patients were judged to have shown "minimal" or "moderate" improvement, and one remained "unchanged" over the year. These patients are considered "survivors," and the influence of their clinical state on adjustment will be the subject of another report. Not included in this report are incidents of minor exacerbations, which we designate as "miniepisodes." (Miniepisodes were not equal in severity to the index episode and responded over two to three weeks to increased surveillance or medication adjustment.) Definitions of type I and II schizophrenic relapse represented a unanimous team decision. Parallel tests of relapse, using rating scale criteria, were also executed. In the few cases where the primary therapist and the team disagreed regarding the judgment of relapse, the case was reviewed by the investigator. In each instance, he agreed with the team that the patient had relapsed. These few equivocal cases were divided among experimental and control conditions.

Patient Characteristics

Of the 103 protocol patients, two thirds are male. The sample is young (mean age, 27 ± 7.7 years), predominantly white (81%), never married (76%), and living with parents (69%). Such characteristics follow, in part, on selecting high EE households (high EE is associated with being male),[26] as well as the requirement that patients be living with a significant other. Forty-seven percent of the sample is Catholic, and most patients have completed high school (38%) or attended college (39%). Occupationally, the prominent classification is that of unskilled worker (39%), with 22% having worked as skilled or semiskilled machine operators, 16% as clerical workers, and about 10% as students or homemakers. Based on these data as well as the educational and occupation achievements of parents, the sample is predominantly lower middle class (ie, Hollingshead social classes III and IV). Although relatively young, patients have been ill for a considerable period of their life. The mean age at first psychotic episode was 21.3 ± 4.3 years. Patients have experienced 2.7 ± 3.1 hospitalizations before the index episode, and 23% are first episodes. Most (78%) had a gradual onset of the index episode. Among the 103 patients, 65 met criteria for definite schizophrenia and two for probable schizophrenia; 30 met criteria for definite schizoaffective disorder and six for probable disorder.

These patient characteristics are not significantly different across treatment cells, with the exception of sex. Forty-nine percent of controls are male and 75% of experimental subjects are male, a discrepancy due in part to the relatively greater refusal of the experimental conditions by potentially eligible female patients. Since female sex has often been reported as a good prognostic indicator,[27] a bias, if it exists, would operate against the experimental treatments. Otherwise, while definite diagnosis of schizophrenia and schizoaffective disorder is similar across cells, five of the six patients with "probable" schizoaffective disorders are control patients, again reflecting the excess of female controls and a possible bias, if any, against experimental conditions.

Results

Treatment Effects on Relapse

Table 4 presents the relapse rates for treatment takers and the entire sample at 12 months after hospital discharge. Regarding the principal sample of those who met criteria for treatment exposure, the unadjusted (marginal), multidimensional, likelihood χ^2 ratios, as well as those adjusted for the effects of other treatment cells (partial takers), indicate the following: (1) there is a significant main effect for family treatment in forestalling relapse (19% relapse); (2) there is a significant main effect for social skills training in forestalling relapse (20% relapse); (3) in the *absence* of evidence that the treatment main effect(s) occurs *only* when combined (a nonsignificant interaction), the effects of family treatment and social skills training are

TABLE 4 First-Year Relapse: Total Sample

	Treatment Takers (N = 90)		Treatment Taker Plus Partial Takers (N = 103)	
	No. Survived	No. (%) Relapsed	No. Survived	No. (%) Relapsed
Family treatment and drug	17	4 (19)	17	5 (23)
Social skills training and drug	16	4 (20)	16	7 (30)
Family treatment, social skills training, and drug	20	0 (0)	21	2 (9)
Drug controls	17	12 (41)	18	17 (49)

	Likelihood χ^2; P		Likelihood χ^2; P	
	Partials	Marginals	Partials	Marginals
Family treatment	6.66; .010	7.23; .007	7.46; .006	8.43; .004
Social skills training	6.09; .014	6.65; .010	3.53; .060	4.50; .034
Interaction	2.23; .135	—	0.12; .734	—

thus *additive* (0% relapse); (4) the international relapse rate among medicated controls is again confirmed (41% relapse).

The results hold for the entire sample of treatment takers and partial takers as well, although the failure of social skills training to forestall the type II relapse of three psychotic patients during the process of engagement renders the partial χ^2 value for this main effect marginally significant.

Table 5 is offered in response to a concern that the effects of psychosocial intervention might be an artifact of greater drug compliance among patients who receive psychosocial therapies.[28] Among patients who were faithful medication compliers during the entire year of study or until they relapsed, family treatment continues to significantly lower relapse, although the main effect for social skills training is only marginal among those meeting criteria for treatment exposure, and not significant in the entire sample. Again, the absence of a significant interaction and the clear reduction of relapse in the combined treatment cell among takers indicate that these effects are additive in nature. Among the drug-compliant treatment tak-

ers, 65% were maintained with fluphenazine decanoate therapy, including 82% of the controls. Those maintained with oral antipsychotic drug therapy were judged "compliant" based on patient and family reports, history, pill counts, and other evidence such as side effects. Fifty-eight percent of relapsed patients were maintained with depot fluphenazine therapy, and 42% with oral neuroleptic therapy.

Nature of Relapse

Among the 31 relapsed patients in the entire sample, 13 have had type I relapses and 15 type II, with no significant differences between experimental and control patients in the type of relapse. (In studies where inpatient stays are longer, subsequent relapse is primarily type I.[6,20]) Three additional relapsed patients did *not* experience a schizophrenic relapse, but were hospitalized for a severe, postpsychotic depression involving suicide attempts in two patients. Of these three patients, two were social skills training subjects and one was a control. Although one might argue that we lessen the prophy-

TABLE 5 First-Year Relapse: Drug-Compliant Patients Only

	Treatment Takers (N = 78)		Treatment Takers Plus Partial Takers (N = 84)	
	No. Survived	No. (%) Relapsed	No. Survived	No. (%) Relapsed
Family treatment and drug	17	2 (11)	17	2 (11)
Social skills training and drug	15	3 (17)	15	4 (21)
	19	0 (0)	19	2 (10)
Drug controls	15	7 (32)	16	9 (36)

	Likelihood χ^2; P		Likelihood χ^2; P	
	Partials	Marginals	Partials	Marginals
Family treatment	6.12; .013	6.32; .012	4.83; .028	5.20; .023
Social skills training	2.80; .094	2.99; .084	0.94; .331	1.32; .251
Interaction	1.33; .249	—	0.25; .616	—

lactic effect of an experimental treatment on schizophrenic relapse by including these patients as relapsers, their outcomes were unequivocally poor, and they represent all remaining study patients who experienced a deteriorated clinical course.

Otherwise, rating scale criteria of schizophrenia relapse underscore the clinical criteria encompassed in the types I and II classifications. Table 6 provides the means and the more reliable median indicators of clinical state for survivors at one year and schizophrenic relapse at the point of termination. The eight schizophrenic symptoms represented in the RDC schizophrenia criteria were scaled in severity from 0 (absent) to 4 (present and severe). Mean differences are all significant (P = .000). It should be noted that the means and SDs of surviving patients are inflated by the presence of the 13 "improved" patients who nevertheless remained persistently psychotic. End-point ratings among nine relapsed patients are missing for a subset of patients who were most often rehospitalized elsewhere in western Pennsylvania. However, reports from family and/or clinical staff verify the clinical deterioration of these patients. Similarly, the 12-month evaluations of nine survivors are missing, whose status was verified in subsequent visits.

Treatment Effects of EE

Since all patients were deemed to be at "high risk" by reason of the high EE status of the household,[11,20] and experimental treatments were designed to lower EE either directly (family treatment) or indirectly (social skills training), the subsequent main and additive effects on relapse led to an analysis of EE household change, by treatment. We sought a confirmation of the implied "mechanism of action," so to speak, that might underlie the psychosocial interventions. While there were 105 repeated CFI schedule evaluations available on individual relatives represented in the entire sample, we focused on the sample of treatment takers for whom main and additive effects were demonstrated and in need of explanation.

Eighty-eight relatives living in 61 of the 90 "taker" households agreed to be re-evaluated at one year, or at the time of pa-

TABLE 6 Rating Scale Criteria of Schizophrenic Relapse

	Survivors	Relapsers
Severity of Research Diagnostic Criteria schizophrenic symptoms (range, 0–32)		
Mean*	3.20 ± 5.15	13.38 ± 6.90
Median	0.46	12.0
No. of Research Diagnostic Criteria schizophrenic symptoms rated "moderately severe" or "severe" (range, 0–8)		
Mean*	0.63 ± 1.40	3.44 ± 1.79
Median	0.19	3.10
Severity of illness (range, 1–7†)		
Mean*	2.65 ± 1.02	5.00 ± 0.91
Median	2.43	5.07
Degree of remission (range, 1–5‡)		
Mean*	2.63 ± 1.15	4.94 ± 0.24
Median	2.37	4.97

*Mean differences between survivors and relapsers were significant at P = .000.   †Range, 1 (not at all) to 3 (mild) to 7 (most extremely ill).   ‡Range, 1 (complete, nonpsychotic) to 5 (incomplete, psychotic).

tient relapse. While only 23% of the relatives in the experimental conditions refused a repeated CFI schedule, unfortunately 52% of control family households declined. (There does not appear to be a negative bias regarding patient relapse in these families, however, since only 24% of patients relapsed in "refusing" households.) In ten of the 15 uncooperative control families and in all 14 of the refusing experimental families, the treatment team was able to make an informed *judgment* of EE change. When it refused a repeated CFI, an experimental family receiving family treatment, for example, was judged to have remained "high" in EE if frequent telephone calls to the clinician or family sessions revealed "emotional temperature" taking of the patient or continuing expressions of hostility and/or criticism. Patient reports of such, and/or unsolicited telephone calls from families of controls and subjects receiving social skills training, led to similar judgments that the household had remained "high" in EE.

Change in EE by Household. Table 7 presents the EE status of households from hospital admission to follow-up. Twenty-two households changed from "high" to "low" EE by formal CFI evaluations and five

by team judgments. Thirty-nine remained "high" by CFI ratings and 19 by team judgments (ten of which were controls). From Table 7, we conclude that (1) there is *no* patient relapse in any household that changes from high EE to low EE, *independent* of treatment condition; (2) among households that remain high in EE, relapse continues to be elevated and is not different among controls (42%) and those who received family treatment alone (33%) or social skills training alone (29%); (3) only the combination of family treatment and social skills training provides a significant prophylactic effect (0%) in households that remain high in EE. We have no results, at the moment, that can adequately explain this phenomenon.

It appears that the main effect of family treatment can be explained in part by its relatively greater ability (as hypothesized) to directly lower household EE in 16 (39%) of the 41 families so treated. However, lowered EE can also occur in a subsample of households not exposed to family treatment (ie, controls and those receiving social skills training alone), where 11 (25%) of 44 households changed from high to low EE. There is no evidence, however, that social skills training indirectly lowers EE as hypothesized, since the proportion of house-

TABLE 7 Household Expressed Emotion Status (Admission to Follow-up) and Patient Relapse Among Treatment Takers (N = 90)

	Households Changed From High to Low in Expressed Emotion				Households That Remained High in Expressed Emotion			
	Camberwell Family Interview Schedule Rating	Team Judgment	Total	% of Patients Relapsed	Camberwell Family Interview Schedule Rating	Team Judgment	Total	% of Patients Relapsed
Controls (N = 29)	5	0	5	0	9	10	19*	42
Social skills training (N = 20)	4	2	6	0	10	4	14	29
Family treatment (N = 21)	7	2	9	0	11	1	12	33
Family treatment and social skills training (N = 20)	6	1	7	0	9	4	13	0

*Five households were missing data.

holds that change from high to low EE is similar to that of controls.

Change in EE by Individual Relative. We explored the pattern of EE at admission and follow-up, by treatment group, for the 88 individual relatives to identify possible relationships to outcome. There were no significant patterns of EE associated with outcome. Table 8 presents the EE characteristics of all 88 individual relatives at admission and follow-up according to the outcome of patients living with the relative. (We include these raw data because the CFI rating is a labor-intensive method, and few investigators might be in the position to accumulate such data in the future.) With 64 "cells" and variable numbers of subject within cells, detailed testing of EE by outcome and treatment group was precluded. However, a few "observations" are instructive: (1) much like the "household" analysis, a greater number of individual relatives change from high to low EE in the family treatment conditions; (2) neither hostility alone nor in combination with emotional overinvolvement characterizes families at admission or

at follow-up; invariably, when hostility occurs, it is in the context of criticism; (3) emotional overinvolvement tends to disappear (31% of relatives at admission, and only 6% at follow-up) and does *not* contribute to relapse.

The only comment that could be made regarding admission EE characteristics and patient outcome is that eventual survivors (contrary to what one might predict) tend to be *over*represented by relatives with high emotional overinvolvement (33%), and eventual relapsed patients are *under*represented (19%) by relatives with high emotional overinvolvement at admission. Regarding follow-up CFI evaluations, the EE characteristic most often associated with relapse is the *combination* of hostility and criticism in the relatives (56% of relapse relatives; 21% of survivors' relatives), a pattern that was equally represented at admission (33%).

Finally, we examined the amount of "face-to-face contact" between patient and relative by treatment and outcome, a phenomenon believed to contribute to relapse among high EE families,[11,20] and one that we

TABLE 8 Expressed Emotion Status* of 88 Relatives at Admission and Follow-up, by Treatment and Their Patients' Outcome

Expressed Emotion Status	No. of Patients (No. Relapsed)							
	Controls (N = 16)		Social Skills Training (N = 19)		Family Treatment (N = 32)		Family Treatment and Social Skills Training (N = 21)	
	Admission	Follow-up	Admission	Follow-up	Admission	Follow-up	Admission	Follow-up
Low expressed emotion	1 (1)	7 (2)	1 (0)	6 (0)	5 (1)	17 (1)	2 (0)	10 (0)
Criticism	9 (5)	3 (2)	5 (1)	5 (0)	9 (1)	6 (2)	3 (0)	3 (0)
Hostility	0 (0)	0 (0)	0 (0)	1 (0)	0 (0)	2 (0)	0 (0)	0 (0)
Criticism/hostility	3 (1)	6 (4)	7 (2)	6 (3)	8 (1)	6 (1)	8 (0)	4 (0)
Emotional overinvolvement	2 (1)	0 (0)	2 (0)	0 (0)	6 (0)	0 (0)	4 (0)	2 (0)
Criticism/emotional overinvolvement	1 (0)	0 (0)	2 (0)	1 (0)	2 (0)	0 (0)	4 (0)	1 (0)
Hostility/emotional overinvolvement	0 (0)	0 (0)	0 (0)	0 (0)	1 (1)	0 (0)	0 (0)	0 (0)
Criticism/hostility/ emotional overinvolvement	0 (0)	0 (0)	2 (0)	0 (0)	1 (1)	1 (1)	0 (0)	1 (0)

*Determined by Camberwell Family Interview Schedule.

thought might explain the absence of relapse in the combined treatment condition. No significant differences in face-to-face contact could be found.

Comment
Limits of Inference Making

We conclude that two disorder-relevant psychosocial interventions, one family centered and the other individually centered, when applied in the context of maintenance chemotherapy can significantly forestall schizophrenic relapse in the first year after hospital discharge. The combination of experimental treatments yields an effect not possible with either treatment alone. The effect of social skills training alone is mitigated somewhat among patients discharged in a psychotic state. Even though clear main effects are demonstrated, it must be emphasized that each treatment strategy represents a "team" approach in its own right: the experimental procedure(s), supportive therapy from the nurse clinician, and maintenance chemotherapy administered by a psychiatrist. Maintenance chemotherapy remains the necessary foundation for psychosocial intervention since the evidence is clear that relapse in the absence of medication averages 68% in one year and increases proportionally among multiepisode patients.[1] There is *no* evidence available to us that the psychosocial interventions tested would be effective without maintenance chemotherapy. The absence of a more complete experimental design (eg, placebo and "no treatment" cells), however, does limit our understanding of the unique contribution from each treatment component in the "systems" design, except, of course, for the experimental condition itself.

Delay of relapse is associated with the reduction of high EE in households, as Leff et al[20] have previously demonstrated—a phenomenon more likely, but by no means entirely, accounted for by family psychoeducation and management. However, "causal" inferences[20] regarding EE and relapse need to be qualified. It is possible that the high EE status of households with a relapsed patient is due to the relapse event itself. In the absence of interim EE evaluations, it is unknown to us whether some or all of these households had, in fact, already changed from high to low EE—and then returned to high EE status at the time of the patient's relapse. Further, preliminary analyses of adjustment (to be published later) suggest that nonrelapsed patients, across treatments, whose households changed from high to low EE are significantly *better* adjusted than nonrelapsed patients whose households remained high in EE. As such, it is as possible to argue that some families changed their EE status because the patient's condition improved as it is to suggest that lowered EE "caused" a better patient outcome.

Further, we would caution against the tendency to admit *only* "high EE" families to psychoeducation and management programs as the primary indicator of "risk."[5-7] Based on evidence from our independent replication study of EE and reexamination of prior studies,[26] we believe that the relationship between EE and schizophrenic relapse has been better established for male schizophrenic patients living in parental homes, a phenomenon that tends, by design, to disproportionately place unmarried male patients under family treatment. However, the considerable relapse we observed among "low EE" female subjects,[26] who frequently suffer from schizoaffective disorder, seems associated with other factors involving real or pending loss (eg, separation or divorce) and should, as such, qualify such patients for family treatment programs as well. Recent independent evidence would also support this recommendation.[29] In addition, we sense a growing movement to provide family "psychoeducation" in a vacuum, ie, as an isolated didactic event, rather than as the foundation for an ongoing relationship wherein theory and facts are *applied* on an individual case basis over time. While there is a clear administrative and fiscal appeal for a more limited effort (ie, families can "manage" more cheaply than paid professionals), we believe that sustained clinical effort and support are required before many families can process, integrate, and effectively apply newly acquired information. However, we recognize that this is an empirical question, one currently under investigation in a National Institute of Mental Health collaborative study.[30]

The absence of relapse in the combined treatment condition among patients and families exposed to treatment is difficult to explain, and the theoretical model of Liberman and Evans[31] is helpful. In this model, "personal" protective factors in the form of enhanced individual coping skills (social skills training), combined with environmental protective factors associated with an improved "family problem-solving" ability (family treatment) decreases both intrinsic vulnerability of the patient, and his environmental stress. This model reflects, in part, the operating theory on which our treatment program was based. We would not infer, however, that positive results are a validation of any underlying theory. The results that we obtained might just as well have followed from factors and processes unknown to us at the moment. What does seem important is the necessity of *some* theory that provides a cognitive mastery and behavioral direction for families, patients, and therapists.

Finally, we wish to emphasize that these early prophylactic effects are more likely related to the *delay* of schizophrenic relapse than to its *prevention*, as Englehardt et al[32] demonstrated years ago. As patients near the end of their second year of treatment, relapse continues to rise in all experimental conditions. Although a main effect of family treatment is being sustained, and much of the relapse is associated with drug noncompliance, we are clearly not preventing schizophrenic relapse. Recently, Leff et al[20] reported the first two-year follow-up of a ninemonth controlled family study and argued that only one (14%) of the seven family therapy patients relapsed when EE or "face-to-face contact" had been reduced, compared with 78% relapse among drug-treated controls. However, when one examines the outcome of their original sample of 12 experimental and 12 control patients, 75% of controls indeed relapsed (seven of these while receiving medication), but 50% of experimental patients also had a poor outcome: two relapsed while receiving drug, two relapsed while not receiving medication, and two committed suicide.

Wallace and Liberman[33] similarly reported a 50% relapse rate at two years among experimental patients who received social skills training while hospitalized and whose families received a behavioral family therapy. (Controls experienced a 79% relapse rate by two years.) Only Falloon et al[34] described a second-year outcome of family intervention significantly better than what one would exponentially predict for drugmaintained patients.[35] In this study, 83% of 18 controls have had a major episode of schizophrenia by 24 months, but only 17% of 18 family-treated patients.[34] Further, controls experienced 54 schizophrenic episodes, of which 41 were "major," while experimental subjects manifested only 36 episodes, of which seven were "major" over the two years of observation.

Comparison With Other One-Year Results of Family Treatment and Social Skills Training

Four controlled *aftercare* studies of family intervention in schizophrenia,[5-7,36] another involving social skills training,[37] and another, a community follow-up of inpatient social skills training and family treatment,[33] have been published in recent years. The first, a pioneering effort by Goldstein et al,[36] was a six-week, postdischarge study of neuroleptic dose and family therapy. While no patient relapsed in the family-therapy/standard-dose group and 24% of patients relapsed in the no-family-therapy/low-dose group, the brief period of treatment exposure and the absence of formal EE ratings permit few direct comparisons with our own and other trials. Otherwise, Leff et al[6] and Falloon et al[5] have published results of their nine-month controlled trials that compared family treatment with drug-treated controls. Köttgen et al[7] have recently published a nine-month study of family *group* therapy vs controls. For the most part, all studies included families judged to be "high" in EE following a CFI assessment. Table 9 presents the nine-month outcomes of these family trials, our own investigation included, together with (exponentially) extrapolated 12-month rates, based on the nine-month data from the three contrasting family studies. Clearly, the low relapse of patients living in families treated in individual sessions is consistent across studies, and remains less than 10% at nine months and equal to or less than 20% at 12 months. The one exception is the more analytically oriented group therapy approach of Köttgen et al,[7] whose patients were also very young.

Equally striking, however, is the experience of drug-treated controls. Among the contrasting studies, nine-month relapse rates with maintenance chemotherapy alone exceed the 12-month 41% relapse rate of our own trial and the characteristic 12-month rate among published, drug-controlled, maintenance studies.[1] Estimates of one-year relapse among controls in the contrasting studies resemble the 68% relapse rate often observed in placebo substitution studies.[1] Leff et al,[20] however, have argued that the presence of a high-EE household places the patient at an increased risk of relapse by nine months (54%), even when maintenance chemotherapy is assured. For the most part, this estimate appears to be based on naturalistic studies,[11] where maintenance treatment was neither provided nor controlled by the investigator. As such, the 28% relapse rate at nine months and the 41% relapse rate at 12 months among our own controls either reflects a prophylactic effect of our "active" control treatment, an effect that further serves to lessen comparisons with the experimental conditions, or indicates that drug controls in the contrasting studies might contain covert drug defaulters. Further, unlike the contrasting studies, we provide evidence that a *patient*-centered, disorder-relevant intervention is as effective as a family-centered approach per se, in the first year after discharge, an observation worth emphasizing in light of the veritable explosion of publications in recent years that selectively endorse family treatment. Indeed, families have been neglected for decades, and a long-overdue response is needed.[38] However, the contribution of a patient-centered approach cannot be ignored, although the focus of individual treatment was often based on family complaints about the patient. Even if the effect of social skills training is not sustained, its combination with family treatment provides an early effect not possible with family treatment alone.

TABLE 9 Nine-Month Relapse (Actual) and 12-Month Relapse (Projected) in High–Expressed Emotion Family Treatment Studies of Schizophrenia

Source, yr	% of Experimental Subjects			% of Control Subjects		
	N	9-mo Relapse	12-mo Relapse	N	9-mo Relapse	12-mo Relapse
Hogarty et al, 1985*	21 family treatment	9	19	29	28	41
	20 social skills training	10	20			
	20 family treatment and social skills training	0	0			
Leff et al,[6,20] 1982 and 1985	12 family treatment	9	12†	12	50	60†
Falloon et al,[5] 1982	18 family treatment	6	8†	18	44	54†
Köttgen et al,[7] 1984	15 group family treatment	33	41†	14	50	60†

*Treatment takers.   †Extrapolated rates.

Otherwise, only one controlled "after-care" study of social skills training could be found in the literature, and this trial supports our own conclusions regarding the efficacy of social skills training. Recently, Bellack et al[37] reported on the differential effects of day hospital treatment vs day hospital and social skills training among a group of schizophrenic patients, most of whom were recently discharged from inpatient care. While all subjects changed after the treatment, the change appeared more "uniform" among social skills subjects. A six-month follow-up revealed selected gains for social skills recipients, but sample attrition, particularly among controls, seems to limit generalizations.

Wallace and Liberman[33] have reported on the nine- and 24-month community outcome of an *inpatient* study of social skills training vs holistic therapy (in the context of maintenance chemotherapy and family treatment), which is worthy of comment. The authors provided evidence of social skills training on reducing relapse and on learning, social competence, and adjustment from the vantage of professional raters, patient confederates, and family at nine months, results that are supported by our own observations. While evidence of generalization appears to accrue to environments and relationships that have been controlled or managed (eg, family and patient-peer relationships) most effects appear attributable to the nine-month follow-up and 50% of patients have relapsed by two years, implying, perhaps, some difficulty in the generalization of coping skills to less familiar or controlled circumstances.

In summary, we are able to state that after three decades of study, there is an increasingly validated message of hope and promise for schizophrenic patients, their families, and clinicians: psychosocial interventions do add something more to the maintenance treatment of schizophrenia than drug therapy alone, at least in the year after hospital discharge. Treatment strategies that place more distance between psychotic episodes are clearly in the public health interest and are demonstrably more cost-effective than inpatient care.[39] However, treatment challenges remain in the decade ahead: (1) strategies are needed for recovered patients that would facilitate engagement of difficult patients (and families) and sustain compliance with maintenance chemotherapy and psychosocial programs over time, and (2) more "patient-specific" therapeutic interventions need to be developed to prepare *recovered* patients for their move toward a fuller life beyond the home. At the moment, our greatest success seems to be in the convalescent months, when family life can be tempered and the patient trained to accommodate and respond to this protected environment. Unfortunately, the functional significance of less apparent schizophrenic vulnerabilities seems not to be understood or managed, in our opinion, at least when later attempts at a more complete and autonomous life beyond the clinic, home, and sheltered workshop are made.

References

1. Hogarty GE: Depot neuroleptics: The relevance of psycho-social factors. *J Clin Psychiatry* 1984;45(pt 2):36–42.

2. Hogarty, GE, Schooler, NR, Ulrich RF, Mussare F, Herron E, Ferro P: Fluphenazine and social therapy in the aftercare of schizophrenic patients: Relapse analyses of a two-year controlled study of fluphenazine decanoate and fluphenazine hydrochloride. *Arch Gen Psychiatry* 1979;36:1283–1294.

3. Schooler NR, Levine J, Severe JB, Brauzer B, DiMascio A, Klerman GL, Tuason VB: Prevention of relapse in schizophrenia: An evaluation of fluphenazine decanoate. *Arch Gen Psychiatry* 1980;37:16–24.

4. Falloon I, Watt DC, Shepperd M: A comparative controlled trial of pimozide and fluphenazine decanoate in the continuation therapy of schizophrenia. *Psychol Med* 1978;8:59–70.

5. Falloon IRH, Boyd JL, McGill CW, Razoni J, Moss HB, Gilderman HA: Family management in the prevention of exacerbations of schizophrenia. *N Engl J Med* 1982;306:1437–1444.

6. Leff J, Kuipers L, Berkowitz R, Eberlein-

VRIES R, STURGEON D: A controlled trial of social intervention in the families of schizophrenic patients. *Br J Psychiatry* 1982;141:121–134.

7. KÖTTGEN C, SONNISCHSEN I, MOLLENHAUER K, JURTH R: Group therapy with the families of schizophrenic patients: Results of the Hamburg Camberwell Family Interview Study III. *Int J Fam Psychiatry* 1984;5:84–94.

8. ANDERSON CM, REISS DJ, HOGARTY GE: *Schizophrenia in the Family: A Practitioner's Guide to Psychoeducation and Management.* New York, Guilford Press, 1986.

9. HOGARTY GE, GOLDBERG SC, SCHOOLER NR: Drug and sociotherapy in the aftercare of schizophrenic patients: III. Adjustment of nonrelapsed patients. *Arch Gen Psychiatry* 1974;31:609–618.

10. VALONE, K, NORTON JP, GOLDSTEIN MJ, DOANE JA: Parental expressed emotion and affective style in an adolescent sample at risk for schizophrenia spectrum disorders. *J Abnorm Psychol* 1983; 92:399–407.

11. HOOLEY, JM: Expressed emotion: A review of the critical literature. *Clin Psychol Rev* 1985;5:119–139.

12. BRADEN W: Vulnerability and schizo-affective psychosis: A two-factor model. *Schizophr Bull* 1984;10:71–86.

13. NUECHTERLEIN KH, DAWSON ME: Information processing and attentional functioning in the developmental course of schizophrenic disorders. *Schizophr Bull* 1984;10:160–203.

14. DAWSON ME, NUECHTERLEIN KH: Psychophysiologic dysfunctions in the developmental course of schizophrenia. *Schizophr Bull* 1984; 10:204–232.

15. LIBERMAN RP, KING LW, DERISI WJ, MCCANN M: *Personal Effectiveness.* Champaign, Ill, Research Press, 1975.

16. WALLACE CJ, NELSON CJ, LIBERMAN RP, AITCHISON RA, LUKOFF D, ELDER JP, FERRIS C: A review and critique of social skills training with schizophrenic patients. *Schizophr Bull* 1980; 6:42–63.

17. HERSEN M, BELLACK AS: Social skills training for chronic psychiatric patients. *Compr Psychiatry* 1976;17:559–580.

18. GREENWALD D, KORNBLITH S, JAVNA C: *A Model of Social Skills Training With Schizophrenic Patients: Pre-publication Report.* 1985.

19. KRAUSS JB, SLAVINSKY AT: *The Chronically Ill Psychiatric Patient and the Community.* London, Blackwell Scientific Publications Ltd, 1982.

20. LEFF J, KUIPERS L, BERKOWITZ R, STURGEON D: A controlled trial of social intervention in the families of schizophrenic patients: Two-year follow-up. *Br J Psychiatry* 1985;146:594–600.

21. SPITZER RL, ENDICOTT J, ROBINS E: *Research Diagnostic Criteria (RDC) for a Selected Group of Functional Disorders,* ed 3. New York, New York State Psychiatric Institute, 1978.

22. HOGARTY GE: Treatment and the course of schizophrenia. *Schizophr Bull* 1977;3:587–599.

23. MCEVOY JP, HOWE AC, HOGARTY GE: Differences in the nature of relapse and subsequent inpatient course between medication-compliant and noncompliant schizophrenic patients. *J Nerv Ment Dis* 1984;172:412–416.

24. VAUGHN CE, LEFF JP: The measurement of expressed emotion in families of psychiatric patients. *Br J Soc Clin Psychol* 1976;15:157–165.

25. LEFF JP, WING JK: Trial of maintenance therapy in schizophrenia. *Br Med J* 1971;3:559–604.

26. HOGARTY GE: Expressed emotion and schizophrenic relapse, in Alpert M (ed): *Controversies in Schizophrenia.* New York, Guilford Press, 1985, pp. 354–363.

27. SEEMAN MV: Gender differences in schizophrenia. *Can J Psychiatry* 1982;27:107–112.

28. KLEIN DF: Psychosocial treatment of schizophrenia, or psychosocial help for people with schizophrenia? *Schizophr Bull* 1980;6:122–130.

29. KÖTTGEN C, SONNISCHSEN I, MOLLENHAUER K, JURTH R: The family relations of young schizophrenic patients: Results of the Hamburg Camberwell Family Interview Study I. *Int J Family Psychiatry* 1984;5:61–70.

30. SCHOOLER, NR, KEITH S: *Pharmacologic and Somatic Treatments Branch, NIMH, Collaborative Study of Fluphenazine Dosage and Family Treatment Protocol.* 1984.

31. LIBERMAN RP, EVANS CC: Behavioral rehabilitation for chronic mental patients. *J Clin Psychopharmacol* 1985;5(suppl):85–145.

32. ENGELHARDT DM, ROSEN B, FREEDMAN N, MARGOLIS R: Phenothiazines in prevention of psychiatric hospitalization: IV. Delay or prevention of hospitalization? *Arch Gen Psychiatry* 1967;16:98–101.

33. WALLACE CJ, LIBERMAN RP Social skills training for patients with schizophrenia: A controlled clinical trial. *Psychiatry Res* 1985; 15:239–247.

34. FALLOON IRH, BOYD JL, MCGILL CW, WILLIAMSON M, RAZANI J, MOSS HB, GILDERMAN AM, SIMPSON GM: Family management in the prevention of morbidity of schizophrenia. *Arch Gen Psychiatry* 1985;42:887–896.

35. HOGARTY, GE, ULRICH RF: Temporal effects of drug and placebo in delaying relapse in schizophrenic outpatients. *Arch Gen Psychiatry* 1977;34:297–301.

36. GOLDSTEIN MJ, RODNICK EH, EVANS JR, MAY

PR, STEINBERG M: Drug and family therapy in the aftercare of acute schizophrenia. *Arch Gen Psychiatry* 1978;35:1169–1177.

37. BELLACK AS, TURNER SM, HERSEN M, LUBER RF: An examination of the efficacy of social skills training for chronic schizophrenic patients. *Hosp Community Psychiatry* 1984;35:1023–1028.

38. HATFIELD AB: The family as partner in the treatment of mental illness. *Hosp Community Psychiatry* 1979;30:338–340.

39. ANDREWS G, HALL W, GOLDSTEIN G, LAPSLEY H, BARTELS R, SILONE D: The economic costs of schizophrenia. *Arch Gen Psychiatry* 1985;42:537–543.

SECTION 3

Mood Disorders

Rare is the person who has not experienced some symptoms of depression. Feelings of sadness affect us all from time to time. In most cases these feelings are fleeting; they last only a day or two at most. But for those who are clinically depressed, the depressed mood is more severe and enduring, markedly interfering with daily life. It is also accompanied by additional symptoms such as changes in appetite and sleep habits, fatigue, lack of interest in previously pleasurable activities, difficulties in concentration, changes in physical activity levels, and feelings of guilt and self-reproach. Sometimes combined with recurrent thoughts of death or suicide, these symptoms form the syndrome we call unipolar depression.

There is another side to depression, however. Some depressed persons also experience periods that are characterized by feelings of elation or euphoria. When these feelings coexist with unusually high levels of activity, rapid speech, distractibility, inflated self-esteem, and decreased need for sleep, the diagnosis is one of mania. Those who experience periods of mania followed by periods of depression are said to be suffering from bipolar disorder.

Although bipolar disorder affects only about 1% of the population, unipolar depression is one of the most common forms of mental disorder. Indeed, it is often referred to as the "common cold of psychopathology" (Seligman, 1973). Weissman,

Myers, and Harding (1978) have estimated that, over the course of a lifetime, approximately 25% of the general population will experience at least one clinically significant episode of depression.

Clinical Heterogeneity

It has long been observed that, like schizophrenia, affective disorders appear to run in families. The first-degree relatives of bipolar patients, for example, have a morbidity risk for this disorder that is more than six times that of the general population. Although familial data cannot invariably be taken as providing evidence for a genetic component to a particular disorder, the genetic evidence appears to be particularly strong in the case of bipolar illness.

Interestingly, the first-degree relatives of bipolar patients are also at elevated risk for developing unipolar depressions. Relatives of unipolar patients, on the other hand, do not appear to have significantly higher rates of bipolar disorder than do persons in the general population. However, Winokur (1979) has observed that alcoholism and sociopathy are overrepresented in the male relatives of women who have early onset (before age 40) depressions. His data have led him to suggest that alcoholism and sociopathy may be part of a "depressive spectrum" of disorders.

173

Taken together, these findings indicate that the diagnosis of unipolar depression may actually cover a range of disorders, each with a different etiology. This may explain why such an apparently diverse array of variables currently attracts the attention of researchers. We will examine two areas of particular importance to current investigations of unipolar depression; neurobiology and the role of cognitions.

Unipolar Depresson
Biological Factors

Biological theories of depression have a long history. As far back as the fourth century B.C., Hippocrates considered depression to be the result of an excess of black bile in the body. Indeed, the word melancholia is derived from the Greek words for black (*melan*) and bile (*choler*). Today, the search for biochemical causes of depression still continues. Now, however, the focus is on neurotransmitters—particularly norepinephrine and serotonin.

Recent developments in biochemical theories of depression are discussed by McNeal and Cimbolic (1986; selection 12) in what is probably the most technical and advanced reading in this compilation. The authors begin by providing a clear and accessible review of biochemical events at the synapse. This is then followed by an examination of the amine theories of depression and a discussion of antidepressant medications. The role of antidepressants is important because their chemical effects have been central to the development of biological theories of depression. As our understanding of the mechanism of action of these medications grows, however, earlier biochemical hypotheses must be expanded and revised. Currently attracting a great deal of interest are the long-term effects of antidepressants on the receptor systems. In many respects therefore, biochemical research in unipolar depression is paralleling biochemical research in schizophrenia. In both cases the

central focus of interest is the postsynaptic membrane.

The Role of Cognitions

For psychologists, the most active area of current research concerns the role of cognitive factors in the development of depression. In large measure, this focus is due to the influence of two specific etiologic theories—Beck's cognitive theory (Beck, 1967) and learned helplessness theory (Abramson Seligman & Teasdale, 1978).

According to Beck's cognitive theory, individuals become depressed because they are inclined to make characteristic errors in logic. These errors, according to the theory, lead them to draw erroneous and negative conclusions about themselves and about their environment. Once activated by situational factors, these maladaptive conclusions or negative schemata conspire to engender the characteristic depressive symptoms of pessimism and feelings of worthlessness. In short, they contribute to a general negative feeling about the self, the world, and the future.

While Beck's theory developed from extensive clinical observations of depressed persons, learned helplessness theory has its roots in early research by Seligman on avoidance learning in dogs. Seligman noticed that when exposed to unavoidable shock in a laboratory setting, many of his experimental animals later failed to avoid controllable shock when the experimental circumstances were changed. In other words, the dogs behaved as if they had "given up." The learned helplessness construct was subsequently extended to explain the behavior of humans exposed to experimenter-induced failure. This extension subsequently revealed some conceptual inadequacies of the theory and led to its reformulation by Abramson, Seligman, and Teasdale in 1978.

Within this reformulation, heavy emphasis is placed on the attributions made in response to negative outcomes. According to the theory, persons who are prone to depression tend to make internal, global, and stable attributions in response to negative outcomes. Thus, a person who performs poorly on a math test, for example, is more likely to become depressed if he or she attributes the failure to an overall lack of intellectual ability rather than to an unstable factor (e.g., feeling unwell on the day of the test), an external factor (e.g., the professor graded it unfairly), or a specific factor (math just isn't my best subject). The causal attribution "I failed because I'm stupid" reflects a negative internal characteristic that is both stable (likely to endure over time) and global (likely to influence behavior in a wide range of domains). For this reason, it is considered to be depressogenic.

The major difference between Beck's cognitive theory and learned helplessness theory concerns their underlying paradigms for cognition. Within Beck's theory, particular attention is given to the forms of conceptual organization (schemata) that *shape the processing* of incoming information. Learned helplessness theory, in contrast, focuses on how incoming information is *explained*. Both models, however, assume that cognitive biases or distortions are central to the development of depression.

As Layne (selection 13) points out, however, there is reason to believe that depression and cognitive distortions do not always go hand in hand. In fact, empirical evidence suggests that the opposite can sometimes be the case. In some situations depressed people may indeed be "sadder but wiser" (Alloy & Abramson, 1979).

Cognitive and cognitive-behavioral theories of depression do not stand or fall, however, on the issue of the accuracy or inaccuracy of depressives' cognitions. The central question is why the cognitions of depressed and nondepressed persons differ at all. In the final analysis, the success of cognitively based models will be judged by the extent to which they generate potentially valuable forms of intervention for depression and can empirically demonstrate that cognitive factors are causes, rather than consequences, of depressive episodes.

Although cognitively based forms of therapy are becoming more and more widely used, there is to date no compelling evidence to suggest that negative or helpless cognitions are anything more than concurrent correlates of dysphoria. In other words, no strong data currently support a cognitive model of the etiology of depression. And yet, it is perhaps premature to conclude that absence of evidence is evidence of absence. This conclusion presupposes that all the variables worthy of investigation have been examined and that no other potentially fruitful avenues of inquiry exist. Many researchers are still very actively involved in efforts to provide an understanding of the role of cognitions and behavior in depresson. And, as is apparent from the articles discussed in this section, empirical and theoretical efforts are growing ever more refined and sophisticated.

In selection 14, for example, Nolen-Hoeksema explores gender differences in depression. In particular, she employs a cognitive vulnerability model that may go some way toward explaining the well-documented 2:1 ratio of depressed women to depressed men. This model is based on empirically demonstrated gender differences in responses to feelings of depression—particularly in the tendency to ruminate on one's emotional state. Women tend to adopt coping strategies that focus attention on their mood; men appear to do things that will have just the opposite effect.

The approach taken by Hammen and her colleagues in selection 15, on the other hand, represents an effort to integrate a cognitive vulnerability model of depression with research on life stress. The association between stressful life events and depression has been known for some time. The strength of the association between these two variables, however, is no more than modest. Using a particularly elegant design, Hammen and her colleagues describe the results of their attempt to predict precisely who would become depressed in their sample of college students and under what conditions. Their strategy was to first classify students according to their areas of vulnerability, and then to follow them prospectively for several months. The result is an interesting and informative article that sheds light on possible interactions between depressive schemata and negative life stress. The article also illustrates the important efforts that are now being made to bring together separate, but potentially related areas of empirical research in order to better understand the phenomenon of depression.

This move toward a more integrative approach is also apparent in recent theoretical developments. Most notable in this regard has been the work of Lewinsohn (selection 16). Lewinsohn begins by considering what we currently know about depression, emphasizing the key empirical and clinical findings that must be explained by any new etiological model. These findings include the central role of dysphoria, gender differences in the prevalence of unipolar disorder, and the heterogeneity of depressive symptoms. Using these as a starting point, Lewinsohn develops a multientry model of depression that appears capable of explaining much of what we already know about the disorder. It also generates a number of relatively specific predictions. For these reasons, Lewinsohn's integrative theory is likely to become a focus of considerable attention for depression researchers in the coming years.

Bipolar Disorder

Although psychological theories have played a dominant role in our understanding of unipolar disorder, most of the contributions to our understanding of bipolar disorder have come from genetic research. A series of reports that have received widespread attention in recent years concern patterns of affective illness—particularly bipolar disorder—among the Amish of Pennsylvania. Unfortunately, we were unable to secure permission to include a valuable introduction to the Amish study (Egeland & Hostetter, 1983) in this selection of readings. Interested readers are therefore referred to the original article. In this, Egeland and Hos-

tetter explain why the Amish are such a unique population for genetic investigations. They then present data concerning the prevalence of unipolar and bipolar disorders in this sample. Particularly interesting is the finding that rates of both disorder are approximately equal. In most other populations, rates of unipolar depression have been found to be approximately 10 times higher than rates of bipolar disorder. Also worthy of mention is the finding that the Amish are one of the few populations in which no marked gender difference in the frequency of unipolar disorder has been found. The possibility that unipolar depression may be underdiagnosed among Amish women is an issue raised in the article (selection 14) by Nolen-Hoeksema.

Perhaps the most exciting data to come from the Amish study, however, relate to the identification of a gene located on the short arm of chromosome 11. This gene appears to be reliably associated with bipolar disorder in the Amish sample. Unfortunately, the original reports of this research are highly technical and are not well-suited to a volume such as this. However, penetrance estimates indicate that approximately 63% of persons who carry the gene will subsequently develop bipolar illness. The Amish data thus provide compelling evidence for a causal role for a specific gene in the development of a psychiatric disorder.

This gene, however, does not provide a full explanation of the etiology of bipolar disorder. Other genetic researchers report that they can find no evidence to link this area of chromosome 11 with bipolar illness in other populations. This points to the likely heterogeneity of the disorder. Although some forms of bipolar illness may be caused by one specific gene, other forms may have different etiologies. It is also important to note that, even in the Amish population, not all persons with the implicated gene exhibit signs of affective illness. This points to the likely role of other (possibly environmental) factors in the phenotypic expression of a particular genotype.

Our section on affective disorders concludes with an investigation of mania and self esteem by Winters and Neale (selection 17). This is an unusual study for a number of reasons. First, it represents a psychological rather than biological or genetic approach to the study of bipolar illness. Although psychologists have made major contributions to our understanding of unipolar depression, they have played almost no role in bipolar research. The Winters and Neale study is unusual also in that it represents an effort to examine empirically the psychodynamic underpinnings of mania with intriguing result.

References and Suggested Additional Reading

ABRAMSON, L. Y., METALSKY, G. I., AND ALLOY, L. B. (1988). The hopelessness theory of depression: Does the research test the theory? In L. Y. ABRAMSON (Ed.), *Social cognition and clinical psychology: A synthesis.* New York: Guilford Press.

ABRAMSON, L. Y., SELIGMAN, M. E. P., AND TEASDALE, J. D. (1978). Learned helplessness in humans: Critique and reformulation. *Journal of Abnormal Psychology, 87,* 49–74.

ALLOY, L. B., AND ABRAMSON, L. Y. (1979). Judgement of contingency in depressed and nondepressed students: Sadder but wiser? *Journal of Experimental Psychology: General, 108,* 441–485.

BECK, A. T. (1967). *Depression: Clinical, experimental and theoretical aspects.* New York: Harper & Row.

BLACKBURN, I. M., EUNSON, K. M. AND BISHOP, S. (1986.) A two-year naturalistic follow-up of depressed patients treated with cognitive therapy, pharmacotherapy and a combination of both. *Journal of Affective Disorders, 10,* 67–75.

EGELAND, J. A., AND HOSTETTER, A. M. (1983). Amish study, I: Affective disorders among the Amish, 1976–1980. *American Journal of Psychiatry, 140,* 1, 56–61.

EGELAND, J. A., et al. (1987). Bipolar affective disorders linked to DNA markers on chromosome 11. *Nature, 325,* 6107, 783–787.

METALSKY, G. I., HALBERSTADT, L. J., AND ABRAMSON, L. Y. (1987). Toward a more powerful test of the diathesis-stress and causal mediation components of the reformulated theory of depression. *Journal of Personality and Social Psychology, 52,* 2, 386–393.

SELIGMAN, M. E. P. (1973). Fall into helplessness. *Psychology Today, 7,* 43–48.

SZASZ, T. (1986). The case against suicide prevention. *American Psychologist, 41,* 7, 806–812.

WEISSMAN, M. M., MYERS, J. K., AND HARDING, P. S. (1978). Psychiatric disorders in a U.S. urban community: 1975–1976. *American Journal of Psychiatry, 135,* 259–262.

WINOKUR, G. (1979). Unipolar depression: Is it divisible into autonomous subtypes? *Archives of General Psychiatry, 36,* 47–52.

12

Antidepressants and Biochemical Theories of Depression

Elizabeth T. McNeal and
Peter Cimbolic

As psychologists, we are aware of biological models of depression, but do not appreciate how the research on this front contributes to our understanding of this illness. This article is directed toward bringing the psychologist closer to recent laboratory findings of the biochemist and neurophysiologist. Early interest in amine uptake systems, notably serotonin and norepinephrine, which dominated the literature for many years, has now shifted to research on more complex amine receptor systems and the importance of amine receptor changes in depression. Though much important work has been done, we still have not developed any singular or comprehensive theory of depression from the biological perspective.

Investigation into the causes of depression has been fraught with difficulty resulting in confusing and often contradictory results. Part of the difficulty may stem from the fact that most investigations of depression have treated it as a univariate singular phenom-

Elizabeth T. McNeal and Peter Cimbolic. Antidepressants and biochemical theories of depression. *Psychological Bulletin*, 1986, Vol. 99, No. 3, pp. 361–374. Copyright © 1986 by the American Psychological Association. Reprinted by permission of the publisher and authors.

ena when, in fact, depression may represent a class of disorders with multiple causal pathways that might themselves be interactional. This would account in part for the conflicting findings. Perhaps the most predominant psychological model of depression is the cognitive formulation first articulated by Beck (1967, 1976). Although the role of cognitive distortion in depression was originally proposed to be etiologically causative, there is growing controversy over the role of cognitive styles in the origin of depression (Coyne & Gotlib, 1983; Hammen, 1985). Aside from the role cognitive distortions play in causing depression, what is less arguable is that, at a minimum, cognitive distortions are seen in depression (Lewinsohn, Steinmetz, Larsen, & Franklin, 1981). Further, there is no lack of evidence that cognitive behavior therapy is an effective treatment for depression (Kovacs, 1980; Rush, Beck, Kovacs, & Hollon, 1977; Simons, Garfield, & Murphy, 1984). However, there is also evidence that certain depressions may be better understood and treated through a biochemical paradigm. Even Beck (1982), acknowledged that some depressions are biochemically or genetically transmitted disorders.

The question then for the clinician becomes which therapies are appropriate for which groups of depressed individuals. Rush (1982) attempted to identify which groups of depressed patients may most benefit from which therapies, and he showed further that some depressed patients are not even appropriate for psychotherapy. Prusoff, Weissman, Klerman, and Rounsaville (1980) have demonstrated that patients diagnosed as having endogenous depression did not respond well to interpersonal psychotherapy. Similarly, Rush (1982) suggested that patients with psychotic depressions should be treated primarily with medications and that verbal therapies should be considered adjunctive in this group of patients. In summary, there is a real need for psychologists to be sensitive to which groups of depressed patients would most benefit from specific therapies, and we cannot assume that patients will be sensitive to these differences in their selection of mental health specialists.

Byrne and Stern's (1981) article represents an attempt to educate the nonmedical therapist about these very issues. They identified which groups of depressed patients are most appropriate for biological interventions versus those for whom psychological interventions should be considered. They further pointed out that as a group, clinical psychologists get little training about the nature of drugs used in the treatment of depression.

Who then should be candidates for antidepressants? Numerous authors and studies have identified symptom clusters that positively respond to antidepressant medication (American Psychiatric Association, 1980; Beckman & Goodwin, 21975; Bielski & Friedel, 1976; Byrne & Stern, 1981; Maas, Fawcett, & Dekirmenjian, 1972; Schatzberg & Rosenbaum, 1980; Schildkraut, 1973). The following appear to be positive predictors for antidepressant therapy: vegetative symptoms, such as changes in appetite and weight; middle and terminal insomnia; mood worse in the morning; acute onset; family history of depression; family history of positive response to antidepressant medications or electroconvulsive therapy (CT); and a previous positive response by the patient. We would expect 70%–80% of this group of patients to improve with antidepressant therapy (Byrne & Stern, 1981; Schoonover, 1983; Rush, 1982). There also appear to be predictors of poor response to

antidepressant medication. These include: chronic symptoms, hypochondriacal features, mood-incongruent psychotic symptoms, family history of schizophrenia, and family or individual history of antidepressant drug failure (Schoonover, 1983).

Another point of interest is that effective antidepressant medication therapy also appears to alleviate many of the cognitive distortions typical of depressed patients (Reda, Carpiniello, Secchiaroli, & Blanco, 1985; Simons et al., 1984). Awareness of the pharmaceutical effects on cognitive processes is of obvious importance to the psychotherapist who provides cognitive interventions.

There also appears to be a growing body of literature comparing and contrasting the efficacy of antidepressant therapy with cognitive therapy and, in summary, they both appear to be effective interventions (Murphy, Simons, Wetzel, & Lustman, 1984; Simons et al., 1984). It now appears that neither cognitive nor biological formulations alone are sufficient etiological models of depression. A cogent and interactive perspective requires the recognition of the complementary rather than competitive roles of biological and cognitive contributions.

The therapeutic efficacy of antidepressant medication has been established. In light of the fact that many depressed patients receive psychopharmacological treatment alone or in combination with psychotherapy, the question that needs to be addressed is not whether antidepressants work but how they may operate in alleviating depression.

Many of the biological theories of depression have been intimately related to the chemical effects of antidepressant medications discovered in the late 1950s. The treatment of manic-depressive illness with lithium and of other depressive disorders with the tricyclic antidepressants revolutionized the psychiatric approach to mental illness. Patients were able to leave psychiatric institutions and be cared for in the home environment. Animal studies with the tricyclic medications showed that these drugs had effects on neurotransmitters in the brain. These effects were thought to be associated with their therapeutic action in humans. Thus drugs were screened for their ability to affect transmitter systems either by decreasing the breakdown of amines in the presynaptic terminal and synapse (the monoamine oxidase inhibitors or MAOIs) or by blocking the uptake of amines into the nerve terminal and thereby prolonging their effects in the synapse (tricyclic antidepressants or TCAs). The biological theories of depression centered largely on the ability of MAOIs and TCAs to alter the release or uptake of monoamines into nerve terminals. The monoamine neurotransmitters include the catecholamines norepinephrine (NE) and dopamine (DA), the indolamine 5-hydroxytryptamine (or serotonin; 5-HT), and acetylcholine (ACh; Prange, 1964; Schildkraut, 1965; Sulser, 1983). Recently, a new generation of drugs has been discovered, some of which do not show these effects. Further, the earlier research was done on the acute effects of these drugs in brain systems, but these acute effects do not appear to fully explain their antidepressant effects. It was later recognized that the chronic effects were quite different and may better help us understand their therapeutic effects. Today then, long-term studies of drug effects are considered more relevant because most antidepressants show a time lag of between 1 and 3 weeks before effects on mood are seen. The earlier hypotheses of depression must be expanded to include these new findings on long-term effects (Charney & Heninger, 1983; Frazer & Mendels, 1980; Sulser, 1983).

The following text has been shortened by the frequent use of abbreviations; they are listed in Table 1 as a reference to facilitate comprehension.

Review of Biochemical Events at the Synapse

To more fully understand the experimental evidence, it may be helpful to first review the functions of the amine neurotransmitter systems in the brain. These events that occur at the synapse, the gap between two or more

neurons, are well understood. Figure 1 illustrates an adrenergic nerve terminal in which NE is the neurotransmitter. Norepinephrine is released into the synapse as a result of a depolarizing impulse carried along the nerve to the nerve terminal. When the impulse arrives at the terminal it causes the release of a specific biochemical or neurotransmitter. The released transmitter enables the nerve to carry its message across the synapse to an adjacent neuronal or nonneuronal cell. Thus an impulse can be carried long distances from nerve to nerve until it reaches its destination (Axelrod, 1974; Hammerschlag & Roberts, 1976).

The catecholaminergic nerve terminal is highly organized. The steps in the synthesis of NE are shown in the illustration. First, the amino acid tyrosine is converted to dihydroxyphenylalanine (DOPA or L-DOPA) by the enzyme tyrosine hydroxylase. The enzyme DOPA decarboxylase then converts DOPA to DA. Dopamine is then taken up into the storage granules where it is converted to NE by the enzyme dopamine β-hydroxylase. When the action potential reaches this nerve terminal, NE is released into the synapse by a process of exocytosis. In exocytosis, the membrane of the storage granule fuses with the nerve terminal membrane and NE is released, along with enzymes in the granule (Axelrod, 1974; Hammerschlag & Roberts, 1976; Snyder, 1976).

In close proximity to the presynaptic or transmitter-releasing terminal is the membrane of another neuronal (or nonneuronal cell), namely the postsynaptic membrane. Located on this postsynaptic membrane are receptor sites where molecules of the neurotransmitter can bind. Receptor binding thus allows a message to be carried from presynaptic to postsynaptic cells. In the noradrenergic synapse, two of the identified postsynaptic binding sites have been named α_1- and β-adrenergic receptors. They span the outside surface of the cell membrane where they are available for binding to NE molecules. The binding of NE to β-postsynaptic adrenergic receptors has been shown to affect the enzyme adenylate cyclase, lo-

TABLE 1 Definitions of Frequently Used Abbreviations in the Text

Abbreviation	Definition
ACh	Acetylcholine: a cholinergic neurotransmitter
AChE	Acetylcholinesterase: enzyme involved in the degradation of ACh
ATP	Adenosine triphosphate: source of energy for the cell
cAMP	Cyclic adenosine monophosphate: compound involved in the phosphorylation of some protein molecules
CAT	Choline acetyltransferase: enzyme that catalyzes the formation of ACh
COMT	Catechol-O-methyltransferase: enzyme involved in the catabolism of catecholamines
CSF	Cerebrospinal fluid: fluid in the ventricles of the brain and within sheaths of the spinal cord
DA	Dopamine: a catecholaminergic neurotransmitter
DOPA (or L-DOPA)	Dihydroxyphenylalanine: precursor of the catecholamines NE and DA
DST	Dexamethasone suppression test: test used to identify depressives based on the nonsuppression of cortisol to the administration of dexamethasone
HA	Histamine: a putative central nervous system neurotransmitter
5-HIAA	5-Hydroxyindoleacetic acid: metabolite of 5-HT
5-HT	5-Hydroxytryptamine or serotonin: an indolamine neurotransmitter
5-HTP	5-Hydroxytryptophan: precursor of serotonin
ISO	Isoproterenol: stimulator of β-noradrenergic receptors
MAO	Monoamine oxidase: enzyme involved in the degradation of monoamines
MAOI	Monoamine oxidase inhibitor: antidepressant that inhibits the degradation of monoamines
MHPG	3-Methoxy-4-hydroxy-phenylglycol: metabolite of NE
NE	Norepinephrine: catecholaminergic neurotransmitter
TCA	Tricyclic antidepressant: drug used in the treatment of depression

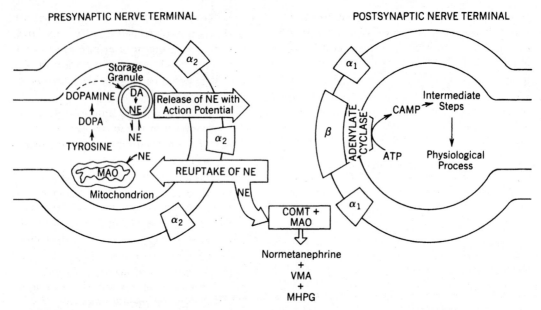

FIGURE 1

Illustration of a noradrenergic synapse. (Adapted from figures presented by Baldessarini, 1983, p. 36, and Kirk & Creveling, 1984, p. 198. DA: dopamine; NE: norepinephrine. Dihydroxyphenylalanine [DOPA] is a precursor of the transmitters DA and NE. The enzymes monoamine oxidase [MAO] and catechol-O-methyltransferase [COMT] are involved in the degradation of NE. 3-

Methoxy-4-hydroxy-phenylglycol [MHPG] and vanillylmandelic acid [VMA] are metabolites in the breakdown of NE. α_1, α_2, and β are receptor sites on the cell membrane. Adenosine triphosphate [ATP] is an energy source for the cell and a precursor to the "second messenger" cyclic adenosine monophosphate [cAMP].)

cated on the inside surface of the cell membrane. Receptor binding can speed up (stimulate) or slow down (inhibit) the conversion of adenosine triphosphate (ATP) to cyclic adenosine monophosphate (cAMP) by the enzyme adenylate cyclase. The binding of NE to a β-postsynaptic adrenergic receptor (in most mammalian brain systems) causes cAMP to be accumulated and the effect is stimulatory. The α_1-postsynaptic adrenergic receptor may not be coupled to adenylate cyclase, but may regulate stores of calcium within the cell through another mechanism. The biochemical cAMP has often been called a "second messenger" because it then directs the cell to carry on various physiological processes. There is also evidence that noradrenergic stimulation of cAMP can occur in presynaptic terminals and that β-receptors exist in some presynaptic nerve endings. This makes interpretation of experimental results

more difficult. For this reason, some conclusions drawn about these systems are open to question (Axelrod, 1974; Cooper, Bloom, & Roth, 1982; Iversen, 1979; Lefkowitz, Caron, Stiles, 1984; Nathanson & Greengard, 1977; Rall, 1972).

The most efficient method of inactivation and the predominant destination of the major portion of released transmitter is through the uptake process. (In dopaminergic neurons, DA instead of NE [the enzyme dopamine β-hydroxylase is lacking here] is released as the transmitter.) Norepinephrine and DA are taken up across the presynaptic membrane, from which they were originally released, and are restored to the storage granules. Many antidepressant drugs block this uptake process and cause a prolonged effect of the neurotransmitter because of its increased contact time with the receptor site. In addition to inactivation by the reuptake process, some of the released neurotransmitter may be inactivated by oxidative deamination by the enzyme monoamine oxidase (MAO). Monoamine oxidase is present in the presynaptic terminal and in the synapse. In the synapse, MAO along with another enzyme, catechol-O-methyltransferase (COMT), metabolize NE into three main products, normetanephrine, vanillylmandelic acid (VMA), and 3-methoxy-4-hydroxy-phenylglycol (MHPG). Urine levels of MHPG have been extensively studied in depressed patients. Along the presynaptic membrane are other receptors for NE, particularly, α_2-adrenergic receptors. When NE accumulates in the synapse, some of the transmitter interacts with α_2-binding sites and conveys information to the presynaptic cell to slow down the synthesis and release of NE. This is a kind of feedback mechanism to turn off release of NE when there is enough present in the synapse. These so-called autoreceptors also exist for DA in a dopaminergic neuron (Axelrod, 1974; Cooper et al., 1982; Iversen, 1979; Maas & Huang, 1980; Snyder, 1976).

The organization of serotonergic nerve terminals is very similar. Release, uptake, and metabolism by MAO are all the same except that the role of MAO is thought to be more important here because there is much newly synthesized 5-HT that spills out of the storage granules and is metabolized by MAO in the presynaptic terminal. Serotonin receptors are known to exist on the presynaptic and postsynaptic membranes but are not as well defined as in the catecholamine system. Two types of receptors have been identified, a 5-HT_1-receptor and a 5-HT_2-receptor, but their physiological functions are not clear. Serotonin is synthesized from the amino acid precursor L-tryptophan. It is converted to 5-hydroxytryptophan (5-HTP) by the enzyme tryptophan hydroxylase and then to 5-HT by a decarboxylase enzyme. The MAO converts 5-HT to 5-hydroxyindoleacetic acid (5-HIAA), the major metabolic product studied in the urine and in cerebrospinal fluid (CSF) of depressed patients. Tricyclic antidepressants all show potent effects in blocking the uptake system of 5-HT, NE, and DA nerve terminals, thus giving rise to the early formulations that these neurotransmitter systems were implicated in depression (Amsterdam & Mendels, 1980; Cooper et al., 1982; Snyder, 1976, 1984; White, Handler, & Smith, 1973).

Acetylcholine nerve terminals resemble those of the other monoamine neurotransmitters. The precursor to this transmitter is choline, and it is converted to ACh by the enzyme choline acetyltransferase (CAT) with the help of a cofactor, acetylcoenzyme A. There is no uptake process for ACh, and it is inactivated in the synapse by the enzyme acetylcholinesterase (AChE), which converts it to choline and acetate. The choline is then taken up across the presynaptic membrane and can be recycled to produce more transmitter. In addition, the uptake of choline is thought to help regulate ACh synthesis. There are ACh receptors located on the postsynaptic membrane, and, in the brain, they are believed to be of the muscarinic subtype. All three of the above-mentioned transmitter systems in the human brain control many functions, such as movement, daily cycles, function of the hypothalamic–pituitary axis, arousal, and sleep, in addition to mood changes (Cooper et al., 1982; MacIntosh, 1976; Snyder, 1984; White et al., 1973).

Amine Theories of Depression

In 1965, Schildkraut and Bunney and Davis presented a catecholamine hypothesis of mood disorders. Depression was associated with a decrease in the levels of brain catecholamines (NE and DA), especially NE. This hypothesis was based on evidence from three different groups of drugs. Reserpine, a drug used to treat hypertension, was known to cause depression in patients who received it. Reserpine releases catecholamines from nerve terminals and therefore depletes the brain of NE and DA along with other amines. In addition, two types of antidepressant drugs (MAOIs and TCAs) increased the activity of catecholamines in the brain. The MAOIs prevent the breakdown of NE by MAO. The TCAs block the uptake of amines released from the nerve, and therefore potentiate the effects of these neurotransmitters. The activity of these drugs was consistent with the hypothesis that decreased brain catecholamine activity caused depression, and antidepressants (by two different mechanisms) reversed this by elevating catecholamine activity in the brain.

Later a variety of approaches were taken to test these hypotheses. Some evidence proved supportive, but some showed that these theoretical formulations were not comprehensive. If increased NE in the brain relieved depression, then giving patients L-DOPA (the amino acid precursor to NE and DA) should raise levels of both transmitters and relieve the depression. Goodwin, Murphy, Brodie, and Bunney (1970) and Mendels, Stinnett, Burns, and Frazer (1975) tried to show the antidepressant effect of L-DOPA. Goodwin et al. found some relief of symptoms in only 4 out of 16 patients, whereas Mendels et al. found no significant improvement in any of their patients. However, another group (Gelenberg, Wojcik, Growdon, Sved, & Wurtman, 1980) did get positive results with tyrosine, another amino acid precursor of NE. They administered tyrosine by mouth and found that depression was alleviated. However, their report was of an effect in only 1 patient.

The indolamine theory of depression was proposed by Glassman (1969). He suggested that although much attention had been placed on the catecholamine hypothesis, there was also evidence that indolamines (particularly serotonin or 5-HT) were important in depression. Much of the evidence presented for this theory was similar to that proposed to support the catecholamine theory. Reserpine was known to deplete stores of 5-HT as well as NE, and MAOIs prevent the breakdown of both of these amines. In addition, TCAs such as imipramine and amitriptyline, which were first found to block the uptake of NE, later proved to be effective

though less potent inhibitors of 5-HT uptake. Other supportive evidence was that administration of the 5-HT precursor tryptophan in combination with an MAOI seemed to give a significantly greater antidepressant effect than the MAOI alone. Glassman reviewed the available clinical and animal research and suggested that the indolamines were at least in part involved in some depressive syndromes. Subsequent studies were reported by Amsterdam & Mendels (1980). One showed improvement in 28 out of 36 chronically depressed patients given tryptophan daily, although others did not confirm these results.

The cholinergic hypothesis proposed that increased brain ACh levels were associated with depression, whereas decreased levels were associated with the manic state. The evidence for this theoretical point came first from Gershon and Shaw (1961), who found that certain insecticides were potent AChE (the enzyme that breaks down ACh) inhibitors. Normal adults exposed to these compounds developed a depressed mood. Subsequent work by K. L. Davis, Hollister, Overall, Johnson, and Train (1976) showed that intravenous injection of physostigmine, a potent AChE inhibitor could cause a depressive-like syndrome in normal people with a variety of aspects of psychomotor retardation present, though with no overall mood alterations. Also, research was done using physostigmine to treat manic patients. Janowsky, El-Yousef, Davis, and Sekerke (1973) administered the drug to 8 patients with manic symptoms in a double-blind study. All showed a decrease in manic symptoms, and 5 of the patients developed a depressed mood. Similarly K. L. Davis, Berger, Hollister, and Defraites (1978) found that mood and thought content reversed from mania toward depression in 6 out of 7 manic patients given physostigmine. They proposed that this was either a direct effect of increased cholinergic activity in the brain or resulted from that increased activity's effect on other neurotransmitter systems in the brain. As Janowsky (1980) has summarized, there are indications for a role of cholinergic mechanisms in depression, but as with the other amine hypotheses, there is also contradicting evidence. Studies with certain anticholinergic agents show that they produce euphoria in some patients, but generally are not good antidepressants. Also, though many TCAs have anticholinergic effects, these effects are present in unequal amounts and are not linked to their therapeutic potency (Maas, 1975). Yet the clinical evidence cited by Gershon and Shaw (1961) with physostigmine indicates that cholinergic transmission may be important in at least some of the symptoms of depression.

Other theorists suggested that an interaction of amine systems may cause depression or that amine-specific subtypes of depression may exist. Mendels et al. (1975) proposed that affective disorders may result from a complex interaction between cholinergic and adrenergic neurotransmitter activity. Depression appears to occur when cholinergic activity is elevated in comparison to adrenergic activity. When the opposite situation is present, mania results. There was also much interest in a suggestion by Maas (1975), that two types of depressives (A and B) could be recognized. Group A was NE-sensitive, and a disorder in NE metabolism or disposition was present, but the 5-HT system was probably not altered. Group B had a disorder in 5-HT transmission, but NE systems were probably intact. Tricyclics were seen as exerting their effects in elevating levels of either of these two neurotransmitter systems by inhibiting uptake. Amitriptyline was considered to have greater effects on the 5-HT system and thus to be useful in treating Group B, and imipramine was considered more effective on the NE system (Group A). Thus, though many scientists have studied single amine systems or proposed the interaction of two, the evidence from all areas supports the idea that complex interactions among all of the amine systems may lead to the symptoms of depression.

The various amine hypotheses have been supported by a variety of different experimental approaches. Many animal studies have been done using amine uptake systems.

The potencies of various antidepressant drugs have been compared in their ability to inhibit uptake of mainly 5-HT, NE and DA into various brain regions. Others have examined the clinical effects of amine precursors, as mentioned previously, and the metabolic products of amines. Recently, much work has been done using neurophysiological and receptor binding techniques demonstrating a difference between chronic versus acute effects of antidepressants, which may explain their efficacy in alleviating depression. This is also consistent with clinical evidence that these drugs take 1–3 weeks to have antidepressant effects. The accumulation of new information has required an expansion of the older monoamine theories of depression.

We next examine the research that has been done on amine metabolites and in a number of new areas concerning the monamines. We also review the antidepressant drugs currently being used clinically or proposed for use. The effects of different antidepressant drugs have been critical to the progress of research in this area. They have been used as pharmacological tools to try to determine the biochemical events that distinguish the depressed from the nondepressed state.

Antidepressant Medications

All of the antidepressants used today have specific effects on monoamine systems in the central nervous system (CNS). The inhibition of uptake of NE by TCAs was reported in the early 1960s by Axelrod and co-workers (Axelrod, Whitby, & Hertting, 1961). Since then, a major focus has been directed toward the screening of compounds for antidepressant activity by testing them as blockers of the monoamine uptake systems. A vast body of literature is available on the ability of TCAs to block the uptake of NE, 5-HT, and DA. Baldessarini (1983, p. 95) has produced a comprehensive list of the effects of antidepressant compounds on the uptake of radiolabeled amines into brain tissue in animal studies. Most compounds show widely differing potencies in their effects on different amine systems. A majority of the commonly used antidepressants such as protriptyline (Vivactyl), desipramine (Norpramin), nortriptyline (Aventyl), imipramine (Tofranil), amitiptyline (Elavil), and doxepin (Sinequan) show better potency at blocking NE uptake than 5-HT uptake. The NE to 5-HT potency ratio is 800 for protriptyline (blockade at NE uptake sites is 800 times greater than the blockade at 5-HT uptake sites), 1,000 for desipramine, 6.7 for nortriptyline, 7.3 for imipramine, 3.5 for amitriptyline, and 10.6 for doxepin when comparisons are made of IC_{50} values (the concentration that inhibits uptake by 50%). In addition, the demethylated or secondary amines protriptyline and nortriptyline are 65 and 4 times, respectively, more potent than the parent compound amitriptyline (a tertiary amine) at blocking NE uptake. Desipramine, a secondary amine, is 30 times more potent than its parent compound imipramine at blocking uptake of NE. Amitriptyline and imipramine, however, are relatively better uptake blockers of 5-HT than are protriptyline, nortriptyline, and desipramine by about four- to five-fold. Because the tertiary amines are demethylated in vivo, a combination of products or products plus the parent compound are present in the brain (Baldessarini, 1983, pp. 90–96; Sourkes, 1976). One must, however, be mindful that the above potencies are based on animal studies, and therefore be cautious in interpreting and extending these findings to humans.

A frequent generalization is that the demethylated amines, such as desipramine, protriptyline, and nortriptyline, are more potent at blocking NE than 5-HT uptake, whereas the tertiary amines such as amitriptyline, imipramine, trimipramine (Surmontil), doxepin, and clomipramine (Anafranil) are more potent blockers of 5-HT relative to NE uptake (Cooper et al. 1982; Simpson, Pi, & White, 1983). However, according to the data presented by Baldessarini (1983, p. 95), the only tertiary amine that shows more po-

tency in blocking 5-HT relative to NE uptake is clomipramine, which is not clinically available in the United States. There is conflicting data in the literature on the potency of many of these drugs at NE versus 5-HT nerve terminals. A point well made by Richelson (1982) is that most of the results from uptake studies are reported as IC_{50} values which cannot be directly compared between studies. The reason for this is that the amount of radioligand being displaced may differ from study to study. Therefore, a more precise measure such as the K_i (or the inhibition constant) value is needed to directly access the potency of a drug in its effects on NE, 5-HT, or NE versus 5-HT uptake. Some preliminary data are now available reporting K_i values from studies of NE uptake into rat brain synaptosomes (Richelson, 1984). Similar data on 5-HT uptake studies, promised in the future by Richelson, should provide a more accurate comparison of drug effects at these two uptake sites.

The following compounds are often described as the second generation antidepressants: trimipramine, amoxapine, maprotiline, trazodone, alprazolam, and nomifensine. Three other compounds, zimelidine, mianserin, and iprindole, have not yet been released in the United States. The new tricyclic trimipramine shows very little activity in inhibiting the uptake of NE, 5-HT, and DA. Amoxapine (Ascendin), another tricyclic compound of the dibenzoxapine family, appears to be almost three times more potent in inhibiting uptake of NE than imipramine and is also potent at 5-HT uptake sites. The tetracyclic maprotiline (Ludiomil) has activity at NE sites about equal to amoxapine, with little 5-HT blocking effect. Another drug, nomifensine (which is unrelated to the tricyclics structurally) is interesting because it has good blocking effects at NE sites and is also a potent blocker of DA uptake sites (Baldessarini, 1983, p. 95; Feighner, 1983; Richelson, 1984). Zimelidine, a bicyclic in structure, is potent in inhibiting 5-HT uptake while having no activity at NE or DA sites. Further, a number of other "atypical" antidepressants are structurally distinct and have different physiological mechanisms from the classic antidepressants. This has caused researchers to assess the limitations of the monoamine uptake theories and their relevance to the etiology of depression. These new compounds have virtually no effect on the uptake of NE, 5-HT, or DA, and do not inhibit MAO. They include mianserin, iprindole, trazodone (Deseryl), and alprazolam (Xanax). Mianserin has some activity against NE but is 3- to 14-fold less potent than imipramine in this effect. The mechanisms of action of iprindole, mianserin, trazodone, and alprazolam remain obscure. However, they all appear to have clear antidepressant effects. Iprindole was among the first of the new generation of antidepressants to challenge the amine hypothesis. Having no effects on any of the three uptake systems, it also has no effect on NE turnover in either acute or chronic treatments. These observations led theorists to look beyond the blockade of presynaptic uptake systems exclusively for effects of antidepressants. Mianserin has been reported to be as effective an antidepressant as imipramine or amitriptyline. It, however, is thought to produce its effects through the blocking of presynaptic α_2-adrenergic receptors, which then results in an increase in NE release. It has also been reported to increase NE turnover in rat brain. However, its overall mechanism of action is an enigma. Trazodone has no effect on NE and DA uptake, but may have some effects on 5-HT uptake in high doses. It does not inhibit MAO. Trazodone has been shown to be a moderate blocker of α_1-postsynaptic receptor sites. Alprazolam is a benzodiazepine, which is therefore related in structure to the widely used antianxiety agent diazepam (Valium). It is reported to have effects similar to MAOIs and tricyclics on REM sleep in depressed patients. Fabre and McLendon (1980) have also reported that it is as effective as imipramine in treating patients with primary depression. Further study is needed, however, to determine the true clinical effects of these medications and their underlying mechanisms of action (Ananth, 1983; Baldessarini, 1983, p. 95; Feighner, 1983;

Kelwala, Stanley, & Gershon, 1983; Richelson, 1984; Sulser, 1983).

A discussion of the antidepressant drugs is not complete without mentioning the MAO inhibitors. The discovery of antidepressant properties of iproniazid, an MAOI, occurred by accident in the early 1950s, around the same time that imipramine was also discovered to have such properties. Both drugs were being used in clinical trials, but not for the treatment of depression. The MAOIs block the action of MAO in the synapse and nerve terminal. They thus prevent the breakdown of amines and enhance their effects. These drugs have been used more in Europe than in the United States and have been shown to be effective antidepressants. Toxic effects from interaction with tyramine-containing foods producing hypertensive crises made them almost obsolete by the late 1960s. However, over the last decade, renewed clinical and research attention has been paid to these drugs. Two forms of MAO are known to exist, A and B. The only three MAOIs available in the United States are the hydrazine compounds phenelzine (Nardil) and isocarboxazid (Marplan), and tranylcypromine (Parnate), an amphetamine-like compound. These drugs are nonselective inhibitors of both forms of the enzyme. Recently, several compounds have been discovered that are highly selective inhibitors. Clorgyline and L-deprenyl have been shown to inhibit MAO-A and MAO-B, respectively. The absence of the "cheese-effect" (or hypertensive response to tyramine-containing foods) of L-deprenyl gives it a safety advantage over other drugs. The antidepressant effects of clorgyline and other MAO-A inhibitors have been fairly well established. Therapeutic effects of L-deprenyl remain controversial, though one controlled study by Mendelwitz and Youdim (1983) showed greater than placebo improvement in 14 unipolar and bipolar patients. The overall clinical significance of the two forms of the enzyme is, as yet, unresolved (Axelrod, 1974; Baldessarini, 1984; Glassman, 1969; Kelwala et al., 1983; Mann et al., 1983).

Metabolic Studies of Monoamines

The clinical studies involving identification of amine metabolites have yielded some interesting but controversial results. Research has shown that 3-methoxy-4-hydroxyphenyglycol (MHPG) is the major metabolite of NE in humans. A number of studies have tested the levels of MHPG in CSF, plasma, and urine. Animal studies suggest that as much as 25% of brain NE may be excreted in the urine as MHPG, whereas human studies suggest that as much as 63% of urinary MHPG may originate in the brain. Therefore most researchers look at urine levels in treated and untreated depressed patients as a measurement of NE activity (Hollister, Davis, & Berger, 1980; Taska & Brodie, 1983). A number of studies in the late 1960s and the 1970s pointed to relations between urinary MHPG and clinical response to TCAs. Maas (1975) has summarized studies that gave consistent findings indicating depressed patients with lower than normal levels of urinary MHPG were good responders to imipramine and desipramine, but not to amitriptyline. On the other hand, patients with normal or higher than normal levels of urinary MHPG were good responders to amitriptyline, but not to imipramine. In addition, other studies showed that patients who responded to a test dose of d-amphetamine with a brightening of mood had lower pretreatment urinary MHPG levels than patients who did not show this effect. Maas then suggested that patients be subgrouped into two categories: Type A, with low urinary MHPG, elevated mood response to imipramine and failure to respond to amitriptyline; and Type B, with normal or high levels of urinary MHPG, no elevated mood with d-amphetamine, and good treatment response to amitriptyline but not imipramine. However, a more recent study (Schatzberg et al., 1982) failed to show a significant difference between the urinary MHPG levels of a group of unipolar depressives and control subjects. Instead, a wide range of levels

among depressives was found, some higher or lower than control and some intermediate. This data is supported by investigators who found similar results in separate controlled studies (Schatzberg et al., 1982, and references therein). So prediction of antidepressant response by testing pretreatment levels of MHPG remains clouded. (Some causes of error variance in MHPG levels are discussed next.)

When MHPG levels are evaluated in response to chronic treatment with tricyclics, the results are also inconsistent. Earlier reports suggested that patients with low urinary MHPG treated with imipramine showed a slight increase or no change in MHPG levels after 4 weeks. This group tended to have a good treatment response. In contrast, patients with no response to imipramine and with normal or high pretreatment levels of urinary MHPG tended to show decreasing levels of urinary MHPG after 4 weeks of treatment. Other studies did not support these results, and studies of imipramine, amitriptyline, nortriptyline, desipramine, and phenelzine (an MAOI) have shown no conclusive correlations between urinary levels of MHPG and clinical responses (Charney, Menkes, & Heninger, 1981; Hollister et al., 1980; Maas et al., 1972).

The finding that appears most consistent is in patients with manic-depressive illness. Here there are lowered MHPG levels in depression and a return to normal levels after recovery or when there is a switch from depression to mania. Some authors suggest that low urinary MHPG levels may be easier to detect in bipolar patients (Maas, 1975; Schatzberg et al., 1982). Muscettola, Potter, Pickar, and Goodwin (1984) suggest there may be a number of methodological reasons for the conflicting findings in this area. One appears to be the variability in MHPG levels due to stress, day-to-day differences, diet, and physical activity, as well as differences in analytical methods used from laboratory to laboratory yielding different findings for the same analyses. Muscettola et al. (1984), after trying to control for these factors by having all patients hospitalized and put on the same diet, studied bipolar and unipolar depressed patients, manic patients, and normal controls. They found a tendency for all depressed patients to have lower urinary levels of MHPG, but they were not statistically different from controls. Manic patients, however, showed significantly higher excreted MHPG levels than depressed patients. The authors also reported only a trend toward low pretreatment MHPG levels to predict positive response to imipramine and desipramine. They stated that it would be premature to use MHPG levels in clinical practice. In summary, the research on MHPG does not present clearly supportive evidence for the catecholamine theory of depression.

The major metabolite of 5-HT is 5-HIAA. It has been measured in urine, but it is thought that CSF readings may be better indicators of brain 5-HT turnover because there is a large peripheral contribution to the urine. In a review of the literature, Baldessarini (1983, pp. 52–56) cited evidence from four studies that showed up to a 70% decrease in CSF 5-HIAA levels in depressed patients compared with controls. Twelve other studies showed a trend in that direction. There have been reports that patients with low pretreatment CSF levels of 5-HIAA show a tendency to respond well to drugs thought by some to primarily affect the 5-HT uptake system, such as amitriptyline (Taska & Brodie, 1983). Although some studies showed predictive value for low pretreatment CSF 5-HIAA patients to respond well to clomipramine and for patients with high pretreatment 5-HIAA to respond to nortriptyline, other studies showed no correlation at all between baseline levels of the metabolite and treatment response to amitriptyline, clomipramine, and imipramine (Amsterdam & Mendels, 1980; Charney et al., 1981). Some authors have suggested that CSF may reflect mainly metabolites that accumulate from the spinal cord and capillaries, rather than from the turnover of 5-HT in the brain (Taska & Brodie, 1983). Even so, a large number of clinical studies have been done on metabolite levels in CSF after long-term antidepressant treatment. In these studies clomipramine, zimelidine, imipramine, amitriptyline, and nortriptyline (in some studies, but not all), have shown an ability to consistently decrease the levels of 5-HIAA in CSF over pretreatment amounts. There is a trend for the effect to be the same with MAOIs but it is not statistically significant. However, the decrease in 5-HIAA levels does not correlate with treatment response. Repeated ECT has no effect on CSF levels (Charney et al., 1981). Although some evidence points to a decrease in 5-HT turnover with antidepressant treatment, whether this effect is clinically significant remains to be seen. Because the indolamine theory of depression would predict low 5-HIAA levels in depression, some of this evidence (showing up to a 70% decrease in depressive levels over controls) is in line with this theory. However, antidepressant treatments would be expected to reverse the situation and increase the turnover of 5-HIAA, which they do not appear to do. Clearly, some important aspects of the 5-HT system need to be more fully understood.

Effects of Antidepressants on Receptor Systems

In recent years, new techniques have been used to elucidate the long-term effects of antidepressants on membrane receptors. These include biochemical assays that measure the effects of receptor-mediated stimulation of cAMP production, receptor binding studies to determine receptor density, and electrophysiological techniques to measure receptor sensitivity. Much information has been accumulated concerning the amine receptor systems and their response to the effects of antidepressant treatments.

β-Adrenergic Receptors

Interest in the area of receptor-mediated events was enhanced when it was discovered that two drugs, reserpine and propranolol, caused an increase in the NE-stimulated cAMP production in rodent brain. Both of these drugs were known to precipitate depressive reactions in humans. When antidepressant drugs were tested, it was found that after long-term but not short-term treatment there was a decrease in the levels of NE-stimulated production of cAMP. The β-adrenergic receptor, a subtype of NE receptors, was a possible site of action for this effect. Also, this was the first demonstration of an effect that was related to long-term and not short-term administration of antidepressant drugs. This was significant because it corresponded well with the action of these drugs in the clinical setting. Because cAMP has been proposed to be a second messenger, which signals a physiological response in the cell after binding of the neurotransmitter to the receptor, the study of cAMP accumulations in brain cells is considered to be a model system for looking at the effects of various neurotransmitters. Norepinephrine-stimulated cAMP production is an indicator of adrenergic receptor activity (Cooper et al., 1982; Daly, 1975; Sulser, 1983).

Part of the effect of NE on the production of cAMP has been found to be mediated through β-adrenergic receptors, as discussed previously. This subtype of receptor is responsible for varying proportions (depending on the particular system studied) of NE's effect on accumulations of cAMP. Evidence from some pharmacological studies indicates that α-adrenergic receptors also contribute to the accumulation of cAMP produced by stimulation with NE in the cerebral cortex (Blumberg, Vetulani, Stawarz, & Sulser, 1976; Daly et al., 1980; Schultz & Daly, 1973).

A large number of antidepressants when administered chronically have been found to reduce the production of cAMP stimulated by NE or isoproterenol (ISO, a pure β-agonist) in in vivo and in vitro studies in animal brain. (Many researchers study this receptor using ISO, a compound that has only β-effects, rather than NE, which has effects on both α- and β-receptors.) These include the typical TCAs such as imipramine, desipramine, and amitriptyline, which block uptake of NE and 5-HT. Also demonstrating this effect are atypical agents such as iprindole and mianserin, which block neither the uptake of NE nor 5-HT; zimelidine, which is a specific 5-HT uptake blocker; the MAOIs, pargyline and clorgyline; and ECT. Thus all currently known forms of antidepressant treatment show a long-term but not a short-term effect on cAMP production. This consistency is not seen when these drugs are compared in their ability to block NE uptake or to change NE turnover in the brain. It has been found that ECT, which has a faster onset of action in humans than most antidepressant drugs, also appears to cause a more rapid reduction in NE-receptor sensitivity. The mechanism of this receptor desensitization is not known. It has been suggested that because a majority of these drugs have been shown to enhance the availability of NE in the synapse, this might cause the loss of sensitivity. Desensitization could occur as a compensatory response to the overabundance of neurotransmitter at the receptor. A desensitization of receptor response has been shown to occur in situations where transmitter levels are increased in nerve tissue, and it has been associated with a decrease in the number of binding sites. However, this would not explain the effects of iprindole and trazodone in causing a decrease in NE-stimulated cAMP levels after long-term treatment. In addition, some antidepressants do not produce consistent down-regulation (or decreases in the sensitivity of NE receptors seen as a decrease in cAMP accumulation) of NE receptors. Fluoxetine, a specific 5-HT uptake inhibitor clearly produces no receptor desensitization. Also, the results with trazodone are conflicting, with evidence for and against its producing desensitization. Still, the overwhelming evidence is that most clinically active drugs and ECT cause down-regulation of the NE receptor system (Frazer & Mendels, 1980; Sulser, 1983).

Linked to the evidence of down-regulation of the NE receptor system is another consistent finding. Antidepressant drugs cause a decrease in the density of β-adrenergic receptors, as evaluated using binding studies in rodent brain. Again these effects are a result of long-term treatment and do not occur with acute administration. Almost all drugs that cause a subsensitivity to NE or ISO stimulation of cAMP also cause a decrease in the number (or density) of β-adrenergic receptors. These changes have been found throughout the brain and include areas such as the cerebral cortex, striatum, hippocampus, cerebellum, and the whole brain. Of the antidepressants considered previously that give consistent evidence of reduced sensitivity to NE, only mianserin fails to show the long-term effect of reducing β-adrenergic receptor density. Mianserin is also unusual in that it is one of the few agents that reduce NE- but not ISO-stimulated cAMP production after long-term administration. Zimelidine, which also shows an effect on NE- but not ISO-stimulated cAMP production, shows inconsistent effects in lowering β-receptor density (some studies say yes, others no). In addition, fluoxetine, which does not produce a subsensitivity to NE, also does not reduce β-receptor density. It will be interesting to see how potent an antidepressant fluoxetine proves to be in humans. Electroconvulsive therapy has also been shown to decrease β-adrenergic receptor density. (Most studies of β-receptor binding have been done using tritiated dihydroalprenolol, a β-receptor antagonist.) An interesting corollary to the above studies is a report that deprivation of REM sleep, which has been associated with antidepressant activity in humans, decreases the density of β-adrenergic receptors (Charney et al., 1981; Maggi, U'Prichard, & Enna 1980; Peroutka & Snyder, 1980; Rosenblatt, Pert, Tallman, Pert, & Bunney, 1979; Sulser, 1983). Thus, the preponderance of evidence is that clinically effective antidepressant drugs (when given chronically), and ECT produce a decrease in NE-stimulated cAMP along with a decrease in β-receptor density.

Physiological studies testing the activity of individual neurons after long-term antidepressant treatment are generally consistent with the biochemical data. They show a decrease in the sensitivity of β-receptors. In rodent brain regions where the physiological responses are believed to be mediated by β-adrenergic postsynaptic receptors (e.g., the cingulate cortex and the cerebellum), clomipramine, desipramine, and maprotoline, as well as tranylcypromine caused a decrease in the responsiveness of neurons to NE. However, another area in which these receptors are located, the hippocampus, was found to show no effect from treatment with a variety of TCAs and iprindole. The effects, when seen, are in most cases reversible. Both β-receptor sensitivity and density return to baseline levels after withdrawal of the treatments. Some evidence exists, however, that these effects may not be specific to antidepressant treatments. Chlorpromazine and amphetamine can also cause an imipramine-like effect on β-adrenergic receptors (Baldessarini, 1983, p. 118; Charney et al., 1981). In summary, the preponderance of data from cAMP accumulation, receptor binding, and neurophysiological studies shows a decrease in both β-postsynaptic density and sensitivity resulting from chronic antidepressant treatments.

α-Adrenergic Receptors

In animal studies, α-adrenergic binding has been studied using the radioligand [^{3}H]WB-4101 and has been shown to correlate with NE-stimulated cAMP accumulation in at least one system (J.N. Davis et al., 1978). Several laboratories have reported no effects on α_1-adrenergic receptor binding in response to long-term treatment with antidepressant drugs (Peroutka & Snyder, 1980; Rosenblatt et al., 1979). However, one laboratory (Rehavi, Ramot, Yavetz, & Sokolovsky, 1980) has identified a "superhigh" affinity site for the α_1-receptor in homogenates of mouse brain. At this site, but not at the lower affinity site, long-term treatment with amitriptyline causes an increase in the receptor density. Thorough study of this superhigh affinity site has not been done by other laboratories, so the results of this one study need to be confirmed.

Many antidepressants, in short-term and long-term treatment, inhibit the binding of WB-4101 to α-receptors in rodent brain. These effects can be correlated with clinical anxiolytic and sedative potencies of the classic tricyclic antidepressants. Alpha-blocking compounds include imipramine, amitriptyline, doxepin, nortriptyline, and mianserin. Iprindole, nomifensine, and zimelidine show poor blocking activity at this site. The concentrations at which imipramine and amitriptyline block α_1-receptors appear to be the same as those at which they block neuronal uptake (Baldessarini, 1983, p. 112; Maggi et al., 1980; Ogren, Ross, Hall, & Archer, 1983; Peroutka & Snyder, 1980). These acute effects would also be present after chronic antidepressant treatment. They may also relate to the physiological data from studies of α_1-receptors.

A summary of the data from electrophysiological studies is presented by Charney et al. (1981). In studies of brain areas where the responses to NE appear to be mediated through postsynaptic α_1-receptors, long-term treatment with antidepressants such as imipramine, desipramine, clomipramine, and iprindole cause an increased responsiveness to NE. A possible mechanism for this supersensitivity could be the blocking effects of these drugs at the receptor. It is known that the uptake blocking effects of (especially) TCAs would cause more NE to be available at the postsynaptic receptor. The increased exposure would cause a decrease in the sensitivity of β-receptors (Frazer & Mendels, 1980). The opposite would occur at the α_1-receptor because of direct blocking effects by antidepressants. Chronic antidepressant treatments increase levels of NE but at the same time can block the α_1-receptor. Thus the receptor cannot interact with the available NE. It acts as if there were a lack of transmitter at the receptor site and becomes supersensitive rather than subsensitive. The low affinity of the antidepressants for direct blocking of the β-receptor as compared with the α_1-receptor is evidence in support of this mechanism (Ogren et al., 1983). It is possible that the increase in sensitivity at α_1-neuronal sites might be expected to be associated with an increase in receptor density by analogy to the β-receptor system, where a decrease in sensitivity is associated with a decrease in receptor density. The evidence for increased receptor density at the superhigh affinity site (Rehavi et al., 1980) is consistent with this reasoning. However, iprindole, as noted previously, which has poor blocking effects at the α_1-receptor site and negligible effects on the NE uptake system, can still cause a supersensitivity of α_1-receptors to stimulation by NE. Thus, the overall mechanism of action of antidepressant drugs on the α_1-receptor remains to be explained.

Many biochemical and electrophysiological studies have been carried out to evaluate the α_2-presynaptic receptor. This receptor has been called the *autoreceptor* and is believed to regulate impulse flow of NE from the presynaptic nerve terminal. Tritiated clonidine has been used to identify α_2-receptors in animal brain. Most antidepressants show little ability to directly block the receptor. Mianserin is a notable exception. It has a high affinity for the α_2-receptor. Amitriptyline also shows some capacity to block α_2-receptor binding. A variety of antidepressant drugs including imipramine, desipramine, iprindole, nomifensine, and zimelidine show essentially no effects in blocking this receptor. Long-term effects of these medications on α_2-adrenergic receptors have given ambiguous results. There is evidence for increased receptor density with imipramine, clomipramine, nortriptyline, mianserin, and iprindole; no change with most of these same drugs; and a decrease with imipramine and clorgyline (Campbell, Murphy, Gallager, & Tallman, 1979; Hall & Ogren, 1981; Reisine, U'Prichard, Wiech, Ursillo, & Yamamura, 1980; Tsukamoto, Asakura, & Hasegawa, 1981). Smith, Garcia-Sevilla, and Hollingsworth (1981) found a decrease in α_2-adrenergic receptor density with chronic amitriptyline treatment in five areas in rat brain using [^{3}H]clonidine as a radioligand. Another group (Cohen, Ebstein, Daly, & Murphy, 1982) also have found a decrease in α_2-receptor density with chronic treatment with clorgyline. This was shown to be coupled to a decrease in the functional response of presynaptic terminals to stimulation by the α_2-agonist clonidine. (These effects were found to precede a decrease in NE-stimulated cAMP response in rat brain.) Electrophysiological studies in the locus ceruleus (which is thought to contain many α_2-receptors) with desipramine and imipramine also show that chronic treatment produces a decrease in sensitivity or functional response (McMillen, Warnack, German, & Shore, 1980; Svensson, 1980; Svensson & Usdin, 1978). If further evidence supports these findings, it means that the feedback system that cuts off release of NE becomes less sensitive with antidepressant treatment. More NE is then released from the nerve terminal. A similar effect would occur with mianserin, which directly blocks the α_2-receptor, as with other drugs that somehow cause a desensitization of the receptor. This has been proposed as a possible mechanism of mianserin's antidepressant effect (as discussed previously). In all, these effects have not been thoroughly studied, and more work needs to be done before the actions of all antidepressants at NE receptors are completely understood.

Other studies on presynaptic α-receptors have been conducted in humans. Alpha binding sites have been identified on human blood platelets and they appear to be of the α_2-subtype, with characteristics similar to those in the brain. Garcia-Sevilla, Zis, Zelnik, and Smith (1981) have reported that chronic antidepressant administration reduces the number of α_2-binding sites on platelet membranes. Pretreatment levels of receptors in these patients were the same as levels in a group of normal controls. The study included 5 patients with endogenous depression or agoraphobia. The decrease in the density of α_2-receptors has been postulated by these researchers to be the mechanism by which long-term tricyclics increase the neuronal release of NE. Another study of human platelets was reported by Wood and Coppen (1981). They found evidence

that the density of α_2-adrenergic receptors in platelets was decreased in a group of 14 depressed female patients suffering from primary depressive illness, as compared with controls. Further work is needed to determine whether the apparent down-regulation of platelet α_2-receptors is a reflection of the depressed state and/or whether it is a clinically relevant effect of antidepressant drugs.

Serotonergic Receptors

Binding studies have been carried out with 5-HT receptors to evaluate the long-term effects of antidepressants. Two types of receptors have been identified in biochemical work in animal brain. Receptors that can be detected by labeling with tritiated 5-HT have been named 5-HT$_1$ receptors and those detected by labeling with tritiated spiperone or spiroperiodol are defined as 5-HT$_2$ receptors. The importance of these receptors has been difficult to assess as they have not been specifically linked to any biological responses. Reports of antidepressant drug effects on receptor densities of 5-HT$_1$ sites have yielded inconsistent results, with no change or decreased density after long-term treatment. Decreases in density have been reported with imipramine, amitriptyline, desipramine, clorgyline, and pargyline, but no changes have also been reported with amitriptyline, desipramine, and iprindole. A variety of TCAs including imipramine, amitriptyline, desipramine, iprindole, and some MAOIs cause a decrease in 5-HT$_2$ receptor populations after chronic but not acute treatments. However, questions of the physiological role of these receptors have been raised because ECT seems to increase receptor density and amphetamine shows the same effect as the antidepressants. There is much support from binding studies in brain that chronic treatment with antidepressants causes a decrease in the density of 5-HT$_2$ receptors, but has little effect on 5-HT$_1$ receptors. These results suggest that effects at 5-HT$_2$ receptors may be related to antidepressant potency whereas those at 5-HT$_1$ receptors are not (Charney et al., 1981; Peroutka & Snyder, 1980; Snyder, 1984; Sulser, 1983; Svensson, 1980).

Neurophysiological evidence is at odds with the binding studies on 5-HT receptors. In five different brain areas, known to contain mostly postsynaptic 5-HT receptors, a variety of tricyclic drugs and iprindole and clomipramine enhanced the sensitivity of 5-HT neurons after long-term administration. In addition, repeated ECT caused the same effect. However, the opposite effect was found for the MAOI clorgyline in one study, and in other studies zimelidine and clomipramine had no effect. The generally increased sensitivity of these receptors may not be an effect found in all brain regions or shared by all antidepressants. However, other evidence from animal behavioral models, thought to be regulated by 5-HT neuronal pathways, indicates an increased sensitivity of 5-HT neurons in several brain areas. Thus there is mostly positive evidence for an increased sensitivity of 5-HT neurons with antidepressant treatment, and this is presumed to occur because of effects at the postsynaptic receptor. A mechanism of action for this may be the blocking effects of antidepressants. These drugs are quite potent blockers of $5-HT_2$ receptors but have little direct effect on $5-HT_1$ receptors. Amitriptyline, nortriptyline, and mianserin are among the most potent blockers of $5-HT_2$ sites (Baldessarini, 1983, p. 112; Charney et al., 1982; Gallager & Bunney, 1979; Ogren et al., 1983). The blocking effects of some of these drugs could cause a supersensitivity of these postsynaptic 5-HT receptors similar to what has been proposed to occur at α_1-adrenergic postsynaptic receptors. Why a decrease in receptor density is seen coupled with an increase in sensitivity is not readily apparent. More research is necessary to clear up this discrepancy.

Other Receptors

Binding studies have also been used to study the receptors for DA, ACh, and histamine (HA), another putative neurotransmitter in brain. Dopamine and HA receptors show no changes after long-term antidepressant treatment. Muscarinic ACh receptors have been reported to show an increase in density after long-term amitriptyline treatment whereas other TCAs and pargyline had no effect. Amitriptyline is highly anticholinergic, a characteristic that causes many of its side effects. For DA there is some neurophysiological and behavioral data to suggest a decrease in sensitivity in supposedly presynaptic autoreceptors. As in the NE system, these receptors are thought to control the production and release of DA. It has been proposed that the drug effects at DA receptors could contribute to the clinical effects of chronic treatment (Charney et al., 1981; Rehavi et al., 1980; Sulser, 1983). In addition, antidepressants directly block binding to histaminergic and muscarinic receptors. However, these effects do not correlate well with their antidepressant potency. Instead they seem to be related to the side effects (Beckmann & Schmauss, 1983; Peroutka & Snyder, 1980; Sulser, 1983).

Neuroendocrine Studies

The neuroendocrine system has for many years been of great interest to researchers in the field of affective illness. The effects of antidepressants on this system have helped to clarify our understanding of depression. It is known that the limbic system in the brain controls mood and has direct effects on the hypothalamus. In the hypothalamus, hormone releasing factors are produced that cause endocrine glands to secrete hormones into the circulation. The brain connections are via neurotransmitter systems. The hypothalamus is vulnerable to such mood changes as depression and stress and to the effects of drugs. Hormone releasing factors produced by the hypothalamus affect the pituitary and the hormones it releases. There are feedback systems between the limbic system, the hypothalamus, the pituitary, and the adrenal cortex, for example, which releases cortisol into the bloodstream. All must be working to keep the body functions in balance (Carroll, 1980).

It has been recognized for some time that depressed patients show increased plasma cortisol levels. In normal people, cortisol secretion during sleep is suppressed. This suppression does not occur in those who are depressed. The lack of inhibition of cortisol secretion is thought to be caused by disturbances in the limbic system. These disturbances lead, in ways not yet understood, to abnormal functioning of the hypothalamic–pituitary–adrenal (HPA) axis. Knowledge of the lack of normal cortisol secretion in depressed patients has led to the development of the dexamethasone suppression test (DST). Dexamethasone is a compound that has effects similar to the body's natural hormone, cortisol. When administered in humans, it causes a feedback response through the HPA axis that leads to suppression of cortisol secretion. In 1976, Carroll proposed the use of this test to detect depression in clinical patients. People who were depressed showed an abnormal early escape from the effects of dexamethasone during an overnight test. The DST was standardized and produced about 45% positive results in inpatients or outpatients with the diagnosis of melancholia. The abnormal DST returned to normal when the patient recovered, showing that the DST is specific to the clinical state of the patient. In addition, a positive DST has been associated with a positive treatment response to tricyclic antidepressant drugs and ECT. The transmitter system responsible for the responses during a DST has not been identified. One suggestion is that decreased postsynaptic NE receptor sensitivity in the hypothalamus is the cause of the inability of this brain region to detect feedback signals from circulating levels of cortisol. The message is not passed on to cut back on cortisol output, so the hypothalamus signals the pituitary to secrete ACTH (adrenocorticotropic hormone), which then acts on the adrenal gland to cause cortisol release. This mechanism could explain both increased levels of circulating cortisol generally found in depressed patients and a lack

of suppression of cortisol with the DST (Brown & Shuey, 1980; Carroll, 1980; Carroll et al., 1981; Sachar et al., 1980; Rubinow, Post, Svard, & Gold, 1984).

Another recent study has shown that an increase in cortisol can be induced with the stimulation of the 5-HT transmitter system (Meltzer et al., 1984). The 5-HT precursor, 5-HTP was administered to unmedicated depressed and manic patients as well as to controls. Serum levels of cortisol increased in all cases, but the increase was significantly greater in both manic and depressed patients than in controls. This study suggests that increased 5-HT receptor sensitivity occurs in the pituitary or hypothalamus in these patients. Decreased 5-HT availability, which would be expected according to some theories to produce increased receptor sensitivity, might be present in mania as well as in depression. Metzler et al. failed to find an association between cortisol response to 5-HTP and a positive DST. This suggests that lack of sensitivity of suppression by dexamethasone is not mediated through 5-HT receptors or related to an abnormality of the 5-HT system. The situation is complex because there is evidence that 5-HT both stimulates and suppresses cortisol secretion. Different serotonergic pathways may account for these results (Meltzer et al., 1984).

A number of investigators have found that thyroid-stimulating hormone (TSH) release is decreased or blunted in depressed patients. This is another parameter of hypothalamic-pituitary activity. When there was sustained improvement of the patients, the TSH response became normal. However, a complex combination of NE and 5-HT functions are thought to be involved. Thus, support for any one amine receptor theory is lacking (Charney et al., 1981).

Some information about α-adrenergic sensitivity has been gained from studies of growth hormone levels in humans. This endocrine response is also affected by the hypothalamic–pituitary axis. Charney et al. (1981) suggested that increases in growth hormone that occur in response to doses of clonidine are decreased in depressed patients when compared with normals. These decreases may normalize after antidepressant treatment. This suggests that α-adrenergic postsynaptic receptor sensitivity is increased after long-term treatment. This finding is consistent with other physiological studies discussed previously that found an increase in sensitivity in postsynaptic α-receptors with chronic treatments (Charney et al., 1981).

Heninger, Charney, and Sternberg (1984) reported that intravenous tryptophan stimulates the release of prolactin. However, when the 5-HT precursor was given to depressed patients, there was a marked blunting of the maximal prolactin response when compared with controls. Also, long-term treatment with the antidepressants amitriptyline and desipramine caused an enhancement of the prolactin response to intravenous tryptophan in 13 depressed patients when compared with baseline levels before treatment. Thus, antidepressants appear to reverse the blunting of the prolactin response found in depression. These data are consistent with suggestions that an abnormality in the 5-HT system is present in depression. The authors suggest that antidepressants increase the sensitivity of postsynaptic 5-HT receptors. However, because the neuroendocrine system is quite complex, it would be necessary to take a number of measurements of this system's function simultaneously to identify the site or sites of dysfunction in depression. Even then, it would be necessary to determine whether they were a cause or an effect of depression.

Conclusion

Over the last few decades, much has been learned about the monoamine systems in depression. Extensive research on the effects of antidepressants on the uptake and metabolism of NE and 5-HT have suggested that these neurotransmitters are involved in some way in at least some depressive syndromes. The evolution of a new generation

of antidepressants that do not show these effects necessitated the development of other theoretical possibilities in order to explain their actions. This also had the effect of redirecting research into studies of the effects of antidepressant treatments on receptor systems in the brain. This work has been very fruitful. We have learned a great deal about the responsiveness of receptor systems to neurotransmitters, especially NE and 5-HT. As it became clear that long-term effects of antidepressants differed from short-term effects, research was also focused in this direction. Chronic treatments with "typical" and "atypical" drugs have yielded some interesting consistencies. Both postsynaptic β-adrenergic receptor density and sensitivity appear to decrease with antidepressant treatments. Also, α_2-adrenergic presynaptic receptors appear to decrease in number in (some) binding studies and according to neurophysiological findings appear to become subsensitive. Also, α_1-adrenergic and 5-HT postsynaptic receptor sensitivities increase in most cases after chronic administration of antidepressants. Though some work has been done on DA, ACh, and HA receptors, the long-term effects of at least the latter two seem to be more related to side effects rather than to desired clinical response. Neuroendocrine studies in humans are a potentially new avenue for the exploration of receptor and neurotransmitter involvement in hormonal responses in depression. They also provide another method to evaluate the effects of antidepressant treatments.

Though much has been learned, this information might be considered just the tip of the iceberg. We still have very little knowledge about the etiology of depression or, more specifically, the various pathways to depression. There is much suggestive evidence that a number of amine transmitter systems are involved in the development of some depressions. Biochemical and neurohormonal data indicate that several neurotransmitter systems may be acting either alone or in combination to produce depressive symptoms. Studies of the effects of antidepressants have contributed much to our knowledge to date, but one must remember that these effects can be misleading. One does not necessarily discover causes of a disease by studying the effects of biochemicals that can "cure" it.

There is accumulating evidence that at least some depressions may result from a number of events that occur because of interactions between neurotransmitter systems. Recent results of a study by Dumbrille-Ross and Tang (1983) have shown that adrenergic as well as serotonergic neurons must be intact to produce the decreased sensitivity of β-adrenergic receptors after chronic imipramine treatment. Also, evidence from neuroendocrine research suggests that some antidepressants may exert effects on 5-HT pathways through intimate connections with NE pathways (Charney, Heninger, & Sternberg, 1984). Others have proposed that ACh pathways may have complex connections with other transmitter systems and the sum of events leads to depression. Some other possibilities beyond the scope of this article are genetic factors that predispose certain people to depressive syndromes and the numerous social and psychological factors that contribute to the illness. It is to be hoped that in time all of this information can be applied toward a more comprehensive theory of depression. The work toward this goal has greatly increased our understanding of these systems and how they may relate to depression. We must remain aware, however, that a singular biochemical pathway may prove to be as elusive as a singular psychological pathway. There may be multiple biochemical as well as psychological pathways to depression.

References

AMERICAN PSYCHIATRIC ASSOCIATION. (1980). *Diagnostic and statistical manual of mental disorders* (3rd ed.). Washington, DC: Author.

AMSTERDAM, J. D., AND MENDELS, J. (1980). Serotonergic function and depression. In J. Mendels and J. D. Amsterdam (Eds.), *The psychology of affective disorders* (pp. 57–71). New York: Karger.

ANANTH, J. (1983). New antidepressants. *Comprehensive Psychiatry, 24,* 116–124.

AXELROD, J. (1974). Neurotransmitters. *Scientific American, 230,* 59–71.

AXELROD, J., WHITBY, L. G., AND HERTTING, G. (1961). Effects of psychotropic drugs on the uptake of H^3-norepinephrine by tissues. *Science, 133,* 383–384.

BALDESSARINI, R. J. (1983). *Biomedical aspects of depression and its treatment.* Washington, DC: American Psychiatric Press.

BALDESSARINI, R. J. (1984). Treatment of depression by altering monoamine metabolism: Precursors and metabolic inhibitors. *Psychopharmacology Bulletin, 20,* 224–239.

BECK, A. T. (1967). *Depression: Clinical, experimental, and theoretical aspects.* New York: Hoeber.

BECK, A. T. (1976). *Cognitive therapy and the emotional disorders.* New York: International Universities Press.

BECK, A. T. (1982). Cognitive therapy of depression: New perspectives. In P. Clayton and J. Barrett (Eds.), *Treatment of depression: Old controversies and new approaches* (pp. 265–290). New York: Raven Press.

BECKMANN, H., AND GOODWIN, F. K. (1975). Antidepressant response to tricyclics and urinary MHPG in unipolar patients: Clinical response to imipramine or amitriptyline. *Archives of General Psychiatry, 32,* 17–21.

BECKMANN, H., AND SCHMAUSS, M. (1983). Clinical investigations into antidepressant mechanisms. I. Antihistaminic and cholinolytic effects: Amitriptyline versus promethazine. *Archiv für Psychiatrie und Nervenkrankheiten, 233,* 59–70.

BIELSKI, R. J., AND FRIEDEL, R. O. (1976). Prediction of tricyclic antidepressant response. *Archives of General Psychiatry, 33* 1479–1489.

BLUMBERG, J. B., VETULANI, J., STAWARZ, R. J., AND SULSE, F. (1976). The noradrenergic cyclic AMP generating system in the limbic forebrain: Pharmacological characterization in vitro and possible role of limbic noradrenergic mechanisms in the mode of action of antipsychotics. *European Journal of Pharmacology, 37,* 337–366.

BROWN, W. A., AND SHUEY, I. (1980). Response to dexamethasone and subtype of depression. *Archives of General Psychiatry, 37,* 747–751.

BUNNEY, W. E., JR., AND DAVIS, J. M. (1965). Norepinephrine in depressive reactions: A review. *Archives of General Psychiatry, 13,* 483–494.

BYRNE, K., AND STERN, S. L. (1981). Antidepressant medication in the outpatient treatment of depression: Guide for nonmedical psychotherapists. *Professional Psychology, 12,* 302–308.

CAMPBELL, I. C., MURPHY, D. L., GALLAGER, D. W., AND TALLMAN, J. F. (1979). Neurotransmitter-related adaptation in the central nervous system following chronic monoamine oxidase inhibition. In T. P. SINGER, R. W. VON KORFF, AND D. L. MURPHY (Eds.), *Monoamine oxidase: Structure, function, and altered functions* (pp. 517–530). New York: Academic Press.

CARROLL, B. J. (1980). Neuroendocrine aspects of depression: Theoretical and practical significance. In J. MENDELS AND J. D. AMSTERDAM (Eds.), *The psychobiology of affective disorders* (pp. 99–110). New York: Karger.

CARROLL, B. J., FEINBERG, M., GREDEN, J. F., TARIKA, J., ALBALA, A. A., HASKETT, R. F., JAMES, N. M., KRONFOL, Z., LOHR, N., STEINER, M., deVIGNE, J. P., AND YOUNG, E. (1981). A specific laboratory test for the diagnosis of melancholia. *Archives of General Psychiatry, 38,* 15–22.

CHARNEY, D. S., AND HENINGER, G. R. (1983). Monoamine receptor sensitivity and depression: Clinical studies of antidepressant effects on serotonin and noradrenergic function. *Psychopharmacology Bulletin, 20,* 213–223.

CHARNEY, D. S., HENINGER, G. R., AND STERNBERG, D. E. (1984). Serotonin function and mechanism of action of antidepressant treatment. Effects of amitriptyline and desipramine. *Archives of General Psychiatry, 41,* 359–365.

CHARNEY, D. S., MENKES, D. B., AND HENINGER, G. R. (1981). Receptor sensitivity and the mechanism of action of antidepressant treatment. *Archives of General Psychiatry, 38,* 1160–1180.

COHEN, R. M., EBSTEIN, R. P., DALY, J. W., AND MURPHY, D. L. (1982). Chronic effects of a monoamine oxidase-inhibiting antidepressant: Decreases in functional α-adrenergic autoreceptors precede the decrease in norepinephrine-stimulated cyclic adenosine 3′:5′-monophosphate systems in rat brain. *Journal of Neuroscience, 2,* 1588–1595.

COOPER, J. R., BLOOM, F. E., AND ROTH, R. H. (1982). *The biochemical basis of neuropharmacology* (4th ed.). New York: Oxford University Press.

COYNE, J. C., AND GOTLIB, I. H. (1983). The role of cognition in depression: A critical appraisal. *Psychological Bulletin, 94,* 472–505.

DALY, J. (1975). Role of cyclic nucleotides in the nervous system. In L. L. Iversen, S. D. Iversen, and S. H. Snyder (Eds.), *Handbook of psychopharmacology* (pp. 47–130). New York: Plenum Press.

DALY, J. W., PADGETT, W., NIMITKITPAISON, Y., CREVELING, C. R., CANTACUZENE, D., AND KIRK, K. L. (1980). Fluoronorepinephrines: Specific agonists for the activation of alpha and beta adrenergic-sensitive cyclic AMP-generating systems in brain slices. *Journal of Pharmacology and Experimental Therapeutics, 212,* 383–389.

DAVIS, J. N., ARNETT, C. D., HOYLER, E., STALVEY, L. P., DALY, J. W., AND SKOLNICK, P. (1978). Brain α-adrenergic receptors: Comparison of [³H]WB 4101 binding with norepinephrine-stimulated cyclic AMP accumulations in rat cerebral cortex. *Brain Research, 159,* 125–135.

DAVIS, K. L., BERGER, P. A., HOLLISTER, L. E., AND DEFRAITES, E. (1978). Physostigmine in mania. *Archives of General Psychiatry, 35,* 119–122.

DAVIS, K. L., HOLLISTER, L. E., OVERALL, J., JOHNSON, A., AND TRAIN, K. (1976). Physostigmine: Effects on cognition and affect on normal subjects. *Psychopharmacologia, 51,* 23–27.

DUMBRILLE-ROSS, A., AND TANG, S. W. (1983). Noradrenergic and serotonergic input necessary for imipramine-induced changes in beta but not S_2 receptor densities. *Psychiatry Research, 9,* 207–215.

FABRE, L. F., AND McLENDON, D. M. (1980). A double-blind study comparing the efficacy and safety of alprazolam with imipramine and placebo in primary depression. *Current Therapeutic Research, 27,* 474–482.

FEIGHNER, J. P. (1983). The new generation of antidepressants. *Journal of Clinical Psychiatry, 44,* 49–55.

FRAZER, A., AND MENDELS, J. (1980). Effects of antidepressant drugs on adrenergic responsiveness and receptors. In J. MENDELS AND J. D. AMSTERDAM (Eds.), *The psychobiology of affective disorders* (pp. 72–82). New York: Karger.

GALLAGER, D. W., AND BUNNEY, W. E. (1979). Failure of chronic lithium treatment to block tricyclic antidepressant-induced 5-HT supersensitivity. *Naunyn-Schmeideberg's Archives of Pharmacology, 307,* 129–133.

GARCIA-SEVILLA, J. A., ZIS, A. P., ZELNIK, T. C., AND SMITH, C. B. (1981). Tricyclic antidepressant drug treatment decreases α_2-adrenoreceptors on human platelet membranes. *European Journal of Pharmacology, 69,* 121–123.

GELENBERG, A. J., WOJCIK, J. D., GROWDON, J. H., SVED, A. F., AND WURTMAN, R. J. (1980). Tyrosine for the treatment of depression. *American Journal of Psychiatry, 137,* 622–623.

GERSHON, L., AND SHAW, F. H. (1961). Psychiatric sequelae of chronic exposure to organophosphorus insecticides. *Lancet, 1,* 1371–1374.

GLASSMAN, A. (1969). Indoleamines and affective disorder. *Psychosomatic Medicine, 31,* 107–114.

GOODWIN, F. K., MURPHY, D. L., BRODIE, H. K. H., AND BUNNEY, W. E. (1970). L-Dopa, catecholamines and behavior: A clinical and biochemical study in depressed patients. *Biological Psychiatry, 2,* 341–366.

HALL, H., AND OGREN, S. O. (1981). Effects of antidepressant drugs on different receptors in the brain. *European Journal of Pharmacology, 70,* 393–407.

HAMMEN, C. L. (1985). Predicting Depression: A cognitive-behavioral perspective. In P. C. KENDALL (Ed.), *Advances in cognitive-behavioral research and therapy* (Vol. 4, pp. 29–71). Orlando, FL: Academic Press.

HAMMERSCHLAG, R., AND ROBERTS, E. (1976). Overview of chemical transmission. In G. J. SIEGEL, R. W. ALBERS, R. KATZMAN, AND B. W. AGRANOFF (Eds.), *Basic neurochemistry* (2nd ed., pp. 167–179). Boston: Little, Brown.

HENINGER, G. R., CHARNEY, D. S., AND STERNBERG, D. E. (1984). Serotonergic function in depression. Prolactin response to intravenous tryptophan in depressed patients and healthy subjects. *Archives of General Psychiatry, 41,* 398–402.

HOLLISTER, L. E., DAVIS, K. L., AND BERGER, P. A. (1980). Subtypes of depression based on excretion of MHPG and response to nortriptyline. *Archives of General Psychiatry, 37,* 1107–10110.

IVERSEN, L. L. (1979). The chemistry of the brain. *Scientific American, 241,* 134–149.

JANOWSKY, D. S. (1980). The cholinergic nervous system in depression. In J. MENDELS AND J. D. AMSTERDAM (Eds.), *The psychobiology of affective disorders* (pp. 83–89). New York: Karger.

JANOWSKY, D. S., EL-YOUSEF, M. K., DAVIS, J. M., AND SEKERKE, H. J. (1973). Parasympathetic suppression of manic symptoms by physostigmine. *Archives of General Psychiatry, 28,* 542–547.

KELWALA, S., STANLEY, M., AND GERSHON, S. (1983). History of antidepressants: Successes and failures. *Journal of Clinical Psychiatry, 44,* 40–48.

KIRK, K. L., AND CREVELING, C. R. (1984). The chemistry and biology of ring-fluorinated biogenic amines. *Medicinal Research Reviews, 4,* 189–220.

KOVACS, M. (1980). The efficacy of cognitive and behavior therapies for depression. *American Journal of Psychiatry, 137,* 1495–1501.

LEFKOWITZ, R. J., CARON, M. C., AND STILES, G. L. (1984). Mechanisms of membrane-receptor regulation. Biochemical, physiological, and clinical insights derived from studies of the adrenergic receptors. *New England Journal of Medicine, 310,* 1570–1579.

LEWINSOHN, P. M., STEINMETZ, J. L., LARSON, D. W., AND FRANKLIN, J. (1981). Depression-related cognitions: Antecedent or consequence? *Journal of Abnormal Psychology, 90,* 213–219.

MAAS, J. W. (1975). Biogenic amines and depression: Biochemical and pharmacological separation of two subtypes of depression. *Archives of General Psychiatry, 32,* 1357–1361.

MAAS, J. W., FAWCETT, J. A., AND DEKIRMENJIAN, H. (1972). Catecholamine metabolism, depressive illness, and drug response. *Archives of General Psychiatry, 26,* 252–262.

MAAS, J. W., AND HUANG, Y. (1980). Norepinephrine neuronal system functioning and depression. In J. MENDELS AND J. D. AMSTERDAM (Eds.), *The psychobiology of affective disorders* (pp. 40–56). New York: Karger.

MACINTOSH, F. C. (1976). Acetylcholine. In G. J. SIEGEL, R. W. ALBERS, R. KATZMAN, and B. W. AGRANOFF (Eds.), *Basic neurochemistry* (2nd ed., pp. 180–202). Boston: Little, Brown.

MAGGI, A., U'PRICHARD, D. C., AND ENNA, S. J. (1980). Differential effects of antidepressant treatment on brain monoaminergic receptors. *European Journal of Pharmacology, 61,* 91–98.

MANN, J. J., AARONS, S. F., FRANCES, A., BERNSTEIN, W., DOUGLAS, C., AND SICKLES, M. (1983). Symptoms of atypical depression as a predictor of response to L-deprenyl. *Psychopharmacology Bulletin, 19,* 333–335.

MCMILLEN, B. A., WARNACK, W., GERMAN, D. C., AND SHORE, P. A. (1980). Effects of chronic desipramine treatment on rat brain noradrenergic responses to α-adrenergic drugs. *European Journal of Pharmacology, 61,* 239–246.

MELTZER, H. Y., UMBERKOMAN-WIITA, ROBERTSON, A., TRICOU, B. J., LOWY, M., AND PERLINE, R. (1984). Effect of 5-hydroxytryptophan on serum cortisol levels in major affective disorders. I. Enhanced response in depression and mania. *Archives of General Psychiatry, 32,* 22–30.

MENDELS, J., STINNETT, J. L., BURNS, D., AND FRAZER, A. (1975). Amine precursors and depression. *Archives of General Psychiatry, 32,* 22–30.

MENDELWITZ, J., AND YOUDIM, M. B. H. (1983). L-Deprenil, a selective monoamine oxidase Type B inhibitor, in the treatment of depression: A double blind evaluation. *British Journal of Psychiatry, 142,* 508–511.

MURPHY, G. E., SIMONS, A. D., WETZEL, R. D., AND LUSTMAN, P. J. (1984). Cognitive therapy and pharmacotherapy. *Archives of General Psychiatry, 41,* 33–41.

MUSCETTOLA, G., POTTER, W. Z., PICKAR, D., AND GOODWIN, F. K. (1984). Urinary-3-methoxy-4-hydroxyphenylglycol and major affective disorders. *Archives of General Psychiatry, 44,* 337–342.

NATHANSON, J. A., AND GREENGARD, P. (1977). "Second messengers" in the brain. *Scientific American, 237,* 108–119.

OGREN, S. O., ROSS, S., HALL, H., AND ARCHER, T. Biochemical and behavioral effects of antidepressant drugs. In G. P. BURROWS, T. R. NORMAN, and B. DAVIES (Eds.), *Drugs in psychiatry: Vol. 1. Antidepressants* (pp. 13–34). Amsterdam: Elsevier.

PEROUTKA, J., AND SNYDER, S. H. (1980). Long-term antidepressant treatment decreases spiroperidal-labeled serotonin receptor binding. *Science, 210,* 88–90.

PRANGE, A. J. (1964). The pharmacology and biochemistry of depression. *Diseases of the Nervous System, 25,* 217–221.

PRUSOFF, B. A., WEISSMAN, M. M., KLERMAN, G. L., AND ROUNSAVILLE, B. J. (1980). Research diagnostic criteria subtypes of depression. *Archives of General Psychiatry, 37,* 796–801.

RALL, T. W. (1972). Role of adenosine 3′,5′-monophosphate (cyclic AMP) in actions of catecholamines. *Pharmacological Reviews, 24,* 399–409.

REDA, M. A., CARPINIELLO, B., SECCHIAROLI, L., AND BLANCO, S. (1985). Thinking, depression, and antidepressants: Modified and unmodified depressive beliefs during treatment with amitriptyline. *Cognitive Therapy and Research, 9,* 135–143.

REHAVI, M., RAMOT, O., YAVETZ, B., AND SOKOLOVSKY, M. (1980). Amitriptyline: Long-term treatment elevates α-adrenergic and muscarinic receptor binding in mouse brain. *Brain Research, 194,* 443–453.

REISINE, T. D., U′PRICHARD, D. C., WIECH, N. L., URSILLO, R. C., AND YAMAMURA, H. I. (1980). Effects of combined administration of amphetamine and iprindole on brain adrenergic receptors. *Brain Research, 188,* 587–592.

RICHELSON, E. (1982). Pharmacology of antidepressants in use in the United States. *Journal of Clinical Psychiatry, 43,* 4–11.

RICHELSON, E. (1984). The newer antidepressants: Structures, pharmacodynamics, and proposed mechanisms of action. *Psychopharmacology Bulletin, 20,* 213–223.

ROSENBLATT, J. E., PERT, C. B., TALLMAN, J. F., PERT, A., AND BUNNEY, W. E. (1979). The effect of imipramine and lithium on α- and β-receptor binding in rat brain. *Brain Research, 160,* 186–191.

RUBINOW, D. R., POST, R. M., SAVAD, R., AND GOLD, P. W. (1984). Cortisol hypersecretion and cognitive impairment in depression. *Archives of General Psychiatry, 4,* 279–283.

RUSH, A. J. (1982). Diagnosing depressions. In A. J. RUSH (Ed.), *Short-term psychotherapies for depression* (pp. 13–15). New York: Guilford Press.

RUSH, A. J., BECK, A. T., KOVACS, M., AND HOLLON, S. (1977). Comparative efficacy of cognitive therapy and imipramine on the treatment of depressed outpatients. *Cognitive Therapy and Research, 1,* 17–37.

SACHAR, E. J., ASNIS, G., NATHAN, S., HALBREICH, U., TABRIZI, M. A., AND HALPERN, F. S. (1980). Dextroamphetamine and cortisol in depression. *Archives of General Psychiatry, 37,* 755–757.

SCHATZBERG, A. F., ORSULAK, P. J., ROSENBAUM, A. H., MARUTA, T., KRUGER, E. R., COLE, J. O., AND SCHILDKRAUT, J. J. (1982). Toward a biochemical classification of depressive disorders, V: Heterogeneity of unipolar depressions. *American Journal of Psychiatry, 139,* 471–475.

SCHATZBERG, A. F., AND ROSENBAUM, A. (1980). Studies on MHPG levels as predictors of antidepressant response. *McLean Hospital Journal, VI,* 138–147.

SCHILDKRAUT, J. J. (1965). The catecholamine hypothesis of affective disorders: A review of supporting evidence. *American Journal of Psychiatry, 122,* 509–522.

SCHILDKRAUT, J. J. (1973). Norepinephrine metabolites as a biochemical criteria for classifying depressive disorders and predicting responses to treatment: Preliminary findings. *American Journal of Psychiatry, 130,* 695–699.

SCHOONOVER, S. C. (1983). Depression. In E. L.

BASSUK, S. C. SCHOONOVER, AND A. J. GELEN-BERG (Eds.), *The practitioner's guide to psychoactive drugs* (pp. 19–74). New York: Plenum Press.

SCHULTZ, J., AND DALY, J. W. (1973). Adenosine 3',5'-monophosphate in guinea pig cerebral cortical slices: Effects of α- and β-adrenergic agents, histamine, serotonin and adenosine. *Journal of Neurochemistry, 21,* 573–579.

SIMONS, A. D., GARFIELD, S. K., AND MURPHY, G. E. (1984). The process of change in cognitive therapy and pharmacotherapy for depression. *Archives of General Psychiatry, 41,* 45–51.

SIMPSON, G. M., PI, E. H., AND WHITE, K. (1983). Plasma drug levels and clinical response to antidepressants. *Journal of Clinical Psychiatry, 44,* 27–33.

SMITH, C. B., GARCIA-SEVILLA, J. A., AND HOLLINGSWORTH, P. J. (1981). α_2-Adrenoreceptors in rat brain are decreased after long-term tricyclic antidepressant drug treatment. *Brain Research, 210,* 413–418.

SNYDER, S. H. (1976). Catecholamines, serotonin, and histamine. In G. J. SIEGEL, R. W. ALBERS, R. KATZMAN, AND B. W. AGRANOFF (Eds.), *Basic neurochemistry* (2nd ed., pp. 203–217). Boston: Little, Brown.

SNYDER, S. H. (1984). Drug and neurotransmitter receptors in the brain. *Science, 224,* 22–31.

SOURKES, T. L. (1976). Psychopharmacology and biochemical theories of mental disorders. In G. J. SIEGEL, R. J. ALBERS, R. KATZMAN, AND B. W. AGRANOFF (Eds.), *Basic neurochemis-try* (2nd ed., pp. 705–736). Boston: Little, Brown.

SULSER, F. (1983). Mode of action of antidepressant drugs. *Journal of Clinical Psychiatry, 44,* 14–20.

SVENSSON, T. H. (1980). Effect of chronic treatment with tricyclic antidepressant drugs on identified brain noradrenergic and serotonergic neurons. *Psychiatrica Scandinavia, 61* (Suppl. 280), 121–131.

SVENSSON, T. H., AND USDIN, T. (1978). Feedback inhibition of brain noradrenergic neurons by tricyclics: α-Receptor mediation after acute and chronic treatment. *Science, 202,* 1089–1091.

TASKA, R., AND BRODIE, H. K. H. (1983). New trends in the diagnosis and treatment of depression. *Journal of Clinical Psychiatry, 44,* 11–33.

TSUKAMOTO, T., ASAKURA, M., AND HASEGAWA, K. (1982). Long-term antidepressant treatment increases α_2-adrenergic receptor binding in rat cerebral cortex and hippocampus. In S. Z. LANGER, R. TAKAHASHI, T. SEGAWA, AND M. BRILEY (Eds.), *New vistas in depression* (pp. 147–151). New York: Pergamon Press.

WHITE, A., HANDLER, P., AND SMITH, E. L. (1973). *Principles of biochemistry* (5th Ed.). New York: McGraw-Hill.

WOOD, K., AND COPPEN, A. (1981). Platelet alpha-adrenoreceptor sensitivity in depressive illness. In J. MENDELWICZ AND H. M. VAN PRAAG (Eds.), *The psychobiology of affective disorders* (pp. 99–110). New York: Karger.

13

Painful Truths About Depressives' Cognitions

Christopher Layne

Cognitive theories assert that depressed persons' cognitions are distorted. Most of the empirical literature directly contradicts this assertion. Using a wide variety of methods to study a wide variety of cognitive processes, experiments consistently find that depressed people suffer significantly *less* cognitive distortion than do both normals and nondepressed psychiatric patients. It was speculated that childhood traumas predispose depression by preventing the normal formation of a defensive screen against painful realities.

Cognitive theories of depression make two main assertions: That depressives' cognitions are relatively pessimistic and that their cognitions are distorted. To date, the former assertion goes unquestioned. However, the latter assertion was questioned by Alloy and Abramson (1979) and again by Mischel (1979), who speculated that depressives are actually more realistic than normals and cited a few experiments in support of this radical departure from cognitive theory. The present paper examines the research that related to the truthfulness or falsity of depressives' cognitions.

Christopher Layne. Painful Truths about Depressives' Cognitions. *Journal of Clinical Psychology*, (1983), Vol. 39, No. 6, pp. 848–853. Copyright © 1983, Clinical Psychology Publishing Corporation. Reprinted by permission.

Pessimism vs. Distortion

Undoubtedly, depressives' cognitions are relatively pessimistic, i.e., less optimistic than those of normals. A variety of experiments have administered questionnaires or inventories and have found that depressives' cognitions are less happy or hopeful than those of nondepressives. Two studies (Lapointe & Crandell, 1980; Nelson, 1977) found that depressed undergraduates endorse a lot of pessimistic beliefs; two other studies (Fibel & Hale, 1978; Prociuk, Breen, & Lussier, 1976) found that depressed undergraduates expressed more pessimism on various hope-questionnaires. Studies with patient populations have obtained almost identical results (Beck, Weissman, Lester, & Trexler, 1974; Erickson, Post, & Paige, 1975; Krantz & Hammen, 1979; Minkoff, Bergman, Beck, & Beck, 1973).

The authors of these questionnaire studies correctly inferred that depressives think more pessimistically than do nondepressives, but they incorrectly inferred that depressives are cognitively distorted. Their unspoken assumption was that normals are rational, realistic beings and that, therefore, any group that thinks differently from them must be irrational.

Unhappy, hopeless thoughts are not irrational if the situation actually is aversive or hopeless. In the above questionnaire studies, group differences may have emerged from the fact that the normals were irrationally optimistic. Another possibility is that the cognitions of both groups were equally realistic. This possibility emerges from the fact that depressives do, in fact, live more difficult lives than do nondepressives—as children (cf. Lloyd, 1980a, for review) and as adults (Dohrenwend & Dohrenwend, 1974: Ilfeld, 1977; Lloyd 1980b). The depressives' relative pessimism may be as realistic a reflection of the present and as realistic a forecast of the future as is the normal's optimism.

The questionnaires used in the above studies are face-valid measures of pessimism, but not realism. None of the questionnaires ever has been validated empirically against an external criterion of realism. For example, the so-called *Irrational* Beliefs Test assumes that it is irrational to believe that: It is impossible to overcome the influence of past history. Such a belief appears pessimistic, but is it irrational? Certainly it possesses no logical errors and it is conceivable that one day it will be confirmed empirically. Depressives may endorse such statements because they are relatively pessimistic, not because they are irrational. Similarly, Krantz and Hammen (1979) assumed that endorsement of a "depressed/distorted" story was a symptom of distortion, when it could have been a symptom of pessimism. Some questionnaires consist of items selected on the basis of their ability to discriminate among various groups of *S*s. But such items do not reveal which of the groups thinks most rationally.

Cognitive distortion must be assessed via external criteria of reality, not by the optimism of normal people. As a depressed person moves from the beginning, through the middle, and to the end of a task, he manifests cognitive distortion only to the extent that his cognitions deviate from external reality. If the gap between depressives' thoughts and reality is wider than that of normals, then depressives clearly are distorted; but if this gap is "normal," or abnormally narrow, then it certainly cannot be concluded that depressives are cognitively distorted.

When objective criteria of rationality are used, a startling finding emerges. The gap between depressives' cognitions and objective reality is frequently normal—i.e., equal to that of nondepressives. But with even greater frequency, the depressives "reality gap" is abnormally narrow, which suggests that depressives are more rational than nondepressives. The evidence follows:

Expectancies

A number of theorists (Beck, 1974; Radloff & Rae, 1979) state that depressives' expectancies are irrational. Depressives supposedly expect fewer rewards and more punishers than are realistic. The expectancies of normals are supposedly realistic.

However, some measures indicate that depressives' expectancies are almost identical to those of normals. Other measures indicate that depressives' expectancies are actually *more* rational than those of normals. A long list of studies shows that depressives' expectancies of success are perfectly normal (Abramson, Garber, Edwards & Seligman, 1978; Klein & Seligman, 1976; McNitt & Thornton, 1978; Miller & Seligman, 1973; Prkachin, Craig, Papageorgis, & Reith, 1977; Rizley, 1978; Sacco & Hokanson, 1978; Smolen, 1978; Wener & Rehm, 1975).

More thorough assessments of expectancies did reveal differences between depressives and nondepressives. Lobitz and Post (1979) obtained two expectancies from each *S*: How well he expected to perform the task and how well he expected other *S*s to perform the task. Results were that nondepressives expected that they would do better than the others, whereas depressives expected that they would only do as well as the others. The subsequent performances of both groups supported the expectancies of the depressives: Both groups performed equally well. The normals' expectations were distorted in that they failed to perform better than the others.

On chance tasks, depressives' expectancies also are less distorted than those of nondepressives. Golin, Terrell, Weitz, and Drost

(1979) examined the illusion of control in inpatients. They assessed expectancies during two games of dice: In one game, the inpatients were allowed to throw their own dice and thus experienced an illusion of control. In the other game, a croupier threw the dice. Of course, the probability of winning was the same in each game. Results were that the nondepressives' expectancies were significantly higher for the illusion-of-control game than for the croupier game, an indication that nondepressives' expectancies were susceptible to the illusion of control. However, the depressives' expectancies were not affected by the illusion. Their expectancies, like the actual probabilities of winning, failed to change.

In sum, depressives' expectancies are never more distorted than those of normals. Depressives can predict upcoming success as accurately as can nondepressives. More importantly, depressives' expectancies are more rationally consistent than those of normals. In both skill and chance tasks, depressives correctly expect that their performances will be equal to those of other people, whereas normals incorrectly expect that their own performances will be better than others'.

Perception

Beck (1974) stated that depressives distort their perceptions of the environment. Supposedly, they filter out positive aspects of the environment and inflate the negative aspects of the environment. They are particularly likely to distort performance feedback, according to Beck.

The opposite is indicated by empirical research. On the Rorschach inkblot test, depressives consistently yield higher form levels and more pure form responses than do nondepressives (e.g., Allison, Blatt, & Zimet, 1968; Holt, 1968). This means that depressives' perceptions match the inkblot better and their perceptions include less movement, shading, and color. People who pro-

duce this kind of Rorschach performance are said to be highly accurate and matter-of-fact in their perceptions.

An experiment by DeMonbreun and Craighead (1977) found that depressives perceive feedback as accurately as do both normals and psychiatric controls. The Es presented Ss with ambiguous feedback and found no group differences in their abilities to identify its valence.

In sum, depressives interpret their perceptions of inkblots more accurately than do nondepressives, and they interpret their perceptions of outcomes no less accurately than do nondepressives. Depressives have not evidenced the perceptual distortion hypothesized by cognitive theories of depression.

Self-monitoring

Both Rehm (1977) and Beck (1974) hypothesized that depressives are unrealistic in their self-monitoring. Beck further indicated that depressives overestimate the frequency of their failures and underestimate the frequency of their successes.

Contrary to these theories, one set of data indicate that depressives and nondepressives both self-monitor significantly inaccurately; three studies showed that depressives self-monitored more accurately than did normals. Roth and Rehm (1980) showed that both depressives and nondepressives departed significantly from objective reality when they self-monitored. However, another study (Lewinsohn, Mischel, Chaplin & Barton, 1980) showed that depressives were more accurate in monitoring their own skilled social behaviors. Moreover, depressives were more accurate in self-monitoring both unskilled social behavior (Roth & Rehm, 1980) and the correctness of responses to a memory recognition task (Rozenski, Rehm, Pry, & Roth, 1977).

Thus, depressives typically monitor their own behavior more accurately than do nondepressives. Nondepressives typically bias their self-monitoring in a self-enhancing way. These findings, like those that involve expectancies and perceptions, directly contradict the hypothesis that depressives are cognitively distorted.

Memory

Beck's (1974) theory clearly indicates that depressives suffer distorted memories. They supposedly forget previous rewards and overestimate the frequency of past punishers.

There is mixed support for these speculations. Depressives do appear to be deficient in their ability to remember high rates of reward (DeMonbreun & Craighead, 1977; Kupier, 1978; Nelson & Craighead, 1977). However, depressives clearly suffer no difficulty in remembering less-desirable outcomes. For example, depressives' memories for low rates of reward were as accurate as normals' (DeMonbreun & Craighead, 1977; Nelson & Craighead, 1977). Nelson and Craighead (1977) also found that depressives' memories for infrequent punishment were superior to those of nondepressives. When punishment was frequent, depressives' memories were as accurate as nondepressives'. Finally, Roth and Rehm's (1980) study revealed that depressives' recall and recognition memories were not significantly different from those of nondepressives. However, on most measures depressives tended to recall and recognize more accurately than did normals.

The data on memory distortion are inconclusive. Three studies found that depressives suffered distorted memories; three found that depressives' memories were as accurate as normals; one found that depressives' memories were significantly superior, and one found consistent, but nonsignificant tendencies for depressives to remember better than nondepressives. It must be concluded that there is no clear evidence that depressives possess inferior memories. While this conclusion is not opposite the assertions of cognitive theories, it is still embarrassing to these theories.

Attributions

Many theories state that depressives are irrational with respect to their causal attributions. Depressives are said to minimize their roles in successes and to maximize their roles in failures (Abramson, Seligman, & Teasdale, 1978; Beck 1974; Rehm, 1977).

However, experiments clearly indicate that depressives are more consistent in their attributions across successes and failures. Rizley (1978) found that depressives saw themselves as equally responsible for their previous successes and failures on a task. Nondepressives attributed high amounts of responsibility to themselves for successes, but low amounts of responsibility to themselves for failures on the same task. This finding was replicated in a second experiment by Rizley and in Kuiper's (1978) study. Finally, four experiments by Alloy and Abramson (1979) consistently found that depressives were much more accurate than nondepressives in judging the degree of contingency between their previous responses and outcomes. The thrust of their article was that depressives were "sadder but wiser."

Once again, the hypothesis that depressives are cognitively distorted is radically contradicted by the evidence. Normals evidence self-serving bias when they attribute the causes of previous outcomes. Depressives exhibit no such bias.

Implications

Contrary to the cognitive theories of depression, empirical research indicates that depressives are cognitively realistic, while nondepressives are cognitively distorted. This phenomenon possesses wide generality: It occurs across a variety of cognitive functions, including expectations, perceptions, self-monitoring, and attributions; the phenomenon occurs across a variety of tasks, including those that require varying degrees of skill and luck and those that involve varying degrees of social and nonsocial stimuli, and it occurs across a variety of outcomes, including various rewards, punishers, neutral outcomes, and no feedback at all.

It is clear that depressives' hyper-realism is not the result of psychopathology in general, but is specific to depression. Many of the above investigations demonstrated that depressives were not only more realistic than normals but that they were also more realistic than various psychiatric control groups (Allison et al., 1968; Golin et al., 1979; Holt, 1968; Lewinsohn et al., 1980; Lobitz & Post, 1979; Roth & Rehm, 1980; Rozenski et al., 1977).

Cognitive theories of depression appear to be dead wrong in their assertion that depressives' cognitions are distorted. Normals appear to be less in touch with reality than are depressives. Normals are even less in touch than are depressed outpatients (Lewinsohn et al., 1980) and even hospitalized inpatients (Rozenki et al., 1977)! With few exceptions, however (Lewinsohn et al., 1980; Rozenski et al., 1977), the empirical literature supports the cognitive theories' assertions that depressives think less optimistically and in less self-serving ways than do normals. The major implication of the empirical literature is that depressives' thoughts are painfully truthful, whereas nondepressives' thoughts are unrealistically positive.

Why are normal's cognitions happily distorted while depressives' cognitions are painfully truthful? Perceptual defensiveness may be at the crux of normals' optimism. Perhaps normals learn to erect a defensive screen against painful perceptions. The defensive screen would lead them to be unrealistically positive in their self-monitoring, their attributions, and their subsequent expectancies. The cognitive biases of normals probably generate increased motivation and, hence, more effective performance. Theorists agree that high expectations produce stronger motivations (e.g., Atkinson, 1964; Logan, 1970; Rotter, Chance, & Phares, 1972; Vroom, 1964). Enhanced motivation may more than compensate for a departure from truth. In the long run, it may be that normals' optimism becomes somewhat self-fulfilling by generating successful performances.

Why are depressives' cognitions painfully truthful? It is *un*likely that depression causes cognitive distortion. A variety of experiments and theories indicate that cognitive variables precede and predispose depression (e.g., Abramson, Seligman, & Teasdale, 1978; Beck, 1974; Radloff & Rae, 1979; Rehm, 1977). It is more likely that painfully truthful cognitions, perhaps in concert with other cognitive deviations, cause depression. Perhaps defenselessness may be at the crux of depressive realism. It is clear that depressives experience many childhood losses (Lloyd, 1980a). From these experiences, the child may learn that the world can be extremely painful. These painful lessons may thwart permanently the erection of a defensive screen against future painful realities. Henceforth, the depressive simply sees things as they are. The accuracy of his cognitions may not compensate adequately for the cognitions' meager effect upon motivation and performance. In the long run, the depressive's painfully truthful cognitions also may become self-fulfilling prophecies.

Implications of the above data for treatment are remarkable. Could it be that some psychotherapies cure depression by helping the depressive erect a defensive screen against reality? Are there intervention strategies that shatter the defensive screen, force the client to face reality, and thereby produce an iatrogenic depression?

References

Abramson, L.Y., Garber, J., Edwards, N.B., and Seligman, M.E.P. Expectancy changes in depression and schizophrenia. *Journal of Abnormal Psychology*, 1978, *87*, 102–109.

Abramson, L.Y., Seligman, M.E.P., and Teasdale, J.D. Learned helplessness in humans: Critique and reformulation. *Journal of Abnormal Psychology*, 1978, *87*, 49–74.

Allison, J., Blatt, S.J., and Zimet, C.N. *The interpretation of psychological tests.* New York: Harper & Row, 1968.

ALLOY, L.B., AND ABRAMSON, L.Y. Judgment of contingency in depressed and nondepressed students: Sadder but wiser? *Journal of Experimental Psychology: General,* 1979, *108,* 441–485.

ATKINSON, J.W. *An introduction to motivation.* Princeton, N.J.: Van Nostrand, 1964.

BECK, A.T. The development of depression: A cognitive model. In R.J. FRIEDMAN AND M.M. KATZ (Eds.), *The psychology of depression.* Washington: Winston, 1974.

BECK, A.T., WEISSMAN, A., LESTER, D., AND TREXLER, L. The measurement of pessimism: The Hopelessness Scale. *Journal of Consulting and Clinical Psychology,* 1974, *42,* 861–865.

DEMONBREUN, B.G., AND CRAIGHEAD, W.E. Distortion of perception and recall of positive and neutral feedback in depression. *Cognitive Therapy and Research,* 1977, *I,* 311–329.

DOHRENWEND, B.P., AND DOHRENWEND, B.S. (EDS.) *Stressful life events: Their nature and effects.* New York: John Wiley, 1974.

ERICKSON, R.C., POST, R.D., AND PAIGE, A.B. Hope as a psychiatric variable. *Journal of Clinical Psychology,* 1975, *31,* 324–330.

FIBEL, B., AND HALE, W.D. The generalized expectancy for success scale—A new measure. *Journal of Consulting and Clinical Psychology,* 1978, *46,* 924–931.

GOLIN, S., TERRELL, F., WEITZ, J., AND DROST, P.L. The illusion of control among depressed patients. *Journal of Abnormal Psychology,* 1979, *88,* 454–457.

HOLT, R.R. (Ed.) *Diagnostic psychological testing* by David Rapaport, Merton Gill, and Roy Schafer. New York: International Universities Press, 1968.

ILFELD, F.W. Current social stressors and symptoms of depression. *American Journal of Psychiatry,* 1977, *134,* 161–166.

KLEIN, D.C., AND SELIGMAN, M.E.P. Reversal of performance deficits and perceptual deficits in learned helplessness and depression. *Journal of Abnormal Psychology,* 1976, *85,* 11–26.

KRANTZ, S. AND HAMMEN, C. Assessment of cognitive bias in depression. *Journal of Abnormal Psychology,* 1979, *88,* 611–619.

KUIPER, N.A. Depression and causal attributions for success and failure. *Journal of Personality and Social Psychology,* 1978, *36,* 236–246.

LAPOINTE, K.A., AND CRANDELL, C.J. Relationship of irrational beliefs to self-reported depression. *Cognitive Therapy and Research,* 1980, *4,* 247–250.

LEWINSOHN, P.M., MISCHEL, W., CHAPLIN, W., AND

BARTON, R. Social competence and depression: The role of illusory self-perceptions. *Journal of Abnormal Psychology,* 1980, *89,* 203–212.

LLOYD, C. Life events and depressive disorder reviewed: I. Events as predisposing factors. *Archives of General Psychiatry,* 1980, *37,* 529–535. (a)

LLOYD, C. Life events and depressive disorder reviewed. *Archives of General Psychiatry,* 1980, *37,* 541–548. (b)

LOBITZ, W.C., AND POST, R.D. Parameters of self-reinforcement and depression. *Journal of Abnormal Psychology,* 1979, *88,* 33–41.

LOGAN, F.A. *Fundamentals of learning and motivation.* Dubuque, Ia.: Wm. C. Brown, 1970.

McNITT, P.C. AND THORNTON, D.W. Depression and perceived reinforcement: A reconsideration, *Journal of Abnormal Psychology,* 1978, *87,* 137–140.

MILLER, W.R., AND SELIGMAN, M.E.P. Depression and the perception of reinforcement. *Journal of Abnormal Psychology,* 1973, *82,* 62–73.

MINKOFF, K., BERMAN, E., BECK, A.T., AND BECK, R. Hopelessness, depression, and attempted suicide. *American Journal of Psychiatry,* 1973, *130,* 455–459.

MISCHEL, W. On the interface of cognition and personality. *American Psychologist,* 1979, *34,* 740–754.

NELSON, R.E. Irrational beliefs in depression. *Journal of Consulting and Clinical Psychology,* 1977, *45,* 1190–1191.

NELSON, R.E AND CRAIGHEAD, W.E. Selective recall of positive and negative feedback, self control behaviors, and depression. *Journal of Abnormal Psychology,* 1977, *86,* 379–388.

PRKACHIN, K.M., CRAIG, K.D., PAPAGEORGIS, D., AND REITH, G. Nonverbal communication deficits and response to performance feedback in depression. *Journal of Abnormal Psychology,* 1977, *86,* 224–234.

PROCIUK, T.J., BREEN, L.J., AND LUSSIER, R.J. Hopelessness, internal-external locus of control, and depression. *Journal of Clinical Psychology,* 1976, *32,* 299–300.

RADLOFF, L.S. AND RAE, D.S. Susceptibility and precipitating factors in depression: Sex differences and similarities. *Journal of Abnormal Psychology,* 1979, *88,* 174–181.

REHM, L.R. A self control model of depression. *Behavior Therapy,* 1977, *8,* 787–804.

RIZLEY, R. Depression and distortion in the attribution of causality. *Journal of Abnormal Psychology,* 1978, *87,* 32–48.

ROTH, D., AND REHM, L.P. Relationships among

self-monitoring processes, memory, and depression. *Cognitive Therapy and Research*, 1980, 4, 149–157.

ROTTER, J.B., CHANCE, J.E., AND PHARES, E.J. (Eds.) *Applications of a social learning theory of personality*. New York: Holt, Rinehart, & Winston, 1972.

ROZENSKI, R.H., REHM, L.P., PRY, G., AND ROTH, D. Depression and self-reinforcement behavior in hospitalized patients. *Journal of Behavior Therapy and Experimental Psychiatry*, 1977, 8, 31–34.

SACCO, W.P., AND HOKANSON, J.E. Expectations of success and anagram performance of depressives in a public and private setting. *Journal of Abnormal Psychology*, 1978, 87, 122–130.

SMOLLEN, R.C. Expectancies, mood, and performance of depressed and nondepressed psychiatric inpatients on chance and skill tasks. *Journal of Abnormal Psychology*, 1978, 87, 91–101.

VROOM, V.H. *Work and motivation*. New York: John Wiley, 1964.

WENER, A.E, AND REHM, L.P. Depressive affect: A test of behavioral hypotheses. *Journal of Abnormal Psychology*, 1975, 84, 221–227.

14

Sex Differences in Unipolar Depression: Evidence and Theory

Susan Nolen-Hoeksema

A large body of evidence indicates that women are more likely than men to show unipolar depression. Five classes of explanations for these sex differences are examined and the evidence for each class is reviewed. Not one of these explanations adequately accounts for the magnitude of the sex differences in depression. Finally, a response set explanation for the sex differences in depression is proposed. According to this explanation, men are more likely to engage in distracting behaviors that dampen their mood when depressed, but women are more likely to amplify their moods by ruminating about their depressed states and the possible causes of these states. Regardless of the initial source of a depressive episode (i.e., biological or psychological) men's more active responses to their negative moods may be more adaptive on average than women's less active, more ruminative responses.

The epidemiology of a disorder can provide important clues to its etiology. When a disorder only strikes persons from one geographical region, one social class, or one

Susan Nolen-Hoeksema. Sex Differences in Unipolar Depression: Evidence and Theory. *Psychological Bulletin,* 1987, Vol. 101, No. 2, pp. 259–282. Copyright © 1987 by the American Psychological Association. Reprinted by permission of the publisher and author.

gender, we can ask what characteristics of the vulnerable group might be making its members vulnerable.

A frequent finding in epidemiological studies of mental disorders is that women are more prone to unipolar affective disorders than are men (Boyd & Weissman, 1981; Weissman & Klerman, 1977). A number of different explanations have been proposed to account for women's greater vulnerability to depression. Previous reviews of these explanations (e.g., Weissman & Klerman, 1977) have been quite brief and uncritical.

In this article, the evidence for sex differences in unipolar depression first is summarized, then the most prominent explanations proposed for these sex differences are discussed in detail. These explanations include those attributing the differences to the response biases of subjects, as well as biological, psychoanalytic, sex role, and learned helplessness explanations.

Although most of the proposed explanations for sex differences in depression have received some empirical support, not one of them has been definitively supported and not one as yet accounts for the magnitude of sex differences in depression. In the final section of this article it is suggested that differences in the ways that men and women respond to their own depressive episodes, whatever the origin of these episodes, may be an important source of the sex differences observed in depression.

Background on the Affective Disorders

According to the third edition of the *Diagnostic and Statistical Manual of Mental Disorders* (*DSM-III;* American Psychiatric Association, 1980), the common symptoms of depression include loss of motivation, sadness, anhedonia, low self-esteem, somatic complaints, and difficulty in concentrating. The opposite of depression is mania. Manic symptoms include greatly increased energy, racing thoughts, pressured speech, wild and extravagant behaviors, and grandiosity. Persons who suffer manic episodes typically also suffer episodes of depression, whereas the majority of persons who suffer depressive episodes never experience mania. Thus in *DSM-III*, the affective disorders are broken down into bipolar affective disorder, which is characterized by alternating episodes of mania and depression, and unipolar depression.

To date, almost all of the discussion of sex differences in depression has been concerned with sex differences in unipolar depression. It has been generally assumed that there are no sex differences in bipolar disorder (e.g., Boyd & Weissman, 1981; Weissman & Klerman, 1977). Yet in a review of the literature on bipolar disorder, Clayton (1981) showed that women predominate among persons given the diagnosis of bipolar disorder, as well as among those with unipolar depression. The only explanation that has been offered for sex differences in bipolar disorder is the suggestion of Winokur and others (see Gershon & Bunney, 1976; Winokur & Tanna, 1969) that both bipolar and unipolar affective disorder are associated with genetic abnormalities linked to the female chromosomes. (This explanation is reviewed in the section on *Biological Explanations.*) Because each of the other explanations of sex differences in depression reviewed here refers only to sex differences in unipolar depression, the data review focuses on studies of unipolar depression.

The *DSM-III* divides unipolar depression into major depressive disorder (MDD) and dysthymic disorder (DD). The diagnosis of MDD is given to patients who have the acute experience of severe depressive symptoms for a period of 2 weeks or more. There are two subtypes of MDD. Major depressive disorder with melancholia is characterized by marked anhedonia, the somatic symptoms of depression (e.g., early morning wakening, psychomotor retardation), and extreme guilt. The subclass "MDD with psychotic features" is used when the patient shows gross impairment in reality testing. The diagnosis of DD is given to a person who chronically experiences moderate-to-severe depressive symptoms for at least a 2-year period. The *DSM-III* classification of depressive disorders departed in a number of ways from its predecessor, the *DSM-II*, and from the classification system used outside the United States, the *International Classification of Diseases* (*ICD;* World Health Organization, 1980). So that studies using different classification systems can be more easily compared, Table 1 lists the types of depression identified by *DSM-III* and matches these labels with the most closely corresponding categories in the *DSM-II* and *ICD* systems.

Evidence for Sex Differences in Unipolar Depression

There are two sources of data on rates of depression in men and women: records of persons treated for diagnosed affective disorders and surveys of the general population in which respondents are asked about symptoms of depression they are experiencing. Many clinicians and researchers argue that clinically severe levels of depression and subclinical levels of depressive symptoms are two distinct types of depression, with different characteristics, causes, and courses (cf. Depue & Monroe, 1978). From this viewpoint, studies in which self-report questionnaires are used to detect depression in a community sample tell us nothing about the epidemiology or etiology of true depressive disorders. Others argue that clinical depres-

TABLE 1 DSM-III Categories for Unipolar Depression and the Corresponding DSM-II and ICD-9 Labels

| | Major Depressive Disorder Subtypes | | | | |
| | | With | Without | | Dysthymic |
Labels	Unspecified	Melancholia	Melancholia	With Psychotic Features	Disorder
DSM-II	Manic-depressive illness, depressed type	Involutional melancholia	Depressive neurosis	Involutional melancholia; psychotic depressive reaction	Depressive neurosis
ICD-9	Manic-depressive reaction, depressed type	Endogenous depression; involutional melancholia	Reactive depression	Depressive psychosis; psychotic depression; reactive depressive psychosis; psychogenic depressive psychosis	Neurotic depression

Note. DSM-II and *DSM-III: Diagnostic and Statistical Manual of Mental Disorders* (2nd ed., 3rd ed; American Psychiatric Association, 1968, 1980). *ICD-9: The International Classification of Diseases* (9th ed.; World Health Organization, 1980).

sion and subclinical depression are simply two points along a continuum of severity in depressive symptoms. In support of this argument, Hirschfeld and Cross (1982) found that clinical and subclinical depressions shared many of the same psychosocial risk factors, such as a high number of bad life events. Hirschfeld and Cross (1982) and Boyd and Weissman (1981) point out, however, that factors such as socioeconomic status, geographic setting (rural vs. urban residence), and sex role stereotypes can affect help-seeking behavior. From this viewpoint, then, it is important to look at both treated cases of depression and surveys of untreated depressive symptoms in any investigation of the epidemiology of depression. With regard to the explanations for sex differences in depression reviewed here, some of the explanations are more applicable either to severe depressions or to moderate levels of depression. Thus, in the present review, studies of treated cases of depression and community studies of depression are reviewed separately.

Very few of the studies described in this article were designed specifically to measure sex differences in depression. Most of the studies were general surveys of psychopathology in particular geographical areas. One goal of this review was to produce summary statistics describing the magnitude of the sex differences in depression across studies (after

M. L. Smith & Glass, 1977). Rachman and Wilson (1980) have raised objections to such meta-analyses, because differences in the quality of methodologies vary greatly across studies. Thus, the conclusions regarding sex differences in depression drawn here are based only on studies that meet the following criteria for adequate methodology: (a) Standardized assessment procedures and/or standardized diagnostic systems are used to identify depression in a sample, (b) sample sizes are reasonably large (i.e., over 50), (c) the selection of the sample was reasonably random, and (d) data on unipolar depression are presented separately from data on bipolar depression. Some studies that did not meet these criteria are reviewed separately, because they provide the only available data on depression in certain countries outside the United States.

Treated Cases of Depression

Table 2 summarizes the data from the methodologically strong studies of treated cases of depression in the United States. Whenever possible, the rates of depression in women and men in each study were adjusted for the number of women and men who participated in the study. All but three of the ratios listed in Table 2 indicate that significantly more women than men were given a diagnosis of depression. The mean female-to-

TABLE 2 Studies of Treated Cases of Depression in the United States

Study	Diagnosis	F:M	Comments
Williams & Spitzer (1983)	Major depression	2.3**	Diagnoses given in the field trials for the *DSM-III*
	Dysthymic disorder	1.9**	
Faden (1977)	Depressive neurosis	1.4**	All admissions to inpatient psychiatric services in the United States, 1974–1975
	Psychotic depression	0.8**	
	Involutional melancholia	1.5**	
	All affective disorders	1.3**	
Rosen, Bahn, & Kramer (1964)	Depressive reaction	1.6**	All admissions to outpatient psychiatric services in the United States, 1961–1962
	Psychotic depression	1.4**	
Pederson, Barry, & Babigian (1972)	Psychotic depression	1.8**	All admissions to inpatient and outpatient psychiatric services in Monroe County, NY, 1961–1962
Lemkau, Tietze, & Cooper (1942)	Depressive reaction	2.2	Admissions to a Baltimore hospital, 1936. Only 11 women and 5 men were given this diagnosis
S. H. Rosenthal (1966)	Depressive reaction	4.6[a]	Admissions to a Massachusetts Mental Health Center, 1965
Weissman, Sholomskas, Pottenger, Prusoff, & Locke (1977)	Current or former depression	4.0**	Outpatients who had a Raskin Scale score of 7 or above. Sample excludes patients also given the diagnosis of alcoholism
Stangler & Printz (1980)	Major depression	0.8	Students at the University of Washington
	Dysthymic disorder	1.7*	

Note. F:M is the ratio of females to males, corrected for the number of females and males in the sample, if possible. Chi-squares were calculated to test for sex differences in the rates of disorder.   [a]The chi-square could not be calculated because of insufficient data.   *p < .05.   **p < .01.

male ratio across all studies in Table 2 was 1.95:1. Thus, across all studies of treated depression in the United States reviewed here, nearly twice as many women as men have been diagnosed as depressed. A *t* test (R. Rosenthal, 1978) performed to test the null hypothesis that the average female-to-male ratio across studies would be 1:1 yielded a $t(14) = 3.26$ ($p < .01$), indicating that the observed sex differences in rates of depression were statistically significant.

Williams and Spitzer (1983) report the only large study to date of the rates of treated depressive disorders according to the *DSM-III* classification system. In the field trials for the *DSM-III*, clinicians in many different treatment settings across the United States used *DSM-III* criteria to diagnose their patients. The female-to-male ratios of 2.1 and 1.9 for MDD and DD, respectively, indicate a clear and significant preponderance of women among depressives (chi-square statistics for both ratios were significant at $p < .01$).

There are three studies in Table 2 in which women do not significantly preponderate among depressives. In Faden's (1977) report of all diagnoses of depression given to psychiatric inpatients in the United States in 1974–1975, significantly more men than women were diagnosed as psychotically depressed. Yet in both Rosen, Bahn, and Kramer's (1964) and Pederson, Barry, and Babigian's (1972) reports of psychiatric diagnoses in large samples, significantly more women than men were diagnosed as psychotically depressed.

Lemkau, Tietze, and Cooper (1942) reported that 11 women and 5 men out of 3,337 psychiatric patients in a Baltimore hospital in 1936 were given the diagnosis of depressive reaction. This yielded a female-to-male ratio for the diagnosis of 2.2, which appears substantial but was not statistically significant because of the low numbers of men and women given the diagnosis.

The only other study in which women did not outnumber men among depressives was that reported by Stangler and Printz (1980). Stangler and Printz's (1980) data are from diagnoses given to University of Washington students seen in the university's psychology clinic. Nineteen of the 320 women in this sample and 14 of the 180 men were diagnosed as having MDD (the difference was nonsignificant). As we shall see later, studies of depressive symptoms reported by college students on questionnaires also have found no sex differences in the level of symptoms. However, note that in Stangler and Printz's study significantly more women than men were given the diagnosis of DD ($p < .05$).

The methodologically stronger studies of treated cases of depression outside the United States are summarized in Table 3. The mean female-to-male ratio in these studies was 2.39, $t(14) = 7.03$, $p < .01$, with all but one (Halevi, Naor, & Cochavy's [1969] study of depressive reactions in Israel) reporting significantly more women than men diagnosed as depressed.

Several of these studies report data from psychiatric registers, which are comprehensive records of all persons treated in psychiatric institutions and private practice in a large geographical area. All but one study (Gershon & Liebowitz, 1975) used the *ICD* criteria for diagnoses. Comparisons of the *ICD* and *DSM-III* systems are shown in Table 1. In Table 3, we see evidence that women significantly outnumber men among unipolar depressives in Denmark, Scotland, England, Wales, Australia, Canada, Iceland, and Israel.

Table 4 presents data from studies that only provided summary data on all affective disorders or that used either idiosyncratic criteria for diagnoses or small samples. The mean female-to-male ratio across these studies was 1.5, $t(24) = 6.26$, $p < .01$. Note that a number of the studies conducted in less modern cultures did not find significant sex differences in depression. Some of these studies had serious flaws, however. The two studies from India (Mohan, 1972; Rao, 1970) and the study of Nigeria (Ezeilo & Onyeama, 1980) were conducted in hospitals built to accommodate 3–4 times more men than women. The data from Egypt (El-Islam, 1969), Iraq (Bazzoui, 1970), and

TABLE 3 Studies of Treated Cases of Depression Outside the United States

Nation	Study	Diagnosis	F:M	Comments
Denmark	Weeke, Bille, Videbech, Dupont, & Juel-Nielsen (1975)	Depressive reaction	3.8*	Psychiatric register, 1960–1964
		Neurotic depression	3.0*	
Scotland	Baldwin (1971)	Neurotic depression	2.4*	Scottish mental hospital admissions, 1977
England and Wales	Martin, Brotherson, & Chave (1957)	Neurotic depression	1.7*	Psychiatric register, 1949–1954
England	Dean, Walsh, Downing, & Shelley (1981)	Psychotic depression	1.8*	Psychiatric register, 1976
Australia	Berah (1983)	Neurotic depression	1.8*	State and general hospital patients, 1978–1981
	Krupinski & Stoller (1962)	Psychotic depression	3.0*	Admissions to a Victoria hospital, 1951–1952
Canada	Canadian Bureau of Statistics (1970)	Neurotic depression	2.2*	First admissions to psychiatric services, 1967
Iceland	Helgason (1977)	Psychotic depression	2.9*	Psychiatric register, 1966–1967
Israel	Halevi, Naor, & Cochavy (1969)	Reactive depression	1.3	Census of 41 psychiatric institutions, 1964
		Psychotic depression	1.8*	
		Involutional melancholia	3.5*	
		All affective disorders	2.3*	
	Gershon & Liebowitz (1975)	Unipolar depression (Feighner criteria)	2.0*	Inpatients at psychiatric hospitals

Note. F:M is the ratio of females to males, corrected for the number of females and males in the sample, if possible. Chi-squares were calculated to test for sex differences in the rates of disorder. ᵃThe chi-square could not be calculated because of insufficient data. *$p < .01$.

Rhodesia (Buchan, 1969) were based on the impressions of one or two psychiatrists, without the use of conventional diagnostic criteria. In addition, Bazzoui (1970) and Rao (1970) point out that access to psychiatric treatment is more restricted for women than for men in many nonmodern countries. So it is not clear that the rates of depression in men and women in these studies illustrate a true absence of sex differences in depression in these countries.

As mentioned earlier, the ratio of female to male depressives varies greatly from country to country. Mazer (1967) demonstrated that in different cultures, criteria for diagnoses are differentially weighted, and certain diagnoses are more frequently applied than others. Even so, there is a consistent tendency for women to preponderate among depressives across a wide variety of nations.

The number of treated cases of a disorder does not represent the true rate of a disorder in a population, because often only the most severe cases of the disorder, or those persons most disruptive to society, or those in the upper socioeconomic classes are treated (Wing, 1976). Further, when psychiatric diagnoses are relied on, idiosyncracies in the application of diagnostic criteria from psychiatrist to psychiatrist (or country to country) can confound the data.

To avoid these problems and others, researchers have sought to measure the rate of depression in the general population, us-

TABLE 4 Weak Studies of Treated Cases of Depression Outside the United States

Nation	Study	Diagnosis	F:M	Comments
Canada	Weissman & Klerman	All affective disorders	1.7[a]	Data from the World
Czechoslovakia	(1977)	All affective disorders	2.1[a]	Health Organization
Denmark		All affective disorders	1.8[a]	Collaborative Study;
Finland		All affective disorders	1.3[a]	rates of females and
France		All affective disorders	1.6[a]	males with sub-types
Norway		All affective disorders	1.5[a]	of affective disorder
Poland		All affective disorders	1.4[a]	were unavailable
Sweden		All affective disorders	1.8[a]	
Switzerland		All affective disorders	1.4[a]	
England and Wales		All affective disorders	1.8[a]	
New Zealand		All affective disorders	1.8[a]	
England	Cooper, Kendell, Gurland, Sartorius, & Farkas (1969)	All affective disorders	1.4	Admissions to a London hospital, $n = 145$
New Zealand	Christie (1968)	All affective disorders	2.1*	Patients given diagnosis of "affective disorder"; $n = 50$; the diagnostic criteria were unclear
The Netherlands	Saenger (1968)	Psychiatric ratings of severe depression	1.3	Persons admitted to a psychiatric hospital and rated by psychiatrist, $n = 289$
Hong Kong	Yap (1965)	Affective disorder initial episode recurrent episodes	1.1	Diagnoses given to 130 patients admitted to a hospital
			1.7**	One-year follow-up of 62 patients
India	Rao (1970)	Endogenous depression	0.6*	Patients treated by the author for depression, $n = 62$
	Mohan (1972)	Affective psychosis	1.4	Patients institutionalized in a hospital that primarily accommodates males, $n = 140$
Egypt	El-Islam (1969)	Nonpsychotic depression	1.0	Patients seen by the author, $n = 157$; the diagnostic criteria were unclear
Iraq	Bazzoui (1970)	Depression	1.2	Hospitalized patients ($n = 42$) and private practice patients ($n = 16$); the diagnostic criteria were unclear
Rhodesia	Buchan (1969)	Depression	1.1	Patients seen by the author, $n = 77$; the diagnostic criteria and method of patient selection were unclear
Nigeria	Ezeilo & Onyeama (1980)	Psychotic depression Neurotic depression	0.8 1.6*	Discharge diagnosis for 969 patients; "no conventional diagnostic inventories available for use."
Kenya	Vadher & Ndetei (1980)	Nonpsychotic depression	2.3*	Patients being treated with chemotherapy for depression, $n = 30$

Note. F:M is the ratio of females to males, corrected for the number of females and males in the sample, if possible. Chi-squares were calculated to test for sex differences in the rates of disorder.   [a]The chi-square could not be calculated because of insufficient data.   *$p < .05$.   **$p < .01$.

ing structured interviews or self-report questionnaires. Reviews of these studies follow.

Community Studies of Depression

Several questionnaires and interviews have been used in studies of depression in U.S. samples. These include the Beck Depression Inventory (BDI; Beck & Beck, 1972), the Center for Epidemiological Studies Depression Scale (CES-D; Radloff, 1977), and the Zung Self-Report Depression Scale (SDS; Zung, 1965), all of which are self-report questionnaires. The originators of each of these questionnaires have designated cutoff scores, and persons scoring above these cutoffs are considered to be seriously depressed. In addition, there are structured interviews, such as the Schedule for Affective Disorders and Schizophrenia (SADS; Endicott & Spitzer, 1978) and the Diagnostic Interview Schedule (DIS; Robbins, Helzer, Croughan, & Ratcliff, 1981). Information gathered in these interviews is used to make diagnoses according to *DSM-III* criteria or the similar Research Diagnostic Criteria (Spitzer, Endicott, & Robins, 1978).

Studies that have used any of these instruments to measure depression in the United States are summarized in Table 5. Most of the studies carried out in large, heterogeneous samples show a significantly greater degree of depression among women. The mean female-to-male ratio in the studies in Table 5 was 1.62, $t(17) = 6.82$, $p < .01$.

Much higher rates of moderate-to-severe symptoms of depression in both men and women are found when self-report inventories are used to detect depression than when structured interviews are used to diagnose depressive disorders. Yet both methods reveal large sex differences in depression. For example, Myers et al. (1984) report a study in which a structured interview, the DIS, was used to diagnose MDD and DD in a general community sample. Myers et al. report that 4% of the women interviewed were diagnosed as having had an MDD at some time during the previous 6-month pe-

riod, whereas 1.7% of the men interviewed were given the same diagnosis (ratio = 2.4, $p < .01$). Women also significantly outnumbered men among adults, with a 6-month prevalence of DD in all age groups and cities. The average percentage of women given this diagnosis was 4%, whereas the average for men was 2% (ratio = 2.0, $p < .01$).

Contrast these data with data from a study by Eaton and Kessler (1981), in which a self-report inventory of depressive symptoms called the CES-D scale was completed by a nationwide sample of 2,867 adults. Eaton and Kessler report that 11% of the men in this study and 21% of the women scored in the severe range of the CES-D (i.e., 15 or above). This is a female-to-male ratio of 1.9 ($p < .01$). Thus, even though the rates of severe depressive symptoms in this study are five times those of diagnosed depressive disorders in men and women in Myers et al.'s study, the female-to-male ratios in the two studies are nearly identical.

The last four studies listed in Table 5 show no significant sex differences in depression. The samples in these studies represent subgroups of the American population, specifically, the Old Order Amish (Egeland & Hostetter, 1983), university students (Hammen & Padesky, 1977), bereaved adults (Bornstein, Clayton, Halikas, Maurice, & Robins, 1973), and elderly adults (Blazer & Williams, 1980). One of the most interesting of these studies is Egeland and Hostetter's 6-year epidemiological study of affective disorders among the Old Order Amish in Pennsylvania. The Old Order Amish are an ultraconservative Protestant religious sect, whose members maintain a closed society separated from the modern world. Egeland and Hostetter established contacts within the Amish community who would inform them when a member of the community appeared "disturbed." This individual would then receive a SADS interview conducted by Egeland or her colleagues, with diagnoses assigned when indicated. Over a 5-year period, 21 women and 20 men were given the diagnosis of major depression, indicating

TABLE 5 Community Studies of Depressive Symptoms in the United States

Study	Criteria for "Depressed"	F:M	Comments
Myers et al. (1984)	Major depression, diagnosed with the DIS	2.4**	DIS administered to 9,000 adults in St. Louis, MO; Baltimore, MD; and New Haven, CT.
	Dysthymic disorder, diagnosed with the DIS	2.0**	
Eaton & Kessler (1981)	Scores >15 on the CES-D	1.9**	Nationwide sample of 2,867 adults
Frerichs, Aneshensel, & Clark (1981)	Scores >15 on the CES-D	1.8**	Los Angeles County adults, n = 1,003
Radloff (1975)	Scores >15 on the CES-D	1.3*	Kansas City blacks, n = 283
		1.4**	Kansas City whites, n = 876
		1.8**	Maryland whites, n = 1,638
Amenson & Lewinsohn (1981)	SADS		Sample of 998 adults living in Oregon
	Current unipolar depression	2.3**	
	Past depressive episodes	1.3**	
Weissman & Myers (1978)	SADS		SADS administered to 511 adults in New Haven, CT
	Current major depression	1.6	
	Current minor depression	1.2	
	Lifetime risk, major depression	2.1**	
	Lifetime risk, minor depression	2.0*	
Blumenthal (1975)	Scores in the severe range on the Zung SDS	1.8**	Sample of 320 married adults
Egeland & Hostetter (1983)	SADS: major depression	1.0	Community of 8,186 Old Order Amish
Hammen & Padesky (1977)	Scores in the severe range on the BDI	1.1	University students, n = 2,272
Bornstein, Clayton, Halikas, Maurice, & Robins (1973)	Feighner criteria	1.1	Sample of 92 bereaved adults
Blazer & Williams (1980)	*DSM-III* criteria for major depression	1.2	Structured interview given to 997 elderly persons

Note. F:M is the ratio of females to males, corrected for the number of females and males in the sample, if possible. Chi-squares were calculated to test for sex differences in the rates of disorder. BDI = Beck Depression Inventory (Beck & Beck, 1972). CES-D = Center for Epidemiological Studies Depression Scale (Radloff, 1977). DIS = Diagnostic Interview Schedule (Robbins, Helzer, Croughan, & Ratcliff, 1981). *DSM-III = Diagnostic and Statistical Manual of Mental Disorders* (3rd ed.; American Psychiatric Association, 1980). SADS = Schedule for Affective Disorders and Schizophrenia (Endicott & Spitzer, 1978). SDS = Self-Report Depression Scale (Zung, 1965).
*$p < .05$.   **$p < .01$.

no sex differences in the rates of unipolar depression in this culture.

The methods Egeland and her colleagues used to ascertain cases of mental disorder may have led to the underdetection of some disorders, however. Because the criterion for being given a SADS interview by the re-searchers was that an individual showed clear disruption in his or her role functioning, disorders in which the individual quietly suffers, such as depression, may have gone unnoticed. This hypothesis is supported by the fact that Egeland found rates of affective disorder that were one-half those found in other studies. In addition, Egeland found equal rates of bipolar and unipolar depression among the Amish, whereas most studies find the rates of unipolar depression to be 10 times the rates of bipolar depression (Clayton, 1981). The symptoms of mania would be more likely to disrupt role functioning than the symptoms of depression. In general, the discrepancies between Egeland's data and data from other studies suggest that unipolar depression may have been underdiagnosed. In particular, because Amish women spend most of their time in the home, detection of moderate-to-severe levels of depression in women may have been very difficult.

The survey study of university students by Hammen and Padesky (1977), which found no sex differences in depression, is in line with Stangler and Printz's (1980) data indicating no sex differences among students treated for depression. One possible explanation for the sex differences in young adults is that depression has an earlier onset in men. That is, it may be that those men who in their lifetimes will become depressed usually do so in young adulthood. After the early 20s, however, the incidence of male depression may decline. Women, on the other hand, may be as vulnerable as men to depression in young adulthood but never show the decrease in vulnerability to depression with age that men show. Data from several studies do not support this explanation. For example, Winokur, Tsuang, and Crowe (1982) found no significant differences between men and women in the median age of onset of unipolar depression in a sample of 225 hospitalized depressives. In addition, Spicer, Hare, and Slater (1973) found that first admissions for depression in England and Wales peaked at an earlier age for women than for men. Thus, it does not appear that the absence of sex differences in depression among college students can be explained by a tendency toward earlier onset of depression in men.

Another possible explanation for the absence of sex differences in depression in college students is that only women with exceptionally good mental health (e.g., who are not depressed) go to college. On the other hand, men who go to college may be more representative of the mental health of men in general, perhaps because men are expected to go to college more than women are, so even depressed men go to college. This hypothesis is supported by data from Radloff's (1975) study on levels of depression in a group of 18- to 25-year-olds that included persons not attending college as well as persons attending college. Radloff found that the mean depression scores of women in this group were significantly higher than men's scores. Similarly, Faden (1977) found that among a group of 18- to 24-year-olds that included both college students and people not in college, significantly more women than men were treated for depression in inpatient psychiatric units in the United States. Thus, it appears that the absence of sex differences in depression in college students does not generalize to the rest of that age group not in college. This supports the hypothesis that college women are self-selected for positive mental health.

Another subgroup of the American population in which no sex differences in rates of depressive symptoms often are found is the bereaved. For example, Bornstein et al. (1973) used the Feighner criteria (Feighner et al., 1972) to diagnose depression in a sample of 65 women and 27 men recently bereaved. One month after their spouse's death, 33% of the men and 36% of the women met the criteria for depression. One year later, 19% of the men and 17% of the women continued to be depressed. In a review of the literature on the physical and mental health of bereaved men and women, Stroebe and Stroebe (1983) concluded that women do not show as much of a decline in physical and mental health after the death of a spouse as men. Stroebe and Stroebe suggest that women are trained to expect the death of their spouse, especially in old age, more than men are. Thus, bereavement may not be as much of a shock for women as for men. In addition, men are not accustomed to having to cope with the daily chores of life, so when they lose their spouses, their daily lives are more disrupted.

Finally, some studies find no sex differences in depression among older Americans. For example, Blazer and Williams (1980) administered a structured interview to 997 elderly persons and found that the rates of MDD in men and women were not significantly different. Similarly, Ensel (1982) found no sex differences in mean scores on the CES-D scale for persons over the age of 50. However, Radloff (1975) did find that women over the age of 65 had higher mean CES-D scores than men over 65. Thus these data on sex differences in depression in the elderly are mixed. In those studies that did not find sex differences, it appears that rates of depression in men increase substantially with age, whereas rates of depression in women remain the same with age or decline slightly. Similarly, in the studies of bereaved adults (described previously), the absence of sex differences in depression appears because the levels of depression in men rise with bereavement to match those of women.

In sum, seven of the studies in Table 5 indicated that women are depressed significantly more often than men, but four studies showed no sex differences in depression. These studies, however, were conducted in nonrepresentative samples of the American population, specifically: the Amish, university students, the elderly, and the bereaved. Excluding these studies, the female-to-male ratio for depressive symptoms in the general U.S. population is 1.8:1.

In Table 6, studies of depression in the general populations of nations outside the United States that used standardized measures and diagnostic criteria are summarized. Again, although the female-to-male ratio varies considerably from one study to the next, the average ratio of 2.08 (excluding Vadher & Ndetei's [1981] study) indicated that significantly more women than men are depressed, $t(12) = 4.15$, $p < .01$.

Note that two of the studies in Table 6 in which there clearly are no sex differences in depression, that is, Leighton et al.'s (1963) study of a tribe in Nigeria and Bash and

Bash-Liechti's (1969) study of rural Iran, were conducted in nonmodern cultures. Further, the rate of depression in these nonmodern areas was much lower than the rate in urban areas of Iran or in the other African studies, which were conducted near cities. This trend might reflect a self-selection among depressives to move into the city, where they could obtain treatment. On the other hand, it could reflect negative influences of urbanization and modernization on mental health. Recall that the rate of affective disorder in Egeland and Hostetter's (1983) study of the Old Order Amish, a strictly nonmodern culture, also was much lower than the rate of depression in the general U.S. population.

Summary. Women are diagnosed as having a depressive disorder significantly more frequently than are men and, with a few exceptions, report more depressive symptoms than do men in most geographical areas of the world. If the ratios for all the stronger studies of depression (i.e., those in Tables 2, 3, 5, and 6) are averaged, the mean female-to-male ratio is 2.02, $t(57) = 8.88$, $p < .01$. The populations in which sex differences in depression have not been consistently found include university students, the bereaved, the elderly, the Old Order Amish, and residents of some rural, nonmodern cultures.

Explanations for the Sex Differences in Depression

Several biological and psychosocial explanations have been proposed to account for the sex differences in depression. Weissman and Klerman (1977) briefly discussed many of these explanations. In this review, the evidence for and against each explanation for the sex differences in depression is evaluated, and conclusions are reached about the level of support for each explanation. First, however, we must examine the possibility that the sex differences in depression are artifacts of differences in the socioeconomic status of men and women, or differences in the will-

TABLE 6 Community Studies of Depressive Symptoms in Countries Outside the United States

Nation	Study	Criteria for "Depressed"	F:M	Comments
Sweden	Essen-Moeller (1956)	ICD: affective disorder	1.8*	Structured interviews, $n = 2,550$
	Essen-Moeller & Hagnell (1961)	ICD: affective disorder	3.0**	Interviewed subjects from Essen-Moeller et al. (1956) 10 years later
Denmark	Sorenson & Stromgren (1961)	ICD: psychogenic depression and depressive neurosis	3.5**	Information taken from public records and interviews, $n = 4,876$
	T. Fremming (1961; cited in Helgason, 1961)	ICD: affective disorder	2.0**	Structured interviews, $n = 4,130$
Iceland	Helgason (1961)	ICD: current affective disorder; lifetime risk of affective disorder	1.8** 1.8**	Structured interviews, $n = 3,843$
Australia	Henderson, Duncan-Jones, Byrne, Scott, & Adcock (1979)	ICD: current depression	2.6	Structured interviews (PSE), $n = 157$
	Byrne (1980)	Scores in the depressed range on the Zung Self-Report Depression Scale	1.4*	Same sample as Henderson et al. (1979)
Uganda	Orley & Wing (1979)	ICD: affective disorder	1.6	Structured interviews (PSE), $n = 206$
Kenya	Vadher & Ndetei (1980)	ICD: affective disorder	18:0	Structured interviews (PSE), $N = 56$
Nigeria	Leighton et al. (1963)	DSM-II: neurotic depression	0.9	Structured interviews with 262 members of the Yoruba tribe
Iran				
Urban	Bash & Bash-Liechti (1974)	ICD: affective disorder	3.6**	Structured interviews, $n = 928$
Rural	Bash & Bash-Liechti (1969)	ICD: affective disorder	1.0	Structured interviews, $n = 482$

Note. F:M is the ratio of females to males, corrected for the number of females and males in the sample, if possible. Chi-squares were calculated to test for sex differences in the rates of disorder. *DSM-II* = *Diagnostic and Statistical Manual of Mental Disorders* (2nd ed.; American Psychiatric Association, 1968). *ICD* = *The International Classification of Diseases* (World Health Organization, 1980). PSE = Present State Examination (Wing, 1976).
*$p < .05$.   **$p < .01$.

ingness of men and women to show the common symptoms of depression.

Artifact Explanations

Artifact Explanation 1: It is an Income Effect, Not a Gender Effect. By most indicators, women's economic status is lower than men's (U.S. Department of Commerce, Bureau of the Census, 1985). Women also do not attain the same levels of education

as men. It could be that the differences observed in rates of depression in men and women are the result of differences in socioeconomic status instead of gender differences. Radloff (1975) and Ensel (1982) tested for this possibility by comparing men's and women's mean scores on the CES-D, controlling for income level, education level, and occupation. In both of these studies, women still had more depressed mean CES-D scores than men after all these socioeconomic indicators were taken into account. These results suggest that observed sex differences in depression are not simply the result of differences in income.

Artifact Explanation 2: Reporting Biases. Some researchers have been concerned that the sex differences in depression result from men's unwillingness to admit to and seek help for depressive symptoms (Padesky & Hammen, 1977; Phillips & Segal, 1969). This hypothesis holds that men and women experience depressive symptoms equally frequently, and to the same degree, but because depressive symptoms are perceived as feminine (Chevron, Quinlan, and Blatt, 1978), men are less likely to admit to them.

A number of studies have failed to support this hypothesis. For example, King and Buchwald (1982) predicted that if this artifact hypothesis was true, men should be less willing than women to disclose symptoms in a public disclosure condition (e.g., an interview with the researcher), whereas fewer sex differences should be found in a private (anonymous) disclosure condition. Instead, King and Buchwald found men no less willing to disclose in the public condition than women, and neither sex was less willing to disclose symptoms in a public disclosure situation than in private. Bryson and Pilon (1984) have replicated these results. Both of these studies, however, used college students for subjects. Recall that there is no tendency toward sex differences in depressive phenomena in this population.

Clancy and Gove (1974) investigated the influence of three types of response bias on the endorsement of items on the Langner Mental Health Scale, which consists of 22 items representing psychological and physiological symptoms of distress (Langner, 1962). These three variables were "perceived desirability" of the items, "need for social approval," and the tendency to "yea-say" or "nay-say." In their random sample of 404 adults (not college students), Clancy and Gove found no significant sex differences in ratings of the undesirability of the

mental health items or in need for social approval. Women, however, were more likely than men to nay-say. Women also had significantly higher scores on the Langner scale. When the relations between the three response bias variables and the mental health scores were controlled for, the sex differences in mental health scores were even larger. These studies were replicated in similar studies by Gove and Geerken (1976) and Gove, McCorkel, Fain, and Hughes (1976).

The claim that women are more willing to seek psychotherapy for depression has also not been consistently supported in the literature. Women do go to medical professionals more often than men (Faden, 1977). In addition, Padesky and Hammen (1977) report a study of college students in which the level of depressive symptoms at which women said they would seek psychotherapy was lower than the level at which men said they would seek help. However, two studies of actual help-seeking behavior have found that men and women with similar levels of self-reported depressive symptoms were equally likely to seek psychiatric help or go to a general practitioner (Amenson & Lewinsohn, 1981; Phillips & Segal, 1969). In addition, Amenson and Lewinsohn (1981) found that men and women with equal levels of self-reported symptoms were equally likely to be diagnosed as depressed in a clinical interview.

In summary, the hypothesis that the lower rates of depression observed in men are due to men's unwillingness to admit to their depressive symptoms has not been consistently supported. Men appear to be just as likely to admit to and seek help for a given level of depression. Still, women appear to experience depression more commonly than men.

Artifact Explanation 3: Kinds of Symptoms. According to this hypothesis, men and women are equally susceptible to depression, but depression in men often takes the form of "acting-out" behaviors instead of sadness, passivity, and crying, which are symptoms commonly included in self-report inventories (Hammen & Peters, 1977). In particular, it has been suggested that the male equivalent of depression is alcoholism (Winokur & Clayton, 1967). Proponents of this argument point to statistics showing that twice as many men as women are diagnosed as alcoholics (e.g, Williams & Spitzer, 1983), and suggest that the rates of alcoholism in men make up for the absence of depression in men. This argument is boosted by evidence that in cultures in which alcohol consumption is strictly prohibited, such as among the Amish, no sex differences in depression are found (Egeland & Hostetter, 1983). In addition, many studies find high rates of depressive symptoms among alcoholic men (cf. Petty & Nasrallah, 1981).

Winokur and his colleagues (Cadoret & Winokur, 1974; Winokur & Clayton, 1967; Winokur, Rimmer & Reich, 1971) argued that depression and alcoholism are genetically linked to each other, with depressive features linked to female chromosomes and alcoholic features linked to male chromosomes. Evidence for a genetic link between depression and alcoholism comes from family history studies that show much higher rates of depression in the families of alcoholics and of alcoholism in the families of depressives than in comparison groups (Cadoret & Winokur, 1974; Cotton, 1979).

Yet there is evidence that depression is as likely a consequence as a cause of alcoholism in men. Petty and Nasrallah (1981), in a critical review of the literature on depression and alcoholism, found a much greater tendency for depression to follow alcoholism, especially in men, than for alcoholism to follow the onset of depressive symptoms. Cadoret and Winokur (1974) report that in patients suffering from both depression and alcoholism, most of the men reported becoming depressed at least 10 years after the onset of alcoholism. The alcoholics who did not become depressed tended to be periodic bingers rather than constant heavy drinkers. Cadoret and Winokur suggest that depres-

sion in male alcoholics is often due to the toxic effects of chronic alcoholism.

Even so, there is clearly some evidence that alcoholism and depression often covary within families and within individuals, and that men tend to show more alcoholism whereas women tend to show more depression. This is not, however, evidence that alcoholism and depression are the same disorder or that alcoholism is a symptom of depression. Instead, these two disorders can be considered two different maladaptive responses to difficult life circumstances. Societal restrictions against women drinking excessively may protect women who are vulnerable to alcoholism from developing the disorder. In the same vein, certain societal demands on men may protect them against depression. This is very different from saying that alcoholism is a symptom of depression. Rather, one should say that both depression and alcoholism could arise given environmental troubles, but societal demands result in sex differences in vulnerabilities to each disorder.

In summary, there apparently is little justification for dismissing the observed sex differences in depression as simply due to differences in men's and women's willingness to show the common symptoms of depression.

Biological Explanations

The pervasiveness of the sex differences in depression across cultures suggests that women's greater vulnerability to depression may be the result of biological characteristics unique to women. Two general types of biological explanations for the sex differences in depression have been proposed. The first group of explanations arises from evidence that women are particularly prone to depression during periods in which they experience significant changes in hormone levels. Several investigators have suggested that depression in women is brought about by changes in the levels of estrogen, progesterone, or other hormones.

The second group of biological explanations of the sex differences in depression attributes the differences to a greater genetic predisposition to depression in women. According to these explanations, women are more likely to inherit the disorder, because the genetic abnormality that leads to depression is somehow linked to the chromosomes that determine gender.

Hormones and Moods. It is widely believed that hormonal fluctuations strongly affect moods in women. Women are believed to be more prone to depression during the premenstrual period, the postpartum period, and menopause, each of which is characterized by changes in the levels of a number of hormones. Specifically, after the onset of puberty, levels of estrogen and progesterone rise and fall sharply during the menstrual cycle (Ganong, 1984). During the first 2 weeks of the cycle, arbitrarily defined as the first 2 weeks after the onset of blood flow, levels of progesterone and estrogen remain quite low. Around the end of the first 2 weeks, the level of estrogen rises and peaks, then declines again. Near the 21st day of the cycle, the level of estrogen peaks again and the level of progesterone peaks for the first time. Then, during the last few days before the onset of the next menstrual flow, the levels of both hormones drop precipitously, and remain low until after the menstrual flow.

Levels of estrogen and progesterone also change dramatically during pregnancy, the postpartum period, and menopause. During pregnancy, both estrogen and progesterone are produced in large amounts. Then, shortly after a woman gives birth (the postpartum period), her estrogen and progesterone levels drop sharply. Similarly, during menopause estrogen and progesterone production decline to very low levels and remain there the rest of a woman's life.

If women commonly experience depression during these periods of hormonal change, this suggests that their greater vulnerability to depression in general may be the result of the negative effects of changes or imbalances in female hormones on moods. The notion that depressions during periods of hormonal fluctuation are common is not well supported, however. Menopausal depression was once thought common, and early *DSM* editions (*DSM-I* and *DSM-II*) called this type of depression involutional melancholia. However, in the *DSM-III*, the category of involutional melancholia was excluded from the classification of affective disorders in response to the absence of evidence for a unique, endogenous type of depression that typically arose in women during middle-to-late adulthood (Weissman, 1979; Winokur, 1973). Indeed, levels of self-reported depressive symptoms seem to drop in women as they pass through menopause (Frieze, Parsons, Johnson, Ruble, & Zellman, 1978).

Estimates of the incidence of postpartum symptoms are high, ranging from 30% to 60% (Sherman, 1971). Yet the great majority of women experiencing postpartum depressive symptoms recover fully from them within 1 day (Pitt, 1973). O'Hara, Rehm, and Campbell (1982) and Atkinson and Rickel (1984) found that most women who remain depressed several weeks postpartum were already depressed before giving birth. Because hormone levels are quite different during pregnancy and postpartum, such data contradict the hormonal explanation for many postpartum depressions. Thus, the data on postpartum and menopausal depressions do not support the notion that hormonal fluctuations often are related to depression in women.

The rate of premenstrual depressions is estimated by some studies to be very high, perhaps as high as 90–100% (Janowsky, Gorney, & Mandell, 1967; see also Sherman, 1971). For example, Schuckit, Daly, Herrman, and Hineman (1975) administered a structured interview to 105 college women, asking about the regular occurrence of depression, anxiety, irritability, and crying during different periods of the menstrual cycle. Sixty-three percent of the students reported that they have at least one of these symptoms regularly during the premenstrual period; 33% of the students said they were often depressed during the premenstrual period.

Recently, research diagnostic criteria for premenstrual depression have been developed by Halbreich, Endicott, and Nee (1983) and Steiner, Haskett, and Carroll (1980). Halbreich et al. introduced the Premenstrual Assessment Form (PAF), a 95-item inventory of psychological and physiological symptoms. Respondents are asked to indicate, retrospectively, the severity with which they experience each symptom during the premenstrual period. Answers to the PAF can be compared to criteria for diagnosing a premenstrual major depressive syndrome; these criteria are quite similar to the *DSM-III* criteria for MDD. Halbreich et al. administered the PAF to 335 women, and found that 43% met the criteria for a premenstrual major depressive syndrome.

From the studies just cited, premenstrual depression appears to be quite common. Indeed, if 43% of the premenstrual women in any given sample, such as the sample in a questionnaire study of depression, were experiencing major depression as a result of being premenstrual, these premenstrual depressions could account for the greater rate of depression in women than men observed in such studies. We can examine this possibility with some simple calculations. Let us first consider the studies that use self-report inventories for depression. Many questionnaire studies that find significant sex differences in rates of depression report that approximately 20% of the female subjects and 10% of the male subjects score in the moderate-to-severe ranges of the depression questionnaires (*DSM-III*, American Psychiatric Association, 1980; Eaton & Kessler, 1981; Frerichs et al., 1981; Radloff, 1975). Imagine that in the absence of premenstrual influences, the true rate of depression among women would be 10%, just as it is in men. Could premenstrual depressive symptoms account for the additional 10% of the female

subjects who score as depressed on the questionnaires? The premenstrual period lasts approximately 5 days in each 28-day cycle (Ganong, 1984). Thus, if we assume that the menstrual cycles of women in any given group are randomly distributed over the month, we can estimate that approximately 20% (5/28) of women participating in any given questionnaire study are premenstrual. In order for premenstrual depression to account for the excess of women scoring as depressed (i.e., an additional 10% of the female sample, compared to the male sample), half (50%) of all women would have to experience moderate-to-severe depressive symptoms during the premenstrual period. That is, 20% (the average percentage of women scoring as depressed) = 10% (the assumed base rate of depression) + 20% [the percentage of women that are premenstrual in any study] × 50%).

Recall that a number of studies have reported that the percentage of women who reported experiencing moderate-to-severe premenstrual emotional symptoms is at least 40% (Halbreich et al., 1983; Janowksy et al., 1967; Schuckit et al., 1975). This is not quite 50%, but a 40% incidence of premenstrual depressions would account for most of the excess depression in women.

However, the validity of questionnaires that ask subjects to retrospectively rate their mood levels during different phases of the menstrual cycle has been seriously questioned (Parlee, 1973). Studies using retrospective questionnaires, apparently greatly overestimate the number of women who actually experience significant depressive symptoms during the premenstrual period. For example, Abplanap, Haskett, and Rose (1979) asked 33 women to complete a daily mood checklist, and once per month to complete the Moos Menstrual Distress Questionnaire (Moos, 1968). The Moos questionnaire asks subjects to rate the degree to which they experienced a number of premenstrual symptoms during different phases of their last menstrual cycle. On the retrospective Moos questionnaire, subjects reported having experienced significantly more symptoms during their last premenstrual period than at any other period in their cycle. However, Abplanap et al. found no relation between cycle phase and daily mood ratings (for similar results, see Persky, O'Brien & Kahn, 1976). Similarly, Schuckit et al. (1975) found that of the 63% of their sample who claimed that they regularly experienced premenstrual increases in negative affect, only 7% (i.e. 4% of their overall sample) actually showed significant increases in depression during the premenstrual period. In sum, the evidence from daily mood ratings suggests that the sex differences in depression observed in community studies are probably not accounted for by the number of women reporting premenstrual depressive symptoms on depression questionnaires.

Yet if daily diaries indicate that most women do not experience significant premenstrual mood changes, why do women report on retrospective questionnaires that they feel more depressed during their premenstrual period than during other times? As Paige (1971) and Ruble and Frieze (1978) point out, even in westernized countries, societal attitudes toward menstruation are still very negative. Menstruating women are expected to hide all signs of blood flow, and the taboos against sex during menstruation are still commonly observed. It is possible that women's negative expectations about their emotional state during the premenstrual and menstrual phases represent their dread of the social inconvenience of these phases. Similarly, the actual increases in anxiety and depression in some women during the premenstrual and menstrual phases may be psychological reactions to the negative social consequences of menstruation and to the physical discomfort of menstruation (e.g., bloating and cramping), and not the direct result of biochemical fluctuations.

One way to test the notion that hormonal changes during the menstrual cycle affect women's moods and that these hormonally based mood changes contribute to the sex

differences in depression would be to conduct a study in which depressive symptoms and cycle phase are measured repeatedly in a large sample. The incidence of premenstrual depression could then be established and the presence of premenstrual depression could be controlled for in comparisons of the rates of depression in men and women.

Although we do not yet have evidence that depressions caused by regular hormonal fluctuations in women contribute to the sex differences in community surveys of depression, it is still possible that abnormalities in hormonal functioning in women account for their higher rate of clinically severe depressions. Many hypotheses have been proposed for exactly how hormonal abnormalities would affect mood in women (see reviews by Janowsky & Rausch, 1985, and Rubinow & Roy-Byrne, 1984). Most of the theories of the effects of hormones on psychopathology have focused on the two ovarian hormones, estrogen and progesterone. Many of the studies of these hypotheses have used samples of women who sought treatment for severe premenstrual syndrome (PMS).

Because each of the periods during which women have been thought to be more vulnerable to depression (e.g., menopause, the premenstrual period, and the puerperium) are characterized by decreased estrogen levels, it has been proposed that estrogen withdrawal triggers depression and other premenstrual symptoms (Backstrom & Mattsson, 1975; Klaiber, Broverman, Vogel, & Kobayshi, 1979). The evidence for this hypothesis is indirect. Klaiber et al. (1979) report reductions of depressive symptoms in depressed women given estrogen therapy. In addition, some women ingesting estrogen in oral contraceptives also show decreases in depression (Bardwick, 1971; Moos, 1968).

Another estrogen-related hypothesis holds that high levels of estrogen in conjunction with low levels of progesterone are what lead to tension and dysphoria. One study found that women suffering from PMS had higher estrogen/progesterone ratios than women not suffering from PMS (Backstrom & Cartensen, 1974), and two other studies found elevated levels of estrogen in women suffering from PMS (Abraham, Elsner, & Lucas, 1978; Munday, Brush, & Taylor, 1981).

Others have argued that declines in levels of progesterone, not estrogen, trigger depressive symptoms. Increases and decreases in levels of progesterone are correlated with increases and decreases in depressive symptoms (Janowsky, Fann, & Davis, 1971). Some studies have found correlations between the degree of depression in some women and the amount of progestin in the oral contraceptives they were using (Culberg, 1972; Grant & Pryse-Davies, 1968; Kutner & Brown, 1972). In addition, several studies have found lower levels of progesterone just prior to menstruation in PMS sufferers compared to controls (Abraham et al., 1978; Backstrom & Cartensen, 1974; Munday et al., 1981; S. L. Smith, 1976).

By what mechanism would estrogen or progesterone withdrawal lead to depression? Levels of estrogen and progesterone in women have been correlated with levels of certain neurotransmitters implicated in depression. For example, in women given estrogen and progesterone therapy, increased serotonin uptake has been noted (Cone, Davis, & Coy, 1981; Ladisich, 1977). Decreased serotonin uptake has been associated with depression in some cases (Baldessarini, 1986); thus it has been suggested that women experience depression during estrogen or progesterone withdrawal because serotonin uptake decreases with the withdrawal (Hackman, Wirz-Justice, & Lichtsteiner, 1972).

Declines in estrogen and progesterone levels also have been associated in some studies with increases in the activity of monoamine oxidase (MAO; Grant & Pryse-Davies, 1968; Janowsky et al., 1971). Monoamine oxidase facilitates the breakdown of norepinephrine, and norepinephrine depletion is associated with depression (J. W. Maas, 1975).

Thus there appears to be considerable evidence that hormonal abnormalities are related to depression in women. Yet there are as many studies that do not support the hormonal theories of female depressions as there are that do (see Janowsky & Rausch, 1985; Rubinow & Roy-Byrne, 1984). For example, the premenstrual decline in estrogen is not the only decrease in estrogen that occurs during the menstrual cycle. Just after a midcycle peak, estrogen levels fall sharply, and this decline is not associated with depressive symptoms (Dalton, 1964). Premenstrual symptoms are also uncommon during that part of the menstrual cycle when estrogen/progesterone ratios are at their highest. In addition, Backstrom, Sanders, and Leask (1983) found no differences in estrogen levels between PMS sufferers and controls.

A number of studies have found that progesterone levels in women who suffer severe premenstrual tension are no different from levels in women who do not (Andersch, Hahn, Andersson, & Isaksson, 1978; Andersen, Larsen, Steenstrup, Svendstrup, & Nielson, 1977). Munday et al. (1981) found that premenstrual symptoms emerged in PMS sufferers before declines in progesterone occurred in the menstrual cycle. Several studies have found that progesterone therapy is no more effective than placebo in alleviating dysphoria and other symptoms of the premenstrual syndrome (Copen, Milne, & Outram, 1969; Jordheim, 1972; Sampson, 1979; S.L. Smith, 1976). After reviewing studies of progesterone therapy and other therapies for premenstrual depression, Rubinow and Roy-Byrne (1984) concluded that "the bulk of the evidence in support of current popular treatments is derived from uncontrolled trials, and, as is true with studies of etiology, the lack of comparability across studies at even the most fundamental levels of population definition and symptom measurement makes the uniform demonstration of any result highly unlikely" (p. 168).

Other researchers have argued that fluctuations in the mineralocorticoids during the premenstrual phase may shift the salt and water balance in the central nervous system, causing emotional symptoms (Dalton, 1964; Janowsky et al., 1967). There is evidence that aldosterone, a mineralocorticoid, may fluctuate in parallel with depressive symptoms during the menstrual cycle (Demarchi & Tong, 1972; Janowsky, Berens, & Davis, 1973). Other studies, however, have found no differences in aldosterone levels in patients exhibiting PMS and normal controls (e.g., Munday et al., 1981).

Other researchers have suggested that depressive symptoms in the premenstrual, postpartum, and menopause phases may result from excess prolactin levels (See Rubinow & Roy-Byrne, 1984) or from fluctuations in the adrenocortical hormones, such as androgens and glucocorticoids (Vermeulen & Verdonck, 1976; M. S. Walker & McGilp, 1978). Yet, again, there is as much evidence against these hypotheses as there is for them (See Janowsky & Rausch, 1985; Rubinow & Roy-Byrne, 1984).

In sum, hypotheses that abnormalities in fluctuations of hormones or other biochemicals in women are associated with severe depression have not been consistently supported. The evidence suggesting that biochemical fluctuations lead to mood changes is indirect, open to multiple interpretations, and contradicted by an equal amount of negative evidence.

Yet it is premature to conclude that hormonal fluctuations have no effects on mood in women, because many studies of hormones and moods have serious methodological flaws. In addition, it must still be explained why sex differences in depression do not emerge until after puberty, when cyclic changes in hormones and other biochemicals begin in women.

One other biological explanation of the sex differences in depression has been proposed. According to this explanation, women's greater vulnerability to both severe and mild depression can be attributed to a genetic predisposition toward depression. A review of the evidence for this explanation follows.

Genetic Factors in the Sex Differences in Depression. Affective disorder runs in families (Gershon, 1983; Weissman, Kidd,

& Prusoff, 1982). This aggregation of affective disorders within families could be due to either genetic or environmental factors shared by family members. Yet in a review of twin studies of affective illness, Allen (1976) found that in dizygotic twins, the average concordance rate for unipolar depression was 11%, but in monozygotic twins the average concordance rate for unipolar depression was 40%. The substantially higher concordance rate for monozygotic twins indicates some sort of genetic transmission of the disorder.

Could it be that the sex differences in depression are due to a greater genetic predisposition to depression in women? A number of investigators have argued that serious affective illness is the result of a mutant gene on the X chromosome (Perris, 1966; Winokur & Tanna, 1969). Because females have 2 X chromosomes, they should be more at risk for depression than men.

One way investigators have tested the X-linkage hypothesis of affective disorder is to examine the correlation between affective disorders and two abnormalities known to result from mutations on the X chromosome, red–green color blindness and the Xg blood group. If affective disorder is caused by mutations on the X chromosome that are in close proximity to the X-chromosome mutations believed to cause color blindness or the Xg blood group, then we should see significant, high correlations between the presence of affective disorder and the presence of either color blindness or the Xg blood group. A number of studies have examined the family pedigrees of persons suffering from affective disorder and have found that relatives who show affective disorder also tend to have the Xg blood group or color blindness (e.g., Mendelwicz, Fleiss, & Fieve, 1972; Reich, Clayton, & Winokur, 1969; Winokur & Tanna, 1969).

However, Gershon and Bunney (1976) note that the family pedigrees used in these studies have often been incomplete and the statistical significance of the relations observed is often marginal. In addition, these linkage studies assume that the loci for affective disorder, color blindness, and Xg blood group occur in close proximity on the X chromosome. However, a large number of studies (reviewed by Gershon & Bunney, 1976) have indicated that the loci for color blindness and the Xg blood group are not near each other.

Another way to test the X-linkage hypothesis is to examine the transmission of affective disorder from parents to children. Specifically, if a father carries the mutant gene on his X chromosome (and therefore manifests affective disorder), all of his daughters will carry the mutant gene, because the father always gives his daughters an X chromosome. Yet none of an affected father's sons will carry the mutation, because the father always gives his sons a Y chromosome. If a mother carries the mutant gene on one of her two X chromosomes, then her daughters and sons have equal chances of carrying the mutant gene. In short, if affective disorder is linked to the X chromosome, we should observe father–daughter pairs of affected individuals, but no father–son pairs (except for sons suffering from reactive depressions). We should observe equal numbers of mother–daughter and mother–son pairs.

However, most family history studies of the X-linkage hypothesis have discovered more father–son pairs of affective disorder individuals than is compatible with transmission via the X chromosome (e.g., Fieve, Go, Dunner, & Elston, 1984; Green, Goetze, Whybrow, & Jackson, 1973). Gershon and Bunney (1976) compiled data from these and several other studies and found that for 106 father–son pairs in which the father had an affective disorder, 10 sons (roughly 10%) showed affective disorder. This prevalence is higher than that in the general population. If the X-linkage hypothesis were true, the prevalence of depression in the sons of fathers with affective disorder would be considerably lower than that in the general population.

More recently, Cloninger, Christiansen, Reich, and Gottesman (1978; see also Kidd & Spence, 1976) argued that most common

psychiatric disorders are unlikely to result from major chromosomal abnormalities or individual abnormal genes. Instead, such disorders are more likely the result of an aggregation of minor genetic abnormalities that interact with environmental variables to make an individual vulnerable to disorder. Cloninger et al. group all the genetic and other familial factors that influence risk for a particular disorder under the label "liability," and argue that only individuals whose liability is above a certain threshold will manifest the disorder. If one sex manifests a disorder less frequently than another, this may be because that sex has a higher threshold for the disorder. For example, men may manifest depression less frequently because they have a higher threshold for developing the disorder. However, the relative invulnerability to depression of men also may be due to nonfamilial environmental factors that protect them. Cloninger et al. argue that we can determine whether observed sex differences in a disorder are probably due to genetic/familial factors or to environmental factors by examining the rates of the disorder in the parents and siblings of affected persons. Specifically, if less depression in men is due to a lesser genetic loading (i.e., higher liability threshold), then we would expect to see more depression in the relatives of depressed men than in the relatives of depressed women. This is because depressed men are more genetically deviant than depressed women, and thus are more likely to transmit their depression to relatives (and to have had their depression transmitted from their parents). However, if the sex differences in depression are due primarily to nonfamilial environmental factors, we should expect no differences in the rates of depression among the relatives of depressed men and women.

Merikangas, Weissman, and Pauls (1985) applied these analyses to family history data from 133 diagnosed unipolar depressives. Complete pedigrees were obtained from all probands, and diagnostic assessments were made of all living relatives of the probands on the basis of SADS interviews (Endicott &

Spitzer, 1978), medical records, and family history information. Merikangas et al. found that the relatives of male and female depressives were equally likely to be diagnosed as depressed. These data indicate that the sex differences in depression are not due to genetic factors, but to environmental factors.

Summary of the Biological Explanations. There is no consistent evidence that the observed sex differences in serious affective disorders are due to a greater genetic predisposition to the disorder in women. The evidence for the influence of fluctuations in female hormones and other biochemicals on mood was more mixed. Some studies provided indirect support for relations between levels of particular biochemicals and moods, but many others did not. The more general notion that depression is common during the premenstrual, postpartum, and menopause periods has not been supported.

Finally, the biological explanations of sex differences in depression, as a class of explanations, do not explain the absence of sex differences in certain subgroups, such as the Amish, university students, and bereaved persons. Psychosocial factors, such as the supportiveness of the Amish culture or the greater impact of a spouse's death on men than on women, more convincingly explain the variations across groups in sex differences in depression.

Psychoanalytic Explanations

According to classic psychoanalytic theory, women are more susceptible to the depressive process than men because of the personality structure that results from women's psychosexual development (Mitchell, 1974). During the Oedipal stage, while castration anxiety is motivating a boy to develop a superego, a girl "realizes" she and all other females have been deprived of a penis and all the power and status that accompany being male. The girl's realization leads to hostility toward her mother for this deprivation, a great decline in her own self-

worth, and the growth of envy of her father and all males.

A girl's fixation on her father, which is the model for later love relationships with men, is a weak one, based on narcissistic love, rather than an object attachment, because it is motivated by a desire to get back a part of herself she feels she has lost. It is this tendency toward narcissistic love relationships, driven by penis envy, that puts women at greater risk for melancholia, according to psychoanalytic theory (Mitchell, 1974). The woman looks to men to make up for her losses, but she is inevitably and frequently disappointed. After such disappointment, she is prone to turning her libidinal energy back in on herself rather than reattaching it to new objects. Her already injured ego is confronted by the hostility she feels against the object just lost, and melancholia is likely to result.

The psychoanalytic description of the development of female personality has received almost no solid experimental support (Lee & Hertzberg, 1978; Sherman, 1971). For example, there is no support for the Oedipal shift in girls from attachment to the mother to attachment to the father (Sherman, 1971). Similarly, there is little evidence of either castration anxiety in boys or penis envy in girls, although many women acknowledge an envy of men's social power.

Later psychodynamic theorists (e.g. Horney, 1967; Menaker, 1979) downplayed notions of biological determinism in personality development, emphasizing instead the interactions between biological roles and cultural restrictions on women's behaviors. These and many more contemporary psychoanalytic writers point to the restrictions placed on female sexual expression, power, and personal freedom by patriarchal cultures as sources of frustration for women. Further, women's roles as child-bearers and child-rearers conflict with their needs for self-development and independence. To the extent that a woman renounces her role as mother, she suffers the disapproval of others, and, according to most of the neo-Freudians, she denies the primary component of female self-definition. These restrictions on female expression, the inferior status of the female role, and the conflicts between the innate desire to bear children and needs for independence all contribute to a greater tendency toward masochism in women (Horney, 1967).

The neo-Freudian accounts of female psychology are rich in their discussions of the interactions between social pressures and biological pressures. Such explanations might do well in accounting for the prevalence of sex differences in depression across many cultures. Characteristically, the theoretical richness of the psychodynamic explanations is counterbalanced by the absence of empirical support for these explanations.

However, a number of suggestions offered by the neo-Freudians on how women's roles as passive wives and mothers affect mental health have been incorporated in contemporary sex role explanations of female psychopathology. These sex role explanations have been empirically tested, and reviews of these tests follow.

Sex Role Explanations

One sex role theory of depression, proposed by Miller (1976) and Scarf (1980), draws heavily on the work of Karen Horney, a neo-Freudian. Horney (1967) argued that many women greatly overvalue love relationships as a result of perceived rejection by their fathers. This overvaluation of love leads to obsessive quests for self-affirmation through involvement in intimate relationships, as well as internalized rage at all competitors (other women) for lovers and at the lovers themselves.

Similarly, Miller (1976) and Scarf (1980) (see also Gilligan, 1982) have argued that a central element of women's roles in society is the nurturance of relationships. Women's greater concern with relationships has been viewed by traditional psychoanalytic theory and moral development theory as an indication that women do not advance to as high a stage of moral development as do men, who are more concerned with issues of justice and rationality. Instead, Miller (1976)

and Gilligan (1982) argue, women's concern with relationships simply represents a different, equally valid approach to moral issues compared to men's approach.

Yet, these theorists suggest, women's concern with relationships makes them more vulnerable to despair and depression. Scarf writes, "It is in terms of highly vested and extraordinarily important loving attachments that most women's secret self-assessments and interior appraisals of self-worth are made" (p. 95). When a love relationship fails, a women loses her self-definition.

What is the evidence that women are more concerned with relationships than are men? Gilligan (1982) has reported a series of studies of men's and women's ways of reasoning about moral issues. Gilligan presents largely anecdotal evidence indicating that women are most likely to worry about how the problem presented to them would affect relationships between the persons involved, whereas men were more likely to invoke rules of justice in solving problems. Gilligan's work has been criticized by L. J. Walker (1984), however, for the far-reaching conclusions she makes on the basis of data from unstructured interviews conducted with small samples.

In an extensive review of studies of sex differences in social behaviors and self-concept, Maccoby and Jacklin (1974) found that, although women and girls describe themselves as more socially oriented than men, their actual behaviors do not show more concern with social relationships than men's behaviors do.

In addition, it is not clear why investing one's self-worth in interpersonal relationships should be more likely to lead to depression than investing it in material and professional success, as men are said to do. Are failed love relationships more frequent events over the life span than failures at work? Why would not men's lack of investment in interpersonal relationships make them more vulnerable to feelings of loneliness and loss?

Horney (1967), Miller (1976), and Scarf (1980) suggest that, because the desire for relationships is an inherent aspect of female personality, women who attempt to succeed in jobs will be continually faced with disturbing conflicts between their natural propensity toward relationships and demands to be independent and competitive in the job. A number of other sex role theorists have been concerned with the incompatible expectations put on a woman when she enters the marketplace (Frieze et al., 1978; Kohn, Wolfe, Quinn, & Snoek, 1965). That is, a woman may be expected to be both passive, unselfish, and supportive in line with her feminine role, and assertive, self-sufficient, and demanding if she is to achieve in her work. These dual sets of expectations are difficult because the woman may feel forced to violate one set, ignore one set, or perhaps live up to both sets of expectations at the same time (Katz, 1975). Deviance from sex role expectations may result in social rejection. For example, Costrich, Feinstein, Kidder, Marecek, & Pascale (1975) found that assertive women were rated as more unattractive and in need of psychotherapy than were assertive men.

Some support for the role conflict hypothesis comes from epidemiological studies of depressive symptoms in the general population. Aneshensel, Frerichs, and Clark (1981) administered the CES-D to 1,000 residents of Los Angeles County. They found that among persons who were married and employed, women reported significantly more depressive symptoms than men; this was not true among unmarried, employed persons, however. This pattern of results is in line with the assertion that having dual roles can be a risk factor for depression in women.

However, Radloff (1975) found that both working wives and nonworking wives reported more depression than working men. In addition, Radloff found that nonworking wives were more depressed than working wives. Rosenfield (1980) and Ensel (1982) report similar patterns of results from data from depression questionnaires. These data do not support the role-conflict hypothesis described previously.

Gove and Tudor (1973) suggested that having two sets of duties or roles in one's life actually protects one against depression. What is wrong (in part) with the traditional female role, according to Gove and Tudor, is that it allows only one source of gratification, the family. Men may be protected against depression because when one source of gratification is taken away, either the family or work, men have that second source to fall back on. Data such as Radloff's (1975), Rosenfield's (1980), and Ensel's (1982), in which women who had both a family and a job were less depressed than nonworking wives, lend partial support to this hypothesis.

Other sex role theories focus on the subjective value of a woman's role in society compared to the value of a man's role. At a very young age, girls are more likely to say they wish they were boys than boys are to say they wish they were girls (Abel & Sahinkaya, 1962; Hartup & Zook, 1960; Parsons, 1978). This undervaluing of the female sex role relative to the male sex role has been attributed to the greater prestige, power, competence, size, and strength associated with men (Kohlberg, 1966).

Gove and Tudor (1973) argue that the traditional female role as homemaker is becoming increasingly boring and undervalued as more modern conveniences are introduced. They suggest that the sex differences in depression (and other neurotic disorders) can be attributed to the lesser value put on the female role, and the resulting lesser gratification women receive from fulfilling that role. The data cited in the present article indicating no sex differences in the Old Order Amish and in university students seem to support this explanation of the sex differences in depression. The male and female roles in Amish society, although different, are both seen as essential to the family and community (Egeland & Hostetter, 1983). In college students, the goals and life-styles of men and women are more similar than they are in noncollege populations (Hammen & Padesky, 1977). Thus, the equality in value given to the male and female roles in these two subcultures might result in the absence of sex differences observed.

Even if a women accepts the traditional female role gladly at one point in her life, chances are her role will change dramatically several times in her life (Ginzberg, 1966; H. S. Maas & Kuypers, 1974). This role discontinuity is due to the different demands put on a woman when she becomes a wife and then a mother, when her children leave home, and when she becomes a widow. Each of these new phases in life demand major reorganizations and reorientations of time, effort, and values. Coupled with the stress of adjusting to new roles may be the loss of a particular gratification from the previous role (e.g., when children leave home; LeMasters, 1957).

These patterns of change in role obligations are said to have no parallel in a man's life cycle (H. S. Maas & Kuypers, 1974). Yet it certainly cannot be said that the roles of men do not make demands that induce stress. Indeed, when men and women are asked to indicate the number of stressful events in their lives, no sex differences are found (Uhlenhuth, Lipman, Balter, & Stern, 1974). It is not so much the number of demands put on women because of their sex role that makes them more vulnerable to low self-esteem or despair, but the conflicts or radical changes in the expectations for women and the society's devaluation of the stereotypical female role.

The biggest problem with sex role accounts of sex differences in mental health is the frequent absence in these accounts of a well-described process by which role conflict or undervaluation might lead to depression or other disorders. It is particularly difficult to explain why sex role pressures would lead some women and not others into depressions so severe they must be hospitalized. Some theorists draw on psychoanalytic notions about the need to express aggression outwardly to explain why the female sex role would predispose to depression (Bardwick, 1971; Chesler, 1972; Chodorow, 1974). That is, women are socialized to control aggressive feelings, which possibly leads to a greater tendency to introject anger. This description of a mechanism by which sex roles predispose to depression suffers from the lack of research for the psychoanalytic introjected hostility theory of depression (Sherman, 1971).

Other psychologists and sociologists suggest that the female sex role contributes to greater feelings of lack of control and helplessness, thereby leading to depression (see Radloff, 1975, for a review). This helplessness hypothesis is described in the next section.

Learned Helplessness Explanation

Learned helplessness has been defined as a set of motivational, cognitive, and affective deficits that occur when uncontrollable negative events are experienced. In humans these deficits include lowered response initiation, an inability to learn new response—outcome contingencies, sadness, and lowered self-esteem. According to the original learned helplessness theory (Maier, Seligman, & Solomon, 1969; Seligman, 1975), these deficits are the result of the expectation that outcomes will be uncontrollable, because no response can be found to control them. In the best-known application of learned helplessness theory, Seligman (1975) pointed out the similarities between depressive symptoms and helplessness deficits, and suggested that some depressions may be due to the expectation that one has no control over important events.

A reformulation of the original helplessness model was proposed by Abramson, Seligman, and Teasdale (1978) to account for inadequacies in the original model in explaining the generality, chronicity, self-esteem loss, and individual differences in human helplessness. The focus of the reformulated model was on the explanations people make for events. People who tend to explain bad events by causes that influence many areas of their lives (global causes), instead of causes that influence only one area (specific causes), will expect to be helpless in many areas of their lives. People who explain bad events by causes that are stable rather than unstable in time will expect to be helpless in the future. People who blame themselves instead of others for bad events will experience a loss of self-esteem. Thus, according to Abramson et al., people who habitually tend to explain bad events by internal, stable, and global causes (and explain good events by external, unstable, and specific causes) will be more vulnerable to depression than people with the opposite style.

Radloff and Monroe (1978) asserted that the epidemiological trends in the incidence of depression in different groups may be best explained by the learned helplessness model. High rates of depression are found among the poor, the undereducated, nonwhites, the unemployed, the ill, and of course, women. In each of these groups other than women, it is easy to see how one might expect his or her actions to be ineffectual in bringing about good events and avoiding bad events. How does learned helplessness explain the preponderance of women among depressives?

First, women may receive more "helplessness training" over their lifetimes than men (LeUnes, Nation, & Turley, 1980). In an extensive review of childrearing practices, Maccoby and Jacklin (1974) found that one of the few practices in which parents consistently treated girls and boys differently was in their attention to girls' and boys' actions. Whereas boys' behaviors and misbehaviors were praised or criticized accordingly, girls' behaviors were largely ignored. Similarly, when boys and girls misbehave in class, teachers are more likely to respond to the misbehavior of boys than that of girls (Dweck, Davidson, Nelson, & Enna, 1978; Serbin, O'Leary, Kent, & Tonick, 1973). Girls seem to have many opportunities to learn that their responses do not control outcomes. Cross-cultural studies indicate that in many cultures, boys are trained to be more self-reliant and active, whereas girls are encouraged to be dependent on others (Maccoby & Masters, 1970; Whiting & Whiting, 1975).

As adults, women can also expect that their actions will be less successful at generating desired outcomes than men's. In several experimental studies, men's performances at laboratory tasks were rated higher than equally good female performances (Deaux & Taynor, 1973; Pheterson, Kiesler, & Goldberg, 1971). Successful women are often rated as less acceptable and likable than unsuccessful women or successful men (Feather & Simon, 1975; Horner, 1968). Goldberg (1968; see also Lavach & Lainer, 1975) found that the achievements of women were rated as less valuable than the achievements of men. Outside of the laboratory, women are less likely to be promoted than men given similar job performances (Rosen & Jerdee, 1974).

On another level, women have more difficulty having their ideas taken seriously by groups than do men (Unger, 1978; Wahrman & Pugh, 1974). In addition, when a woman attempts to gain power over a situation by asserting that she has greater expertise, greater information, greater authority, or a greater right to make a decision than a man, she is often seen as being "out of place" (Johnson, 1976).

Besides experiencing more events that could give them a sense of helplessness, women may also be more prone to the maladaptive explanatory style the reformulated helplessness theory identifies as a risk factor for depression. A number of studies of children and college students have found that women are more likely to attribute success on academic tasks and other positive events to luck or the favors of others, and to attribute failures to a lack of ability and other stable, global factors (Breen, Vulcano, & Dyck, 1979; Dweck, 1975; Dweck & Repucci, 1973; Nicholls, 1975; Wiegers & Frieze, 1977). Such attribution patterns are associated with a greater tendency to become helpless after failing at tasks.

Although a wide range of studies have supported the hypothesis that a maladaptive explanatory style is a risk factor for depression (for a review see Peterson & Seligman, 1984), most of the studies of the reformulated model have used populations in which sex differences in levels of depression are usually not found (e.g., university students, children, and hospitalized depressives). There have been no studies using a nonstudent adult sample to test whether sex differences in explanatory style account for sex differences in depression.

Of course, it is neither necessary nor sufficient under the helplessness theory to have a maladaptive explanatory style in order to become depressed. It is sufficient that one expects to be helpless in controlling the environment. As discussed previously, there is considerable evidence that women in many areas of the world are trained to have this expectation. Thus, learned helplessness theory could explain the preponderance of women among depressives across cultures. Direct tests of the helplessness theory account of sex differences in depression have not been done, however.

One test of this explanation of sex differences in depression would include measuring the number of uncontrollable events in the lives of a sample of (nonstudent) women and men, and assessing their explanatory styles and their levels of depression. The learned helplessness explanation of sex differences in depression would be supported if it was shown that a greater degree of uncontrollability and a more maladaptive explanatory style in women account for any sex differences observed in depression in the sample. A more important study would be a longitudinal study in which explanatory style, uncontrollable life events, and depression are first assessed in a large group of children and then reassessed frequently as the children go through puberty, adolescence, young adulthood, and older adulthood. The learned helplessness theory would predict that the emergence of sex differences in depression after puberty should be preceded by a divergence in men's and women's explanatory styles and uncontrollable life experiences, with women developing more maladaptive explanatory styles and beginning to experience more uncontrollable events than men. Similarly, if women become less vulnerable to depression in older adulthood (cf. Frieze et al.,

1978), then this change in vulnerability should be preceded by improved explanatory style and a reduced number of uncontrollable events.

Summary

Five different explanations of the sex differences observed in depression have been reviewed. From the evidence currently available, not one of these explanations has been strongly supported.

In the final section of this article, a new explanation for the sex differences in depression is proposed. It is argued that, regardless of the initial source of a depressive episode, how an individual responds to his or her own depressed state may contribute to the severity, chronicity, and recurrence of an episode. Specifically, it is argued that the men's responses to their dysphoria are more behavioral and dampen their depressive episodes, whereas women's responses to their depressive episodes are more ruminative and amplify them.

Response Sets for Depressive Episodes

Most people occasionally experience mild-to-moderate episodes of depressive symptoms. For some of us, these episodes last only a few hours or days. Yet we somehow bring ourselves out of such episodes before we reach the point where we would say we are depressed on a questionnaire or would seek professional help. For others, however, initially mild depressive symptoms often become more severe, until they are moved to acknowledge it to those who ask or even to seek therapy.

There is reason to believe that the ways we respond to or cope with our moods affect the severity and chronicity of those moods (Rippere, 1977). In particular, persons who tend to respond to their own episodes of depression by engaging in activities designed to distract them from their mood appear to recover faster from depressive episodes than those who tend to be inactive and to ruminate about the causes and implications of their depressed moods (cf. Beck, Rush, Shaw, & Emery, 1979; Teasdale, 1985; Zullow, 1984).

Evidence is emerging from a number of studies that men and women show different patterns of responding to their own feelings of depression. The general results of these studies, which are described in more detail in the following sections, are that men, when depressed, tend to engage in activities designed to distract themselves from their mood. Women, when depressed, tend to be less active and to ruminate more about the possible causes of their mood and the implications of their depressive episodes.

Some may want to argue that such differences reduce the sex differences in depression to artifacts of response bias (cf. Funabiki, Bologna, Pepping, & Fitzgerald, 1980). I propose, however, that women's response tendencies toward depression are actually a *cause* of their greater tendency toward depression, whereas men's response tendencies actually lessen their rates of depression. That is, the more ruminative response style of women amplifies and prolongs their depressive symptoms, whereas the more active response style of men dampens and shortens their depressive symptoms. Indeed, men and women may not even need to have different vulnerabilities to the onset of depression for the sex differences in rates of depression to emerge. The sex differences in response tendencies for depressed moods and the effects of these differential responses on the severity and chronicity of depressed moods in themselves could account for the observed sex differences in rates of depression.

First, let us examine the evidence for sex differences in response tendencies for depressive episodes.

Sex Differences in Responses to Depressive Symptoms. In order to investigate the possible sex differences in responses to depressed moods, Nolen-Hoeksema (1986) presented college students with a "list of things people do when depressed" and asked them to rate how likely they would be to engage in the behaviors or thoughts described when depressed. The subjects were instructed to be sure to "rate these items according to what you think you *would* do, not what you *should* do." The men in the sample had significantly higher scores than women on 4 of 37 items: "I avoid thinking of reasons why I'm depressed," "I do something physical," "I play a sport," and "I take drugs." Each of these responses would tend to distract the individual from his depressed mood. The women in the sample scored significantly higher than the men on "I try to determine why I'm depressed," "I talk to other people about my feelings," and "I cry to relieve the tension." These responses tend to focus and maintain the individual's attention on her mood.

Quite similar sex differences in responses to depressed mood have been found in other studies (Chino & Funabiki, 1984; Funabiki et al., 1980; Kleinke, Staneski, & Mason, 1982). For example, Kleinke et al. (1982) found that male college students were more likely than female students to say they coped with depression by thinking about other things, ignoring their problem, or engaging in physical activity. Female students were more likely to say they would cut down on responsibilities and activities when depressed, confront their feelings, and blame themselves for being depressed. Again, the men's responses to their mood tended to be active and designed to relieve the mood by distraction, whereas the women's responses tended to be less active and more likely to focus attention on their mood.

These sex differences in activity levels during depression may emerge during childhood. In a study of self-reported depressive symptoms in 168 children from 8 to 11 years old, Nolen-Hoeksema, Girgus, and Seligman (1986) found that the depressive symptoms distinguishing depressed girls from nondepressed girls were different from those distinguishing depressed boys from nondepressed boys. Discriminant function analyses of the children's answers to the Children's

Depression Inventory (CDI; Kovacs, 1980) revealed that depressed boys more often endorsed items indicating misbehavior, such as "I never do what I am told," "I do bad things," and "I get into fights all the time." Depressed girls did not tend to have high scores on these misbehavior items. Instead, the depressed girls endorsed items indicating negative self-evaluation, self-preoccupation, and loneliness, such as "I hate myself," "I'll never be as good as other kids," and "I feel alone." (Both boys and girls scoring in the depressed range on the CDI had high scores on items indicating sadness, pessimism, and indecision.) These sex differences in most prominent depressive symptoms do not translate directly into sex differences in responses to depressed affect. Yet they do indicate that even in childhood, depressed boys tend to be active, whereas depressed girls tend to be more contemplative or self-focused.

Dweck and Gilliard (1975) provide observational evidence to support the more general notion that when stressed, men respond actively but women are more contemplative, even in childhood. They gave boys and girls experiences with unsolvable tasks and asked the children to state their expectancies for future success after each trial or only after the first and last trials. Their results indicate that asking for expectancy statements after each trial of failure was associated with decreases in persistence at later trials and in expectations for success at future trials in both boys and girls. When the experimenter asked for expectancy statements only after the first trial, the boys did not show decreased persistence on later trials. However, the girls showed decreases in persistence that were as large as those in the condition in which expectancy statements were asked for after every trial. That is, the girls appeared to engage naturally in self-evaluation and rumination about the future, regardless of whether or not they were asked to, whereas boys did not.

In summary, there is evidence that in both children and adults, the responses of males to stress and feelings of sadness tend to be active and often designed to distract them from their mood. The responses of females to their episodes of depression tend to be inactive and likely to focus their attention back on the mood and the self. These sex differences in responses to one's own affective state contribute to the sex differences observed in rates of depression. That is, men's active response style toward depression dampens the severity of their depressed mood and shortens the episodes of depression. Yet women's ruminative, inactive response style amplifies and prolongs their episodes of depression.

Effects of Response Style on Depressed Moods. There are at least three mechanisms by which a ruminative, inactive response set for depression should amplify and prolong an episode, whereas an active response set for depression should dampen and shorten an episode. First, rumination interferes with attention, concentration, and the initiation of instrumental behaviors (Diener & Dweck, 1978; Heckhausen, 1980; Kuhl, 1982; Sarason, 1975). Kuhl (1981) has argued that these difficulties lead to increased failures and a greater sense of helplessness in controlling one's environment, and thereby contribute to depression. On the other hand, engaging in active behaviors when depressed increases the individual's chances for controlling the environment and obtaining positive reinforcers, thereby dampening an existing depressed mood.

Support for this argument comes from a study by Kuhl (1981). He classified subjects as either "state oriented" or "action oriented" on the basis of their responses to a questionnaire asking what they would do in response to a variety of bad events. Then he exposed these subjects to uncontrollable failures at cognitive tasks (i.e., the standard learned helplessness training). The state-oriented subjects showed more helpless behaviors on subsequent tasks than did the action-oriented subjects. Kuhl found that the state-oriented subjects did not appear to become helpless during training because they came into the training with a generalized belief that they could not succeed at the tasks. Rather the state-oriented subjects' excessive rumination about their failures during the helplessness training appeared to interfere with learning in subsequent tasks, thereby leading to poor performance on these tasks, compared to the action-oriented subjects. With regard to depression, Kuhl argues that state-oriented persons may be more likely to focus on their mood state when depressed and that this focus interferes with instrumental behavior. The individual then experiences increased failure and loss of control, which act as helplessness training.

A second mechanism by which a tendency to become ruminative when depressed would amplify depression, whereas a tendency to become active would dampen it, is suggested by Bower (1981) and Teasdale (1983, 1985). Bower, Teasdale, and others have demonstrated that mood state has a powerful effect on an individual's recall of past events, social perceptions, and ability to learn new material. Persons who are depressed or who have been made sad by affect induction procedures (cf. Velten, 1968) show greater access to negative memories and easier learning of negatively toned new material. For example, Teasdale and Fogarty (1979) induced a happy or sad mood in college students by having the subjects read a series of self-referent statements appropriate in tone and content to the mood to be induced. Self-reports of mood by subjects confirmed that the procedures did induce the intended affect. Then the subjects were given a series of positively toned or negatively toned stimulus words and were asked to tell the experimenter what past experience each stimulus word brought to mind as quickly as the experience was recalled. The latency of retrieval for pleasant and unpleasant memories was measured. The time required to retrieve pleasant memories, relative to that needed to retrieve unpleasant memories, was significantly longer for the subjects with induced depression than for the subjects with induced happiness. Teasdale and Fogarty argued that these results indicate

that mood state affects the accessibility of pleasant and unpleasant memories, with depressed mood enhancing the accessibility of unpleasant memories and impairing the accessibility of pleasant memories.

Bower (1981) and Teasdale (1985) describe a vicious cycle between mood and memory that would maintain and deepen a depressed mood. The depressed mood activates a storehouse of negative memories, which amplify the current depressed mood and lead one to interpret current events in light of memories of past failures and losses. The depressed mood is thereby exacerbated and extended.

An individual who tends to be inactive and ruminative in response to a depressed mood should be more likely to become caught in the vicious cycle between mood and memory described by Teasdale and Bower. This cycle would both amplify and maintain the depressed mood. An individual who tends to respond to a depressed mood by becoming active should be more likely to distract him- or herself from the mood and negative cognitions, thereby breaking the cycle and dampening the depressive episode.

Finally, ruminative response sets during depressive episodes may increase the likelihood that an individual will consider depressogenic explanations for current negative events (Diener & Dweck, 1981; Kuhl, 1981; Zullow, 1984), thereby increasing expectations of helplessness and hopelessness. That is, ruminating about one's current state generates depressing explanations that increase depression (e.g., "I am depressed because I really blew it at the meeting today"). Such explanations, according to the reformulated helplessness theory (Abramson et al., 1978), increase the individual's expectations that he or she will continue to have problems in the future. Another type of vicious circle is set up, in which the individual's expectations of uncontrollability lead to decreases in positive, goal-oriented behavior, and the resulting failures enhance the individual's sense of helplessness and depression (Radloff & Rae, 1979).

Support for this mechanism comes from

Diener and Dweck's (1978) study with children. They gave children solvable or unsolvable puzzles and asked them to vocalize whatever they were thinking while working on the puzzles and after each puzzle. Diener and Dweck found that some children had many thoughts about their past and future performances and others did not seem to think much at all about explanations and expectations. Both the ruminating and the nonruminating children expressed some depressive explanations for their failures. Yet the ruminating children invoked these depressing explanations more frequently than the nonruminators. In addition, after trials with unsolvable puzzles, the ruminators showed more helplessness on future tasks than did the nonruminators. Diener and Dweck argued that the more frequent invocation of depressing explanations by the ruminating children led to the greater helplessness deficits seen in them. Additional evidence for this argument comes from a study by Zullow (1984), who found that college students who showed both a ruminative style and a tendency to explain events in pessimistic terms (cf. Abramson et al., 1978) were more prone to depression than were students who only showed rumination or a tendency toward pessimistic explanations.

In sum, I have argued that a ruminative response set for depression may amplify depressive episodes, relative to an active response set for depression, by (a) interfering with instrumental behavior, thereby increasing failures and a sense of helplessness; (b) increasing the accessibility of negative memories; and (c) increasing the chances that an individual will consider depressing explanations for his or her depression. Women appear to engage in more rumination and less distracting activity than men during depressive episodes. The sex differences in rates of depression arise because women's ruminative response styles amplify and prolong their depressive episodes, by the mechanisms described previously, whereas men's active response styles dampen their depressive episodes.

Origins of Response Styles. Why would women be more ruminative and men more active in their response to depressed moods? Being active and ignoring one's moods are part of the masculine stereotype. Being emotional and inactive are part of the feminine stereotype. From a very young age, children describe themselves and others in terms of sex role stereotypes, even before their actual behavior conforms to the stereotype (Brown, 1956; Nadelman, 1974; Schell & Silber, 1968). Parents reinforce behaviors consistent with these stereotypes; parents seem particularly concerned that boys not show feminine or sissy behaviors (Maccoby & Jacklin, 1974). Thus, the active response style of men toward their depressed moods may result simply from conformity to the sanctions against emotionality in men. Rumination in women may not be encouraged directly by parents or others; parents and teachers do not appear to reward girls for passivity and contemplation—they simply do not reward them as much for activity as they do boys (Dweck et al., 1978; Serbin et al., 1973). In addition, because women are told that they are naturally emotional, they may come to believe that depressed moods are unavoidable and cannot be easily dismissed when present. Such an attitude would decrease the probability of women taking simple actions to distract themselves from their moods.

Implications for Interventions and the Prevention of Depression in Women. If a ruminative response style amplifies women's vulnerability to depression, then the recommended interventions for depressed women should be ones that help to distract them from their mood and increase activity. In addition, it would be important to educate the depressed client about the distorting effects of mood on thinking and memory so that she realizes the difficulties involved in thinking clearly about problems and situations while depressed. Several of the interventions suggested by cognitive-behavioral therapies for depression (i.e., Beck et al., 1979; Teasdale 1985) would be particularly appropriate for the treatment of depression in women. These interventions provide the client with exercises to disentangle herself from the effects of mood on thinking as well as a structured approach to problem solving that helps her deal with existing problems in the most rational way possible. A ruminating depressive would be encouraged to engage in some activity when depressed in order to distract herself from the mood. She could also be discouraged from allowing herself to worry constantly. Beck, Emery, and Greenberg (1985) and others have recommended setting aside a half-hour at the end of the day to do one's worrying. The ruminator often finds her worries diminished in size and number by the time the "worry hour" arrives. In addition, the depressive should be encouraged never to make a decision or try to solve a problem when she is depressed, because she has particular access to negative memories and depressing attributions for events. Instead, she should do something to distract herself to relieve the mood state, then go back to the decision or problem to think about it.

To help prevent depression when grown, girls should be encouraged to be as active in response to their moods as boys are encouraged to be. This does not imply that women should be encouraged to become cold or unfeeling, or that they should fill their lives with distractions to avoid thinking about their real problems. I agree with Hammen and Peters's (1977) concern that sex role demands might prevent a seriously depressed man from seeking the help he needs. In addition, though, sex role expectations for women might encourage them to pay too much attention to their own hedonics. Seriously depressed women may be more likely to be detected than seriously depressed men. Yet mildly depressed women may be more likely to become moderately or seriously depressed than mildly depressed men.

In addition, it is clear that sometimes feelings of depression should not be ignored. Often such feelings are indications that something is seriously wrong in one's life. Denying the signs of existing difficulties can be maladaptive. However, constant attention to one's own hedonics can also be maladaptive.

Conclusion

Many of the explanations for sex differences in depression reviewed here are part of the popular mythology about the mental health of women. This is especially true of the notions that hormonal fluctuations strongly affect moods in many women and that women have a natural preoccupation with interpersonal relationships. However, this review has revealed that most of the explanations for depression in women have little empirical support. Suggestions for future research on several of the existing explanations have been offered throughout this review. In addition, a new response set explanation for the sex differences in depression was proposed. This new explanation also requires further investigation.

One laboratory test of the new response set explanation would be to measure the tendency toward a ruminative versus an active response set for depression in a sample of men and women; then standard procedures (e.g., Velten, 1968) could be used to induce a depressed mood in the subjects. The chronicity and severity of the induced mood in the men and women would then be compared. According to the proposed response set explanation, women should ruminate more than men, and this ruminative response set should be related to more chronic and severe depressed moods in women.

Another way of testing the response set explanation would be to conduct a longitudinal field study in which the response sets for depression and depressive symptoms are measured repeatedly over an extended period of time in a nonstudent sample. The response set explanation would predict that women should show more rumination during depression and that this style would be related to more frequent, more chronic, and more severe depressive episodes in women as compared to men.

One large study could be done that would simultaneously test several of the proposed explanations of sex differences in depression. This study would be longitudinal, beginning with a large sample of prepubescent children. The response sets for depression, explanatory style, uncontrollable life events, and depressive symptoms would be measured repeatedly (perhaps semiannually) and information concerning the onset of menses and the menstrual cycle phase would be gathered from the girls once they reached puberty. These variables then could be compared for their ability to predict the depressive episodes that women and men experience over their life spans and the emergence of sex differences in depression.

References

ABEL, H., AND SAHINKAYA, R. (1962). Emergence of sex and race friendship preferences. *Child Development, 33,* 939–943.

ABPLANAP, J. M., HASKETT, R. F., AND ROSE, R. M. (1979). Psychoendocrinology of the menstrual cycle. I. Enjoyment of daily activities and moods. *Psychosomatic Medicine, 41,* 587–604.

ABRAHAM, G. E., ELSNER, C. W., AND LUCAS, L. A. (1978). Hormonal and behavioral changes during the menstrual cycle. *Senologia, 3,* 33–38.

ABRAMSON, L. Y., SELIGMAN, M. E. P., AND TEASDALE, J. D. (1978). Learned helplessness in humans: Critique and reformulation. *Journal of Abnormal Psychology, 87,* 49–74.

ALLEN, M. G. (1976). Twin studies of affective illness. *Archives of General Psychiatry, 33,* 1476–1478.

AMENSON, C. S., AND LEWINSOHN, P. M. (1981). An investigation into the observed sex differences in prevalence of unipolar depression. *Journal of Abnormal Psychology, 90,* 1–13.

AMERICAN PSYCHIATRIC ASSOCIATION. (1968). *Diagnostic and statistical manual of mental disorders* (2nd ed.). Washington, DC: Author.

AMERICAN PSYCHIATRIC ASSOCIATION. (1980). *Diagnostic and statistical manual of mental disorders* (3rd ed.). Washington, DC: Author.

ANDERSCH, B., HAHN, L., ANDERSSON, M., AND ISAKSSON, B. (1978). Body water and weight in patients with premenstrual tension. *British Journal of Obstetrics and Gynaecology, 85,* 546–551.

ANDERSEN, A. N., LARSEN, J. F., STEENSTRUP, O. R., SVENDSTRUP, B., AND NIELSEN, J. (1977). Effect of bromocriptine on the premenstrual syndrome. *British Journal of Obstetrics and Gynaecology, 84,* 370–374.

ANESHENSEL, C. S., FRERICHS, R. R., AND CLARK, V. A. (1981). Family roles and sex differences in depression. *Journal of Health and Social Behavior, 22,* 379–393.

ATKINSON, A. J., AND RICKEL, A. U. (1984). Postpartum depression in primiparous patients. *Journal of Abnormal Psychology, 93,* 115–119.

BACKSTROM, T., AND CARTENSEN, H. (1974). Estrogen and progesterone in plasma in relation to premenstrual tension. *Journal of Steroid Biochemistry, 5,* 257–260.

BACKSTROM, T., AND MATTSON, B. (1975). Correlations of symptoms in premenstrual tension to oestrogen and progesterone concentrations in blood plasma. *Neuropsychobiology, 1,* 80–86.

BACKSTROM, T., SANDERS, D., AND LEASK, R. (1983). Mood, sexuality, hormones and the menstrual cycle: II. Hormone levels and their relationship to the premenstrual syndrome. *Psychosomatic Medicine, 45,* 503–507.

BALDESSARINI, R. J. (1986). A summary of biomedical aspects of mood disorders. In J. C. Coyne (Ed.), *Essential papers on depression* (pp. 459–492). New York: New York University Press.

BALDWIN, J. A. (1971). *The mental hospital in the psychiatric service: A case register study.* New York: Oxford University Press.

BARDWICK, J. M. (1971). *The psychology of women: A study of bio-cultural conflicts.* New York: Harper & Row.

BASH, K. W., AND BASH-LIECHTI, J. (1969). Studies on the epidemiology of neuro-psychiatric disorders among the rural population of the province of Kuhzestan, Iran. *Social Psychiatry, 4,* 137–143.

BASH, K. W., AND BASH-LIECHTI, J. (1974). Studies on the epidemiology of neuro-psychiatric disorders among the population of the city of Shiraz, Iran. *Social Psychiatry, 9,* 163–171.

BAZZOUI, W. (1970). Affective disorders in Iraq. *British Journal of Psychiatry, 117,* 185–203.

BECK, A. T., AND BECK, R. W. (1972). Screening depressed patients in a family practice: A rapid technique. *Postgraduate Medicine, 52,* 81–85.

BECK, A. T., EMERY, G., AND GREENBERG, R. L. (1985). *Anxiety disorders and phobias: A cognitive perspective.* New York: Basic Books.

BECK, A. T., RUSH, J., SHAW, B., AND EMERY, G. (1979). *Cognitive therapy of depression.* New York: Guilford Press.

BERAH, E. F. (1983). Sex differences in psychiatric morbidity: An analysis of Victorian data. *Australian and New Zealand Journal of Psychology, 17,* 266–273.

BLAZER, D., AND WILLIAMS, C. D. (1980). Epidemiology of dysphoria and depression in an elderly population. *American Journal of Psychiatry, 137,* 439–444.

BLUMENTHAL, M. D. (1975). Measuring depressive symptomatology in a general population. *Archives of General Psychiatry, 32,* 971–978.

BORNSTEIN, P. E., CLAYTON, P. J., HALIKAS, J. A., MAURICE, W. L., AND ROBINS, E. (1973). The depression of widowhood after 13 months. *British Journal of Psychiatry, 122,* 561–566.

BOWER, G. H. (1981). Mood and memory. *American Psychologist, 36,* 129–148.

BOYD, J. H., AND WEISSMAN, M. M. (1981). Epidemiology of affective disorders: A re-examination and future directions. *Archives of General Psychiatry, 38,* 1039–1046.

BREEN, L. J., VULCANO, B., AND DYCK, D. B. (1979). Observational learning and sex roles. *Psychological Reports, 44,* 135–144.

BROWN, D. G. (1956). Sex-role preference in young children. *Psychological Monographs, 70* (14, Whole No. 421).

BRYSON S. E., AND PILON, D. J. (1984). Sex differences in depression and the method of administering the Beck Depression Inventory. *Journal of Clinical Psychology, 40,* 529–534.

BUCHAN, T. (1969). Depression in South African patients. *South African Medical Journal, 43,* 1055–1058.

BYRNE, D. G. (1980). The prevalence of symptoms of depression in an Australian general population. *Australian and New Zealand Journal of Psychiatry, 14,* 65–71.

CADORET, R., AND WINOKUR, G. (1974). Depression in alcoholism, *Annals of the New York Academy of Sciences, 23,* 34–39.

CANADIAN BUREAU OF STATISTICS. (1970). *Mental health statistics; Vol. 2. Institutional admissions and separations, 1967.* Ottawa: The Queen's Printer.

CHESLER, P. (1972) *Women and madness.* Garden City, NY: Doubleday.

CHEVRON, E. S., QUINLAN, D. M. AND BLATT, S. J. (1978). Sex roles and gender differences in the expression of depression. *Journal of Abnormal Psychology, 87,* 680–683.

CHINO, A. F., AND FUNABIKI, D. (1984). A cross-validation of sex differences in the expression of depression. *Sex Roles, 11,* 175–187.

CHODOROW, N. (1974). Family structure and feminine personality. In M. Z. ROSALDO AND L. LAMPHERE (Eds.), *Women, culture, and society* (pp. 43–66). Stanford, CA: Stanford University Press.

CHRISTIE, K. M. (1968). *A first assessment of costs and benefits associated with drug usage in New Zealand mental hospitals.* Auckland: New Zealand Institute of Economic Research.

CLANCY, K. AND GOVE, W. (1974). Sex differences in mental illness: An analysis of response bias in self-reports. *American Journal of Sociology, 80,* 205–216.

CLAYTON, P. J. (1981). The epidemiology of bipolar affective disorder. *Comprehensive Psychiatry, 22,* 31–43.

CLONINGER, C. R., CHRISTIANSEN, K. O., REICH, T., AND GOTTESMAN, I. (1978). Implications of sex differences in the prevalence of antisocial personality, alcoholism, and criminality for familial transmission. *Archives of General Psychiatry, 35,* 941–951.

CONE, R. I., DAVIS, G. A., AND COY, R. W. (1981). Effects of ovarian steroids on serotonin metabolism within grossly dissected and microdissected brain regions of the ovariectomized rat. *Brain Research Bulletin, 7,* 639–644.

COOPER, J. E., KENDELL, R. E., GURLAND, B. J., SARTORIUS, N., AND FARKAS, T. (1969). Cross-national study of diagnosis of the mental disorders: Some results from the first comparative investigation. *American Journal of Psychiatry, 125* (Suppl.), 21–29.

COPEN, A. J., MILNE, H. B., AND OUTRAM, D. H. (1969). Dytide, norethisterone, and placebo in the premenstrual syndrome: A double-blind comparison. *Clinician Trials, 6,* 33–36.

COSTRICH, N., FEINSTEIN, J., KIDDER, L., MARECEK, J., AND PASCALE, L. (1975). When stereotypes hurt: Three studies of the penalties for sex role reversals. *Journal of Experimental and Social Psychology, 11,* 520–530.

COTTON, N. S. (1979). The familial incidence of alcoholism: A review. *Journal of Studies on Alcohol, 40,* 89–116.

CULBERG, J. (1972). Mood changes and menstrual symptoms with different gestagen-estrogen combinations. *Acta Psychiatrica Scandinavica* (suppl. 236), 1–86.

DALTON, K. (1964). *Premenstrual syndrome.* Springfield, IL: Charles C. Thomas.

DEAN, G., WALSH, D., DOWNING, H., AND SHELLEY, E. (1981). First admissions of native-born and immigrants to psychiatric hospitals in southeast England, 1976. *British Journal of Psychiatry, 139,* 506–512.

DEAUX, K., AND TAYNOR, J. (1973). Evaluation of male and female ability; Bias works two ways. *Psychological Reports, 32,* 261–262.

DEMARCHI, G. W., AND TONG, J. E. (1972). Menstrual, diurnal, and activation effects on the resolution of temporally paired flashes. *Psychophysiology, 9,* 362–367.

DEPUE, R. A., AND MONROE, S. M. (1978). Learned helplessness in the perspective of the depressive disorders: Conceptual and definitional issues. *Journal of Abnormal Psychology, 87,* 3–20.

DIENER, C. L., AND DWECK, C. S. (1978). Analysis of learned helplessness: Continuous changes in performance, strategy, and achievement cognitions following failure. *Journal of Personality and Social Psychology, 36,* 451–462.

DWECK, C. S. (1975). The role of expectations and attributions in the alleviation of learned helplessness. *Journal of Personality and Social Psychology, 31,* 674–685.

DWECK, C. S., DAVIDSON, W., NELSON, S., AND ENNA, B. (1978). Sex differences in learned helplessness: II. The contingencies of evaluative feedback in the classroom and III. An experimental analysis. *Developmental Psychology, 14,* 268–276.

DWECK, C. S., AND GILLIARD, D. (1975). Expectancy statements as determinants of reactions to failure: Sex differences in persistence and expectancy change. *Journal of Personality and Social Psychology, 32,* 1077–1084.

DWECK, C. S., AND REPUCCI, N. D. (1973). Learned helplessness and reinforcement responsibility in children. *Journal of Personality and Social Psychology, 25,* 109–116.

EATON, W. W. AND KESSLER, L. G. (1981). Rates of symptoms of depression in a national sample. *American Journal of Epidemiology, 114,* 528–538.

EGELAND, J. A., AND HOSTETTER, A. M. (1983). Amish study: I. Affective disorders among the Amish, 1976–1980. *American Journal of Psychiatry, 140,* 56–61.

EL-ISLAM, M. F. (1969). Depression and guilt: A study at an Arab psychiatric clinic. *Social Psychiatry, 4,* 56–58.

ENDICOTT, J., AND SPITZER, R. L. (1978). A diagnostic interview: The Schedule for Affective Disorders and Schizophrenia. *Archives of General Psychiatry, 35,* 837–844.

ENSEL, W. M. (1982). The role of age in the relationship of gender and marital status to depression. *Journal of Nervous and Mental Disease, 170,* 536–543.

ESSEN-MOELLER, E. (1956). Individual traits and morbidity in a Swedish rural population. *Acta Psychiatrica Neurologica Scandinavica* (Suppl. 100), 1–160.

ESSEN-MOELLER, E., AND HAGNELL, O. (1961). The frequency and risk of depression within a rural population group in Scania. *Acta Psychiatrica Scandinavica* (Suppl. 162), 28–32.

EZEILO, B. N., AND ONYEAMA, W. (1980). Marital status and psychiatric illness: A Nigerian perspective. *Psychopathologie Africaine, 16,* 309–319.

FADEN, V. B. (1977). *Primary diagnoses of discharges from nonfederal general hospital psychiatric inpatient units, U. S., 1975* (Mental Health Statistical Note 137). Rockville, MD: Department of Health, Education, and Welfare Publications.

FEATHER, N. T., AND SIMON, J. G. (1975). Reactions to male and female success and failure in sex-linked cultures. *Journal of Personality and Social Psychology, 31,* 20–31.

FEIGHNER, J. P., ROBINS, E., GUZE, S. B., WOODRUFF, R. A., WINOKUR, G., AND MUNOZ, R. (1972). Diagnostic criteria for use in psychiatric research. *Archives of General Psychiatry, 26,* 57–63.

FIEVE, R. R., GO, R., DUNNER, D. K., AND ELSTON, R. (1984). Search for biological/genetic markers in a long-term epidemiological and morbid risk study of affective disorders. *Journal of Psychiatric Research, 18,* 425–445.

FREIRICHS, R. R., ANESHENSEL, C. S., AND CLARK, V. A. (1981).Prevalence of depression in Los Angeles County. *American Journal of Epidemiology, 113,* 691–699.

FRIEZE, I. H., PARSONS, J. E., JOHNSON, P. B., RUBLE, D. N., AND ZELLMAN, G. L. (1978). *Women and sex roles: A social psychological perspective.* New York: Norton.

FUNABIKI, D., BOLOGNA, N. C., PEPPING, M., AND FITZGERALD, K. C. (1980). Revisiting sex differences in the expression of depression. *Journal of Abnormal Psychology, 89,* 194–202.

GANONG, W. F. (1984). Physiology of reproduction and pregnancy. In R. C. Benson (Ed.), *Current obstetric and gynecologic diagnosis and treatment* (pp. 60–87). Los Altos, CA: Lange Medical Publications.

GERSHON, E. S. (1983). The genetics of affective disorders. In L. Grinspoon (Ed.), *Psychiatry update* (pp. 434–457). Washington, DC: American Psychiatric Press.

GERSHON, E. S., AND LIEBOWITZ, J. H. (1975). Sociocultural and demographic correlates of affective disorders in Jerusalem. *Journal of Psychiatric Research, 12,* 37–50.

GERSHON, E.S, AND LIEBOWITZ, J. H. (1975). Sociocultural and demographic correlates of affective disorders in Jerusalem. *Journal of Psychiatric Research, 12,* 37–50.

GILLIGAN, C. (1982). *In a different voice.* Cambridge, MA: Harvard University Press.

GINZBERG, E. (1966). *Life styles of educated women.* New York: Columbia University Press.

GOLDBERG, S. (1968). Are women prejudiced against women? *Transactions, 5,* 28–30.

GOVE, W. R., AND GEERKEN, M. R. (1976). Response bias in surveys of mental health: An empirical investigation. *American Journal of Sociology, 82,* 1289–1317.

GOVE, W., McCORKEL, J., FAIN, T., AND HUGHES, M. (1976). Response bias in community surveys of mental health: Systematic bias or random noise? *Social Science and Medicine, 10,* 497–502.

GOVE, W. R., AND TUDOR, J. F. (1973). Adult sex roles and mental illness. *American Journal of Sociology, 78,* 812–835.

GRANT, E. C. G., AND PRYSE-DAVIES, J. (1968). Effect of oral contraceptives on depressive mood changes and endometrial monoamine oxidase and phosphates. *British Medical Journal, 3,* 777–780.

GREEN, R., GOETZE, V., WHYBROW, P., AND JACKSON, R. (1973). X-linked transmission of manic-depressive illness. *Journal of the American Medical Association, 223,* 1289.

HACKMAN, E., WIRZ-JUSTICE, A., AND LICHTSTEINER, M. (1972). The uptake of dopamine and serotonin in the rat brain during progesterone decline. *Psychopharmacologia, 32,* 183–191.

HALBREICH, U., ENDICOTT, J., AND NEE, J. (1983). Premenstrual depressive changes. *Archives of General Psychiatry, 40,* 535–542.

HALEVI, H. S., NAOR, E., AND COCHAVY, Z. (1969). *Census of mental inpatients, 1964.* Jerusalem: Ministry of Health.

HAMMEN, C. L., AND PADESKY, C. A. (1977). Sex differences in the expression of depressive responses on the Beck Depression Inventory. *Journal of Abnormal Psychology, 86,* 609–614.

HAMMEN, C. L., AND PETERS, S. D. (1977). Differential responses to male and female depressive reactions. *Journal of Consulting and Clinical Psychology, 45,* 994–1001.

HARTUP, W. W., AND ZOOK, E. A. (1960). Sex-role preferences in three-and four-year-old children. *Journal of Consulting Psychology, 24,* 420–426.

HECKHAUSEN, H. (1980). Task-irrelevant cognitions during an exam: Incidence and effects. In H. W. KROHNE AND L. LAUX, (Eds.), *Achievement, stress, and anxiety.* Washington, DC: Hemisphere.

HELGASON, T. (1961). The frequency of depressive states in Iceland as compared with other Scandinavian countries. *Acta Psychiatrica Scandinavica* (Suppl. 162), 81–90.

HELGASON, T. (1977). Psychiatric services and mental illness in Iceland: Incidence study (1966–1967) with a 6–7 year follow-up. *Acta Psychiatrica Scandinavica* (Suppl. 268), 1–140.

HENDERSON, S., DUNCAN-JONES, P., BYRNE, D. G., SCOTT, R., AND ADCOCK, S. (1979). Psychiatric disorder in Canberra: A standardized study of prevalence. *Acta Psychiatrica Scandinavica, 60,* 355–374.

HIRSCHFELD, R. M. A., AND CROSS, C. K. (1982). Epidemiology of affective disorders: Psychosocial risk factors. *Archives of General Psychiatry, 39,* 35–46.

HORNER, M. S. (1968). *Sex differences in achievement motivation and performance in competitive and non-competitive situations.* Unpublished doctoral dissertation, University of Michigan, Ann Arbor.

HORNEY, K. (1967). *Feminine psychology.* New York: Norton.

JANOWSKY, D. S., BERENS, S. C., AND DAVIS, J. M. (1973). Correlations between mood, weight, and electrolytes during the menstrual cycle: A renin-angiotensin-aldosterone hypothesis of premenstrual tension. *Psychosomatic Medicine, 35,* 143–154.

JANOWSKY, D. S., FANN, W. E., AND DAVIS, J. M. (1971). Monoamines and ovarian hormone-linked sexual and emotional changes: A review. *Archives of Sexual Behavior, 1,* 205–218.

JANOWSKY, D. S., GORNEY, R., AND MANDELL, A. J. (1967). The menstrual cycle. Psychiatric and ovarian-adrenocortical hormone correlates: Case study and literature review. *Archives of General Psychiatry, 17,* 459–469.

JANOWSKY, D. S., AND RAUSCH, J. (1985). Biochemical hypotheses of premenstrual tension syndrome. *Psychological Medicine, 14*, 3–8.

JOHNSON, P. (1976). Women and power: Toward a theory of effectiveness. *Journal of Social Issues, 32*, 99–110.

JORDHEIM, O. (1972). The premenstrual syndrome: Clinical trials of treatment with a progestogen combined with a diuretic compared with both a progestogen alone and with a placebo. *Acta Obstetrica Gynecologica Scandinavica, 51*, 77–80.

KATZ, M. (1975, August). *Sex role training and coping behavior in a role conflict situation: Homemaking-career conflicts.* Paper presented at the 83rd Annual Convention of the American Psychological Association, Chicago, IL.

KIDD, K. K., AND SPENCE, M. A. (1976). Genetic analyses of pyloric stenosis suggesting a specific maternal effect. *Journal of Medical Genetics, 13*, 290–294.

KING, D. A., AND BUCHWALD, A. M. (1982). Sex differences in subclinical depression: Administration of the Beck Depression Inventory in public and private disclosure situations. *Journal of Personality and Social Psychology, 42*, 963–969.

KLAIBER, E. L., BROVERMAN, D. M., VOGEL, W., AND KOBAYSHI, V. (1979). Estrogen therapy for severe persistent depressions in women. *Archives of General Psychiatry, 6*, 550–554.

KLEINKE, C. L., STANESKI, R. A., AND MASON, J. K. (1982). Sex differences in coping with depression. *Sex Roles, 8*, 877–889.

KOHLBERG, L. (1966). A cognitive-developmental analysis of children's sex-role concepts and attitudes. In E. E. Maccoby (Ed.), *The development of sex differences* (pp. 82–172.) Stanford, CA: Stanford University Press.

KOHN, R. L., WOLFE, D. M., QUINN, R. P., AND SNOEK, J. D. (1965). *Organizational stress: Studies in role conflict and ambiguity.* New York: Wiley.

KOVACS, M. (1980). Rating scales to assess depression in school-aged children. *Acta Paedopsychiatria, 46*, 305–315.

KRUPINSKI, J., AND STOLLER, A. (1962). Survey of institutionalized mental patients in Victoria, Australia, 1882–1959. II. Analyses in terms of diagnoses. *Medical Journal of Australia, 1*, 1314–1315.

KUHL, J. (1981). Motivational and functional helplessness: The moderating effect of state versus action orientation. *Journal of Personality and Social Psychology, 40*, 155–170.

KUTNER, S. J., AND BROWN, W. L. (1972). Types of oral contraceptives, depression and premenstrual symptoms. *Journal of Nervous and Mental Disease, 55*, 153–162.

LADISICH, W. (1977). Influence of progesterone on serotonin metabolism: A possible causal factor for mood changes. *Psychoneuroendocrinology, 2*, 257–266.

LANGNER, T. (1962). A twenty-two item screening score of psychiatric symptoms indicating impairment. *Journal of Health and Human Behavior, 3*, 269–266.

LAVACH, J. F., AND LAINER, H. B. (1975). The motive to avoid success in 7th, 8th, 9th, and 10th grade high achieving girls. *Journal of Educational Research, 68*, 216–218.

LEE, D., AND HERTZBERG, J. (1978). Theories of feminine personality. In I. H. FRIEZE, J. E. PARSONS, P. B. JOHNSON, D. N. RUBLE, AND. G. L. ZELLMAN (Eds.), *Women and sex roles: A social psychological perspective* (pp. 28–44). New York: Norton.

LEIGHTON, A. H., LAMBO, T. A., HUGHES, C. C., LEIGHTON, D. C., MURPHY, J. M., AND MACKLIN, D. B. (1963). *Psychiatric disorder among the Yoruba.* Ithaca; NY: Cornell University Press.

LEMASTERS, E. E. (1957). Parenthood as crisis. *Marriage and Family Living, 19*, 352–355.

LEMKAU, P., TIETZE, C., AND COOPER, M. (1942). Complaint of nervousness and the psychoneuroses: An epidemiological viewpoint. *American Journal of Orthopsychiatry, 12*, 214–223.

LEUNES, A. D., NATION, J. R., AND TURLEY, N. M. (1980). Male-female performance in learned helplessness. *Journal of Psychology, 104*, 255–258.

MAAS, H. S., AND KUYPERS, J. A. (1974). *From thirty to seventy: A forty-year longitudinal study of changing lifestyles and personal development.* San Francisco, CA: Jossey-Bass.

MAAS, J. W. (1975). Biogenic amines and depression. *Archives of General Psychiatry, 32*, 1357–1361.

MACCOBY, E. E., AND JACKLIN, C. N. (1974). *The psychology of sex differences.* Stanford, CA: Stanford University Press.

MACCOBY, E. E., AND MASTERS, J. (1970). Attachment and dependency. In P. Mussen (Ed.), *Carmichael's manual of child psychology* (Vol. 2, pp. 1–101). New York: Wiley.

MAIER, S. F., SELIGMAN, M. E. P., AND SOLOMON, R. L. (1969). Pavlovian fear conditioning and learned helplessness. In B. A. Campbell and

R. A. Church (Eds.), *Punishment and aversive behavior* (pp. 299–343). New York: Appleton-Century-Crofts.

MARTIN, F. M., BROTHERSON, J. H. F., AND CHAVE, S. P. W. (1957). Incidence of neurosis in a new housing estate. *British Journal of Preventative and Social Medicine, 11,* 196–202.

MAZER, M. (1967). Psychiatric disorders in general practice: The experience of an island community. *American Journal of Psychiatry, 124,* 609–615.

MENAKER, E. (1979). The therapy of women in the light of psychoanalytic theory and the emergence of a new view. In L. Lerner (Ed.), *Masochism and the emergent ego: Selected papers of Esther Menaker.* New York: Human Services Press.

MENDLEWICZ, J., FLEISS, J. L., AND FIEVE, R. R. (1972). Evidence for X-linkage in the transmission of manic-depressive illness. *Journal of the American Medical Association, 222,* 1624.

MERIKANGAS, K. R., WEISSMAN, M. M., AND PAULS, D. L. (1985). Genetic factors in the sex ratio of major depression. *Psychological Medicine, 15,* 63–69.

MILLER, J. B. (1976). *Toward a new psychology of women.* New York: Beacon Press.

MITCHELL, J. (1974). *Psychoanalysis and feminism.* New York: Random House.

MOHAN, B. (1972). *Social psychiatry in India: A treatise on the mentally ill.* Calcutta: The Minerva Association.

MOOS, R. H. (1968). The development of a menstrual distress questionnaire. *Psychosomatic Medicine, 30,* 853–867.

MUNDAY, M., BRUSH, M. G., AND TAYLOR, R. W. (1981). Correlations between progesterone, oestradiol and aldosterone levels in the premenstrual syndrome. *Clinical Endocrinology, 14,* 1–9.

MYERS, J. K., WEISSMAN, M. M., TISCHLER, G. L., HOLZER, C. E., LEAF, P. J., ORVASCHEL, H., ANTHONY, J. E., BOYD, J. H., BURKE, J. D., KRAMER, M. AND STOLTZMAN, R. (1984). Six-month prevalence of psychiatric disorders in three communities. *Archives of General Psychiatry, 41,* 959–967.

NADELMAN, L. (1974). Sex identity in American children: Memory, knowledge, and preference tests. *Developmental Psychology, 10,* 413–417.

NICHOLLS, J. G. (1975). Causal attributions and other achievement-related cognitions: Effects of task outcome, attainment value, and sex.

Journal of Personality and Social Psychology, 31, 379–389.

NOLEN-HOEKSEMA, S. (1986). Unpublished data, University of Pennsylvania, Philadelphia.

NOLEN-HOEKSEMA, S., GIRGUS, J. S., AND SELIGMAN, M. E .P. (1986). *Sex differences in depressive symptoms in children.* Unpublished manuscript, University of Pennsylvania, Philadelphia.

O'HARA, M. W., REHM, L. P., AND CAMPBELL, S. B. (1982). Predicting depressive symptomatology: Cognitive-behavioral models and postpartum depression. *Journal of Abnormal Psychology, 91,* 457–461.

ORLEY, J., AND WING, J. K. (1979). Psychiatric disorders in two African villages. *Archives of General Psychiatry, 36,* 513–520.

PADESKY, C., AND HAMMEN, C. (1977). *Help-seeking for depression: Sex differences in college students.* Unpublished manuscript. University of California, Los Angeles.

PAIGE, K. E. (1971). Effects of oral contraceptives on affective fluctuations associated with the menstrual cycle. *Psychosomatic Medicine, 33,* 515–537.

PARLEE, M. B. (1973). The premenstrual syndrome. *Psychological Bulletin, 80,* 454–465.

PARSONS, J. E. (1978). Classic theories of sex-role socialization. In I. H. FRIEZE, J. E. PARSONS, P. B. JOHNSON, D. N. RUBLE, AND G. L. ZELLMAN (Eds.), *Women and sex roles: A social psychological perspective* (pp. 95–113). New York: Norton.

PEDERSON, A. M., BARRY, D. J., AND BABIGIAN, H. M. (1972). Epidemiological considerations of psychotic depression. *Archives of General Psychiatry, 27,* 193–197.

PERRIS, C. (1966). A study of bipolar (manic-depressive) and unipolar recurrent depressive psychosis. *Acta Psychiatrica Scandinavica* (Suppl. 194), 1–89.

PERSKY, H., O'BRIEN, C. P., AND KAHN, M. R. (1976). Reproductive hormone levels, sexual activity and moods during the menstrual cycle. *Psychosomatic Medicine, 38,* 62–63.

PETERSON, C., AND SELIGMAN, M. E. P. (1984). Causal explanations as a risk factor for depression: Theory and evidence. *Psychological Review, 91,* 347–374.

PETTY, F., AND NASRALLAH, H. A. (1981). Secondary depression in alcoholism: Implications for future research. *Comprehensive Psychiatry, 22,* 587–595.

PHETERSON, G. I., KIESLER, S. B., AND GOLDBERG, P. A. (1971). Evaluation of the performance of women as a function of their sex, achievement, and personal history. *Journal of Personality and Social Psychology, 19,* 114–118.

PHILLIPS, D. L., AND SEGAL, B. E. (1969). Sexual status and psychiatric symptoms. *American Sociological Review, 34,* 58–72.

PITT, B. (1973). Maternity blues. *British Journal of Psychiatry, 122,* 431–433.

RACHMAN S. J., AND WILSON, G. T. (1980). *The effects of psychological therapy: Second enlarged edition.* New York: Pergamon Press.

RADLOFF, L. (1975). Sex differences in depression: The effects of occupation and marital status. *Sex Roles 1,* 249–265.

RADLOFF, L. S. (1977). The CES-D scale: A self-report depression scale for research in the general population. *Journal of Applied Psychological Measurement,1,* 385–401.

RADLOFF, L. S., AND MONROE, M. K. (1978). Sex differences in helplessness with implications for depression. In L. S. HANSEN AND R. S. RAPOZA (Eds.), *Career development and the counseling of women* (pp. 199–221). Springfield, IL: Charles C. Thomas.

RADLOFF, L. S., AND RAE, D. S. (1979). Susceptibility and precipitating factors in depression: Sex differences and similarities. *Journal of Abnormal Psychology, 88,* 174–181.

RAO, A. V. (1970). A study of depression as prevalent in south India. *Transcultural Psychiatric Research Review, 7,* 166–167.

REICH, T., CLAYTON, P., AND WINOKUR, G. 1969. Family history studies: V. The genetics of mania. *American Journal of Psychiatry, 125,* 1358–1369.

RIPPERE, V. (1977). "What's the thing to do when you're feeling depressed?"—A pilot study. *Behavior Research and Therapy, 15,* 185–191.

ROBBINS, L. N., HELZER, J. E., CROUGHAN, J., AND RATCLIFF, K. S. (1981). National Institute of Mental Health Diagnostic Interview Schedule: Its history, characteristics, and validity. *Archives of General Psychiatry, 38,* 381–389.

ROSEN, B. M., BAHN, A. K., AND KRAMER, M. (1964). Demographic and diagnostic characteristics of psychiatric clinic outpatients in the U.S.A., 1961. *American Journal of Orthopsychiatry, 34,* 455–468.

ROSEN, B., AND JERDEE, T. H. (1974). Effects of applicant's sex and difficulty of job on evaluations of candidates for managerial positions. *Journal of Applied Psychology, 59,* 511–512.

ROSENFIELD, S. (1980). Sex differences in depression: Do women always have higher rates? *Journal of Health and Social Behavior, 21,* 33–42.

ROSENTHAL, R. (1978). Combining results of independent studies. *Psychological Bulletin, 85,* 185–193.

ROSENTHAL, S. H. (1966). Changes in a population of hospitalized patients with affective disorders, 1945–1965. *American Journal of Psychiatry, 123,* 671–681.

RUBINOW, D. R., AND ROY-BYRNE, P. (1984). Premenstrual syndromes: Overview from a methodologic perspective. *American Journal of Psychiatry, 141,* 163–172.

RUBLE, D., AND FRIEZE, I. (1978). Biosocial aspects of reproduction. In I. H. FRIEZE, J. E. PARSONS, P. B. JOHNSON, D. N. RUBLE, AND G. L. ZELLMAN (Eds.), *Women and sex roles: A social psychological perspective* (pp. 191–209). New York: Norton.

SAENGER, G. (1968). Psychiatric outpatients in America and the Netherlands: A transcultural comparison. *Social Psychiatry, 3,* 149–164.

SAMPSON, G. A. (1979). Premenstrual syndrome: A double-blind controlled trial of progesterone and placebo. *British Journal of Psychiatry, 135,* 209–215.

SARASON, I. G. (1975). Anxiety and self-preoccupation. In I. G. SARASON AND C. D. SPIELBERGER (Eds.), *Stress and anxiety* (pp. 27–44). Washington, DC: Hemisphere.

SCARF, M. (1980). *Unfinished business: Pressure points in the lives of women.* New York: Ballantine Books.

SCHELL, R. E., AND SILBER, J. W. (1968). Sex role discrimination among young children. *Perceptual and Motor Skills, 27,* 379–389.

SCHUCKIT, M. A., DALY, V., HERRMAN, G., AND HINEMAN, S. (1975). Premenstrual symptoms and depression in a university population. *Diseases of the Nervous System, 36,* 516–517.

SELIGMAN, M. E. P. (1975). *Helplessness; On depression, development and death.* San Francisco: Freeman.

SERBIN, L. A., O'LEARY, K. D., KENT, R. N., AND TONICK, I. J. (1973). A comparison of teacher response to the preacademic and problem behavior of boys and girls. *Child Development, 44,* 796–804.

SHERMAN, J. A. (1971). *On the psychology of women: A survey of empirical studies.* Springfield, IL: Charles C. Thomas.

SMITH, M. L., AND GLASS, G. V. (1977). Meta-analysis of psychotherapy outcome studies. *American Psychologist,* 752–760.

SMITH, S. L. (1976). The menstrual cycle and mood disturbances. *Clinical Obstetrics and Gynecology, 19,* 391–397.

SORENSON, A., AND STROMGREN, E. (1961). The Samso investigation. *Acta Psychiatrica Scandinavica* (Suppl. 162), 63–68.

SPICER, C. C., HARE, E. H., AND SLATER, E. (1973). Neurotic and psychotic forms of depressive illness: Evidence from age-incidence in a national sample. *American Journal of Psychiatry, 130,* 535–541.

SPITZER, R. L., ENDICOTT, J., AND ROBINS, E. (1978). Research diagnostic criteria: Rationale and reliability. *Archives of General Psychiatry, 35,* 773–782.

STANGLER, R. S., AND PRINTZ, A. M. (1980). *DMS-III:* Psychiatric diagnosis in a university population. *American Journal of Psychiatry, 137,* 937–940.

STEINER, M., HASKETT, R. F., AND CARROLL, B. J. (1980). Premenstrual tension syndrome: The development of research diagnostic criteria and new rating scales. *Acta Psychiatrica Scandinavica, 62,* 177–190.

STROEBE, M. S., AND STROEBE, W. (1983). Who suffers more? Sex differences in health risks of the widowed. *Psychological Bulletin, 93,* 279–301.

TEASDALE, J. D. (1983). Negative thinking in depression: Cause, effect or reciprocal relationship? *Advances in Behavior Research and Therapy, 5,* 3–26.

TEASDALE, J. D. (1985). Psychological treatments for depression: How do they work? *Behavior Research and Therapy, 23,* 157–165.

TEASDALE, J. D., AND FOGARTY, S. J. (1979). Differential effects of induced mood on retrieval of pleasant and unpleasant events from episodic memory. *Journal of Abnormal Psychology, 88,* 248–257.

UHLENHUTH, E. H., LIPMAN, R. S., BALTER, M. B., AND STERN, M. (1974). Symptom intensity and life stress in the city. *Archives of General Psychiatry, 31,* 759–764.

UNGER, R. K. (1975). *Status, power, and gender: An examination of parallelisms.* Paper presented at the conference on New Directions for Research on Women, Madison, WI.

U.S. DEPARTMENT OF COMMERCE, BUREAU OF THE CENSUS. (1985). *Statistical abstracts of the United States, 1985.* Washington, DC: Author.

VADHER, A., AND NDETEI, D. M. (1981). Life events and depression in a Kenyan setting. *British Journal of Psychiatry, 139,* 134–137.

VELTEN, E. (1968). A laboratory task for induction of mood states. *Behavior Research and Therapy, 6,* 473–482.

VERMEULEN, A., AND VERDONCK, L. (1976). Plasma androgen levels during the menstrual cycle. *American Journal of Obstetrics and Gynecology, 125,* 491–494.

WAHRMAN, R., AND PUGH, M. D. (1974). Sex, nonconformity, and influence. *Sociometry, 37,* 137–147.

WALKER, L. J. (1984). Sex differences in the development of moral reasoning: A critical review. *Child Development, 55,* 677–691.

WALKER, M. S., AND MCGILP, S. (1978). Excretory patterns of urinary free 11-hydroxycorticosteroids and total oestrogens throughout the normal menstrual cycle. *Annals of Clinical Biochemistry, 15,* 201–202.

WEEKE, A., BILLE, M., VIDEBECH, T., DUPONT, A., AND JUEL-NIELSEN, N. (1975). Incidence of depressive syndromes in a Danish county. *Acta Psychiatrica Scandinavica, 51,* 28–41.

WEISSMAN, M. M. (1979). The myth of involutional melancholia. *Journal of the American Medical Association, 242,* 742–744.

WEISSMAN, M. M., KIDD, K. K., AND PRUSOFF, B. A. (1982) Variability in rates of affective disorders in relatives of depressed and normal probands. *Archives of General Psychiatry, 39,* 1397–1403.

WEISSMAN, M. M., AND KLERMAN, G. L. (1977). Sex differences in the epidemiology of depression. *Archives of General Psychiatry, 34,* 98–111.

WEISSMAN, M. M., AND MYERS, J. K. (1978). Affective disorders in a United States community: The use of research diagnostic criteria in an epidemiological survey. *Archives of General Psychiatry, 35,* 1304–1311.

WEISSMAN, M. M., SHOLOMSKAS, D., POTTENGER, M., PRUSOFF, B. A., AND LOCKE, B. Z. (1977). Assessing depressive symptoms in five psychiatric populations: A validation study. *American Journal of Epidemiology, 106,* 203–214.

WHITING, B. B., AND WHITING, J. W. M. (1975). *Children of six cultures: A psychocultural analysis.* Cambridge, MA: Harvard University Press.

WIEGERS, R. M., AND FRIEZE, I. H. (1977). Gender, female traditionality, achievement level, and cognitions of success and failure. *Psychology of Women Quarterly, 2,* 125–137.

WILLIAMS, J. B. W., AND SPITZER, R. L. (1983). The issue of sex bias in *DSM-III. American Psychologist, 38,* 793–798.

WING, J. K. (1976) A technique for studying psychiatric morbidity in inpatient and outpatient series and general population samples. *Psychological Medicine, 6,* 667–671.

WINOKUR, G. (1973). Depression in the menopause. *American Journal of Psychiatry, 130,* 92–93.

WINOKUR, G., AND CLAYTON, P. (1967). Family history studies: II. Sex differences and alcoholism in primary affective illness. *British Journal of Psychiatry, 113,* 973–979.

WINOKUR, G., RIMMER, J., AND REICH, T. (1971). Alcoholism: IV. Is there more than one type of alcoholism? *British Journal of Psychiatry, 118,* 525–531.

WINOKUR, G., AND TANNA, V. L. (1969). Possible role of X-linked dominant factor in manic-depressive disease. *Diseases of the Nervous System, 30,* 89–93.

WINOKUR, G., TSUANG, M. T., AND CROWE, R. R. (1982). The Iowa 500: Affective disorder in relatives of manic and depressed patients. *American Journal of Psychiatry, 139,* 209–212.

WORLD HEALTH ORGANIZATION. (1980). *The international classification of diseases* (9th ed.). Geneva: Author.

YAP, P. M. (1965). Phenomenology of affective disorders in Chinese and other cultures. In A. V. S. DEREUCH AND R. PORTER (Eds.), *Transcultural psychiatry* (pp. 84–105). Boston: Little, Brown.

ZULLOW, H. (1984). *The interaction of rumination and explanatory style in depression.* Unpublished master's thesis, University of Pennsylvania, Philadelphia.

ZUNG, W. W. K. (1965). A self-rating depression scale. *Archives of General Psychiatry, 12,* 63–70.

15

Depressive Self-Schemas, Life Stress, and Vulnerability to Depression

Constance Hammen, Terry Marks, Arlene Mayol, and Robert deMayo

A vulnerability model of depression was tested by hypothesizing that depressogenic self-schemas that interact with schema-congruent negative life events will be associated with depression. Ninety-three college students were followed prospectively for four monthly assessments of both interview- and questionnaire-measured stressful life events, and clinical interview- and questionnaire-measured depression. An information-processing schema model of vulnerability was used to define subgroups of 46 dependent and 32 self-critical schematic individuals at the beginning of the study; the schema groups were based on clinical subtypes discussed both by Beck and by psychodynamically oriented theorists. As predicted, the dependent subgroup showed significantly stronger associations between depression and schema-relevant interpersonal life events than between depression and schema-irrelevant negative achievement events. The predicted opposite pattern for self-critical schematics was observed, but was less often statistically significant. The results are discussed in the terms of the need for integration of cognitive and life-stress models of depression.

Constance Hammen, Terry Marks, Arlene Mayol, and Robert deMayo. Depressive Self-Schemas, Life stress, and Vulnerability to Depression. *Journal of Abnormal Psychology*, 1985, Vol. 94, No. 3, pp. 308–319. Copyright © 1985 by the American Psychological Association. Reprinted by permission of the publisher and authors.

Depression research that integrates developments in life-stress approaches and cognitive approaches is virtually nonexistent, despite numerous calls for such efforts (e.g., Billings & Moos, 1982; Brown & Harris, 1978; Paykel, 1979; Warheit, 1979). Although life-stress research has become increasingly sophisticated in specifying depressive reactions to general classes of events such as those with negative impact (Brown & Harris, 1978; Paykel, 1979), correlations between measures of stress and depression remain modest, and clarification of the mechanisms of individual differences in responses has not been pursued vigorously. Meanwhile, the cognitive theories of depression that have been so productive in stimulating research (Abramson, Seligman, & Teasdale, 1978; Beck, Rush, Shaw, & Emery, 1979) have generally attended only indirectly to the ways in which such intraindividual mechanisms interact with stressful events to produce depression. It would appear to be time to integrate cognitive vulnerability mechanisms with stressful life-event properties to predict which persons become depressed under which stressful circumstances.

Recent developments in information processing and social cognition have been applied to depression and may be useful candidates in the search for depression vulnerability processes that interact with situational factors to produce depression. Research readily documents the link between affect and information processing (Bower, 1981; Isen, Shalker, Clark, & Karp, 1978), and the schema concept contributes the idea of enduring structures by which information is attended to, interpreted, stored, and retrieved (Fiske & Linville, 1980; Markus, 1977). As Kihlstrom and Nasby (1981) put it, "Schemata guide the individual's cognitive construction and reconstruction of specific percepts and memories, thereby influencing his or her behavior in that domain" (p. 293). As applied to depression, Kuiper and colleagues (Derry & Kuiper, 1981; Kuiper, Olinger, & MacDonald, 1988) and Teasdale and colleagues (Clark & Teasdale, 1982; Teasdale, 1983; Teasdale & Fogarty, 1979) have shown that depressed persons show facilitated recall of negative personal information, and the obverse occurs for nondepressed persons. However important such studies are for demonstrating the cognitive biasing effects due to depression, they share two limitations, to date, as indicators of vulnerability to depressive reactions to stressful life events. First, depressive cognition appears to be mood state dependent. Hammen, Miklowitz, and Dyck (in press) have found that longitudinal analyses of depressive self-schema responding (recall of negative personal information) reflect current mood; when no longer depressed, individuals' schema responding resembles that of stable nondepressed persons. These results agree with those of others who show that depressive responses to cognition questionnaires become nondepressed when the person is no longer depressed (e.g., Hamilton & Abramson, 1983; Lewinsohn, Steinmetz, Larson, & Franklin, 1981). The second difficulty with recent cognitive theories of depression is that the current information-processing approaches do not pursue a link with vulnerability to stressful life events.

What is needed, therefore, is a way to assess depression vulnerability schemas that is relatively independent of current mood. Moreover, the schema should have implications for vulnerability to specific stressful life events so that it is possible to predict that schema-consistent negative events will be associated with depression, whereas schema-inconsistent negative events will not. The present study attempted these goals. The method of schema assessment was based on Markus's (1977) original notion that availability in memory of behavioral examples of a construct may be used to index the strength of the schema. As Kihlstrom and Nasby (1981) pointed out, it is unlikely that schemas are fully represented in individuals' awareness, so that indirect techniques such as memory analysis may be needed. Thus, the relative accessibility of certain content in memory may be used to index presence of a schema that organizes the information and facilitates recall.

In the present study, methods of behavioral example recall were used to define schemas for *dependence* and *self-criticism*. There were several reasons for this choice of schema subtypes. First, they can be assessed independent of current mood. Second, and most theoretically important, they provide a hypothesized interaction with specific types of stressful life events. Recent work by Beck (e.g., Beck, 1982), and from an entirely different perspective by Blatt and colleagues (Blatt, D'Afflitti, & Quinlan, 1976; Blatt, Quinlan, Chevron, McDonald, & Zuroff, 1982) and Arieti and Bemporad (1980) hypothesize at least two major types of depressives: a dependent or sociotropic type especially responsive to negative events affecting interpersonal relationships, and a self-critical or autonomous type who responds with depression to negative events in the achievement domain.[1] It is speculated

---

[1] We do not intend to imply that these types are identical across the different theories or that the present study defines them entirely in the manner the original authors meant. Rather, we use these clinical theories as a general basis for defining our own schema subtypes for purposes of testing hypotheses about schema by event relations.

that dependent types derive their well-being and sense of self-worth from receiving support, understanding, and connection from others. Their primary orientation is toward seeking closeness and intimacy with other people, so that their self-concept may be particularly threatened by perceived rejection, loss, or abandonment in the interpersonal domain. Self-critical individuals derive their sense of self-worth through accomplishing goals in the achievement domain. Thus, their self-concept may be particularly threatened by perceived failure or goal frustration in the achievement realm. Therefore, information-processing schema theory was used to hypothesize a vulnerability mechanism whereby persons identified as relatively more schematic for dependency would experience negative interpersonal events as relatively more depressing than negative achievement events, and that relatively self-critical schematic persons would show the opposite pattern.

The present study additionally attempts to avoid three of the major methodological weaknesses of contemporary life-stress research. First, the design is a prospective one, involving definition of schema type at one point in time and then following individuals monthly over a 4-month period for depression status and occurrence of stressful life events. Many life-stress/depression studies rely on long-term retrospective reports of symptoms and event occurrence, thus obscuring the timing and accuracy of the data obtained. Thus, the present design improves the reliability and completeness of reported events by using brief reporting periods. Second, both questionnaire and interview assessment of stressful life events were obtained during the longitudinal period. It has been argued that exclusive reliance on questionnaire data may be confounded with mood and distress state, and such methods often include items that are themselves symptoms of depression. Therefore, we used questionnaire methods based on the carefully developed Psychiatric Epidemiology Research Interview Life Events Scale (PERI; Dohrenwend, Kransoff, Askenasy, & Doh-renwend, 1978) and others, and also used Brown's interview methods for assessing events in context so that their impact may be evaluated independent of the individual's subjective reaction to them (Brown & Harris, 1978). Third, reliance on questionnaire measures of mood status outcome has sometimes obscured the question of specificity of depressive reactions to stressors and their clinical significance. Therefore, both questionnaire and clinical interview methods of symptom assessment were used during the course of the study to evaluate specifically depressive outcomes and their clinical status.

As a final methodological note, we selected college students as the population for testing the present hypotheses for several reasons: They have relatively high rates of clinically significant depression (e.g., Hammen, 1980) and stress; they have relatively homogeneous demographic characteristics in terms of age, socioeconomic status, and marital status; and they share common stressors, so as to limit extreme variability in life conditions. Finally, their availability and willingness to cooperate in an extensive prospective study are essential.

Method

Participants

Ninety-four undergraduates were screened from 375 students in the Introductory Psychology research pool who participated in initial testing. The 94 were selected to represent an array of depressed and nondepressed students scoring high and low on the Beck Depression Inventory (BDI; Beck, Ward, Mendelson, Mock, & Erbaugh, 1961), to be studied prospectively over 5 months, spanning two academic quarters, on a variety of mood, clinical, experimental, and life-stress measures, only some of which are pertinent to the present study (See Hammen, Marks, de Mayo, & Mayol, 1984). Twenty-seven were men (29%) and 67 were women (71%); the majority were in their freshman year (70%), and their ethnic backgrounds mirrored that of the University of California, Los Angeles, as a whole: approximately 72% Caucasian, and the remainder distributed among Asian, Hispanic, and black groups.

Depression Status at Screening. As part of the initial screening, participants were given the BDI (Beck et al., 1961), a scale that has been shown to correlate highly with psychiatrist ratings of student depression (Bumberry, Oliver, & McClure, 1978) and with interviewer-administered Hamilton Rating Scale for Depression scores in a college sample (Hammen, 1980). Of the final sample of 94, 41 initially scored 14 or higher on the BDI ($M = 18.8$, $SD = 4.3$), placing them in the moderately depressed range, and the other 53 scored 7 or below ($M = 3.8$, $SD = 2.4$). This method of selection was not intended to identify an exclusively "depressive" subgroup, but rather one that would provide a diverse sample likely to include a range of depressive experiences over the prospective period.

Two to 3 weeks after initial screening, each participant was interviewed for diagnostic status, using the Schedule for Affective Disorders and Schizophrenia-Lifetime version (SADS —L; Endicott & Spitzer, 1978). Diagnostic decisions may be used to characterize the sample: .39 of the initially high BDI group had a current diagnosis of major, minor, or intermittent depression, whereas .04 of the initially nondepressed had a current diagnosis (both had a minor depression).

Assessment of Schema Subtypes

Within 2–4 weeks of the initial screening and again 2 months after that, participants were seen individually for assessment of schema subtypes. Procedures were modeled on methods described by Markus (1977), Teasdale, Taylor, and Fogarty (1980), and Bower (1981) for retrieval of information stored in memory. The assumption is made that schema-consistent information will be relatively accessible in memory compared with schema-noncongruent information

and can be used to index the strength of a schema for that information. Participants were given a booklet asking them to provide as many specific examples of events as they could recall that had happened to them in the past month with instructions to respond to each of the following:

1. Examples of times they had felt *bad* about themselves or the way their lives were going (example, "I got a bad grade on my chemistry midterm"),

2. Examples of times they had felt *good* about themselves or about the way their lives had been going (example, "got together with an old friend"),

3. Examples of times they felt helpless, rejected, or dependent on others for emotional needs (example, "when G. didn't call me after the holidays"), and

4. Examples of times they felt critical of themselves or guilty for something they did or did not do (example, "I didn't push myself hard enough in practice").

A separate page was provided for each of the four categories, and the pages were presented in counterbalanced order. Instructions and examples were provided by the experimenter to ensure that the forms were completed fully. Participants also completed the BDI at the conclusion of the session. Procedures for the second testing 2 months later were identical.

Classification of Schema Subtypes. For purposes of this research, schemas were operationally defined as a preponderance of a specific type of content across the four behavioral examples tasks. For each task, judges rated each example given for whether it contained interpersonal or achievement (or other) content. Items that involved another person or persons in a social context were considered interpersonal items, and those pertaining to academic, work, or other achievement situations were considered to be achievement events. Content themes were rated regardless of the negative or positive quality of the behavioral examples. Interrater reliability was determined on a subsample of 20 subjects, and independent judges achieved 93% agreement on interpersonal instances, and 100% on achievement, for an overall reliability of .97.

On the average, individuals provided three to four examples each of good and bad things that happened to them, and about two examples each of times they felt rejected/helpless and self-critical/guilty. After each behavioral example from memory was content coded, the ratio of the number of interpersonal to achievement items reported was determined for each of the four memory stimuli: times the person felt bad, good, helpless/rejected, and self-critical/guilty. Categorization as a dependent or self-critical schematic was operationally determined by comparing the number of the ratio scores greater than one (more interpersonal events than achievement events) and the numbers of ratio scores less than one (more achievement events than interpersonal events). If the person had more ratio scores above one than below one, she or he was classified as dependent, and if the reverse was true, as self-critical. If there were equal numbers of ratios above and below one, the person was considered mixed.

Prior work with self-schemas has shown that current mood state may strongly affect information retrieved from memory, and that, at least when requests are made for affectively colored memories such as positive and negative experiences, different information may be obtained when the same person is in a different mood (e.g., Clark & Teasdale, 1982; Hammen et al., 1984; Hammen et al., 1986). Therefore, it was important to determine the stability of schema classification over time, inasmuch as the schema concept as employed in the current research assumes that it is not dependent on the person's mood. The same schema task readministered approximately 2 months later was scored and classified identically. The reliability of the classifications of dependent, self-critical, or mixed at the two testings was determined by calculating weighted kappa (Cohen, 1968). The kappa coefficient was

.30 ($p<.001$), indicating modest but significant stability of classification, even though a subsample of 19 subjects displayed a notably different mood state at the two testings. Mood instability across the two testings was defined as a change in BDI scores of at least 5 points, which moved the person from the category of nondepressed (BDI < 10) to depressed (BDI > 9) or the reverse. A chi-square analysis comparing mood stability groups (change vs. no change) by classification stability across the two testings (same classification vs. different classification) was nonsignificant, $\chi^2(1) = 1.49, p > .05$. Overall, therefore, the classification procedure yielded relatively reliable categories over the two testings, and mood change did not appear to contribute significantly to changes in schema categorization.

In order to classify participants in the most reliable fashion possible, data from both the testings were employed. As with the individual classifications at the Time 1 and Time 2 testings, the final classification was determined by a preponderance in the eight ratio scores favoring either achievement or interpersonal content. Whereas .32 of all subjects were classified as mixed at one of the two testings, in the final determination only 10 were considered mixed, suggesting that more data points over the two testings permit clearer classification. These 10 were omitted from further analyses. There were 46 dependent schematics, and 32 self-critical schematics in the final sample. An additional 6 persons missed either the Time 1 or Time 2 schema procedure and were therefore not included. A chi-square analysis of the two schema groups by gender indicated no significant difference in the sex distributions of the groups, $\chi^2(1) = 0.19, p > .05$.

As a check on the classification based on data from the two testings, the groups were compared on the number of ratio scores that favored achievement, and those that favored social themes. As required by the classification system, the dependent schematics had significantly more interpersonal themes than did the self-critical schematics, $t(75) = 9.86, p < .001$, and their interpersonal themes exceeded their achievement themes, $t(45) = 11.88$, $p < .001$. Conversely, the self-critical schematics displayed more retrieval of achievement content circumstances than did the dependent schematics, $t(45) = 9.86$, $p < .001$, and their achievement themes exceeded their interpersonal themes, $t(30) = 7.16$, $p < .001$.

Follow-Up Assessment of Depression and Stressful Life Events

After the schema assessment procedure, once each month for 4 months following the screening and an initial diagnostic interview, participants completed a questionnaire packet (returned by mail) and a telephone interview. The questionnaire packets included a 120-item Life Events Survey (developed for this study). It was developed by combining a number of commonly used life-events lists: the Life Stress Inventory (Cochrane & Robertson, 1973), the PERI Life Events Scale (Dohrenwend et al., 1978), and the Life Experiences Survey (Sarason, Johnson, & Siegal, 1978). Items that might be confounded with depressive symptomatology were omitted. The major goal was to obtain an extensive list of events that would apply specifically to a college student population, and prove useful as a repeated measure of ongoing stressors. Subjects rated each item that had occurred in the last month on a 7-point degree-of-impact scale anchored at *extremely negative impact* and *extremely positive impact*. The packets also included the BDI.

The telephone interview included two portions: One was a diagnostic evaluation of any depressive episode occurring in the past month, using the Research Diagnostic Criteria (RDC; Spitzer & Endicott, 1975), and the other, a life-events assessment covering the past month.

Diagnostic Evaluation. For aspects of the project that were not relevant to the present study, participants had received a full diagnostic assessment using the SADS–L (Endicott & Spitzer, 1978; Spitzer & Endi-

cott, 1975). The SADS–L is a structured interview format based on the RDC that has been shown to be highly reliable for current and past psychiatric status. In preparation for such interviewing, the project staff of clinical psychology graduate students completed a 3-month training program that also included training interviews on undergraduates who were similar to those selected for the study. A reliability study based on 32 cases in the training phase yielded 100% agreement between independent rater pairs for current primary diagnosis. During the present study, a separate reliability study with independent raters on 30 cases yielded an overall kappa coefficient of .93 for current diagnoses, and 98% agreement within one scale point on SADS-based extracted Hamilton scores for depression severity. The monthly follow-up interviews followed a similar format and were typically conducted by the same person who did the initial SADS–L, so that we have every confidence that the telephone interviews yielded reliable RDC diagnoses.

Life-Stress Interview An interview format for assessing event occurrence and contextual threat was developed based on Brown's methods (Brown & Harris, 1978; Costello, 1982). The goal is to elicit sufficient information about each of several areas of life functioning to be able to evaluate event occurrence and its date and context, regardless of the person's own emotional reaction to it. All relevant background information is elicited, and a detailed written report is completed by the interviewer. Participants made a subjective threat rating on a 4-point scale (from *no threat* to *severe threat*) for each circumstance. Each follow-up interview covered the past month. The written descriptions of each event, with any of the participants' subjective reactions excluded, were evaluated by a rating team unaware of the subject's status. The team made ratings of objective short-term and long-term threat on the 4-point scale, based on assessment of the context in which this event occurred. The team also rated whether an event would most likely be considered objectively positive, negative, or ambiguous, and whether the event's occurrence was probably independent of the subject, probably dependent on the subject, or ambiguous (possibly both dependent and independent). For analyses of reliability of these ratings, two separate teams independently rated all the events for each follow-up interview. The overall kappa coefficients between teams' ratings were .79 for short-term threat, .84 for long-term threat, and .75 for independence rating, all highly significant.

Attrition.   Across the follow-up evaluations, only one person missed more than one interview. Because he had also missed one of the schema assessments, he was dropped from analyses. Of the mail (questionnaire) follow-ups, 87% were completed, and the majority of participants (55 of 78 in the final schema sample) completed all of the follow-ups. In order to maintain the largest possible sample sizes for data analyses, missing data points for each individual were filled by assigning the average value of the person's available scores for each variable.

Dependent Variables for Follow-Up Period

Depression Status.   There were three possible depression outcome variables. One was mean BDI score across the four follow-ups. A second was number of times the BDI score reached 14 or above over the 4 months (ranging from 0–4 times). This was included as a measure of consistency of mood, because a simple mean BDI could reflect extreme but inconsistent changes. A third measure was the number of times in the four follow-ups the person met the RDC for possible major or minor depression (ranging from 0–4 times). This was included to assess the clinical syndrome of depression rather than the particularly subjective symptoms assessed by the BDI. Note that this is not a measure of number of discrete episodes for those with depression lasting more than one month, but is rather the number of months

during which criteria were met for a diagnosis.

Life-events scores were computed separately for questionnaire and interview sources. All negative impact events (those rated by subjects on the negative end of the scale) were totaled across the four monthly follow-ups for each person. Event totals are reported, rather than subjectively weighted scores, because recent research has shown unit weighting to be highly comparable empirically to either subjective weights or "life change unit" weights and, also, relatively freer of the potential confounding of independent (event impact) and dependent (distress outcome) variables. The number of negative interpersonal and negative achievement events was computed according to event item numbers (e.g., all events covering work and academic life were considered achievement, whereas those covering family, social, and romantic relationships were considered interpersonal). Items covering health, finances, accidents, and other miscellany were omitted from these classifications.

Similar procedures were followed in classifying interview-assessed events. The rating team had given each event an item number that best corresponded to the same event on the Life Events Survey.

Results
Overall Characteristics of Schema Groups

Table 1 presents the descriptive characteristics of the schema groups in terms of depression and experience of stressful life events. No systematic differences were predicted, and statistical analyses of the depression scores of the two groups indicated no significant differences in levels of depression, either at the initial schema assessment or during the follow-up. There was a tendency of the self-critical group to report more diagnosable depressions during the follow-up

TABLE 1 Characteristics of Schema Groups

Measure	Group	
	Dependent	Self-Critical
Depression variables		
BDI at first schema assessment		
M	7.37	6.16
SD	7.88	5.96
Mean BDI across follow-ups		
M	5.63	5.82
SD	6.32	6.17
Mean number diagnoses across follow-ups		
M	0.39	0.75
SD	0.77	1.01
Negative life events[a]		
Interview total		
M	3.34	3.94
SD	2.56	2.79
Achievement		
M	1.04	1.48
SD	1.40	1.43
Interpersonal		
M	1.58	1.39
SD	1.87	1.35
Questionnaire total		
M	10.99	10.03
SD	13.30	7.29
Achievement		
M	3.33	3.95
SD	4.48	3.91
Interpersonal		
M	4.81	3.52
SD	6.15	2.83

Note. Dependent group *n* = 46; self-critical *n* = 32. BDI = Beck Depression Inventory.
[a]Summed across four follow-ups. Totals are not the sum of interpersonal and achievement events because other classes of negative events are included in totals. Inclusion is based on participants' subjective rating of negative impact.

period, but the effect was not significant, $t(76) = 1.78, p = .08$.

In terms of reported negative life events during the follow-up, the two groups did not differ significantly on total events or on interpersonal and achievement events, whether assessed by interview or questionnaire.

Depression as a Function of Schema Type and Event Type

The central hypothesis of the study was that depressive outcomes would be more strongly associated with schema-congruent negative events than with schema-incongruent negative events. This hypothesis was examined first with data from the follow-up interviews and then with data from the follow-up questionnaires.

The hypothesis was tested with a series of Pearson correlations for each group between depression measures and event measures, which are presented in Table 2. The significance of differences in correlations between independent groups was tested to examine the magnitude of correlations between depression and achievement events for each group, and between depression and interpersonal events for each group. One-tailed tests were employed because directional predictions were specified. Next, within-group correlations were compared, using the LISREL V procedure (Jöreskog & Sörbom, 1981) to test the equality of correlations of depression with achievement and interpersonal events.

The interview-elicited negative life-event data indicate clearly that dependent schematics show a stronger association between depression and interpersonal events than do the self-critical schematics, achieving statistically significant differences on two of the three depression measures. The dependent schematics also show significantly stronger correlations between depression and interpersonal events than between depression and achievement events; all of the within-group comparisons were statistically significant. The self-critical schematics displayed stronger correlations between depression and achievement events than did the dependent schematics on all the measures of depression, as predicted, with the difference

TABLE 2 Correlations between Depression and Event Types by Schema Group

| | Group | | |
	Dependent	Self-critical	Between-group Comparison
	Life-stress interview		
Mean BDI across follow-ups			
Achievement events	−.01	.31	$z = 1.38$, *ns*
Interpersonal events	.48	.09	$z = 1.80$, $p < .05$
	$\chi^2(1) = 6.37$, $p = .01$[a]	$\chi^2(1) < 1$	
BDI > 14 across follow-ups[b]			
Achievement events	−.10	.51	$z = 2.76$, $p < .01$
Interpersonal events	.41	−.08	$z = 2.15$, $p < .05$
	$\chi^2(1) = 6.94$, $p < .01$	$\chi^2(1) = 6.83$, $p < .01$	
Diagnosable depressions across follow-ups[c]			
Achievement events	−.16	.21	$z < 1$, *ns*
Interpersonal events	.53	.48	$z < 1$, *ns*
	$\chi^2(1) = 13.65$, $p < .001$	$\chi^2(1) = 1.31$, *ns*	
	Life-events questionnaire		
Mean BDI across follow-ups			
Achievement events	.55	.38	$z < 1$, *ns*
Interpersonal events	.65	.23	$z = 2.25$, $p < .05$
	$\chi^2(1) < 1$, *ns*	$\chi^2(1) < 1$, *ns*	
BDI > 14 across follow-ups			
Achievement events	.48	.42	$z = 1$, *ns*
Interpersonal events	.62	.32	$z = 1.65$, $p = .05$
	$\chi^2(1) = 2.05$, $p > .10$	$\chi^2(1) < 1$, *ns*	
Diagnosable depressions across follow-ups			
Achievement events	.22	.03	$z < 1$, *ns*
Interpersonal events	.44	.16	$z = 1.30$, *ns*
	$\chi^2(1) = 5.24$, $p = .02$	$\chi^2(1) < 1$, *ns*	

Note. Dependent group $n = 46$; self-critical group $n = 32$. BDI = Beck Depression Inventory.
[a]Hypotheses regarding the equality of the within-group correlations were tested using the LISREL V procedure (Jöreskog & Sörbom, 1981). A significant chi-square permits rejection of the null hypothesis of equality of the correlations.
[b]The actual distribution of elevated BDI scores across the follow-ups was as follows: .77 had none, .11 had one, .05 had two, and .035 each had 3 and 4 elevations, respectively.
[c]The following distributions of major or minor diagnosable depression across the follow-ups were observed: .67 had none, .19 had one, .10 had two, 0.35 had 3, and .01 had 4.

achieving statistical significance on the measure of number of BDI elevations. Similarly, the within-group comparisons showed stronger correlations as predicted between depression and achievement events than between depression and interpersonal events on two of the three depression measures, and the effect was significant for the number of BDI elevations.

With regard to the questionnaire measure of negative events, the dependent schematics showed the predicted higher correlations of depression and interpersonal events than those displayed by the self-critical schematics; two of the three between-groups comparisons were statistically significant. Also as predicted, the dependent schematics showed stronger correlations between depression and interpersonal events than between depression and achievement events, with the effect reaching statistical significance on two of the three comparisons. The self-critical schematics, on the other hand, had higher correlations for achievement events than for interpersonal events on two of the three depression measures, but the effects were not significant. Also, they did not display the expected stronger correlations between depression and achievement events than those shown by the dependent schematics.

Because 24 significance tests are presented in Table 2 that are not entirely independent of one another, it is appropriate to adjust the test-wise alpha level to reduce the probability of Type I errors. One such method would divide .05 by three significance tests within each of several groups of comparisons (e.g., 4 sets of three comparisons within each schema group by life-event method across depression measures; 4 sets of three comparisons between schema groups on event type across depression measures by life-event method). The resulting alpha value of .0167 results in support for the hypotheses concerning the dependent schematics, and some support for hypotheses about self-critical groups. The findings hold for the interview method, but not the questionnaire method, of assessing life events.

Mechanisms of Schema Action

Although the design of the study does not permit explication of the manner in which schemas may interact with events to produce depression, several issues were explored. First, is there a simple quantitative effect, such that more schema-consistent negative events occur that might eventuate in depression? Second, is there a qualitative effect, such that schema-consistent events are highly personally "loaded" and given high subjective threat ratings, and that depression corresponds to the subjective appraisal of upset? A third possibility is that persons in schema subgroups "cause" schema-consis-

tent events to occur. Fourth, are the reports of schema-consistent events biased, such that schema-congruent events may be more salient and recalled better, thus producing spurious correlations with depression?

Quantity of Schema-consistent Events. As noted in the descriptive information presented in Table 1, there were no significant differences between schema groups in their reports of achievement and interpersonal events. The dependent schematics reported more interpersonal events than achievement events, and the difference was statistically significant for the questionnaire-assessed events, $t(45 = 2.58, p = .01$, but not significant for interview-assessed events, $t(45) = 1.65, p = .10$, two-tailed. The self-critical schematics, on the other hand, reported more achievement than interpersonal events but the differences were nonsignificant.

Subjective Appraisal of Events. It might be predicted that schemas would lead to the assessment of schema-consistent events as relatively more upsetting. Individuals' mean subjective threat ratings for negative interpersonal and achievement events were compared across schema subtypes, as well as within subtypes. The groups did not differ significantly on appraisals of negative achievement or interpersonal events for either the questionnaire or interview-based data. Also, within-subjects comparisons of achievement and interpersonal mean impact ratings were nonsignificant for each schema group, although both groups tended to appraise interpersonal events more negatively than achievement events. Thus, there was no support for the idea that schemas may induce a bias in appraisal of threat that is specific to schema-consistent events.

Do Schemas "Cause" Events to Occur? Judges' ratings of the independence/ dependence of event occurrence based on the contextual threat interviews permitted analyses of whether schema-congruent events may have been relatively more likely caused in part by qualities of the person. The proportions of achievement negative events and interpersonal negative events that were considered independent of the person or which were considered possibly dependent (a mixture of independent and dependent) were evaluated. The third category of independence, events judged to be entirely caused by the person's behavior or characteristics, was omitted from analyses because it was extremely rare.

The two schema groups did not differ significantly on their proportions of events judged to be independent in causation, whether interpersonal or achievement events. Also, the groups did not differ in their proportions of achievement and interpersonal events judged to be possibly dependent (mixed). Within-group analyses showed that both groups reported that more of their interpersonal events were judged to be independent in occurrence than were achievement events ($p < .01$); the obverse was that both groups reported that more of their possibly dependent events had achievement than interpersonal content. On the whole, therefore, there was no evidence of content-specific patterns of event causation.

Recall Accuracy of Schema-consistent Events. An analysis was conducted to learn if recall accuracy is affected by event content; that is, does the schema enhance recall of schema-consistent events compared to schema inconsistent events? A separate study on half the sample had been conducted on recall accuracy by comparing subjects' and informants' (usually the roommate) reports of events for the subject in the past month. The reliabilities of interview-assessed events for the dependent and self-critical groups were compared for their interpersonal and achievement events. The kappa coefficients were .39 ($p < .05$) for achievement events and .43 ($p < .01$) for interpersonal events in the dependent group. For the self-critical group comparable figures were .41 ($p < .01$) and .37 ($p < .01$). Thus, there were no overall differences in recall accuracy within groups. However, the kap-

pas were somewhat modest, even though significant, and it may be that schema-enhanced recall is a more subtle process not captured in the present analyses.

Discussion

The results of the study provide some support for the utility of a schema by negative event approach to depression/vulnerability. The research is the first we know that provides data to test a frequently hypothesized association between cognitive vulnerability and stressful life-event characteristics. The research brings together two heretofore independent lines of investigation of depression. Using a schema conceptualization for defining and assessing common clinical subtypes of depression, it was predicted in advance that certain persons would experience more depression when they experienced negative interpersonal events than negative achievement events, whereas other individuals were predicted to show the opposite pattern. The correlations obtained in the present longitudinal study offer preliminary support for the predictions.

The results that were obtained offered stronger support for hypotheses regarding the association between depression and interpersonal events for the dependent schematics than for the hypotheses regarding the self-critical group. Fewer statistically significant associations between depression and achievement-related events were observed for self-critical schematics. One possible explanation is that the smaller sample size for this group resulted in a less sensitive test of hypotheses. Another possibility is that participants' student status rendered academic events highly salient and also more normative across both schema groups, thereby reducing the strength of results for the self-critical group. A non-student sample may be necessary for a more distinct achievement schema group where such experiences centrally define the sense of self. Results also indicated greater support for hypotheses when interview assessment of life events was employed, with far less support with questionnaire events. We suspect that this pattern stems from differences in the accuracy and reliability of the two methods. The questionnaire method tended to elicit multiple responses to what was essentially aspects of the same event, whereas the interview method permitted classification of the core event only. This "inflation" of events may have been more pronounced for interpersonal content for both groups, inasmuch as there were more such items on the questionnaire. It must also be considered that more subjects missed questionnaire follow-ups than interviews, so that their event counts, which included their mean scores entered for missing values, were less accurate. Finally, it should be noted that the results are attenuated when a more conservative alpha level is used to adjust for the large number of comparisons. Replications of this work are clearly warranted in order to increase confidence in the reliability of the findings.

Previously, the life-events research domain has generally yielded weak but significant correlation between events and depressive outcome. It may now be speculated that the usual concept of stress is too vague and the typical procedure of giving equal weight to schema-congruent and schema-incongruent events in correlations with depression serves to diminish overall correlations. Several life-stress researchers have explicitly assigned a role to individual perception of events. Brown (Brown & Harris, 1978) cogently argued for the role of individual *meaning* in predicting the impact of negative events. However, for all practical purposes, his concept of meaning has been synonymous with objective impact, and other investigators have not explored *meaning* empirically at all. We use a schema model in which meaning is operationalized in terms of individuals' appraisals of events as making them feel helpless/dependent or self-critical/guilty. We suggest that further efforts toward differentiating event impact in terms of individuals' typical ways of con-

structing it may provide more precise methods of evaluating the stressfulness of events.

Most cognitive mediation theories of depression, on the other hand, have paid scant attention to event occurrence or characteristics, focusing nearly exclusively on intraindividual processes such as depressive cognitive styles or "distortions." We suggest that the concept of depressive causal analyses or distorted interpretations need not necessarily be invoked, or even if germane to a particular type of event does not necessarily apply across all negative situations. Rather, individuals appear to have, for the most part, domains of functioning that are relatively more and less vulnerable to the stimulation of depressive experiences. This concept is not new; Beck and Seligman and colleagues (e.g., Abramson et al., 1978) have alluded to such a process, but have not explicitly integrated evaluation of stressful events into their empirical studies. Moreover, previous work on depression vulnerability has used measures of depressive cognition that appear to be symptoms or concomitants (Kuiper et al., 1988) of depression that change significantly when persons are no longer depressed (Hamilton & Abramson, 1983; Hammen et al., 1984; Lewinsohn et al., 1981). The present method of assessing vulnerability content schemas offers promise for measuring relatively stable themes that have implications for impinging stressful events.

The present results are interpreted in information-processing terms. The schema process implies that schema-consistent events are especially likely to be meaningful, attended to, evaluated in terms of implications for well-being, stored in memory, and accessible in recall. For instance, we may speculate that for a dependent schematic person, interpersonal events are more salient, likely to be appraised as making the person feel good, or if negative, feel rejected and helpless, and because of their salience in memory, serve as the basis for self-concept and predictions about the future. However, the present study yielded no direct evidence bearing on the specific mechanisms by which schemas may be associated with depression outcomes. Further research is needed to clarify this process.

The subtypes that were employed in the present work warrant comment. The types were drawn largely from commonly discussed clinical subtypes of depressives, such as those characterized by Beck (1982), Blatt et al. (1976, 1982) and Arieti and Bemporad (1980). As noted, our current operationalization of the types is not meant to be a direct representation of any of these investigators' types. The work of Blatt and colleagues may be most similar; they have used a Depressive Experience Questionnaire to characterize dependent, self-critical, and efficacious subtypes, and have shown that clinical judges were able to accurately predict the classification of 56% of patients based on clinical records of certain symptomatology, early childhood experiences, and life situations. However, precipitating life events were only one factor taken into consideration. Their psychodynamic perspective is in many ways compatible with the current one, although their view places more emphasis on speculations about the origin of maladaptive coping experiences than on the cognitive mechanisms of perceiving current stressors.

Finally, although the results represent a promising beginning step in building the complex cognition-event model of depression that has often been speculated about but rarely pursued systematically, limitations need to be noted. The correlational nature of our data linking stress and depression are acknowledged. Although the schema data were collected before the events occurred, the direction of causality between events and depression remains a matter of speculation. Generalizations to other populations besides young adult college students and to the clinically depressed need to be demonstrated rather than assumed. Also, the specificity of the schema-event relation for depression has not been demonstrated; it is possible that other psychopathological outcomes besides depression also occur. We have acknowledged that there are certainly other ways to assess and categorize schema subtypes; indeed, the present methods are rather gross and unrefined, including behavioral examples that were mixtures of minute incidents, daily hassles, and ongoing strains. An ideal schema-assessment procedure might attempt to avoid overlap between such procedures and event-assessment methods. However, the current procedures did not simply involve the recreation of the schema classification method during the life-event assessment because the majority of items on the schema recall task were not items on the life-event schedule. The event-classification system employed here was also unrefined, relying on general item content and ignoring the possibility that there are achievement aspects of interpersonal events, and interpersonal aspects of achievement events. Our methods relied on telephone interviews that were based on measures shown to be reliable but the actual effect of non-face-to-face interviewing is unknown. Also the interviewer conducted both the diagnostic evaluation and life-stress assessment, although she or he was unaware of the schema status of the participant and unaware of the schema hypotheses. Finally, we feel that it is also important to mention that a complete model of depression will need to include additional psychosocial factors such as coping resources and responses, social resources, and chronic stressors that are beyond the scope of the present work (e.g., Billings, Cronkite, & Moos, 1983). Despite these limitations, the present data are an encouraging beginning in pursuit of the process by which individual vulnerability encountering negative events may lead to depression.

References

Abramsom, L., Seligman, M., and Teasdale, J. (1978). Learned helplessness in humans: Critique and reformulation. *Journal of Abnormal Psychology, 87,* 49–75.

Arieti, S., and Bemporad, J. (1980). The psychological organization of depression. *American Journal of Psychiatry, 136,* 1369–1365.

BECK, A. T. (1982). Cognitive therapy of depression: New perspectives. In P. Clayton and J. Barrett (Eds.), *Treatment of depression: Old controversies and new approaches* (pp. 265–290). New York: Raven Press.

BECK, A., RUSH, A., SHAW, B., AND EMERY, G. (1979). *Cognitive therapy of depression.* New York: Guilford Press.

BECK, A., WARD, C., MENDELSON, M., MOCK, J., AND ERBAUGH, J. (1961). An inventory for measuring depression. *Archives of General Psychiatry, 4,* 53–63.

BILLINGS, A., CRONKITE, R., AND MOOS, R. (1983). Social-environmental factors in unipolar depression: Comparisons of depressed patients and nondepressed controls. *Journal of Abnormal Psychology, 92,* 119–133.

BILLINGS, A., AND MOOS, R. (1982). Psychosocial theory and research on depression: An integrative framework and review. *Clinical Psychology Review, 2,* 213–237.

BLATT, S., D'AFFLITTI, J., AND QUINLAN, D. (1976). Experiences of depression in normal young adults. *Journal of Abnormal Psychology, 85,* 383–389.

BLATT, S., QUINLAN, D., CHEVRON, E., McDONALD, C., AND ZUROFF, D. (1982). Dependency and self-criticism: Psychological dimensions of depression. *Journal of Consulting and Clinical Psychology, 59,* 113–124.

BOWER, G. (1981). Mood and memory. *American Psychologist, 36,* 129–148.

BROWN, G., AND HARRIS, T. (1978). *Social origins of depression: A study of psychiatric disorder in women.* New York: Free Press.

BUMBERRY, W., OLIVER, J., AND McCLURE, J. (1978). Validation of the Beck Depression Inventory in a university population using psychiatric estimate as the criterion. *Journal of Consulting and Clinical Psychology, 46,* 150–155.

CLARK, D. M., AND TEASDALE, J. D. (1982). Diurnal variation in clinical depression and accessibility of memories of positive and negative experiences. *Journal of Abnormal Psychology, 91,* 87–95.

COCHRANE, R., AND ROBERTSON, A. (1973). The Life Events Inventory: A measure of the relative severity of psychosocial stressors. *Journal of Psychosomatic Research, 17,* 135–139.

COHEN, J. (1968). Weighted kappa: Nominal scale agreement with provision for scaled disagreement or partial credit. *Psychological Bulletin, 70,* 213–220.

COSTELLO, C. (1982). Social factors associated with depression: A retrospective community study. *Psychological Medicine, 12,* 329–339.

DERRY, P., AND KUIPER, N. (1981). Schematic processing and self reference in clinical depression. *Journal of Abnormal Psychology, 90,* 286–297.

DOHRENWEND, B. S, KRANSOFF, L., ASKENASY, A., AND DOHRENWEND, B. P. (1978). Exemplification of a method for scaling life events: The PERI Life Events Scale. *Journal of Health and Social Behavior, 19,* 205–229.

ENDICOTT, J., AND SPITZER, R. (1978). A diagnostic interview: The Schedule of Affective Disorders and Schizophrenia. *Archives of General Psychiatry, 35,* 837–844.

FISKE, S., AND LINVILLE, P. (1980). What does the schema process buy us? *Personality and Social Psychology Bulletin, 6,* 543–557.

HAMILTON, E., AND ABRAMSON, L. (1983). Cognitive patterns and major depressive disorder: A longitudinal study in a hospital setting. *Journal of Abnormal Psychology, 92,* 173–184.

HAMMEN, C. L. (1980). Depression in college students: Beyond the Beck Depression Inventory. *Journal of Consulting and Clinical Psychology, 48,* 126–128.

HAMMEN, C., MARKS, T., DeMAYO, R., AND MAYOL, A. (1984). *Self-schemas and risk for depression: A prospective study.* Manuscript submitted for publication.

HAMMEN, C., MIKLOWITZ, D., AND DYCK, D. (1986). Stability and severity parameters of depressive self-schema responding. *Journal of Social and Clinical Psychology, 41,* 23–45.

ISEN, A., SHALKER, T., CLARK, M., AND KARP, L. (1978). Affect, accessibility of material in memory, and behavior: A cognitive loop? *Journal of Personality and Social Psychology, 36,* 1–12.

JÖRESKOG, K.G., AND SÖRBOM, D. (1981). *Analysis of linear structural relationships by maximum likelihood and least squares methods: User's guide.* Chicago: International Educational Services.

KIHLSTOM, J. F., AND NASBY, W. (1981). Cognitive tasks in clinical assessment: An exercise in applied psychology. In P.C. Kendall and S.D. Hollon (Eds.), *Assessment strategies for cognitive-behavioral interventions* (pp. 287–318). New York: Academic Press.

KUIPER, N. A., OLINGER, L. J., AND MacDONALD, M. R. (1988). Depressive schemata and the processing of personal and social information. In L. Alloy (Ed.), *Cognitive processes in depression.* New York: Guilford.

LEWINSOHN, P., STEINMETZ, J., LARSON, D., AND FRANKLIN, J. (1981). Depression-related cognitions: Antecedent or consequence? *Journal of Abnormal Psychology, 90,* 213–219.

MARKUS, H. (1977). Self-schemata and processing of information about the self. *Journal of Personality and Social Psychology, 35,* 63–78.

PAYKEL, E. S. (1979). Recent life events in the development of the depressive disorders. In R.A. Depue (Ed.), *The psychobiology of the depressive disorders: Implications for the effects of stress.* New York: Academic Press.

SARASON, I. G., JOHNSON, J. H., AND SIEGAL, J. M. (1978). Assessing the impact of life changes: Development of the life experiences survey. *Journal of Consulting and Clinical Psychology, 46,* 932–946.

SPITZER, R. L., AND ENDICOTT, J. (1975). *Schedule for Affective Disorders and Schizophrenia (SADS)* (2nd ed.). New York: New York State Psychiatric Institute, Biometrics Research.

TEASDALE, J. (1983). Negative thinking in depression: Cause, effect, or reciprocal relationship? *Advances in Behavior Research and Therapy, 5,* 3–25.

TEASDALE, J., AND FOGARTY, S. (1979). Differential effects of induced mood on retrieval of pleasant and unpleasant memories from episodic memory. *Journal of Abnormal Psychology, 88,* 248–257.

TEASDALE, J., TAYLOR, R., AND FOGARTY, S. (1980). Effects of induced elation-depression on the accessibility of memories of happy and unhappy experiences. *Behavior Research and Therapy, 18,* 339–346.

WARHEIT, G. (1979). Life events, coping, stress, and depressive symptomatology. *American Journal of Psychiatry, 136,* 502–507.

16

An Integrative Theory of Depression

Peter M. Lewinsohn, Harry Hoberman, Linda Teri, and Martin Hautzinger

Introduction

Over the last 15 years there has been a dramatic proliferation of theories of the etiology of depression. Contemporary theories of depression generally postulate a unitary and linear mechanism that is assumed to be causal of depression. According to these theories, if a given phenomenon (X) is present, an episode of depression should occur; that is, X is sufficient and necessary for the occurrence of depression. In part, the variety of theoretical models reflects the heterogeneity of the symptomatology of depressed individuals, with different theorists emphasizing different dimensions of the depressive experience as being critical to the onset of the disorder.

Currently, the most influential theoretical approaches in the etiology of depression may roughly be divided into the following emphases: reinforcement, interpersonal interaction, cognitions, and biochemical factors. Early models of depression based on reinforcement include those of Skinner (1953),

Peter M. Lewinsohn, Harry Hoberman, Linda Teri, and Martin Hautzinger. An Integrative Theory of Depression. In S. Reiss and R. R. Bootzin (Eds.). *Theoretical Issues in Behavior Therapy*. New York: Academic Press, 1985, pp. 331–359. Copyright © 1985 by Academic Press, Inc. Reprinted by permission.

Ferster (1965), and Lazarus (1968). Lewinsohn (1975; Lewinsohn, Weinstein, and Shaw, 1969) places the focus of causality on the quality of an individual's interactions with his or her environment; a decrease in response-contingent reinforcement (a decrease in pleasant events or an increase in unpleasant events) is assumed to lead to dysphoria, which is seen as the key manifestation of depression. McLean (1976), Coyne (1976b), and Weissman and her associates (Klerman & Weissman, 1982; Weissman & Paykel, 1974) emphasize the importance of interpersonal interactions and relationships. Cognitive perspectives of depression are represented by the writings of Beck (1967; Beck, Rush, Shaw, & Emery, 1979), Ellis and Harper (1961), Rehm (1977), and Seligman (1975), who suggest that depression results from negative cognitive structures that distort an individual's experience in a negative manner. Seligman emphasizes a perceived lack of control over the environment and aspects of the individual's attributional style in the onset of depression (Abramson, Seligman, & Teasdale, 1978). Ellis and Harper (1961) hypothesize that individual's irrational beliefs cause them to overreact emotionally to situations and to become depressed. Rehm (1977), and Kanfer and Hagerman (1981) view the concept of self-control as critical, so that depression is related to the manner in which people self-monitor, evaluate, and reward their behavior.

Biochemical theories of depression have focused on changes in the levels of neurotransmitters in areas of the brain subserving emotionality, sleep regulation, and motor activity. Thus, Schildkraut (1965), Bunney and Davis (1965) and Schildkraut and Kety (1967) advanced the biogenic amine hypothesis. According to this hypothesis, depression is associated with a functional deficit of one or more neurotransmitter amines at critical synapses in the central nervous system.

Clearly, a rich and varied collection of theories of unipolar depression have been proposed, and for each some supportive experimental evidence exists. (A complete review of research findings for the different psychosocial theories is presented in Blaney [1977]; Doerfler [1981]; and Lewinsohn, Teri, & Hoberman [1982].) Biochemical theories are reviewed in Sachar (1975) and Zis and Goodwin (1982). However, it seems fair to say that in any given study the theoretical predictions have accounted for only a relatively small proportion of the total variance. Moreover, many of these studies suffer from serious methodological problems (Blaney, 1977; Doerfler, 1981; Eastman, 1976). Perhaps most importantly, causal relationships have rarely been tested, let alone proven. The experimental research on depression has relied almost exclusively on studies that examine the covariation of depression level with theory-indicated variables. For example, while characteristic thought and behavior patterns have been shown to be associated with depression (e.g., Lewinsohn, Steinmetz, Larson, & Franklin, 1981), it is impossible to know whether these correlational findings are of etiological significance. Certain critical phenomena may indeed precede the onset of depression, and in some way contribute to its occurrence, but it is equally possible that the cognitive and behavioral changes are in fact the consequences of being depressed. From the point of view of developing an accurate understanding of the etiology of depression, the current state of affairs is tantalizing but confusing.

Two interrelated steps would seem to be necessary in order to obtain greater clarity about the etiology of depression. The first would involve a change in research methodology. While considerable progress has been made in the delineation of the psychological abnormalities associated with depression, most of these findings are based on studies of people who are already depressed. Consequently, it is impossible to determine whether the distinguished characteristics of depressives antedate or result from the disorder. As several writers have pointed out (e.g., Hirschfeld & Cross, 1982; Lloyd, 1980) longitudinal, prospective studies are essential for understanding whether variables are antecedents, concomitants, or consequences of depression. It is abundantly clear that a number of factors do covary with depression; the issue now is to identify the temporal, if not causal, relationship between these factors and depressive disorders. The second step would involve a change in the conceptualization of the nature of etiological agents in psychopathology. As already discussed, most theorists have consistently advocated unidimensional, linear models of depressive onset. Such an approach to conceptualizing the causation of disorders, mental or physical, has been criticized on a number of accounts by contemporary epidemiologists; there is a substantial body of empirical evidence and theoretical justification that suggests that disorders have more than one cause (Kleinbaum, Kupper, & Morganstern, 1982). Further, writers such as Susser (1966) have suggested that the most common causes of pathological conditions may be contributory, not necessary, nor by themselves, sufficient. By accepting a multidetermined model of depression, theorists would thereby allow for a synthesis of the variety of factors shown to be associated with depression.

More multifaceted theoretical statements on the etiology of depression have been presented. Foremost among these writers have been Akiskal and McKinney (1973, 1975). In a series of papers, Akiskal and McKinney have suggested that all of the different theoretically privileged variables (chemical, experiential, and behavioral) can be seen to induce depression by affecting a common pathway perhaps in the diencephalon.

Akiskal and McKinney's view would seem to be that all of the depression theorists may be right, with a heterogeneity of causes producing the same end result, namely a depressive episode. Billings and Moos (1982) have also proposed an integrative framework for summarizing the available data on depression. They too emphasize a multiplicity of causes in the onset of depression and view depression as resulting from the interplay of stressors, personal and environmental resources, and an individual's appraisal and coping responses to the specific stressor. A somewhat different view of the causation of depression has been postulated by Craighead (1981). While agreeing with the two aforementioned groups of theorists as to the multiplicity of etiological factors in depression, Craighead also suggests that it may be more clinically useful to view the end result of the depressive process as polydimensional rather than unitary. Thus, the different phenomenological dimensions of depression may each have their own causes and etiological patterns. This conceptualization implies that there may well be subtypes of depressives who correspond to the variety of causal factors indicated by the various theories of depression, for example, negative cognition depressives, low positive reinforcement depressives, learned helplessness depressives, and so on. Although these integrative perspectives on depression differ somewhat from one another, they represent important contributions to a more sophisticated understanding of the etiology of depression.

Although these more recent theoretical statements represent important contributions, they also possess certain limitations. To begin with, they are far more descriptive than explanatory. While these theories suggest that theoretically privileged variables can and should be integrated with one another, they fail to provide an adequate explanation of how such variables might interact with one another and what the nature of the etiological mechanisms might be. Further, these theories fail to show how the multiple-cause models account for the diverse phenomena and findings known about depression.

The purpose of this article is severalfold. First, an attempt is made to identify the significant research findings on depression that an adequate theory of depression needs to be able to explain. Second, a new theory of the etiology of depression is presented which attempts to provide an explanation of the environmental and personal mechanisms that interact to produce an episode of depression. Finally, the heuristic value of the new theory in explaining the various findings about depression are explored.

Key Findings Any Theory of Depression Should Explain

Perhaps the primary value of a theoretical model for depression is to provide a cohesive and internally consistent framework for integrating the available knowledge about depression and to generate new and testable hypotheses. Our current theorizing is heavily influenced by certain findings that we feel have especially important theoretical implications. These include

1. The symptom heterogeneity of depression.

2. The centrality of dysphoria in depression.

3. The multiplicity of the behavioral and cognitive changes that are associated with depression.

4. The high prevalence (point and lifetime) and incidence of depression in the general population.

5. The relationship between age and the prevalence of depression.

6. The elevated prevalence of depression in females and in persons who have had a previous episode of depression.

7. The fact that persons with a previous history of depression do not differ from controls on depression-related variables.

8. The time-limited nature of depression.

9. Effectiveness of many different kinds of interventions and the nonspecificity of treatment effects.

10. The unique role of stress and of low social supports as triggers (precipitating factors) for the occurrence of depression.

The Symptom Heterogeneity of the Depression Syndrome

On the basis of well-designed descriptive studies and reviews of the clinical literature (Levitt & Lubin, 1975) a fairly concise picture of the depression syndrome has emerged. It is clear that:

1. The depression syndrome is constituted by a large number of diverse symptoms that include emotional (e.g., feelings of dysphoria, sadness), cognitive (e.g., feelings of guilt, low self-esteem, difficulties with memory and concentration), behavioral (e.g., passivity, psychomotor retardation, social-interactional problems, agitation), and somatic (e.g., sleeplessness, headaches, aches and pains, loss of energy, fatigue) manifestations.

2. Individual patients differ in the number and the degree of severity with which they experience these symptoms.

Even though it is possible and convenient to reduce the large number of depression symptoms to a smaller number of clusters by means of statistical procedures (e.g., Grinker, Miller, Sabshin, Nunn, & Nunnally, 1961; Paykel, Prusoff & Klerman, 1971; Rosenthal & Gudeman, 1967), the fact remains that there are large individual differences in the specific symptoms shown by depressed individuals. These individual differences are

clearly recognized by DSM-III (APA, 1980) with its stipulation that to meet criteria for a diagnosis of depression, patients must show n out of N symptoms. There have also been numerous attempts to account for this individual variation in depression symptoms by postulating the existence of subtypes of depression, such as the endogenous versus reactive categorization (Feinberg & Carroll, 1982; Gillespie, 1929), the anxious, hostile, retarded, and agitated subtypes (Overall & Hollister, 1980), and distinctions based on pharmacotherapy response (Overall & Hollister, 1966). Unfortunately, these attempts have been relatively unsuccessful and no generally acceptable typology for unipolar depression has yet emerged. In addition, none of these typologies are based on singly or jointly sufficient features and they do not generate subgroups of depressed patients who are homogeneous with respect to the defining characteristics. Rather, these categorizations are based on the fact that, to some extent, all depression symptoms are intercorrelated (that is, of course, the reason they are included in the depression syndrome) and that some symptoms are more highly correlated with some than with other symptoms. (For excellent reviews of the difficulties that have been encountered in generating a depression typology, the reader is referred to papers by Andreasen [1982] and Akiskal, Hirschfeld, and Yerevanian [1983].)

Centrality of Dysphoria in Depression

Another key finding that has emerged from descriptive studies is that dysphoria is the only depression symptom that comes close to being invariant; that is, it appears in almost all depressed patients. Dysphoria has been reported to be present in more than 90% of depressed patients (Ayd, 1961; Levitt & Lubin, 1975; Woodruff, Murphy, & Herjanic, 1967). The unique importance of dysphoria for the definition of the depression syndrome is clearly recognized by DSM-III, which comes close to making persistent dysphoria a necessary condition for a diagnosis of depression. If dysphoria is a key manifestation of depression, it should be given a central position in depression theory.

The Multiplicity of the Behavioral and Cognitive Changes which are Associated with Depression

Another important finding from depression research is the pervasiveness of the impact of depression on the individual's functioning. These largely negative repercussions occur in multiple spheres, affecting behavior, cognitions, and biochemical functioning.

At the level of overt behavior, people who are depressed are less active (Libet & Lewinsohn, 1973); tend not to enjoy pleasant activities (MacPhillamy & Lewinsohn, 1974), and consequently are probably less motivated; are more sensitive to aversive contingencies (Lewinsohn, Lobitz, & Wilson, 1973; Lewinsohn & Talkington, 1979) and therefore are probably more likely to avoid situations; manifest social skill difficulties that affect their behavior in social interactions (Gotlib, 1982; Hautzinger, 1980; Hinchcliffe, Hooper, & Roberts, 1978; Libet & Lewinsohn, 1973; Youngren & Lewinsohn, 1980); have a negative social impact (Coyne, 1976a); Hammen & Peters, 1977; 1978; Lewinsohn, Mischel, Chaplin, & Barton, 1980); and have fewer close friends and intimates (Brown & Harris, 1978; Costello, 1982). Not surprisingly, their adjustment in important life roles is seriously reduced (Weissman & Paykel, 1974).

At the level of cognitions, depressed individuals have higher expectancies for negative outcomes and lower expectancies for positive outcomes (Lewinsohn, Larson, & Muñoz, 1982), subscribe to irrational beliefs (Muñoz, 1977; Nelson, 1977), and blame themselves for failures (Seligman, Abramson, Semmel, & von Baeyer, 1979). Depressed individuals also have enhanced recall for hedonically negative information (Kuiper, 1978; Lloyd & Lishman, 1975; Wener & Rehm, 1975).

Clearly, to be depressed puts a severe load on the individual's ability to cope. Theories of depression need to account for the seriousness and for the pervasiveness of these effects. Apparently all areas of functioning are affected in a global way.

The High Prevalence (Point and Life Time) of Depression in the General Population

While specific estimates vary somewhat, probably due to different methods of assessment and sampling procedures, it is clear that, compared with most other disorders, depression is a very common problem. It has been called the common cold of mental disorders (Seligman, 1975). On the basis of the available information it may safely be estimated that at least 4% of the adult population is sufficiently depressed at any given time to meet rigorous diagnostic criteria (Lehmann, 1971; Weissman & Myers, 1978), and that approximately 10% of the population will develop an episode of depression within a one year period (Amenson & Lewinsohn, 1981). The lifetime prevalence of depression (i.e., the percentage of individuals likely to experience an episode of depression at some time during their lifetime) may be estimated to be between 25–50% (Amenson & Lewinsohn, 1981; Myers & Weissman, 1980).

The very high rate of occurrence of depression strongly suggests that its antecedents or its predisposing characteristics must be common or multiple.

The Relationship between Age and the Prevalence of Depression

While the available data are relatively weak and conclusions therefore must be tentative, it appears that the prevalence of depression is relatively low in early childhood (Kashani & Simonds, 1979). The prevalence of depression increases during adolescence and probably peaks between the ages of 20 and 40 (Lewinsohn, Hautzinger, & Duncan, 1984). Beyond this age the prevalence of depression seems to remain stable and perhaps even to decrease slightly (Teri & Lewinsohn, 1981). This counter-intuitive decrease of depression beyond a certain age has been found in several studies (Comstock & Helsing, 1976; Craig & Van Natta, 1979; Hirschfeld & Cross, 1982; Teri & Lewinsohn, 1981). Theories of depression, therefore, must allow for what appears to be a curvilinear relationship between age and depression.

The Elevated Prevalence of Depression in Females and in Persons Who Have Had a Previous Episode of Depression

The elevated prevalence of depression among females is probably one of the best-documented findings in the depression literature with two to three times as many females as males reported to have depression (Weissman & Klerman, 1977). This finding extends across the entire adult age span (Teri & Lewinsohn, 1985).

Epidemiological findings have placed this finding in a somewhat new perspective. Amenson and Lewinsohn (1981) in a longitudinal, prospective study of approximately 1000 community participants replicating the elevated prevalence, found that the incidence of new cases of depression (i.e., in people without a previous history of depression) was quite comparable for men (7.1%) and for women (6.9%). Women did not have longer lasting episodes than men, nor did they become depressed earlier in life. The major gender difference was obtained for persons with a history of previous depression. Women with a history of previous depression were much more likely to become depressed again than were men with a history of previous depression (21.8% vs. 12.9%). This increased susceptibility for women to become depressed again was present even after the effects of a host of potentially relevant psychosocial factors were statistically removed. Thus for men a history of previous depression doubled their risk for depression; for women the risk factor tripled. In related findings, Keller, Shapiro, Lavori, and Wolfe (1982) and Gonzales, Lewinsohn, and Clarke (1985) also found that about 30% of depressed patients who were recovered after treatment had another epi-

sode within one year. The finding that some segments of the population are more vulnerable for depression suggests the importance of including a predisposing factor or vulnerability construct in depression theory.

The Fact That Persons with a Previous History of Depression Do Not Differ from Controls on Depression-Related Variables

A number of studies (Hamilton & Abramson, 1983; Lewinsohn, et al., 1981; Youngren, 1978; Youngren & Lewinsohn, 1980; Zeiss & Lewinsohn, 1985) indicate that persons with a history of depression do not show depression-related cognitive and behavioral manifestations after they are depressed. The correlates of depression do not seem to represent stable characteristics of such persons. Yet, as pointed out earlier, these same individuals are at substantially elevated risk for future depression. What may be suggested by these findings is that not only do people differ in their vulnerability to depression but this vulnerability may only be activated under certain conditions.

The Time-Limited Nature of Depression

Two additional findings seem especially salient for depression theory: (1) Most people have relatively short-lived episodes; and (2) Most people are able to terminate their depression without professional assistance.

In a study on the duration of episodes of depression, the frequency distribution of episode duration values was found to be very skewed (Lewinsohn, Fenn, Stanton, & Franklin, 1985); about 25% of episodes of unipolar depression last less than one month; 50% last less than 3 months; and only 25% one year or longer. The fact that most episodes are of relatively short duration confirms clinical observation (Beck, 1967) that depression usually is a time-limited disorder. Furthermore, most people who experience an episode of depression do not seek treatment (Vernon & Roberts, 1982). The psychological processes that enable people to terminate their depression in such a short period of time are being studied (Hautzinger & Hoffman, 1979; Parker & Brown, 1979), and the findings suggest that a range of different strategies are employed. Clearly, treatment is not a necessary condition for depression improvement. At the same time, there are a substantial number of individuals (approximately 15–30%) who do have long episodes or who do not seem to benefit from treatment (Weissman, Prusoff, & Klerman, 1978).

The fact that some people are able to effectively use a wide range of behaviors to terminate their depression suggests that depression can be influenced from many directions. Consequently, a theory of depression probably needs multiple points of entry for potential reversal.

The Effectiveness of Many Different Kinds of Interventions and the Nonspecificity of Treatment Effects

An impressively wide array of different interventions have been found to be efficacious for depression. Cognitive therapy is aimed at changing depressive thought processes (e.g., Beck et al., 1979; Fuchs & Rehm, 1977); behavioral treatments are aimed at improving social skills (Hersen, Bellack, & Himmelhoch, 1980; Sanchez, Lewinsohn, & Larson, 1980; Zeiss, 1977), increasing pleasant activities, teaching time management and relaxation skills (Lewinsohn, 1976), or training in general problem-solving skills (McLean & Hakstian, 1979); and antidepressant medications (Rush, Beck, Kovacs, & Hollon, 1977; Morris & Beck, 1974) are aimed at restoring a theorized biochemical imbalance. In spite of this theoretically provocative diversity, empirical support for the therapeutic efficacy of all of these treatments has been provided (Lewinsohn & Hoberman, 1982; Paykel, 1982; Rehm, 1981; Rehm & Kornblith, 1979) and differences between treatment outcomes have generally been small and often not significant (e.g., Wilson, Goldin & Charbonneau-Powis, 1983).

These studies pose several interesting challenges for depression theory. Since most of the treatments were theoretically derived, that is, specifically designed to modify the specific conditions assumed by the theory to be a critical antecedent for depression, how can they all be effective? Furthermore, the treatments while effective in ameliorating depression, do not seem to be specific in impacting hypothesized target behaviors (and cognitions) at which they are aimed (e.g., Zeiss, Lewinsohn, & Munõz, 1979).

These findings suggest that a theory of depression should allow for multiple points of causal entry and multiple modes of improving depression. Further, the findings suggest that the functional systems (i.e., cognitive, behavioral, and somatic) that are affected by depression, tend to change together; that is, they move en masse.

Stress and Low Social Supports as Triggers of Depression

The association among stress, weak social supports, and depression has, of course, been known for some time (Paykel et al., 1969). Recent prospective studies (e.g., Lewinsohn & Hoberman, 1982) have gone a step farther in showing that the occurrence of stressful life events actually precedes the occurrence of depression. In particular the literature suggests that stressors related to marital distress, social exits, and work problems bear an especially strong relationship to the later development of depression. The central importance of stress in the chain of events leading to depression has been recognized by several theorists (Aneshensel & Frerichs, 1982; Billings & Moos, 1982; Brown & Harris, 1978).

Current Psychological Theories of Depression

Having identified what we consider to be the most salient research findings that a theory of unipolar depression needs to address, it is now appropriate to move toward an elaboration of a model of the etiology of depression. Before presenting the structure of this new theory, however, it is important to briefly reconsider the bases of the two major types of psychological theories of depression. Cognitive theories of depression, particularly those of Beck (1967) and Abramson et al., (1978), are fairly explicit in postulating that certain depressogenic cognitive patterns cause people to interpret their experiences in ways that cause them to become depressed. These predisposing cognitive patterns are assumed to be relatively stable characteristics of the person; that is, individuals who become depressed possess a stable depressogenic cognitive style that predisposes them to depressive episodes. Thus Beck (1967, p. 290) has stated: "During the developmental period, the depression-prone individual acquires certain negative attitudes regarding himself, the outside world, and his future . . . The idiosyncratic attitudes represent persistent cognitive patterns, designated as schemas." Similarly, Seligman has reported on a prospective study that attempted to assess whether students who possess a depressogenic attributional style would score as more depressed after a later failure; that is, it was predicted that the "combination of a *preexisting* internal, stable, and global way of construing causality for negative events followed by an actual encounter with failure will be sufficient to cause depression (1981, p. 125; emphasis added).

Unfortunately, the available research has failed to demonstrate that individuals who become depressed can be distinguished on the basis of the kinds of preexisting cognitive styles suggested by Beck and other cognitive theorists. While patterns of depressive cognitions do indeed co-occur with dysphoria— that is, they definitely are concomitants of depression—there is accumulating evidence that these patterns are not apparent either before or after a depressive episode. Lewinsohn et al., (1981) reported on the results of a longitudinal, prospective study of the onset of depression. All participants were assessed on a number of cognitions (expec-

tations for positive and negative outcomes, attributions, and irrational negative beliefs) at the beginning of the study and were later evaluated to determine if an episode of depression occurred. Participants who became depressed during the course of the study were compared with those who did not become depressed and with those who were depressed at entry into the study. The results of this study indicated that persons who were later to become depressed did not differ on the cognitive measures from those who remained undepressed. The types of cognitions endorsed by the major cognitive theories were found to be concomitants but not antecedents of depression. Additionally, the cognitive patterns of persons who had been depressed at some time in the past (but who were not depressed during the course of the study) were not distinguishable from those who remained undepressed. Thus individuals who have been depressed or who are about to become depressed are not characterized by a stable depressogenic cognitive style. Similarly, Peterson, Schwartz, and Seligman (1981) found no evidence for a particular attributional style to be predictive of later depressive symptoms, and, also consistent with our findings, Wilkinson and Blackburn (1981) showed that the cognitions of recovered depressed patients could not be differentiated from those of normal or psychiatric controls. In short, there is little evidence for the contention in cognitive theories that a particular cognitive content is a causal factor in the initial development of a depressive episode.

Behavioral or reinforcement theories of depression have postulated the nature of person–environment interactions as causing depression. In particular, theories such as Lewinsohn's (Lewinsohn, Youngren, & Grosscup, 1979) have emphasized that changes in the quality of a person's reinforcement (e.g., a decrease in positive or an increase in negative reinforcement) lead to depression. As was indicated earlier, such changes do indeed covary with depression. However, in the results of a longitudinal, prospective study by Lewinsohn and Hoberman (1982), neither the frequency of pleasant nor unpleasant events predicted the later occurrence of depression, suggesting that the number of such events are not antecedents of depressive episodes. With regard to reinforcement, only the aversiveness of unpleasant events emerged as predicting later depression and the number of macrostressors (which could be considered a measure of negative reinforcement) predicted depressive onset. Thus it is clear that the premises of the reinforcement theory of depression were not entirely supported.

An Integrative Theory of Depression

The findings that major predictions of cognitive and reinforcement theories have not been demonstrated to be antecedents for depression provides cause for thought. Can it be that neither cognitions nor the quality of person–environment interactions are related to the etiology and maintenance of depression? We think not. Rather we propose that cognitions and reinforcement are both important variables in the onset of

depression. However, we would argue that past cognitive and reinforcement positions have offered too simplistic views; in particular, we contend that while the cognitive models have overemphasized cognitive dispositional factors, the reinforcement models have, in truth, overemphasized situational factors. Consequently, we offer a model of the etiology and maintenance of depression that attempts to capture what we see as the complexity and interactive nature of psychopathogenic factors. This model is presented schematically in Figure 1. The model represents an attempt to integrate the findings of our epidemiological and treatment outcome studies with an increasing body of work in social psychology in the phenomenon of self-awareness (e.g., Carver, Blaney & Scheier, 1979a, b; Duvall & Wicklund, 1972; Scheier, Carver, & Gibbons, 1981). The proposed etiological model should be regarded as tentative and not etched in concrete. It simply represents the phenomena and conditions that we think are often involved in the development and maintenance of depression. We do not imply that the chain of causation is fixed and invariant; rather, the model attempts to incorporate a

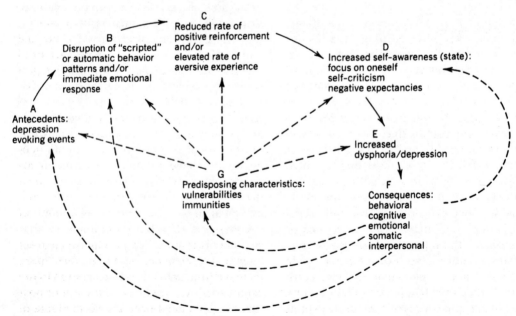

Figure 1
Schematic representation of variables involved in the occurrence of unipolar depression.

number of different characteristics and processes that can influence and in turn are influenced by the occurrence of depression.

We view the occurrence of depression as a product of both environmental and dispositional factors. More specifically, we see depression as the end result of environmentally initiated changes in behavior, affect, and cognitions. In accord with previous behavioral theories of depression, we view environmental or situational factors as the primary triggers of the depressogenic process. Like cognitive theorists, we view cognitions as significant moderators of the effects of the environment, that is, as critical for determining whether situational conditions are going to result in depression. In particular, we believe that when attention is shifted increasingly toward the self versus the environment as a consequence of the individual's unsuccessful efforts to cope with disruptive life conditions, the preconditions for depression are set in motion.

The chain of events leading to the occurrence of depression is postulated to begin with the occurrence of an evoking event or antecedent (A), which is empirically defined as any event that increases the probability for the future occurrence of depression. In the literature to date, all of these evoking events fall under the general rubric of stressors, including macrostressors (e.g., losing one's job), microstressors (e.g., being criticized), and chronic difficulties (e.g., marital discord). The relationship between such stressors and depression is a well-documented finding in the depression literature. Both retrospective studies (e.g., Brown & Harris, 1978; Costello, 1982; and Paykel et al., 1969) and prospective studies (Lewinsohn & Alexander, 1983; Lewinsohn & Hoberman, 1982; Lewinsohn & Teri, 1984) have demonstrated an increase in the incidence of life events, or the presence of chronic difficulties, in the months preceding an episode of depression. In particular, the literature suggests that stressors related to marital distress, social exits, and work problems exhibit an especially strong relationship to the later development of depression.

Antecedents of the Occurrence of Depression

The occurrence of antecedents are assumed to initiate the depressogenic process to the extent that they disrupt substantial, important, and relatively automatic behavior patterns of an individual (B). Langer (1978) has suggested that much of everyday behavior is "scripted" (e.g., Schank & Abelson, 1975) and consequently automatic, requiring very little mental effort. An implication of Langer's position is that much of what occurs to people on an everyday basis is generally expected and predictable (or at least is perceived that way). Thus as Coyne (1982) has postulated, most individuals get by in their lives with well-established behavior patterns because of the regularities in their environment. The presence of a stressor or chronic difficulty acts to disrupt the regularity of an individual's life, particularly those aspects of the individual's behavioral repertoire that are typical and crucial to a person's everyday interactions with the environment. Stressful life events are assumed to lead to depression to the extent that they are disruptive of personal relationships, job tasks, and automatic behaviors. Thus promotion, moving to a new (albeit better) job or environment, could become an A, as can rejection or the ending of a relationship unless the person is able to quickly develop other behavior patterns to replace those that have been disrupted.

A further consequence of the presence of an evoking event and its subsequent disruption of patterned behavior is an initial negative emotional reaction. The degree or intensity of this initial negative affect will be a function of the salience or importance of the evoking event or the degree of disruption of everyday behavior (Taylor & Fiske, 1978).

Such disruptions and the emotional upset they typically engender are assumed to be related to the occurrence of depression to the extent that they lead to a reduction of positive reinforcement or to an elevated rate of aversive experience (C); that is, they shift the balance of the quality of a person's interactions with the environment in a negative direction (e.g., Lewinsohn et al., 1979).

As the effects of evoking events exert their impact on an individual's obtained level of reinforcement, persons attempt to reduce that impact (Coyne, Aldwin, & Lazarus, 1981). In fact, these endeavors to cope with the deleterious effects of stressors are conceptualized as being an important component of the stress process (Lazarus & Launier, 1978). Stressors and their effects are rarely discrete experiences and depending upon the salience of the evoking event and the degree of life disruption, individuals typically are forced to deal with such events over a period of time. These efforts will be successful to different degrees, depending upon both environmental and dispositional factors (G).

The inability to reverse the impact of the stress (e.g., through decreasing negative reinforcement or increasing positive reinforcement and consequently, producing a resumption of patterned behavior or neutral or positive affect) is hypothesized to lead to a heightened state of self-awareness (D). We would suggest that two phenomena will focus a person's attention on him or herself. First, the initial negative emotional response that follows the evoking event and the subsequent emotional impact of the person's inability to reverse the impact of the stress increases self-awareness. As Wegner and Giuliano (1980) have demonstrated, physiological arousal elicits self-focused attention. In addition we hypothesize that a reduction in positive reinforcement or increase in negative experience will also produce an increment in self-focused attention.

The concept of self-awareness or self-focused attention was introduced by Duval and Wicklund (1972) who suggested that attention at a specific point in time can be directed in either of two directions—outwardly, toward the environment, or inwardly, toward the self—and that certain events will increase the degree to which attention will be focused on the self or be externally focused. One of Duval and Wicklund's major points was that when attention is focused internally (that is when a state of self-awareness exists), individuals become more aware of their thoughts, feelings, values, and standards. A reconceptualization of self-focused attention by Carver and Scheier (1981) suggests that self-awareness produces a heightened consciousness of whatever self-elements are salient in a specific situation. A substantial literature has accumulated that explores a variety of effects of self-focused attention. It is this body of research that forms the basis for the assumption that self-awareness, a cognitive process, is the critical factor in mediating the effects of reduced positive reinforcement on depression.

As has been noted by several investigators (Ganellen & Blaney, 1981; Ingram & Smith, 1984; Smith & Greenberg, 1981; Teasdale, 1983), the effects of increasing self-awareness are amazingly similar to many of the cognitive and behavioral phenomena of depression. First, increased self-awareness has been shown to cause individuals to become increasingly self-critical (Duval & Wicklund, 1972) and to produce an increase in the discrepancy between ratings of ideal self and the perceived self (Ickes, Wicklund, & Ferris, 1973). Second, when a state of self-awareness is induced, individuals are increasingly likely to attend to performance norms or standards for behavior (Carver & Scheier, 1983). Thus, as individuals attempt to cope with their disrupted lives, they will compare themselves to certain standards. If the comparison to standards is unfavorable (as it is likely to be in initial coping efforts and over time with unsuccessful coping efforts) Carver and Scheier's (1983) theory of self-attention predicts that a negative affective reaction will ensue. A third consequence of heightened self-awareness will be to impact on an individual's attributions for events. Conditions of heightened self-awareness result in greater acceptance of responsibility for outcomes, that is, internal attributions (Buss & Scheier, 1976; Duval & Wicklund, 1972; Hull & Levy, 1979). Self-focused attention also potentiates negative expectancies (Carver, Blaney, & Scheier,

1979a, 1979b). In short, self-focused attention produces many of the cognitive alterations that have been emphasized by cognitive theorists.

Self-focused attention also has behavioral consequences. Increased self-awareness in the face of negative outcome expectancies has been shown to be associated with behavioral withdrawal (Carver et al., 1979, 1979b) and with social difficulties (Christensen, 1982; Fenigstein, 1979). Research has also shown that under conditions of self-focused attention, negative expectancies lead to reduced effort and persistence (e.g., Carver et al., 1979a, 1979b; Kernis, Zuckerman, Cohen, & Spadafora, 1982; Scheier & Carver, 1977) and reducing self-awareness increases performance (Brockner & Hulton, 1978). Another important consequence of a heightened state of self-awareness is an intensification or magnification of affective reactions. Experimentally induced self-focused attention has been shown (Scheier & Carver, 1977) to produce more extreme depression or elation following mood-induction procedures and to produce negative affect in psychiatric patients (Gibbons, Smith, Brehm, & Schroeder, 1980).

In short, the elicitation of a state of self-awareness increases the individual's awareness of his or her failure to live up to his or her expected standards of coping, and engenders a state of self-denigration, behavioral withdrawal, and dysphoria.

We hypothesize that feeling increasingly self-aware (D) and dysphoric (E) breaks through an individual's self-protective and self-enhancing self-perceptions (e.g., Alloy & Abramson, 1979; Lewinsohn, et al., 1980) and thus leads to many of the cognitive, behavioral, and emotional changes (F) that have been shown to be correlated with depression. These changes (F) are presumed to be quite consequential and to play an important role in the maintenance and exacerbation of the depressive state. The negative effects of dysphoria on a host of cognitive processes have been shown on a series of studies (Clark & Teasdale, 1982; Davis, 1979; Derry & Kuiper, 1981; Isen, Shalker, Clark, & Karp, 1978; Lloyd & Lishman, 1975; Natale & Hantas, 1982; Rogers, Kuiper, & Kirker, 1977; Teasdale, 1983; Teasdale & Fogarty, 1979; Teasdale & Russell, 1983; Teasdale & Taylor, 1981; Teasdale, Taylor, Fogarty, 1980). Briefly these studies have shown that in a state of dysphoria negative thoughts and memories become more accessible and that negative information about the self is processed more efficiently, a complete reversal from the way information about the self is processed in nondepressed individuals. In other words, the induction of depressed mood drastically changes the way in which subjects interpret their previous and their current experiences and augments the dysphoria.

Thus, as dysphoria escalates we would argue that a very basic transition occurs in cognitions regarding the self. Specifically, we suggest that the self-schema is changed. Research in cognitive social psychology has indicated that knowledge is structured in schemas or schemata. A *schema* is defined as a structured body of information that is stored in long-term memory and that is capable of organizing and clustering new incoming environmental and personal information (Davis, 1979). The self-schema (Derry & Kuiper, 1981; Rogers et al., 1977) is assumed to be the particular body of information about the individual that interacts with incoming data so as to organize the processing and retention of self-related information. It is this self-schema that we hypothesize has changed. Specific instances of this change in the self-schema are hypothesized to represent negative self-evaluations, low rates of self-reinforcement, pessimism about the future, internal and global attributions for failure experiences, cognitive distortion of the type described by Beck et al., (1979), and preoccupation with negative experiences from the past.

We also hypothesize that being self-aware and dysphoric acts to reduce the individual's social competence and contributes to the negative impact on others (Coyne, 1976a; Hammen & Peters, 1978). Consistent with this focus on self-awareness, Jacobson and

Anderson (1982), for example, found that depressed subjects are more likely to refer to themselves in social conversation when self-references were not directly solicited. They suggest that depressed people are preoccupied with themselves and that they therefore focus on themselves even at times when the normal flow of conversation suggests a more natural focus on the interacting partner. We suggest that it is these types of behaviors that cause depressed people to elicit social rejection in social interaction (Coyne, 1976a; Hammen & Peters, 1978; Strack & Coyne, 1983). Our hypothesis that many of the social skill deficits shown by depressed individuals are secondary to being depressed is consistent with observations that social skill of recovered depressed persons is indistinguishable from that of nondepressed persons (Zeiss & Lewinsohn, 1985; Youngren, personal communication, 1977).

In short, then, an episode of depression is likely to result as a consequence of a chain of events beginning with the occurrence of antecedent-eliciting events leading to a heightened state of self-focused attention. In turn, a continuing increase in self-awareness provides a basis for a large number of affective, behavioral, and cognitive transformations that exacerbate dysphoria and act to induce and maintain an episode of depression.

Immunities and Vulnerabilities

Additionally, the proposed model allows for predisposing characteristics of various kinds either to increase or to decrease the risk for a depressive episode. The need to incorporate a moderator variable of this kind is dictated by the fact that there seem to be individual differences and environmental variables that systematically increase (vulnerabilities) or decrease (immunities) the probability for the occurrence of depression. These vulnerabilities and immunities are assumed to be relatively stable characteristics of the person or of the person's environment. The concept of vulnerability was first introduced by Zubin (1976). The central idea was that under a given set of circumstances some individuals are more (or less) likely to develop a psychopathological disorder. Predisposing characteristics are assumed to influence not only the probability for the occurrence of a depressive episode but also to influence whether an episode is going to be of short or long duration.

On the basis of our own research as well as that of other researchers in the field, the following person and environment characteristics can be suggested to act as predisposing vulnerabilities: (1) being female, (2) being age 20–40, (3) having a previous history of depression, (4) having low coping skills, (5) having increased sensitivity to aversive events, (6) being poor, (7) being highly self-conscious (Fenigstein, Scheier & Buss, 1975), (8) having a low threshold for the evocation of the depressogenic self-schemata, (9) having low self-esteem, (10) being high on interpersonal dependency (Hirschfeld, Klerman, Chodoff, Korchin, & Barrett, 1976), and (11) having children below the age of 7 (Brown & Harris, 1978). The following may be hypothesized to act as protective immunities: high learned resourcefulness (Rosenbaum, 1980); high self-perceived social competence (Lewinsohn et al., 1980); high frequency of pleasant events; and the availability of a close and intimate confidant (Brown & Harris, 1978).

As indicated in Figure 1, predisposing characteristics are assumed to affect all elements of the model. While an accounting of the many ways in which each of the suggested predisposing characteristics can affect the path of depressive onset is beyond the limit of this paper, a few illustrative examples can be provided. An individual with good coping skills would be more likely to be able to reverse the depressogenic cycle by implementing new behaviors to deal with the disruption (B), or by decreasing self-awareness by finding distractions and thereby staying focused on external events. The ease with which the individual can become angry may also in this context constitute an immunity in that by becoming angry the individual remains focused on external events and avoids becoming self-aware.

The behavior of the significant others in the person's environment may constitute a vulnerability to the extent that they selectively reinforce the depressed individual's symptoms and complaints. Under such conditions one would expect the depression to become an operant; that is, it is now being maintained by the environment and therefore will perpetuate and become part of the individual's life style. Conversely, the action of significant others may act as an immunity for an episode of depression to the extent that they are able to provide help with restoring disrupted behavior patterns or call attention to instances of competence, for example.

Feedback Loops

The model allows for additional "feedback loops" that are seen as important for determining the level of severity and the duration of an episode of depression. Thus, becoming depressed (F) and thinking and behaving in the depressed mode would be expected to interfere with the individual's problem-solving skills (G) and, consequently, their ability to reverse the disruption (B) and the effects of the disruption (C). Similarly, when an individual has become depressed, his or her behavior becomes more complaining, less friendly, more withdrawn and passive, and more aversive to others (Coyne, 1976a; Hammen & Peters, 1977). This may serve to increase the likelihood for the occurrence of additional depression-evoking events (A); for example, the spouse becomes more dissatisfied and threatens to leave the patient; the boss begins questioning the patient's competence. Being depressed (F) would also be expected to reduce the individual's energy level and enjoyment of pleasant activities, to increase sensitivity to aversive events and self-awareness, and consequently to influence the overall ability to reverse the depressogenic chain.

The feedback loops set the stage for a vicious cycle but also for a benign cycle. By reversing any of the components of the model, the depression will be progressively and increasingly ameliorated.

Explanatory Power of the Model

We believe that our model, in addition to taking into account much of what is empirically known about depression, provides potential explanations for a number of important aspects of depression. For example, the model allows for the heterogeneity and the multiplicity of depression symptoms because the effects of increased self-awareness and of dysphoria appear to be so global and include such a wide range of behavioral, physiological, and cognitive manifestations. The model allows for many points of entry into the chain of events leading to depression and thus allows for a multiplicity of causes, each of which is contributory but none of which is essential.

The model suggests that the prevalence and incidence of depression should be high because there are so many points of entry and because there probably are many relatively common (e.g., everyday) antecedents. Conversely, our model implies that while episodes of depression are common, most will be of a short duration because there are a large number of person-initiated and environmental changes that can act to reverse the depressogenic cycle.

The model assigns a central role to dysphoria because dysphoria is assumed to be necessary for the evocation of the consequences (F), that is, the shift into the depressive mode of thinking and behaving. While there has been some debate about whether depression can exist in the absence of dysphoria (the so-called "masked depressions," for example, Glaser, 1967; Sugar, 1967; Toolan, 1969), our assumption is that without dysphoria only a very incomplete syndrome will exist since neither the changes in processing of information about the self nor the depression-induced social behavior changes will have occurred.

People can ameliorate their depression by changing the consequences of depression, distracting themselves, reducing self-awareness, increasing pleasant activities, decreasing unpleasant activities, trying to enhance one's general coping skills and becoming more effective in eliminating the disruption or perhaps even the antecedent events, or moving to a different environment that does not have the antecedent event and that calls for behavior patterns that are part of the individual's nondepressive repertoire.

The fact that any number of psychological, biological, and eclectic interventions for depression are successful may be explained by the large number of person-initiated and environmental changes that can act to reverse the depressogenic cycle. Interventions would be expected to be effective to the extent that they affect one of the links of the model in a crucial and powerful way or because the intervention impacts many of the points and thus has a large cumulative effect. Because the feedback loops are so extensive, there are many ways to get a reverse process started. The fact that most current therapies are actually multimodal is consistent with this argument. There is, of course, no reason why a person can't do all of these things by themselves—and most people do (Parker & Brown, 1979; Rippere, 1977; Vernon & Roberts, 1982).

The model also is capable of generating relatively specific and testable predictions. To wit, our model predicts that (1) the likelihood that antecedents increase the probability for depression should be proportional to the degree to which they disrupt important behavior patterns; (2) disruptions should increase the probability for the occurrence of depression to the extent that they result in a decrease in positive and an increase in negative person–environment interactions; and (3) a reduced rate of positive reinforcement or an elevated rate of aversive experience increases self-awareness.

Theories of unipolar depression are important not only because of the prevalence and seriousness of the clinical syndrome, but, at a more general level, because of their potential relevance for larger theories of behavior. Depression clearly involves interactions between overt and covert behavior; among emotions, cognitions, and behavior; and between current situational conditions and the more remote effects of the individual's past. Thus, theories of depression provide a testing ground for many of the more important issues in psychology.

Concluding Comments

We want to emphasize that our conceptualization is meant to be a working model. We do not expect that the directions of all of the arrows in Figure 1 will necessarily be correct. We may have suggested too many or too few linkages; future research will hopefully clarify these issues. A primary virtue of the model is that it is testable and that it emphasizes the importance of the temporal study of the chain of events and the processes that lead to depression.

This is certainly an exciting time in depression theory. Through the mid-60s what might be considered the first phase of psychological theories of depression was dominated by psychoanalytic thinking and was a relatively static period during which people in the field felt they had most of the answers. During the late 60s and through the 70s (Phase 2), linear theories focused on a single causal agent to the exclusion of others. These theories stimulated a great deal of productive conceptual and empirical activity. The field is now moving into the next phase that promises to do justice to the complexity of the clinical phenomena of depression and of the underlying psychological processes. These newer theories appear to be multifactorial. They assume that a number of different causes are important, none of which are necessary or sufficient but all of which interact in important ways.

References

ABRAMSON, L. Y., SELIGMAN, M. E, AND TEASDALE, J. D. (1978). Learned helplessness in humans: Critique and reformation. *Journal of Abnormal Psychology, 7,* 49–74.

AKISKAL, H. S., HIRSCHFELD, R. M. A., AND YEREVANIAN, B. I. (1983). The relationship of personality to affective disorders. *Archives of General Psychiatry, 40,* 801–810.

AKISKAL, H. S, AND MCKINNEY, W. T. (1973). Depressive disorders: Toward a unified hypothesis. *Science, 182,* 20–29.

AKISKAL, H. S., AND MCKINNEY, W. T. (1975). Overview of recent research in depression, integration of ten conceptual models into a comprehensive clinical frame. *Archives of General Psychiatry, 32,* 285.

ALLOY, L. B., AND ABRAMSON, L. Y. (1979). Judgment of contingency in depressed and nondepressed students: Sadder but wiser? *Journal of Experimental Psychology, 90,* 1–13.

AMENSON, C. S., AND LEWINSOHN, P. M. (1981). An investigation into the observed sex difference in prevalence of unipolar depression. *Journal of Abnormal Psychology, 90,* 1–13.

AMERICAN PSYCHIATRIC ASSOCIATION. (1980). *Diagnostic and Statistical Manual of Mental Disorders* (3rd ed.). Washington, DC: Author.

ANDREASEN, N. C. (1982). Concepts, diagnosis and classification. In E. S. PAYKEL (Ed.), *Handbook of affective disorders* (pp. 24–44). London: Churchill-Livingstone.

ANESHENSEL, C. S., AND FRERICHS, R. R. (1982). Stress, support, and depression: A longitudinal causal model. *Journal of Community Psychology, 10,* 363–376.

AYD, F. J., JR. (1961). *Recognizing the depressed patient.* NY: Grune & Stratton.

BECK, A. T. (1967). *Depression: Clinical, experimental and theoretical aspects.* NY: Harper & Row.

BECK A. T., RUSH, A. J., SHAW, B. F., AND EMERY, G. (1979). *Cognitive therapy of depression.* NY: Guilford Press.

BILLINGS, A. G., AND MOOS, R. N. (1982). Psychosocial theory and research on depression: An integrative framework and review. *Clinical Psychology Review, 2,* 213–237.

BLANEY, P. H. (1977). Contemporary theories of depression: Critique and comparison. *Journal of Abnormal Psychology, 86,* 203–223.

BROCKNER, J., AND HULTON, A. J. B. (1978). How to reverse the vicious cycle of low self-esteem: The importance of attentional focus. *Journal of Experimental Social Psychology, 14,* 564–578.

BROWN, G. W., AND HARRIS, T. (1978). *Social origins of depression: A study of psychiatric disorder in women.* NY: Free Press.

BUNNEY, W. E., AND DAVIS, J. M. (1965). Norepinephrine in depressed reactions. *Archives of General Psychiatry, 13,* 483–494.

BUSS, A., AND SCHEIER, M. (1976). Self-consciousness, self-awareness and self-attribution. *Journal of Research in Personality, 10,* 463–468.

CARVER, C. S., BLANEY, P. H., AND SCHEIER, M. F. (1979a). Focus of attention, chronic expectancy, and responses to a feared stimulus. *Journal of Personality and Social Psychology, 37,* 1186–1195.

CARVER, C. S., BLANEY, P. H., AND SCHEIER, M. F. (1979b). Reassertion and giving up: The interactive role of self-directed attention and outcome expectancy. *Journal of Personality and Social Psychology, 37,* 1859–1870.

CARVER, C. S., AND SCHEIER, M. F. (1978). Self-focusing effects of dispositional self-consciousness, mirror presence, and audience presence. *Journal of Personality and Social Psychology, 36,* 324–332.

CARVER, C. S., AND SCHEIER, M. F. (1981). *Attention and self-regulation: A control-theory approach to human behavior.* NY: Springer.

CARVER, C. S., AND SCHEIER, M. F. (1983). A control theory approach to human behavior, and implications for problems of self-management. In P. KENDALL (Ed.), *Advances in cognitive-behavioral research and therapy* (Vol. 2, pp. 129–194). NY: Academic Press.

CHRISTENSEN, D. (1982). The relationship between self-consciousness and interpersonal effectiveness and a new scale to measure individual differences in self-consciousness. *Personality and Individual Differences, 3,* 177–188.

CLARK, D. M., AND TEASDALE, J. D. (1982). Diurnal variation in clinical depression and accessibility of memories of positive and negative experiences. *Journal of Abnormal Psychology, 91,* 87–95.

COMSTOCK, G. W., AND HELSING, K. J. (1976). Symptoms of depression in two communities. *Psychological Medicine, 6,* 551–563.

COSTELLO, C. G. (1982). Social factors associated with depression: A retrospective community study. *Psychological Medicine, 12,* 329–339.

COYNE, J. C. (1976a). Depression and the response of others. *Journal of Abnormal Psychology, 85,* 186–193.

COYNE, J. C. (1976b). Toward an interactional description of depression. *Psychiatry, 39,* 28–40.

COYNE, J. C. (1982). A critique of cognitions as causal entities with particular reference to depression. *Cognitive Therapy and Research, 6,* 3–13.

COYNE, J. C., ALDWIN, C., AND LAZARUS, R. S. (1981). Depression and coping in stressful episodes. *Journal of Abnormal Psychology, 90,* 439–447.

CRAIG, T., AND VAN NATTA, P. A. (1979). Influence of demographic characteristics on two measures of depressive symptoms. *Archives of General Psychiatry, 35,* 149–154.

CRAIGHEAD, W. E. (1981). Behavior therapy for depression: Issues resulting from treatment studies. In L. P. REHM (Ed.), *Behavior therapy for depression: Present status and future directions.* NY: Academic Press.

DAVIS, H. (1979). The self-schema and subjective organization of personal information in depression. *Cognitive Therapy and Research, 3,* 415–425.

DERRY, P. A., AND KUIPER, N. A. (1981). Schematic processing and self-reference in clinical depression. *Journal of Abnormal Psychology, 90,* 286–297.

DOERFLER, L. A. (1981). Psychological research on depression: A methodological review. *Clinical Psychology Review, 1,* 119–137.

DUVAL, S., AND WICKLUND, R. (1972). *A theory of objective self-awareness.* NY: Academic Press.

EASTMAN, C. (1976). Behavioral formulations of depression. *Psychological Review, 83,* 277–291.

ELLIS, A., AND HARPER, R. A. (1961). *A guide to rational living.* Hollywood, CA: Wilshire.

FEINBERG, M., AND CARROLL, B. J. (1982). Separation of subtypes of depression using discriminant analyses. I. Separation of unipolar endogenous depression from nonendogenous depression. *British Journal of Psychiatry, 140,* 384–391.

FENIGSTEIN, A. (1979). Self-consciousness, self-attention, and social interaction. *Journal of Personality and Social Psychology, 37,* 75–86.

FENIGSTEIN, A., SCHEIER, M. F., AND BUSS, A. H. (1975). Public and private self-consciousness assessment and theory. *Journal of Consulting and Clinical Psychology, 43,* 522–527.

FERSTER, C. B. (1965). Classification of behavior pathology. In L. KRASNER AND L. P. ULLMAN (Eds.), *Research in behavior modification* (pp. 6–26). NY: Holt, Rinehart & Winston.

FUCHS, C. Z., AND REHM, C. P. (1977). A self-control behavior therapy program for depression. *Journal of Consulting and Clinical Psychology, 45,* 206–215.

GANELLEN, R., AND BLANEY, P. H. (1981, August). *A cognitive model of depressive onset.* In new theoretical approaches to the psychology of depression. Annual convention of the American Psychological Association, Los Angeles.

GIBBONS, F., SMITH, T., BREHM, S., AND SCHROEDER, D. (1980). *Self-awareness and self-confrontation: The role of focus of attention in the process of psychotherapy.* Unpublished manuscript. University of Kansas, Lawrence.

GILLESPIE, R. D. (1929). The clinical differentiation of types of depression. *Guy's Hospital Reports, 75,* 306–344.

GLASER, K. (1967). Masked depression in children and adolescents. *American Journal of Psychotherapy, 21,* 565–574.

GONZALES, L., LEWINSOHN, P. M., AND CLARKE, G. (1985). Longitudinal follow-up of unipolar depressives: An investigation of predictors of relapse. *Journal of Consulting and Clinical Psychology, 53,* 461–469.

GOTLIB, I. H. (1982). Self-reinforcement and depression in interpersonal interaction: The role of performance level. *Journal of Abnormal Psychology, 91,* 3–13.

GRINKER, R. R., SR., MILLER, J., SABSHIN, M., NUNN, R., AND NUNNALLY, J. C. (1961). *The phenomena of depressions.* NY: Hoeber.

HAMILTON, E. W., AND ABRAMSON, L. Y. (1983). Cognitive patterns and major depressive disorder: A longitudinal study in a hospital setting. *Journal of Abnormal Psychology, 92,* 173–184.

HAMMEN, C. L., AND PETERS, S. D. (1977). Differential responses to male and female depressive reactions. *Journal of Consulting and Clinical Psychology, 45,* 994–1001.

HAMMEN, C. L., AND PETERS, S. D. (1978). Interpersonal consequences of depression: Responses to men and women enacting a depressed role. *Journal of Abnormal Psychology, 87,* 322–332.

HAUTZINGER, M. (1980). *Verbalverhalten Depressiver und ihrer Socialpartner.* Dissertation, Technischen Universität Berlin.

HAUTZINGER, M., AND HOFFMAN, N. (Eds.). (1979). *Depression und Umwelt.* Salzburg, Austria: Otto Muller Verlag.

HERSEN, M., BELLACK, A. S., AND HIMMELHOCH, J. M. (1980). Skills training with unipolar depressed women. In J. P. CURRAN AND P. M. MONTI (Eds.), *Social competence and psychiatric disorders: Theory and practice.* NY: Guilford.

HINCHCLIFFE, M. K., HOOPER, D., AND ROBERTS, F. J. (1978). *The melancholy marriage.* NY: John Wiley and Sons.

HIRSCHFELD, R. M. AND CROSS, C. K. (1982). Epidemiology of affective disorders: Psychosocial risk factors. *Archives of General Psychiatry, 39,* 35–45.

HIRSCHFELD, R., KLERMAN, G. L., CHODOFF, P., KORCHIN, S., AND BARRET, J. (1976). Dependency, self-esteem, clinical depression. *Journal of the American Academy of Psychoanalysis, 4,* 373–388.

HULL, J. G., AND LEVY, A. S. (1979). The organizational functioning of the self: An alternative to the Duval and Wicklund model of self-awareness. *Journal of Personality and Social Psychology, 37,* 756–768.

ICKES, J., WICKLUND, A., AND FERRIS, C. (1973). Objective self-awareness and self-esteem. *Journal of Experimental Social Psychology, 9,* 202–219.

INGRAM, R. E., AND SMITH, T. S. (1984). Depression and internal versus external locus of attention. *Cognitive Therapy and Research, 8,* 139–152.

ISEN, A. M., SHALKER, T. E., CLARK, M., AND KARP, L. (1978). Affect, accessibility of material in memory, and behavior: A cognitive loop? *Journal of Personality and Social Psychology, 36,* 1–12.

KANFER, F. H., AND HAGERMAN, S. (1981). The role of self-regulation. In L. REHM (Ed.), *Behavior therapy for depression: Present status and future directions.* (Chap. 4). NY: Academic Press.

KASHANI, J. G., AND SIMONDS, J. (1979). The incidence of depression in children. *American Journal of Psychiatry, 136,* 1203–1205.

KELLER, M. B., SHAPIRO, R. W., LAVORI, P. W., AND WOLFE, N. (1982). Relapse in major depressive disorder: Analysis of the life table. *Archives of General Psychiatry, 39,* 911–915.

KENDELL, R. E. (1976). The classification of depression: A review of contemporary confusions. *British Journal of Psychiatry, 129,* 15–28.

KERNIS, M. H., ZUCKERMAN, M., COHEN, A., AND SPADAFORA, S. (1982). Persistence following failure: The interactive role of self-awareness and the attributional basis for negative expectancies. *Journal of Personality and Social Psychology, 43,* 1184–1191.

KLEINBAUM, D. G., KUPPER, L. L., AND MORGAN-

STERN, H. (1982). *Epidemiologic research: Principles and quantitative methods.* Belmont, CA: Lifetime Learning.

KLERMAN, G. L., AND WEISSMAN, M. M. (1982). Interpersonal psychotherapy: Theory and research. In A. J. RUSH (Ed.), *Short-term psychotherapies for depression.* NY: Guilford Press.

KUIPER, N. A. (1978). Depression and causal attributions for success and failure. *Journal of Personality and Social Psychology, 36,* 236–246.

LANGER, E. J. (1978). Rethinking the role of thought in social interaction. In J. HARVEY, W. ICKES, AND R. F. KIDD (Eds.), *New directions in attribution research* (Vol. 2). Hillsdale, NJ: Erlbaum.

LAZARUS, A. A. (1968). Learning theory and the treatment of depression. *Behavior Research and Therapy, 6,* 83–89.

LAZARUS, R. S., AND LAUNIER, R. (1978). Stress-related transactions between person and environment. In L. A. PERVIN AND M. LEWIS (Eds.), *Internal and external determinants of behavior.* NY: Plenum.

LEHMAN, H. E. (1971). Epidemiology of depressive disorders. In R. R. FIEVE (Ed.), *Depression in the 70's: Modern theory and research.* Princeton, NJ: Excerpta Medica.

LEVITT, E. G., AND LUBIN, B. (1975). *Depression.* NY: Springer.

LEWINSOHN, P. M. (1975). The behavioral study and treatment of depression. In M. HERSEN, R. M. EISLER, AND P. M. MILLER (Eds.), *Progress in behavioral modification* (Vol. 1). NY: Academic Press.

LEWINSOHN, P. M. (1976). Activity schedules in the treatment of depression. In C. E. THORESEN AND J. D. KRUMBOLTZ (Eds.), *Counseling methods* (pp. 74–83). NY: Holt, Rinehart & Winston.

LEWINSOHN, P. M., AND ALEXANDER, C. (1983). *Depression and learned helplessness.* Paper presented at the Annual Meeting of the Association for the Advancement of Behavior Therapy, Washington, DC.

LEWINSOHN, P. M., FENN, D., STANTON, A., AND FRANKLIN, J. (1985). *The relationship of age at onset to duration of episode in unipolar depression.* Unpublished manuscript, University of Oregon, Eugene.

LEWINSOHN, P. M., HAUTZINGER, M., AND DUNCAN, E. (1984). *Is there an age elevated risk for unipolar depression?* Unpublished mimeo, University of Oregon, Eugene.

LEWINSOHN, P. M., AND HOBERMAN, H. M. (1982). Depression. In A. S. BELLACK, M. HERSEN, AND

A. E. KAZDIN (Eds.), *International handbook of behavior modification and therapy.* NY: Plenum.

LEWINSOHN, P. M., LARSON, D. W., AND MUÑOZ, R. F. (1982). Measurement of expectancies and other cognitions in depressed individuals. *Cognitive Therapy and Research, 6,* 437–446.

LEWINSOHN, P. M. LOBITZ, W. C., AND WILSON, S. (1973). Sensitivity of depressed individuals to aversive stimuli. *Journal of Abnormal Psychology, 81,* 259–263.

LEWINSOHN, P. M. MISCHEL, W., CHAPLIN, W., AND BARTON, R. (1980). Social competence and depression: The role of illusory self-perceptions. *Journal of Abnormal Psychology, 89,* 203–212.

LEWINSOHN, P. M., STEINMETZ, J., LARSON, D., AND FRANKLIN, J. (1981). Depression related cognitions: Antecedent or consequence? *Journal of Abnormal Psychology, 90,* 213–219.

LEWINSOHN, P. M., AND TALKINGTON, J. (1979). Studies on the measurement of unpleasant events and relations with depression. *Applied Psychological Measurement, 3,* 83–101.

LEWINSOHN, P. M., TERI, L., AND HOBERMAN, H. (1983). Depression: A perspective on etiology, treatment, and life span issues. In M. ROSENBAUM, D. FRANKS, AND Y. JAFFE (Eds.), *Perspectives on behavior therapy in the eighties.* NY: Springer.

LEWINSOHN, P. M., WEINSTEIN, M., AND SHAW, D. (1969). Depression: A clinical-research approach. In R. D. RUBIN AND C. M. FRANK (Eds.), *Advances in behavior therapy.* NY: Academic Press.

LEWINSOHN, P. M., YOUNGREN, M. A., AND GROSSCUP, S. J. (1979). Reinforcement and depression. In R. A. DEPUE (Ed.), *The psychobiology of depressive disorders: Implications for the effects of stress.* NY: Academic Press.

LEWIS, A. J. (1938). States of depression: Their clinical and etiological differentiation. *British Medical Journal, 2,* 875–878.

LIBET, J., AND LEWINSOHN, P. M. (1973). The concept of social skill with special references to the behavior of depressed persons. *Journal of Consulting and Clinical Psychology, 40,* 304–312.

LLOYD, C. (1980). Life events and depressive disorder reviewed: Events as predisposing factors. *Archives of General Psychiatry, 37,* 529–535.

LLOYD, G., AND LISHMAN, W. A. (1975). Effect of depression on the speed of recall of pleasant and unpleasant experiences. *Psychological Medicine, 5,* 173–180.

MACPHILLAMY, D. J., AND LEWINSOHN, P. M. (1974). Depression as a function of levels of desired and obtained pleasure. *Journal of Abnormal Psychology, 83,* 651–657.

McLEAN, P. D. (1976). Therapeutic decision making in the behavioral treatment of depression. In P. O. DAVIDSON (Ed.), *The behavioral management of anxiety, depression, and pain.* NY: Bruner/Mazel.

McLEAN, P. D. (1979). *Matching of treatments to subject characteristics.* Paper presented at the NIMH conference "Research recommendations for the behavioral treatment of depression," Pittsburgh, PA.

McLEAN, P. D., AND HAKSTIAN, A. R. (1979). Clinical depression: Comparative efficacy of outpatient treatments. *Journal of Clinical and Counseling Psychology, 47,* 818–836.

MORRIS, J. B., AND BECK, A. T. (1974). The efficacy of anti-depressant drugs: A review of research (1958 to 1972). *Archives of General Psychiatry, 30,* 667–674.

MUÑOZ, R. F. (1977). A cognitive approach to the assessment and treatment of depression. *Dissertation Abstracts International, 38,* 2873B.

MYERS, J. K., AND WEISSMAN, M. M. (1980). Use of a self-report symptom scale to detect depression in a community sample. *American Journal of Psychiatry, 137,* 1081–1084.

NATALE, M., AND HANTAS, M. (1982). Effect of temporary mood states on selective memory about the self. *Journal of Personality and Social Psychology, 42,* 927–934.

NELSON, R. E. (1977). Irrational beliefs in depression. *Journal of Consulting and Clinical Psychology, 45,* 1190–1191.

OVERALL, J. E., AND HOLLISTER, L. E. (1966). Nosology and depression and differential response to drugs. *The Journal of the American Medical Association, 195,* 946–948.

OVERALL, J. E., AND HOLLISTER, L. E. (1980). Phenomenological classification of depressive disorders. *Journal of Clinical Psychology, 36,* 372–376.

PARKER, G., AND BROWN, L. (1979). Repertoires of response to potential precipitants of depression. *Australian and New Zealand Journal of Psychiatry, 13,* 327–333.

PAYKEL, E. S. (Ed.) (1982). *Handbook of affective disorders.* NY: Guilford Press.

PAYKEL, E. S., MYERS, J. K., DIENELT, M. N., KLERMAN, G. L., LINDENTHAL, J. J., AND PEPPER, M. P. (1969). Life events and depression: A controlled study. *Archives of General Psychiatry, 21,* 753–760.

PAYKEL, E. A., PRUSOFF, B., AND KLERMAN, G. L. (1971). The endogenous–neurotic continuum in depression: Rater independence and factor distributions. *Journal of Psychiatric Research, 8,* 73–90.

PETERSON, C., SCHWARTZ, S., AND SELIGMAN, M. E. P. (1981). Self-blame and depressive symptoms. *Journal of Personality and Social Psychology, 41,* 253–259.

REHM, L. P. (1977). A self-control model of depression. *Behavior Therapy, 8,* 787–804.

REHM, L. P., AND KORNBLITH, G. I. (1979). Behavior therapy for depression: A review of recent developments. In M. HERSEN, R. M. EISLER, AND P. M. MILLER (Eds.), *Progress in behavior modification* (Vol. 7). NY: Academic Press.

RIPPERE, V. (1977). Common sense beliefs about depression and antidepressive behavior: A study of social consensus. *Behavior Research and Therapy, 15,* 465–473.

ROGERS, T. B., KUIPER, N. A., AND KIRKER, W. S. (1977). Self-reference and the encoding of personal information. *Journal of Personality and Social Psychology, 35,* 677–688.

ROSENBAUM, M. (1980). A schedule for assessing self-control behaviors: Preliminary findings. *Behavior Therapy, 11,* 109–121.

ROSENTHAL, S. H., AND GUDEMAN, J. E. (1967). The endogenous depressive pattern: An empirical investigation. *Archives of General Psychiatry, 16,* 241–249.

RUSH, A. J., BECK, A. T., KOVACS, M., AND HOLLON, S. (1977). Comparative efficacy of cognitive therapy and pharmacotherapy in the treatment of depressed outpatients. *Cognitive Therapy and Research, 1,* 17–37.

SACHAR, E. J. (1975). Neuroendocrine abnormalities in depressive illness. In E. J. SACHAR (Ed.), *Topics in psychoendocrinology* (pp. 135–156). NY: Grune & Stratton.

SANCHEZ, V. C., LEWINSOHN, P. M., AND LARSON, D. W. (1980). Assertion training: Effectiveness in the treatment of depression. *Journal of Clinical Psychology, 36,* 526–529.

SCHANK, R., AND ABLESON, R. P. (1975). *Scripts, plans and knowledge.* Prepared for presentation at the 4th International Conference on Artificial Intelligence. Tbilisi, USSR.

SCHEIER, M. F., AND CARVER, C. S. (1977). *Learned helplessness or egotism: Do expectancies matter?* Carnegie-Mellon University, Pittsburgh.

SCHEIER, M. F., CARVER, C. S., AND GIBBONS, F. X. (1981). Self-focused attention and reactions to fear. *Journal of Research in Personality, 15,* 1–15.

SCHILDKRAUT, J. J. (1965). The catecholamine hypothesis of affective disorders: A review of supporting evidence. *American Journal of Psychiatry, 122,* 509–522.

SCHILDKRAUT, J. J., AND KETY, S. S. (1977). Biogenic amines and emotion. *Science, 156,* 21–30.

SELIGMAN, M. E. P. (1975). *Helplessness.* San Francisco, CA: W. H. Freeman.

SELIGMAN, M. E. P. (1981). A learned helplessness point of view. In L. P. REHM (Ed.), *Behavior therapy for depression* (pp. 123–142). NY: Academic Press.

SELIGMAN, M. E. P., ABRAMSON, L. Y., SEMMEL, A., AND VON BAEYER, C. (1979). Depressive attributional style. *Journal of Abnormal Psychology, 88,* 242–247.

SKINNER, B. F. (1953). *Science and human behavior.* NY: Macmillan.

SMITH, T. W., AND GREENBERG, J. (1981). Depression and self-focused attention. *Motivation and Emotion, 5,* 323–329.

STRACK, S., AND COYNE, J. C. (1983). Social confirmation of dysphoria: Shared and private reactions. *Journal of Personality and Social Psychology, 44,* 798–806.

SUGAR, M. (1967). Disguised depressions in adolescents. In G. L. USDEN (Ed.), *Adolescence: Care and Counseling* (pp. 77–93). Philadelphia: J. P. Lippincott.

SUSSER, M. (1966). *Causal thinking in the health sciences: Concepts and strategies of epidemiology.* NY: Oxford University Press.

TAYLOR, S. E., AND FISKE, S. T. (1978). Getting inside the head: Methodologies for process analysis in attribution and social cognition. In J. HARVEY, W. ICKES, AND R. KIDD (Eds.), *New directions in attributional research* (Vol. 3). Hillsdale, NJ: Erlbaum.

TEASDALE, J. D. (1983). Affect and accessibility. *Phil. Trans. R. Soc. Lond., B302,* 403–412.

TEASDALE, J. D., AND FOGARTY, S. J. (1979). Differential effects of induced mood on retrieval of pleasant and unpleasant events from episodic memory. *Journal of Abnormal Psychology, 88,* 248–257.

TEASDALE, J. D., AND RUSSELL, M. L. (1983). Differential effects of induced mood on the recall of positive, negative, and neutral words. *British Journal of Clinical Psychology, 22,* 163–171.

TEASDALE, J. D., AND TAYLOR, R. (1981). Induced

mood and accessibility of memories: An effect of mood state or of mood induction procedure? *British Journal of Clinical Psychology, 20,* 426–442.

TEASDALE, J. D., TAYLOR, R., AND FOGARTY, S. J. (1980). Effects of induced elation-depression on the accessibility of memories of happy and unhappy experiences. *Behavior Research and Therapy, 18,* 339–346.

TERI, L., AND LEWINSOHN, P. M. (1985). *Depression and age: The relationship of age, gender, and method of assessment on the symptom pattern of depression.* Unpublished mimeo. University of Oregon, Eugene.

TOOLAN, J. M. (1969). Depression in children and adolescents. In G. CAPLAN AND S. LeBOVICI (Eds.), *Adolescence: Psychosocial perspective.* NY: Basic Books.

VERNON, S. W., AND ROBERTS, R. E. (1982). Prevalence of treated and untreated psychiatric disorders in three ethnic groups. *Social Science and Medicine, 16,* 1575–1582.

WEGNER, D. N., AND GIULIANO, T. (1980). Arousal-induced attention to self. *Journal of Personality and Social Psychology, 38,* 719–726.

WEISSMAN, M. M., AND KLERMAN, G. (1977). Sex differences and the epidemiology of depression. *Archives of General Psychiatry, 34,* 98–111.

WEISSMAN, M. M., AND MYERS, J. K. (1978). Affective disorders in a US urban community. *Archives of General Psychiatry, 35,* 1304–1311.

WEISSMAN, M. M., AND PAYKEL, E. S. (1974). *The depressed woman.* Chicago: University of Chicago Press.

WEISSMAN, M. M., PRUSOFF, B. A., AND KLERMAN, G. L. (1978). Personality and the prediction of long-term outcome of depression. *American Journal of Psychiatry, 135,* 797–800.

WENER, A. E., AND REHM, L. P. (1975). Depressive affect: A test of behavioral hypotheses. *Journal of Abnormal Psychology, 84,* 221–227.

WILKINSON, I. M., AND BLACKBURN, I. M. (1981).

Cognitive style in depressed and recovered depressed patients. *British Journal of Clinical Psychology, 20,* 283–292.

WILSON, P. H., GOLDIN, J. C., AND CHARBONNEAU-POWIS, M. (1983). Comparative efficacy of behavioral and cognitive treatments of depression. *Cognitive Therapy and Research, 7,* 111–124.

WOODRUFF, R. A., JR., MURPHY, G. E., AND HERJANIC, M. (1967). The natural history of affective disorders. 1. Symptoms of 72 patients at the time of index hospital admission. *Journal of Psychiatric Research, 5,* 255–263.

YOUNGREN, M. A. (1978). *The functional relationship of depression and problematic interpersonal behavior.* Unpublished doctoral dissertation, University of Oregon, Eugene.

YOUNGREN, M. A., AND LEWINSOHN, P. M. (1980). The functional relationship between depression and problematic interpersonal behavior. *Journal of Abnormal Psychology, 89,* 333–341.

ZEISS, A. M. (1977). Interpersonal behavior problems of the depressed: A study of outpatient treatment. *Dissertation Abstracts International, 38,* 2895B–28956B.

ZEISS, A. M., LEWINSOHN, P. M., AND MUÑOZ, R. (1979). Nonspecific improvement effects in depression using interpersonal, cognitive, and pleasant events focused treatments. *Journal of Consulting and Clinical Psychology, 47,* 427–439.

ZEISS, A. M., AND LEWINSOHN, P. M. (in preparation). *Social skill of formerly depressed individuals.* University of Oregon, Eugene.

ZIS, A. P., AND GOODWIN, F. K. (1982). The amine hypothesis. In E. S. PAYKEL (Ed.), *Handbook of affective disorders* (pp. 179–190). NY: Guilford Press.

ZUBIN, J. (1976). The role of vulnerability in the etiology of schizophrenic episodes. In L. J. WEST AND D. E. FLINN (Eds.), *Treatment of schizophrenia: Progress and prospects.* NY: Grune and Stratton.

17

Mania and Low Self-Esteem

Ken C. Winters and John M. Neale

The present study tested the theory that although bipolar patients do not report low self-esteem, they do possess a cognitive schema of low self-esteem. Equal-sized groups (n = 16) of remitted bipolars, remitted unipolars, and normals completed a self-report battery of tests of self-esteem, social desirability, and self-deception, and a task designed to assess whether self-esteem influences inferences about the causes of imagined events. Remitted bipolars scored the same as normals and higher than remitted depressives on self-esteem, and they scored higher than the other groups on both social desirability and self-deception. Furthermore, remitted bipolars' inferences about the causes of failures resembled those of a depressive, suggesting the presence of a low self-worth schema. The data are consistent with the view that bipolar patients have negative feelings of self which are not revealed on usual self-report inventories. Also, because the remitted depressives showed a "depressive attributional style" on the inference task, issues concerning the mood dependence of depressive cognitions were discussed.

Ken C. Winters and John M. Neale. Mania and Low Self-Esteem. *Journal of Abnormal Psychology,* 1985, Vol. 94, No. 3, pp. 282–290. Copyright © 1985 by the American Psychological Association. Reprinted by permission of the publisher and authors.

Psychologists' interest in depression has accelerated over the last decade, perhaps due to the development of psychological theories of the disorder (e.g., Abramson, Seligman, & Teasdale, 1978; Beck, 1967; Lewinsohn, 1974). Most of this interest, however, has focused on unipolar depression and is based on a conceptual framework that addresses the differences between depressive and normal states. In contrast, research on bipolar disorder (cycling of depression and mania) has remained largely within the province of physiologically oriented theory, leaving a large gap in our understanding of psychological mechanisms in mania.

The available literature concerning psychological underpinnings of mania is, for the most part, limited to psychodynamic accounts. In general, these theories suggest that mania is a defense against an unpleasant psychological state such as unacceptable id impulses (e.g., Klein, 1968) or the psychic pain associated with object loss and its associated depression (Freeman, 1971; Lewin, 1951). However, the proposed psychic states against which the manic is defending have not been empirically identified nor has the "defensive" aspect of the theory been directly tested.

We propose that self-esteem is a promising variable for study in bipolar patients. Fluctuations in reported self-esteem are indeed prominent features of both poles of the disorder—low self-esteem in depression and high self-esteem (grandiosity) in mania. Following the general framework suggested by earlier psychodynamic theories, we hypothesize that low self-esteem may characterize the manic in both phases of the disorder. In the manic phase, however, low self-esteem is not directly expressed. Furthermore, because self-esteem is usually regarded as a relatively stable characteristic, we hypothesize that low self-esteem is also present (although perhaps attenuated from what would be observed during a depressive episode) but not directly expressed between episodes of the bipolar disorder.

Indirect support for this viewpoint is provided by data indicating that on self-report inventories remitted manics appear "normal" (e.g., MacVane, Lange, Brown, & Zayat, 1978) yet frequently experience marital problems (e.g., Brodie & Leff, 1971) and difficulties at work (Dunner & Hall, 1980). Moreover, from a clinical perspective, manic patients' interpersonal behavior has been described in ways that are consistent with a low self-esteem formulation. For example, manics are often described as poor candidates for psychotherapy. Dooley (1921) described the typical therapy picture wherein the manic forms therapy relationships easily because of an eagerness to please and gratefulness for the therapist's interest. However, as analysands, manics tend to be shallow and show little talent for introspection, which could reflect avoidance of distressing information about the self. Rado (1928) noted that manics have low self-regard and crave others' approval almost obsessively. Similar views of bipolars have been noted by others (Ablon, Davenport, Gershon, & Adland, 1975; Cohen, Baker, Cohen, Fromm-Reichmann, & Weigert, 1954; Donnelly, Murphy, & Goodwin, 1976; Gibson, Cohen, & Cohen, 1959; Jacobson, 1953; Janowsky, El-Yousef, & Davis, 1974; Janowsky, Leff, & Epstein, 1970).

The present study examined whether bipolars, even when not depressed, have feelings of low self-esteem. Although a thorough examination of the hypothesis would require a longitudinal study of bipolars during both manic and depressive states, as a first step we decided to test a group of bipolars who were in remission. Because it may be difficult to obtain meaningful participation in psychological tasks from a floridly symptomatic manic, and also because the hypothesis suggests that feelings of low self-esteem are relatively stable, testing the hypothesis on remitted manics was viewed as an appropriate beginning. First, remitted manics' self-reports were examined with a battery of inventories that measured self-esteem, defensiveness, and self-deception (i.e., unwillingness to admit certain undesirable and uncomfortable feelings and attitudes). The hypothesis suggests that remitted manics will express both a normal level of self-esteem and a high degree of defensiveness and self-deception. The implication of this pattern of results is that the report of a normal level of self-esteem may not be veridical.

In the second part of the study, we attempted to measure the hypothesized low self-esteem of bipolars in a subtle way, using a pragmatic inference task. A pragmatic inference is merely a conclusion that is drawn by an individual from stated information; however, the conclusion consists of information that was not stated directly and need not logically follow from the original statement (Harris & Monaco, 1978). Although people can distinguish between given information and inferred information under detailed immediate questioning, such distinctions generally are lost at later recall. This confusion between stated and inferred information is consistent with the view that people go beyond the information given and make tacit assumptions about causality, actors, instruments, and actions (Johnson, Bransford, & Solomon, 1973), and that these assumptions can be shaped by specific domain-related prior knowledge (e.g., Minsky, 1975). Furthermore, there is growing evidence to suggest that dispositional characteristics, such as self-esteem, can affect information processing in a task such as this (e.g., Markus, 1977).

The pragmatic inference paradigm was

used to investigate patterns of causal attributions in remitted manics. Subjects were read aloud short scenarios characterized by ambiguous causes of events (i.e., both an internal and external cause were imbedded) and were required to make inferences about causal attributions implied within the story. Based on the hypothesis that remitted manics have feelings of low self-esteem it was predicted that they will infer that positive events are due to external factors (e.g., luck) and negative events to internal ones (e.g., self).

A remitted unipolar depressive group was also included in the study because they characteristically express low self-esteem, even in remission (Altman & Wittenborn, 1980), and do not typically show high levels of defensiveness. Furthermore, the inclusion of this group allows us to examine a current issue concerning the relation of mood to depressive-like cognitions. Most germane to this issue is Hamilton and Abramson's (1983) findings that "depressive attributional style" was present when depressives were symptomatic but was largely absent when the patients were tested later just prior to discharge, presumably when the symptoms were in remission. They measured attributional style using the Attributional Style Questionnaire (ASQ; Seligman, Abramson, Semmel, & von Baeyer, 1979). The ASQ requires the subject to state causes for a variety of hypothetical success and failure events. The task measures attributional style in a relatively transparent way and, therefore, may encourage self-presentation bias. Being tested just before discharge could encourage a depressed patient to self-present in a positive light, thus accounting for Hamilton and Abramson's finding of the disappearance of the depressive-like attributional style. Our pragmatic inference task differs from the ASQ in that (a) both success and failure are embellished in each story, (b) subjects are required to answer questions about facts and inferences not related to causality, and (c) the task is presented as a nonspecific memory task. Therefore, our inference task may provide an opportunity to assess attributional style in a way that is less sensitive to response biasing.[1]

Method
Subjects

Forty-eight subjects—16 bipolar outpatients, 16 unipolar depressive outpatients, and 16 normals—between the ages of 18 and 65 were included in the study. The bipolars and depressives were recruited from two local outpatient clinics (Downstate Medical Center in Brooklyn, New York, and Health Sciences Center, State University of New York at Stony Brook). Only those with a discharge *Diagnostic and Statistical Manual of Mental Disorders*, 3rd edition (DSM-III; American Psychiatric Association, 1980) diagnosis from their most recent hospitalization of bipolar disorder (either mixed or manic) or major depression (single episode or recurrent) were considered. In addition, bipolars were required to have had at least one previous episode of depression. One bipolar and one depressive who were approached refused participation. Diagnosis for this study con-

---

[1]Two additional cognitive tasks were also used but are not discussed in this report because they did not provide an adequate test of the hypothesis. One was a dichotic shadowing paradigm in which adjectives varying in their relation to self-esteem (low esteem-content, high esteem-content, and neutral content) were presented to subjects in the unattended ear while a series of numbers were shadowed in the attended ear. Subjects were subsequently tested for recognition of the unattended adjectives. The prediction was that the manics would recognize more low self-esteem-content adjectives than high self-esteem and neutral-content adjectives. However, the unipolar depressives who were also tested did not display this pattern, even though they were characterized by self-reported low self-esteem. Therefore, we conclude that the task failed to test the theory adequately. The second task used a verbal-slips induction paradigm (Motley & Baars, 1976) to test the prediction that manics would commit more verbal slips that connote low self-esteem as opposed to verbal slips unrelated to self-esteem. However, the rate of verbal slips by all subjects was extremely low, and the task proved to be unreliable (coefficients alpha for low self-esteem items = .21; for neutral items = .19).

formed to the DSM-III. To ensure that these criteria were met, all prospective subjects were administered the Schedule for Affective Disorders and Schizophrenia (SADS); Spitzer & Endicott, 1978) by the first author. Interviews focused on (a) the month prior to the interview, (b) the month preceding the patient's most recent hospitalization, and (c) past history of psychopathology. Information about past psychopathology is important to distinguish between bipolar disorder and major depression; present symptomatology was assessed to ensure that all subjects were indeed in remission. Cases were independently diagnosed by one of the authors and an advanced graduate student. Two categories were of interest: bipolar disorder in remission and major depression in remission. Exclusion from the study occurred if (a) there was disagreement between diagnosticians ($n = 1$), or (b) the individual's current symptomatology was

severe enough to meet DSM-III criteria for the disorder ($n = 2$). Normals (hospital staff and local clerical workers) were excluded if they had a history of psychiatric or psychological treatment, organicity, or addiction ($n = 0$).

Demographic and symptom data for the current (i.e., remitted) period and for the period covering the most recent hospitalization are presented in Table 1. Separate symptom data are reported for categories of items on the SADS that relate to depression and mania and for individual items that most closely pertain to self-esteem (negative worth and grandiosity). Negative worth refers to feelings of worthlessness and low self-worth; grandiosity refers to the delusional or nondelusional belief of elevated power, knowledge, or ability in oneself. The category that comprises the sum of other depressive symptoms includes subjective feelings of depression, feelings of self-reproach,

TABLE 1 Characteristics of Sample

Data	Remitted Bipolars		Remitted Depressives		Normals		F or t
	M	SD	M	SD	M	SD	
Demographics							
Age	47.4	13.4	42.1	12.4	43.4	11.5	0.39
Educational level[a]	3.8	1.5	4.8	0.9	3.6	1.7	1.56
Occupation rating[b]	4.4	1.4	5.5	0.9	4.3	1.1	2.90
No. previous hospitalizations	4.0	3.3	2.3	1.1			10.40*
No. years since most recent hospitalization	2.9	2.6	2.4	1.7			2.34
Current symptom ratings[c]							
Negative worth	0.3	0.2	0.6	0.7			1.32
Sum of other depression symptoms	0.8	0.2	1.3	0.8			3.04*
Grandiosity	0.3	0.5	0.2	0.3			.76
Sum of other manic symptoms	0.8	0.7	0.6	0.6			.74
Symptom ratings of previous hospitalization[c]							
Negative worth	2.3	0.5	4.9	1.3			4.6*
Sum of other depressive symptoms	20.3	3.1	42.2	4.1			9.2*
Grandiosity	5.1	1.0	1.1	0.3			8.9*
Sum of other manic symptoms	49.3	4.1	13.2	2.6			13.4*

Note. For all groups, $n = 16$. Women composed 75% of remitted bipolar group and normals, and 68.8% of remitted depressives. [a]Ratings based on scale from Current and Past Psychopathology Scales (CAPPS; Spitzer & Endicott, 1968): 1 = professional, 7 = <7 years of school. [b]Ratings based on scale from CAPPS: 1 = high executive or major professional, 8 = adult not working at job, school, or housework. [c]Based on ratings from SADS: 0 = not present, 6 = severe. *$p < .01$.

discouragement, suicidal tendencies, sleep disturbance, subjective feeling of lack of energy, appetite change, indecisiveness, loss of concentration, and loss of interest in usually pleasurable activities. The category that consists of the sum of the other manic symptoms includes elevated or expansive mood, less sleep than usual, more energy than usual, increase in goal-directed behavior, expression of irritability, motor hyperactivity, pressured or accelerated speech, and involvement in activities with high potential for painful consequences.

No between-group differences were found on age, highest completed school grade, highest occupational level obtained, and number of years since most recent hospitalization. For the current symptom ratings, the scores for the two clinical groups were very low. On one measure—sum of the other depressive symptoms—the remitted depressives were scored reliably higher than remitted bipolars. The low scores on current symptoms indicate that patients were in remission. The remitted bipolar group had significantly more previous hospitalizations than the remitted depressive group, $t(30) = 10.4$, $p < .01$, which is consistent with previous findings (e.g., Depue & Monroe, 1978). For symptom data on the month preceding the patient's most recent hospitalization, remitted manics and remitted depressives differed significantly ($p < .01$) on negative worth, sum of other depression symptoms, grandiosity, and sum of other manic symptoms. These findings indicate that symptomatology agreed with diagnoses.

Materials and Task Descriptions

Self-Report Battery. The self-report battery consisted of three instruments: O'Brien and Epstein's (1974) Self-Report Inventory II (SRI-II), the Marlowe-Crowne Social Desirability Scale (M-C SD; Crowne & Marlowe, 1964), and the Self-Deception Questionnaire (SDQ; Sackeim & Gur, 1979). All items were distributed randomly and rescaled to fit one format (4-point Likert scale, anchored by *false, mostly false, mostly true,*

and *true*). Subjects were instructed to indicate how accurate or inaccurate each item would be as a self-description.

The SRI-II consists of 98 items that are divided into nine scales related to self-esteem: general esteem, power over self, power over others, likeability, competence, morality, health, functioning, and appearance. All scales have positive and negative questions. The split-half reliabilities for all subscales are quite adequate (ranging from .64 to .95), and all intercorrelations among subscales are positive with the majority falling within the .20 to .60 range (O'Brien, 1980).

The M-C SD scale consists of 33 items, of which 18 are keyed *true* and 15 *false*. Crowne and Marlowe (1964) reported that this scale has an internal consistency of .88 (Kuder-Richardson formula 20) and a test–retest reliability of .84 (1-month interval). Although high scores on the M-C SD have been commonly interpreted as a measure of social-desirability response set, extended work with this scale has led to its use as a measure of defensiveness (Crowne & Marlowe, 1964; Weinberger, Schwartz, & Davidson, 1979).

The SDQ consists of 20 items. Positive endorsements are judged to be universally true but psychologically threatening (e.g., "Have you ever made a fool of yourself?"). In a sample of 55 undergraduates, Sackeim and Gur (1979) found that the SDQ has a test–retest reliability of .81 (4- and 10-week intervals), and that it correlated positively with other measures of deception.

Pragmatic Inference. Stimuli for this task consisted of 12 short scenarios, some of them adapted from items on the ASQ (Seligman et al., 1979). These scenarios—half of which reflect successful outcomes and the other half failure outcomes—consist of short paragraphs that describe a situation in which both an internal and external locus of causality is implied. For example, one scenario describes a situation in which a person is unemployed and having difficulty finding new work; the cause is hinted to be either

TABLE 2 Means and Standard Deviations for the Measures of Self-Esteem, Social Desirability, and Self-Deception

Measure	Remitted Bipolars		Remitted Depressives		Normals	
	M	SD	M	SD	M	SD
Self-esteem	233.8	18.7	187.0	10.6	240.0	17.1
Social desirability	90.6	14.8	81.1	10.7	81.5	7.9
Self-deception	50.8	7.9	44.6	3.9	42.4	6.4

Note. Higher values for each scale represent more of the concept being assessed.

poor work record (internal) or a poor job market (external). The themes for the remaining scenarios were: Your new business becomes successful; you are complimented on your appearance at work; a neighbor shuns you by not asking for your advice; a co-worker acts hostile toward you; a stranger down on hard times befriends you; a first date goes poorly; you throw a successful party; people react negatively to a speech you give; the boss compliments your work performance; you receive favorable remarks from the professor on your term paper; you are given a pay raise at work. Scenarios were randomly ordered. After each scenario was read aloud, subjects were instructed to respond on paper to four multiple-choice questions pertaining to the story. In one question (target), subjects were asked to select which cause they remembered as the main contributing factor in the outcome of the scenario; in another they were asked for memory of implied information not related to causality, and in two other questions they were asked for memory of stated facts. Pilot work was conducted on a group of col-

lege students so that the probability of endorsing either an internal or an external cause for each target item would not differ statistically from .5. After some modification and repiloting, all target items met this criterion. An example of one scenario and its follow-up questions is provided in the following example:

You have been looking unsuccessfully for a job as a factory worker. Unemployment is a problem in the economy, especially in your field. Sales are hurting because of foreign imports. You decide to talk to a friend about the situation, who reminds you that you have had difficulties with management because of tardiness and a poor performance record. Indeed, the last job in which you were laid off almost ended earlier when the boss threatened to fire you. Your search for a job is frustrating and you go 4 weeks without finding a job.

1. With whom do you discuss your situation? (factual)
   A. A relative
   B. A friend

TABLE 3 *t* Values for the Planned Contrasts

Measure	Bipolars vs. Depressives	Bipolars vs. Normals	Depressives vs. Normals
Self-esteem	8.3**	−1.1	−9.5**
Social desirability	2.4*	2.2*	−0.1
Self-deception	2.8**	3.7**	1.0

Note. df = 30.   *$p < .05$.   **$p < .01$.

TABLE 4 Pearson Product-Moment Correlations Among the Self-Report Measures

Group	Esteem and Social Desirability	Esteem and Self-deception
Remitted bipolar	.60*	.58*
Remitted depressive	−.22	.26
Normal	−.07	.32

*p < .05.

TABLE 5 Means and Standard Deviations on the Pragmatic Inference Task

	Remitted Bipolars		Remitted Depressives		Normals	
Question Topic	M	SD	M	SD	M	SD
Mean recall of stated facts						
Success scenarios	11.6	1.8	11.4	2.2	11.8	1.0
Failure scenarios	11.2	2.8	11.6	1.5	12.0	0.0
Tacit assumptions of causality						
Success scenarios	2.8	0.9	2.3	1.0	2.6	1.1
Failure scenarios	3.3	0.8	3.0	0.6	2.3	0.8

2. In what type of field were you previously employed? (noncausal inference)
A. Automobile industry
B. Computer industry

3. How long do you go without finding work? (factual)
A. Four weeks
B. Four months

4. Why do you have trouble finding work? (causal inference)
A. Poor work record
B. Poor job market

Procedure

After psychiatric subjects were interviewed (SADS) and their hospital records were re-

TABLE 6 t Values for the Planned Contrasts on Pragmatic Inference Task

Question Topic	Bipolars vs. Depressives	Bipolars vs. Normals	Depressives vs. Normals
Stated facts			
Success scenarios	0.1	0.1	0.2
Failure scenarios	0.2	0.3	0.1
Tacit assumptions			
Success scenarios	0.4	0.7	0.2
Failure scenarios	−0.5	3.1**	2.3*

Note. df = 30.   *p < .05.   **p < .01.

TABLE 7 Pearson Product-Moment Correlations Between the Pragmatic Inference Task and the Self-Report Inventory II

| | Tacit Assumptions on the PIT | | |
Group	Success	Failure	Total
Remitted bipolar	−.18	.12	−.04
Remitted depressive	−.15	−.42*	−.32
Normal	−.53*	−.38	−.56*
Pooled correlation for normals and depressives[a]	−.37*	−.42*	−.48*

Note. PIT = pragmatic inference task.   [a]Calculated by applying the z transformation, averaging the z scores, and converting back to r.

viewed to determine if inclusion criteria for the study were met, the interviewer escorted them to a testing room and administered first the self-report battery on self-esteem, defensiveness, and self-deception and then the pragmatic inference task (along with the other cognitive tasks noted earlier). The inference task was presented as a test of memory. Control subjects were given a brief diagnostic interview to rule out the presence of any psychiatric problems and then administered the materials in a testing room in the same manner as the psychiatric subjects.

Results

Self-Report Measures

A series of planned comparisons was conducted to evaluate the following two sets of hypotheses. First, on self-esteem remitted bipolars and normals will not differ, and both will score higher than remitted depressives; these predictions are based on the assumption that although both remitted bipolars and remitted depressives actually have low self-esteem, manics will not present themselves in a manner consistent with their "true" feelings. Second, on social desirability and self-deception remitted bipolars will score higher than remitted depressives and normals, and remitted depressives and normals will not differ; these predictions are based on the clinical lore that depressives are not defensive, and that bipolars are defensive

in their self-presentations. Each of these predictions was confirmed.[2] (See Tables 2 and 3 for means, standard deviations, and t values.)

To determine whether defensiveness was related to self-esteem, Pearson product–moment correlations were computed between the self-esteem total score and the two defensiveness scales within each diagnostic group. For the remitted bipolars, there were significant positive correlations between self-esteem and social desirability ($r = .60$), and self-esteem and self-deception ($r = .58$). All other correlations were nonsignificant. Fisher's r to z transformation was used to test the significance of the differences between correlations. For the remitted bipolars, the correlation between self-esteem and social desirability was greater than this correlation in the other two groups ($p < .05$, one-tailed); the magnitude of the correlations between self-esteem and self-deception did not differ significantly among the groups (see Table 4).

Pragmatic Inference Task

On the pragmatic inference task, we predicted that remitted bipolars and depressives

---

[2]For the self-esteem measure, the same pattern of results was found for four of the nine subscales: general esteem, power over others, likeability, and competence. Normals scored higher than remitted bipolars on power over self and health ($p < .05$) and higher than remitted unipolars on morality and functioning ($p < .05$). Remitted bipolars scored higher than remitted depressives and normals on appearance ($p < .05$)

would be more likely than normals to select an external cause for success and an internal cause for failure. Analyses were first performed to evaluate recall of stated facts. Mean recall was extremely high for all groups, and there were no between-group differences (see Table 5). For success events, the dependent variable is the number of events given an external attribution; for failure events, the dependent variable is the number of events given an internal attribution. Coefficients alpha for the causality items were adequate: success events = .59, failure events = .69. Planned contrasts on failure scenarios indicated that remitted bipolars and remitted depressives chose significantly more internal causes than did normals, $t(30) = 3.1$, $p < .01$; $t(30) = 2.3$, $p < .05$, respectively (see Table 6). There were no between-group differences on success scenarios (see Table 5).[3]

Validity of the Pragmatic Inference Task

We computed Pearson product-moment correlations between the pragmatic inference task and the SRI-II, a reliable and valid measure of self-esteem (Table 7). Our hypothesis is that the inference task and SRI-II ought to be negatively correlated in normals and unipolars, but uncorrelated in bipolars because their SRI-II scores are assumed to be invalid. For the bipolars, none of the correlations between pragmatic inferences and SRI-II approached significance. For the other groups moderately strong relations emerged. However, the correlations for the bipolars were not reliably smaller ($p < .05$) than those for any other group, although there were several trends in this direction.

Discussion

The pattern of scores for the remitted bipolars on the self-report instruments and the pragmatic inference task is consistent with the theory that bipolar disorder is associated with unreported feelings of low self-esteem. Remitted bipolars scored the same as normals and higher than remitted depressives on self-esteem and higher than both groups on social desirability and self-deception. Like the remitted depressives, they attributed significantly more negative events to internal causes than did normals. Insofar as the tendency to infer that failures are due to internal causes reflects a cognitive "schema" of low self-esteem, it can be inferred that remitted bipolars, like remitted depressives, have lower self-esteem than do normals, yet they do not report this to be the case on a self-report inventory.[4] Furthermore, in the bipolar group, there was no relation between the pragmatic inference task and the SRI-II, and yet there was a strong relation between the measures of defensiveness and the SRI-II. This pattern did not occur in the other two groups. Therefore, these results suggest that the remitted bipolars were defensive about self-esteem and that the pragmatic inference task may have bypassed this defensiveness.

One interpretation of the data is that the bipolar, like the depressive, is aware of feelings of low self-esteem yet, in contrast to the depressive, avoids the discomfort produced by these feelings by self-reporting normal esteem. The possibility that bipolars are defensive about self-esteem is consistent with psychodynamic notions that disordered individuals often project a self-image that serves to reduce uncomfortable self-attitudes (see Winters & Neale, 1983). However, whether the process of recognizing feelings

---

[3]Mean ratings on attribution questions for success scenarios for all groups were slightly less than the mean score expected (3.0) if all items had precisely met criteria for optimal item probability (.5). This result occurred because most of these six attribution questions when considered individually tended to have an item probability slightly less, but not significantly different, than .5.

---

[4]The lack of a diagnostic effect on pragmatic inferences for success events is not inconsistent with some literature on attributional style in depressives. For example, Seligman, Abramson, Semmel, and von Baeyer (1979) found that differences between depressives and normals were generally absent for success scenarios.

of low self-esteem and self-reporting normal esteem occurs at a conscious or unconscious level cannot be determined from the data.

It is important, however, to qualify these interpretations with the caution that our study is a preliminary examination that admittedly requires replication with a longitudinal design. The low self-esteem hypothesis implies that during a manic phase self-report of esteem would be high, whereas indexes of cognitive schema would reveal low self-esteem. Conversely, during a depressive phase, self-report and cognitive schema would indicate low self-esteem. A within-subjects design that tested bipolars during both phases of the disorder would address these predictions. A critical question related to this issue concerns why low self-esteem is sometimes expressed overtly in the form of depression and why it is sometimes effectively avoided. Furthermore, we appreciate the need for more research to delineate the specific cognitive processes that are involved in schema-based inferences. Whether the nature of this process involves encoding or retrieval effects, or some other cognitive process such as response biasing, is indeed an important question for future work.

Finally the performance of the remitted depressives deserves discussion. They reported lower esteem than did normals and remitted bipolars, which is consistent with other findings that suggest the presence of depressive-like traits (e.g., negative opinion of self after a clinical episode has passed (e.g., Altman & Wittenborn, 1980). However, our finding that depressive-like cognitions are present during remission is not consistent with Hamilton and Abramson's (1983) study. The results of their study indicated that depressive attributional style was absent during remission. These findings were interpreted as suggesting that depressive attributional style may be mood dependent. Our results from the pragmatic inference task suggest that a depressive-like schema may persist following remission of clinical symptoms. The previously discussed differences between our task and the ASQ seem crucial; that is, Hamilton and Abram-

son's failure to find depressive attributional style may simply reflect response biasing due to the context of being tested just before discharge from the hospital. If self-presentation bias is avoided, depressive cognitive schemas may be relatively stable.

References

ABLON, S. L., DAVENPORT, Y. B., GERSHON, E. S., AND ADLAND, M. L. (1975). The married manic. *American Journal of Orthopsychiatry, 45,* 854–866.

ABRAMSON, L. Y, SELIGMAN, M. E. P., AND TEASDALE, J. D. (1978). Learned helplessness in humans: Critique and reformulation. *Journal of Abnormal Psychology, 87,* 49–74.

ALTMAN, J. H., AND WITTENBORN, J. R. (1980). Depression-prone personality in women. *Journal of Abnormal Psychology, 89,* 303–308.

AMERICAN PSYCHIATRIC ASSOCIATION. (1980). *Diagnostic and statistical manual of mental disorders* (3rd ed.). Washington, DC: Author.

BECK, A. T. (1967). *Depression: Clinical, experimental and theoretical aspects.* New York: Harper & Row.

BRODIE, H. K. H., AND LEFF, M. J. (1973). Bipolar depression—a comparative study of patients' characteristics. *American Journal of Psychiatry, 28,* 221–228.

COHEN, M. B., BAKER, G., COHEN, R. A., FROMM-REICHMANN, R., AND WEIGERT, E. V. (1954). An intensive study of twelve cases of manic-depressive psychosis. *Psychiatry, 17,* 103–138.

CROWNE, D. P., AND MARLOW, D. (1964). *The approval motive: Studies in evaluative dependence.* New York: Wiley.

DEPUE, R. A., AND MONROE, S. M. (1978). The unipolar–bipolar distinction in the depressive disorders. *Psychological Bulletin, 85,* 1001–1030.

DONNELLY, E. F., MURPHY, D. L., AND GOODWIN, F. K. (1976). Cross-sectional and longitudinal comparisons of unipolar and bipolar depressed groups. *Journal of Consulting and Clinical Psychology, 44,* 233–237.

DOOLEY, L. (1921). A psychoanalytic study of manic-depressive psychosis. *Psychoanalytic Review, 8,* 32–72.

DUNNER, D. L., AND HALL, K. S. , (1980). Social adjustment and psychological precipitants in mania. In R. H. BELMAKER AND H. M. VAN

PRAAG (Eds.), *Mania: An evolving concept* (pp. 337–347). Jamaica, NY: Spectrum.

FREEMAN, T. (1971). Observations on mania. *International Journal of Psychoanalysis, 52,* 479–486.

GIBSON, R. W., COHEN, M. B., AND COHEN, R. A. (1959). On the dynamics of the manic-depressive personality. *American Journal of Psychiatry, 115,* 1101–1107.

HAMILTON, E. W., AND ABRAMSON, L. Y. (1983). Cognitive patterns and major depressive disorder: A longitudinal study in a hospital setting. *Journal of Abnormal Psychology, 92,* 173–184.

HARRIS, R. J., AND MONACO, G. E. (1978). Psychology of pragmatic inference: Information processing between the lines. *Journal of Experimental Psychology, 107,* 1–22.

JACOBSON, E. (1953). Contribution to the metapsychology of cyclothymic depression. In P. GREENACRE (Ed.), *Affective disorders* (pp. 212–234). New York: International University Press.

JANOWSKY, D. S., EL-YOUSEF, M. K., AND DAVIS, J. M. (1974). Interpersonal maneuvers of manic patients. *American Journal of Psychiatry, 131,* 250–255.

JANOWSKY, D. S., LEFF, M., AND EPSTEIN, R. S. (1970). Playing the manic game. *Archives of General Psychiatry, 22,* 252–261.

JOHNSON, M. K., BRANSFORD, J. D., AND SOLOMON, S. K. (1973). Memory for tacit implications of sentences. *Journal of Experimental Psychology, 98,* 203–225.

KLEIN, M. (1968). A contribution to the psychogenesis of manic-depressive states. In W. GAYLIN (Ed.), *The meaning of despair* (pp. 182–223). New York: Science House.

LEWIN, B. (1951). *The psycho-analysis of elation.* London: Hogarth.

LEWINSOHN, P. M. (1974). A behavioral approach to depression. In R. J. FREIDMAN AND M. M. KATZ (Eds.), *The psychology of depression: Contemporary theory and research* (pp. 157–178). Washington, DC: Winston-Wiley.

MACVANE, J. R., LANGE, J. D., BROWN, W. A., AND ZAYAT, M. (1978). Psychological functioning of bipolar manic-depressives in remission. *Archives of General Psychiatry, 35,* 1351–1354.

MARKUS, H. (1977). Self-schemata and processing information about the self. *Journal of Personality and Social Psychology, 35,* 63–78.

MINSKY, M. (1975). A framework for representing knowledge. In P. H. Winston (Ed.), *The psychology of computer vision.* New York: McGraw-Hill.

MOTLEY, M. T., AND BAARS, B. J. (1976). Laboratory induction of verbal slips: A new method of psycholinguistic research. *Communication Quarterly, 24,* 28–34.

O'BRIEN, E. J. (1980). *The Self-Report Inventory: Development and validation of a multidimensional measure of the self-concept and sources of self-esteem.* Unpublished manuscript. University of Massachusetts.

O'BRIEN, E. J., AND EPSTEIN, S. (1974, August). *Naturally occurring changes in self-esteem.* Paper presented at the annual meeting of the American Psychological Association, New Orleans, LA.

RADO, S. (1928). The problem of melancholia. *International Journal of Psychoanalysis, 9,* 420–438.

SACKEIM, H. A., AND GUR, R. C. (1979). Self-deception, other deception, and self-reported psychopathology. *Journal of Consulting and Clinical Psychology, 47,* 213–215.

SELIGMAN, M. E. P., ABRAMSON, L. Y., SEMMEL, A., AND VON BAEYER, C. (1979). Depressive attributional style. *Journal of Abnormal Psychology, 88,* 242–247.

SPITZER, R. L., AND ENDICOTT, J. (1968). *The current and past psychopathology scales* (CAPPS). New York: Biometrics Research.

SPITZER, R. L., AND ENDICOTT, J. (1978). *Schedule for affective disorders and schizophrenia* (SADS) (3rd ed.). New York: Biometrics Research.

WEINBERGER, D. A., SCHWARTZ, G. E., AND DAVIDSON, R. J. (1979). Low-anxious and repressive coping styles: Psychometric patterns and behavioral and physiological response to stress. *Journal of Abnormal Psychology, 88,* 369–380.

WINTERS, K. C., AND NEALE, J. M. (1983). Delusions and delusional thinking in psychotics: A review of the literature.*Clinical Psychology Review, 3,* 227–253.

SECTION 4

Anxiety Disorders and Reactions to Stress

We live in stressful times. Needs are not always immediately gratified, and difficult choices are an integral part of our lives. Everyone knows what it is like to be under pressure. External demands from peers, parents, professors, and others are all too familiar. We also place many demands on ourselves—demands that in some cases may seriously tax our coping resources.

It is therefore hardly surprising that, after decades of neglect, the study of anxiety and stress-related disorders is once again attracting attention. Psychopathology researchers during the 1950s and 1960s were preoccupied with developing an understanding of schizophrenia. In the 1970s, affective disorders formed their principal focus of interest. Finally, well into the 1980s, the spotlight has fallen on the anxiety disorders. This increase in attention has hardly come too soon. Anxiety-reducing medications are among the most frequently prescribed drugs in the United States.

The Problem of Classification

Precisely how anxiety disorders should be classified still remains highly controversial. Early taxonomies, prominent until the beginning of this century, used Greek and Latin prefixes to generate names for unusual fears of objects and situations. This gave rise to a seemingly endless list of so-called phobias, including such interestingly named conditions as melissophobia (fear of bees) and triskaidekaphobia (fear of the number 13). This method of naming fears was of limited utility, however, because it lacked any underlying system or principle of organization—the hallmark of any useful taxonomy. The mere naming of the feared object also contributed little to an understanding of the phenomenon.

Current classification systems, however, are also not without their critics. According to DSM-III-R, the characteristic features of anxiety disorders are symptoms of anxiety and avoidance behavior. The resulting cluster of anxiety disorders consequently includes panic disorder (with and without agoraphobia), agoraphobia (without panic disorder), social phobia, simple phobia, obsessional compulsive disorder, generalized anxiety disorder, and post-traumatic stress disorder. European psychiatrists and psychologists, however, find this grouping somewhat arbitrary and have criticized the DSM for not adhering to a more consistent underlying classificatory principle. They note that hypochondriasis, which has at its core the fear of having a serious disease, is not classified as an anxiety disorder but as a somatoform disorder. The inclusion of posttraumatic stress-disorder (PTSD) as an anxiety disorder is also somewhat controversial. This is because the predominant symptom of PTSD is not anxiety or avoidance behavior but the reliving of a traumatic event. Whether PTSD should be classified not as an anxiety disorder but as a dissociative condition is currently the subject of some debate.

Phobia

The most prevalent anxiety disorder is phobia. Most people would feel nervous or fearful on the edge of a cliff or in the presence of an uncaged snarling tiger. In these contexts fear and anxiety serve a protective function of preparing us for fight or flight. Phobias, in contrast, involve fear or anxiety that is both handicapping and out of proportion to the objective risk of a situation or stimulus object. They are characterized by extreme and persistent fear of a circumscribed stimulus (such as a snake or a rat), a situation (e.g., witnessing blood or tissue injury), or activity (e.g., eating or speaking in public).

Data from the Epidemiologic Catchment Area (ECA) study (selection 4) indicate that approximately 4% of the general population have some form of clinically significant phobia. The prevalence of phobia is particularly high in women, and phobia is the most common psychiatric diagnosis for females of all ages. Because most phobic individuals experience only minimal impairment in their day-to-day functioning when not confronting the feared stimulus, however, they rarely seek help for their fears.

The same is not true of those with panic disorder. This disorder, which is found in only about 1% of the population, is the most common problem found in persons seeking treatment for anxiety. Particularly likely to solicit help are individuals whose panic attacks limit their ability to leave home and go into public places.

Agoraphobia

Commonly assumed to denote fear of open spaces, the word agoraphobia actually derives from the Greek term "agora," meaning an assembly or marketplace. Agoraphobics, the majority of whom are women, experience difficulty in a variety of situations—crossing bridges, riding on buses or trains, being in theaters, churches, crowded elevators, or busy stores. Their difficulties usually begin between the ages of 15 and 35 (Marks, 1987) and rapidly generalize to a wide range of stimuli. Their central problem usually concerns going out alone.

In the absence of treatment, the course of agoraphobia tends to be chronic. Breier, Charney, and Heninger (1986) reported that the majority of their patient sample of agoraphobics experienced no complete remissions subsequent to the development of the disorder. Depression, other anxiety disorders, and alcoholism, were also common in these patients. In many cases, however, these other problems predated the initial panic attack. This suggests that they are not invariably the consequences of panic disorder or agoraphobia.

All the patients studied by Breier and colleagues had both a history of spontaneous panic attacks and a current diagnosis of agoraphobia. In approximately 75% of their sample the agoraphobia began within 1 year of a first panic attack. These observations support the view, currently reflected in DSM-III-R, that agoraphobia may develop as a consequence of panic disorder. Future episodes of panic are feared, and situations thought to be capable of triggering panic attacks are carefully avoided.

Panic

Spontaneous panics, by their very nature, are triggered by a cue for panic that is obscure. Most patients report that their attacks come "out of the blue." The possibility that cognitive factors might be of central importance, however, is raised in an interesting article by Clark (selection 18). Clark argues that panic attacks are the result of a gross misinterpretation of normal bodily sensations. These sensations typically involve anxiety responses such as palpitations, breathlessness, and dizziness. If these normal manifestations of anxiety are misinterpreted and perceived as much more dangerous than they really are (e.g., as signs of an impending heart attack), levels of apprehension will rise. This apprehension then produces a further increase in physical sensations. Continued escalation of this sequence of events culminates in a panic attack.

Clark's cognitive model of panic is important for a number of reasons. First, it is consistent with the major clinical features of the disorder. Panic patients frequently report that the first thing they become aware of during a panic episode is a change in physical sensation. Clark's model is also well able to explain why infusions of sodium lactate, which is frequently used to induce panic attacks in the laboratory and which causes a number of changes in physical function, might have its effects. Finally, the model has implications for treatment. Although it is too early to judge the success of behavioral and cognitive–behavioral approaches to panic based on this model, it is clear that this is likely to be an active area of research in the coming years.

Obsessive–Compulsive Disorder

The word obsession comes from the Latin *"obsidere,"* meaning to besiege (Marks, 1987). This well describes exactly what the unpleasant and repetitive thoughts, impulses, and ideas do to the mind of the obsessive. In the majority of clinical cases, obsessions are also accompanied by repetitive, stereotyped, and purposeful acts. These are known as compulsions and are designed to neutralize the obsessive material or else to prevent some feared situation from occurring.

Unlike most phobias, which typically occur in females, obsessive–compulsive disorder occurs with equal frequency in men and women. Like other anxiety disorders, the condition usually develops during adolescence or young adulthood, with 81% of cases beginning between the ages of 10 and 40 (Black, 1974). It is not until several years after the onset of symptoms, however, that the typical patient seeks treatment.

Obsessive–compulsive patients divide fairly evenly into what are called "cleaners" and "checkers." In the former group, fears usually center around contamination. Contact with an object considered contaminated leads to prolonged washing and cleaning. Marks (1987) describes a 23-year-old patient who washed her hands 125 times a day, used three bars of soap, took 3-hour showers, and washed her hair repeatedly for fear of contamination with a cancer-causing germ.

Ritualistic checkers, on the other hand, worry that death, disease, or destruction will befall either themselves or others. To avert such harm they check repeatedly. Checked items include stoves, windows, electrical appliances, and doors. Many rituals are repeated a particular number of times. In some cases, elaborate counting rituals develop, as in the example that follows, which is taken from Marks (1987).

I count the number of letters in the words spoken to me in any conversation, and I can tell you instantaneously the exact total of letters up to 350 or so. When you say "Good morning, John" I make an immediate mental note that this has 15 letters. When you asked me "does your counting obsession interfere with your conversations with people" I answered "not really" but before I answered I noticed that your question contained 64 letters. I also must count the number of letters on every street

sign. That does Interfere sometimes, especially when I am in a hurry to get somewhere in the car and there are lots of signs in the streets. If there are 3 numbers in a house or store window I must multiply them. For example, I see 275 on a building. I multiply 2 × 7 × 5 very rapidly. It equals 70.

It remains possible, of course, that compulsive checkers check repeatedly because of a genuinely poorer ability to remember their actions. In order to determine if compulsive checking is associated with memory failure, Sher, Frost, and Otto (selection 19) compared checking and nonchecking college students on a variety of cognitive tasks. In keeping with prediction, compulsive checkers were found to have poorer memory for prior action than did noncheckers. An obvious next step is to examine to what extent these memory deficits are found in clinical samples, and to what extent they are associated with the severity of the checking disorder.

Dissociative and Somatoform Disorders

Within DSM-III-R, somatoform and dissociative conditions are not considered anxiety disorders. Their essential features are physical symptoms that have no demonstrable organic basis (somatoform disorders) and disturbances in identity, memory, or consciousness (dissociative disorders). Although obvious symptoms of anxiety are typically not apparent in such patients, some form of intrapsychic anxiety is assumed to be present. Both somatoform and dissociative disorders are widely viewed as being reactions to stress.

Multiple Personality

Multiple personality is perhaps the most striking dissociative disorder. It is also the most controversial. According to the DSM, the essential feature of this diagnosis is the existence (within the same person) of two or more distinct personalities or personality states. These function independently, are generally not aware of each other, and are in control of the individual at different times. In many cases the behavior patterns of the several personalities are quite different.

Multiple personality disorder has received a great deal of attention in recent years. This stems in part from use of the diagnosis in the widely publicized defense of accused murderer Kenneth Bianchi. Bianchi was arrested in 1979 and charged with the murder of several California women. However, while being examined under hypnosis as part of a pretrial psychiatric evaluation, a new identity emerged. This personality, who called himself Steve, claimed responsibility for the murders. He also said that Ken (whom he hated) knew nothing about what had happened.

In the months that followed, a number of experts were brought in to evaluate the legitimacy of Bianchi's claim. Some (e.g., Watkins, 1984) accepted Bianchi as a genuine case of multiple personality. Others (e.g., Orne et al., 1984) were less convinced. Although Bianchi was eventually found guilty, debate over his diagnosis still continues in psychological and psychiatric circles. Two things are clear: (1) multiple personality is an extremely difficult disorder to diagnose, and (2) the difficulties inherent in making the diagnosis are exacerbated in the forensic context because of the obvious advantages to accused criminals of convincing a jury that they are not responsible for an act.

In selection 20, Spanos, Weekes, and Bertrand examine an analogue of the Bianchi case from a social psychological perspective. In a particularly inventive design, 48 college students were asked to play the role of an accused murderer. The experimental manipulations varied in the degree to which subjects were cued for the symptoms of multiple personality. Among the college students receiving the so-called "Bianchi treatment," more than 80% adopted a different name and manifested major signs of multiple personality disorder. These results are used by Spanos and colleagues to argue for the possible role of contextual cues and social legitimization in the development of the disorder.

The Spanos article emphasizes the subtle social influence factors that may operate between therapist and patient to generate a belief in both that a multiple personality disorder exists. The inclusion of this article, however, should not be taken to mean that we consider all cases of multiple personality to be iatrogenic. Also worthy of mention is an article by Putnam and colleagues (1986), which takes a very different position. Based on an extensive survey of 100 cases of multiple personality diagnosed according to the DSM-III, this report concludes that the phenomenon is a true clinical entity characterized by particular signs and symptoms such as depression and attempts by one personality to destroy the other. Certain kinds of life experiences, specifically physical and sexual abuse in childhood, also seem implicated in most cases of the development of the disorder. A prevalent hypothesis is that dissociation becomes the child's only reliable escape from such traumatic experiences.

One means through which defensive reactions might be achieved is described by Sackeim and his colleagues in selection 21. They describe, with reference to hysterical and hypnotic blindness, a model capable of explaining why persons who report to be blind often perform well on visual tasks. The model has implications for conversion disorders and, at a more general level, for the dissociation between awareness and behavior.

Stress and Coping

The final focus in this section is on stress and stress-resistance. In a recent study Holahan and Moos (1986) examined the personality factors and coping styles associated with psychological and physical adjustment. Using a 1-year longitudinal design, they demonstrated that feelings of self-confidence, an easy-going personality, and a tendency not to use avoidance-based forms of coping afforded both men and women some protection from the negative psychological consequences of life stress. In women, these stress-resistance variables were also associated with lower levels of physical complaints.

Holahan and Moos's demonstration of a link between psychological and physical well-being under conditions of high stress and a disinclination to use avoidance coping is particularly interesting in the light of Pennebaker and Beall's work on inhibition and disease (selection 22). Pennebaker and Beall asked undergraduates to write about personally traumatic events for 15-minutes on four consecutive evenings. Although writing about the events was associated with relatively higher blood pressure and negative mood immediately following the essay, subjects made fewer visits to a health center in the 6 months following the experiment. Although only preliminary at this stage, Pennebaker and Beall's data suggest that confronting a traumatic event, despite its short-term negative consequences, may be associated with positive health benefits in the longer term.

References and Suggested Additional Readings

BARLOW, D. H. (1988). *Anxiety and its disorders: The nature and treatment of anxiety and panic.* New York: Guilford Press.

BLACK, A. (1974). The natural history of obsessional neurosis. In H. R. Beech (Ed.), *Obsessional states.* London: Methuen.

BREIER, A., CHARNEY, D. S., AND HENINGER, G. R. (1986). Agoraphobia with panic attacks: Development, diagnostic stability, and course of illness. *Archives of General Psychiatry, 43,* 1029–1036.

HOLAHAN, C. J., AND MOOS. (1986). Personality, coping, and family resources in stress resistance: A longitudinal analysis. *Journal of Personality and Social Psychology, 51, 2,* 389–395.

MARKS, I. M. (1987). *Fears, phobias and rituals.* New York: Oxford University Press.

ORNE, M. T., DINGES, D. F., AND ORNE, E. C. (1984). On the differential diagnosis of multiple personality in the forensic context. *International Journal of Clinical and Experimental Hypnosis, 32,* 118–169.

PUTNAM, F. W., GUROFF, J. J., SILBERMAN, E. K., BARBAN, L., AND POST, R. M. (1986). The clinical phenomenology of multiple personality disorder: Review of 100 recent cases. *Journal of Clinical Psychiatry, 47,* 6, 285–293.

TUMA, A. H., AND MASER, J. D. (1985). *Anxiety and the anxiety disorders.* Hillsdale, N. J.: Lawrence Erlbaum Associates.

WATKINS, J. G. (1984). The Bianchi (L. A. Hillside Strangler) case: Sociopath or multiple personality? *International Journal of Clinical and Experimental Hypnosis, 32,* 67–101.

18

A Cognitive Approach to Panic

David M. Clark

Summary: A cognitive model of panic is described. Within this model panic attacks are said to result from the catastrophic misinterpretation of certain bodily sensations. The sensations which are misinterpreted are mainly those involved in normal anxiety responses (e.g. palpitations, breathlessness, dizziness etc.) but also include some other sensations. The catastrophic misinterpretation involves perceiving these sensations as much more dangerous than they really are (e.g. perceiving palpitations as evidence of an impending heart attack). A review of the literature indicates that the proposed model is consistent with the major features of panic. In particular, it is consistent with the nature of the cognitive disturbance in panic patients, the perceived sequence of events in an attack, the occurrence of 'spontaneous' attacks, the role of hyperventilation in attacks, the effects of sodium lactate and the literature on psychological and pharmacological treatments. Finally, a series of direct tests of the model are proposed.

Introduction

Ever since Freud's (1894) classic essay on anxiety neurosis, it has been accepted that panic attacks are a frequent accompaniment of certain types of anxiety disorder. How-ever, it is only relatively recently that panic attacks have become a focus of research interest in their own right. This shift in emphasis is largely a result of the work of Donald Klein. In a series of studies which started in the 1960s, Klein and his colleagues (Klein, 1964; Zitrin, Klein and Woerner, 1980; Zitrin, Woerner and Klein, 1981; Zitrin, Klein, Woerner and Ross, 1983) appeared to demonstrate that anxiety disorders which are characterized by panic attacks respond to imipramine while anxiety disorders which are not characterized by panic attacks fail to respond to imipramine. This 'pharmacological dissociation' led Klein (1981) to propose that panic anxiety is *qualitatively* different from non-panic anxiety. A view which was subsequently endorsed by the writers of DSM-III (APA, 1980) when they created the two diagnostic categories of 'panic disorder' and 'agoraphobia with panic' and used the presence or absence of panic attacks as a major criteria for distinguishing between different types of anxiety disorder. Following the publication of DSM-III, there has been an enormous increase in research on panic attacks. Perhaps because drug studies were the major stimulus for the creation of the

David M. Clark. A Cognitive Approach to Panic. Reprinted by permission from *Behavior Research and Therapy*, 1986, Vol. 24, No. 4, pp. 461–470. Copyright © 1986, Pergamon Journals, Ltd.

diagnostic category of panic disorder, most recent research has concentrated on biological approaches to the understanding of panic. However, there are a number of reasons for supposing that panic attacks might be best understood from a cognitive perspective. After a brief description of the phenomenology of panic attacks, the present article presents a cognitive approach to the understanding of panic. A literature review indicates that the proposed cognitive model is consistent with existing information on the nature of panic and the article concludes with a set of specific predictions which could be used to test the model.

The Phenomenology of Panic Attacks

A panic attack consists of an intense feeling of apprehension or impending doom which is of sudden onset and which is associated with a wide range of distressing physical sensations. These sensations include breathlessness, palpitations, chest pain, choking, dizziness, tingling in the hands and feet, hot and cold flushes, sweating, faintness, trembling and feelings of unreality. Panic attacks occur in both phobic and non-phobic anxiety disorders. Within phobics, attacks occur in feared situations (such as a supermarket for an agoraphobic) but some attacks occur in 'safe' situations such as at home. Some attacks follow a clearly identifiable precipitating event or short period of anxious rumination but other attacks are perceived by patients as occurring 'out of the blue'. The latter are commonly termed 'spontaneous' panic attacks. The majority of people who suffer frequent panic attacks fall into the DSM-III categories of panic disorder or agoraphobia with panic. In order to be diagnosed as suffering from panic disorder an individual must have had at least three panic attacks in the last 3 weeks and these attacks must not be restricted to circumscribed phobic situations. In order to be diagnosed as suffering from agoraphobia with panic, an individual must show marked fear and avoidance of the agoraphobic cluster of situations and also have a history of panic attacks.

A Cognitive Model of Panic Attacks

Paradoxically, the cognitive model of panic attacks is perhaps most easily introduced by discussing work which has focused on neurochemical and pharmacological approaches to the understanding of panic. This work has established that in patients, panic attacks can be provoked by a wide range of pharmacological and physiological agents including: infusions of lactate (Appleby, Klein, Sachar and Levitt, 1981; Leibowitz, Fyer, Gorman, Dillon, Appleby, Levy, Anderson, Levitt, Palij, Davies and Klein, 1984), yohimbine (Charney, Beninger and Breier, 1984) and isoproterenol (Rainey, Pohl, Williams, Knitter, Freedman and Ettedgui, 1984); oral administration of caffeine (Charney, Beninger and Jatlow, 1985); voluntary hyperventilation (Clark, Salkovskis and Chalkley, 1985) and inhalation of carbon dioxide (van den Hout and Griez, 1984). These agents rarely provoke panic attacks in individuals without a history of panic. However, they produce some of the bodily sensations which are associated with panic attacks in most individuals. The success of the agents at producing panic attacks in panic patients and their less marked effects on normals have been taken to indicate that certain biochemical changes have a direct panic-inducing effect, and that individuals who are vulnerable to the agents have a biochemical disorder. These conclusions have provided a rationale for the further exploration of drug treatments for panic (Chouinard, Annabie, Fontaine and Solyom, 1982; Zitrin, 1983) and also for studies which attempt to identify neurochemical abnormalities in panic patients (Charney et al., 1984; Nesse, Cameron, Curtis, McCann and Huber-Smith, 1984).

However, two recent studies (Clark and Hemsley, 1982; van den Hout and Griez,

1982) suggest an alternative, psychological, explanation for the panic-inducing effects of these diverse agents. These studies investigated the effects of two panic-inducing agents—hyperventilation (Clark and Hemsley, 1982) and CO_2 inhalation (van den Hout and Griez, 1982)—in normal Ss. It was found that individuals varied considerably in their affective response to the procedures and there was tentative evidence that the extent to which individuals experienced the procedures as pleasurable or aversive was determined by cognitive factors such as expectation and the recall of previous experiences with the induced sensations. This suggests that the various pharmacological and physiological agents which have been shown to promote panic in patients may not have direct panic-inducing effects but instead may provoke panic only if the bodily sensations which they induce are interpreted in a particular fashion. This is the central notion behind the cognitive theory of panic which is described below.

It is proposed that panic attacks result from the catastrophic misinterpretation of certain bodily sensations. The sensations which are misinterpreted are mainly those which are involved in normal anxiety responses (e.g. palpitations, breathlessness, dizziness etc.) but also include some other bodily sensations. The catastrophic misinterpretation involves perceiving these sensations as much more dangerous than they really are. Examples of catastrophic misinterpretations would be a healthy individual perceiving palpitations as evidence of impending heart attack; perceiving a slight feeling of breathlessness as evidence of impending cessation of breathing and consequent death; or perceiving a shaky feeling as evidence of impending loss of control and insanity.

Figure 1 illustrates the sequence of events that it is suggested occurs in a panic attack.*

---

*Although derived independently, the present model has similarities with the models of panic which have recently been proposed by Beck, Emery and Greenberg (1985) and by Griez and van den Hout (1984).

A wide range of stimuli appear to provoke attacks. These stimuli can be external (such as a supermarket for an agoraphobic who has previously had an attack in a supermarket) but more often are internal (body sensation, thought or image). If these stimuli are perceived as a threat, a state of mild apprehension results. This state is accompanied by a wide range of body sensations. If these anxiety-produced sensations are interpreted in a catastrophic fashion, a further increase in apprehension occurs. This produces a further increase in body sensations and so on round in a vicious circle which culminates in a panic attack.

The model shown in Fig. 1 can deal both with panic attacks which are preceded by a period of heightened anxiety and also with panic attacks which are not preceded by a period of heightened anxiety but instead appear to come 'out of the blue'. In the case of attacks which are preceded by heightened anxiety two distinct types of attack can be distinguished. In the first the heightened anxiety which precedes the attack is concerned with the anticipation of an attack. This is often the case when agoraphobics experience an attack in a situation (such as a supermarket) where they have previously panicked. On entering such a situation they

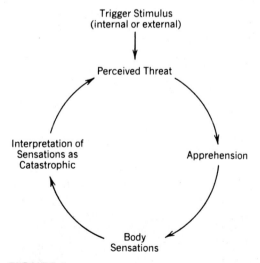

FIGURE 1.

A cognitive model of panic attacks.

tend to become anxious in anticipation of a further attack, then selectively focus on their body, notice an unpleasant body sensation, interpret this as evidence of an impending attack and consequently activate the vicious circle which produces an attack. In other cases the heightened anxiety which precedes an attack may be quite unconnected with anticipation of an attack. For example, an individual may become nervous as a result of the particular topics which are being discussed in a dispute with a spouse, notice their bodily reaction to the argument, catastrophically interpret these sensations and then panic.

In the case of panic attacks which are not preceded by a period of heightened anxiety, the trigger for an attack often seems to be the perception of a bodily sensation which itself is caused by a different emotional state (excitement, anger) or by some quite innocuous event such as suddenly getting up from the sitting position (dizziness), exercise (breathlessness, palpitations) or drinking coffee (palpitations). Once perceived the body sensation is interpreted in a catastrophic fashion and then a panic attack results. In such attacks patients often fail to distinguish between the triggering body sensation and the subsequent panic attack and so perceive the attacks as having no cause and coming 'out of the blue'. This is understandable given the patients' general beliefs about the meaning of an attack. For example, if an individual believes that there is something wrong with his heart, he is unlikely to view the palpitation which triggers an attack as different from the attack itself. Instead he is likely to view both as aspects of the same thing—a heart attack or near miss.

In Fig. 1 it is hypothesized that the misinterpretation of bodily symptoms of anxiety is always involved in the vicious circle which culminates in a panic attack. However, other sensations can also play a role in panic, particularly as triggering stimuli. We have already mentioned sensations such as breathlessness and palpitations which sometimes are produced by anxiety but other times can initially be produced by innocuous events or positive emotions. In addition, occasionally panic attacks are triggered by sensations which are never part of an anxiety response. For example, floaters in the visual field are not symptoms of anxiety. However, if an individual was concerned about the possibility of a deterioration in sight then perception of a floater could trigger a panic. The individual might interpret the floater as a sign of impending visual deterioration, become anxious, as a product of this anxiety experience blurred vision, this would further reinforce the belief that there was something seriously wrong with his or her vision and so activate a vicious circle of misinterpretation and increasing blurred vision which culminates in a panic attack.

So far our discussion of the sensations whose misinterpretation results in a panic attack has mainly concentrated on sensations which arise from the perception of internal physical processes (e.g. palpitations). These are the most common sensations involved in the production of panic attacks. However, sensations which arise from the perception of mental processes can also contribute to the vicious circle which culminates in a panic attack. For example, for some patients the belief that they are about to go mad is partly based on moments when their mind suddenly goes blank. These moments are interpreted as evidence of impending loss of control over thinking and consequent insanity.

A final aspect of the cognitive model which requires comment concerns the temporal stability of patients' catastrophic interpretations of bodily sensations. For some patients the panic-triggering sensations and their interpretations of those sensations remain fairly constant across time. However, in other patients both the sensations and interpretations change over time. For example, some patients appear to have a rather vague belief that they are going to suffer from some serious illness, this leads them to misinterpret a very wide range of bodily sensations and the particular misinterpretations will vary depending on which bodily sensations are noticed, what illnesses they have information about and what illnesses they have already been able to discount.

A Brief Review of Research on Panic Attacks

Having presented a cognitive model of panic, I will now briefly review the literature on panic to determine the extent to which it is consistent with the proposed model.

1. Ideational Components of Panic Anxiety

If the above model is correct, one would expect that the thinking of patients who suffer from panic attacks would be dominated by thoughts which relate to the catastrophic interpretation of bodily sensations. A recent interview study has provided data which is broadly consistent with this hypothesis. Hibbert (1984a) compared the ideation of non-phobic patients who experienced panic attacks ($n = 17$) and non-phobic patients who did not experience panic attacks ($n = 8$). Panic patients were significantly more likely than non-panic patients to have thoughts concerned with the anticipation of illness, death or loss of control (includes going mad'), but did not differ from non-panic patients in the frequency of thoughts concerned with general feelings of being unable to cope or with the anticipation of social embarrassment. In discussing these results Hibbert (1984a, p. 622) concluded that "the ideational content of those experiencing panic attacks can be understood as a reaction to the somatic symptoms, a connection insisted upon by all but 2 of the patients".

2. Perceived Sequence of Events in a Panic Attack

As the cognitive model specifies that panic attacks result from the catastrophic interpretation of bodily sensations, one would expect that a bodily sensation would be one of the first things which individuals notice

during an attack. Two studies have asked patients about the perceived sequence of events in an attack and both have provided results consistent with this expectation. Hibbert (1984a) and Ley (1985) both found that panic patients frequently report that the first thing they notice during an episode of anxiety is a physical feeling. In addition, Hibbert (1984a) found that this sequence of events was reported significantly more often by patients with panic attacks than by patients without panic attacks (53 and 0%, respectively).

3. The Role of Hyperventilation in Panic Attacks

The bodily sensations which are produced by voluntary hyperventilation are very similar to those experienced in naturally occurring panic attacks. This observation has led a number of writers (Clark, 1979; Clark and Hemsley, 1982; Gibson, 1978; Hibbert, 1984b; Kerr, Dalton and Gliebe, 1937; Lewis, 1957; Lum, 1976; Wolpe, 1973) to suggest that hyperventilation may play an important role in the production of panic attacks. Consistent with this suggestion it has been shown that in some panic patients (i) voluntary hyperventilation produces a panic-like state (Clark et al., 1985) and (ii) hyperventilation accompanies naturally occurring panic attacks (Hibbert, 1986; Salkovskis, Warwick, Clark and Wessels, 1986c), panic attacks produced by contrived psychological stress (Salkovskis, Clark and Jones, 1986a) and panic attacks induced by sodium lactate (Liebowitz, Gorman, Abby, Levitt, Dillon, Gail, Appleby, Anderson, Palij, Davies and Klein, 1985b). These observations suggest that hyperventilation plays a role in some panic attacks. However, it is clear that hyperventilation *per se* does not produce panic. As already mentioned, studies of the effects of hyperventilation in normals (Clark and Hemsley, 1982; Svebak and Grossman, 1986) have shown that individuals vary considerably in their affective response to hyperventilation with some individuals actually finding the experience enjoyable. It is therefore suggested that hyperventilation only induces panic if the bodily sensations which it induces are (a) perceived as unpleasant and (b) interpreted in a catastrophic fashion.

4. Lactate-induced Panic

Infusions of sodium lactate are the most frequently used technique for inducing panic attacks in the laboratory. Between 60–90% of panic patients and 0–20% of normals and non-panic anxious patients experience an attack when given an i.v. infusion of 0.5–1.0 M racemic sodium lactate (Appleby et al., 1981; Liebowitz et al., 1984, 1985a; Rainey et al., 1984). Even when Ss do not panic, lactate infusions are accompanied by a wide range of physiological and biochemical changes. Liebowitz et al. (1985b) reported that lactate produces significant increases in heart rate, systolic blood pressure, pyruvate, prolactin and bicarbonate, and significant decreases in cortisol, pCO_2, phosphate and ionized calcium. As some of these changes in bodily function are likely to be perceived, the cognitive model could account for the panic-inducing effects of lactate by proposing that individuals who panic do so because they catastrophically interpret the induced sensations. This is consistent with Liebowitz et al.'s (1985b, p. 718) observation that individuals who panic during lactate infusion perceive bodily changes such as tremor and parasthesias well before the onset of panic. The fact that more patients than controls panic on lactate would mainly be explained by supposing that patients have, as a relatively enduring characteristic, a particularly marked tendency to interpret certain bodily sensations in a catastrophic fashion. However, in some studies part of the difference in response between patients and controls may be due to differences in the instructions given to the two groups. For example, in their pre-infusion instructions, Appleby et al. (1981) told patients that they "might experience a panic attack" (p. 413) but told controls that they "might experience an attack with symptoms analogous to

those of 'public speaking' " (p. 413). As the controls presumably had never experienced a panic attack but probably had been slightly nervous during public speaking these instructions are likely to lead controls to expect a less-frightening experience than patients. Such differences in expectation can have marked effects on the affect produced by biochemical interventions (cf. van den Hout and Griez, 1982).

5. Effects of Psychological Treatment

The proposal that panic attacks result from the catastrophic interpretation of certain bodily sensations suggests both a cognitive–behavioural and a behavioural approach to the treatment of panic attacks. The cognitive–behavioural approach would involve identifying patients' negative interpretations of the bodily sensations which they experience in panic attacks, suggesting alternative non-catastrophic interpretations of the sensations and then helping the patient to test the validity of these alternative interpretations through discussion and behavioural experiments. The behavioural approach would capitalize on the observation that fear of specific stimuli can often be treated by repeated, controlled exposure to those stimuli and would consist of graded exposure to the body sensations which accompany panic. Recently both of these approaches have been tried and the initial results are highly encouraging.

Clark et al. (1985) adopted the cognitive–behavioural approach and concentrated on one particular alternative interpretation—the view that the bodily sensations which patients experience in a panic attack are the result of stress-induced hyperventilation rather than the more catastrophic things which patients usually fear (impending heart attack, insanity, loss of control). The treatment had five stages:

1. Brief voluntary hyperventilation. This was intended to induce a state which patients recognized as similar to their panic attacks.

2. Explanation and discussion of the way hyperventilation induces panic. On the basis of the results of the brief period of voluntary hyperventilation, it was suggested to patients that during a panic attack they may be overbreathing. This then produces a wide range of bodily sensations which they interpret in a catastrophic fashion leading to greater anxiety, more overbreathing and so on round in a vicious circle which culminates in a panic attack. Patients attempted to fit their own recent experience of panic attacks into this model and where doubts were expressed these were carefully considered. Attacks which initially appeared inconsistent with the model were carefully discussed. After reviewing details of these attacks with the therapist, the patient was often able to see ways in which the model could account for the attacks.

3. Training in a pattern of slow, controlled breathing to use in a coping technique during attacks.

4. Training in more appropriate cognitive responses to bodily symptoms. These responses were based on the discussion described above.

5. Identification and modification of panic triggers. By reviewing panic diaries, it was often possible to identify hitherto unrecognized triggers for panic. This helped some patients to see their panic attacks as more understandable, made them less frightening and suggested control techniques. Examples of triggers identified in this way were high caffeine intake, misinterpretation of the bodily symptoms of a hangover, postural hypotension, phase in the menstrual cycle and fleeting, bizarre images.

To date, two evaluations of this treatment approach have been reported. In the first evaluation (Clark et al., 1985) patients were selected who perceived a similarity between the effects of overbreathing and naturally occurring panic attacks. Substantial reductions in panic attack frequency were observed during the first few weeks of treatment. These initial gains, which occurred in the absence of exposure to feared external situations, were improved upon with further treatment and maintained at 2-yr follow-up. In the second evaluation (Salkovskis, Jones and Clark, 1986b), an unselected group of panic patients were studied. Again a substantial reduction in attack frequency was observed. In addition, there was some evidence that outcome was positively correlated with the extent to which patients perceived a marked similarity between the effects of voluntary overbreathing and naturally occurring attacks. Neither study employed a waiting-list control group. However, it is unlikely that the observed improvements are due to spontaneous remission as, in both studies, a stable baseline was established before treatment, and significant improvements from baseline took place in a treatment period shorter than the baseline. It therefore appears that the cognitive–behavioural package is an effective treatment for panic, especially in patients who perceive a marked similarity between hyperventilation and naturally occurring panic. Patients who fail to perceive a marked similarity between the effects of hyperventilation and naturally occurring panic would probably benefit from the inclusion of additional procedures which concentrate on other, non-catastrophic explanations of bodily sensations (cf. Clark, 1986).

Griez and van den Hout (1983, 1986) adopted the behavioural approach to treatment and used inhalations of 35% CO_2/65% O_2 as a way of repeatedly exposing patients to the bodily sensations which accompany panic attacks. Inhalation of 35% CO_2/65% O_2 is a highly effective technique for inducing the bodily sensations of panic (van den Hout and Griez, 1984). Its effects appear to result from the sudden drop in pCO_2 (hyperventilation) which follows exhalation of the gas rather than from the increase in pCO_2 (hypercapnia) which accompanies inhalation (van den Hout and Griez, 1984). When used as a treatment, inhalations are introduced in a graded fashion. Initially, Ss take small inhalations, as their anxiety drops they are encouraged to take a full-depth inhalation and eventually take several full-depth inhalations each session. Griez and van den Hout (1986) evaluated the short-term effectiveness of this treatment using a cross-over design in which 2 weeks of CO_2 therapy was compared with 2 weeks of propranolol. CO_2 inhalation therapy was associated with significant reductions in panic attack frequency and fear of autonomic sensations. Propranolol failed to have significant effects on either of these measures. However, the difference in change scores between treatments only reached significance on the measure of fear of autonomic sensations. In view of the unusually brief duration of therapy, it is possible that Griez and van den Hout's (1986) results are an underestimate of the effectiveness of CO_2 inhalation therapy. Although the therapy was associated with substantial drops in panic attack frequency, most patients were not panic-free at the end of 2 weeks and it is possible that further improvements would have been observed if the therapy had been extended over a longer and more normal period of time.

At this stage, neither Clark et al.'s (1985) cognitive–behavioural treatment nor Griez and van den Hout's (1984) behavioural treatment have been compared against an alternative psychological treatment in order to control for non-specific therapy ingredients. Until this is done it is not possible to say whether the apparent effectiveness of the treatments is due to their specific emphasis on fear of internal sensations. However, it is encouraging to note that both treatments appear to be effective with panic disorder patients as these patients form a group for whom there is no generally accepted psychological treatment. In Clark et al.'s (1985) study, these patients (termed 'non-situationals') did extremely well. Indeed, most were panic-free by the end of treatment.

In contrast to panic disorder, there is a generally accepted psychological treatment for agoraphobia with panic. Numerous studies (cf. Mathews, Gelder and Johnston, 1981) have shown that graded, in vivo exposure to feared external situations is an effective treatment for agoraphobic avoidance and situational fear. Early studies did not include direct measures of panic but it was assumed that panic attacks would decline as situational fear declined and recent studies have confirmed this assumption (Marks, Grey, Cohen, Hill, Mawson, Ramm and Stern, 1983; Michelson, Marchione and Mavissakalian, 1985; Mavissakalian and Michelson, 1986). The question therefore arises of whether the cognitive–behavioural and behavioural treatments described above have anything to add to graded, in vivo exposure. Several authors (Freud, 1895; Goldstein and Chambless, 1978; Hallam, 1978; Klein, 1981; Westphal, 1872) have argued that in many cases agoraphobia is best viewed as a fear of panic rather than a fear of specific situations. This suggests that treatments which directly tackle panic may produce more generalized change. In particular, they may be more effective than graded exposure alone in reducing the frequency of 'spontaneous' panic attacks and panic attacks which occur in patient's homes. Certainly there is room for further improvement in these areas. In a recent study, Michelson et al. (1985) found that 45% of patients given the DSM-III diagnosis of agoraphobia with panic were still experiencing panic attacks at home without obvious environmental provocation after 3 months of in vivo, therapist-assisted exposure to feared situations.

6. The Role of Biological Factors in Panic

By specifying that the catastrophic interpretation of certain bodily sensations is a necessary condition for the production of a panic attack, the cognitive model provides a different perspective to that offered by biological models of panic and also provides a rationale for psychological approaches to treatment. However, it would be wrong to assume that biological factors have no role to play in panic attacks. In principle, there are, at least three ways in which biological factors might increase an individual's vulnerability to the vicious circle shown in Fig. 1.

First, biological factors may contribute to the triggering of an attack. As already mentioned, panic attacks are often triggered by a perceived body sensation such as breathlessness or palpitations, and such sensations appear to be reported more frequently by panic patients than by other patients or normals. Body sensations are particularly likely to be noticed when there is a change in bodily processes (Pennebaker, 1982). It is therefore possible that the increase in perceived body sensations observed in panic patients occurs because such patients experience more, or more intense, benign fluctuations in body state than others.

Second, biological factors are likely to influence the extent to which a perceived threat produces an increase in bodily sensations, as shown in Fig. 1. The reduced efficiency of central adrenergic α_2-autoreceptors, which it has been suggested is characteristic of panic patients (Charney et al., 1984), would be an example of such an effect. Noradrenergic neutrons in the locus coerulus and other brain-stem areas play an important role in the control of the autonomic nervous system. The α_2-adrenergic autoreceptor has an inhibitory influence on presynaptic noradrenergic neurons. A deficiency in this autoreceptor would mean that release of noradrenaline would not be damped down by presynaptic inhibition and individuals with such a deficiency would experience larger than normal surges in noradrenaline and sympathetic nervous system activation in response to a perceived threat. A further example of a biological influence on the extent to which a perceived threat produces an increase in body sensations comes from the literature on hyperventilation. As already mentioned, in some patients the bodily sensations which occur in a panic attack are partly a result of hyperventilation and the effects of hyperventilation vary with resting levels of pCO_2 which in turn vary with phase in the menstrual cycle (Damos-Mora, Davies, Taylor and Jenner, 1980).

Finally, the extent to which bodily sensations which accompany anxiety are interpreted in a catastrophic fashion will largely be determined by psychological factors. However, biological factors may also have a role to play in this aspect of the vicious circle. For example, the hypothesized deficiency in central α_2-adrenergic autoreceptors would mean that individuals would be more likely to experience sudden surges in sympathetic activity and surges in activity may be more likely to be interpreted in a catastrophic fashion than gradual build-ups.

7. Effects of Pharmacological Treatment

Within the model shown in Fig. 1, there are several ways in which drugs could be effective in reducing the frequency of panic attacks. Blockade of, or exposure to the bodily sensations which accompany anxiety, and a reduction in the frequency of bodily fluctuations which can trigger panic could all have short term effects on panic. However, if patients' tendency to interpret bodily sensations in a catastrohic fashion is not changed, discontinuation of drug treatment should be associated with a high rate of relapse.

So far, three drugs (propranolol, diazepam and imipramine) have been investigated in controlled trials which include measures of panic. Propranolol appears to be ineffective, even when given in doses which are sufficient to effect β-blockade (Noyes, Anderson, Clancy, Crowe, Slymen, Ghoneim and Hinrichs, 1984; Griez and van den Hout, 1986). This is perhaps because β-blockade reduces the cardiovascular apsects of panic but appears to leave some of the other bodily sensations unaffected (Gorman, Levy, Liebowitz, McGrath, Appleby, Dillon, Davies and Klein, 1983). Noyes et al. (1984) found that high doses of diazepam (up to 30 mg) were effective in reducing panic frequency over a period of 2 weeks but they failed to provide data on the long-term effectiveness of diazepam. However, other studies (Catalan and Gath, 1985) have raised serious doubts about the long-term effectiveness of diazepam as a treatment for anxiety. In contrast to propranolol and diazepam, more positive results have been obtained with imipramine. Three controlled trials (Zitrin et al., 1980, 1983; McNair and Kahn, 1981) have found that imipramine is more effective than an inert placebo in reducing the frequency of panic attacks in agoraphobics with panic and a further trial (Telch, Agras, Taylor, Roth and Gallen, 1985) obtained a trend towards a significant difference between imipramine and placebo ($P <$ 0.1). However, two further studies with agoraphobics (Marks et al., 1983; Mavissakalian and Michelson, 1986) failed to find differences between imipramine and placebo on measures of panic. In those studies in which imipramine has been more effective than placebo it has always been combined with graded exposure to feared situations. This raises the possibility that imipramine may not have direct anti-panic effects, but instead simply potentiates the effects of self-initiated and/or therapist-initiated graded exposure. Consistent with this suggestion, Telch et al. (1985) found that imipramine had no effect on panic when given in conjunction with counter-exposure instructions. However, in the only study to investigate the effects of imipramine in panic disorder (as opposed to agoraphobia with panic), Garakani, Zitrin and Klein (1984) found that imipramine without the addition of psychological treatment was associated with a marked reduction in panic attacks. This study was a case series and so did not include a placebo control group. Until a study is reported which includes such a group, it will remain unclear whether imipramine has a specific anti-panic effect in panic disorder.

Summary and Predictions

It has been suggested that panic attacks result from the catastrophic interpretation of certain bodily sensations. The sensations which are misinterpreted are mainly those which are involved in normal anxiety responses (e.g. palpitations, breathlessness, dizziness etc.) but also include some other sensations. The catastrophic misinterpretation involves perceiving these sensations as much more dangerous than they really are (e.g. perceiving palpitations as evidence of

an impending heart attack). Encouragingly, a review of the literature indicates that the proposed model is consistent with the nature of the cognitive disturbance in panic patients, the perceived sequence of events in an attack, the occurrence of 'spontaneous' attacks, the role of hyperventilation in attacks, the effects of sodium lactate and the literature on psychological and pharmacological treatments. However, at this stage, no studies have been reported which provide a direct test of the cognitive model. Final evaluation of the model must therefore await studies which test its central predictions. These predictions are:

1. Compared to other anxious patients and normal controls, patients who suffer from panic attacks will be more likely to interpret certain bodily sensations in a catastrophic fashion.*

2. Pharmacological agents which provoke panic (such as sodium lactate) do so only when the somatic sensations produced by the agent are interpreted in a catastropic fashion, and the panic-inducing effects of these agents can be blocked by instructional manipulations.

3. Treatments which fail to change patients tendency to interpret bodily sensations in a catastrophic fashion will have higher rates of relapse than treatments which succeed in changing interpretations.

References

APA; American Psychiatric Association (1980) *Diagnostic and Statistical Manual of Mental Disorders.* 3rd edn. APA, Washington, D.C.

APPLEBY I. L., KLEIN D. F., SACHAR E. J. AND LEVITT M. (1981) Biochemical indices of lactate-induced panic: a preliminary report. In *Anxiety:*

---

*In testing this prediction it may be important to distinguish between immediate and long-term threat. It is likely that interpretations of sensations which lead patients to believe they are in immediate danger of a catastrophy such as dying or going mad will be particularly characteristic of panic while interpretations which imply some distant danger may be more characteristic of hypochondriasis.

New Research and Changing Concepts (Edited by KLEIN D. F. AND RABKIN J.). Raven Press, New York.

BECK A. T., EMERY G. AND GREENBERG R. L. (1985) *Anxiety Disorders and Phobias: a Cognitive Perspective*. Basic Books, New York.

CATALAN J. AND GATH D. H. (1985) Benzodiazepines in general practice: time for a decision. *Br. med. J.* **290**, 1374–1376.

CHARNEY D. S., BENINGER G. R. AND BREIER A. (1984) Noradrenergic function in panic anxiety: effects of yohimbine in healthy subjects and patients with agoraphobia and panic disorder. *Archs gen. Psychiat.* **41**, 751–763.

CHARNEY D. S., BENINGER G. R. AND JATLOW P. I. (1985) Increased anxiogenic effects of caffeine in panic disorders. *Archs gen. Psychiat.* **42**, 233–243.

CHOUINARD G., ANNABIE L., FONTAINE R. AND SOLYOM L. (1982) Alprazolam in the treatment of generalised anxiety and panic disorders: a double-blind placebo-controlled study. *Psychopharmacology.* **77**, 229–233.

CLARK D. M. (1979) Therapeutic aspects of increasing pCo_2 by behavioural means. Unpublished M. Phil. Thesis. Univ. of London.

CLARK D. M. (1986) Cognitive therapy for anxiety. *Behav Psychother.* In press.

CLARK D. M. AND HEMSLEY D. R. (1982) The effects of hyperventilation: individual variability and its relation to personality. *J. Behav. Ther. exp. Psychiat.* **13**, 41–47.

CLARK D. M., SALKOVSKIS P. M. AND CHALKLEY A. J. (1985) Respiratory control as a treatment for panic attacks. *J. Behav. Ther. exp. Psychiat.* **16**, 23–30.

DAMAS-MORA J., DAVIES L., TAYLOR W. AND JENNER F. A. (1980) Menstrual respiratory changes and symptoms. *Br. J. Psychiat,* **136**, 492–497.

FREUD S. (1984) The justification for detaching from neurasthenia a particular syndrome: the anxiety-neurosis. Reprinted in: Freud S. (1940) *Collected Papers.* Vol. 1, Hogarth Press, London.

FREUD S. (1895) Obsessions and phobias: their psychical mechanisms and their etiology. Reprinted in: FREUD S. (1940) *Collected Papers,* Vol. 1. Hogarth Press, London.

GARAKANI H., ZITRIN C. M. AND KLEIN D. F. (1984) Treatment of panic disorder with imipramine alone. *Am. J. Psychiat.* **141**, 446–448.

GIBSON H. B. (1978) A form of behaviour therapy for some states diagnosed as "affective disorder". *Behav. Res. Ther.* **16**, 191–195.

GOLDSTEIN A. J. AND CHAMBLESS D. L. (1978) A re-analysis of agoraphobia. *Behav. Ther.* **9**, 47–59.

GORMAN J. M., LEVY G. F., LIEBOWITZ M. R., McGRATH P., APPLEBY I. L., DILLON D. J., DAVIES S. O. AND KLEIN D. F. (1983) Effect of β-adrenergic blockade on lactate induced panic. *Archs gen. Psychiat.* **40**, 1079–1082.

GRIEZ E. AND VAN DEN HOUT M. A. (1983) Treatment of phobophobia by exposure to CO_2 induced anxiety symptoms *J. nerv. ment. Dis.* **171**, 506–508.

GRIEZ E. AND VAN DEN HOUT M. A. (1984) Carbon dioxide and anxiety: an experimental approach to a clinical claim. Unpublished Doctoral Dissertation. Rijksaniversiteit, Maastricht, The Netherlands.

GRIEZ E. AND VAN DEN HOUT M. A. (1986) CO_2 inhalation in the treatment of panic attacks. *Behav. Res. Ther.* **24**, 145–150.

HALLAM R. S. (1978) Agoraphobia: a critical review of the concept. *Br. J. Psychiat.* **133**, 314–319.

HIBBERT G. A. (1984a) Ideational components of anxiety: their origin and content. *Br. J. Psychiat.* **144**, 618–624.

HIBBERT G. A. (1984b) Hyperventilation as a cause of panic attacks. *Br. med. J.* **288**, 263–264.

HIBBERT, G. A. (1986) Ambulatory monitoring of transcutaneous pCO_2. In *Proceedings of the 15th European Conference on Psychosomatic Research* (Edited by LACEY L. AND STURGEON J.). Libby, London.

VAN DEN HOUT M. A. AND GRIEZ E. (1982) Cognitive factors in carbon dioxide therapy. *J. psychosom. Res.* **26**, 209–214.

VAN DEN HOUT M. A. AND GRIEZ E. (1984) Panic symptoms after inhalation of carbon dioxide. *Br. J. Psychiat.* **144**, 503–507.

VAN DEN HOUT M. A. AND GRIEZ E. (1985) Peripheral panic symptoms occur during changes in alveolar carbon dioxide. *Compreh. Psychiat.* **26**, 381–387.

KERR W. J., DALTON J. W. AND GLIEBE P. A. (1937) Some physical phenomena associated with anxiety states and their relation to hyperventilation. *Am. intern. Med.* **11**, 961–992.

KLEIN D. F. (1964) Delineation of two-drug responsive anxiety syndromes. *Psychopharmacologiea* **5**, 397–408.

KLEIN D. F. (1981) Anxiety reconceptualised. In *Anxiety: New Research and Changing Concepts* (Edited by KLEIN D. F. AND RABKIN J.). Raven Press, New York.

LEWIS B. I. (1954) Chronic hyperventilation syndrome. *J. Am. med. Ass.* **31**, 1204–1208.

LEY R. (1985) Agoraphobia, the panic attack and

the hyperventilation syndrome. *Behav. Res. Ther.* **23**, 79–82.

LIEBOWITZ M. R., FYER A. J., GORMAN J. M., DILLON D., APPLEBY I. L., LEVY G., ANDERSON S., LEVITT M., PALIJ M., DAVIES S. O. AND KLEIN D. F. (1984) Lactate provocation of panic attacks: I. Clinical and behavioural findings. *Archs gen. Psychiat.* **41**, 764–770.

LIEBOWITZ M. R., ABBY J. F., GORMAN J. M., DILLON D., DAVIES S., STEIN J. M., COHEN B. S. AND KLEIN D. F. (1985a) Specificity of lactate infusions in social phobia versus panic disorders. *Am. J. Psychiat.* **142**, 947–950.

LIEBOWITZ M. R., GORMAN J. M., ABBY J. F., LEVITT M., DILLON D., GAIL L., APPLEBY I. L., ANDERSON S., PALIJ M., DAVIES S. O. AND KLEIN D. F. (1985b) Lactate provocation of panic attacks: II. Biochemical and physiological findings. *Archs gen. Psychiat.* **42**, 709–719.

LUM L. C. (1976) The syndrome of habitual chronic hyperventilation. In *Modern Trends in Psychosomatic Medicine*, Vol. 3 (Edited by HILL O. W.). Butterworths, London.

McNAIR D. M. AND KAHN R. J. (1981) Imipramine compared with a benzodiazepine for agoraphobia. In *Anxiety: New Research and Changing Concepts* (Edited by KLEIN D. F. AND RABKIN J.). Raven Press, New York.

MARKS I. M., GREY S., COHEN S. D., HILL R., MAWSON D., RAMM E. M. AND STERN R. S. (1983) Imipramine and brief therapist-aided exposure in agoraphobics having self exposure homework: a controlled trial. *Archs gen. Psychiat*, **40**, 153–162.

MATHEWS A. M., GELDER M. G. AND JOHNSTON D. W. (1981) *Agorophobia: Nature and Treatment*. Guilford Press, New York.

MAVISSAKALIAN M. AND MICHELSON L. (1986) Agoraphobia: relative and combined effectiveness of therapist-assisted *in vivo* exposure and imipramine. *J. clin. Psychol.* In press.

MICHELSON L., MARCHIONE K. AND MAVISSAKALIAN M. (1985) Cognitive and behavioural treatments of agoraphobia: clinical, behavioural and psychophysiological outcome. *J. consult. clin. Psychol.* **53**, 913–926.

NESSE R. M., CAMERON O. G., CURTIS G. C., McCANN D. S. AND HUBER-SMITH M. J. (1984) Adrenergic function in patients with panic anxiety. *Archs gen. Psychiat.* **41**, 771–776.

NOYES R., ANDERSON D. J., CLANCY J., CROWE R. R., SLYMEN D. J., GHONEIM M. M. AND HINRICHS J. V. (1984) Diazepam and propranolol in panic disorder and agoraphobia. *Archs gen. Psychiat*, **41**, 287–292.

PENNEBAKER J. W. (1982) *The Psychology of Physical Symptoms*. Springer Verlag, New York.

RAINEY J. M., POHL R. B., WILLIAMS M., KNITTER E., FREEDMAN R. R. AND ETTEDGUI E. (1984) A comparison of lactate and isoproterenol anxiety states. *Psychopathology* **17**, 74–82.

SALKOVSKIS P. M., CLARK D. M. AND JONES D. R. O. (1986a) A psychosomatic mechanism in anxiety attacks: the role of hyperventilation in social anxiety and cardiac neurosis. In *Proceedings of the 15th European Conference on Psychosomatic Medicine* (Edited by LACEY H. AND STURGEON J.). Libby, London.

SALKOVSKIS P. M., JONES D. R. O. AND CLARK D. M. (1986b) Respiratory control in the treatment of panic attacks: replication and extension with concurrent measurement of behaviour and pCO_2. *Br. J. Psychiat.* In press.

SALKOVSKIS P. M., WARWICK H. M.. C., CLARK D. M. AND WESSELS D. J. (1986c) A demonstration of acute hyperventilation during naturally occurring panic attacks. *Behav. Res. Ther.* **24**, 91–94.

SVEBAK S. AND GROSSMAN P. (1986) How aversive is hyperventilation? Submitted for publication.

TELCH M. J., AGRAS W. S., TAYLOR C. B., ROTH W. T. AND GALLEN C. C. (1985) Combined pharmacological and behavioural treatment for agoraphobia. *Behav. Res. Ther.* **23**, 325–336.

WESTPHAL C. (1872) Die Agoraphobie: eine neuropathische Erscheinung. *Arch Psychiat. NervKrankh.* **3**, 138–171.

WOLPE J. (1973) *The Practice of Behaviour Therapy*, 2nd edn. Pergamon Press, New York.

ZITRIN C. M. (1983) Differential treatment of phobias: use of imipramine for panic attacks. *J. Behav. Ther. exp. Psychiat.* **14**, 11–18.

ZITRIN C. M., KLEIN D. F. AND WOERNER M. G. (1980) Treatment of agoraphobia with group exposure *in vivo* and imipramine. *Archs gen. Psychiat.* **37**, 63–72.

ZITRIN M. C., WOERNER M. G. AND KLEIN D. F. (1981) Differentiation of panic anxiety from anticipatory anxiety and avoidance behaviour. In *Anxiety: New Research and Changing Concepts*. (Edited by KLEIN D. F. AND RABKIN J.). Raven Press, New York.

ZITRIN C. M., KLEIN D. F., WOERNER M. G. AND ROSS D. C. (1983) Treatment of phobias. I. Comparison of imipramine hydrochloride and placebo. *Archs gen. Psychiat.* **40**, 125–133.

19

Cognitive Deficits in Compulsive Checkers: An Exploratory Study

Kenneth J. Sher, Randy O. Frost, and Randall Otto

Summary: Compulsive-checking behavior can be conceptualized as resulting, in part, from a memory failure. In order to determine if memory difficulties are associated with compulsive checking, the performance of college-student checkers were compared with the performance of non-checkers on a number of cognitive tasks hypothesized to be relevant to understanding checking behavior. Using the Checking and Cleaning subscales of the Maudsley Obsessional–Compulsive Inventory, four groups of subjects were identified: (1) Cleaning Checkers ($N = 13$); (2) Noncleaning Checkers ($N = 13$); (3) Cleaning Noncheckers ($N = 13$); and (4) Noncleaning Noncheckers ($N = 15$). It was hypothesized that the cognitive deficits studied would characterize individuals with checking compulsions, but not persons with non-checking compulsions (i.e. Cleaning Noncheckers) or normal controls (i.e. Noncleaning Noncheckers). Compulsive checkers were found to have a poorer memory for prior actions than non-checkers and were also found to underestimate their ability at distinguishing memories of real and imagined events, a process referred to as reality monitoring. Both of these deficits were specific to compulsive checkers and can be viewed as contributing to the likelihood that an individual will engage in checking behavior. If an individual has difficulty in recalling whether an intended action has been executed, they may be inclined to engage in checking behavior to insure the intended action is carried out. Similarly, a tendency to underestimate reality-monitoring ability could result in increased checking behavior as the individual attempts to reduce his/her uncertainty over whether a previous behavior actually occurred or merely was thought to occur. It is concluded that the study of cognitive deficits in compulsive checking is a potentially fruitful avenue for further inquiry.

Kenneth J. Sher, Randy O. Frost, and Randall Otto. Cognitive Deficits in Compulsive Checkers: An Exploratory Study. Reprinted by permission from *Behavior Research and Therapy*, 1983, Vol. 21, No. 4, pp. 357–363. Copyright © 1983, Pergamon Journals, Ltd.

Introduction

Genetic, emotional and environmental factors have all been implicated in the genesis and maintenance of compulsive checking and other obsessive–compulsive behaviors (Beech, 1974; Carr, 1974; Rachman and Hodgson, 1980; Salzman and Thaler, 1981). However, the processes responsible for checking phenomena are far from understood. While cognitive factors have been hypothesized to play a key role in compulsive behavior (e.g. Carr, 1974), the possible role of memory dysfunction has not been well studied. This is somewhat surprising in that as pointed out by Reed (1977),

perhaps the most central feature of obsessional disorder seems to involve *pathologically* faulty memory. The doubts and indecisions which lie at the heart of the disorder are often of the 'Did I or didn't I?' variety, which is often manifested in compulsive checking and ritualization. (p. 177)

In the only relevant investigation of memory and obsessive–compulsive behavior of which we are aware, Reed (1977) compared the performance of patients with obsessive–compulsive personality disorder and matched control patients with other personality disorder and found:

a. No difference in long-term memory recall (WAIS Information subtest);

b. Significantly better performance by obsessive–compulsives on a test of attention (WAIS Digit Span subtest); and

c. No difference on the ability to remember soluble problems but significantly better performance by obsessive–compulsives at recalling insoluble problems.

In addition to these experimental tasks, Reed had his subjects recall a recent event and then describe the phenomenology of the recollection process. Reed reported that although the obsessive–compulsives seemed to give longer and more detailed reports, their description of the recollection process tended to be from the viewpoint of a third person while the controls' descriptions tended to emphasize their original subjective experience. Although Reed's findings suggest a difference in cognitive functioning between obsessive–compulsive and other personality-disordered persons, his findings do not point to any specific deficit that could be linked closely to compulsive-checking behavior.

There are several potential ways in which distorted memory processes may play a role in compulsive checking. The first is that compulsive checkers may simply be poorer at memory for prior actions, necessitating repeated checks. If so, in an experimental setting it should be more difficult for com-

pulsive checkers to remember a set of actions engaged in over the course of an experiment. Such a deficit in memory for motor-based actions is suggested by Reed's (1977) finding that obsessive–compulsives describe recollection processes in terms of exclusively visual imagery in contrast to controls who use images from all modalities, including kinesthetic. The first hypothesis of this study then, is that compulsive checkers are deficient in their memory for actions (experimental tasks engaged in during the experiment).

A more complex relationship between memory processes and compulsive checking is suggested by the recent work of Johnson and Raye (1981) on what they refer to as "reality monitoring". Reality monitoring is the process of distinguishing memories of internal origin (imagined occurrences) from those of external origin (actual occurrences). For compulsive checkers it may be that either prior to or following the execution of a purposeful action (e.g. turning off the stove), the individual also imagines or visualizes the execution of the action. If the individual has a deficit in reality monitoring, s/he might believe the memory for the act to be of internal (imagined) and not external (actual) origin. The result would be the belief that turning off the stove was only imagined and not actually done, thus instigating a check.* At least three different types of deficits relating to reality monitoring could result in checking behavior. First, compulsive checkers may have poorer reality-monitoring ability. That is, they may be deficient at distinguishing memories of actual from imagined events. Second, compulsive checkers may have a bias toward judging that memories have their origin in the internal

---

*An alternative conception can also be put forth in which the individual imagines *the failure to execute the action*. In this case the reality-monitoring task is to determine if this memory for failing to execute the action is real or imagined. If the S has a deficit in reality monitoring, s/he would be more likely to judge that the imagined failure actually occurred and thus institute a check.

world (imagined). That is, when confronted with a reality-monitoring decision (e.g. "Did I leave the stove or did I only imagine I did?") checkers may be biased toward deciding that the memory corresponds to an internal and not an external occurrence, thus necessitating a check.† Finally, regardless of their actual reality-monitoring performance, checking may be instigated if checkers tend to underestimate their ability to reality monitor. Thus, although a checker might be able to accurately determine that s/he had performed the action (e.g. turned off the stove) and not simply imagined it, s/he does not trust this determination and thus is inclined to check or redo the prior action.

The major purpose of the study then, was to test several hypotheses regarding memory deficits among compulsive checkers. First, it was hypothesized that checkers would show poorer memory for actions than noncheckers. Second, checkers should have poorer reality-monitoring ability. Third, checkers should show a bias toward believing memories were imagined rather than real. Finally, regardless of their reality-monitoring ability and decision bias, checkers should underestimate their performance on the reality-monitoring task.

Method

Subjects

From an initial pool of 358 students enrolled in an Introductory Psychology class, 4 groups of *S*s were constituted on the basis of scores on the Maudsley Obsessional–Compulsive Inventory (MOCI; Rachman and Hodgson, 1980). The first group was composed of *S*s scoring 5 or more on both

the Cleaning and Checking subscales (Cleaning Checkers, $N = 13$). The second group comprised *S*s scoring 2 or less on the Cleaning subscale and 5 or more on the Checking subscale (Noncleaning Checkers, $N = 13$). A group of Cleaning Noncheckers ($N = 13$) was composed of *S*s scoring 5 or more on the Cleaning subscale and 2 or less on the Checking subscale. Finally, a group of normals (Noncleaning Noncheckers, $N = 15$) included *S*s scoring 2 or below on both the Cleaning and Checking subscales. Thus *S*s scoring 3 or 4 on either the Checking or Cleaning subscales were not included in the present study. The cutoff score of 5 on the Checking subscale classified 12.8% of the sample as Checkers. The cutoff score of 5 on the Cleaning subscale classified 12.2% of the sample as Cleaners. No differences were anticipated between Cleaners and Noncleaners on memory processes. Cleaners were included as a control for compulsive-nonchecking phenomena. Without such a control any differences between Checkers and Noncheckers could be attributed to nonspecific abnormality (since they were drawn from the extreme of a distribution) or general compulsiveness rather than checking *per se*. It should be noted that *S*s for this experiment were drawn from a normal undergraduate-student population.

Because the Checking subscale of the MOCI has not been validated as a screening instrument for detecting checkers in college-student samples, it was necessary to demonstrate that college students scoring high on the Checking subscale of the MOCI actually engage in more checking than students scoring low on the Checking subscale. To do this a brief questionnaire was developed to measure the frequency of everyday checking behaviors. The 7 items on the questionnaire included: checking to make sure you have your wallet; checking to make sure you have your keys; checking examination questions before handing in a test; checking to make sure your car or house door is locked; checking letters before mailing; checking to see if zippers are closed; and checking electrical appliances to make sure

---

†As suggested previously, an alternative hypothesis is that the individual imagines a failure to execute an action. In this case a bias toward deciding that the memory was of external origin could lead to checking behavior.

they are turned off. Ss indicated the frequency of checking behavior for each of these items on a 4- or 5-point scale.

Experimental Tasks

Subjects were asked to complete 7 separate tasks during the course of the experiment. The tasks included (1) reality monitoring; (2) recognition; (3) letter cancelling; (4) indicator tracking; (5) a fear survey schedule; (6) a questionnaire concerning attitudes toward responsibility; and (7) a questionnaire on frequency of everyday checking (already described). After completing all 7 tasks, Ss were given a piece of blank paper and a pencil and asked to name or briefly describe each of the tasks they participated in during the experiment. The total number of tasks recalled served as a measure of memory for actions.

The reality-monitoring task was adapted from ones described by Johnson and Raye (1981). The task involved having Ss view stimuli of two types on a CRT display: (1) a cue word with its opposite (e.g. hot:cold); and (2) a cue word with the first letter of its opposite (e.g. north:s . . .). Ss were instructed to 'read' the opposite word when presented with a stimulus of the first type, and to 'think' the implied opposite word when presented with a stimulus of the second type. After viewing a sample series of stimuli of both types Ss were presented with a series of 48 trials (24 type 1 stimuli and 24 of type 2). Each stimulus was presented for 2 sec, one after another. Following the 48 viewing trials, Ss were presented with test words, one at a time, and instructed to indicate whether they had previously 'read' it (i.e. the entire word was viewed) or 'thought' it (i.e. only the first letter was viewed). Ss then were asked to estimate their performance by indicating the percentage of test words they correctly identified from 50% (chance) to 100% (perfect performance).

The cue words employed were all common (frequency of 100 occurrences/million words on the Thorndike–Lorge word norms; Thorndike and Lorge, 1944). Additionally, a cue word–opposite word pair was selected only if the opposite had been found to be a strong associate of the cue word (greater than 50% of respondents gave as first response on word-association test) in at least one study surveyed by Shapiro and Palermo (1968).

Reality-monitoring ability was measured in two ways: (1) the total percent correct (the mean of the proportion of 'read' words correctly identified and the proportion of 'thought' words correctly identified); and (2) a d' statistic derived by signal-detection theory (Swets, 1964). For the computation of d', 'read' words correctly identified as 'read'' served as the hit-rate, and the 'thought' words incorrectly identified as 'read' words served as the false-alarm rate. A measure of bias was calculated by the proportion of times the S indicated that the test word has been 'read'. The Ss' estimates of the percentage of test words they correctly identified with the actual performance covaried out served as a measure of the extent to which Ss underestimated their performance.

As a control for general ability at recognition tasks, a simple recognition task was employed. In this task Ss viewed a series of 24 high-frequency words, one at a time, on a CRT with the same display time and interstimulus-interval used in the reality-monitoring task. After viewing all 24 words, Ss then viewed a series of 48 test words, one at a time, and were instructed to indicate whether the word was 'old' (i.e. one of the stimulus words) or 'new'. As in the reality-monitoring task, Ss estimated their performance on a scale from 50–100%. Both the proportion of words correctly identified and a d' measure of recognition ability were calculated. The proportion of times that a S indicated that a test word was 'old' served as a measure of bias.

The remainder of the tasks were included with only tentative predictions regarding Checkers vs Noncheckers. An Indicator Tracking Task required Ss to perform a series of numerical calculations on a CRT (counting backwards from 1000 by 7s) while at the same time keeping track of the status of an indicator which went 'on' or 'off' at random intervals. This task required Ss to remember an event which occurred independent of and consecutive with a demanding cognitive task. A letter-cancelling task required Ss to read a short passage and cross out all the e's. Measures of total time spent on the task and total number of cancellations were collected. Ss also completed a Fear Survey Schedule (FSS; Wolpe and Lang, 1964). This schedule was used since Rachman and Hodgson (1980) suggest that compulsions (especially cleaning) are similar to the type of avoidance seen in phobias. It was expected that both Cleaners and Checkers would show higher FSS scores than Noncleaners and Noncheckers, and that Cleaners would show more types of phobias than Checkers. A questionnaire designed to measure attitudes toward responsibility, criticism and guilt was also administered. The items were derived consistent with the hypothesis that checking is motivated by fear of criticism and guilt (Rachman and Hodgson, 1980). It was expected that both Checkers and Cleaners would report more dislike of criticism, more negative reactions to guilt and less eagerness to take on major responsibilities (i.e. buying a house etc.).

Data Analysis

In all analyses 2 (Checkers, Noncheckers) × 2 (Cleaners, Noncleaners) ANOVAs were used except in those which involved Ss' performance estimates. For Ss' estimates of their performance on the reality-monitoring and recognition tasks 2 × 2 ANCOVAs were conducted using the actual performance as the covariate.

Results

To determine the extent to which the MOCI detected checkers among a sample of normal college students, it was necessary to examine the results of the 7-item checking questionnaire. The items on the test were all intercorrelated, $\alpha = 0.73$. Significant main

effects for Checking (P's < 0.05) indicated that Checkers, as identified by the MOCI, reported significantly more checking behavior than Noncheckers on 6 of the 7 individual items. In addition, Checkers reported significantly more checking behavior on the scale composed of the weighted sum of all 7 items, $F(1,50) = 10.26$, $P < 0.005$. In contrast, on only 1 of the 7 items was there a significant difference between Cleaners and Noncleaners, and on the composite scale there was no significant Cleaning effect, $F(1,50) = 2.79$, $P > 0.10$. Thus the Checking subscale of the MOCI appears to have identified a group of individuals who report more everyday checking behaviors, and distinguished them from a group of Compulsive Noncheckers.

Of the four experimental hypotheses, two were supported by the present data. On the memory for actions measure there was a significant main effect for Checking, $F(1,48) = 4.41$, $P < 0.05$. Checkers ($\bar{X} = 5.5$, SD = 1.19) had a poorer memory for prior actions than Noncheckers ($\bar{X} = 6.1$, SD = 0.92). This deficit was specific to Checkers. There was no significant effect for Cleaning and no significant interaction.

Regarding the hypotheses related to reality-monitoring ability, there were no significant differences between Checkers and Noncheckers on either measure of reality-monitoring ability (d' and proportion of words correctly identified). Also, there were no significant differences between Checkers and Noncheckers on the measure of response bias. Thus, the second and third hypotheses were not supported by these data.

Concerning the hypothesis that checkers would underestimate their performance on the reality-monitoring task, there was a significant main effect for Checking, $F(1,48) = 4.11$, $P < 0.05$, in the ANCOVA on the estimated performance on the reality-monitoring task. Checkers underestimated their performance on the reality-monitoring task compared to Noncheckers (Checkers $\bar{X} = 0.615$, SD = 0.098; Noncheckers $\bar{X} = 0.676$, SD = 0.124). This

TABLE 1 Means and SDs for major dependent measures

	Checkers		Noncheckers	
Measures	Cleaners (N = 13)	Noncleaners (N = 13)	Cleaners (N = 13)	Noncleaners (N = 15)
Memory for actions				
$\overline{X}$	5.42	5.62	5.77	6.40
SD	1.44	0.96	0.83	0.91
d' on reality-monitoring task				
$\overline{X}$	0.547	0.806	0.430	0.601
SD	0.631	0.551	0.333	0.791
Proportion correct on reality-monitoring task				
$\overline{X}$	0.598	0.643	0.577	0.605
SD	0.116	0.091	0.061	0.134
Response bias on reality-monitoring task				
$\overline{X}$	0.458	0.358	0.448	0.500
SD	0.215	0.124	0.194	0.294
Performance estimate on reality-monitoring task (unadjusted)*				
$\overline{X}$	0.635	0.596	0.688	0.667
SD	0.090	0.105	0.157	0.096

*Means for performance estimate when adjusted for covariate (proportion correct on reality-monitoring task) differ from the reported (unadjusted) means by no more than 0.003.

effect was specific to Checkers since there was no comparable effect for Cleaners. Further, this effect was specific to perceived ability to discriminate actual from imagined occurrences since there was no comparable checking effect on performance estimates for the recognition-control task.

There were no significant effects for Checking on the indicator-tracking task or on the letter-cancelling task. Checkers tended to report more fear of responsibility; $F(1,50) = 2.83$, $P < 0.10$, and reported more guilt than Noncheckers, $F(1,50) = 9.18$, $P < 0.005$ on the attitude questionnaire. Checkers also had significantly higher FSS scores than Noncheckers ($\overline{X}$s = 182.5 and 155.2; SDs = 41.5 and 38.8, respectively).

Unexpectedly, Cleaners only tended to have higher FSS scores than Noncleaners, $F(1,50) = 3.78$, $P = 0.057$ ($\overline{X}$s = 179.7 and 157.8, respectively). There were no significant differences between Cleaners and Noncleaners on the attitude questionnaire or on their ability to keep track of the binary states of the indicator (indicator tracking).

Cleaners did spend more time on the letter-cancelling task, $F(1,50) = 4.07$, $P = 0.049$, but did not cancel any more letters than Noncleaners.

Discussion

The present study found that college students who score high on the Checking subscale of the MOCI report greater everyday checking behavior, have poorer recall of prior actions, and tend to underestimate their ability to make reality-monitoring decisions. If an individual has difficulty in recalling whether an intended action has been executed, they may be inclined to engage in checking behavior to insure the intended action has been carried out. Similarly, a tendency to underestimate reality-monitoring ability could result in increased checking behavior as the individual attempts to reduce his/her uncertainty over whether a previous behavior actually occurred or merely was thought to have occurred. The fact that these results were found for checkers but not for a group of compulsive noncheckers (cleaners) suggests that the differences are specific to checking and may relate to the development of that behavior.

To our knowledge, the finding that checkers tend to be deficient in their memory for actions has not been reported previously. This finding may be of potential importance for understanding the genesis and maintenance of checking behavior, and may ultimately be useful in attempting clinical assessments of individuals with problematic checking behavior. The stage of processing at which this deficit occurs (encoding, storage, retrieval) has not yet been identified, nor have the psychological factors which influence this apparent memory problem. Reed's (1977) hypothesis that obsessionals have a deficit at redintegration—the process of reconstructing the memory of the whole on the basis of the parts—and that this redintegrative deficit may covary with depression in obsessive–compulsive individuals is clearly one possibility. At this point the exact deficits and factors that determine them are open research questions.

Whether the tendency to underestimate performance on the reality-monitoring task is specific to tasks involving reality-monitoring decisions or is related to a more global 'doubting' factor is difficult to determine. In the present study, however, checkers did not exhibit a similar tendency when asked to determine whether they had previously seen certain stimuli on a simple recognition task. Although the stimuli words on the recognition task were matched with the words on the reality-monitoring task for word frequency, the tasks were not matched in the strict sense suggested by Chapman and Chapman (1973, 1978). Thus, although the underestimation of performance was specific to the reality-monitoring task, the finding must be cautiously interpreted. The tendency to underestimate reality-monitoring ability may reflect a general tendency to doubt the effectiveness of one's behavior when confronted with a difficult task. This is in line with other theorists beginning with Freud (1909/1955) and Maudsley (1895)

who have hypothesized that doubting is a key component in many obsessive–compulsive behaviors. Additional research will be needed to determine more precisely the form and content of doubting and the relationship of doubting to a more primary memory deficit.

Two hypotheses regarding the relationship between reality monitoring and checking behavior were not supported. Checkers were not found to be deficient in their reality-monitoring ability nor were they shown to exhibit a response bias towards judging that memories are imagined. However, it is perhaps premature to conclude that checking behavior is unrelated to reality-monitoring ability. First, the reality-monitoring task employed in the current study was quite difficult with 20% scoring at or below chance (50%). Thus, there may have been a floor effect which precluded finding significant differences between groups. Second, and perhaps more important, the reality-monitoring task employed exclusively verbal stimuli. Checking behavior as it typically occurs involves motor action and it could be that checkers are deficient in distinguishing memories for actual actions from memories for imagined actions. The present finding of deficient memory for actions in checkers certainly suggests that assessment of action based memories are particularly relevant for studying checking behavior. The specificity of a deficit in motor based actions is suggested by Reed's (1977) work which found that obsessive–compulsives described the recollection process in terms of exclusively visual imagery in contrast to controls who described or implied the use of images of all modalities, including *kinesthetic*. Development of an appropriate reality-monitoring task based on actual and imagined motor actions, while difficult, would probably be of greater relevance for understanding checking behavior.

The study of cognitive deficits in compulsive checkers appears to be a fruitful avenue of inquiry for understanding the etiology and maintenance of checking behavior. The findings from the checking questionnaire indicate that even among a nonclinical sample the MOCI can identify a sample of persons who report engaging in frequent checking behavior, and who show memory deficits and performance estimates which might help explain checking behavior. Checking behavior is not only a symptom of obsessive–compulsive disorder but is a prevalent but little studied aspect of the 'psychopathology of everyday life.'

References

BEECH H. (1974) *Obsessional States.* Methuen, London.

CARR A. (1974) Compulsive neurosis: a review of the literature. *Psychol. Bull.* **81,** 311–318.

CHAPMAN L. J. AND CHAPMAN J. P. (1973) *Disordered Thoughts in Schizophrenia.* Appleton-Century-Crofts, New York.

CHAPMAN L. J. AND CHAPMAN J. P. (1978) The measurement of differential deficit. *J. psychiat. Res.* **14,** 303–311.

FREUD S. (1909) Notes upon a case of obsessional neurosis. In STRACHEY J. (Ed. and Trans.; 1955) *The Standard Edition of the Complete Psychological Works of Sigmund Freud,* Vol. 9. Hogarth Press, London.

JOHNSON M. AND RAYE C. (1981) Reality monitoring. *Psychol. Bull.* **88,** 67–85.

MAUDSLEY H. (1895) *The Pathology of the Mind,* revised edn. Macmillan, London.

RACHMAN S. AND HODGSON R. (1980) *Obsessions and Compulsions.* Prentice-Hall, Englewood Cliffs, New Jersey.

REED G. S. (1977) Obsessional personality disorder and remembering. *Br. J. Psychiat.* **130,** 177–183.

SALZMAN L. AND THALER F. H. (1981) Obsessive–compulsive disorders: a review of the literature. *Am. J. Psychiat.* **138,** 286–296.

SHAPIRO S. I. AND PALERMO D. S. (1968) An atlas of normative free association data. *Psychol. Monogr. (Suppl.)* **2**(12). (Whole No. 28).

SWETS J. A. (1964) *Signal Detection and Recognition by Human Observers.* Wiley, New York.

THORNDIKE E. L. AND LORGE I. (1944) *The Teacher's Word Book of 30000 Words.* Bureau of Publications. Teachers College, New York.

WOLPE J. AND LANGE P. (1964) A fear survey schedule for use in behavior therapy. *Behav. Res. Ther.* **2,** 27–30.

20

Multiple Personality: A Social Psychological Perspective

Nicholas P. Spanos, John R. Weekes, and Lorne D. Bertrand

The part of an accused murderer remanded for pretrial psychiatric evaluation was role played by 48 college students. Role players were assigned to interview treatments that varied in how extensively they cued for symptoms of multiple personality. The most explicit treatment (i.e., Bianchi treatment, n = 16) included a hypnotic interview that was used in diagnosing a suspect in the "Hillside strangler" rape–murder cases as suffering from multiple personality. A less explicit hypnotic treatment (n = 16) and a nonhypnotic treatment (n = 16) were administered to the remaining role players. Most subjects in the Bianchi treatment displayed the major signs of multiple personality (e.g., adoption of a different name, spontaneous posthypnotic amnesia). In a later session subjects who role played as multiple personalities performed very differently on psychological tests administered separately to each role-played identity. Those who failed to enact the multiple personality role performed similarly when tested twice. Findings are discussed in terms of a social psychological formulation that emphasizes the roles of active cognizing, contextual cuing, and social legitimation in the genesis of multiple personality.

Nicholas P. Spanos, John R. Weekes, and Lorne D. Bertrand. Multiple Personality: A Social Psychological Perspective. *Journal of Abnormal Psychology,* 1985, Vol. 94, No. 3, pp. 362–376. Copyright © 1985 by the American Psychological Association. Reprinted by permission of the publisher and authors.

People who are diagnosed as multiple personalities (i.e., multiples) present themselves as possessing two or more distinct identities. They convey this impression by exhibiting a relatively integrated interpersonal style when calling themselves by one name, and different and distinct interpersonal styles when calling themselves by other names (Ullmann & Krasner, 1975). For instance, when self-presenting as "Joe" the patient may interact with others in a generally belligerent and aggressive manner. However, when self-presenting as "Harry" he interacts in a meek, passive, dependent style. Typically, cases of multiple personality involve displays of amnesia (Sutcliff & Jones, 1962; Taylor & Martin, 1944). For example, when behaving as "Harry" the person may claim to know nothing about "Joe," but when behaving as "Joe" he claims to know all about "Harry" as well as all about himself.

Although relatively rare throughout most of this century, cases of multiple personality have become increasingly common in the last decade (Boor, 1982; Greaves, 1980; Orne, Dinges, & Orne, 1984; Saltman & Solomon, 1982). For instance, Bliss, Larson, and Nakashima (1983) recently reported that 27 out of 45 patients admitted to a single inpatient psychiatric service with auditory hallucinations were discovered to be multiple personalities. Between 1934 and 1971, however, fewer than half this number of multiple personality cases were reported in the entire American psychiatric literature (Rosenbaum, 1980). Along related lines it is worth noting that some psychotherapists seem much more likely than others to make contact with such patients. According to Gruenewald (1971) most psychotherapists do not see even a single such patient in their entire career. It is somewhat surprising, therefore, that some investigators (e.g., Allison & Schwarz, 1980; Bliss, 1980, 1984a; Braun, 1984; Kluft, 1982) have each dealt with more than 50 such patients.

Some contemporary investigators contend that the incidence of multiple personality has not really increased (Allison & Schwarz, 1980; Watkins & Johnson, 1982). From this perspective, multiple personality was previously (and often continues to be) misdiagnosed as schizophrenia, psychopathy, and a variety of other disorders (Allison & Schwarz, 1980; Rosenbaum, 1980; Watkins & Johnson, 1982). Nonetheless, multiple personality is beginning to be recognized as a legitimate and distinct disorder and, as a result, it is correctly diagnosed more frequently. According to this view, only a relatively few psychotherapists possess the training and experience required to recognize the often subtle indicators of this disorder, and it is these few therapists who correctly diagnose a disproportionately large number of these cases (Watkins & Johnson, 1982).

According to many investigators who adopt a psychodynamic perspective, the most important antecedents of multiple personality involve early developmental traumas such as sexual abuse, severe physical punishment, and ambivalent and inconsistent treatment by parents (Allison, 1974; Gruenewald, 1977, 1984; Herzog, 1984). Although adult stresses may trigger some manifestations of the disorder, these are considered insufficient in the absence of predisposing developmental antecedents to produce multiple personalities. From this perspective, multiple personality patients are implicitly conceptualized as the passive ineffectual victims of unconscious processes that temporarily "take control" and become manifest as new identities.[1]

A social psychological conceptualization suggests instead that people learn to enact the role of the multiple personality patient (Spanos, in press; Sutcliff & Jones, 1962; Ullmann & Krasner, 1975). These patients are conceptualized as actively involved in using available information to create a social impression that is congruent with their perception of situational demands and with the interpersonal goals they are attempting to achieve. According to this perspective, psychotherapists often play a particularly important part in the generation and maintenance of this role enactment. Although it may be done unwittingly, therapists sometimes encourage patients to adopt the mul-

---

[1]Several case studies indicated that the various personality enactments of multiples were associated with distinct electroencephalograph (EEG) patterns and/or differences in visual-evoked responding (VER; Braun, 1983; Lamore, Ludwig & Cain, 1977; Ludwig, Brandsma, Wilbur, Benfeldt & Jameson, 1972). These results, however, are far from clear or consistent. For instance, Lamore, Ludwig and Cain reported VER differences between the four personality enactments of a single multiple, and concluded that it was "as if four different people had been tested" (p. 40). However, their data indicate as much variability within as between the various personality enactments. Moreover, Ludwig, Brandsma, Wilbur, Benfeldt, and Jameson (1972) and Coons, Milstein, and Marley (1982) found no VER differences between the personality enactments of multiples. Ludwig, Brandsma, Wilbur, Benfeldt, and Jameson (1972) and Coons, Milstein, and Marley (1982) reported EEG differences between the personality enactments of each of their patients. It is important, however, that Coons, Milstein, and Marley also found that a nonpatient control who simulated different personalities produced even more marked between-personality EEG differences than did the actual patients. Coons, Milstein, and Marley concluded that EEG differences between the personality enactments of multiples "involve changes in intensity of concentration, mood, and degree of muscle relaxation, and duration of recording involved in such studies. It is not as if each personality is a different individual with a different brain. Instead, to put it simply, the EEG changes reflect changes in emotional state" (p. 825).

tiple personality role, provide them with information about how to enact that role convincingly, and, perhaps most important, provide "official" validation for the different identities that their patients enact (Sutcliff & Jones, 1962).

The social psychological perspective does not hold that psychotherapists are the only source of information that patients have about multiple personality. In fact, information about this disorder is widespread in our culture, and as a result, the major components of the role are probably fairly well-known. For instance, popular movies and television shows like "The Three Faces of Eve" and "Sybil," and a number of popular biographies like *Sybil* (Schreiber, 1973), *The Five of Me* (Hanksworth & Schwarz, 1977), and *The Minds of Billy Milligan* (Keyes, 1981), provide detailed examples of the symptoms and course of multiple personality. Moreover, these sources usually make the role of multiple personality appear relatively attractive by portraying the protagonist as a person with a dramatic set of symptoms who overcomes numerous obstacles and eventually gains dignity, esteem, and much sympathetic attention from significant, high-status others.

The authors of the well-known book *The Three Faces of Eve* (Thigpen & Cleckley, 1957) recently commented on the attractions of the multiple personality role and on the lengths to which some individuals go to have their self-diagnoses legitimated by psychiatric authority (Thigpen & Cleckley, 1984). Following publication of their book the authors were inundated with telephone calls and letters from people who had diagnosed themselves as multiple personalities and who presented themselves in terms of this diagnosis by having each "personality" introduce itself over the phone in a different voice, by having each write a different portion of a letter in its own unique handwriting, and so on. According to Thigpen and Cleckley (1984) many of these people

appeared to be motivated (either consciously or unconsciously) by a desire to draw attention to themselves. Certainly, a diagnosis of multiple personality attracts a good deal more attention than most other diagnoses. Some patients appear to be motivated by secondary gain associated with avoiding responsibility for certain actions. (p. 64)

In short, knowledge concerning the multiple personality role is probably fairly widespread. For some people the idea that they suffer from this disorder may even provide a viable and face-saving account for personal failings and problems. Nevertheless, people are relatively unlikely to enact such a deviant and complex role without some assurance that their enactments will be treated seriously. When such assurance is provided by psychotherapists, some patients combine their general knowledge of the role with the information gleaned from their therapeutic interactions to enact the "symptoms" of multiple personality (Spanos, in press; Sutcliff & Jones, 1962).

Evidence from Clinical Reports

Direct evidence concerning the role of the therapist in shaping manifestations of multiple personality is difficult to obtain because most clinical reports do not provide the necessary details about therapist/client interactions. Nevertheless, even the limited data available suggest that therapists sometimes implicitly encourage manifestations of multiple identity, and then validate these manifestations by treating them as signs of new and unique personalities (Sutcliff & Jones, 1962). For instance, before exhibiting signs of a second personality, a patient named Linda claimed that she had difficulty remembering a sexual interaction that had been described to her by her husband. At this point one of her therapists "instructed Linda to close her eyes and asked to speak to the 'one who carried out the act.' " (Smith, Buffington, & McCard, 1982). Only after this intervention did the patient refer to Linda in the third person and begin referring to herself by a different name. Prince (1930) actually provided the names for the various personalities of his most famous patient. He designated them BI, BII, BIII, and BIV. Later he went still further, "Desiring to have some distinctive term of address for BIII, I gave her the name of 'Chris' " (p. 30).

Official validation for a patient's alternate identities is implicitly provided by the common therapeutic practice of conversing at length with the various "personalities" and obtaining from each information about their origins, functions, and habits, as well as information about what "they" know and don't know about each other (Bliss, 1980; Kluft, 1982; Sutcliff & Jones, 1962). Validation is extended still further when the aid of one "personality" is enlisted in the therapeutic endeavor. "So too the therapist occasionally was able to enlist Eve Black's support in some remedial aid directed toward the problem of her body's cohabitant" (Thigpen & Cleckley, 1957, p. 140). The practice of enlisting the aid of various "personalities" is employed extensively by Allison and Schwarz (1980), who believe that all multiple personality patients possess an entity called an *inner self helper* (ISH), which functions to work with the therapist in producing personality reintegration. "I have had conversations with the ISH aspect of my patients, and I've discovered that they regard themselves as agents of God, with the power to help the main personality" (Allison & Schwarz, 1980, p. 109).

Kohlenberg (1973) demonstrated the importance of contextual variables in multiple personality by testing a single patient who was diagnosed as manifesting three different personalities. Baseline rates of occurrence were assessed for the behaviors associated with each identity, and afterwards, the behavioral manifestations of one identity were selectively reinforced. The behaviors associated with the reinforced identity showed a dramatic increase in frequency of occurrence. During later extinction trials the frequency of these behaviors decreased to baseline levels.

Relatively few patients manifest clear signs of multiple personality at the beginning of therapy. Instead, such signs tend to become increasingly evident as therapy progresses. Manifestations of multiple personality seem to occur most frequently when hypnotic procedures are employed in therapy and, as noted by Sutcliffe and Jones (1962), patients who displayed the most elaborate and long-lasting evidence of multiple identities were those who were exposed to protracted hyponotherapy. These findings are consistent with the hypothesis that patients learn to enact the multiple personality role as they gain increasing exposure to information that defines the components of the role and that validates its enactment.

From the social psychological perspective, hypnotic procedures are conceptualized as rituals that, in the context of psychotherapy, may serve to legitimate the transition from manifestations of one identity to manifestations of another (Sarbin & Coe, 1979; Spanos, 1986). Hypnosis is popularly conceptualized as a procedure for uncovering hidden or unconscious aspects of personality. Moreover, psychotherapy patients frequently learn to conceptualize their problems as resulting from unconscious mental forces or "parts" that can be revealed with the aid of special, disinhibiting rituals like hypnosis. Thus, psychotherapy patients who are "hypnotized" are afforded tacit encouragement to describe wishes, feelings, and remembrances that remain unacknowledged in other contexts. When to all of this is added tacit (sometimes even explicit) encouragement to interpret troublesome or uncharacteristic aspects of current and past behavior in terms of one or more indwelling but unconscious selves, it is not surprising that some patients manifest evidence of such "selves" when hypnosis legitimates their appearance (Orne et al., 1984; Spanos, 1986).

It is worth noting that the social psychological perspective does not hold that multiple personality patients are necessarily faking their enactments. The multiple identities created by these individuals are both implicitly encouraged and then consistently validated by high-status experts. Thus, it should come as no surprise that those who carry out such enactments sometimes adopt the interpretation of their behavior that is so strongly and consistently reinforced by significant others.

In summary, even the limited clinical material reviewed thus far indicates that clinicians sometimes encourage and validate their patients' enactments of multiple identities, and patients respond to such encouragement by shaping their enactments in terms of perceived contextual demands. Recently a California court case involving the diagnosis of multiple personality highlighted the potential importance of the clinician/patient interaction in shaping manifestations of this disorder.[2]

The Hillside Strangler Case

In 1979, Kenneth Bianchi was arrested and implicated in the rape murders of several California women (the Hillside strangler murders). Despite much evidence of guilt, Bianchi maintained his innocence and was remanded for pretrial psychiatric evaluation. While undergoing evaluation, Bianchi submitted to a hypnotic interview and during this procedure manifested evidence of multiple personality. Bianchi's interview was videotaped and transcribed, and thereby provides an unusual amount of information about the clinician/client interactions asso-

ciated with the occurrence of a "new" identity.

The clinicians began by defining the purpose of the interview as uncovering what the patient was really like, and by defining hypnosis as a tool that can reveal hidden aspects of the personality (Schwarz, 1981, pp. 139–140). After administering a hypnotic induction procedure the clinician defined the situation as one in which a hidden personality was to emerge.

I've talked a bit to Ken but I think that perhaps there might be another part of Ken that I haven't talked to. And I would like to communicate with that other part. And I would like that other part to come to talk to me ... And when you're here, lift the left hand off the chair to signal to me that you are here. Would you please come, Part, so I can talk to you ... Part, would you come and lift Ken's hand to indicate to me that you are here ... Would you talk to me Part, by saying 'I'm here'? (pp. 142–143)

Following the last question, Bianchi (B) answered "yes" and engaged with the clinician (C) in the following interchange.

C: Part, are you the same as Ken or are you different in any way?

B: I'm not him.

C: You're not him. Who are you? Do you have a name?

B: I'm not Ken.

C: You're not him? Okay: Who are you? Tell me about yourself. Do you have a name I can call you by?

B: Steve. You can call me Steve. (Schwarz, 1981, pp. 139–140)

While enacting the identity of Steve, Bianchi stated that he hated Ken because Ken was nice and that he (Steve), with the help of his cousin, had murdered a number of women. He also indicated that Ken knew nothing about his (Steve's) existence, and nothing about the murders. Following ter-

---

[2]Several experiments (e.g., Kampman, 1976; Watkins & Watkins, 1980) indicate that highly hypnotizable "normal" college students can be induced via hypnotic suggestions to present themselves as possessing multiple *indwelling selves*. Some investigators (e.g., Hilgard, 1977; Watkins & Watkins, 1980) have argued that these indwelling selves existed prior to the experimental instructions that "called them forth." On the other hand, much evidence (reviewed by Spanos, 1983; Spanos, in press) indicates that the "selves" enacted in these studies are experimental creations with characteristics determined by demands in the test situation.

mination of the hypnotic procedures Bianchi displayed "spontaneous amnesia" for the portion of the interview involving "Steve" (Schwarz, 1981).

According to the examining clinician the hypnotic interview had simply served to bring a preexisting but hidden identity to the surface (Watkins, 1984). Along these lines, a number of prominent defense psychiatrists testified that, in their opinion, Bianchi had been suffering from multiple personality at the time that he committed the murders (Watkins, 1984). Alternatively, the social psychological perspective suggests that Bianchi's enactment of a new identity was cued by information culled during the hypnotic interview, coupled with background information about psychiatric disorders and hypnosis common to many people in our culture. This position was favored by prosecution psychiatrists (cf. Orne et al., 1984) and by many of the police officers familiar with the proceedings (Schwarz, 1981).

The Present Experiment

We used the structure of the Bianchi case to develop an experiment that tested hypotheses derived from the social psychological account of multiple personality. College students were instructed to play the role of an accused murderer named Harry Hodgins (for male subjects) or Betty Hodgins (for females). Subjects were told that Harry/Betty had been remanded for psychiatric evaluation, and that they were to role play being Harry/Betty throughout a psychiatric interview that might involve hypnosis. Subjects were given no information about the specific symptoms to manifest and were told nothing about multiple personality.

Subjects were assigned to three interview treatments that varied in the extent to which they provided cues for manifesting multiple personality. The initial portion of the interview was, however, the same for all subjects. It began by asking Harry/Betty about their guilt, and then asked about their relations with peers and parents. Subjects in one treat-

ment were then administered a brief hypnotic induction and an interview procedure that was taken almost verbatim from the Bianchi interview. As in the Bianchi interview, subjects were explicitly asked the question, "Part, are you the same thing as Harry (Betty) or are you different?" Subjects in a second hypnotic treatment were informed that personality was complex and sometimes involved walled off thoughts and feelings. They were further informed that hypnosis could help "get behind the wall" and that during hypnosis the experimenter/ "psychiatrist" would be able to talk to a different part of them. However, they were not asked "Part, are you the same thing as Harry/Betty or are you different?" Nonhypnotic controls were also told that personality was complex and involved walled off thoughts and feelings. However, they were told nothing about hypnosis or about the experimenter/"psychiatrist" being able to contact another part of them.

Bianchi initially denied his guilt, and we anticipated that most of our subjects would do the same. Furthermore, we anticipated that most subjects who failed to manifest a "new" personality during the interview would continue to deny guilt. On the other hand we expected that, like Bianchi, many of those who enacted a new identity would confess guilt and attribute it to the new identity.

Multiple personality patients who have been administered psychological tests have usually responded differently when enacting each identity (Jeans, 1976; Ludwig et al., 1972; Miller, 1984; Osgood & Luria, 1957; Osgood, Luria, Jeans & Smith, 1976; Smith et al., 1982; Thigpen & Cleckley, 1957). Because these test differences have often been dramatic and consistent, some investigators have suggested that they cannot be accounted for in terms of role playing (Greaves, 1980; Ludwig, Brandsma, Wilbur, Benfeldt, & Jameson, 1972; Smith et al., 1982; Watkins, 1984).

Our subjects role played during a second session that involved the administration of two personality inventories. Both of these inventories have been used previously with multiple personality patients (e.g., sentence completion, semantic differential). Both tests were administered twice. If subjects had previously enacted a multiple personality, their "new" identity was contacted and instructed to complete the tests. The second administration of the tests was given after subjects had "returned" to enacting Harry/Betty. Subjects who previously failed to enact a multiple personality completed the tests twice in succession as Harry/Betty. We anticipated that subjects who enacted two identities would exhibit significantly larger test differences across the two administrations than would subjects who enacted only one identity.

Method

Subjects

Twenty four male and 24 female Carleton University undergraduates (ages 18–24) volunteered to play the role of an accused murderer in a two-session experiment. All of the subjects had been previously tested for hypnotic suggestibility on the Carleton University Responsiveness to Suggestion Scale (CURSS: Spanos, Ratke, Hodgins, Stam, & Bertrand, 1983). However, performance on the CURSS was not a selection criterion for the present study. All of the subjects received course credit for their participation.

Procedure

Subjects were randomly assigned to three treatments with the restriction of an equal number of males (n = 8) and an equal number of females (n = 8) in each treatment.

Session One

All of the subjects were seen individually, first by an assistant and then by an experimenter who played the role of interviewing psychiatrist. The assistant informed subjects that they were to play the role of accused murderer Harry (Betty) Hodgins. Males were

informed that Harry had been accused of brutally killing three women, named Ann, Jenny, and Mary. Females were informed that Betty was accused of killing three young boys, named Billy, Johnny, and Tommy. Subjects were further told that, despite much evidence of guilt, a *not guilty* plea had been entered for the accused, and the accused had been remanded for psychiatric evaluation. Subjects were then asked to participate in a simulated psychiatric interview. They were instructed to role play Harry/Betty throughout the interview and to use any knowledge they had about criminals and any information that they could pick up from the setting, to give a convincing performance. They were further informed that the experimenter/ "psychiatrist" might suggest the use of hypnosis and, if so, that they were to role play throughout this procedure as well.

Subjects were then escorted to a different room and introduced to a male "psychiatrist," who was neatly dressed and prominently displayed a name badge on his white lab coat. The "psychiatrist's" office included a desk on which were displayed several texts on psychiatry and psychotherapy. The office also contained a videocamera and recorder, and permission to record the session was obtained. The "psychiatrist" informed subjects that it was institutional policy to videotape all interviews with court-referred patients.

The "psychiatrist" began the interview by asking, "Please tell me why you are here?" He then asked the accused about each of his or her alleged victims (e.g., "Tell me about Ann and what happened to her"). Subjects' answers were scored dichotomously as admitting or denying guilt. Subjects were also asked about their relationships with women or children, their childhoods, and their relationships with their parents.

Following these questions, the interview procedure diverged as a function of subjects' treatment assignment.

Bianchi Treatment. Subjects in this treatment were informed that it was possible to find out more about people under hypnosis, and permission to hypnotize them was obtained. Subjects were "hypnotized" by asking them to focus on the end of a pen that was lowered toward the floor. They were told that, as the pen lowered, their eyes would close and they would become hypnotized. Following the hypnotic procedure the "psychiatrist" addressed the subject with a monologue taken almost verbatim from the Bianchi interview (Schwarz, 1981, pp. 142–144). For instance, "I've talked a bit to Harry (Betty) but I think perhaps there might be another part of Harry (Betty) that I haven't talked to, another part that maybe feels somewhat differently from the part that I've talked to. And I would like to communicate with that other part." As in the Bianchi interview, subject's "part" was addressed directly and instructed to lift the accused's hand to signal its presence. As in the Bianchi interview, the "psychiatrist" asked "Would you talk to me Part, by saying 'I'm here'?" Whatever subjects' response they were asked, "Part, are you the same thing as Harry (Betty) or are you different in any way?" Following their response to this question they were administered the following standard queries.

1. Who are you?
2. Tell me about yourself.
3. Do you have a name I can call you by?
4. Tell me about yourself (repeat name used by subject in answering last question), what do you do?

Subjects were classified as adopting or not adopting a different name (a name other than Harry or Betty) on the basis of their response to Question 3. Subjects' answers to Questions 1, 2, and 3 were classified dichotomously as making or not making clear reference to two different identities.

In the remainder of the interview, subjects were again asked about each of their alleged victims (e.g., "Tell me about Ann") and were again classified as admitting or denying guilt. Subjects were also asked the following questions, "Tell me about Harry (Betty), what's he (she) like?" Subjects' answers

were classified as identifying Harry (Betty) with the self, for example, "I've already told you about myself. What else do you want to know?", or identifying Harry (Betty) as different from self, for example, "Harry's a nice person."

Subjects who adopted a name other than Harry or Betty were told that the experimenter would be able to contact their other part in the future by hypnotizing them and calling for the part by name. These subjects were also told that when they were awakened, the "psychiatrist" would again be talking to Harry (Betty). Finally, subjects were "awakened" and asked, "What do you remember about when you were hypnotized?" Those who indicated remembering nothing beyond the pen lowering and feeling relaxed were classified as "spontaneously amnesic."

Hidden Part Treatment. These subjects were exposed to the pen lowering hypnotic procedure described above and then administered the following instructions.

Personality is complex and involves many different ways of thinking and feeling about things. Sometimes part of us thinks about and feels things that other parts of us don't even know about . . . sometimes we have very strong feelings and frightening thoughts that we block off from our conscious mind. These thoughts and feelings still exist, but they are walled off in a different part of our mind. Sometimes these walled-off thoughts and feelings are quite complex and it's almost like there are different people inside of us with different feelings and ideas. (During hypnosis, it is possible to get behind the mental wall to the blocked off parts of the mind. I am going to put my hand on your shoulder, and when I do, I will be in contact with another part of you. I will get behind the wall and will be talking to the part of you that experiences strong feelings and frightening thoughts.)

Following these instructions the "psychiatrist" placed his hand on the subject's shoulder and asked the standard inquiries (starting with Question 1) under the preceding treatment.

No-hypnosis Control. These subjects were not administered a hypnotic procedure. However, they were administered that portion of the "hidden part" treatment instructions shown above that is not in parentheses. They were also administered the same standard inquiry as subjects in the other treatments.

Two judges who were naive to subjects' treatment group rated their transcribed testimony for the following characteristics (a) pretreatment guilt/innocence, (b) posttreatment guilt/innocence, (c) same/different name, (d) spontaneous amnesia/no amnesia, (e) one/two identities, and (f) Harry (Betty) identified with self/other. Interrater agreement was uniformly high and ranged from 92% to 100%.

Session Two

When subjects arrived for their second session, they were again instructed by the assistant to role play Harry or Betty and were again escorted to the "psychiatrist's" office. Subjects in the two hypnosis conditions were again "hypnotized" with the pen-lowering procedure. Subjects who had adopted a different name in the earlier session were presented with the cue for reinstating their other "part" (i.e., I want to talk to _____). Subjects' "part" was addressed directly and instructed to complete two psychological tests (a sentence completion test and a semantic differential inventory). After completing the tests these subjects were informed that when they awakened, the "psychiatrist" would again be talking to Harry (Betty). Once "awakened" Harry (Betty) was instructed to complete the same tests. Subjects in the hypnotic conditions who had not adopted a different name during the earlier session were "hypnotized" and instructed to complete the tests while

under hypnosis. They were then "awakened" and instructed to again complete the tests. Subjects in the no-hypnosis condition were instructed to complete the tests twice in succession. Following completion of the second set of tests, subjects were debriefed, thanked for their participation, and dismissed.

Sentence Completion Test. This questionnaire consisted of the following five partial sentences: (a) I am _____, (b) My mother is _____, (c) The thing I like least about myself is _____, (d) Sexual thoughts _____, and (e) When I get angry _____. Subjects were instructed to complete each sentence in writing. Two judges who were blind to subjects' treatment rated each subject's response to each sentence as the same or different across the two administrations of the test. The raters were instructed to classify sentences as "different" on the basis of clear differences in meaning as opposed to differences in spelling and sentence structure. Interrater agreements concerning same/different classifications were high for each sentence and ranged from $r(46) = .83$, to $r(46) = .96$. For each subject the number of "different" ratings obtained was summed to yield a single score that ranged from *no differences between sentences* (0) to *all sentences different* (5).

Semantic Differential. Subjects were instructed to rate 11 concepts on 10 bipolar 7-point scales. The 11 concepts (e.g., love, me, sex) and 10 scales had been employed by Osgood and Luria (1957) to evaluate the three identities of the famous patient described by Thigpen and Cleckley (1957) in *The Three Faces of Eve*. The standard semantic differential instructions and testing format were employed.

For each subject under each concept the score obtained on each bipolar scale during the first test administration was subtracted from the corresponding bipolar scale score on the second administration. The signs of these difference scores were eliminated and, within concepts, the absolute differences were summed to yield 11 concept difference scores for each subject.

Time to Read Instructions. The typed instructions attached to the semantic differential test booklets were 1⅓ pages long. These instructions were identical on both administrations of the test. Subjects who take the test twice in the same session usually take substantially more time reading the instructions the first time than the second time. The experimenter "psychiatrist" used a hidden stop watch to unobtrusively time the number of seconds it took subjects to read these instructions on each administration of the test. For each subject reading time in seconds on the second test was subtracted from reading time on the first. The *smaller* the difference score, the more similar the reading times on the two tests.

Results

Session One

Second Names and Amnesia. As Table 1 indicates, reports of a second name and displays of "spontaneous amnesia" differed significantly across the treatments. More specifically, when asked "Do you have a name I can call you by?" 81% of the subjects in the Bianchi treatment and 31% of those in the hidden part treatment adopted a name other than Harry or Betty. Relatedly, 63% of the subjects in both the Bianchi and hidden part treatments, but none of the subjects in the control treatment, displayed spontaneous amnesia.

The covariation between reports of a second name and displays of spontaneous amnesia were assessed by combining the subjects in the Bianchi and hidden part treatments and eliminating control subjects from the analysis. Fifteen (83%) of the 18 subjects who adopted a second name also displayed amnesia, whereas only 5 (36%) of the 14

who failed to report a second name displayed amnesia, $\chi^2(1) = 7.62$, $p < .01$.[3]

Denial and Admission of Guilt. As shown in Table 1, the number of subjects who initially admitted guilt was small and did not differ significantly across treatments. Following treatment administration, however, subjects in the Bianchi and hidden part conditions were more likely than were control subjects to admit guilt. It is interesting that none of the control subjects changed their testimony in this regard following treatment administration.

Among the 27 subjects in the Bianchi and hidden part treatments who initially denied guilt, 11 both adopted a different name and displayed amnesia. Ten of these 11 subjects (90.9%) admitted guilt during enactment of their second identity.

Below is an example of testimony from a subject who admitted guilt while enacting the role of a second identity.

> **She (Jenny) was with Ann, and she was a threat to me. She was a threat to Harry. I care about Harry, but even though he won't let me be part of him I know that there's trouble for him . . . Well she got in my way when I was leaving and I pushed her. I had to hit her.**

Two Identities. Immediately following treatment instructions, subjects were asked "Who are you?" and on two later occasions they were asked "Tell me about yourself."

---

[3]Chi-square analyses on each dependent variable indicated no within-treatment differences between males and females. There were no significant differences between treatments in CURSS scores. Moreover, among subjects in the Bianchi and hidden part treatments, those who displayed multiple identity (different name plus amnesia) and those who did not, failed to differ significantly on CURSS scores. When interpreting these results it is important to keep in mind that subjects were instructed to role play a defendant undergoing hypnosis. They were not instructed to, themselves, become "hypnotized."

TABLE 1 Summary of Interview Data for Each Treatment

Data	Treatment			Chi-square Analysis
	Bianchi	Hidden Part	Control	
Different name	13	5	0	$\chi^2(2) = 27.93, p < .001$
Same name	3	11	16	
Amnesia	10	10	0	$\chi^2(2) = 17.14, p < .001$
No amnesia	6	6	16	
Initially denied	13	14	14	$\chi^2(2) < 1, ns$
Initially admitted	3	2	2	
Later denied	6	7	14	$\chi^2(2) = 9.65, p < .01$
Later admitted	10	9	2	
Different identity	10	3	0	$\chi^2(2) = 18.16, p < .001$
No different identity	5	13	16	
Harry/Betty different self	13	13	6	$\chi^2(2) = 10.56, p < .01$
Harry/Betty same self	2	3	10	

Subjects were classified as to whether or not they made clear reference to two identities when answering any of these questions. Table 1 indicates that the frequency of such references differed significantly across treatments.[4] Most of these references were made by subjects in the Bianchi treatment, and none were made by control subjects. Subjects in the Bianchi and hidden part treatments were combined and then divided into those who did or those who did not adopt a different name when asked "Do you have a name I can call you by?" Twelve of the 17 (70.6%) subjects who adopted a different name also referred to two identities when asked "Tell me about yourself." Alternatively, only 1 of the 14 (7.1%) subjects who did not adopt a different name referred to two identities when asked to "Tell me about yourself"; $\chi^2(1) = 10.80, p < .001$. The following are three examples of answers that made reference to two different identities.

1. I'm sort of like Harry's friend, 'cause Harry didn't have very many friends when he was little.

2. I'm inside of Harry. I control Harry's outer feelings, sometimes I make him express feelings.

3. I've always been with Betty since I can remember. She doesn't know I'm here, but I know I'm here.

Typical answers that did not refer to different identities were as follows.

1. I'm a nurse. I work in a hospital.
2. I'm 19, 5'11". I weigh 180 pounds.

Tell Me About Harry (Betty), What's He (She) Like? Table 1 shows a significant difference among treatments in the number of subjects whose answers to this question identified Harry (Betty) with themselves rather than different from themselves. Control subjects were more likely than those in the other two treatments to implicitly identify Harry with themselves in their answers. Collapsing across treatments, 100% of the subjects who adopted a different name referred to Harry as different from themselves, whereas only 13 out of the 30 (43.3%) subjects who failed to adopt a different name

---

[4]Because of equipment malfunction the testimony of one subject in the Bianchi treatment was not tape-recorded in its entirety. This subject was scored for pre- and posttreatment guilt/innocence, same/different name and amnesia/no amnesia. However, he could not be scored for one/two identities or Harry identified with self/other.

referred to Harry as different from themselves, $\chi^2(1) = 15.09$, $p < .001$.

Session Two

Our major interest was to compare differences across test administrations for subjects who enacted both of the major symptoms of multiple personality (i.e., adoption of a different name and amnesia) against subjects who enacted neither symptom. Thus, 11 multiples (second name plus amnesia) were compared to 23 nonmultiples who displayed neither a second name nor amnesia on sentence completion test differences, semantic differential difference scores, and reading time difference scores. Excluded from these analyses were subjects who admitted guilt initially ($n = 7$), those who adopted a second name without amnesia ($n = 1$), and those who displayed amnesia without a second name ($n = 5$).

Sentence Completion. Role-playing multiples, $M = 3.91$, $SD = 1.51$, wrote significantly more sentences that were different across the two test administrations than did nonmultiples, $M = 1.0$, $SD = 1.24$, $F(1, 32) = 35.41$, $p < .001$. Below are examples of five sentences rated as different. In each case, the first sentence was written while the subject enacted the alternate identity (AI), and the second was written when the subject role played Harry (H) or Betty (B).

1. AI: *My mother is* a scum bag probably just like yours.

   H: *My mother is* a clean, very good woman.

2. AI: *When I get angry* I like to physically hurt people.

   H: *When I get angry* my mind seems to go blank and I can't remember what I've done. The only way I know is by people telling me.

3. AI: *Sexual thoughts* Betty is too quiet and shy. She never sees men the way I know she wants to. I love to hold men, feel them, make love to them.

   B: *Sexual thoughts* I push them out of my mind. They are sinful. My father always told me they were wrong.

4. AI: *I am* not going to be told what to do.

   H: *I am* an average person.

5. AI: *When I get angry* I get violent. You wouldn't like me when I get angry.

   H: *When I get angry* I don't know what happens. I really don't know.

Many of the sentences rated as the same across the two administrations of the test were worded identically. Even when differences in wording occurred, the meanings remained the same. Below are two examples of sentences with different wordings that were rated as the same. Both examples were given by nonmultiples.

1. B: *When I get angry* I usually try to keep it inside around others, and I prefer to go jogging or go for a walk to release tension and to help me solve the problem.

   B: *When I get angry* I usually keep it inside until I'm alone and can vent it in a harmless way such as jogging.

2. H: *Sexual thoughts* Well of course I like women.

   H: *Sexual thoughts* I love women.

Semantic Differential. Difference scores on the semantic differential were analyzed with a 2×11 split-plot analysis of variance, with one between-subjects factor (multiple personality/no multiple personality) and one within-subjects factor (11 concepts). The main effect for groups was highly significant, $F(1,32) = 37.79$, $p < .001$, and indicated that multiples obtained higher semantic differential difference scores, $M = 14.19$, than did nonmultiples, $M = 5.50$. The interaction did not approach significance.

Reading Time. Nonmultiples, $M = 67.74$, had significantly larger reading time differences between test administrations than did multiples, $M = 46.91$, $F(1,32) = 4.69$, $p < .05$. In other words nonmultiples took less time than did multiples to read test instructions on the second administration of the semantic differential.

Discussion

Context, Rules, and Multiple Identities

More than 80% of the subjects given the Bianchi interview adopted a different name, and all of them referred to their primary identity (Harry/Betty) in the third person. In addition, the majority of these subjects responded to general questions by indicating "spontaneously" that they were possessed of two identities, and followed termination of hypnosis by displaying "spontaneous amnesia" for their second identity. Not as many subjects in the hidden part treatment displayed the major components of multiple personality. Even here, however, almost one third of the subjects enacted these "symptoms." It is important that none of the control subjects either adopted a different name or displayed spontaneous anmesia.

All but one of the role-playing multiples who initially denied guilt admitted it while enacting their second identity. On the other hand, nonmultiples who initially denied guilt continued to do so throughout the interview. These findings indicate that the multiple personality role was viewed by subjects as a credible vehicle for negotiating a difficult personal dilemma. When "caught dead to rights," adopting the role of a multiple enabled subjects to acknowledge the evidence against them while disavowing personal responsibility for wrongdoing. Because nonmultiples had no such strategy available to them, their most reasonable option was to continue denying guilt despite all the evidence to the contrary.

Subjects who enacted the multiple personality role in their first testing session maintained this role successfully in their second session. Like clinical patients given this diagnosis, our role-playing multiples showed marked and consistent differences between identities on the semantic differential and sentence completion tests. It is important that role-playing multiples responded differently than did control subjects on nonsuggested and relatively subtle indicators of multiple identity, as well as on more obvious indicators. For instance, role-playing multiples displayed amnesia "spontaneously" in their first session and, in their second, validated their amnesic displays by taking significantly longer than did nonmultiples to read test instructions that had been given earlier to their other identity.

Watkins (1984) hypothesized that naive subjects exposed to the type of interview employed with Bianchi would be unable to fake the symptoms of multiple personality. Contrary to this hypothesis, our findings indicate rather clearly that when given the appropriate inducements, enacting the multiple personality role is a relatively easy task. The important inducements include perceived gain for adopting the role (e.g., escaping legal punishment, interpersonal rewards from significant others), and exposure to procedures (like the Bianchi interview) that make salient the major components of the role, encourage its adoption, and legitimate its enactment. The rules for enacting this role were conveyed clearly by the structure of the Bianchi treatment. Subjects given this treatment were implicitly instructed to do the following: (a) Behave as if you are two separate people who inhabit the same body. (b) Act as if the *you* I have been talking to thus far is one of those people, and that the *you* I have been talking to does not know about the existence of the other person. (c) When I provide a signal for contacting the other person, act as though you are that other person. To the extent that subjects (or patients) behave in terms of these rules, the "classic" symptoms of multiple personality follow by implication and do not have to be individually taught through direct instruction or further suggestion. For instance, it follows from these rules that Identity B will discuss Identity A in the third person, that Identity A will disavow activities attributed to B and will display "amnesia" for the period of B's "take over", and that Identities A and B will perform differently on psychological tests.

Clinical reports (Ludwig et al., 1972; Smith et al., 1982; Thigpen & Cleckley, 1957; Watkins & Johnson, 1982) frequently indicate that the identities of multiple personality patients are extreme opposites in terms of tastes, preferences, emotionality, and behavior. If Identity A is passive B is aggressive, if A is frigid B is seductive, and so on. In our data, this tendency toward opposites was clear both in the open-ended testimony of role-playing multiples and in their sentence completion and semantic differential test performance.

Typically, this tendency toward opposites is explained by arguing that wishes unacceptable to the primary personality are expressed by the secondary personality (Allison & Schwarz, 1980; Thigpen & Cleckley, 1957). We do not deny that adoption of the multiple personality role becomes a way for clients to "have their cake and eat it too" (Spanos, 1986). Nevertheless, the tendency toward opposites may also be motivated by more basic considerations of cognitive economy.

Following the rules for being a multiple means remembering which experiences, behaviors, and preferences go with Identity A and which go with Identity B. The memory load involved in this enterprise can be appreciably lightened by making Identity A and Identity B stereotypical opposites. Under these circumstances behavior can be guided by relatively simple higher order decision rules, for example, when A acts like a prototypical "sweet innocent," when B acts like a prototypical bitch. As long as Mr. Hyde's characteristics remain markedly different from those of Dr. Jeckyll, Mr. Hyde will have little difficulty differentiating his experiences and memories from those of Dr. Jeckyll. Moreover, those who meet Mr. Hyde are unlikely to confuse him with or interact with him as Dr. Jeckyll.

Control subjects, like those in the other two treatments, were informed that people have hidden thoughts and feelings "almost like there are different people inside." Despite such instructions none of the control subjects enacted a second identity. To understand why this pattern occurred, it is important to keep in mind that the interview procedure administered to control subjects failed to provide any vehicle that legitimated a transition to a different identity. There was no point in the interaction between "psychiatrist" and control subject where the enactment of a new identity could be naturally "fit in." On the other hand, in both the Bianchi and hidden part treatments, hypnosis was defined as a procedure for contacting subjects' other part. By initiating such "contact" the "psychiatrist" encouraged the enactment of a new "part." Multiple personality enactments occurred most frequently in the Bianchi treatment, and it was in this treatment that the enactment of a full-fledged new identity was given particularly clear and consistent legitimation. Here, subjects' "part" was addressed directly, instructed to "lift the hand from the chair" and asked to answer "I'm here." Finally, the idea that the "part" would be legitimated as a literal "new person" was driven home by asking. "Part, are you the same thing as Harry (Betty) or are you different in any way?"

Psychotherapy and Multiple Personality

It is important to note that Ken Bianchi's case was unusual in a number of respects. For instance, multiple personality is diagnosed much more frequently in females than in males (Allison & Schwarz, 1980; Boor, 1982; Coons, 1980; Greaves, 1980; Sutcliffe & Jones, 1962), and with a few exceptions (e.g., Keyes, 1981) such patients have not been accused of serious crimes. For these reasons, it might be argued that the results of the present study are limited in scope, and that situational factors only play an important role in those rare cases of multiple personality where the patient can obtain some obvious gain (e.g., a not guilty by reason of insanity verdict) by adopting this role. From a social psychological perspective, such a restriction on the role of situational factors greatly underestimates the importance of psychotherapists in shaping the perceptions and attributions of their clients. Psychotherapy can be conceptualized as an interpersonal process geared to changing the assumptions, attitudes, and beliefs that clients hold about themselves and others (e.g., Frank, 1973). Typically, therapists are seen by clients as competent, high-status experts whose opinions are highly valued and whose suggestions are taken very seriously. Moreover, clients are frequently unhappy, insecure people who are very concerned about the status of their relationship with their therapist, and who are strongly invested in presenting themselves in a way that will win their therapist's interest, concern, and approval. Under these circumstances, mutual shaping between therapists "on the lookout" for signs of multiple personality and clients involved in conveying an appropriate impression, may lead to enactments of multiple personality that confirm the initial suspicions of the therapist and that, in turn, lead the therapist to encourage and to validate more elaborate displays of the disorder (Sutcliffe & Jones, 1962).

Some investigators who suspect multiple personality take pains to guard against suggesting or encouraging the enactment of multiple identities (e.g., Horton & Miller, 1972). On the other hand, other investigators argue for the use of hypnotic procedures in suspected cases, in an attempt to "bring forth" other personalities (Allison & Schwarz, 1980; Bliss, 1980, 1984b; Brandsma & Ludwig, 1974; Watkins, 1984). Allison and Schwarz stated that clients are frequently reluctant to accept that they are multiple personalities and, under these circumstances, should be actively persuaded by the therapist to accept this diagnosis. Allison and Schwarz, Bliss, and Watkins recommended hypnosis for identifying the number of indwelling identities and for communicating with the identities separately in order to discover their individual characteristics. In short, clinicians vary quite dramatically in

the extent to which they deem it appropriate to encourage and legitimate enactments of multiple identity. It is little wonder, therefore, that some therapists are much more likely than others to "discover" cases of multiple personality, or that the recent upsurge in the number of such patients parallels increased interest in the disorder and increased sensitivity to "signs" that call for interview procedures like those used with Bianchi.[5]

From a social psychological perspective the amnesia displayed by multiple personality patients constitutes strategic enactment. This does not mean that such displays of forgetting are necessarily faked. It does suggest, however, that these patients maintain control over memory processes and enact displays of forgetting by exercising such control in a goal-directed manner. The displays of forgetting exhibited by these pa-

---

[5]For some investigators (cf. Orne, Dinges & Orne, 1984) the diagnosis of multiple personality should involve evidence that a patient's different identities existed prior to psychiatric intervention. In practice, however, this criterion is difficult to apply meaningfully because, in many cases, the only evidence for the pretherapy existence of different identities comes from reports made by the patient during therapy. Even when other evidence is available it is often ambiguous and open to alternative interpretation (cf. the divergent opinions of Orne, Dinges & Orne, 1984, and Watkins, 1984, concerning evidence for the pretreatment existence of multiple identities in the Bianchi case). From a social psychological perspective, acceptance of the pretherapy existence criterion may encourage a misleading categorization of cases into *genuine* (evidence of pretherapy multiple identity) and *nongenuine* (no such clear evidence). According to the social psychological perspective, people may learn how to be a multiple from sources other than therapy (e.g., television shows). Moreover, they may initially enact various components of this role for, and seek legitimation of their enactments from, audiences other than mental health professionals (e.g., friends, family). In clinical cases of multiple personality it is, obviously, important to delineate pretherapy as well as posttherapy variables that are relevant to the genesis and maintenance of the patients' enactments. Nevertheless, it is not clear that cases involving evidence of pretherapy multiple identity enactments should be considered somehow more genuine than are those in which the relevant self-conceptions and other role components were learned and first enacted in the therapist's office.

tients are selective and context dependent (when enacting Identity B, the patient recalls events that he or she failed to recall while enacting Identity A). Such displays are guided by the impressions that subjects are attempting to convey in self-presenting as first one identity and then as another. Similar selective and context-dependent displays of forgetting occur when amnesia is suggested to experimental subjects in hypnotic situations. A good deal of recent evidence (e.g., Spanos, Radtke & Bertrand, 1984) indicates that hypnotic amnesia constitutes a strategic attempt to control memory processes in order to guide recall (and failures to recall) in terms of the unfolding demands of the hypnotic test situation.

Clinical anecdotes (e.g., Allison & Schwarz, 1980; Bliss, 1980; Ross, 1984) indicate that hypnotic interventions that legitimate remembering without discrediting earlier enactments of amnesia, often induce a "sharing" of memories among the several identities enacted by multiples. For example, posthypnotic suggestion that the primary personality will gradually become aware of a previously "hidden" secondary personality, or hypnotic suggestions encouraging the various "personalities" to share their memories, are often associated with increased recall of previously "hidden" memories by the primary personality. From a social psychological perspective, of course, hypnotic procedures do not possess intrinsic properties that enhance recall or prompt the "fusion" of "dissociated identities." Instead, such interventions provide a legitimating context for redefining the situation as one in which displays of "cross-personality" remembering are now considered role appropriate.

In the Bianchi case, the possibility of escaping a murder charge was a highly salient inducement for enacting the multiple personality role. From a social psychological perspective, it is unlikely that patients who adopted this role under the pressure of such a salient external inducement would (at least initially) assign much credibility to their enactments (Jones, 1979). However, in typical psychotherapy situations the inducements

for behaving in terms of a therapist's suggestions are much more subtle and, thereby, less easily identified and reflected upon. Under these circumstances, many psychotherapy clients who are led to enact the multiple personality role probably become convinced by their own enactments and by the validation that these enactments elicit from their therapists.

A social psychological approach to multiple personality does not deny that long-standing attributes and cognitive styles may predispose some people to adopt this role more easily and more convincingly than others. For instance, a number of clinical reports describe multiples as highly imaginative people, and as people with rich fantasy lives who, as children, created imaginary companions. By the same token, recent studies also indicate that multiples tend to obtain high scores on tests of hypnotic susceptibility (Bliss, 1984a, 1984b). Taken together, these findings appear to describe people who have spent a good deal of time covertly rehearsing and becoming absorbed in a range of "make believe" roles and activities. It would not be surprising if such people were particularly adept at enacting the role of a "new identity" when contextual inducements called for such enactment.

Enacting multiple identities involves more than behaving as different people at different times. It also requires reinterpreting the past in a manner that is consistent with the notion of possessing multiple selves. Typically, this involves attributing uncharacteristic, shameful, or disavowed aspects of earlier behavior to one or more alternate identities. Such reinterpretation may occur with relative ease in people who have had much practice at imagining themselves in different roles or as different people, and can draw upon these fantasies as a means of fleshing out their new identities.

References

ALLISON, R. B. (1974). A new treatment approach for multiple personalities. *American Journal of Clinical Hypnosis, 17,* 15–32.

ALLISON, R. B., AND SCHWARZ, T. (1980). *Minds in many pieces: The making of a very special doctor.* New York: Rawson, Wade.

BLISS, E. L. (1980). Multiple personalities: A report of 14 cases with implications for schizophrenia and hysteria. *Archives of General Psychiatry, 37,* 1388–1397.

BLISS, E. L. (1984a). A symptom profile of patients with multiple personalities, including MMPI results. *Journal of Nervous and Mental Disease, 171,* 197–202.

BLISS, E. L. (1984b). Hysteria and hypnosis. *Journal of Nervous and Mental Disease, 172,* 203–206.

BLISS, E. L., LARSON, E. M., AND NAKASHIMA, S. R. (1983). Auditory hallucinations and schizophrenia. *Journal of Nervous and Mental Disease, 171,* 30–33.

BOOR, M. (1982). The multiple personality epidemic: Additional cases and inferences regarding diagnosis, etiology, dynamics and treatment. *Journal of Nervous and Mental Disease, 170,* 302–304.

BRANDSMA, J. M., AND LUDWIG, A. M. (1974). A case of multiple personality: Diagnosis and treatment. *International Journal of Clinical and Experimental Hypnosis, 22,* 216–233.

BRAUN, B. G. (1983). Psychophysiologic phenomena in multiple personality and hypnosis. *American Journal of Clinical Hypnosis, 26,* 124–137.

BRAUN, B. G. (1984). Hypnosis creates multiple personality: Myth or reality? *International Journal of Clinical and Experimental Hypnosis, 32,* 191–197.

COONS, P. M. (1980). Multiple personality: Diagnostic considerations. *Journal of Clinical Psychiatry, 41,* 330–336.

COONS, P. M., MILSTEIN, V., AND MARLEY, C. (1982). EEG studies of two multiple personalities and a control. *Archives of General Psychiatry, 39,* 823–825.

FRANK, J. D. (1973). *Persuasion and healing.* New York: Schoken Books.

GREAVES, G. B. (1980). Multiple personality of 165 years after Mary Reynolds. *Journal of Nervous and Mental Disease, 168,* 577–595.

GRUENEWALD, D. (1971). Hypnotic techniques without hypnosis in the treatment of a dual personality. *Journal of Nervous and Mental Disease, 153,* 41–46.

GRUENEWALD, D. (1977). Multiple personality and splitting phenomena: A reconceptualization. *Journal of Nervous and Mental Disease, 164,* 385–393.

GRUENEWALD, D. (1984). On the nature of multiple personality: Comparisons with hypnosis. *International Journal of Clinical and Experimental Hypnosis, 32,* 170–190.

HANKSWORTH, H., AND SCHWARZ, T. (1977). *The five of me.* New York: Pocket Books.

HERZOG, A. (1984). On multiple personality: Comments on diagnosis, etiology, and treatment. *International Journal of Clinical and Experimental Hypnosis, 32,* 210–221.

HILGARD, E. R. (1977). *Divided consciousness.* New York: Wiley.

HORTON, P., AND MILLER, D. (1972). The etiology of multiple personality. *Comprehensive Psychiatry, 13,* 151–159.

JEANS, J. F. (1976). An independent validated case of multiple personality. *Journal of Abnormal Psychology, 85,* 247–386.

JONES, E. E. (1979). The rocky road from acts to dispositions. *American Psychologist, 34,* 107–117.

KAMPMAN, R. (1976). Hypnotically induced multiple personality: An experimental study. *International Journal of Clinical and Experimental Hypnosis, 24,* 215–227.

KEYES, D. (1981). *The minds of Billy Milligan.* New York: Bantam.

KLUFT, R. P. (1982). Varieties of hypnotic interventions in the treatment of multiple personality. *American Journal of Clinical Hypnosis, 24,* 230–240.

KOHLENBERG, R. J. (1973). Behavioristic approach to multiple personality: A case study. *Behavior Therapy, 4,* 137–140.

LAMORE, K., LUDWIG, A. M., AND CAIN, R. L. (1977). Multiple personality: An objective case study. *British Journal of Psychiatry, 131,* 35–40.

LUDWIG, A. M., BRANDSMA, J. M., WILBUR, C. B., BENFELDT, F., AND JAMESON, D. H. (1972). The objective study of a multiple personality: Or, are four heads better than one? *Archives of General Psychiatry, 26,* 298–310.

MILLER, R. D. (1984). The possible use of autohypnosis as a resistance during hypnotherapy. *International Journal of Clinical and Experimental Hypnosis, 32,* 236–247.

ORNE, M. T., DINGES, D. F., AND ORNE, E. C. (1984). On the differential diagnosis of multiple personality in the forensic context. *International Journal of Clinical and Experimental Hypnosis, 32,* 118–169.

OSGOOD, C. E., AND LURIA, Z. (1957). Introduction. In C. H. THIGPEN AND H. M. CLECKLEY, *The three faces of Eve.* New York: Fawcett.

Osgood, C. E., Luria, Z., Jeans, R. F., and Smith, S. W. (1976). The three faces of Evelyn: A case report. *Journal of Abnormal Psychology, 85,* 247–286.

Prince, M. (1930). *The dissociation of a personality.* London: Longmans, Green.

Rosenbaum, M. (1980). The role of the term *schizophrenia* in the decline of diagnoses of multiple personality. *Archives of General Psychiatry, 37,* 1383–1385.

Ross, C. A. (1984). Diagnosis of multiple personality during hypnosis: A case report. *International Journal of Clinical and Experimental Hypnosis, 32,* 222–235.

Saltman, V., and Solomon, R. S. (1982). Incest and multiple personality. *Psychological Reports, 50,* 1127–1141.

Sarbin, T. R., and Coe, W. C. (1979). Hypnosis and psychopathology: Replacing old myths with fresh metaphors. *Journal of Abnormal Psychology, 88,* 506–562.

Schreiber, F. R. (1973). *Sybil.* New York: Warner.

Schwarz, J. R. (1981). *The Hillside Strangler: A murderer's mind.* New York: New American Library.

Smith, R. D., Buffington, P. W., and McCard, R. H. (1982). *Multiple personality: Theory: diagnosis, and treatment.* New York: Irvington.

Spanos, N. P. (1983). The hidden observer as an experimental creation. *Journal of Personality and Social Psychology, 44,* 170–176.

Spanos, N. P. (1986). Hypnosis, nonvolitional responding and multiple personality: A social psychological perspective. In B. Maher and W. Maher (Eds.). *Progress in experimental personality research* (Vol. 14, pp. 1–62). New York: Academic Press.

Spanos, N. P. (in press). Hypnosis, demonic possession and multiple personality: Strategic enactments and disavowals of responsibility for actions. In C. Ward (Ed.). *Altered states of consciousness and mental health: A cross cultural perspective.*

Spanos, N. P., Radtke, H. L., and Bertrand, L. D. (1984). Hypnotic amnesia as a strategic enactment: Breaching amnesia in highly susceptible subjects. *Journal of Personality and Social Psychology, 47,* 1155–1169.

Spanos, N. P., Radtke, H. L., Hodgins, D. C., Stam, H. J., and Bertrand, L. D. (1983). The Carleton University Responsiveness to Suggestion Scale: Normative data and psychometric propeties. *Psychological Reports, 53,* 523–535.

Sutcliffe, J. P., and Jones, J. (1962). Personal identity, multiple personality and hypnosis. *International Journal of Clinical and Experimental Hypnosis, 10,* 231–269.

Taylor, W. S., and Martin, M. F. (1944). Multiple personality. *Journal of Abnormal and Social Psychology, 39,* 281–300.

Thigpen, C. H., and Cleckley, H. M. (1957). *The three faces of Eve.* New York: Fawcett.

Thigpen, C. H., and Cleckley, H. M. (1984). On the incidence of multiple personality disorder. *International Journal of Clinical and Experimental Hypnosis, 32,* 63–66.

Ullmann, L. P., and Krasner, L. (1975). *A psychological approach to abnormal behavior.* Englewood Cliffs, NJ: Prentice-Hall.

Watkins, J. G. (1984). The Bianchi (L.A. Hillside Strangler) case: Sociopath or multiple personality? *International Journal of Clinical and Experimental Hypnosis, 32,* 67–101.

Watkins, J. G., and Johnson, R. J. (1982). *We, the divided self.* New York: Irvington.

Watkins, J. G., and Watkins, H. (1980). Ego states and hidden observers. *Journal of Altered States of Consciousness, 5,* 3–18.

21

A Model of Hysterical and Hypnotic Blindness: Cognition, Motivation, and Awareness

Harold A. Sackeim, Johanna W. Nordlie, and Ruben C. Gur

Clinical and experimental analyses of hysterical conversion reactions of blindness are reviewed. A model is offered to account for the visually controlled behavior of the psychogenically blind. The model attributes a central role to motivational factors in determining selective nonawareness of cognition. A case study of hypnotic blindness is presented that illustrates the utility of the model. The model has implications for interpretations of other hypnotic phenomena and for views concerning the relations between cognition and awareness.

There have been long-standing debates in psychology and philosophy concerning the relations between cognition and awareness (e.g., Descartes, 1641/1967; Dixon, 1971; James, 1890/1950; Sartre, 1958; Wundt, 1912/1973). Hypnotic phenomena have been critical to this controversy by providing possible examples of information processing that is not subject to awareness. As increasing numbers of psychologists accept the view that the relations between cognition and awareness are contingent as opposed to necessary (e.g., Nisbett & Wilson, 1977), there has been a resurgence of interest in the concept of dissociation as fundamental to interpretations of the nature of hypnosis (Hilgard, 1973, 1976, 1977). However, the notion that selective awareness or nonawareness of cognition can be determined by motivational factors still remains controversial. Psychopathological disorders have long been a source of speculation concerning the role of motivation in influencing the awareness of cognition (e.g., Breuer & Freud, 1895/1955; Charcot, 1890). In particular, hysterical conversion reactions have been instructive of the processes by which motivational factors can produce dissociations in awareness.

We will review the experimental literature on visual functioning in hysterical blindness. On the basis of this review we will propose a model of the processes that underlie such functioning. Similarities between hysterical and hypnotic blindness will be discussed. A case study of two hypnotically blind subjects and one simulating subject that bears on the utility of the model in accounting for psychogenic blindness will be presented. The model attributes a central

Harold A. Sackeim, Johanna W. Nordlie, and Ruben C. Gur. A Model of Hysterical and Hypnotic Blindness: Cognition, Motivation, and Awareness. *Journal of Abnormal Psychology,* 1979, Vol. 88, No. 5, pp. 474–489. Copyright © 1979 by the American Psychological Association. Reprinted by permission of the publisher and authors.

role to motivational factors in determining the awareness of cognition. The features of the model suggest novel alternative accounts of dissociation and of "hidden observer" effects that have been demonstrated in experiments on hypnotic analgesia (e.g., Hilgard, Morgan, & Macdonald, 1975).

Clinical Studies of Hysterical Conversion Disorders

Clinical analysis of psychological functioning in hysterical conversion reactions has long been a source for theoretical claims about the structure of consciousness and the role of unconscious mentation in psychopathology (Breuer & Freud, 1895/1955; Charcot, 1890; Freud, 1895/1962; Janet, 1929). Freud's discovery that hysterics' somatic difficulties (e.g., paralysis) remitted during hypnosis and often reappeared when hypnosis was lifted led him to argue that the somatic difficulties in these patients were psychogenically based. His findings that the remission of these difficulties was associated with the recovery of memory of early traumatic experiences, that the remembering of these experiences produced intense affective states, and that the patients often demonstrated amnesia for these memories when hypnosis was lifted were taken as evidence that the memories were significant factors in the etiology of the disorders and that the nonawareness of these mentations was under motivational control. Indeed, in summarizing the conclusions they reached through treating these patients with apparent somatic complaints, Breuer and Freud (1895/1955) wrote, "Hysterics suffer mainly from reminiscences" (p. 7).

The validity of these conclusions as they apply to hysteria and, more generally, to the study of consciousness is subject to debate. The traditional psychoanalytic view has been that patients with hysterical conversion reactions and those with hysterical personality disorders overlap in the dynamic, genetic, and structural factors presumed to be etiologically significant in producing the dis-

orders (Fenichel, 1945). Yet, it is now commonly accepted that the two diagnostic categories are only loosely related (Chodoff, 1974). Studies have indicated that patients with conversion reactions are more likely to receive collateral diagnoses of other personality disorders than that of the hysterical type (e.g., Chodoff & Lyons, 1958; Guze, Woodruff, & Clayton, 1971; Stephens & Kamp, 1962). At least in Western countries, diagnoses of hysterical conversion reactions are relatively rare (Slater, 1965; Stephens & Kamp, 1962; Templer & Lester, 1974). Controlled studies have shown that alarmingly high proportions of individuals who receive the diagnosis of hysterical conversion die from or develop signs of physical disease of the central nervous system (Slater & Glithero, 1965; Whitlock, 1967), indicating that despite its infrequency the diagnosis of hysterical conversion reaction is often misapplied.

Even if it is granted that the somatic complaints diagnosed as hysterical by Breuer and Freud were of doubtful organic origin, there are questions as to the adequacy of the evidence generated from observation of these patients to support the general conclusions that Breuer and Freud derived. Conclusions based on the results of clinical interactions raise issues concerning observer bias (Rosenthal, 1969), expectations of subjects, and demand characteristics (Orne, 1962). It should be recalled that Freud first generated the concepts of resistance and transference from the treatment of these hysteric patients. Implicit in the theoretical framework generated to explain conversion reactions is the assumption that the hysteric truly believes that loss of functioning has occurred and is not simply malingering (Brady, 1966; Freud, 1895/1962). In the clinical situation it is a matter of subjective judgment as to whether an organically intact individual who presents, for example, loss of sight or hearing is giving a veridical report of conscious experience or is lying.

Although the psychoanalytic account of hysterical conversion reactions remains prominent, recently other theories of the processes underlying such reactions have been offered (e.g., Szasz, 1975; Ullman & Krasner, 1969). These theories differ from the psychoanalytic model in the degree to which they emphasize unconscious motivation, as opposed to malingering, as central to explanations of the symptomatic behavior. For instance, Ullman and Krasner claimed simply that the sensory disturbances seen in conversion disorders are feigned in order to achieve secondary gains. Szasz, taking an intermediate position, agreed with Freud (1895/1962) that somatic symptoms in such cases are translations of psychological conflicts, but he also argued that patients may or may not be aware that they are using symptoms for the purpose of communication. Determining whether patients are malingering when presenting conversion disorders should prove critical in evaluating the merits of these theories.

Experimental Studies of Hysterical Blindness

There have been a few experimental investigations of processing of information in patients with sensory disturbances diagnosed as hysterical conversion reactions. Although this article specifically examines studies of hysterical blindness, the results of such investigations are in line with studies of other conversion disorders such as deafness (e.g., Malmo, Davis, & Barza, 1952–1953). Five studies have tested the degree to which patients with hysterical conversion reactions of blindness deny visual functioning.

Brady and Lind (1961) trained a patient who reported total blindness to press a button on a schedule of differential reinforcement of low rate of responding (DRL) under which responses spaced between 18 and 21 seconds apart were reinforced. Introduction of slight visual cues signalling that an immediate response would be reinforced resulted in *deterioration* in performance. This procedure was continued and the patient's performance returned to baseline levels. However, it was discovered that in sessions

following those showing the deterioration, the patient had covered his eyes and therefore could not attend to the cues. After this discovery the visual cues were increased in intensity and the patient was informed of their presence. This procedure again resulted in an initial deterioration in performance. However, despite the fact that the patient continued to report total blindness, performance improved and surpassed initial baseline values. The procedure was continued and the patient spontaneously reported recovery of sight.

Grosz and Zimmerman (1965; Zimmerman & Grosz, 1966) conducted a follow-up investigation of the same patient. The patient's recovery of sight was apparently short-lived and the patient again reported total blindness. In this study the patient was presented with a three-choice discrimination task for geometrical shapes. During control sessions in which correct choices were randomized, the patient performed at chance level. During sessions in which responses to one of the three stimuli were consistently reinforced, the patient correctly responded at levels well below chance. The patient maintained this level of performance for over 100 experimental sessions. In the latter part of the study, a confederate of the experimenters established rapport with the patient and informed the patient that "the doctors reckon that the patient can see because he makes fewer correct responses than a blind man would make" (p. 259). The patient was also told the correct number of responses necessary to perform at a chance level. Subsequent to this manipulation, latency of response increased and the patient's performance improved to chance level. At no point during this study did the patient report a change in his blindness.

Following the report by Grosz and Zimmerman (1965), Miller (1968) attempted a replication on another patient who presented functional blindness of the left eye. Over a series of trials the patient was shown groups of three geometrical shapes in which two shapes were always identical. The patient was asked to select the odd shape. Each eye was examined separately and the patient achieved perfect performance when tested with her right eye. In each of two sessions the patient's identifications were well below chance when the left eye was tested. Prior to a third session the patient demanded an explanation of the testing. At that point the experimenter informed the patient of the purpose of testing, including the notion that truly blind individuals should perform at chance levels. The patient continued with the task for an additional 20 trials, maintaining below chance performance. Then, with outbursts of emotion, she refused to continue. Overall, Miller's finding of below chance performance was in line with the results of Brady and Lind (1961) and Grosz and Zimmerman (1965). The failure of the manipulation to influence performance was attributed to the fact that the statement concerning chance level responding was made by the experimenter and under conditions in which the patient had demanded an explanation of the purpose of testing.

Theodor and Mandelcorn (1973) conducted a similar investigation of a patient diagnosed as presenting a conversion reaction of tunnel vision. The patient's visual field in each eye was tubular and measured less than 5°-centrally. The consulting neurologist, psychiatrist, and ophthalmologist agreed that the visual disturbance reflected a conversion reaction. The patient was administered a two-alternative forced-choice task requiring identification of the presence or absence of a visual target during discrete trial intervals. In a control series of 10 trials, the target was presented 2° temporal to fixation, well within the patient's range of vision. The patient's responses were all correct. A series of 100 trials was then administered with the target 45° from fixation, well within the area in which the patient claimed blindness. The patient performed significantly below chance level (30% correct).

Grosz and Zimmerman (1970) used the same procedure as in their previous study (1965) to assess visual functioning in a patient who presented a conversion reaction

of partial blindness. The patient was unable to read print of any size, although she was able to identify objects and count fingers at some distance. Testing comprised 600 trials distributed over five sessions, the first of which was a control session in which no visual stimuli were presented during the three-choice identification task. In this session, despite the absence of stimuli, the patient made responses on 35 of 120 trials. On the remaining 480 trials, the patient produced correct identifications on all but one occasion. These results were in striking contrast to the findings of the other investigations (Brady & Lind, 1961; Grosz & Zimmerman, 1965; Miller, 1968; Theodor & Mandelcorn, 1973), all of which found that, at least initially, hysterically blind subjects were below chance in their identifications of visual targets. Also noteworthy was Grosz and Zimmerman's finding that the patient's response latency increased markedly as testing progressed, changing from a mean of 1.5 seconds in the control session to nearly a minute per trial in the final session. The near-perfect performance notwithstanding, the patient showed significant somatic and emotional distress as testing progressed.

A Model of Hysterical Conversion Reactions

The results of the five studies on the four patients diagnosed as presenting hysterical conversion reactions demonstrate that the behavior of these patients was considerably under the control of visual stimuli. This agrees with the findings of other investigations that show, for instance, that a hysterically blind patient may be classically conditioned to visual targets (e.g., Cohen, Hilgard, & Wendt, 1933). For three of the patients (Brady & Lind, 1961; Grosz & Zimmerman, 1965; Miller, 1968; Theodor & Mandelcorn, 1973) the extent to which they denied behaviorally that they were functioning visually indicated that they were reacting to visual stimulation. Furthermore, the findings of Brady and Lind and Grosz and Zimmerman suggest that the extent to which visual functioning was behaviorally denied was subject to motivational manipulations. The remaining patient (Grosz & Zimmerman, 1970) demonstrated visual functioning in a more straightforward manner by correctly identifying visual targets at a high level of accuracy and clearly did not engage in behavioral denial.

If one accepts the assumption that these patients were not malingering or consciously lying about their perceptual experience, then the results of these investigations suggest a particular model of the psychological processes that underlie hysterical conversion reactions. We will first present an account of the cases of below chance performance (see Figure 1). The hysterically blind individual is not aware of visual cues, and perceptual representations are blocked from awareness. However, the hysterically blind individual may not only report nonawareness of visual stimuli but may act in a fashion contrary to what one would expect given conscious awareness of stimulation and veridical reports of that experience. Therefore, information must be extracted from the visual percept and transformed or denied. The operations that the hysterically blind perform on the information extracted from the percept also occur outside of awareness. The hysterically blind individual does not report that although he or she did not see anything, he or she had a feeling as to the nature of a stimulus and then behaved in an opposite manner. Given the assumption that these patients have provided veridical reports of their conscious experience, the experimental studies of visual behavior indicate that for at least some hysterically blind patients a two-stage defensive operation is likely to be involved in the processing of visual information.

The results indicating that the extent to which patients behaviorally denied visual functioning was subject to experimental manipulation suggest that the two stages of defensive operations, blocking and denial, are independent. Brady and Lind (1961) found

that when the patient was informed of the presence of visual cues, after initial deterioration, the patient's performance improved to levels above baseline values. This change in behavior occurred before the patient reported recovering sight. Similarly, the manipulation used by Grosz and Zimmerman (1965) resulted in a change from below chance to chance level performance without any reported change in the patient's visual experience. The independence of the two stages and the role of motivational factors in moderating their influence is also suggested by the frequently stated clinical observation that hysterically blind individuals avoid walking in front of cars, tripping over furniture, and so on, although they report no awareness of engaging in such specific avoidance behaviors (e.g., Janet, 1929).

The suggestion that the two stages of defensive operations, blocking and denial, are independent is critical to an account of the visually controlled behavior of Grosz and Zimmerman's (1970) second patient. This patient identified visual targets at high levels of accuracy while maintaining claims of blindness. Assuming veridicality of the patient's report, in such cases perceptual representations are blocked from awareness. These representations undergo processing and the information extracted is not subject to denial. Rather, appropriate decisions are made concerning inputs, and these decisions appear in awareness (see Figure 1).

The question must be raised as to why one type of patient manifests denial and another type does not. Our hypothesis that motivational circumstances influence levels of denial offers one explanation. For instance, all the patients described above, except for Grosz and Zimmerman's (1970) second patient, had only one physical complaint, blindness. Demonstrating that they were incapable of sight may have been particularly important for them. Grosz and Zimmerman's second patient had multiple complaints, including backache, headache, and difficulties with speech. Another possibility is that although individuals may differ in their ability to dissociate (e.g., Hilgard,

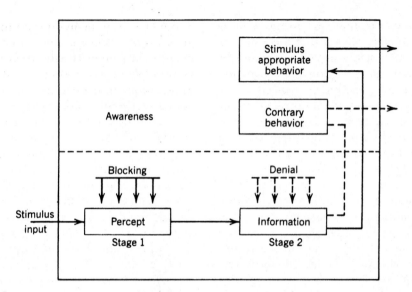

FIGURE 1

A model of visual functioning in psychogenic blindness under strong and weak motivational sets for blindness. (Motivational sets do not differ in regard to their effects in Stage 1. The effects of denial [e.g., in cases of strong motivation for blindness] result in below chance performance in identifying visual targets and are illustrated by the dotted lines in Stage 2. In the absence of denial or when the power of Stage 2 denial is lessened [e.g., in cases of weak motivation for blindness], the psychogenically blind are more accurate in their visual identifications. This is illustrated by solid lines in Stage 2.)

1977) or to block perceptual representations from awareness, even people high in this ability may differ in their capacity to employ denial. For instance, Sackeim and Gur (1978, 1979; Gur & Sackeim, 1979) have presented evidence that individuals differ in tendencies to engage in self-deception. Blum (1975; Blum & Porter, 1973; Blum, Porter, & Geiwitz, 1978), on the basis of studies of hypnotic negative visual hallucinations, viewed the capacity to inhibit processing of perceptual inputs as a skill varying among individuals. Likewise, in the psychoanalytic literature, a distinction has been made between those patients with hysterical conversion reactions who engage in repression or blocking and those patients who in addition employ denial (e.g., Chodoff, 1954). Only a subgroup of patients with this disorder present "la belle indifférence" (e.g., Templer & Lester, 1974). Chodoff (1954) argued that patients manifesting this minimization of and inattention to symptoms be-

longed to the group that makes use of both types of defense. It is noteworthy that the patient tested both by Brady and Lind (1961) and by Grosz and Zimmerman (1965) displayed this minimization. "The patient did not seem greatly alarmed by his loss of sight, but instead had an attitude of patient forebearance" (Brady & Lind, 1961, p. 332). This may be contrasted with the attitude of Grosz and Zimmerman's (1970) second patient, who was described as distressed about her condition. Therefore, differences in the extent to which the hysterically blind behaviorally deny visual processing may be due to differences in motivational circumstances or differences in the capacity for or characteristic use of denial as a defense.

The fundamental features of the proposed model of visual information processing in the hysterically blind are compatible with current cognitive theories of the normal visual information-processing system (Kahneman, 1968; Neisser, 1967; Turvey, 1973). It is generally held that processing of visual inputs is mediated by a hierarchically organized temporal sequence of events that involves initial stages of iconic representation and subsequent stages of extraction and transformation of information. Initially, perceptual inputs are rather literally represented. They are then subject to selection and categorization recording, which may result either in overt responses to the input or in short-term storage. The proposed model posits that in the hysterically blind, the perceptual representations are blocked from awareness, and under some motivational circumstances the information that is extracted from the representations may be subject to a denial operation that results in incorrect identifications of visual stimuli.

Hysteria or Malingering

The value of the proposed model hinges on whether the hysterically blind individual provides a veridical report of conscious experience. As is the case with findings from clinical interactions, the experimental analyses of behavior of hysterically blind patients provide little objective evidence in regard to this issue. Brady (1966) questioned whether absolute distinctions could be made between cases of hysterical conversion reactions and cases of malingering. Grosz and Zimmerman (1965) concluded, "Now, short of the patient admitting deliberate deceit, there is, of course, no way of proving either hysteria or malingering . . . both the diagnosis of hyseria and of malingering lean rather heavily on highly subjective judgments" (p. 257). However, these conclusions may be in error. The independence of the two stages of defensive operations in the proposed model and the susceptibility of at least the second stage to motivational manipulations suggest that manipulations could be found that would result in differing types of behavior in presumed hysterics and malingerers. For example, a manipulation that in the hysteric lessened the efficiency or power of Stage 2 denial but left Stage 1 blocking unchanged

should result in the hysteric claiming blindness for visual inputs but correctly identifying visual stimuli at high levels of accuracy. In other words the hysteric would not have access to the visual percept but would have access to the information extracted from the percept. This type of behavior was exemplified by Grosz and Zimmerman's (1970) second patient and by the patient tested by Brady and Lind (1961) following the motivational manipulation.

The malingerer, on the other hand, should not demonstrate a dissociation between reports of blindness and correct identification of stimuli. Because the denial used by the malingerer is under conscious control, a consciously malingering patient would be unlikely to maintain claims of blindness while simultaneously giving correct identifications of visual stimuli. Therefore, motivational manipulations should influence the accuracy of visual identifications in the hysterically blind but not in the malingerer.

In proposing that Stage 2 denial is independent of Stage 1 blocking of visual representations from awareness, it is assumed that it is possible for people to claim veridically that they are blind and nevertheless correctly identify visual inputs. Is this likely? Weiskrantz, Warrington, Sanders, and Marshall (1974) reported instances of this type of behavior in brain-damaged patients. Lesions in Area 17 of the visual cortex often result in circumscribed scotomas. These patients are blind in restricted regions of their visual fields. Weiskrantz et al. examined a patient with a unilateral lesion in this area and scotoma in the left visual field. The patient was tested extensively on a series of six visual discrimination and identification tasks. Despite consistent reports of blindness to stimuli presented within the range of the scotoma, the patient performed at above chance levels on each task. For instance, the patient would guess successfully as to whether stimuli were Xs or Os while maintaining that he could not perceive the stimuli. It was established through experimenter and electrographic monitoring of eye fixation that the patient did not achieve above chance performance by a shift of fixation. Furthermore, the patient was able to maintain above chance levels of performance at stimulus durations below the latency for initiation of a saccade. Weiskrantz et al. labeled this phenomenon "blind-sight."

The introspective report of this patient concerning his performance is of considerable interest. The patient maintained that although he was blind and could not see stimuli presented within the range of the scotoma, he had feelings about the nature of the stimuli.

> **When he was shown his results he expressed surprise and insisted several times that he thought he was just guessing. When he was shown a video film of his reaching and judging orientation of lines, he was openly astonished. In an interview just afterwards he commented that he could see none of the stimuli and that he would have told us if he could have seen any, "because otherwise he would have been cheating himself." Needless to say, he was questioned repeatedly about his vision in his left half field and his most common response was that he saw nothing at all. If pressed, he might say that he perhaps had a "feeling" that the stimulus was either pointing this or that way, or was "smooth" (the O) or "jagged" (the X). On one occasion in which "blanks" were randomly inserted in a series of stimuli in a reaching experiment, he afterwards spontaneously commented he had a feeling that maybe there was no stimulus present on some trials. But always he was at a loss for words to describe any conscious perception, and repeatedly stressed that he saw nothing at all in the sense of "seeing," and that he was merely guessing. (Weiskrantz et al., 1974, p. 721)**

The behavior of this brain-damaged patient in the visual identification tasks and his introspective report about his experience accord well with the basic features of the proposed model. He had no awareness of visual representations; however, his above chance performance indicated that stimulus-bound decisions took place and were dependent on extensive processing of visual inputs. The model may also provide an explanation for the great uncertainty the patient had concerning the accuracy of his decisions. Ordinarily, when we look at a visual target we have access not only to the decisions we reach concerning its nature, but we also have available visual representations of the target by which to validate those decisions. Without awareness of such representations, decisions reached on the basis of visual processing might have the subjective qualities of feelings or guesses.

Further evidence for the independence of visual processing from awareness of visual representation comes from the literature on subliminal perception (cf. Dixon, 1971; Sackeim, Packer, & Gur, 1977). Marcel (in press; Marcel & Patterson, 1978) has provided perhaps the most clear-cut demonstration of this phenomenon. He presented normal subjects with words followed at varying intervals by visual masks. Subjects were required to guess whether a word had been presented at all, whether the word was an orthographically similar or dissimilar word, and whether the word was a semantically related or unrelated word. Marcel found that with progressively shortened target-mask intervals, the decision concerning whether a word had been presented was the first to drop to chance levels of accuracy. At shorter intervals, the accuracy of decisions concerning whether a visually similar word had been presented fell to chance. Finally, at still shorter intervals, decisions about semantically related words reached chance levels of accuracy. Subjects were able to process visual inputs semantically at target-mask intervals so brief that they were at chance level in deciding whether a word had ever been presented.

Thus, in quite different contexts Weiskrantz et al. (1974) and Marcel (in press) have provided instances of dissociation between the processing of visual inputs and the awareness of visual representations. Our model suggests that a similar dissociation underlies visual functioning in the psychogenically blind, although it is produced through different means. It would seem possible, then, that in the absence of strong motivation to deny visual functioning, the psychogenically blind would identify visual stimuli at high levels of accuracy while maintaining phenomenological blindness. In this respect they should certainly differ from malingerers. Under strong motivational sets for blindness, we hypothesize that at least some of the psychogenically blind submit the decision reached on the basis of visual processing to a second defensive operation of denial. This would account for their below chance performance under testing conditions. It has not been empirically determined whether malingerers who are attempting to appear blind also perform at below chance levels in visual identification tasks.

Hypnosis and Hysteria

The question as to whether the performance of hypnotically blind subjects on visual identification tasks is similar to that of hysterically blind patients comes to the fore. Hypnosis has been employed to establish symptomatic behavior in general (e.g., Reyher, 1967; Sommerschield & Reyher, 1973; Gur, Sackeim, Packer, & Liran, Note 1) and in particular to mimic the symptomatic behavior found in hysterical conversion reactions of analgesia (Hilgard, Morgan, & Macdonald, 1975), deafness (Crawford, Macdonald, & Hilgard, Note 2), tunnel vision (Blum, 1975; Miller & Leibowitz, 1976), monocular blindness (Pattie, 1935), and binocular blindness (James, 1890/1950; Loomis, Harvey, & Hobart, 1936; Ludholm, & Lowenbach, 1942–1943). Can hypnotic blindness therefore serve as an experimental analogue of hysterical blindness?

Parallels between hypnosis and hysterical conversion reactions frequently have been suggested (Chertok, 1975; Frankel, 1978; Gill & Brenman, 1959; Hilgard, 1977). In-

deed, in discussing hysterical blindness and hypnotically induced blindness, William James (1890/1950) concluded that the same type of psychological organization underlies both phenomena. His formulation of this organization shows a striking resemblance to the basic features of the model proposed here.

We have, then, to deal in these cases neither with a blindness of the eye itself, nor with a mere failure to notice, but with something much more complex; namely, an active counting out and positive exclusion of certain objects. It is as when one "cuts" an acquaintance, "ignores" a claim, or "refuses to be influenced" by a consideration. But the perceptive activity which works to this result is disconnected from the consciousness which is personal, so to speak, to the subject, and makes of the object concerning which the suggestion is made, its own private possession and prey. (pp. 212–213)

Meares (1957) argued that hypnosis produces a shift in defensive styles toward those presumed characteristic of hysterics. More generally, the dissociations in conscious experience that are claimed to characterize the hysteric (Breuer & Freud, 1895/1955; Janet, 1929) are also claimed to be central components of hypnotic phenomena (Hilgard, 1973, 1976). Given this interest in drawing conceptual links between hypnosis and hysterical conversion reactions, it may be surprising that there has been little systematic investigation of whether the two phenomena are mediated by similar processes.

Charcot's (1890) view that hypnosis involves a temporary hysterical reaction and that only hysterics are susceptible to hypnosis has not received support. Differences in normal samples on measures of hysterical personality style, such as the *Hy* scale of the Minnesota Multiphasic Personality Inventory, are not associated with hypnotic susceptibility (Hilgard, 1965; Schulman & London, 1963; Secter, 1961). What little evidence there is suggests that although hysterical patients may be more susceptible to hypnosis than other neurotics, they are not markedly more susceptible than normals (Ehrenreich, 1949; Gill & Brenman, 1959). However, as mentioned earlier, there are only weak associations between diagnoses of hysterical conversion reaction and other diagnostic categories of hysteria (e.g., Chodoff, 1974). A recent study (Bendefeldt, Miller, & Ludwig, 1976) found that a group of patients with various types of hysterical conversion reactions showed greater waking suggestibility than a matched control group of patients with other psychiatric disorders. The significance of this finding may be questioned, since one of the five criteria used by Bendefeldt et al. to diagnose hysterical conversion reactions was the "presence of increased susceptibility to external suggestion" (p. 1251). To our knowledge, there has not been any investigation that compared patients with hysterical conversion reactions to controls on standard measures of hypnotic susceptibility.

Another way to examine this issue may be to determine whether the sensorimotor disturbances in hysterical conversion reactions can be reversed with hypnosis. Case reports of the successful use of hypnosis in this disorder and in hysterical dissociative reactions are readily available (e.g., Frankel, 1978; Winer, 1978). However, it is likely that unsuccessful attempts to reverse conversion symptoms would not be reported. Again, there have been no systematic investigations in this area.

Studies that compare the performance of patients with hysterical conversion reactions to that of subjects with hypnotically induced sensorimotor disturbances may provide the most compelling data in the assessment of the relations between the two phenomena. For example, Malmo and colleagues (Malmo, Boag, & Raginsky, 1954; Malmo, Davis, & Barza, 1952–1953) compared the electromyographic responses to loud tones of two hypnotically deaf subjects with those of a hysterically deaf patient. The two hypnotic subjects were also tested under waking conditions. The hysteric patient showed a clear startle response following the first tone. This was associated with an intense emotional outburst, and the patient also began to weep. On subsequent trials, the patient showed little electromyographic response to the tones. Of the two hypnotic subjects, only one claimed complete deafness for the tones. This subject, like the hysteric, showed a startle response on the first trial and an absence of response on all subsequent trials. The other hypnotic subject, despite reporting having heard sounds on occasional trials, showed a lack of response across all trials. Under waking conditions the two previously hypnotized subjects demonstrated a gradual decline in response to tones as trials progressed. Malmo et al. (1954) concluded that similar processes mediated the electromyographic response of the hysterically and hypnotically deaf subjects. They suggested that the inhibition of responsiveness occurred faster than one would expect simply on the basis of normal habituation.

There have been no studies that directly compared the visually controlled behavior of hysterically and hypnotically blind subjects. With one exception (Miller & Leibowitz, 1976), reports concerning visual processing in hypnotically induced blindness have been case studies or inadequately controlled investigations. The findings from such studies generally support the view that the behavior of the hypnotically blind is similar to that of the hysterically blind. For instance, Pattie (1935) presented an extensive analysis of a subject who was strongly encouraged to be monocularly blind during hypnosis. Initial results of a series of tests of this subject's visual functioning did not differentiate the subject's condition from genuine blindness. When the subject demonstrated visual processing by failing a complicated filter test, the experimenter confronted the subject with a charge of malingering. The intensity of the subject's denial of having malingered and the concomitant affective reaction convinced the investigator that the malingering behavior had not been subject to conscious control. Pattie concluded that for this subject the "tendencies to malinger were repressed and dissociated" (p. 239).

Blum, Porter, and Geiwitz (1978) investigated the accuracy of identifying features of a stimulus array in two hypnotic subjects in whom negative visual hallucinations had been suggested for those features. They found that under some conditions the subjects' performance was below chance levels. In particular, subjects' performance deteriorated when they were given longer intervals between warning and target stimuli. As in the model proposed here, Blum et al. suggested that during negative visual hallucinations, sensory registration of inputs and processing of sensory representations take place and are subject to inhibitory mechanisms prior to the stage of verbal report.

Despite the fact that previous investigators have been successful in employing hypnosis to produce reports of analgesia, deafness, tunnel vision, and other types of blindness in normal subjects, only one controlled study has explicitly examined whether the denial of visual processing typical of the hypnotized subject is similar to that found in the hysterically blind (Miller & Leibowitz, 1976). They investigated the processing of visual information in four subjects with hypnotically induced tunnel vision and in four simulating subjects. Subjects were asked to identify the presence or absence of a light under hypnotic narrowing of the visual field, hypnosis without narrowing, and awake conditions. The light was presented at three luminance levels, and sensitivity and response criteria measures were computed. For both groups, sensitivity was influenced by luminance levels, as expected. Both groups of subjects also performed differently depending on experimental conditions. The hypnotic narrowing condition produced the lowest sensitivity levels for both groups. However, hypnotic and simulating subjects did not differ in sensitivity levels. Surprisingly, both groups performed at levels above chance in every experimental condition. There was no difference between the groups in response

criteria, nor did experimental conditions exert an effect.

Methodological problems may account for the failure of Miller and Leibowitz to find differences between hypnotic and simulating groups and for the above chance performance of both groups. The simulating subjects were highly susceptible to hypnosis, and this introduces the question of whether these subjects became hypnotized during the study (Orne, 1972). The manipulation of narrowing of the visual field raises the question as to whether shifts in fixation were responsible for the above chance performance. Perhaps of greatest significance is the fact that Miller and Leibowitz's subjects were given considerable practice with feedback at the beginning of each session. The purpose of the practice trials was to give subjects an opportunity to stabilize response criteria. However, it is possible that the feedback procedure also influenced subjects' subsequent performance on experimental trials. The inconclusive findings of Miller and Leibowitz are contrasted with the case studies that suggest similarities in the visually controlled behavior of the hysterically and hypnotically blind.

A Case Study

A large group of undergraduate volunteers ($n = 265$) was tested on the group adaptation of the Stanford Hypnotic Susceptibility Scale, Form C (Weitzenhoffer & Hilgard, 1962), and subjects with extreme scores were tested again on the Stanford Profile Scale, Form II (Hilgard, Lauer, & Morgan, 1963), administered individually. Two highly susceptible subjects were chosen for participation in the study from among those scoring in the top 3% of both assessments. One low scoring subject who fell within the bottom 5% of those tested was assigned to a simulating condition. In the experimental sessions, subjects were administered a hypnotic induction procedure by an experimenter blind to their group assignments. Following the induction, total blindness was

suggested to the subjects. In each session
subjects were presented with 100 trials of a
visual identification task. They were shown
a line drawing of either a happy or a sad
face (cf. Sackeim et al., 1977) and were requested to guess whether the face was definitely happy, probably happy, probably sad,
or definitely sad. Subjects were to participate
in six experimental sessions. Procedural
variations not relevant to the proposed
model were introduced in the third and
fourth sessions, and data for these sessions
will not be discussed here. Prior to participating in the experimental sessions, one
highly susceptible subject was given instructions by a second experimenter inducing
strong motivation for blindness. It was repeatedly emphasized to the subject that it
was critical to the nature of the project that
she be blind throughout the experimental
sessions. The visual identification task was
presented as a test of blindness. The other
hypnotic subject was given instructions inducing weak motivation for blindness and
was simply informed that blindness would
be suggested to her and that she should do
her best to comply with the suggestion. The
subject low in susceptibility was given simulating instructions following the procedure
outlined by Orne (1972) and was also informed of the instructions of weak motivation for blindness.

Only one experimental session could be
conducted with the hypnotic subject in the
strong motivation for blindness condition.
This subject completed 66 trials of the identification task and reported that she felt uneasy and had developed a headache. The
session was suspended at that point and the
subject did not wish to return for further
experimentation. The subject's Receiver Operating Characteristic curve for her performance on the identification task is presented
in Figure 2. Her curve falls below the diag-
onal, indicating that her overall sensitivity
was below chance. Interestingly, the distributions of correct and incorrect responses for
identifications of low confidence (i.e., probably happy or sad) and for high confidence

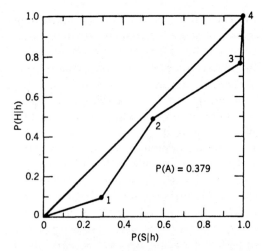

FIGURE 2
The receiver operating characteristic (ROC)
curve for the performance of a hypnotic subject under the strong motivation for blindness
condition. (The point marked 1 corresponds
to the cumulative probabilities of hits,
$p(H/h)$, and false alarms, $p(S/h)$, for "definitely happy" identifications. The point
marked 2 corresponds to "probably happy"
identifications. The point marked 3 corresponds to "probably sad" identifications, and
the point marked 4 corresponds to "definitely
sad" identifications, $P(A)$ is a nonparametric
measure of sensitivity and refers to the percentage of area falling under the ROC
curve.)

identifications (i.e., definitely happy or sad)
were different. The subject was correct on 27
out of 45 (60%) occasions when she used
the two "probable" categories. This rate of
correct responses did not differ from chance
($z = 1.34, p > .1$, two-tailed). On the other
hand, the subject made correct identifications on only 4 out of 21 (19%) trials in
which the two "definite" categories were
used ($z = 2.85, p < .01$, two-tailed). The
difference between the proportions of correct
identifications for responses using the
"probable" categories and for responses using the two "definite" categories was also
significant, ($z = 3.87, p < .001$, two-tailed).
In short, this subject was most likely to make
a misidentification when she claimed to be

most certain of her decision. Certainty judgments had not been obtained in previous studies with hysterically blind patients, and these results suggest that such a procedure may be of value.

In a postexperimental interview, the subject stated that she was blind throughout the session. She claimed that she saw neither the visual targets nor anything else in the room. She reported that her identifications were pure guesses, and she had no explanation for her pattern of results. The honesty of the subject's report is supported in part by the fact that twice during the experimental sessions she raised her hand to indicate that the blindness was lifting. At those points the task was suspended and the experimenter deepened the trance and readministered the blindness suggestion.

The hypnotic subject tested in the weak motivation for blindness condition also maintained that she was completely blind during the sessions. In the four sessions the subject was perfectly accurate in her identifications. Using both probable and definite response categories, the subject failed to misidentify a stimulus in 400 trials.

In the postexperimental interview the subject insisted that she did not see anything in the room, including the visual targets. In fact, she maintained that her eyes were closed in three of the sessions. The introspective report of this subject concerning her performance was remarkably similar to that of the brain-damaged patient studied by Weiskrantz et al. (1974).[1] The former subject stated, "Oh, but I didn't seem to miss the visual too much because when Amy [the experimenter] would ask me what one of the pictures was I would—without really being reticent about what I was saying—I would say, 'My eyes are closed, how could I know this is a happy face?' [But] I would just say, 'Well it feels like a happy face.'"

---

[1]The experimental sessions, as well as the postexperimental interviews, were completed before the authors were aware of the report by Weiskrantz et al. (1974).

The subject reported that during the identification task she was guessing and that she always tried to take the best guess. Prior to being shown her results she estimated that she was probably correct on 60% of the trials. She attributed this moderate level of above chance performance to the fact that she felt that she could "sense" but not see. When the subject was confronted with her results, she was clearly astonished and could not account for her perfect performance. The subject's report of blindness was supported in part by her raising her hand to indicate that the blindness was lifting in two differing sessions.

The performance of the simulating subject differed in the first session compared to the remaining three. During the first experimental session, the subject correctly identified stimuli at a level below chance (31%, $z = 3.80$, $p < .001$, two-tailed). She was equally inaccurate in her high and low confidence responses. In the remaining experimental sessions, her performance was consistently at chance level. The subject reported in the postexperimental interview that she was neither hypnotized nor blind in any of the sessions. She stated that she had attempted to perform at a chance level and produce as many right as wrong identifications. When the subject was informed of the results of the first session, she seemed surprised. She stated that she was somewhat nervous during the first session and had wondered whether the experimenter would discover that she was simulating. The subject stated that after the first session she tended to look away from the screen and that may have helped her produce random responses.

The findings provide some initial support for the proposed model of visual functioning in hypnotic blindness. Both hypnotically blind subjects demonstrated that their identifications were under considerable visual control. As expected, the hypnotically blind subject in the strong motivation condition showed this by performing at a level below chance. The weak motivation for blindness condition differed from the strong motivation condition in that the subject in the former set was told in a more matter-of-fact way that total blindness would be suggested. She was told that blindness could be experienced as a pleasant, relaxing state. Furthermore, the visual identification task was not presented directly as a test of her blindness, as was the case for the subject in the strong motivation condition. In four experimental sessions the hypnotic subject in the weak motivation condition achieved perfect accuracy in performance, despite her claim of total blindness. These findings are in line with the hypothesis that in the absence of strong motivation to deny visual functioning, the psychogenically blind individual will not have access to sensory representations (Stage 1 blocking) but will correctly identify inputs on the basis of processing of those representations. When there is strong motivation to deny visual functioning, not only will the psychogenically blind be unaware of sensory representations but the decisions they reach concerning the nature of inputs will be subject to a second defensive operation of denial.

The results of the one simulating subject suggest that it is unlikely that people who attempt to fake blindness would correctly identify visual inputs at high levels of accuracy. When the experimenter who conducted the sessions was asked who were the possible simulators, she was certain that the hypnotically blind subject who achieved perfect performance had been simulating. However, one should exercise caution in drawing conclusions on the basis of these findings. The behavior of hypnotic subjects is too variable to allow much confidence in the results obtained from such small samples. This case material is significant because it suggests methods by which to test whether hypnotic blindness can serve as an analogue of hysterical blindness and how both phenomena differ from malingering. A more extensive investigation is called for in which the behavior of hysterical and hypnotically blind subjects is examined under the same procedures and compared with the behavior of simulating controls.

Discussion

In the past, hysteria and hypnosis have been viewed as similar phenomena. In reexamining this issue we have proposed that a fruitful avenue for investigation may be to determine whether hypnotically induced sensorimotor disturbances and hysterical conversion reactions are mediated by comparable processes. We have offered a model that accounts for the visually controlled behavior in both types of psychogenic blindness. In addition to the methods illustrated in the pilot study, other procedures may be suggested to test this model. For instance, we attributed differences in rates of misidentification of visual targets among the hysterically and hypnotically blind to differences in motivational factors regulating levels of denial and/or to individual differences in the capacity or propensity to use denial as a characteristic defense. These hypotheses may be tested by manipulating motivational circumstances, as in the pilot study. They may also be examined by relating differences in symptomatology and in the nature of secondary gains to variations in rates of misidentification. Those patients who are consistently below chance in their identifications would be expected to show other signs of denial, such as "la belle indifférence." These patients and comparable hypnotically blind subjects should also score high on psychometric measures of the utilization of denial (e.g., Gleser & Ihilevich, 1969; Sackeim & Gur, 1979). Any type of hypnotic negative visual hallucination may serve as an experimental analogue of hysterical conversion reactions of partial or total blindness.

Investigation of visually controlled behavior in the hysterically and hypnotically blind has implications for several areas of inquiry. Our model stipulates that the psychogenically blind are not malingering or consciously lying in claiming phenomenological blindness. The model suggests a method by which to discriminate between malingering and psychogenic blindness. Implicit in this view is the claim that when the psychogenically blind identify visual inputs at levels below chance they are engaging in self-deception. In order to be so wrong, they must first be right. These individuals are not aware of correctly identifying inputs, and the denial of recognition also occurs outside of their awareness. These individuals have reached two decisions about the nature of inputs: They are aware of only one decision or guess, and their selective nonawareness is determined by motivational factors. This type of behavior fulfills the criteria Sackeim and Gur (1978, 1979; Gur & Sackeim, 1979) have argued are necessary and sufficient for the ascription of the term *self-deception*.

The view that people can have cognitions of which they are not aware was at one time quite controversial (e.g., Bruner & Postman, 1949; Howie, 1952; Luchins, 1950). Indeed, it had been suggested that phenomena like subliminal perception and perceptual defense were conceptual impossibilities, because they entailed that people could perceive and not perceive at the same time. Our account of psychogenic blindness claims that the processes at one time considered to be conceptually impossible do in fact occur. Furthermore, the behavior of the psychogenically blind suggests that the selective nonawareness of cognition can be under motivational control.

Our account of psychogenic blindness also provides an alternative account of related phenomena, such as "hidden observer" effects. Hilgard, Morgan, and Macdonald (1975) found that hypnotically induced analgesia was effective in reducing reported pain. However, when the hidden observer in subjects is used as a source of information through automatic talking, writing, or key pressing, reported pain is heightened, although generally it does not reach waking-state levels. Similar work with hypnotic deafness (Crawford, Macdonald, & Hilgard, Note 2) has shown that under standard instructions for deafness, hypnotic subjects report lack of awareness of auditory stimulation, but at least partial hearing is reported when the hidden observer is ac-

cessed. Hilgard (1973, 1976) interpreted these findings within the general framework of a neodissociation theory of hypnosis. He argued that hypnosis produces shifts in hierarchies of cognitive control and, in particular, introduces dissociative barriers between control systems. For example, the control system responsible for the report of no pain and that responsible for the hidden observer's report of some pain are independent. Therefore, Hilgard assumed that the same inputs were independently processed by two control systems. Furthermore, he claimed that the results of processing within each control system could be subject to awareness, as exemplified by the same subject reporting no pain and some pain. In this respect, this model differs from traditional psychodynamic perspectives that emphasize dissociations between conscious and unconscious experience.

Our model of visual information processing in psychogenic blindness may provide the following account of Hilgard's observations. The results reported by Hilgard et al. (1975) on pain reduction indicate that standard suggestions of analgesia initially result in Stage 1 blocking of sensory representations of pain from awareness. These representations are subject to further Stage 2 processing. Because the hidden observer experiments did not employ motivational manipulations that would encourage Stage 2 transformation or denial, subjects can report the presence of some pain. By this interpretation, the significant difference between the original and the hidden observer reports of pain is that they are based on different stages in a unitary stream of processing.

The subjective self-reports of hypnotic subjects fit well with this view. Just as hypnotically or hysterically blind subjects under low motivation for blindness conditions may report total blindness while identifying visual stimuli at levels above chance, the hypnotically analgesic subject reports feeling no pain but knows that pain is occurring. Our model posits a critical dissociation between the awareness and nonawareness of stages in a unitary stream of processing and is therefore more akin to psychodynamic perspectives. Hilgard's model posits a critical dissociation between multiple systems simultaneously processing inputs. Whether our proposed model provides a more parsimonious and heuristically valuable account of hidden observer phenomena is a matter for future investigation.

The findings from studies of the psychogenically blind bear on general considerations of the relations between cognition and awareness. The influence of awareness on the processing of information has been a matter of concern in hypnosis research (e.g., Knox, Crutchfield, & Hilgard, 1975; Stevenson, 1976) and in other areas (e.g., Neisser, 1967). Study of the psychogenically blind should contribute to the understanding of this general problem. For instance, the psychogenically blind may prove to be a useful population in which to examine the role of awareness and nonawareness in the processes underlying perceptual constancy and visual illusion effects. Finally, a number of cognitive psychologists have argued that the final products in the processing of information are necessarily subject to awareness and that when we are aware of cognition, these final stages constitute awareness (Mandler, 1975; Miller, 1962; Neisser, 1967; Nisbett & Wilson, 1977). "Conscious awareness is itself rather late in the sequence of mental processing" (Posner & Boies, 1971, p. 407). One would be hard pressed to argue that the psychogenically blind subjects, as well as the subjects of Weiskrantz et al. (1974) and of Marcel and Patterson (1978), were phenomenologically aware of seeing, even though they all demonstrated extensive visual processing. If our model is valid, phenomenological awareness of sight is not dependent on the final products of information processing but rather is tied to initial sensory representations.

Reference Notes

1. Gur, R. C., Sackeim, H. A., Packer, I. K., and Liran, J. *Hypnosis as a tool for studying motivational*

effects on cognition. Paper read at the 85th annual convention of the American Psychological Association, San Francisco, August 1977.

2. Crawford, H., Macdonald, H., and Hilgard, E. R. *Hidden observer in hypnotic deafness and hypnotic analgesia.* Paper read at the 85th annual convention of the American Psychological Association, San Francisco, August 1977.

References

Bendefeldt, F., Miller, L. L., and Ludwig, A. M. Cognitive performance in conversion hysteria. *Archives of General Psychiatry,* 1976, *33,* 1250–1254.

Blum, G. S. A case study of hypnotically induced tubular vision. *International Journal of Clinical and Experimental Hypnosis,* 1975, *23,* 111–119.

Blum, G. S., and Porter, M. L. The capacity for selective concentration on color versus form of consonants. *Cognitive Psychology,* 1973, *5,* 47–70.

Blum, G. S., Porter, M. L., and Geiwitz, P. J. Temporal parameters of negative visual hallucination. *International Journal of Clinical and Experimental Hypnosis,* 1978, *26,* 30–44.

Brady, J. P. Hysteria versus malingering: A response to Grosz and Zimmerman. *Behavior Research and Therapy,* 1966, *4,* 321–322.

Brady, J. P., and Lind, D. L. Experimental analysis of hysterical blindness. *Archives of General Psychiatry,* 1961, *4,* 331–339.

Breuer, J., and Freud, S. Studies on hysteria. In J. Strachey (Ed. & trans.), *The complete works of Sigmund Freud* (Vol. 2). London: Hogarth, 1955. (Originally published, 1895.)

Bruner, J. S., and Postman, L. Perception, cognition, and behavior. *Journal of Personality,* 1949, *18,* 14–31.

Charcot, J. M. *Oeuvres complètes.* Paris: Aux Bureaux du Progrès Médical, 1890.

Chertok, L. Hysteria, hypnosis, psychopathology. *Journal of Nervous and Mental Disease,* 1975, *161,* 367–378.

Chodoff, P. A reexamination of some aspects of conversion hysteria. *Psychiatry,* 1954, *17,* 75–81.

Chodoff, P. The diagnosis of hysteria: An overview. *American Journal of Psychiatry,* 1974, *131,* 1073–1078.

Chodoff, P., and Lyons, H. Hysteria, the hysterical personality, and "hysterical" conversion. *American Journal of Psychiatry,* 1958, *115,* 734–740.

COHEN, L. H., HILGARD, E. R., AND WENDT, G. R. Sensitivity to light in a case of hysterical blindness studied by reinforcement inhibition and conditioning methods. *Yale Journal of Biology and Medicine*, 1933, *6*, 61–67.

DESCARTES, R. Meditations on first philosophy. In E. S. HALDANE AND G. R. T. ROSS (Eds. and trans.), *The philosophical works of Descartes.* Cambridge, England: Cambridge University Press, 1967. (Originally published, 1964.)

DIXON, N. F. *Subliminal perception: The nature of a controversy.* London: McGraw-Hill, 1971.

EHRENREICH, G. A. The relationship of certain descriptive factors to hypnotizability. *Transactions of the Kansas Academy of Science*, 1949, *52*, 24–27.

FENICHEL, O. *The psychoanalytic theory of neurosis.* New York: Norton, 1945.

FRANKEL, F. H. Hypnosis and related clinical behavior. *American Journal of Psychiatry*, 1978, *135*, 664–668.

FREUD, S. On the psychical mechanism of hysterical phenomena: A lecture. In J. STRACHEY (Ed. & trans.), *The complete psychological works of Sigmund Freud* (Vol. 3). London: Hogarth, 1962. (Originally published, 1895.)

GILL, M. M., AND BRENMAN, M. *Hypnosis and related states.* New York: International Universities Press, 1959.

GLESER, G. C., AND IHILEVICH, D. An objective instrument for measuring defense mechanisms. *Journal of Consulting and Clinical Psychology*, 1969, *33*, 51–60.

GROSZ, H. J., AND ZIMMERMAN, J. Experimental analysis of hysterical blindness: A follow-up report and new experimental data. *Archives of General Psychiatry* 1965, *13*, 255–260.

GROSZ, H. J., AND ZIMMERMAN, J. A second detailed case study of functional blindness: Further demonstration of the contribution of objective psychological laboratory data. *Behavior Therapy*, 1970, *1*, 115–123.

GUR, R. C., AND SACKEIM, H. A. Self-deception: A concept in search of a phenomenon. *Journal of Personality and Social Psychology*, 1979, *37*, 147–169.

GUZE, S. B., WOODRUFF, R. A., AND CLAYTON, P. J. A study of conversion symptoms in psychiatric outpatients. *American Journal of Psychiatry*, 1971, *128*, 643–646.

HILGARD, E. R. *Hypnotic susceptibility.* New York: Harcourt, Brace & World, 1965.

HILGARD, E. R. A neodissociation interpretation of pain reduction in hypnosis. *Psychological Review*, 1973, *80*, 396–411.

HILGARD, E. R. Neodissociation theory of multiple cognitive control systems. In G. E. Schwartz and D. Shaprio (Eds.), *Consciousness and self-regulation: Advances in research* (Vol. 1).New York: Plenum Press, 1976.

HILGARD, E. R. *Divided consciousness: Multiple controls in human thought and action.* New York: Wiley, 1977.

HILGARD, E. R., LAUER, L. W., AND MORGAN, A. H. *Manual for Stanford Profile Scales of Hypnotic Susceptibility, Forms I and II.* Palo Alto, Calif.: Consulting Psychologists Press, 1963.

HILGARD, E. R., MORGAN, A. H., AND MACDONALD, H. Pain and dissociation in the cold pressor test: A study of hypnotic analgesia with "hidden reports" through automatic key pressing and automatic talking. *Journal of Abnormal Psychology*, 1975, *84*, 280–289.

HOWIE, D. Perceptual defense. *Psychological Review*, 1952, *59*, 308–315.

JAMES, W. *The principles of psychology.* New York: Dover, 1950. (Originally published, 1890.)

JANET, P. *The major symptoms of hysteria.* New York: Macmillan, 1929.

KAHNEMANN, D. Method, findings, and theory in studies of visual masking. *Psychological Bulletin*, 1968, *70*, 404–426.

KNOX, V. J., CRUTCHFIELD, L., AND HILGARD, E. R. The nature of task interference in hypnotic dissociation: An investigation of automatic behavior. *International Journal of Clinical and Experimental Hypnosis*, 1975, *23*, 305–323.

LOOMIS, A. L., HARVEY, E. N., AND HOBART, G. A. Brain potentials during hypnosis. *Science*, 1936, *83*, 239–241.

LUCHINS, A. S. On an approach to social perception. *Journal of Personality*, 1950, *19*, 64–84.

LUDHOM, H., AND LOWENBACH, H. Hypnosis and the alpha activity of the electroencephalogram. *Character and Personality*, 1942–1943, *11*, 145–149.

MALMO, R. B., BOAG, T. J., AND RAGINSKY, B. B. Electromyographic study of hypnotic deafness. *International Journal of Clinical and Experimental Hypnosis*, 1954, *2*, 305–317.

MALMO, R. B., DAVIS, J. F., AND BARZA, S. Total hysterical deafness: An experimental case study. *Journal of Personality.* 1952–1953, *21*, 188–204.

MANDLER, G. Consciousness: Respectable, useful, and probably necessary. In R. Solso (Ed.), *Information processing and cognition: The Loyola Symposium.* Hillsdale, N.J.: Erlbaum, 1975.

MARCEL, A. J. Conscious and unconscious reading: The effects of visual masking on word perception. *Cognitive Psychology,* in press.

MARCEL, A. J., AND PATTERSON, K. E. Word recognition and production: Reciprocity in clinical and normal studies. In J. Requin (Ed.), *Attention and performance* (Vol. 7). Hillsdale, N.J.: Erlbaum, 1978.

MEARES, A. A working hypothesis as to the nature of hypnosis. *A. M. A. Archives of Neurology and Psychiatry,* 1957, *77,* 549–555.

MILLER, E. A note on the visual performance of a subject with unilateral functional blindness. *Behavior Research and Therapy,* 1968, *6,* 115–116.

MILLER, G. A. *Psychology: The science of mental life.* New York: Harper & Row, 1962.

MILLER, R. J., AND LEIBOWITZ, H. W. A signal detection analysis of hypnotically induced narrowing of the peripheral visual field. *Journal of Abnormal Psychology,* 1976, *85,* 446–454.

NEISSER, U. Cognitive psychology. New York: Appleton-Century-Crofts, 1967.

NISBETT, R. E., AND WILSON, T. D. Telling more than we know: Verbal reports on mental processes. *Psychological Review,* 1977, *84,* 231–259.

ORNE, M. T. On the social psychology of the psychological experiment: With particular reference to demand characteristics and their implications. *American Psychologist,* 1962, *17,* 776–783.

ORNE, M. T. On the simulating subject as a quasi-control group in hypnosis research: What, why, and how. In E. Fromm & R. E. Shor (Eds.), *Hypnosis: Research developments and perspectives.* Chicago: Aldine-Atherton, 1972.

PATTIE, F. A. A report on an attempt to produce uniocular blindness by hypnotic suggestion. *British Journal of Medical Psychology,* 1935, *15,* 230–241.

POSNER, M. I., AND BOIES, S. J. Components of attention. *Psychological Review,* 1971, *78,* 391–408.

REYHER, J. Hypnosis in research in psychopathology. In J. E. Gordon (Ed.), *Handbook of clinical and experimental hypnosis.* New York: Macmillan, 1967.

ROSENTHAL, R. Interpersonal expectations: Effects of experimenter's hypothesis. In R. Rosenthal & R. L. Rosnow (Eds.), *Artifact in behavioral research.* New York: Academic Press, 1969.

SACKEIM, H. A., AND GUR, R. C. Self-deception, self-confrontation, and consciousness. In G. E.

Schwartz & D. Shapiro (Eds.), *Consciousness and self-regulation: Advances in research* (Vol. 2). New York: Plenum, 1978.

SACKEIM, H. A., AND GUR, R. C. Self-deception, other-deception, and self-reported psychopathology. *Journal of Consulting and Clinical Psychology,* 1979, *47,* 213–215.

SACKEIM, H. A., PACKER, I. K., AND GUR, R. C. Hemisphericity, cognitive set, and susceptibility to subliminal perception. *Journal of Abnormal Psychology,* 1977, *86,* 624–630.

SARTRE, J. P. *Being and nothingness: An essay on phenomenological ontology* (H. Barnes, Trans.). London: Meuthen, 1958.

SECTER, I. I. Personality factors of the MMPI and hypnotizabilitty. *American Journal of Clinical Hypnosis,* 1961, *3,* 185–188.

SCHULMAN, R. E., AND LONDON, P. Hypnotic susceptibility and MMPI profiles. *Journal of Consulting Psychology,* 1963, *27,* 157–160.

SLATER, E. T. O. Diagnosis of "hysteria." *British Medical Journal,* 1965, *1,* 1395–1399.

SLATER, E. T. O., AND GLITHERO, E. A follow-up of patients diagnosed as suffering from hysteria. *Journal of Psychosomatic Research,* 1965, *9,* 9–13.

SOMMERSCHIELD, H. AND REYHER, J. Posthypnotic conflict, repression, and psychopathology. *Journal of Abnormal Psychology,* 1973, *82,* 278–290.

STEPHENS, J. H. AND KAMP, M. On some aspects of hysteria: A clinical study. *Journal of Nervous and Mental Disease,* 1962, *134,* 305–315.

STEVENSON, J. A. Effect of posthypnotic dissociation on the performance of interfering tasks. *Journal of Abnormal Psychology,* 1976, *85,* 398–407.

SZASZ, T. S. *Pain and pleasure: A study of bodily feelings.* New York: Basic Books, 1975.

TEMPLER, D. I., AND LESTER, D. Conversion disorders: A review of research findings. *Comprehensive Psychiatry,* 1974, *15,* 285–293.

THEODOR, L. H., AND MANDELCORN, M. S. Hysterical blindness: A case report and study using a modern psychophysical technique. *Journal of Abnormal Psychology,* 1973, *82,* 552–553.

TURVEY, M. T. On peripheral and central processes in vision: Inferences from an information-processing analysis of masking with patterned stimuli. *Psychological Review,* 1973, *80,* 1–52.

ULLMAN, L. P. AND KRASNER, L. *A psychological approach to abnormal behavior.* Englewood Cliffs, N.J.: Prentice-Hall, 1969.

WEISKRANTZ, L., WARRINGTON, E. K., SANDERS,

M. D., AND MARSHALL, J. Visual capacity in the hemianopic field following a restricted occipital ablation. *Brain,* 1974, *97,* 709–728.

WEITZENHOFFER, A. M. AND HILGARD, E. R. *Stanford Hypnotic Susceptibility Scale, Form C.* Palo Alto, Calif.: Consulting Psychologists Press, 1962.

WHITLOCK, F. A. The aetiology of hysteria. *Acta Psychiatrica Scandinavica,* 1967, *43,* 144–162.

WINER, D. Anger and dissociation: A case study of multiple personality. *Journal of Abnormal Psychology,* 1978, *87,* 368–372.

WUNDT, W. *An introduction to psychology.* New York: Arno, 1973. (Originally published, 1912.)

ZIMMERMAN, J. AND GROSZ, H. J. "Visual" performance of a functionally blind person. *Behavior Research and Therapy,* 1966, *4,* 119–134.

22

Confronting a Traumatic Event: Toward an Understanding of Inhibition and Disease

James W. Pennebaker and
Sandra Klihr Beall

According to previous work, failure to confide in others about traumatic events is associated with increased incidence of stress-related disease. The present study served as a preliminary investigation to learn if writing about traumatic events would influence long-term measures of health as well as short-term indicators of physiological arousal and reports of negative moods. In addition, we examined the aspects of writing about traumatic events (i.e., cognitive, affective, or both) that are most related to physiological and self-report variables. Forty-six healthy undergraduates wrote about either personally traumatic life events or trivial topics on 4 consecutive days. In addition to health center records, physiological measures and self-reported moods and physical symptoms were collected throughout the experiment. Overall, writing about both the emotions and facts surrounding a traumatic event was associated with relatively higher blood pressure and negative moods following the essays, but fewer health center visits in the 6 months following the experiment. Although the findings and underlying theory should be considered preliminary, they bear directly on issues surrounding catharsis, self-disclosure, and a general theory of psychosomatics based on behavioral inhibition.

James W. Pennebaker and Sandra Klihr Beall. Confronting a Traumatic Event: Toward an Understanding of Inhibition and Disease. *Journal of Abnormal Psychology*, 1986, Vol. 95, No. 3, pp. 274–281. Copyright © 1986 by the American Psychological Association. Reprinted by permission of the publisher and authors.

Individuals seek to understand major upheavals in their lives. Although a natural way of understanding traumas is by talking with others, many upsetting events cannot easily be discussed. For example, victims of family or sexual abuse, or perpetrators of illegal or illicit acts, are often reticent to divulge these experiences because of guilt or fear of punishment. In order not to betray their true feelings or experiences, they must inhibit their overt behaviors, facial expressions, and language. In addition to the work of inhibiting behavior following a trauma, individuals may actively attempt not to think about aspects of the concealed information because of its aversive and unresolved nature. In short, individuals who are unable to confide in others about extremely upsetting events must work to inhibit their behaviors, thoughts, and feelings.

In recent years, evidence has accumulated indicating that not disclosing extremely personal and traumatic experiences to others over a long period of time may be related to disease processes. For example, across several surveys, college students and adults who reported having experienced one of several types of childhood traumatic events (e.g., sexual or physical abuse, death or divorce of parents) were more likely to report current health problems if they had not disclosed the trauma to others than if they had divulged it (Pennebaker & Hoover, 1986; Susman, 1986). These results were obtained independent of measures of social support (see Pennebaker, 1985, for review). Similarly, a survey of spouses of suicide and accidental-death victims revealed that those individuals most likely to become ill in the year following the death were the ones who had not confided in others about their experiences (Pennebaker & O'Heeron, 1984). Survey results indicate that the less individuals confided, the more they ruminated about the death.

A question that emerges from these studies is What aspects of confiding a traumatic event reduce physiological levels and disease rates? On a strict interpersonal level, discussing a trauma allows for social comparison (e.g., Wortman & Dunkel-Schetter, 1979) and coping information from others (e.g., Lazarus, 1966). From a cognitive perspective, talking about, or in some way confronting a traumatic event, may help the individual to organize (Meichenbaum, 1977), assimilate (Horowitz, 1976), or give meaning (Silver & Wortman, 1980) to the trauma. These approaches assume that a major upheaval undermines the world view of the person. Confronting the event, then, should help the individual categorize the experience into a meaningful framework.

Many investigators have argued that discussing an event may also serve a cathartic function (e.g., Scheff, 1979). In one of the few well-controlled clinical studies examining catharsis, Nichols (1974) found that patients undergoing somatic–emotional discharge therapy (in which subjects actively express emotions) were more likely to achieve their therapeutic goals than were matched control subjects who received traditional insight therapy. Other studies that have employed venting, in which subjects hit a pillow or write about fantasies associated with aggression, have produced mixed

results in subsequent reports of anger (see Nichols & Zax, 1977, for review).

Catharsis and the cathartic method, as developed by Freud (1904/1954) and Breuer and Freud (1895/1966), stress the fundamental links between cognition and affect surrounding a significant or threatening experience. If the experience is particularly disturbing, the memory or ideation may be suppressed, whereas the emotion or affect associated with the event continues to exist in consciousness in the form of anxiety. The cathartic method, or talking cure, was effective in that the forgotten memories were recalled and linked to the anxiety. Breuer and Freud (1895/1966) noted that hysterical symptoms were most likely to disappear after the patient had described the event in fine detail. Although very few studies have directly tested the original catharsis ideas, some recent work suggests that the linking of the cognitive and affective components of a given phobia helps to reduce the magnitude of the phobia (Tesser, Leone, & Clary, 1978).

Our own views assume that to inhibit one's behavior requires physiological work. To not talk about or otherwise confront major upheavals that have occurred in one's life is viewed as a form of inhibition. Actively inhibiting one's behavior, thoughts, and/or feelings over time places cumulative stress on the body and thus increases the probability of stress-related diseases (cf. Selye, 1976). It would follow that if individuals actively inhibit divulging personal or traumatic events, or both, allowing them to do so in a benign setting could have the positive effect of reducing long-term stress and stress-related disease. The original purpose of the present project was to learn if merely writing about a given traumatic event would reduce stress associated with inhibition in both the short run and over time. Our second purpose was to attempt to evaluate the aspects of dealing with a past trauma that were most effective in reducing stress.

Because we were interested in examining the effects of divulging traumatic events independent of social feedback, subjects in the present experiment were required to write rather than talk about upsetting experiences. On 4 consecutive nights, subjects wrote about either a trivial preassigned topic (control condition) or a traumatic experience in their own life from one of three perspectives. Analogous to the venting view of catharsis, trauma–emotion subjects were instructed to write each night about their feelings concerning their traumatic experiences without discussing the precipitating event. In line with a strict cognitive approach, the trauma–fact subjects were required to write about traumatic events without discussing their feelings. Similar to the cathartic method, the trauma–combination subjects wrote about both the traumatic events and their feelings about them. Heart rate, blood pressure, and self-reports were collected during each session. Finally, health center records and mailback surveys were collected from 4 to 6 months following the experiment in order to determine long-term health consequences of the study.

Method

Overview

Within the 4×4 (Condition $\times$ Session) between–within design, 46 undergraduates were randomly assigned to write one of four types of essays for 15 min each night for 4 consecutive evenings. Those in the control condition ($n = 12$) were assigned different trivial topics each night; those in the trauma–emotion cell ($n = 12$) wrote about their feelings associated with one or more traumas in their life; trauma–fact subjects ($n = 11$) wrote about the facts surrounding traumatic events; and trauma–combination subjects ($n = 11$) wrote about both their feelings and the facts surrounding the traumas. Before and following the writing of each essay, subjects had their blood pressure, heart rate, and self-reported moods and physical symptoms collected. Four months after completion of the study, subjects completed questionnaires about their health and

general views of the experiment. In addition, records for both prior to and 6 months following the experiment were collected from the health and counseling centers.

Subjects

Forty-six introductory psychology students (34 women and 12 men) participated as part of a course requirement. The data of all of the subjects were included. For 2 subjects, who were unable to attend one of the four experimental sessions, mean physiological measures and self-reports were substituted for the missing day. Four months after the experiment, all of the subjects were mailed follow-up questionnaires along with self-addressed stamped envelopes. Four subjects (one in each condition) failed to return their questionnaires.

Procedure

On the initial day of the experiment, subjects were individually told that they would be required to write, for four consecutive sessions, either about a preassigned topic or about one or more traumatic experiences that had occurred in their lives. After agreeing to participate, subjects completed a battery of individual difference scales including the Cognitive and Social Anxiety Questionnaire (CSAQ; Schwartz, Davidson, & Goleman, 1978), the Marlowe–Crowne Social Desirability Scale (Crowne & Marlowe, 1964), a general physical symptom inventory (the PILL; Pennebaker, 1982), and a questionnaire that tapped a number of health-relevant behaviors. After completing the questionnaires, subjects were randomly assigned to one of the four conditions and were given the appropriate experimental instructions by the first experimenter.

Those subjects assigned to the control condition were told to write about a different trivial topic each evening (a description of their living room, during the first session, the shoes that they were wearing, for the second session, and a tree and the room in which they were sitting, during the third and fourth sessions, respectively). Prior to writing during each session, the experimenter noted that the person was to describe the assigned item as objectively as possible. The trauma–emotion subjects were asked to write about a personally upsetting experience and to describe the feelings they had about the experience. It was emphasized that they were to write only about their feelings, with no mention of what actually happened. Subjects in the trauma–fact condition were asked to describe an upsetting personal experience in a narrative fashion, being careful to concentrate their writing on the vent itself, without referring to their feelings at all. The trauma–combination subjects were instructed both to describe an upsetting event and to report any feelings they had about it.

Subjects in the three trauma groups were told they could write about the same traumatic event each session or choose a different upsetting event each day, as long as they followed the guidelines given by the experimenter. Finally, subjects in all conditions were told that for exploratory purposes, it would be appreciated if they would place each night's essay in a box by the door prior to leaving. Although the essays would be marked by subject number, subjects were assured that their names would not be associated with any aspect of their data. It should be emphasized that all of the subjects were greeted for each session by the first experimenter who reiterated the specific instructions for each condition.

After receiving the general experimental instructions from the first experimenter, subjects were introduced to the second experimenter, who remained blind to condition throughout the study. The second experimenter escorted the subjects to a private cubicle. Once seated in the cubicle, the subjects were asked to complete a short questionnaire that assessed the degree to which they were experiencing each of nine physical symptoms (e.g., headache, racing heart, tense stomach) and eight moods (e.g., sad, guilty, contented) along unipolar 7-point scales, ranging from *not at all* (1) to *a great deal* (7). On completing the questionnaire, the second experimenter measured systolic

and diastolic blood pressure using a Conphar mercury sphygmomanometer. Subjects' pulses were measured manually by the experimenter at the radial artery. After recording pulse and blood pressure, the experimenter handed the subjects a blank note pad and instructed them to begin writing about their topic for the next 15 min, until the experimenter returned. The experimenter exited and shut the doors to assure the subjects' privacy.

The experimenter returned 15 min later. After measuring and recording blood pressure and pulse, the experimenter handed subjects a postexperimental questionnaire that assessed the degree to which they were experiencing each of the same symptoms and moods that were measured prior to writing the essay. In addition, subjects were asked to respond to questions that asked, along 7-point scales, how personal their essay had been and the degree to which they had revealed their emotions in their essay. Subjects also responded, along a 7-point scale, to the question, "Overall, how much have you told other people about what you wrote today?" Following the sessions, subjects were thanked, requested to place their essay in the box, and reminded to return at a prearranged time the following day.

Following the final experimental session, each of the subjects was extensively debriefed for more than 20 min. During the debriefing session, subjects were told about the manipulations and measures that had been used in the experiment. Although explicit predictions about the outcome of the various trauma manipulations were not divulged, subjects were informed that one possible outcome of the experiment was that writing about traumatic experiences could have beneficial health effects in both the short run and the long run. It was repeatedly emphasized, however, that the project was empirical and that "we do not know how it will come out." The extended debriefing was necessary for both ethical reasons and to encourage subjects to sign a consent form giving the experimenters access to their health records for the following 2 years. All of the subjects also agreed to complete future questionnaire surveys that would be mailed to them.

The experiment was conducted November 14–17, 1983. In mid-March 1984, all of the subjects were mailed the same health questionnaire that they had completed on the first day of the experiment, assessing health habits, self-reported health center visits, number of days their activities had been restricted due to illness, and so forth, since participating in the experiment. In addition, subjects were asked to rate the degree to which they had thought about the study since participating in it, the degree to which they had discussed the study with others, and the degree to which they felt the study had had an impact on them. Finally, subjects were encouraged to write their long-term impressions of the study since having participated in it.

At the end of May 1984, Student Health Center and Counseling and Testing Center personnel were given names and subject numbers for each of the participants in the study. Personnel in each office listed the number of visits the student had made for illness, injury, checkups, psychiatric, or other reasons for the time periods August 27–November 13 and November 14–May 15. Personnel in both centers, who were blind to condition, returned the coded data with names and other identifying information removed.

Results

Overall, the study has four general classes of variables. The first class dealt with the essays themselves, including what the subjects wrote about, the way they approached the essays, and their perceptions of the essays. The second type of variable relates to the subjects' responses to the essays. That is, we sought to learn about changes in the subjects' physiological levels, moods, and symptom reports from before to after writing each essay across the 4 days. The third broad issue

concerned the long-term effects of the experiment. For example, did the study influence the various health-related variables or have any lasting psychological or behavioral impact, or both? A final group of variables of interest includes several individual difference factors, such as sex of subject, and measures of anxiety, symptom-reporting, and so forth. Specifically, we sought to learn if any of these variables relate to any of our manipulated factors.

Content of Essays

Following each session, subjects rated their own essay as to the degree to which (a) it was personal, (b) it revealed their emotions, and (c) they had shared it with other people. For each item, a 4×4 (Condition $\times$ Session) between–within repeated measures analysis of variance (ANOVA) was computed. In response to the question "How personal was the essay that you wrote today?" on a 7-point scale ranging from *not at all* (1) to *a great deal* (7), a significant condition main effect obtained, $F(3, 42) = 12.9$, $p < .001$. No other effects attained significance. As can be seen in Table 1, all three trauma groups reported writing more personal essays than did control subjects. Further, contrasts using the mean-square error term indicated no significant diferences between any of the trauma groups. In response to the item "How much did you reveal your emotions in what you wrote today?" the condition main effect attained significance, $F(3, 42) = 26.4$, $p < .001$. As expected, contrasts indicated that the trauma–emotion and trauma–combination subjects revealed their emotions to a greater degree than did either the trauma–facts or control subjects.

As a general check on the degree to which subjects had previously inhibited divulging their writing topics, subjects were asked to rate the degree to which they had told other people about what they had written following each session. The highly significant condition main effect, $F(3, 42) = 8.70$, $p < .001$, was attributable to the subjects in the control condition who had rarely dis-

TABLE 1 Means of Essay-Related Variables by Condition

Variables	Condition			
	Control	Trauma–emotion	Trauma–fact	Trauma–combination
Essay-related dimensions				
Personal	2.8_a	5.2_b	4.4_b	4.9_b
Reveal emotion	2.5_a	5.3_b	2.5_a	5.4_b
Subjects writing personal essay previously not discussed (%)	16.6_a	75.0_b	63.6_b	54.6_b
Words per essay	252_a	301_{ab}	296_{ab}	340_b
Self-references per essay (%)	2.4_a	11.3_b	7.1_c	8.4_c
Self-report and physiological measures				
Systolic blood pressure change	-3.9_a	-0.8_{ab}	-3.0_a	$+0.4_b$
Negative moods change	-1.0_a	$+1.7_{bc}$	$+0.6_{ab}$	$+3.8_c$
N	12	12	11	11

Note. The personal and reveal emotion means are based on subjects' self-reports of their own essays averaged across all four sessions. Ratings were based on 7-point scales, where 7 = *essay was personal or revealed emotion to a great extent.* Change scores are computed by subtracting the pre-essay score from the post-essay score. A positive number, then, indicates an increase in blood pressure or negative emotion following the essay. For none of the above variables are there significant initial differences. Means with different subscripts are different at $p \leq .05$.

cussed the trivial events that had been assigned to them (means for the four conditions: control = 1.58; trauma–emotion = 2.83; trauma–fact = 3.84; trauma–combination = 3.86; pairwise comparisons among the three trauma condition means did not attain significance). To directly evaluate the inhibition interpretation, a comparison was made between ratings of how personal each night's writing topic had been with the degree to which it had previously been disclosed to others. One difficulty with relying on each subject's mean reports averaged across all 4 nights was that many subjects wrote about extremely traumatic topics, that they had not previously disclosed, on only 1 of the 4 nights. Consequently, the ratings of previous disclosure were subtracted from ratings of how personal the essay had been for each session for each subject in all conditions. If the difference between these two 7-point scales was

+4 or higher on any of the 4 nights, the subject was classified as an individual who was disclosing a previously inhibited experience.

The percentage of subjects who were classified as writing about a personal experience that had not been disclosed to others is included in Table 1. An overall one-way ANOVA on the classification was statistically significant, $F(3, 42) = 3.49$, $p = .02$. Pairwise comparisons indicate that subjects in the three trauma cells wrote more personal essays and more essays on topics not previously discussed than did those in the control condition.

Following each writing session, all of the subjects were asked to place their essay in a box. Of the 184 possible essays among the 46 subjects, all but 10 were returned. Each essay was coded as to number of words written, percentage of self-references (i.e., use of I, me, we, us), number of mark-outs, and—

for the trauma groups only—the general theme of the essay (e.g., death of family member, public humiliation, break-up with boyfriend/girlfriend).

As is depicted in Table 1, subjects in the trauma–combination condition tended to write the most and subjects in the control cell the least. Although neither the session nor the Condition × Session effects attained significance, the overall condition main effect was marginally significant $F(3, 42) = 2.67$, $p < .06$. Subjects in the trauma–emotion condition were far more likely to use first person in their essays than were those in the control or other trauma cells (condition main effect, $F(3, 41) = 50.6$, $p < .001$). Finally, no main effects or interactions emerged in terms of the number of mark-outs per word ratio across condition.

Of the 127 trauma essays, 27% dealt with the death of a close friend, family member, or pet; 20% involved boyfriend/girlfriend problems (usually the breaking of a relationship); and 16% centered on fights among or with parents or friends. Other percentages of topics were, major failure, such as not being elected cheerleader (8%); public humiliation, such as overhearing friends laughing about them (8%); leaving home to go to college (7%); being involved in car accident (5%); an alcohol or drug problem (5%); their own health problems (4%); sexual abuse, such as incest or rape (3%); and other, or unclassifiable (13%). The percentages total more than 100% because some of the topics could be classified in two separate categories. One-way ANOVAs comparing the three trauma conditions indicated no consistent differences in type of topics written about. Note, however, that a significantly higher percentage of trauma–emotion essays could not be categorized ($p = .03$). The only individual difference variable related to essay topic was sex of subject: women were more likely to write about losing a boyfriend/girlfriend; men were more likely to focus on the death of a pet (both $ps < .05$).

It is difficult to convey the powerful and personal nature of the majority of trauma condition essays with statistical analyses. One woman wrote about teaching her brother to sail; on his first solo outing, he drowned. The father of a male subject separated from his mother when the subject was about 9 years old. Prior to leaving home, the father told the subject that the divorce was the subject's fault (because his birth had disrupted the family). When she was 10 years old, one female subject had been asked to clean her room because her grandmother was to be visiting that night. The girl did not do so. That night, the grandmother tripped on one of the girl's toys, broke her hip, and died of complications during surgery a week later. Another subject depicted her seduction by her grandfather when she was about 12 years old. Another, who had written about relatively trivial topics during the first sessions, admitted during the last evening that she was gay. A male subject reported that he had considered suicide because he thought that he had disappointed his parents.

Two additional observations are in order. First, there was no discernable pattern about the depth or emotionality of the subject's topic from one night to another. For some subjects, the first session produced the most profound essay, whereas for others the final session did. Often a particularly emotional essay would be followed by a startlingly superficial one. No individual difference measures were related to the patterning or overall depth of essay topic. Second, a mere reading of the topics by each subject overlooks the person's reaction to it. For example, approximately one third of the essays dealing with the death of a close friend or family member indicated that the subjects were not particularly upset by the loss of the person. Rather, the death made them aware of their own mortality.

Responses to Essays

Before and after each day's essay writing, the heart rate and blood pressure of each of the subjects were measured by the experimenter. Also before and after writing the essay subjects completed a brief questionnaire that assessed the degree to which they were experiencing each of nine physical symptoms and eight moods.

Physiological Measures. Because heart rate and systolic and diastolic blood pressure reflect a general cardiovascular response, all three measures were simultaneously subjected to a 4 × 4 × 2 × 3 (Condition × Session × Pre- versus Post-Essay Reading × Physiological Index [heart rate, systolic and diastolic blood pressure]) between−within repeated measures multivariate analysis of variance (MANOVA). Across all three physiological indexes, a Condition × Session × Pre-Post interaction attained significance, $F(9, 116) = 1.99$, $p = .046$. In addition, the type of physiological index interacted with both session, $F(6, 37) = 11.7$, $p < .001$, and Condition × Pre-Post, $F(6, 80) = 2.26$, $p < .046$. No other main effects or interactions were significant.

Separate repeated measures ANOVAS on each of the physiological measures indicated that all of the above effects were attributable to changes in systolic blood pressure. That is, a 4 × 4 × 2 (Condition × Session × Pre-Post) between−within ANOVA yielded a significant session main effect indicating a general lowering of blood pressures over the course of the experiment for subjects in all conditions, $F(3, 40) = 16.6$, $p < .001$. In addition, a marginally significant Condition × Pre−Post interaction, $F(3, 42) = 2.56$, $p = .068$, and a Condition × Session × Pre−Post interaction, $F(9, 116) = 2.23$, $p = .025$, were obtained. As depicted in Table 1, the Condition × Pre−Post interaction reflects the fact that subjects in the control and trauma−fact cells demonstrated significantly larger decreases in blood pressure following the writing sessions. The triple interaction is primarily attributable to the trauma−combination condition subjects, who initially evidenced a large increase in blood pressure from before to after the essay. After the first session, however, the trauma−combination subjects demonstrated moderate decreases in blood pressure from before

to after the writing session. Separate repeated measures (ANOVAS) on heart rate and diastolic blood pressure yielded no significant condition main effects or interactions.

Self-reports. Before and after each essay, subjects responded to a questionnaire asking them to rate the degree to which they were currently experiencing each of nine symptoms and eight moods—ranging from *not at all* (1) to *a great deal* (7). Because previous research has indicated that the symptoms (racing heart, upset stomach, headache, backache, dizziness, shortness of breath, cold hands, sweaty hands, pounding heart) such as these are correlated, the items were summed to yield an overall symptom index (see Pennebaker, 1982, for scalar properties of comparable symptom and mood indexes). Similarly, the summed mood items (nervous, sad, guilty, not happy, not contented, fatigued, anxious) composed a general negative mood index.

A 4 × 4 × 2 (Condition × Session × Pre- versus Post-Essay) repeated measures ANOVA on the self-reported symptom index yielded no main effects or interactions. A comparable analysis on the negative mood index resulted in a significant pre−post main effect, $F(1, 42) = 4.49$, $p = .04$, such that subjects tended to report more negative moods after writing each day's essay. In addition, a significant Pre−Post × Session interaction emerged, $F(3, 40) = 3.07$, $p = .04$, such that over time, subjects' negative moods increased after writing each essay. Finally, the Condition × Pre−Post interaction attained significance, $F(3, 42) = 2.83$, $p = .05$. As seen in Table 1, these effects reflect the fact that subjects in the trauma conditions reported more negative moods after writing the essays, whereas control subjects typically felt more positive.

The means presented in Table 1 depict the general changes in blood pressure and self-reported negative moods from before to after writing each day's essay. It is of interest that across each of these measures the means of the trauma−emotion and trauma−combination conditions are similar, as are the trauma–fact and control cells. Indeed, contrasts using the mean-square error term comparing these two sets of cells indicate that they are all significantly different. Further, in referring back to Table 1, this general pattern holds for the degree to which subjects revealed emotions and the percentage of self-references used in their essays. The implications of these similarities in response to a relatively brief stimulus are discussed later.

Long-Term Effects

At the conclusion of the school year, Student Health Center personnel recorded the number of times that each subject had visited the health center for each of the following reasons: illness, injury, check-up, psychiatric, or other. The number of visits were recorded separately for number of visits prior to the experiment (i.e., from the beginning of the school year in late August to mid-November) and following the experiment (mid-November through mid-May). Counseling center records were recorded for number of visits for psychological versus other reasons (e.g., vocational) for both prior to and following the experiment. Approximately 4 months following the completion of the laboratory study, subjects were mailed a questionnaire that included a number of health and health-related items that had been assessed on the beginning day of the experiment. The items on the follow-up survey asked subjects about health problems that had occurred since the completion of the laboratory study. Finally, two additional questions were included that asked subjects how much they had thought about and had been affected by their participation in the study. Further, subjects were encouraged to write, in their own words, their perceptions of the experiment. All but four of the subjects completed and returned the questionnaire.

Health and Counseling Center Visits. The number of visits to the health center for illness was subjected to a 4 × 2 (Condition × Before versus After the Experiment) repeated measures ANOVA. Although neither main effect approached significance, the predicted Condition × Before–After interaction was obtained, $F(3, 42) = 2.74$, $p = .055$. As can be seen in Table 2, the change in health center visits for illness was due to an overall increase in all conditions except the trauma–combination cell. Separate repeated measures ANOVAs for the number of health center visits due to injury, psychiatric, or other reasons yielded no significant effects. Over the course of the year, only 1 subject visited the counseling center for psychological reasons and 2 for vocational help. Analyses of variance on these data produced no significant effects.

Follow-up Questionnaire Data. Although only 42 of the original 46 subjects returned the follow-up questionnaires, their health data were similar to the health center findings. Subjects were asked at the beginning of the experiment in November and on the follow-up questionnaire to report the number of days their activities had been restricted due to illness (since the beginning of school, during the November administration, and since the experiment for the follow-up questionnaire). A repeated measures ANOVA yielded a trend for the Condition × Time interaction, $F(3, 38) = 2.19$, $p = .10$, suggesting that those in the control condition reported the most days and those in the trauma–combination the least (see Table 2). On both administrations of the questionnaire, subjects were asked to check if they had experienced each of eight specific health problems (ulcers, high blood pressure, constipation/diarrhea, colds or flu, migraine headaches, acne or skin disorders, heart problems, or other major difficulties). The summed health problem index was then subjected to a repeated measures ANOVA. Overall, subjects in the trauma–combination and trauma–emotion conditions reported reductions in health problems relative to those in the control and trauma–fact cells, $F(3, 38) = 3.05$, $p = .04$. For none of the above measures were there significant con-

TABLE 2 Summary of Long-Term Effects

Variables	Condition			
	Control	Trauma–emotion	Trauma–fact	Trauma–combination
No. of health center visits				
Prior to study	0.33	0.33	0.27	0.54
Following study	1.33_{ab}	1.58_a	1.45_{ab}	0.54_b
Change in visits	1.00_a	1.25_a	1.18_a	0.00_b
Self-reported health measures				
Change in no. of days restricted activity for illness	4.00_a	1.18_{ab}	1.90_{ab}	0.70_b
Change in no. of illnesses	0.18_a	-0.73_b	0.10_a	-0.60_b
Amount of thought about study	1.82_a	2.73_b	1.40_a	2.70_b
Degree of longlasting effects	1.36	2.45	1.70	2.40

Note. The health center visit means are based on all subjects ($N = 46$). All other variables are based on follow-up self-reports ($n = 42$). See text for significance levels of overall one-way analyses of variance. Means with different subscripts are significantly different, $p \leq .05$. No significant initial differences by conditions were obtained for any of the above variables.

dition effects at Time 1. In addition, subjects were asked about several health-related behaviors, such as aspirin consumption, and alcohol, tobacco, and caffeine use for both prior to and following the experiment. No significant differences were obtained on any measure.

All of the subjects were asked to rate the degree to which they had thought about or had been affected by the experiment. In response to the question, "Since the end of the experiment back in November, how much have you thought about what you wrote," on a scale ranging from *not at all* (1) to *a great deal* (7), a marginally significant condition main effect obtained, $F(3, 38) = 2.58$, $p = .06$. As seen in Table 2, those in the trauma–emotion and trauma–combination conditions were more likely to have thought about their essays than those in the trauma–facts or control cells.

Finally, subjects responded to the question, "Looking back on the experiment, do you feel as if it has had any longlasting ef-

fects? Please answer this in your own words as well as rating it on a 1 to 7 scale." Although the overall one-way ANOVA was not statistically significant, $F(3, 38) = 1.43$, $p = .25$, the Means × Condition interaction is presented in the table. Overall, 7 of the 31 trauma subjects rated the long-lasting effect as a 4 or higher along the 7-point scale. The responses to the open-ended question were uniformly positive. Because of the potentially sensitive nature of this paradigm, we feel that it is useful to present the responses of each of these subjects:

Trauma–emotion subjects. It helped me think about what I felt during those times. I never realized how it affected me before.

It helped to write things out when I was tense, so now when I'm worried I sit and write it out . . . later I feel better.

I had to think and resolve past experiences . . . One result of the experiment

is peace of mind, and a method to relieve emotional experiences. To have to write emotions and feelings helped me understand how I felt and why.

Trauma–fact subject. **It made me think a little deeper about some of the important parts of my life.**

Trauma–combination subjects. **It made me think a lot—But I'm still in the same situation.**

If one writes down things that worry one, there is a tendency to feel better.

Although I have not talked with anyone about what I wrote, I was finally able to deal with it, work through the pain instead of trying to block it out. Now it doesn't hurt to think about it.

Other Relevant Data

All of the subjects completed a number of individual difference measures at the beginning of the experiment, including the Marlowe–Crowne Social Desirability Scale, the Cognitive and Somatic Anxiety Scales, and the PILL, which taps the general frequency of occurrence of 54 common symptoms and sensations. Collapsing across condition, these measures were not consistently related to any of the primary dependent measures in the experiment. Although women reported writing about events that were more personal than did men, $r(44) = .41$, $p < .01$, no other sex differences were obtained. Finally, intercorrelations among the changes in physiological levels and self-reports during the experiment with changes in health yielded no consistent significant effects.

Discussion

The results of the experiment should be viewed as promising rather than definitive. Writing about earlier traumatic experience was associated with both short-term increases in physiological arousal and long-

term decreases in health problems. Although these effects were most pronounced among subjects who wrote about both the trauma and their emotions associated with the trauma, there was substantial overlap in effects with those subjects who wrote only about their emotions associated with traumatic events. Subjects who were instructed to write only about previous traumatic events—without referring to their own emotions—were similar to control condition subjects on most physiological, health, and self-report measures.

Despite the general pattern of results, several weaknesses underscore the importance of future replication. Some of the measures yielded contradictory or only marginally significant effects. The number of subjects was quite small. Subjects were not selected in any way for having a debilitating undisclosed past trauma; therefore, it was impossible to evaluate the degree to which such subjects carried the results. In addition, two possible confounds associated with demand characteristics and changes in coping strategies may have influenced the health center data. These alternative explanations, as well as a number of issues surrounding catharsis, self-disclosure, coping strategies, and behavioral inhibition, are discussed next.

Recall that subjects were debriefed following the final essay-writing session. Although subjects were told about the experimental design, we were honest in admitting that we had no idea which, if any, condition would be most related to health. It is possible that subjects regulated their health center visits and follow-up questionnaire reports to some degree on the basis of our debriefing information.

One unforeseen mechanism that may also have affected the results was that we apparently provided some subjects with a new strategy for coping with both traumatic and significant daily events. It was clear that among those subjects who responded in writing to our follow-up questionnaire, some had begun writing about their experiences on their own after having participated in the experiment. Although we suspect that this behavior occurred with greater frequency in the trauma–emotion and trauma–combination cells, we cannot evaluate its direct impact on health.

Although these alternative explanations must be considered seriously, several of the experimental findings offer important directions for future research. For all but the objective health center data, the trauma–emotion and trauma–combination subjects were strikingly similar. Both groups evidenced higher blood pressure and more negative moods, relative to the other groups, each day after writing the essay; and both groups thought a great deal about the study in the months following the study. The results from both of these conditions cause one to argue against a simple venting or discharge theory of catharsis, which would predict that the expression of emotion should make the person more relaxed or happy, or both. Despite these relatively brief negative effects, both groups showed some long-term benefits. For example, self-reports concerning the change in number of different illnesses reported indicated an improvement in health for both groups. Similar trends emerged for self-reported days of restricted activity due to illness. Unfortunately, we cannot evaluate whether the long-term similarity between the two groups for these self-report measures reflects expectancy effects or true self-perceptions. Clearly, writing about the emotional side of a traumatic event was upsetting and physiologically arousing. However, the arousal per se may not have produced any long-term changes.

Perhaps one of the more unexpected findings was that having subjects write about the objective aspects of the traumatic events alone was neither arousing nor particularly upsetting. Indeed, this is reminiscent of the finding with subjects in studies by Lazarus and his colleagues (e.g., Lazarus, Opton, Nomikos, & Rankin, 1965), in which hearing a nonemotional and/or intellectual description of an upsetting scene greatly reduced physiological responses to that event.

Despite the fact that there were no short-term adverse effects from writing the non-emotional description of one's own traumatic experiences, there appear to be few, if any, long-term benefits in any objective or subjective indexes of health. It should be emphasized that these results are not necessarily inconsistent with the views of theorists who argue that the resolution of a trauma is associated with the cognitive work of organizing, assimilating, or finding meaning to the events surrounding the trauma (e.g., Horowitz, 1976; Silver, Boon, & Stones, 1983; Swann & Predmore, 1985). Rather, our findings point to the importance of emphasizing the emotions that coincide with the objective (or, at least, perceived) trauma.

Although the results of the experiment support what has been hypothesized by theorists in psychology and psychosomatics for decades, the exact mechanisms linking confiding and disease have not been sufficiently identified. The early ideas of Freud and Breuer were partially confirmed, in that tying both the cognitions and affect surrounding traumatic events was optimally effective in maintaining long-term health. Unlike their early claims, however, these effects were not immediate. It must be admitted, however, that subjects wrote only briefly each night. Either longer writing times or collecting our self-reports and physiological measures several minutes or hours after each night's essay, or both, may have demonstrated different results.

An interesting variation on this idea, posited by Jourard (1971), argues that self-disclosure allows for one's feelings and thoughts to become more concrete, which ultimately results in greater self-knowledge. Disease results, according to Jourard, when the motive toward self-understanding is blocked. Although we cannot evaluate the role of a possible blocked motive related to understanding, the concept of making thoughts and feelings concrete may be critically important. In this study, subjects did not receive social support or social comparison information. In none of the essays did subjects write about developing some type of coping strategies for the future. No love, positive feedback, or other mechanism commonly used to explain psychotherapy was at work.

The ideas of Jourard closely parallel many of our ideas about behavioral inhibition. We have argued that the act of inhibiting behavior is physiologically stressful (cf. Pennebaker & Chew, 1985). Previous surveys indicate that not confiding in others about a traumatic event—which we view as a form of behavioral inhibition—is associated with disease. As our study has indicated, one need not orally confide to another. Rather, the mere act of writing about an event and the emotions surrounding it is sufficient to reduce the long-term work of inhibition.

We have raised more questions than we have answered. The general pattern of results—although promising—must be replicated under more stringent conditions. Further, the role of inhibition must be demonstrated more precisely. Although writing about traumas appears to have positive long-term health effects, we must pinpoint the aspect of this exercise that is beneficial. Possibilities include making an event concrete, linking the affective and cognitive aspects, the reduction of forces associated with behavioral inhibition over time, and so forth. The ultimate resolution of these issues should have direct bearing on our understanding of social, cognitive, and psychosomatic processes.

References

BREUER, J., AND FREUD, S. (1966). *Studies on hysteria.* New York: Avon. (Original work published 1895)

CROWNE, D. P., AND MARLOWE, D. (1964). *The approval motive: Studies in evaluative dependence.* New York: Wiley.

FREUD, S. (1954). *The origins of psychoanalysis.* New York: Basic Books. (Original work published 1904)

HOROWITZ, M. J. (1976). *Stress response syndromes.* New York: Jacob Aronson.

JOURARD, S. M. (1971). *Self-disclosure: An experimental analysis of the transparent self.* New York: Wiley.

LAZARUS, R. (1966). *Psychological stress and the coping process.* New York: McGraw-Hill.

LAZARUS, R., OPTON, E., NOMIKOS, M., AND RANKIN, N. (1965). The principle of short-circuiting of threat: Further evidence. *Journal of Personality, 33,* 622–635.

MEICHENBAUM, D. (1977). *Cognitive-behavior modification: An integrative approach.* New York: Plenum Press.

NICHOLS, M. P. (1974). Outcome of brief cathartic psychotherapy. *Journal of Consulting and Clinical Psychology, 42,* 403–410.

NICHOLS, M. P., AND ZAX, M. (1977). *Catharsis in psychotherapy.* New York: Gardner Press.

PENNEBAKER, J. W. (1982). *The psychology of physical symptoms.* New York: Springer-Verlag.

PENNEBAKER, J. W. (1985). Traumatic experience and psychosomatic disease: Exploring the roles of behavioral inhibition, obsession, and confiding. *Canadian Psychology, 26,* 82–95.

PENNEBAKER, J. W., AND CHEW, C. H. (1985). Deception, electrodermal activity, and inhibition of behavior. *Journal of Personality and Social Psychology, 49,* 1427–1433.

PENNEBAKER, J. W., AND HOOVER, C. W. (1986). Inhibition and cognition: Toward an understanding of trauma and disease. In R. J. DAVIDSON, G. E. SCHWARTZ, AND D. SHAPIRO (Eds.), *Consciousness and self-regulation* (Vol. 4, pp. 107–136). New York: Plenum Press.

PENNEBAKER, J. W., AND O'HEERON, R. C. (1984). Confiding in others and illness rates among spouses of suicide and accidental-death victims. *Journal of Abnormal Psychology, 93,* 473–476.

SCHEFF, T. J. (1979). *Catharsis in healing, ritual, and drama.* Berkeley: University of California Press.

SCHWARTZ, G. E., DAVIDSON, R. J., AND GOLEMAN, D. (1978). Patterning of cognitive and somatic processes in the self-generation of anxiety: Effects of meditation versus exercise. *Psychosomatic Medicine, 40,* 321–328.

SELYE, H. (1976). *The stress of life.* New York: McGraw-Hill.

SILVER, R. L., BOON, C., AND STONES, M. H. (1983). Searching for meaning in misfortune: Making sense of incest. *Journal of Social Issues, 39,* 81–102.

SILVER, R. L., AND WORTMAN, C. B. (1980). Coping

with undesirable life events. In J. GARBER AND M. E. P. SELIGMAN (Eds.), *Human helplessness: Theory and applications* (pp. 279–375). New York: Academic Press.

SUSMAN, J. R. (1986). *The relationship of expressiveness styles and elements of traumatic experience to self-reported illness.* Unpublished master's thesis, Southern Methodist University.

SWANN, W. B., AND PREDMORE, S. C. (1985). Intimates as agents of social support: Sources of consolation or despair? *Journal of Personality and Social Psychology, 49,* 1609–1617.

TESSER, A., LEONE, C., AND CLARY, E. G. (1978). Affect control: Process constraints versus catharsis. *Cognitive Therapy and Research, 2,* 265–274.

WORTMAN, C. B., AND DUNKEL-SCHETTER, C. (1979). Interpersonal relationships and cancer: A theoretical analysis. *Journal of Social Issues, 35,* 120–155.

SECTION 5

Substance Abuse and Interpersonal Disorders

The articles in this section are remarkable in their diversity. They describe a heterogeneous group of clinical conditions. Some of these are officially listed as DSM Axis-I diagnoses; others are Axis-II conditions. The common thread that links these apparently diverse articles, however, is simple: The conditions they describe are more likely to be viewed as problems by others than they are by the individuals themselves. All psychiatric and psychological disorders reflect to some extent the value judgments of society. This is especially true for the disorders described in this section.

Personality Disorders

DSM-III-R currently recognizes 11 different forms of personality disorder. Some of these, such as antisocial personality disorder, have been studied fairly extensively. Others, such as narcissistic personality disorder and passive–aggressive personality disorder, are conditions about which we know relatively little. All personality disorders, however, are widely considered to be recognizable by early adulthood. They are also believed to reflect relatively stable behavioral patterns.

DSM-III was the first diagnostic system to formally recognize the possible coexistence of clinical conditions and personality disorders. The provision of Axis II represents an acknowledgment that information about premorbid personality factors might be relevant in the development, course, and also treatment of Axis-I psychopathology. Separation of the patient's more enduring or trait-like characteristics from his/her episodic or state-like clinical characteristics also relieves the diagnostician from the responsibility of choosing one condition over the other in cases where a personality disorder and a clinical syndrome coexist.

The reliability with which personality disorders can be diagnosed, however, still presents a major problem. As Frances, himself a member of the DSM advisory committee on personality disorders, points out in selection 23, the boundaries between different personality disorders are often more apparent than real. The boundary between normal functioning and personality disorder generally is also far from precise. The DSM employs such terms as "maladaptive" and "inflexible" in its operational definitions. It fails, however, to tell the diagnostician exactly what these terms mean. As a result, diagnostic agreement for personality disorders as a class tends to be relatively low.

There is also little agreement about precisely which personality disorders should be recognized by the DSM. Particularly controversial has been the recent proposal to add two new diagnoses, self-defeating personality disorder and sadistic personality disorder, to the existing psychiatric nomenclature.

375

Self-Defeating and Sadistic Personality Disorder

The essential feature of self-defeating personality disorder is a pervasive pattern of self-defeating behavior that is present in a wide variety of contexts. The diagnosis is designed to describe persons who tend to avoid or undermine pleasurable experiences, who are often drawn to situations or relationships that will result in suffering, and who resist the helpful efforts of others.

Sadistic personality disorder, on the other hand, describes a pervasive pattern of cruel, demeaning, and aggressive behavior directed toward others. This behavior tends to be more situation-specific than is the case with other personality disorders. It is more likely to characterize relationships with family members and subordinates than relationships with high status persons and authority figures.

The proposed inclusion of self-defeating and sadistic personality disorder into the DSM generated much heated debate. Feminists in particular were outraged by the diagnoses. They argued that the self-defeating label would be used primarily to describe women who remained in abusive relationships. The men who abused them, on the other hand, would be diagnosed as suffering from sadistic personality disorder. The concern was that attachment of these diagnostic labels would create the false impression that (1) abused women are in some way responsible for what happens to them and that (2) abusive men (because they are psychiatrically disordered) should be absolved of blame for their violent behavior.

Self-defeating and sadistic personality disorder are not currently listed as official DSM-III-R diagnoses. Instead, they appear in a special appendix to DSM-III-R. This appendix describes diagnostic categories that have been proposed for inclusion in the classification system but that are thought to be in need of further study. At present, it is too early to tell if these two new and highly controversial diagnoses will ultimately find their way into mainstream psychiatric terminology.

Antisocial Personality Disorder

The traits associated with personality disorders are often ego-syntonic. Put another way, they are not regarded by the person who has them as being undesirable or problematic. The DSM notes that this is particularly likely to be true of persons with sadistic personality disorder. The same can also be said of persons diagnosed with antisocial personality disorder.

The essential feature of antisocial personality disorder is a long-standing pattern of irresponsible and antisocial behavior. This must begin before age 15 and continue into adulthood. During childhood or early adolescence the antisocial pattern is characterized by such behaviors as lying, vandalism, truancy, and aggression toward others. Adult antisocial features (which must have occurred after reaching age 18) include failure to honor financial obligations, child neglect, theft, destruction of property, and other illegal behaviors.

Antisocial personality disorder differs from most other forms of personality disorder in that it can be diagnosed with a high degree of reliability. Until recently, however, there was concern about the discriminant validity of the antisocial classification. As operationalized in DSM-III, the diagnosis of antisocial personality hovered dangerously close to a description of criminality. Moreover, there was a widespread tendency for the term antisocial to be used interchangeably with terms such as sociopath or psychopath. This was potentially misleading because the diagnostic criteria for antisocial personality disorder in DSM-III omitted many of the important hallmarks of the psychopath, as described by Cleckley (1976). Conspicuous by their absence were such clinical criteria as superficial charm, absence of feelings of responsibility, and an inability to learn from experience. In 1987, however, lack of remorse was included among the antisocial diagnostic criteria listed in DSM-III-R. This addition has gone some way toward bringing the constructs of antisocial personality and psychopathy into closer alignment.

Cleckley's concept of the psychopath is well illustrated in Sandler's (selection 24) portrait of con artist Edgar Berube. Despite a profound lack of family resemblance, the charismatic Berube managed to persuade fraternity brothers at the University of New Hampshire that he was the son of Senator Edward Kennedy. Some years later, while posing as the grandson of oil magnate Armand Hammer, Berube was indicted on 38 counts of forgery, theft, and passing bad checks. He was subsequently jailed, but, after serving only a few months of his 7-year sentence, he was released from prison. It took prison officials a month to realize that the release papers had been forged by Berube himself.

Sandler's article documents Berube's cyclical pattern of deception, discovery, and subsequent deception in a new location. As such, it provides a description of psychopathic behavior that fits in well with the experimental work of Siegel (selection 25). Using a sample of psychopathic and nonpsychopathic criminal offenders, Siegel demonstrates experimentally that the former are less able (or willing) to suppress behavior in the face of negative consequences. This difference between psychopaths and nonpsychopaths is particularly marked under circumstances in which the probability of punishment is uncertain. In other words, psychopaths appear to behave as if they believe that they have some form of "magical immunity." Whether this is a cause or a consequence of their behavior, however, is unclear. After all, psychopaths may come to believe that many of their behaviors will go unpunished because many of their behaviors may indeed have had no negative consequences—at least in the short-term. Although Edgar Berube was always caught eventually, the simple fact is that the probability of his being punished for any *single* transgression was extremely low.

Drug and Alcohol Abuse

One of the most serious problems facing society today is substance abuse. Most of us can readily bring to mind names of actors, athletes, and rock stars whose lives have been cut short by psychoactive drugs. Moreover, the range of drugs that can be abused or on which individuals can become dependent grows with each revision of the DSM. DSM-III, for example, saw the inclusion of phencyclidine (PCP) abuse; DSM-III-R now lists cocaine dependence in addition to cocaine abuse.

Like clothing styles, drug-abuse patterns appear to change over time. Some recent changes are documented by Kozel and Adams in selection 26. Marijuana abuse, for example, was at its peak in the 1970s. In 1978, almost 11% of high-school seniors reported that they used marijuana daily. By 1985, the daily use figure had dropped to below 5%. The opposite pattern is found for cocaine abuse, however. Between 1974 and 1985 the number of people who had ever tried cocaine rose from 5.4 million to 22.2 million.

The most commonly abused substance, however, is alcohol. In the last generation, per capita alcohol consumption has risen by almost 50%. Between 10 and 15 million Americans now have a drinking problem, making alcohol abuse the most serious drug problem in the United States today.

The role of biological factors in the development of alcoholism is reviewed by Schuckit in selection 27. This article begins with a discussion of studies suggesting that alcoholism tends to run in families. Schuckit then goes on to describe evidence supporting a genetically based interpretation of the data—at least for a subgroup of alcoholics. This leads naturally to a consideration of populations at elevated risk for alcoholism and a consideration of the mechanisms through which vulnerability might be expressed.

A number of Schuckit's findings are worthy of mention here. Men with no family history of alcoholism tend to report feeling more intoxicated after drinking a standard amount of alcohol than do men with a family history of alcoholism. The cognitive and psychomotor performance of these high-risk individuals also supports their subjective reports of lower levels of intoxication. For example, after a standard dose of ethanol, they sway less. Speculating from these findings, Schuckit suggests that the decreased intensity of reaction to low doses of alcohol characteristic of the at-risk subjects may make it difficult for them to discern when they are becoming drunk. They may therefore be less able to take steps to prevent this from happening.

In addition to identifying persons at risk for developing alcoholism, genetic factors may also explain why some persons are particularly unlikely to develop drinking problems. Many Asians, for example, lack an enzyme important in alcohol metabolism. As a result, they experience facial flushing, palpitations, and nausea after drinking. These immediately negative consequences of alcohol ingestion are thought to explain the generally low prevalence of alcoholism in Asian populations.

Most people, however, do not experience particularly negative or unpleasant reactions to low doses of alcohol. Indeed, the "tension reduction" hypothesis, widely accepted in recent years, proposes that alcohol, through its ability to lower stress levels, actually has reinforcing properties.

The stress reduction–alcohol relationship is not invariably found, however, and in selection 28 Steele and his colleagues attempt to understand precisely why this is so. Using a new and theoretically very appealing approach, they empirically demonstrate the important mediating role of distracting activity. The logic behind their study is simple. Alcohol impairs the ability to use multiple cues simultaneously. After being exposed to a psychologically stressful event, alcohol should therefore enhance any benefits that may be derived from a distracting task. This is because alcohol's damage to cognition should render it difficult to ruminate about a negative event *and* attend to a distracting stimulus at the same time. Attention is therefore turned away from the self and the individual feels better. Steele's findings also suggest that the unhappy individual who attempts to drown his or her sorrows alone may run the risk of feeling even worse.

Sexual Deviations

Our final focus in this section is on a group of disorders known as paraphilias. The essential feature of paraphilias is arousal to non-normative sexual objects or situations. DSM-III-R recognizes nine forms of paraphilia, including fetishism, exhibitionism, voyeurism, and frotteurism (rubbing against a nonconsenting person). Conspicuous by their absence, however, are rape and incest.

In general, very little is known about the paraphilias. Sexual deviations are rarely diagnosed in general clinical settings, and prevalence estimates are largely unavailable. What is clear, however, is that virtually all cases of paraphilia involve males. Indeed, some diagnoses (e.g., transvestic fetishism or "cross dressing") are reserved solely for men. In order to be given the diagnosis, the paraphiliac must have acted on his urges or be markedly distressed by them.

One of the most disturbing forms of sexual deviation is pedophilia. This is because it involves young children, who, in order to get help, must confront adults who may be unable or in some cases unwilling to believe their stories. This is all the more likely because, as Lanyon points out in selection 29, the pedophile is usually someone the victim (and presumably his/her family) knows. Pedophilia is also a distressing disorder because, like rape and incest, it often leaves long-lasting psychological scars on its victims. For this reason, the more we can learn about its cause and treatment, the better able we will be to halt the development of psychopathology in yet another generation.

References and Suggestions for Additional Reading

CLECKLEY, H. (1976). *The Mask of Sanity* (5th ed.). St. Louis, MO: Mosby.

HULL, J. G. (1981). A self-awareness model of the causes and effects of alcohol consumption. *Journal of Abnormal Psychology, 90*, 6, 586–600.

Journal of Consulting and Clinical Psychology

(1986). Special series: Current issues in the evaluation and treatment of sexual disturbances. *54*, 2.

LYKKEN, D. T. (1957). A study of anxiety in the sociopathic personality. *Journal of Abnormal and Social Psychology, 55,* 6–10.

LYKKEN, D. T. (1982). Fearlessness: Its carefree charm and deadly risks. *Psychology Today,* September, 21–28.

SHER, K. J. AND LEVENSON, R. W. (1982). Risk for alcoholism and individual differences in the stress-response-dampening effect of alcohol. *Journal of Abnormal Psychology, 91,* 5, 350–367.

23

The DSM-III Personality Disorders Section: A Commentary

Allen Frances

The author reviews the *DSM-III* section on personality disorders, discusses several of its more controversial diagnoses, and suggests some possible alternatives. He attributes the continued low reliability of personality diagnoses, compared with the other major sections of *DSM-III*, to two inherent obstacles: the lack of clear boundaries demarcating the personality disorders from normality and from one another, and the confounding influence of state and role factors. Nonetheless, the *DSM-III* multiaxial system highlights the importance of personality diagnosis and, together with the provision of clearly specified diagnostic criteria, achieves a considerably improved reliability compared with previous nomenclatures.

The multiaxial diagnostic system introduced by *DSM-III* serves to highlight the importance of the personality disorders and to recognize their frequent coexistence with, and possible contribution to, the other psychiatric disorders. *DSM-III* provides separate axes—Axis I for all other clinical syndromes and Axis II for personality disorders—to en-

sure that the personality disorders not be overlooked "when attention is directed to the usually more florid Axis I disorder" (1). This concern arises from accumulating evidence that the quality and quantity of preexisting personality disturbance may indeed influence the predisposition, manifestation, course, and response to treatment of various Axis I conditions (2–7). The separation of Axes I and II has contributed to the increased diagnostic reliability achieved by the whole system. Evaluators are now encouraged to label both the clinical syndrome and the personality disorder (when both are present), rather than being forced to arbitrarily and unreliably make a choice between them.

This paper discusses some of the obstacles to the establishment of a reliable nomenclature of personality diagnosis. It also provides a critical review of the *DSM-III* section on personality disorders, particularly several of its more controversial diagnoses. As a member of the Advisory Committee on Personality Disorders to the APA Task Force on Nomenclature and Statistics, I acknowledge considerable bias in my presentation. Undoubtedly, I have blind spots that favor some of the choices made in *DSM-III* and may also be taking this last opportunity to argue against choices that I disliked. No one who worked on *DSM-III* had the quixotic goal of achieving any lasting or perfect solutions. It is my hope that a continued discussion of the controversies and decisions that resulted

Allen Frances. The *DSM-III* Personality Disorders Section: A Commentary. *American Journal of Psychiatry*, 1980, Vol. 137, No. 9, pp. 1050–1054, 1980. Copyright © 1980, by the American Psychiatric Association. Reprinted by permission.

in *DSM-III* will encourage the research and debate required for an improved *DSM-IV.*

Limitations to Reliability

Previous clinical systems of personality diagnosis were plagued by very low reliability (8). Although *DSM-III* has improved on this considerably, the personality disorders as a group still attain the lowest reliability of any major category in the classification (9). There are at least two inherent reasons for this: 1) most of the personality disorders are probably no more than the severe variants of normally occurring personality traits that are distributed continuously and without clear boundaries to indicate pathology, and 2) personality assessment is inevitably confounded by intercurrent state and role factors. I will discuss these obstacles in turn.

In order to classify disorders into separate types, one ideally requires that they be distinct and mutually exclusive and that the number of cases falling at the boundary between disorders be relatively few (10). Although the organic, schizophrenic, and affective disorders all retain their fair share of fuzziness, these categories are to some extent discontinuous from one another and discrete from normality. In comparison, the various personality disorders are not at all clearly distinct from normal functioning or from each other (or even, as is discussed below, from Axis I conditions). *DSM-III* states, "It is only when personality traits are inflexible and maladaptive and cause either significant impairment in social or occupational functioning or subjective distress that they constitute personality disorders." Although in most instances *DSM-III* attempts to carefully and operationally define its criteria, it provides no definitions or quantifications for the terms "inflexible," "maladaptive," or "significant." It would indeed be difficult to make these concepts operational. Since each clinician is left to his or her own judgment in deciding whether a particular degree of personality impairment should be regarded as disorder or merely a normal trait, this decision is made with only fair reliability.

In addition, the various personality disorders are, to some extent, correlated and continuous with each other (11). Some of the diagnostic criteria appear, in more or less similar language, under more than one category. *DSM-III* does attempt to soften the potential rigidity and inapplicability of the category system to personality diagnosis by allowing for multiple and mixed diagnoses. Although this undoubtedly constitutes the only possible current compromise, there is another method of personality diagnosis that may receive increasing attention in the future. The alternative to the *DSM-III* categorical classification would be the use of a dimensional system. This method has been extensively studied by psychologists. Among the best-known factor scales are those of Eysenck (12), Cattell (13), Leary (14), and McLemore and Benjamin (15); the MMPI is a widely used nonfactorial scale.

A dimensional system avoids many problems of the categorical approach. It is, at least theoretically, the more applicable method for describing normally distributed traits that can be quantified and measured. As this applies to *DSM-III*, the patient might be rated (perhaps on a scale of 1 to 10) for each personality characteristic rather than being diagnosed within one or another distinct personality type. This procedure might greatly improve the description of patients who are on the boundary between normality and disorder or between one and another personality disorder. The dimensional system successfully renders continuities and saves information that is lost in the forced choice of just one or the other category. It also lessens the reification of categories and the accompanying halo effect on clinicians, who may perceive patients as neatly fitting into one or another category while perhaps ignoring those traits outside the anticipated cluster.

There are substantial reasons why *DSM-III* continues to apply the more traditional categorical approach in the face of these undeniable advantages to personality diagnosis of a dimensional system. Kendell (10) has observed that clinicians naturally think in terms of categories even if research scientists tend to prefer dimensions. Dimensions may provide more information than can be conveniently used and often seem too complicated for routine clinical discourse. The creation of categories serves to reduce information overload, abstract what is most crucial, and convey a more vivid, if less accurate, picture of the patient. It is good to realize that the evolution of diagnostic nosologies must be one of the most conservative of clinical endeavors; radical departures tend to be ignored. It would certainly be premature to demand widespread conversion to a dimensional system at this time. However, it is possible that with the future widespread availability of computers, psychiatry will prefer a dimensional system, at least for personality diagnosis.

The second inherent limitation to the reliability of the diagnosis of personality disorders results from the difficulty in distinguishing and untangling trait from state and role factors. The *DSM-III* definition of personality disorder does address and, in theory, solves these problems. Personality traits are defined as enduring patterns exhibited in a wide range of activities, recognizable by adolescence or earlier, and continuing throughout adult life. In actual practice, however, it is often quite impossible on cross-sectional evaluation to decide to what extent the current behavior and clinical picture represent an enduring and lifelong pattern or to what extent they are being strongly influenced by the patient's current state and/or role expectations. The interaction of trait and state is inherently confounding and difficult to analyze. It may be impossible to eliminate completely the possible influence of Axis I conditions in the assessment of personality disorders. Many studies have ignored the fact that the patient's current mood inevitably tends to contaminate the evaluation of his or her long-standing traits. The Eysenck neuroticism scale, supposedly a personality measure, has been found to be very sensitive to mood changes and may be more a measure of depression than of personality impairment (16). Only repeated evaluations and careful history taking (perhaps also using relatives) can minimize the contamination of current state factors. The multiaxial system is a useful advance in its recognition of the possible mutual influence of personality and Axis I disorders and its provision of independent ratings for each.

The trait-role overlap is almost as difficult to disentangle. Within an overall personality pattern, each individual is certainly capable of a range of behaviors that are differentially selected depending on the contingencies, expectations, or role assignments of the particular current social environment. Personality disorder is by definition a pervasive and inflexible set of maladaptive behaviors that occur widely and not exclusively in response to a specific set of circumstances. A pathological reaction that is elicited by only one particular and unusual stimulus (e.g., an Army recruit's disobedience in boot camp) would be defined as an adjustment, not a personality, disorder. In order to qualify for the often carelessly applied diagnosis of passive-aggressive personality disorder, the behavior in question would have to be general, long-standing, maladaptive, and not merely an isolated role response to one difficult situation. In any given evaluation of personality, the consultant must judge whether the patient's behavior is deeply ingrained or whether it is merely a particular reaction to the current environment, including, incidentally, the often unfamiliar and stressful environment of the psychiatric evaluation.

A Critical Review

The following remarks constitute a critical review of the *DSM-III* section on personality disorders. The criticisms must be understood in the general context of my overall enthusiastic approval of this section. For several years I have had opportunities to use it for clinical, teaching, and research purposes and have found it to be clinically and heuristically helpful and a vast improvement over *DSM-II*. The following discussion assumes and probably requires some familiarity with the *DSM-III* section on personality disorders, which might profitably be read simultaneously.

Additions and Deletions

Four of the *DSM-II* personality disorders have either been eliminated from the *DSM-III* classification or transferred to other of its sections. The diagnosis of asthenic personality had been rarely used anyway and was probably indistinguishable from chronic mild depression. The diagnosis of inadequate personality dealt with the patient's functional level rather than describing a distinct behavior pattern. These two diagnoses were retired, probably without mourners. The diagnosis of explosive disorder was transferred out of the personality disorders section because its *DSM-III* definition requires an intermittent rather than a continuous course. There was some support for including a diagnosis of impulsive personality for patients whose outbursts are consistent with deeply ingrained overall personality functioning. As a compromise, impulsive personality has been listed as one of the possible other personality disorders but without specific criteria. The transfer of cyclothymic disorder to the affective section will be discussed in more detail below. The rationale for most of the five new categories of personality disorders—the schizotypal, borderline, narcissistic, avoidant, and dependent—will also be discussed.

Clusters

There is a comment in the introduction to the section that the personality disorders are grouped into 3 clusters: 1) the paranoid, schizoid, and schizotypal disorders are characterized by odd or eccentric behavior; 2) the histrionic, narcissistic, antisocial, and borderline disorders are characterized by dramatic, emotional, or erratic behavior; and 3) the avoidant, dependent, compulsive, or passive-aggressive disorders are characterized by anxious or fearful behavior. The reader should understand that this clustering does not arise from any particular evidence. In fact, most of the criteria clusters that define the 11 defined personality disorders are based only on clinical intuition and impression that has yet to be confirmed by factor analysis or other forms of validation (i.e., follow-up, family, psychological test, or response to treatment studies). Allport and Odbert (17) gathered 4,500 personality adjectives that were listed in the dictionary. There is no particular reason to believe that the 11 personality types described in *DSM-III* are the most appropriate number or grouping of personality traits or that the criteria best cluster as they now stand. On a more optimistic note, there is some evidence that the factor analyses of items derived from self-report questionnaires turn up approximately the same syndromes as had been derived intuitively by clinicians (18, 19).

Handling of Spectrum Disorders

There is some inconsistency and an overcompensation for past historical errors in the classification of the schizophrenic and affective spectrum disorders. In order to keep psychotic conditions together and to narrow the diagnosis of schizophrenia, which has been applied overinclusively in the United States (20), *DSM-III* places the presumed nonpsychotic spectrum disorder (schizotypal personality) within the personality disorders section. This is in itself a useful advance, but, simultaneous to the taming of schizophrenia, *DSM-III* may have become paradoxically overinclusive with the affective disorders. The presumed affective spectrum disorders—cyclothymic and dysthymic—do not join the schizophrenia spectrum disorder in the personality section but instead are listed with the major affective disorders. This placement of cyclothymic disorder is agreeable enough because there is fairly compelling evidence of its close relationship to the major affective disorders (21). The inclusion of dysthymic disorder (chronic depressive disorder or depressive neurosis) is a much more controversial and worrisome decision. Dysthymic disorder probably includes an extremely heterogeneous group of patients. They may have vegetative symptoms indicative of an affective disorder; psychological conflicts that make them pessimistic, self-defeating, and unhappy; a chronically difficult life situation; or various mixtures of the above.

DSM-III would have been more consistent had it selected one way to handle both the schizophrenic and the affective spectrum disorders. If dysthymic disorder must be included in the affective section, it should have required as an essential criterion the presence of vegetative symptoms; this is not the case now. Nonvegetative chronic depression should have appeared separately under one or another title (I would have preferred depressive or masochistic personality) in the personality disorders section.

New Categories of Schizotypal and Borderline Personality Disorders

The introduction of two new categories, the schizotypal and borderline personality disorders, represents a major clarification of what has been a very confusing classification. The separation of these two different, but at times overlapping, types of "borderline" disorders should improve the level of clinical discourse and research. The manner in which the criteria were derived and tested has been well described (11) and need not be reviewed here.

Perpetuation of the Term "Borderline Personality Disorder"

The perpetuation of this term caused considerable controversy and resulted only from the lack of wide acceptance of any substitute term. Many feel that the concept of borderline has been so variously and loosely applied that it has lost all precise meaning and shape. It is no longer clear what it "borders" on, especially since the border to schizophrenia is now occupied by the schizotypal personality disorder and the border to affective illness by the cyclothymic and dysthmic disorders. There are, in fact, three additional ways that the term "borderline personality"

has been used: 1) descriptively, to define by symptomatic similarities a particular syndrome of unstable personality (this is the sense of the DSM-III usage), 2) psychodynamically, to define an inferred level of personality organization somewhere between the psychotic and neurotic levels of integration and with characteristic deficits in psychic structure (which may coexist with any of the descriptive personality types), and 3) as a rating of severity of impairment indicating the presence of any marked character disorder (regardless of its particular descriptive or structural characteristics).

It is yet to be determined to what extent these three uses correlate with one another in the groups they define. Since the diagnosis borderline personality has attained such an unusual popularity, it is probably helpful to have a definite set of criteria on which to base a more precise discussion and research investigation. The major dispute regarding the criteria that were chosen concerned the advisability of an additional essential feature—that the patient must have displayed transient, self-limited deficits in reality testing. This suggestion would have considerably narrowed the borderline personality group and rendered it more homogeneous. It was voted down pending the accumulation of data on the relationship between transient psychotic episodes and the rest of the syndrome of instability.

Antisocial Personality Disorder

Surprisingly, this was the most controversial of all the personality disorders. The DSM-III diagnostic criteria specifying antisocial personality are indeed clear and reliable and have been the most carefully studied (22), but they may have missed the most important clinical point. Using criteria comparable to those in DSM-III, approximately 80% of all criminals are diagnosed as antisocial (23). Many investigators have suggested the inclusion of additional items that might indicate the individual's capacity for loyalty to others, guilt, anticipatory anxiety, and learning from past experiences. Some distinction between antisocial and dyssocial patterns of behavior was included in both *DSM-I* and *DSM-II* and is reflected in the current definition of childhood conduct disorders in *DSM-III* (24). These are divided into the socialized and undersocialized subtypes—a separation that seems to have some usefulness in predicting adult behavior. It has also been shown that if criminals are evaluated with more traditional and less inclusive criteria, only 30% are diagnosed as having antisocial personalities (25). For clinicians who work in prisons, it would seem to be more useful to have criteria that distinguish those criminals who are capable of loyalty, anxiety, and guilt from those who are not, since the behavior and management of each group are likely to be quite different. There was also considerable concern that the *DSM-III* criteria would be too easily and universally attained by individuals growing up in rough and deprived areas.

Schizoid and Avoidant Personality Disorders

The distinction between these two disorders is a new one. Individuals with these disorders might closely resemble each other, although the individual with an avoidant personality is much more likely to have achieved at least one close relationship. By definition, the major difference between the categories resides in the patient's motivation for relative social isolation. The patient with an avoidant personality craves closeness but avoids it because of fears of criticism and rejection. The patient with a schizoid personality is beyond desire. Some people have argued that this judgment cannot be made reliably and depends on inference. They suggest that the two conditions be combined. This may become necessary, but my own clinical impression is that it is well worth trying to distinguish the two disorders. The avoidant and schizoid patients are likely to be markedly different in their family history, predisposition to schizophrenia, ability to

form therapeutic or other relationships, and need for the response to treatment.

There was also a dispute involving the use of the word "schizoid." In earlier drafts of *DSM-III*, it was replaced by the term "introverted," but this was quite upsetting to Jungian analysts and factor psychologists, for whom "introverted" does not imply the presence of disorder and is, rather, a normal type. Some people felt that the motivation beneath the avoidant personality disorder should have been defined more broadly to include fears about shame, humiliation, losing control, and making a fool of oneself. The patient with an avoidant personality is often likely to meet the criteria for the dependent personality; once a relationship is formed it is clung to tenaciously.

Narcissistic Personality Disorder

This is a new category whose necessity was suggested by an increasing psychoanalytic literature and by the isolation of narcissism as a personality factor in a variety of psychological studies. The distinguishing features in a psychoanalytic definition of narcissistic character might include 1) deficits in libidinal object constancy, 2) an incomplete internalization of maturation of psychic structures and regulatory mechanisms, particularly those having to do with self-esteem, and 3) aberrant or immature grandiosity. In making this diagnosis, the psychodynamic clinician might assess whether the patient experiences others as fully realized and separate objects or as self-objects and whether the transference that evolves in treatment takes on either a grandiose or idealizing configuration. Unfortunately, it is difficult to put these concepts into a descriptive and operational form that can be applied in one or two interviews by psychiatrists who may not have psychodynamic training or inclination. Instead, the *DSM-III* criteria for narcissistic personality disorder define descriptive and behavioral features that require only limited inferences about psychic structures, object constancy, and motivations. It is not clear to what extent the descriptive and psychodynamic definitions correlate and whether they will select the same patient groups.

Conclusions

The two major innovations of *DSM-III*—the multiaxial system and the provision of specific diagnostic criteria—are significant contributions to improved diagnosis of personality disorders. The next step in improving reliability is a clearer specification, even if an arbitrary one, of the precise quantity of impairment that defines a disorder. In addition, the individual personality disorders themselves need to be studied in various ways. The current *DSM-III* clustering of criteria is primarily based only on clinical intuition and should be validated with large studies to determine how the various criteria cluster in actual patients. It will be interesting to learn whether certain of the current disorders are highly correlated with each other and could perhaps be collapsed or whether new combinations might emerge. It is not clear whether the current criteria will successfully define relatively homogeneous groups of patients, e.g., the borderline personality disorder may include patients on an affective disorder spectrum, others with problems of impulse control, others with a masochistic need for punishment, and still others with a deficient self-concept. The validation of personality types as well as the investigation of their relationship to other *DSM-III* disorders are important and fascinating areas for future research.

References

1. AMERICAN PSYCHIATRIC ASSOCIATION: Diagnostic and Statistical Manual of Mental Disorders, 3rd ed. Washington, DC, APA, 1980
2. HIRSCHFELD R, KLERMAN G: Personality attributes and affective disorders. Am J Psychiatry 136:67–70, 1979
3. WEISSMAN M, PRUSOFF B, KLERMAN G: Personality and prediction of long-term outcome of depression. Am J Psychiatry 135:797–800, 1978
4. TAYLOR M, ABRAMS R: Acute mania: clinical and genetic study of responders and nonresponders to treatments. Arch Gen Psychiatry 32:863–865, 1975
5. KUPFER D, PICKAR D, HIMMELHOCH J, et al: Are there two types of unipolar depression? Arch Gen Psychiatry 32:866–871, 1975
6. BIELSKI R, FRIEDEL R: Prediction of tricyclic antidepressant response. Arch Gen Psychiatry 33:1479–1489, 1976
7. GARMEZY N: Process and reactive schizophrenia: some conceptions and issues, in Classification in Psychiatry and Psychopathology. Edited by KATZ M, COLE J, BARTON W. Chevy Chase, Md., US Department of Health, Education, and Welfare, 1965
8. KREITMAN N, SAINSBURY P, MORRISSEY J, et al: The reliability of psychiatric assessment: an analysis. J Ment Sci, 107:887–908, 1961
9. SPITZER R, FORMAN J, NEE J: DSM-III field trials: I. Initial interrater diagnostic reliability. Am J Psychiatry 136:815–817, 1979
10. KENDELL R: The Role of Diagnosis of Psychiatry. Oxford, Blackwell, 1979
11. SPITZER R, ENDICOTT J, GIBBON M: Crossing the border into borderline personality and borderline schizophrenia: the development of criteria. Arch Gen Psychiatry 36:17–24, 1979
12. EYSENCK H: The Scientific Study of Personality. New York, Macmillan Publishing Co, 1965
13. CATTELL R: The Scientific Analysis of Personality. Chicago, Aldine Publishing Co, 1965
14. LEARY T: Interpersonal Diagnosis of Personality: A Functional Theory and Methodology of Personality Evaluation. New York, Ronald Press, 1957
15. McLEMORE C, BENJAMIN L: Whatever happened to interpersonal diagnosis? A psychosocial alternative to DSM-III. Am Psychol 34:17–34, 1979
16. LIEBOWITZ M, STALLONE F, DUNNER D, et al: Personality features of patients with primary affective disorder. Acta Psychiatr Scand 60:214–224, 1979
17. ALLPORT G, ODBERT H: Trait-names: a psycholexical study. Psychological Monographs 47:1–171, 1936
18. LAZARE A, KLERMAN G, ARMOR D: Oral, obsessive, and hysterical personality patterns. Arch Gen Psychiatry 14:624–630, 1966
19. LAZARE A, KLERMAN G, ARMOR D: Oral-ob-

sessive and hysterical personality patterns: replication of factor analysis in an independent sample. J Psychiatr Res 7:275–290, 1970

20. KENDELL R, COOPER J, GOURLAY A, et al: Diagnostic criteria of American and British psychiatrists. Arch Gen Psychiatry 25:123–130, 1971

21. AKISKAL H, DJENDEREDJIAN A, ROSENTHAL R, et al: Cyclothmyic disorder: validating criteria for inclusion in the bipolar affective group. Am J Psychiatry 134:1227–1233, 1977

22. ROBINS L: Deviant Children Grown Up. Baltimore, Williams & Wilkins Co, 1966

23. GUZE S, GOODWIN D, CRANE, J: Criminality and psychiatric disorders. Arch Gen Psychiatry 20:583–591, 1969

24. JENKINS R: The psychopathic or antisocial personality. J Nerv Ment Dis 131:318–334, 1960

25. HARE R: Psychopathy, in Handbook of Biological Psychiatry, vol III. Edited by VAN PRAAG H, LEDER H, RAFAELSON O. New York, Marcel Dekker 70–77, 1985

24

Portrait of a Con Artist

Tim Sandler

On October 2, 1984, a prison guard escorted Edgar Peter Berube from his protective-custody cell through the corridors of New Hampshire State Prison in Concord. After paperwork was completed, another guard took Berube outside to an electronic gate. The gate slowly opened, and after serving only nine months on a minimum sentence of seven years, Berube stepped into his brother's car and was driven to his mother's home in Somersworth, New Hampshire. Once there, he announced he would be taking a bus to Hingham, Massachusetts, where he would begin a drug rehabilitation program—a condition of his "early release." After three days in Somersworth, Berube told his mother he needed $250 to enter the program. She gave him a check. He wrote down a forwarding phone number and left. Berube never arrived at the program, nor was he expected. He wasn't expected because his release was unauthorized; prison officials say Berube himself forged the release documents from inside the prison.

It took a full month before officials realized that the release had been unauthorized. A warrant was issued for Berube's arrest, and a nationwide manhunt began. Berube was arrested in Colorado in mid-November 1984. He is now back in New Hampshire State Prison, serving his previous sentence and awaiting trial on charges of forgery and escape.

Just how the release was arranged is unclear. What is clear, however, is that Berube is a resourceful man with considerable appeal. The news reports of his escape attracted widespread attention—and even something approaching admiration. As details of the release unfolded last fall, Merrimack County prosecutor Michael Johnson was exasperated, though he couldn't help but recognize Berube's charisma. "Mr. Berube has developed into something of a folk hero," Johnson said at the time. "He is the biggest con artist New England has seen in a long time . . . your all-American flimflam man."

In 1982 Johnson was responsible for having Berube, then a student at New England College in Henniker, indicted on 38 counts of forgery, theft, and passing bad checks. Posing at the college as the grandson of oil magnate Armand Hammer, Berube had, by his own account, embezzled almost $100,000 before he was caught. Court proceedings on those charges were continued for several months, and Berube was free on bail when he enrolled at Beloit College in Wisconsin. There, according to the district attorney's office in Beloit, he passed himself off as a member of the wealthy DuPont family and arranged to withdraw money from a money market fund he had set up in New York. According to the Beloit district attorney's office, there was no money in that fund.

By then Berube had assumed and perfected a bizarre pattern of behavior. It was a role firmly established by 1978, when fraternity brothers at the University of New Hampshire in Durham say it was not rare to see Berube being dropped off at their house in a chauffeur-driven limousine—not particularly unusual for the son of Senator Edward Kennedy, they thought.

These are only some highlights of a brilliant but flawed life. The origins of Berube's derailment are numerous, but his thinking was surely influenced by the pressures and fantasies of his culture. The lure of fame and fortune was irresistible, and it made way for a life-time of deception and self-delusion. By the age of 16, Berube had surreptitiously appropriated $2,000 from his parents, according to psychiatric records. In the next dozen years he succeeded in preying on friends, relatives, and employers, deceiving psychiatrists, attorneys, and judges. His early release in 1984 may well embody his deception of the entire criminal justice system.

Although Johnson acknowledges, "You can't help but be awed by his determination and incorrigibleness," Johnson's irritation with Berube has fermented to indignation. "He's a con man and a criminal who steals a lot of money from people by pretending to be young, aristocratic, and harmless," Johnson says. "He is very charming, persuasive, and intelligent when he wants to be, and people trust him. Then he steals from them. As I've said all along, he's a man trying to take a short cut to the American dream."

Others see more than just a criminal in Berube. Says clinical psychologist David Diamond, who began treating 15-year-old Berube in 1971, "On several levels there is a self-destructive element to this whole thing. He's obviously hurting at some level and trying to compensate for that by making himself into an important person so the slights of his past are washed away by his exploits. He's not living a normal life. He

wouldn't have gotten into this pattern unless he was dealing with important psychiatric issues. And in this case, I think it's fair to say that what you're dealing with is a psychopathic personality."

It has been less than a year since Berube was recaptured. Wearing standard blue prison garb and handcuffs, Berube is led from his maximum-security cell in New Hampshire State Prison to a small, stark conference room. He sits at a wooden table and is watched by guards through a picture window from the unit manager's office. The guards like Berube; they joke with him and about him; they consider him neither dangerous nor a threat. Yet they remain wary.

At 29, Berube looks middle-aged. He is bald, thin at the arms, loose at the waist and neck. But his voice seems to be from another body. It has the confidence and zeal of a young salesman. It is a voice of persuasion.

In a series of interviews at the prison from early February to early April 1985, Berube is animated and thoughtful, episodically irritable and evasive. His confident and vivid accounts of his career are sometimes deadly accurate, other times easily disproved. Intentional or not, there is a convincing liar in Berube. Although he is stripped of his props, his formidable performing skills are intact. Berube's thirst for excitement is particularly evident as he recounts the more salient details of his past. He readily acknowledges his uncanny ability to slide through the cracks of both psychiatric and criminal justice systems. Berube is not interested in talking about ordinary or personally revealing details. Still, he quietly acknowledges that his conduct has been born more out of psychological necessity than simple ethical disregard.

Asked whether his adult conduct was a pattern that emerged from his family life, Berube parries. "Whatever goes on in the house stays in the house," he says. "That's the way I was brought up." But social histories written at the New Hampshire State Hospital do give a portrait of a young man as con artist. (Those histories and other psychiatric records going back to 1971 were released to the author by Berube for purposes of this article.)

Berube told caseworkers that he was raised with three brothers in Somersworth—a humble, rusty, working-class community. His parents, Yolanda and Romeo Berube, were French-Canadian immigrants. His mother came from a wealthy family, his father from a blue-collar family. The difference in economic backgrounds, Berube told case workers, surfaced in his parents' intense desire for status and the appearance of wealth. As he told social worker Teresa M. Butkus, he, too, entertained that desire.

"At the age of 13 or 14 something happened," Butkus wrote in a 1974 report, "and he began getting into serious trouble with money. He had the image of being a rich kid but actually wasn't. People were always borrowing money from him and when he didn't have it he wrote false checks to get it. . . . Popularity became very important to him as he tried to find friends who were popular (school athletes) and then buy their friendship." (Reached in Augusta, Maine, where she is now an adoption supervisor for the state Department of Human Services, Butkus says of Berube, "He was a very bright guy who seemed to have a real need to pull things over on people and then get caught so everyone would know. I'm not sure where that need comes from.")

About the same time, Berube says, quarrels erupted between him and his parents about the company he kept. According to Berube, his father, for years a Somersworth police officer, had his first heart attack after one of those arguments. Berube blamed himself privately, and, he told caseworkers, his mother blamed him openly. And, he says, he took her disfavor seriously.

Therapy with Diamond, at the urging of Berube's parents, did not avert his impulse to steal money from them. According to psychiatric records, he took about $2,000 all told, most of which, Berube told Diamond, he gave to a needy friend.

Rejection by his parents and a longing to pull together a disintegrating family were strong concerns of Berube, Diamond wrote in a letter to a probation officer in 1979. In a 1974 letter to Butkus, Diamond wrote, "The only way he has found to get 'love' is to get in trouble, get caught and then be forgiven." Today Diamond looks back and recognizes Berube's ability to control the persona he presented: "I think he must have conned me a couple of times, too."

In late 1971 Berube stopped seeing Diamond after a year, but was referred to him again a year later after being charged with fraudulently cashing $750 worth of his aunt's checks. After that arrest, authorities discovered Berube had crafted an article appearing in a local newspaper announcing he was the recipient of a $2,500 college scholarship.

In an October 1973 letter to Berube's attorney, Wayne Murray, Diamond recommended long-term, intensive psychotherapy for Berube and referred him to a psychiatrist named G. S. Nothmann for testing. Under Nothmann's care, Berube was given prescriptions for medication and was given the Minnesota Multiphasic Personality Inventory. The MMPI report confirmed Diamond's analysis: "The test results on this patient are strongly suggestive of a major emotional disorder. The test pattern resembles those of psychiatric outpatients who later require inpatient care."

"Although he may express firm intentions to change his behavior, the pattern is a persistent one and the long range prognosis is not encouraging. Assisting him to a better adjustment will probably require modification of his environment, warm support, and firm limits." (Reached in Dover, New Hampshire, Nothmann now says he cannot comment on a former patient.)

Cautions emphasized in both Nothmann's and Diamond's reports, however, were largely overlooked when Berube was admitted to the New Hampshire State Hospital's Forensic Unit for additional pretrial evaluation in January 1974. It was there that Butkus, according to Berube, took him under her wing. Berube told Butkus how he was taken advantage of in school, how he won an award in high school for being the ugliest student in the class, and how he was ignored and misunderstood by his parents. Butkus' reports painted a picture of a sensitive, artistic, and affected young man. His sympathy-inspiring persona made an impression on Butkus: "Edgar seems to be looking very desperately for someone to love or be loved." Today, Butkus says, "That's the way he presented himself at the time—he didn't have anyone who cared about him. I still think he had a tremendous amount of potential that didn't get tapped."

Under Butkus' guidance, Berube received a high school equivalency degree and took more tests at the Vocational Rehabilitation Development Center in Manchester, New Hampshire. According to another psychiatric report, Berube scored 122 on his IQ test, placing him in the superior intelligence range.

Berube was cleared of the check forgery charges after a tentative plan was developed by Butkus and Murray that included outpatient psychiatric treatment and living in a boarding house. Vocational Rehabilitation also arranged to give Berube financial assistance for admission and tuition at New England College. The plan reflected an earlier conclusion made by Butkus: "I feel that he is quite competent and not dangerous to anyone." Berube was discharged on March 27, 1974.

At the time, Berube's brother Robert was living in Concord, New Hampshire, and he offered Edgar a place to stay after his release. "I really tried to help him," the elder Berube told a reporter from the *Concord Monitor* in a 1982 interview. Berube left after staying one night, taking with him his brother's identification cards. "He got all the IDs in order to go to Boston to use my name to get loans and credit," Robert Berube told the reporter, adding that he thwarted his brother's attempts when banks in Boston called to check his credit.

Edgar Berube started at New England College in the fall of 1974 but was dismissed shortly afterward for having falsified his application. "It was a misunderstanding," Berube now says earnestly, talking of the ap-

plication. "I wrote on a questionnaire that my father worked as a maintenance supervisor at the University of New Hampshire, and when it was checked they couldn't find a record of it. But it *was* true."

Somersworth High School principal Robert Langelier tells a different story. In a recent telephone interview, he recalls that in September 1974, New England College returned a transcript of Berube's apparently because of a question. The transcript stated he had good grades and attendance; Langelier says the transcript was falsified.

In the summer of 1975, after his dismissal from New England College, Berube moved to a small room in a Boston boarding house. According to Berube, he paid $20 a week to a landlord who believed he was renting to a young man called Ed Rockefeller.

Talking of this today, Berube smiles. "When I first moved to Boston I had left home," he says, "and I wanted to make it on my own. I was determined to do something without assistance. What had the most impact on me was that people without money were surviving the best way they could. Everyone where I lived was using different names. I'm very adept and quick at learning things, which I think is one of my pitfalls, and at the time I was experimenting with what would work."

To begin with, Berube says, he "set up three different residences at boarding rooms in Boston, Cambridge, and Newton. After that I went to the welfare department, under my own name, and applied for assistance three times. All I did was see three different counselors." At his separate addresses, Berube says, he received a total of $180 a month—as well as additional money for a nonexistent disability.

Berube began working at Hugo's Lighthouse restaurant in Cohasset and befriended the owner. The owner, Berube says, was generous with him and paid for his evening extension courses at Harvard University. Among the courses he tells of taking in the 1975–1976 semester were Finance, Monetary Economics, and Espionage and Ethics. In the latter course, he recalls "a very tweedy-type professor who worked for the OSS, then the CIA. He smoked a pipe, had a foreign accent, the whole bit.''

Harvard Continuing Education has no record of an Edgar Berube taking any courses. It does list an Edward Berube for that semester, but the courses do not match those described by Berube. The department also has no record of courses taken by Dave Barry, the name Berube says he used the following semester.

Berube's first tangle with Boston police came in July 1975, after he stole a $776 federal government check from a neighbor. He deposited it in his own account. Charged with larceny and forgery, Berube appeared in Boston Municipal Court. He was convicted and received six months in the House of Correction; the sentence was suspended, and he was put on probation.

At about the same time, Berube was answering charges of larceny by check in Cambridge District Court. In that case, he pleaded guilty and was again put on probation.

The arrests proved educational. "I was using my own name then" on checks, Berube recalls, "and whenever I was caught, which wasn't hard, I was always asked why I used my own name. The police laughed at how easy it was to find me. I hadn't really thought about coming up with different names and IDs for that."

Berube signed himself Lewis A. Antony in 1977. "It was scary at first," he says now, "rembering names, numbers, et cetera." At the same time, he says, he tested the financial waters of the banks in the Boston area. "That's when I learned about banks, deposits, computer tellers, and floating systems. I would play with local checks versus federal checks to see how long it would take for them to come back. I also found that if you split a check, they record it as cash and don't put it on hold. So I would get part of the cash up front, then I would go to the bank the next day and ask for the balance and withdraw it. It all seemed so pathetically easy. It didn't make sense that 200 million other people weren't doing it. I thought, "If I can do that, then the sky is the limit.""

But in saying so today, Berube neglects to explain that once he passed the checks, he was eventually charged with at least 14 counts of larceny, larceny by false pretense, and forgery, in three Suffolk County courts. Included in the charges was $2,500 worth of payroll checks forged from Hugo's Lighthouse, where the memory of Berube lingers.

"Of all the boys who have worked here over the years, Eddie stands out," banquet manager Joanne Winters told a *Boston Globe* reporter last fall. "He was a little preppy, very personable. He always brought coffee to the women who did payroll, so of course they loved him." The money Berube illegally obtained during his three years in Boston went in part toward summer trips to Europe, Berube says.

In February 1978, Berube's father died of complications resulting from a heart attack. A blizzard buried the East, and Edgar Berube was stranded in Boston, missing the funeral. When he did return to Somersworth, he left at least 19 felonies and misdemeanors behind him and $14,000 in debts, according to court documents. Court records show that Berube completed probation on only one of his charges; a Boston probation clerk says outstanding warrants on probation defaults alone could net him at least two years in prison. The remaining cases were never resolved.

His father's death was traumatic, although, Berube says, "I never shed a tear. But from that point on I've tried to engage myself with the most difficult tasks. I spent an enormous amount of time studying up on things, only to leave them. I had to keep my mind occupied for 24 hours a day."

Several months later, after being put on probation again for a New Hampshire forgery, Berube's deceptions took on another dimension. He surfaced in Durham at the University of New Hampshire. There, he became Edward Kennedy III.

Berube's UNH identity was at first a ploy for admittance into a fraternity, he says. "When I used the name, I had no intention of pursuing it. I thought it would require an act of God to get into the fraternity, so I said,

'I'm Edward Kennedy.' I told them I would be taking courses at UNH, which I wasn't, and I signed a contract as a summer boarder as Edward Kennedy III. Doing it was a matter of necessity and, I guess, curiosity."

The ruse quickly snowballed. "I told three people at the beginning. The rest was carried by word of mouth," Berube recalls. Soon he was confronted with questions. At first uneasy, he simply answered inquiries about the Kennedys with a simple "family business."

"The more I didn't confirm anything, the more people would confirm it for me," Berube recalls in an interview. "People were satisfied because they think that's what being in the Kennedy family is supposed to be—mysterious." Yet Berube studied the role. He says he researched the Kennedys in *Forbes, Who's Who,* and a dozen books giving background, financial data, and significant events on the Kennedys.

"Then it was almost like I had a dossier on my mind," Berube says. "It became a matter of pressing a button for a certain date, name, event, and ad-libbing in between the facts. Everybody has different buttons you push to make them laugh, cry, smile, whatever. It's a matter of putting that into the way you act and react to situations." Just the same, Berube admits, "There were people who doubted. If you put A, B, and C together, things were very contradictory."

Daniel Manley, now a painting contractor, was one of those with misgivings. A student at UNH and chef at the Tin Palace restaurant, where Berube was employed from the start of his stay in Durham, Manley worked shoulder-to-shoulder with Berube. "I considered him a good friend," Manley says. "He confided in me, I thought, more than others." Manley remembers Berube sitting in the restaurant kitchen telling him his real name was Edward Kennedy III, not Edgar Berube. Manley thought it was a joke until Berube showed him a student identification card that had his picture with the Kennedy name, and another piece of Kennedy identification.

Though they were friends, Manley remained suspicious. By then he was more comfortable questioning Berube: If he was a Kennedy, why wasn't he using his real name? Berube told him the fake name was a cover, for security reasons.

Why was a Kennedy slinging burgers at the Tin Palace? Manley remembers asking. To keep a low profile, Berube responded, and because the Kennedys believe in getting a feel for what it's like to earn money instead of having it handed to them all the time.

But, Manley remembers telling Berube, you don't look like a Kennedy. You're out of shape, you're ugly, you're balding. I'm dying of cancer, Manley remembers Berube saying solemnly. The balding and his condition, Berube said, were from the treatment.

After a few weeks, Berube began using props to lend credence to his claims. Manley recalls. "He came into work one day in the fall and dropped hints that it was his birthday. Later on he was going through a notebook and nonchalantly handed me a card signed: 'Love, Caroline and John.'"

Berube's first clear performance error wasn't long after. Berube had told Manley he transferred from Cornell to UNH to save his family from unnecessary pain, worrying about his cancer. He figured the farther he was from them, the less grief family members would feel. At Cornell, he told Manley, he was on the tennis and lacrosse teams. Manley asked him if he wanted to play tennis with him one day. Berube agreed.

But Berube played poorly. Says Manley, "I thought, 'This guy is lying.' After the game the first thing he said was, 'Let's go out to dinner.' He knew. Then he flashed some money, which was typical. He would intensify his scheme on those who questioned him. People who questioned him were the ones he gave to—he increased buying you dinners, entertaining you, and even giving you money. He tried to reduce your curiosity, your desire and ability to question. That's what his con was."

Berube continued to make himself known as a Kennedy. Talk of his Aunt Jackie was accompanied by extravagant meals in Boston and tickets to sold-out rock concerts.

According to Manley, a student reported that Berube once arranged a trip to a New England Patriots game. An off-white limousine drove Berube and friends, leading a caravan of cars. They sat at the 50-yard line. (Berube, on the other hand, says they sat at the 20-yard line.) Again, according to news accounts and to Berube, no one but Berube paid a cent.

The same student remembers Berube picking up a $1,200 tab at a posh Boston hotel. Berube says it was closer to $300, but he concedes that when the waiter would not accept Berube's credit card because the card's $600 limit had been exceeded, Berube took him aside and suggested the waiter call his father, Senator Edward Kennedy, to straighten out the problem. The waiter accepted the card.

Manley finally made up his mind about Berube's credibility during a conversation with him on the way to a Berube-sponsored jaunt to a Boston Red Sox game. Manley and his roommates asked Berube specific questions about which Kennedy he was directly related to. Berube faltered, then changed his story and said he was the son of Joe Kennedy. (In fact, Joe Kennedy Jr. was killed in World War II and had no children.) Manley remembers a silence. The subject was dropped. The roommates knew Joe Kennedy had had no son. After that, says Manley, Berube kept his distance.

For others, there was still something to gain in believing Berube. "The bottom line of it for those who took this seriously was that people wanted a percentage of this," Berube says defensively. "I relied on their bragging as a marketing tool. I think a couple of them even said they went to the Hyannis compound for a weekend. To me, it's still the most fascinating thing. It proved the point that people look at heroes or legends and will put common sense aside to be a part of them. They were so hungry, so eager. It was a case of them wanting to be in Never-Never Land, Camelot Country. People say I had an identity problem—I think the students were just as bad." Recounting this, Berube sits back in his chair, shakes his head, and laughs, imagining the pictures on the living room walls of parents who photographed their sons and daughters with their arms around "Ed Kennedy."

The money bolstering Berube's reputation didn't come only from his wages at the Tin Palace. During his four-month stay in Durham, Berube says, he set up seven savings and checking accounts in three regional cities. He used each as a vehicle for kiting checks. Opening each account with about $300, he then waited for checks to be printed. Afterward, he wrote checks to himself, cash, or Edward Kennedy III. Other times he split deposited checks into new accounts. And as in Boston, he walked away with cash. When he overdrew one account, he wrote a check from another to cover it; sometimes it was good, sometimes it wasn't. He also forged applications for credit cards, using the name Edward Kennedy III, and drew money from them. And finally, he resorted to cashing stolen checks from fraternity members.

Although Berube says, "I had money to buy what I wanted when I wanted to buy it," he knew he was living on borrowed time. "I was robbing Peter to pay Paul to shut up John."

He soon lost control and perspective. "I knew the checks would bounce, but I wasn't worried. What it came down to was that I got into a role reversal where I immersed myself so deep that it came to a point that I didn't concern myself with the consequences."

One December evening in 1978 at a sorority party, Berube says, he drank all he could and swallowed 20 sedatives. He collapsed down a flight of stairs, and an ambulance took him to Wentworth-Douglass Hospital in Dover. Fraternity brothers told nurses he was a Kennedy. Berube had visited the hospital twice before as Edward Kennedy; his file was reopened. But unexpectedly, Berube says, a hospital official phoned the Kennedy Compound in Hyannis and was told there was no Edward Kennedy III, only an Edward Kennedy Jr., who was in Miami. Two sets of conflicting identification were also found on Berube. His ruse unraveled.

As front-page headlines in local papers touted Berube's exploits, he was indicted in two New Hampshire counties in connection with 17 felonies and misdemeanors for theft, forgery, and theft by deception. He again avoided a jury trial. In return for guilty pleas for more than 10 of the charges, most were continued for sentence pending his good behavior. On two of the felonies, he was ordered to serve one year in the Strafford County House of Correction and to pay almost $7,000 in restitution while on two years' probation.

Before the sentence, Berube was readmitted to the New Hampshire State Hospital Forensic Unit for a four-day evaluation. After examining notes from two interviews with Berube, psychiatric consultant Warren W. Burns, M.D., concluded in a February 1979 evaluation of Berube's sanity at the time of the alleged offenses, "His judgment appears to be poor." But, Burns wrote, "The alleged offenses do not appear to be related to or the product of mental illness." (Today Burns says that he doesn't remember Berube.)

Berube was discharged to the House of Correction. He completed his sentence the next year. Several months later, according to Berube, he again falsified New England College admission forms and was accepted for the fall 1980 semester. Once he arrived at the small college, word spread that he was the grandson of Occidental Petroleum founder Armand Hammer.

At New England College, Berube found proving his assumed identity was not as difficult as it had been at the University of New Hampshire. Being the grandson of Armand Hammer was a less impressive and less demanding role than being Edward Kennedy III. Individuals with comparable backgrounds were common at a private school like New England College. Berube even continued to use his given name.

"I didn't strain myself like I did for the Kennedy thing; they just took the ball and ran with it. That's not to say I didn't do any

research. I went to the library to look things up, and I had myself put on an Occidental Petroleum mailing list."

Berube continued to finance his image as he had a UNH. With money from financial aid and from a civil suit filed against Strafford County House of Correction for a fall down some stairs, Berube was able to put his money where his mouth was. "Oxy will pay for it" was commonly heard among friends and acquaintances whose meals and, in several cases, cross-country trips were paid for by Berube.

New England College spokesman Arnold Coda will not confirm Berube's accomplishments at the school, but other students say he was known among his peers as a diligent student leader with a knack for management. Students elected him a student government senator his first year, and he later became senate treasurer and president. His familiarity with finances and banking proved an asset. Along with organizing numerous charitable fund-raisers, Berube helped dig the student newspaper out of a large fiscal hole. Students also remember his ingenuity when it came to replacing cuts in the senate budget. His grades were high, and in 1982, Berube says, he won the school's Crimson Award for Outstanding Leadership. "I did a lot of things for the students on that campus." Talking in prison of how New England College officials now slight his achievements, he hangs his head, and his eyes fill with tears.

The college administration has filed a demand for an account of funds. Berube managed in the senate budget, and Coda will not discuss the details of the financial issues. But Berube does: While he conducted student affairs, he continued attending to personal interests. In 1981 the financial aid department received two letters drafted by Berube, according to the *New Hampshire Times* and to Berube. Both were written on Occidental Petroleum stationery that Berube had had printed. The first was purportedly signed by his mother and said she wished to donate $100 a month to the school beyond her son's academic costs. After a few $100 checks were received, the donations stopped. The second letter said Berube was the recipient of a $5,000 Occidental scholarship. Berube was being honored, the letter said, for being one of the five outstanding students in the nation. No check for the scholarship was ever received by the college, Berube says.

Berube knew that receiving letters from the likes of Occidental Petroleum was not out of the ordinary for New England College. He learned that even before his arrival, Hammer's philanthropy, including a substantial contribution to the school's library, had reached the college. Berube figured he was on safe ground.

By all outward appearances, Berube looked poised. Only a few close to him caught glimpses of a different Berube. "He was a very sensitive and quite an emotional person who would crack into tears fairly easily given some sort of stress," recalls his academic adviser. H. R. Monford Sayce.

At New England College, Berube began wearing a wig to cover his balding, and the cancer story circulated once more. He made convincing efforts to perpetuate it. "He claimed he was going for treatment," Sayce says. "He broke down crying a couple of times in my office. He did the same to other faculty members. It was a bid for sympathy. But it had reached the point that he needed people to believe his tales. It became a consuming passion to the extent that he not only believed them, he lived them and became them, which made it hard to detect the flaws."

Because of Berube's emotional outbursts, a member of the New England College faculty phoned Berube's mother and discovered discrepancies in Berube's stories. He was never directly confronted by the staff, but, Sayce says, Berube sensed their suspicion and withdrew his confidences.

Sayce speculates that compounding Berube's fervor and apprehension was his increasing cocaine use. First casually, ultimately compulsively, Berube began using cocaine in the summer of 1981. At first the cocaine was free, compliments of Berube's landlord in Henniker, George Russell. According to Berube, Russell provided unlimited amounts of the drug. Eventually, in return, Russell expected Berube to act as a distributor among students at the college. Lavishly and generously, Berube used, sold, and gave away the cocaine, according to friends and to Berube.

Berube soon had difficulty finding the money to pay for the cocaine Russell fronted him, and he was looking at tens of thousands of dollars in debts. "I was known as a coke connoisseur," Berube recalls, "and I was living a pretty excessive lifestyle. That also meant I owed a lot of money. By April 1982 I owed $14,000 to George Russell alone—more to other people."

According to Berube, from May through August 1982 he wrote a series of bad checks to Russell for the cocaine. Russell continued to front Berube the cocaine because of Berube's threats to "blow the lid off the whole thing," Berube says now. Armand Hammer's name, he adds, helped extend his credit.

Berube looked for a way out. By then, he had been elected senate president and appointed president of the New England College Pub, a privately owned tavern, and Berube had at his disposal the bank accounts of both. Under his own name and Armand Hammer's, Berube systematically opened bank accounts across the state. Deeper in debt, he wrote checks from his own accounts, using the Pub and senate accounts as guarantors. When his checks bounced, the money was taken from the other two accounts. He deposited the money he received in other accounts and again began kiting. "By the end," Berube says, "I used 31 bank accounts to write about $100,000 in checks."

In the summer of 1982 Berube felt the walls closing in. "I knew I couldn't have continued covering for another year," he says. "I was getting increasingly paranoid. It was like, you know, you're acting strange, you can see it, but you can't deal with changing it."

Instead of changing, Berube decided to eliminate part of the problem. During the fall of that year he went to the US Drug Enforcement Agency office in Concord, New Hampshire, and told officials the details of George Russell's business ventures. Berube introduced an undercover agent to Russell. The agent made a number of sizable cocaine buys. Russell was consequently arrested, convicted of distribution of cocaine, and sentenced to five years in federal prison.

Berube says, uncharacteristically, that at the time he was too disoriented to make a deal with agents in return for the cooperation. Shortly thereafter, in November 1982, he was arrested by Concord police—and ultimately charged with more than three dozen forgery, theft, and bad-check counts. Along with the New England College and Pub accounts, the charges ranged from forging other students' names on checks to buying plane tickets to West Palm Beach, Florida, with a check supposedly made out by Armand Hammer, according to court records. The court released Berube on $5,000 personal recognizance bail.

In addition, Concord National Bank, New England College Pub, and former New England College student Andrea Anderson filed civil suits against Berube. According to Berube's attorney, Norman Gile, and a bank official, summary judgments were made against Berube totaling more than $51,000.

As litigation began, Berube decided to finish school. From his mother's home he applied to Iowa State University. He was accepted and started classes in January 1983. Berube says he soon began pledging a fraternity, chairing the homecoming finance committee, and working for the university's financial aid department. But in June 1983 his arrests were discovered, and he was asked to leave the school.

Berube says that before leaving, he crafted another college transcript for himself and wrote a letter, purporting to be from Yolanda DuPont, inquiring about donation procedures, and applied to Beloit College in Wisconsin. Saying he was a member of the DuPont family, Berube recalls, he was accepted in a week, and he moved to a Holiday Inn in Beloit. He was not particularly concerned with his academic career. "The only reason I went there was because I needed money," Berube says now. "I knew court and other expenses were coming up."

In the meantime, he missed a pretrial hearing in Merrimack County Superior Court, and a warrant was issued for his arrest in New Hampshire. After enrolling at Beloit and receiving college identification establishing him as a Beloit resident, Berube withdrew nonexistent funds totaling almost $3,000. (Wisconsin authorities confirm Berube's account, and they have charged Berube with theft by fraud. A warrant has been issued for his arrest.) Anticipating court dates, he returned to his mother's home in Somersworth, where he was later arrested.

During a pretrial hearing on the 38 forgery, theft, and bad-check counts in November 1983, Berube told Superior Court Judge William F. Cann of an $8,000 per month cocaine habit while at New England College and of a drug-abuse history dating back to the mid-1970s. His claims were backed by psychiatrist Henry Wolstat, who wrote a letter to the court saying Berube was drug-dependent and suicidal. (Reached this month in Portsmouth, New Hampshire, Dr. Wolstat declined to comment on Berube's case.)

When negotiations were completed, Berube pleaded guilty to 10 class A felony counts of forgery, theft, and bad checks totaling $53,956. He was sentenced December 15, 1983, by Judge Cann to two $7\frac{1}{2}$- to 15-year sentences—the second suspended upon good behavior and on the condition he seek help for his drug problem.

In June 1984 the Classification Department of the New Hampshire State Prison received two documents intended for Edgar Berube's file. The first was apparently a motion to reduce Berube's sentence; the second appeared to be an order from Judge Cann actually reducing the sentence to $1\frac{1}{2}$ to three years. The papers were processed.

At the end of September another document supposedly issued by Cann was put in Berube's file. It was a "decision" that read, in part, "I order that the defendant be discharged from the sentence imposed and that the defendant be discharged to the drug treatment program Turnabout." Berube was released.

After visiting his mother, Berube took a bus to Boston, where he obtained identification saying he was Peter T. Kern, heir to a family food fortune, and a PGA golfer. Berube was eventually tracked to Seattle, Washington, where he reportedly used a document bearing a seal he had had made to withdraw $5,000 from an account he opened at the Rainier Bank. Berube had fled to Colorado by the time the bank officials began investigating the loss and contacted the Boston law firm of Ropes & Gray, because the seal on the document contained the firm's name and location. John England, an official at Ropes & Gray, happened to recognize that the zip code on the seal was incorrect and apparently associated that mistake with another case Berube had been involved in. England contacted Mer-

rimack County prosecutor Michael Johnson. Berube was recaptured soon thereafter.

In a telephone interview with the *Globe* in November 1984, from jail in Colorado, where he was awaiting extradition, Berube said he did not forge the documents and claimed his release was legal.

At one time, authorities wondered if Berube acted alone. Johnson, however, claims he did, with the help of typewriter correction fluid, old court documents, and a prison typewriter. He adds that Berube had access to the prison law library and a copying machine.

Still, the questions of exactly how the documents got to the Classification Department remain. By mail? Delivered by hand? How? By whom? The answers probably won't be known before November, the earliest time attorneys say Berube will be tried on four counts of forgery and one count of escape.

25

Probability of Punishment and Suppression of Behavior in Psychopathic and Nonpsychopathic Offenders

Richard A. Siegel

To investigate the hypothesis that psychopathic offenders would show less suppression of behavior as a function of punishment at varying levels of probability, three groups of subjects were selected. Fifty criminal offenders were divided into two groups of psychopathic and nonpsychopathic offenders based on clinical ratings. A third group of nonoffenders was also used. A probability-learning card game was developed that consisted of 10 different levels of punishment probability, with the punishment based on the response-cost technique of removing reinforcers (chips redeemable for money). A measure of suppression was obtained from the reduction of subjects' response rates. Results are reported that show psychopathic offenders to produce the least suppression and the lowest winnings, with these findings attributed to the psychopaths being least responsive when the probability of punishment is most uncertain. Additional data are presented to indicate that these results are best explained in terms of cognitive factors, with the element of magical or superstitious logic proposed as a major pathognomic characteristic of psychopathy.

In recent years, there has been an increasing amount of interest in experimental studies of conditioning and learning in psychopathic criminal offenders. Drawing upon the clinical formulations of Cleckley (1964), much of the emphasis has been on psychopaths' reported inability to profit from experience and their lack of response to punishment. Thus, Hare (1970), for example, has reviewed many of his own studies and those of other investigators and has concluded that ample evidence exists to support the hypothesis that psychopaths are deficient in such processes as autonomic arousal, aversive conditioning, and avoidance learning in comparison with other, nonpsychopathic offenders. Consistent with such studies, Eysenck (1964) has proposed that constitutional weaknesses in the psychophysiological processes underlying autonomic arousal may be the key pathogenic factor in psychopathy.

Most of these studies have been conducted within the framework of either classical conditioning or negative reinforcement–avoidance learning models. However, they have obvious implications for a theory

Richard A. Siegel. Probability of Punishment and Suppression of Behavior in Psychopathic and Nonpsychopathic Offenders. *Journal of Abnormal Psychology*, 1978, Vol. 87, No. 5, pp. 514–522. Copyright © 1978 by the American Psychological Association. Reprinted by permission of the publisher and the author.

of punishment constructed within the guidelines proposed by Azrin and Holz (1966), who have proposed a definition of punishment in terms of the power of a stimulus to produce a reduction in the future probability of a response. Church (1963) and Estes (1969) have argued that conditioned emotional reactions are the basis of punishment, so if deficits in autonomic arousal and conditionability interfere with the acquisition of conditioned emotional reactions, it would follow that such deficits would also be associated with diminished suppression in response to punishment. Since there is abundant evidence of such deficits in psychopathic offenders, one can predict that punishment would produce less suppression with these individuals.

However, there are reasons to believe that the suppressive effect of punishment on psychopathic offenders may be a more complex phenomenon. Even though the investigations of autonomic conditioning have produced results consistent with clinical descriptions of the psychopath as incorrigible (Maher, 1966) and unaffected by the sanctions of criminal justice (Cleckley, 1964), many of these same clinical formulations also emphasize the manipulative and deceptive tactics of psychopaths that are designed to avoid or escape impending punishment.

One factor that might reconcile these seemingly contradictory views is suggested by a study showing that many delinquent boys, aware of the uncertain odds of being apprehended by the police, would often conclude that they would not in fact be caught, a belief described as based on a "magical immunity mechanism" (Claster, 1967). Thus, it can be argued that psychopaths do indeed respond to punishment when it is a virtual certainty but fail to respond when it is uncertain, believing instead in their own immunity. This factor, which we can call the probability of punishment, is clearly relevant to the real world of crime and punishment, where prevailing rates of arrest and conviction are low enough that the probability of punishment is highly uncertain. Zimring (1971), in his analysis of the concept of deterrence in criminal justice, has called for

more research into what he terms deterrence-related personality traits, among which he includes the subjective appreciation of the probability or credibility of punishment.

In a study of the effects of probability of punishment with psychopathic offenders, Hare (1966) showed that inclusion of this variable produces differences between psychopathic and nonpsychopathic subjects in their preference for immediate versus delayed pain. However, in that study the experimental factor was pain, not punishment in the sense proposed by Azrin and Holz (1966). Thus, the effects of varying probabilities of punishment on the suppression of behavior of psychopaths have not yet been systematically investigated. The present study was designed to test the hypothesis that psychopathic offenders will show increasingly less suppression as a consequence of punishment as the probability of punishment becomes increasingly uncertain than either nonpsychopathic offenders or nonoffenders.

Method

Subjects

The offender subjects were patients at the Treatment Center for Sexually Dangerous Persons, a facility jointly operated by the Massachusetts Departments of Corrections and Mental Health, in Bridgewater, Massachusetts. These patients were all men with a history of conviction for various aggressive sexual offenses who had been committed to the treatment center indefinitely. Most of them had a record of multiple arrests and convictions for both sexual and nonsexual crimes. After the experimental procedure was approved by an institutional Human Rights Committee, all patients were informed of the nature and purpose of the research and were invited to participate. Out of a total population of 97, 57 patients consented to participate as subjects.

The classification method employed was similar to that used in the several studies by

Hare (1970). A checklist was constructed consisting of 14 of Cleckley's (1964) 16 criteria for psychopathy (the other 2, absence of psychosis and good intelligence, were excluded because the former was a selection criterion and the latter was used separately to equate the two offender groups). This checklist was then filled out by each patient's principal therapist, with each item presented on a 7-point scale from 1 (never) to 7 (always). This yielded a psychopathy score with a possible range from 14 to 98.

Two checks on reliability were conducted: a test–retest procedure, with therapists filling out the checklist a second time 3 weeks after the first, and an interrater reliability procedure using a second therapist for each patient. Because second therapists were available for only a portion of the patient sample, and because some therapists declined to fill out ratings more than once on a patient, the samples for these reliability checks were considerably smaller than the total sample. The reliability correlations obtained were +.85 ($n = 12$) for test–retest and +.72 ($n = 22$) for interrater reliability.

Of the original 57 who consented to participate, 7 subjects with a history of psychosis or mental retardation or who had been at the treatment center too brief a time for ratings to be made were excluded, leaving a final sample of 50. This sample was divided into two groups of 25 each: those above the median psychopathy score of 53 forming the psychopathic (P) offender group, and those at or below the median forming the nonpsychopathic (NP) offender group, with mean psychopathy scores of 65.8 and 45.0, respectively.[1]

To compare these two groups, mean ages, months at the treatment center, and IQ were

calculated. The latter were obtained from therapists' estimates on a 7-point scale, since IQ data in case records were highly variable in terms of type of test used, date of test administration, and availability of scores. The respective results were 31.5, 60.6, and 3.5 for Group P, and 30.7, 59.9 and 3.8 for Group NP. None of the differences between groups was significant. The age of these subjects was very similar to that of the subjects used by Hare (1966, 1970) in his studies, and the IQ was apparently only slightly lower.

A partial check on the validity of this classification of subjects as psychopathic and nonpsychopathic was made possible by the fact that at the time of this study the mental health staff of the center had just completed a tier classification of all patients into minimum, moderate, and maximum privilege status based on their current adjustment at the institution. Nineteen of the subjects in Group P (76%) were classified as minimum, whereas only 4 from Group NP (16%) were so classified ($\chi^2 = 9.02, p < .025$). Since the factors employed in the tier-classification procedure was closely related to the criteria used in this study's ratings for psychopathy, these data support the validity of that measure.

A sample of nonoffenders was drawn from two sources. Nineteen college undergraduates from psychology courses at the University of Lowell were recruited on a volunteer basis, and six male staff workers from the treatment center and from the Veterans Administration Hospital at Bedford, Massachusetts were similarly obtained. At each institution, potential subjects were provided the same descriptive information about the study as had been given the patients at the treatment center. The mean age for this nonoffender (NO) group was 28.9, not significantly different from the means for Groups P and NP. The age distribution for all three groups was roughly bimodal, with one subgroup in the 18–24 year range and another in the 35–45 year range. A test of the correlation of age with the dependent variables of this study yielded nonsignificant results. IQ estimates were not obtained for

---

[1] In the actual data analyses of this study, the independent variable of *psychopathy* was treated as both a groups variable (psychopathic, nonpsychopathic, and nonoffender) and also as a continuous variable in correlation analyses, using the actual psychopathy scores obtained from the clinical ratings. These correlational analyses, while yielding results in the predicted directions, never achieved statistical significance, and thus they have not been reported.

Group NO, nor were there any ratings for psychopathy.

Materials

For this study, a probability game was developed based on the probability-learning studies of Myers, Fort, Katz, and Suydam (1963) and the response–cost method of punishment employed by Weiner (1962). The materials for this game consisted of 11 specially arranged decks of standard playing cards and a set of standard poker chips. The choice of ordinary and familiar materials reflected a deliberate attempt to maximize subjects' interest and ease with the experiment.

Since the response-cost method of punishment functions through the removal of a reinforcer, the playing cards were divided into two categories: those that would signal the delivery of the reinforcer (the poker chips), and those that would signal the removal of the reinforcer. For ease of recognition, the number cards (ace through 10) were designated as reward cards, and the face cards (jack, queen, and king) were designated as punishment cards. Each of the eleven decks consisted of 40 cards, with percentages of punishment cards varying in 10% increments from 0% to 100%. The poker chips used as the reinforcement were set at a value of 1 cent each and were redeemed for cash or credit at the end of the experiment for each subject.

Procedure

The design for this experiment was a 3×11 analysis of variance with repeated measures. Subjects from all three groups were tested through all 11 conditions of probability of punishment, with offender and nonoffender subjects tested during alternate weeks. For the offenders, the experimenter was kept blind as to their group status.

The experimental procedure was identical for all subjects. To obtain their informed consent, subjects were first told that this was a study to investigate the relationship between "various personality characteristics" and subjects' "response to a game that involves their skill in estimating odds where they will win or lose money based on their method of playing the game." The treatment center subjects were also told that their decision to participate or not, as well as all results of the experiment, would be confidential, and would in no way affect their status at the institution. Following this, subjects were then given an explanation of the rules of the game, as follows:

I have a game we're going to play in which you have a chance to win some money, which you will be allowed to keep. We will be using these chips, which are worth one cent apiece. At the end of the game I'll cash you in.

We will begin with this deck of cards [the zero percent deck]. I am going to place the deck in front of you face down. Each time you turn over the top card you will receive one chip. This is our way of providing you a stake for the game so you don't have to put up your own money. . . .

We are going to continue the game with ten more decks of cards. However, these decks consist of both number cards (ace through ten) as in the first deck, and also face cards (jack, queen, and king). Each time you turn over a number card you will be rewarded with one chip, but each time you turn over a face card you will be punished by losing one chip.

Each of the ten decks we will use is different. Some of the decks contain a lot of number cards and few face cards, which means you could win a lot, while others contain a lot of face cards and fewer number cards, which means you could lose a lot. We will use all ten decks in this game, but you do not have to play all the cards in a deck. Once I put a deck in front of you and tell you to begin, you start to turn the cards over one at a time. You may continue to play through the deck, turning over all the cards, or you may decide to stop at any time. When you have either played through the deck or indicated that you wish to stop, we will go on to the next

deck, and so on until we have played all ten decks.

These 10 decks were presented to subjects in random order, with the subjects allowed to choose each deck. All decks were shuffled by the experimenter before being played. Although a predetermined balanced order of decks and cards might have been more precise, this procedure was adopted to increase the subjects' belief in the fairness of the game. A post hoc check on order of decks revealed no significant differences between groups.

At two points during the game, subjects were asked two questions. The first concerned their recall of the percentage of punishment cards turned over in the deck they had just played. The second asked them to estimate the chances that the next card from that deck would be a punishment card. These questions were asked immediately after the playing of the 30% and 70% decks.

After completion of the game, subjects counted their chips and were cashed in. The entire procedure lasted approximately 25 minutes.

Measure of Suppression

The dependent variable of this study is the degree of suppression of subjects' card-playing behavior at different probabilities of punishment. Since each deck consisted of 40 cards, the number of cards in each deck not played by a subject represents the number of potential responses suppressed. The ratio of this number to the maximum of 40 yielded a measure of the suppression percentage. However, in keeping with the usual emphasis in operant research on the rate of responding, an intermediate step was followed. For each subject, the time needed to play all 40 cards in the first deck (which was always the 0% deck) was used as a baseline time. For the remaining 10 decks, subjects were allowed to take as much time as they wanted, but only the number of cards not played within the baseline time limit was used to calculate the actual *suppression rate*.

The data on total cards not played, regardless of time, were also retained, but since these data yielded almost identical results, they are not presented here to avoid redundancy.

Two additional measures were derived from the game. Net *winnings* was the total of chips earned by each subject at the end of the game. *Tolerance for punishment* was the sum of all 10 decks of the longest consecutive sequence of punishment cards played in each deck.

Results

As a test of the general hypothesis that psychopathic offenders will show less suppression to punishment than either nonpsychopathic offenders or nonoffenders, the mean of the suppression rates for all 10 decks was calculated for each subject, and then the group means for P, NP, and NO. A 1 × 3 analysis of variance was significant, $F(2, 72) = 9.80$, $p < .01$. Differences between means were tested using Scheffé's test of multiple comparisons, and as predicted, the mean suppression rate for Group P (38.44) was significantly lower than the means for Groups NP and NO (49.60 and 51.00; $p < .001$).

These results are consistent with the findings of Hare (1970) that psychopathic offenders are less responsive to punishment than nonpsychopathic offenders and that nonpsychopathic offenders and nonoffenders tend to be very similar in their responses.

The specific hypothesis of this study, that psychopathic offenders would show more nearly equivalent amounts of suppression at the highest and lowest levels of probability of punishment but would show significantly less suppression at moderate levels in comparison to nonpsychopathic offenders and nonoffenders, was tested by employing the suppression rates for each of the decks in a 3 × 11 trend analysis of variance. The linear, quadratic and residual trends were analyzed, with the interaction of Groups × Trials (probability levels) as the critical term. The mean suppression rates for Groups

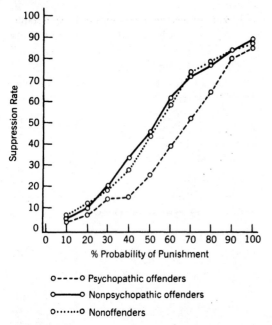

o----o Psychopathic offenders

o———o Nonpsychopathic offenders

o·······o Nonoffenders

FIGURE 1

Suppression as a function of probability of punishment for psychopathic, nonpsychopathic, and nonoffender groups.

P, NP, and NO for each probability level are represented graphically in Figure 1. There was a significant interaction of Groups × Levels, $F(2, 72) = 8.86$, $P < .005$.

As can be seen in Figure 1, Group P does in fact show the greatest deficit in suppres-

sion at the moderate levels of probability (between 40% and 70%), while being virtually equivalent to the other groups when the probability of punishment is more certain (10%, 20%, 30%, and 100%). Individual 1 × 11 trend analyses for the quadratic trend with Groups NP and NO were not significant, $F(1, 24) = .13$ and $.01$, respectively, but were significant for Group P, $F(1, 24) = 20.52$, $p < .001$. Table 1 presents the means, standard deviations, and Fs from a 1 × 3 analysis of variance for suppression rate scores at each of the 10 probability levels with all three groups. The largest differences between groups are found at the 50%, 60%, and 70% levels.

Using tolerance for punishment as a further measure of suppression, a 1 × 3 analysis of variance was significant, $F(2, 72) = 5.12$, $p < .01$. Scheffé's test of multiple comparisons on the means for P, NP, and NO (42.7, 35.5, and 35.2) showed psychopathic subjects most willing to tolerate long consecutive sequences of punishment cards.

Subjects' scores for winning, which can be regarded as a measure of their degree of success in playing the game, also produced significant differences between groups, $F(2, 72 = 3.59$, $p < .05$. Scheffé's test for differences between the means of Group P, NP, and NO (81.2, 91.2, and 88.6) showed psy-

TABLE 1 Mean Suppression Rate Scores for Levels of Probability (in Percent) for Psychopathic, Nonpsychopathic, and Nonoffender Groups

Level	Psychopathic		Nonpsychopathic		Nonoffender		
	M	SD	M	SD	M	SD	F[a]
10	3.56	7.85	6.96	10.94	7.28	9.22	1.20
20	6.52	14.93	9.64	14.43	10.96	14.29	.61
30	14.12	19.77	20.00	25.11	19.80	17.88	.61
40	15.72	16.60	33.00	29.99	27.64	22.94	3.45*
50	25.36	24.23	45.92	28.43	44.92	28.46	4.57**
60	39.52	32.85	60.00	24.82	58.28	25.42	4.12**
70	51.64	31.27	71.56	12.10	72.72	20.25	6.86***
80	64.04	26.52	76.60	11.23	78.84	14.75	4.56**
90	80.32	11.99	83.48	6.08	83.48	6.25	1.14
100	85.60	6.94	88.48	4.71	87.60	9.10	1.07

[a]$df = 2, 72$.   *$p < .05$.   **$p < .025$.   ***$p < .01$.

TABLE 2 Mean Scores for Recalled and Estimated Probabilities (in Percent) for Psychopathic, Nonpsychopathic, and Nonoffender Groups

	Psychopathic		Nonpsychopathic		Nonoffender		
Probability	M	SD	M	SD	M	SD	F^a
Recalled							
30	31.22	26.85	32.77	20.91	30.26	21.66	.68
70	72.43	18.49	70.62	15.77	73.51	17.27	.92
Estimated							
30	27.77	22.46	30.78	19.65	26.99	20.24	1.78
70	55.21	23.29	69.11	17.73	71.20	19.88	3.52*

$^a df = 2, 72.$ $^*p < .05.$

chopathic subjects winning the least, a function of their responses at levels above 50% punishment. Since Group P subjects showed greater diminishing of suppression at the higher levels than at the lower levels, the net effect was to reduce their net winnings below the levels for Groups NP and NO. Thus, if we use winnings as an index of adaptiveness, psychopathic offenders are not only deviant in their response to varying levels of probability of punishment, they are also maladaptive, since their style of responding costs them money. This is illustrated by the fact that on 12 occasions, Group P subjects

played 10 or more punishment cards in succession, which happened only twice for Group NP.

In an attempt to offer at least a partial explanation for why these differences between groups exist, we can look at two additional sets of data. The first set comes from the results of the two questions that subjects were asked during the game, presented in Table 2. The first question, asking subjects for their recall of the number of punishment cards played, shows no differences between groups, indicating that failure of memory cannot account for the differences in playing

TABLE 3 Mean Ratings for Psychopathy Criteria for Psychopathic and Nonpsychopathic Groups

	Psychopathic		Nonpsychopathic		
Criterion	M	SD	M	SD	t^a
Anxiety	3.67	1.93	4.53	1.51	1.72
Unreliability	3.58	1.55	2.30	1.32	3.09**
Manipulation	3.54	1.34	2.53	1.41	2.65*
Guilt	3.33	1.28	3.88	1.61	1.31
Antisocial behavior	3.42	1.26	2.50	1.32	2.48*
Impulsivity	5.92	1.76	3.78	1.37	4.71***
Egocentricity	4.42	1.55	3.08	1.24	3.32**
Shallowness	5.00	1.89	3.98	1.39	2.14*
Lack of insight	5.42	1.44	3.58	1.49	4.37***
Nonconformity	4.55	1.39	3.33	1.17	3.30**
Loss of control with alcohol	5.18	2.08	2.89	1.77	4.12***
Depression	3.33	1.20	2.83	1.33	1.37
Impersonal sex	5.55	1.23	4.18	1.54	3.42**
Need for immediate gratification	5.92	1.44	3.93	1.30	5.05***

^{a}Two-tailed t value at $p < .05 = 2.01.$ $^*p < .05.$ $^{**}p < .01.$ $^{***}p < .001.$

the game. The second question, however, does produce differences between groups for their estimate of the probability of being punished on the next card from the 70% deck. Subjects in Group P consistently underestimated their probability of being punished, which conforms to Claster's (1967) description of the magical immunity mechanism and to Cleckley's (1964) discussion of the magical and quasi-delusional thought processes typical of psychopathy.

The second set of data, presented in Table 3, was derived from the 14 individual criteria of psychopathy used to classify subjects into groups. The means of the therapists' ratings for each of these criteria were calculated for Groups P and NP, and these means, along with the standard deviations and t values, are given in Table 3. As can be seen, the three criteria involving affect (nervous, guilty, depressed) are not significantly different between groups. In contrast, those criteria showing the greatest differences (impulsive, lack of insight, loss of control when intoxicated, and need for immediate gratification) can all be thought of as involving a cognitive/behavioral framework similar to that advocated by Mahoney (1977).

Discussion

The results of this study provide very strong evidence in support of the central hypothesis that the diminished responsiveness to punishment among psychopathic offenders is greatest when the probability of punishment is highly uncertain. Although this hypothesis was derived in part from the experimental work of Hare (1975), the results taken as a whole represent an important departure from his model. First, this study failed to show any significant difference between psychopathic subjects and others when the probability of punishment was a near certainty. Second, the data for the individual criteria of psychopathy failed to show any special importance to affective factors (anxiety, guilt, depression) that can be thought of as related to the psychophysiological

dimension that Hare has emphasized. Even though the correlational nature of these data make any causal inference very tentative, the apparent importance of the cognitive/behavioral dimension cannot be overlooked.

This last point takes on added interest in the light of the results from the questions on subjects' estimates of the future probability of punishment. Cleckley (1964) and Maher (1966) have described the quality of "superstitious" logic that may play a major role in the deviant response to punishment of psychopaths. Some informal, anecdotal data collected during the experimental procedure illustrate this point. As the subjects played the game, they frequently made spontaneous comments, and these were recorded as nearly verbatim as possible. Five subjects made comments that were unmistakably superstitious; for example, one subject, after turning over a queen, said, "I never have any luck with the ladies, I think I'll quit." All five of these subjects were from Group P. A sixth subject employed what he called his "ESP" by feeling the cards before turning them, while another subject refused to play even one card from one deck because he didn't "like the feel of it," and both these subjects were also from Group P.

The use of the operant framework in this study in contrast to the classical conditioning framework employed by Hare (1975) also deserves further comment, since it seems to lead to two definite advantages. First, it allows for a more direct investigation of punishment in terms of the variable most important to criminal justice, suppression (or deterrence), rather than in terms of underlying or intermediate variables like autonomic arousal or conditioned emotional reactions. Second, the nature of the operant method provides a check on factors that can often contaminate autonomic conditioning studies. The use of an observable response such as the turning of cards, which can be easily counted, eliminates the uncertain variability of psychophysiological measures (Hare, 1972). The use of a baseline time measure eliminates the effect of variations in individual responding, and the absence of differences in suppression at the highest and lowest levels of probability excludes the possibility of individual differences between subjects in the perceived strength of the reinforcer or the punishment.

There is, however, one way in which the results of this study are very much in keeping with the model used by Hare (1975). His work has been one of the major reasons why the often criticized concept of psychopathy has begun to reestablish scientific credibility. This present study, by also producing strongly significant differences between psychopathic offenders and other groups, adds further support to the viability of the concept of psychopathy.

There are some words of caution that should be mentioned at this point. As Hare (1975) and Widom (1977) have pointed out, this study, like so many others, is limited by its use of only institutionalized male offenders; whether these results would also apply to noninstitutionalized or female offenders cannot be inferred. Moreover, it is certainly possible that the treatment center population is not typical of offenders in the usual correctional facilities—a point that may account for the lack of importance of the affective factors evident in Table 3.

Furthermore, the predicted relationship between psychopathy and diminished response to punishment describes only a correlation between these two characteristics, so that any presumption of causality is premature. However, Maher (1966) and Ullman and Krasner (1975) have both reviewed social learning models of psychopathy derived from studies showing erratic and inconsistent discipline to be common in the family background of psychopaths, and such a form of discipline might be seen as the precursor of later deviant responses to punishment.

Finally, there are the limitations inherent in the specific methodology used. One cannot simply assume that a subject's method of playing a game under experimental conditions for token amounts of money would predict a person's strategy in dealing with real-life situations. In addition, this study employed immediate reward and punishment, with the magnitude of reward and punishment equivalent. The effects of increasing the size of the possible loss or gain, of delaying either the reward or punishment, or of altering the ratio between them cannot yet be determined but should prove a fruitful basis for future research.

References

AZRIN, N. H., AND HOLZ, W. C. Punishment. In W. K. HONIG (Ed.), *Operant behavior*. New York: Appleton-Century-Crofts, 1966.

CHURCH, R. M. The varied effects of punishment on behavior. *Psychological Review*, 1963, *70*, 369–402.

CLASTER, D. S. Comparison of risk-perception between delinquents and nondelinquents. *Journal of Criminal Law, Criminology, and Police Science*, 1967, *58*, 80–86.

CLECKLEY, H. *The mask of sanity* (4th ed.). St. Louis, Mo.: Mosby, 1964.

ESTES, W. K. Outline of a theory of punishment. In B. A. CAMPBELL AND R. M. CHURCH (Eds.), *Punishment and aversive behavior*. New York: Meredith, 1969.

EYSENCK, H. J. *Crime and personality*. London: Methuen, 1964.

HARE, R. D. Preference for delay of shock as a function of its intensity and probability. *Psychonomic Science*, 1966, *5*, 393–394.

HARE, R. D. *Psychopathy: Theory and research*. New York: Wiley, 1970.

HARE, R. D. Psychopathy and physiological responses to adrenalin. *Journal of Abnormal Psychology*, 1972, *79*, 138–147.

HARE, R. D. Psychopathy. In P. VENABLES AND M. CHRISTIE (Eds.), *Research in psychophysiology*. New York: Wiley, 1975.

MAHER, B. A. *Principles of psychopathology*. New York: McGraw-Hill, 1966.

MAHONEY, M. J. Reflections on the cognitive-learning trend in psychotherapy. *American Psychologist*, 1977, *32*, 5–13.

MYERS, J. L., FORT, J. G., KATZ, L., AND SUYDAM, M. M. Differential monetary gains and losses and event probability in a two-choice situation. *Journal of Experimental Psychology*, 1963, *66*, 521–522.

ULLMANN, L., AND KRASNER, L. *A psychological approach to abnormal behavior* (2nd ed.). Englewood Cliffs, N.J.: Prentice-Hall, 1975.

WEINER, H. Some effects of response cost upon humans' operant behavior. *Journal of the Experimental Analysis of Behavior*, 1962, *5*, 201–208.

WIDOM, C. S. A methodology for studying non-institutionalized psychopaths. *Journal of Consulting and Clinical Psychology*, 1977, *45*, 674–683.

ZIMRING, F. E. *Perspectives on deterrence*. Rockville, Md.: Department of Health Education and Welfare Publication No. (ADM) 74–10, 1971.

26

Epidemiology of Drug Abuse: An Overview

Nicholas J. Kozel and Edgar H. Adams

Issues regarding the use of epidemiology in drug abuse research are discussed and systems for monitoring national trends and identifying risk factors are described. Data indicate a general decline in marijuana use among youth, a cohort aging effect among heroin and marijuana users, and increased prevalence and health consequences associated with cocaine use.

The application of epidemiology to the study of drug abuse is relatively recent. Despite the long history of drug abuse in society, the use of the epidemiologic approach to study this complex public health problem began in earnest less than two decades ago. It was during the outbreak of heroin abuse in the late 1960's that the use of the term "epidemic" to describe drug abuse came into vogue. Although most of the scientific community recognized both the validity and the benefit inherent in using the tools of the epidemiologist in understanding and addressing the problem of drug abuse during

Nicholas J. Kozel and Edgar H. Adams. Epidemiology of Drug Abuse: An Overview. *Science*, Vol. 234, pp. 970–974, November 21, 1986. Copyright © 1986 by the American Association for the Advancement of Science. Reprinted by permission of the publisher and authors.

that era (1–8), the introduction of the technique was not without its critics (9, 10).

One focus of concern during that time was that the initial introduction of drugs into the body was voluntary. This was contrasted with diseases involuntarily contracted that were being investigated by the traditional medical epidemiology model. It was argued by some that since drug abuse was a self-imposed condition, it was automatically excluded from the jurisdiction of the epidemiologist, whose imperative was to study infectious disease. In response, Greene made a strong case that heroin addiction was a communicable disease in the classical sense, with the drug itself being the infectious agent, the host and reservoir being man, and the drug-using peer as the vector (11).

Another major concern of the day was the potential for indiscriminate use of quarantine (in this case also known as incarceration) as a preventative against the spread of drug abuse to the general population. This argument centered on the conclusion, held inevitable by some, that drug abusers once identified would be automatically imprisoned. Neither of these objections stimulated much action beyond debate and posed no serious impediment to the efficacious introduction of epidemiology to the study of drug abuse.

There was also much discussion about whether drug abuse more closely paralleled a chronic relapsing disease or an acute disease pattern. The popular view was that drug abuse was a unidimensional phenomenon, that is, no distinction was made between the type of drugs used, etiology, and populations at risk. There was an attempt to classify drug-using behavior into one of two apparently distinct categories. More recently, the recognition of the wide differences in classes of drugs abused and the diversity of abuser populations point up even further distinctions in the underlying motivations for initial use and resultant adverse health consequences. Over the years drug abuse has moved from the position of being challenged as an appropriate object for epidemiologic study to challenging the creativity of epidemiology itself.

Recent history shows that in contrast to the issues in which drug abuse differs from other types of epidemiologic investigation, the areas of similarity are immediately evident. Drug abusers demonstrate patterns of behavior that can be measured, incidence curves can be drawn, rates of prevalence can be computed, attack rates can be calculated, risk factors can be identified, etiologies and consequences can be determined, and prevention programs can be implemented.

As with most social behavior, the etiology of drug abuse is complex, varying through time, by geographic region, and by demographic characteristics. The underlying causes of drug abuse are as diverse as the populations that they affect. Peer pressure, curiosity, depression, hedonism, attempts to increase or improve performance, rebellion, alienation, and a wide variety of other reasons have been cited as responsible for abuse of substances ranging from solvents to stimulants to opiates. Changes have been observed in the types of drugs abused both in national waves as well as regional and localized ripples, from marijuana in the 1960's through heroin in the 1970's to cocaine in the 1980's.

Risk factors change and are subject to the same demographic and geographic variations that affect other aspects of drug abuse. The factors that placed populations at high risk for heroin abuse in the late 1960's and early 1970's have changed dramatically in the 1980's. In the earlier period, the profile of a heroin addict was a male in the middle to late teens who was initiated into heroin use during the previous several years, disproportionately from minority groups, and living in an inner city area. In the mid-1980's, the heroin addict population still is composed primarily of males, but in their early to mid-30's, the majority of whom have a history of heroin abuse that extends back to the late 1960's and early 1970's. They are, in fact, the earlier use cohort.

Not only are certain populations at risk for abuse of specific types of drugs, but drug abuse itself constitutes an antecedent condition for other adverse health consequences. Thus, intravenous drug abusers are at high risk for contracting acquired immune deficiency syndrome (AIDS) as well as a host of other diseases. The consequences of drug abuse vary just as widely and change just as substantially over time. Changes in patterns of abuse, such as engaging in more dangerous routes of administration, increasing dosage units, or using drugs in combination, increase vulnerability to toxic effect. For example, the recent domestic cultivation of sinsemilla marijuana has introduced much higher levels of tetrahydrocannabinol into the marijuana-abusing population, thus increasing the amount of psychoactive substance ingested and the probability of acute adverse health consequences. In addition, social and psychological problems resulting from chronic cocaine abuse have been identified that were totally unsuspected just a few years ago. In fact, the compulsive drug-seeking behavior associated with cocaine abuse has led to a redefinition of the term "addiction," which previously had been restricted to the physical withdrawal symptoms resulting from opiate and depressant dependence.

Measurement Issues

Measurement of the drug abuse problem is complicated by the fact that drug abuse is an illicit behavior and that populations of interest may not be studied by traditional research methodologies. In addition, drug abuse itself may be considered a deviant behavior or it may be considered a disease (that is, addiction), or, as mentioned above, it may be regarded as an antecedent to a disease, such as AIDS, subacute bacterial endocarditis, and others. In the first case, the population at risk is the general population of the United States. In the second case, the population at risk might be defined as those who had abused a certain drug more than a given number of times and, in the third case, the population at risk might be defined as intravenous (IV) drug abusers.

Analytical epidemiology has been used on many occasions to document specific risk factors associated with drug abuse (12–14), but findings in this paper are based on data from national drug abuse surveillance programs. One of the most effective measurement tools employed in the descriptive epidemiology program for drug abuse is surveys. Repeated cross-sectional surveys are used to monitor trends, changes in the attitude of the population, and the prevalence of drug use. Two such surveys, the National Household Survey on Drug Abuse and the High School Senior Survey, are sponsored by the National Institute on Drug Abuse (NIDA). These surveys use probability samples, thus allowing extrapolation to the general population.

The annual High School Senior Survey collects information from approximately 16,000 to 18,000 public and private high school seniors located in approximately 130 high schools in the contiguous United States. These survey data are used to monitor trends in drug abuse and, through a longitudinal study of a subsample of each class, to monitor maturational factors associated with drug abuse. The measures and procedures employed have been standardized and applied consistently in data collection since 1975.

Although the exclusion of dropouts and absentees from the study may result in somewhat conservative estimates of drug abuse in the high school senior class population, the stability of the survey provides an ex-

cellent measurement of drug abuse trends, including both prevalence and incidence data as well as changes in attitudes and beliefs about drugs. In addition, the follow-up design in the survey provides information on drug abuse subsequent to high school graduation, which is vital to determination of age-related risk factors. For example, these data indicate that while the extent of marijuana abuse does not change significantly after high school, the abuse of cocaine increased dramatically. This finding, in addition to findings from other studies, has been used to suggest that the age of risk for cocaine abuse may be different from that for other drugs (15).

The National Household Survey on Drug Abuse, a general population survey of household members aged 12 and above, has been conducted every 2 to 3 years since 1971. This survey excludes populations in institutionalized settings (prisons, military bases, colleges) as well as transient and nonresidential populations. Therefore, estimates of drug abuse may be conservative. Still this household survey remains the single most important measure of drug abuse in our general population. In addition to monitoring trends by age, sex, and other demographic variables, the size of the database permits analysis of a variety of questions on drug abuse. For example, data from the 1982 survey suggested that current abuse of marijuana as well as annual prevalence (use in the past year) of marijuana abuse had decreased for both males and females between 1979 and 1982. These decreases were greater for males, pointing to the possibility that incidence rates during the period may have been higher for females (16). More detailed analysis of the 1982 survey data regarding first use of marijuana for the previous year indicated that the incidence of marijuana abuse was higher among females than males in the age group 12 to 25 (Table 1). The incidence rates in Table 1 represent new use of marijuana as a percentage of the population at risk and exclude those who have used marijuana previously.

In another study, the National Household Survey on Drug Abuse database was used in

TABLE 1 Population Using Marijuana for the First Time in the Preceding Year and Incidence Rates for Marijuana Use. Data from 1982.

Age Group	First Use (%)		Incidence	
	Males	Females	Males	Females
12 to 17	4.0	8.0	5.3	9.6
18 to 25	0.7	1.4	2.3	3.3
Sample Size	1404	1460	845	938

an attempt to define the population at risk for cocaine abuse. Analysis of the household data suggested that, not only were cocaine abusers likely to have abused marijuana prior to abuse of cocaine, but the probability of abusing cocaine increased with the frequency and recency of marijuana abuse (17). The inclusion of drug problem and dependency scales in the most recent survey will enable researchers to assess risks according to levels of abuse. For example, a recent study of high-risk cocaine abusers (defined as having abused cocaine at least 12 times in the previous year) indicated that the number of self-reported dependency symptoms increased with frequency of abuse (18).

There are two more data systems that are used by NIDA. The Drug Abuse Warning Network (DAWN) reports consequences of drug abuse as reflected by emergency room episodes for drug-related problems and medical examiner cases for drug-related fatalities. The Client Oriented Data Acquisition Process (CODAP) reports treatment data.

Both data systems have been used to monitor drug abuse trends and health consequences. For example, DAWN data have been used to measure recent changes in reported cocaine morbidity and mortality, increases in speedballing (the use of heroin and cocaine in combination), and increases in the median age of heroin abusers. In addition, DAWN data were used to monitor the spread of the combination of pentazocine and tripelennamine, known on the street as "T's and blues." With the reformulation of pentazocine to include the narcotic antag-

onist naloxone, DAWN reflected a subsequent decline in the number of emergency cases and fatalities related to T's and blues (19).

An example of the use of CODAP data is a recent analysis of admissions for treatment in the Southwest which showed that the abuse of inhalants is particularly serious among the Hispanic population in that area. With a sample controlled for age it was found that 60% of Hispanics admitted to drug abuse treatment programs had less than a 12th-grade education. This figure rose to 85% when only inhalant abusers were examined (20). While each of the trend indicator or measurement systems cited has recognized methodological limitations, each provides a particular view of drug abuse behavior or consequences and together form a reasonably solid foundation for tracking epidemiologic trends.

Patterns and Trends of Selected Drugs of Abuse

Heroin

In many respects, heroin is one of the most difficult drugs to investigate. In spite of its visible presence during the past 20 years as a national social and health problem, its association with crime and the recent relation established between IV drug abuse (predominantly IV heroin abuse) and AIDS, heroin abuse continues to be a relatively rare event and involves a population that seeks to remain hidden. These circumstances virtually

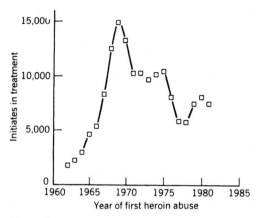

FIGURE 1.

Incidence of heroin abuse. Data are based on admissions to a panel of federally funded treatment programs.

preclude the use of traditional research methods, such as general surveys, in studying incidence, prevalence, and consequences of abuse.

Treatment data reported to CODAP, however, have been used to identify relative changes in incidence through calculation of year of first heroin use. Because of the difficulty in identifying denominator data, raw counts rather than rates have to suffice for incidence trend analysis. Figure 1 shows that epidemics of heroin abuse occurred in the United States during the mid-1960's, the mid-1970's, and the early 1980's.

The data show that the epidemics which occurred in the 1960's and 1970's were national in scope, whereas the epidemics of the 1980's were more localized in geographic location. In the latter case, the country in which the heroin originated was identified as an important link to the area of the United States affected (21).

In comparison with incidence analysis, problems are even more complex in estimating the prevalence of heroin abuse. Over the years, various methods have been used, including snowball techniques and multiplier methods as well as mathematical and systems analysis models (22). In spite of the inherent difficulties of definition and measurement, various estimates of the heroin

addict population have been surprisingly similar and consistent for the last decade, for the most part ranging between 400,000 and 600,000.

Although heroin prevalence appears to have remained relatively stable in recent years, changes have occurred in characteristics of abusers, most notably an aging effect, as evidenced in both treatment and DAWN emergency room data. For example, the percentage of all heroin-related nonfatal emergencies reported to DAWN, which involved persons 30 years of age or older, increased from 36% in 1979 to 58% in 1983, whereas a similar increase from 41 to 56% occurred during the same time period among heroin treatment admissions. These age data make a strong case, when combined with declining incidence data, that the preponderance of current heroin abusers were initiated into heroin abuse between the mid-1960's and mid-1970's.

A variety of risk factors and health consequences have been related to heroin abuse over the years. Most recently, reports of the growing availability of "black tar" heroin, a type of heroin purported to be of high purity and low price, may be responsible for recent increases in heroin-related morbidity and mortality (23). Additional risk factors include abuse of heroin in combination with other substances. A particularly lethal combination in recent years has been the ingestion of heroin in temporal proximity to the consumption of alcohol (12). The most dramatic issue of the day, though, is the association between IV drug abuse and AIDS. Not only has the percentage of AIDS cases associated with IV drug abuse been increasing, but in some areas, such as New York and New Jersey, IV drug abusers are threatening to become the majority risk group, and this group is viewed as representing the potential bridge to the general population.

Marijuana

The most widely abused illegal drug in the country today is marijuana. The 1982 National Household Survey on Drug Abuse indicated that an estimated 56 million people in the United States had used marijuana at least once and slightly more than 20 million were estimated to have consumed it during the month before the survey (16, 24). By 1985, lifetime prevalence increased to 62 million, while use in the past month decreased to 18 million. These estimates represent a substantial percentage of the national population, but the lifetime (ever used), annual, and past month prevalence trends show a decline or leveling among all age groups during the most recent measurement points (Table 2).

The increase in the 26 and older age category was found to be the result of a cohort effect—that is, the entry of the 23- to 25-year-old age cohort into the 26 and older age group between 1979 and 1982. The net change in the older adult group was not statistically significant (17).

These national household trends are reflected in data from high school senior classes which reached their apex in marijuana use with the classes of 1978 and 1979 and have since declined through 1984 and leveled off in 1985 (Table 3). A clue to the

reasons underlying the surge in marijuana abuse during the 1970's and its subsequent decline also may be garnered from the High School Senior Survey. The point at which marijuana abuse had reached its peak was the same point at which perceived harmfulness was at its nadir. For example, in 1978 monthly prevalence among high school seniors was at 37% and almost 11% used marijuana daily. At the same time, only 12% of seniors nationwide believed that there was great risk of harm associated with occasional use, and 35% perceived great risk with regular use. By 1985 monthly prevalence declined to 26% and daily use to below 5%, whereas perceived risk for occasional use rose to 25% and for regular use to 70%.

Thus, the belief that marijuana use, even once or twice, poses no great risk is highly correlated with an increase in prevalence trends and probably had its genesis in the social status afforded the drug during the 1960's and early 1970's and the lack at that time of conclusive findings regarding short- or long-term health consequences (25). Now it is clear that marijuana has a serious impact on social functioning as well as

TABLE 2 Trend in Estimated Prevalence of Marijuana Use among Three Age Groups, 1971–1982.

Prevalance	Population Using Marijuana (%)						
	1972	1974	1976	1977	1979	1982	1985
12- to 17-year-olds							
Ever used	14.0	23.0	22.4	28.0	30.9	26.7	23.7
Used in past year		18.5	18.4	22.3	24.1	20.6	20.0
Used in past month	7.0	12.0	12.3	16.6	16.7	11.5	12.3
Sample size	880	952	986	1272	2165	1581	2287
18- to 25-year-olds							
Ever used	47.9	52.7	52.9	59.9	68.2	64.1	60.5
Used in past year		34.2	35.0	38.7	46.9	40.4	37.0
Used in past month	27.8	25.2	25.0	27.4	35.4	27.4	21.9
Sample Size	772	849	882	1500	2044	1283	1804
26 years and older							
Ever used	7.4	9.9	12.9	15.3	19.6	23.0	27.2
Used in past year		3.8	5.4	6.4	9.0	10.6	9.5
Used in past month	2.5	2.0	3.5	3.3	6.0	6.6	6.2
Sample size	1613	2221	1708	1822	3015	2760	3947

TABLE 3 Trend in Estimated Prevalence of Marijuana Use Among High School Senior Classes, 1975–1985.

| Prevalance | High School Seniors Using Marijuana (%) | | | | | | | | | | |
---	1975	1976	1977	1978	1979	1980	1981	1982	1983	1984	1985
Ever used	47.3	52.8	56.4	59.2	60.4	60.3	59.5	58.7	57.0	54.9	54.2
Used in past year	40.0	44.5	47.6	50.2	50.8	48.8	46.1	44.3	42.3	40.0	40.6
Used in past month	27.1	32.2	35.4	37.1	36.5	33.7	31.6	28.5	27.0	25.2	25.7
Used daily in past month	6.0	8.2	9.1	10.7	10.3	9.1	7.0	6.3	5.5	5.0	4.9
Sample size	9,400	15,400	17,100	17,800	15,500	15,900	17,500	17,700	16,300	15,900	16,000

health. Behaviorally, use of marijuana, especially long-term heavy use, has been directly related to subsequent abuse of other illicit drugs (26). Marijuana has been called a "gateway" drug and, indeed, the single best predictor of cocaine use is frequent use of marijuana during adolescence (27).

Clinical effects of marijuana also have been documented, specifically the effect of marijuana on the nervous system as well as the cardiovascular, respiratory, and other major body systems (28). In addition, long-term marijuana abuse, just as long-term cigarette smoking, can produce serious chronic effects over time and recent evidence suggests that marijuana abuse adversely affects performance (29). With these considerations in mind, the Institute of Medicine has called for further epidemiologic study in the form of cohort and case-control studies to identify the long-term health consequences of marijuana abuse (28).

Cocaine

In 1973, the Strategy Council on Drug Abuse stated that morbidity associated with cocaine abuse did not appear to be great. It also stated that at the time there were virtually no confirmed cocaine overdose deaths and that a negligible number of people were seeking medical help or treatment for problems associated with cocaine abuse (30). In 1972, approximately 48% of young adults between 18 and 25 years of age had tried marijuana, but only 9% had ever tried cocaine. Between 1974 and 1985, lifetime prevalence of cocaine use increased from 5.4 million to 22.2 million. Estimates of current

prevalence, use in the past 30 days, increased from 1.6 million in 1977 to 4.3 million in 1979, remained stable through 1982, and increased to 5.8 million in 1985. Data from the High School Senior Survey also show increases in current use of cocaine among high school seniors in the past 2 years. By 1985, 6.7% of high school seniors had used cocaine in the past 30 days. Additional data collected in five waves of the Gallup Poll in late 1984 and mid-1985 did not indicate dramatic increases in the use of cocaine overall, but did suggest increases in current use in males aged 26 to 34. Annual prevalence did not appear to increase.

As with marijuana, increases in lifetime prevalence of cocaine abuse were noted in the 1982 National Survey. Unlike marijuana, however, the increases in cocaine abuse in the 26 and older population were, in fact, due to new users in that population (17), suggesting that the age of risk for abuse of cocaine differs from other drugs. Further evidence of the different age risks for cocaine abuse is provided by an 8-year-follow-up sample of students from the High School Senior Survey. In this study, all prevalence measures rose substantially with age. By 1985, lifetime cocaine prevalence was 40% for 27-year-olds who were seniors in 1976. Use in the past year was 20% compared with approximately 13% among graduating high school seniors in the class of 1985. Interestingly, both annual prevalence and current prevalence among college students and the total sample up to 4 years after high school has been relatively stable between 1980 and 1985 (Table 4).

Overall, the data suggest relative stability

TABLE 4 Trend in Annual Prevalence of Cocaine Use Among Follow-Up Populations, 1 to 4 Years After High School, 1980–1985.

Sample	Used Cocaine in Past 12 Months (%)					
	1980	1981	1982	1983	1984	1985
Total	18.0	18.1	19.2	17.5	17.5	17.2
Full-time college students	16.9	15.9	17.2	17.2	16.4	17.3
Sample Size	2855	2862	2861	2821	2790	2690

in the annual prevalence pool estimated at approximately 12 million, but an increase in use in the past month. As previously mentioned, data from the Gallup Poll suggest increases in use in the past 30 days in the 26- to 34-year-old population. This is consistent with previous follow-up data from the High School Senior Survey and from other studies that suggest a general progression of frequency of use of cocaine. The 26- to 34-year-old population ranged in age from 16 to 24 in 1976 when marijuana abuse had yet to peak, and the cocaine epidemic was just beginning. Of note, a recent sample of 100 cases of high-risk cocaine abusers, defined as having used cocaine at least 12 times in the previous year, indicates that 60% of this population had been smoking marijuana for more than 10 years.

Even with the current increase in abuse of cocaine in the older population, the rise does not match the epidemic increases noted in the late 1970's. However, sharp increases have been noted in treatment admissions, emergency room cases, and mortality associated with cocaine abuse. Between 1981 and 1985, the number of DAWN nonfatal emergencies associated with cocaine increased threefold from 3296 to 9946, and cocaine-related deaths showed a similar threefold increase from 195 to 580. Recent reports of heart attacks in relatively healthy individuals have been attributed to the abuse of cocaine and have heightened awareness of the severe consequences of a drug once thought to be benign (31–33).

The rise in treatment admissions parallels the trend noted for emergency room and medical examiner cases. In 1977, primary cocaine abuse accounted for 1.8% of all admissions to federally funded treatment facilities. By 1981, they accounted for 5.8%, and in 1984 the 15 states still submitting treatment data to NIDA reported that primary cocaine admissions accounted for almost 14% of total clients. If secondary cocaine problems were included, more than a fourth (28.7%) of treatment clients reported to NIDA had a problem with cocaine.

Route of administration is particularly important with cocaine. In the past, inhaling (or snorting) the drug has been the predominant mode of administration, whereas inhaling the vapors of cocaine, that is, freebasing, was virtually nonexistent. Although the reported incidence of heart attacks in cocaine snorters clearly demonstrates that intranasal abuse of cocaine is not safe, researchers have suggested that more potent physiological and psychological consequences may occur from either the smoking or IV route.

On the basis of treatment data, it appears that freebasing cocaine has increased from less than 1% in 1977 to almost 5% in 1981 and 18% in 1984. Similarly, emergency room data show that in 1977 less than 1% of cases were associated with smoking cocaine compared with 6% in 1984 and 14% during the first quarter of 1986.

The increase in smoking cocaine in the first quarter of 1986 may reflect the introduction of a form of freebase cocaine known as "crack." An important aspect of "crack" is that it is sold on the street in the freebase form. In the past the user had to convert the cocaine from hydrochloride, the form that is snorted, to freebase. This new marketing tactic may bring about an increase in freebasing and subsequent casualties. In addition, the marketing of "crack" in 65- to 100-milligram doses for $10 rather than in gram lots for $100 initially removes the price barrier that has prohibited many, especially the young, from experimenting with cocaine. These are viewed as ominous signs with the potential to develop into a major public health problem.

Conclusion

Our knowledge of drug abuse has advanced substantially in a very short time. Much can be said about risk factors associated with other types of drug abuse. The variety and range of substances involved and the dynamic social nature of drug abuse sets it in a cycle of almost constant change. In addition, drug epidemics often are localized and involve specific subpopulations that make surveillance based on national data systems difficult. At the same time, the multifaceted nature of the problem has allowed us to apply investigative techniques for a variety of disciplines in public health, medicine, and the social sciences. Significantly, epidemiology has become a staple in the methodological armamentarium of drug abuse research.

References

1. R. L. DuPont and M. H. Greene, *Science* **181**, 716 (1973).

2. L. G. Hunt and C. D. Chambers, *The Heroin Epidemics* (Spectrum, New York, 1976).

3. P. H. Hughes, E. C. Senay, R. Parker, *Arch. Gen. Psychiatry.* **27**, 585 (1972).

4. M. H. Greene, J. L. Luke, R. L. DuPont, *Med Ann. D.C.* **43**, 175 (1974).

5. D. X. Freedman and E. C. Senay, *J. Am. Med. Assoc.* **223**, 1155 (1973).

6. R. L. DuPont, *N. Engl. J. Med.* **285**, 320 (1971).

7. P. H. Hughes and G. A. Crawford, *Arch. Gen. Psychiatry.* **27**, 149 (1972).

8. J. C. Ball and C. D. Chambers, Eds., *The Epidemiology of Opiate Addiction in the United States* (Thomas, Springfield, IL, 1970).

9. E. D. Drucker and V. W. Sidel, "The communicable disease model of heroin addiction—a critique," paper presented at the meeting of the American Public Health Association, San Francisco, 4 to 8 November 1973.

10. P. Jacobs, "Epidemiology abuse: Epidemiological and psychosocial models of drug abuse," paper presented at the National Drug Abuse Conference, New Orleans, 4 to 7 April 1975.

11. M. H. Greene, *Am. J. Public Health* (Suppl.) **64**, 1 (1974).

12. A. J. Ruttenber and J. L. Luke, *Science* **226**, 14 (1984).

13. Centers for Disease Control, *Morb. Mortal. Wkly. Rep.* **30**, 185 (1981).

14. C. Vandelli et al., *Drug Alcohol Depend.* **14**, 129 (1984).

15. L. D. Johnston, P. M. O'Malley, J. G. Bachman, *Drug Use among American High School Students, College Students, and Other Young Adults—National Trends Through 1985* (National Institute on Drug Abuse, Rockville, MD, *1986).*

16. National Institute on Drug Abuse, *National Survey on Drug Abuse: Main Findings 1982* (National Institute on Drug Abuse, Rockville, MD, 1983).

17. E. H. Adams et al., *Adv. Alcohol Drug Abuse,* in press.

18. E. H. Adams and B. A. Rouse, "Populations at risk for cocaine use and subsequent consequences," paper to be presented at the meeting of the American Psychiatric Association, Washington, DC, 18 to 22 November 1986.

19. C. Baum, J. P. Hsu, R. C. Nelson, *Public Health Rep.,* in press.

20. E. H. Adams, "An overview of drug use in the United States and along the U.S.–Mexico border," paper presented at the U.S.–Mexico Border Public Health Association meeting, Monterrey, Mexico, 28 to 30 April 1986.

21. National Institute on Drug Abuse, *Epidemiology of Heroin: 1964–1984* (National Institute on Drug Abuse, Rockville, MD, 1985).

22. M. D. Brodsky, *Natl. Inst. Drug Abuse Res. Monogr. Ser.* 57 (1985), p. 94.

23. National Institute on Drug Abuse, *Community Epidemiology Work Group Proceedings* (National Institute on Drug Abuse, Rockville, MD 1986).

24. National Institute on Drug Abuse, *Population Projections—Based on the National Survey on Drug Abuse, 1982* (National Institute on Drug Abuse, Rockville, MD, 1983).

25. National Commission on Marihuana and Drug Abuse, *Marihuana: A Signal of Misunderstanding* (Government Printing Office, Washington, DC, 1972).

26. R. R. Clayton and H. L. Voss, *Natl. Inst. Drug Abuse Res. Monogr. Ser.* 39 (1981), p. 46.

27. D. B. Kandel, D. Murphy, D. Karus, *Natl. Inst. Drug Abuse Res. Monagr. Ser.* 61 (1985), p. 76.

28. Institute of Medicine, *Marijuana and Health* (National Academy Press, Washington, DC, 1982).

29. J. A. Yesavage, V. O. Leirer, M. Denari, L. E. Hollister, *Am. J. Psychiatr.* **142**, 1325 (1985).

30. Strategy Council on Drug Abuse, *Federal Strategy for Drug Abuse and Drug Traffic Prevention 1973* (Government Printing Office, Washington, DC, 1973).

31. J. S. Schachne, B. H. Roberts, P. D. Thompson, *N. Engl. J. Med.* **310**, 1665 (1984).

32. P. F. Pasternack, S. B., Calvin, F. G., Bauman, *Am. J. Cardiol.* **55**, 847 (1985).

33. L. L. Cregler and H. Mark, *ibid.* **57**, 1185 (1986).

27

Biological Vulnerability to Alcoholism

Marc A. Schuckit

This article reviews the role of biological factors in the risk for alcoholism. The discussion notes the importance of the definition of primary alcoholism and highlights data indicating that this disorder is genetically influenced. The major emphasis is on studies of men at high risk for the future development of alcoholism. The most promising trait markers of a biological vulnerability to alcoholism include a decreased intensity of reaction to modest ethanol doses for sons of alcoholics compared with control subjects, a decreased amplitude of certain brain waves of the event-related potential, and a different pattern of background cortical electroencephalograms for young men at high risk for future alcoholism.

The adequate definition of alcoholism is an important concern for all studies of etiology in alcoholism. Briefly, the ideal rubric would offer unambiguous and objective criteria that are easy to apply in research and treatment settings (Goodwin & Guze, 1984). Although no perfect definition of alcoholism exists, most diagnoses require individuals to have

Marc A. Schuckit. Biological Vulnerability to Alcoholism. *Journal of Consulting and Clinical Psychology*, 1987, Vol. 55, No. 3, pp. 301–309. Copyright © 1987 by the American Psychological Association. Reprinted by permission.

been drinking heavily over an extended period of time and to have subsequently suffered multiple major life problems. This usually entails daily drinking with an inability to stop for long periods, along with repeated efforts to control intake, and consumption often meets or exceeds a fifth of spirits or its equivalent in wine or beer per day. This pattern, often present for years before diagnosis, is accompanied by evidence of impaired social or occupational functioning and is often associated with evidence of tolerance or physical symptoms of withdrawal from alcohol (American Psychiatric Association, 1980).

Because research concerning the biological factors involved in the predisposition toward alcoholism is in the early stages, most investigators have chosen to focus on relatives of severely alcoholic individuals with the hope that genetic factors may be most obvious and easy to identify. Thus, alcoholism in relatives often requires not only that they fulfill the definition but also that the alcoholic family member have suffered severe alcohol-related consequences, such as job loss or divorce, or have received treatment for alcoholic detoxification or rehabilitation. Future work will have to determine the generalizability of results to relatives of less severely alcoholic individuals. Thus, the present focus of studies is on a biological vulnerability toward relatively severe alcoholism. Most investigations do not analyze biological influences in the decision to begin drinking during teenage years or in the occurrence of temporary and relatively mild problems that might be observed as part of growing up in a heavy-drinking society (a problem in perhaps 40% or more of young men; Cahalan & Cisin, 1968; Fillmore & Midanik, 1984).

Another issue of importance in the definition of alcoholism is the distinction between primary and secondary illness. In primary alcoholism, the severe life problems associated with heavy and persistent drinking develop in individuals with no major preexisting psychiatric illness (Schuckit, 1983a, 1984a). Thus, alcoholics who develop their alcohol-related life problems after the emergence of manic depressive disease or antisocial personality disorder (i.e., secondary alcoholics) are usually excluded from these investigations for fear that genetic factors influencing the primary disorder (e.g., manic depressive disease) might obscure the genetic factors that predispose the subject toward alcoholism. There is evidence from longitudinal follow-up studies that primary alcoholics demonstrate significantly different clinical histories and 1-year outcomes than secondary alcoholics (Schuckit, 1985c).

Importance of Genetics

Regardless of the definition of alcoholism that is used, there is evidence that alcoholism is a genetically influenced disorder. This conclusion is supported by work from family, twin, and adoption studies in humans as well as in animals. Family studies have revealed a threefold to fourfold increased risk for this disorder in sons and daughters of alcoholics, without clear evidence of a heightened vulnerability toward other primary psychiatric diseases (Cotton, 1979; Schuckit, 1986). However, demonstrating the familial nature of alcoholism does not clearly support the contribution of genetics because most children are raised by their biological parents.

Research with twins evaluates the relative contributions of genetics and environment by comparing the risk for alcoholism in identical and fraternal twins of alcoholics (Schuckit, 1981). Because both types of twins share major childhood environmental events, an alcoholism risk closely related to environment would show identical twins and fraternal twins of alcoholics to be at equally high risk. However, because identical twins share 100% of their genes and fraternal twins share only 50%, alcoholism that is genetically influenced should be significantly higher in the identical twin of an alcoholic than in the fraternal twin.

Several twins investigations have examined the similarity of drinking quantity and frequency in twins in the general population. Two of these studies have concluded that genetic factors appear to contribute to drinking patterns but, perhaps reflecting the emphasis on a "normal" population, do not contribute to adverse consequences (Jonsson & Nilsson, 1968; Partanen, Bruun, & Markkanen, 1966). Other investigators have demonstrated that genetic factors might be important in the rate of absorption or elimination of alcohol, with a high level of heritability shown for the alcohol elimination rate (0.8–0.98) and for the appearance and destruction of its first breakdown product, acetaldehyde (0.6–0.8) (Radlow & Conway, 1978; Vesell, Page, & Passancanti, 1971). However, pointing out how the rate of alcohol metabolism can be affected by the use of other drugs, by dietary and drinking habits, and by smoking history, another study reported a heritability level of 0.57 for the absorption and 0.46 for the elimination of alcohol (Kopun & Propping, 1977).

There is a series of ancedotal reports of the adult drinking habits of monozygotic (MZ) twins separated sometime early in life. Because of their retrospective and anecdotal nature, these studies offer few definite conclusions, and most of the data relate to drinking practices rather than to alcoholism. A review of the literature shows as many as 100 studied cases of separated twins in which the authors have noted a level of similarity in the separated twins' choice to drink, experience of life problems related to alcohol intake, and usual drinking patterns (Jonsson & Milsson, 1968; Newman, Freeman, & Holzinger, 1937; Shields, 1962).

Several twins studies have directly addressed the concordance rate for alcoholism in MZ versus dizygotic (DZ) twins. Kaij studied 174 male twin pairs containing at least one twin who was registered with an alcohol problem at a temperance board. As many as 90% of the twins were interviewed, and zygosity was established by anthropological markers and blood typing (Kaij, 1960). Under relatively crisp criteria for alcoholism, the concordance rate was 58% in MZ twins and 28% in DZ twins. In addition, a Veterans Administration twin register study also reported a higher MZ than DZ concordance rate (26% vs. 12%; Hrubec & Omenn, 1981), but a recent British investigation of 61 twin pairs revealed no MZ/DZ differences on concordance as measured by the Schedule for Affective Disorders and Schizophrenia (SADS-L) (Gurling, Oppenheim, & Murray, 1984; Murray et al., 1983).

In summary, twins studies offer some evidence of heritability in the decision to drink and in the frequency and quantity of alcohol imbibed. Most studies dealing directly with alcoholism have also shown a significantly higher level of concordance for this disorder in MZ twins versus DZ twins, and studies of MZ twins separated early in life have been anecdotally consistent with the importance of genetic factors.

The third type of genetic study of humans evaluates the risk for alcoholism in biological children of alcoholics who were adopted out and raised separately from their real parents (i.e., adoption studies). Whether using a half-sibling methodology or actual adoption records, these investigations have also consistently revealed a threefold to fourfold higher risk for alcoholism in adopted-out sons of alcoholics, even when they were raised by nonalcoholic adoptive parents (Cadoret, Cain, & Grove, 1980; Goodwin, 1985; Schuckit, Goodwin, & Winokur, 1972). In one of the most frequently cited studies,

Goodwin, Schulsinger, Hermansen, Guze, and Winokur (1973) documented an 18% rate of alcoholism among 55 Danish adopted-away sons of alcoholics by the age of 30 compared with a 5% rate of alcoholism among 78 adopted-away control subjects. Further evaluation showed that the amount of alcoholism in the offspring of alcoholics did not differ significantly whether they were raised by an alcoholic parent or not (Goodwin et al., 1974). Using a similar approach, Bohman, Sigvardsson, and Cloninger (1981) also noted a fourfold higher rate of alcoholism in Sweden among 29 adopted-away daughters of alcoholic mothers (10.3%) than among 577 control subjects (2.8%).

Human research is also attempting to identify important subgroups among primary alcoholics. For example, one preliminary series of studies has identified at least two possible subtypes. The first is likely to be more severe, to be seen in men, and to be closely allied with criminality (i.e., male-limited type), whereas the second is equally likely to be seen in either sex and appears to be more responsive to environmental factors (i.e., milieu-limited type) (Cloninger, Bohman, & Sigvardsson, 1981; Cloninger, Bohman, Sigvardsson, & von Knorring, 1984). Although the results of these investigations must be considered preliminary, they highlight the probability that not all alcoholics are likely to be equally sensitive to the same genetic influences. These studies also demonstrate how much work still needs to be done and emphasize how the search for markers of a predisposition to alcoholism is likely to identify multiple factors that are differentially relevant in different alcoholic subgroups. These results also point out the importance of environmental factors in alcoholic problems.

Cloninger and colleagues have used family, twin, and adoption studies to estimate the rate of heritability for alcoholism. Utilizing some earlier twin and family studies, they have estimated an overall heritability rate of about 64%, but the figure may actually be as high as 90% for the hypothesized male-limited subtype (Cloninger et al.,

1984; Cloninger, von Knorring, Sigvardsson, & Bohman, 1983).

Animal studies have also contributed to our understanding of how biological factors might influence the decision to drink, the level of central nervous system (CNS) sensitivity to the effects of ethanol, and the voluntary intake of enough alcohol to cause intoxication (Deitrich & Spuhler, 1984; Meisch, 1982). At least one recently developed animal model addressed biological factors that might interact to yield enough voluntary oral intake to cause intoxication, tolerance, and physical dependence (Li, 1984; Schuckit, Li, Cloninger, & Deitrich, 1985). Although the focus in this article is on human research, these studies have demonstrated that factors important to alcohol consumption and subsequent problems can be genetically influenced, even in subhuman mammals. These models may be important in future attempts to increase our knowledge of neurochemical and physiologic systems that contribute to specific markers for the alcoholism risk.

Thus, one can conclude that there is generally consistent evidence supporting the importance of genetic factors in the development of alcoholism. Alcoholism is probably a polygenic and multifactorial problem, with genetically influenced biological factors that interact with environmental events (Cloninger, Reich, & Yokoyama, 1983) to contribute significantly to the risk for development. There is little direct documentation of the environmental factors mediating the risk, but Cloninger's work indicates the possible importance of early-life home instability, a relatively low-status occupation for the father, and the subject's need for an extended neonatal hospital stay. Additional factors that, by common sense, might be important include the availability of alcoholic beverages in society (e.g., the price of liquor and number of liquor outlets), social attitudes toward drunkenness, and peer pressures toward excessive drinking.

The studies outlined here have searched for trait markers of a vulnerability toward alcoholism (Schuckit, 1985d). These markers should be easily measured properties that are present before the illness develops and can be observed during remission from active problems. The markers might be fortuitous and indirectly associated with a predisposition, perhaps because the genes influencing the marker are located on the same chromosome, relatively close to the genes influencing the development of alcoholism. On the other hand, it is possible that the trait markers observed will actually be directly involved in the mechanisms that increase the alcoholism risk.

Studies of Men with a Vulnerability Toward Alcoholism

Trait markers are observable either before alcoholism develops or while the illness is in remission. Unfortunately, heavy drinking and its associated lifestyle (with the increased risk for trauma and nutritional deficiencies) is capable of producing in some people biological, physiological, and emotional or cognitive changes that might continue for extended periods of time after abstinence (Schuckit, 1984a). Thus, observing alcoholics even after 20 years of abstinence could reveal cirrhosis, brain damage, evidence of a peripheral neuropathy, or other problems that did not predate the alcoholism and are not appropriate trait markers of a vulnerability toward this disorder. As a result, most investigators have attempted to identify trait markers by observing individuals at high risk for the future development of alcoholism but who have not yet developed major alcohol-related life problems.

Methodological Considerations

There are at least three possible approaches to the study of populations at high risk for the development of alcoholism. First, and most important, are studies of children of alcoholics who have been adopted out and reared by nonalcoholic adoptive parents. These children are then followed with repeated evaluations over time to observe differences from control subjects in the way hypothesized markers actually associate with alcoholism. Unfortunately, such detailed evaluations of the adopted-away children of alcoholics are expensive and difficult to carry out because few appropriate groups have been made available for study. Two such cohort investigations of the offspring of alcoholics have reported limited data: One studied children who were adopted out between 1924 and 1927 in Copenhagen, and another used adoption records in Iowa (Cadoret, Cain, & Grove, 1980; Jacobsen & Schulsinger, 1981; Utne, Hensen, Winkler, & Schulsinger, 1977).

The second approach is to intensively study a limited number of families of alcoholics, searching for markers that are present in alcoholic relatives but are absent in nonalcoholic relatives. Such investigations can provide useful information about the probable pattern of inheritance in alcoholism. However, these studies often require personal interviews and the testing of multiple generations within families, and results must be interpreted while controlling for the effects of prior drinking patterns, age, and so on. As a result, these expensive and time-consuming investigations rarely gather data from more than a limited number of families. Therefore, this approach is probably best reserved for use after preliminary data have identified the markers that are most appropriate for future investigation.

Most studies of populations at high risk for alcoholism have utilized cohorts or groups of normal individuals chosen because of their date of birth, their educational institution, or their use of public resources or contact with police agencies. The goal has been to identify and study individuals at high risk for future alcoholism before the disorder has actually developed. One large cohort of 9,000 children from complication-free, full-term births (some with an alcoholic biological parent) in Copenhagen between 1951–1961 is presently being evaluated (Gabrielli & Mednick, 1983; Pollock, Volavka, & Goodwin, 1983; Schulsinger, 1972). In a re-

lated approach, United States investigations of populations at elevated risk for alcoholism have evaluated biological sons of alcoholics who were identified at various ages. In most cases, sons were chosen so higher risk and lower risk groups could be followed over time to observe the actual development of alcoholism. The selection of men reflects the expectation that men will show higher rates of vulnerability to alcoholism (Schuckit & Morrisey, 1979) and the possibility that results from ethanol challenges could vary with the phase of the menstrual cycle or with the consumption of birth control pills, which could jeopardize study results if women were used (Jones & Jones, 1976).

Some studies of populations at high risk for alcoholism have evaluated prepubertal boys in order to observe them before actual exposure to ethanol, but these have risked missing the markers that appear only after puberty or follow the exposure to modest drinking (Begleiter, Porjesz, Bihari, & Kissin, 1984; Behar, Berg, & Rapoport, 1983). Other investigations have selected older subjects, usually in their late teens to midtwenties, populations that offer investigators the opposite pattern of assets and liabilities (Schuckit, 1985b).

In the approach used in our laboratory since 1978, a mailed questionnaire has been used to identify young, drinking but not yet alcoholic men at elevated risk for the development of alcoholism. The questionnaire utilizes a highly structured format to gather information on demography and pattern of alcohol and drug intake as well as on associated problems; personal, medical, and psychiatric histories; and family history of major psychiatric disorders, including alcoholism and drug abuse. The definition of psychiatric illness follows the *Diagnostic and Statistical Manual of Mental Disorders* (*DSM-III*; American Psychiatric Association, 1980), with modifications of alcoholism and drug abuse criteria that require evidence of major life problems related to substances (Schuckit, 1984a). From these mailings, the sons of primary alcoholics who were themselves drinkers but who had not experienced major life problems from alcohol or drugs and who had no past history of medical or psychiatric disorders were selected as higher risk or family history positive (FHP) subjects. Each FHP man was matched with a lower risk family history negative (FHN) individual on age, sex, race, educational level, quantity and frequency of drinking, substance intake history, height-to-weight ratio, and smoking history.

Men selected for study were subsequently tested individually in the laboratory on three occasions, where they consumed placebo, 0.75 ml/kg of ethanol, or 1.1 ml/kg of ethanol. The subjects were unaware of the hypotheses being tested, and the two family history groups had very similar scores on the effects they expected from three drinks (Schuckit, 1984c). The ethanol was given as a 20% by volume solution (for active beverages) in a sugar-free, noncaffeinated beverage, which was drunk over a 10-min period. Before the challenge, laboratory personnel determined the subject's baseline level of functioning on a variety of cognitive and psychomotor tests, mood and anxiety scales, and hormonal levels. After drinking the beverage, individuals were observed over a 4-hr period, during which their reactions to the two doses of ethanol and the placebo were established.

Other studies of high-risk populations have used slightly different methods. For example, Tarter, Hegedus, Goldstein, Shelly, and Alterman (1984) evaluated cognitive and psychomotor test performance without ethanol challenges in a series of boys in their midteens who were in trouble with the law. A group in Oklahoma utilized labor unions, social organizations, and churches to identify both male and female children of alcoholics (Schaeffer, Parsons, & Yohman, 1984). In another series of studies, Begleiter et al. (1984) utilized community volunteers in their preteen years to study the electrophysiological attributes of young sons of alcoholic fathers, and a similar approach was used by Behar et al. (1983). As a result, children of various ages and socioeconomic groups with alcoholic parents have been identified through a variety of methodol-

ogies and have been studied either at baseline or after an ethanol challenge.

Populations at Elevated Risk for Alcoholism

Preliminary findings have indicated several potential trait markers of a vulnerability toward alcoholism. However, even after a potential marker has been identified and replicated in other laboratories, there are many important research steps that must be taken. First, the association between the marker that has been identified in sons of alcoholics and the future development of alcoholism must be established through follow-up investigations. Second, the genetic basis of the biological marker must be established. Third, the actual mechanism for the expression of the vulnerability needs to be studied. Despite these caveats, early work has identified at least one possible behavioral trait marker (a decreased intensity of reaction to ethanol) and several electrophysiological markers that may prove to be important.

Decreased Intensity of Reaction to Ethanol. Our investigations, as well as the results from two laboratories in the United States and Denmark, have documented the ethanol reactions of sons of alcoholics and carefully matched control subjects. Subjective levels of intoxication were measured on an analogue scale at baseline and again at several intervals after drinking. Subjects were required to rate the intensity of different aspects of intoxification, including overall drug effect, dizziness, nausea, level of "high," and so on.

Before challenges, the FHP and FHN subjects expressed similar expectations of the effects of ethanol; after drinking, both groups developed similar patterns of blood alcohol concentrations over time (Mednick, 1983; O'Malley & Maisto, 1985; Schuckit, 1980, 1984c, 1985a). Despite these similarities and identical self-reports for the two groups following placebo, the FHP men rated themselves as significantly less intoxicated than did the FHN men after drinking 0.75 ml/kg of ethanol (see Figure 1). A similar but non-

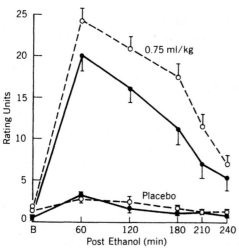

FIGURE 1

Mean self-ratings on a 0 (*none*) to 36 (*great*) scale measuring the drug effect of placebo and 0.75 ml/kg of ethanol for 23 matched pairs with positive (closed circles) and negative (open circles) family histories. (Bars indicate standard errors and B indicates baseline. This figure was taken from "Subjective Responses to Alcohol in Sons of Alcoholics and Controls" by M. A. Schuckit, 1984, *Archives of General Psychiatry, 41*, pp. 879–884. Copyright 1984 by the American Medical Association. Reprinted by permission.)

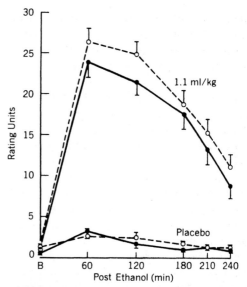

FIGURE 2

Mean self-ratings on a 0 (*none*) to 36 (*great*) scale measuring the drug effect of placebo and 1.1 ml/kg of ethanol for 23 matched pairs with positive (closed circles) and negative (open circles) family histories. (Bars indicate standard errors and B indicates baseline. This figure was taken from "Subjective Responses to Alcohol in Sons of Alcoholics and Controls" by M. A. Schuckit, 1984, *Archives of General Psychiatry, 41*, pp. 879–884. Copyright 1984 by the American Medical Association. Reprinted by permission.)

significant trend was noted after subjects drank a 1.1 ml/kg ethanol dose (Figure 2). Overall, FHN subjects scored 39% higher on the "drug effect" item over the 4 hr after the lower dose challenge and scored 24% higher after the higher dose. In both settings, the maximum group difference was observed 60–120 min after the drink had been consumed.

In our own laboratory, FHP subjects also demonstrated smaller decrements in cognitive and psychomotor performance after drinking. For example, to measure the level of sway in the upper body, we asked subjects to stand still, with hands at the sides and feet together. Although there were no group differences at baseline or after consuming placebo (as shown in Figure 3), the FHN subjects showed significantly greater increase in body sway after drinking the 0.75 ml/kg dose of ethanol (Schuckit, 1985a). Using the raw data, we found a significant

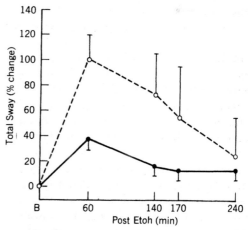

FIGURE 3

Percent increase in body sway or standing steadiness following 0.75 ml/kg of ethanol for 23 matched pairs with positive (closed circles) and negative (open circles) family histories. (Bars indicate standard errors and B indicates baseline. ETOH = ethanol.)

Time × Family History interaction, $F(3, 197) = 3.84$, $p = .01$, although the family-history effect alone was not quite significant ($p = .06$). Similarly, preliminary analyses of changes in hormones sensitive to an ethanol challenge have revealed a less intense response in FHP subjects for cortisol and prolactin after drinking, although these data analyses were carried out without placebo controls, and attempts to replicate these findings have not yet been published (Schuckit, 1984b; Schuckit, Parker, & Rossman, 1983).

If we speculate on the meaning of the results, we may assume that a decreased intensity of reaction to low doses of ethanol would make it more difficult for individuals to discern when they are becoming drunk. However, the greater similarity in levels of intoxication after higher doses of alcohol showed that men in both family groups were capable of experiencing a similar drug effect. An impaired ability to fully experience the effects of moderate alcohol doses could make it harder to know when to stop drinking during an evening; it may be more difficult to use relatively subtle cues to learn when to quit before becoming too drunk. This is an example of a biologically influenced factor that might not cause alcoholism but, in conjunction with a heavy drinking milieu, could predispose an individual toward a higher risk for alcohol-related life problems.

Possible Electrophysiological Markers. Studies of sons of alcoholics have tentatively indicated two types of brain waves as markers associated with a predisposition toward alcoholism. The first, event-related potentials (ERPs), are computer-averaged brain waves measuring electrophysiological brain reactions to stimuli (Porjesz & Begleiter, 1983). One part of the ERP, a positive wave observed at approximately 300 ms after a stimulus (the P300), occurs in normal individuals after they experience an anticipated but rare event. The P300 is thought to correlate with an individual's ability to selectively attend to an anticipated stimulus. Following up on observations of a nonreversible flattened amplitude of P300s in alcoholics, Begleiter et al. (1984) documented a similarly decreased P300 wave in the preadolescent sons of alcoholics. Our own laboratory has recently replicated this trend for a lower amplitude P300 wave, and an earlier study with Elmasian, NeVille, Woods, Schuckit, and Bloom (1982) questioned whether FHP and FHN subjects might demonstrate P300 amplitudes that respond differently to ethanol and placebo challenges. Another study evaluated other possible ERP differences between family history groups (Schmidt & Neville, 1984).

In a second finding, alcoholics have been shown to demonstrate relatively low levels of slow waves (e.g., alpha waves) on background cortical electroencephalograms (EEGs) before ethanol, and they might show a greater increase in this wave after an ethanol challenge (Gabrielli et al., 1982; Pollock et al., 1983; Volavka, Pollock, Gabrielli & Mednick, 1982). Following up on these results, studies of populations at high risk for the development of alcoholism have revealed similar EEG patterns in the sons of alcoholics. Thus, it is possible that ethanol has different reinforcing properties in individuals at high risk for alcoholism: Perhaps it corrects for a lower level of alpha activity and, thus, produces more feelings of relaxation (Schuckit, Engstrom, Alpert, & Duby, 1981).

In summary, follow-up studies on electrophysiological differences between alcoholics and control subjects have identified two possible trait markers for alcoholism in the sons of alcoholics. Some of these findings, however, are preliminary and require replication. Future investigations must evaluate the relations between physiological findings and other potential markers of a predisposition toward alcoholism, including the apparently decreased reaction to ethanol in these young men.

Cognitive and Psychomotor Impairment. The series of studies carried out in our laboratory has documented no major cognitive or psychomotor differences between sons of alcoholics and control subjects before an ethanol challenge. However, our subjects have been highly functioning young men, and it is possible that some sons of alcoholics may show cognitive or psycho-motor deficits but that these individuals were not a part of our sample (i.e., our sample contained students or university employees). Therefore, it is of interest to examine the results of studies using sons of alcoholics who have been identified at a younger age through their associations with juvenile authorities. Comparisons of FHP and FHN subjects from this population have shown lower verbal IQs for the FHP subjects as well as decreased auditory word span performance, lower levels of reading comprehension, a higher number of errors on the Categories Test of the Halstead-Reitan Neuropsychological Test battery, and problems with constructional praxis and abstract problem-solving (Gabrielli & Mednick, 1983; Knop, Goodwin, Teasdale, Mikkelsen, & Schulsinger, 1984; Schaeffer et al., 1984; Tarter, Hill et al., 1984).

A related finding has associated the risk for alcoholism with signs of hyperactivity or impulsivity during childhood (Goodwin, Schulsinger, Hermansen, Guzi, & Winokur, 1975; Knop et al., 1984; McCord, 1981; Mednick, 1983). However, childhood hyperactivity can reflect nonspecific stressors, such as living with an alcoholic parent, and might be temporary and distinct from a true hyperactive child syndrome or from attention deficit disorder (Schuckit, Petrich, & Chiles, 1978). A number of other studies following cohorts over time have not demonstrated a close association between impulsivity or hyperactive child syndrome and the future development of alcoholism (Tarter, Hegedus, & Gavaler, 1985; Vaillant, 1984; Vaillant & Milofsky, 1982). In addition, in our own laboratory, FHP subjects were no more likely to have demonstrated hyperactivity in childhood or to have shown more signs of impulsivity on personality tests than FHN subjects (Saunders & Schuckit, 1981).

In summary, some men may show an association between cognitive and psycho-motor test performance problems, signs of

hyperactivity in childhood, and the future development of alcoholism. However, these behavior problems are not apparent in the sons of alcoholics who function moderately well, and the relation between these variables and future alcoholism may not be strong enough to be identified through prospective cohort studies of the general population.

Personality Profiles and the Future Development of Alcoholism

During the course of heavy drinking and the months following recovery, alcoholics are likely to show many abnormalities on personality tests (Schuckit & Haglund, 1982). However, many of these results may reflect the actions of ethanol as well as the mood swings and life crises inherent in an alcoholic lifestyle, and abnormal results may become normal with continued abstinence. In addition, some personality traits that remain after drinking may reflect other primary psychiatric diagnoses, such as antisocial personality disorder, and not alcoholism per se (Schuckit, 1973).

It is, thus, not surprising that observations of personality attributes in young men at high risk for the future development of alcoholism show few consistent results. In our own laboratory studies of highly functioning young men, few baseline group differences were observed on scores of neuroticism, extraversion, state anxiety, or locus of control; on scales of the Minnesota Multiphasic Personality Inventory (MMPI); or on indirect measures of personality, such as the portable Rod Frame Test (Morrison & Schuckit, 1983; Saunders & Schuckit, 1981; Schuckit, 1982, 1983b; Schuckit & Penn, 1985). However, no definitive answers are available because of limitations in the number of pairs studied, because of the difficulty of proving an absence of a significant difference between groups, and because of the highly select nature of some of the populations investigated. The personality differences between alcoholic and control subjects (MacAndrew, 1979) do justify further evaluations.

Biochemical Markers

A number of unique patterns of blood proteins can be observed in alcoholics even after continued abstinence. These include at least one major enzyme of ethanol degradation, enzymes important in the metabolism of brain neurotransmitters, and some blood antigens.

Most ethanol in the body is broken down by the enzyme alcohol dehydrogenase (ADH) to acetaldehyde, a psychoactive substance that is subsequently destroyed by the enzyme aldehyde dehydrogenase (ALDH; Li, 1977). The patterns of form (or isoenzymes) for both ALDH and ADH are genetically controlled. Although the pattern might change in normal individuals with age and although the amount of enzyme can be strongly influenced by drinking, the types of isoenzymes are not likely to be significantly altered by drug intake.

There are at least four isoenzymes of ALDH in the human liver, each with different biochemical properties (Greenfield & Pietruszko, 1977). The ALDH isoenzyme most sensitive to low doses of acetaldehyde varies markedly in different ethnic groups and is missing in 30%–50% of Orientals (Harada, Agarwal, Goedde, & Ishikawa, 1983; Suwaki & Ohara, 1985). In the absence of this isoenzyme form, ethanol oxidation results in significantly higher levels of blood acetaldehyde after drinking, with a subsequent syndrome of facial flushing, palpitations, and nausea that resembles a mild ethanol-disulfiram interaction. Orientals missing this enzyme are less likely than their cohorts to drink heavily and appear to have a lower rate of alcoholism (Suwaki & Ohara, 1985). Thus, one genetically controlled enzyme does influence the chance of developing alcoholism within Oriental subgroups, although this finding may have limited applicability to non-Oriental populations. There is little evidence of significant differences among Occidental groups on their ALDH isoenzyme pattern.

Second, monamine oxidase (MAO), an enzyme important in the degradation of brain neurotransmitters, has been reported to have abnormal activity levels in people with a variety of psychiatric disorders and personality types. The activity level of this enzyme is said to be low in alcoholics, although it is not clear whether it returns to normal after an extended period of abstinence (Sullivan, Cavenar, Maltbie, Lister, & Zung, 1979). There is preliminary evidence that sons of alcoholics may also demonstrate lower levels of MAO activity, although most studies have demonstrated only a trend and not a significant difference from control populations (Scher, 1983; Schuckit, Shaskan, & Duby, 1982).

Finally, based on comparisons of alcoholic and control subjects, a number of other blood proteins are of interest. These include the brain protein Pt1-Duarte (Comings, 1979) and a possible linkage in repulsion between the D gene of the Rh system, the SS phenotype for complement C3, and alcoholism (Hill, Goodwin, Cadoret, Osterland, & Doner, 1980). Each of these potential markers requires further evaluation in relatives of alcoholics as well as in populations at high risk for the development of alcoholism before definitive conclusions can be drawn.

Conclusion

This article has reviewed information on the biological vulnerability toward alcoholism. Most of the work is based on the premise that alcoholism is a genetically influenced disorder. In evaluating the studies, however, it is important to remember the likelihood that biological factors explain only one important part of the risk for alcoholism. The final development of this disorder probably depends on the interaction between biological and environmental factors. The emphasis on biology in this article reflects both the discipline of the author and the ease with which biological factors can be measured and thus identified early in the course of a series of studies.

At this point in the research, the methodologies being used are of as much interest as the results themselves. In general, researchers have taken advantage of persistent differences between alcoholic and control subjects to identify foci for studies of populations at high risk for the development of alcoholism. Potential trait markers of greatest interest are those that not only differentiate alcoholic from control subjects but also retain their efficacy with extended abstinence. It is these measures that are generally used to compare the children of alcoholics with the children of control subjects.

The results of any of the studies of populations at high risk for alcoholism are affected by research approach. Different markers might be identified in young prepubertal children than in older or highly functioning children of alcoholics. Results may also be affected by the definition of alcoholism used and by whether children of primary or secondary alcoholics were evaluated.

Despite the diversity of methodologies, several important leads toward identifying the trait markers associated with a vulnerability toward alcoholism are apparent. Sons of alcoholics appear to show a decreased intensity of reaction to modest doses of ethanol, to have lower amplitude ERP P300 brain waves, and to show unusual patterns of wave form frequencies on background cortical EEGs. Other interesting and potentially important findings require further evaluation.

Once a behavior or test result is accepted as being significantly different in populations at high risk for alcoholism than in control subjects, much work remains before the actual presence of a trait marker for alcoholism can be established. Thus, this article has described a series of research projects that are in their infancy, and much important work remains to be done.

These findings contain a number of clinical and research implications. First, the studies outlined in this article underscore the probability that biological and genetic factors are important in a vulnerability toward alcoholism. Taken together with family, twins, and adoption studies, the results can be used to highlight the importance of biological influences and to emphasize the probability that alcoholism is not just a moral weakness.

Second, the series of studies contains implications for the prevention of alcoholism. The fourfold increased risk for alcoholism in children of alcoholics emphasizes how vulnerable this particular group is to the development of alcohol-related life problems. These individuals might be chosen as the focus of some intensive prevention efforts in the future.

Third, the present results hold a number of implications for the future. It is the hope of many investigators that identification of the biological factors associated with a vulnerability toward alcoholism will help clinicians develop more specific and effective prevention and treatment efforts. Further progress will also help to identify those sons and daughters of alcoholics who have inherited the traits that increase their vulnerability. These individuals can then be followed over time in order to identify the social and cultural factors that maximize the chances for expression of the vulnerability and the factors that provide protective action.

In conclusion, interesting and important research is now being carried out to help identify the biological vulnerabilities to alcoholism. Recent years have witnessed great progress in this field, and research strategies appear to be bearing fruit. Although no generally accepted biological marker of a vulnerability toward alcoholism has yet been identified (with the possible exception of the ALDH isoenzyme pattern), the results of research have been most promising. We recognize the deficiencies inherent in any brief overview and encourage the reader to reexamine our references and to follow the literature in this field as it unfolds further in the coming years.

References

AMERICAN PSYCHIATRIC ASSOCIATION. (1980). *Diagnostic and statistical manual of mental disorders* (3rd. ed.). Washington, DC: Author.

BEGLEITER, H., PORJESZ, B., BIHARI, B., AND KISSIN, B. (1984). Event-related brain potentials in boys at risk for alcoholism. *Science, 227,* 1493–1496.

BEHAR, D., BERG, C. J., AND RAPOPORT, J. L. (1983). Behavior and physiological effects of ethanol in high-risk and control children: A pilot study. *Alcoholism: Clinical and Experimental Research, 7,* 404–410.

BOHMAN, M., SIGVARDSSON, S., AND CLONINGER, C. R. (1981). Maternal inheritance of alcohol abuse: Cross-fostering analysis of adopted women. *Archives of General Psychiatry, 38,* 965–969.

CADORET, R. J., CAIN, C. A., AND GROVE, W. M. (1980). Development of alcoholism in adoptees raised apart from alcoholic biologic relatives. *Archives of General Psychiatry, 37,* 561–563.

CAHALAN, D. AND CISIN, I. H. (1968). American drinking practices: Summary of findings from a national probability sample. *Quarterly Journal of Studies on Alcohol, 29,* 130–151.

CLONINGER, C. R., BOHMAN, M., AND SIGVARDSSON, S. (1981). Inheritance of alcohol abuse: Cross-fostering analysis of adopted men. *Archives of General Psychiatry, 36,* 861–868.

CLONINGER, C. R., BOHMAN, M., SIGVARDSSON, S., AND VON KNORRING, A. L. (1984). Psychopathology in adopted-out children of alcoholics. In M. GALANTER (Ed.), *Recent developments in alcoholism* (pp. 37–51). New York: Plenum Press.

CLONINGER, C. R., REICH, T., AND YOKOYAMA, S. (1983). Genetic diversity, genome organization, and investigation of the etiology of psychiatric diseases. *Psychiatric Developments, 3,* 225–246.

CLONINGER, C. R., VON KNORRING, A. L. SIGVARDSSON, S., AND BOHMAN, M. (1983, March). *Inheritance of alcohol abuse.* Presented at the International Conference on Pharmacological Treatments for Alcoholism: Looking to the Future, organized by the Alcoholism Education Centre and the Institute of Psychiatry, University of London, England.

COMINGS, D. E. (1979). The genetic heterogeneity of human brain proteins and their diagnosis in living patients. *Nature, 277,* 28–32.

COTTON, N. S. (1979). The familial incidence of alcoholism: A review. *Journal of Studies on Alcohol, 40,* 89–116.

DEITRICH, R. A., AND SPUHLER, K. (1984). Genetics of alcoholism and alcohol actions. In R. SMART AND E. M. SELLERS (Eds.), *Research advances in alcohol and drug problems* (Vol. 8, pp. 47–98). New York: Plenum Press.

ELMASIAN, R., NEVILLE, H., WOODS, D., SCHUCKIT, M. A., AND BLOOM, F. (1982). Event-related brain potentials are different in individuals at high risk for developing alcoholism. *Proceedings of the National Academy of Sciences, United States, 79,* 7900–7903.

FILLMORE, K. M. AND MIDANIK, L. (1984). Chronicity of drinking problems among men: A longitudinal study. *Journal of Studies on Alcohol, 45,* 228–236.

GABRIELLI, W. F. AND MEDNICK, S. A. (1983). Intellectual performance in children of alcoholics. *Journal of Nervous and Mental Diseases, 171,* 444–447.

GABRIELLI, W. F., MEDNICK, S. A., VOLAVKA, J., POLLOCK, V. E., SCHULSINGER, F., AND ITIL, T. M. (1982). Electroencephalograms in children of alcoholic fathers. *Psychophysiology, 19,* 404–407.

GOODWIN, D. W. (1985). Alcoholism and genetics. *Archives of General Psychiatry, 42,* 171–174.

GOODWIN, D. W. AND GUZE, S. B. (1984). *Psychiatric diagnosis.* New York: Oxford University Press.

GOODWIN, D. W., SCHULSINGER, F., HERMANSEN, L., GUZE, S., AND WINOKUR, G. (1973). Alcohol problems in adoptees raised apart from alcoholic biological parents. *Archives of General Psychiatry, 28,* 238–243.

GOODWIN, D. W., SCHULSINGER, F., HERMANSEN, L., GUZE, S. B., AND WINOKUR, G. (1975). Alcoholism and the hyperactive child syndrome. *Journal of Nervous and Mental Diseases, 160,* 349–353.

GOODWIN, D. W., SCHULSINGER, F., MOLLER, N., HERMANSEN, L., WINOKUR, G., AND GUZE, S. B. (1974). Drinking problems in adopted and nonadopted sons of alcoholics. *Archives of General Psychiatry, 31,* 164–169.

GREENFIELD, N. J. AND PIETRUSZKO, R. (1977). Two aldehyde dehydrogenases from human liver: Isolation via affinity chromatography and characterization of the isoenzymes. *Biochemical Biophysical Acta, 483,* 35–45.

GURLING, H. M. D., OPPENHEIM, B. E., AND MURRAY, R. M. (1984). Depression, criminality and psychopathology associated with alcoholism: Evidence from a twin study. *Acta Genet Med Gemellol, 33,* 333–339.

HARADA, S., AGARWAL, D. P., GOEDDE, H. W., AND ISHIKAWA, B. (1983). Aldehyde dehydrogenase isoenzyme variation and alcoholism in Japan. *Pharmacology, Biochemistry and Behavior, 18,* 151–153.

HILL, S. Y., GOODWIN, D. W., CADORET, R., OSTERLAND, C. K., AND DONER, S. M. (1980). Association and linkage between alcoholism and eleven serological markers. *Journal of Studies on Alcohol, 36,* 981–989.

HRUBEC, Z. AND OMENN, G. S. (1981). Evidence of genetic predisposition to alcohol cirrhosis and psychosis: Twin concordances for alcoholism and its biological end points by zygosity among male veterans. *Alcoholism: Clinical and Experimental Research, 5,* 207–212.

JACOBSEN, B. AND SCHULSINGER, F. (1981). The Danish adoption register. In S. A. MEDNICK AND A. E. BAERT (Eds.), *Prospective longitudinal research: An empirical basis for the primary prevention of psychosocial disorders* (pp. 225–230). Oxford, England: Oxford University Press.

JONES, B. M., AND JONES, M. K. (1976). Women and alcohol: Intoxication, metabolism, and the menstrual cycle. In M. GREENBLATT AND M. A. SCHUCKIT (Eds.), *Alcoholism problems in women and children* (pp. 103–136). New York: Grune & Stratton.

JONSSON, E. AND NILSSON, T. (1968). Alcoholism in monozygotic and dizygotic twins. *Nord Hyg Tidskr, 49,* 21.

KAIJ, L. (1960). *Studies on the etiology and sequels of abuse of alcohol.* Lund, Sweden: University of Lund, Department of Psychiatry.

KNOP, J., GOODWIN, D., TEASDALE, T. W., MIKKELSEN, U., AND SCHULSINGER, F. (1984). A Danish prospective study of young males at high risk for alcoholism. In D. W. GOODWIN, D. TEILMANN, VAN DUSEN, AND S. A. MEDNICK (Eds.), *Longitudinal research in alcoholism* (pp. 107–122). Boston: Kluwer-Nijhoff.

KOPUN, M. AND PROPPING, P. (1977). The kinetics of ethanol absorption and elimination in twins and supplementary repetitive experiments in singleton subjects. *European Journal of Clinical Pharmacology, 11,* 337–344.

LI, T. K. (1977). Enzymology of human alcohol metabolism. In A. MEISTER (Ed.), *Enzymology of human alcohol metabolism* (pp. 19–56). New York: Wiley.

LI, T. K. (1984, December). *An animal model of alcoholism.* Paper presented at the American College of Neuropsychopharmacology, San Juan, Puerto Rico.

MACANDREW, C. (1979). On the possibility of the psychometric detection of persons who are prone to the abuse of alcohol and other substances. *Addictive Behaviors, 4,* 11–20.

MCCORD, J. (1981). Alcoholism and criminality: Confounding and differentiating factors. *Journal of Studies on Alcohol, 42,* 739–748.

MEDNICK, S. A. (1983, May). *Subjects at risk for alcoholism: Recent reports.* Paper presented at the 14th Annual Medical Scientific Conference of the National Alcoholism Forum, Research Society on Alcoholism, Houston, TX.

MEISCH, R. (1982). Animal studies of alcohol intake. *British Journal of Psychiatry, 141,* 113–120.

MORRISON, C. AND SCHUCKIT, M. A. (1983). Locus of control in young men with alcoholic relatives and controls. *Journal of Clinical Psychiatry, 44,* 306–307.

MURRAY, R. M., CLIFFORD, C., GURLING, H. M. D., TOPHAM, A., CLOW, A., AND BERNADT, M. (1983). Current genetic and biological approaches to alcoholism. *Psychiatric Developments, 2,* 179–192.

NEWMAN, H. H., FREEMAN, F. N., AND HOLZINGER, K. J. (1937). *Twins: A study of heredity and environment.* Chicago: University of Chicago Press.

O'MALLEY, S. S. AND MAISTO, S. A. (1985). The effects of family drinking history on responses to alcohol: Expectancies and reactions to intoxication. *Journal of Studies on Alcohol, 46,* 289–297.

PARTANEN, J., BRUUN, K., AND MARKKANEN, T. (1966). *Inheritance of drinking behavior: A study on intelligence, personality, and use of alcohol of adult twins.* Helsinki, Finland: Finnish Foundation for Alcohol Studies.

POLLOCK, V. E., VOLAVKA, J., AND GOODWIN, D. W. (1983). The EEG after alcohol administration in men at risk for alcoholism. *Archives of General Psychiatry, 40,* 857–861.

PORJESZ, B. AND BEGLEITER, H. (1983) Brain dysfunction and alcohol. In B. KISSIN AND H. BEGLEITER (Eds.), *The pathogesis of alcoholism* (pp. 415–483). New York: Plenum Press.

RADLOW, R. AND CONWAY, T. L. (1978, August), *Consistency of alcohol absorption in human subjects.* Paper presented at the American Psychological Association, Toronto, Canada.

SAUNDERS, G. R. AND SCHUCKIT, M. A. (1981). Brief communication: MMPI scores in young men with alcoholic relatives and controls. *Journal of Nervous and Mental Disease, 168,* 456–458.

SCHAEFFER, K. W., PARSONS, O. A., AND YOHMAN,

J. R. (1984). Neuropsychological differences between male familial and nonfamilial alcoholics and nonalcoholics. *Alcoholism: Clinical and Experimental Research, 8,* 347–358.

SCHER, K. J. (1983). Platelet monoamine oxidase activity in relatives of alcoholics. *Archives of General Psychiatry, 40,* 466.

SCHMIDT, A. L. AND NEVILLE, H. J. (1984, June). *Event-related brain potentials (ERPs) in sons of alcoholic fathers.* Paper presented at the meeting of the International Society for Biological Research, Santa Fe, NM.

SCHUCKIT, M. A. (1973). Alcoholism and sociopathy—diagnostic confusion. *Journal of Studies on Alcohol, 34,* 157–164.

SCHUCKIT, M. A. (1980). Self-rating alcohol intoxication by young men with and without family histories of alcoholism. *Journal of Studies on Alcohol, 41,* 242–249.

SCHUCKIT, M. A. (1981). Twin studies on substance abuse. In L. GEDDA, P. PARISI, AND W. NANCE (Eds.), *Twin research 3: Epidemiological and clinical studies* (pp. 61–70). New York: Alan R. Liss.

SCHUCKIT, M. A. (1982). Anxiety and assertiveness in sons of alcoholics and controls. *Journal of Clinical Psychiatry, 43,* 238–239.

SCHUCKIT, M. A. (1983a). Alcoholism and other psychiatric disorders. *Hospital and Community Psychiatry, 34,* 1022–1027.

SCHUCKIT, M. A. (1983b). Extroversion and neuroticism in young men. *American Journal of Psychiatry, 140,* 1223–1224.

SCHUCKIT, M. A. (1984a). *Drug and alcohol abuse: A clinical guide to diagnosis and treatment* (2nd ed.). New York: Plenum Press.

SCHUCKIT, M. A. (1984b). Differences in plasma cortisol after ethanol in relatives of alcoholics and controls. *Journal of Clinical Psychiatry, 45,* 374–379.

SCHUCKIT, M. A. (1984c). Subjective responses to alcohol in sons of alcoholics and controls. *Archives of General Psychiatry, 41,* 879–884.

SCHUCKIT, M. A. (1985a). Ethanol-induced changes in body sway in men at high alcoholism risk. *Archives of General Psychiatry, 42,* 375–379.

SCHUCKIT, M. A. (1985b). Studies of populations at high risk for alcoholism. *Psychiatric Developments, 3,* 31–63.

SCHUCKIT, M. A. (1985c). The clinical implications of primary diagnostic groups among alcoholics. *Archives of General Psychiatry, 42,* 1043–1049.

SCHUCKIT, M. A. (1985d). Trait (and state) mark-

ers of a predisposition to psychopathology. In L. L. Judd and P. Groves (Eds.), *Psychological foundations of clinical psychiatry* (pp. 1–19). Philadelphia, PA: Lippincott.

SCHUCKIT, M. A. (1986). Alcoholism and affective disorders: Genetic and clinical implications. *American Journal of Psychiatry, 143,* 140–147.

SCHUCKIT, M. A., ENGSTROM, D., ALPERT, R., AND DUBY, J. (1981). Differences in muscle-tension response to ethanol in young men with and without family histories of alcoholism. *Journal of Studies on Alcohol, 42,* 918–924.

SCHUCKIT, M. A., GOODWIN, D. A., AND WINOKUR, G. A. (1972). A study of alcoholism in half siblings. *American Journal of Psychiatry, 128,* 1132.

SCHUCKIT, M. A. AND HAGLUND, R. M. J. (1982). An overview of the etiologic theories on alcoholism. In N. ESTES AND E. HEINEMANN (Eds.), *Alcoholism: Development, consequences, and interventions* (pp. 16–31). St. Louis, MO: Mosby.

SCHUCKIT, M. A., LI, T. K., CLONINGER, E. R., AND DEITRICH, R. A. (1985). Genetics of alcoholism. *Alcoholism: Clinical and Experimental Research, 9,* 475–492.

SCHUCKIT, M. A. AND MORRISEY, E. R. (1979). Psychiatric problems in women at alcoholic detoxification. *American Journal of Psychiatry, 136,* 611–617.

SCHUCKIT, M. A., PARKER, D. C., AND ROSSMAN, L. R. (1983). Prolactin responses to ethanol in men at elevated risk for alcoholism and controls. *Biological Psychiatry, 18,* 1153–1159.

SCHUCKIT, M. A. AND PENN, N. E. (1985). Performance on the rod and frame for men at elevated risk for alcoholism and controls. *American Journal of Drug and Alcohol Abuse, III,* 113–118.

SCHUCKIT, M. A., PETRICH, J., AND CHILES, J. (1978). Hyperactivity: Diagnostic confusion. *Journal of Nervous and Mental Disease, 166,* 79–87.

SCHUCKIT, M. A., SHASKAN, E., AND DUBY, J. (1982). Platelet MAO activities in the relatives of alcoholics and controls: A prospective study. *Archives of General Psychiatry, 39,* 137–140.

SCHULSINGER, F. (1972). Psychopathy: Heredity and environment. *International Journal of Mental Health, 1,* 190–206.

SHIELDS, J. (1962). *Monozygotic twins.* London: Oxford University Press.

SULLIVAN, J. L., CAVENAR, J. O., MALTBIE, A. A., LISTER, P., AND ZUNG, W. W. K. (1979). Familial biochemical and clinical correlates of alcoholics with low platelet monoamine oxidase activity. *Biological Psychiatry, 14,* 385–389.

SUWAKI, J. AND OHARA, H. (1985). Alcohol-induced facial flushing and drinking behavior in Japanese men. *Journal of Studies on Alcohol, 46,* 196–198.

TARTER, R. E., HEGEDUS, A. M., AND GAVALER, J. S. (1985). Hyperactivity in sons of alcoholics. *Journal of Studies on Alcohol, 46,* 259–261.

TARTER, R. E., HEGEDUS, A. M., GOLDSTEIN, G., SHELLY, C., AND ALTERMAN, A. (1984). Adolescent sons of alcoholics: Neuropsychological and personality characteristics. *Alcoholism: Clinical and Experimental Research, 8,* 216–222.

TARTER, R., HILL, S., JACOB, T., HEGEDUS, A., AND WINSTEN, K. J. (1984, June). *Neuropsychological comparison of sons of alcoholic depressed and normal fathers.* Paper presented at the meeting of the International Society for Biological Research Association, Santa Fe, NM.

UTNE, H. E., HENSEN, F. V., WINKLER, K., AND SCHULSINGER, F. (1977). Alcohol elimination rates in adoptees with and without alcoholic parents. *Journal of Studies on Alcohol, 38,* 1219–1223.

VAILLANT, G. E. (1984). The course of alcoholism and lessons for treatment. In L. GRINSPOON (Ed.), *Psychiatry update* (pp. 311–319). Washington, DC: American Psychiatric Press.

VAILLANT, G. E. AND MILOFSKY, E. S. (1982). Natural history of male alcoholism. *Archives of General Psychiatry, 39,* 127–133.

VESELL, E. S., PAGE, J. G., AND PASSANCANTI, G. T. (1971). Genetic and environmental factors affecting ethanol metabolism in man. *Clinical Pharmacological Therapy, 12,* 192–201.

VOLAVKA, J., POLLOCK, V., GABRIELLI, W. F., AND MEDNICK, S. A. (1982). The EEG in persons at risk for alcoholism. In M. GALANTER (Ed.), *Currents in alcoholism* (Vol. 8, pp. 116–123). New York: Grune & Stratton.

28

Drinking Your Troubles Away: The Role of Activity in Mediating Alcohol's Reduction of Psychological Stress

Claude M. Steele, Lillian Southwick, and Robert Pagano

Two experiments tested the hypothesis that alcohol's reduction of psychological stress depends to an important degree on whether the drinker is also engaged in distracting activity. In the first study, the factor of whether or not subjects had received alcohol (dose of 1 mg/ kg) was crossed, in a 2 × 2 design, with the factor of whether they rated pleasant art slides or did nothing during a period that immediately followed their having received negative feedback on an IQ test (taken earlier). As predicted, a significant interaction effect showed that mood improvement during this recovery period was greatest in the alcohol/slides condition—the only condition in which absolute mood improvement reached significance. Study 2 replicated this effect, and it provided evidence that ruled out several alternative explanations of the alcohol–activity effect. The results are discussed in terms of their implication that alcohol's reduction of psychological stress stems largely from its impairment of cognitive processes that, in conjunction with distracting activity, blocks out stress-inducing thoughts.

Claude M. Steele, Lillian Southwick, and Robert Pagano. Drinking Your Troubles Away: The Role of Activity in Mediating Alcohol's Reduction of Psychological Stress. *Journal of Abnormal Psychology*, 1986, Vol. 95, No. 2, pp. 173–180. Copyright © 1986 by the American Psychological Association. Reprinted by permission of the publisher and the authors.

In Conger's statement of the "tension-reduction" hypothesis (1951, 1956), he assumed that alcohol directly reduced stressful tension and that this effect, in turn, reinforced drinking. Alcoholism, or addictive drinking, he reasoned, could develop as an outgrowth of this reinforcement effect. As tests of this effect began to accumulate, however, it became clear that alcohol's relationship to stress was more complex than Conger had assumed (cf. Cappell & Herman, 1972; Marlatt, 1976). Sometimes alcohol reduced stress (e.g., Carpenter, 1957; Levenson, Sher, Grossman, Newman, & Newlin, 1980; Polivy, Schueneman, & Carlson, 1976); sometimes it had no effect (e.g., Wilson & Abrams, 1977); and sometimes it even increased stress reactions (e.g., Abrams & Wilson, 1979). Although it is difficult to distinguish the effects of inconsistent methodologies from truly inconsistent effects, it is clear at this point that alcohol has no direct, tension-reducing effect that generalizes across all types of stress, people, and situations.

This fact, however, disproves only the most global version of the tension-reduction hypothesis. As Wilson, Perold, and Abrams (1981) have noted, the more useful question for current researchers is "Under what conditions, at which doses, in what people, and on which measures does alcohol reduce tension?" Rather than reducing stress through some single, direct effect, it is quite possible that alcohol reduces stress through a variety of processes in which specific effects of alcohol interact with other variables to affect stress reactions. The present research examines one such process in which the stress-reducing effects of alcohol are hypothesized to stem from alcohol's impairment of cognitive functioning.

Unlike its effects on stress, alcohol consistently impairs perceptual and cognitive functioning; the ability to use several cues at the same time (Medina, 1970; Moskowitz & DePry, 1968); the ability to abstract and conceptualize (e.g., Kastl, 1969; Tarter, Jones, Simpson, & Vega, 1971); the cognitive elaboration needed to encode meaning from incoming information (e.g., Birnbaum, Johnson, Hartley, & Taylor, 1980); the ability to use active and systematic encoding strategies (Rosen & Lee, 1976); the ability to encode large numbers of situational cues (e.g., Washburne, 1956); and so on. It is argued that through these effects—in particular, alcohol's narrowing of perception to more immediate cues and its weakening of abstracting and conceptual ability—alcohol restricts attention and information processing to the most immediate aspects of experience, to the most salient internal and external stimuli (cf. Pernanen, 1976; Steele, Critchlow, & Liu, 1985; Steele & Southwick, 1985; Zeichner & Pihl, 1979). During intoxication, then, one has less ability to process information that is not tied to immediate internal and external experience. Taken as a working hypothesis, this idea has implications for alcohol's ability to improve affect following a psychologically stressing event.

Our logic is as follows: If, after some psychological stressor, one is engaged in a distracting activity, alcohol's damage to cognition should make it necessary to turn one's limited capacity to the immediate demands of the activity and away from internal thoughts stemming from the stressor, thereby reducing stress. In essence, the impairment caused by alcohol should combine with the demands of distracting activity to crowd out cognitions related to the stressor, blocking their impact and enhancing affect. In this reasoning, alcohol's enhancement of affect is mediated indirectly through a general effect of alcohol—its impairment of cognitive processing—and distracting activity, and not through a direct effect of alcohol on affective processes. Neither alcohol nor activity alone should reduce this kind of stress as effectively. Without the cognitive impairment of alcohol intoxication, one could easily have enough functioning cognitive capacity to be engaged in a pleasant, distracting activity and still be worrying over an earlier stressor. Cold sober, one can easily watch television and brood over a problem. Similarly, in the absence of a distracting activity, alcohol's damage to thinking (especially its impairment of the abstracting and thought-generative processes that enable self-justification and other cognitive defenses) could cause one to focus more rigidly on internally salient, stressor-related thoughts—a "crying in one's beer" effect.

We note that by shrinking the focus of thought to one's immediate activity, alcohol could increase negative affect when that activity is negative. The intoxication of arguing spouses, for example, might increase negative affect by restricting attention to the immediate conflict (cf. Pernanen, 1976). Thus, for the combined effect of alcohol and activity to reduce worry and improve affect, our argument assumes, the activity itself must be at least affectively neutral.

We also note that our reasoning does not oppose alcohol's ability to directly influence affect. Evidence on the biphasic physiological effects of alcohol shows that soon after ingestion, small amounts of alcohol can cause positive affect (e.g., Mello, 1968; McCollam, Burish, Maisto, & Sobell, 1980). Nonetheless, the inconsistency of alcohol's effects on stress shows that this direct effect is not enough to always reduce stress. Apparently, alcohol's direct effects must interact with other factors to alleviate stress. Our research examines one such indirect process.

Finally, the focus of our model is on the disturbing worry that can follow a psychologically stressful event. Because this type of stress is general and psychological, it should be manifested most clearly at the psychological level in the overall quality of subjects' affect. Thus, a measure of the overall positivity of affect was the primary dependent variable in this research. Related negative moods (e.g., depression, hostility, and anxiety) and positive moods were also measured.

Study 1

While either intoxicated or sober, all of the subjects in this experiment experienced esteem-threatening feedback on a frustrating adult IQ test that they had taken earlier. Half of the subjects in the alcohol and no-alcohol conditions then engaged in a mildly pleasant slide-rating task (presumably distracting their attention away from the stressor) while the other half sat alone with nothing to do (presumably allowing their attention to focus on the stressor) ostensibly allowing the collection of base rate physiological measures.[1] This experiment thus took the form

---

[1] It is possible, of course, that the reduction of psychological stress (indicated by enhanced mood) would also be manifested at the physiological level as a reduction in physiological arousal following the stressor. To explore this possibility, subjects' heart rate and skin conductance were measured throughout the course of this experiment. These measures, however, gave rise to inconsistent results. Thus, to reduce the length and complexity of the present report, these results were omitted.

of a 2 × 2 factorial design in which the variable of whether or not subjects received alcohol in their drinks was crossed with whether or not subjects were given an activity to perform (slide rating) during the recovery period that followed the IQ test and feedback. Subjects' affect was monitored throughout the experiment so that the degree to which it was worsened by the IQ test and negative feedback and the degree to which it improved during the recovery period immediately following the feedback (i.e., the period in which subjects either rated slides or waited) could be assessed. Based on our model, we expected that the condition in which subjects both rated slides and were intoxicated following the stressor would produce significantly more improvement in positive affect during the recovery period than any of the other conditions. A fifth condition, no-stress control, was also included in which subjects consumed alcohol and rated slides but did not take the esteem-threatening IQ test or receive negative feedback. This condition enabled us to determine whether these activities could directly enhance mood, even in the absence of a preceding stressor.

Method

Subject Selection and Design. An advertisement in the student newspaper and postings around campus recruited subjects for an experiment on "alcohol and task performance." The ad offered $7.50 for participation in a 2½-hour experiment and provided a number to call. Respondents left their name and number on a telephone answering tape and were recontacted for a screening interview. To qualify for participation, subjects had to be 21 years or older, University of Washington students, and experienced with alcohol but without a history of substance abuse, negative reactions to alcohol, or legal complications involving alcohol use. Subjects who passed the screening were scheduled for an experimental session and were told not to eat or consume an alcoholic beverage for 4 hours prior to their arrival. Over the course of the experiment, 9 subjects had to be dropped because they drank less than three-fourths of the designated amount of alcohol, 1 subject was dropped because of noncompliance with the experimental procedure, and 1 subject was dropped because he had had an alcohol-related arrest. In all, 71 subjects (31 women and 40 men) participated in this experiment in afternoon and evening sessions when subjects were most willing to drink. All subjects were conducted through the experiment one at a time and were randomly assigned to experimental conditions. A drinking-habits measure derived from Cahalan, Cisin, and Crossley (1969) and administered to 55 of our subjects (the measure was inadvertently omitted from the postexperimental questionnaires of the remaining subjects) showed that the mean drinking-habits rating for our sample was 2.96 on the following scale: 1 = *never drink;* 2 = *drink at least once a year, but less than once a month;* 3 = *drink at least once a month, but no more than three or four drinks each time;* 4 = *drink nearly every day or weekly, often five or more drinks each time.*

Procedure. On arrival, subjects completed an informed consent form detailing the procedures of the study, were weighed, and had their identification checked. The experimenter explained that this study was part of a program of research to identify the kind of judgments that alcohol was most likely to impair, and that the purpose of the present pilot study was to evaluate procedures for use in later experiments. The experimenter explained that because anxiety and other mood states affect judgments of the sort examined in today's study, physiological and questionnaire measures of mood states would be taken throughout the experiment. The major steps of the study were then reiterated (these had first been detailed in the informed consent form).

1. *Mood and Self-esteem Measures.* Subjects first completed a pretest mood measure, the Multiple Affect Adjective Checklist (MAACL; Zuckerman & Lubin, 1965), and a self-esteem measure (Pervin & Lilly, 1967).

Pretesting had shown that the moods of high-esteem subjects tended to recover faster from the negative IQ performance and feedback than the moods of subjects with moderate and low self-esteem. This tendency held for all of the self-threatening stress induction procedures that were pretested. Apparently high-self-esteem subjects have more resources with which to recover from these stresses than lower self-esteem subjects. At any rate, to the extent that individual differences in self-esteem influence how much subjects' moods recover from the IQ stressor, they reduce the sensitivity of our mood recovery measure to treatment effects. To address this problem, we administered a self-esteem measure before treatments. This measure could then be used as a covariate or blocking variable in subsequent data analyses, thus removing from the test of treatment effects variation due to esteem-based differences in mood recovery.

2. *IQ Test.* Subjects were next given a 17-item intelligence test comprising the more difficult items from a self-administered IQ test developed by Eysenck (1962). Pretesting had shown that most subjects missed at least 10 of the 17 items. The act of taking this test gave subjects immediate, face-valid evidence of their poor performance (that would later be confirmed by direct feedback), thus initiating the stress reaction. Instructions stated that 20 min would be allowed for completion of the task, that guesses would not be penalized, and that although no one would be expected to do all of the items correctly in the time allowed, "most of the problems are solvable with a bit of patience." The subject was left alone for 20 min before the experimenter returned, collected the test, and stated that as a courtesy to subjects the test would be scored immediately and feedback would be provided to all subjects later on in the experiment. The subject then completed another MAACL.

3. *Drink Administration and Absorption.* During the initial phone contact, and again in the informed consent form and introduction, all subjects were told that they would receive alcohol in this experiment and that the amount would be based on body weight. Subjects in the alcohol conditions received several chilled drinks made up in a 1:5 ratio of 80-proof vodka to tonic with a small amount of lime juice added. Drink quantities were set by a prepared chart based on an alcohol dose of 1 ml (100% ethanol)/kg of body weight. On the basis of previous research (e.g., Babor, Berglas, Mendelson, Ellingboe, & Miller, 1983; McCollam et al., 1980; Sutker, Tabakoff, Goist, & Randall, 1983), this dosage was estimated to bring subjects' blood alcohol level to approximately .08% within 35–40 min of the beginning of drinking, the point at which stress recovery was measured. Subjects in the placebo conditions received an equivalent volume of tonic water and lime juice. Pretesting and prior research has shown that subjects cannot distinguish between alcohol and placebo drinks prepared in this fashion at a better than chance level (e.g., Marlatt, Demming, & Reid, 1973).

The drinks were administered by the polygraph operator in order to keep the experimenter blind to subjects' beverage condition (experimenters were also kept blind to the experimental hypothesis). Subjects were given 15 min to consume their drinks and were encouraged to drink faster at the halfway point, if necessary. A 20-min absorption period followed during which subjects could read from the *Book of Lists* and *Architectural Digest*.

4. *IQ Feedback.* To reinforce the stressful impact of the IQ test itself, at the end of the absorption period, the experimenter returned with the subject's test form and stated:

> **I scored your test, and you didn't do too well. You only got 7 out of the 17 items correct, which would put you in the bottom quarter of the scores we have been getting on the test. Here, I can show you a few you got wrong.**

Using the answer sheet, the experimenter then told the subject the correct answers and

gave standard justifications for the first 10 incorrect items (alternative "correct" answers were used if the subjects actually missed fewer than 10). This particular IQ-feedback manipulation of self-esteem was adapted from procedures developed by Hull and Young (1983). Following this feedback, the MAACL was administered again.

5. *Recovery Period.* In the activity conditions, subjects were told they would next be making aesthetic judgments of art slides. It was assumed that viewing and rating these slides would distract subjects' attention and thought from stressful thoughts about their IQ performance. In the no-activity condition, it was explained that as control subjects (they were given this same "control" identity at the outset of the experiment) they would undergo a 15-min waiting period during which they were to sit quietly to enable base rate physiological measures in the absence of activity. Activity subjects were asked to rate, as carefully as possible, a series of art slides as to their attractiveness and intellectual and emotional impact. The slides used in this task were selected, on the basis of pretesting, to be mildly positive in affective tone. Subjects in both conditions were then left alone to rate slides or sit quietly for 15 min, following which all subjects completed the MAACL.

Dependent Measures. *Affect.* The ability of alcohol and activity to block out stressful cognitions should improve overall affect following a psychological stressor. It might do this by reducing negative moods as well as by strengthening positive moods. Thus, the primary dependent measure was a measure of overall affect, based on both positive and negative moods. This measure was derived from the MAACL by subtracting the number of affectively negative mood adjectives endorsed from the number of affectively positive adjectives endorsed. (Whether an adjective was negative, positive, or neutral was decided by two judges who agreed on 92% of the adjectives and resolved differences through discussion. Neutral items were not used in this index.)[2] Positive scores indicate overall positive affect; negative scores indicate overall negative affect. In pretesting we compared this index with the pleasure subscale of the Russell and Mehrabian (1975) mood index (the subscale most related to the positive–negative dimension of overall affect) both before and after the administration of a psychological stressor similar to the one used in the present experiment. Before the stressor the two scales correlated .69 ($n = 13, p < .01$), and after the stressor they correlated .87 ($n = 13, p < .001$). This degree of association between the MAACL index and another measure of affect (despite the inherent unreliability of the Russell–Mehrabian subscale, composed, as it is, of only six items) supports the adequacy of the MAACL as a measure of this aspect of mood. Also, although our model does not make strong predictions regarding specific negative mood states, the MAACL includes subscale measures of negative mood states, depression, hostility, and anxiety, that enable exploratory analyses. Finally, an additional subscale comprising only the positive adjectives from the MAACL (as identified by our judges' ratings) was computed to explore condition effects on just positive moods. The test–retest reliability of each scale was assessed by correlating scores from the first and second administration of each scale in the present experiment. These were .96 for the anxiety subscale, .95 for the depression subscale, .96 for the hostility subscale, .70 for the overall measure of affect, and .79 for the positivity subscale.

Postexperimental Questionnaire. This measure included two items to check subjects' reactions to the IQ feedback ("How well do you think you did on the IQ test?" and "To what extent are you satisfied with your performance on the IQ test?"), a measure of their suspiciousness about the feedback ("Did you have any suspicions about the accuracy of the feedback you received about your performance on the IQ test?"), and a measure of subjects' beliefs as to the content of their drinks ("Please estimate the number of ounces of alcohol in your drinks" and "How intoxicated are you?").

After completing this questionnaire, subjects were fully debriefed, paid, and detached from the physiological equipment, and had their blood alcohol levels measured. They were released if it was below .05 (most subjects) and otherwise were sent home in cabs.

Results

Sex of subject had no significant effects on any dependent measure, allowing us to collapse over this variable in these analyses. Incomplete questionnaires occasionally caused minor differences in the number of subjects among some measures. These were unrelated to conditions, however.

Overall Affect. Before the question of recovery from stress can be addressed, it must be shown that our procedures caused a stressful reaction in subjects prior to the recovery period. Table 1 presents the means for overall affect broken down by times of measurement and condition. There it can be seen that the IQ test and feedback greatly worsened subjects' overall affect from the beginning of the experiment to the point just after the feedback. A 2 × 2 × 2 analysis of variance (ANOVA) with alcohol, activity, and a time of measurement factor comprising these two measurement points revealed that only time of measurement significantly affected subjects moods during this phase of the experiment, $F(1, 51) = 39.1, p < .0001$. The IQ test and feedback successfully lowered subjects' moods prior to the recovery period.

---

[2]The items scored as positive were MAACL items numbered 2, 3, 6, 8, 10, 11, 19, 21, 22, 24, 27, 31, 34, 40, 42, 44, 45, 47, 48, 49, 52, 53, 54, 56, 57, 59, 60, 66, 67, 70, 71, 74, 76, 80, 81, 88, 89, 90, 91, 93, 99, 100, 101, 104, 105, 108, 112, 114, 118, 121, 126, 127, and 132. The items scored as negative were numbered 4, 5, 9, 12, 13, 14, 15, 16, 17, 18, 23, 25, 28, 29, 30, 32, 33, 35, 36, 37, 38, 39, 41, 43, 46, 50, 51, 55, 58, 61, 62, 63, 64, 65, 68, 69, 72, 73, 75, 77, 78, 79, 82, 83, 84, 85, 86, 87, 96, 97, 98, 102, 103, 106, 107, 109, 110, 111, 113, 115, 116, 117, 119, 120, 122, 123, 124, 125, 130, and 131.

TABLE 1   Unadjusted Means for Measures of Affect by Condition

Measure	Alcohol		No Alcohol		No Feedback Control
	Slides	No Slides	Slides	No Slides	
Overall affect					
Pretest	18.4	19.6	24.6	20.1	16.1
Postfeedback	4.4	11.5	15.0	8.9	16.3
Postrecovery	8.7	9.7	14.0	8.9	17.4
n	14	13	16	12	16
Depression					
Pretest	11.9	10.5	9.7	10.1	13.1
Postfeedback	17.4	15.9	12.9	15.1	14.4
Postrecovery	16.3	16.4	13.9	15.2	16
n	13	13	15	12	16
Hostility					
Pretest	6.8	6.8	6.3	5.9	6.9
Postfeedback	11.2	8.5	7.9	9.8	6.2
Postrecovery	9.6	9.3	8.3	9.4	6.7
n	13	13	15	12	16
Anxiety					
Pretest	6.1	5.9	5.6	6.8	7.2
Postfeedback	7.5	6.9	6.6	7.8	10.6
Postrecovery	8.2	6.9	7.2	8.0	6.1
n	13	13	15	12	16
Positive affect					
Pretest	20.7	22.3	28.5	25.0	20.6
Postfeedback	9.6	15.8	20.7	12.8	19.1
Postrecovery	12.1	15.3	19.8	12.6	18.9
n	14	13	16	12	16

Note. The overall affect scale ranged from −70 to +53. The *n* for each measure was the number of subjects for whom the requisite measure was available. The means for affect positivity include data from two more subjects than the means for the mood subscales because the data for two subjects were lost between the times these two measures were coded.

We predicted that the combination of alcohol intoxication and slide rating would cause more recovery of affect following the stressful IQ test and feedback than either alcohol or slide rating alone. Recovery was operationalized as the improvement in affect positivity from the point immediately preceding the recovery period to the point immediately following it. Change scores corresponding to this difference were the units of analysis. Using self-esteem (described earlier) as a covariate, a 2 (alcohol) × 2 (activity) analysis of covariance (ANCOVA) on these change scores yielded a significant Alcohol × Slides interaction, $F(1, 43) = 5.62$, $p < .022$. Table 2 presents mean change scores, adjusted for the esteem covariate. There it can be seen that, as predicted, the greatest improvement in overall mood occurred in the alcohol/slides condition. The predicted components of this interaction—that the alcohol/slides condition would differ from the other three experimental conditions—were tested using the Bonferroni *t* procedure (cf. Edwards, 1985) to maintain the experimentwise error rate for this set of

TABLE 2 Adjusted Means and Confidence Intervals (CIs) for the Change in Overall Affect

Condition	n	M	95% CI[a]
Alcohol/slides	11	6.52	0.08, 12.27
Alcohol/no slides	12	−1.94	−9.02, 5.15
No alcohol/slides	13	−1.92	−4.79, 0.96
No alcohol/no slides	12	0.87	−2.53, 4.28
No-feedback control	17	0.98	−1.61, 3.58

Note. The overall affect scale ranged from −70 to +53. The *n* for each measure was the number of subjects for whom the requisite measure was available. (Seven subjects had to be excluded from these analyses because their self-esteem scales, used as the covariate, were incomplete.)
[a]Numbers are opposite ends of the confidence interval.

three contrasts at $p < .05$. Using this procedure, the alcohol/slides condition caused significantly more improvement in overall affect than the no-alcohol/slides condition, $t(22) = 2.74$, but only marginally more than the other conditions, $t(21) = 2.16$ and $t(21) = 1.98$ for the no-alcohol/no-slides and the alcohol/no-slides contrasts, respectively. The 95% confidence intervals for the condition means presented in Table 2 show that only the interval around the alcohol/slides mean did not include zero, indicating that only this condition produced significant positive changes in subjects' moods. (The assumptions of the ANCOVA—homogeneity of regression coefficients and a lack of condition effects on the covariate—were tested and supported using the procedures described by Hull & Nie, 1980, p. 77). Finally, rating slides while being intoxicated is apparently not sufficient to directly enhance affect. Subjects in the control condition who rated slides while they were intoxicated but were not exposed to the IQ stressor did not show significant mood improvement during the recovery period, $F < 1$ (see Table 2). The stress-reducing effect of alcohol and slides thus did not stem from its direct enhancement of affect.

MAACL Subscales. The same analyses that were performed on the overall affect scores were also performed on the depression, hostility, and anxiety subscales as well as the positive-adjective subscale of the MAACL. Table 1 presents the critical means for these measures. That the IQ test and feedback significantly worsened these moods in subjects was indicated by significant time of measurement effects comparing subjects' scores at the beginning of the experiment with their scores after the feedback. For depression this effect was $F(1, 51) = 33.3$, $p < .0001$; for hostility it was $F(1, 51) = 19.6$, $p < .001$; for anxiety it was $F(1, 51) = 7.4$, $p < .01$; and for affect positivity it was $F(1, 51) = 48.9$, $p < .0001$. Improvement in these mood states during the recovery period was analyzed using the same change score analysis described for overall affect. Although the pattern of condition means for these measures was similar to that for overall affect, no significant effects emerged; the *F*s were generally less than 1.

Drinking Expectancies and Postexperimental Measures. Both alcohol and no-alcohol subjects believed they had consumed some alcohol as indicated by their estimates of the number of ounces of alcohol in their drinks ($Ms = 3.29$ and 1.24, respectively) and by their mean ratings of how intoxicated they were at the end of the experiment ($Ms = 3.83$ and 1.73, respectively; 31 indicates maximum intoxication). Nonetheless, as is typical in experiments using this dose of alcohol (cf. Levenson et al., 1980) subjects receiving alcohol had significantly stronger drinking expectancies than subjects receiving no alcohol, $F(1, 32) = 18.97, p < .001$, for intoxication ratings, and $F(1, 29) = 12.46, p = .001$, for estimated ounces.

The primary test of the effectiveness of the stress manipulation (i.e., the IQ test and feedback) is its effect on the affect measures reported earlier. Several items were included, however, to measure subjects' perceptions of their test performance and the feedback. On the average, subjects rated themselves as performing at the 50th percentile of the students taking the test, a rating not as low as the feedback (25th percentile) but probably lower than the percentile they expected or desired. They rated their test performance satisfaction as 2.87 on a 7-point scale for which higher numbers indicated greater satisfaction, indicating a general lack of performance satisfaction. A significant Alcohol × Slides interaction emerged for this scale, $F(1, 46) = 8.12, p < .01$, but the pattern of condition means (alcohol/slides, 2.33; alcohol/no-slides, 3.92; no-alcohol/slides, 3.00; and no-alcohol/no-slides, 2.25) is different than that for the stress measures, indicating no readily interpretable relation between the two condition effects. Subjects were also asked whether they had any suspicions about IQ feedback; 37.5% said yes, 58.3% said no, and 4.3% did not answer. These types of respondents were distributed approximately equally across conditions. We note that this question places a strong demand on subjects to display suspicion and that in the open-ended part of the question in which subjects were asked to spell out their suspicions, no subject revealed that he/she understood the hypothesis, the real purpose of the IQ stressor, or the purpose of the experiment, which was to examine the alcohol–stress relationship.

Discussion

The results of this experiment suggest that alcohol's ability to restore a favorable mood after depressing events can depend on whether subjects also have something to do to occupy their thinking. Rating art slides while being intoxicated tended to cause more affective recovery from evaluative stress than the other treatments and was the only treatment in which subjects' moods showed significant positive change. Although this interaction was in the same direction for the subscales of the MAACL, it reached significance only for the overall affect measure. This pattern of results, then, fits the interpretation that the ability of alcohol intoxication to relieve distressing worry depends on the coexistence of accompanying activity. Having to fight through an alcohol haze (from a less than ataxic dose of alcohol) to think and process information presumably leaves one still able to engage in immediate activity, but less able to also think and worry about a prior stressor. The plausibility of this indirect process is further supported by the finding that alcohol and slides, in the absence of stress, did not directly increase affect.

Despite the suggestiveness of these findings, they fall short of providing complete support for our hypothesis in several ways. Although the stress-reducing effect of alcohol and activity together was significantly greater than that for activity alone, it was only marginally better than the other conditions, alcohol alone or the combination of no alcohol and no slides, failing to provide definitive evidence that activity significantly augments alcohol's stress-reducing effect. One purpose of our second experiment, then, was to provide a more sensitive test of this aspect of our reasoning.

Another problem of interpretation arises because the group whose mood improved the most during the recovery period—alcohol/slides subjects—also had the lowest moods at the beginning of that period (see Table 1). Thus, the greater mood improvement in that condition during the recovery period could reflect greater regression of their mood scores to a higher mean level of mood in the experiment, or could reflect that these subjects had more room on the response scale with which to show change. Several considerations oppose these interpretations. For subjects' postfeedback moods, neither the overall condition effect

($p < .15$) nor the comparisons among condition means reached significance, meaning that prerecovery moods in the alcohol/slides condition were not significantly lower than these moods in the other conditions. Also, although the possibility of regression cannot be ruled out altogether, the moods of the other groups were also relatively low at this point in the procedure yet showed no improvement or got worse. The possibility that alcohol/slides subjects improved more because they had more room on the scale to show it does not fit the fact that subjects in the other conditions also had ample room to change on the scale (it ranged from -70 to $+53$) but did not. These arguments notwithstanding, another purpose of the second experiment was to establish the replicability of the stress-reducing effect found in the alcohol/slides condition. Another source of concern over the replicability of this effect is that the statistical significance of the analyses in this study depended on the use of the self-esteem covariate. As noted, pretesting had shown that high-self-esteem subjects tended to recover faster from the IQ stressor than moderate- and low-esteem subjects, independent of treatment effects. The self-esteem covariate was thus included to remove this extraneous variation from the test of predicted effects. Nonetheless, another purpose of the second experiment was to establish (through the use of more subjects in each condition and the ability to test effects over two experiments) that the critical stress-reducing effect of alcohol and slides was not dependent on the use of this covariate.

One explanation cannot be ruled out by replication alone. Following the IQ test and feedback, alcohol's narrowing of attention and impairment of generative thought may have caused alcohol/slides subjects to dwell on the possibility of further failure on the next "intellectual" task, the slide-rating task, and to become more anxious as a result. In turn, these subjects may have experienced a stronger sense of relief and thus more mood enhancement during the recovery period, when they realized that the second intellectual task was, in fact, not threatening.

Clearly, relief over the nonthreatening nature of the second intellectual task was not enough to cause mood recovery by itself because subjects in the no-alcohol/slides condition also could have experienced relief in this way yet showed no mood improvement. Still, if alcohol helped restrict subjects' attention to the anticipation of further failure in the alcohol/slides condition, it may have increased their anxiety prior to the recovery period and, in turn, their relief when they found that the task was not threatening. The fact that moods were especially low for the alcohol/slides subjects just before the slide task encourages this explanation.

Study 2
Method

As noted, the primary purpose of this second experiment was to replicate the stress-reducing effect of alcohol and slide rating found in Study 1 and to determine whether this effect reduced stress significantly more than alcohol alone. To this end, it replicated exactly the alcohol/no-slides and alcohol/slides conditions of Study 1. If, as we have hypothesized, the combination of alcohol and activity is uniquely effective at reducing psychological stress, then the alcohol/slides condition should produce significantly better mood recovery than the alcohol/no-slides condition. A third condition examined the extent to which the unthreatening nature of the slide task—by providing relief from an alcohol-accentuated expectation of further failure—may have contributed to mood improvement in the alcohol/slides condition of Study 1. This condition replicated all of the procedures of the alcohol/slides condition except that at the outset of the experiment, subjects were not told there would be a second intellectual task. They learned of the slide-rating task only as it began. If the expectation of this task mediated the greater mood recovery among alcohol/slides subjects of Study 1, the alcohol/slides subjects in the present study who expected no second task should not show significant mood recovery.

Sixty-two subjects (40 men and 22 women) were recruited through ads in the university newspaper in the same manner as described in Study 1 and were randomly assigned to experimental conditions: an alcohol/slides/expectancy condition ($n = 21$), in which the second intellectual task was expected; an alcohol/slides/no-expectancy condition ($n = 20$), in which the second task was not expected; and the alcohol/no-slides/no-expectancy condition ($n = 21$). The mean rating of this sample of subjects on the drinking habits questionnaire was 3.12.

Results and Discussion

Sex of subject had no significant effect on any dependent measure in the study, allowing us to collapse over this variable in these analyses. Each analysis includes all those subjects for whom the requisite dependent measures were available.

Overall Affect. A 3 (condition) $\times$ 2 (time of measurement) ANOVA in which levels of the time factor were the point at the beginning of the experiment and the point just prior to the recovery period revealed only a significant time of measurement effect, $F(1, 56) = 27.5$, $p < .0001$, showing that subjects' moods dropped sharply in response to the IQ test and feedback (see Table 3).

In this experiment, being intoxicated and rating slides proved superior to just being intoxicated as an antidote to depressed affect, a suggested but not reliable effect in the first study. As in Study 1, mood recovery was analyzed as the change in mood during the recovery period. A one-way ANOVA on these scores showed that the overall effect of treatments was marginally significant, $F(2, 59) = 2.77$, $p < .07$. As in Study 1, the Bonferroni t procedure was used to test planned contrasts. As predicted, the alcohol/slides/expectancy condition of this experiment, which provided an exact replication of the alcohol/slides condition of Study 1, pro-

duced significantly more mood recovery ($M = 7.71$) than the alcohol/no-slides/no-expectancy condition ($M = 2.19$), which replicated the alcohol/no-slides condition of Study 1, $t(40) = 2.43$. (This scale ranged from -70 to $+53$.) A test of this contrast over both studies, using a method described by Rosenthal (1978, p. 187) for combining p levels associated with independent tests of the same hypothesis, was highly significant, $p < .0003$. Also, although there was a clear tendency toward greater mood recovery among alcohol/slides/no-expectancy subjects than among alcohol/no-slides/no-expectancy subjects ($M = 7.05$), this difference did not reach significance, $t(35) = 1.77$. Nonetheless, the confidence intervals around the condition means revealed that, regardless of whether subjects expected a second task, mood improvement was significantly greater than zero in both alcohol/slides conditions but not in the alcohol/no-slides condition. Only the combination of alcohol and slides produced significant mood recovery in this study. This experiment thus demonstrates the replicability of this effect, and does so, we also note, without the use of the self-esteem covariate used in Study 1. (Self-esteem was not significantly related to the dependent measures in this study.)

In Study 1 the alcohol/slides subjects had lower mood scores at the beginning of the recovery period than subjects in the other conditions, raising the possibility that their greater improvement was somehow an artifact of lower prerecovery moods (e.g., the regression and relief arguments). These arguments were plausible because this difference in moods, though not significant, was fairly substantial. In the present study the alcohol/slides/expectancy subjects still had slightly lower moods at the beginning of the recovery period than the other conditions, but this difference was small and nonsignificant, $F < 1$ (see Table 3). Most important, the alcohol/slides/no-expectancy condition—by producing significant mood recovery even though its prerecovery mood (11.95) was slightly higher than the prere-

TABLE 3 Unadjusted Means for the Affect Measures by Condition

Measure	Alcohol/Slides		Alcohol/No Slides/ No Expectancy
	Expectancy	No Expectancy	
Overall affect			
Pretest	16.7	22.6	17.5
Postfeedback	7.9	11.3	11.6
Postrecovery	15.6	18.4	13.8
n	21	20	21
Depression			
Pretest	12.3	9.8	12.6
Postfeedback	16.0	14.9	18.0
Postrecovery	16.4	13.5	17.0
n	21	20	21
Hostility			
Pretest	7.0	6.1	7.0
Postfeedback	13.4	9.0	10.1
Postrecovery	8.4	7.2	12.4
n	21	20	21
Anxiety			
Pretest	6.7	4.6	6.8
Postfeedback	8.2	7.2	8.8
Postrecovery	7.3	5.6	10.5
n	21	20	21
Positive affect			
Pretest	21.0	24.5	20.4
Postfeedback	12.6	15.6	14.7
Postrecovery	18.5	20.5	18.5
n	21	20	21

Note. The overall affect scale ranged from -70 to $+53$.

covery mood in the alcohol/no-slides/no-expectancy condition (11.7) where mood recovery was not significant—showed conclusively that an especially low prerecovery mood was not in any way necessary for alcohol and activity to cause mood recovery. The same finding also rules out the relief alternative explanation. Subjects in the alcohol/slides/no-expectancy condition of this experiment showed significant mood recovery even though they expected no second task and could not have felt relief over learning about one.

MAACL Subscales. As in Study 1, although recovery of these moods mirrored the condition effects for the overall affect measure, none of these effects reached significance, even though the 3 (condition) $\times$ 2 (time of measurement) ANOVAs showed that the IQ test and feedback had significantly lowered each of these moods from the beginning of the experiment to the beginning of the recovery period: $F(1, 59) = 14.2$, $p < .001$, for anxiety; $F(1, 59) = 17.5$, $p < .001$, for depression; and $F(1, 59) = 10.6$, $p < .001$, for hostility; and $F(1, 56) = 40.7$, $p < .0001$, for affect positivity.

Subjects' acceptance of the IQ test and feedback was similar to that reported for Study 1, and no condition effects emerged for any of these measures.

General Discussion

We reasoned that while one's cognitive processes are impaired by alcohol, the demands of a simple cognitive task should help reduce negative reactions to a prior psychological stressor by making it harder to think and worry about the stressor. Either alcohol, or the task alone, the argument goes, should not block out stressor-related cognitions as effectively and thus should not afford as much relief from worry. Two experiments showed that only the combination of intoxication and slide rating significantly improved subjects' overall affect following the stress of poor IQ test performance. These data thus provide the first evidence that activity may be a necessary catalyst of alcohol's ability to reduce this kind of stress and, in so doing, help to explain why and under what circumstances drinking alcohol can be reinforcing as a stress reducer.

Although alcohol and activity consistently improved overall affect following a psychological stressor in these two experiments, these factors did not produce significant recovery of the specific negative moods measured by the MAACL (anxiety, depression, and hostility) nor of the positive moods measured by this scale. Why did these factors cause less improvement in specific moods than in overall affect? One possible explanation can be ruled out by available data: The greater number of adjectives on the overall affect scale might have made this measure more reliable than the smaller specific state subscales and thus more sensitive to real condition differences. The test–retest reliabilities for these measures, however, were actually higher for the specific subscales (ranging from .96 to .79) than for the overall scale (.70), ruling out differential reliabilities as the cause of these results. One other explanation remains plausible: Our measure of overall affect involves a pooling of all negative and all positive moods on the scale and thus may be more likely to tap the range of mood changes that occurred during the recovery period than could the specific mood scales, each of which sampled a smaller range of moods. The present experiments, unfortunately, do not provide the evidence needed to evaluate this possibility.

Although we have argued that alcohol and activity enhance affect after psychological stress by blocking out of awareness cognitions related to the stressor, we must emphasize that we do not have direct evidence that such a blocking-out effect mediated the present results. We believe that we have ruled out a number of alternative explanations. Still, the present research supports our reasoning primarily as a working hypothesis, one that must be established through converging lines of research. We also note that the present experiments have demonstrated the stress-reducing effects of alcohol and activity for a time period that encompasses only an ascending blood alcohol level. Our reasoning in this research—based, as it is, on the assumption of alcohol's impairment of cognition rather than its direct effects on affect—predicts that the effects and activity would generalize to periods of descending blood alcohol levels as well, because cognition is also impaired during this limb of the blood alcohol level curve. Confirmation of this possibility, however, awaits further research. With these limitations in mind, the present findings suggest the importance, perhaps even necessity, of activity as a mediator of alcohol's enhancement of affect following a psychological stressor.

References

Abrams, D. B. and Wilson, T. G. (1979). Effects of alcohol on social anxiety in women: Cognitive versus physiological processes. *Journal of Abnormal Psychology, 88,* 161–173.

Babor, T. F., Berglas, S., Mendelson, J. H., Ellingboe, J., and Miller, K. (1983). Alcohol, affect, and the disinhibition of verbal behavior. *Psychopharmacology, 80,* 53–60.

Birnbaum, I. M., Johnson, M. K., Hartley, J. T., and Taylor, T. H. (1980). Alcohol and elaborate schemes for sentences. *Journal of Experimental Psychology: Human Learning and Memory, 66,* 293–300.

CAHALAN, D., CISIN, I. H., AND CROSSLEY, H. M. (1969). *American drinking practices: A national study of drinking behavior and attitudes* (Monograph No. 6). New Brunswick, NJ: Rutgers Center for Alcohol Studies.

CAPPELL, H. AND HERMAN, C. P. (1972). Alcohol and tension reduction. *Quarterly Journal of Studies on Alcohol, 33,* 33–64.

CARPENTER, J. A. (1957). Effects of alcoholic beverages on skin conductance: An exploratory study. *Quarterly Journal of Studies on Alcohol, 18,* 1–18.

CONGER, J. J. (1951). The effects of alcohol on conflict behavior in the albino rat. *Quarterly Journal of Studies on Alcohol, 12,* 1–29.

CONGER, J. J. (1956). Alcoholism: Theory, problem, and challenge: II. Reinforcement theory and the dynamics of alcoholism. *Quarterly Journal of Studies on Alcohol, 17,* 296–305.

EDWARDS, A. L. (1985). *Experimental design in psychological research* (5th ed.). New York: Holt, Rinehart & Winston.

EYSENCK, H. J. (1962). *Know your own IQ.* New York: Penguin Books.

HULL, C. H. AND NIE, N. H. (Eds.). (1980). *SPSS update 7–9: New procedures and facilities for releases 7–9.* New York: McGraw-Hill.

HULL, J. G. AND YOUNG, R. D. (1983). Self-consciousness, self-esteem, and success–failure as determinants of alcohol consumption in male social drinkers. *Journal of Personality and Social Psychology, 44,* 1097–1109.

KASTL, A. J. (1969). Changes in ego functioning under alcohol. *Quarterly Journal of Studies on Alcohol, 30,* 371–380.

LEVENSON, R. W., SHER, K. J., GROSSMAN, L. M., NEWMAN, J., AND NEWLIN, D. B. (1980). Alcohol and stress response dampening: Pharmacological effects, expectancy, and tension reduction. *Journal of Abnormal Psychology, 89,* 528–538.

MARLATT, G. A. (1976). Alcohol, stress, and cognitive control. In I. G. SARASON AND C. D. SPIELBERGER (Eds.), *Stress and anxiety* (Vol. 3, pp. 271–296). Washington, DC: Hemisphere.

MARLATT, G. A., DEMMING, B., AND REID, J. B. (1973). Loss of control drinking in alcoholics: An experimental analogue. *Journal of Abnormal Psychology, 81,* 233–241.

MEDINA, E. L. (1970). The role of the alcoholic in accidents and violence. In R. E. POPHAM (Ed.), *Alcohol and alcoholism* (pp. 350–355). Toronto, Canada: University of Toronto Press.

MELLO, N. K. (1968). Some aspects of behavioral pharmacology of alcohol. *Proceedings of the American College of Neuropsychopharmacology, 8,* 787–809.

McCOLLAM, J. B., BURISH, T. G., MAISTO, S. A., AND SOBELL, M. B. (1980). Alcohol's effects on physiological arousal, self-reported affect, and sensations. *Journal of Abnormal Psychology, 89,* 224–233.

MOSKOWITZ, H. AND DEPRY, D. (1968). Differential effect of alcohol on auditory vigilance and divided attention. *Quarterly Journal of Studies on Alcohol, 29,* 54–67.

PERNANEN, K. (1976). Alcohol and crimes of violence. In B. KISSIN AND H. BEGLEITER (Eds.), *The biology of alcoholism, Vol. 4: Social aspects of alcoholism* (pp. 351–444). New York: Plenum.

PERVIN, L. A. AND LILLY, R. S. (1967). Social desirability and self-ideal self-ratings on the semantic differential. *Educational and Psychological Measurement, 27,* 845–853.

POLIVY, J., SCHUENEMAN, A. L., AND CARLSON, K. (1976). Alcohol and tension reduction: Cognitive and physiological effects. *Journal of Abnormal Psychology, 85,* 595–600.

ROSEN, L. J. AND LEE C. L. (1976). Acute and chronic effects of alcohol use on organizational processes in memory. *Journal of Abnormal Psychology, 85,* 309–317.

ROSENTHAL, R. (1978). Combining results of independent studies. *Psychological Bulletin, 85,* 185–193.

RUSSELL, J. A. AND MEHRABIAN, A. (1975). The mediating role of emotions in alcohol use. *Journal of Studies on Alcohol, 39,* 1508–1536.

STEELE, C. M. AND SOUTHWICK, L. (1985). Alcohol and social behavior. I: The psychology of drunken excess. *Journal of Personality and Social Psychology, 88,* 18–34.

STEELE, C. M., CRITCHLOW, B., AND LIU, T. J. (1985). Alcohol and social behavior II: The helpful drunkard. *Journal of Personality and Social Psychology, 48,* 35–46.

SUTKER, P. B., TABAKOFF, B., GOIST, K. C., AND RANDALL, C. L. (1983). Acute alcohol intoxication, mood states and alcohol metabolism in women and men. *Pharmacology Biochemistry and Behavior, 18,* 349–354.

TARTER, R. E., JONES, B. M., SIMPSON, C. D., AND VEGA, A. (1971). Effects of task complexity and practice on performance during acute alcohol intoxication. *Perceptual and Motor Skills, 37,* 307–313.

WASHBURNE, C. (1956). Alcohol, self, and the group. *Quarterly Journal of Studies on Alcohol, 17,* 108–123.

WILSON, G. T., AND ABRAMS, D. B. (1977). Effects of alcohol on social anxiety and physiological arousal: Cognitive versus pharmacological processes. *Cognitive Therapy and Research, 1,* 195–210.

WILSON, G. T., PEROLD, E. A., AND ABRAMS, D. A. (1981). The effects of expectations of self-intoxication and partner's drinking on anxiety in dyadic social interaction. *Cognitive Therapy and Research, 5,* 251–264.

ZEICHNER, A. AND PIHL, R. O. (1979). Effects of alcohol and behavior contingencies on human aggression. *Journal of Abnormal Psychology, 88,* 153–160.

ZUCKERMAN, M. AND LUBIN, B. (1965). *Manual for the Multiple Affect Adjective Checklist.* San Diego, CA: Educational and Industrial Testing Service.

29

Theory and Treatment in Child Molestation

Richard I. Lanyon

This paper reviews the state of current knowledge on child molestation, as distinguished from child rape. The traditional view that deviant sexual behavior is based in a character disorder is contrasted with the functional view, which makes no assumptions about etiology. Descriptive characteristics of child molesters are presented; in particular, preference molesters or pedophiles, who prefer children, are distinguished from situational molesters, whose basic preference is for adult partners, but who choose children as a function of circumstances. Structured assessment devices are needed for making this distinction and also for assessing molesters' potential for violence. From a clinical perspective, the family-systems approach is widely considered to be the treatment of choice for incestuous families. For eliminating the deviant behavior and impulses of offenders themselves, the empirical treatment literature shows that behavioral methods using covert sensitization have considerable promise, at least for situational molesters.

Child molesters tend to be defined as older persons whose conscious sexual desires and responses are directed, at least in part, toward dependent, developmentally immature children and adolescents who do not fully comprehend these actions and are unable to give informed consent (Groth, Hobson, & Gary, 1982; Mrazek, 1984; Schechter & Roberge, 1976). Because such behavior is widely believed to constitute a serious risk for the children's well-being and further development (psychological, moral, and/or physical), such behavior is prohibited in our culture, and there are strong social sanctions against it.

Despite these sanctions, child molestation occurs with alarming frequency. Because of the traditional taboos surrounding the discussion and study of sexual matters, especially deviant behavior, the scientific investigation of this topic is a relatively recent enterprise. To gain a broader understanding of the current state of knowledge, it is helpful to examine briefly the topic of sexual deviations in general.

There are two major views in the literature as to how sexually deviant behavior is best conceptualized. The traditional view has its roots in the classical literature of Krafft-Ebing (1886/1965), Freud (1905/1953), and Ellis (1942), and has two basic premises: (a) that all sexually deviant behaviors are theoretically and etiologically similar, and (b) that they represent a single type of psychopathology, specifically, a form of character disorder. Two results have stemmed

Richard I. Lanyon. Theory and Treatment in Child Molestation. *Journal of Consulting and Clinical Psychology*, 1986, Vol. 54, No. 2, pp. 176–182. Copyright © 1986 by the American Psychological Association. Reprinted by permission of the publisher and the author.

from this perspective. First, there have been a number of attempts to delineate a single theory of sexual psychopathology, usually involving psychoanalytic concepts and difficulties in psychosexual development. No specific theory has been agreed upon, however. Second, because sexual psychopathology is viewed as a character disorder, the behaviors have been regarded as highly resistant to change, so that treatment is lengthy and is based on restructuring of the character. This view is reflected in the writings and recommendations of Burgess, Groth, Holmstrom, and Sgroi (1978), Rada (1978), and others. It also tends to be the view held by the judicial system, by the social service agencies, and by the general public.

The second major view of sexual deviations is a more recent development and has its roots in the relatively atheoretical, elemental behavioral approaches to human disorders. Those who hold this view make no assumptions about etiology, and treatability is a purely empirical question. In particular, it is not assumed that a particular form of psychopathology (or any psychopathology) underlies the disorder and must be treated in order for the sexual behavior to change. Recommended interventions involve behavior therapy procedures for bringing about symptomatic changes and focus primarily on developing (or improving) adaptive sexual functioning and eliminating specific deviant behaviors, thoughts, and feelings. Proponents of this view include Abel, Blanchard, and Becker (1978) and Barlow (1974).

The behavioral or functional view does not imply that all or even most sexually deviant men or women are treatable in a practical sense, or that they are usually free of character disorder or other psychopathology. However, it is argued that such intrapsychic difficulties have not been shown to play a causal role in the development and maintenance of the deviant sexual behavior and that although they may hamper treatment, they are not the root of the disorder and do not necessarily require treatment for the sexual problem to be alleviated.

The empirical literature on sexual devia-

tions is of three kinds: descriptive studies, laboratory studies in an experimental vein, and treatment studies. Although some of this work has been guided by theoretical notions, most of it has been undertaken with a minimum of assumptions about the nature of the phenomena.

The impetus for embarking on descriptive surveys came from the work of Kinsey and his colleagues (Kinsey, Pomeroy, & Martin, 1948; Kinsey, Pomeroy, Martin, & Gebhard, 1953) on normative sexual behaviors, which led to at least three surveys on deviant sexuality (Gebhard, Gagnon, Pomeroy, & Christianson, 1965; Karpman, 1954; Mohr, Turner, & Jerry, 1964). An interesting result of these and other works, in addition to their function of demonstrating that deviant sexuality could be studied empirically, was that most sex offenders were found to be not remarkably different from other troubled people except in the deviant sexual behavior itself and in the failure of some types of offenders to establish satisfactory emotional and sexual relationships with their opposite sex peers.

These conclusions are consistent with the view that the differences are deep-seated and, therefore, difficult to approach therapeutically. They are also consistent with the view that sex offenders may not be very different from other troubled persons and that the sexual behavior can and should be studied in its own right. The latter view has given rise to a growing experimental literature that has attempted to map the differences in physiological arousal patterns among different types of sex offenders, as compared with nonoffenders. This literature is reviewed in detail by Langevin (1983).

The empirical development of behaviorally based treatments for sexual deviations occurred as an integral part of the behavior therapy movement. Early developments involved the use of aversive procedures alone and shared in the negative publicity received by early aversive behavior modification techniques. More recently, comprehensive behavioral models have been proposed (e.g., Abel et al., 1978; Barlow, 1974), and there is now a growing literature of behavioral treatment outcome studies. Reviews of particular aspects of this literature have tended to be optimistic in their conclusions (e.g., Adams & Sturgis, 1977; Blair & Lanyon, 1981; Kelly, 1982). All these empirical developments can be viewed as indicating the coming-of-age of deviant sexuality as a scientifically reputable topic that is potentially capable of being mapped, understood, and approached with viable treatment modalities.

Description and Classification

We now review the descriptive literature on child molestation. Because of space limitations, the review is necessarily selective, but it attempts to be representative. More focused reviews have been recently published by Howells (1981), Langevin (1983), and Kelly (1982). Excluded here are discussions of female offenders, a topic on which almost no data exist; characteristics of victims, the problems created for them, and their treatment; assessment issues; and questions of morals and values, as to how such men should be regarded by society.

Myths

A number of widely held beliefs about child sexual abusers have been shown to have no substance. Most prominent is the stereotype that child molesters are socially marginal persons or "dirty old men." Indeed, the molester is most commonly a respectable, otherwise law-abiding person, who may escape detection for exactly that reason. Furthermore, the median age of first offense is reported to be as young as 16 (Groth et al., 1982). Second, most molestation is done by men who are not strangers, but who are known to the victim, and in fact are often related to the victim (Conte & Berliner, 1981). Third, data and experienced clinical opinion suggest that children do not fabricate accounts of being molested except in

rare instances, presumably when there are clear motivations to do so (Meiselman, 1978; Summit, 1983).

Violence

This review is limited to a consideration of child sexual abuse in which there is no direct physical coercion or violence. Cases including violence constitute about 10% to 15% of child sexual abuse cases (DeFrancis, 1969; Mrazek, Lynch, & Bentovim, 1981), but they receive disproportionate publicity and lead the public to believe that they are typical of child sexual abuse cases in general. Groth et al. (1982) have termed these men *child rapists* and believe that they are etiologically and motivationally more similar to rape than to child molestation. These authors have suggested that the term *child molestation* be used only when the pressures used are psychological ones and the harm done to the child is psychological rather than physical.

The question of potential for violence is obviously important in determining the appropriate disposition and treatment of sex offenders. Avery-Clark and Laws (1984) showed that physiological measures of sexual arousal could discriminate less dangerous from more dangerous sex offenders, and the work of Abel, Becker, Murphy, and Flanagan (1981) represents an empirical start toward developing procedures for distinguishing child molesters from child rapists. Particularly useful would be valid assessment devices that did not rely on physiological measurement and therefore could be used on a broad basis.

Frequency

As might be expected in view of the definitional problems and the secrecy surrounding this disorder, estimates of frequency from direct reports are generally believed to be serious underestimates. No data could be found on the incidence of child molestation as a disorder among adults. Following Mrazek's (1984) review of victimization among children, it would appear that perhaps 10% to 15% of children and adolescents suffer at least one incident of sexual victimization from an adult, and approximately twice as many girls as boys. Abusive behavior ranges from genital fondling to attempted or actual oral–genital contact and intercourse. In regard to sex of victim, available data appear to indicate that close to three-quarters of male abusers choose female victims exclusively (Frisbie, 1969; Langevin, 1983), about one-quarter choose male victims, and a small minority choose both sexes (Frisbie & Dondis, 1965; Groth & Birnbaum, 1978).

Sexual History

It is here that a distinction of considerable importance has been made. It appears to have originated with Karpman (1954), who distinguished molesters who have a stable erotic *preference* for children from those who utilize children as *surrogates* for adult sexual partners. Groth more recently made this distinction a cornerstone of his theoretical position on the development of child molestation and offered a list of characteristics that are said to differentiate the two types (Groth et al., 1982). These authors proposed the terms *fixated*, referring to arrested psychosexual development, and *regressed*, referring to psychopathologically regressive behavior under stress after more-or-less normal psychosexual development.

Howells (1981) likewise supported the distinction, preferring the atheoretical terms *preference* and *situational* molesters. Preference molesters are described by the sources just cited as having a primary sexual orientation to children and as being relatively disinterested in adult partners for the fulfillment of both sexual and emotional needs. They are usually unmarried, and any marriage or other apparent heterosexual relationship is usually either for convenience, as a cover, or for access to desired children. Victims are usually male children, whose role tends to be that of a substitute for an adult female partner. Preference molesters usually do not view their behavior as inappropriate and believe that society should stop harassing them and permit them to

meet their needs. Offenses are usually pre-planned, are an ongoing and persistent part of the offender's life, have a compulsive quality to them, and do not appear to be precipitated by stress.

Situational molesters, on the other hand, generally have a more-or-less normal history of heterosocial and heterosexual development and skills, although often with some deficits in these skills, particularly in intimate relationships. Their primary sexual and emotional interests are unequivocally toward adult partners, and they view their child-related urges as abnormal and as a problem. Significant life stresses are usually present, and episodes of molestation or urges to do so can often be tied to these stresses. The behavior is often impulsive, is generally not premeditated to any extent, and is episodic rather than persistent.

Empirical data to support this classification system was reported by Groth and Birnbaum (1978), who showed that 175 convicted child sexual abusers could be classified either as preference (83) or situational (92) and found significant differences on many of these factors. There is a question as to whether the classification was done independently of the results, however. It would seem reasonable to assume that the preference versus situational distinction might more profitably be approached as a dimension rather than as a dichotomy, and the development of a scale to quantify such a dimension is currently being undertaken by the present author.

It should be clear that if there are indeed three broad categories of child sexual abusers (including child rape), then the results of most of the existing research in this area, which has treated child sexual abusers as a single group, are of uncertain meaning. At the very least, future studies should be designed so as to take these categories into consideration.

Other Classifications

One traditional classification is that of incestuous versus nonincestuous situations.

Some reviewers now believe that except insofar as incest additionally involves complex family dynamics, this is not a useful distinction in understanding the offender. For example, there is empirical evidence to suggest that both groups are similar in sexual preference patterns (Abel et al., 1981). A second classification is homosexual versus heterosexual molesters (e.g., Howells, 1981; Langevin, 1983), with its implication that male molesters of male victims are basically homosexual in orientation (and perhaps should be encouraged toward that goal in treatment). However, most molesters of boys state that they do not have adult homosexual preferences, and laboratory studies of sexual arousal suggest that this is indeed the case (e.g., Freund & Langevin, 1976). The preference versus situational distinction correlates positively with the homosexual versus heterosexual classification.

A third type of classification involves the use of the word *pedophile*. The *Diagnostic and Statistical Manual of Mental Disorders* (DSM-III, American Psychiatric Association, 1980) restricts its use to refer to men for whom children provide the "repeatedly preferred or exclusive method of achieving sexual excitement" (p. 271) and excludes those men who are sexually drawn to children but who would readily choose an adult female peer if circumstances permitted. Once again, the preference versus situational distinction seems to capture the difference between pedophiles and nonpedophilic molesters as described in DSM-III.

A fourth aspect of classification has to do with the role of physiological sexual arousal in the definition of a child molester. On the one hand, the DSM-III definition requires such arousal, at least for its category of pedophile. Similarly, the experimental laboratory literature (Langevin, 1983) and certain treatment procedures are based on the use of physical arousal measures as the most central dependent variable and, in some cases, as the only criterion of deviancy. On the other hand, Groth et al. (1982) and others have argued persuasively that child molestation and other sex offenses are best char-

acterized as sexual behavior in the service of primarily nonsexual needs, such as affection and love (and in the case of rapists, power or anger). Also, it is the writer's clinical observation that some molesters (and rapists and exhibitionists) achieve physical arousal with difficulty or not at all, so that for these men it is not a meaningful part of their deviant behavior pattern. Thus, it is perhaps safer to avoid the use of arousal as the sole criterion for deviancy and to await further research on this question.

Personality and Psychopathology

There is an extensive clinical psychoanalytic literature that offers a wide variety of ideas about the etiology of child molestation and the nature of molesters (e.g., Howells, 1981; Kraemer, 1976; Rosen, 1979). These ideas are perhaps best regarded as sources of hypotheses for further research. Consistencies among them include the significance of nonsexual (e.g., affectional or mastery) components of the molester's motivation, the idealization of childhood that is said to be a central aspect of the preference molester's motivation, and the context of anxiety-laden adult heterosexuality.

A number of studies have utilized objective test procedures, such as the Minnesota Multiphasic Personality Inventory (e.g., Atwood & Howell, 1971; McCreary, 1975; Toobert, Bartelme, & Jones, 1959), the Edwards Personal Preference Schedule (Fisher, 1969; Fisher & Howell, 1970), the Kelly Repertory Grid (Howells, 1978), and the semantic differential (Frisbie, Vanasek, & Dingman, 1967). No consistent findings emerge from these and similar studies except to support the view that molesters' sexual identification is not significantly feminine and that they tend to be somewhat more shy, passive, and unassertive than average (Langevin, 1983). Studies focusing exclusively on incestuous men have shown somewhat different trends (e.g., Meiselman, 1978), portraying them as often domineering and controlling, at least within the family itself.

Questions to do with psychological and

psychosexual development and maturity have been inadequately addressed empirically. It is in this area in particular that preference and situational molesters should be separated for independent study. Overall, it is a frequent finding that molesters have some degree of social difficulty; however, it has been suggested that because the molesters studied are those who have been caught, the more socially skillful ones go undetected (Howells, 1981).

The studies in this section have addressed adult molesters. From the viewpoint of early intervention, primary attention should be given to adolescent offenders, the younger the better. Unfortunately, few data exist on adolescents, who as a group have interpersonal needs and characteristics that differ obviously from those of adults. Also relevant is the common belief that most or even all molesters are themselves victims of childhood molestation and that this is an important developmental component of their problem and must be addressed in treatment. This question appears not to have been studied systematically, although clinically it would appear that at the least, molesters report having been victimized with a frequency that is much greater than average.

Physico-Chemical Studies

There are few studies in this area, and results tend to be unremarkable. Rada, Laws, and Kellner (1976) found that plasma testosterone levels were within normal limits. Mental retardation and senility (Mohr et al., 1964) and other brain pathology (Regestein & Reich, 1978) have not been shown to be relevant factors in child sexual abuse.

Cognitive Studies

An area of potential relevance, though virtually unstudied, is the nature of molesters' cognitions about children. An interesting study by Howells (1978) using the Kelly Repertory Grid showed that for child sexual abusers, the differences between cognitions of adults and children were not the same as for normals. Because molesters (and pref-

erence molesters, in particular) report atypical cognitions about children, it would seem important to document systematically these differences in cognitions, both sexual and nonsexual, and to investigate possible causal relations.

Effects of Alcohol

Alcohol has at times been reported to be a causal factor in child molestations (e.g., Rada, 1978). However, other writers (e.g., Howells, 1981) believe that the association is overemphasized and that molesters are overeager to blame alcohol (and other factors such as job or marital stress) because it provides a more socially acceptable explanation than a personal deficiency. More research is needed in this area.

Treatment

Four different treatment approaches to child molestation have been reported; physiological, psychoanalytic, family systems, and behavioral.

Physiological Approaches

Castration. The surgical removal of the testicles is considered barbaric in this country but has been utilized in Europe on a voluntary basis for treatment of sex offenders, including child molesters. A review of several outcome studies on the long-term effects of castration (Heim & Hursch, 1979) showed a reported dramatic reduction in sex offenses, but the studies involved methodological difficulties such as sole reliance on self-report and lack of control data for recidivism rates. There are other data to indicate that sex drive is by no means reliably reduced by this method (Langevin, 1983). In addition, a wide variety of undesirable physical side effects and psychological side effects were reported. It is concluded that castration remains an undemonstrated method for the treatment of any type of sex offender.

Chemotherapy. The use of chemotherapy involving antiandrogens for sex offenders has considerable appeal for many segments of the public but is a highly controversial topic (e.g., Fisher, 1984). On the one hand, clinical reports (e.g., Spodak, Falck, & Rappeport, 1978) have shown mixed outcomes, and side effects are reported as problematic (Langevin, 1983). Also, the changes (reduction in the strength of arousal) are temporary, and sexual arousal to inappropriate stimuli is reported to return when the drug is terminated.

On the other hand, researchers employing drug treatments remain enthusiastic about their potential (e.g., Berlin & Meinecke, 1981), and there is the belief that new and more sophisticated drugs such as cyproterone hold particular promise for reducing deviant but not normal arousal. A middle-of-the-road position might be that at the present time, drug treatment should perhaps be considered for a small minority of offenders for whom other treatments have consistently failed or are unsuitable.

Psychoanalytic Approaches

Individual psychoanalytic therapy was virtually the sole treatment method for child molestation prior to the 1960s. Early accounts have been reviewed by Karpman (1954) and by Lorand and Balint (1956). Such treatments were typically addressed to the interplay of personality dynamics, which were said to account for both the etiology of the problem and its change during treatment. Later writers reported essentially the same approach to treatment (e.g., Kopp, 1962). Group psychoanalytic therapy has also been reported as an approach for child molestation (Hartman, 1965; Quinsey, 1977; Resnik & Peters, 1967). There are no systematic outcome data for these approaches. The opinions of Groth et al. (1982), after treating many child sex offenders from a general psychoanalytic perspective, were that "it would be misleading to suggest that we have reached a state of clinical knowledge that insures successful re-habilitation of adults who sexually molest children" (p. 140) and that the problem "is something the offender will need to work with every day of his life" (p. 143).

Family-Systems Approaches

With the development of systems approaches to the conceptualization and treatment of family problems in general, there has been a rapid increase of interest in using such an approach to incestuous child molestation. Indeed, a survey of recent writings on incest shows this to be the most widely recommended and utilized method (Burgess et al., 1978; Mrazek & Kempe, 1981; Sgroi, 1982). The major assumptions are that the psychodynamic interplay among family members is of prime importance and should be a basic focus of treatment, that the father needs to accept responsibility for his acts, that the mother also needs to accept her share of the responsibility, that peer support and self-awareness in the sense of the Alcoholics Anonymous model of alcoholism is needed, and that the process of change is an insight-oriented one. Treatment is accomplished by a combination of individual therapy for each family member, followed by therapy for each dyad and then family therapy, plus group therapy and self-help support groups.

One well-known family-systems program is the Child Abuse Treatment Program of Santa Clara County (Giarretto, 1982), where out of more than 4,000 cases, mostly father–daughter incest, 90% of the children were reportedly returned to the families with less than 1% recidivism. An independent analysis of this program by Kroth (1979) showed a slightly lower but meaningful percentage of success by subjective criteria: Fathers were returned to the home after a median period of 90 days, and 92% of fathers did eventually return to their homes. Mrazek (1984) offered the caution that the outcomes in other programs appeared to be less positive.

It is emphasized that the present article addresses men who molest children, whereas family-systems treatment is concerned with the functioning of all family members and of the family as a whole. It is clear that in an incestuous family situation, the victim, the offender, the wife, and possibly other family members have significant difficulties requiring treatment and that the family functioning also requires attention. For these purposes, the family-systems approach is the current state-of-the-art. However, systematic research is needed to identify its effective components because it is usually very costly in terms of therapeutic time. Another empirical need is to document the extent of its success in eliminating the man's deviant sexual behaviors, thoughts, and feelings.

Behavioral Approaches

The application of behavior therapy approaches to child sexual abusers has also developed actively in the last 20 years. Because this work has been recently reviewed systematically by Kelly (1982), such a review is not necessary here. Kelly identified 32 behavioral studies since 1960, 14 of which involved sufficient control procedures, quantification, and methodological sophistication to enable meaningful conclusions to be drawn from the findings. Most of these studies utilized some form of aversion procedure, the most frequent of which was aversive imagery (covert sensitization), either alone or in combination with other procedures.

For example, Maletzky (1980) treated 38 molesters of male children with covert sensitization in which aversive odors were paired with deviant sexual fantasies. Homework included aversive imaginal procedures, changes in masturbation fantasies, and manipulation of the environment. Of the 38 subjects, a nationwide search showed only four legal charges in a 3-year follow-up period. Other outcome data showed major reductions in frequency of self-reported deviant urges and masturbation fantasies and positive changes in penile plethysmograph records. Case-by-case data were not reported. In a different type of controlled-study, Brownell, Hayes, and Barlow (1977)

used covert sensitization to eliminate child-related sexual behavior and urges, plus an orgasmic reconditioning procedure to increase heterosexual responsiveness. Positive changes as measured by self-report and plethysmography were stable over a 6-month follow-up period.

Kelly's (1982) conclusion was that the therapeutic behavioral reorientation of child molesters has now been clearly demonstrated. This conclusion appears warranted despite a number of problems and cautions with the outcome literature, such as the adequacy and objectivity of measurement procedures, bias in publication (positive studies are more likely to be accepted), and the fact that data as to which subjects respond most successfully are not available. In particular, no distinction was made in this literature between situational and preference molesters (or pedophiles as defined by DSM-III). Because the number of deviant aspects and also their nature are more extensive for preference than situational molesters, it is likely that the successful treatment outcomes have tended to be with situational, rather than preference, molesters.

The behavior therapy outcome literature has suffered from a consistent underemphasis on the development of adaptive ways of meeting sexual and affectional drives and on the need to deal with interpersonal and systems issues within the marital or family unit. In many cases that present for treatment in a typical practical setting, the family-systems and related problems (financial, alcohol-related, multiple crisis, police involvement, etc.) are so severe that they are beyond the capacity of the treatment setting to resolve. In these cases, the fact that aversive imagery can be successful in eliminating deviant characteristics is essentially irrelevant because the clinician is unable to set the stage for its successful use.

Clinical Suggestions

The following paragraphs state the author's tentative suggestions for a systematic treatment program for child molesters. They are based on an integration of the research and clinical literature on child molestation with 10 years of personal experience in treating such clients. Although the steps are presented in a particular order, there will necessarily be substantial overlap in practice as a number of aspects of treatment proceed simultaneously. This material is intended simply as a basis for discussion and hypotheses, and not as a set of proven procedures.

1. Any crises or immediate life problems are dealt with or stabilized. This may at times include a psychiatric evaluation for the possibility of medication to provide temporary relief from strong anxiety or depression. It may also include the therapist's involvement in family or legal matters. It is at this step that many cases, particularly those presenting at low-cost or public treatment facilities, cannot be processed further because adequate treatment resources are not available.

2. Sex education is provided as required.

3. If there is an existing adult sexual relationship that will continue, direct counseling and sex therapy are employed with the couple to alleviate any difficulties in the relationship and to ensure that the sexual and emotional aspects of the relationship are satisfying for both partners. If the offense is incestuous, then the full involvement of the family system in treatment is usually needed. These interventions are ongoing throughout the entire period of therapy.

4. If there is no ongoing adult sexual relationship, the client is encouraged to develop one. If he does not have the skills, or if he experiences disabling anxiety in this area, these problems should be approached first. This is often a long and difficult aspect of treatment because many clients still have the complex anxieties and attitudes, often unrecognized, that prevented them from developing these skills during the usual period in their lives, namely, adolescence.

5. The behavior therapy procedure of aversive imagery is employed to eliminate the deviant behaviors and also thoughts and impulses about them. Included are permanent self-management skills and follow-up at gradually increasing intervals.

The following factors would appear to be related to good prognosis: (a) manageability of life crises and financial needs; (b) good heterosocial and heterosexual skills and experiences, plus a cooperative and committed adult sexual partner, or the willingness and motivation to learn such skills and find such a partner; (c) motivation and willingness to persist in treatment and follow therapeutic instructions; (d) relative freedom from other disorders such as alcoholism or drug addiction, psychosis, or substantial neurosis or character disorder; and (e) relative freedom from constrictive religious or moral beliefs about normal adult sexuality.

Conclusions

The literature on child molestation has yielded some tentative conclusions and hypotheses. The conclusions may be summarized as follows:

1. There are alternatives to the view that child molestation is necessarily based in a character disorder and must be treated accordingly.

2. There is a substantial research literature, mostly of an atheoretical nature, on descriptive aspects and on treatment.

3. An important distinction is made between preference molesters, or pedophiles, whose basic preference is for children, and situational molesters, whose basic preference is for adults.

4. It is also important to distinguish molesters, who control their victims by psychological means, from child rapists, who employ physical coercion and violence. Valid assessment devices are needed to identify those offenders who have the potential for violence.

5. There is little to suggest that analytic psychotherapy is a successful treatment procedure. For incestuous situations, the family-systems approach is widely used and is generally considered clinically to be the most useful, although adequate empirical data are not yet available.

6. For eliminating the offender's deviant behaviors, thoughts, and feelings, behavior therapy procedures involving aversive procedures (and covert sensitization, in particular) have shown a relatively high success rate. These data should be considered to apply as yet only to the most readily treated group, situational molesters.

7. Family-systems approaches have tended to underemphasize the need to address directly the offender's deviant behaviors and impulses; behavioral approaches have tended to underemphasize the necessity for attending to the offender's interpersonal context.

8. Future research should attend to the situational/preference dimension and also to the role of cognitive factors in the etiology and maintenance of child molestation.

References

ABEL, G. G., BECKER, J. V., MURPHY, W. D., AND FLANAGAN, B. (1981). Identifying dangerous child molesters. In R. B. Stuart (Ed.), *Violent behavior; Social learning approaches to prediction, management, and treatment* (pp. 116–137). New York: Brunner/Mazel.

ABEL, G. G., BLANCHARD, E. B., AND BECKER, J. V. (1978). An integrated treatment program for rapists. In R. T. RADA (Ed.), *Clinical aspects of the rapist* (pp. 161–214). New York: Grune & Stratton.

ADAMS, H. E., AND STURGIS, E. T. (1977). Status of behavioral reorientation techniques in the modification of homosexuality: A review. *Psychological Bulletin, 84,* 1171–1188.

AMERICAN PSYCHIATRIC ASSOCIATION. (1980). *Diagnostic and statistical manual of mental disorders* (3rd ed.). Washington, DC: Author.

ATWOOD, R., AND HOWELL, R. (1971). Pupillometric and personality test scores of female aggressing pedophiliacs and normals. *Psychonomic Science, 22,* 115–116.

AVERY-CLARK, C. A., AND LAWS, D. R. (1984). Differential erection response patterns of sexual child abusers to stimuli describing activities with children. *Behavior Therapy, 15,* 71–83.

BARLOW, D. H. (1974). The treatment of sexual deviation: Toward a comprehensive behavioral approach. In K. S. CALHOUN, H. E. ADAMS AND K. M. MITCHELL (Eds.), *Innovative treatment methods in psychopathology* (pp. 121–147). New York: Wiley.

BERLIN, F. S., AND MEINECKE, C. F. (1981). Treatment of sex offenders with antiandrogenic medication: Conceptualization, review of treatment modalities, and preliminary findings. *American Journal of Psychiatry, 138,* 601–607.

BLAIR, C.D., AND LANYON, R. I. (1981). Exhibitionism: Etiology and treatment. *Psychological Bulletin, 89,* 439–463.

BROWNELL, K. D., HAYES, S. C., AND BARLOW, D. H. (1977). Patterns of appropriate and deviant sexual arousal: The behavioral treatment of multiple sexual deviations. *Journal of Consulting and Clinical Psychology, 45,* 1144–1155.

BURGESS, A. W., GROTH, A. N., HOLSTROM, L. L. AND SGROI, S. S. (1978). *Sexual assault of children and adolescents.* Lexington, MA: Heath.

CONTE, J. R., AND BERLINER, L. (1981). Sexual abuse of children: Implications for practice. *Social Casework, 62,* 601–606.

DEFRANCIS, V. (1969). *Protecting the child victims of sex crimes committed by adults.* Denver, CO: American Humane Association.

ELLIS, H. (1942). *Studies in the psychology of sex* (2 vols.). New York: Random House.

FISHER, G. (1969). Psychological needs of heterosexual pedophiliacs. *Diseases of the Nervous System, 30,* 419–421.

FISHER, G., AND HOWELL, L. (1970). Psychological needs of homosexual pedophiliacs. *Diseases of the Nervous System, 31,* 623–625.

FISHER, K. (1984, May). Old attitudes slow treatment gains for sex offenders. *APA Monitor,* pp. 23–24.

FREUD, S. (1953). Three essays on the theory of sexuality. In S. Freud, *The complete psychological works of Sigmund Freud.* (standard ed., Vol. 7, pp. 123–243). London: Hogarth Press. (Original work published 1905).

FREUND, K., AND LANGEVIN, R. (1976). Bisexuality in homosexual pedophilia. *Archives of Sexual Behavior, 5,* 415–423.

FRISBIE, L. (1969). *Another look at sex offenders in*

California (Research Monograph No. 12). Sacramento: California Department of Mental Hygiene.

FRISBIE, L. V., AND DONDIS, E. H. (1965). *Recidivism among treated sex offenders* (Research Monograph No. 5). Sacramento: California Department of Mental Hygiene.

FRISBIE, L. V., VANASEK, F. J. AND DINGMAN, H. F. (1967). The self and the ideal self: Methodological study of pedophiles. *Psychological Reports, 20,* 699–706.

GEBHARD, P. H., GAGNON, J. H., POMEROY, W. B., AND CHRISTIANSON, C. V. (1965). *Sex offenders: An analysis of types.* New York: Harper & Row.

GIARRETTO, H. (1982). A comprehensive child sexual abuse treatment program. *Child Abuse and Neglect, 6,* 263–278.

GROTH, A. N., AND BIRNBAUM, H. J. (1978). Adult sexual orientation and attraction to underage persons. *Archives of Sexual Behavior, 7,* 175–181.

GROTH, A. N., HOBSON, W. F., AND GARY, T. S. (1982). The child molester: Clinical observations. In J. Conte & D. A. Shore (Eds.), *Social work and child sexual abuse* (pp. 129–144). New York: Haworth.

HARTMAN, V. (1965). Notes on group psychotherapy with pedophiles. *Canadian Psychiatric Association Journal, 10,* 283–288.

HEIM, N., AND HURSCH, C. J. (1979). Castration for sex offenders: A review and critique of recent European literature. *Archives of Sexual Behavior, 8,* 281–304.

HOWELLS, K. (1978). Some meanings of children for pedophiles. In M. Cook & G. Wilson (Eds.), *Love and attraction* (pp. 57–82). London: Pergamon Press.

HOWELLS, K. (1981). Adult sexual interest in children: Considerations relevant to theories of etiology. In M. Cook & K. Howells (Eds.), *Adult sexual interest in children* (pp. 55–94). London: Academic Press.

KARPMAN, B. (1954). *The sexual offender and his offenses.* New York: Julian Press.

KELLY, R. J. (1982). Behavioral reorientation of pedophiliacs: Can it be done? *Clinical Psychology Review, 2,* 387–408.

KINSEY, A. C., POMEROY, W. B., AND MARTIN, C. E. (1948). *Sexual behavior in the human male.* Philadelphia: Saunders.

KINSEY, A. C., POMEROY, W. B., MARTIN, C. E., AND GEBHARD, P. H. (1953). *Sexual behavior in the human female.* Philadelphia: Saunders.

KOPP, S. B. (1962). The character structure of sex offenders. *American Journal of Psychotherapy, 16,* 64–70.

KRAEMER, W. (1976). *The normal and abnormal love of children.* London: Sheldon Press.

KRAFFT-EBING, R., VON. (1965). *Psychopathia sexualis.* New York: Putnam. (Original work published 1886).

KROTH, J. A. (1979). Family therapy impact on intra-familial child sexual abuse. *Child Abuse and Neglect, 3,* 297–302.

LANGEVIN, R. (1983). *Sexual strands.* Hillsdale, NJ: Erlbaum.

LORAND, A. S., AND BALINT, M. (Eds.). (1956). *Perversions: Psychodynamics and therapy.* New York: Random House.

MALETZKY, B. (1980). Self-referred versus court-referred sexually deviant patients: Success with assisted covert sensitization. *Behavior Therapy, 11,* 306–314.

McCREARY, C. P. (1975). Personality differences among child molesters. *Journal of Personality Assessment, 39,* 591–593.

MEISELMAN, K. (1978). *Incest: A psychological study of causes and effects with treatment recommendations.* San Francisco: Jossey-Bass.

MOHR, J. W., TURNER, R. W., AND JERRY, M. B. (1964). *Pedophilia and exhibitionism.* Toronto: University of Toronto Press.

MRAZEK, F. J. (1984). Sexual abuse of children. In B. LAHEY AND A. E. KAZDIN (Eds.), *Advances in child clinical psychology* (Vol. 6, pp. 199–215). New York: Plenum Press.

MRAZEK, P. B., AND KEMPE, C. H. (Eds.). (1981). *Sexually abused children and their families.* New York: Pergamon Press.

MRAZEK, P. B., LYNCH, M., AND BENTOVIM, A. (1981). Recognition of child sexual abuse in the United Kingdom. In P. B. MRAZEK AND C. H. KEMPE (Eds.), *Sexually abused children and their families* (pp. 35–49). Oxford: Pergamon Press.

QUINSEY, V. L. (1977). The assessment and treatment of child molesters: A review. *Canadian Psychological Review, 18,* 204–220.

RADA, R. T. (1978). Sexual psychopathology: Historical survey and basic concepts. In R. T. Rada (Ed.), *Clinical aspects of the rapist* (pp. 1–19). New York: Grune & Stratton.

RADA, R., LAWS, D., AND KELLNER. R. (1976). Plasma testosterone levels in the rapist. *Psychosomatic Medicine, 38,* 257–268.

REGESTEIN, Q. R. AND REICH, P. (1978). Pedophilia occurring after the onset of cognitive impairment. *Journal of Nervous and Mental Disease, 166,* 794–798.

RESNIK, H. L. P., AND PETERS, J. J. (1967). Outpatient group therapy with convicted pedophiles. *International Journal of Group Psychotherapy, 17,* 151–158.

ROSEN, I. (1979). *Sexual deviation* (2nd ed.). Oxford: Oxford University Press.

SCHECHTER, M. D., AND ROBERGE, L. (1976). Sexual exploitation. In R. E. HELFER AND C. H. KEMPE (Eds.), *Child abuse and neglect: The family and the community* (pp. 127–142). Cambridge: Ballinger.

SGROI, S. M. (1982). *Handbook of clinical intervention in child sexual abuse.* Lexington, MA: Heath.

SPODAK, M. K., FALCK, Z. A., AND RAPPEPORT, J. R. (1978). The hormonal treatment of paraphilias with depo-provera. *Criminal Justice and Behavior, 5,* 304–311.

SUMMIT, R. C. (1983). The child sexual abuse accommodation syndrome. *Child Abuse and Neglect, 7,* 177–193.

TOOBERT, S., BARTELME, K. F., AND JONES, E. S. (1959). Some factors related to pedophilia. *International Journal of Psychiatry, 4,* 272–279.

Psychopathology in Children

The study of childhood maladjustment and psychopathology has undergone radical change in recent years. A crude index of the nature and extent of this change emerges from a contrast between the original version of DSM published in 1952 and the most recent DSM-III-R published in 1987. DSM-I contained no major diagnostic categories reserved exclusively for children and considered most childhood disorders as mere downward extensions in age of adult psychiatric disorders. DSM-III-R, in contrast, contains 11 major categories of disorders first evident in infancy, childhood, or adolescence and reflects a much more differentiated view of cognitive, social, and emotional differences between children and adults. The current taxonomy is by no means a final statement on childhood psychopathology. To the contrary, it signals the earliest stages of a concentrated, multidisciplinary effort to understand the nature, origins, and sequelae of childhood disorders. Subsequent revisions of the DSM will no doubt reflect and contribute to advances in this area.

Historically, the study of normal and abnormal development in childhood have been separate fields of inquiry. Childhood disorders were by and large considered the proper domain of child psychiatry, and the study of normal social, emotional, and cognitive development was the domain of child/developmental psychologists. Separate advancements in these and related fields, how-ever, made it increasingly clear that there was much to be gained by combining interests, perspectives, resources, and research strategies (Cicchetti, 1989). This recognition, in turn, gave rise to the gradual emergence of a new discipline—developmental psychopathology.

Developmental Psychopathology

Developmental psychopathologists do not share a particular theoretical orientation or research strategy. What they do share is an interest in understanding the factors that mediate and/or modify the development and maintenance of psychological and psychiatric disorders. Not all adult disorders have their origins in childhood, and many childhood disturbances do not continue into adulthood. Therefore, developmental psychopathologists study both normal and disturbed populations and are concerned with continuities and discontinuities in abnormal functioning across the life span.

Michael Rutter's article, entitled "Child Psychiatry: The Interface between Clinical and Developmental Research" (selection 30) provides an excellent point of departure for our section on childhood disorders. It begins with a brief examination of the origins of developmental psychopathology as a discipline and describes some of its distinctive features as a route to understanding both childhood and adult disorders. Rutter then explores in considerable detail how a developmental perspective on psychopathology has contributed to our understanding of childhood depression, autism, schizophrenia, and the effects of adverse experiences in childhood on psychological development.

Depression

Until recently, the existence of depression in children was a highly controversial issue. Some had argued that although children can feel sad, they cannot become clinically depressed (Anthony, 1975). This view was endorsed by many psychoanalytically oriented researchers and clinicians, who subscribed to the traditional Freudian theory that the superego must be developed in order for depression to occur. And because, according to analytic theory, young children do not yet have adequately developed superegos, they should be incapable of becoming depressed.

Still others (e.g., Glaser, 1968) had argued in support of the concept of "masked" depression, wherein problematic behaviors such as delinquency, fears, and learning difficulties are considered to be "depressive equivalents." Clearly, however, this approach—which has subsequently been abandoned—held considerable potential for confusion. If a wide range of behavior deviations in children can be interpreted as manifestations of depressive symptomatology, how can a differential diagnosis ever be made?

In more recent years, the majority of clinicians and researchers have come to accept that depression does occur in children. The controversy now concerns whether traditional adult criteria should be used to diagnose childhood depression. As Rutter points out (selection 30), the fact that depressed children can meet DSM criteria should not be taken to mean that depressed

children are merely small versions of depressed adults. A number of developmental considerations clearly suggest that this is not the case. These include the twofold increase in the frequency of depression after puberty, the dramatic rise in the suicide rate between ages 10 and 20, and the striking reversal of the ratio of depressed males to depressed females—again after puberty. Rutter's article also draws attention to the fact that depression in children is closely associated with a number of other problems. These include conduct problems, school difficulties, and disturbed peer relationships.

Hyperactivity

Hyperactivity (or attention-deficit hyperactivity disorder as it is now officially called) is characterized by developmentally inappropriate degrees of inattention, impulsiveness, and motor behavior. Most commonly found in boys, the disorder is estimated to occur in as many as 3% of children (DSM-III-R, 1987). Hyperactive children are easily distracted by extraneous stimuli. They also find it hard to sustain involvement in tasks or play activities, to wait their turn, and to follow through on instructions. In many cases these behaviors lead to difficulties in school and problems with peers. Although inability to pay attention is characteristic of hyperactive children, other groups also exhibit attentional deficits. This is particularly true of the learning disabled. An important question is therefore: Are certain types of attentional deficits unique to hyperactive children, or do they exhibit attentional problems that overlap with those found in other diagnostic groups?

In an effort to address this issue, Tarnowski, Prinz, and Nay (selection 31) compared hyperactive, learning disabled, and mixed diagnosis boys on a variety of different tasks. Some of these tasks were designed to assess sustained attention, whereas others focussed on the assessment of selective attention. A sample of nonhyperactive, nonlearning disabled boys was also included for comparison purposes.

An interesting pattern of results was found. Deficits in sustained attention were found only in the hyperactive children. Selective attention problems, on the other hand, were more characteristic of the learning disabled than the hyperactive children. Perhaps not surprisingly, children with both hyperactivity and learning disability showed evidence of both selective and sustained attentional deficits. The results of Tarnowski's group therefore support the view that attention deficits—specifically deficits in sustained attention—are an important and perhaps diagnosis-specific feature of hyperactivity.

Eating Disorders

Our final focus in this section is on eating disorders. DSM-III currently recognizes four different eating disorders. Some, such as pica (ingestion of nonnutritive substances such as hair or paint) and rumination disorder (repeated regurgitation), are found in very young children of both sexes. Others, such as anorexia and bulimia nervosa are most likely to develop during adolescence and typically affect females rather than males.

Strong desires to prevent weight gain are characteristic of both anorexia and bulimia. In anorexia, this gives rise to a voluntary restriction of food intake and a resulting loss of body weight. Bulimic individuals, on the other hand, may be underweight, overweight, or of normal weight. What distinguishes them is a recurrent pattern of binge eating followed by either self-induced vomiting, excessive laxative use, fasting, or vigorous exercise.

Two features serve to make the inclusion of an article on bulimia nervosa particularly important. First, unlike anorexia (accounts of which can be traced back to the Middle Ages), bulimia appears to be a new disorder. According to Boskind-White and White (1986), the original name, bulimarexia, was introduced in 1976 when an unusual pattern of behavior was observed in a large number of women students seeking treatment at Cornell University. Second, the occurrence of bulimia appears to be limited to the United States and Europe (Westermeyer, 1985). Not surprisingly, these factors have led many to a consideration of sociocultural factors in the development of the disorder.

In our final article of this section, Striegel-Moore, Silberstein, and Rodin (selection 32) raise a number of questions central to an understanding of bulimia. Noting that approximately 90% of bulimic individuals are women they ask, Why women? Second, because being female is clearly not the only risk factor for developing bulimia, they ask, Which women? Finally, in recognition of the recent inclusion of bulimia into the psychiatric nomenclature, they ask, Why now? The result is a thoughtful integration of a large number of diverse research findings that should be of high interest to both the male and female student of psychopathology.

References and Suggestions for Additional Reading

ANTHONY, E. J. (1975). Childhood depression. In ANTHONY, E. J. AND BENEDEK, T. (Eds.). *Depression and human existence.* Boston: Little, Brown.

BLECHMAN, E. A., McENROE, M. J., CARRELLA, E. T., AND AUDETTE, D. P. (1986). Childhood competence and depression. *Journal of Abnormal Psychology, 95,* 3, 223–227.

BOSKIND-WHITE, M. AND WHITE, W. C. (1986). Bulimarexia: A historical-sociocultural perspective. In Brownell, K. D. & Foreyt, J. P. (1986). *Handbook of eating disorders.* New York: Basic Books.

BROWNELL, K. D. & FOREYT, J. P. (1986). *Handbook of eating disorders.* New York: Basic Books.

CICCHETTI, D. (1989). An historical perspective on the discipline of developmental psychopathology. In J. ROLF, A. MASTEN, D. CICCHETTI, K. NUECHTERLEIN, AND S. WEINTRAUB (Eds.). *Risk and protective factors in the development of psychopathology.* New York: Cambridge University Press.

GLASER, K. (1968) Masked depression in children and adolescents. *American Journal of Psychotherapy, 21,* 565–574.

HODGES, K. K. AND SIEGEL, L. J. (1985). Depres-

sion in children and adolescents. In BECKMAN, E. E. AND LEBER, W. R. *Handbook of depression: Treatment, assessment, and research.* Homewood, Il: Dorsey Press.

WESTERMEYER, J. (1985). Psychiatric diagnosis across cultural boundaries. *American Journal of Psychiatry, 142,* 7, 798–805.

30

Child Psychiatry: The Interface between Clinical and Developmental Research

Michael L. Rutter

Synopsis: Developmental psychopathology constitutes a research strategy that is concerned with questions about continuities and discontinuities over time (the developmental perspective) and over the span of behavioural variation (the psychopathological perspective). The utility of this approach is discussed in relation to childhood depression, autism and schizophrenia, and the effects of adverse life experiences.

Introduction

Child psychiatry is a relatively young discipline. Although psychiatric disorders in children had been described by Maudsley as long ago as 1867, the first clinical services specifically allocated for children with psychiatric problems were not set up until the 1920s, the first textbook appeared about a decade later, and recognition as a separate subspeciality with its own programme of training came much more recently. Child psychiatry's roots lie in the interdisciplinary Mental Hygiene movement, in psychoanal-

Michael L. Rutter. Child Psychiatry: The interface between Clinical and Developmental Research. *Psychological Medicine,* 1986, Vol. 16, pp. 151–169. Copyright © 1986 by Cambridge University Press. Reprinted by permission.

ysis, in educational psychology and in services for delinquents (Cameron, 1956; Kanner, 1959; Warren, 1974). It is easy to see the marks of those early influences in the practice of child psychiatry today: interdisciplinary approaches are characteristic; work with schools as well as families is integral; psychiatric conditions are seen to span disorders of conduct as well as disturbances of emotion; and psychodynamic theories and methods of treatment are given emphasis.

Nevertheless, when Kanner (1959) reviewed trends in child psychiatry just over a quarter of a century ago he warned that all was not well; methods of working had become ossified, there was too little contact with medicine and too often systems of thought were inflexible. During the last two decades there has come a widespread acceptance of the unfortunate consequences of some aspects of child psychiatry's upbringing, a recognition that has been accompanied by major changes in clinical concepts and patterns of care. Both within the discipline (Philips et al. 1983) and outside it (Guze, 1983) there is agreement that the establishment of community services away from University centres led to intellectual malnutrition and academic isolation. Moreover, there is unanimity on the need for research that is closely integrated with clinical practice and training. For obvious reasons, this plea for research has usually been accompanied by an emphasis on epidemiological and longitudinal studies and on the need for nosological investigations likely to lead to improved systems of diagnosis and classification (see DHSS, 1980).

But what should constitute the scientific underpinnings of child psychiatry? The question is crucial if child psychiatry is to have any credentials as a distinctive discipline. Of course, child psychiatry is part of general psychiatry and shares with it many of its distinctive features. Both are heavily reliant on the basic sciences—neurobiological and behavioural. But is child psychiatry just the psychiatry of little people? Guze (1983), a sympathetic critic, seemed to imply so in his essay on 'Child psychiatry: taking stock', in that he made little mention of development, and his lengthy list of related disciplines did not include developmental psychology. On the other hand, the American Academy of Child Psychiatry in its 'Project Future' (Philips et al. 1983) placed 'developmental psychopathology' as one of its two areas of research warranting special emphasis (nosology, epidemiology and outcome studies was the other). Unfortunately, the remnants of child psychiatry's infancy were to be seen in its equation of development with psychoanalytical theory; equally, the mark of adolescent rebellion was evident in its relative disregard of the contributions of other disciplines (Rutter, 1984d).

Nevertheless, it has to be the case that child psychiatry requires an understanding of the developmental process; children are developing organisms and not just small adults. Sometimes adult psychiatrists have equated a developmental approach with a focus on the role of early life experiences, but that constitutes a most misleadingly restricted view of development. As Eisenberg (1977) noted, development encompasses the roots of behaviour in prior maturation and physical influences (both internal and external) as well as the residues of earlier experiences. Equally, it involves not just the sequelae of the past but also the modulations of those sequelae by the circumstances of the present.

It should be added that a developmental perspective is necessary in adult as well as in child psychiatry (Rutter, 1980). That is not to suggest that all adult disorders have their origins in childhood or even that psychiatric conditions arising during the years of adulthood can only be understood by reference to the process of development as it took place in childhood. That would be absurd; many mental illnesses arise for reasons that are unconnected with happenings in childhood. This is of interest and importance in its own right. A developmental perspective must take account of continuities *and* discontinuities between childhood and adult life. Research findings are clear cut in their indication that *both* occur (see Kagan, 1984; Rutter, 1984a, b, c; Sroufe & Rutter, 1984).

Of course, one may ask what normal development has to do with illness? Is it not likely that the factors underlying disorder will prove to be different from those that account for adaptive functioning, that abnormal development will not parallel normal growth? Indeed, in many cases, that is probable. But the very posing of these questions begins to provide a structure for the scientific basis of child psychiatry—namely, what has come to be called 'developmental psychopathology' (Rutter & Garmezy, 1983).

Developmental Psychopathology

It should be made clear that developmental psychopathology comprises an agenda for the future more than accomplishments of the past. Until very recently research on child development and research on child psychiatric disorders were rather separate endeavours (Achenbach, 1978). Nevertheless, that is changing—as much by shifts in the focus of developmental research as by any alterations in child psychiatry (see Cicchetti, 1984). Developmental psychopathology has no single unifying theoretical perspective. That is not because theories are unimportant—to the contrary they are essential as a means of ordering ideas and of making sense out of factual findings. Nor is it because the prevailing theories are necessarily wrong in what they propose. Rather, it is that no one theory even begins to approximate a complete explanation for developmental processes—normal or abnormal (Rutter, 1980). So, if developmental psychopathology does not constitute a theory, what is it? More than anything, it is characterized by the types of questions it poses rather than by the specific answers it provides. Thus, developmentalists raise queries about the processes and mechanisms underlying developmental transitions and about the implications that follow their occurrence; about whether or not there are age-dependent variations in susceptibility to stress; whether the development of depression or delinquent activities at one age is dependent on prior occurrences at an earlier age; and whether there are points in development at which personality becomes stabilized. Psychopathologists focus on individual differences, asking about heterogeneity in the developmental process and in behavioural outcomes. The prime focus is on the question of the extent to which normal variation extends into disorder. Is psychotic depression an extreme variant of normal misery or does it differ in kind? Is antisocial personality disorder the end of the continuum of normal delinquent activities or does it represent a qualitative discontinuity?

Developmental psychopathology has as its distinctive feature the combination of these two approaches. The questions raised concern both continuities and discontinuities over time (the developmental perspective) and continuities and discontinuities over the span of behavioural variation (the psychopathological perspective). The conjunction of the two is used as the prime research strategy to gain an understanding of the developmental process and the origins and course of psychiatric disorders. Such understanding is crucial for the rational planning of treatment strategies (Maughan & Rutter, 1985*b*; Rutter, 1979*b*, 1982).

It has to be said that the achievements to date of a developmental psychopathology approach are modest, as might be expected

from the fact that the advantages of this way of looking at research problems are only just beginning to be appreciated. Nevertheless, already research findings are forcing reconceptualizations of development and of disorder. These are illustrated here by the findings from three different areas of investigation that exemplify different facets of developmental psychopathology research: depressive disorders in childhood, autism and schizophrenia, and the effects of adverse experiences.

Depressive Disorders in Childhood

During the last decade or so there has been a considerable change in psychiatric concepts of childhood depression (see Cantwell & Carlson, 1983; Rutter et al. 1985). Up to the mid-1970s the prevailing view was that depressive conditions rarely occurred in children (or that, when they arose, they did so in a 'masked' form). Then, following the use of various standardized questionnaire and interview techniques, it became accepted that depressive disorders meeting adult criteria can and do appear in childhood. As so often happens, once the phenomenon had been recognized, it came to be seen ever more widely. Thus, there have been claims that depression constitutes one of the commonest causes of child psychiatric referrals (making the situation closely comparable to that in adult life). Moreover, it has been thought by some workers that, because adult-type research diagnostic criteria can be applied to childhood depression, this means that the problem has been solved; depressive conditions in young people are equivalent to those in adults and can be studied in the same way. But is that really so?

Developmental considerations clearly indicate that it is not. In the first place, there are huge age differences in the occurrence of depressive and depression-related conditions (Rutter, 1985*a, b*). These are most dramatically shown in suicide figures where the rate rises more than a hundred-fold between the ages of 10 and 20 years (McClure, 1984; Shaffer, 1985). Suicide before the age of 10 is so rare as to be almost non-existent; then after the age of 14 or so there is a rapid rise in incidence. Parasuicide rates similarly increase very sharply over the adolescent age period (Hawton & Goldacre, 1982). Once again, there is a huge jump in frequency during the teenage years, although parasuicide differs from suicide in reaching a peak in early adult life rather than old age.

Psychiatric clinic data show further age trends of note. Mania and bipolar affective disorders become substantially more common during the teens, although they can arise in earlier childhood. Depressive conditions also double in frequency over the years surrounding puberty. For example, using an operationally defined cluster of depressive symptomatology, Pearce (1978, and personal communication) found that whereas only 1 in 9 pre-pubertal clinic attenders showed such a cluster, a quarter of post-pubertal children attending the same psychiatric clinic did so—a more than two-fold increase in rate. Interestingly, his data also showed a change in sex ratio—from a male preponderance before puberty to a female one after puberty.

General population studies provide further evidence. Kaplan and his colleagues (1984), using the Beck inventory, showed that depressive feelings became substantially more frequent during the mid and late teens compared with their rates during earlier adolescence. The Isle of Wight data (Rutter et al. 1976; Rutter, 1979*a*) showed the same. However, they also suggested that the rise may be more a function of pubertal status than of chronological age. Fig. 1 shows the puberty differences for three measures of depressive feelings as assessed in boys all of whom were aged $14\frac{1}{2}$–$15\frac{1}{2}$ years.

There are important limitations to all the studies cited; nevertheless, it is clear that the years of adolescence are accompanied by quite startling changes in affective phenomenology. It is not enough to assert that depression of a type typical of adult life can

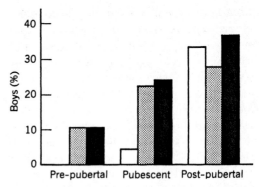

FIGURE 1

Depressive feelings and stage of puberty. □, Marked misery (interview report); ▨, self-depreciation (interview report); ■ miserable (questionnaire self-report).

occur in childhood (although clearly it can); we must go on to ask why there are such major age changes in both depressive feelings and clinical disorders—why young children seem to be relatively protected and why vulnerability appears to increase during adolescence.

However, in seeking to answer that question it is crucial to recognize that, although there are major age trends in various forms of affective disorder, nevertheless feelings of misery and unhappiness are quite common in early and middle childhood. For example, in the Isle of Wight study of 10–12 year old children (Rutter et al. 1970) two-fifths of the boys and three-fifths of the girls with psychiatric disorder were reported by their parents to show misery. Moreover, misery could not be viewed as just a normal emotional manifestation, as it was reported some 4–6 times as often in the psychiatric group as in the general population. Thus, dysphoric mood is a common psychopathological feature. Why, then is it said that depression as a disorder or condition is less common in childhood than in adult life? There appear to be three main reasons. First, compared with depression in adults, the feelings of misery in childhood are more often labile and influenced by circumstances, and less often accompanied by depressive-type cognitions of guilt, self-depreciation, and feelings of hopelessness about the future. Secondly, it is less common for the misery to be accompanied by such depression-associated vegetative features as early morning wakening, loss of weight and psychomotor retardation. Thirdly, it is usual for the misery to be associated with a wide range of other psychosocial problems, but perhaps especially conduct disturbance and educational difficulties. Accordingly, the main question concerns this rather heterogeneous group of psychiatric disorders in which dysphoric mood is prominent but yet which fail fully to meet the traditional adult criteria for major depressive disorder. Are these the childhood equivalents of adult depression, in which the manifestations have been modified as a result of psychological immaturity? Or, rather, are these basically different conditions with the dysphoria simply part of some other form of psychiatric disorder (such as a conduct disorder) or an understandable reaction to adverse circumstances (such as educational failure or isolation from peers)?

The very raising of these questions draws our attention to the methodological problems. To begin with, it seems that, up to the age of 8 years or so, children find it difficult to consider their own affect separate from particular environmental contexts and equally difficult to differentiate normal sadness from autochthonous dysphoria (Kovacs, 1985). Similarly, children's limited ability to reflect on their own cognitive processes constrains their ability to report depressive cognitions. The usual approach to this problem is to ask children about depression in a way that differs from that used with adults. For example, the K-SADS-P (Chambers et al. 1985) suggests that the feeling of being lonely or of missing someone should be used as synonymous with depressive mood; similarly, the Weinberg criteria treat 'negative and difficult to please' as indicative of dysphoric mood, and desire to 'run away or leave home' as evidence of self-depreciatory ideation (see Cantwell, 1983). But are these isomorphic? Certainly, it is not self-evident that they should be taken as equivalents.

Perhaps the most basic need in the study of childhood depression is to determine how the manifestations of depression vary with age. In a frustrating fashion, the satisfactory investigation of developmental trends awaits the availability of reliable and valid measures of depressive affect and cognition, while the creation of measures applicable to all age groups awaits knowledge on the developmental features that influence the manifestations of depression. The dilemma cannot be circumvented; it is necessary to grasp the nettle and to seek to deal with the substantive and methodological issues in parallel. That will constitute the first goal of developmental and epidemiological studies in this area—namely, to delineate the changes with age in the various components of depression (affect, cognition, somatic features, and impaired social functioning), as considered both separately and in terms of patterns. However, it will be appreciated that such investigations must go beyond the developmental study of the clinical manifestations of depression; it is necessary also to examine some of the possible bases for such age changes. For instance, it has been suggested that young children are less likely to suffer from depression because of their limited capacities in social and metacognition. It appears that young children differ from adolescents in that they are less likely to respond to task failure with generalized feelings of helplessness, they are less likely to develop negative self-perceptions and less likely to think about the long-term future (see Rutter, 1985b). Accordingly, the second goal is the determination of age changes in those aspects of cognition that might be involved in the psychological processes leading to depression. Of course, in these investigations it will be crucial to relate changes in rates of depression not only to chronological age and to cognitive maturity, but also to hormonal levels and sexual maturity. Ideally, biochemical markers of depression should also be examined; if depression occurs as often in childhood as in adult life but does so in masked form, such markers should be linked with these atypical depressive disorders in childhood but not in adult life. Unfortunately, that task must be for the future as sufficiently sensitive and specific markers of depression (either trait or state) have yet to be identified (Puig-Antich, 1985).

An entirely different hypothesis to explain age differences in depression proposes that children are relatively protected from depression because they are less likely to experience life stressors or less likely to perceive them as carrying long-term threat, or because they are more likely to be buffered from stress through affectional support from the family. Investigations, therefore, are being undertaken to determine whether or not there are developmental trends in appraisal of or responses to acute stress and chronic adversity that may help to explain age differences in depressive manifestations.

Longitudinal studies provide a rather different approach to the same problem. Insofar as depression constitutes a meaningful and distinctive psychiatric condition it might be supposed that there should be some uniformity in the form of the symptomatology or the course of the disorder over time in relation to recurrences. Zeitlin (1985) used this strategy in examining the records of Maudsley Hospital patients seen both as children and later as adults. Depressive disorders at the two age periods were operationally defined in terms of the constellation of symptoms identified in Pearce's (1978) investigation of child patients. Two findings stood out. First, nearly all the children who exhibited the depressive syndrome in childhood also did so in adult life (see Fig. 2). The continuity over time was strikingly strong. However, it should be noted that depression was a very common clinical picture in adult life and most depressed adults had *not* shown psychiatric problems in childhood. Secondly, although there was strong continuity looking forwards from childhood depression, the same was not true looking back from adult life. Whereas non-depressive neurotic disorders were highly consistent in their symptom patterns between childhood and adult life, this was not so for

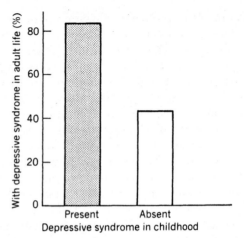

FIGURE 2

Links between depressive syndromes in childhood and adult life (looking forwards). Data from Zeitlin (1985).

depressive disorders (see Fig. 3). Only two-fifths of adults with a depressive syndrome had shown a pure emotional disorder in childhood (depressive or non-depressive) and a third had exhibited antisocial behaviour without any type of emotional disturbance.

Zeitlin's data underline the universal observation that depression in childhood is very frequently associated with a mixed as-

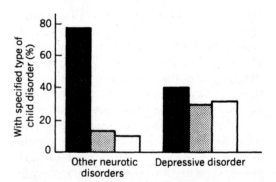

FIGURE 3

Childhood antecedents of depressive and non-depressive neurotic disorders (looking back). Data from Zeitlin (1985). ■, "Pure' emotional disorder in childhood; ▨, mixed disorder in childhood; □, delinquency/conduct disorder in childhood.

sortment of problems, including poor relationships with peers, conduct disturbance, and educational difficulties (see Puig-Antich, 1982; Puig-Antich et al. 1985). We are left with the problem of how to interpret the temporal consistency of depressive symptomatology. Does the consistency mean that depressive disorders in childhood usually include a great admixture of other symptoms, so that the diagnosis should be made on the *presence* of depressive phenomena, rather than the absence of other problems? Or, alternatively, does it imply that most of these mixed pictures are not 'true' depressive syndromes at all; is it merely that personality features lend a dysphoric colouring to other psychiatric disorders?

A prospective study is needed to resolve that issue. For that purpose, Pearce's original series of depressed children, together with carefully matched controls with non-depressive psychiatric disorders, are being re-examined in adult life blind to the childhood diagnosis. Adult outcome will be used as a validating criterion for childhood depression but, in addition, the data will be used to determine how far continuities over time reflect the persistence of environmental risk factors rather than syndrome constancy. A family history of major affective disorder constitutes another validating criterion. The fact that Weissman and her colleagues (1984) showed that the familial loading was greater in adults when the onset was in early, rather than middle, adult life makes this a particularly powerful tool for examining continuities and discontinuities between child and adult depression. However, the demonstration of a genetic factor in depression does not necessarily mean that children's relative protection from depression will be genetically determined. In adult life depression has been shown to have a variety of aetiological factors and it appears, for example that women's greater predisposition to depression is *not* genetically determined (Merikangas et al. 1985). Age differences in the manifestation of depression need to be investigated from psycho-social, cognitive, and biological perspectives.

Autism and Schizophrenia
Autism

Depression provides an example of a disorder where many of the questions concern possible linkages with apparently similar psychiatric conditions arising in adult life. The second example, autism, is different in that the condition only arises in childhood. For some years after Kanner (1943) first described the syndrome of autism it was widely thought to constitute the earliest form of schizophrenia. The assumption was understandable in that both involved severe distortions in social functioning and it was natural to seek to extrapolate down the age span from what was known regarding adult mental illnesses. Nevertheless, subsequent research has strongly suggested that autism and schizophrenia do *not* constitute the same condition. The probable discontinuity between the two is shown by the data on the distribution of age of onset for psychotic and psychotic-like conditions in childhood and adolescence (Rutter, 1974). Such conditions tend either to arise in the infancy period (when most fall into the autistic-type pattern) or in adolescence (when most fall into the schizophrenic-type pattern)—see Fig. 4

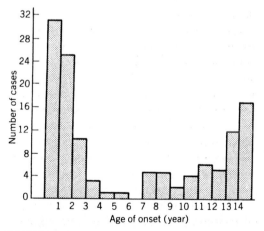

FIGURE 4

Distribution of cases of child psychosis by age of onset from Makita (1966) and Kolvin (1971).

(based on data from Makita, 1966; Kolvin, 1971). It is decidedly less common for there to be an onset in middle childhood. Subsequent research (see Rutter, 1972) has gone on to indicate a host of other differences between autism and schizophrenia—with respect to symptomatology (even in adult life autistic individuals rarely exhibit delusions or hallucinations), to course (the remitting, relapsing pattern of schizophrenia is not found in autism), to family history (a loading for schizophrenia is unusual in autism), and many other features. Apart from a few diehards (Tanguay, 1984), most research workers now accept that autism is distinct from schizophrenia.

Research has, therefore, moved in other directions. Following the experimental investigations of Hermelin & O'Connor (1970) and our own clinical studies (see Rutter, 1983a) it became apparent that cognitive deficits constituted a crucial part of the autistic syndrome. Initially, it had been supposed that autistic children lacked speech and failed to perform intellectually because they were socially withdrawn, or emotionally distressed, or unmotivated. It is now clear that this is not the case. Autistic children's malfunction is a consequence of basic deficits or incapacities in a range of cognitive functions.

The widespread recognition of that fact has been accompanied by an important change in the prevailing concepts of autism. It is no longer thought of as a psychosis (with the implication of a *loss* of reality sense) but rather as a developmental disorder (with the implication that there has been a failure to progress developmentally) (see Rutter & Schopler, 1986). This is, of course, reflected in the DSM-III terminology (APA, 1980), in which autism is now classified as a pervasive developmental disorder. The acceptance that autism involved a developmental disorder of cognition led naturally to research in which autism was compared, first with global mental retardation and, secondly, with specific developmental disorders of receptive language. In both sets of studies numerous differences were found (see Rutter, 1983a). Autism differed from both the other diagnostic

groups in its particular pattern of cognitive deficits and in its developmental course. But, also, it differed in various biological correlates. For example, although autism is frequently accompanied by intellectual impairment the medical syndromes associated with autism differ from those associated with non-autistic mental handicap (Wing & Gould, 1979). For example, Down's syndrome is the commonest single cause of severe mental handicap but yet it is rare for it to lead to autism. Conversely, congenital rubella (Chess et al. 1978) and infantile spasms (Riikonen & Amnell, 1981) are quite commonly associated with autism. Three inferences stem from these observations on the medical correlates of autism. First, they suggest the importance of organic brain pathology in autism; secondly, they suggest that there is some specificity to the neuropathology that leads to autism rather than other forms of mental handicap; and, thirdly, they emphasize the likely aetiological heterogeneity of autism (as congenital rubella and infantile spasms have little in common with one another).

Neurodevelopmental issues are also highlighted by the findings on longitudinal course. Our own follow-up into early adult life (Rutter, 1970) showed that 15 out of 63 autistic children developed epileptic fits and that in two-thirds of these cases the onset was in adolescence. Deykin & MacMahon (1979), in a larger scale investigation, confirmed this finding in both its key features. Autistic children have a rate of epileptic seizures many times higher than that in the general population. But, interestingly, the age of onset is also distinctive (Fig. 5). Ordinarily, seizures are most likely to develop during the infancy period; autism stands out as different, with its peak age of onset in adolescence. The meaning of this finding is not yet known; however, it differentiates autism from the rest of mental handicap and underlines the fact that organic brain disorders already present in infancy may have much later sequelae (Rutter, 1983b).

The next set of data points to the importance of genetic factors. Folstein (Folstein &

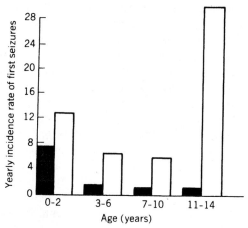

FIGURE 5

Age-specific incidence rates for onset of seizures. Based on Deykin & MacMahon (1979). ■, General population; □, autistic children.

Rutter, 1977) investigated 21 same-sex twin pairs, the sample comprising the total number obtained from a nationwide search. The monozygotic pairs showed a 36% pairwise concordance rate for autism (compared with 0% in DZ pairs) and an 82% concordance for cognitive abnormalities (compared with 10% in DZ pairs). The findings suggested that, probably, it is not autism as such that is inherited but rather some broader predisposition to language and cognitive abnormalities. The same conclusion flows from sibling studies. For example, August et al. (1981) found that 15% of the sibs of autistic children compared with 3% of sibs of Down's syndrome individuals had language disorders, learning disabilities or mental retardation; Minto et al.'s (1982) data suggested, in addition, that there may be more subtle verbal deficits in sibs; and our own findings (Bartak et al. 1975) showed that the family history of speech delay applies to higher functioning, as well as mentally handicapped, autistic children.

During the last few years there has been an important advance in chromosomal studies with the identification of the so-called 'fragile X' phenomenon. It appears that this is a rare occurrence in normal individuals but it is present in some 5% of mentally re-

tarded children and some 5–15% of autistic children—findings so far being contradictory on whether or not the rate of fragile sites is higher in autism (Blomquist et al. 1985; Watson et al. 1984).

It is striking that the early research into autism demonstrated how different it was from mental handicap and from the developmental disorders of language, whereas the recent genetic research has shown that, in spite of the differences, there are also important connections. The situation is one that is central to developmental psychopathology—namely, the continuities and discontinuities between different types of disorder and between disorder and normality. The objective of delineating the nature and pattern of these continuities and discontinuities constitutes the main focus of our current research into autism. However, before outlining those investigations one further line of enquiry should be mentioned: that is, the study of autistic children's social functioning.

The early studies into autism showed the importance of basic cognitive deficits. Accordingly, hypotheses on the nature of autism tended to suggest that the abnormalities in social functioning might be secondary to some general deficit in abstracting meaning from the environment. However, it was never clear how this might come about; there was a lack of knowledge on the specifics of the social abnormalities characteristic of autism; and there was a need to relate such social abnormalities to the course of normal development of social relations. Recent research has begun to fill that gap. First, there are some relevant negative findings. Thus, it has been shown that the social deficits are not a function of a lack of self-recognition (Spiker & Ricks, 1984) or of an impairment in the taking of visuospatial perspectives (Hobson, 1984). Rather, it seems that autism is associated with an inability to appreciate the thinking of others (Baron-Cohen et al. 1985) and with marked difficulties in the discrimination of socioemotional cues (Hobson, 1986). One task that Hobson used involved matching short videotape sequences to schematic drawings; the content of the tapes varied in order to provide differentiations between inanimate objects (the 'things' condition), between emotions (happy, sad, etc.), and between people according to age and sex (the 'people' condition). In brief, the findings showed that, compared with both normal and mentally retarded subjects of comparable mental age, the autistic children had marked difficulties with the socio-emotional discriminations but not with those that concerned inanimate objects (see Fig. 6). The inference is that there is some particular difficulty in autistic children's appreciation of socio-emotional cues. The finding is important in showing a deficit in a skill that is present very early in development—even infants are known to respond to differences in people's facial expression (Zahn-Waxler et al. 1984).

It is apparent that future research will have to proceed along several different avenues. First, we need to learn more about the development of autistic children's cognitive abilities and the connections between different types of deficits. This is particularly necessary in relation to the autistic individuals without severe mental handicap—many of whom gain extensive language skills but yet remain grossly impaired in their social functioning. Further questions concern cognitive functioning in relation to the development of seizures in adolescence, and the investigation of possible sex differences in cognitive patterns (an important issue in view of the infrequency with which autism occurs in girls). Secondly, genetic strategies are required not only to elucidate the role of genetic factors in autism but, more particularly, to delineate the nature of heterogeneity within autism. For this purpose, the twin pairs first studied by Folstein are being reinvestigated together with a new twin sample of similar size. The issues being tackled include: (1) the extent to which concordance is a function of the fragile X phenomenon; (2) the better delineation of the social and cognitive deficits in the non-autistic co-twins; and (3) the study of whether or not autism is associated with schizophrenia (or other psychiatric) conditions developing in adult life. We are also investigating whether there is anything distinctive about the pattern of autism or of mental handicap associated with the fragile X through a large-scale study of autistic and mentally retarded individuals.

A family-genetic design comparing autistic with Down's syndrome individuals is being used to take further the finding that autism seems sometimes to be associated with more subtle cognitive and social deficits in other family members. Several issues re-

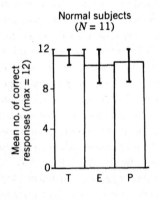
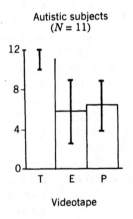
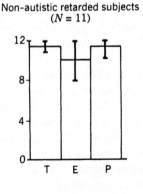

Videotape

FIGURE 6

Overall performance on separate videotapes of 'things' (T), 'emotions' (E) and 'people' (P) (age and gender).

quire to be tackled. To begin with, at present, there is considerable uncertainty on exactly which cognitive and social deficits are associated with autism; hence, there is a need to clarify what differentiates those that are part of the autistic spectrum from those that are not—a characteristic question in the field of developmental psychopathology. The research tactic of using within-individual and within-family patterning will be employed for this purpose. A closely inter-linked problem, of course, concerns the question of heterogeneity within autism; that is, how to tell which cases of autism involve genetic factors and which do not. Obviously, that constitutes the main focus of our genetic family study.

The assumption behind these studies is that there are likely to be 'lesser variants' of autism. This is suggested by the parallels between autism and so-called Asperger's syndrome (Wing, 1981) or schizoid disorder of childhood (Wolff & Barlow, 1979), conditions with apparently similar social abnormalities but without the grosser intellectual handicaps often associated with autism. It is also indicated by the twin and family findings which show that autism is sometimes connected with milder cognitive and social abnormalities in non-autistic co-twins and other family members. The challenge is to determine how such subtle deficits may be differentiated from the broad run of (presumably much more common) social and cognitive abnormalities that have nothing to do with autism. It is typical of the developmental psychopathology approach that there should be a focus on this interface between normality and abnormality and between different types of social malfunction. For this purpose, our research efforts have concentrated on the development of appropriate psychometric measures to tap possible subtle deficits of a type that parallels those in autism but which are compatible with normal functioning.

Schizophrenia

As noted above, the bimodal distribution of age of onset serves to separate autism and schizophrenia. Most schizophrenic psychoses are first manifest in early adult life not childhood and, at first sight, it is not obvious that a developmental approach would be fruitful. Nevertheless, there are good reasons for supposing that it would be productive (Rutter, 1984b). The first point is that, since the early reports by Bleuler and Kraepelin, it has been clear that some half of schizophrenic psychoses with an onset in adult life have been preceded by overtly abnormal, albeit non-psychotic, behaviour in childhood. During the last 25 years or so a variety of research strategies has served to delineate the specific behavioural features that characterize these childhood precursors of adult schizophrenia (Rutter, 1984b; Rutter & Garmezy, 1983). They comprise three rather different aspects: (1) neurodevelopmental abnormalities in the form of clumsiness, visuospatial difficulties and verbal impairment; (2) attention deficits characterized by poor signal–noise discrimination; and (3) abnormalities in interpersonal relationships shown by odd unpredictable behaviour, social isolation and rejection by peers together with (in males) solitary antisocial behaviour in the home.

Several research issues stem from these findings. First, it is evident that these features do not amount to a readily recognizable clinical picture; moreover, it is obvious that each feature reflects a much broader category of problems. Numerous children show developmental delay or social difficulties or attentional deficits. The question is what is distinctive about those that are associated with schizophrenia. The issue may be tackled in several different ways. Thus, Hanson et al. (1976) noted that it was the *combination* of these three disparate features that seemed characteristic. However, there is also a need for comparative investigations. For example, are the attentional deficits associated with schizophrenia the same as, or different from, those associated with the hyperkinetic syndrome or with learning disabilities? Similarly, how do the social deficits associated with schizophrenia compare with those found in autism?

A second research topic concerns the need

to investigate aetiological heterogeneity within the syndrome of schizophrenia. During recent years, for example, there has been interest in the demonstration that some schizophrenics show enlarged ventricles on CAT scans. This has led to attempts to determine whether this abnormality is associated with items such as clinical picture, course and outcome, neurological 'soft signs', and cognitive deficits (Kolakowska et al. 1985; Williams et al. 1985; Owens et al. 1985). Some associations have been reported but, to date, they have not served to identify a definable subgroup, apart from the important observation that enlarged ventricles appear to be much more common in schizophrenics without a positive family history (Murray et al. 1985). The implication is that the brain abnormalities stem from environmental factors—possibly from perinatal intraventricular haemorrhage (see Stewart, 1983). Curiously, however, almost no use has been made of the presence or absence of abnormalities of behaviour in childhood. These abnormalities are found in only about a half of schizophrenics; do they link up with genetic or environmental predisposition, with CAT scan findings, or with clinical features in adult life? Indeed, is the group with childhood abnormalities itself homogeneous? A recent paper by Lewis & Mezey (1985) suggests not. They report 6 cases of schizophrenic-like psychoses in individuals who had shown childhood disturbance, including developmental delay, in which septum pellucidum cavities were noted on CAT scans. However, it should be added that evidence of aetiological heterogeneity should not necessarily be taken as synonymous with syndrome separation. The possibility of multifactorial causation (either additive or synergistic) needs to be borne in mind, as there is evidence that it may well apply in schizophrenia (Schulsinger et al. 1984), as also in autism (Folstein & Rutter, 1977).

The discussion of autism began with its separation from schizophrenia. It is necessary now to end the consideration of schizophrenia with the observation of the apparent importance of developmental disturbances in some cases. Such disturbances may involve both social and language abnormalities and we are left with the need for a better differentiation of the cognitive and social deficits associated with autism from those linked with schizophrenia.

Effects of Adverse Experiences in Childhood

The third area of developmental psychopathology research differs in its focus: that is, the effect of adverse experiences in childhood. In considering that vast field of research the focus will be on the particular issues of special interest with respect to developmental psychopathology. However, before proceeding it is necessary to note some findings from earlier studies. The first issue, of course, was whether there are any detectable sequelae of adverse experiences. That question meant asking whether the statistical associations found between various adversities and child psychiatric disorder could be artefacts stemming from genetic influences, from the effects of children on their parents (rather than the other way round), or from the operation of some third variable. It is evident from a review of research findings that all three effects do indeed apply (see Rutter, 1985c d). Thus, Graham & Stevenson's (1985) large-scale general population twin study clearly points to the important contribution of genetic factors. Nevertheless, the available evidence also indicates that there are true environmental effects on both behaviour and cognitive development.

The second major issue was whether the effects applied to persistent psychiatric disorders or whether they solely concerned short-term situational responses to stressful situations. We tackled this question in our comparison of London and the Isle of Wight (see Rutter, 1979a). The findings showed that behavioural disturbances were twice as common in London and that the increased psychiatric risk was a function of a higher rate of family adversities in the metropolis (Rutter et al. 1975*a*, *b*). Also, however, the excess of disorders in London children was most marked in the case of those manifest at both 10 and 14 years: that is, the area effect applied most markedly to persistent disorders (see Fig. 7).

The same pattern was evident in our study of the children of mentally ill parents (Rutter & Quinton, 1984, 1985). Fig. 8 shows the findings on behavioural disturbances shown on the teacher questionnaire (i.e. a measure outside the family situation); it is evident that the difference between cases and controls applied to persistent, rather than fluctuating, behavioural disturbances. In short, the effect of parental mental disorder was on disorders that were both pervasive over situations and persistent over time. It may be concluded that there are environmental effects that go far beyond transient situational reactions (other evidence suggests the findings were not mainly genetic in origin).

The third major question concerned the identification of which environmental influences have which effects (see Garmezy & Rutter, 1985; Rutter, 1981*a*, *b*, 1985*c*, *d*, *e*; Rutter & Madge, 1976; Rutter & Giller, 1983). The topic is too large to allow of a succinct summary but certain general statements can be made. First, the evidence is

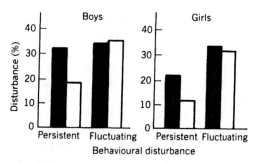

FIGURE 8

Child disturbance in cases and controls (teacher questionnaires). Data from Rutter & Quinton (1984). ■, Children of psychiatric patients; □, controls.

much stronger regarding the effects of chronic adversities than of acute stressors. On the whole, where acute events have been followed by long-term consequences it seems that this has happened because the acute event led to lasting changes in patterns of interaction. For example, Dunn & Kendrick's (1982) study of reactions to the birth of a sibling suggests such a process. Also, Goodyer et al.'s (1985) findings suggest that, on the whole, acute life events do not have the same close temporal association with the onset of psychiatric disorder that has been found for adult depression. However, it has to be said that there has been remarkably little study of the effects of acute stressors in childhood. That constitutes one important item on our research agenda for current work.

Secondly, much more is known regarding environmental influences on conduct disorders than on emotional disturbances. With conduct disorders the main effects seem to stem from family discord, disrupted and discontinuous early parenting, deviant parental behaviour and lack of effective supervision. Thirdly, the predominant influences on cognitive development are not the same as those for socio-emotional or behavioural development. There is a fair degree of specificity in environmental effects. Fourthly, to an important extent (perhaps particularly for emotional disorder and personality variations), the influences stem from within-fam-

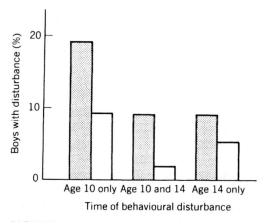

FIGURE 7

Behavioural disturbance among boys in London and the Isle of Wight. ▨, Inner London; □, Isle of Wight.

ily differences (i.e. from ways in which parents treat different children differently) as much as from global family features that impinge on all children similarly. Lastly, although the evidence on this point is decidedly weak, it appears that environmental effects may be most strongly operative in children who are genetically vulnerable. With these findings as a general background three issues of particular importance with respect to developmental psychopathology will be considered. (1) How do experiences operate, that is what do they do to the organism (see Rutter, 1984c)? (2) What accounts for the universal finding of huge individual differences in children's responses to stress and adversity (see Rutter, 1985f)? (3) Under what circumstances do early life experiences have long-lasting sequelae (Rutter 1984c)?

Mode of Operation of Experiences

The question of how experiences exert their effects has been tackled in several different ways, but the findings are consonant in their emphasis on certain issues. First, it is clear that many effects concern specific interactions, relationships, or circumstances rather than any enduring feature of the child as an individual. For example, it is evident that the measure of the security or insecurity of a child's relationship with a parent is a dyadic and not an individual feature; the quality of a child's relationship with one parent is of little or no predictive value for the quality of his relationship with the other parent (Lamb, 1978; Main & Weston, 1981). Similarly, Hay (1984) noted that whether or not children yielded in conflicts with peers was more a function of the peer relationship than of the individual child (that is, prior conflicts were of no predictive value if the children changed partners).

On the other hand, there is abundant evidence that these dyadic qualities *do* have other effects which extend over time and over other situations. Thus, Hay (1984) found that, among preschool children, the loser of a dispute between peers was more likely than the winner to initiate the next conflict. It appears that a child's feelings or thoughts about an experience may determine future actions. Dodge (1983) also showed that children's responses to other children were influenced by the history of past experiences with or by the reputation of the other child. Again, cognitions seem important. The role of reputation has been shown in other research, too; people interpret experiences according to their attribution of intention (see Parke & Slaby, 1983). Interestingly, aggressive boys are more likely than other boys to attribute hostile intentions to others—as a result, they elicit as well as initiate more negative interactions (Dodge, 1980). Patterson's (1982) data indicate that such processes are also associated with altered responsiveness to environmental conditions; thus, he found that aggressive boys were less susceptible to discipline. Kagan (1984) put it this way: 'it is not what (parents) do to children . . . that matters, but rather the intention the child imputes to those who act on and with him' (p. xvi); 'the person's interpretation of experience is simultaneously the most significant product of an encounter and the spur to the next' (p. 279). Perhaps that is overstating the position in order to clarify the point, but still it does seem that the cognitive processing of experiences is crucial to many of their effects. What happens to the organism is not so much any change in personality 'structure' but rather an alteration in self-concept or self-confidence, in attitudes and attributions, in styles of interaction, and in feelings of self-efficacy. Of course, cognitive sequelae are not all-important, but they do constitute a crucial feature of environmental effects that was rather neglected until recently. The consideration may help to explain why some people emerge from stress situations with a strengthened resistance to stress (as a result of increased self-confidence and enhanced problem-solving skills that stem from having coped successfully), whereas others emerge with a sensitization or increased vulnerability (as a result of demoralization and feelings of impotency that stem from having perceived themselves as not coping).

It is uncertain whether such cognitive mediations play the main role in the effects associated with the quality of early patterns of attachment. However, it is probable that several rather different mechanisms are involved. For example, Dunn & Kendrick (1982) found that first-born girls who had an intense playful relationship with their mother were more likely than other girls to have a poor relationship with their younger siblings. Perhaps this effect reflected rivalry and jealousy, with jealously greater when the prior mother–child relationship was a strong and affectionate one. Whatever the explanation, the finding serves as a reminder that relationships may be reciprocal and contrasting; it is not simply a matter of children learning a specific pattern of behaviour that then generalizes. The function of early parent–child relationships is also brought out in Sroufe et al.'s (1983) finding that children with secure attachments were *more* independent later; conversely, insecure attachments predisposed to overdependency. In other words, close attachment seemed to foster confidence and autonomy. A more extreme example is provided by Tizard's studies of institution-reared infants (Tizard, 1977; Tizard & Hodges, 1978). Their experiences of multiple caretaking in the early years were associated with an increased likelihood of inattentive, poorly modulated social behaviour and task performance at primary school (see also Roy, 1983). Moreover, children who spent their first few years in an institution but who were subsequently adopted changed their pattern of behaviour at home but not at school.

Individual Differences

The topic of individual differences in children's responses to stress and adversity is an equally important one, although similarly little investigated up until recently. At one time workers tended to dismiss variations in response as simply a function of genetically determined individual differences in vulnerability to psychological stressors. However, a review of the evidence indicates that this constitutes a most inadequate explanation (although doubtless it plays a part). Rather, the empirical findings point to the likely importance of both protective factors and interactive processes (Rutter, 1985*f*). Interactive processes do not mean just multiplicative synergistic effects (although they occur) but rather that many variables operate indirectly through their effects on interpersonal interactions both dyadic and polyadic rather than directly through any lasting change in the individual (see Rutter, 1983*c*, 1985*f*). The term also implies that many protective influences operate by virtue of their initiating chain reactions over time. It was these considerations that led Bronfenbrenner (1979) to argue that the main effects are in the interaction.

An example is provided by Quinton's long-term follow-up of women institutionalized in childhood (Quinton et al. 1984; Rutter & Quinton, 1984). The institution-reared women showed a worse psychosocial outcome in adult life compared with controls, but there was great heterogeneity, with some women functioning very well. The single most important factor associated with a good outcome was a harmonious marriage to a supportive non-deviant man. The finding raises the question of why some women made 'good' marriages whereas others did not. The key factor in that connection proved to be whether or not they 'planned' their marriage (see Fig. 9). A lack of planning was operationally defined in terms of marriage after an acquaintance of less than 6 months, together with marriage under pressure or to escape an intolerable situation. The results showed that 'planners' were much less likely to choose deviant spouses and that far fewer of the institution-reared women (compared with controls) were planners (either for marriage or for other aspects of their lives—Quinton, 1984). Thus, it appeared that an institutional upbringing predisposed to a lack of planning that then made an unsatisfactory marriage more likely which, in turn, predisposed to worse psychosocial functioning as assessed in other contexts. However, that leaves unanswered

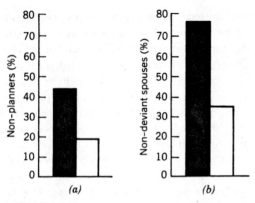

FIGURE 9

Institutional rearing, planning and choice of spouse. (a) Institutional rearing and planning: ■, institution reared; □, controls. (b) Planning and choice of spouse: ■, 'planners'; □, 'non-planners'.

the prior question of why some institution-reared women *did* plan their lives. The most important factor appeared to be positive experiences at school (see Fig. 10). The implication is that the girls' success, pleasure and achievement in one area of their lives led to feelings of self-esteem and self-efficacy that

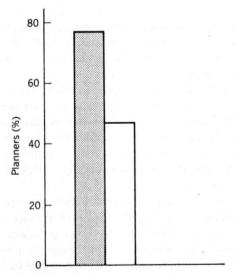

FIGURE 10

Positive school experiences and planning for marriage: ▨, 2 or more positive school experiences (N = 49); □, 0 or 1 positive school experience (N = 22).

led to more effective coping in other situations.

The child's own characteristics have also been shown to play an important role in determining individual differences in children's responses to adversity; this has been evident, for example, with respect to both sex and temperamental variations. In part, it is likely that temperamental features operate through their influence on children's reactions to life circumstances; thus, probably this applies to the important differences in physiological reactivity studied by Kagan and his colleagues (1984). Also, however, it is crucial that temperamental features influence how other people respond to the child. This is shown in Fig. 11 in terms of Graham's finding that, within families with a mentally ill parent, children with difficult temperaments were more likely to elicit parental criticism, irritation and hostility (Graham et al. 1973; Rutter, 1978).

Long-lasting Sequelae

The third topic of special interest with respect to developmental psychopathology concerns the question of how and under what circumstances early life experiences lead to long-lasting sequelae, either adaptive or maladaptive. The few examples of research findings given illustrate three of the main considerations: namely, the cognitive

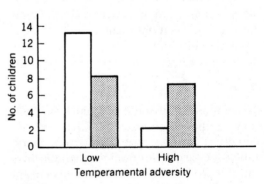

FIGURE 11

Temperamental adversity and parental criticism. □, Low parental criticism; ▨, high parental criticism.

processing of the experiences, the effects on patterns of interpersonal interaction, and the crucial role of chains of indirect effects (see Rutter, 1984a, c). With regard to cognitive processing, the further point needs to be made that understanding can be either protective or the reverse. Thus, infants under the age of 6 months show less distress following hospital admission because they have yet to develop the capacity for selective attachments and hence do not experience separation in the same way. On the other hand, children over the age of 4 years or thereabouts are also less prone to show emotional disturbance in relation to hospital admission because their understanding has advanced to the point that they are able to maintain relationships through a period of separation and because they are better able to appreciate why they are in hospital and what is happening. For toddlers their understanding is sufficient to make them vulnerable but not enough to provide protection. A somewhat related point is that a distinction needs to be drawn between emotional response to an experience and the meaning attributed to it. Thus, babies cry when given an injection but it is not until about 8 or 9 months of age that they cry in *anticipation* when the nurse approaches with the syringe. Similarly, infants show definite responses to variations in adults' emotional expression and are affected by parental depression but this does not mean that the experience has the same meaning that it will do in an older child (see Zahn-Waxler et al. 1984).

As discussed elsewhere (Rutter, 1984a, c), numerous mechanisms operate to determine continuities and discontinuities in the developmental process and hence to determine the extent to which there are long-term sequelae of adverse childhood experiences. However, four considerations require emphasis. First, to an important extent the links over time reflect connections between adverse environments rather than changes in the child himself. This is both because people act to select their own environments and because particular experiences serve to open

up or close down opportunities. The effects of institutional rearing on choice of spouse constitutes an example of selection. Our studies of schools provide an illustration of the role of opportunities. Quite powerful effects of the school environment on children's behaviour and attainment were found (Rutter et al. 1979). There were no direct effects of schooling on later employment, but there were important indirect effects (Gray et al. 1980). Young people with disturbed behaviour were less likely to stay at school to sit exams; their lack of exam success then resulted in their obtaining relatively unskilled jobs; in this way, chain reactions led to more lasting indirect effects.

The second point is that it matters greatly what people *do* about their situations. Thus, our longitudinal studies of London primary school children showed that black children tended to have lower scholastic attainments than their white counterparts (Maughan et al. 1985). However, black teenagers (especially girls) showed better school attendance and were more likely to stay on at school after the end of compulsory education. As a result of this greater educational persistence or commitment, their final examination results on leaving school were closely comparable with those of white adolescents at the same schools, in spite of their worse performance earlier in their school careers (Maughan & Rutter, 1985a).

The third point is that environmental influences continue to operate throughout life; personality functioning is far from set in early childhood. The effects of marriage provide a striking example of a major influence that can go far to modify the effects of childhood experiences.

The last point is that important experiences occur at school as well as at home, and in the peer group as well as in the family, as illustrated by some of the research findings mentioned. It is for that reason that our research in the past has concentrated on school as well as family influences; it will continue to do so in the future. A further relevant issue is the repeated demonstration of the close inter-connections between cognitive disabilities and psychiatric disorder—shown in the Isle of Wight studies in the association with reading retardation (Rutter et al. 1970) and by Richman et al. (1982) in the associations with language disorders in the preschool period. Such links need to be studied with both general population and high risk samples.

The effect of adverse life experiences has been a major research focus for us over many years and it will continue to be so in the future. However, as illustrated in the examples from Quinton's studies of institution-reared children and of children with mentally ill parents, the approach has been one that takes these developmental psychopathology issues as its main concern. We are as interested in developmental discontinuities as with continuities, in protective factors as much as adversities, and in long-term as well as short-term adaptations and maladaptations.

Conclusions

The examples given illustrate the advantage of combining clinical and developmental perspectives in the study of psychiatric disorder and of the developmental process. In conclusion, a few of the implications that follow from this developmental psychopathology approach should be noted. With respect to psychiatry, the main point is a scepticism regarding the prevailing assumption that we know how disorders should be conceptualized and classified—an assumption that has led both to highly structured, hierarchical, operationally defined systems of diagnosis and classification, and to mechanical, non-clinical questionnaire-type interviews to generate such diagnoses. Of course, the development of rigorous measures and of agreed specified diagnostic criteria has been a major step forward. Nevertheless, in many areas such approaches assume a level of knowledge not yet available. Worse, they suppose that we can ignore continua that span different types of disorder or that link normality with abnormality. Instead, it is

suggested that these should constitute a main focus for study—not because it is thought that necessarily there are continuities but because it will be helpful to determine whether or not they exist.

Finally, in common with other commentators (see especially Bronfenbrenner, 1979; Kagan, 1984; Maccoby, 1984), it is argued that our concepts of what is involved in personality development must undergo rather radical transformation. The infancy years are not determinative; there is no structure of personality as traditionally conceived, but there is coherence and organization of functioning; cognitive processes play a major role in emotional and behavioural responses; temperamental features are influential but operate through interactions as much as individual reactivity; much behaviour is context-related; many of the links in development are social rather than individual; continuities over time are usually indirect rather than direct; and fluidity in functioning continues right into adult life.

A developmental psychopathology perspective has already been successful in posing some useful questions. Whether or not it will go on to provide any worthwhile answers to those questions remains the challenge for the future.

References

ACHENBACH, T. M. (1978). Psychopathology of childhood: research problems and issues. *Journal of Consulting and Clinical Psychology, 46,* 759–776.

AMERICAN PSYCHIATRIC ASSOCIATION. (1980). *Diagnostic and Statistical Manual of Mental Disorders—DSM-III* (3rd edition). APA: Washington, D.C.

AUGUST, G. J., STEWART, M. A. AND TSAI, L. (1981). The incidence of cognitive disabilities in the siblings of autistic children. *British Journal of Psychiatry, 138,* 416–422.

BARON-COHEN, S., LESLIE, H. M. AND FRITH, U. (1985). Does the autistic child have a 'theory of mind'? *Cognition, 27,* 321–342.

BARTAK, K., RUTTER, M. AND COX, A. (1975). A comparative study of infantile autism and specific developmental receptive language disorder: I. The children. *British Journal of Psychiatry, 126,* 127–145.

BLOMQUIST, H. K., BOHMAN, M., EDVINSSON, S. O., GILLBERG, C., GUSTAVSON, K.-H., HOLMGREN, G. AND WAHLSTROM, J. (1985). Frequency of the fragile X syndrome in infantile autism. *Clinical Genetics, 27,* 113–117.

BRONFENBRENNER, U. (1979). *The Ecology of Human Development Experiments by Nature and Design.* Harvard University Press: Cambridge, Mass.

CAMERON, K. (1956). Past and present trends in child psychiatry. *Journal of Mental Science, 102,* 599–603.

CANTWELL, D. P. (1983). Depression in childhood: clinical picture and diagnostic criteria. In *Affective Disorders in Childhood and Adolescence: An Update* (ed. D. P. CANTWELL AND G. A. CARLSON), pp. 3–18. MTP Press: Lancaster.

CANTWELL, D. P. AND CARLSON, G. A. (1983). Issues in classification. In *Affective Disorders in Childhood and Adolescence: An Update* (ed. D. P. CANTWELL AND G. A. CARLSON), pp. 19–38. MTP Press: Lancaster.

CHAMBERS, W. J., PUIG-ANTICH, J., HIRSCH, M., PAEZ, P., AMBROSINI, P. J., TABYIZI, M. A. AND DAVIES, M. (1985). The assessment of affective disorders in children and adolescents by semistructured interview. *Archives of General Psychiatry, 42,* 696–702.

CHESS, S., FERNANDEZ, P. B. AND KORN, S. J. (1978). Behavioural consequences of congenital rubella. *Journal of Pediatrics, 93,* 699–703.

CICCHETTI, D. (1984). The emergence of developmental psychopathology. *Child Development, 55,* 1–7.

DEPARTMENT OF HEALTH AND SOCIAL SECURITY (1980). *Two Reports on Research into Services for Children and Adolescents.* HMSO: London.

DEYKIN, E. Y. AND MacMAHON, B. (1979). The incidence of seizures among children with autistic symptoms. *American Journal of Psychiatry, 136,* 1310–1312.

DODGE, K. A. (1980). Social cognition and children's aggressive behavior. *Child Development, 51,* 162–172.

DODGE, K. A. (1983). Behavioral antecedents of peer social status. *Child Development, 54,* 1386–1399.

DUNN, J. AND KENDRICK, C. (1982). *Siblings: Love, Envy, and Understanding.* Grant McIntyre: London.

EISENBERG, L. (1977). Development as a unifying concept in psychiatry. *British Journal of Psychiatry, 131,* 225–237.

FOLSTEIN, S. AND RUTTER, M. (1977). Infantile autism: a genetic study of 21 twin pairs. *Journal of Child Psychology and Psychiatry, 18,* 297–321.

GARMEZY, N. AND RUTTER, M. (1985). Acute stress reactions. In *Child and Adolescent Psychiatry: Modern Approaches* (ed. M. RUTTER AND L. HERSOV), pp. 152–176. Blackwell Scientific: Oxford.

GOODYER, I., KOLVIN, I. AND GATZANIS, S. (1985). Recent undesirable life events and psychiatric disorder in childhood and adolescence. *British Journal of Psychiatry, 147,* 517–523.

GRAHAM, P. J. AND STEVENSON, J. (1985). A twin study of genetic influences on behavioral deviance. *Journal of the American Academy of Child Psychiatry, 24,* 33–41.

GRAHAM, P. J., RUTTER, M. AND GEORGE, S. (1973). Temperamental characteristics as predictors of behavior disorders in children. *American Journal of Orthopsychiatry, 43,* 328–339.

GRAY, G., SMITH, A. AND RUTTER, M. (1980). School attendance and the first year of employment. In *Out of School: Modern Perspectives in Truancy and School Refusal* (ed. L. HERSOV AND I. BERG), pp. 343–370. Wiley: Chichester.

GUZE, S. B. (1983). Child psychiatry: taking stock. In *Childhood Psychopathology and Development* (ed. S. B. GUZE, F. J. EARLS AND J. E. BARRETT), pp. 203–210. Raven Press: New York.

HANSON, D. R., GOTTESMAN, I. I. AND HESTON, L. L. (1976). Some possible childhood indicators of adult schizophrenia inferred from children of schizophrenics. *British Journal of Psychiatry, 129,* 142–154.

HAWTON K. AND GOLDACRE, M. (1982). Hospital admissions for adverse effects of medicinal agents (mainly self-poisoning) among adolescents in the Oxford region. *British Journal of Psychiatry, 141,* 166–170.

HAY, D. F. (1984). Social conflict in early childhood. In *Annals of Child Development,* Vol. 1 (ed. G. J. WHITEHURST), pp. 1–44. JAI Press: Greenwich, Conn.

HERMELIN, B. AND O'CONNOR, N. (1970). *Psychological Experiments with Autistic Children.* Pergamon: Oxford.

HOBSON, R. P. (1984). Early childhood autism and the question of egocentrism. *Journal of Autism and Developmental Disorders, 14,* 85–104.

HOBSON, R. P. (1986). The autistic child's appraisal of expressions of emotion: an experimental investigation. *Journal of Child Psychology and Psychiatry, 27,* 321–342.

KAGAN, J. (1984). *The Nature of the Child*. Basic Books: New York.

KAGAN, J. REZNICK, J. S. CLARKE, C., SNIDMAN, N. AND GARCIA-COLL, C. (1984). Behavioral inhibition to the unfamiliar. *Child Development*, 55, 2212–2225.

KANNER, L. (1943). Autistic disturbances of affective contact. *Nervous Child*, 2, 217–250.

KANNER, L. (1959). The thirty-third Maudsley lecture: trends in child psychiatry. *Journal of Mental Science*, 105, 581–593.

KAPLAN S. L., HONG, G. K. AND WEINHOLD, C. (1984). Epidemiology of depressive symptomatology in adolescents. *Journal of the American Academy of Child Psychiatry*, 23, 91–98.

KOLAKOWSKA, T., WILLIAMS, A. O., ARDERN, M., REVELEY, M. A., JAMBOR, K., GELDER, M. G. AND MANDELBROTE, B. M. (1985). Schizophrenia with good and poor outcome. I. Early clinical features, response to neuroleptics and signs of organic dysfunction. *British Journal of Psychiatry*, 146, 229–239.

KOLVIN, I. (1971). Psychoses in childhood—a comparative study. In *Infantile Autism: Concepts, Characteristics and Treatment* (ed. M. RUTTER), pp. 7–26. Churchill Livingstone: London.

KOVACS, M. (1985). A developmental perspective on methods and measures in the assessment of depressive disorders: the clinical interview. In *Depression in Young People: Developmental and Clinical Perspectives* (ed. M. RUTTER, C. IZARD AND P. READ), pp. 435–478. Guilford Press: New York.

LAMB, M. E. (1978). Qualitative aspects of mother– and father–infant attachments. *Infant Behaviour and Development*, 1, 265–275.

LEWIS, S. W. AND MEZEY, G. C. (1985). Clinical correlates of septum pellucidum cavities: an unusual association with psychosis. *Psychological Medicine*, 15, 43–54.

McCLURE, G. M. C. (1984). Recent trends in suicide amongst the young. *British Journal of Psychiatry*, 144, 134–138.

MACCOBY, E. E. (1984). Socialization and developmental change. *Child Development*, 55, 317–328.

MAIN, M. AND WESTON, D. R. (1981). The quality of the toddler's relationship to mother and to father: related to conflict behaviour and the readiness to establish new relationships. *Child Development*, 52, 932–940.

MAKITA, K. (1966). The age of onset of childhood schizophrenia. *Folia Psychiatrica Neurologia Japonica*, 20, 111–121.

MAUGHAN, B. AND RUTTER, M. (1985a). Black pupils' progress in secondary school. II. Examination attainments. *British Journal of Developmental Psychology*, 3, 113–121.

MAUGHAN, B. AND RUTTER, M. (1985b). Education: improving practice through increasing understanding. In *Children, Youth and Families: The Action Research Relationship* (ed. R. RAPOPORT) pp. 26–50. Cambridge University Press: Cambridge (in the press).

MAUGHAN, B., DUNN, G. AND RUTTER, M. (1985). Black pupil's progress in secondary school. I. Reading progress 10–14. *British Journal of Developmental Psychology*, 3, 113–121.

MERIKANGAS, K. R., WEISSMAN, M. M. AND PAULS, D. L. (1985). Genetic factors in the sex ratio of major depression. *Psychological Medicine*, 15, 63–70.

MINTON, J., CAMPBELL, M., GREEN, W. H., JENNINGS, S. AND SAMIT, C. (1982). Cognitive assessment of siblings of autistic children. *Journal of the American Academy of Child Psychiatry*, 21, 256–261.

MURRAY, R. M., LEWIS, S. W. AND REVELEY, A. M. (1985). Towards an aetiological classification of schizophrenia. *Lancet* i, 1023–1026.

OWENS, D. G. C., JOHNSTONE, E. C., CROW, T. J., FRITH, C. D., JAGOE, J. R. AND KREEL, L. (1985). Lateral ventricular size in schizophrenia: relationship to the disease process and its clinical manifestations. *Psychological Medicine*, 15, 27–42.

PARKE, R. D. AND SLABY, R. G. (1983). The development of aggression. In *Socialization, Personality, and Social Development*, Vol. 4, *Handbook of Child Psychology* (4th edn) (ed. E. M. HETHERINGTON), pp. 547–641. Wiley: New York.

PATTERSON, G. R. (1982). *Coercive Family Process*. Castalia Publishing: Eugene, Oregon.

PEARCE, J. (1978). The recognition of depressive disorder in children. *Journal of the Royal Society of Medicine*, 71, 494–500.

PHILIPS, I., COHEN, R. L. AND ENZER, N. B. (1983). *Child Psychiatry: A Plan for the Coming Decades*. American Academy of Child Psychiatry: Washington, D.C.

PUIG-ANTICH, J. (1982). Major depression and conduct disorder in prepuberty. *Journal of the American Academy of Child Psychiatry*, 21, 118–128.

PUIG-ANTICH, J. (1985). Effects of age and puberty on psychobiological markers of depressive illness. In *Depression in Young People: Developmental and Clinical Perspectives* (ed. M. RUTTER,

C. Izard and P. Read), pp.341–396. Guilford Press: New York.

Puig-Antich, J., Lukens, E., Davies, M., Goetz, D., Brennan-Quattrock, J. and Todak, G. (1985). Psychosocial functioning in prepubertal major depressive disorders. *Archives of General Psychiatry, 42*, 500–517.

Quinton, D. (1984). Adverse childhood experiences and the psychosocial functioning of women in early adulthood. Ph.D. Thesis: University of London.

Quinton, D., Rutter, M. and Liddle, C. (1984). Institutional rearing, parenting difficulties, and marital support. *Psychological Medicine, 14*, 102–124.

Richman, N., Stevenson, J. and Graham, P. J. (1982). *Preschool to School: A Behavioural Study.* Academic Press: London.

Riikonen, R. and Amnell, G. (1981). Psychiatric disorders in children with earlier infantile spasms. *Developments in Medicine and Child Neurology, 23*, 747–760.

Roy, P. (1983). Is continuity enough? Substitute care and socialization. Paper presented at the Spring Scientific Meeting, Child and Adolescent Psychiatry Specialist Section, Royal College of Psychiatrists, London, March 1983.

Rutter, M. (1970). Autistic children: infancy to adulthood. *Seminars in Psychiatry, 2*, 435–450.

Rutter, M. (1972). Childhood schizophrenia reconsidered. *Journal of Autism and Childhood Schizophrenia, 2*, 315–337.

Rutter, M. (1974). The development of infantile autism. *Psychological Medicine, 4*, 147–163.

Rutter, M. (1978). Family, area and school influences in the genesis of conduct disorders. In *Aggression and Antisocial Behaviour in Childhood and Adolescence* (ed. L. Hersov, M. Berger and D. Shaffer), pp. 95–113. *Journal of Child Psychology and Psychiatry* Book Series No. 1. Pergamon: Oxford.

Rutter, M. (1979a). *Changing Youth in a Changing Society: Patterns of Adolescent Development and Disorder.* Nuffield Provincial Hospitals Trust: London. (Harvard University Press: Cambridge, Mass. 1980.)

Rutter, M. (1979b). Autism: psychopathological mechanisms and therapeutic approaches. In *Cognitive Growth and Development: Essays in Memory of Herbert G. Birch* (ed. M. Bortner), pp. 273–299. Brunner/Mazel: New York.

Rutter, M. (1980). Introduction. In *Scientific Foundations of Developmental Psychiatry* (ed. M. Rutter), pp. 1–7. Heinemann Medical: London.

Rutter, M. (1981a). *Maternal Deprivation Reassessed.* Penguin: Harmondsworth.

Rutter, M. (1981b). Stress, coping and development: some issues and some questions. *Journal of Child Psychology and Psychiatry, 22*, 323–356.

Rutter, M. (1982). Psychological therapies: issues and prospects. *Psychological Medicine, 12*, 89–94.

Rutter, M. (1983a). Cognitive deficits in the pathogenesis of autism *Journal of Child Psychology and Psychiatry, 24*, 513–531.

Rutter, M. (ed.) (1983b). *Developmental Neuropsychiatry.* Guilford Press: New York.

Rutter, M. (1983c). Statistical and personal interactions: facets and perspectives. In *Human Development: An Interactional Perspective* (ed. D. Magnusson and V. Allen), pp. 295–319. Academic Press: New York.

Rutter, M. (1984a). Continuities and discontinuities in socio-emotional development: empirical and conceptual perspectives. In *Continuities and Discontinuities in Development.* (ed. R. Emde and R. Harmon), pp. 41–68, Plenum: New York.

Rutter, M. (1984b). Psychopathology and development: I. Childhood antecedents of adult psychiatric disorder. *Australian and New Zealand Journal of Psychiatry, 18*, 225–234.

Rutter, M. (1984c). Psychopathology and development: II. Childhood experiences and personality development. *Australian and New Zealand Journal of Psychiatry, 18*, 314–327.

Rutter, M. (1984d). 'Project Future': the way forward for child psychiatry? *Journal of the American Academy of Child Psychiatry, 23*, 577–581.

Rutter, M. (1985a). The developmental psychopathology of depression. In *Depression in Young People: Developmental and Clinical Perspectives* (ed. M. Rutter, C. Izard and P. Read), pp. 3–30. Guilford Press: New York.

Rutter, M. (1985b). Depressive feelings, cognitions and disorders: a research postscript. In *Depression in Young People: Developmental and Clinical Perspectives* (ed. M. Rutter, C. Izard and P. Read.), pp. 491–519. Guilford Press: New York.

Rutter, M. (1985c). Family and school influences on behavioural development. *Journal of Child Psychology and Psychiatry, 26*, 349–368.

Rutter, M. (1985d). Family and school influences on cognitive development. *Journal of Child Psychology and Psychiatry, 26*, 683–704.

Rutter, M. (1985e). Family and school influences: meanings, mechanisms and implications. In *Longitudinal Studies in Child Psychology and Psychiatry: Practical Lessons from Research Experience* (ed. A. R. NICOL), pp. 357–403. Wiley: Chichester.

RUTTER, M. (1985*f*). Resilience in the face of adversity: protective factors and resistance to psychiatric disorder. *British Journal of Psychiatry, 147,* 598–611.

RUTTER, M. AND GARMEZY, N. (1983). Developmental psychopathology. In *Socialization, Personality, and Social Development,* Vol. 4, *Handbook of Child Psychology* (ed. E. M. HETHERINGTON), pp. 775–911. Wiley: New York.

RUTTER, M. AND GILLER, H. (1983). *Juvenile Delinquency: Trends and Perspectives.* Penguin: Harmondsworth.

RUTTER, M. AND MADGE, N. (1976). *Cycles of Disadvantage: A Review of Research.* Heinemann Educational: London.

RUTTER, M. AND QUINTON, D. (1984). Parental psychiatric disorder: effects on children. *Psychological Medicine, 14,* 853–880.

RUTTER, M. AND QUINTON, D. (1985). Parental mental illness as a risk factor for psychiatric disorders in childhood. In *Psychopathology in the Perspective of Person-Environment Interaction* (ed. D. MAGNUSSON AND A. OHMAN). Academic Press: New York.

RUTTER, M. AND SCHOPLER, E. (1986). Autism and pervasive developmental disorders: concepts and diagnostic issues. In *Assessment, Diagnosis and Classification in Child and Adolescent Psychiatry* (in the press).

RUTTER, M., TIZARD, J. AND WHITMORE, K. (eds.) (1970). *Education, Health and Behaviour.* Longmans: London. (Reprinted 1981, Krieger: Huntington, N.Y.)

RUTTER, M., COX, A., TUPLING, C., BERGER, M. AND YULE, W. (1975*a*). Attainment and adjustment in two geographical areas. I. The prevalence of psychiatric disorder. *British Journal of Psychiatry, 126,* 493–509.

RUTTER, M., YULE, B., QUINTON, D., ROWLANDS, O., YULE, W. AND BERGER, M. (1975*b*). Attainment and adjustment in two geographical areas. III. Some factors accounting for area differences. *British Journal of Psychiatry, 126,* 520–533.

RUTTER, M., TIZARD, J., YULE, W.,GRAHAM, P. AND WHITMORE, K. (1976). Research report: Isle of Wight Studies 1964–1974. *Psychological Medicine, 6,* 313–332.

RUTTER, M., MAUGHAN, B., MORTIMORE, P., OUS-

TON, J. with SMITH, A. (1979). *Fifteen Thousand Hours: Secondary Schools and their Effects on Children.* Open Books: London. Harvard University Press: Cambridge, Mass.

RUTTER, M., IZARD, C. AND READ, P. (eds.) (1985). *Depression in Young People: Developmental and Clinical Perspectives.* Guilford Press: New York.

SCHULSINGER, F., PARNAS, J., PETERSEN, E. T., SCHULSINGER, H., TEASDALE, T. W., MEDNICK, S., MOLLER, L. AND SILVERTON, L. (1984). Cerebral ventricular size in the offspring of schizophrenic mothers. *Archives of General Psychiatry, 41,* 602–606.

SHAFFER, D. (1985). Developmental factors in child and adolescent suicide. In *Depression in Young People: Developmental and Clinical Perspectives* (ed. M. RUTTER, C. IZARD AND P. READ), pp. 383–396. Guilford Press: New York.

SPIKER, D. AND RICKS, M. (1984). Visual self-recognition in autistic children: developmental relationships. *Child Development, 55,* 214–225.

SROUFE, L. A. AND RUTTER, M. (1984). The domain of developmental psychopathology. *Child Development, 55,* 17–29.

SROUFE, L. A., FOX, N. E. AND PANCAKE, V. R. (1983). Attachment and dependency in developmental perspective. *Child Development, 54,* 1615–1627.

STEWART, A. (1983). Severe perinatal hazards. In *Developmental Neuropsychiatry* (ed. M. RUTTER), pp. 15–31. Churchill Livingstone: London.

TANGUAY, P. E. (1984). Toward a new classification of serious psychopathology in children. *Journal of the American Academy of Child Psychiatry, 23,* 373–384.

TIZARD, B. (1977). *Adoption: A Second Chance.* Open Books: London.

TIZARD, B. AND HODGES, J. (1978). The effect of early institutional rearing on the development of eight-year-old children. *Journal of Child Psychology and Psychiatry, 19,* 99–118.

WARREN, W. (1974). The third Kenneth Cameron memorial lecture. Bethlem Royal and Maudsley Hospitals, London, July 1974.

WATSON, M. S., LECKMAN, J. F., ANNEX, B., BREG, W. R., BOLES, D., VOLKMAR, F. R., COHEN, D. J. AND CARTER, C. (1984). Fragile X in a survey of 75 autistic males. *New England Journal of Medicine, 310,* 1462.

WEISSMAN, M. M., WICKRAMARATNE, P., MERIKANGAS, K. R. LECKMAN, J. F., PRUSSOF, B. A., CARUSO, K. A., KIDD, K. K. AND GAMMON, C. D. (1984). Onset of major depression in early adulthood: increased familial loading and specificity. *Archives of General Psychiatry, 41,* 1136–1143.

WILLIAMS, A. O., REVELEY, M. A., KOLAKOWSKA, T., ARDERN, M. AND MANDELBROTE, B. M. (1985). Schizophrenia with good and poor outcome. II. Cerebral ventricular size and its clinical significance. *British Journal of Psychiatry, 146,* 239–246.

WING, L. (1981). Asperger's syndrome: a clinical account. *Psychological Medicine, 11,* 115–130.

WING, L. AND GOULD, J. (1979). Severe impairments of social interaction and associated abnormalities in children: epidemiology and classification. *Journal of Autism and Developmental Disorders, 9,* 11–30.

WOLFF, S. AND BARLOW, A. (1979). Schizoid personality in childhood: a comparative study of schizoid, autistic and normal children. *Journal of Child Psychology and Psychiatry, 20,* 19–46.

ZAHN-WAXLER, C., CUMMINGS, E. M. AND COOPERMAN, G. (1984). Emotional development in childhood. In *Annals of Child Development,* Vol. 1 (ed. G. J. WHITEHURST), pp. 45–106. JAI Press: Greenwich, Conn.

ZEITLIN, H. (1985). *The Natural History of Psychiatric Disorder in Childhood.* Institute of Psychiatry, Maudsley Monograph. Oxford University Press: London.

31

Comparative Analysis of Attentional Deficits in Hyperactive and Learning-disabled Children

Kenneth J. Tarnowski, Ronald J. Prinz, and Susan M. Nay

Children with attention deficit disorder with hyperactivity (ADDH), learning disability (LD), ADDH–LD, and normal children were compared on measures of sustained attention, selective attention, and span of apprehension. Unique patterns of attentional deficits were associated with each of the diagnostic groups. The ADDH children with and without learning disabilities exhibited sustained attention deficits. The LD groups evidenced selective attention deficits on a speeded classification task. The LD and ADDH–LD groups evidenced recall difficulties on a paired-associate task, regardless of distractor presence. The three clinical groups performed more poorly than did the normal group on the span of apprehension measure. Although attentional deficits were most pervasive in the ADDH–LD group, multivariate composites of attentional variables were sensitive to the ADDH and LD dimensions. The implications of the findings for diagnosis and assessment are discussed.

Problems of attentional performance characterize two childhood disorders, attention deficit disorder with hyperactivity (ADDH) and learning disabilities (LD; Douglas & Peters, 1979; Rosenthal & Allen, 1978). There is a real need, however, for clarification regarding the attentional constructs, such as sustained and selective attention, that distinguish ADDH, LD, and mixed-diagnosis children.

The most prevalent method of assessing sustained attention has been with the Continuous Performance Test (CPT; Rosvold, Mirsky, Sarason, Bransome, & Beck, 1956), a laboratory task requiring a child to track an infrequent auditory or visual stimulus embedded in a series of monotonous and irrelevant stimuli. The CPT reliably differentiates hyperactive from normal children and is sensitive to methylphenidate pharmacotherapy (Sostek, Buchsbaum, & Rapoport, 1980; Sykes, Douglas, & Morganstern, 1972), whereas application to LD samples has yielded equivocal findings. For example, Swanson (1981) reported that the CPT differentiated learning-disabled from normal children. However, some of the LD

Kenneth J. Tarnowski, Ronald J. Prinz, and Susan M. Nay. Comparative Analysis of Attentional Deficits in Hyperactive and Learning-disabled Children. *Journal of Abnormal Psychology*, Vol. 95, 1986, No. 4, pp. 341–345. Copyright © 1986 by the American Psychological Association. Reprinted by permission of the publisher and the authors.

children in Swanson's sample may also have qualified for an ADDH diagnosis. This type of diagnostic confounding prevents the determination of diagnosis-specific attentional dysfunction.

Investigations of selective attention via the central–incidental paradigm (Hagen, 1967) have been prevalent with LD samples. Consistently, normal children recall greater amounts of centrally designated information in comparison with learning-disabled children (Dawson, Hallahan, Reeve, & Ball, 1980; Hallahan, Kauffman, & Ball, 1973). In administering this measure with and without incidental stimuli as intratask distractors. Peters (1977) did not find selective attention deficits for ADDH children. Furthermore, distractors did not adversely affect performance. In sum, selective attention deficits as assessed with the central–incidental paradigm have been found for LD children but remain uncertain for ADDH children.

Although Hagen's (1967) measure has proven to be a useful discriminator with LD samples, task performance appears to be a function of selective attending as well as short-term visual memory skills. The contribution of memorial skills to selective attending has been shown to be effectively minimized with the use of speeded classification tasks (Gardner, 1970). Multidimensional stimuli are presented, and the speed with which stimuli are classified according to a single stimulus dimension is measured. The ability to selectively attend to a specified stimulus dimension is assessed under varying processing loads that are manipulated via the systematic introduction of one or more irrelevant stimulus dimensions. Speeded classification performance has been found to differentiate LD from normal children (Copeland & Wisniewski, 1981), although the status of well-defined ADDH children on this task remains unknown.

Finally, investigators have emphasized the need to distinguish between peripheral and central aspects of attentional functioning (Lahey, Kupfer, Beggs, & Landon, 1982). In order to reduce the contribution of peripheral scanning processes to attentional performance, recent child studies have used a span of apprehension task. The span of apprehension is a feature extraction measure that has proven useful in differentiating ADDH and LD from normal children (Blackwell, McIntyre, & Murray, 1983; Denton & McIntyre, 1978).

Measures of sustained attention, selective attention, and span of apprehension offer potentially significant indices of attentional deficit in ADDH and LD children, although the pattern across measures for these diagnostic groups is confusing. The equivocal findings in the ADDH and LD attentional literature might be due to diagnostically mixed samples. A significant portion of ADDH children are LD and vice versa (Lambert & Sandoval, 1980; Safer & Allen, 1976). If attentional difficulties are specific to each diagnostic category, then investigators need to consider "pure" groups to address this issue.

In this study, we compared four groups: (a) ADDH children who were not LD, (b) LD children who were not ADDH, (c) children who were ADDH and LD, and (d) children who were neither ADDH nor LD. The groups were compared on five attentional tasks to determine overall multivariate discrimination and to isolate diagnostic-specific measures of attention. On the basis of the attentional literature with ADDH and LD children (Douglas & Peters, 1979; Rosenthal & Allen, 1978), we hypothesized that deficits in sustained attention would be confined to the ADDH groups, that selective attention deficits would be identified in the LD groups, and that a compounding of attentional problems would characterize children with a dual ADDH–LD diagnosis.

Method

Subjects

A clinical sample of boys, ages 7 to 9 years, was selected from 165 families seeking assessment and treatment services through a university-based program for children with behavior and learning problems. Three clinical groups were identified: (a) the ADDH group (n = 14) included boys with a primary diagnosis of ADDH and no concomitant learning disability; (b) the LD group (n = 12) included boys with a primary LD problem but not a diagnosis of ADDH; and (c) the ADDH–LD group (n = 12) included boys with a confirmation of ADDH and LD.

An ADDH diagnosis required a score of 15 or greater on the Abbreviated Teacher Rating Scale (ATRS; Goyette, Conners, & Ulrich, 1978) and confirmation of *Diagnostic and Statistical Manual of Mental Disorders*, 3rd edition (DSM-III; American Psychiatric Association, 1980) ADDH criteria. Parental interview confirmed onset (before age 6) and duration (greater than 12 months), whereas parent and teacher completion of the SNAP checklist (Stephens, Pelham, & Skinner, 1984) confirmed DSM-III symptomatology.

An LD confirmation required that the child was performing below grade level in either mathematics or reading and have at least 1 *SD* discrepancy (using z transfor-

mations from age norms) between Wechsler Intelligence Scale for Children–Revised (WISC–R; Wechsler, 1974) IQ and mathematics/reading performance on the Peabody Individual Achievement Test (PIAT; Dunn & Markwardt, 1970).

Of 165 families seeking services, 55 boys were excluded because of age, 15 because their IQ was not in the 85–120 range, 6 because the family failed to show up for the initial appointment, and 38 because of seizure or head-trauma history, suspected psychosis, visual or auditory disability, or failure to meet diagnostic criteria. No family with a qualifying boy dropped out.

A comparison sample of normal boys (n = 13) was drawn from the community. The normal boys had an IQ–achievement discrepancy of not greater than 0.75 *SD*, did not have behavior problems at home or school, and had a WISC–R IQ of 85–120. Of 25 boys, 12 failed to meet these criteria.

To preserve group distinction, boys in the LD group had to have an ATRS score below 15, and boys in the ADDH group had to have an IQ–achievement discrepancy of less than 1 *SD*. Planned comparisons verified group

TABLE 1 Group Means and Standard Deviations for Diagnostic and Descriptive Characteristics

	Group							
	ADDH		ADDH–LD		LD		Normal	
	(n = 14)		(n = 12)		(n = 12)		(n = 13)	
Variable	M	SD	M	SD	M	SD	M	SD
	Diagnostic variables							
ATRS	19.7	3.6	20.1	3.3	8.0	4.2	3.8	3.9
IQ–achievement discrepancy	0.08	0.60	1.03	0.59	0.91	0.49	−0.11	0.49
	Descriptive variables[a]							
Child's age (in months)	101.3	13.1	98.7	12.2	104.9	11.1	102.8	9.7
Grade level	2.7	1.3	2.3	1.1	2.8	0.9	2.9	1.0
WISC–R IQ	101.6	9.3	108.5	12.2	104.3	6.7	108.6	9.8
Mother's education	14.4	2.8	13.4	2.0	14.3	2.7	15.5	2.2
Socioeconomic status[b]	5.6	2.2	5.4	1.7	4.7	2.2	5.9	1.8

Note. ADDH = attention deficit disorder with hyperactivity; (ADDH)–LD = with learning disability; ATRS = Abbreviated Teacher Rating Scale; WISC–R = Wechsler Intelligence Scale for Children–Revised. [a]One-way analyses of variance for all five descriptive variables were nonsignificant ($p < .05$). [b]10-point occupational status scale for head of household (Duncan, 1961).

separation. The LD group was significantly ($p < .01$) lower than the ADDH–LD and ADDH groups on the ATRS, $F(3, 47) = 62.3$, $p < .0001$. The ADDH group was significantly lower than the ADDH–LD and LD groups on the IQ–achievement discrepancy, $F(3, 47) = 14.0$, $p < .0001$, but did not differ significantly from the normal group. Group means and standard deviations are found in Table 1. The four groups did not differ significantly ($p < .05$) with respect to child's age and grade level, WISC–R IQ, maternal education, and occupational status. Group means and standard deviations are also found in Table 1.

Approximately 20% of the children in the ADDH and ADDH–LD groups were receiving stimulant medication, which was discontinued for 24 hr prior to each session.

Measures

Continuous Performance Test. Sustained attention was assessed with the CPT (Rosvold et al., 1956). The task consisted of 600 presentations of single digits (0–9) for 100 ms, with an interstimulus interval of 1500 ms. A correct response required pressing a lever for every occurrence of a *4* that was preceded by a *6*. D-prime (sensitivity) and beta (response bias) were scored for the CPT.

Central–incidental Task. The central–incidental task (CI-1) was administered using procedures similar to those from Dawson et al. (1980). Each of seven cards depicting an animal and a household object were presented for 2 s and placed face down in a row. The child was instructed to note the order in which the animals appeared and to ignore the household objects. Each trial ended with an opportunity for the child to indicate the row position of the card that matched a probe card. An incorrect choice required additional selections until the correct card was identified. The central portion of the task consisted of 14 seven-card trials, although each animal and serial position was probed twice. The second half of the task assessed incidental learning. Children were asked to match each of seven pictures of household objects to the pictures of animals. Central percentage correct and tries needed, and incidental percentage correct were scored for the CI-1.

Central Task. The central (C2) task is the CI-1 task without incidental stimuli as embedded distractors. Central percentage correct and tries needed were scored for C2.

Speeded Classification. The speeded classification (SC) task measures selective attention while minimizing the contribution of memory to task performance (Copeland & Wisniewski, 1981; Strutt, Anderson, & Well, 1975). For each of 12 decks (24 cards/deck) the child sorted cards as rapidly and accurately as possible according to the specified dichotomous dimension of form (circle/square), line orientation (horizontal/vertical), or star position (high/low). Decks contained one, two, or no irrelevant dimensions. Any deck sorted with more than three errors required re-sorting. The SC task was scored for total errors and sort time.

Span of Apprehension. The span of apprehension task (SA; Denton & McIntyre, 1978) was chosen as a measure of central processing because the task maintains constant stimulus features across trials, minimizes memory demands, precludes peripheral scanning through brief exposure, and permits subject pacing. Four-by-four matrices of letters containing either a T or an F in a noncorner position were presented for 100 ms. Remaining matrix positions were filled with blanks and either zero, three, five, or nine nontarget letters, yielding four matrix configurations of increasing complexity. Two sets of four 10-trial blocks were presented. Children verbally indicated T or F after each trial.

Span of apprehension was computed by the formula $SA = D(2 Pc - 1)$, where D is the number of letters in the matrix and Pc is the percentage correct.

Procedure

During the first of two sessions, the WISC–R and PIAT were administered to the child while parents were interviewed. The order and session of administration for the CI-1, C2, SA, and SC tasks were randomized across children. The CPT, which is sensitive to fatigue effects, was always administered at the beginning of the second session. An assigned tester administered all attentional tasks, but remained blind to information about the child's diagnostic status and family. Practice items requiring 90% mastery preceded each of the five attentional tasks.

Results

A significance level of .05 was adopted for all multivariate and univariate tests. With the four groups classified in terms of presence/absence of ADDH and LD diagnoses, a 2 × 2 (ADDH × LD) multivariate analysis of variance (Wilk's criterion) was performed on the 10 dependent variables. The analysis

yielded significant main effects for ADDH, $F(10, 38) = 2.04$, and LD, $F(10, 38) = 2.59$, whereas the ADDH × LD interaction was not significant, $F(10, 38) = .062$. Means, standard deviations, and univariate main effects for the 10 variables are presented in Table 2.

The ADDH main effects were contributed primarily by three significant variables: CPT D-prime, CI-1 central percentage correct, and SC total sort time. For the LD main effects, CI-1 central percentage correct and tries needed, C2 central percentage correct and tries needed, and SC total sort time were significant. Groups did not differ with respect to CPT beta, a response bias measure.

Although span of apprehension did not produce significant ADDH or LD main effects, planned comparisons contrasting the three diagnostic groups (pooled) with the normal group were significant for correct recognitions, $t(47) = 2.85$, $p < .01$, and span of apprehension, $t(47) = 2.42, p < .01$.

The ADDH and LD main effects were found for the CI-1 task, whereas an LD effect emerged for the C2. Given the differential

TABLE 2 Univariate F Ratios with Group Means and Standard Deviations for Additional Variables

| | | | Group Main Effects | | | | | | | |
| | ADDH | LD | ADDH | | ADDH–LD | | LD | | Normal | |
Task Variable	F-ratio	F-ratio	M	SD	M	SD	M	SD	M	SD
CPT										
D-prime	10.29*	1.63	2.77	0.90	2.38	1.47	3.31	0.83	3.64	0.64
Beta	0.09	0.32	6.04	4.81	4.36	4.24	5.70	3.91	5.41	4.29
CI-1										
Central % correct	4.69*	6.56*	0.36	0.15	0.31	0.17	0.34	0.16	0.52	0.17
Central tries needed	3.29	8.70*	38.07	9.25	41.67	9.00	40.83	9.80	30.08	6.28
Incidental % correct	2.07	0.40	0.56	0.31	0.48	0.31	0.65	0.33	0.65	0.38
C2										
Central % correct	1.50	16.32*	0.45	0.19	0.33	0.14	0.33	0.17	0.56	0.13
Central tries needed	3.58	18.21*	33.29	12.06	45.25	10.13	39.58	8.34	28.92	5.85
SC										
Total errors	0.02	0.25	13.86	20.38	10.58	9.38	15.75	25.84	7.31	14.47
Total sort time	4.87*	4.20*	452.50	138.05	503.75	212.91	446.50	49.41	342.39	83.80
SA										
Span of apprehension	1.40	2.10	2.79	0.73	2.75	1.16	2.75	0.88	3.37	0.48

Note. CPT = Continuous Performance Test; CI-1 = central-incidental task with embedded distractors: C2 = central task without embedded distractors; SC = speeded classification task; SA = span of apprehension task.   *$p <$ .05.

pattern of ADDH and LD main effects for these tasks, a significant ADDH × Task interaction was expected but not found. Inspection of the means in Table 2 indicates that the performance of the LD, ADDH–LD, and normal groups changed little across the tasks. Although the performance of the ADDH group did not equal that of the normal group for either task, only the ADDH group evidenced significant improvement upon removal of the task-embedded distractors in C2, $t(13) = 3.00$, $p < .01$.

In a separate analysis, feature effects for the SC task were analyzed under conditions where test stimuli contained either zero, one, or two embedded irrelevant dimensions in a 2 × 2 × 2 (ADDH × LD × Number of Irrelevant Dimensions) repeated measures analysis of variance using sorting time as the dependent variable. The irrelevant dimensions main effect, $F(2, 94) = 27.66$, $p < .0001$, and the LD × Irrelevant Dimensions interaction, $F(2, 94) = 6.43$, $p < .005$, were significant.

Discussion

The analyses revealed that (a) ADDH children with and without LD, demonstrated sustained attention deficits, whereas LD and normal children did not display this deficiency; (b) the three clinical groups demonstrated significantly slower sort times on the SC task in comparison to the normal group; (c) the LD groups evidenced disrupted attentional performance on the SC task as a function of the number of irrelevant stimuli present; (d) both LD groups evidenced central recall difficulties whether distractors were present (CI-1) or absent (C2), suggesting the presence of memory difficulties in these groups; (e) the ADDH (non-LD) group did not demonstrate central recall deficits under the no-distraction condition but did show recall problems under the distraction condition, suggesting susceptibility to intratask distractors; (f) the SA performance of the three clinical groups was poorer than that of the normal group; (g) attentional def-

icits were compounded in the ADDH–LD group, which evidenced all of the deficits of the LD group, as well as those of the ADDH (non-LD) group; and (h) a multivariate composite of attentional variables differentiated the ADDH dimension from the learning disability dimension.

As predicted, deficits in sustained attention were confined exclusively to the ADDH groups, regardless of the presence of learning disability. The absence of response bias (beta) differences suggests that group differences for sustained attention were not attributable to response set or motivational state (Sostek et al., 1980). The results replicated other investigations of sustained attention in hyperactive children (e.g., Sykes et al., 1972) and also contributed to the small but expanding literature on the adoption of a signal detection approach to assessment of attention deficit (Nuechterlein, 1983; O'Dougherty, Nuechterlein, & Drew, 1984; Sostek et al., 1980; Swanson, 1981).

In contrast to findings by Swanson (1981), CPT sustained attention did not differentiate LD children. Swanson found that an LD sample, which did not explicitly exclude ADDH children, exhibited poorer sustained attention than a comparison group of normal children.

The finding that LD groups exhibited comparable deficits with and without distractors on the central–incidental tasks suggests functioning characterized by memory difficulties (Pelham, 1979; Torgesen, 1977). However, the selective attention deficits of LD children cannot be explained simply as a function of memory deficits because their performance on the speeded classification task, which minimizes memorial demands, was also found to be deficient.

The finding that ADDH groups experienced greater central recall difficulties only in the presence of embedded distractors (CI-1) argues strongly for susceptibility to distraction. Although conflicting evidence exists concerning distractibility in ADDH (Douglas & Peters, 1979), our finding supports the proposal by Rosenthal and Allen (1978, 1980) that distractibility in ADDH is more likely to emerge under conditions where distractors are embedded within task stimuli (intratask distractors) in contrast to those occurring externally (extratask distractors).

Difficulties in selective attention on the SC task emerged for the LD groups. Because the sorting times of the clinical groups were markedly slower than those of the normal group, sorting errors were not simply a function of rapid and impulsive responding but rather reflected deficient attentional processing or perhaps motor dysfunction. However, clear evidence for selective attention deficit was confined to the LD groups given that only the LD × Irrelevant Dimensions interaction was significant. Findings for the SC task are similar to those of Copeland and Wisniewski (1981) for LD children and extend the use of this instrument to well-defined ADDH populations.

The SA findings were similar to those for SC sort time in that performance by the three clinical groups was consistently worse than that of the normal group. Denton and McIntyre (1978) reported a span of apprehension deficit in hyperactive children. Recently, Blackwell et al. (1983) found similar deficits for LD samples. In a series of studies, McIntyre and colleagues (Blackwell et al., 1983; McIntyre, Blackwell, & Denton, 1978) demonstrated that the SA deficit for ADDH and LD children is one of a more rapidly decaying afterimage and/or dysfunctional information pick-up rate. Although the span of apprehension distinguishes between peripheral and central aspects of attentional functioning, the measure would appear to provide little discrimination between ADDH and LD samples.

The findings of this study have implications for the manner in which ADDH and LD are conceptualized and assessed. Contemporary nosological systems acknowledge the possibility of a dual diagnosis of ADDH and LD for a given child (e.g., DSM-III). We found that children with both disorders exhibited a pattern of attentional deficits that was different from those with a singular diagnosis. Although Halperin, Gittleman, Klein, and Rudel (1984) failed to find support for the proposal that hyperactive and hyperactive–learning disabled children are distinct subgroups contained within ADDH, they did not use sensitive attentional measures in their evaluation. The multidimensional attentional assessment conducted in our study supports the validity of such a distinction.

A diagnostically distinct ADDH syndrome emerged in our study. Rutter (1983), among others, has argued that empirical support is still lacking despite the widespread acceptance of hyperactivity (ADDH) as a diagnostically validated syndrome. One issue is the extent to which attentional problems are unique to ADDH. If similar attentional problems are associated with a number of childhood diagnostic categories, the validity of a diagnostic syndrome such as ADDH that includes attentional problems as a defining feature is in question. For example, Dykman and colleagues (Ackerman, Dykman, Holcomb, & McCray, 1982; Ackerman, Dykman, & Ogelsby, 1983) reported that measures of cognitive style (e.g., Matching Familiar Figures) have generally failed to distinguish ADDH, ADD, LD, and ADDH–LD children. The pattern of attentional problems found in our study preserved the diagnostic integrity of ADDH. Although LD and other non-ADDH-disordered children might show deficits on some attentional variables, the collective pattern of deficits permits differential diagnosis of ADDH.

In conclusion, results provide support for diagnostic-specific deficits in attentional functioning. Further examination of the attentional processes of homogeneous groups contained in the ADDH and LD diagnostic dimensions appears warranted. A more detailed understanding of the cognitive dysfunctions associated with these groups should function to enhance the continued development of assessment and intervention strategies.

References

ACKERMAN, P. T., DYKMAN, R. A., HOLCOMB, P. J., AND McCRAY, D. S. (1982). Methylphenidate effects on cognitive style and reaction time in four groups of children. *Psychiatry Research, 7,* 199–213.

ACKERMAN, P. T., DYKMAN, R. A., AND OGELSBY, D. M. (1983). Sex and group differences in reading and attention disordered children with and without hyperkinesis. *Journal of Learning Disabilities, 16,* 407–415.

AMERICAN PSYCHIATRIC ASSOCIATION (1980). Diagnostic and statistical manual of mental disorders (3rd ed.). Washington, DC: Author.

BLACKWELL, S. L., MCINTYRE, C. W., AND MURRAY, M. E. (1983). Information processed from brief visual displays by learning-disabled boys. *Child Development, 54,* 927–940.

COPELAND, A. P., AND WISNIEWSKI, N. M. (1981). Learning disability and hyperactivity: Deficits in selective attention. *Journal of Experimental Child Psychology, 32,* 88–101.

DAWSON, M. M., HALLAHAN, D. P., REEVE, R. E., AND BALL, D. W. (1980). The effect of reinforcement and verbal rehearsal on selective attention in learning disabled children. *Journal of Abnormal Child Psychology, 8,* 133–144.

DENTON, C. L., AND MCINTYRE, C. W. (1978). Span of apprehension in hyperactive boys. *Journal of Abnormal Child Psychology, 6,* 19–24.

DOUGLAS, V. I., AND PETERS, K. G. (1979). Toward a clearer definition of the attentional deficit of hyperactive children. In G. A. HALE AND M. LEWIS (Eds.), *Attention and cognitive development* (pp. 173–247). New York: Plenum Press.

DUNCAN, O. D. (1961). A socioeconomic index for all occupations. In A. J. REISS (Ed.), *Occupations and social status.* New York: Free Press of Glencoe.

DUNN, L. M., AND MARKWARDT, F. C. (1970). *Peabody Individual Achievement Test.* Minneapolis, MN: American Guidance Service.

GARDNER, W. R. (1970). The stimulus in information processing. *American Psychologist, 25,* 350–358.

GOYETTE, C. H., CONNERS, C. K., AND ULRICH, R. F. (1978). Normative data on revised Conners parent and teacher rating scales. *Journal of Abnormal Child Psychology, 6,* 221–236.

HAGEN, J. W. (1967). The effect of distraction on selective attention. *Child Development, 38,* 685–694.

HALLAHAN, D. P., KAUFFMAN, J. M., AND BALL, D. W. (1973). Selective attention and cognitive tempo of low achieving and high achieving sixth grade males. *Perceptual and Motor Skills, 36,* 579–583.

HALPERIN, J. M., GITTELMAN, R., KLEIN, D. F., AND

RUDEL, R. G. (1984). Reading-disabled hyperactive children: A distinct subgroup of attention deficit disorder with hyperactivity? *Journal of Abnormal Child Psychology, 12,* 1–14.

LAHEY, B. B., KUPFER, D. L., BEGGS, V. E., AND LANDON, D. (1982). Do learning-disabled children exhibit peripheral deficits in selective attention? An analysis of eye movements during reading. *Journal of Abnormal Child Psychology, 10,* 1–10.

LAMBERT, N., AND SANDOVAL, J. (1980). The prevalence of learning disabilities in a sample of children considered hyperactive. *Journal of Abnormal Child Psychology, 8,* 33–50.

MCINTYRE, C. W., BLACKWELL, S. L., AND DENTON, C. L. (1978). Effect of noise distractibility on the spans of apprehension of hyperactive boys. *Journal of Abnormal Child Psychology, 6,* 483–493.

NUECHTERLEIN, K. H. (1983). Signal detection in vigilance tasks and behavioral attributes among offspring of schizophrenic mothers and among hyperactive children. *Journal of Abnormal Psychology, 92,* 4–28.

O'DOUGHERTY, M., NUECHTERLEIN, K. H., AND DREW, B. (1984). Hyperactive and hypoxic children: Signal detection, sustained attention, and behavior. *Journal of Abnormal Psychology, 93,* 178–191.

PELHAM, W. E. (1979). Selective attention deficits in poor readers? Dichotic listening, speeded classification, and auditory and visual central and incidental learning tasks. *Child Development, 50,* 1050–1061.

PETERS, K. G. (1977). *Selective attention and distractibility in hyperactive and normal children.* Unpublished doctoral dissertation, McGill University.

ROSENTHAL, R. H., AND ALLEN, T. W. (1978). An examination of attention, arousal, and learning dysfunctions of hyperkinetic children. *Psychological Bulletin, 85,* 689–715.

ROSENTHAL, R. H., AND ALLEN, T. W. (1980). Intratask distractibility in hyperkinetic and nonhyperkinetic children. *Journal of Abnormal Child Psychology, 8,* 175–187.

ROSVOLD, H. E., MIRSKY, A. F., SARASON, I., BRANSOME, E. D., AND BECK, L. H. (1956). A continuous performance test of brain damage. *Journal of Consulting Psychology, 20,* 343–352.

RUTTER, M. (1983). Behavioral studies: Questions and findings on the concept of a distinctive syndrome. In M. RUTTER (Ed.), *Developmental neuropsychiatry* (pp. 259–279). New York: Guilford Press.

SAFER, D. J., AND ALLEN, R. P. (1976). *Hyperactive*

children: Diagnosis and management. Baltimore, MD: Baltimore University Park Press.

Sostek, A. J., Buchsbaum, M. S., and Rapoport, J. L. (1980). Effects of amphetamine on vigilance performance in normal and hyperactive children. *Journal of Abnormal Child Psychology, 8,* 491–500.

Stephens, R. S., Pelham, W. E., & Skinner, R. (1984). The state dependent and main effects of methylphenidate and pemoline on paired-associates learning and spelling in hyperactive children. *Journal of Consulting and Clinical Psychology, 52,* 104–113.

Strutt, G. F., Anderson, D. R., and Well, A. D. (1975). A developmental study of the effects of irrelevant information on speeded classifi-cation. *Journal of Experimental Child Psychology, 20,* 127–135.

Swanson, L. (1981). Vigilance deficit in learning disabled children: A signal detection analysis. *Journal of Child Psychology and Psychiatry, 22,* 393–399.

Sykes, D. H., Douglas, V. I., and Morganstern, G. (1972). The effect of methylphenidate (Ritalin) on sustained attention in hyperactive children. *Psychopharmacologia, 25,* 262–274.

Torgesen, J. (1977). Memorization processes in reading-disabled children. *Journal of Educational Psychology, 69,* 571–578.

Wechsler, D. (1974). *Wechsler Intelligence Scale for Children–Revised.* New York: Psychological Corporation.

32

Toward an Understanding of Risk Factors for Bulimia

Ruth H. Striegel-Moore,
Lisa R. Silberstein, and Judith Rodin

Abstract: The purpose of this article is to integrate diverse research efforts in an attempt to move toward an understanding of risk factors for bulimia. For this task, three questions in particular require attention. Because 90% of bulimics are women, a first question to address is, Why women? Second, despite the high prevalence of dieting and weight concerns among women in general, it is still a minority who evidence the clinical syndrome of bulimia, leading to the question, Which women in particular? These questions are considered from a range of perspectives—sociocultural, developmental, psychological, and biological. Third, the rapidly increasing prevalence of bulimia in recent years raises yet another question, Why now? Our analysis points to research questions that must be examined before we can expand our understanding of the etiology of bulimia.

In its end-of-the-year review, *Newsweek* referred to 1981 as "the year of the binge purge syndrome" (Adler, 1982, p. 29). This designation reflected the public's growing awareness of a significant sociocultural phe-

Ruth H. Striegel-Moore, Lisa R. Silberstein, and Judith Rodin. Toward an Understanding of Risk Factors for Bulimia. *American Psychologist*, 1986, Vol. 41, No. 3, pp. 246–263. Copyright © 1986 by the American Psychological Association. Reprinted by permission of the publisher and the authors.

nomenon, namely, the seemingly sudden and dramatic rise of bulimia. One year earlier, bulimia had become recognized as a psychiatric disorder in its own right in the Diagnostic and Statistical Manual of Mental Disorders (DSM-III; American Psychiatric Association, 1980); this development has facilitated standardized assessment. In the last few years there has been a proliferation of literature on bulimia, as researchers and clinicians have attempted to describe the clinical picture of the disorder, to outline treatment approaches, and to identify factors associated with it.

Even though the investigative forays into bulimia have really just begun, it now seems both possible and useful to draw together the current and sometimes disparate existing pieces of knowledge about the disorder and to propose working hypotheses about its etiology. A few efforts have already been made in this direction (Garner, Rockert, Olmsted, Johnson, & Coscina, 1985; Hawkins & Clement, 1984; Johnson, Lewis, & Hagman, 1984; Russell, 1979; Slade, 1982). Our own conceptualization of this disorder both permits better understanding of the risk factors already proposed and implicates additional variables in the etiology of bulimia. We hope that as we delineate possible risk factors of bulimia, it will become clearer where our current knowledge is most lacking and therefore where research is needed. An understanding of etiology will, we hope, also facilitate the clinical treatment of bulimia.

As we think about bulimia and its recent rise, three questions in particular demand attention. First, bulimia is primarily a woman's problem, with research consistently indicating that approximately 90% of bulimic individuals are female[1] (Halmi, Falk, & Schwartz, 1981; Katzman, Wolchik, & Braver, 1984; Leon, Carroll, Chernyk, & Finn, 1985; Pope, Hudson, Yurgelun-Todd, & Hudson, 1984; Pyle et al., 1983; Wilson, 1984). Hence, a key factor that places someone at risk for developing bulimia is being a woman. One major question that demands an answer then is, simply, Why women?

Second, it appears that weight concerns and dieting are so pervasive among females today that they have become normative (Rodin, Silberstein, & Striegel-Moore, 1985). An overwhelming number of women currently feel too fat (regardless of their actual weight) and engage in repeated dieting efforts (Drewnowski, Riskey, & Desor, 1982; Garner, Olmsted, & Polivy, 1983; Herman & Polivy, 1975; Huon & Brown, 1984; Mann et al., 1983; Moss, Jennings, McFarland, & Carter, 1984; Nielsen, 1979; Nylander, 1971; Polivy & Herman, 1985; Pyle et al., 1983; Wooley & Wooley, 1984). Despite the prevalence of dieting and weight concerns among women in general, it is still a minority who develop the clinical syndrome of bulimia, thus prompting another essential question: Which women in particular?[2] In our discussion, we will be conceptualizing a continuum ranging from unconcern with weight and normal eating, to "normative discontent" with weight and moderately disregulated/restrained eating, to bulimia (Rodin, Silberstein, & Striegel-Moore, 1985). The question of "which women in particular" can be seen, therefore, as a question of which women will move along this continuum from normative concerns to bulimia.

Third, it is not women in all times and places but rather women of *this* era in Western society who are developing bulimia. Therefore, a third question is, Why now? This question has received very little empirical attention. However, the seemingly sudden and dramatic rise of bulimia over the past few years suggests that we need to consider the possible role of sociohistorical factors.

One critical aspect to the challenge of developing an etiological model of bulimia is the heterogeneity of the women who develop the disorder. Bulimic women differ with regard to their eating behavior and body weight, with some women exhibiting anorexia nervosa as well as bulimia either in the past or at present, others maintaining weight within the normal range, and others currently or in the past being obese (Beumont, George, & Smart, 1976; Garfinkel & Garner, 1982; Garner, Garfinkel, & O'Shaughnessy, 1985; Gormally, 1984; Loro & Orleans, 1981). Bulimic women can be divided into those who purge (by means of vomiting or abuse of cathartics) and those who do not resort to purging as a way of controlling their weight (Casper, Eckert, Halmi, Goldberg, & Davis, 1980; Garfinkel, Moldofsky, & Garner, 1980; Grace, Jacobson, & Fullager, 1985; Halmi et al., 1981). Furthermore, bulimic women vary greatly regarding the nature and extent of associated psychopathology. Some bulimic women do not exhibit any other psychiatric symptoms aside from those subsumed under the diagnosis of bulimia (Johnson, Stuckey, Lewis, & Schwartz, 1982), whereas others show multiple types of psychopathology (Garner & Garfinkel, 1985; Garner, Garfinkel, & O'Shaughnessy, 1985; Hudson, Laffer, & Pope, 1982; Hudson, Pope, & Jonas, 1984;

---

[1] At present, there are insufficient data to discuss the etiology of the disorder in the 10% of bulimics who are men. Some of the risk factors specified for women may relate to men as well. Some speculation on what groups of men are most vulnerable will be considered briefly in the last section of the article.

[2] Many investigators suggest that eating disorders should be conceptualized as a spectrum spanning anorexia nervosa, bulimia, and compulsive overeating (Andersen, 1983; Szmukler, 1982; Yager, Landsverk, Lee-Benner, & Johnson, 1983). In this relatively early stage of conceptualization, it seems useful to limit our scope to bulimia. However, we will sometimes draw on the existing literature about other eating disorders when relevant. A task for the future is clearly to delineate more precisely the commonalities and differences among the eating disorders and to develop a conceptual framework that integrates them.

Lacey, 1982; Wallach & Lowenkopf, 1984). The implications of this heterogeneity for identifying risk factors are crucial. A particular risk factor that may be central to the etiology of the disorder in some women may be minor or even irrelevant in the development of bulimia in other women. Furthermore, this heterogeneity argues against unidimensional models of bulimia. Any model of bulimia (e.g., biochemical or addiction models) still must consider the three questions that we are now posing.

The questions—Why women? Which women in particular? Why now?—compose the starting point for our discussion of factors placing individuals at risk for bulimia. These questions compel us to consider bulimia from a range of perspectives—sociocultural, developmental, psychological, and biological. Examining each of these perspectives in turn, we will consider the first two questions in tandem. From each perspective, we must try first to identify factors that might place women at greater risk than men for bulimia and second to understand which women in particular might be at greater risk. Subsequently, we will consider our third question, Why now?

Sociocultural Variables

Central to an etiological analysis are the sociocultural factors that place women at greater risk than men for bulimia. We and others have reviewed data suggesting that risk increases because our society values attractiveness and thinness in particular, therefore making obesity a highly stigmatized condition (Boskind-White & White, 1983; Garner, Rockert, Olmsted, Johnson, & Coscina, 1985; Hawkins & Clement, 1984; Johnson et al., 1984; Rodin, Silberstein, & Striegel-Moore, 1985; Russell, 1979). Numerous studies suggest that this attitude affects people of all ages and that these social norms are applied more strongly to women than to men (see Rodin, Silberstein, & Striegel-Moore, 1985, for review). We begin the present analysis by asking which women in particular are affected by these sociocultural attitudes regarding attractiveness and

weight, and then we suggest other significant social norms, not previously discussed, that may enhance the risk for bulimia in women.

Which Women in Particular? How might the high value placed on thinness and the stigmatization of obesity in women have a greater impact on some women than on others, thus placing them at greater risk for bulimia? At a basic level, women at greatest risk for bulimia should be those who have accepted and internalized most deeply the sociocultural mores about thinness and attractiveness. In other words, the more a woman believes that "what is fat is bad, what is thin is beautiful, and what is beautiful is good," the more she will work toward thinness and be distressed about fatness. To explore this hypothesis, we developed a series of attitude statements based on these sociocultural values (e.g.,"attractiveness increases the likelihood of professional success"). As predicted, bulimic women expressed substantially greater acceptance of these attitudes than nonbulimic women (Striegel-Moore, Silberstein, & Rodin, 1985a). Another study found that bulimic women aspired to a thinner ideal body size than did normal controls (Williamson, Kelley, Davis, Ruggiero, & Blouin, 1985).

But how do women come to internalize these attitudes differently? One source of influence is the subculture within which they live. Although attitudes about thinness and obesity pervade our entire society, they also are intensified within certain strata. Women of higher socioeconomic status are most likely to emulate closely the trendsetters of beauty and fashion (Banner, 1983), and therefore not surprisingly, they exhibit greater weight preoccupation (Dornbusch et al., 1984). Obesity traditionally has been least punished (and of greatest prevalence) in the lower socioeconomic classes (Goldblatt, Moore, & Stunkard, 1965). Although as yet there are no epidemiological studies drawing representative samples across social classes, we would expect that a differential emphasis on weight and appearance constitutes an important mediating variable in a relationship between social class and bulimia.

Certain environments also appear to increase risk. For example, boarding schools and colleges have been thought to "breed" eating disorders such as bulimia (Squire, 1983). Consistent with this hypothesis, one study found a dramatically higher weight gain in freshmen women during their first year in college than in women of similar socioeconomic background who did not go to college (Hovell, Mewborn, Randle, & Fowler-Johnson, 1985). Several factors may account for this observation. As predominantly middle- and upper-class environments, campuses represent those socioeconomic classes at greater risk, as just discussed. Furthermore, as stressful and semiclosed environments, campuses may serve to intensify the sociocultural pressures to be thin. The competitive school environment may foster not only academic competition but also competition regarding the achievement of a beautiful (i.e., thin) body. Women's appearance is of greater importance in dating than is men's (Berscheid, Dion, Walster, & Walster, 1971; Harrison & Saeed, 1977; Janda, O'Grady, & Barnhart, 1981; Krebs & Adinolfi, 1975; Stroebe, Insko, Thompson, & Layton, 1971; Walster, Aronson, Abrahams, & Rottmann, 1966), and we have preliminary evidence that schools in which dating is heavily emphasized have higher prevalence rates of bulimia than schools in which the emphasis on dating is less prominent (Rodin, Striegel-Moore, & Silberstein, 1985).

Other kinds of subcultures also appear to amplify sociocultural pressures and hence place their members at greater risk for bulimia. Prime examples are those subcultures in which optimal weight is specified, explicitly or implicitly, for the performance of one's vocation or avocation. Members of professions that dictate a certain body weight—for example, dancers, models, actresses, and athletes—evidence significantly greater incidence of anorexia and related eating pathology than individuals whose job performance is unrelated to their appearance and weight (Crago, Yates, Beutler, & Arizmendi, 1985; Druss & Silverman, 1979; Garner & Garfinkel, 1978, 1980; Joseph, Wood, & Goldberg, 1982; Yates, Leehey, & Shisslak, 1983). Although fewer data are available regarding the occurrence of bulimia in these subcultural groups, clinical evidence suggests that it has a high incidence level as well (Vincent, 1979). Eating pathology in these professions seems linked not to their stressful nature so much as to their emphasis on weight and appearance (Garner & Garfinkel, 1980), and the pathology typically begins after the person has entered the subculture (Crago et al., 1985).

Comparative studies of athletes would help to shed light on the role of culturally mandated weight and appearance specifications as a risk factor. Our model predicts that a higher incidence of bulimia would be found in sports emphasizing a svelte body—such as gymnastics or figure skating—or attaining a certain weight class—such as wrestling—than in sports where thinness is less clearly mandated, such as tennis or volleyball. The sparse literature on the effects of athletic participation in general on body image is potentially contradictory. On the one hand, research examining self-esteem variables suggests that athletic involvement enhances self-image, sociability, and feelings of self-worth (e.g., Vanfraechem & Vanfraechem-Raway, 1978). On the other hand, studies examining weight and dieting behavior suggest that athletic activity is associated with dissatisfaction with body weight and body image, repeated dieting attempts, and dysphoric episodes (e.g., Smith, 1980). The ways in which a focus on physical strength and skills might affect body image and eating behaviors, as well as the ways in which weight concerns influence exercise patterns, are issues worthy of further study.

The Central Role of Beauty in the Female Sex Role Stereotype

Beauty ideals have varied considerably in Western cultures over the course of past centuries (Banner, 1983; Beller, 1977; Brownmiller, 1984; Rudofsky, 1971), and women have been willing to alter their bodies to conform to each historical era's ideal of beauty (Ehrenreich & English, 1978). It has been proposed that being concerned with one's appearance and making efforts to enhance and preserve one's beauty are central features of the female sex role stereotype (Brownmiller, 1984). Our language reflects the intimate connection between femininity and beauty: The word *beauty*, a derivative of the Latin word *bellus*, was originally used only in reference to women and children (Banner, 1983). This female connotation of the word beauty still exists today: The most recent revision of Webster's dictionary (Guralnik, 1982) lists as one of its definitions of beauty "a very good-looking woman."

Several studies have documented that physically attractive women are perceived as more feminine (Cash, Gillen, & Burns, 1977; Gillen, 1981; Gillen & Sherman, 1980; Unger, 1985) and unattractive women as more masculine (Heilman & Saruwatari, 1979). It has also been shown that the mesomorphic male silhouette is associated with perceived masculinity, whereas the ectomorphic female silhouette is associated with perceived femininity (Guy, Rankin, & Norvell, 1980). Hence, thinness and femininity appear to be linked.

Interestingly, there also appears to be a relationship between certain types of eating behavior and femininity. In one study, women who were described as eating small meals were rated significantly more feminine, less masculine, and more attractive than women who ate large meals, whereas descriptions of meal size had no effect on ratings of male targets (Chaiken & Pliner, 1984). Another study suggested that women may actually restrict their food intake in the service of making a favorable impression on men (Chaiken & Pliner, 1984).

Do dieting behavior and the pursuit of the svelte body thus constitute a pursuit of femininity? For women who endorse the traditional female sex role stereotype, we would conjecture that being attractive and thin are important because, by definition, these attributes figure prominently in the traditional roles and values of womanhood. However, women who have achieved occupational success and have abandoned many traditional dictums for female behavior and roles also, it appears, worry about their weight and pursue thinness (Lakoff & Scherr, 1984). One possible reason is that thinness represents the antithesis of the ample female body associated with woman as wife and mother (Beck, Ward-Hull, & McLear, 1976). A second reason may be found in the women's orientation to success. These women set high standards for themselves, and thinness represents a personal accomplishment. At the same time, thinness may serve an instrumental and somewhat paradoxical end of furthering a woman's success in a man's world, because femininity gives a woman a "competitive edge" (Brownmiller, 1984). It also may be difficult for women to abandon femininity wholesale—and *looking* feminine, even while displaying "unfeminine" ambition and power, may serve an important function in a woman's sense of self as well as in how she appears, literally, to others.

Which Women in Particular? Given the central role of beauty in the female sex role stereotype and the association of thinness with femininity and beauty, for which women might these dimensions increase the risk of bulimia? It might be expected that those women endorsing the female sex role most strongly would most value and pursue thinness. Clinical impressions of bulimic clients do suggest that these women show stereotypically "feminine" behavior characteristics (e.g., being dependent, unassertive, eager to please, and concerned with social approval); this suggestion leads to the hypothesis that bulimia is the result of a struggle to live up to an ideal of femininity (Boskind-Lodahl, 1976; Boskind-Lodahl & Sirlin, 1977; Boskind-White & White, 1983; Hawkins & Clement, 1984; Johnson et al., 1984). However, studies considering the relationship between bulimia and femininity, at least as measured by current masculinity–femininity scales (Bem, 1974; Spence & Helmreich, 1978), have yielded inconsistent results (Dunn & Ondercin, 1981; Hatsukami, Mitchell, & Eckert, 1981; Katzman & Wolchik, 1984; Norman & Herzog, 1983; Rost, Neuhaus, & Florin, 1982; Williamson, Kelly, Davis, Ruggiero, & Blouin, 1985). Some of these studies show a relationship, and some show no relationship between bulimia and feminine values and behaviors.

Our data suggest one way to understand the conflicting findings on the association between femininity and bulimia. We found that whereas femininity scores on the Personal Attributes Questionnaire (PAQ; Spence & Helmreich, 1978) did not relate to measures of body image and eating pathology, masculinity scores were inversely related to measures of body dissatisfaction and eating pathology (Striegel-Moore, Silberstein, & Rodin, 1985b). Masculinity as measured on the PAQ reflects such traits as being decisive, self-confident, active, and independent; in short, this construct represents a sense of competence and self-confidence. As we will explore later, self-confidence does seem to be inversely related to bulimia, although the causal direction is unclear. Femininity on the PAQ is represented by such traits as being gentle, emotional, and aware of others' feelings; it is interesting but not surprising that the presence of such traits is not consistently predictive of eating pathology.

In a recent article, Spence (1985) argued that the constructs of masculinity and femininity guiding research during the past decade have been inadequately defined. She pointed out that the terms *masculinity* and *femininity* appear to have two distinct and different meanings. First, they have an empirical meaning and are used as labels for specific qualities or events that are perceived as being more closely associated with males or females. Second, they represent theoretical constructs that refer to a person's phenomenological sense of maleness or femaleness. To date, Spence (1985) argued, no valid measure has been developed that captures these constructs. One suggestion for future measures of femininity/masculinity is to include items relevant to physical appearance.

Developmental Processes

A developmental perspective clarifies many issues relevant to our inquiry about the factors placing women at risk for bulimia. In this section we ask what aspects of female development might make women more vulnerable than men, and some women more vulnerable than others, to developing bulimia.

Childhood

Following from our discussion of sociocultural attitudes, it is not surprising that from early childhood girls learn from diverse agents of socialization that appearance is especially important to them as girls and that they should be concerned with it. From their families, little girls learn that one of their functions is to "pretty up" the environment, to serve as aesthetic adornment (Barnett & Baruch, 1980). Young girls learn that being attractive is intricately interwoven with pleasing and serving others and, in turn, will secure their love. Beyond the family environment, schools also teach the societal message. Significantly more of the positive feedback that boys receive from their teachers is addressed specifically to the intellectual aspects of their performance than is true for girls, whereas girls are more often praised for activities related to intellectually irrelevant aspects, such as neatness (i.e., taking care of appearances; Dweck, Davidson, Nelson, & Enna, 1978).

The mass media and children's books also teach girls about the importance of appearance. From their survey of children's readers, Women on Words and Images (1972) revealed that girls in these primers were constantly concerned about how they look, whereas boys never were. Indeed, attending to one's appearance was a major activity for the girl characters, whereas the boys were more likely to solve problems and play hard.

Television teaches girls a singular feminine ideal of thinness, beauty, and youth, set against a world in which men are more competent and also more diverse in appearance (Federal Trade Commission, 1978; Lewis & Lewis, 1974; Schwartz & Markham, 1985).

Girls appear to internalize readily these societal messages on the importance of pursuing attractiveness. Developmental studies have documented that girls are more concerned than boys about looking attractive (Coleman, 1961; Douvan & Adelson, 1966). Parents, teachers, and peers all describe girls as more focused than boys on their looks, and children's fantasies and choice of toys also reflect this interest (Ambert, 1976; Nelsen & Rosenbaum, 1972; Oakley, 1972; Wagman, 1967). Whereas boys tend to choose toys involving physical and mechanical activity, girls select toys related to aesthetic adornment and nurturance (Ambert, 1976; Oakley, 1972).

In the mid-1980s bulimia does not appear to be emerging during childhood. However, it is striking how much of the groundwork seems to be laid during these early years. Two kinds of sex differences in self-concept, which will be especially pertinent to our discussion of adolescence, are already evident in grade-school children. First, when asked to describe themselves, girls as young as seven refer more to the views of other people in their self-depictions than do boys (McGuire & McGuire, 1982). For girls more than for boys it seems that self-concept is an interpersonal construct. The implications of this will be considered soon.

Second, although the role of body image in children's self-concepts has not been studied extensively, body build and self-esteem measures have been found to be correlated for girls but not boys in the fourth, fifth, and sixth grades (Guyot, Fairchild, & Hill, 1981). Furthermore, even among these grade-school children, weight was found to be critical in the relationship between body image and self-concept: The thinner the girl, the more likely she was to report feeling attractive, popular, and successful academically. In addition, studies have found that even as

children, females are more dissatisfied with their bodies than are males. Although nonobese girls have a more positive attitude than obese girls toward their bodies, they still express more concerns about their appearance than both nonobese and obese boys (Hammar, Campbell, Moores, Sareen, Gareis, & Lucas, 1972; Tobin-Richards, Boxer, & Petersen, 1983). Indeed Tobin-Richards, Boxer, and Petersen (1983) found that perceived weight and body satisfaction were negatively correlated with weight for girls, whereas boys valued being of normal weight and expressed equal dissatisfaction with being underweight or overweight.

Adolescence

Although girls learn from early childhood to be attentive to their appearance and even to worry about their weight, the major developmental challenge that amplifies a variety of risk factors for bulimia is adolescence. We will consider first the physical changes ushered in at puberty, because the extensive biological changes associated with this period render perceptions of the body highly salient in the adolescent's overall self-perceptions. Coming to terms with the vital adolescent question "Who am I?" involves forming a new body image and integrating the new physical self into one's self-concept.

In the context of the current sociocultural norms already described, pubertal development may create a particular problem for girls. Before puberty, girls have 10% to 15% more fat than boys, but after puberty girls have almost twice as much fat as boys (Marino & King, 1980). The reason is that girls gain their weight at puberty primarily in the form of fat tissue. In contrast, boys' weight spurt is predominantly due to an increase in muscle and lean tissue (Beller, 1977; Tanner, 1978). Given our cultural beauty ideal of the "thin, prepubertal look" for women (Faust, 1983), and the tall, muscular look for men, it is not surprising that adolescent girls express lower body esteem than adolescent boys (Simmons & Rosenberg, 1975) and greater dissatisfaction with their weight

(Dornbusch et al., 1984). Whereas physical maturation brings boys closer to the masculine ideal, for most girls it means a development away from what is currently considered beautiful. Consistent with this tenet is the finding that when boys report dissatisfaction with their weight, their discontent is due to a desire to be heavier, whereas girls want to be thinner (George & Krondl, 1983; Simmons & Rosenberg, 1975; Tobin-Richards, Boxer, & Petersen, 1983).

Crisp and Kalucy (1974) and Rosenbaum (1979) found that adolescent girls were highly concerned about their looks and expressed awareness of the great value society places on physical attractiveness in women. These adolescents had a very differentiated view of their own bodies and appraised critically its various components. Interestingly, girls in the Rosenbaum (1979) study judged themselves more harshly than they thought their peers would. And consistent with our review thus far, these girls listed weight as their leading concern about their appearance. In a survey of 195 female high school juniors and seniors, 125 girls reported that they made conscious efforts to restrict their food intake in order to maintain or lose weight (Jakobovits, Halstead, Kelley, Roe, & Young, 1977).

In addition to the concrete physical changes that adolescents undergo, adolescence is clearly an era replete with challenges of both an intrapersonal and an interpersonal nature. The literature of adolescent psychology describes three primary tasks that both male and female adolescents have to master: achieving a new sense of self (involving the integration of accelerating physical growth, impending reproductive maturity, and qualitatively advanced cognitive skills); establishing peer relationships, in particular heterosexual relationships; and developing independence (Aldous, 1978; Blyth & Traeger, 1983; Douvan & Adelson, 1966; Erikson, 1968; Havighurst, 1972; Simmons, Blyth, & McKinney, 1983; Steele, 1980; Tobin-Richards et al., 1983; Wittig, 1983). Our consideration of sex differences in the ways adolescents negotiate these tasks is informed by work on the psychology of

gender. Several authors have argued that women define themselves primarily in relation and connection to others, whereas for men, individuation and a sense of agency are more central in forming a sense of self (Chodorow, 1978; Gilligan, 1982; Miller, 1976).

Turning to the first task, it is consistent with Chodorow's (1978) theory that the self-images of adolescent girls seem to be more interpersonally oriented than are those of boys (Carlson, 1965; Dusek & Flaherty, 1981; Hill, Thiel, & Blyth, 1981; McGuire & McGuire, 1982). Girls also appear to be more self-conscious and insecure than boys (Bush, Simmons, Hutchinson, & Blyth, 1978; Hill & Lynch, 1983). Compared to boys, girls seem to worry more about what other people think of them, care more about being liked, and try to avoid negative reactions from others (Simmons & Rosenberg, 1975). Hill and Lynch (1983) argued that, in response to feeling insecure and in an effort to avoid negative evaluation by others, the adolescent girl becomes increasingly sensitive to and compliant with social demands and sex-role-appropriate standards. The strong message to teenage girls regarding the importance of beauty and thinness (as evidenced, for example, in the teen fashion magazines) thus intersects with heightened sensitivity to sociocultural mandates as well as to personal opinions of others. It is not surprising, then, that the adolescent girl becomes concerned with and unhappy about her pubertal increase in fat.

Following from this, we would expect that the second task of adolescence—forming peer relationships, and heterosexual relationships in particular—would also be relatively more problematic for girls than for boys. Studies support this hypothesis (Douvan & Adelson, 1966; Rosenberg & Simmons, 1975). For example, Simmons and Rosenberg (1975) found that girls were more likely than boys to rank popularity as more important than being independent or competent, and these authors found that this emphasis on popularity is correlated with a less stable self-image and a greater susceptibility to others' evaluations. Given that attractive (i.e., thin) females are rewarded in the interpersonal and especially the heterosexual domain, the wish to be popular and the pursuit of thinness may become synonymous in the mind of the teenage girl.

The third task of adolescence, establishing independence, also seems to pose a different challenge to girls than to boys. According to Gilligan (1982), females' relational orientation becomes particularly problematic for them at adolescence, when tasks of separation and individuation emerge. Gilligan reported that adolescent girls conceptualize dependence as a positive attribute, with isolation its polar opposite; however, in a world that views dependence as problematic, the girls often begin to feel confused, insecure, and inadequate.

We can speculate about ways in which the adolescent girl's increasing preoccupation with weight and dieting behavior is tied to the issue of independence. When other aspects of life seem out of control, weight may appear to be one of the few areas that, allegedly, can be self-controlled (Hood, Moore, & Garner, 1982). Because our society views weight loss efforts as a sign of maturity (Steele, 1980), dieting attempts may reflect a girl's desire to show *others*, as well as herself, that she is growing up. Hence, dieting may be a part of, a metaphor for, or a displacement of movements toward independence. Alternatively, the attempts to lose weight may be a refuge from the developmental challenges regarding independence that are posed to the adolescent. Losing weight may represent an effort to defy the bodily changes signaling maturity and adulthood. A successful diet will indeed preserve the prepubertal look, perhaps reflecting a desire to remain in childhood (Bruch, 1973; Crisp, 1980; Leon, Lucas, Colligan, Ferdinande, & Kamp, 1985; Selvini-Palazzoli, 1978).

Adulthood

The themes of adolescence—self-concept, interpersonal relationships, and dependence/independence—clearly continue into the adult years. We will now follow these issues as women enter late adolescence and adulthood and again delineate how these tasks continue to be different for men and women.

First, let us consider the body image of adult women and men. Given a persistent indoctrination into the sociocultural emphasis on female appearance, it is not surprising that women come to use very exact barometers for measuring their own bodies. In a sample of college students, Kurtz (1969) found that women possessed a more clearly differentiated body concept—that is, they discriminated more finely among various features of the body—than men. Similarly, females have clearly defined "templates" of the ideal, extremely thin female figure (Fallon & Rozin, 1985; Fisher, 1964; Jourard & Secord, 1955) and show much less variability than males in their view of acceptable size and weight (Harris, 1983).

With these two images in mind—their own body image and the ideal body image—women measure themselves against the ideal, and most emerge from such comparisons with discrepancies that are viewed as flaws and causes for self-criticism. Fallon and Rozin (1985) asked a sample of men and women to locate their actual figure as well as their ideal figure on a display of different-sized body shapes. For females, there was a significant discrepancy between their current and their ideal figures, with a thinner figure viewed as ideal. For males, there was no significant difference between self and ideal. These sex differences have been found repeatedly in other studies as well (Leon, Carroll, et al., 1985; Striegel-Moore, McAvay, & Rodin, in press; Rodin, Striegel-Moore, & Silberstein, 1985).

There is evidence suggesting that this self–ideal discrepancy may be exaggerated for women, not only because the beauty ideal for women has become increasingly thin, but also because women tend to overestimate their body size. Many studies document women's consistent exaggeration of body size, both of the figure as a whole and of specific body parts—typically the fat-bearing areas such as waist and hips. Importantly, these estimation differences appear specific to female subjects' own bodies, because they accurately judge the size of other people's bodies and of physical objects (Button, Fransella, & Slade, 1977; Casper, Halmi, Goldberg, Eckert, & Davis, 1979; Crisp & Kalucy, 1974; Fries, 1975; Garner, Garfinkel, Stancer, & Moldofsky, 1976; Halmi, Goldberg, & Cunningham, 1977). In a study comparing the estimation errors of men and women, men were significantly more accurate than women in estimates of their own body size (Shontz, 1963).

An issue integrally related to self-concept that has been implicit in our discussion thus far is the association between body image and self-esteem. Many self-concept theories (for an overview, see Harter, 1985) have proposed that dissatisfaction with a particular domain of one's self will result in overall lower self-esteem. In particular, it is argued that the effect of shortcomings in one domain on an individual's general level of self-esteem is determined by the relative importance of that domain in the person's self-definition. Hence, failure to succeed in an area of relatively minor importance to an individual will prove far less damaging to self-worth than inadequacy in a domain of central importance.

Surprisingly few studies have investigated the influence of body image on self-esteem. In studies that have examined this relationship, moderate, significant correlations have been found (Franzoi & Shields, 1984; Lerner, Karabenick, & Stuart, 1973; Lerner, Orlos, & Knapp, 1976; Mahoney, 1974; Secord & Jourard, 1953). Given the greater societal emphasis on attractiveness in women than in men, we would expect physical appearance to have relatively more influence on a woman's general sense of self-esteem than on a man's. Empirical studies, however, have produced conflicting results.

Some studies have supported the tenet that women's body image satisfaction is more highly correlated with self-esteem than is men's (Lerner et al., 1973; Martin & Walter, 1982; Secord & Jourard, 1953), whereas other studies have found the reverse to be true (Mahoney, 1974; Franzoi & Shields,

1984). Perhaps these contradictory findings are due to the fact that body image satisfaction has a different meaning for men and women (Franzoi & Shields, 1984). Several studies have suggested that whereas men tend to see their bodies as primarily functional and active, women seem to view their bodies along aesthetic and evaluative dimensions (Kurtz, 1969; Lerner et al., 1976; Story, 1979).

The relationship between weight, as a particular component of body image, and self-esteem in women deserves further investigation. We conjecture that dissatisfaction with weight relates to chronic low self-esteem and that, in addition, weight plays a role in more short-term and volatile fluctuations of self-esteem. In a large-scale *Glamour* magazine survey, 63% of the respondents reported that weight *often* affected how they felt about themselves, and another 33% reported that weight *sometimes* affected how they felt about themselves (Wooley & Wooley, 1984).

Thus far, we have been considering adulthood as a single entity. As theory and research on adult development have increased, earlier views of adulthood as a sustained, stable period have been replaced by conceptualizations of the entire life span as part of an ongoing developmental process (Erikson, 1968; Levinson, Darrow, Klein, Levinson, & McKee, 1978; Neugarten, 1969, 1970). Our knowledge of weight concerns, dieting, and bulimia is limited by the relatively restricted range of samples that have been studied: The majority of research has focused on the narrow band between 10th grade in high school and senior year of college. However, some initial observations about later adulthood can be made.

First, puberty is clearly not the only period in a woman's life when her biology will potentiate fat increase. During pregnancy, a healthy woman may gain 5 to 11 pounds in fat alone (National Research Council, 1970; Hytten & Leitch, 1971; Pitkin, 1976), and it is often the case that many women have difficulty losing adipose tissue after the baby is born (Beller, 1980; Cederlof & Kay, 1970;

Helliovaara & Aromaa, 1981). There is some evidence from cross-sectional studies that menopause may be another event in a woman's life that promotes weight gain (e.g., McKinlay & Jeffreys, 1974), although longitudinal studies are needed to confirm this assumption. Although the precise role of sex hormones in weight regulation is still not fully understood, levels of estrogen and progesterone have been related to hunger and food intake (Dalvit-MacPhillips, 1983; Dippel & Elias, 1980).

Women also have a lower resting metabolic rate than men and thus require fewer calories for their life-sustaining functions. This sex difference is due in part to size differences between men and women, but it is also due to the higher ratio of fat to lean tissue in women. Adipose tissue is more metabolically inert than lean tissue and thus contributes to women's lower resting metabolic rate. With aging, sex differences in metabolic rate may actually increase, along with a relatively larger decrease in lean body mass and concomitant increase in fat tissue in women compared to men (Bray, 1976; Forbes & Reina, 1970; Parizkowa, 1973; Wessel, Ufer, Van Huss, & Cederquist, 1963; Young et al., 1961; Young, Blondin, Tensuan, & Fryer, 1963).

Second, it appears that middle age does not free women from assuming that their attractiveness is a key factor in their happiness. In a large-scale study of American couples, Blumstein and Schwartz (1983) observed that looks continued to be critical well beyond the early years of relationships. In particular, wives were keenly aware of the importance of their appearance to their husbands. Although the authors did not explicitly separate weight from other aspects of appearance, their case reports suggest that weight gain is a central way in which physical appearance changes over time and is a primary cause of concern.

What happens in later life? In a current longitudinal study of people over age 62, we found that the second greatest personal concern expressed by women in the sample, following memory loss, was change in body weight. Weight concerns were rarely expressed by men in the sample (Rodin, 1985). As just described, women tend to become fatter as they age, as a result of biological changes. In addition, some evidence suggests that the process of aging diminishes a woman's perceived attractiveness more than it does a man's (Hatfield & Sprecher, 1986), a phenomenon dubbed by Sontag (1972) as the double standard of aging in our society.

In sum, although the data on the topic are sparse, it seems that women's battle with weight, both psychological and physical, lasts a lifetime. Clinically, we find that bulimia can have its onset well after the adolescent and young adult years. From both a clinical and a theoretical viewpoint, the study of women's concerns with weight and eating problems should examine women across the life span.

Which Women in Particular? Having looked at the developmental trajectory followed by women in general in our society, we now consider which women during their developmental course will be pushed beyond a normative discontent into the disordered eating range.

Timing of development. One developmental factor that may affect risk for bulimia is the timing of biological development. Life-span theory suggests that being "out-of-phase" (Neugarten, 1972) with one's cohorts presents a particular stressor and increases the likelihood of a developmental crisis. Research on puberty has suggested sex differences in the impact of early versus late maturation, which may be important in identifying risk factors for bulimia. Male early developers have been found to be more relaxed, less dependent, and more self-confident. They also enjoy a more positive body image and a greater sense of attractiveness than do late-developing boys (Clausen, 1975; Jones, 1965; Tobin-Richards et al., 1983).

For girls, results on the outcomes of early maturation are less clear. Although early-maturing girls have been found to enjoy greater popularity among male peers (Simmons, Blyth, & McKinney, 1983) and greater self-confidence (Clausen, 1975) than girls who develop on time or later, early-developing girls also have been reported to be less popular among female peers, to experience greater emotional distress, to perceive themselves as less attractive, and to hold a lower self-concept than their peers (Peskin, 1973; Simmons et al., 1983). Furthermore, pubertal growth may carry more explicit sexualized meanings for girls than for boys, and parents may respond to their daughters' signs of early sexual maturation with more fear and subsequent greater protectiveness than to their sons' sexual maturation (Hamburg, 1974; Seiden, 1976).

In terms of body dissatisfaction, early-developing girls seem to be particularly unhappy with their weight (Simmons et al., 1983; Tobin-Richards et al., 1983). This finding is not surprising, given that early-developing girls tend to be fatter than their peers (and tend to remain so once they have completed their pubertal growth). In Simmon et al.'s (1983) sample, weight and body image satisfaction were inversely correlated for all girls, regardless of maturational status. In fact, when weight was corrected for, the differences in body image satisfaction of early-, middle-, and late-developing girls disappeared. Bruch (1981) suggested that early development may be a risk factor in anorexia nervosa. Although there are no empirical data on this issue, we conjecture that maturing faster than her peers may place a girl at risk for bulimia as well.

Personality. From our depiction of female development, it becomes clear that women have a primarily relational orientation. We conjecture that if a woman's orientation toward others' needs and opinions eclipses a sense of her own needs and opinions, she will be at risk for mental health problems in general. Whereas psychiatry has long noted women's vulnerability to hysteria, agoraphobia, or depression, in our current society, women also will be at risk for bulimia. Indeed, clinicians depict bulimic women as ex-

hibiting a strong need for social approval and avoiding conflict, and as experiencing difficulty in identifying and asserting needs (Arenson, 1984; Boskind-Lodahl, 1976; Boskind-White & White, 1983). Initial research has found that bulimic women have higher need for approval than control women (Dunn & Ondercin, 1981; Katzman & Wolchik, 1984) and also score higher on a measure of interpersonal sensitivity (Striegel-Moore, McAvay, & Rodin, 1984).

One question that arises, then, is whether there is a personality profile that places some women at greater risk for bulimia. Although the methodology of assessing personality traits in individuals who already exhibit the clinical syndrome does not permit causal inferences, let us briefly examine the major findings of this line of research. Group profiles of the Minnesota Multiphasic Personality Inventory (MMPI) obtained for bulimic women were found to show significant elevations on the clinical scales Depression, Psychopathic Deviate, Psychasthenia, and Schizophrenia (Hatsukami, Owen, Pyle, & Mitchell, 1982; Leon, Lucas et al., 1985; Orleans & Barnett, 1984; Wallach & Lowenkopf, 1984).

Presenting MMPI data in the form of group profiles ignores the heterogeneity of profiles within a sample. Hatsukami et al. (1982) reported that the two most common codetypes (which together accounted for only 25% of their sample) may represent two subgroups of bulimics, one with more obsessive–compulsive problems and the other with addictive behaviors. Importantly, for 20% of the bulimic subjects, none of the clinical scales were significantly elevated; it is possible that this represents another subgroup of bulimics who do not show psychopathology in areas other than their eating disorder.

Many researchers have identified one substantial subgroup of bulimic women to be those who also report problems with alcohol or drug abuse (Leon, Carroll, et al., 1985; Mitchell, Hatsukami, Eckert, & Pyle, 1985; Pyle et al., 1983; Walsh, Roose, Glassman, Gladis, & Sadik, 1985). These observations have led some experts to conclude that bulimia is basically a substance-abuse disorder (Brisman & Siegel, 1984; Wooley & Wooley, 1981), with food either one of many substances or the only substance that is abused. A view of bulimia as a substance-abuse disorder is supported by the high incidence of substance abuse found among the members of bulimic women's immediate families (Leon, Carroll, et al., 1985; Strober, Salkin, Burroughs, & Morrell, 1982). We conjecture that the constellation of personality factors that predispose a woman to substance abuse would place her at risk also for bulimia, including an inability to regulate negative feelings, a need for immediate need gratification, poor impulse control, and a fragile sense of self (Brisman & Siegel, 1984; Goodsitt, 1983).

Another characteristic of bulimic women that has attracted considerable attention has been the high prevalence of depressive symptoms (Fairburn & Cooper, 1982; Hatsukami, Eckert, Mitchell, & Pyle, 1984; Johnson & Larson, 1982; Johnson et al., 1982; Katzman & Wolchik, 1984; Mitchell et al., 1985; Norman & Herzog, 1983; Pyle, Mitchell, & Eckert, 1981; Russell, 1979; Wallach & Lowenkopf, 1984; Walsh et al., 1985; Williamson et al., 1985; Wolf & Crowther, 1983). Between 35% and 78% of bulimic patients have been reported to satisfy the DSM-III criteria for a diagnosis of affective disorder during the acute stage of illness (Gwirtsman, Roy-Byrne, Yager, & Gerner, 1983; Hatsukami et al., 1984; Herzog, 1982; Hudson et al., 1982; Hudson et al., 1984; Pope, Hudson & Jonas, 1983). This high incidence of depressive symptoms in bulimia has led to the hypothesis that bulimia is a variant of an affective disorder. However, these studies were conducted with patients, and such individuals generally report a high incidence of depressive symptoms regardless of the presenting problem (e.g., Kashani & Priesmeyer, 1983; Rabkin, Charles, & Kass, 1983). Furthermore, the symptoms of a major depressive episode or

dysthymic disorder and bulimia overlap considerably, a point that has been made with respect to anorexia (Altschuler & Weiner, 1985).

Whether or not bulimia is a type of affective disorder, several possible links between bulimic and depressive symptoms may obtain. There is some evidence that depressive symptoms increase during or after binge eating and purging episodes (Johnson et al., 1982; Johnson & Larson, 1982; Russell, 1979). For some bulimic women, the binge/purge cycle serves a self-punishing purpose (Johnson et al., 1984), which is consonant with the depressive constellation. Alternatively, eating may be an antidote to depression, used as self-medication and self-nurturance. There also may be an association between depression and the onset of the binge/purge cycle. Perhaps when weight-conscious women become depressed, their customary restraint of eating weakens, thus increasing the likelihood of binging. We have described earlier the apparent association between body dissatisfaction and low self-esteem, which is a common marker of depression. At present, the question remains unanswered whether depression is a symptom secondary to bulimia, or whether a depressive syndrome places a woman at greater risk for bulimia.

Behaviorally oriented researchers have begun to examine the possibility that inadequate coping skills constitute a risk factor for bulimia (Hawkins & Clement, 1984). Several clinicians and researchers have argued that a deficit of coping skills renders a bulimic woman less able to deal effectively with stress, and binging is an expression of her inability to cope (Boskind-White & White, 1983; Hawkins & Clement, 1984; Katzman & Wolchik, 1984; Loro, 1984; Loro & Orleans, 1981).

In addition, researchers have found that women who experience more stress are at greater risk for binge eating (Abraham & Beumont, 1982; Fremouw & Heyneman, 1984; Pyle et al., 1981; Strober, 1984; Wolf & Crowther, 1983). We postulate that stress is not a specific risk factor but rather, in concert with the other risk factors we have discussed, may play a role in a woman's likelihood of developing bulimia. Research is needed to determine whether bulimic women, compared with other women, encounter a higher level of life stress, subjectively experience stressors as more stressful, or are less skilled in coping with stress.

Biological Factors
Genetic Determinants of Weight

In attempts to understand bulimia, it is crucial to examine biological and genetic factors. As discussed in the section on development, women are genetically programmed to have a proportionately higher body fat composition than men—a sex difference that appears to hold across all races and cultures (Bennett, 1984; Tanner, 1978), and the differences between the sexes in fatness increases dramatically, on the average, across the life span.

Substantial individual differences in body build and weight are genetically determined. Identical twins, even when reared apart, are significantly more similar in weight than are fraternal twins or siblings (Borjeson, 1976; Bray, 1981; Brook, Huntley, & Slack, 1975; Fabsitz, Feinleib, & Hrubec, 1978; Feinleib et al., 1977; Medlund, Cederlof, Floderus-Myrhed, Friberg, & Sorensen, 1976; Stunkard, Foch, & Hrubec, 1985). Adopted children resemble their biological parents in weight far more than they resemble their adoptive parents (Stunkard, Sorensen, et al., 1985).

One path by which heredity may influence weight is by determining the ways in which food is metabolized. Individual differences in metabolic rate seem to be of great significance in determining the efficiency of caloric expenditure (Rimm & White, 1979). Indeed, even individuals matched for age, sex, weight, and activity level can differ dramatically from each other in the amount of calories they eat while maintaining identical levels of body weight (Rose & Williams, 1961).

Which Women in Particular? We conjecture that those women who are genetically programmed to be heavier than the svelte ideal will be at higher risk for bulimia than those women who are naturally thin. Clinical and empirical evidence suggests that a woman who is heavier than her peers may be more likely to develop bulimia (Boskind-White & White, 1983; Fairburn & Cooper, 1983; Johnson et al., 1982; Yager, Landsverk, Lee-Benner, & Johnson, 1985).

It has been suggested that in addition to the genetic predisposition to a specific body weight, a predisposition to an eating disorder may be genetically transmitted. Research on this issue is in an early stage, but initial findings suggest familial clustering of eating disorders. Studies have documented a significantly higher incidence of both anorexia nervosa and bulimia among the first-degree female relatives of anorexic patients than in the immediate families of control subjects (Gershon et al., 1983; Strober, Morrell, Burroughs, Salkin, & Jacobs, 1985). Monozygotic twins have a considerably higher concordance rate than dizygotic twins for anorexia (Crisp, Hall, & Holland, 1985; Garfinkel & Garner, 1982; Holland, Hall, Murray, Russell, & Crisp, 1984; Nowlin, 1983; Vandereyken & Pierloot, 1981). Following from this line of research with anorexic women, the question of the inheritability of bulimia now needs to be examined with bulimic patients.

The Disregulation of Body Weight and Eating through Dieting

A significant number of women, then, face a frustrating paradox: Although society prescribes a thin beauty ideal, their own genes predispose them to have a considerably heavier body weight. Current society promotes dieting as the pathway to thinness, and as we would expect, significantly more women than men report dieting at any time (e.g., Nielsen, 1979; Nylander, 1971). Before age 13, 80% of girls report that they have already been on a weight-loss diet, as compared to 10% of boys (Hawkins, Turell, & Jackson, 1983).

On the basis of studies investigating the physiological changes that occur as a result of dieting, many researchers now believe that dieting is not only an ineffective way to attain long-term weight loss but that it may in fact contribute to subsequent weight gain and binge eating (Polivy & Herman, 1985; Rodin, 1981; Rodin, Silberstein, & Striegel-Moore, 1985; Wardle, 1980; Wooley & Wooley, 1981). A substantial decrease in daily caloric intake will result in a reduced metabolic rate, which thus impedes weight loss (Apfelbaum, 1975; Boyle, Storlien, Harper, & Keesey, 1981; Garrow, 1978; Westerterp, 1977). The suppression of metabolic rate caused by dieting is most pronounced when basal metabolic rate is low from the outset (Wooley, Wooley, & Dyrenforth, 1979). Because women have lower metabolic rates than men, women are particularly likely to find that, despite their efforts, they cannot lose as much weight as they would like. Upon resuming normal caloric intake, a person's metabolic rate does not immediately rebound to its original pace, and in fact, a longer period of dieting will prolong the time it takes for the metabolic rate to regain its original level (Even, Nicolaidis, & Meile, 1981). Thus, even normal eating after dieting may promote weight gain.

Numerous other physiological changes due to food restriction have been reported (Bjorntorp & Yang, 1982; Faust, Johnson, Stern, & Hirsch, 1978; Fried, Hill, Nickel, & DiGirolamo, 1983; Gruen & Greenwood, 1981; Miller, Faust, Goldberger, & Hirsch, 1983; Walks, Lavan, Presta, Yang, & Bjorntorp, 1983). All of these alterations contribute to increased efficiency in food utilization and an increased proportion of fat in body composition. Hence, dieting ultimately produces effects opposite to those intended. In addition to these biological ramifications, dieting also produces psychological results that are self-defeating. Typically, a dieter feels deprived of favorite foods, and when "off" the diet, she is likely to overeat (Herman & Mack, 1975; Polivy & Herman, 1985).

Which Women in Particular? We propose that a prolonged history of repeated dieting attempts constitutes yet another risk factor for bulimia. Animal research suggests that regaining weight occurs significantly more rapidly after a second dieting cycle than after a first (Brownell, Stellar, Stunkard, Rodin, & Wilson, 1984). We conjecture that those women who have engaged in repeated dieting attempts will be the least successful at achieving their target weights by dieting. These women may be most vulnerable, then, to attempting other weight loss strategies, including purging.

The literature on the physiological and psychological effects of dieting suggests a seemingly paradoxical picture: The more restrictively a person diets, the more likely she or he will be to crave foods (particularly foods not allowed as part of the diet) and to give in to those cravings eventually. Indeed, several studies have found a high correlation between restraint and binge eating (Hawkins & Clement, 1980, 1984; Leon, Carroll, et al., 1985; Striegel-Moore et al., 1985b). From their review of this research, Polivy and Herman (1985) concluded that food restriction may be an important causal antecedent to binging. In support of this view, the clinical literature suggests that in many cases bulimia was preceded by a period of restrictive dieting (Boskind-Lodahl & Sirlin, 1977; Dally & Gomez, 1979; Johnson et al., 1982; Mitchell et al., 1985; Russell, 1979; Wooley & Wooley, 1985).

Affective Instability

Affective instability has been proposed as another biogenetic risk factor of bulimia (Hawkins & Clement, 1984; Johnson, Lewis, & Hagman, 1984; Strober, 1981). It is widely recognized that women have a higher incidence of affective disorders than men. If a predisposition to affective instability increases an individual's risk of bulimia, then it would represent another answer to the questions of both why women rather than men become bulimic and which women in particular.

Several family studies have revealed a high incidence rate of affective disorders among first-degree relatives of bulimic patients (Gwirtsman et al., 1983; Herzog, 1982; Hudson et al., 1982; Hudson et al., 1983; Pyle et al., 1983; Slater & Cowie, 1971; Strober et al., 1982; Yager & Strober, 1985), with one exception (Stern et al., 1984). Studies considering the incidence of bulimia in first-degree relatives of patients with an affective disorder would constitute another test of the hypothesized familial association between affective disorders and bulimia (Altschuler & Weiner, 1985). Two studies addressing this question, however, did not find increased incidence of eating disorders among the first-degree relatives of patients with an affective disorder, a result that argues against a *simple* hypothesis that affective disorders and eating disorders are merely alternate expressions of the same disposition (Gershon et al., 1983; Hatsukami et al., 1984; Strober, 1983; Yager & Strober, 1985). In the absence of twin studies, adoption studies, and sophisticated family aggregation studies, at present no conclusions regarding genetic transmission of bulimia via an affective disorder link can be made.

creased if the family places heavy emphasis on appearance and thinness; if the family believes and promotes the myth that weight is under volitional control and thus holds the daughter responsible for regulating it; if family members, particularly females (mother, sisters, aunts), model weight preoccupation and dieting; if the daughter is evaluated critically by members of the family with regard to her weight; if the daughter is reinforced for her efforts to lose weight; and if family members compete regarding the achievement of the ideal of thinness.

Furthermore, a risk to develop bulimia may derive from how the family system operates. Clinicians have described families with a bulimic member as sharing similarities with "psychosomatic families" (Minuchin, Rosman, & Baker, 1978), including enmeshment, overprotectiveness, rigidity, and lack of conflict resolution. In addition, bulimic patients' families are reported to exhibit isolation and heightened consciousness of appearance, and they attach special meaning to food and eating (Schwartz et al., 1985). Research evaluating these assumptions is still in its infancy (Johnson & Flach, 1985; Kagan & Squires, 1985; Kog, Vandereycken, & Vertommen, in press; Kog, Vertommen, & DeGroote, in press; Sights & Richards, 1984; Strober, 1981).

Family Variables

With a few exceptions (e.g., Boskind-White & White, 1983; Schwartz, 1982; Schwartz, Barrett, & Saba, 1985; Yager, 1982), the bulimia literature has largely ignored the potential role of family characteristics that might predispose some women to bulimia. Prospective studies are completely missing, and there is no comprehensive theoretical framework that would allow delineation of the relevant variables to be included in a prospective investigation of families.

In light of our review, we conjecture that certain family characteristics may amplify the sociocultural imperatives described earlier. For example, we hypothesize that a daughter's risk for bulimia is relatively in-

Why Now?

In the final section, we attempt to speculate on what makes bulimia so likely at this particular time. We recognize that ease of diagnosis per se, after inclusion of the disorder in the DSM-III (American Psychiatric Association, 1980), may have contributed to the apparent increase, but we wish to focus on other sociocultural and psychological mediators that contribute to the increased risk of bulimia in this era.

Shift Toward Increasingly Thin Standard

In recent years, the beauty ideal for women has moved toward an increasingly thin standard, which has become more uniform and has been more widely distributed due to the advent of mass media. Changes in measurements over time toward increasing thinness have been documented in Miss America contestants, Playboy centerfolds, and female models in magazine advertisements (Garner, Garfinkel, Schwartz, & Thompson, 1980; Snow & Harris, 1985). During the same time period, however, the average body weight of women under 30 years of age has actually increased (Metropolitan Life Foundation, 1983; Society of Actuaries, 1959, 1979).

Lakoff and Scherr (1984) suggested that models on television and in magazines are seen as realistic representations of what people look like, as compared with painted figures who are more readily acknowledged to be artistic creations. Even though the magazine model or television actress has undergone hours of makeup preparation as well as time-consuming and rigorous workout regimens to achieve the "look," her audience thinks that the model's public persona is what she really looks like. Her "look" is then rapidly and widely disseminated, so that the public receives a uniform picture of beauty.

Effects of Media Attention on Dieting and Bulimia

We hypothesize that current sociocultural influences teach women not only what the ideal body looks like but also how to try to attain it, including how to diet, purge, and engage in other disregulating behaviors. The mass-market weight control industry almost prescribes these rituals. For example, the bestseller *Beverly Hills Diet Book* (Mazel, 1981) advocated a form of bulimia in which binges are "compensated" by eating massive quantities of raw fruit to induce diarrhea (Wooley & Wooley, 1982). In addition to the mass media making available what one might call manuals for "how to develop an eating disorder," females more directly teach each other how to diet and how to binge, purge, and starve. Schwartz, Thompson, and Johnson (1981) found that a college woman who purges almost always knows another

female student who purges, whereas a woman who does not purge rarely knows someone who does.

A positive feedback loop is thus established: The more women there are with disordered eating, the more likely there are to be even more women who develop disordered eating. We certainly do not mean to imply that psychopathology is merely learned behavior—but we suggest that the public's heightened awareness of eating disorders and a young woman's likelihood of personal exposure to the behaviors may be a significant factor in the increased emergence of eating disorders in the last several years.

We have already noted how family members may model for other members both attitudes and behaviors concerning weight and eating. Interestingly, as Boskind-White and White (1983) described, the women now presenting with bulimia are the daughters of the first Weight Watchers' generation. A question for future study is, What will the daughters of the generation of bulimic women be like?

Fitness

In the past decade, along with the fitness movement, there has been a redefinition of the ideal female body, which is characterized now not merely by thinness but by firm, shapely muscles (while avoiding too much muscularity) as well. Although the possible health benefits from increased exercise are very real, the current emphasis on fitness may itself be contributing to the increased incidence of bulimia. The strong implication is that anyone who "works out" can achieve the lean, healthy-looking ideal and that such attainment is a direct consequence of personal effort and therefore worthy of pride and admiration. Conversely, the inability to achieve the "aerobics instructor look" may leave women feeling defeated, ashamed, and desperate. The pursuit of fitness becomes another preoccupation, compulsion, even obsession for many. Again, we note that women's bodies are predisposed to have a fairly high proportion of fat; indeed, female hormones are disregulated when the percentage of body fat drops below a certain level. The no-fat ideal reflects an "unnatural" standard for many women.

If the pursuit of fitness represents a step even beyond pursuit of thinness, so too does the upsurge of cosmetic surgery. From suction removal of fat to face-lifts, women in increasing numbers are seeking to match the template of beauty with ever more complicated (and expensive) procedures. The message, again, seems to be that beauty is a matter of effort and that failure to attain the beauty ideal makes one personally culpable.

Shifting Sex Roles

Perhaps, ironically, in this era when women feel capable and empowered to pursue success in professional arenas, they have a heightened sense that their efforts should attain success in the domain of beauty as well. It seems that being occupationally successful does not relieve a woman of the need to be beautiful. Indeed, the pursuit of beauty and thinness may sometimes compromise women's success in other domains, for it takes time, attention, and money and is a drain on self-esteem.

In this transitional time of rapidly shifting sex roles, it seems likely that girls more than boys are experiencing the stresses of changing roles, perhaps placing girls at greater risk for psychological distress in general. These changing roles may intersect with all of the risk factors for bulimia we have been discussing and therefore may be an important part of the answer to Why now? The messages communicated to girls are complex and quite often confusing: Work hard at school, but be sure to be popular and pretty; be a lawyer, but be feminine. Little research has been done that can illuminate these kinds of issues. Clinically, we find that bulimic women often express confusion about their roles; an interesting question for research is whether this distinguishes them from other women in general and from other women psychotherapy clients.

Steiner-Adair (1986) studied adolescent girls' images of the ideal woman and their personal goals for themselves and looked at the relationship of these views with performance on the Eating Attitudes Test (EAT), a measure of disordered eating (Garner & Garfinkel, 1979). Interestingly, all girls had a similar picture of the ideal "superwoman" (career, family, beauty), but those girls who saw the "superwoman" as consonant with their own goals had elevated eating pathology scores, whereas the non-eating-disordered girls had more modest goals for themselves. Hence, a girl's ability to put distance between the societal ideal and her own expectations for herself was associated with decreased evidence of eating disturbance. This seems analogous to our findings of a significant correlation between agreement with statements reflecting sociocultural messages regarding attractiveness, and a measure of disordered eating (Striegel-Moore, Silberstein, & Rodin, 1985a). Gilligan (1982) has argued that the process of female development in our androcentric society makes it difficult for girls and women to find and use their own "voice." We would contend that when women instead adopt the socioculturally defined voice and strive to match the unrealistically successful as well as the unrealistically thin public model, the consequences may be unhealthy.

Conclusions

We have tried to understand bulimia and point to important gaps in our knowledge by examining three questions: Why women? Which women in particular? Why now? We addressed these questions by drawing on a diverse literature in social and developmental psychology, psychology of gender, clinical psychiatry and psychology, and biological psychiatry and medicine. As we conclude our analysis of risk factors in women, it is instructive to ask how men may fit into this picture.

Though significantly fewer men than women currently show evidence of bulimia (a ratio of 1:10), bulimic men do exist and, we hypothesize, will increase in number in the near future. Indeed, bulimic men are an important group to study in the context of our risk factor model, because although men and women may share certain sociocultural, psychological, and biological risk factors, there clearly are gender differences in the variables placing an individual at risk.

Surely our society's fitness consciousness applies to men as much as, and perhaps even more than, to women. It is possible that the sexes pursue fitness for different reasons, with women focusing more on the effects exercise has on physical appearance, whereas men pursue strength and muscularity (Garner, Rockert, Olmsted, Johnson, & Coscina, 1985). However, the workout body type for men has become, it seems, a more widely aspired-to-ideal, and similarly to women, more and more men today are fighting to ward off the effects of aging on their appearance. As men become more fashion conscious and more weight conscious, we would expect them to diet more. Already, diet soft drinks, light beers, and other diet products are being marketed for a male as well as a female audience. Because men rarely have the long history of dieting efforts that women do, men typically are more successful in their weight-loss efforts. However, if they succumb to repeated cycles of gaining and losing, we hypothesize that these patterns will lead to the same effects in men as they have in women and could therefore potentiate bulimia.

Beyond the general pressure on men to be conscious of physical fitness and appearance that may result in an increased risk for men to develop bulimia, certain male subcultures (similar to female subcultures) emphasize weight standards and thus place certain men at greater risk for bulimia. If our hypothesis is correct that environments that emphasize weight standards foster the development of bulimia, then we would expect to find a higher incidence of bulimia in men who participate in such environments than in men who do not. In fact, initial research does show that athletes such as wrestlers and jockeys evidence higher incidence of bulimia (Rodin, Striegel-Moore, & Silberstein, 1985) than athletes in sports that do not prescribe a certain body weight. Clinical evidence suggests that homosexual men, whose subculture promotes a thin body ideal and a heightened attentiveness to appearance and fashion (Kleinberg, 1980; Lakoff & Scherr, 1984; Mishkind, Rodin, Silberstein, & Striegel-Moore, 1986), may also be at increased risk for bulimia (Herzog, Norman, Gordon, & Pepose, 1984).

The present analysis has underscored questions that remain to be investigated. As we conclude, let us briefly outline some of these agendas for future study. Initial research suggests that a description of bulimia as a single entity does not reflect adequately the heterogeneity of the population. In particular, we need diagnostic categories that allow differentiation among subgroups, which would then permit an investigation of the differential relationships among those subgroups and the various risk factors. An additional step involves clarifying the relationships among bulimia, anorexia, and obesity, and the risk factors involved in each of those syndromes. Another question deserving further attention is the place of bulimia in the spectrum of psychiatric disorders in general and in the affective disorders in particular. In addition, we need to understand the risk factors that bulimia may share with other psychiatric syndromes that have been disproportionally represented by women, such as depression and agoraphobia.

Having emphasized the importance of female socialization as a major contributing factor in bulimia, we also need to examine how changes in the female sex role stereotype may affect the incidence of bulimia. Furthermore, reaching an understanding of the risk factors for bulimia in men could help expand and refine our understanding of risk factors in women as well as in men. Finally, although we have focused our attention on identifying factors that place women at risk for bulimia, it will be equally important to delineate variables that serve a protective function.

Another important task is to develop strategies for the prevention of bulimia. Numerous risk factors have been described that do not lend themselves easily to modification. Many have to do with social values and mores. Unfortunately, large-scale social changes are slow and difficult to effect. Other risk factors involve genetic determinants. Even if some factors that lead to bulimia are genetically determined or transmitted, however, the fact that they are expressed as an eating disorder rather than in some other clinical manifestation can be understood only by referring to the present sociocultural milieu and to female sex role socialization practices. As strategies for change in these areas are developed, shifts in the incidence and prevalence of bulimia may be expected to follow.

References

ABRAHAM, S., AND BEUMONT, P. J. V. (1982). How patients describe bulimia or binge eating. *Psychological Medicine, 12,* 625–635.

ADLER, J. (1982, January). Looking back at '81. *Newsweek,* pp. 26–52.

ALDOUS, J. (1978). *Family careers: Developmental change in families.* New York: Wiley.

ALTSCHULER, K. Z., AND WEINER, M. F. (1985). Anorexia nervosa and depression: A dissenting view. *American Journal of Psychiatry, 142,* 328–332.

AMBERT, A. M. (1976). *Sex structure.* Don Mills, Canada: Langman.

AMERICAN PSYCHIATRIC ASSOCIATION (1980). *Diagnostic and statistical manual of mental disorders* (3rd ed.). Washington, DC: Author.

ANDERSEN, A. E. (1983). Anorexia nervosa and bulimia: A spectrum of eating disorders. *Journal of Adolescent Health Care, 4,* 15–21.

APFELBAUM, M. (1975). Influence of level of energy intake on energy expenditure in man. Effects of spontaneous intake, experimental starvation and experimental overeating. In G. A. Bray (Ed.), *Obesity in perspective* (OBHEW Publication No. NIH 75-708, Vol. 2, pp. 145–155). Washington, DC: U.S. Government Printing Office.

ARENSON, G. (1984). *Binge eating. How to stop it forever.* New York: Rawson.

BANNER, L. W. (1983). *American beauty.* New York: Knopf.

BARNETT, R. C., AND BARUCH, G. K. (1980). *The competent woman: Perspectives on development.* New York: Irvington.

BECK, J. B., WARD-HULL, C. J., AND McLEAR, P. M. (1976). Variables related to women's somatic preferences of the male and female body. *Journal of Personality and Social Psychology, 34,* 1200–1210.

BELLER, A. S. (1977). *Fat and thin: A natural history of obesity.* New York: Farrar, Straus & Giroux.

BELLER, A. S. (1980). Pregnancy: Is motherhood fattening? In J. R. KAPLAN (Ed.), *A woman's conflict* (pp. 139–158). Englewood Cliffs, NJ: Prentice-Hall.

BEM, S. L. (1974). The measurement of psychological androgyny. *Journal of Consulting and Clinical Psychology, 42,* 155–162.

BENNETT, W. I. (1984). Dieting: Ideology versus physiology. *Psychiatric Clinics of North America, 7,* 321–334.

BERSCHEID, E., DION, K. K., WALSTER, E., AND WALSTER, G. (1971). Physical attractiveness and dating choice. A test of the matching hypothesis. *Journal of Experimental Social Psychology, 7,* 173–189.

BEUMONT, P. J., GEORGE, G.C., AND SMART, D. E. (1976). "Dieters" and "vomiters and purgers" in anorexia nervosa. *Psychological Medicine, 6,* 617–622.

BJORNTORP, P., AND YANG, M. U. (1982). Refeeding after fasting in the rat: Effects on body composition and food efficiency. *American Journal of Clinical Nutrition, 36,* 444–449.

BLUMENSTEIN, P. W., AND SCHWARTZ, P. (1983). *American couples.* New York: Morrow.

BLYTH, D. A., AND TRAEGER, C. M. (1983). The self-concept and self-esteem of early adolescents. *Theory Into Practice, 22,* 91–97.

BORJESON, M. (1976). The aetiology of obesity in children. *Acta Paediatrica Scandinavica, 65,* 279–287.

BOSKIND-LODAHL, M. (1976). Cinderella's stepsisters. *Signs: Journal of Women, Culture and Society, 2,* 342–358.

BOSKIND-LODAHL, M., AND SIRLIN, J. (1977). The gorging-purging syndrome. *Psychology Today, 10,* 50–52, 82–85.

BOSKIND-WHITE, M., AND WHITE, W. C. (1983). *Bulimarexia: The binge/purge cycle.* New York: Norton.

BOYLE, P. C., STORLIEN, L. H., HARPER, A. E., AND KEESEY, R. E. (1981). Oxygen consumption and locomotor activity during restricted feeding and realimentation. *American Journal of Physiology, 241,* R392–397.

BRAY, G. A. (1976). *The obese patient.* Philadelphia: Saunders.

BRAY, G. A. (1981). The inheritance of corpulence. In L. A. CIOFFI, W. P. T. JAMES, AND T. B. VAN ITALLIE (Eds.), *Weight regulatory system: Normal and disturbed mechanisms* (pp. 185–195). New York: Raven Press.

BRISMAN, J., AND SIEGEL, M. (1984). Bulimia and alcoholism: Two sides of the same coin? *Journal of Substance Abuse Treatment, 1,* 113–118.

BROOK, C. G. D., HUNTLEY, R. M. C., AND SLACK, J. (1975). Influence of heredity and environment in determination of skinfold thickness in children. *British Medical Journal, 2,* 719–721.

BROWNELL, K. D., STELLAR, E., STUNKARD, A. J., RODIN, J., AND WILSON, G. T. (1984). *Behavioral and metabolic effects of weight loss and regain in animals and humans.* Unpublished manuscript, University of Pennsylvania, Philadelphia.

BROWNMILLER, S. (1984). *Femininity.* New York: Linden Press/Simon & Schuster.

BRUCH, H. (1973). *Eating disorders: Obesity, anorexia nervosa and the person within.* New York: Basic Books.

BRUCH, H. (1981). Developmental considerations of anorexia nervosa and obesity. *Canadian Journal of Psychiatry, 26,* 212–217.

BUSH, D. E., SIMMONS, R., HUTCHINSON, B., AND BLYTH, D. (1978). Adolescent perceptions of sex roles in 1968 and 1975. *Public Opinion Quarterly, 41,* 459–474.

BUTTON, E. J., FRANSELLA, F., AND SLADE, P. D. (1977). A reappraisal of body perception disturbance in anorexia nervosa. *Psychological Medicine, 7,* 235–243.

CARLSON, R. (1965). Stability and change in the adolescent's self-image. *Child Development, 36,* 659–666.

CASH, T. F., GILLEN, B., AND BURNS, D. S. (1977). Sexism and "beautyism" in personnel consultant decision making. *Journal of Applied Psychology, 62,* 301–310.

CASPER, R. C., ECKERT, E. D., HALMI, K. A., GOLDBERG, S. C., AND DAVIS, J. M. (1980). Bulimia: Its incidence and clinical importance in patients with anorexia nervosa. *Archives of General Psychiatry, 37,* 1030–1035.

CASPER, R. C., HALMI, K. A., GOLDBERG, S. C., ECKERT, E. D., AND DAVIS, J. M. (1979). Disturbances in body image estimation as related to other characteristics and outcome of anorexia nervosa. *British Journal of Psychiatry, 134,* 60–66.

CEDERLOF, R., AND KAY, L. (1970). The effect of childbearing on body weight. A twin control study. *Acta Psychiatrica Scandinavica,* (Suppl.) *219,* 47–49.

CHAIKEN, S., AND PLINER, P. (1984). *Women, but not men, are what they eat: The effect of meal size and gender on perceived femininity and masculinity.* Unpublished manuscript, Vanderbilt University, Nashville, TN.

CHODOROW, N. (1978). *The reproduction of mothering: Psychoanalysis and the sociology of gender.* Berkeley: University of California Press.

CLAUSEN, J. A. (1975). The social meaning of differential physical and sexual maturation. In S. E. DRAGASTIN AND G. H. ELDER, JR. (Eds.), *Adolescence in the life cycle: Psychological change and social context* (pp. 24–48). Washington, DC: Hemisphere.

COLEMAN, J. S. (1961). *The adolescent society.* New York: Free Press.

CRAGO, M., YATES, A., BEUTLER, L. E., AND ARIZMENDI, T. G. (1985). Height–weight ratios among female athletes: Are collegiate athletics the precursors to an anorexic syndrome? *International Journal of Eating Disorders, 4,* 79–87.

CRISP, A. H. (1980). *Anorexia nervosa: Let me be.* London: Academic Press.

CRISP, A. H., HALL, A., AND HOLLAND, A. J. (1985). Nature and nurture in anorexia nervosa: A study of 34 pairs of twins, one pair of triplets and an adoptive family. *International Journal of Eating Disorders, 4,* 5–27.

CRISP, A. H., AND KALUCY, R. S. (1974). Aspects of the perceptual disorder in anorexia nervosa. *British Journal of Medical Psychology, 47,* 349–361.

DALLY, P. J., AND GOMEZ, J. (1979). *Anorexia nervosa.* London: William Heinemann Medical Books.

DALVIT-MACPHILLIPS, S. P. (1983). The effect of the human menstrual cycle on nutrient intake. *Physiology and Behavior, 31,* 209–212.

DIPPEL, R. L., AND ELIAS, J. W. (1980). Preferences for sweets in relationship to use of oral contraceptives in pregnancy. *Hormones and Behavior, 14,* 1–6.

DORNBUSCH, S. M., CARLSMITH, J. M., DUNCAN, P. D., GROSS, R. T., MARTIN, J. A., RITTER, P. L., AND SIEGEL-GORELICK, B. (1984). Sexual maturation, social class, and the desire to be thin among adolescent females. *Developmental and Behavioral Pediatrics, 5,* 308–314.

DOUVAN, E., AND ADELSON, J. (1966). *The adolescent experience.* New York: Wiley.

DREWNOWSKI, A., RISKEY, D., AND DESOR, J. A. (1982). Feeling fat yet unconcerned: Self-reported overweight and the restraint scale. *Appetite: Journal for Intake Research, 3,* 273–279.

DRUSS, R. G., AND SILVERMAN, J. A. (1979). Body image and perfectionism of ballerinas: Comparison and contrast with anorexia nervosa. *General Hospital Psychiatry, 1,* 115–121.

DUNN, P., AND ONDERCIN, P. (1981). Personality variables related to compulsive eating in college women. *Journal of Clinical Psychology, 37,* 43–49.

DUSEK, J. B., AND FLAHERTY, J. F. (1981). The development of the self-concept during the adolescent years. *Monographs of the Society for Research in Child Development, 46,* 1–67.

DWECK, C. S., DAVIDSON, W., NELSON, S., AND ENNA, B. (1978). Sex differences in learned helplessness: II. The contingencies of evaluative feedback in the classroom, and III. An experimental analysis. *Developmental Psychology, 14,* 268–276.

EHRENREICH, B., AND ENGLISH, D. (1978). *For her own good: 150 years of the experts' advice to women.* New York: Anchor Press/Doubleday.

ERIKSON, E. H. (1968). *Identity: Youth and crisis.* New York: Norton.

EVEN, P., NICOLAIDIS, S., AND MEILE, M. (1981). Changes in efficiency of ingestants are a major factor of regulation of energy balance. In L. A. CIOFFI, W. P. T. JAMES, AND T. B. VAN ITALLIE (Eds.), *The body weight regulatory system: Normal and disturbed mechanisms* (pp. 115–123). New York: Raven Press.

FABSITZ, R., FEINLEIB, M., AND HRUBEC, Z. (1978). Weight changes in adult twins. *Acta Geneticae Medicae et Gemellologiae, 17,* 315–332.

FAIRBURN, C. G., AND COOPER, P. J. (1982). Self-induced vomiting and bulimia nervosa: An undetected problem. *British Medical Journal, 284,* 1153–1155.

FAIRBURN, C. G., AND COOPER, P. J. (1983). The epidemiology of bulimia nervosa. *International Journal of Eating Disorders, 2,* 61–67.

FALLON, A. E., AND ROZIN, P. (1985). Sex differences in perceptions of body shape. *Journal of Abnormal Psychology, 94,* 102–105.

FAUST, M. S. (1983). Alternative constructions of adolescent growth. In J. BROOKS-GUNN AND A. C. PETERSEN (Eds.), *Girls at puberty* (pp. 105–125). New York: Plenum Press.

FAUST, J. M., JOHNSON, P. R., STERN, J. S., AND HIRSCH, J. (1978). Diet-induced adipocyte number increase in adult rats: A new model of obesity. *American Journal of Physiology, 235,* E279–286.

FEDERAL TRADE COMMISSION. (1978). FTC staff report on television advertising to children. Washington, DC: Author.

FEINLEIB, M., GARRISON, R. J., FABSITZ, R., CHRISTIAN, J. C., HRUBEC, Z., BORHANI, N. O., KANNEL, W. B., ROSENMAN, R., SCHWARTZ, J. T., AND WAGNER, J. O. (1977). The NHLBI twin study of cardiovascular disease risk factors: Methodology and summary of results. *American Journal of Epidemiology, 106,* 284–295.

FISHER, S. (1964). Sex differences in body perception. *Psychological Monographs, 78,* 1–22.

FORBES, G., AND REINA, J. C. (1970). Adult lean body mass declines with age: Some longitudinal observations. *Metabolism, 19,* 653–663.

FRANZOI, S. L., AND SHIELDS, S. A. (1984). The body esteem scale: Multidimensional structure and sex differences in a college population. *Journal of Personality Assessment, 48,* 173–178.

FREMOUW, W. J., AND HEYNEMAN, E. (1984). A functional analysis of binge episodes. In R. C. HAWKINS II, W. J. FREMOUW, AND P. F. CLEMENT (Eds.), *The binge-purge syndrome* (pp. 254–263). New York: Springer.

FRIED, S. K., HILL, J. O., NICKEL, M., AND DI-GIROLAMO, M. (1983). Prolonged effects of fasting-refeeding on rat adipose tissue lipoprotein lipase activity. Influence of caloric restriction during refeeding. *Journal of Nutrition, 113,* 1861–1869.

FRIES, H. (1975). Anorectic behavior: Nosological aspects and introduction of a behavior scale. *Scandinavian Journal of Behavior Therapy, 4,* 137–148.

GARFINKEL, P. E., AND GARNER, D. M. (1982). *Anorexia nervosa. A multidimensional perspective.* New York: Brunner/Mazel.

GARFINKEL, P. E., MOLDOFSKY, H., AND GARNER, D. M. (1980). The heterogeneity of anorexia nervosa. *Archives of General Psychiatry, 37,* 1036–1040.

GARNER, D. M., AND GARFINKEL, P. E. (1978). Sociocultural factors in anorexia-nervosa. *Lancet, 2,* 674.

GARNER, D. M., AND GARFINKEL, P. E. (1979). The Eating Attitudes Test: An index of the symptoms of anorexia nervosa. *Psychological Medicine, 9,* 273–279.

GARNER, D. M., AND GARFINKEL, P. E. (1980). Sociocultural factors in the development of anorexia nervosa. *Psychological Medicine, 10,* 647–656.

GARNER, D. M., AND GARFINKEL, P. E. (Eds.). (1985). *Handbook of psychotherapy for anorexia nervosa and bulimia.* New York: Guilford.

GARNER, D. M., GARFINKEL, P. E., AND O'SHAUGHNESSY, M. (1985). The validity of the distinction between bulimia with and without anorexia nervosa. *American Journal of Psychiatry, 142,* 581–587.

GARNER, D. M., GARFINKEL, P. E., SCHWARTZ, D., AND THOMPSON, M. (1980). Cultural expectations of thinness in women. *Psychological Reports, 47,* 483–491.

GARNER, D. M., GARFINKEL, P. E., STANCER, H. C., AND MOLDOFSKY, H. (1976). Body image disturbances in anorexia nervosa and obesity. *Psychosomatic Medicine, 38,* 327–336.

GARNER, D. M., OLMSTED, M. P., AND POLIVY, J. (1983). Development and validation of a multidimensional eating disorder inventory for anorexia nervosa and bulimia. *International Journal of Eating Disorders, 2,* 15–34.

GARNER, D. M., ROCKERT, W., OLMSTED, M. P., JOHNSON, C., AND COSCINA, D. V. (1985). Psychoeducational principles in the treatment of bulimia and anorexia nervosa. In D. M. GARNER AND P. E. GARFINKEL (Eds.), *Handbook of psychotherapy for anorexia nervosa and bulimia* (pp. 513–572). New York: Guilford.

GARROW, J. (1978). The regulation of energy expenditure. In G. A. BRAY (Ed.), *Recent advances in obesity research* (Vol. 2, pp. 200–210). London: Newman.

GEORGE, R. S., AND KRONDL, M. (1983). Perceptions and food use of adolescent boys and girls. *Nutrition and Behavior, 1,* 115–125.

GERSHON, E. S., HAMOVIT, J. R., SCHREIBER, J. L., DIBBLE, E. D., KAYE, W., NURNBERGER, J. I., ANDERSEN, A., AND EBERT, M. (1983). Anorexia nervosa and major affective disorders associated in families: A preliminary report. In S. B. GUZE, F. J. EARLS, AND J. E. BARRETT (Eds.), *Childhood psychopathology and development* (pp. 279–284). New York: Raven Press.

GILLEN, B. (1981). Physical attractiveness: A determinant of two types of goodness. *Personality and Social Psychology Bulletin, 7,* 277–281.

GILLEN, B., AND SHERMAN, R. C. (1980). Physical attractiveness and sex as determinants of trait attributions. *Multivariate Behavioral Research, 15,* 423–437.

GILLIGAN, C. (1982). *In a different voice: Psychological theory and women's development.* Cambridge, MA: Harvard University Press.

GOLDBLATT, P. B., MOORE, M. E., AND STUNKARD, A. J. (1965). Social factors in obesity. *Journal of the American Medical Association, 192,* 1039–1044.

GOODSITT, A. (1983). Self-regulatory disorders in eating disorders. *International Journal of Eating Disorders, 2,* 51–61.

GORMALLY, J. (1984). The obese binge eater: Diagnosis, etiology, and clinical issues. In R. C. HAWKINS, II, W. J. FREMOUW, AND P. F. CLEMENT (Eds.), *The binge-purge syndrome* (pp. 47–73). New York: Springer.

GRACE, P. S., JACOBSON, R. S., AND FULLAGER, C. J. (1985). A pilot comparison of purging and non-purging bulimics. *Journal of Clinical Psychology, 41,* 173–180.

GRUEN, R. K., AND GREENWOOD, M. R. C. (1981). Adipose tissue lipoprotein lipase and glycerol release in fasted Zucker (fa/fa) rats. *American Journal of Physiology, 241,* E76–E83.

GURALNIK, D. B. (Ed.). (1982). *Webster's new world dictionary* (2nd ed.). New York: Simon & Schuster.

GUY, R. F., RANKIN, B. A., AND NORVELL, M. J. (1980). The relation of sex-role stereotyping to body image. *Journal of Psychology, 105,* 167–173.

GUYOT, G. W., FAIRCHILD, L., AND HILL, M. (1981). Physical fitness, sport participation, body build and self-concept of elementary school children. *International Journal of Sport Psychology, 12,* 105–116.

GWIRTSMAN, H. E., ROY-BYRNE, P., YAGER, J., AND GERNER, R. H. (1983). Neuroendocrine abnormalities in bulimia. *American Journal of Psychiatry, 140,* 559–563.

HALMI, K. A., FALK, J. R., AND SCHWARTZ, E. (1981). Binge-eating and vomiting: A survey of a college population. *Psychological Medicine, 11,* 697–706.

HALMI, K. A., GOLDBERG, S., AND CUNNINGHAM, S. (1977). Perceptual distribution of body image in adolescent girls: Distortion of body image in adolescence. *Psychological Medicine, 7,* 253–257.

HAMBURG, B. (1974). Early adolescence: A specific and stressful stage of the life cycle. In G. COELHO, D. A. HAMBURG, AND J. E. ADAMS (Eds.), *Coping and adaptation* (pp. 101–126). New York: Basic Books.

HAMMAR, R. D., CAMPBELL, V. A., MOORES, N. L., SAREEN, C., GAREIS, F. J., AND LUCAS, B. (1972). An interdisciplinary study of adolescent obesity. *Journal of Pediatrics, 80,* 373–383.

HARRIS, M. B. (1983). Eating habits, restraint, knowledge and attitudes toward obesity. *International Journal of Obesity, 7,* 271–288.

HARRISON, A. A., AND SAEED, L. (1977). Let's make a deal: Analysis of revelations and stipulations in lonely hearts advertisements. *Journal of Personality and Social Psychology, 35,* 257–264.

HARTER, S. (1985). Processes underlying the construction, maintenance and enhancement of the self-concept in children. In J. SULS AND A. GREENWALD (Eds.), *Psychological perspectives on the self* (Vol. 3, pp. 137–181). Hillsdale, NJ: Erlbaum.

HATFIELD, E., AND SPRECHER, S. (1986). *Mirror, mirror: The importance of looks in everyday life.* New York: SUNY Press.

HATSUKAMI, D., ECKERT, E., MITCHELL, J. E., AND PYLE, R. (1984). Affective disorder and substance abuse in women with bulimia. *Psychological Medicine, 14,* 701–704.

HATSUKAMI, D. K., MITCHELL, J. E., AND ECKERT, E. (1981). Eating disorders: A variant of mood disorders? *Psychiatric Clinics of North America, 7,* 349–365.

HATSUKAMI, D., OWEN, P., PYLE, R., AND MITCHELL, J. (1982). Similarities and differences on the MMPI between women with bulimia and women with alcohol or drug abuse problems. *Addictive Behaviors, 7,* 435–439.

HAVIGHURST, R. J. (1972). *Developmental tasks and education.* New York: McKay.

HAWKINS, R. C. II, AND CLEMENT, P. F. (1980). Development and construct validations of a self-report measure of binge eating tendencies. *Addictive Behaviors, 5,* 219–226.

HAWKINS, R. C. II, AND CLEMENT, P. F. (1984). Binge eating: Measurement problems and a conceptual model. In R. C. HAWKINS II, W. J. FREMOUW, AND P. F. CLEMENT (Eds.) *The binge-purge syndrome* (pp. 229–253). New York: Springer.

HAWKINS, R. C., JR., TURELL, S., AND JACKSON, L. J. (1983). Desirable and undesirable masculine and feminine traits in relation to students' dietary tendencies and body image dissatisfaction. *Sex Roles, 9,* 705–724.

HEILMAN, M. E., AND SARUWATARI, L. R. (1979). When beauty is beastly: The effects of appearance and sex on evaluations of job applicants for managerial and non-managerial jobs. *Organizational Behavior and Human Performance, 23,* 360–372.

HELLIOVAARA, M., AND AROMAA, A. (1981). Parity and obesity. *Journal of Epidemiology and Community Health, 35,* 197–199.

HERMAN, C. P., AND MACK, D. (1975). Restrained and unrestrained eating. *Journal of Personality, 43,* 647–660.

HERMAN, C. P., AND POLIVY, J. (1975). Anxiety, restraint, and eating behavior. *Journal of Abnormal Psychology, 84,* 666–672.

HERZOG, D. (1982). Bulimia in the adolescent. *American Journal of Diseases of Children, 136,* 985–989.

HERZOG, D. B., NORMAN, D. K., GORDON, C., AND PEPOSE, M. (1984). Sexual conflict and eating disorders in 27 males. *American Journal of Psychiatry, 141,* 989–990.

HILL, J. P., AND LYNCH, M. E. (1983). The intensification of gender-related role expectations during early adolescence. In J. BROOKS-GUNN AND A. C. PETERSEN (Eds.), *Girls at puberty* (pp. 201–228). New York: Plenum Press.

HILL, J. P., THIEL, K. S., AND BLYTH, D. A. (1981). *Grade and gender differences in perceived intimacy with peers among seventh- to tenth-grade boys and girls.* Unpublished manuscript, Boys Town Center for the Study of Youth Development, Richmond, VA.

HOLLAND, A. J., HALL, A., MURRAY, R., RUSSELL, G. F. M., AND CRISP, A. H. (1984). Anorexia nervosa: A study of 34 twin pairs and one set of triplets. *British Journal of Psychiatry, 145,* 414–419.

HOOD, J., MOORE, T. E., AND GARNER, D. M. (1982). Locus of control as a measure of ineffectiveness in anorexia nervosa. *Journal of Consulting and Clinical Psychology, 50,* 3–13.

HOVELL, M. F., MEWBORN, C. R., RANDLE, Y., AND FOWLER-JOHNSON, S. (1985). Risk of excess weight gain in university women: A three-year community controlled analysis. *Addictive Behaviors, 10,* 15–28.

HUDSON, J. I., LAFFER, P. S., AND POPE, H. G., JR. (1982). Bulimia related to affective disorder by family history and response to the dexamethasone suppression test. *American Journal of Psychiatry, 137,* 605–607.

HUDSON, J. I., POPE, H. G., JR., AND JONAS, J. M. (1984). Treatment of bulimia with antidepressants: Theoretical considerations and clinical findings. In A. J. STUNKARD AND E. STELLAR (Eds.), *Eating and its disorders* (pp. 259–273). New York: Raven Press.

HUDSON, J. I., POPE, H. G., JR. JONAS, J. M., LAFFER, P. S., HUDSON, M. S., AND MELBY, J. C. (1983). Hypothalamic-pituitary-adrenal axis hyperactivity in bulimia. *Psychiatry Research, 8,* 111–117.

HUON, G., AND BROWN, L. B. (1984). Psychological correlates of weight control among anorexia nervosa patients and normal girls. *British Journal of Medical Psychology, 57,* 61–66.

HYTTEN, F. E., AND LEITCH, I. (1971). *The physiology of human pregnancy.* Oxford: Blackwell Scientific Publications.

JAKOBOVITS, C., HALSTEAD, P., KELLEY, L., ROE, D. A., AND YOUNG, C. M. (1977). Eating habits and nutrient intakes of college women over a thirty-year period. *Journal of the American Dietetic Association, 71,* 405–411.

JANDA, L. H., O'GRADY, K. E., AND BARNHART, S. A. (1981). Effects of sexual attitudes and physical attractiveness on person perception of men and women. *Sex Roles, 7,* 189–199.

JOHNSON, C., AND FLACH, A. (1985). Family characteristics of 105 patients with bulimia. *American Journal of Psychiatry, 142,* 1321–1324.

JONNSON, C. L., AND LARSON, R. (1982). Bulimia: An analysis of moods and behavior. *Psychosomatic Medicine, 44,* 341–353.

JOHNSON, C., LEWIS, C., AND HAGMAN, J. (1984). The syndrome of bulimia. *Psychiatric Clinics of North America, 7,* 247–274.

JOHNSON, C. L., STUCKEY, M. R., LEWIS, L. D., AND SCHWARTZ, D. M. (1982). Bulimia: A descriptive survey of 316 cases. *International Journal of Eating Disorders, 2,* 3–16.

JONES, M. C. (1965). Psychological correlates of somatic development. *Child Development, 36,* 899–911.

JOSEPH, A., WOOD, J. K., AND GOLDBERG, S. C. (1982). Determining populations at risk for developing anorexia nervosa based on selection of college major. *Psychiatry Research, 7,* 53–58.

JOURARD, S. M., AND SECORD, P. F. (1955). Body-cathexis and the ideal female figure. *Journal of Abnormal and Social Psychology, 50,* 243–246.

KAGAN, D. M., AND SQUIRES, R. L. (1985). Family cohesion, family adaptability, and eating behaviors among college students. *International Journal of Eating Disorders, 4,* 267–280.

KASHANI, J. H., AND PRIESMEYER, M. (1983). Differences in depressive symptoms and depression among college students. *American Journal of Psychiatry, 140,* 1081–1082.

KATZMAN, M. A., AND WOLCHIK, S. A. (1984). Bulimia and binge eating in college women: A comparison of personality and behavioral characteristics. *Journal of Consulting and Clinical Psychology, 52,* 423–428.

KATZMAN, M. A., WOLCHIK, S. A., AND BRAVER, S. L. (1984). The prevalence of frequent binge eating and bulimia in a nonclinical sample. *International Journal of Eating Disorders, 3,* 53–62.

KLEINBERG, S. (1980). *Alienated affections: Being gay in America.* New York: St. Martin's Press.

KOG, E., VANDEREYCKEN, W., AND VERTOMMEN, H. (in press). Towards verification of the psychosomatic family model. A pilot study of 10 families with an anorexia/bulimia patient. *International Journal of Eating Disorders.*

KOG, E., VERTOMMEN, H., AND DEGROOTE, T. (in press). Family interaction research in anorexia nervosa: The use and misuse of a self-report questionnaire. *International Journal of Family Psychiatry.*

KREBS, D., AND ADINOLFI, A. A. (1975). Physical attractiveness, social relations, and personality style. *Journal of Personality and Social Psychology, 31,* 245–253.

KURTZ, R. M. (1969). Sex differences and variations in body attitudes. *Journal of Consulting and Clinical Psychology, 33,* 625–629.

LACEY, J. H. (1982). The bulimic syndrome at normal body weight: Reflections on pathogenesis and clinical features. *International Journal of Eating Disorders, 2,* 59–66.

LAKOFF, R. T., AND SCHERR, R. L. (1984). *Face value: The politics of beauty.* Boston: Routledge & Kegan Paul.

LEON, G. R., CARROLL, K., CHERNYK, B., AND FINN, S. (1985). Binge eating and associated habit patterns within college student and identified bulimic populations. *International Journal of Eating Disorders, 4,* 43–57.

LEON, G. R., LUCAS, A. R., COLLIGAN, R. C., FERDINANDE, R. J., AND KAMP, J. (1985). Sexual, body-image, and personality attitudes in anorexia nervosa. *Journal of Abnormal Child Psychology, 13,* 245–258.

LERNER, R. M., KARABENICK, S. A., AND STUART, J. L. (1973). Relations among physical attractiveness, body attitudes, and self-concept in male and female college students. *Journal of Psychology, 85,* 119–129.

LERNER, R. M., ORLOS, J. B., AND KNAPP, J. R. (1976). Physical attractiveness, physical effectiveness and self-concept in late adolescents. *Adolescence, 11,* 313–326.

LEVINSON, D. J., DARROW, C. N., KLEIN, E. B., LEVINSON, M. H., AND MCKEE, B. (1978). *The seasons of a man's life.* New York: Knopf.

LEWIS, C. E., AND LEWIS, N. A. (1974). The impact of television commercials on health-related beliefs and behavior in children. *Pediatrics, 53,* 431–435.

LORO, A. D. (1984). Binge eating: A cognitive-behavioral treatment approach. In R. C. HAWKINS II, W. J. FREMOUW, AND P. F. CLEM-

ENTS (Eds.), *The binge-purge syndrome* (pp. 183–210). New York: Springer.

LORO, A. D., AND ORLEANS, C. S. (1981). Binge eating in obesity: Preliminary findings and guidelines for behavioral analysis and treatment. *Addictive Behaviors, 6,* 155–166.

MAHONEY, E. R. (1974). Body-cathexis and self-esteem: Importance of subjective importance. *Journal of Psychology, 88,* 27–30.

MANN, A. H., WAKELING, A., WOOD, K., MONCK, E., DOBBS, R., AND SZMUKLER, G. (1983). Screening for abnormal eating attitudes and psychiatric morbidity in an unselected population of 15-year-old schoolgirls. *Psychological Medicine, 13,* 573–580.

MARINO, D. D., AND KING, J. C. (1980). Nutritional concerns during adolescence. *Pediatric Clinics of North America, 27,* 125–139.

MARTIN, M., AND WALTER, R. (1982). Korperselbstbild und neurotizismus bei kindern und jugendlichen [Body image and neuroticism in children and adolescents]. *Praxis der Kinderpsychologie und Kinderpsychiatrie, 31,* 213–218.

MAZEL, J. (1981). *The Beverly Hills diet.* New York: Macmillan.

McGUIRE, W. J., AND McGUIRE, C. V. (1982). Significant others in self-space: Sex differences and developmental trends in the social self. In J. SULS (Ed.), *Social psychological perspectives on the self* (pp. 71–96). Hillsdale, NJ: Erlbaum.

McKINLAY, S., AND JEFFREYS, M. (1974). The menopausal syndrome. *British Journal of Preventive and Social Medicine, 28,* 108–115.

MEDLUND, P., CEDERLOF, R., FLODERUS-MYRHED, B., FRIBERG, L., AND SORENSEN, S. (1976). A new Swedish Twin Registry. *Acta Medica Scandinavica* (Suppl. 600).

METROPOLITAN LIFE FOUNDATION. (1983). *Statistical Bulletin, 64,* 2–9.

MILLER, J. B. (1976). *Toward a new psychology of women.* Boston, MA: Beacon Press.

MILLER, W. H., FAUST, I. M., GOLDBERGER, A. C., AND HIRSH, J. (1983). Effects of severe long-term food deprivation and refeeding on adipose tissue cells in the rat. *American Journal of Physiology, 245,* E74–E80.

MINUCHIN, S., ROSMAN, B. L., AND BAKER, L. (1978). *Psychosomatic families: Anorexia nervosa in context.* Cambridge, MA: Harvard University Press.

MISHKIND, M. E., RODIN, J., SILBERSTEIN, L. R., AND STRIEGEL-MOORE, R. H. (in press). The embodiment of masculinity: Cultural, psychological, and behavioral dimensions [Special issue on men's studies]. *American Behavioral Scientist.*

MITCHELL, J. E., HATSUKAMI, D., ECKERT, E. D., AND PYLE, R. L. (1985). Characteristics of 275 patients with bulimia. *American Journal of Psychiatry, 142,* 482–485.

MOSS, R. A., JENNINGS, G., McFARLAND, J. H., AND CARTER, P. (1984). The prevalence of binge eating, vomiting, and weight fear in a female high school population. *Journal of Family Practice, 18,* 313–320.

NATIONAL RESEARCH COUNCIL, FOOD AND NUTRITION BOARD, Committee on Maternal Nutrition. National Research Council. (1970). *Maternal nutrition and the course of pregnancy.* Washington, DC: National Academy of Sciences.

NELSEN, E. A., AND ROSENBAUM, E. (1972). Language patterns within the youth subculture: Development of slang vocabularies. *Merrill-Palmer Quarterly, 18,* 273–285.

NEUGARTEN, B. L. (1969). Continuities and discontinuities of psychological issues into adult life. *Human Development, 12,* 121–130.

NEUGARTEN, B. L. (1970). Dynamics of transition of middle age to old age: Adaptation and the life cycle. *Journal of Geriatric Psychiatry, 41,* 71–87.

NEUGARTEN, B. L. (1972). Personality and aging process. *Gerontologist, 12,* 9.

NIELSEN, A. C. (1979). Who is dieting and why? Chicago, IL: Nielsen Company, Research Department.

NORMAN, D. K., AND HERZOG, D. B. (1983). Bulimia, anorexia nervosa, and anorexia nervosa with bulimia. *International Journal of Eating Disorders, 2,* 43–52.

NOWLIN, N. (1983). Anorexia nervosa in twins: Case report and review. *Journal of Clinical Psychiatry, 44,* 101–105.

NYLANDER, J. (1971). The feeling of being fat and dieting in a school population: Epidemiologic interview investigation. *Acta Sociomedica Scandinavica, 3,* 17–26.

OAKLEY, A. (1972). *Sex, gender and society.* New York: Harper & Row.

ORLEANS, C. T., AND BARNETT, L. R. (1984). Bulimarexia: Guidelines for behavioral assessment and treatment. In R. C. HAWKINS II, W. J. FREMOUW, AND P. F. CLEMENT (Eds.), *The binge-purge syndrome* (pp. 144–182). New York: Springer.

PARIZKOVA, J. (1973). Body composition and exercise during growth and development. In G.

L. Rarick (Ed.), *Physical activity: Human growth and development* (pp. 98–124). New York: Academic Press.

Peskin, H. (1973). Influence of the developmental schedule of puberty on learning and ego functioning. *Journal of Youth and Adolescence, 2,* 273–290.

Pitkin, R. M. (1976). Nutritional support in obstetrics and gynecology. *Clinical Obstetrics and Gynecology, 19,* 489–513.

Polivy, J., and Herman, C. P. (1985). Dieting and binging: A causal analysis. *American Psychologist, 40,* 193–201.

Pope, H. G., Jr., Hudson, J. I., and Jonas, J. M. (1983). Antidepressant treatment of bulimia: Preliminary experience and practical recommendations. *Journal of Clinical Psychopharmacology, 3,* 274–281.

Pope, H. G., Jr., Hudson, J. I., Yurgelun-Todd, D., and Hudson, M. S. (1984). Prevalence of anorexia nervosa and bulimia in three student populations. *International Journal of Eating Disorders, 3,* 45–51.

Pyle, R. L., Mitchell, J. E., and Eckert, E. D. (1981). Bulimia: A report of 34 cases. *Journal of Clinical Psychiatry, 42,* 60–64.

Pyle, R. L., Mitchell, J. E., Eckert, E. D., Halvorson, P. A., Neuman, P. A., and Goff, G. M. (1983). The incidence of bulimia in freshman college students. *International Journal of Eating Disorders, 2,* 75–85.

Rabkin, J. G., Charles, E., and Kass, F. C. (1983). Hypertension and DSM-III depression in psychiatric outpatients. *American Journal of Psychiatry, 140,* 1072–1074.

Rimm, A. A., and White, P. L. (1979). Obesity: Its risks and hazards. In G. A. Bray (Ed.), *Obesity in America* (pp. 103–124). Washington, DC: Department of Health, Education, and Welfare.

Rodin, J. (1981). The current status of the internal–external obesity hypothesis: What went wrong. *American Psychologist, 1,* 343–348.

Rodin, J. (1985, June 30). *Yale health and patterns of living study: A longitudinal study on health, stress, and coping in the elderly.* Unpublished progress report. Yale University, New Haven, CT.

Rodin, J., Silberstein, L. R., and Striegel-Moore, R. H. (1985). Women and weight: A normative discontent. In T. B. Sonderegger (Ed.), *Nebraska symposium on motivation: Vol. 32. Psychology and gender* (pp. 267–307). Lincoln: University of Nebraska Press.

Rodin, J., Striegel-Moore, R. H., and Silberstein, L. R. (1985, July). *A prospective study of bulimia among college students on three U.S. campuses.* First unpublished progress report. Yale University, New Haven, CT.

Rose, G. A., and Williams, R. T. (1961). Metabolic studies on large and small eaters. *British Journal of Nutrition, 15,* 1–9.

Rosenbaum, M. (1979). The changing body image of the adolescent girl. In M. Sugar (Ed.), *Female adolescent development* (pp. 234–252). New York: Brunner/Mazel.

Rosenberg, F. R., and Simmons, R. G. (1975). Sex differences in the self-concept during adolescence. *Sex Roles, 1,* 147–160.

Rost, W., Neuhaus, M., and Florin, I. (1982). Bulimia nervosa: Sex role attitude, sex role behavior, and sex role-related locus of control in bulimiarexic women. *Journal of Psychosomatic Research, 26,* 403–408.

Rudofsky, B. (1971). *The unfashionable human body.* New York: Doubleday.

Russell, G. (1979). Bulimia nervosa: An ominous variant of anorexia nervosa. *Psychological Medicine, 9,* 429–448.

Schwartz, D. M., Thompson, M. G., and Johnson, C. L. (1981). Anorexia nervosa and bulimia: The socio-cultural context. *International Journal of Eating Disorders, 1,* 20–36.

Schwartz, L. A., and Markham, W. T. (1985). Sex stereotyping in children's toy advertisements. *Sex Roles, 12,* 157–170.

Schwartz, R. C. (1982). Bulimia and family therapy: A case study. *International Journal of Eating Disorders, 2,* 75–82.

Schwartz, R. C., Barrett, M. J., and Saba, G. (1985). Family therapy for bulimia. In D. M. Garner and P. E. Garfinkel (Eds.), *Handbook of psychotherapy for anorexia nervosa and bulimia* (pp. 280–307). New York: Guilford.

Secord, P. F., and Jourard, S. M. (1953). The appraisal of body-cathexis: Body-cathexis and the self. *Journal of Consulting Psychology, 17,* 343–347.

Seiden, A. M. (1976). Sex roles, sexuality and the adolescent peer group. *Adolescent Psychiatry, 4,* 211–225.

Selvini-Palazzoli, M. (1978). *Self-starvation: From individuation to family therapy in the treatment of anorexia nervosa.* New York: Aronson.

Shontz, F. C. (1963). Some characteristics of body size estimation. *Perceptual and Motor Skills, 16,* 665–671.

Sights, J. R., and Richards, H. C. (1984). Parents

of bulimic women. *International Journal of Eating Disorders, 3,* 3–13.

SIMMONS, R. G., BLYTH, D. A., AND MCKINNEY, K. L. (1983). The social and psychological effects of puberty on white females. In J. BROOKS-GUNN AND A. C. PETERSEN (Eds.), *Girls at puberty* (pp. 229–278). New York: Plenum Press.

SIMMONS, R. G., AND ROSENBERG, F. (1975). Sex, sex roles, and self-image. *Journal of Youth and Adolescence, 4,* 229–258.

SLADE, P. (1982). Towards a functional analysis of anorexia nervosa and bulimia nervosa. *British Journal of Clinical Psychology, 21,* 167–179.

SLATER, E., AND COWIE, V. (1971). *The genesis of mental illness.* London: Oxford University Press.

SMITH, N. J. (1980). Excessive weight loss and food aversion in athletes simulating anorexia nervosa. *Pediatrics, 66,* 139–142.

SNOW, J. T., AND HARRIS, M. B. (1985). *An analysis of weight and diet content in five women's interest magazines.* Unpublished manuscript, University of New Mexico, Albuquerque.

SOCIETY OF ACTUARIES. (1959). *Build and blood pressure study.* Washington, DC: Author.

SOCIETY OF ACTUARIES AND ASSOCIATION OF LIFE INSURANCE MEDICAL DIRECTORS' OF AMERICA (1979). *Build and blood pressure study.* Chicago, IL: Author.

SONTAG, S. (1972). The double standard of aging. *Saturday Review, 54,* 29–38.

SPENCE, J. T. (1985). Gender identity and its implications for the concept of masculinity and femininity. In T. B. SONDEREGGER (Ed.), *Nebraska Symposium on Motivation: Vol. 32, Psychology and gender* (pp. 59–95). Lincoln: University of Nebraska Press.

SPENCE, J. T., AND HELMREICH, R. L. (1978). Gender, sex roles, and the psychological dimensions of masculinity and femininity. In J. T. SPENCE AND R. L. HELMREICH, *Masculinity and femininity* (pp. 3–18). Austin: University of Texas Press.

SQUIRE, S. (1983). *The slender balance: Causes and cures for bulimia, anorexia, and the weight-loss/weight-gain seesaw.* New York: Putnam.

STEELE, C. I. (1980). Weight loss among teenage girls: An adolescent crisis. *Adolescence, 15,* 823–829.

STEINER-ADAIR, K. (1986). The body politic: Normal female adolescent development and the development of eating disorders. *Journal of the American Academy of Psychoanalysis, 14,* 95–114.

STERN, S. L., DIXON, K. N., NEMZER, E., LAKE, M. D., SANSONE, R. A., SMELTZER, D. J., LANTZ, S., AND SCHRIER, S. S. (1984). Affective disorder in the families of women with normal weight bulimia. *American Journal of Psychiatry, 141,* 1224–1227.

STORY, I. (1979). Factors associated with more positive body self-concepts in preschool-children. *Journal of Social Psychology, 108,* 49–56.

STRIEGEL-MOORE, R. H., MCAVAY, G., AND RODIN, J. (1984, September). *Predictors of attitudes toward body weight and eating in women.* Paper presented at the meeting of the European Association for Behavior Therapy, Brussels, Belgium.

STRIEGEL-MOORE, R. H., MCAVAY, G., AND RODIN, J. (1986). Psychological and behavioral correlates of feeling fat in women. *International Journal of Eating Disorders, 5,* 935–947.

STRIEGEL-MOORE, R. H., SILBERSTEIN, L. R., AND RODIN, J. (1985a, March). *Psychological and behavioral correlates of binge eating: A comparison of bulimic clients and normal control subjects.* Unpublished manuscript, Yale University, New Haven, CT.

STRIEGEL-MOORE, R. H., SILBERSTEIN, L. R., AND RODIN, J. (1985b, August). *The relationship between femininity/masculinity, body dissatisfaction, and bulimia.* Paper presented at the meeting of the American Psychological Association, Los Angeles, CA.

STROBER, M. (1981). The significance of bulimia in juvenile anorexia nervosa: An exploration of possible etiological factors. *International Journal of Eating Disorders, 1,* 28–43.

STROBER, M. (1983, May). *Familial depression in anorexia nervosa.* Paper presented at the meeting of the American Psychiatric Association, New York, NY.

STROBER, M. (1984). Stressful life events associated with bulimia in anorexia nervosa. *International Journal of Eating Disorders, 3,* 2–16.

STROBER, M., MORRELL, W., BURROUGHS, J., SALKIN, B., AND JACOBS, C. (1985). A controlled family study of anorexia nervosa. *Journal of Psychiatric Research, 19,* 239–246.

STROBER, M., SALKIN, B., BURROUGHS, J., AND MORRELL, W. (1982). Validity of the bulimia-restrictor distinction in anorexia nervosa. *Journal of Nervous and Mental Disease, 170,* 345–351.

STROBE, W., INSKO, C. A., THOMPSON, V. D., AND LAYTON, B. D. (1971). Effects of physical attractiveness, attitude similarity, and sex on various aspects of interpersonal attraction.

Journal of Personality and Social Psychology, 18, 79–91.

STUNKARD, A. J., FOCH, T. T., AND HRUBEC, Z. (1985). *A twin study of human obesity.* Unpublished manuscript, University of Pennsylvania, Philadelphia.

STUNKARD, A. J., SORENSEN, T. I. A., HANIS, C., TEASDALE, T. W., CHAKRABORTY, R., SCHULL, W. J., AND SCHULSINGER, F. (1985). *An adoption study of human obesity.* Unpublished manuscript, University of Pennsylvania, Philadelphia.

SZMUKLER, G. L. (1982). Anorexia-nervosa: Its entity as an illness and its treatment. *Pharmacology and Therapeutics, 16,* 431–446.

TANNER, J. M. (1978). *Foetus into man: Physical growth from conception to maturity.* Cambridge, MA: Harvard University Press.

TOBIN-RICHARDS, M. H., BOXER, A. M., AND PETERSEN, A. C. (1983). The psychological significance of pubertal change. Sex differences in perceptions of self during early adolescence. In J. BROOKS-GUNN AND A. C. PETERSEN (Eds.), *Girls at puberty* (pp. 127–154). New York: Plenum Press.

UNGER, R. K. (1985). Personal appearance and social control. In M. SAFIR, M. MEDNICK, I. DAFNA, AND J. BERNARD (Eds.), *Woman's worlds: From the new scholarship* (pp. 142–151). New York: Praeger.

VANDEREYKEN, W., AND PIERLOOT, R. (1981). Anorexia nervosa in twins. *Psychotherapy and Psychosomatics, 35,* 55–63.

VANFRAECHEM, J. H. P., AND VANFRAECHEM-RAWAY, R. (1978). The influence of training upon physiological and psychological parameters in young athletes. *Journal of Sports Medicine, 18,* 175–182.

VINCENT, L. M. (1979). *Competing with the Sylph: Dancers and the pursuit of the ideal body form.* New York: Andrews & McMeel.

WAGMAN, M. (1967). Sex differences in types of daydreams. *Journal of Personality and Social Psychology, 3,* 329–332.

WALKS, D., LAVAN, M., PRESTA, E., YANG, M. U., AND BJORNTORP, P. (1983). Refeeding after fasting in the rat: Effects of dietary-induced obesity on energy balance regulation. *American Journal of Clinical Nutrition, 37,* 387–395.

WALLACH, J. D., AND LOWENKOPF, E. L. (1984). Five bulimic women. MMPI, Rorschach, and TAT characteristics. *International Journal of Eating Disorders, 3,* 53–66.

WALSH, B. T., ROOSE, S. P., GLASSMAN, A. H., GLADIS, M., AND SADIK, C. (1985). Bulimia and depression. *Psychosomatic Medicine, 47,* 123–131.

WALSTER, E., ARONSON, V., ABRAHAMS, D., AND ROTTMANN. L. (1966). Importance of physical attractiveness in dating behavior. *Journal of Personality and Social Psychology, 4,* 508–516.

WARDLE, J. (1980). Dietary restraint and binge eating. *Behavioral Analysis and Modification, 4,* 201–209.

WESSEL, J. A., UFER, A., VAN HUSS, W. D., AND CEDERQUIST, D. (1963). Age trends of various components of body composition and functional characteristics in women aged 20–69 years. *Annals of the New York Academy of Sciences, 110,* 608–622.

WESTERTERP, K. (1977). How rats economize—energy loss in starvation. *Physiological Zoology, 80,* 331–362.

WILLIAMSON, D. A., KELLEY, M. L., DAVIS, C. J., RUGGIERO, L., AND BLOUIN, D. C. (1985). Psychopathology of eating disorders: A controlled comparison of bulimic, obese, and normal subjects. *Journal of Consulting and Clinical Psychology, 53,* 161–166.

WILSON, G. T. (1984). Toward the understanding and treatment of binge eating. In R. C. HAWKINS II, W. J. FREMOUW, AND P. F. CLEMENT (Eds.), *The binge-purge syndrome* (pp. 264–289). New York: Springer.

WITTIG, M. A. (1983). Sex role development in early adolescence. *Theory Into Practice, 22,* 105–111.

WOLF, E., AND CROWTHER, J. H. (1983). Personality and eating habit variables as predictors of severity of binge eating and weight. *Addictive Behaviors, 8,* 335–344.

WOMEN ON WORDS AND IMAGES. (1972). *Dick and Jane as victims: Sex stereotyping in children's readers.* (Available from Women on Words and Images, Box 2163, Princeton, NJ 08540)

WOOLEY, O. W., WOOLEY, S. C., AND DYRENFORTH, S. R. (1979). Obesity and women–II. A neglected feminist topic. *Women Studies International Quarterly, 2,* 81–89.

WOOLEY, S. C., AND WOOLEY, O. W. (1981). Overeating as substance abuse. *Advances in Substance Abuse, 2,* 41–67.

WOOLEY, S., AND WOOLEY, O. W. (1982). The Beverly Hills eating disorder: The mass marketing of anorexia nervosa. *International Journal of Eating Disorders, 1,* 57–69.

WOOLEY, S. C., AND WOOLEY, O. W. (1984, February). Feeling fat in a thin society. *Glamour,* 198–252.

WOOLEY, S. C., AND WOOLEY, O. W. (1985). Intensive outpatient and residential treatment for bulimia. In D. M. GARNER AND P. E. GARFINKEL (Eds.), *Handbook of psychotherapy for anorexia nervosa and bulimia* (pp. 391–430). New York: Guilford.

YAGER, J. (1982). Family issues in the pathogenesis of anorexia nervosa. *Psychosomatic Medicine, 44*, 43–60.

YAGER, J., LANDSVERK, J., LEE-BENNER, K., AND JOHNSON, C. (1985). *The continuum of eating disorders: An examination of diagnostic concerns based on a national survey.* Unpublished manuscript, Neuropsychiatric Institute, University of California, Los Angeles.

YAGER, J., AND STROBER, M. (1985). Family aspects of eating disorders. In A. FRANCIS AND R. HALES (Eds.), *Annual review of psychiatry,* (Vol. 4, pp. 481–502). Washington, DC: American Psychiatric Press.

YATES, A., LEEHEY, K., AND SHISSLAK, C. M. (1983). Running—An analogue of anorexia? *New England Journal of Medicine, 308,* 251–255.

YOUNG, C. M., BLONDIN, J., TENSUAN, R., AND FRYER, J. H. (1963). Body composition studies of "older" women, thirty–seventy years of age. *Annals of the New York Academy of Science, 110,* 589–607.

YOUNG, C. M., MARTIN, M. E. K., CHIHAN, M., McCARTHY, M., MANNIELO, M. J., HARMUTH, E. H., AND FRYER, J. H. (1961). Body composition of young women: Some preliminary findings. *Journal of the American Dietetic Association, 38,* 332–340.

Psychological Intervention

One of the most challenging aspects of the field of psychopathology is the prevention and treatment of the kinds of problems that we have become familiar with in the readings covered thus far. How does one intervene in another's troubled life? What words of comfort can be given to a deeply depressed patient whose only thoughts are self-destruction? And, once improvement has been made, how can this be maintained in the absence of regular and reassuring contact with the therapist? Indeed, how do the ministrations of a clinical psychologist or psychiatrist differ from the words of comfort that we all may occasionally seek from a confidant or member of the clergy?

These are but some of the difficult questions surrounding the study and practice of psychological intervention, usually referred to as *psychotherapy*. Shorn of its theoretical complexities, any given psychotherapy can be defined as ". . . a situation in which one human being (the therapist) tries to act in such a way as to enable another human being to act and feel differently. . . ." (Wachtel, 1977, p. 271). This is a useful, yet vague definition. Consider that there are hundreds of schools of therapy, from Gestalt therapy to psychoanalysis to behavior therapy. Each approach has its enthusiastic adherents, both patients and therapists; each has detractors equally as vocal. How are we to understand the subject?

Toward A Therapeutic Rapprochement?

One way to organize our thinking about this diverse and sometimes perplexing field is to categorize therapies into *insight* versus *action* therapies (London, 1986). Insight therapies, like psychoanalysis and client-centered therapy, hold that greater awareness of the reasons for feelings and behavior is both necessary and sufficient for beneficial change. Action therapies, on the other hand, focus more directly on modifying feelings and behaviors, with a de-emphasis on insight. Yet there is much overlap, both conceptual and practical. Indeed, most therapists view themselves as "eclectics," that is, as borrowing more or less freely from different approaches.

A behaviorally oriented therapist, for example, might pay close attention to a patient's dreams for clues about the source of his or her problems. Once discovered, the therapeutic approach might then be via a behavioral procedure such as guided exposure. Or a psychoanalyst might exhort a patient fearful of father figures to behave differently through the employment of role-play situations (a tactic frequently employed by behavior therapists) but then devote most of the therapy time to an analysis of the patient's dreams following the enactment of

527

counterphobic behavior. It is a truism to experts in psychotherapy that, although theoretical frameworks are important—guiding research and practice—by themselves they do not completely describe or explain what experienced therapists actually *do* (Lazarus & Davison, 1971). Therapists in fact often behave in ways that are not entirely consistent with their theories. This is probably a good thing, because far less is known about psychotherapy than we would like or hope. Despite the fact that millions of dollars have been spent over the years to fund ambitious inquiries into whether certain therapies work, we still know relatively little about the precise mechanisms of therapeutic change. This situation is not unique to psychotherapy research, however. It should be noted that many more millions have been spent on biologically oriented research over this same time period; and here too, we are still some distance from a thorough understanding of the complex phenomena under investigation. But both kinds of research are necessary and useful if society is to take seriously its collective commitment to improving quality of life.

The first article in this section is a creative piece by Messer (selection 33) that is unusual in a number of respects. First, Messer distinguishes how psychoanalytically and behaviorally oriented therapists work. He then goes on to show what each therapeutic orientation might offer to the other. This represents the kind of integrative direction that is becoming increasingly popular among therapists—as evidenced both by publications (e.g., Goldfried & Davison, 1976; Wachtel, 1977) and by an organization called the Society for Explorations in Psychotherapy Integration. For example, Messer suggests that analytic therapists might do well to focus on more concrete goals and be more directive with their patients (as behavior therapists are); and that behavior therapists might move more deliberately than they typically do, appreciating (as their analytic counterparts appreciate) that patients do not always know what they want or, if they do, do not always readily inform

the therapist. The vehicle Messer uses to make his points is the analytically oriented supervision of a case being treated by a behavior therapist. The investigation of "therapeutic choice points" helps illustrate several possibilities for rapprochement. Such a study also enhances our understanding of the thinking processes of a therapist as he or she tries to deal humanely and effectively with the bewildering complexity of a psychologically troubled human being.

Treatment and Prevention of Fear

As we have seen from earlier readings (e.g., selection 4), simple phobias have a fairly high prevalence in the general population. Phobias are also problems that are frequently treated by therapists. In the last few decades, research has indicated that behavioral interventions appear to be particularly effective for these kind of problems. Biran and Wilson (1981), for example, found that encouraging in vivo (real-life) exposure to fearsome situations was more effective than a method that was more cognitive in nature—one that had subjects analyze the irrationalities presumed to underlie their fears and then combat these presumed cognitive "culprits" with more realistic self-talk.

That exposure may also be valuable in the *prevention* of fearful behavior is further suggested by the article of Mineka and Cook (selection 34). This article provides an example of the value of analog research in enhancing our understanding of human behavior. In a cleverly designed and executed experiment with rhesus monkeys, Mineka and Cook found that it was possible to protect animals from the acquisition of an unrealistic fear by providing them with prior exposure to nonfearful animals interacting fearlessly with the potentially phobic object—in this case a nonpoisonous snake. An implication that the authors tentatively draw is that parents who are afraid of something that they desire their children not to come to fear might seek to provide "immunizing" experiences of the kind found useful in this experiment. If they can arrange to have their children watch fearless models interacting comfortably with whatever the parents themselves loathe and avoid, future phobic behavior on the part of their offspring might be circumvented.

Marital Conflict

It is important to point out that by no means every person who seeks or is referred for therapy is suffering from psychiatric disorders of the types focused on in this book. One of the most prevalent types of distress encountered by therapists concerns marital conflicts—long considered to be an extremely difficult problem to treat. In recognition of the prevalence of marital problems and the importance of psychotherapy for the maritally distressed, we have included an article on the treatment of marital difficulties.

In selection 35, Johnson and Greenberg describe an interesting comparison between two rather different approaches. The first is an experiential, humanistic approach that emphasizes the uncovering and communication of feelings. The second represents a more directive problem-solving behavioral approach. This is designed to help couples construe their marital conflict as arising from unsolved but solvable problems and places relatively little emphasis on emotional dimensions. Of interest here is that a comparison of the two forms of intervention in a sample of 45 distressed couples revealed a clear superiority of the emotion-focused treatment, not only at the termination of therapy but also at 8-week follow-up.

Maintaining Therapeutic Gains

The continued superiority of the emotion-focused treatment group in Johnson and Greenberg's study is particularly impressive. As difficult as it is to help a patient change, it is perhaps even more difficult to help him

or her maintain the change. All too often, patients relapse subsequent to the termination of therapy. In recognition of the importance of relapse prevention in psychotherapy, our final article is a review by Brownell and his colleagues (selection 36). Here, the central concern is how patients can be prevented from returning to previous modes of ineffective functioning.

Many forces can impinge on a person and can draw out the old ways of being. Fortunately, clinical researchers like Marlatt (one of the co-authors of this selection) have been looking into what might cause relapse and how it might be prevented. It appears that the way a patient explains his or her lapse is central to whether the slip signals an inexorable return to pretherapy misery or whether the patient will bounce back from the lapse. Research suggests that if the lapse can be attributed to a temporary external cause—such as the alcoholic who takes a drink after an unusually upsetting event—the patient is likely to be able to get past the episode and return to sobriety. In contrast, if falling off the wagon is viewed as reflecting an inherent personality defect, a return to the wished-for abstinence is much less likely.

References and Suggestions for Additional Reading

Barlow, D. H. (Ed.) (1985). *Clinical handbook of psychological disorders.* New York: Guilford Press.

Biran, M., and Wilson, G. T. (1981). Treatment of phobic disorders using cognitive and exposure methods: A self-efficacy analysis. *Journal of Consulting and Clinical Psychology, 49,* 886–899.

Goldfried, M. R., and Davison, G. C. (1976). *Clinical behavior therapy.* New York: Holt, Rinehart & Winston.

Haaga, D. A., and Davison, G. C. (1986). Cognitive change methods. In F. H. Kanfer, and A. P. Goldstein (Eds.), *Helping people change* (3rd ed.) (pp. 236–282) Elmsford, NY: Pergamon Press.

HAAGA, D. A. AND DAVISON, G. C. (1989). Outcome studies of rational emotive therapy. In M. E. BERNARD AND R. DI GIUSEPPE (Eds.), Inside rational emotive therapy: A critical appraisal of the theory and therapy of Albert Ellis. New York: Academic Press.

HOLLON, S. D., AND BECK, A. T. (1986). Cognitive and cognitive-behavioral therapies. In S. L. GARFIELD, AND A. E. BERGIN (Eds.), *Handbook of psychotherapy and behavior change* (3rd ed.) (pp. 443–482) New York: Wiley.

LAZARUS, A. A., AND DAVISON, G. C. (1971). Clinical innovation in research and practice. In A. E. BERGIN AND S. L. GARFIELD (Eds.), *Handbook of psychotherapy and behavior change: An empirical analysis.* (pp. 196–213) New York: Wiley.

LONDON, P. (1986). *The modes and morals of psychotherapy* (2nd ed.). New York: McGraw-Hill.

WACHTEL, P. L. (1977). *Psychoanalysis and behavior: Toward an integration.* New York: Basic Books.

33

Behavioral and Psychoanalytic Perspectives at Therapeutic Choice Points

Stanley B. Messer

Abstract: Recent trends in behavior therapy and psychoanalytic therapy suggest some confluence of attitudes even though each type of therapy retains its own distinctive form. Differences and emerging similarities in the conception and practice of these two therapies were clarified during the author's supervision of a behavior therapist conducting psychoanalytic therapy. This article compares possible behavioral interventions with psychoanalytic interventions at choice points in therapy and discusses the rationale for each, along with newly proposed intersecting directions, in the following areas (a) Goal setting (Are goals determined by the client or therapist?); (b) promoting action versus exploring mental content; (c) challenging versus understanding irrational cognitions; (d) modifying cognitive schemata versus elaborating unconscious fantasies; (e) dissipating versus releasing emotions; and (f) the therapeutic relationship (Is it actual or projected?). Based on this analysis, suggestions are made for the psychoanalytic therapist and the behavior therapist who is inclined to incorporate perspectives or attitudes of the other. The implications of doing so for the visions of reality of each type of therapy are discussed.

I am a student but not a scholar of behavior therapy. One need not be a scholar, however, to recognize that behavior therapy, having regained the mind it lost, has become far friendlier than it once was to the cognitive concepts of psychoanalysis. This flirtation is not mere conditioned eyelash batting but penetrates even to the heart of the flirted-with object, namely, unconscious processes. In a book devoted to a reconsideration of unconscious factors, Meichenbaum and Gilmore (1984) have argued, for example, that cognitive events, processes, and structures each imply an unconscious domain that cognitive–behavior therapists must recognize and understand. Mahoney (1980), too, has stressed the tacit dimension in human functioning and its nonverbal, unrealistic underpinning in childhood.

Coming on the heels of this interest in unconscious information processing is a growing stress on the role of affect in the behavior therapies (Van Den Bergh & Eelen, 1984), based largely on the work of Zajonc and Bower. Drawing on Zajonc's (1980) theory of the relative independence of cognitive and affective systems, Rachman (1981) advocated that behavior therapists

Stanley B. Messer. Behavioral and Psychoanalytic Perspectives at Therapeutic Choice Points. *American Psychologist*, 1986, Vol. 41, No. 11, pp. 1261–1272. Copyright © 1986 by the American Psychological Association. Reprinted by permission of the publisher and the author.

give feeling states and their modification more careful study. In another vein, Bower (1981) has demonstrated that people learn more about events, and recall more experiences, that are congruent with their mood. Thus, behavior therapists have been advised to attend first to depressive patients' affect and then to their cognitions (Wilson, 1982).

Indications of change are apparent in psychoanalytic theory and therapy as well. Some psychoanalytic therapists are willing to delineate goals together with their clients at the outset of therapy and to propose a psychodynamic focus for treatment—a problem-solving attitude long familiar to behavior therapists (Malan, 1976; Mann & Goldman, 1982; Strupp & Binder, 1984). Many psychoanalysts now give more weight to reality considerations, such as the actual quality of interaction with the therapist (Kohut, 1977) versus the analyst as a blank screen, as well as to the effect of real events on people's lives (Shengold, 1979) and people's adaptive efforts to deal with those events (Blanck & Blanck, 1979; Langs, 1976). More importance is placed on emphasizing clients' responsibility for, and ability to affect and control expression of their emotions (Schafer, 1983), their actions (Appelbaum, 1982), and even their personality characteristics (Schwartz, 1984). The possibilities envisaged for mastery and self-control constitute a link to similar viewpoints held by behavior therapists (Kanfer, 1971; Meichenbaum, 1977). It is of no small significance that the new editor of a leading psychoanalytic journal has acknowledged, in an editorial statement, that "much has been learned from behaviorism and cognitive therapies" (Shapiro, 1985, p. 8).

Although this article focuses on psychoanalytic therapy and behavior therapy only, both surely owe a debt to humanistic therapies like those of Maslow and Rogers, particularly in conceptualizing the nature of the client–therapist relationship. Although in the 1960s and 1970s, techniques were considered all that mattered in producing successful outcomes in behavior therapy, this point of view is now regarded as a "fiction" (Kazdin, 1979). The respect for the client that the therapist conveys, the degree of trust engendered (A. A. Lazarus & Fay, 1984), and other characteristics of the relationship have been given new prominence (see DeVoge & Beck, 1979; Ford, 1978). Similarly, psychoanalytic therapists, harkening back to Freud's (1913/1959) emphasis on establishing rapport with and offering sympathetic understanding to the patient, now talk more of giving hope of relief from suffering and of limiting the domain of the role of abstinence (Leider, 1984). Wolf (1983), a disciple of Kohut, has pointed to the therapeutic effects of the analyst's self-revelations. In an article that compared the contributions of Rogers and Kohut, Kahn (1985) noted each author's emphasis on empathy and on valuing the client. It is clear that both psychoanalytic and behavior therapy, in the spirit of the humanistic therapies, have become more attuned to the healing powers of the psychotherapeutic relationship itself.

A recent experience supervising a behavior therapist conducting psychoanalytic therapy helped me clarify the differences between psychoanalytic therapy and behavior therapy and the emerging areas of consensus. The therapist, at times, was inclined to proceed in a direction dictated by the values of behavior therapy, whereas I counseled her to take the route advocated by psychoanalytic therapy. However, at each of these forks in the therapeutic road, we discussed the rationale for making one choice rather than the other.

In the following sections I contrast some possible behavioral interventions with psychoanalytic interventions at the choice points in therapy and try to clarify the reasons for each. (These two broad theoretical and therapeutic orientations are not unitary, of course, but encompass various subdivisions, such as traditional–behavioral, cognitive–behavioral, psychoanalytic, and short-term psychodynamic, which are indicated where appropriate). I then draw upon the recent psychotherapy literature to document trends in both therapies that illustrate the mutual influence taking place. It is interesting to note that although therapists typically declare a single orientation as their primary reference point, 65% of therapists in a survey by Larson (1980) acknowledged contributions from other orientations. It should be emphasized that the two therapies continue to maintain their distinctive identities, despite some absorption of other perspectives. This article will serve the quest of some for a more integrative therapy, whereas for others, the apposition provided may sharpen their understanding and appreciation of their current theoretical leanings and clarify why they choose to practice therapy as they do.

Subjects

The Therapist

The therapist was a clinical psychologist with 15 years of clinical experience, particularly in behavior therapy. She was familiar with client-centered and psychoanalytic concepts but had not carried out a long-term psychoanalytic therapy, which she wanted to do to expand her clinical repertoire.

The Supervisor

I was the supervisor in this situation. I am a clinical psychologist with formal training in psychoanalytic psychotherapy and 15 years of experience practicing, teaching, and supervising it. I am familiar with the theory and practice of behavior therapy and have carried out, under supervision, some behavioral therapies as well.

The Client

The client, Bill, was a 20-year-old college student about to enter his senior year. He lived at home with his parents and a 23-year-old, athletic brother. Bill's main complaint in seeking psychotherapy was "concern about homosexual feelings," which he was afraid to reveal, particularly because his parents would not accept them. He stated,

"I don't know if this is right for me. I'm frustrated and confused about my future and my well-being if I choose this way of life or not."

What brought him to the clinic at this time was a recent incident in which he became sexually aroused by a female friend. He was with her at a party at which they both had a lot to drink. He felt sexual toward her, and the next day he experienced guilt and discomfort when he was with her. Shortly after this, he told her about his gay feelings, which she accepted, and they remain friends. He had had few such heterosexual feelings in the past.

Bill had not engaged in either homosexual or heterosexual acts, but he reported frequently fantasizing about having sex with very masculine men. He had both male and female friends. He described himself as having general doubts about his adequacy and worth; for example, he regarded himself as physically unattractive (a perception inconsistent with conventional standards). Recently, Bill had run into a former roommate to whom he was sexually attracted. Bill wanted to be closer to him, but also saw a risk involved in pursuing a closer relationship. He asked the therapist what he should do.

It should be noted that, in keeping with current views, our emphasis was not on the diagnosis or treatment of homosexuality, but on the sexual-orientation disturbance Bill complained of.

Therapeutic Choice Points

Goal Setting: Client or Therapist Determined?

The client's dilemma as presented in the evaluation sessions raises the question of how goals are set in therapy. There appears to be a sharp contrast between how therapeutic goals are arrived at in psychoanalytic therapy and how they are arrived at in behavior therapy. Wilson and O'Leary (1980), following Bandura (1969) and Ullman and

Krasner (1965), stated that in behavior therapy, "choosing therapeutic objectives is a matter of value judgment and ought to be determined primarily by the client" (p. 285). In a general sense the psychoanalyst might agree, but in practice the way in which therapeutic objectives are arrived at by each kind of therapist is quite different. The behavior therapist is much more prepared to accept at face value and at the outset what clients state that they want.[1] Thus, when Bill said he would like to get closer to a male former roommate because of his sexual appeal, his therapist was prepared to help him immediately achieve greater comfort with closeness to men. The idea of the client's setting the goal is derived from the logical positivist position that behavior therapy is scientifically based and, presumably, value free. This attitude toward goal setting can also be viewed as related to behavior therapy's democratic and humanistic ideological underpinnings (Woolfolk & Richardson, 1984).

Psychoanalytic therapists are less democratic (but not necessarily less humanistic). The customer, in their eyes, is not always right. Imbued with the notion of unconscious conflict, and a symptom/disease distinction, they are much more likely to take a "wait and see" attitude toward a client's initially stated objective. Bill's homosexual inclinations, after all, may have been a flight from women (and there was evidence of this) or a concern with his male adequacy (as his negative comparison with his older, athletic brother suggested), or both. On the other hand, he may indeed have been a confirmed homosexual whose need in therapy was support for a new life-style. In traditional psychoanalytic therapy, the client agrees not so much to a specific goal that may be difficult to formulate precisely, but

to a process of exploring and clarifying what the options may be.

What has been happening in the area of behavioral assessment that brings it closer to psychoanalytic assessment? Fishman and Lubetkin (1983), two behavior therapists, contended that "the manifest problem serves as a cover for a more severe problem" (p. 27) and that clients derive a secondary gain from their overt problems. They suggested that many behavior therapists are too wedded to the "prima facie" complaints that clients bring to therapy, and they recommended that therapists attend to what they called the "behavioral dynamics" of the problem, meaning "underlying processes such as feelings of worthlessness, inadequacy, dependency, inferiority and so on" (p. 27).

Woolfolk and Richardson (1984) have also criticized traditional approaches to behavioral assessment in referring to the absence in behavior therapy of normative concepts of health and sickness or growth and stagnation. They framed the problem in this way:

> **The great difficulty for behavior therapists is in remaining faithful to their system while simultaneously managing to encompass client aims within a therapeutic dialectic, to challenge the client's goals, or to view certain of the objectives that people bring into therapy as manifestations of outright causes of their difficulties. (p. 783)**

In essence, this is what the psychoanalytic therapist would advocate—a dialogue, a questioning of client goals, and a view of the stated problem or objectives as partly symptomatic.

Has there been any modification of the psychoanalytic commitment to open-ended dialogue and assessment? Influenced, perhaps, by the notion of behavioral contracting and the necessity for briefer therapies, some psychoanalytic therapists now advocate delineating a dynamic focus, together with the client, at therapy's outset (see Rasmussen &

---

[1] Multimodal therapy, which evolved out of clinical behavior therapy, recognizes that clients often present a complaint as a "calling card," which should not be mistaken for the more central issue (A. A. Lazarus, 1981).

Messer, 1986; Winokur, Messer, & Schacht, 1981). This focus has been variously expressed in the language of intrapsychic conflict (impulse–defense configurations; Davanloo, 1980), interpersonal difficulties (maladaptive patterns of behavior; Strupp & Binder, 1984), or the self (chronically endured pain; Mann & Goldman, 1982). Individual goals are set in advance, making possible a more pragmatic problem-solving approach (psychodynamic style) and the evaluation of outcome in a systematic way (Malan, 1976). Furthermore, this approach brings the client into the goal-setting process in a more active and consensual fashion.

Promoting Action Versus Exploring Mental Content

In supervision, the therapist wondered aloud about the possibility of teaching Bill how to approach his former roommate to whom he was sexually attracted, and in this way helping him to decide if he really was homosexual. The attitude underlying this approach is the therapist as educator, one who facilitates the movement of the client in a direction that he or she indicates a desire to move. From a psychoanalytic perspective, there are several problems in promoting direct action at this early point in therapy. To begin with, in teaching the client how to approach a man, the therapist is explicitly or implicitly encouraging the client in a specific direction regarding his sexuality (cf. Halleck, 1976), one that could have a strong negative impact on his self-image and self-esteem. It is one thing to think about acting in a certain way and quite another to do it. Actions, as the saying goes, speak louder than words—even for the actor. From an analytic viewpoint, the therapist should position herself attitudinally midway between Bill's homosexual and heterosexual impulses. This would mean, of course, not teaching him heterosexual skills at this point either. The behavior therapist may ask, why, then, not teach him both sets of skills and in this way still remain equidistant from both sets of sexual inclinations?

The answer lies in the relative weight given by behaviorists and psychoanalysts to mental conflict in human affairs. To press the client to act in either or both directions is to underplay a major cognitive facet of his problem, namely, the inability to resolve his ambivalence. Although the client at this time was inclined to befriend a former roommate and have a sexual liaison, more fundamentally he appeared to be confused about just what it was he wanted and seemed immobilized by the anxiety that came into play as he approached one alternative or the other. Dollard and Miller (1950) referred to this dilemma as an approach–avoidance conflict, and Wachtel (1977) has pointed to its ubiquity in the clinical situation. What one fears influences what one wants; from a psychoanalytic point of view, the anxiety that comes to the fore in both homosexual and heterosexual situations for our client, should be attended to carefully and clarified before therapy proceeds (Wachtel, 1982). In discussing homosexuality in particular, Halleck (1976) expressed the following viewpoint:

> **It is one thing to offer treatment to a patient who has had the opportunity to weigh the extent to which his motivation to change is determined by internal psychological processes as opposed to external oppression. It is something entirely different to offer treatment to a patient who has never been given an opportunity to achieve such awareness. (p. 169)**

There is another potential problem with the more didactic, directive approach to skill training. It conveys the message to the client that he or she *needs* to be directed, which would be particularly troublesome to someone with a high internal locus of control. Viewed from within a behavioral framework, the resistance generated in such a person could affect the maintenance of the desired behavior (Goldfried, 1983).

The Scylla of behavior therapists' encouraging immediate client action, however, is paralleled by the Charybdis of psychoanalysts' fostering client passivity. The psychoanalyst Rangell (quoted in Appelbaum, 1975) chided his colleagues in the following manner:

> **I have seen a wrongly moralistic anti-action attitude which creeps into some analyses fortify the patient's own phobic avoidance of action and lead in some cases to almost a paralysis of the latter and a taboo even against the necessary actions of life. (p. 290)**

Clients come to believe (as do, in fact, some psychoanalytic therapists) that insight and interpretations inevitably lead to change (London, 1986). There is the possibility of confusion between responsible action and neurotic behavior, in which positive, growth-enhancing, mastery-related action is mistakenly viewed as similar to unreflective, feeling-avoidant acting out (Appelbaum, 1982). The exploration of mental content, after all, is infinite and too often can be accompanied by decreasing or null returns.

Recently, some psychoanalytic psychologists, cognizant perhaps of behavioral theory and therapy, have recommended that a client's reluctance to act be viewed as resistance and interpreted accordingly. Fried (1982) defined the "working through" phase of psychoanalytic therapy as comprising, among other things, the active search for new directions. She stated, "Anyone who collects insights step-by-step, but does not do anything with them—that is, does not *use* them by casting around for and adopting behavioral change—is not engaged in the serious labor of working through (p. 244). Applying the framework of neo-Freudian, interpersonal theory, Wachtel (1977) went even further in advocating the active incorporation of behavioral techniques, such as assertiveness training or systematic desensitization, into a basically psychodynamic therapy. (See Messer & Winokur, 1984a, 1984b, and Wachtel, 1984a, 1984b, for a debate on the merits of this more radical approach.) Perhaps the real issue is when to emphasize interpretation and when to promote, in one fashion or another, direct action.

Challenging Versus Understanding Irrational Cognitions: The Role of Reality

> **Bill was frequently self-derogatory and noted that in the presence of others he felt he had to beat them to the punch by putting himself down. In one instance Bill said to the therapist that he sometimes thought no one would want him because he was not lovable.**

One neobehavioral approach would be to respond paradoxically (A. A. Lazarus, 1981) by exaggerating Bill's own statements to underscore their irrationality (e.g., "Yeah, you're thinking, who would want to be with a balding, skinny sissy like me"). In response to Bill's bemoaning his physical appearance, a cognitive–behavioral therapist might encourage him to look in a mirror and evaluate himself objectively or have him ask other people for such an evaluation. Such interventions seem designed to help the client get a more realistic perspective on his or her physical and psychological attributes—one more in tune with how he or she really looks and acts according to more objective criteria (Goldfried & Robins, 1982).

> **The therapist, instead of using paradox or cognitive disputation, followed standard psychoanalytic procedure: When Bill complained about his physical characteristics, she asked him what came to mind. Immediately, an image of his older brother—the masculine high school football hero—loomed large, and he talked at some length about how he always felt like a 99-pound weakling compared with him.**

The preceding clinical vignettes illustrate two prominent differences between the perspective of the behavioral therapist and that of the psychoanalytic therapist. The behavior therapist takes an objective and rational stance toward the client's complaints and urges that the client do likewise. The behavior therapist might believe that there is no objective, rational reason for Bill to regard himself as he does and would want to help him see this by parodying his view of himself and by urging him to look at his reflection in the mirror in a more realistic fashion. In addition, the therapist might get Bill to have others offer him realistic feedback, in the hope that he could be disabused of the notion that he is too thin, too effeminate, or too weak looking. This approach to therapy is reflected in Mahoney's (1974) suggestion, based on Kelly's (1955) earlier work, that clients be trained as personal scientists: "We should model and teach an intimate empiricism replete with skills training in problem analysis, hypothesis generation, evaluative experimentation and so on" (p. 274). Similarly, Ellis (1970) stated that "the rational–emotive therapist . . . can almost always put his finger on a few central irrational philosophies of [the client]. . . . He can often induce him . . . to replace them with scientifically testable hypotheses about himself and the world."

Psychoanalytic therapists, by contrast, place much higher value on the client's subjective and irrational views. They would encourage Bill to immerse himself further in his subjective, negative view of himself to see where this led. They would not reassure him, nor hold up the leavening mirror of reality. Rather, they would try to help him expose the roots of his irrationality in childhood experiences, which typically reveal the climate that necessitated the client's maladaptive outlook and behavior.

Both behavior therapists and psychoanalytic therapists ultimately aim to help clients gain a more realistic and rational perspective on their problems, and there may be more commonality here than first meets the eye. The heightened self-awareness accomplished through psychoanalytic exploration eventually leads to more objective appraisal and rational problem analysis, as takes place in behavior therapy. However, the way it is achieved is different; whether the result is the same is moot.

Some behavior therapists are now considering the importance of understanding the formation of irrational beliefs, an approach that is similar to the psychoanalytic tradition. A dissatisfaction with the cognitive–behavioral approach to rationality was recently expressed most cogently by Mahoney (1980). He questioned the equation of rationality with "a naively simplistic form of 'good reasoning'" (p. 169) and the notion that rational thinking is always the most adaptive and reality oriented. Furthermore, he challenged the idea that recognizing one's irrationality is sufficient to purge it and that one can readily replace it with more adaptive ideas. Instead, he advocated exploring the sources of a belief in nonverbal fantasies and tracing its roots to earlier, even childhood, experiences.

Although psychoanalysis continues to focus on fantasy, the intrapsychic, and irrationality, it has become much more mindful of the role of external reality and the client's rational and adaptive efforts to deal with it, which behavior therapy has long emphasized. Robert Langs (1973), a prolific writer on psychoanalytic psychotherapy, has described the role of reality in this way:

> **We already know that human beings function basically by reacting and adapting to stimuli; only if we correctly ascertain the stimulus can we correctly understand their responses on any level. . . . Context defines the problem with which the patient is dealing, the reality event (or internal upheaval) which has prompted the patient's adaptive responses. (p. 311)**

Advocates of self-psychology, such as Kohut (1977, 1982), and object-relations theorists, such as Winnicott (1965, 1971), have also emphasized the critical role of environment (vs. primarily drive-related fantasy) in personality development, especially the role of the parents in providing a facilitative emotional milieu and empathic attunement to the infant's needs.

Masson, a historian of psychoanalysis, in a series of controversial articles and books

(1984a, 1984b, 1985), challenged the traditional psychoanalytic notion that childhood fantasies, rather than actual childhood events, are primary in the etiology of neurosis. Masson (1984b) claimed that when Freud and his followers abandoned the seduction theory—that parents had actually done something sexual to their children—"they also abandoned an important truth: that sexual, physical and emotional violence is a real and tragic part of the lives of many children" (p. 59). Extending a similar viewpoint to therapy, Shengold (1979), a psychoanalyst, has recommended that clients who were mistreated as children must know what they have suffered, at whose hands, and how it has affected them. These authors emphasized adaptation to external, objective reality and not just exploration of internal, psychic fantasy and distortion.

Modifying Cognitive Schemata Versus Elaborating Unconscious Fantasies

In a session that took place after Bill had been in therapy for a year, he talked about his fearful attitude toward his mother. When he was in the house recently with his girlfriend (the one toward whom he sometimes feels sexual), he was worried that because he was wearing short shorts, his mother may have thought something sexual went on and would disapprove. Suddenly, he remembered an event from the time he was five: "I was in the garage with two girls. I exposed myself to them and my mother found me. It's all black after that. I feel sick to my stomach and weak in my knees as I tell you this. I was also terrified at the time."

In the following session, Bill, who was involved in college theatre productions, reported that he was in the backstage dressing room and there was a girl in her pantyhose and bra. He felt disgusted and immediately had an image of himself feeling that same way about his mother. He remembered that when he was a little boy, he had opened the door to her bedroom; she was naked and became upset with him. There was also a skunklike odor that he attached to the scene and that he assumed was the smell of female genitals. He also remembered quite vividly her big breasts and pubic hair.

A social-learning conception of these events and memories might focus on the role of Bill's mother in adopting a punitive attitude toward sex in general and to Bill's burgeoning sexuality in particular. He was terrified of her response to his exposing himself to the girls, felt disgust after his mother was upset that he saw her naked, and associated female genitals with an unpleasant odor. A conditioned emotional response had been instituted. It is not surprising, then, that Bill expected a similar negative response from his mother to the current suggestive situation of his being alone with a woman while wearing short shorts.

A traditional behavior therapist, employing notions of reciprocal inhibition, might propose to desensitize Bill to these unpleasant situations so that he could react with calm rather than fear to his mother's disapproval. Similarly, through counterconditioning, Bill could learn to disconnect the response of disgust to the stimulus of a woman in bra and panties. One can imagine a behavior therapist constructing a desensitization hierarchy consisting of scenes related to Bill's being with a woman in a variety of increasingly sexual situations up to and including seeing her naked and ultimately being sexual with her.

Cognitively oriented behavior therapists might view Bill as operating according to a cognitive rule, schema, or structure that has profoundly affected his life. In essence, one of Bill's implicit personal constructs (Kelly, 1970) or core organizing principles (Meichenbaum & Gilmore, 1984) might have been that women are frightening, disapprove of his sexuality, have smelly genitals, and are best avoided, a construct that led to his sexual-orientation disturbance. Cognitively oriented therapists would probably have pointed out to Bill the irrational nature of this implicit and unfortunate guide for living. They would have helped him see how it had functioned to keep him at a distance from women, whom he had, in fact, desired all along.

Traditional psychoanalytic therapists would not so much discount the preceding behavioral and cognitive analyses as they would emphasize another aspect of the situation, which would lead them to proceed differently. What, they might wonder, was stirred up in Bill both cognitively and affectively when he saw his mother with her breasts and pubic hair exposed? Was he disgusted only because of her being upset, or was there something brewing in him that led to the feeling of disgust? In other words, the psychoanalytic therapist, always alert for inner motives at play, would look for a hidden drive, wish, or feeling as a possible cause of Bill's behavior: for example, might Bill as a child have felt sexual toward his mother? Might his opening of the closed door to her room have been not entirely innocent and accidental? What effect would such feelings have had on his attitude and his relationship with his father?

In psychoanalytic parlance, the therapist would be on the lookout for an unconscious fantasy that had been guiding Bill's behavior—in this case, one with an oedipal tone. The object of the therapist would be to help Bill reconstruct this fantasy, whose major characteristics are that it is unconscious, childhood based, and wish fulfilling, and consists of an organized mental representation or structure (Beres, 1962). The first and last characteristics—that it is unconscious and structured—are shared with the concept of cognitive schema. Insofar as childhood origins and drive-related (sexual or aggressive) or wish-fulfilling features of the unconscious fantasy are stressed, the two constructs part company (cf. Sarason, 1979). The wish-fulfilling nature of unconscious fantasy (e.g., "I want to possess mother but am afraid of father") prompts the therapist to help the client elaborate the fantasy more completely. The purpose of his or her interpretations is to bring the fantasy to con-

sciousness and verbal expression. Ironically, an unconscious fantasy, as described in the classical psychoanalytic literature, is viewed as having a more palpable reality than a cognitive schema. Meichenbaum and Gilmore (1984), for example, refer to the core organizing principle as a theoretical construct or "a useful fiction" whose existence cannot be proved but only inferred. The psychoanalyst, it is true, also infers the unconscious fantasy on the basis of memories, dreams, neurotic symptoms, and other behavior, but ultimately aims at having it be exposed.

How does the ongoing process of elaborating such a fantasy proceed?

In the same session as Bill's reminiscence about seeing his mother naked, he recalled that as a child he would have a bad dream in which his father would get into bed with him and sleep with him. "In the dream my father would be nice, but my mother would get mad. I used to think of him as an ogre during the day because he was so quiet, but he was nice to me at night. I had a dream this week I didn't want to tell you. I dreamed I was sleeping with my father and that, in the morning, my mother was upset and asked me what my father did to me. She meant I had anal intercourse. I denied it. When I woke I was very upset because I wondered if it was really something that happened to me when I was younger."

Why, one might ask, in a session about Bill's seeing his mother naked, was there suddenly an emphasis on sleeping with his father, a concern about having anal intercourse with him? One hypothesis would be that he fantasized submitting sexually to his father to alleviate his guilt and anxiety about his sexual interest in his mother. Another possibility would be that he could only be close to his father by imagining submitting to him sexually because of his father's being so distant from him. The important point for present purposes is that the client was encouraged to continue to associate and, in this way, provided more of the pieces that made up the unconscious fantasy.[2]

It may be added, parenthetically, that the expression of unconscious fantasies often has behavioral consequences. Following this session, Bill decided that he was going to move out of his parents' house, which he felt he needed to do to be a truly independent man.

Unconscious processing, even if not "the dynamic unconscious," is becoming an accepted phenomenon among experimental cognitive psychologists (e.g., Marcel, 1983) and slowly but surely among cognitive behavior therapists (e.g., Mahoney, 1980). Nevertheless, the difference between the automatic or unconscious processing of words, word clusters, or percepts, and the kind of elaborate processing that must be involved in the formation of an unconscious fantasy is considerable. Silverman and his colleagues and students have conducted a program of research that deliberately links the curative action of behavior therapy and the unconscious fantasy. They have tried to demonstrate that what is referred to as the "nonspecific effects" of behavior therapy may be accounted for, in part, by the activation of unconscious fantasies (Mendelsohn & Silverman, 1984). Thus, in training a young man to be more assertive with his father, the behavior therapist may mediate behavior change by sanctioning a forbidden wish that makes up the unconscious fantasy ("I want to kill my father") and by preparing the client for the expression and gratification of milder forms of the wish. This approach can be contrasted with the effort of the psychoanalytic therapist to expose the wish and show how it has inhibited the client from speaking up to his father.

In the traditional psychoanalytic approach to the process of reconstructing an unconscious fantasy, the pieces of the fantasy are brought to the surface much like the shards in an archaeological dig. The therapist's job is to brush away the dirt and debris surrounding the fragments of associative memory to help reconstruct the fantasy (Jacobsen & Steele, 1978). Behavior therapists and others have long complained that a construct such as the unconscious fantasy is more the product of therapists' synthetic abilities and imagination coupled with clients' suggestibility than it is a template or structure of the mind. Spence (1984), criticized the construct from within psychoanalytic ranks and asked the following question:

> **Do therapists, listening with evenly hovering attention "really hear" what the patient is saying between the lines and function mainly as archaeologists in putting together pieces of the past (historical truth), or do they supply a significant amount of their own creativity and ingenuity in what they select, how they choose to phrase and rephrase it, and in how they choose the proper narrative frame? (p. 86)**

Spence (1982) demonstrated that therapists do not and cannot listen with truly evenly hovering attention, but can only do so with preformed ideas from theory or personal experience. Such a formulation casts doubt on the objective status of the unconscious fantasy and its veridical reconstruction, and indicates something akin to Meichenbaum and Gilmore's "useful fiction" or, phrased in another way, an intersubjective dialogue between client and therapist. As one might imagine, this perspective is being hotly contested and debated in psychoanalytic circles (see Geha, 1984; Spence, 1984, and the accompanying commentaries).

Dissipating Versus Releasing Emotions: The View of Affect

The preceding clinical vignettes can be used to illustrate certain differences in emphasis in psychoanalytic and behavioral attitudes

---

[2] It should be noted that, in line with psychoanalytic therapists' taking environmental events more seriously (as described in the preceding section), the possibility that some actual sexual contact had taken place must be considered.

toward the expression of affect. The cognitive–behavioral approach does not ignore affect, but typically treats it as an aspect of behavior to be managed, reduced, or explained (Messer & Winokur, 1980, 1984b). Thus, a traditional behavior therapist, as pointed out earlier, might have chosen to desensitize Bill to his fearful anticipation of his mother's response to a sexually suggestive situation and to his fear of his girlfriend's sexuality. A cognitive–behavioral therapist would have pointed to the irrational nature of his fear and the sort of cognitions that sustained it. The therapist might have employed cognitive techniques, such as thought stopping or modification of self-statements.

Affect is accorded a very central and quite different role in psychoanalytic theory and practice. One psychoanalytic model that highlights its preeminence views affect as an organizer and coordinator of various physiological and psychological systems that are part of behavior (Noy, 1982). This model is similar to R. S. Lazarus's (1982, 1984) theory, which posits that the experience of emotion involves a fusion of thought, action impulses, and somatic disturbances (see also Bower, 1981; Leventhal, 1980). With clients like Bill, psychoanalytic therapists first encourage expression of a spectrum of feelings and physiological reactions (e.g., his fear, disgust, nausea, and incestuous sexual feelings). They attempt to bring a range of emotional reactions to the surface (often through interpretation of defenses and resistance) and are less likely to curtail the process in favor of reducing or immediately managing negative affects. The purpose is to extend clients' emotional awareness and sensitivity, to help them experience the corrective effect of expressing such embarrassing feelings without aversive consequences, and to expand their range of behavioral choice by freeing them from feelings that were festering within. Ultimately, the goal is to help the client reestablish cognitive control over the internal chaos of conflicting emotions. Note that the aim is not extinction, as in flooding or implosive techniques (Stampfl & Levis, 1976); rather, it is to help the client regulate and reconcile the different affects that exist in a confused, regressed state (Kris, 1952). In this sense, "the psychoanalytic process is both cognitive and affective, and the usefulness of either one, or the blending of the two, varies with circumstances" (Appelbaum, 1982, p. 1005).

Recently, there has been a change in the attitude of behavior therapists toward the significance and role of emotion. In an Association for Advancement of Behavior Therapy (AABT) panel (1983) on relations among cognition, emotion, and behavior, each of the participants (Gal, Lang, Matthews, and Rachman) emphasized the importance of emotion and the necessity that behavior therapists pay closer attention to it. Rachman, for example, drew out the implications of Zajonc's (1980, 1984) theory that feeling and thinking are under the influence of partially independent systems, and that affective reactions and evaluations may precede cognitive and perceptual encoding. Rachman argued that irrational emotions should not always be viewed by the behavior therapist as caused by faulty reasoning. They should be modified directly and not necessarily be verbal means (see also Rachman, 1981). What is aimed at is an emotional processing to absorb the disturbance and allow it to decline (Rachman, 1980).

In contrast to Rachman's approach, which tends to compartmentalize affect and treat it as a separate system, Lang's bioinformational theory of emotional imagery posits a coupling, albeit a loose one, of the behavioral, physiological, and cognitive components of an affect. Behavior change, then, "depends not on simple exposure to fear stimuli but on the generation of the relevant affective cognitive structure, the prototype for overt behavior, which is subsequently modified into a more functional form" (Lang, 1979, p. 501). As Lang said at the AABT meeting, accessing emotion is the difficult but critical part of therapy. Similarly, Matthews stressed that for a technique such as systematic desensitization to work, a certain level of anxiety must be operative, which the therapist may have to elicit. "Getting in touch with one's emotions may be for some persons a necessary first step—one that enables them to profit from the various therapeutic techniques that cognitive–behaviorists have developed" (Bowers, 1980, p. 183; see also Safran & Greenberg, in press, for a full elaboration of this viewpoint). These attitudes are similar in that they insist on greater attention to, or allow the emergence of, emotional responses before behavioral techniques are instituted.

Although psychoanalysis has always viewed affect and insight in a complementary fashion, the importance of therapy's providing an affective experience has been highlighted more recently, especially by those who practice short-term dynamic therapy in their attempt to attain more rapid problem resolution and by those working with clients whose difficulties are thought to be related to preverbal experiences (Blanck & Blanck, 1979). Following the lead of Alexander and French (1946), who saw psychoanalytic therapy as offering a "corrective emotional experience," modern-day therapists who provide brief therapy, such as Sifneos (1979) and Davanloo (1980), actually provoke anxiety, anger, and other affects to intensify clients' emotional involvement in therapy and to help them experience the irrational aspects of their fears. As stated by Davanloo (1980), "One persistently confronts the patient, asking what he really feels rather than interpreting it to him" (p. 46).

In his most recent psychoanalytic theorizing, Schafer (1983) viewed people as active in relation to their affects, rather than passive and reactive. He emphasized clients' responsibility for their affects and their greater potential for mastering and controlling them. The consequence for the conduct of therapy is that "analysts do not hesitate to raise questions as to why someone feels a certain way and why he or she even makes sure to feel that way or not feel that way" (Schafer, 1983, p. 102). Schafer pointed out that if therapists proceed in this fashion, clients cannot disown affects or see them as separate from themselves; nor can they as readily disclaim responsibility for experienc-

ing or inhibiting them. Note how this point of view is consistent with the behavioral emphasis on self-control and management of affect.

The Therapeutic Relationship: Actual or Projected?

When it seemed timely, Bill was encouraged to freely express his thoughts and feelings about his therapist. In one instance he said that he wanted to see her only as a "therapist," not as a "person," and certainly not as a "woman." He wanted to keep her at arm's length, much as he was doing, he realized, with his girlfriend. In another session, Bill referred to the therapist as a "bitch" who pushed him to examine what he preferred not to think about. In this way, it seems, she was like his domineering mother in his eyes. In the same session, he professed appreciation and love for his therapist, for her willingness to listen to him and help him, and he admitted to his growing dependency on her.

Traditionally, behavior therapists have paid much less attention to the therapeutic relationship than they have to the application of behavioral techniques. More recently, a consensus has emerged that a positively toned, warm, and caring relationship in an atmosphere of trust may be an important facet of behavior therapy (Brady et al., 1980; Goldfried, 1982; A. A. Lazarus & Fay, 1984; Meichenbaum & Gilmore, 1982; Wilson, 1982). In addition, A. A. Lazarus (1981) has emphasized the desirability of setting up the therapy relationship on an egalitarian footing. Aside from its potential intrinsic healing powers, a positive relationship serves the purpose of winning the cooperation of the client in putting into effect the suggestions, programs, and technical procedures that the behavior therapist introduces (Wilson & Evans, 1977).

The traditional stance of psychoanalytic therapists such as Fenichel, Hartmann, Rappaport, and most recently Brenner (1979) has been to emphasize technical and personal neutrality, the notion of the therapist as a blank screen or mirror reflecting only what is shown to him or her. There have always been psychoanalysts who stressed the therapist's benignity and humannness (e.g., Ferenczi, Rank, Reik, and most recently Stone, 1961); however, it is only in recent years that this more humanistic view of the psychoanalytic therapist's role has achieved ascendance (Malcolm, 1981), paralleling the shift that has occurred in behavior therapy. Whether it is described as a holding environment (Winnicott, 1965), empathy (Kohut, 1977), or the real relationship (Roland, 1967; Tuttman, 1982), this view acknowledges the important role of the client–therapist relationship itself. The focus shifts to the therapist's real interpersonal role and its analysis, and to a recognition of the mutual social influence of client and therapist (Gill, 1983; Hoffman, 1983; Strupp & Binder, 1984). From this perspective, transference is not so much a distortion as it is a rigid way of construing and responding to a real interaction.

Although psychoanalytic practitioners accept the role played by therapist support and caring, they see it as only one element of a total relationship (Dewald, 1982). The therapeutic alliance, as psychoanalysts call the cooperative working relationship, is used not only to further the patient's amenability to free association (parallel to the patient's cooperation with a behavioral regimen), but also to foster the expression of a whole gamut of feelings and fantasies about the therapist that inevitably arise in an intense two-person interaction. Accordingly, in the case vignettes presented earlier, Bill was able to express his loving, hateful, and dependent feelings toward his therapist and came to see how they tended to reflect attitudes he held toward significant people in his life, such as his mother and his girlfriend.

What is being referred to will be recognized as transference reactions. One may note a link between the posited value of such feelings and the work of Bower (1981), who has demonstrated that people learn more

about events, and recall more experiences, that are congruent with their mood. If a current mood tends to provide easier access to consciousness of other mood-congruent events, it can be understood, in cognitive and experimental terms, how currently experienced transferential feelings allow for ready access to similar feelings about significant others. Clarification and interpretation of transferential behavior bring together the past and the present and involve the person in an *in vivo* experience that has an immediacy of impact, with great therapeutic potential (Strupp, 1979). Behavior therapists have not given systematic attention to "the ways in which patients may try to please or defeat the therapist, seduce or objectify the therapist, be passive in relation to, or a controller of, the therapist" (Pervin, 1982, p. 10; for some beginning efforts by behavior therapists in this direction, see Arnkoff, 1982). Similarly, behavior therapists, with a few exceptions (e.g., Goldfried & Davison, 1976), have not paid much attention to their own reaction to clients, which could be useful in helping them understand what their clients may be eliciting in others.

Implications for the Practice of Behavior Therapy and Psychoanalytic Therapy

Based on the foregoing analysis, for behavior therapists inclined to incorporate psychoanalytically toned interventions, the following suggestions can be made:

1. Clients cannot be the sole arbiter of therapeutic goals and particularly not at the outset of therapy. It is the behavior therapist's task to help clients explore their professed therapeutic objectives to determine whether those objectives are truly suitable within the context of their life and the total clinical picture. The therapist's judgment must enter in an unabashed way, which may involve the therapist's challenging the initial objectives the client brings to therapy.

2. The behavior therapist should spend more time exploring clients' mental content, particularly conflictual dispositions. This suggestion is not intended to imply that the behavior therapists should never encourage action, but that the therapist delay such interventions so as to explore the internal (cognitive and affective) reality before promoting action in one direction or another.

3. Behavior therapists should not always regard irrational cognitions as requiring immediate objective feedback and a scientific, problem-solving attitude. Irrationality should be respected and viewed as a natural outgrowth of life experiences and the inner needs that shaped them and, thus, as having a logic all its own. Some attempt should be made to understand the real life events, the subjective experience, and the internal cognitive and affective processes that led to the development of the irrational thoughts. The client's experience of describing such elements may well alter the illogical cognitions. If not, more active problem-solving approaches can be applied.

4. In discerning schemas or core organizing principles and giving feedback to clients about them, behavior therapists should be attuned to their possible (a) unconscious character, (b) childhood origins, and (c) base in conflicting feelings, typically hostility, love, and dependency. In other words, behavior therapists may want to try to elaborate their clients' unconscious fantasies before choosing the point of entry for the behavioral modification.

5. Clients' emotions need as close attention as their cognitions and behavior, both independently and in connection with thoughts and actions. Negative emotions, in particular, should not be viewed as needing only to be reduced or curtailed; rather, their expression should be encouraged in order to help the client regulate and integrate them.

6. In addition to striving for a positive relationship with clients, behavior therapists should be on the alert for ambivalent and negative reactions that clients may have to them, or that they may have to their clients,

in therapy. These observations can be invaluable in alerting behavior therapists to the way their clients perceive, respond to, and affect others, as well as in helping therapists to overcome client resistance when progress is not evident.

For psychoanalytic therapists inclined to be influenced by the attitudes of behavior therapists, the following suggestions can be made:

1. For some clients, a focus of therapy should be established early on, with their expressed consent. Goals can be delineated and eventually evaluated. This approach would serve to prevent the drift that can occur in an open-ended psychoanalytic therapy and would allow systematic evaluation of results.

2. It should be recognized that the value of insight is often reflected in action. Although action can be a defensive substitute for feeling, it may also be a way of putting insight to work in a constructive and growth-enhancing way. Part of the working-through phase of psychoanalytic therapy can be a trying out of new ways of behaving; this will bring residual anxieties to the fore, which can then be explored further, if necessary.

3. If psychoanalytic therapists view unconscious fantasies as constructions rather than reconstructions, as "useful fictions" rather than veridical cognitive structures, they need not discover the one correct underlying fantasy. The therapist, from this perspective, must lead clients to a vision of themselves and events that is different from their current view. Narrative truth emerges from the dialogue between therapist and client, which provides an organizing influence in the client's life. There are clearly multiple avenues for constructing and interpreting such a narrative (for example, oedipal, separation–individuation).

4. In an empathic manner, the psychoanalytic therapist should acknowledge the role of external reality, both present and past, and the client's adaptive efforts to deal with it in addition to exploring its personal, idiosyncratic meanings. Helping certain clients see how they were caught in a dilemma as children and how they inevitably reacted by skewing some aspect of their psychic life provides them with hope for change in their present, usually quite different, circumstances as adults.

5. The ability of clients to control their affect, both its inhibition and its expression, should be given more credence. Stated differently, clients can be viewed somewhat less as passive reactors to unconscious forces, and somewhat more as conscious creators or maintainers of their current pathological situation, including their cognition, affect, and behavior.

6. Psychoanalytic therapists should allow their human qualities to shine through, as advocated by humanistic as well as neobehavioral therapists, particularly their caring for and support of the client. They should keep in mind their actual role and behavior and their impact on the client in understanding the transferential elements of the relationship.

The Changing Visions of Behavior Therapy and Psychoanalytic Therapy

Messer and Winokur (1980, 1981) have proposed that psychoanalysis and behavior therapy hold different perspectives and visions of reality (from among the comic, tragic, romantic, and ironic outlooks), which set certain limits to the integration of these therapies but do not preclude it. Most recently they have tried to specify the ways in which integration is possible, but have also pointed to the trade-offs and compromises in world view that such an approach entails (Messer, 1983, 1986; Messer & Winokur, 1984b, 1986).

There are several implications of adopting the suggestions presented in the preceding section for the visions of behavior therapy and psychoanalytic therapy. To begin with, behavior therapists would have to give up

the appeal of clearly defined goals and their resolution in a focused and relatively uncomplicated way. The comic vision of familiar, controllable, and predictable aspects of situations and people would be tempered, and a more tragic view, including the inevitability of suffering, pain, and conflict, would be adopted. If behavior therapists were to increase exploration of mental content and elicit more childlike fantasies, irrational beliefs, and feelings, it would require a greater appreciation of the romantic and ironic visions of life, the former with its emphasis on the heroic, uncertain, adventuresome search, and the latter with its emphasis on paradox, that is, things often not being what they seem. In addition, the suggestions entail a relative shift from a world of consensual reality to one of greater subjectivity and introspection. The advantages of behavior therapy's close ties to the ethos of modernism—rationality, pragmatism, and technolgy—would be reduced, but a more richly textured view of human functioning would ensue.

For their part, psychoanalytic therapists would have to adopt a somewhat more comic view of reality, one that regards problems as more definable, more externally based, and more controllable. Some romantic aspects of psychoanalysis, including emphasis on the open-ended, inner-oriented quest, would be curtailed. Psychoanalytic therapy's tragic view would be softened insofar as the possibility of mastery and self-control would be emphasized, and the power of the relationship to heal would be brought to the fore. The ironic view, requiring relative therapist detachment, would yield to a more involved and affective therapist role. The result would be a more pragmatic, scientific, and meliorative psychotherapy (cf. London, 1986).

Such shifts in each therapy's vision of reality will not be universally acclaimed. Certain psychoanalytic therapists and behavior therapists, by virtue of their personal dispositions, beliefs, and values, will continue to prefer the purer vision and ideology that each therapy originally encompassed (see Arkowitz & Messer, 1984, for examples). For some behavior therapists (e.g., Franks, 1984), the potential decrease of scientific precision, parsimony, and the direct curative attitude of the comic vision is too high a price to pay for the possible yield of integration. For some psychoanalytic therapists, the potential gain of scientific exactness, parsimony, and melioration is more than offset by the decrease in open-ended exploration in the romantic and tragic modes. However, there are many therapists of both orientations who undoubtedly will welcome the kind of change occurring in each therapy. For them, the mutual influence of one therapy on the other, the convergence of certain perspectives, and the particular shift of visions and values that this entails constitute a creative challenge both to the theory of each therapy and to its practice.

References

ALEXANDER, F., AND FRENCH, T. M. (1946). *Psychoanalytic therapy: Principles and application.* New York: Ronald Press.

APPELBAUM, S. A. (1975). The idealization of insight. *International Journal of Psychoanalytic Psychotherapy, 4,* 272–302.

APPELBAUM, S. A. (1982). Challenges to traditional psychotherapy from the "new therapies." *American Psychologist, 37,* 1002–1008.

ARKOWITZ, H., AND MESSER, S. B. (Eds.). (1984). *Psychoanalytic therapy and behavior therapy: Is integration possible?* New York: Plenum Press.

ARNKOFF, D. B. (1982). Common and specific factors in cognitive therapy. In M. J. LAMBERT (Ed.), *Psychotherapy and patient relationships* (pp. 85–125). Homewood, IL: Dorsey Press.

ASSOCIATION FOR ADVANCEMENT OF BEHAVIOR THERAPY. (1983, December). *The relationships between cognition, emotion, and behavior: Implications for treatment.* Panel discussion conducted at the meeting of the Association for Advancement of Behavior Therapy, Washington, DC.

BANDURA, A. (1969). *Principles of behavior modification.* New York: Holt, Rinehart & Winston.

BERES, D. (1962). The unconscious fantasy. *Psychoanalytic Quarterly, 31,* 309–328.

BLANCK, G., AND BLANCK, R. (1979). *Ego psychology* (Vol. 2). New York: Columbia University Press.

BOWER, G. (1981). Mood and memory. *American Psychologist, 36,* 129–148.

BOWERS, K. S. (1980). "De-controlling" cognition and cognitive control. In M. J. MAHONEY (Ed.), *Psychotherapy process: Current issues and future directions* (pp. 181–184). New York: Plenum Press.

BRADY, J. P., DAVISON, G. C., DEWALD, P. A., EGAN, G., FADIMAN, J., FRANK, J. D., GILL, M. M., HOFFMAN, I., KEMPLER, W., LAZARUS, A. A., RAIMY, V., ROTTER, J. B., AND STRUPP, H. H. (1980). Some views on effective principles of psychotherapy. *Cognitive Therapy and Research, 4,* 269–306.

BRENNER, C. (1979). Working alliance, therapeutic alliance, and transference. *Journal of the American Psychoanalytic Association, 27*(Suppl.). 137–158.

DAVANLOO, H. (Ed.). (1980). *Short-term dynamic psychotherapy.* New York: Aronson.

DEVOGE, J. T., AND BECK, S. (1979). The therapist-client relationship in behavior therapy. In M. HERSEN, R. M. EISLER, AND P. M. MILLER (Eds.), *Progress in behavior modification* (Vol. 6, pp. 203–248). New York: Academic Press.

DEWALD, P. A. (1982). Psychoanalytic perspectives on resistance. In P. L. WACHTEL (Ed.), *Resistance: Psychodynamic and behavioral approaches* (pp. 45–68). New York: Plenum Press.

DOLLARD, J., AND MILLER, N. E. (1950). *Personality and psychotherapy.* New York: McGraw-Hill.

ELLIS, A. (1970). *The essence of rational psychotherapy: A comprehensive approach to treatment.* (Available from Institute for Rational Living, 45 East 65th St., New York, NY 10021).

FISHMAN, S. T., AND LUBETKIN, B. S. (1983). Office practice of behavior therapy. In M. HERSEN (Ed.), *Outpatient behavior therapy: A clinical guide* (pp. 21–41). New York: Grune & Stratton.

FORD, J. D. (1978). Therapeutic relationship in behavior therapy: An empirical analysis, *Journal of Consulting and Clinical Psychology, 46,* 1302–1314.

FRANKS, C. M. (1984). On conceptual and technical integrity in psychoanalysis and behavior therapy: Two fundamentally incompatible systems. In H. ARKOWITZ AND S. B. MESSER (Eds.), *Psychoanalytic therapy and behavior therapy: Is integration possible?* (pp. 223–247). New York: Plenum Press.

FREUD, S. (1959). Further recommendations in

the technique of psychoanalysis: On beginning the treatment. In *Collected papers* (Vol. 2, pp. 342–365). New York: Basic Books. (Original work published 1913).

FRIED, E. (1982). On "working through" as a form of self-innovation. In S. SLIPP (Ed.), *Curative factors in dynamic psychotherapy* (pp. 243–258). New York: McGraw-Hill.

GEHA, R. E. (1984). On psychoanalytic history and the "real" story of fictitious lives. *International Forum for Psychoanalysis, 1,* 221–291.

GILL, M. M. (1983). The point of view of psychoanalysis: Energy discharge or person? *Psychoanalysis and Contemporary Thought, 6,* 523–551.

GOLDFRIED, M. R. (1982). Resistance and clinical behavior therapy. In P. L. WACHTEL (Ed.), *Resistance: Psychodynamic and behavioral approaches* (pp. 95–114). New York: Plenum Press.

GOLDFRIED, M. R. (1983, December). *The clinical applicability of behavior therapy.* Panel discussion conducted at the meeting of the Association for Advancement of Behavior Therapy, Washington, DC.

GOLDFRIED, M. R., AND DAVISON, G. C. (1976). *Clinical behavior therapy.* New York: Holt, Rinehart & Winston.

GOLDFRIED, M. R., AND ROBINS, C. (1982). On the facilitation of self-efficacy. *Cognitive Therapy and Research, 6,* 361–379.

HALLECK, S. L. (1976). Another response to "Homosexuality: The ethical challenge." *Journal of Consulting and Clinical Psychology, 44,* 167–170.

HOFFMAN, I. (1983). The patient as interpreter of the analyst's experience. *Contemporary Psychoanalysis, 19,* 389–422.

JACOBSEN, P. B., AND STEELE, R. S. (1978). From present to past: Freudian archaeology. *International Review of Psychoanalysis, 6,* 349–362.

KAHN, E. (1985). Heinz Kohut and Carl Rogers: A timely comparison. *American Psychologist, 40,* 893–904.

KANFER, F. H. (1971). The maintenance of behavior by self-generated stimuli and reinforcement. In A. JACOBS AND L. B. SACHS (Eds.), *Psychology of private events* (pp. 39–59). New York: Academic Press.

KAZDIN, A. (1979). Fictions, factions, and functions of behavior therapy. *Behavior Therapy, 10,* 629–654.

KELLY, G. A. (1955). *The psychology of personal constructs.* New York: Norton.

KELLY, G. A. (1970). A brief introduction to personal construct theory. In D. BANNISTER (Ed.), *Perspectives in personal construct theory* (pp. 1–29). New York: Academic Press.

KOHUT, H. (1977). *The restoration of the self.* New York: International Universities Press.

KOHUT, H. (1982). Introspection, empathy, and the semi-circle of mental health. *International Journal of Psychoanalysis, 63,* 395–407.

KRIS, E. (1952). *Psychoanalytic explorations in art.* New York: International Universities Press.

LANG, P. J. (1979). A bio-informational theory of emotional imagery. *Psychophysiology, 16,* 495–512.

LANGS, R. (1973). *The technique of psychoanalytic psychotherapy* (Vol. 1). New York: Aronson.

LANGS, R. (1976). *The bipersonal field.* New York: Aronson.

LARSON, D. (1980). Therapeutic schools, styles, and schoolism: A national survey. *Journal of Humanistic Psychology, 20,* 3–20.

LAZARUS, A. A. (1981). *The practice of multi-modal therapy.* New York: McGraw-Hill.

LAZARUS, A. A., AND FAY, A. (1984). Behavior therapy. In T. B. KARASU (Ed.), *The psychiatric therapies* (pp. 483–538). Washington, DC: American Psychiatric Association.

LAZARUS, R. S. (1982). Thoughts on the relations between emotion and cognition. *American Psychologist, 37,* 1019–1024.

LAZARUS, R. S. (1984). On the primacy of cognition. *American Psychologist, 39,* 124–129.

LEIDER, R. J. (1984). The neutrality of the analyst in the analytic situation. *Journal of the American Psychoanalytic Association, 32,* 573–586.

LEVENTHAL, H. (1980). Toward a comprehensive theory of emotion. In L. BERKOWITZ (Ed.), *Advances in experimental social psychology* (Vol. 13, pp. 139–207). New York: Academic Press.

LONDON, P. (1986). *The modes and morals of psychotherapy* (2nd ed.). New York: Holt, Rinehart & Winston.

MAHONEY, M. J. (1974). *Cognition and behavior modification.* Cambridge, MA: Ballinger.

MAHONEY, M. J. (1980). Psychotherapy and the structure of personal revolutions. In M. J. MAHONEY (Ed.), *Psychotherapy process: Current issues and future directions* (pp. 157–180). New York: Plenum Press.

MALAN, D. H. (1976). *The frontier of brief psychotherapy.* New York: Plenum Press.

MALCOLM, J. (1981). *The impossible profession.* New York: Knopf.

MANN, J., AND GOLDMAN, R. (1982). *A casebook in time-limited psychotherapy.* New York: McGraw-Hill.

MARCEL, A. J. (1983). Conscious and unconscious perception: An approach to the relations between phenomenal experience and perceptual processes. *Cognitive Psychology, 15,* 238–300.

MASSON, J. M. (1984a). *The assault on truth.* New York: Farrar, Straus, & Giroux.

MASSON, J. M. (1984b, February). Freud and the seduction theory. *Atlantic Monthly,* pp. 33–60.

MASSON, J. M. (Ed. & Trans.). (1985). *The complete letters of Sigmund Freud to Wilhelm Fliess 1887–1904.* Cambridge, MA: Belknap Press of Harvard University Press.

MEICHENBAUM, D. H. (1977). *Cognitive behavior modification.* New York: Plenum Press.

MEICHENBAUM, D., AND GILMORE, J. B. (1982). Resistance from a cognitive–behavioral perspective. In P. L. WACHTEL (Ed.), *Resistance: Psychodynamic and behavioral approaches* (pp. 133–156). New York: Plenum Press.

MEICHENBAUM, D., AND GILMORE, J. B. (1984). The nature of unconscious processes: A cognitive–behavioral perspective. In K. BOWERS AND D. MEICHENBAUM (Eds.), *The unconscious reconsidered* (pp. 273–298). New York: Wiley.

MENDELSOHN, E., AND SILVERMAN, L. H. (1984). The activation of unconscious fantasies in behavioral treatments. In H. ARKOWITZ AND S. B. MESSER (Eds.), *Psychoanalytic therapy and behavior therapy: Is integration possible?* (pp. 255–293). New York: Plenum Press.

MESSER, S. B. (1983). Integrating psychoanalytic and behavior therapy: Limitations, possibilities and trade-offs. *British Journal of Clinical Psychology, 22,* 131–132.

MESSER, S. B. (1986). Eclecticism in psychotherapy: Underlying assumptions, problems, and trade-offs. In J. C. NORCROSS (Ed.), *Handbook of eclectic psychotherapy* (pp. 379–397). New York: Brunner/Mazel.

MESSER, S. B., AND WINOKUR, M. (1980). Some limits to the integration of psychoanalytic and behavior therapy. *American Psychologist, 35,* 818–827.

MESSER, S. B., AND WINOKUR, M. (1981). What about the question of integration? A reply to Apfelbaum and to Ellis. *American Psychologist, 36,* 800–802.

MESSER, S. B., AND WINOKUR, M. (1984a). Psychoanalytic therapy versus psychodynamic therapy: Commentary on Paul L. Wachtel. In H. ARKOWITZ AND S. B. MESSER (Eds.), *Psychoanalytic therapy and behavior therapy: Is integration possible?* (pp. 53–57). New York: Plenum Press.

MESSER, S. B., AND WINOKUR, M. (1984b). Ways of knowing and visions of reality in psychoanalytic therapy and behavior therapy. In H. ARKOWITZ AND S. B. MESSER (Eds.), *Psychoanalytic therapy and behavior therapy: Is integration possible?* (pp. 59–100). New York: Plenum Press.

MESSER, S. B., AND WINOKUR, M. (1986). Eclecticism and the shifting visions of reality in three systems of psychotherapy. *International Journal of Eclectic Psychotherapy, 5,* 115–124.

NOY, P. (1982). A revision of the psychoanalytic theory of affect. In the CHICAGO INSTITUTE OF PSYCHOANALYSIS (Ed.), *The annual of psychoanalysis* (Vol. 10, pp. 139–186). New York: International Universities Press.

PERVIN, L. (1982, November). *Conceptual and applied limitations of behavior therapy: A dynamic systems perspective.* Paper presented at the meeting of the Association for the Advancement of Behavior Therapy, Los Angeles.

RACHMAN, S. (1980). Emotional processing. *Behavior Research and Therapy, 18,* 51–60.

RACHMAN, S. (1981). The primacy of affect: Some theoretical implications. *Behavioral Research and Therapy, 19,* 279–290.

RASMUSSEN, A., AND MESSER, S. B. (1986). A comparison and critique of Mann's time-limited psychotherapy and Davanloo's short-term dynamic psychotherapy. *Bulletin of the Menninger Clinic, 50,* 163–184.

ROLAND, A. (1967). The reality of the psychoanalytic relationship and situation in the handling of transference resistance. *International Journal of Psychoanalysis, 48,* 504–510.

SAFRAN, J. D., AND GREENBERG, L. L. (in press). Hot cognition and psychotherapy process: An information processing/ecological approach. In P. C. KENDALL (Ed.), *Advances in cognitive–behavioral research and therapy* (Vol. 5). New York: Academic Press.

SARASON, I. G. (1979). Three lacunae of cognitive therapy. *Cognitive Therapy and Research, 3,* 223–235.

SCHAFER, R. (1983). *The analytic attitude.* New York: Basic Books.

SCHWARTZ, W. (1984). The two concepts of action and responsibility in psychoanalysis. *Journal of the American Psychoanalytic Association, 32,* 557–572.

SHAPIRO, T. (1985). Editorial: Psychoanalysis, philosophy, and the public. *Journal of the American Psychoanalytic Association, 33,* 5–9.

SHENGOLD, L. L. (1979). Child abuse and deprivation: Soul murder. *Journal of the American Psychoanalytic Association, 27,* 533–559.

SIFNEOS, P. (1979). *Short-term dynamic psychotherapy: Evaluation and technique.* New York: Plenum Press.

SPENCE, D. P. (1982). *Narrative truth and historical truth.* New York: Norton.

SPENCE, D. P. (1984). Five readers reading. *International Forum for Psychoanalysis, 1,* 85–101.

STAMPFL, T. G., AND LEVIS, D. J. (1976). Implosive therapy: A behavioral therapy. In J. T. SPENCE, R. C. CARSON, AND J. W. THIBAUT (Eds.), *Behavioral approaches to therapy* (pp. 89–110). Morristown, NJ: General Learning Press.

STONE, L. (1961). *The psychoanalytic situation.* New York: International Universities Press.

STRUPP, H. (1979). A psychodynamicist looks at modern behavior therapy. *Psychotherapy: Theory, Research, and Practice, 6,* 124–131.

STRUPP, H. H., AND BINDER, J. L. (1984). *Psychotherapy in a new key: A guide to time-limited dynamic psychotherapy.* New York: Basic Books.

TUTTMAN, S. (1982). Regression: Curative factor or impediment in dynamic psychotherapy? In S. SLIPP (Ed.), *Curative factors in dynamic psychotherapy* (pp. 177–198). New York: McGraw-Hill.

ULLMAN, L. P., AND KRASNER, L. (1965). *Case studies in behavior modification.* New York: Holt, Rinehart & Winston.

VAN DEN BERGH, O., AND EELEN, P. (1984). Unconscious processing and emotions. In M. A. REDA AND M. J. MAHONEY (Eds.), *Cognitive psychotherapies* (pp. 173–210). Cambridge, MA: Ballinger.

WACHTEL, P. L. (1977). *Psychoanalysis and behavior therapy.* New York: Basic Books.

WACHTEL, P. L. (1982). What can dynamic therapies contribute to behavior therapy? *Behavior Therapy, 13,* 594–609.

WACHTEL, P. L. (1984a). On theory, practice and the nature of integration. In H. ARKOWITZ AND S. B. MESSER (Eds.), *Psychoanalytic therapy and behavior therapy: Is integration possible?* (pp. 31–52). New York: Plenum Press.

WACHTEL, P. L. (1984b). Tragedy, irony and human assistance: Commentary on Stanley B. Messer and Meir Winokur. In H. ARKOWITZ AND S. B. MESSER (Eds.), *Psychoanalytic therapy and behavior therapy: Is integration possible?* (pp. 101–105). New York: Plenum Press.

WILSON, G. T. (1982). Psychotherapy process and procedure: The behavioral mandate. *Behavior Therapy, 13,* 291–312.

WILSON, G. T., AND EVANS, I. M. (1977). The therapist–client relationship in behavior therapy. In A. S. GURMAN AND A. M. RAZIN (Eds.), *The therapist's contribution to effective psychotherapy: An empirical approach* (pp. 544–565). New York: Pergamon Press.

WILSON, G. T., AND O'LEARY, K. D. (1980). *Principles of behavior therapy.* Englewood Cliffs, NJ: Prentice-Hall.

WINNICOTT, D. W. (1965). *The maturational processes and the facilitating environment.* New York: International Universities Press.

WINNICOTT, D. W. (1971). *Playing and reality.* Middlesex, England: Penguin.

WINOKUR, M., MESSER, S. B., AND SCHACHT, T. (1981). Contributions to the theory and practice of short-term dynamic psychotherapy. *Bulletin of the Menninger Clinic, 45,* 125–142.

WOLF, E. S. (1983). Concluding statement. In A. GOLDBERG (Ed.), *The future of psychoanalysis: Essays in honor of Heinz Kohut* (pp. 495–505). New York: International Universities Press.

WOOLFOLK, R. L., AND RICHARDSON, F. C. (1984). Behavior therapy and the ideology of modernity. *American Psychologist, 39,* 777–786.

ZAJONC, R. B. (1980). Feeling and thinking: Preferences need no inferences. *American Psychologist, 35,* 151–175.

ZAJONC, R. B. (1984). On the primacy of affect. *American Psychologist, 39,* 117–123.

34

Immunization against the Observational Conditioning of Snake Fear in Rhesus Monkeys

Susan Mineka and Michael Cook

The effects of extensive prior exposure to snakes on subsequent observational conditioning of snake fear in rhesus monkeys were examined. Three groups of monkeys (n = 8 per group) were given one of three kinds of pretreatment: (a) An immunization group spent six sessions watching a nonfearful monkey behave nonfearfully with snakes; (b) a latent inhibition group spent six sessions by themselves behaving nonfearfully with snakes with total exposure time to snakes equal to that for the immunization group; and (c) a pseudoimmunization group spent six sessions watching a monkey behave nonfearfully with neutral objects. All groups were then given six sessions of observational conditioning in which they watched fearful monkeys behave fearfully with snakes. When subsequently tested for acquisition of snake fear, the pseudoimmunization and latent inhibition groups showed significant acquisition, but 6 out of 8 subjects in the immunization group did not. Thus, it seems that for a majority of subjects, prior exposure to a nonfearful model behaving nonfearfully with snakes can effectively immunize against the subsequent effects of exposure to fearful models behaving fearfully with snakes. The implications of these results for possible modes of preventing the acquisition of human fears and phobias are discussed.

Susan Mineka and Michael Cook. Immunization against the Observational Conditioning of Snake Fear in Rhesus Monkeys. *Journal of Abnormal Psychology*, 1986, Vol. 95, No. 4, pp. 307–318. Copyright © 1986 by the American Psychological Association. Reprinted by permission of the publisher and the authors.

Recent research using a primate model for the vicarious acquisition of phobic fears has provided support for the hypothesis that a substantial proportion of humans' fears and phobias may be acquired through observational conditioning. In these experiments (Cook, Mineka, Wolkenstein, & Laitsch, 1985; Mineka, Davidson, Cook, & Keir, 1984), adolescent and adult rhesus monkeys rapidly acquired an intense fear of snakes simply through observing wild-reared adult model monkeys (related or unrelated to the observers) behave fearfully in the presence of snake stimuli. The level of fear acquired by the observers was essentially asymptotic after only 8 min (spread over two sessions) of watching the model monkeys behave fearfully in the presence of snakes. That this demonstration provided a good model for the vicarious acquisition of phobic fears in humans was further supported by the observation that the fear was not context specific and was manifest in at least two of Lang's (1968, 1971) three fear-response systems: behavioral avoidance and behavioral distress. In addition, the fear showed no signs of diminution at 3-month follow-up.

Although these results support the hypothesis that human fears and phobias may also be acquired through observational conditioning, the apparent speed and ease of acquisition of fear found with these procedures raises at least one important concern. If such fears can be acquired in humans with as brief exposure to models behaving fearfully as occurs in monkeys, then one might well expect the incidence of specific fears or phobias to be quite high in friends and relatives of individuals exhibiting intense specific fears or phobias. One might also expect a higher concordance rate between parents' and children's fears than has typically been reported (see Emmelkamp, 1982; Marks, 1987, for reviews). The observer monkeys used in experiments to date, however, have differed in one very important way from many humans who may have experiences observing models behaving fearfully with specific objects. In particular, the observer monkeys in these experiments had very little prior exposure to snake stimuli (13-min average with a range of 8 to 21 min possible during pretests) prior to their observational conditioning experiences. By contrast, humans may often have much more extensive experience with an object prior to seeing a model behave fearfully with that object. Such prior experience can occur through exposure to the object alone, increasing the familiarity of the object and thereby perhaps reducing the object's salience. Alternatively, or in addition, people may have been exposed to another person behaving nonfearfully with that object (i.e., a nonfearful model). The goal of the present experiment was to determine, using a primate model, whether these two types of prior exposure to a specific stimulus do indeed reduce the effectiveness of subsequent observational conditioning using models who are fearful of that stimulus.

Put in somewhat different terms, the goal of the present experiment was to determine whether there is an effective way to immunize subjects against the potent effects of observational conditioning experiences. The topic of immunization against specific forms of emotional disturbance or psychopathology has long been of interest to experimental psychopathologists, although it has not received a great deal of direct attention for most disorders. There are, however, several notable exceptions to this dearth of attention on the topic of immunization. For example, Seligman and his colleagues have addressed the issue of immunization against hopelessness depression through extensive prior exposure to controllable stimulation (e.g., Seligman, 1975). Others have also hypothesized that gaining a sense of mastery or control over one's environment may minimize fearful reactions to strange, novel, and threatening events, especially early in development (for reviews see Mineka, 1985a, 1985b; Mineka, Gunnar, & Champoux, in press; Mineka & Hendersen, 1985). As important as it is, however, such experience with mastery and control probably has quite generalized effects in immunizing against reactions to a wide range of stressful experiences, and perhaps against various forms of psychopathology as well. What is unknown is whether there are practical ways to directly immunize against the acquisition of specific anxiety disorders, such as, for example, specific phobias.

One way to look for ideas about possible methods of immunization is to examine effective forms of therapy for specific phobias. Procedures that are effective in treating a disorder might well, if used prior to the onset of the disorder, be expected to prevent its onset. (See Barrios & Shigetomi, 1980, and Poser & King, 1975, for related discussions.) In reviewing the treatment literature, two potential methods emerge, which parallel the two mentioned earlier as likely to be involved in explaining why more people do not rapidly acquire the fears of their friends and relatives. First, it is well known that extensive exposure to a feared object or situation is a critical ingredient in effective behavior therapy techniques (Emmelkamp, 1982; Foa & Kozak, 1985; Marks, 1987; Rachman, 1985). This would suggest that extensive prior exposure to an object alone might immunize against the subsequent acquisition of fear to that object. Indeed, consistent with this prediction, Jaremko (1978) reported that an analogue form of desensitization administered to college students prior to the classical conditioning of electrodermal responses resulted in significant interference in conditioning.

A second potential mode of immunization stems from the work of Bandura and his colleagues, who have argued that having the phobic patient watch a nonfearful model behave nonfearfully with the phobic object can often enhance the effectiveness of the therapy over exposure to the object alone (e.g., Bandura, Blanchard, & Ritter, 1969; Bandura, Grusec, & Menlove, 1967). It is true that not all studies have supported the proposition that modeling significantly enhances the effects of in vivo exposure therapy alone when total exposure time to the feared object is carefully controlled (see Bourque & Ladouceur, 1980; Emmelkamp, 1982, for reviews). Nevertheless, definitive conclusions on this point from the behavior therapy literature are sufficiently unclear at this time that it is possible that exposure to a nonfearful model behaving nonfearfully with an object might provide superior immunization against the acquisition of fear to that object compared with simple exposure to that object. And indeed, there are several findings in support of this suggestion. Poser and King (1975), for example, took children who were assessed as being fairly neutral about snakes and exposed them to a film of a model interacting nonfearfully with snakes. Subsequently, these children approached a snake more closely than did children who had simply seen a film of the snake with no model. In addition, Melamed and her colleagues have shown that children who watched a film of a similar-aged peer undergoing a dental restorative treatment subsequently showed less fear and distress during their own dental work than did children who saw a demonstration film that lacked a peer model (Melamed, Yurcheson, Fleece, Hutcherson, & Hawes, 1978; cf. Melamed & Siegel, 1975, for related findings on preparing children for surgery).

These two potential modes of immunization found in the behavior therapy literature—exposure alone versus exposure to a nonfearful model—also have conceptual foundations in the classical conditioning literature. First, extensive prior exposure to a conditioned stimulus (CS) presented alone results in a retardation of conditioning when the CS is subsequently paired with an unconditioned stimulus (UCS), a phenomenon known as *latent inhibition* (Lubow, 1973; Lubow & Moore, 1959). Latent inhibition is most often considered to result from a loss of CS salience or associability that occurs during the preexposure to the CS when it predicts nothing of importance (Mackintosh, 1974, 1983; Rescorla, 1975). Thus, one might well expect that extensive preexposure to snake stimuli would result in retarded acquisition of snake fear when subjects subsequently undergo observational conditioning experiences with fearful models, presumably because of a loss of salience or associability of the snake stimuli.

The second suggestion for a possible mode of immunization—prior exposure to a nonfearful model—has a less firmly established conceptual foundation in the conditioning literature, just as in the behavior therapy literature. Intuitively, if exposure to a nonfearful model provided more interference with subsequent acquisition of fear than did exposure alone, this would seem to involve an active learning of safety. In the classical conditioning literature, the most closely related concept appears to be that of conditioned inhibition. In conditioned inhibition, CSs that signal the absence of an aversive UCS acquire the capacity to actively inhibit conditioned fear responses (e.g., Pavlov, 1927; Rescorla & LoLordo, 1965) and, according to some, may make the subject feel safe (e.g., Seligman & Binik, 1977). However, such active inhibitory conditioning, or learning of safety, is thought to occur only when CSs signal the absence of the UCS in a context where UCSs do sometimes occur (cf. Wagner & Rescorla, 1972). Thus, watching a nonfearful model behave nonfearfully in a context where fear or aversive stimulation never occurs would not be expected to provide the necessary conditions for conditioned inhibition or learned safety to occur. Thus, the classical conditioning literature provides no strong empirical grounds from which to predict that watching a model behave nonfearfully will immunize more effectively than will simple exposure alone, as long as exposure to the nonfearful model is occurring in a context where aversive stimulation does not occur. Nonetheless, there are the findings of Poser and King (1975) and of Melamed et al. (1978) suggesting the superiority of modeling as a method of immunization. Furthermore, there are the occasional, although inconsistent, findings from the social learning literature referred to above regarding the therapeutic superiority of exposure to nonfearful models over exposure to the object alone. Therefore, it seemed worth investigating whether prior exposure to nonfearful models may be a more effective immunization procedure than prior exposure to the object alone (latent inhibition).

Thus, the present experiment compares these two methods of preexposure to snake stimuli for their effectiveness in reducing the effects of subsequent observational conditioning of snake fear in monkeys. Three groups of laboratory-reared monkeys who were not initially afraid of snakes received one of three different kinds of pretreatment. The immunization group spent six sessions watching nonfearful models behaving nonfearfully with snake stimuli, the latent inhibition group spent six sessions by themselves reaching for food in the presence of the snake stimuli (thus being equated with the immunization group for total exposure to snake stimuli), and the pseudoimmunization group spent six sessions watching models behave nonfearfully with nonsnake stimuli. Subsequent to these three different pretreatments, all groups received six sessions of discriminative observational conditioning in which they watched fearful models respond fearfully with snake stimuli and nonfearfully with neutral objects. (This procedure was identical to that of Mineka et

al., 1984, and Cook et al., 1985.) The three groups were then compared for their acquisition and retention of snake fear.

Method

Subjects (Observers)

Subjects were 24 laboratory-reared rhesus monkeys (*Macaca mulatta*), all living at the University of Wisconsin Primate Laboratory in single-animal cages. The subjects—9 males and 15 females—ranged in age from 4 to 12 years.

Models

Models were 3 wild-reared and 3 laboratory-reared rhesus monkeys living in either single-animal or group cages. The wild-reared models (1 female and 2 males) ranged in age from approximately 27 to 31 years. They had been imported from India 21–27 years prior to the study. They had all demonstrated a fear of snakes in earlier studies (Mineka et al., 1984; Mineka, Keir, & Price, 1980) and were therefore assigned to the fearful model group. The 3 laboratory-reared models (1 male and 2 females) were all housed in single-animal cages, and they ranged in age from 13 to 19 years. (It was not possible to equate the wild- and laboratory-reared models on age because of the unavailability of younger wild-reared monkeys or older laboratory-reared monkeys.) During pretests the laboratory-reared models all failed to show a fear of snakes and snakelike stimuli and were therefore assigned to the nonfearful model group.

Apparatus

The following objects were used to determine each subject's reactions: (a) a 3¼-ft-long (99.1 cm) live boa constrictor (*Constrictor constrictor*), approximately 1¾ in. (4.4 cm) in diameter; (b) a 41¾-in.-long (106 cm) sinuous, brown, rubber toy snake, approximately 1 in. (2.5 cm) in diameter; (c) a 24-in.-long (61 cm) sinuous, green, rubber toy snake, approximately 1 in. (2.5 cm) in diameter; (d) a 3-ft-long (91.4 cm) sinuous, black, rubber electrical cord, approximately $\frac{3}{8}$ in. (1 cm) in diameter; (e) a 3¾-ft-long (114.3 cm) sinuous, yellow, rubber electrical cord, approximately ¼ in. (0.6 cm) in diameter; and (f) four "neutral" objects, which were wood blocks of different shapes and colors.

Testing was carried out in two settings. The first was a Wisconsin General Test Apparatus (WGTA). In this apparatus, the experimenter sits behind a one-way mirror, unobserved by the monkey. A gray tray with an uncovered Plexiglas box (53.4 cm long × 15.2 cm high × 21.3 cm wide) on it was moved toward the monkey, who was in a holding cage several feet away (98.5 cm long × 52.6 cm high × 51.4 cm wide). All stimulus objects were placed inside the uncovered Plexiglas box; a food reward was placed on a ledge at the top of the back wall of the box (the wall furthest from the monkey). A moveable cage blind could be lowered by the experimenter, preventing the monkey from viewing the Plexiglas box, the stimulus, and the food reward. (See Harlow, 1949, for a more detailed description.)

The second testing apparatus was the Sackett Self-Selection Circus (Sackett, 1970), which consists of a hexagonal center compartment surrounded by six rhomboidal-shaped outer compartments. The center compartment was separated from each outer compartment by a guillotine-type door that could be pneumatically raised and lowered. The side walls separating the six outer compartments from each other were made of 0.32-cm plywood. In the present experiment, four of the six outer compartments were used as "stimulus" compartments; each had a guillotine door and an outer wall (i.e., the wall furthest from the center compartment and opposite the guillotine door) constructed of Plexiglas. A fifth outer compartment was used as a start compartment. Its guillotine door was made of plywood to prevent subjects from looking into or out of the start compartment; its outer wall was also opaque. (The sixth compartment was

not used; its guillotine door was also made of plywood.) Each of the stimulus objects used in Sackett Circus testing was placed inside a cage (53 cm long × 35 cm high × 30 cm wide) with one side (53 cm × 35 cm) made of Plexiglas. The cage was placed so this Plexiglas side faced the outer Plexiglas wall of the stimulus compartment, and thus the monkey inside the stimulus compartment could view the stimulus through two layers of Plexiglas. The real snake, however, was placed in a Plexiglas box (same dimensions as the Plexiglas box used in WGTA testing) within the cage and so was seen through three layers of Plexiglas.

Fluorescent light fixtures attached just outside the outer Plexiglas wall of each stimulus compartment provided light. A video camera was placed directly above the hexagonal center compartment so that the apparatus could be seen on a monitor in an adjacent room.

Procedure

WGTA Adaptation and Pretest. Before testing, each monkey was adapted to the WGTA apparatus and procedure. Although some monkeys had previous WGTA experience, they were readapted to ensure comparable performance. A trial consisted of (a) placing one of the neutral objects inside the Plexiglas box; (b) placing a food reward (either a Froot Loop or a raisin, depending on individual preference) on the ledge of the Plexiglas box; and (c) moving the tray with the Plexiglas box on it toward the monkey, raising the blind (so the moneky could now see the box, stimulus object, and treat), and starting a timer. The trial ended (the timer was stopped) when the monkey touched the food reward. This procedure required the monkey to reach over the stimulus in the open box in order to obtain the food reward. Monkeys were considered to be adapted when they reached for and touched the food reward within 10 s on 18 of 20 consecutive trials. Most monkeys required many days of adaptation before reaching criterion.

All monkeys received a pretest in the

WGTA. The pretest procedure was similar to that employed during adaptation, with the following exceptions: (a) In addition to the neutral objects, test stimuli during the pretest included the real and toy snakes and the yellow and black cords: all were placed inside the open Plexiglas box during their presentation to the monkey. (b) Trials during the pretest were all 60 s long instead of ending when the monkey touched the food reward, as during adaptation. Thus, the food-reach latency was recorded when the monkey touched the food reward, but the trial continued until 60 s had elapsed. Failure of the monkey to touch the food reward during the trial resulted in a recorded latency of 60 s. (c) In addition to recording the latency of the food-reach response, the occurrence of any of 12 disturbance behaviors was recorded during the 60-s trials. The disturbance behaviors were scored using a modified 1–0 frequency system (Sackett, 1978). A 60-s trial was subdivided into three 20-s intervals; if a particular disturbance behavior occurred one or more times during a given 20-s interval, that behavior was given a score of 1 for that interval. Because there were three intervals per trial, each behavior could receive a score of 0 to 3 for a given trial. The maximum composite score for behavioral disturbance on any given trial was thus 36 (3 intervals × 12 disturbance behaviors).

The disturbance behaviors recorded were identical to those previously shown to occur in this situation (Cook et al., 1985; Mineka et al., 1984; Mineka & Keir, 1983; Mineka et al., 1980): fear withdraw (sudden retreat to and/or flattening of the body against the back of the cage); cage clutch (holding onto the side or the back of the cage); cage shake (obvious moving or shaking of the cage); spasm/tic (vigorous shaking or jerking of the hands or upper body); eye aversion (rapidly looking away from the stimulus); stare (prolonged, fixed gaze into the box from the back of the cage); fear grimace (stretching the lips over the gums, exposing the teeth); threat (lips thrust forward, ears retracted or flattened against the head); ear flap (ears flat-

tened against the head but without the lips thrust forward as with a threat); lip smack (lips repeatedly moving up and down, chattering of teeth); vocalization; and piloerection (fur raised up on the shoulders and torso).

Finally, because the boa was free to move about on those trials it was presented, an evaluation was made of its movement. An ordinal scale of 0 to 3 was employed, with 0 indicating no movement at all and 3 indicating that the snake was coming out of the Plexiglas box. Movement by the boa during its presentation was relatively infrequent, occurring only 25 times over the course of the experiment (mean movement for these 25 trials was 1.64).

A pretest session consisted of 22 trials, composed of two 11-trial sequences. For a given sequence, the three snake and two cord stimuli were each presented once interspersed by 6 neutral object trials, 2 of which came at the outset of the sequence. Thus, each snake or cord stimulus was presented twice during the pretest. The order of the snake and cord trials was identical to that described in previously published experiments (Cook et al., 1985; Mineka et al., 1984).

Because, over the course of the experiment, three investigators were responsible for recording the occurrence/nonoccurrence of fear behaviors during WGTA sessions, it was necessary to assess interrater agreement. The four interrater agreement sessions were procedurally identical to the WGTA pretests described above. The sessions involved 3 different monkeys who had acquired a fear of snakes through observational learning. Because of space limitations, only two of the three investigators were present to record fear behaviors during any given trial. Over 88 trials (4 sessions × 22 trials per session), 65 fear behaviors were recorded by one or both of the raters who were present. The interrater agreement for these 65 fear behavior occurrences was 85%; that is, only 10 of these 65 recorded behaviors were noted by only one of the two raters present. If all the instances for which the observers agreed no fear behaviors occurred were included in this analysis, interrater agreement would exceed 99%. (Agreement concerning movement of the real snake, which was presented on 8 of the 88 trials, was 100%.)

Sackett Circus Adaptation and Pretest. For each Sackett Circus session, the monkey was confined to the start compartment for the first 5 min. During this time, the four stimulus objects were put in their appropriate cages outside the four stimulus compartments. After the 5-min period elapsed, the five guillotine doors separating the center compartment from the start compartment and the four stimulus compartments were simultaneously opened. When the monkey exited from the start compartment (almost always within 10 s), the plywood guillotine door of that compartment was lowered to prevent reentry. The monkey was then free to enter or reenter any of the four stimulus compartments or to stay in the center for the next 5 min. At this point all the guillotine doors were lowered, terminating the trial. An experimenter, observing the monkey on a monitor in the adjacent room, recorded the amount of time spent inside each of the four stimulus compartments.

Prior to the Circus pretest, monkeys were given adaptation sessions in order to (a) familiarize them with the apparatus and procedure and (b) ensure that they displayed no compartment preference. In these sessions, only four neutral objects (i.e., wood blocks) were used as stimulus objects. Sessions continued for each monkey until a criterion of four consecutive sessions of "no preference" was met: spending 10%–40% of the total entry time in each compartment. All monkeys required at least five sessions to meet this criterion.

All monkeys then received three Circus pretests. The procedure employed during the pretests was identical to that during adaptation sessions except that instead of four neutral objects, the stimuli used were the real and toy snakes and one of the four neutral objects.

Pretreatment Sessions. Subjects (observers) were randomly assigned to one of three groups ($n = 8$ per group) that received the pretreatments described below:

1. Subjects in the *latent inhibition group* received six latent inhibition sessions in the WGTA. The procedure followed during each of the sessions was identical to that used during the WGTA pretest session (i.e., 22 trials per session, 10 involving the presentation of the three snake and two cord stimuli). As during the WGTA pretest, the subjects' food-reach latency and disturbance behavior scores were recorded for each trial.

2. Each subject in the *immunization group* was paired with one of the nonfearful models and underwent six immunization sessions in the WGTA. During each session the nonfearful model underwent the exact equivalent of a WGTA pretest, with food-reach latency and disturbance behaviors being recorded. Unlike during the pretest, however, the immunization subject with whom the model was paired was present during the immunization session. The immunization subject was confined in a cage (53 cm long × 35 cm high × 30 cm long) with one side (53 cm × 35 cm) made of Plexiglas. The cage was situated next to the cage holding the nonfearful model so that the immunization subject could observe the nonfearful model and his/her reactions to the various stimuli (i.e., the nonfearful model's food-reach latency and level of behavioral disturbance). Because there were only 3 nonfearful models, each immunization subject did not have a unique model. Specifically, each of the 3 models modeled for either 2 or 3 of the 8 observers.

3. Each subject in the *pseudoimmunization group* was paired with one of the fearful models and underwent six pseudoimmunization sessions in the WGTA. The procedure employed during these pseudoimmunization sessions was identical to that used in the immunization sessions except that only neutral objects were used (i.e., no snake or cord stimuli were ever presented to the fearful models during these sessions). Again, each fearful model modeled for 2 or 3 of the 8 subjects.

Observational Conditioning. Following pretreatment sessions, each of the 24 subjects in the three observer groups was paired with a fearful model. Immunization subjects were necessarily paired with two different models over the course of the experiment, a nonfearful model during the treatment and a fearful model during observational conditioning. Pseudoimmunization subjects, who were paired with fearful models in both of these two phases, were therefore assigned a different model during conditioning than the one assigned during pseudoimmunization. Fearful models modeled for 2 or 3 of the observers in each of the observer groups. (Collapsing over the three observer groups, each fearful model modeled for 7–9 observers.)

Model–observer pairs underwent six observational conditioning sessions in the WGTA, the procedure of each similar to immunization sessions. Specifically, while the model was confined to the WGTA holding cage and presented a series of stimuli (trials), the observer was confined in the cage so he/she could watch the food-reach latencies and fear behaviors exhibited by the model. These six sessions differed from the six immunization/pseudoimmunization sessions in the following particulars: (a) In addition to recording the food-reach latency and disturbance behaviors of the model, the disturbance behaviors shown by the observer monkey were also recorded. (It should be noted, however, that the fear behavior scores of models and observers are not strictly comparable. Because the cage holding the observer was much smaller than the cage holding the model, some of the 12 fear behaviors were difficult or impossible for the observer to exhibit specifically, cage clutch, cage shake, and fear withdrawal.) (b) Trials were of 40-s rather than 60-s duration. Thus, for a given subject on a given trial, the maximum possible food-reach latency was 40 s rather than 60 s, and the maximum possible behavioral disturbance score was 24 rather

than 36. (c) Unlike the WGTA pretests and immunization sessions, the yellow and black cords were not used; test stimuli were limited to the real and toy snakes and the neutral objects previously used in WGTA testing. (d) Sessions were 15 rather than 22 trials in length. The order of the 15 trials was 6 neutral object trials, 6 trials with the real and toy snakes, and 3 neutral object trials. Thus, unlike during the WGTA pretest and the immunization sessions, snake stimuli trials were not separated from each other by neutral object trials. (The rationale for this procedure is described in detail by Cook et al., 1985, and Mineka et al., 1984, as is the specific ordering of snake trials for the conditioning sessions.)

Sackett Circus and WGTA Posttests. On the day following the second, fourth, and sixth conditioning sessions, observers were tested in the Sackett Circus to determine whether snake fear, if acquired, would manifest itself in a situation other than where the conditioning took place (i.e., the WGTA). These three Circus posttests were procedurally identical to the pretests, with the subject having 5 min to freely enter and leave each of the stimulus compartments adjacent to the neutral object and the three snake stimuli (real, brown, and green toy snakes). Following the third posttest in the Circus, a final WGTA session (identical in procedure to the WGTA pretest) was conducted to test for behavioral avoidance and behavioral disturbance in the situation where observational conditioning occurred.

For each subject, the Circus and WGTA pretests, the pretreatment and conditioning sessions, and the Circus and WGTA posttests were conducted over a 6- to 8-week period. Typically, pretesting in the WGTA and Circus took place during the first week. Pretreatment sessions took place over the next 2 weeks. A cycle of two conditioning sessions and a Circus posttest took place the following week, with this cycle being repeated two more times during the next 2 weeks. The final WGTA test was conducted 1–3 days subsequent to the last Circus posttest.

Follow-up Testing. To test for retention of acquired fear, all observers received follow-up sessions in the Circus and WGTA approximately 3 months following the final conditioning session. The procedures used during Circus and WGTA follow-up were identical to those used in the Circus and WGTA pretests and posttests. The Circus follow-up session preceded the WGTA follow-up session by about 2–3 days.

A summary of the procedure is provided in Table 1.

Data Analysis

For WGTA analyses, scores for each snake stimulus were derived by summing latencies

TABLE 1 Overview of Procedure

Experimental Phase	Procedure
Adaptation	Observers were adapted in Circus using neutral stimuli to ensure lack of compartment preference. Both models and observers were adapted in WGTA using neutral stimuli to ensure stable, rapid responding for food treats.
Pretests	Models and observers were administered a pretest in WGTA consisting of 22 60-s trials, 6 with snake and 16 with nonsnake stimuli. Models and observers were also given three pretests in Circus with snake and neutral stimuli.
Pretreatment	1. Latent inhibition subjects were administered six latent inhibition sessions. Each session consisted of 22 60-s trials, 6 with snake and 16 with nonsnake stimuli.
	2. Six immunization sessions were administered to each nonfearful-model–immunization observer pair. Each session consisted of an observer watching a model respond on 22 60-s trials, 6 with snake and 16 with nonsnake stimuli.
	3. Six pseudoimmunization sessions were administered to each fearful-model–pseudoimmunization-observer pair. Each session consisted of an observer watching a model respond on 22 60-s trials, all with neutral stimuli.
Observational conditioning	Six observational conditioning sessions were administered to each fearful-model–observer pair. Each session consisted of an observer watching a fearful model on 15 40-s trials, 6 with snake and 9 with nonsnake stimuli.
Circus posttests	Circus tests with snake and neutral stimuli were administered to observers following Sessions 2, 4, and 6 of conditioning. The procedure was identical to that used during Circus pretests.
WGTA posttest	Observers were administered a posttest in WGTA following the last Circus posttest. The procedure was identical to that used during WGTA pretest.
Three-month follow-up	Observers were administered follow-up tests in Circus and WGTA approximately 3 months following conditioning. Procedures were identical to those used during pretests and posttests.

Note. WGTA = Wisconsin General Test Apparatus.

(and disturbance behavior scores) over the two trials on which the stimulus was presented during a session. Past research employing this paradigm (Cook et al., 1985; Mineka et al., 1984; Mineka & Keir, 1983; Mineka et al., 1980) indicated that responding to the cord stimuli did not significantly differ from responding to the neutral stimuli. Therefore, analyses for the present experiment derived composite neutral stimulus scores by summing over the two yellow cord trials, the two black cord trials, and the first two neutral object trials of a session, and dividing by 3. For the pretest, latent inhibition, immunization, pseudoimmunization, posttest, and follow-up sessions in the WGTA, the maximum attainable latency score was 120 s (60 s per trial). The maximum attainable disturbance behavior score was 72 (36 per trial). (Due to a shorter trial length, maximum latency and disturbance behavior scores during observational conditioning were 80 s and 48, respectively.) In all Circus analyses, total amount of time spent in each of the different stimulus compartments (hereinafter referred to as *compartment time*) was the dependent measure.

In all statistical analyses the rejection level was set at $\alpha = .05$, unless otherwise noted. When analysis of variance (ANOVA) results involving repeated measures violated the assumption of compound symmetry, the degrees of freedom shown are those recommended by Greenhouse and Geisser (1959). It should be noted, however, that because this procedure assumes maximal violation, it tends to overcorrect (i.e., the procedure is overly conservative).

All post-hoc comparisons were Duncan's multiple-range tests ($\alpha = .05$). Comparisons were performed only if the appropriate simple main effect corresponding to the means to be contrasted was significant ($\alpha = .05$). Comparisons involving repeated measures always used separate error terms for each of the individual comparisons. Separate error terms for contrasts based on independent groups were used only when heterogeneity of variance was indicated (Levene test, $\alpha = .05$).

Results

The results revealed rapid, strong, and persistent observational conditioning of snake fear in the pseudoimmunization group. By contrast, 6 of the 8 monkeys in the immunization group showed little or no sign of observational conditioning of snake fear. The latent inhibition group showed moderate levels of observational conditioning, intermediate between the levels shown by the other two groups. Before describing the results of the posttests in detail, the results of the pretest, pretreatment, and observational conditioning sessions will be presented.

Models and Observers at Pretest

At pretest, both WGTA and Circus measures reflected an initial lack of snake fear by the laboratory-reared monkeys (nonfearful models and latent inhibition, immunization, and pseudoimmunization observers) but an intense fear of snakes by the wild-reared monkeys (fearful models). Because the results so closely parallel those published in the past comparing the responses of wild- and laboratory-reared rhesus monkeys (Cook et al., 1985; Mineka et al., 1984; Mineka et al., 1980), details of the analyses are not presented here. As in previous experiments, only the fearful models showed differential responding to the different stimuli, with longer latencies and more disturbance behaviors in the WGTA to the three snake stimuli than to the neutral objects. Latencies and disturbance behaviors for the other four groups did not differ across the stimulus objects. Analysis of the Circus results revealed that the fearful models spent more time with the neutral object than with the three snake stimuli, whereas the remaining groups spent comparable amounts of time with all four objects.

Pretreatment Sessions

The WGTA measures (food-reach latency and disturbance behavior) during the six pretreatment sessions indicated a lack of fear (i.e., short latencies and few disturbance behaviors) for (a) latent inhibition monkeys responding to snake and neutral stimuli during latent inhibition sessions, (b) nonfearful models responding to snake and neutral stimuli during immunization sessions, and (c) fearful models responding to neutral stimuli during pseudoimmunization sessions. For all groups, means for food-reach latency in the presence of snake and neutral stimuli were all less than or equal to 8.06 s; means for disturbance behaviors were all less than or equal to 0.31.

Observational Conditioning Sessions

Fearful Model Behavior. Although variability existed, the food-reach latencies and disturbance behaviors of the fearful models during the six observational conditioning sessions clearly indicated a fear of snake stimuli and a concomitant lack of fear of neutral stimuli. The means and standard deviations for the two measures are shown in Table 2.

Observer Behavior (Latent Inhibition, Immunization, and Pseudoimmunization Groups). Observer disturbance behaviors during the six conditioning sessions were analyzed by a 3 × 6 × 4 (Groups × Sessions × Stimulus Objects) mixed-design ANOVA. The ANOVA revealed a significant main effect for objects. $F(3,63) = 75.59$, which was the result of the following pattern of differences: neutral stimulus < green toy snake < brown toy snake < real snake. As

TABLE 2 Means and Standard Deviations for Model and Observer Performance during Observational Conditioning

Dependent Measure	Stimulus			
	Real Snake	Brown Toy	Green Toy	Neutral
Fearful models ($n = 3$)				
Latency				
M	76.23	68.79	57.31	6.36
SD	6.62	10.94	19.51	1.51
Disturbance behavior				
M	5.01	3.16	1.62	0.08
SD	1.32	1.36	1.38	0.13
Latent inhibition observers ($n = 8$)				
Disturbance behavior				
M	1.69	0.56	0.27	0.04
SD	1.17	0.43	0.28	0.07
Immunization observers ($n = 8$)				
Disturbance behavior				
M	1.63	0.79	0.21	0.17
SD	0.79	0.58	0.26	0.24
Pseudoimmunization observers ($n = 8$)				
Disturbance behavior				
M	2.27	0.88	0.48	0.10
SD	0.90	0.60	0.41	0.09

Note. Maximum latency score possible = 80 s; maximum disturbance behavior score possible = 48. Scores for each object were averaged across the six observational conditioning sessions.

discussed above (see *Procedure*), because the apparatus imposed an artificially low ceiling on observer disturbance behavior scores during conditioning, a statistical comparison of these scores either with their own disturbance scores during the WGTA pretest or with the disturbance scores of the fearful models during conditioning would not be meaningful. Nevertheless, the reactions of the observers to snake presentations during conditioning (as indexed by behavioral disturbance) could be characterized as qualitatively similar to the fearful reactions of their models to snake presentations during pretests and conditioning (indicated by behavioral avoidance and behavioral disturbance) and as dissimilar to the observers' earlier nonfearful reactions to snake stimuli during the pretests (indicated by a lack of behavioral avoidance and lack of behavioral disturbance). Table 2 shows the means and standard deviations for each of the three observer groups for disturbance behavior during conditioning to each of the four stimuli.

Observers at Pretest, Posttest, and Follow-Up

During the pretest, the three groups were indistinguishable, all showing a lack of snake fear on all three dependent measures. During the posttest, however, latent inhibition and pseudoimmunization observers revealed that they had acquired a strong fear of snakes, as indicated by a differential pattern of responding to the different objects on all three measures. By contrast, 6 of 8 immunization observers showed very little or no snake fear on the three measures. Furthermore, there were indications that the mean level of snake fear in the latent inhibition group was slightly less than in the pseudoimmunization group, although these differences were not significant. During the follow-up, snake fear was maintained in the latent inhibition and pseudoimmunization groups, and it remained largely absent in 6 of 8 immunization observers.

Sackett Circus. To determine whether there were any trends in the acquisition of snake fear across the three Circus posttests, a $3 \times 3 \times 4$ (Groups $\times$ Sessions $\times$ Stimulus Objects) mixed-design ANOVA was performed. The analysis revealed only a significant main effect for objects, $F(1, 21) = 36.94$, which was the result of observers spending significantly more time with the neutral stimulus than with the snake stimuli. Observers also spent more time with the green toy snake than with the real snake. Thus, as in previous experiments (Cook et al., 1985; Mineka et al., 1984), the level of acquired fear appeared to be asymptotic at the time of the first Circus posttest.

A $3 \times 3 \times 4$ (Groups $\times$ Tests $\times$ Stimulus Objects) mixed-design ANOVA compared observer compartment times at pretest, posttest, and follow-up. (Pretest and posttest values were averaged across their individual sessions because previous ANOVAS failed to show significant effects involving the sessions factor at either of these test stages.) A significant main effect for objects was found, $F(1, 21) = 31.66$, along with a significant Tests $\times$ Objects interaction, $F(1, 21) = 10.89$.

Although the $3 \times 3 \times 4$ factorial design lacked the power to demonstrate the predicted Groups $\times$ Tests $\times$ Objects triple interaction, a planned comparison, which contrasted those cells of the design most critical to the experimental hypothesis, was performed and found to be significant. The constructed comparison ignored both of the toy snakes, focusing on differences in response to the real snake and the neutral stimulus. Furthermore, as there were a priori reasons for believing that the immunization procedure would prove more effective than the latent inhibition procedure in retarding acquisition of snake fear, only the immunization observers were contrasted with the pseudoimmunization (control) observers. Also, because acquisition of snake fear was more critical than maintenance, pretest values were compared with posttest but not with follow-up values. In sum, the comparison examined the difference in reaction to the real snake and neutral stimulus, which should be greater for the pseudoimmunization than for the immunization observers

TABLE 3 Duncan's Post-Hoc Within-Group Comparisons for Pseudoimmunization, Latent Inhibition, and Immunization Groups at Posttest in the Sackett Circus and WGTA

Group/Stimulus	Real Snake	Brown Toy	Green Toy	Neutral
Circus compartment time				
Pseudoimmunization				
Real Snake	—	*ns*	.05	.05
Brown toy		—	*ns*	.05
Green toy			—	.05
Latent inhibition				
Real snake	—	*ns*	.05	.05
Brown toy		—	*ns*	.05
Green toy			—	.05
Immunization				
Real snake	—	*ns*	*ns*	*ns*
Brown toy		—	*ns*	*ns*
Green toy			—	*ns*
WGTA latency				
Pseudoimmunization				
Real snake	—	*ns*	*ns*	.05
Brown toy		—	*ns*	.05
Green toy			—	.05
Latent inhibition				
Real snake	—	.05	*ns*	.05
Brown toy		—	*ns*	.05
Green toy			—	.05
Immunization				
Real snake	—	*ns*	*ns*	*ns*
Brown toy		—	*ns*	*ns*
Green toy			—	*ns*
WGTA disturbance behavior				
Pseudoimmunization				
Real snake	—	.05	.05	.05
Brown toy		—	*ns*	.05
Green toy			—	.05
Latent inhibition				
Real snake	—	.05	.05	.05
Brown toy		—	*ns*	.05
Green toy			—	.05
Immunization				
Real snake	—	*ns*	*ns*	*ns*
Brown toy		—	*ns*	*ns*
Green toy			—	*ns*

Note. WGTA = Wisconsin General Test Apparatus.

during the posttest, but not during the pretest. Specifically, the coefficients for the comparison were derived from the following formula:

$$[(R_{post} - N_{post}) - (R_{pre} - N_{pre})]_{pseudo}$$
$$- [(R_{post} - N_{post}) - (R_{pre} - N_{pre})]_{immun},$$

where R is the real snake, N is the neutral stimulus, pre and post are the pretest and posttest, respectively, and pseudo and immun refer to the pseudoimmunization and immunization groups, respectively. As noted above, for Circus compartment times, this planned comparison was significant, $F(1, 21) = 7.99$.

Having demonstrated with this planned comparison that the three-way interaction was significant, post-hoc comparisons were performed to identify the locus of the effect. They showed, in general, that differences in responsivity to the stimuli emerged at posttest for the pseudoimmunization and latent

inhibition groups, which were indicative of snake fear (i.e., less compartment time with snake stimuli and more time with the neutral stimulus), but not for the immunization group. Fear was maintained in the pseudoimmunization and latent inhibition observers at follow-up but was still absent in the immunization observers. Although within-group comparisons of compartment time with the stimuli at posttest and follow-up supported the foregoing conclusion, an examination for between-groups differences during the posttest and follow-up at each separate object did not, for the most part, reveal significant results. (Tables 3 and 4 summarize the post-hoc comparisons at posttest for the Circus dependent measure. Because analogous comparisons for the follow-up were highly similar, they are not represented.) The failure of group differences to emerge may have been due, at least in part, to variability in observer performance, especially in the immunization group, where

TABLE 4   Duncan's Post-Hoc Between-Groups Comparisons for Pseudoimmunization, Latent Inhibition, and Immunization Groups at Posttest in the Sackett Circus and WGTA

Stimulus	Comparison		
	Immunization vs. Latent Inhibition	Pseudo-immunization vs. Latent Inhibition	Pseudo-immunization vs. Immunization
Circus compartment time			
Real snake	*ns*	*ns*	*ns*
Brown toy	*ns*	*ns*	*ns*
Green toy	*ns*	*ns*	*ns*
Neutral	*ns*	*ns*	*ns*
WGTA latency			
Real snake	*ns*	*ns*	.05
Brown toy	*ns*	*ns*	.05
Green toy	*ns*	*ns*	.05
Neutral	*ns*	*ns*	*ns*
WGTA disturbance behavior			
Real snake	*ns*	*ns*	*ns*
Brown toy	*ns*	.05	.05
Green toy	*ns*	.05	.05
Neutral	*ns*	*ns*	*ns*

Note. WGTA = Wisconsin General Test Apparatus.

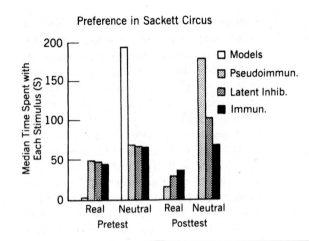

FIGURE 1
Median compartment times (in seconds) in the Sackett Circus for the fearful models at pretest and the pseudoimmunization, latent inhibition, and immunization groups at pretest and posttest, separately, for the real snake and for the neutral object (wood block).

6 of 8 observers showed virtually no sign of snake fear at posttest and follow-up, although the remaining 2 observers acquired and maintained high levels of snake fear. For this reason, Figure 1 illustrates the median, rather than mean, compartment times with the real snake and neutral stimulus for the three observer groups during the pretest and posttest and for the fearful models during the pretest. To illustrate the bimodal nature of the results for the immunization group, Table 5 shows the responses of individual immunization observers to the real snake during posttest and follow-up in both the Circus and the WGTA.

WGTA. Food-reach latencies during pretest, posttest, and follow-up were analyzed by a 3 × 3 × 4 (Groups × Tests × Stimulus Objects) mixed-design ANOVA. There were significant main effects for tests, $F(1, 21) = 22.93$, and objects, $F(1, 21) = 35.52$, and a significant Tests × Objects interaction, $F(1, 21) = 14.09$. Again, although the three-way Groups × Tests × Objects interaction was not significant, the planned comparison for

TABLE 5 Responses of Individual Immunization Monkeys to the Real Snake during Posttest and Follow-Up in the WGTA and Circus

	Dependent measure					
	WGTA Latency		WGTA Disturbance Behavior		Circus Compartment Time	
Subject	Posttest	Follow-up	Posttest	Follow-up	Posttest	Follow-up
Z79	7.2	4.5	1	0	57.4	73.3
AG46	4.0	5.7	0	0	53.5	50.7
AE14	15.4	10.4	2	2	36.9	55.8
AC38	10.1	7.2	0	1	34.1	49.3
AC30	40.3	45.8	3	2	48.5	70.5
AF63	47.6	41.1	2	1	36.5	75.3
AH80	120.0	120.0	12	10	6.5	9.3
AG19	120.0	120.0	10	9	9.6	7.3

Note. Maximum latency score possible = 120 s; maximum disturbance behavior score possible = 72. Sackett Circus posttest scores were averaged across the three posttests. WGTA = Wisconsin General Test Apparatus.

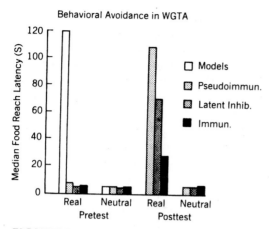

FIGURE 2

Median food-reach latencies (in seconds) in the Wisconsin General Test Apparatus (WGTA) for the fearful models at pretest and the pseudoimmunization, latent inhibition, and immunization groups at pretest and posttest, separately, for the real snake and for the neutral objects (black and yellow cords and wood blocks).

WGTA latency (same formula as for the Circus planned comparison) was significant, $F(1, 21) = 6.87$. Post-hoc comparisons (see Tables 3 and 4) reflected a pattern similar to that found with Circus compartment time: Pseudoimmunization and latent inhibition observers showed longer food-reach latencies to snake stimuli than to neutral stimuli at posttest (i.e., an increase in fear of snakes relative to the pretest); the immunization observers continued to show short latencies to all stimuli at posttest. This pattern was maintained at follow-up. Additionally, there were significant group differences at posttest in WGTA latency. Specifically, pseudoimmunization observers exhibited significantly longer latencies (more fear) than immunization observers for the snake stimuli. Latent inhibition observers displayed intermediate latencies that were not significantly different from those of the other two groups. Figure 2 illustrates the median WGTA latencies for the real snake and neutral stimulus for the three observer groups during the pretest and posttest and for the fearful models during the pretest.

Observer disturbance behavior was ana-

lyzed by a 3 × 3 × 4 (Groups × Tests × Stimulus Objects) mixed-design ANOVA. The analysis revealed significant main effects for tests and objects, $Fs(1, 21) = 33.89$ and 36.78, respectively. There were also significant Groups × Tests and Tests × Objects two-way interactions, $Fs(1, 21) = 3.09$ and 20.19, respectively, and a significant Groups × Tests × Objects three-way interaction, $F(1, 21) = 2.19$. Additionally, the planned comparison for this dependent measure was significant, $F(1, 21) = 9.82$. Post-hoc comparisons (see Tables 3 and 4) again revealed acquired snake fear, indicated by the greater number of fear behaviors elicited by snake stimuli relative to neutral stimuli during the posttest for the pseudoimmunization and latent inhibition groups, but not the immunization group. This pattern was maintained at follow-up. Additionally, as in the case of WGTA latency, there were significant group differences at posttest. Pseudoimmunization observers exhibited significantly more disturbance behaviors than latent inhibition and immunization observers for the toy snakes. Figure 3 illustrates the median num-

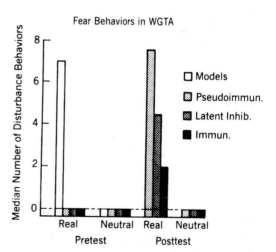

FIGURE 3

Median levels of disturbance behaviors in the Wisconsin General Test Apparatus (WGTA) for the fearful models at pretest and the pseudoimmunization, latent inhibition, and immunization groups at pretest and posttest, separately, for the real snake and for the neutral objects (black and yellow cords and wood blocks).

ber of disturbance behaviors in the WGTA for the real snake and neutral stimulus for the three observer groups during the pretest and posttest and for the fearful models during the pretest.

Relation between Performance During Observational Conditioning and Posttests

There was a great deal of variability in the level of snake fear acquired by observers. For example, 6 of 8 immunization observers and 1 of 8 latent inhibition observers showed only minimal signs of observational conditioning. Mineka et al. (1984) and Cook et al. (1985), using an observational condi-

tioning paradigm identical to the one used in the present experiment, noted that a significant amount of variability in level of observer snake fear at posttest could be accounted for by the behavior of the *models* during observational conditioning. For example, collapsing across Experiments 1 and 2 of Cook et al. (1985), the level of model disturbance behavior during conditioning was positively correlated with level of observer disturbance behavior during the WGTA posttest, $r(16) = .76$ (i.e., higher fear displayed by models during conditioning was associated with higher fear displayed by observers during the WGTA posttest).

To help uncover the source of individual differences in learning, the present experi-

TABLE 6 Intercorrelations between Model and Observer Performance during Observational Conditioning and Observer Performance during WGTA and Circus Posttests

Dependent Measure	Observational Conditioning		Posttests		
	Model Disturbance Behavior	Observer Disturbance Behavior	Circus Time	WGTA Latency	WGTA Disturbance Behavior
Model latency during conditioning					
Latent inhibition	.84	.48	−.22	.14	.40
Immunization	.81	.27	−.19	.25	.32
Pseudoimmunization	.79				
		.77	−.71	.60	.62
Model disturbance behavior during conditioning					
Latent inhibition	—	.33	−.16	−.18	.09
Immunization	—	−.23	.35	−.25	−.24
Pseudoimmunization					
	—	.84	−.30	.63	.52
Observer disturbance behavior during conditioning					
Latent inhibition	—	—	−.41	.72	.94
Immunization	—	—	−.83	.73	.83
Pseudoimmunization					
	—	—	−.51	.49	.51

Note. All measures were collapsed over the three snake stimuli, ignoring the neutral stimuli. Observational conditioning measures were collapsed over the six conditioning sessions. Sackett Circus posttest scores were averaged across the three posttests. WGTA = Wisconsin General Test Apparatus.

ment employed the same correlational approach. Measures in the analysis were (a) three observer posttest measures (WGTA food-reach latencies and disturbance behaviors, and Circus compartment times); (b) observer disturbance behaviors during observational conditioning; and (c) model latencies and disturbance behaviors during observational conditioning. All measures were collapsed across the three snake stimuli (ignoring the neutral stimuli), and Circus posttest and observational conditioning measures were also collapsed across their individual sessions. Separate correlation matrices were calculated for each of the three observer groups. The results are summarized in Table 6.

As noted previously, each model was paired with more than one observer. Because a model's performance for one observer was not independent of his/her performance with the other observers, application of tests of significance to the obtained correlation coefficients were not appropriate in a strict sense. (For reference purposes, $r(6) \geq .71$ is significant, $\alpha = .05$.) Several conclusions emerge from the data:

First, for the pseudoimmunization group, there were moderately strong relations between measures of model performance during observational conditioning and measures of observer performance during conditioning and the posttests. For example, model fear levels during conditioning were positively correlated with observer levels of disturbance during conditioning, $rs(6) \geq .77$. In addition, model latencies during conditioning were positively correlated with pseudoimmunization observer latencies and disturbances during posttests, $rs(6) \geq .60$, and negatively correlated with pseudoimmunization Circus compartment times during posttests, $r(6) = -.71$. (In each case higher model fear was associated with higher pseudoimmunization observer fear.) For the latent inhibition and immunization groups, the comparable correlations were much weaker. For example, model fear during observational conditioning was not strongly related either to observer disturbance during

conditioning, $rs(6) \leq |.48|$, or to observer fear during the posttests, $rs(6) \leq |.40|$.

By contrast, the relationship between *observer* disturbance behavior during observational conditioning and fear during WGTA posttests was stronger for the latent inhibition and immunization groups than for the pseudoimmunization group. For the pseudoimmunization group, $rs(6) \leq .51$; for the latent inhibition group, $rs(6) \geq .72$; and for the immunization group, $rs(6) \geq .73$. In other words, observer fear during observational conditioning was more predictive of fear during the posttest for the latent inhibition and immunization groups than for the pseudoimmunization group.

Discussion

The results of the present experiment provide strong support for the hypothesis that prior exposure to a model behaving nonfearfully with snake stimuli can serve to immunize monkeys against the effects of later exposure to a different model behaving fearfully with snake stimuli. Six out of 8 monkeys in the immunization group showed little or no sign of acquisition of snake fear following the observational conditioning procedure. This is in spite of the fact that an identical procedure has been effective in conditioning fear for 70%–85% of monkeys in other experiments (Cook et al., 1985; Mineka et al., 1984; the pseudoimmunization group of the present experiment). That the immunization group was immunized against the observational conditioning of snake fear was most evident in the analyses that looked for differential responding to the snake and neutral stimuli in the WGTA and Circus at pretest, posttest, and follow-up. Such comparisons showed that the immunization group did not respond differentially to snake and nonsnake stimuli at any of these three stages and did not show significant changes in responding to snake stimuli across the three tests. If snake fear had been acquired and maintained, differential responding to snake versus neutral stimuli should have been exhibited at posttest and follow-up as it was in the latent inhibition and pseudoimmunization groups.

Ideally, support for the effectiveness of the immunization procedure would also be found in significant between-groups comparisons at posttest and/or follow-up for the snake stimuli. The present analyses provided partial support for this prediction as well. The immunization group showed shorter food-reach latencies during the WGTA posttest with all three snake stimuli than did the pseudoimmunization group and fewer disturbance behaviors than did the pseudoimmunization group during toy snake presentations. That more significant group differences did not emerge seems attributable to the fact that 2 of the 8 subjects in the immunization group did show substantial observational conditioning of snake fear.

By contrast, the effectiveness of a latent inhibition pretreatment involving a period of exposure to snake stimuli equal to that received by the immunization group, but without a nonfearful model, did not significantly reduce the effects of observational conditioning. The latent inhibition group did show differential responding to snake and nonsnake stimuli at posttest and follow-up and did show changes in responding to snake stimuli from pretest to posttest and follow-up. They did not show significantly less fear than the pseudoimmunization group on any of the three indices of fear at posttest and follow-up (except for showing fewer disturbance behaviors at posttest in the presence of the toy snakes than the pseudoimmunization group). Nevertheless, Figures 1–3 all suggest that the level of acquired fear in the latent inhibition group was somewhat less than in the pseudoimmunization group and that with a larger number of subjects significant effects of latent inhibition on retarding fear acquisition might have emerged. Furthermore, it should also be noted that, unlike the pseudoimmunization group, the latent inhibition group never differed significantly from the immunization group at posttest or follow-up. This again

suggests indirectly that the latent inhibition pretreatment had a small but nonsignificant effect on reducing the level of acquired fear.

Summarizing the discussion thus far, the present results do not provide a definitive answer to the question of whether exposure to a model behaving nonfearfully with snake stimuli is more effective than simple exposure to snake stimuli alone in retarding subsequent observational conditioning. The present results do suggest that the immunization procedure with a nonfearful model does effectively immunize a majority of subjects and that the latent inhibition procedure does not significantly interfere with conditioning, at least using the present procedures. However, at least in part because of large within-group variability for the immunization group, one cannot conclusively state that the immunization procedure is more effective than the latent inhibition procedure. This is somewhat reminiscent of findings in the behavior therapy literature, which often hint that modeling techniques are superior to straightforward exposure techniques. However, as reviewed in the introduction, these results are inconsistent and, when combined together, do not provide convincing evidence for the therapeutic superiority of modeling. There is, however, one difference between the present results on immunization and those in the therapy literature. In the behavior therapy literature, both modeling and straightforward exposure are generally found to be effective therapeutic techniques when compared with no-treatment control groups. By contrast, our immunization procedure essentially prevented learning in 6 of 8 subjects whereas the latent inhibition procedure did not have a significant effect on retarding learning.

Several other interesting aspects of the present results should also be noted. The question of the source of individual differences in the acquisition of fear has been of interest since the original report of Mineka et al. (1984) that only 5 of 6 adolescent/young adult monkeys acquired a fear of snakes after watching one of their parents behave fearfully with snakes. In that experiment, as well as in Experiment 1 of Cook et al. (1985), strong evidence was provided that the primary source of individual variability in the level of fear the observers acquired lies in how much fear the models exhibited during observational conditioning. For example, in both of those experiments, the total number of disturbance behaviors exhibited by the models over the course of conditioning was highly correlated ($rs \geq .95$) with the amount of fear exhibited by the observers in the WGTA posttest. In addition, as in the present experiment, Cook et al. (1985) monitored the level of disturbance behavior exhibited by observers during conditioning and found that this also was highly correlated with the model's level of fear during conditioning and with their own level of acquired fear in the posttest. Individual differences were also striking in the present experiment, especially for the immunization group in which 2 subjects showed no effects of immunization and 6 subjects were very effectively immunized. Examination of possible sources of these individual differences is therefore of considerable interest and, as seen below, raises some interesting questions about how the immunization procedure may be operating.

The results presented in Table 5 show that only one of the three groups in the present experiment—the pseudoimmunization group—showed a pattern of correlational results similar to that found by Mineka et al. (1984) and Cook et al. (1985). Interestingly, of the three groups in this experiment, the pseudoimmunization group was most analogous, in terms of treatment received, to the groups of the previous experiments. Thus, for the pseudoimmunization group, the models' level of fear during conditioning was strongly related to the observers' level of disturbance during conditioning ($rs \geq .77$) and to the observers' level of fear in the posttest ($rs \geq .52$, for the WGTA posttest), although the relationships were somewhat less strong than in the two previous experiments. By contrast, for the latent inhibition and immunization groups, the models' level of fear

during conditioning was generally unrelated to that of the observers, either during conditioning ($rs \leq |.48|$) or during the posttest ($rs \leq |.40|$). For these latter groups, only the observers' level of fear during conditioning was predictive of their fear during the posttest ($rs \geq .72$, for the WGTA posttest). Thus, it seems that one effect of the latent inhibition and immunization pretreatments was to weaken the effect that the model's fear had on the observer's fear during conditioning, leaving other unknown factors to determine how disturbed the observers became during conditioning.

A full understanding of the mechanisms underlying the immunization effect produced in this experiment will require further research. Nevertheless, the results do provide some possible answers to some of the questions raised in the introduction. In particular, they demonstrate that although observational conditioning can indeed be a very powerful method for acquiring new fears, prior learning experiences with that same stimulus can, indeed, interfere with the observational conditioning process. Thus, to the extent that analogous effects occur in humans, it becomes far less surprising that the concordance rate between the fears of parents and their children, or between the fears of people living in close proximity to one another, is not higher than has often been reported (see Emmelkamp, 1982, and Marks, 1987, for reviews). In addition, our results suggest that parents who are concerned that their children might acquire their own fears through observational conditioning may be able to prevent this from occurring. Again, assuming that analogous effects are likely to occur in humans, our results suggest that giving one's children extensive exposure to a nonfearful model interacting with one's feared object should frequently accomplish this immunization. The present results do not, of course, address the issue of how much prior exposure is necessary to immunize against differing amounts of observational conditioning experiences. Such interesting questions await future research.

References

BANDURA, A., BLANCHARD, E., AND RITTER, B. (1969). The relative efficacy of desensitization and modeling approaches for inducing behavioral, affective, and attitudinal changes. *Journal of Personality and Social Psychology, 13*, 173–199.

BANDURA, A., GRUSEC, J., AND MENLOVE, F. (1967). Vicarious extinction of avoidance behavior. *Journal of Personality and Social Psychology, 5*, 16–23.

BARRIOS, B., AND SHIGETOMI, C. (1980). Coping skills training: Potential for prevention of fears and anxieties. *Behavior Therapy, 11*, 431–439.

BOURQUE, P., AND LADOUCEUR, R. (1980). An investigation of various performance-based treatments with acrophobics. *Behaviour Research and Therapy, 18*, 161–170.

COOK, M., MINEKA, S., WOLKENSTEIN, B., AND LAITSCH, K. (1985). Observational conditioning of snake fear in unrelated rhesus monkeys. *Journal of Abnormal Psychology, 94*, 591–610.

EMMELKAMP, P. (1982). *Phobic and obsessive-compulsive disorders: Theory, research, and practice.* New York: Plenum Press.

FOA, E., AND KOZAK, M. (1985). Treatment of anxiety disorders: Implications for psychopathology. In A. TUMA AND J. MASER (Eds.), *Anxiety and the anxiety disorders* (pp. 421–452). Hillsdale, NJ: Erlbaum.

GREENHOUSE, S., AND GEISSER, S. (1959). On methods in the analysis of profile data. *Psychometrika, 24*, 95–112.

HARLOW, H. (1949). The formation of learning sets. *Psychological Review, 56*, 51–65.

JAREMKO, M. (1978). Prophylactic systematic desensitization: An analogue test. *Journal of Behavior Therapy and Experimental Psychiatry, 9*, 5–9.

LANG, P. (1968). Fear reduction and fear behavior: Problems in treating a construct. In J. SHLEIN (Ed.), *Research in psychotherapy* (Vol. 3, pp. 90–102). Washington, DC: American Psychological Association.

LANG, P. (1971). The application of psychophysiological methods to the study of psychotherapy and behavior modification. In A. BERGIN AND S. GARFIELD (Eds.), *Handbook of psychotherapy and behavior change: An empirical analysis* (pp. 75–125). New York: Wiley.

LUBOW, R. (1973). Latent inhibition. *Psychological Bulletin, 79*, 398–407.

LUBOW, R., AND MOORE, A. (1959). Latent inhibition: The effect of nonreinforced preexposure to the conditioned stimulus. *Journal of Comparative and Physiological Psychology, 52*, 415–419.

MACKINTOSH, N. (1974). *The psychology of animal learning.* London: Academic Press.

MACKINTOSH, N. (1983). *Conditioning and associative learning.* New York: Oxford University Press.

MARKS, I. (1987). *Fears, phobias, and rituals.* London: Oxford University Press.

MELAMED, B., AND SIEGEL, L. (1975). Reduction of anxiety in children facing hospitalization and surgery by use of filmed modeling. *Journal of Consulting and Clinical Psychology, 43*, 511–521.

MELAMED, B., YURCHESON, R., FLEECE, E., HUTCHERSON, S., AND HAWES, R. (1978). Effects of film modeling on the reduction of anxiety-related behaviors in individuals varying in level of previous experience in the stress situation. *Journal of Consulting and Clinical Psychology, 46*, 1357–1367.

MINEKA, S. (1985a). Animal models of anxiety-based disorders: Their usefulness and limitations. In A. TUMA AND J. MASER (Eds.), *Anxiety and the anxiety disorders* (pp. 199–244). New York: Erlbaum.

MINEKA, S. (1985b). The frightful complexity of the origins of fears. In F. BRUSH AND J. OVERMIER (Eds.), *Affect, conditioning, and cognition: Essays on the determinants of behavior* (pp. 55–73). Hillsdale, NJ: Erlbaum.

MINEKA, S., DAVIDSON, M., COOK, M., AND KEIR, R. (1984). Observational conditioning of snake fear in rhesus monkeys. *Journal of Abnormal Psychology, 93*, 355–372.

MINEKA, S., GUNNAR, M., AND CHAMPOUX, M. (in press). The effects of control in the early social and emotional development of rhesus monkeys. *Child Development.*

MINEKA, S., AND HENDERSEN, R. (1985). Controllability and predictability in acquired motivation. *Annual Review of Psychology, 36*, 495–530.

MINEKA, S., AND KEIR, R. (1983). The effects of flooding on reducing snake fear in rhesus monkeys: 6-month follow-up and further flooding. *Behaviour Research and Therapy, 21*, 527–535.

MINEKA, S., KEIR, R., AND PRICE, V. (1980). Fear of snakes in wild- and lab-reared rhesus monkeys. *Animal Learning and Behavior, 8*, 653–663.

PAVLOV, I. (1927). *Conditioned reflexes.* London: Oxford University Press.

POSER, E., AND KING, M. (1975). Strategies for the prevention of maladaptive fear responses. *Canadian Journal of Behavior Science, 7,* 279–294.

RACHMAN, S. (1985). The treatment of anxiety disorders: A critique of implications for psychopathology. In A. TUMA AND J. MASER (Eds.), *Anxiety and the anxiety disorders* (pp. 453–461). Hillsdale, NJ: Erlbaum.

RESCORLA, R. (1975). Pavlovian excitatory and inhibitory conditioning. In W. ESTES (Ed.), *Handbook of learning and cognitive processes* (Vol. 2, pp. 7–35). Hillsdale, NJ: Erlbaum.

RESCORLA, R., AND LOLORDO, V. (1965). Inhibition of avoidance behavior. *Journal of Comparative and Physiological Psychology, 59,* 406–412.

SACKETT, G. (1970). Unlearned responses, differential rearing experiences, and the development of social attachments by rhesus monkeys. In L. ROSENBLUM (Ed.), *Primate behavior: Development in field and laboratory research* (Vol. 1, pp. 112–140). New York: Academic Press.

SACKETT, G. (1978). Measurement in observational research. In G. SACKETT (Ed.), *Observing behavior: Vol. 2, Data collection and analysis methods* (pp. 25–43). Baltimore: University Park Press.

SELIGMAN, M. (1975). *Helplessness: On depression, and development, and death.* San Francisco: W. H. Freeman.

SELIGMAN, M., AND BINIK, Y. (1977). The safety-signal hypothesis. In H. DAVIS (Ed.), *Operant-Pavlovian interactions* (pp. 165–180). Hillsdale, NJ: Erlbaum.

WAGNER, A., AND RESCORLA, R. (1972). Inhibition in Pavlovian conditioning: Application of a theory. In R. BOAKES AND M. HALLIDAY (Eds.), *Inhibition and learning* (pp. 301–336). New York: Academic Press.

35

Differential Effects of Experiential and Problem-Solving Interventions in Resolving Marital Conflict

Susan M. Johnson and
Leslie S. Greenberg

The present study compared the relative effectiveness of two interventions in the treatment of marital discord: a cognitive–behavioral intervention, teaching problem-solving skills, and an experiential intervention, focusing on emotional experiences underlying interaction patterns. Forty-five couples seeking therapy were randomly assigned to one of these treatments or to a wait-list control group. Each treatment was administered in eight sessions by six experienced therapists whose interventions were monitored and rated to ensure treatment fidelity. Results indicated that the perceived strength of the working alliance between couples and therapists and general therapist effectiveness were equivalent across treatment groups and that both treatment groups made significant gains over untreated groups on measures of goal attainment, marital adjustment, intimacy levels, and target complaint reduction. Furthermore, the effects of the emotionally focused treatment were superior to those of the problem-solving treatment on marital adjustment, intimacy, and target complaint level. At follow-up, marital adjustment scores in the emotionally focused group were still significantly higher than those in the problem-solving group.

Susan M. Johnson and Leslie S. Greenberg. Differential Effects of Experiential and Problem-Solving Interventions in Resolving Marital Conflict. *Journal of Consulting and Clinical Psychology*, 1985, Vol. 53, No. 2, pp. 175–184. Copyright © 1985 by the American Psychological Association. Reprinted by permission of the publisher and the authors.

The more dynamic approaches to marital therapy seem to have produced much practice but little research and have made unique contributions to the understanding of relationship processes but not to the technology of treatment interventions (Gurman, 1978). These approaches have tended in practice to be eclectic and pragmatic rather than rigorous in the specification of interventions designed to modify marital interactions. Jacobson (1978a) suggested that it is crucial for other approaches to follow the example set by their behavioral colleagues and to specify and empirically validate their interventions.

Considerable attention has recently been given to the role of affect in psychotherapy in general (Greenberg & Safran, 1984; Mahoney, 1984; Rachman, in press) and in marital therapy in particular (Fincham & O'Leary, 1982; Margolin & Weinstein, 1983).

It is becoming increasingly clear that a complete approach to therapy needs to deal not only with cognitive and behavioral processes but also with affective processes. The experiential and dynamic approaches focus extensively on affective processes but have not always clearly specified the interventions used. This is particularly true in experiential marital therapy. A set of affective interventions was therefore specified in order to test the efficacy of an integrated affective systemic approach to marital therapy (Greenberg & Johnson, 1987).

Most of the comparative research in marital therapy has been concerned with comparing the effectiveness of different components of the behavioral approach. The one nonanalogue study comparing behavioral interventions with another form of therapy is that of Liberman, Levine, Wheeler, Sanders, and Wallace (1976), who compared the effects of communication training plus contingency contracting group interventions and an insight approach. Results were inconclusive; both groups improved on self-report measures, but only the behavioral group improved on problem-solving skills. Methodological problems such as the lack of a control group, no random assignment, and a small therapist sample biased in favor of the behavioral treatment makes even these inconclusive results tentative.

The present study was implemented to evaluate an emotionally focused treatment (EF) according to a treatment manual (Greenberg & Johnson, 1987) and to compare the effectiveness of this treatment with an untreated wait-list control (C) and the problem-solving (PS) intervention outlined by Jacobson and Margolin (1979). This PS treatment seems to epitomize the present behavioral approach to marital therapy, which includes cognitive components, and has been extensively and rigorously researched during the last decade (Jacobson, 1977, 1978b, 1979).

Thus, couples seeking assistance for problems in conflictual relationships were randomly assigned to one of the two treatment groups (EF or PS) and to one of the six therapists implementing each treatment or to the wait-list control group. Treated couples received eight sessions of conjoint marital therapy and were measured at assessment, after treatment, and at 2-month follow-up. Control groups were assessed after a 2-month waiting period and then were treated.

Method

Subjects

Couples requesting counseling in response to a newspaper article were screened by phone and in an assessment interview. The article described the research project as one that provided counseling for couples to help them resolve problems and gave a phone number to call. To be included, couples had to be presently living together and to have been cohabiting for a minimum of 1 year, to have no immediate plans for divorce, to have received no psychiatric treatment within the last 2 years, to be free of alcohol or drug problems and primary sexual dysfunction, not to be presently involved in other psychologically oriented treatment, and at least one partner had to score in the distressed range (under 100) on the Dyadic Adjustment Scale (DAS; Spanier, 1976).

Two couples were excluded because they had been living together less than a year; five couples were excluded because they had already separated and were living apart; seven couples were excluded because they had recently been or were currently receiving psychiatric treatment for problems such as depression; two couples were excluded because one of the partners was reportedly alcoholic; three couples were excluded because they reported their marital problem as primarily involving sexual dysfunction; six couples were excluded during the assessment interview because their scores on the DAS were above the criteria set for distress; three couples were excluded because of their extremely low DAS scores, that is, a couple score of 65 and below (Spanier, 1976, reports 70 as the mean for divorced couples);

two couples objected to the taping of sessions; and one couple was excluded because of extensive upcoming vacations.

Forty-five couples entered the study, 15 in each treatment group and 15 in the control group. The mean length of partnerships was 8.6 years (range = 1–24 years), and the average educational level of spouses was 15 years. There was an average of 1.75 children per family (range = 0–7 children), and 22% of the spouses had been married previously. Seven couples had received previous marital therapy. When these demographic variables were analyzed, no significant differences were found among the three groups.

Therapists

Twelve therapists participated. Six therapists (two men and four women) administered each treatment. Therapists in both groups possessed an average of 4 years clinical experience that included marital therapy implemented within the framework of the model they used in this study. All therapists were trained in and professed an orientation congruent with the model of therapy they were asked to implement. All therapists had at least a master's degree in clinical or counseling psychology or in social work. Each group of therapists was given 12 hr of additional training by an experienced trainer in the implementation of the therapy manual describing the approach they were using. Therapists were also given brief telephone consultations and 2 hr of group supervision during the study; both groups received the same amount of assistance.

Measures

The Test of Emotional Styles (ES: Allen & Hamsher, 1974). This test measures three factors of emotional style, Orientation, Expressiveness, and Responsiveness, and was used to check for group equivalence on these three factors in order to ensure that treatment effects would not be confounded with a group bias toward emotional experience. Allen and Hamsher reported convergent and divergent validity and internal consistency data; reliability for the three factors just listed were .92, .90, and .85, respectively.

The Couples Therapy Alliance Scale (AS: Pinsof & Catherall, 1983). This instrument was completed by each client in private after the third therapy session and is a measure of the client's view of the therapeutic relationship, based on the work of Bordin (1979). The measure contains three components: bond between therapist and client, agreement as to therapeutic goals, and engagement in tasks relevant to the process of therapy. These three components are viewed in relation to Self, Other, and the Relationship in three separate subscales. The client responds to the 28 items on a Likert-type 5-point scale. This instrument was intended to control for the relationship factors that have been shown to be important in predicting therapeutic outcomes. Because it is still in the process of revision, item analyses were conducted, and the reliability (internal consistency) for this sample was .96 for the total test and .88, .92, and .85, respectively, for each of the subtests (Self, Other, and Relationship).

Dyadic Adjustment Scale (Spanier, 1976). This widely used self-report questionnaire can be scored as an index of global marital adjustment (total score) or can be broken down into four subscales, Consensus (13 items), Satisfaction (10 items), Cohesion (5 items), and Affectional Expression (4 items). It is at present the instrument of choice for the assessment of marital adjustment in terms of reliability and validity. Spanier reports a reliability of .96 (Cronbach's alpha). Most items involve a 5- or 6-point Likert-type scale defining the amount of agreement or frequency of an event. When subjected to an item analysis the reliability (internal consistency) for the total test for this sample (N = 45) was .84, and the subtest reliabilities were .73, .78, .79, and .58, respectively.

Target Complaints (TC; Battle et al., 1966). This measure was recommended by

Waskow and Parloff (1975) as a core battery instrument for use in outcome research and consists of a 5-point scale on which each client is asked to rate the amount of change on the presenting problem. Battle et al. gave evidence as to the validity and reliability of this measure and reported a reliability (test–retest) of .68.

Goal Attainment Scaling (GAS; Kiresuk & Sherman, 1968).

This procedure is a means of obtaining from clients specific, observable, and qualifiable individual goals for therapy and of measuring the attainment of these goals. Five levels of attainment—worse than expected results, less than expected results, expected results, somewhat better than expected results, and much better than expected results—were specified during assessment in terms of three specific behaviors and one emotional response.

The Personal Assessment of Intimacy in Relationships Inventory (PAIR; Schaefer & Olson, 1981).

This instrument consists of 36 items arranged in six subscales, Emotional, Social, Sexual, Intellectual, and Recreational Intimacy, and Conventionality; this last subscale was designed to measure social desirability factors. The test was constructed so that a difference score is obtained between perceived and expected levels of intimacy, but only the perceived scores were used in this study. Couples indicate agreement or disagreement on a 5-point Likert-type scale. Schaefer and Olson (1981) reported reliabilities for all subtests in the .70 range. The reliabilities for this sample were .69, .64, .79, .57, .72, and .67, respectively. As suggested by Clayton (1975), the Conventionality subscale was viewed in this study as a measure of functional relationship idealization.

A posttreatment interview was conducted to gather descriptive data as to how couples experienced the process of therapy. Control couples completed an Activities While Waiting Questionnaire to check for other possible therapeutic factors that might have occurred during the waiting period.

Manipulation Checks

To ensure treatment validity, the interventions used by the therapists in the treatment sessions were monitored and rated by two trained graduate student raters who viewed the videotapes of selected sessions and who were not informed as to which treatment they were observing. The raters categorized the therapist interventions into the categories of the implementation checklist that was devised for this study.

This checklist comprises six categories of interventions. One category contains 3 general interventions that were common to both treatments, such as information gathering. The five other categories were problem definition, dealing with attacking behavior, facilitating listening, directing the process of therapy, and facilitating problem resolution. In these five categories, 10 differential interventions taken from each of the two treatment manuals were described; for example, contrasting interventions in the problem-definition category might be (a) the therapist defines the problem in terms of emotions underlying interactional positions (EF) or (b) the therapist defines the problem in terms of manifest behaviors and lack of skill (PS).

Two 10-min segments from the middle and final third of 120 sessions were observed and rated. These sessions were selected randomly from the total 240 sessions. Each couple was thus observed for 80 min during therapy. An intervention was defined as a complete therapist statement; in all, 1,866 interventions were coded. Of these, only 47 (2.5%) were coded in categories that were inappropriate to the treatment condition being observed. Interrater reliability was calculated on 406 observations (20.8%) taken from 25 randomly chosen sessions. The two raters agreed on 93% of the interventions observed. Cohen's kappa (1960), which considers the proportion of agreement after chance agreement has been removed from consideration, was .99 for cross-treatment agreements and .95 for interventions within treatments. These statistics suggest that the treatments were implemented according to the treatment manuals and were able to be differentiated easily and reliably.

Procedure

After telephone screening and assessment interviews, couples were informed of research requirements and were given pretests. Treatment couples were randomly assigned to treatment and therapist and were seen weekly for eight 1-hr sessions. All sessions were videotaped and audiotaped. Couples completed the Alliance Scale after the third session. At the end of treatment or the waiting period, couples were reassessed; treatment couples were informed of the follow-up procedures, and wait-list couples were assigned to a therapist for treatment. Treatment couples were contacted by phone 8 weeks after termination, and follow-up questionnaires were sent to them in the mail. There were no dropouts from this study. This unusual lack of attrition may be due to the excellent quality of the therapists in this study and the alliance ($M = 117.45$, maximum possible $= 140$) they were able to create with their clients.

Experimental Conditions

The problem-solving treatment used in this study is based on the concept that couples may be taught to become more skilled at negotiation and positive control strategies so that coercive tactics will be unnecessary and also may be taught to control the negative communication practices that have become habits in their relationship. Although this approach is concerned with teaching behavior management, there is also a focus on the enhancement of positive exchanges. As Margolin and Weinstein (1983) pointed out, such a skill-oriented stance places a value on rational rather than emotional processes, the expression of feeling being confined in therapy mostly to the clarification of the impact of one partner's behavior on the other. Rules for effective communication, problem definition, and problem solution, including the making of contractual agreements, are taught, modeled, and rehearsed. Problems are defined in terms of specific manifest behaviors, and couples are taught communication skills, such as paraphrasing, that help them to manage conflict in their relationship. The therapist's role is mainly that of teacher and coach. The treatment manual for this intervention may be found in Jacobson and Margolin (1979). The effectiveness of this treatment as opposed to other components of the behavioral approach, such as contingency contracting, has been demonstrated (Jacobson, 1977).

The emotionally focused treatment represents an integrated affective systemic approach to marital therapy (Greenberg & Johnson, in press) and is based on the experiential tradition of psychotherapy, which emphasizes the role of affect and intrapsychic experience in change (Gendlin, 1974; Greenberg & Safran, 1984; Perls, Hefferline, & Goodman, 1951; Rogers, 1951), and the systemic tradition, which emphasizes the role of communication and interactional cycles in the maintenance of problem states (Sluzki, 1978; Watzlawick, Beavin, & Jackson, 1967). In this model, clients are viewed as active perceivers constructing meanings on the basis of their current emotional state and experiential organization and are seen as having healthy needs and wants that can emerge in the safety of the therapeutic environment. It is not partner's feelings and wants that are considered the problem, but rather the disowning, or disallowing, of these experiences that leads to ineffective communication and escalating interactional cycles.

From this perspective, problems are seen as being maintained by self-sustaining, reciprocal, negative interaction patterns, the most basic of which appears to be a pursuer–distancer or attack–withdraw pattern that springs from and sustains each partner's distress and negative perceptions of the other.

The therapist in this approach therefore identifies the negative interaction cycles and guides the couple in accessing the unacknowledged feelings underlying each person's position in this cycle. Particular attention is paid to underlying vulnerabilities, fears, and unexpressed resentments. This process of accessing and expressing previously unacknowledged feelings is to be distinguished from the ventilation of superficial or defensive reactions and from talking about feelings on a rational level; it is a synthesis of new emotional experience in the present (Greenberg & Safran, 1984). The therapist uses the methods of Gestalt therapy and innovations from client-centered therapy (Rice, 1974) to access and heighten specific underlying responses. The therapist then reframes the problem in terms of these emotional responses and encourages clients to identify with their disowned feelings and needs and to accept and respond to their partner's needs. Finally, the therapist helps the couple to consolidate their new positions in relation to their partner and focuses on the strengthening of trust and intimacy that arises from this process. The treatment goal here is the creation of a new emotional experience to promote new interactional positions.

The wait-list control group was told that a therapist could not be assigned to them at present and that there would be a maximum required wait of 8 weeks before the treatment could begin. At the end of 7 weeks clients in the group were contacted, and a time was set for a reassessment of the present status of the relationships and the first therapy session. The Activities While Waiting Questionnaire was given to monitor other possible therapeutic activities during this period, such as reading self-help books, and a minimal amount of such potentially therapeutic activity was reported.

Results

Preliminary analyses consisted of item and test analyses as well as tests for group equivalence on demographic variables and the Test of Emotional Styles. No significant group differences were found on the three subscales of this test for male or female spouses. Also, no significant differences were found between the means of the two treatment groups

on any of the subscales or on the total score for the alliance measure ($p < .20$). These results suggest that both groups had therapeutic alliances of a similar quality and found the treatments equally relevant to their concerns. Differential therapist effects were also tested by a series of one-way analyses of variance (ANOVAS; Therapist × Individual Score on Each Postmeasure) in which therapists were treated as a fixed factor. The critical signifiance level corrected by the Bonferroni procedure (Hays, 1981) would be .0027, however these results were not significant even at the .01 level. Thus, there was no evidence of differential therapist performance.

Pretreatment Measures

Preliminary univariate analyses on all DAS and PAIR subscales and an overall multivariate test found no significant differences between groups, $F(20, 68) = .83$, $p < .66$. Total adjustment scores (DAS) for couples, not included in the multivariate analysis of variance (MANOVA) because of lack of independence, were not significantly different in the three experimental groups, $F(2, 42) = .06$, $p < .94$. The mean on this variable for the couples in the EF group was 92.8 ($SD = 8.8$); for PS couples the mean was 91.7 ($SD = 8.1$) and for the controls 91.9 ($SD = 10.7$). Couples' distress level was then consistent across groups.

Treatment Effects

Because the total DAS score could not be included in a multivariate analysis, an ANOVA was conducted, $F(2, 42) = 16.79$, $p < .001$, and post hoc comparisons using Tukey's procedure found that all groups were significantly different from each other.

The results of a MANOVA conducted on treatment outcome variables are presented in Table 1. The overall F statistic was as follows: $F(24, 64) = 1.24$, $p < .001$. To guard against the problem of escalating Type I error rate, the Bonferroni procedure was used to calculate the critical significance level for each univariate test. After post hoc Tukey statistics

TABLE 1 Multivariate Analysis of Variance: Means for Treatment Outcome Variables

Variable	Group			
	EF	PS	C	F(2, 42)
DAS				
Consensus	48.13	47.53	40.8	8.25*
Satisfaction	38.43	34.10	31.70	8.60*
Cohesion	17.27	13.80	11.90	13.91*
Affectional expression	8.87	7.0	7.13	5.12
PAIR				
Emotional	64.13	51.33	45.60	4.68
Social	65.33	56.40	52.26	2.74
Sexual	69.33	62.80	59.06	0.92
Intellectual	70.26	58.66	43.33	20.29*
Recreational	72.0	64.67	57.27	3.98
Conventionality	64.80	45.07	38.40	7.74*
TC	3.70	3.07	1.17	69.89*
GAS	60.0	57.33	42.33	31.11*

Note. EF = emotionally focused, PS = problem solving, C = wait-list control, DAS = Dyadic Adjustment Scale, PAIR = Personal Assessment of Intimacy in Relationships Inventory, TC = Target Complaints, GAS = Goal Attainment Scaling.   *$p < .001$.

were calculated on each variable with a significant *F* ratio, the results were as follows:

1. Both treatment group means were significantly higher than controls on the DAS subscale, Consensus; on TC and GAS; and on the PAIR subscale, Intellectual Intimacy.

2. Only the EF treatment group means were significantly different from controls on the DAS subscales, Satisfaction and Cohesion, and on the PAIR subscale, Conventionality.

3. The EF treatment group scored significantly higher than did the PS group on the total DAS score and on the DAS subscales, Satisfaction and Cohesion; on the PAIR subscales, Intellectual Intimacy and Conventionality (here interpreted as Idealization); and on TC improvement. Thus, the EF and PS groups did not differ significantly on the DAS subscale, Consensus, or on GAS, although both differed from controls on these measures.

Although the subscales Affectional Expression ($p < .01$) and Emotional Intimacy ($p < .015$) did not reach the .004 level of significance, the trend here was in favor of the EF treatment. The results at termination show both treatments are more effective than a wait-list control and also show differential effects consistently in favor of the EF treatment.

Follow-Up Measures

All treatment couples except one returned the follow-up data ($n = 29$). The focus of the follow-up was to determine whether differential effects found at treatment termination would also be found 8 weeks later. Because the total DAS score could not be included in a MANOVA, a repeated measures ANOVA was conducted, and a significant difference was found between groups, $F(1, 27) = 9.4, p < .005$. The mean for the EF group was 112.4 ($SD = 11.2$) and for the PS group, 101.1 ($SD = 8.9$). No significant time effect or Time × Group interaction was found.

The results of a repeated measures MANOVA conducted on the variables that differentiated between groups at the end of treatment, that is, on Satisfaction, Cohesion, Intellectual Intimacy, Conventionality, and TC, are shown in Table 2; the overall multivariate $F(5, 23) = 3.67$, $p < .014$. Thus, the general difference between groups found at treatment termination held at follow-up. The critical significance level for univariate statistics was set at .01 (Bonferroni correction). No significant time effect or Time × Group interaction was found. The Conventionality variable failed to differentiate between the two groups; the EF group appeared to regress on this variable ($p < .03$). The Intellectual Intimacy and TC variables just failed to reach significance at the .01 level ($p < .014$, for both). However, the EF

group means on the Satisfaction and Cohesion variables continued to be significantly higher ($p < .007$ and $p < .001$). This analysis was repeated after treatment with the variables that did not differentiate between treatments in order to check for sleeper effects; however, the multivariate F statistic was not significant. The group means at pretest, posttest, and follow-up assessment are presented in Figure 1.

Individual Analyses

Additional analyses were conducted on individual scores, and these are briefly reported here. No significant differences between groups were found on any of the pretreatment variables when male and female scores were considered separately. The additional information of interest given by these analyses is as follows: If posttreatment

TABLE 2 Repeated Measures Analysis: Follow-Up Mean Scores on Differentiating Variables

Variable	Time	Group EF (n = 15)	PS (n = 14)	F(1, 127)
DAS				
Satisfaction	1	38.6	34.0	8.48[a],*
	2	38.3	34.1	0.03[b]
				0.21[c]
Cohesion	1	17.6	13.9	15.89[a],*
	2	16.9	13.6	2.11[b]
				0.25[c]
TC	1	3.8	3.3	6.87[a]
	2	3.7	3.1	0.97[b]
				0.00[c]
PAIR				
Intellectual	1	70.3	58.3	6.87[a]
	2	68.7	58.6	0.06[b]
				0.12[c]
Conventionality	1	64.8	45.0	5.38[a]
	2	55.5	44.6	2.47[b]
				2.19[c]

Note. EF = emotionally focused, PS = problem solving, DAS = Dyadic Adjustment Scale, TC = Target Complaints, PAIR = Personal Assessment of Intimacy in Relationships Inventory. [a]Group F statistic. [b]Time F statistic. [c]Time × Group interaction. *$p < .01$.

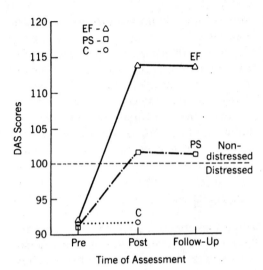

Figure 1

Group means on total Dyadic Adjustment Scale (DAS) scores at pretest, posttest, and follow-up. (EF = emotionally focused, PS = problem solving, C = wait-list control.)

total DAS scores are considered individually, only means for men were significantly different in all three groups; the EF mean was the highest and the control mean, the lowest; for women, both treatment group means were significantly higher than that for controls, but the difference among them was not significant. Significant differences between treatment groups for the variable Conventionality (interpreted as Idealization), which was significant in the analysis of couple scores, were found on male means only. For female partners only, Emotional Intimacy and Affectional Expression were significantly higher in the EF group; these variables did not reach significance in the couples analysis. Intellectual Intimacy did not differentiate between treatment groups in individual analyses, although significant differences were found between C and EF groups when female scores were considered and between both treatment groups and controls when male scores were considered. At follow-up, significant differences between groups were found on the DAS total scores when men and women were considered separately ($p < .006$ and $p < .011$, respectively); in both cases EF individual scores were higher. When female

scores were considered, Satisfaction and Cohesion failed to reach the critical level for significance, whereas the means for men were significantly different at the .01 level.

Descriptive Data

The main results of the posttreatment interview, which probed couples' experience of therapy, were that couples' experience of therapy was consistent with the two therapy manuals; clients in the PS group spoke of having more skills and engaging in negotiations more often, and those in the EF group spoke of experiencing underlying feelings and perceiving each other differently. The Activities While Waiting Questionnaire results for the control group suggested that the waiting period was uncontaminated by other significant therapeutic events. As to deterioration, there were no significant decreases of total DAS scores in the treatment groups; the largest drop from earlier scores was a drop of 7.5 computed on an EF couple at follow-up. One separation was reported after follow-up by a couple in the PS group, but this was by mutual consent and was amicable. If couples' posttreatment total DAS scores are viewed in terms of effect size (Smith & Glass, 1977), this statistic computes at 2.19 for the EF group and 1.12 for the PS group. The mean effect of the EF treatment in this sample is more than two standard deviations from the mean of the control group after the waiting period. Were couples nondistressed at the end of therapy? The mean total DAS score for the EF treatment couples after treatment ($M = 112.7$) is within 2 points of Spanier's norm for married couples ($M = 114.8$), and this level was the same at follow-up; also, seven of the EF couples scored above this norm at termination and follow-up. The mean for PS couples after treatment was 102.4, and for controls after the waiting period, 91.5.

Discussion

In this study, both treatments significantly improved the quality of dyadic relationships.

The study therefore replicates the past research on the effectiveness of the PS treatment, which in this study increased the total DAS level, as well as the amount of Consensus and Intellectual Intimacy between partners, and facilitated improvement in the Target Complaint that brought couples to therapy and the attainment of relationship goals, as measured by the GAS.

The results of this study demonstrate the effectiveness of the affective systemic emotionally focused treatment, which increased total DAS level and the Consensus, Satisfaction, and Cohesion elements of this scale, as well as the amount of Intellectual Intimacy and Conventionality (Idealization) between partners and facilitated improvement in TC and GAS. This suggests that focusing on inner experience as it is translated into relationship events during interaction may be a powerful tool for changing the nature of relationships.

Differential outcome effects for the two treatments were found. The results and the trends in these results were consistently in favor of the EF group. The EF group means were significantly higher on total DAS score, on the Satisfaction and Cohesion aspects of this score, on Intellectual Intimacy and Conventionality, and on TC improvement. At follow-up, the first three measures just mentioned continued to differentiate between groups.

It is interesting to note that the EF couples' improvement on Consensus and GAS was consistent with that made by PS couples even though these are variables that may be expected to be especially responsive to the PS treatment. This would seem to suggest that the EF treatment also had an effect on a couple's ability to negotiate and change specific behaviors in spite of the fact that these areas were not focused on in terms of skill training or contracting. It may be that the increase in trust and responsiveness, which is the goal of the EF treatment, has an effect in these areas. The clarification of positions taken in relation to each other may be as useful as training in negotiating rules. As Gurman suggested (1981), poor social skills in a relationship often reflect relationship rules of minimal disclosure and self-exposure.

The differential increase in Satisfaction and Cohesion attained by EF couples may reflect the fact that this treatment attempts to address what Gurman (1978) referred to as the felt needs of the couple directly, especially if positive affect is considered the most important characteristic of a good marriage, as Broderick (1981) suggested. Hahlweg, Schindler, Revenstorf, & Brengelmann (1984) found that the emotional-affective quality of the relationship predicted successful outcome in therapy and suggested that whereas a behavioral approach facilitates the improvement of manifest behaviors such as problem solving, it is perhaps less well suited to deal with the internal experiences affecting the emotional qualities of a marriage. The increased idealization of spouse and relationship found in the EF group seems in light of individual scores to be mainly a reflection of idealization on the part of the male spouses. It may be that because a man is generally less oriented toward emotion, the opportunity to access and express emotion results in a more positive and romantic estimation of his spouse. This effect would seem to be short lived because it was not found to be significant at follow-up. Intellectual Intimacy was also higher in the EF group, implying that the generation of openness and trust perhaps generalizes to the discussion of rational issues. The increased reduction of the TC in the EF group may be considered evidence for the importance of emotional experience in therapeutic change. If such experience provides a framework for the creation of meaning in a relationship and overrides other cues, then the modification of such experience directly addresses the sense of deprivation and pain that is reflected in the target complaint or core struggle.

The fact that assignment to treatment was random, that implementation was monitored, and that therapeutic alliance was consistent across groups adds credibility to the claim that differential effects in outcome were due to the interventions used rather than confounding factors such as client motivation or therapist and client relationship factors. The responses on the task dimension of the Alliance Scale, consistent across treatment groups, suggest that both treatments were equally credible and relevant to participants.

One potential limitation of this study was the use of the first author as one of the EF therapists. This author did not administer any posttests, however, and there are no data to suggest differential therapist effects or differential therapist–client alliances. Nevertheless, it would have been preferable to have kept these roles separate. Also, although every attempt was made to operationalize both treatments in a parallel and equitable fashion, the researchers were possibly biased toward the EF treatment because they had developed this treatment. To ensure external validity, this study should therefore be replicated by other investigators.

The mean level of distress for the couples in this study ($M = 92.1$, $SD = 9.1$, range $= 71–105$) on the pretest total DAS score suggests that this sample is most accurately considered as moderately distressed rather than severely distressed. However, as Jacobson, Follette, and Elwood (1984) pointed out, even though the inclusion of some mildly distressed couples may appear to ease the task of therapy, it also increases the difficulty of demonstrating treatment effects. The fact that couples were solicited also prompts a question as to how representative this sample was of a clinical population. However, most of the couples involved had considered or were considering separation, and all were willing to engage in tedious and demanding research procedures to obtain and complete treatment.

The fact that therapists are nested under treatment has disadvantages and advantages (O'Leary & Turkewitz, 1978). In light of the fact that no evidence exists for differential therapist effectiveness and the large number of therapists used (12), the advantages (the fact that all therapists were committed to and were trained in the approach they implemented and thus were more able to produce a pure sample of each therapy) appear to outweigh the disadvantages. No significant differences were found between the two groups of therapists on variables such as years of clinical experience or training or the quality of the relationship they were able to create with their clients as measured by the Alliance Scale (Pinsof & Catherall, 1983). However, because of the limited statistical power present in the analysis of differential therapist effects it is possible that treatment differences were in some way a reflection of the different sets of therapists.

The study could be viewed as being limited by the fact that all measures were self-report. However, this kind of measurement seems to be particularly appropriate in the sense that marital satisfaction or well-being is a qualitative, subjective factor rather than an externally quantifiable phenomena, and thus it is the perception of behaviors that is salient to marital satisfaction. Also, in recent studies, Jacobson et al. (1984) suggested that observational coding systems are relatively insensitive to relationship changes produced during behavioral marital therapy. The Goal Attainment measure could be viewed as more objective in that it was specifically tied to observable behaviors, although the individual still subjectively judged whether those behaviors did in fact occur in the relationship. The difficulty of attaining relevant objective measures is also an issue in this field, and it has been suggested that use of coding measures will be justified only when it has been demonstrated that such systems measure constructs that are not adequately measured by less expensive means (Jacobson et al., 1984).

Concerning the issue of social desirability factors on measures such as the PAIR and the DAS, it is logical to presume that any demand characteristics were randomly distributed across both groups and therefore were not confounded with differences between groups. As suggested by O'Leary and Turkewitz (1978), research procedures were set up in such a way as to minimize the client's investment in impression management, for example, ensuring that therapists were absent when questionnaires were completed.

Future research should be conducted to examine in depth the process of conflict resolution in the emotionally focused therapy. This will shed light on how change occurs in this treatment and on the role of affect in the creation of more positive relationships in marital therapy.

References

ALLEN, J. G., AND HAMSHER, J. H. (1974). The development and validation of a test of emotional styles. *Journal of Consulting and Clinical Psychology, 42,* 663–668.

BATTLE, C. C., IMBER, S. D., HOEHN-SARIC, R., STONE, A. R., NASH, E. R., AND FRANK, J. D. (1966). Target complaints as criteria of improvement. *American Journal of Psychotherapy, 20,* 184–192.

BORDIN, E. (1979). The generalizability of the psychoanalytic concept of the working alliance. *Psychotherapy: Theory, Research and Practice, 16,* 222–229.

BRODERICK, J. (1981). A method for derivation of areas for assessment in marital relationships. *The American Journal of Family Therapy, 9,* 25–34.

CLAYTON, R. R. (1975). *The family, marriage and social change.* Lexington, MA: Heath.

COHEN, J. (1960). A coefficient of agreement for nominal scales. *Educational Psychological Measurement, 20,* 37–46.

FINCHAM, F., AND O'LEARY, D. K. (1982). *Affect in the eighties: A new direction in behavioral marital therapy.* Paper presented at the 90th Annual Convention of the American Psychological Association, Washington, DC.

GENDLIN, E. T. (1974). Client-centered and experiential psychotherapy. In D. A. WEXLER AND L. NORTH RICE (Eds.), *Innovations in client-centered therapy* (pp. 211–246). New York: Wiley.

GREENBERG, L., AND JOHNSON, S. M. (1987). Emotionally focused couples therapy: An integrated affective systemic approach. In N. S. JACOBSON AND A. S. GURMAN (Eds.), *The clinical handbook of marital therapy.* New York: Guilford Press.

GREENBERG, L., AND SAFRAN, J. (1984). Integrating affect and cognition: A perspective on the process of therapeutic change. *Cognitive Therapy and Research, 8,* 559–578.

GURMAN, A. S. (1978). Contemporary marital therapies: A critique and comparative analysis of psychoanalytic, behavioral and systems theory approaches. In T. J. PAOLINO AND B. S. MCCRADY (Eds.), *Marriage and marital therapy* (pp. 445–566). New York: Brunner/Mazel.

GURMAN, A. S. (1981). Integrative marital therapy. Toward the development of an interpersonal approach. In S. H. BUDMAN (Ed.), *Forms of brief therapy* (pp. 415–453). New York: Guilford Press.

HAHLWEG, K., SCHINDLER, L., REVENSTORF, D., AND BRENGELMANN, J. C. (1984). The Munich marital therapy study. In K. HAHLWEG AND N. S. JACOBSON (Eds.), *Marital interaction: Analysis and modification* (pp. 3–26). New York: Guilford Press.

HAYS, W. L. (1981). *Statistics.* New York: Holt Rinehart & Winston.

JACOBSON, N. S. (1977). Problem solving and contingency contracting in the treatment of marital discord. *Journal of Consulting and Clinical Psychology, 45,* 92–100.

JACOBSON, N. S. (1978a). A review of the research on the effectiveness of marital therapy. In T. J. PAOLINO AND B. S. MCCRADY (Eds.), *Marriage and marital therapy* (pp. 395–444). New York: Brunner/Mazel.

JACOBSON, N. S. (1978b). Specific and nonspecific factors in the effectiveness of a behavioral approach to the treatment of marital discord. *Journal of Consulting and Clinical Psychology, 46,* 442–452.

JACOBSON, N. (1979). Increasing positive behavior in severely distressed marital relationships: The effects of problem solving training. *Behavior Therapy, 10,* 311–326.

JACOBSON, N. S., FOLLETTE, W. C., AND ELWOOD, R. W. (1984). Outcome research in behavioral marital therapy: A methodological and conceptual reappraisal. In K. HAHLWEG AND N. S. JACOBSON (Eds.), *Marital interaction: Analysis and modification* (pp. 113–129). New York: Guilford Press.

JACOBSON, N. S., AND MARGOLIN, G. (1979), *Marital therapy: Strategies based on social learning and behavior exchange principles.* New York: Brunner/Mazel.

KIRESUK, T. J., AND SHERMAN, R. E. (1968). Goal attainment scaling: General method for evaluating comprehensive community mental health programs. *Community Mental Health Journal, 4,* 443–453.

LIBERMAN, R. P., LEVINE, J., WHEELER, E., SANDERS, N., AND WALLACE, L. J. (1976). Marital therapy in groups: A comparative evaluation of behavioral and interactional formats. *Acta Psychiatrica Scandinavica Monograph, Supplement 226*, 1–34.

MAHONEY, M. (1984). Integrating cognition, affect and action: A comment, *Cognitive Therapy and Research, 8*, 585–589.

MARGOLIN, G., AND WEINSTEIN, C. D. (1983). The role of affect in behavioral marital therapy. In L. R. WOLBERG AND M. C. ARONSON (Eds.), *Group and family therapy* (pp. 334–355). New York: Brunner/Mazel.

O'LEARY, D. K., AND TURKEWITZ, H. (1978). Methodological errors in marital and child treatment research. *Journal of Consulting and Clinical Psychology, 46*, 747–758.

PERLS, F., HEFFERLINE, R., AND GOODMAN, P. (1951). *Gestalt therapy,* New York: Julian Press.

PINSOF, W., AND CATHERALL, D. (1983). *The Couples Therapy Alliance Scale manual.* Chicago, IL: The Chicago Center for Family Studies, Northwestern University.

RACHMAN, S. (1984). A re-assessment of the "Primacy of Affect." *Cognitive Therapy and Research, 8*, 579–584.

RICE, L. (1974). The evocative function of the therapist. In D. WEXLER AND L. RICE (Eds.), *Innovations in client centered therapy* (pp. 289–312). New York: Wiley-Interscience.

ROGERS, C. R. (1951). Client-centered therapy. Boston: Houghton & Mifflin.

SCHAEFER, M. T., AND OLSON, D. H. (1981). Assessing intimacy: The PAIR inventory. *Journal of Marital and Family Therapy. 1*, 47–60.

SLUZKI, C. (1978). Marital therapy from a systems theory perspective. In T. J. PAOLINO AND B. S. MCCRADY (Eds.), *Marriage and marital therapy* (pp. 366–394). New York: Brunner/Mazel.

SMITH, M. L., AND GLASS, G. V. (1977). Meta-analysis of psychotherapy outcome studies. *American Psychologist, 32*, 752–760.

SPANIER, G. (1976). Measuring dyadic adjustment. *Journal of Marriage and the Family, 38*, 15–28.

WASKOW, I. E., AND PARLOFF, M. B. (Eds.). (1975). *Psychotherapy change measures.* Rockville, MD: National Institute of Mental Health.

WATZLAWICK, P., BEAVIN, J. H., AND JACKSON, D. D. (1967). *Pragmatics of human communication: A study of interactional patterns, pathologies, and paradoxes.* New York: Norton.

36

Understanding and Preventing Relapse

Kelly D. Brownell, G. Alan Marlatt, Edward Lichtenstein, and G. Terence Wilson

Abstract: This article examines relapse by integrating knowledge from the addictive disorders of alcoholism, smoking, and obesity. Commonalities across these areas suggest at least three basic stages of behavior change: motivation and commitment, initial change, and maintenance. A distinction is made between lapse and relapse, with lapse referring to the process (slips or mistakes) that may or may not lead to an outcome (relapse). The natural history of relapse is discussed, as are the consequences of relapse for patients and the professionals who treat them. Information on determinants and predictors of relapse is evaluated, with the emphasis on the interaction of individual, environmental, and physiological factors. Methods of preventing relapse are proposed and are targeted to the three stages of change. Specific research needs in these areas are discussed.

The problem of relapse remains an important challenge in the fields dealing with health-related behaviors, particularly the addictive disorders. This is true for areas of

Kelly D. Brownell, G. Alan Marlatt, Edward Lichtenstein, and G. Terence Wilson. Understanding and Preventing Relapse. *American Psychologist*, 1986, Vol. 41, No. 7, pp. 765–782. Copyright © 1986. Reprinted by permission of the publisher and authors.

obesity (Brownell, 1982; Rodin, 1981; Stunkard & Penick, 1979; Wilson, 1980), smoking (Lando & McGovern, 1982; Lichtenstein, 1982; Ockene, Hymowitz, Sexton, & Broste, 1982; Pechacek, 1979; Shiffman, 1982) and alcoholism (Marlatt, 1983; Miller & Hester, 1980; Nathan, 1983; Nathan & Goldman, 1979).

The purpose of this article is to focus on relapse by integrating the perspectives of four researchers and clinicians who have worked with one or more of the addictive disorders (Brownell, 1982; Lichtenstein, 1982; Marlatt, 1983; Wilson, 1980). We will discuss the natural history of relapse, its determinants and effects, and methods for prevention. We hope that our collective experience and different perspectives will aid in developing a model for evaluating and preventing relapse.

Commonalities and Differences in the Addictions

Compelling arguments can be marshaled for both commonalities and differences in the addictive disorders. Many differences exist, both among the disorders and among persons afflicted with the same disorder. For example, genetic contributions to both alcoholism (McClearn, 1981; Schuckitt, 1981) and obesity (Stunkard et al., 1986) suggest separate pathways for their development. There may be key differences in the pharmacology of nicotine and alcohol (Ashton & Stepney, 1982; Best, Wainwright, Mills, & Kirkland, in press; Gilbert, 1979; Myers, 1978; Pomerleau & Pomerleau, 1984), and food abuse fits even less neatly with concepts of physical dependency, withdrawal, and tolerance. Treatment goals also vary, with abstinence the target in some cases and moderation in others.

Individual differences within the addictions are also impressive. Variable treatment responses are an example. There are also striking differences in patterns of use. Some smokers, alcoholics, and overeaters engage in steady substance use, whereas others binge. Combinations of physiological, psychological, social, and environmental factors may addict different people to the same substance. Finally, different processes may govern the initiation and maintenance of the disorders.

There is also increasing emphasis on commonalities. One reason is that rates for relapse appear so similar. In 1971, Hunt, Barnett, and Branch found nearly identical patterns of relapse in alcoholics, heroin addicts, and smokers. The picture is the same today (Marlatt & Gordon, 1985). There may also be common determinants of relapse (Cummings, Gordon, & Marlatt, 1980). These factors suggest important commonalities in the addictive disorders. Progress may be aided by viewing these disorders from multiple perspectives (Levison, Gerstein, & Maloff, 1983; Marlatt & Gordon, 1985; Miller, 1980; Nathan, 1980).

The notion of commonalities gained support from expert panels assembled by two government agencies. The National Institute on Drug Abuse (NIDA) convened a panel of researchers in alcoholism, obesity, smoking, and drug abuse and found both conceptual and practical similarities in the areas (NIDA, 1979). Similar conclusions appeared in a more extensive report by the National Academy of Sciences (Levison et al., 1983). Both reports noted the importance of relapse and suggested the utility of combining perspectives from different areas of the addictions.

The question of whether the addictions are more similar than different is difficult to answer. It may be the case, for example, that there are common psychological adaptations to different physiological pressures. Nicotine dependence may be the central issue for a smoker, excessive fat cells for a dieter, and disordered alcohol metabolism for an alcoholic, but there may be common social or psychological provocations for relapse, emotional reactions to initial slips, and problems in reestablishing control. Our hope is to *expand* the information to be focused on relapse by considering both similarities and differences. In so doing, both conceptual and practical ideas may emerge that would not be suggested by the knowledge available in any one area.

Rates and Definition

Relapse rates for the addictions are assumed to be in the range of 50% to 90% (Hunt et al., 1971; Hunt & Matarazzo, 1973; Marlatt & Gordon, 1980, 1985). This underscores the importance of the problem. However, defining specific rates is difficult. Hidden within these averages is large variability. The rates depend on characteristics of the addiction, individual variables, the success of treatment, and so forth.

The figures generally cited for relapse could overestimate or underestimate actual rates. Most data are from clinical programs, so rates are based on those who have received formal treatment. These figures could overstate the problem because only difficult cases are seen and because only one attempt to change is studied (Schachter, 1982). Persons attempting to change on their own may be more successful and may relapse less frequently (Schachter, 1982). The vast majority of persons who change do so on their own (Ockene, 1984). These data could understate the case because clinical programs are most likely to provide effective treatments. In addition, various criteria are used to define relapse. For example, relapse in alcohol studies could be defined as days intoxicated, days hospitalized or jailed, days drinking out of control, or the use of any alcohol. This points to the need for standard definitions and for the study of the natural history of relapse.

Lapse and Relapse—Process Versus Outcome

There are two common definitions of relapse, each reflecting a bias regarding its nature and severity (Marlatt & Gordon, 1985). *Webster's New Collegiate Dictionary* of 1983 gives both definitions. The first is "a recurrence of symptoms of a disease after a period of improvement." This refers to an *outcome* and implies a dichotomous view because a person is either ill and has symptoms or is well and does not. The second definition is "the act or instance of backsliding, worsening, or subsiding." This focuses on a *process* and implies something less serious, perhaps a slip or mistake.

The choice of the process or outcome definition has important implications for conceptualizing, preventing, and treating relapse. We suggest that *lapse* may best describe a process, behavior, or event (Marlatt & Gordon, 1985). *Webster's* defines *lapse* as "a slight error or slip . . . a temporary fall esp. from a higher to a lower state." A lapse is a single event, a reemergence of a previous habit, which may or may not lead to the state of relapse. When a slip or mistake is defined as a lapse, it implies that corrective action can be taken, not that control is lost completely. There is support for this distinction in smokers (Coppotelli & Orleans, 1985; Mermelstein & Lichtenstein, 1983) and in dieters (Dubbert & Wilson, 1984). In these cases, different determinants were found for lapses (slips) and relapses.

The challenge with this approach is defining when one or more lapses become a relapse. One former smoker may lose control with the first transgression, whereas another may smoke one cigarette each month and never lose control. A lapse, therefore, could be defined concretely as use of the substance in the case of smoking and alcoholism or violation of program guidelines for a dieter. The individual's *response* to these lapses determines whether relapse has occured. This

varies from person to person and may be best defined by perceived loss of control. Reliable measures do not yet exist for this assessment. Research in this area is important for the field.

The Nature and Process of Relapse

Surprisingly little is known about relapse in its natural state. Most data are from clinical programs where different treatments are used with different populations, so it is difficult to isolate the factors that influence relapse. In addition, few researchers have done careful evaluations of patients when they are most likely to relapse, that is, after treatment has ended. Periodic follow-ups in groups are the only contacts with patients in most studies, so repeated, intensive assessments are needed. There would be great value in learning more about the nature and process of relapse.

The Need for a Natural History

A metaphor that describes traditional thought on relapse is of a person existing perilously close to the edge of a cliff. The slightest disruption can precipitate a fall from which there is no return. A person is always on the brink of relapse, ready to fall at any disturbance. There may be physiological, psychological, or social causes of the disturbance, but the outcome is just as final. The first slip creates momentum so that a complete relapse is certain.

This metaphor may be inadequate. It does not explain why a relapse occurs under the same circumstances that the person managed before. An eating binge may precipitate relapse in a dieter, but such an individual has probably recovered from similar binges in the past. A smoker may relapse after being offered a cigarette, but there are cases where this same person refused the cigarette or prevented the lapse from becoming a relapse. Also, the metaphor is based on observations of people who have relapsed, not those who have not; therefore, successful recovery is seldom seen.

Information on natural history could address the question of whether the probability of relapse increases or decreases with time. If relapse occurs when treatment "wears off," the probability should increase with time. If the metaphor used above is valid, the chance of relapse should increase with time simply because more disturbances could occur. One can speculate, however, that a person learns to cope effectively as time passes and that those who "survive" beyond the initial period are those who will succeed. To the extent withdrawal symptoms precipitate relapse, particularly in smoking and alcoholism, the likelihood of relapse should decrease as the body adapts to the absence of the addictive substance.

It is in this context that the concept of a "safe" point arises. This is a point in time before which relapse is likely and beyond which relapse is unlikely. In the work of Hunt et al. (1971) on heroin addiction, smoking, and alcoholism, relapse curves stabilized after the first three months. It is appealing to conclude that individuals who abstain for three months are likely to succeed thereafter, but more recent evidence does not support a specific safe point (Lichtenstein & Rodrigues, 1977; Wilson & Brownell, 1980). Defining such a point would have important conceptual and practical implications, so more study on this topic could pay high dividends. Interpreting relapse curves may be the first step.

Relapse curves are one type of survival curve. As such, the figures must be interpreted with several facts in mind (Elandt-Johnson & Johnson, 1980; Marlatt & Gordon, 1985; Sutton, 1979). Group averages do not represent individuals. Marlatt, Goldstein, and Gordon (1984) found that abstinence rates for smokers after quitting on the basis of a New Year's resolution were 21% both 4 and 12 months later, implying that relapse rates stabilize and show a safe point at 4 months. However, different individuals formed the 21% these two times; some persons moved from abstinence to relapse

whereas equal numbers moved in the opposite direction. Second, the cumulative nature of the curves implies that a person who relapses will remain so; survival curves are negatively accelerating by their nature. Schachter (1982) noted that cure for many persons follows several relapses. Third, the probability of survival for the entire group increases with time because the persons at highest risk are most likely to leave the sample. Life table analyses have been designed to deal with these issues (Elandt-Johnson & Johnson, 1980). Therefore, it may be possible in future research to develop a time line for the relapse process and to determine whether there are "safe" points.

Some information does exist on the natural history of the addictions. Vaillant's (1983) report on the long-term progress of 110 alcohol abusers, 71 of whom were "alcohol dependent," shows the complexity of the issue. Vaillant's book, and an article by Vaillant and Milofsky (1982), showed the importance of cultural and ethnic factors in alcoholism. Many personal and environmental factors influenced the propensity to drink excessively. It was clear from these data that a lapse does not necessarily become a relapse and that this transition has many determinants.

Schachter (1982) interviewed 161 persons from the Psychology Department at Columbia University and from a resort community. In their retrospective accounts, they reported much higher rates of success at dieting and smoking cessation than suggested by the literature. Almost all successes were achieved without professional aid. Although Schachter's methods have been questioned (Jeffery & Wing, 1983; Prochaska, 1983), he made several important points. He noted that cure rates are based on clinical samples and that self-quitters may differ from therapy-assisted quitters, a notion supported by DiClemente and Prochaska (1982). Second, he found that many of the successful quitters had made numerous attempts to change before finally succeeding.

Marlatt and Gordon (1980, 1985) have examined the natural history of the relapse itself. Beginning with a high-risk situation, their cognitive–behavioral model addresses the coping process (Figure 1). The absence of a coping response leads to decreased self-efficacy (Bandura, 1977a, 1977b), then use of the substance, and then the cognitive phenomenon they label the "abstinence violation effect." This phenomenon involves the loss of control that follows violation of self-imposed rules. The end result of this process is increased probability of relapse. Recent data from an analysis of relapse episodes in smokers showed a significant difference in attributions for slips between subjects who slipped (smoked at least 1 cigarette) and regained abstinence and those who relapsed (Goldstein, Gordon, & Marlatt, 1984). Persons who relapsed made more internal, characterological attributions for the slip. This model is useful in conceptualizing the relapse process from the point at which the person is in a high-risk situation.

Marlatt and Gordon's (1985) model allows for multiple determinants of high-risk situations but emhasizes cognitive processes thereafter. Other factors of a physiological or environmental nature may also be important. For example, the use of nicotine or alcohol after a period of abstinence may create a physiological demand for additional use. An environmental example is that of a smoker whose lapse occurs in a social setting where others are smoking. The resulting cues may provoke further use. Grunberg and colleagues have found powerful effects of nicotine on the regulation of body weight and food preferences in both humans and animals (Grunberg, 1982; Grunberg & Bowen, 1985; Grunberg, Bowen, Maycock, & Nespor, 1985; Grunberg, Bowen, & Morse, 1984). Stopping smoking can create physiological pressure to change food intake and gain weight. This in turn has psychological and environmental consequences that can precipitate relapse. Therefore, it is important to consider the interaction of individual, environmental, and physiologial factors in all stages of the change process.

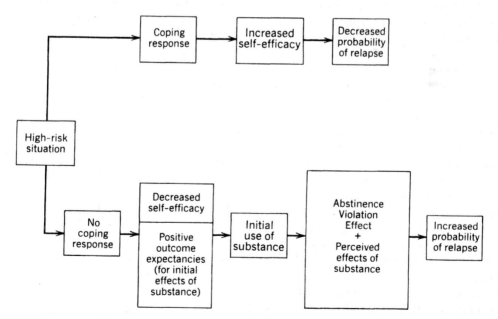

FIGURE 1

A cognitive-behavioral model of the relapse process beginning with the exposure to a high-risk situation.

Note. Reprinted from *Relapse Prevention: Maintenance Strategies in Addictive Behavior Change* (p. 38) by G. A. Marlatt and J. R. Gordon, 1985, New York: Guilford Press. Copyright 1985 by Guilford Press. Reprinted by permission.

There is much to be learned about the natural history of relapse. More descriptive information is needed on lapses and their associations with relapse. This research is not easy because the work must be prospective and because qualitative and quantitative work must be combined. As an example, Lichtenstein (1984) followed treated smokers at 1-, 2-, 3-, 6-, and 12-month intervals with telephone calls. Relapses were preceded by slips for 41 subjects; 19 subjects reported slips but did not relapse. More information of this nature would be useful.

Stages of Change

Several attempts have been made to divide the change process into stages (DiClemente & Prochaska, 1982; Horn, 1976; Marlatt & Gordon, 1985; Prochaska, 1979; Prochaska & DiClemente, 1982, 1983, 1984; Rosen & Shipley, 1983). There seems to be a convergence of opinion that at least three fundamental stages exist.

Horn (1976) first proposed four stages of change in smoking cessation (a) contemplating change, (b) deciding to change, (c) short-term change, and (d) long-term change. This is similar to the three-stage models suggested by DiClemente and Prochaska (1982), Rosen and Shipley (1983), and Marlatt and Gordon (1985), which involve the decision and commitment to change, initial change, and maintenance of change.

Prochaska and DiClemente have done the most thorough work in this area by evaluating stage models of smoking cessation and therapy in general. Prochaska (1979) reviewed 300 therapy outcome studies and proposed five stages, three of which involved "verbal processes" and two "behavioral processes." DiClemente and Prochaska (1982) used this model to compare smokers who quit on their own to those who used commercial programs. They proposed the three stages mentioned above and described six verbal and four behavioral processes within the stages. In their recent work, Prochaska and DiClemente (1983, 1984) suggested five stages: (a) precontemplation, (b) contemplation, (c) action, (d) maintenance, and (e) relapse.

More work is needed to test the utility of the various stage models. They are similar in many respects. Each has at least one stage where motivation and commitment are central, followed by initial change and then the maintenance of change, so we will use these three fundamental stages to organize the description of relapse prevention later in this article. Whichever stage model prevails, we feel that relapse must be considered in light of the stages that precede it. This will draw attention to the early determinants of relapse and the importance of the many factors that influence long-term success.

A stage model may also be helpful for relapse itself. A model might include the time prior to a lapse, the lapse itself, and the period in which the person does or does not relapse. The work of Lichtenstein, Antonuccio, and Rainwater (1977), Cummings et al. (1980), and Shiffman (1982, 1984) suggests the utility of such an approach.

An important conceptual advance has been the emphasis of Prochaska and DiClemente (1982, 1984) on a circular rather than linear model of change. Linear models have stages that occur in a specific sequence, with relapse occurring at the last stage. A circular model shows relapse leading back to an earlier stage from which an individual may make another attempt to change. Relapse can be viewed in a less negative light from this perspective, as an individual may acquire information or skills that may be helpful later. This is consistent with Schachter's (1982) notion that success for most individuals comes after several relapses. Taking this to the extreme, one could suggest that relapse is a *necessary* step on the path to success. We do not support this extreme, but we do feel that relapse may provide valuable experience and that persons who relapse should be instructed accordingly.

The Consequences of Relapse

Relapse could provoke a variety of responses in the individual. It is generally assumed that these responses are negative, but this may not be true in all cases. This is an important issue because these responses may determine the likelihood of success in subsequent attempts to change.

It would appear at first glance that relapse has negative emotional effects. Disappointment, frustration, and self-condemnation are apparent in people who relapse. Family and friends are unhappy and sometimes angry. Yet, learning may occur before or during the relapse, so some benefit may exist. One study tracked depression in subjects who lost weight and then regained it (Brownell & Stunkard, 1981). Depression scores dropped as weight declined, but returned halfway to baseline as half of the weight was regained. Although these subjects were not successful maintainers, the net change in mood was still positive.

There may also be physiological effects of relapse. When a person stops smoking, the body begins the healing process, and risk for premature death declines (U.S. Department of Health and Human Services, 1983). Because there is a dose–response relationship between smoking and disease, bouts of abstinence may incur some benefit, so the smoker who relapses may be better off medically than one who never quit. This is highly speculative, but it does show that this issue deserves more attention.

The picture may be different in the weight loss area, where relapse may have detrimental metabolic and health effects. A recent study found that repeated cycles of weight loss and regain in animals was associated with increased metabolic efficiency (Brownell, Greenwood, Shrager, & Stellar, 1986). As a result, the animals lost weight at half the rate when they were put on a diet a second time even though intake was the same on both diets. When allowed to eat freely, the animals regained at three times the rate on the second diet than on the first diet. Dieting and relapse made subsequent dieting more difficult. Epidemiology studies with humans show positive effects of weight loss on blood pressure, cholesterol, glucose tol-

erance, and so forth (Simopolous & Van Itallie, 1984). However, when an equal amount of weight is regained, the negative effects on blood pressure and cholesterol may be greater than the positive effects when the weight is lost (Ashley & Kannel, 1974).

Relapse: Failure or Incremental Learning? We wonder whether repeated attempts to change followed by relapse increase or decrease the chance for later success. There is evidence that persons who have dieted many times have a poor prognosis (Jeffrey et al., 1984; Jeffery, Snell, & Forster, 1985), although Dubbert and Wilson (1984) did not find this result. A relapse could be a failure that strengthens the person's view that the problem is beyond his or her best efforts. However, relapse may have positive consequences if the experience somehow prepares the individual for later success. This more optimistic view is consistent with Schachter's (1982) suggestion that multiple attempts occur before many people succeed. A person who relapses may be acquiring information about his or her weaknesses and may learn ways to prevent lapses in the future.

This view of incremental learning could be useful to both professionals and patients. If relapse can be a constructive experience, experimentation with programmed relapse might be warranted (Marlatt & Gordon, 1985). This approach involves planning and executing a relapse that would not occur otherwise, to teach patients to recover with self-management techniques. This approach will be discussed in more detail below.

An area that has received little attention is the effect of patients who relapse on the professionals who treat them. Following patients through the emotional roller coaster of success and relapse is discouraging and can make professionals pessimistic with new patients. Whether this pessimism is justified depends on perspective. It is a failure viewed in the short term, but some long-term effect may occur. Most patients will make other attempts, and some will succeed.

Determinants and Predictors of Lapse and Relapse

We make several assumptions here. The first is that there are similarities in relapse across the addictive disorders (Marlatt & Gordon, 1985). Our second assumption is that different processes govern initial change and maintenance (Bandura, 1977a). This assumption has been substantiated by research on alcoholism (Cronkite & Moos, 1980; Marlatt & Gordon, 1985), smoking (Lichtenstein, 1982; Pomerleau, Adkins, & Pertschuk, 1978; Shiffman, 1982, 1984), and obesity (Brownell, 1982; Dubbert & Wilson, 1984; Wilson, 1978). The third assumption is that the risk for relapse is determined by an interaction of individual, situational, and physiological factors.

The initial attempts to classify relapse situations were made by Marlatt (1978), Marlatt and Gordon (1980), and Cummings et al. (1980). The Cummings et al. analysis evaluated 311 initial relapse episodes in drinking, smoking, compulsive gambling, excessive eating, and heroin addiction. Several determinants emerged, which can be broadly grouped into individual (intrapersonal) and situational (environmental) categories. These two categories are supported by work on smoking (Mermelstein & Lichtenstein, 1983; Shiffman, 1982, 1984) and obesity (Dubbert & Wilson, 1984). We feel it important to add physiological variables, as their importance is becoming more clear (Best et al., in press; Brownell, 1982; Lichtenstein, 1982; Myers, 1978; Nathan & Wiens, 1983; Pomerleau & Pomerleau, 1984).

Individual and Intrapersonal Factors

Negative Emotional States. Stress, depression, anxiety, and other emotional states are related to relapse. Cummings et al. (1980) found that negative emotional states accounted for 30% of all relapses. Shiffman (1982, 1984) evaluated reports of relapse in 264 ex-smokers who called a telephone hotline service (Stay Quit Line). Subjects were interviewed soon after the relapse, so reports were recent even if based only on self-report. Most of the subjects (71%) had negative affects preceding the relapse, with the most common mood state being anxiety, followed by anger or frustration, and depression (Shiffman, 1982). Ossip-Klein, Shapiro, and Stiggens (1984) have also used a telephone hotline to study relapse in smokers. Mermelstein, Cohen, and Lichtenstein (1983) found that 43% of relapses occur under stress. Pomerleau et al. (1978) reported that those who smoke to reduce negative affect are at increased risk for relapse. A careful study of smokers by Abrams et al. (1986) supported these notions by using physiological, behavioral, and self-report data.

In a study with smokers, Mermelstein and Lichtenstein (1983) studied both lapses (slips) and relapses. Lapses were more commonly associated with situational factors, whereas relapses occurred during negative emotional states or stress events. When the data from these studies with different addictive behaviors are combined, it is clear that negative emotional states greatly increase the chance of relapse. More specifically, negative moods may increase the chance that a lapse will become a relapse.

Inadequate Motivation. It is surprising that so little work has been done on motivation and commitment. It would seem that all persons who set out to change are motivated, particularly those who enter professional programs. However, there are degrees of motivation, and it is common for a person to begin the change process in a burst of enthusiasm without appreciation for the long-term effort involved. In other cases, the motivation may be more external than internal, when social pressure forces a symbolic if not real attempt to change.

There are three relevant aspects of the motivation issue. The first is the need to evaluate motivation so that high-risk subjects can be detected. To our knowledge, this has not been done in the addictions area. Second, screening for motivation is important if treatment should be targeted at those with a chance for success. Third, methods may be available for increasing motivation, to improve a person's "readiness" for change (Marlatt & Gordon, 1985; Prochaska & DiClemente, 1984). The second and third issues have implications for treatment, as we will discuss.

Response to Treatment. There is some evidence that initial responses to treatment predict later success. Weight loss in the first weeks of treatment has been related to success (Foreyt et al., 1982; Graham, Taylor, Hovell & Siegel, 1983; Jeffery, Wing, & Stunkard, 1978). Pomerleau et al. (1978) found that early compliance (self-monitoring) was related to positive outcome in smokers, and Glasgow, Shafer, and O'Neill (1981) found that self-reported compliance was related to success in self-quitters. Inability to stop smoking on the assigned target date (usually midway in treatment) is a poor prognostic sign (Lichtenstein, 1982).

One of us (KDB) has observed informally a paradoxical relationship between early program adherence and outcome in persons on very low-calorie diets, a rigid program that is nearly a complete fast (Wadden, Stunkard, & Brownell, 1983). Patients are asked not to "cheat" on the diet. Those who struggle with adherence to a moderate degree seem to do better in the long run than those who adhere perfectly from the outset. The perfect adherers seem to have trouble recovering from the inevitable slip that the early perfection merely postpones. It is possible that high motivation initially can mask strong pressures to relapse, but once internal and external pressures wear away restraint, a lapse is likely to become a relapse. Patients who struggle to a moderate degree with adherence throughout a program may do well later because they can cope with temporary setbacks.

Coping Skills. Shiffman (1984) found that both cognitive and behavioral coping responses were associated with success in smokers calling the hotline mentioned earlier. The most common behavioral responses were consumption of food and drink and other distracting activities. Several aspects of "self-talk" were the most common cognitive responses. Shiffman found positive associations between outcome and seven behavioral and five cognitive methods of coping, but the various coping strategies were about equally effective.

There is evidence in the weight control area showing the utility of a cognitive "threshold" for weight regain in persons who have lost weight (Brownell, 1984a; Wilson, 1985). Stuart and Guire (1978) examined successful maintainers in Weight Watchers and found them likely to have a personal regain threshold of three pounds or less before they instituted self-correcting actions. Bandura and Simon (1977) found that subjects who used proximal rather than distal goals were most successful at maintenance. One aspect of the proximal goals was a weight increase threshold.

Another factor that may relate to long-term success are the coping skills associated with self-efficacy (Bandura, 1977b). Self-efficacy is a person's belief that he or she can respond effectively to a situation by using available skills. This concept is at the root of the relapse prevention approach of Marlatt and Gordon (1985) and has been applied to alcoholism (Chaney, O'Leary, & Marlatt, 1978), smoking, (Brown, Lichtenstein, McIntyre, & Harrington-Kostur, 1984; Hall, Rugg, Tunstall, & Jones, 1984; Killen, Maccoby, & Taylor, 1984), and obesity (Perri, McAdoo, Spevak, & Newlin, 1984; Perri, Shapiro, Ludwig, Twentyman, & McAdoo, 1984). Several studies have found measures of self-efficacy associated with positive outcome (Colletti, Supnick, & Payne, 1985; Condiotti & Lichtenstein, 1981; Killen et al., 1984; Supnick & Colletti, 1984).

Physiological Factors

Physiological factors may be a central determinant of relapse. Genetic factors appear to be important for alcoholism, smoking, and obesity (McClearn, 1981; Pomerleau, 1984; Schuckitt, 1981; Stunkard et al., 1986). In the cases of alcoholism and smoking, other physiological influences are related to withdrawal, to the reinforcing properties of alcohol or nicotine, or to conditioned associations between specific cues and physiological responses (Abrams & Wilson, 1986; Hodgson, 1980; Ludwig, Wikler, & Stark, 1974; Pomerleau, 1984; Pomerleau & Pomerleau, 1984; Poulos, Hinson, & Siegel, 1981; Siegel, 1979). A patient's use of terms like *urge* and *craving* may reflect some of these pressures.

Siegel (1979) and others (Ludwig et al., 1974) proposed that alcoholics show conditioned reactions to environmental, emotional, and physiological stimuli that have been associated with previous withdrawal. Conditioned compensatory responses are thought to elicit craving for alcohol. Poulos et al. (1981) suggested that treatment must deal with extinction of these cues.

Degree of physical dependency must also be considered in alcohol abuse (Hodgson, 1980; Marlatt & Gordon, 1985; Miller & Hester, 1980). Several studies by Hodgson and colleagues found that alcoholics with serious physical dependency have stronger cravings and respond differently than mildly dependent subjects to ingestion of alcohol (Hodgson, Rankin, & Stockwell, 1979; Stockwell, Hodgson, Rankin, & Taylor, 1982). Dependency may also influence the goals and course of treatment. Chronic alcohol use is associated with several cognitive impairments, so skill acquisition may be more difficult (Wilkinson & Sanchez-Craig, 1981). If controlled drinking is a viable goal of treatment, it would be so for only a subgroup of problem drinkers: abstinence is the clear goal for severe alcohol dependence (Marlatt, 1983; Miller & Hester, 1980; Nathan & Goldman, 1979).

Similarly powerful factors may be associated with smoking (Abrams & Wilson, 1986; Pomerleau & Pomerleau, 1984). A review by McMorrow and Foxx (1983) showed how changes in smoking behavior accompany changes in blood nicotine level. Pomerleau (1984) found that nicotine stimulates release of beta-endorphin, increases heart rate, and possibly improves memory and attention; therefore he characterized nicotine as a powerful chemical reinforcer. Furthermore, the degree of physical dependence has implications for treatment. Two studies found that smokers who are highly dependent on nicotine benefit most from treatment with nicotine chewing gum (Fagerstrom, 1982; Hall et al., 1985).

Different but also influential physiological factors may be involved in obesity. Food does not seem addictive in the manner of cigarettes and alcohol, yet the physical pressures to regain lost weight may be extremely powerful (Bennett & Gurin, 1982; Bray, 1976; Brownell, 1982; Wooley, Wooley, & Dyrenforth, 1979). Such pressures could involve the lipid repletion of fat cells and alterations of several factors including body composition, metabolic rate, thermogenic response to food, and enzyme activity, each of which may be related to a body weight "set point" in which the organism defends a biological ideal against fluctuations, including weight loss.

Given these important physiological factors, it may be informative to examine the subjective impressions of their likely manifestations, namely cravings, urges, and withdrawal. Studies in these areas have shown inconsistent findings. The Cummings et al. (1980) study found that "urges and temptations" were associated with only 6% of the relapse situations and that "negative physical states" were associated with only 7% of the situations. Mermelstein et al. (1983) found that craving was the major factor in only 9% of relapses in smokers. In contrast, Shiffman (1982) found that approximately half of the relapse situations in smokers occurred in conjunction with withdrawal symptoms. Even though Shiffman interpreted this result as showing that withdrawal symptoms are less important than expected, they would appear from his data to be powerful precipitating events.

Environmental and Social Factors

There is compelling evidence that environmental and social factors, incuding specific external contingencies, play an important role in the addictive disorders. These can be interactions among individuals (social support), environmental or setting events, or programs that manipulate contingencies.

Social Support. Social factors are important determinants of susceptibility to diseases, including heart disease, cancer, and psychiatric disturbances (Cobb, 1976; Cohen & Syme, 1985). They are important in a person's ability to make stressful decisions and to adhere to a therapeutic program (Janis, 1983) and have been related to success in the addictive disorders (Best, 1980; Colletti & Brownell, 1982; Moos & Finney, 1983).

Research in this area has taken two forms: the evaluation of social support as a predictor variable and the modification of social factors to boost treatment effectiveness. Treatment will be discussed below. The work with predicting success with social variables has been fruitful.

Support from family and friends is one of the few variables that is associated with long-term success at weight reduction (Brownell, 1984a; Miller & Sims, 1981; Wilson, 1985). Studies on smoking suggest the same association (Coppotelli & Orleans, 1985; Mermelstein et al., 1983). Whether a spouse is a smoker and is attempting to quit relates negatively to ability to stop smoking (Lichtenstein, 1982). Perceived general support (not specific to quitting) also relates to the maintenance of nonsmoking or reduced smoking (Mermelstein et al., 1983). Moos and Finney (1983) summarized studies in the alcohol area showing that marital and family cohesion enhance response to treatment in follow-ups of as long as two years. In their review of the relapse area, Marlatt and Gordon (1985) and Cummings et al. (1980) pointed to the importance of social factors across areas of the addictions.

Interpersonal conflict can be viewed as the converse of social support, and studies have shown that it is a prognostic sign for relapse. In the study by Cummings et al. (1980), nearly half (48%) of the relapse episodes occurred in association with inter-

personal determinants, with one third of these coming from conflict. It appears, therefore, that stressful interpersonal relationships can hinder and that supportive relationships can help. This emerges from the literature despite inconsistent methods of measuring support. The supportive person may be helpful not only in establishing a benevolent environment but by assisting with specific behavior changes (Coppotelli & Orleans, 1985). One challenge is to evaluate the nature of supportive behaviors and the reasons certain behaviors support some persons and not others.

One possible avenue for social support is from commercial or self-help groups. Such groups abound and exist in all areas of the addictions (Gartner & Reissman, 1984). Groups like Alcoholics Anonymous, Weight Watchers, Overeaters Anonymous, and SmokEnders deliver programs to millions and reach many more people than do professional programs. Their potential is tremendous, both to teach skills and provide social support. Is this potential realized?

It is difficult to evaluate many self-help and commercial groups. They vary greatly in cost, approach, size, geographic distribution, and so forth. Different chapters of the same group sometimes differ as much with one another as they do with outside groups. It is clear that many people benefit from these approaches, both in terms of initial results and maintenance (Gartner & Reissman, 1984). Guidelines are needed to refine the active components of these groups and to determine which people are best suited for self-help approaches.

Environmental Stimuli and External Contingencies. Events in the environment can set the stage for relapse. These typically take the form of social pressure from others, exposure to the undesirable behavior during social events like parties, and cues from situations formerly associated with the addictive behavior.

Shiffman (1982) found that social events preceded one fourth of the relapse crises of smokers and that activities previously associated with smoking (eating and drinking) were frequent antecedent events. Marlatt and Gordon (1980, 1985) also found these to be important factors. Mermelstein and Lichtenstein (1983) reported that lapses were most likely under social cues, a social celebration, or the consumption of alcohol.

Numerous programs have shown that contingency management and the systematic manipulation of environmental factors can enhance motivation. Programs using financial incentives have been useful in promoting weight loss in both adults and children (Epstein, Wing, Koeske, Andraski, & Ossip, 1981; Jeffery, Forster, & Snell, 1985; Jeffery, Gerber, Rosenthal, & Lindquist, 1983). Reward systems have also been used with some success in smoking (Lichtenstein, 1982). The careful work of Bigelow, Stitzer, and colleagues has shown powerful effects of contingency management on drug abuse, alcohol intake, and smoking (Bigelow, Stitzer, Griffiths, & Liebson, 1981; Stitzer & Bigelow, 1984). Such work presents specific components of treatment that may help prevent relapse.

External contingencies have most often been manipulated in the alcohol area. Hunt and Azrin (1973) used an intensive community reinforcement program in which family, social, and vocational reinforcers were altered systematically. Among the treatment components were marital and family counseling, skills training, assistance with daily needs such as obtaining a driver's license, a social club for clients, and contingency contracting. Compared to control clients, those who received this program remained more sober, had better employment records, and showed several other tangible indications of improvement. Azrin (1976) then modified this approach using Antabuse and an early warning system for relapse. Employee Assistance Programs (EAP) are another example of environmental contingencies influencing alcoholics (Nathan, 1983, 1984). Participating in treatment and remaining sober may be a condition for employment. Some programs for impaired professionals require treatment for continued practice.

Individual, Environmental, and Physiological Factors: An Interaction

The risk for lapse and relapse is determined by an interaction of individual, environmental, and physiological factors. This is an area in which the distinction of lapse and relapse is particularly useful, as there may be different determinants and antecedents in each case. Mermelstein and Lichtenstein (1983) showed in their findings that lapses tended to be associated with social factors and that relapses were associated with individual factors (negative emotional states and stress events). Shiffman (1982) theorized that a situational analysis could predict increased risk for relapse but that coping skills would determine whether this risk becomes reality. Other theorists have pointed to powerful physiological cravings to help explain both addiction and relapse (Abrams & Wilson, 1986; Brownell, 1982; Pomerleau & Pomerleau, 1984).

If lapse and relapse are viewed on a time line, individual, environmental, and physiological factors may exert their influence at different stages. Physiological factors may promote lapse and may set into play a series of reactions to an initial lapse that may increase the likelihood of relapse. The environmental and social factors can provide the setting, stimuli, and encouragement from others to lapse. As the choice point for the lapse approaches, coping skills can prevent the lapse. Whether the lapse recurs and ends in relapse probably results from a complex interaction of these factors, each of which may assume more or less importance depending on the individual and his or her environment.

Prevention of Lapse and Relapse

Traditional Approaches Versus the Prevention Model

Traditional attempts to facilitate long-term maintenance fall in three categories. The first has been to extend treatment by adding "booster" sessions. As the name implies, patients are to be "immunized" against pressures to relapse with the initial treatment, and periodic boosters are needed to maintain the protection. Booster sessions have been used most extensively in the obesity and smoking areas and have been consistently ineffective (Lichtenstein, 1982; Wilson, 1985).

A second approach has been to add more components to the treatment package, the most common being relaxation, contingency management, and assertion training. This has not been effective. Marlatt and Gordon (1985) stated, "All of this is heavy artillery— yet all it may do is project the cannonball a little bit further before it finally hits the ground" (p. 45). Adding new components to a package may help, but not enough to prevent relapse.

Adding components may also complicate a package and compromise the results of otherwise effective treatment. This result would be predicted from the literature showing that compliance is related inversely to the complexity of a regimen (Epstein & Cluss, 1982; Sackett & Haynes, 1976). There is some support for this in two obesity studies in which the combination of an appetite suppressant with behavior therapy was no more effective (Craighead, 1984) or even less effective (Craighead, Stunkard, & O'Brien, 1981) than behavior therapy alone.

A third traditional approach to preventing relapse is to adopt a model of lifelong treatment. This model is inherent in Alcoholics Anonymous, where participants are always "recovering" and never "recovered." This same philosophy applies to Overeaters Anonymous and to some extent to the lifetime membership offered by Weight Watchers. It may be true that chronic disorders require chronic treatment. According to our model of relapse prevention, lifelong treatment has both advantages and disadvantages. On the negative side, imparting the message that a person can control but not cure an addiction may establish a climate in which lapses create strong expectations of relapse. On the positive side, lifelong programs do not have the disadvantage of stan-

dard programs in which intensive treatment is followed by no treatment, the point at which relapse may be likely. These approaches must be considered viable, if for no other reason than that millions of persons have profited from their use. Program evaluation studies are difficult because of their long-term nature and the problems in doing research on commercial and self-help groups. It is, however, a pressing need for the field.

We propose that the prevention of lapse and relapse correspond to the stages of their natural history. The approach described below is based on the three stages described earlier: motivation and commitment, initial change, and maintenance. We attempt to integrate what is known about individual, environmental, and physiological determinants of lapse and relapse.

Stage 1: Motivation and Commitment

At this stage, individuals commit themselves to change and make the first steps toward the modification of maladaptive behavior. There are two aspects of this process that are pertinent to relapse. One is the development of methods to enhance motivation. The second is screening to identify an individual's likelihood of success. Central to both is the ability to assess motivation and other factors related to prognosis. This is a pressing area for research, as good methods do not exist.

Enhancing Motivation. Many candidates for programs are motivated, but many are not. A major challenge is to enhance motivation when it is low in order to maximize readiness for change. Little systematic work has been done in this area. Education about the dangers of the addiction, support from others, therapist characteristics, and feedback about physical status are among the possible methods for increasing motivation, but even these factors have not been studied in detail. The field stands to profit from research targeted at this initial stage in the change process.

One possible approach for enhancing motivation is to use contingency-management procedures. Monetary incentives have been studied most thoroughly; the deposit-refund system is most common. In this system, patients are required to deposit money, sometimes on a sliding scale, that is then returned for attendance at meetings or for a specified behavior change (Hagen, Foreyt, & Durham, 1976; Jeffery et al., 1983). This approach reduces attrition (Hagen et al., 1976; Wilson & Brownell, 1980), but it is not clear whether it enhances motivation prior to treatment. The deposit-refund may simply deter people who are not motivated from entering treatment, which gives it possible utility as a screening device.

It is surprising that so little has been done on methods for enhancing motivation. The work of Prochaska and his colleagues is a move in this direction (Prochaska, 1979; Prochaska & DiClemente, 1983, 1984). These studies have helped define stages of change. The knowledge from these and similar studies may suggest methods for enhancing motivation in the early stages. Such methods could have wide application in public health programs where the goal is to encourage attempts to change.

One important aspect of this early stage is preparing the individual for the possibility of lapse and even relapse (Lando, 1981). A fine line must be drawn between preparing a person for mistakes and giving "permission" for mistakes to occur by inferring that they are inevitable. Two metaphors may be useful in this context. One is of a fire drill (Marlatt & Gordon, 1985). A person must practice to escape a fire even though fires are rare. The second metaphor is of a forest ranger whose dual tasks are to prevent and contain fires (Brownell, 1985). The best course is to prevent fires, but when they do occur, one must move swiftly before the fire consumes the entire forest.

Screening to Determine Prognosis. Screening prior to a program may have two potential benefits. First, screening may help match individuals to programs. Second, screening may focus professional efforts on those most likely to succeed.

Many potential remedies are available for the addictions. They range from no-cost efforts at self-change to expensive commercial and clinical programs. In between these extremes lie community programs, the media, self-help books, self-help groups, advice from a health care provider, and many others. Each approach works for some people. Screening could be valuable if individuals could be matched to the approach with the greatest impact at lowest cost. Developing criteria for this matching is a major need for the field.

The second use of screening is to make use of predictions of who will do well and who will not. The primary implication of the search for predictors is that persons who are likely to do poorly can be identified and can receive special treatment. This idea is appealing but is not yet practical. This approach assumes that there is something beyond standard treatment. In clinical programs, standard treatment *is* the most intensive and effective treatment known, so what else is to be done? In less intensive approaches, say self-help groups or community programs, referral to a more intensive approach may be the answer. However, there are several other tacit assumptions with this approach. One is that such persons will succeed if only the right procedures are used. This assumes the variance in outcome rests with the program rather than with the individual, which perpetuates the medical model of disease and cure. The other is that the cost of such efforts is justified.

Another perspective on screening would shift the focus from those at greatest risk for failure to those with greatest chance for success. Screening might be used to target a program to those most likely to benefit and to prevent the negative consequences of failure for those at high risk, assuming that the consequences of relapse are more negative than positive. The rationale for this has been discussed previously in the weight loss area (Brownell, 1984b). One reason is that failure, or the more likely occurrence of initial success followed by relapse, may add to a legacy of inadequacy and demoralize the patient. Second, the initial success followed by relapse may have negative physiological consequences, particularly for dieters. Third, the failure may convince the person that the problem is intractable, which may decrease the chance that treatment will be pursued later when motivation is higher. Fourth, if treatment is delivered in groups, "negative contagion" can occur when patients who are not doing well discourage those who are. Fifth, the morale of professionals suffers when a patient fails. Sixth, working with patients who are likely to fail leaves fewer resources for those who may succeed.

The object would be to screen for individual, environmental, or physiological factors that cannot be remedied easily. One factor is motivation. It is difficult to motivate a person who does not have a strong commitment to change. There are instances of programs motivating groups of people, say in a worksite or community (Brownell, Cohen, Stunkard, Felix, & Cooley, 1984; Pechacek, Mittelmark, Jeffery, Loken, & Luepker, 1985), but reliable methods for motivating individuals have not been developed. Another factor relates to a person's skills. Some skills deficits may be difficult to overcome.

Physiological factors may be among the most important objects of screening. Our earlier discussion raised some of the possible variables to be measured, including physical dependency, metabolic factors, withdrawal, and genetic loading. It is clear, therefore, that screening will be a multifaceted activity that will require assessment of many variables.

The concept of screening is easier to support in principle than to apply in practice. Its strength lies in the ability to separate false positives from false negatives. Using no screening increases false positives, that is, people who will eventually fail are permitted into a program. A screening procedure can produce false negatives (persons who would succeed are screened out unfairly). It is important to consider these along with the associated ethical issues (which will be discussed).

Two Methods for Screening. Little attention has been given to screening, so we can offer only preliminary ideas. One is a behavioral test of motivation, and the other is the use of predictor variables. The next few years will probably offer physiological variables for screening, but only the tentative suggestions made above are possible currently.

There are several possibilities for behavioral tests of motivation. The deposit-refund system has been effective in reducing attrition in obesity programs (Hagen et al., 1976; Wilson & Brownell, 1980) and has been used in smoking programs as well (Lichtenstein, 1982). This system is usually conceptualized as a means for sustaining motivation during a program, but it may also serve to screen out people with low levels of motivation before a program. Another behavioral test is to institute a "screening phase" prior to treatment. Patients must meet established criteria prior to entrance to the program. One of us (KDB) uses this in a weight control program by requiring patients to lose one pound per week for two weeks and to complete self-monitoring diaries. These criteria, combined with the deposit-refund system, are not difficult to meet for most patients, but individuals who are not motivated may not join a program where such a commitment is necessary. These are just examples of behavioral tests for motivation. More research may identify better methods.

The second (even less precise) method for screening is to use some combination of predictor variables to identify subjects at high risk for relapse. Marlatt et al. (1984) found that a motivational rating of desire to quit distinguished individuals who could not stop smoking for even a day from those who could quit for longer periods. As our discussion above shows, identifying predictors of relapse is not sufficiently advanced to warrant screening. With more research, however, this may be possible.

This discussion pertains to clinical programs where treatment is intensive and costly. Large-scale programs, say in work sites or communities, may be inexpensive, so the aim shifts from having a strong impact on small groups to spreading lesser impact over large numbers (Brownell, 1986; Davis, Faust, & Ordentlich, 1984; Stunkard, 1986). In this case, the cost of screening may not be warranted.

The Ethics of Screening. Screening used in this fashion raises complex ethical issues. The decision of who can enter a program would no longer be based on who registers first or who can pay the fee, but there would be a conscious effort to deliver treatment to individuals with specific characteristics. This affords the opportunity for treatment to some and denies it to others. Although such an approach has not been studied, it is likely that certain subgroups of the population would fall disproportionately into the "nonmotivated" category. These subgroups might be characterized by sex, race, religion, or ethnic background, all groups that Western culture protects against discrimination.

Whether such screening can be justified ethically may depend on many factors. One is the ability to help those at high risk. In the absence of proven technology for this purpose, does screening become more important? Another issue is cost. Is the extra cost of aiding a high-risk person justifiable? Some extra cost may be justified, but how much? What allocation of these resources will have the greatest impact on society, or should society be the primary concern? A third factor will be the sensitivity and specificity of screening procedures. A screening that produces few false negatives may be warranted if the social, psychological, and health costs of false positives are high, but how many false negatives can be tolerated?

These questions are too complex to address in detail here. We do feel that screening and identification of those with high and low chances for success is an issue of major importance. Who receives treatment is not currently determined by a systematic examination of the issues. It may happen in a systematic way, but for reasons that we do not understand and that may not be rational. Avoiding the questions only sidesteps the ethical issues but does not make the process of delivering treatment more ethical. We hope more research will be done in this area.

Stage 2: Initial Behavior Change

This stage of treatment is the intensive period that lies between screening and the maintenance phase. This period may be several weeks in smoking programs and three to six months in alcohol and obesity programs. This may not be the time for greatest risk of relapse, because patients are generally motivated and are gratified with their changes. However, high-risk situations do occur; therefore, this time is ideal for the acquisition and practice of skills specific to relapse (Marlatt & Gordon, 1985). Some of these have been described in detail elsewhere (Marlatt & Gordon, 1980, 1985), so the basic rationale for the use and timing of the procedures will be given here.

The choice of specific treatment procedures is important, as is the timing of their use. The tendency is to squeeze all components into the initial treatment period and to use maintenance to review material presented earlier. This can burden the subject early in a program and may focus on skills when the skills are not required. Therefore, the right mixture of relapse prevention strategies in both initial treatment and maintenance may be one key to positive outcome.

We suggest three areas to be covered in initial treatment (a) decision making, (b) cognitive restructuring, and (c) coping skills. These are the procedures aimed specifically at the prevention of lapse and relapse and are to be done in addition to the techniques specific to the treatment of smoking, alcoholism, or obesity. They emerge from our conceptual approach described earlier and from existing information on predictors of relapse and the success of relapse prevention programs. A fourth area, cue elimination, has preliminary support in both theory and practice and may become more important as research progresses.

The focus on these three areas does not imply that they form the sole source of treatment. We do feel that specific techniques aimed at relapse are desirable in all stages of the change process and that relapse prevention techniques may aid any treatment program. For example, treatment for a dieter might consist of a habit change program of behavior modification, a supplemented fast, or even surgery. An alcoholic may receive Antabuse, may attend Alcoholics Anonymous, or may receive a skills training program. In each case, specific approaches can be applied to the lapse and relapse processes and may improve the prognosis for long-term change.

Additional areas will undoubtedly be added to these three as knowledge on relapse expands. We do not wish to imply that these are the only targets for relapse prevention or even that they will be consistently effective. These are what the literature permits us to propose. Contingency management will probably be added to the list soon, as studies begin to target these techniques to relapse. Physiological factors may also emerge as important targets, but specific physiological interventions aimed at relapse are not

evident from current knowledge. The number of studies on relapse is increasing rapidly. Our hope is that these will suggest refinement of the areas we suggest and will identify new areas for emphasis.

The first of the three areas involves decision-making skills. These prepare a person for analyzing the individual and environmental determinants of relapse. This analysis allows the person to decide which coping skills should be summoned for dealing with a particular situation. Cognitive restructuring is also central to this approach, as it teaches individuals to interpret events, attitudes, and feelings in a rational way and to respond constructively to crises. Such a scheme for analyzing the lapse and relapse sequence and of specifying methods of decision making, coping, and cognitive restructuring is shown in Figure 2. This presents examples of how an individual would

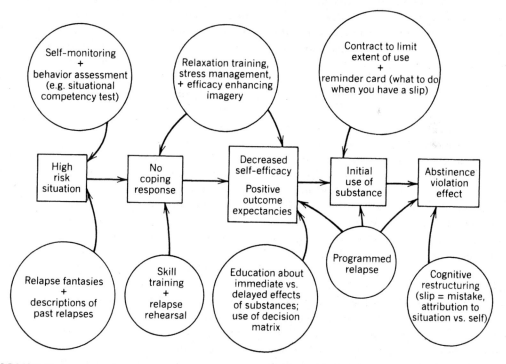

FIGURE 2

An example of decision-making and coping skills applied to the lapse and relapse process.

Note. Reprinted from *Relapse Prevention: Maintenance Strategies in Addictive Behavior Change* (p. 54) by G. A. Marlatt and J. R.

Gordon, 1985, New York: Guilford Press. Copyright 1985 by Guilford Press. Reprinted by permission. The boxes represent the stages in the process and the circles represent examples of interventions targeted at each stage.

use the framework described here to prepare for high-risk situations.

Cue extinction is receiving more attention as a possible means of preventing lapse and relapse. Based on the theoretical work of Siegel (1979) and others (Ludwig et al., 1974), there has been increasing emphasis on extinguishing the associations between cues and cravings (Abrams & Wilson, 1986). There may be individual, environmental, or physiological associations with substance use, and their extinction may be particularly important early in the change process when withdrawal is an issue. This is an area of potential importance, so more research is needed to test the theory and to develop clinical applications.

Research is needed to refine the techniques within these categories and to determine whether these categories are most appropriate for emphasis during initial behavior change. Shiffman's (1984) study of relapse in smokers is helpful in this regard, as he discovered that a combination of cognitive and behavioral coping skills was associated with maintenance.

Stage 3: Maintenance

Most programs include some treatment during the maintenance phase, but this period has been virtually ignored as a point of intervention. With the exception of booster sessions, which are a reiteration of earlier material, few studies have used the maintenance phase as the time for targeting the lapse and relapse process. This is unfortunate, as clinical judgment would dictate emphasis in just this period. There are three areas of intervention that may be appropriate for the maintenance phase: (1) continued monitoring, (b) social support, and (c) general life-style change. Again, more areas may emerge as research continues, but these three are suggested by existing research.

It is widely believed that long-term vigilance, either via some form of self-evaluation or contact with a professional, is important in the therapeutic process. It is our impression that individuals profit from monitoring

that extends beyond initial treatment. Treatment studies suggest that maintenance improves as contacts with professionals increase during follow-up, both in smoking (Colletti & Supnick, 1980) and obesity (Perri, McAdoo et al., 1984; Perri, Shapiro et al., 1984). This must be reconciled, however, with the general ineffectiveness of booster sessions. In addition, this raises the issue of when treatment ends and maintenance begins. Additional contacts may simply extend treatment and delay relapse rather than prevent it in any fundamental way. Whether these contacts actually influence relapse may depend on the nature of the contact and the type of material presented.

Marlatt and Gordon (1985) proposed social support as a component of relapse prevention. Social support is a predictor of long-term success, but attempts to intervene in the social environment have produced inconsistent results (Brownell, 1982; Brownell, Heckerman, Westlake, Hayes, & Monti, 1978; Lichtenstein, 1982). We believe that social factors are crucial in the behavior change process (Cohen & Syme, 1985) but that variations in social relationships make it unlikely that any single approach will work consistently. For instance, attempts to enlist the aid of a spouse may have positive effects in some marriages and negative effects in others. It is not surprising that parametric studies with groups show no effects for such programs. This is also an area where developmental work is needed so that the potential of social support can be exploited.

General life-style change may also be helpful (Marlatt & Gordon, 1985). The theory is that a source of gratification can be substituted for the absence of the addictive disorder. This notion is consistent with clinical experience, but little research has been done. Likely candidates are relaxation training, meditation, and exercise. Of these, exercise has several intriguing possibilities, as we will discuss.

A controversial but thus far ineffective approach to maintenance is programmed lapse. This approach involves a planned lapse in a therapeutic setting and might include an eating binge for a dieter, smoking for an ex-smoker, or drinking for a problem drinker. This would be done only after the person has received extensive instruction in the cognitive and behavioral coping skills mentioned above. The purpose is to have the inevitable lapse occur under supervision and to demonstrate that self-management skills can be used to prevent the lapse from becoming a relapse. It may also be a useful paradoxical technique; because the therapist controls the lapse, perceptions about lack of control may change.

Cooney and colleagues tested this approach with smokers (Cooney & Kopel, 1980; Cooney, Kopel, & McKeon, 1982). After 5 weeks of cessation, subjects smoked one cigarette in a controlled session. Most were surprised by how unpleasant the cigarette was and were confident they would not smoke later. These subjects had greater self-efficacy ratings than subjects receiving only the cessation program, but there were no differences in abstinence rates at a 6-month follow-up. In fact, there was a trend for programmed lapse subjects to relapse earlier.

This approach must be tested further before clinical use. The potential for harm is great, as the very cognitive patterns the procedure is designed to counter may promote uncontrolled relapse. Physiological factors may also create pressure to relapse. In addition, the studies with smokers by Cooney and colleagues did not produce favorable results. It might be a mistake, however, to dismiss the use of programmed lapse without more thorough evaluation.

A Special Role for Exercise? The wonders of exercise have been touted to the point of provoking a backlash, but there may be a special role for physical activity in the addictive disorders. Exercise has a natural role in the weight control field, but there is increasing evidence that its generalized effects may also benefit patients in the smoking and alcoholism areas.

Exercise is emerging as one of the most important components of treatment in the weight control area (Brownell & Stunkard, 1980; Thompson, Jarvie, Lahey, & Cureton, 1982). It is one of the few factors correlated with long-term success (Cohen, Gelfand, Dodd, Jensen, & Turner, 1980; Graham et al., 1983; Katahan, Pleas, Thackery, & Wallston, 1982; Miller & Sims, 1981; Stuart & Guire, 1978). Studies in which exercise is an independent variable show improved maintenance of weight loss (Dahlkoetter, Callahan, & Linton, 1979; Harris & Hallbauer, 1973; Stalonas, Johnson, & Christ, 1978).

Three studies suggest the benefits of exercise for smokers. Koplan, Powell, Sikes, Shirley, and Campbell (1982) sent questionnaires to 2,500 runners one year after they completed the 10 km Peachtree Road Race in Atlanta. Fully 81% of men and 75% of women who smoked cigarettes when they started running had stopped smoking after beginning. Giving up smoking was significantly more common among current runners than among those who had stopped running in the year following the race. In the Ontario Exercise-Heart Collaborative Study, 733 men recovering from myocardial infarction were followed for three years of an exercise program (Oldridge et al., 1983). For the 46.5% of the men who dropped out, the two strongest predictors of dropout were smoking and blue collar occupation. Shiffman (1984) found that exercise was used as a coping response in smokers who avoided relapse.

The only study in the alcoholism area also produced encouraging findings. Murphy, Marlatt, and Pagano (1986) trained heavy drinkers in aerobic exercise (running) or meditation. The running condition was associated with the most significant reductions in drinking rates during both treatment and follow-up.

If exercise can be used to prevent relapse, there are several possible mechanisms. It may be a general life-style activity that brings gratification, and possibly a positive addiction (Glasser, 1976), to the person who needs adaptive substitutes for the undesirable behavior (Marlatt & Gordon, 1985). It may influence self-concept or self-efficacy, which may generalize to the behavior change program. It may provide some stimulus control by removing the person to a safe setting or may provide a peer group that supports healthy behavior. There may also be physiological effects that influence the appetitive processes directly or that may change psychological functioning. These possibilities deserve further exploration.

Effects of Existing Programs

The use of relapse prevention programs is in its infancy, but many of the existing studies show positive effects. In addition to the contingency management studies mentioned above, which showed positive long-term results, several studies have used variations of the model proposed by Marlatt and Gordon (1980). Chaney et al. (1978) first used some elements of relapse prevention with alcoholics. They found no differences in absolute abstinence between the relapse prevention group and two control groups, but there were significant differences in favor of the relapse prevention group for duration and severity of drinking.

Hall et al. (1984) used a skills training program for relapse prevention in smokers. Subjects receiving this training had greater abstinence rates than subjects who did not at 6 and 52 weeks from the beginning of the study. The program had its greatest effect on light smokers. Killen et al. (1984) also found positive effects for relapse prevention with smokers. Brown et al. (1984) used a cognitive relapse prevention program with smokers and found promising results in a pilot study but no effects in a controlled study. Supnick and Colletti (1984) tested the Marlatt and Gordon (1980) model with smokers and found that a problem-solving component was associated with lower relapse rates but that a relapse-coping component was not.

Several studies have tested relapse prevention with dieters. Abrams and Follick (1983) found improved long-term results by adding a relapse prevention package to a behavioral program administered in a work setting. Sternberg (1985) found similar results in a clinical setting, but using basically the same approach, Collins, Rothblum, and Wilson (1986) found no effect. Two studies, one by Perri, McAdoo et al. (1984) and another by Perri, Shapiro et al. (1984), found

positive effects for a relapse prevention package. Perri, McAdoo et al. (1984) found better long-term results for a multicomponent maintenance program than for a control approach using booster sessions. Perri, Shapiro et al. (1984) then tested various approaches to maintenance and found that relapse prevention boosted long-term results but only when mail and telephone contacts were added.

It is too early to draw specific conclusion's about these studies. They vary widely in populations and in the procedures labeled "relapse prevention." Most are modeled conceptually after Marlatt and Gordon's (1980, 1985) principles, but the application in treatment is different from setting to setting. Some studies can be faulted for small sample sizes, short follow-up periods, modest treatment effects, and so forth, so it is not surprising to find mixed results. The studies with results in favor of relapse prevention, however, outnumber those with negative results, so at the very least, more vigorous testing of the model is warranted.

We hope researchers will continue to test a wide range of relapse prevention procedures rather than risk the problem seen in behavioral research for obesity, in which a "package" was developed and compared to other approaches. Its statistical superiority was more important than clinical realities, and the package became standard fare (Brownell, 1982; Foreyt et al., 1982; Wilson, 1978). Instead of searching for better approaches, investigators tested small refinements in the package. We should avoid early adoption of a relapse prevention package and avoid the focus only on comparative studies to the exclusion of the less rewarding but more important developmental studies that will generate useful ideas for clinical testing.

Recommendations for Research

Interest in lapse and relapse is relatively recent, so needs for additional research abound. The area is ripe for studies on issues ranging from the natural history of relapse to methods that patients might employ in high-risk situations.

Table 1 presents a list of research needs suggested from the various sections of this article. The topics include both theoretical and practical issues. We hope this will stimulate work in what is an important area of behavior change.

Table 1 Research Needs in the Areas of Lapse and Relapse

Areas	Questions to be Answered
Natural history	1. Is a relapse incremental learning or a failure experience? 2. Does the chance of relapse increase or decrease with time? 3. What are the stages of the lapse and relapse processes? 4. Is there a "safe" point beyond which a person will not relapse? 5. How frequent are lapses, and do they precede relapse?
Effects of lapse and relapse	1. What are the effects on mood? 2. Do lapse and relapse influence self-efficacy? 3. Do others' reactions influence lapse and relapse? 4. What are the physiological effects of lapse and relapse? 5. How do professionals deal with relapse in their patients?
Determinants and predictors	1. Do various treatments influence probability of relapse? 2. Does early response to treatment predict relapse? 3. Is past history of success and relapse predictive? 4. What are the roles of withdrawal symptoms, cravings, and urges? 5. What are the roles of conditioning and compensatory responses? 6. What are the mechanisms of social support? 7. Do physiological factors influence risk? 8. Can relapse be predicted after treatment but before maintenance?
Prevention of lapse and relapse	1. What criteria can be used to screen patients? 2. Does screening influence false positive and false negative rates? 3. What is the role of exercise? 4. Are cue extinction procedures helpful? 5. Is there any role for programmed relapse? 6. What are the relevant coping strategies? 7. Can motivation be enhanced at various points in treatment? 8. Is lifelong treatment necessary?

Conclusions

Relapse remains one of the most important problems associated with the addictive disorders. Previous work suggested that relapse rates and the shapes of relapse curves are similar across the addictions. This article attempts to move beyond this by identifying commonalities in the *process* of relapse, and by pointing to the need for more information on the natural history, determinants, consequences, and prevention of lapse and relapse. We conceptualize behavior change as occurring in three stages (motivation and commitment, initial change, and maintenance of change) and propose specific methods for dealing with relapse at each stage. Writing this article strengthened our view that each area of the addictions has much to offer the others; therefore, we support more interaction among researchers and clinicians across the areas.

References

ABRAMS, D. B., AND FOLLICK, M. J. (1983). Behavioral weight loss intervention at the worksite: Feasibility and maintenance. *Journal of Consulting and Clinical Psychology, 51,* 226–233.

ABRAMS, D. B., MONTI, P. M., PINTO, R. P., ELDER, J. P., BROWN, R. A., AND JACOBUS, S. I. (1986). *Psychosocial stress and coping in smokers who quit.* Unpublished manuscript.

ABRAMS, D. B., AND WILSON, G. T. (1986). Habit disorders: Alcohol and tobacco dependence. In A. J. FRANCES AND R. E. HALES (Eds.) *The American Psychiatric Association Annual Review* (Vol. 5, pp. 606–626). Washington, DC: American Psychiatric Association.

ASHLEY, F. W., AND KANNEL, W. B. (1974). Relation of weight change to change in atherogenic traits: The Framingham study. *Journal of Chronic Disease, 27,* 103–114.

ASHTON, H., AND STEPNEY, R. (1982). *Smoking: Psychology and pharmacology.* London: Tavistock.

AZRIN, N. H. (1976). Improvements in the community-reinforcement approach to alcoholism. *Behaviour Research and Therapy, 14,* 339–348.

BANDURA, A. (1977a). *Social learning theory.* Englewood Cliffs, NJ: Prentice-Hall.

BANDURA, A. (1977b). Self-efficacy: Toward a unifying theory of behavior change. *Psychological Review, 84,* 191–215.

BANDURA, A., AND SIMON, K. M. (1977). The role of proximal intentions in self-regulation of refractory behavior. *Cognitive Therapy and Research, 1,* 177–193.

BENNETT, W., AND GURIN, J. (1982). *The dieter's dilemma: Eating less and weighing more.* New York: Basic Books.

BEST, J. A. (1980). Mass media, self-management, and smoking modification. In P.O. DAVIDSON AND S. M. DAVIDSON (Eds.), *Behavioral medicine: Changing health lifestyles* (pp. 371–390). New York: Brunner/Mazel.

BEST, J. A., WAINWRIGHT, P. E., MILLS, D. E., AND KIRKLAND, S. A. (in press). Biobehavioral approaches to smoking control. In W. LINDEN (Ed.), *Biological barriers in behavioral medicine.* New York: Karger.

BIGELOW, G., STITZER, M. L., GRIFFITHS, R. R., AND LIEBSON, I. A. (1981). Contingency management approaches to drug self-administration and drug abuse: Efficacy and limitations. *Addictive Behaviors, 6,* 241–252.

BRAY, G. A. (1976). *The obese patient.* Philadelphia: Saunders.

BROWN, R. A., LICHTENSTEIN, E., MCINTYRE, K. O., AND HARRINGTON-KOSTUR, J. (1984). Effects of nicotine fading and relapse prevention on smoking cessation. *Journal of Consulting and Clinical Psychology, 52,* 307–308.

BROWNELL, K. D. (1982). Obesity: Understanding and treating a serious prevalent, and refractory disorder. *Journal of Consulting and Clinical Psychology, 50,* 820–840.

BROWNELL, K. D. (1984a). Behavioral, psychological, and environmental predictors of obesity and success at weight reduction. *International Journal of Obesity, 8,* 543–550.

BROWNELL, K. D. (1984b). The psychology and physiology of obesity: Implications for screening and treatment. *Journal of the American Dietetic Association, 84,* 406–414.

BROWNELL, K. D. (1985). *The LEARN Program for weight control.* Unpublished treatment manual, University of Pennsylvania.

BROWNELL, K. D. (1986). Public health approaches to obesity and its management. *Annual Review of Public Health, 7,* 521–533.

BROWNELL, K. D., COHEN, R. Y., STUNKARD, A. J., FELIX, M. J., AND COOLEY, N. B. (1984). Weight loss competitions at the work site: Impact on weight, morale, and cost-effectiveness.

American Journal of Public Health, 74, 1283–1285.

BROWNELL, K. D., GREENWOOD, M. R. C., SHRAGER, E. E., AND STELLAR, E. (1986). Dieting induced efficiency: Metabolic and behavioral adaptations to cycles of weight loss and regain. Manuscript submitted for publication.

BROWNELL, K. D., HECKERMAN, C. L., WESTLAKE, R. J., HAYES, S. C., AND MONTI, P. M. (1978). The effect of couples training and partner cooperativeness in the behavioral treatment of obesity. *Behaviour Research and Therapy, 16,* 323–333.

BROWNELL, K. D., AND STUNKARD, A. J. (1980). Physical activity in the development and treatment of obesity. In A. J. STUNKARD (Ed.), *Obesity* (pp. 300–324). Philadelphia: Saunders.

BROWNELL, K. D., AND STUNKARD, A. J. (1981). Couples training, pharmacotherapy, and behavior therapy in treatment of obesity. *Archives of General Psychiatry, 38,* 1223–1229.

CHANEY, E. F., O'LEARY, M. R., AND MARLATT, G. A. (1978). Skill training with alcoholics. *Journal of Consulting and Clinical Psychology, 46,* 1092–1104.

COBB, S. (1976). Social support as a moderator of life stress. *Psychosomatic Medicine, 38,* 300–314.

COHEN, E. A., GELFAND, D. J., DODD, D. K., JENSEN, J., AND TURNER, C. (1980). Self-control practices associated with weight loss maintenance in children and adolescents. *Behavior Therapy, 11,* 26–37.

COHEN, S., AND SYME, L. (1985). *Social support and health.* New York: Academic Press.

COLLETTI, G., AND BROWNELL, K. D. (1982). The physical and emotional benefits of social support: Applications to obesity, smoking, and alcoholism. In M. HERSEN, R. M. EISLER, AND P. M. MILLER (Eds.), *Progress in behavior modification* (Vol. 13, pp. 110–179). New York: Academic Press.

COLLETTI, G., AND SUPNICK, J. A. (1980). Continued therapist contact as a maintenance strategy for smoking reduction. *Journal of Consulting and Clinical Psychology, 48,* 665–667.

COLLETTI, G., SUPNICK, J. A., AND PAYNE, T. J. (1985). The Smoking Self-Efficacy Questionnaire: A preliminary validation. *Behavioral Assessment, 7,* 249–254.

COLLINS R. L., ROTHBLUM, E., AND WILSON, G. T. (1986). The comparative efficacy of cognitive and behavioral approaches to the treatment of obesity. *Cognitive Therapy and Research, 10,* 299–317.

CONDIOTTI, M. M., AND LICHTENSTEIN, E. (1981).

Self-efficacy and relapse in smoking cessation programs. *Journal of Consulting and Clinical Psychology, 49,* 648–658.

COONEY, N. L., AND KOPEL, S. A. (1980). *Controlled relapse: A social learning approach to preventing smoking recidivism.* Paper presented at the meeting of the American Psychological Association, Montreal.

COONEY, N. L., KOPEL, S. A., AND McKEON, P. (1982). *Controlled relapse training and self-efficacy in ex-smokers.* Paper presented at the meeting of the American Psychological Association, Washington, DC.

COPPOTELLI, H. C., AND ORLEANS, C. T. (1985). Spouse support for smoking cessation maintenance by women. *Journal of Consulting and Clinical Psychology, 53,* 455–460.

CRAIGHEAD, L. W. (1984). Sequencing of behavior therapy and pharmacotherapy for obesity. *Journal of Consulting and Clinical Psychology, 52,* 190–199.

CRAIGHEAD, L. W., STUNKARD, A. J., AND O'BRIEN, R. (1981). Behavior therapy and pharmacotherapy for obesity. *Archives of General Psychiatry, 38,* 763–768.

CRONKITE, R., AND MOOS, R. (1980). The determinants of posttreatment functioning of alcoholic patients: A conceptual framework. *Journal of Consulting and Clinical Psychology, 48,* 305–316.

CUMMINGS, C., GORDON, J. R., AND MARLATT, G. A. (1980). Relapse: Prevention and prediction. In W. R. MILLER (Ed.), *The addictive disorders: Treatment of alcoholism, drug abuse, smoking, and obesity* (pp. 291–322). New York: Pergamon.

DAHLKOETTER, J., CALLAHAN, E. J., AND LINTON, J. (1979). Obesity and the unbalanced energy equation: Exercise vs. eating habit change. *Journal of Consulting and Clinical Psychology, 47,* 898–905.

DAVIS, A. L., FAUST, R., AND ORDENTLICH, M. (1984). Self-help smoking cessation and maintenance programs: A comparative study with 12-month follow-up by the American Lung Association. *American Journal of Public Health, 74,* 1212–1219.

DiCLEMENTE, C. C., AND PROCHASKA, J. O. (1982). Self-change and therapy change of smoking behavior. A comparison of processes of change in cessation and maintenance. *Addictive Behaviors, 7,* 133–142.

DUBBERT, P. M., AND WILSON, G. T. (1984). Goal-setting and spouse involvement in the treatment of obesity. *Behaviour Research and Therapy, 22,* 227–242.

ELANDT-JOHNSON, R. C., AND JOHNSON, N. L. (1980). *Survival models and data analysis*. New York: Wiley.

EPSTEIN, L. H., AND CLUSS, P. A. (1982). A behavioral medicine perspective on adherence to long-term medical regimens. *Journal of Consulting and Clinical Psychology, 50*, 950–971.

EPSTEIN, L. H., WING, R. R., KOESKE, R., ANDRASIK, F., AND OSSIP, D. J. (1981). Child and parent weight loss in family-based behavior modification programs. *Journal of Consulting and Clinical Psychology, 49*, 674–685.

FAGERSTROM, K. O. (1982). A comparison of psychological and pharmacological treatments in smoking cessation. *Journal of Behavioral Medicine, 5*, 343–351.

FOREYT, J. P., MITCHELL, R. E., GARNER, D. T., GEE, M., SCOTT, L. W., AND GOTTO, A. M. (1982). Behavioral treatment of obesity: Results and limitations. *Behavior Therapy, 13*, 153–163.

GARTNER, A., AND REISSMAN, F. (Eds.). (1984). *The self-help revolution*. New York: Human Sciences Press.

GILBERT, D. G. (1979). Paradoxical tranquilizing and emotion-reducing effects of nicotine. *Psychological Bulletin, 86*, 643–661.

GLASGOW, R. E., SCHAFER, L., AND O'NEILL, H. K. (1981). Self-help books and amount of therapist contact in smoking cessation programs. *Journal of Consulting and Clinical Psychology, 49*, 659–667.

GLASSER, W. (1976). *Positive addiction*. New York: Harper & Row.

GOLDSTEIN, S., GORDON, J. R., AND MARLATT, G. A. (1984). *Attributional processes and relapse following smoking cessation*. Paper presented at the meeting of the American Psychological Association, Toronto.

GRAHAM, L. E., II, TAYLOR, C. B., HOVELL, M. F., AND SIEGEL, W. (1983). Five-year follow-up to a behavioral weight loss program. *Journal of Consulting and Clinical Psychology, 51*, 322–323.

GRUNBERG, N. E. (1982). The effects of nicotine and cigarette smoking on food consumption and taste preferences. *Addictive Behaviors, 7*, 317–331.

GRUNBERG, N. E., AND BOWEN, D. J. (1985). Coping with the sequelae of smoking cessation. *Journal of Cardiopulmonary Rehabilitation, 5*, 285–289.

GRUNBERG, N. E., BOWEN, D. J., MAYCOCK, V. A., AND NESPOR, S. M. (1985). The importance of sweet taste and caloric content in the effects of nicotine on specific food consumption. *Psychopharmacology, 87*, 198–203.

GRUNBERG, N. E., BOWEN, D. J., AND MORSE, D. E. (1984). Effects of nicotine on body weight and food consumption in rats. *Psychopharmacology, 83*, 93–98.

HAGEN, R. L., FOREYT, J. P., AND DURHAM, T. W. (1976). The dropout problem: Reducing attrition in obesity research. *Behavior Therapy, 7*, 463–471.

HALL, S. M., RUGG, D., TUNSTALL, C., AND JONES, R. T. (1984). Preventing relapse to cigarette smoking by behavioral skill training. *Journal of Consulting and Clinical Psychology, 52*, 372–382.

HALL, S. M., TUNSTALL, C., RUGG, D., JONES, R. T., AND BENOWITZ, N. (1985). Nicotine gum and behavioral treatment in smoking cessation. *Journal of Consulting and Clinical Psychology, 53*, 256–258.

HARRIS, M. G., AND HALLBAUER, E. S. (1973). Self-directed weight control through eating and exercise. *Behaviour Research and Therapy, 11*, 523–529.

HODGSON, R. J. (1980). The alcohol dependence syndrome: A step in the wrong direction? *British Journal of Addiction, 75*, 255–263.

HODGSON, R. J., RANKIN, H. J., AND STOCKWELL, T. R. (1979). Alcohol dependence and the priming effect. *Behaviour Research and Therapy, 17*, 379–387.

HORN, D. A. (1976). A model for the study of personal choice health behavior. *International Journal of Health Education, 19*, 89–98.

HUNT, G. W., AND AZRIN, N. H. (1973). A community-reinforcement approach to alcoholism. *Behaviour Research and Therapy, 11*, 91–104.

HUNT, W. A., BARNETT, L. W., AND BRANCH, L. G. (1971). Relapse rates in addiction programs. *Journal of Clinical Psychology, 27*, 455–456.

HUNT, W. A., AND MATARAZZO, J. E. (1973). Three years later: Recent developments in the experimental modification of smoking behavior. *Journal of Abnormal Psychology, 81*, 107–114.

JANIS, I. L. (1983). The role of social support in adherence to stressful decisions. *American Psychologist, 38*, 143–160.

JEFFERY, R. W., BJORNSON-BENSON, W. M., ROSENTHAL, B. S., LINDQUIST, R. A., KURTH, C. C., AND JOHNSON, S. C. (1984). Correlates of weight loss and its maintenance over two years of follow-up in middle-aged men. *Preventive Medicine, 13*, 155–168.

JEFFERY, R. W., FORSTER, J. L., AND SNELL, M. K. (1985). Promoting weight control at the worksite: A pilot program of self-motivation using payroll based incentives. *Preventive Medicine, 14*, 187–194.

JEFFERY, R. W., GERBER, W. M., ROSENTHAL, B. S., AND LINDQUIST, R. A. (1983). Monetary contracts in weight control: Effects of group and individual contracts. *Journal of Consulting and Clinical Psychology, 51*, 242–248.

JEFFERY, R. W., SNELL, M. K., AND FORSTER, J. L. (1984). Group composition in the treatment of obesity: Does increasing group heterogeneity improve treatment results? *Behaviour Research and Therapy, 23*, 371–373.

JEFFERY, R. W., AND WING, R. R. (1983). Recidivism and self-cure of smoking and obesity: Data from population studies. *American Psychologist, 37*, 852.

JEFFERY, R. W., WING, R. R., AND STUNKARD, A. J. (1978). Behavioral treatment of obesity: State of the art in 1976. *Behavior Therapy, 6*, 189–199.

KATAHAN, M., PLEAS, J., THACKERY, M., AND WALLSTON, K. A. (1982). Relationship of eating and activity self-reports to follow-up weight maintenance in the massively obese. *Behavior Therapy, 13*, 521–528.

KILLEN, J. D., MACCOBY, N., AND TAYLOR, C. B. (1984). Nicotine gum and self-regulation training in smoking relapse prevention. *Behavior Therapy, 15*, 234–248.

KOPLAN, J. P., POWELL, K. E., SIKES, R. K., SHIRLEY, R. W., AND CAMPBELL, C. C. (1982). An epidemiologic study of the benefits and risks of running. *Journal of the American Medical Association, 248*, 3118–3121.

LANDO, H. (1981). Effects of preparation, experimenter contact, and a maintained reduction alternative on a broad-spectrum program for eliminating smoking. *Addictive Behaviors, 6*, 361–366.

LANDO, H., AND McGOVERN, P. (1982). Three-year data on a behavioral treatment for smoking: A follow-up note. *Addictive Behaviors, 7*, 177–181.

LEVISON, P. K., GERSTEIN, D. R., AND MALOFF, D. R. (Eds.). (1983), *Commonalities in substance abuse and habitual behaviors.* Lexington, MA: Lexington.

LICHTENSTEIN, E. (1982). The smoking problem: A behavioral perspective. *Journal of Consulting and Clinical Psychology, 50*, 804–819.

LICHTENSTEIN, E. (1984). Systematic follow-up of slips and relapses after smoking cessation. Manuscript in preparation.

LICHTENSTEIN, E., ANTONUCCIO, D. O., AND RAINWATER, G. (1977). *Unkicking the habit: The re-sumption of cigarette smoking.* Paper presented at the meeting of the Western Psychological Association, Seattle.

LICHTENSTEIN, E., AND RODRIGUES, M-R. P. (1977). Long-term effects of rapid smoking treatment for dependent cigarette smokers. *Addictive Behaviors, 2*, 109–112.

LUDWIG, A. M., WIKLER, A., AND STARK, L. H. (1974). The first drink: Psychobiological aspects of craving. *Archives of General Psychiatry, 30*, 539–547.

MARLATT, G. A. (1978). Craving for alcohol, loss of control, and relapse: A cognitive-behavioral analysis. In P. E. NATHAN, G. A. MARLATT, AND T. LOBERG (Eds.), *Alcoholism: New directions in behavioral research and treatment* (pp. 271–314). New York: Plenum.

MARLATT, G. A. (1983). The controlled-drinking controversy: A commentary. *American Psychologist, 38*, 1097–1110.

MARLATT, G. A., GOLDSTEIN, S., AND GORDON, J. R. (1984). Unaided smoking cessation: A prospective analysis. Manuscript in preparation.

MARLATT, G. A., AND GORDON, J. R. (1980). Determinants of relapse: Implications for the maintenance of behavior change. In P. O. DAVIDSON AND S. M. DAVIDSON (Eds.), *Behavioral medicine: Changing health life-styles* (pp. 410–452). Elmsford, NY: Pergamon.

MARLATT, G. A., AND GORDON, J. R. (Eds.). (1985). *Relapse prevention: Maintenance strategies in addictive behavior change.* New York: Guilford.

McCLEARN, G. (1981). Genetic studies in animals. *Alcoholism: Clinical and Experimental Research, 5*, 447–448.

McMORROW, M. J., AND FOXX, R. M. (1983). Nicotine's role in smoking: An analysis of nicotine regulation. *Psychological Bulletin, 2*, 302–327.

MERMELSTEIN, R., COHEN, S., AND LICHTENSTEIN, E. (1983). *Psychosocial stress, social support, and smoking cessation maintenance.* Paper presented at the annual meeting of the American Psychological Association, Anaheim, CA.

MERMELSTEIN, R. J., AND LICHTENSTEIN, E. (1983). *Slips versus relapses in smoking cessation: A situational analysis.* Paper presented at the meeting of the Western Psychological Association, San Francisco.

MILLER, P. M. (1980). Theoretical and practical issues in substance abuse and treatment. In W. R. MILLER (Ed.), *The addictive behaviors: Treatment of alcoholism, drug abuse, smoking, and obesity* (pp. 265–290). New York: Pergamon.

MILLER, P. M., AND SIMS, K. L. (1981). Evaluation

and component analysis of a comprehensive weight control program. *International Journal of Obesity, 5*, 57–66.

MILLER, W. R., AND HESTER, R. K. (1980). Treating the problem drinker: Modern approaches. In W. R. MILLER (Ed.), *The addictive behaviors: Treatment of alcoholism, drug abuse, smoking, and obesity* (pp. 11–142). New York: Pergamon.

MOOS, R. H., AND FINNEY, J. W. (1983). The expanding scope of alcoholism treatment evaluation. *American Psychologist, 38*, 1036–1044.

MURPHY, T., MARLATT, G. A., AND PAGANO, R. (1986). The effect of aerobic exercise and meditation on alcohol consumption in male heavy drinkers. *Addictive Behaviors, 11*, 175–186.

MYERS, R. D. (1978). Psychopharmacology of alcohol. *Annual Review of Pharmacology and Toxicology, 18*, 125–144.

NATHAN, P. E. (1980). Etiology and process in the addictive behaviors. In W. R. MILLER (Ed.), *The addictive behaviors: Treatment of alcoholism, drug abuse, smoking, and obesity* (pp. 241–264). New York: Pergamon.

NATHAN, P. E. (1983). Failures in prevention: Why we can't prevent the devastating effect of alcoholism and drug abuse. *American Psychologist, 38*, 459–467.

NATHAN, P. E. (1984). Alcoholism prevention in the work place: Three examples. In P. M. MILLER AND T. E. NIRENBERG (Eds.), *Prevention of alcohol abuse* (pp. 235–261). New York: Plenum.

NATHAN, P. E., AND GOLDMAN, M. S. (1979). Problem drinking and alcoholism. In O. F. POMERLEAU AND J. P. BRADY (Eds.), *Behavioral medicine: Theory and practice* (pp. 255–278). Baltimore, MD: Williams & Wilkins.

NATHAN, P. E., AND WIENS, A. N. (1983). Alcoholism: Introduction and overview. *American Psychologist, 38*, 1035.

NATIONAL INSTITUTE ON DRUG ABUSE. (1979). *Behavioral analysis and treatment of substance abuse.* NIDA Research Monograph 25, U.S. Department of Health, Education, and Welfare.

OCKENE, J. K. (1984). Toward a smoke-free society. *American Journal of Public Health, 74*, 1198–1200.

OCKENE, J. K., HYMOWITZ, N., SEXTON, M., AND BROSTE, S. K. (1982). Comparison of patterns of smoking behavior change among smokers in the Multiple Risk Factor Intervention Trial (MRFIT). *Preventive Medicine, 11*, 621–638.

OLDRIDGE, N. B., DONNER, A. P., BUCK, C. W., JONES, N. L., ANDREW, G. M., PARKER, J. O., CUNNINGHAM, D. A., KAVANAUGH, T., RECHNITZER, P. A., AND SUTTON, J. R. (1983). Predictors of dropout from cardiac exercise rehabilitation: Ontario exercise-heart collaborative study. *American Journal of Cardiology: 51*, 70–74.

OSSIP-KLEIN, D. J., SHAPIRO, R. M., AND STIGGINS, J. (1984). Freedom Line: Increasing utilization of a telephone support service for ex-smokers. *Addictive Behaviors, 9*, 227–230.

PECHACEK, T. P. (1979). Modification of smoking behavior. In *Smoking and health: A report of the Surgeon General.* DHEW Pub. No. PHS 19-50066, Washington, DC: U.S. Government Printing Office.

PECHACEK, T. P., MITTELMARK, M., JEFFERY, R. W., LOKEN, B., AND LUEPKER, R. (1985). *Quit and win: Direct incentives for smoking cessation.* Manuscript submitted for publication.

PERRI, M. G., MCADOO, W. G., SPEVAK, P. A., AND NEWLIN, D. B. (1984). Effect of a multicomponent maintenance program on long-term weight loss. *Journal of Consulting and Clinical Psychology, 52*, 480–481.

PERRI, M. G., SHAPIRO, R. M., LUDWIG, W. W., TWENTYMAN, C. T., AND MCADOO, W. G. (1984). Maintenance strategies for the treatment of obesity: An evaluation of relapse prevention training and posttreatment contact by mail and telephone. *Journal of Consulting and Clinical Psychology, 52*, 404–413.

POMERLEAU, O. F. (1984). Reinforcing properties of nicotine: Smoking and induced vasopressin and beta-endorphin release, antioception and anxiety reduction. *Pavlovian Journal of Biological Science, 19*, 107.

POMERLEAU, O. F., ADKINS, D., AND PERTSCHUK, M. (1978). Predictors of outcome and recidivism in smoking cessation treatment. *Addictive Behaviors, 3*, 65–70.

POMERLAU, O. F., AND POMERLEAU, C. S. (1984). Neuroregulators and the reinforcement of smoking: Towards a biobehavioral explanation. *Neuroscience and Biobehavioral Reviews, 8*, 503–513.

POULOS, C. X., HINSON, R. E., AND SIEGEL, S. (1981). The role of Pavlovian processes in drug tolerance and dependence: Implications for treatment. *Addictive Behaviors, 6*, 205–212.

PROCHASKA, J. O. (1979). *Systems of psychotherapy: A transtheoretical analysis.* Homewood, IL: Dorsey.

PROCHASKA, J. O. (1983). Self-changers versus therapy changers versus Schachter. *American Psychologist, 37*, 853–854.

PROCHASKA, J. O., AND DICLEMENTE, C. C. (1982). Transtheoretical therapy: Toward a more integrated model of change. *Psychotherapy: Theory, Research, and Practice, 19*, 276–288.

PROCHASKA, J. O., AND DICLEMENTE, C. C. (1983).

Stages and processes of self-change of smoking: Toward an integrative model of change. *Journal of Consulting and Clinical Psychology, 51,* 390–395.

PROCHASKA, J. O., AND DiCLEMENTE, C. C. (1984). *The transtheoretical approach: Crossing traditional boundaries of therapy.* Homewood, IL: Dow Jones/Irwin.

RODIN, J. (1981). Current status of the internal–external hypothesis for obesity: What went wrong? *American Psychologist, 36,* 361–372.

ROSEN, T. J., AND SHIPLEY, R. H. (1983). A stage analysis of self-initiated smoking reductions. *Addictive Behaviors, 8,* 263–272.

SACKETT, D. L., AND HAYNES, R. B. (Eds.), (1976). *Compliance with therapeutic regimens.* Baltimore, MD: Johns Hopkins University Press.

SCHACHTER, S. (1982). Recidivism and self-cure of smoking and obesity. *American Psychologist, 37,* 436–444.

SCHUCKITT, M. A. (1981). The genetics of alcoholism. *Alcoholism: Clinical and Experimental Research, 5,* 439–440.

SHIFFMAN, S. (1982). Relapse following smoking cessation: A situational analysis. *Journal of Consulting and Clinical Psychology, 50,* 71–86.

SHIFFMAN, S. (1984). Coping with temptations to smoke. *Journal of Consulting and Clinical Psychology, 52,* 261–267.

SIEGEL, S. (1979). The role of conditioning in drug tolerance and addiction. In J. D. KEEHEN (Ed.), *Psychopathology in animals: Research and treatment implications.* New York: Academic Press.

SIMOPOULOS, A. P., AND VAN ITALLIE, T. B. (1984). Body weight, health, and longevity. *Annals of Internal Medicine, 100,* 285–295.

STALONAS, P. M., JOHNSON, W. G., AND CHRIST, M. (1978). Behavior modification for obesity: The evaluation of exercise, contingency management and program adherence. *Journal of Consulting and Clinical Psychology, 2,* 225–235.

STERNBERG, B. S. (1985). Relapse in weight control: Definitions, processes, and prevention strategies. In G. A. MARLATT AND J. R. GORDON (Eds.), *Relapse prevention: Maintenance strategies in addictive behavior change* (pp. 521–545). New York: Guilford.

STITZER, M. L., AND BIGELOW, G. E. (1984). Contingent reinforcement for carbon monoxide reduction: Within-subject effects of pay amount. *Journal of Applied Behavior Analysis. 17,* 477–484.

STOCKWELL, T. R., HODGSON, R. J., RANKIN, H. J., AND TAYLOR, C. (1982). Alcohol dependence, beliefs, and the priming effect. *Behaviour Research and Therapy, 20,* 513–522.

STUART, R. B., AND GUIRE, K. (1978). Some correlates of the maintenance of weight loss through behavior modification. *International Journal of Obesity, 2,* 225 –235.

STUNKARD, A. J. (1986). The control of obesity: Social and community perspectives. In K. D. BROWNELL AND J. P. FOREYT (Eds.), *The physiology, psychology, and treatment of the eating disorders.* New York: Basic Books.

STUNKARD, A. J., AND PENICK, S. B. (1979). Behavior modification in the treatment of obesity: The problem of maintaining weight loss. *Archives of General Psychiatry, 36,* 810–816.

STUNKARD, A. J., SORENSON, T. I. A., HANIS, C., TEASDALE, T. W., CHAKRABORTY, R., SCHULL, W. J., AND SCHULSINGER, F. (1986). An adoption study of human obesity. *New England Journal of Medicine, 314,* 193–198.

SUPNICK, J. A., AND COLLETTI, G. (1984). Relapse coping and problem solving training following treatment for smoking. *Addictive Behaviors, 9,* 401–404.

SUTTON, S. R. (1979). Interpreting relapse curves. *Journal of Consulting and Clinical Psychology, 47,* 96–98.

THOMPSON, J. K., JARVIE, G. J., LAHEY, B. B., AND CURETON, K. J. (1982). Exercise and obesity: Etiology, physiology, and intervention. *Psychological Bulletin, 91,* 55–79.

U.S. DEPARTMENT OF HEALTH AND HUMAN SERVICES. (1983). *The health consequences of smoking: Cardiovascular disease: A report of the Surgeon General.* Washington, DC: Author.

VAILLANT, G. E. (1983). *The natural history of alcoholism: Causes, patterns, and paths to recovery.* Cambridge, MA: Harvard University Press.

VAILLANT, G. E. AND MILOFSKY, E. S. (1982). The etiology of alcoholism: A prospective viewpoint. *American Psychologist, 37,* 494–503.

WADDEN, T. A., STUNKARD, A. J., AND BROWNELL, K. D. (1983). Very low calorie diets: Their efficacy, safety, and future. *Annals of Internal Medicine, 99,* 675–684.

WILKINSON, D. A., AND SANCHEZ-CRAIG, M. (1981). Relevance of brain dysfunction to treatment objectives: Should alcohol-related cognitive deficits influence the way we think about treatment? *Addictive Behaviors, 6,* 253–260.

WILSON, G. T. (1978). Methodological considerations in treatment outcome research on obesity. *Journal of Consulting and Clinical Psychology, 46,* 687–702.

WILSON, G. T. (1980). Behavior therapy for obesity. In A. J. STUNKARD (Ed.), *Obesity* (pp. 325–344). Philadelphia: Saunders.

WILSON, G. T. (1985). Psychological prognostic

factors in the treatment of obesity. In J. Hirsch and T. B. Van Itallie (Eds.), *Recent advances in obesity research* (Vol. 4, pp. 301–311). London: Libbey.

Wilson, G. T., and Brownell, K. D. (1980). Behavior therapy for obesity: An evaluation of treatment outcome. *Advances in Behaviour Research and Therapy, 3,* 49–86.

Wooley, S. C., Wooley, O. W., and Dyrenforth, S. R. (1979). Theoretical, practical, and social issues in behavioral treatments of obesity. *Journal of Applied Behavior Analysis, 12,* 3–26.